ENCYCLOPEDIA

of

POST-COLONIAL

LITERATURES

in English

ENCYCLOPEDIA
of
POST-COLONIAL LITERATURES
in English

Volume 1

EDITED BY

Eugene Benson
University of Guelph, Canada

and

L.W. Conolly
Trent University, Canada

London and New York

First published in 1994
by Routledge
11 New Fetter Lane, London EC4P 4EE
29 West 35th Street, New York, NY 10001

Reprinted 2001

Routledge is an imprint of the Taylor & Francis Group

Printed and bound in Great Britain by TJI Digital, Padstow, Cornwall

British Library Cataloguing in Publication Data
A catalogue record for this book is available from the British Library.

Library of Congress Cataloging-in-Publication Data
A catalog record for this book has been requested.

ISBN 0–415–05199–1 (set)
0–415–11344–X (Volume 1)
0–415–11345–8 (Volume 2)

CONTENTS

INTRODUCTION xxv
ACKNOWLEDGEMENTS xxix
CONTRIBUTORS xxxii
Abad, Gemino Henson 1
Abbas, Khwaja Ahmad 1
ABORIGINAL LITERATURE 2
Aboriginal Literature (Australia) 2
Aboriginal Literature (Canada) 4
Aboriginal Song and Narrative (Australia) 9
Aborigines in Literature (Australia) 10
Aboud, James C. 12
Abrahams, Lionel 12
Abrahams, Peter 13
Abruquah, Joseph Wilfred 15
Achebe, Chinua 15
Acorn, Milton 18
Adams, Arthur H. 18
Adams, Glenda 19
Adamson, Robert 19
Adcock, Fleur 20
Africa in Canadian Literature 21
African Connections 24
Agard, John 25
Ahmad, Sayeed 26
Aidoo, Ama Ata 27
Alexander, Meena 28
Alfon, Estrella D. 28
Ali, Ahmed 29
Alkali, Zaynab 32
Alley, Rewi 32
Allfrey, Phyllis Shand 33
Aluko, Timothy Mofolorunso 34
Amadi, Elechi 34
Amanuddin, Syed 35
Amerindians in Caribbean Literature 36
Anand, Mulk Raj 37
Anantanarayanan, Madhavaiah 39
Andersen, Johannes Carl 40
Anderson, Balfour 40
Anderson, Ethel 41
Anderson, Jessica 41
Anderson, Vernon 42
Angira, Jared 43
ANTHOLOGIES 43
Anthologies (Australia) 43
Anthologies (Canada) 46
Anthologies (The Caribbean) 49
Anthologies (East Africa) 50
Anthologies (India) 52
Anthologies (Malaysia and Singapore) 53
Anthologies (New Zealand) 54
Anthologies (Pakistan) 56
Anthologies (The Phillipines) 57
Anthologies (South Africa) 58
Anthologies (South Pacific) 60
Anthologies (Sri Lanka) 61
Anthologies (West Africa) 61
Anthony, Frank Sheldon 64
Anthony, Michael 64
Anyidoho, Kofi 66
Arcellana, Francisco 66
Archibald, Douglas Rupert 67
Arguilla, Manuel E. 68
Armah, Ayi Kwei 69
Asare, Bediako 70
Ashton-Warner, Sylvia 71
Association for Commonwealth Literature and Language Studies 71
Association of Nigerian Authors 73
Astley, Thea 73
Atwood, Margaret 75
Aurobindo, Sri 77
Australia 80
Australia Council 83

Australia in Canadian Literature in English 84
Autobiography 86
Avison, Margaret 86
AWARDS 87
Awards (Australia) 87
Awards (Canada) 88
Awards (India) 89
Awards (New Zealand) 90
Awards (The Phillipines) 91
Awards (Singapore) 93
Awards (South Africa) 93
Awards (West Africa) 94
Awoonor, Kofi 95
Ayyar, Ayilam Subramania Panchapakesa 96

Bail, Murray 98
Baird, Irene 98
Ballantyne, David 99
Bandler, Faith 100
Bangladesh 100
Baratham, Gopal 103
Barker, Lady Mary Ann 103
Barnard, Marjorie Faith 104
Bascom, Harold A. 105
Basu, Romen 105
Baugh, Edward Alston Cecil 107
Baughan, Blanche Edith 107
Bautista, Cirilo F. 108
Baxter, James Keir 108
Baynton, Barbara 110
Beaglehole, John Cawte 111
Bean, C. E. W. 112
Beaver, Bruce 112
Bekederemo 113
Belgrave, Valerie 115
Bennett, Alvin Gladstone 116
Bennett, Louise 116
Benson, Mary 117
Berry, James 118
Best, Elsdon 119
Bethell, Mary Ursula 120
Bharati, Sarabhai 120
Bhatnagar, Om Prakash 121
Bhattacharya, Bhabani 122
Bhushan, V. N. 124
Biography 124
Birney, Earle 124
bissett, bill 126
Bissoondath, Neil 127
Black, Stephen 127
Black Writers in Britain 128
Blainey, Geoffrey 130
Blaise, Clark 131
Bland, Peter 132
Blight, John 132
Boey Kim Cheng 133
Boldrewood, Rolf 133
Bolt, Carol 134
Bond, Ruskin 135
Bosman, Herman Charles 136
Botswana 138
Bowering, George 140
Boyd, Martin 141
Brainard, Cecelia Manguerra 142
Braithwaite, E. R. 143
Brand, Dionne 143
Brasch, Charles Orwell 144
Brata, Sasthi 145
Brathwaite, Edward Kamau 146
Breeze, Jean Binta 148
Brennan, Christopher John 148
Brett, Lily 150
Brew, Kwesi 150
Brewster, Elizabeth 151
Bringhurst, Robert 152
Brink, André 152
British Influences on Caribbean Literature 154
BROADCASTING 155
Broadcasting (Australia) 155
Broadcasting (Bangladesh) 157
Broadcasting (Canada) 157
Broadcasting (India) 159
Broadcasting (Pakistan) 160
Broadcasting (St Helena) 161
Broadcasting (South Pacific) 162

Brodber, Erna 162
Brooke, Frances 163
Brown, Wayne Vincent 164
Bruce, Charles 165
Bruce, Mary (Minnie) Grant 166
Brutus, Dennis Vincent 166
Buckler, Ernest 167
Buckley, Vincent 168
Bukenya, Austin 169
Bulletin 169
Bulosan, Carlos 170
Bunting, John Reginald 171
Burke, Eddie 171
Burn, David 172
Butler, Frederick Guy 173
Buzo, Alexander 174

Callaghan, Morley 176
Callender, Timothy 177
Cambridge, Ada 178
Cameron, Norman Eustace 179
Cameroon 179
Campbell, Alistair Te Ariki 182
Campbell, David 183
Campbell, George 183
Campbell, Hazel Dorothy 184
Campbell, Maria 185
Campbell, Marion 185
Campbell, Roy 186
Campbell, William Wilfred 188
Canada 188
Canada Council, The 194
Canadian Connections with Caribbean Literature 194
Canadian North, The 195
Cappiello, Rosa 196
Carew, Jan 197
Carey, Peter 197
Cargill, Morris 198
Caribbean, The 199
Caribbean in Canadian Literature, The 201
'Caribbean Voices' 204
Carman, Bliss 205
Carman, Dulce 205
Carr, Emily 206
Carter, Martin Wylde 207
Cartey, Wilfred 208
Casey, Gavin 209
Cato, Nancy 210
CENSORSHIP 210
Censorship (Overview) 210
Censorship (Australia) 212
Censorship (Canada) 213
Censorship (St Helena) 215
Censorship (Singapore) 216
Censorship (South Africa) 216
Censorship (South Pacific) 218
Censorship (West Africa) 219
Chandler, A. Bertram 220
Chatterjee, Upamanyu 221
Chattopadhyaya, Harindranath 221
Chaudhuri, Nirad C. 222
Chen, Willi 224
Cheney-Coker, Syl 224
Cheong, Colin 225
Chettur, G. K. 225
Chettur, S. K. 226
Chiang, Michael 227
Chifunyise, Stephen 227
CHILDREN'S LITERATURE 228
Children's Literature (Overview) 228
Children's Literature (Australia) 230
Children's Literature (Canada) 231
Children's Literature (The Caribbean) 234
Children's Literature (East Africa) 236
Children's Literature (India) 237
Children's Literature (New Zealand) 238
Children's Literature (The Phillipines) 241
Children's Literature (Singapore) 242
Children's Literature (South Africa) 243
Children's Literature (South Pacific) 244
Children's Literature (West Africa) 245
Chimombo, Steve 248
Ching, Frank 248
Chinodya, Shimmer 249
Chinweizu 249
Chipasula, Frank 250
Clark, J. P. 250

Clark, Manning 250
Clarke, A. M. 251
Clarke, Austin 252
Clarke, George Elliott 252
Clarke, Marcus 253
Cleary, Jon 254
Cliff, Michelle 254
Clift, Charmian 255
Cloete, Stuart 256
Clouts, Sydney David 256
Coetzee, John Maxwell 258
Cogswell, Frederick William 260
Cohen, Leonard Norman 261
Cohen, Matt 261
Collins, Merle 262
Collymore, Frank 262
Confederation Poets (Canada) 264
Connor, Ralph 264
Conton, William 265
Convict Literature (Australia) 266
Cook, Michael 267
Coomaraswamy, Ananda K. 268
Cope, Jack 269
Copway, George 270
Corris, Peter 270
Couani, Anna 271
Coulter, John 271
Courage, James Francis 272
Couvreur, Jessie 273
Cowan, James 273
Cowan, Peter 273
Cowasjee, Saros 274
Cowley, Joy 275
Craig, Christine 275
Craig, Dennis Roy 276
Crawford, Isabella Valancy 276
Crime and Mystery Fiction (Australia) 277
Crime and Mystery Fiction (Canada) 278
Crime and Mystery Fiction (India) 280
Crime and Mystery Fiction (New Zealand) . 281
CRITICISM 282
Criticism (Overview) 282
Criticism (Australia) 284
Criticism (Canada) 286
Criticism (The Caribbean) 292
Criticism (India) 294
Criticism (Malaysia) 298
Criticism (New Zealand) 299
Criticism (Pakistan) 301
Criticism (The Philippines) 302
Criticism (Singapore) 305
Criticism (South Africa) 306
Criticism (South Pacific) 309
Criticism (Sri Lanka) 311
Criticism (West Africa) 311
Cross, Ian 314
Crump, Barry 314
Cullinan, Patrick Roland 315
CULTURAL JOURNALISM 315
Cultural Journalism (Australia) 315
Cultural Journalism (Canada) 317
Cultural Journalism (India) 318
Cultural Journalism (Singapore) 321
Cumper, Patricia 321
Curnow, Allen 322
Currimbhoy, Asif 323

Dabydeen, Cyril 325
Dabydeen, David 325
D'Aguiar, Fred 326
Dalisay, Jose Yap 327
Dallas, Ruth 327
D'Alpuget, Blanche 328
Dangarembga, Tsitsi 329
Dangor, Achmat 329
Dark, Eleanor 330
DaRoy, Ester V. 331
Daruwalla, Keki Nasserwanji 331
Das, Gurcharan 332
Das, Kamala 332
Das, Mahadai 334
Das, Manoj 334
Dathorne, Oscar Ronald 335
Davey, Frank 336
Davies, Robertson 337
Davin, Dan(iel) 339
Davis, A. H. 340
Davis, Jack 340

Dawe, Bruce 341
Dawes, Neville 342
D'Costa, Jean Constance 343
de Boissière, Ralph 344
de Graft, Joe Coleman 345
De Groen, Alma 345
Dei-Anang, Michael Francis 346
de la Roche, Mazo 347
de Lisser, Herbert George 348
Demetillo, Ricaredo 349
De Mille, James 350
Dennis, C. J. 351
de Roo, Anne 351
Derozio, Henry Louis Vivian 352
Desai, Anita 352
Desai, Boman 354
Desani, Govindas Vishnoodas 355
Deshpande, Gauri 356
Deshpande, Shashi 357
de Souza, Eunice 358
De Ungria, Ricardo 359
Devanny, Jean 360
Dewdney, Christopher 360
Dhlomo, Herbert Isaac Ernest 361
Dhlomo, Rolfes Robert Reginald 362
Dhondy, Farrukh 362
Dikobe, Modikwe 363
Dimalanta, Ophelia Alcantara 364
Dixon, McDonald Ernest 364
Djoleto, Amu 365
Dobson, Rosemary 365
Domett, Alfred 366
DRAMA 367
Drama (Overview) 367
Drama (Australia) 370
Drama (Canada) 373
Drama (The Caribbean) 377
Drama (East Africa) 381
Drama (Hong Kong) 382
Drama (India) 383
Drama (Malaysia) 386
Drama (Malta) 387
Drama (New Zealand) 388
Drama (Pakistan) 397
Drama (The Philippines) 398
Drama (Singapore) 399
Drama (South Africa) 401
Drama (South Pacific) 406
Drama (Sri Lanka) 407
Drama (West Africa) 408
Dransfield, Michael 414
Drayton, Geoffrey 415
Drewe, Robert 416
Drum 416
Duckworth, Marilyn 418
Dudek, Louis 419
Duder, Tessa 419
du Fresne, Yvonne 420
Duggan, Eileen 420
Duggan, Maurice 421
Duncan, Sara Jeannette 422
Duodo, Cameron 424
du Plessis, Menán 424
Durack, Mary 425
Dutt, Narendrenath 425
Dutt, Romesh Chunder 425
Dutt, Toru 426
Dutton, Geoffrey 427

Early Novel (India) 429
Easmon, Raymond Sarif 429
East-West Encounter (India) 429
Ebejer, Francis 432
Eden, Dorothy 432
Edgell, Zee 433
Edmond, Lauris Dorothy 433
Edmond, Murray 434
Ee Tiang Hong 435
Ekwensi, Cyprian O. D. 436
Eldershaw, Flora 437
Elliott, Sumner Locke 438
Ellis, Zoila Maria 438
Emecheta, Buchi 439
Engel, Marian 440
Enriquez, Emigdio Alvarez 441
Equiano, Olaudah 441
Eri, Sir Serei Vincent 442
EROTICA 443

Erotica (Australia) 443
Erotica (Canada) 444
Escoffery, Gloria 445
Espina Moore, Lina 446
Espino, Federico Licsi 447
ESSAYS 448
Essays (Australia) 448
Essays (Canada) 450
Essays (The Philippines) 454
Essays (West Africa) 455
Essex Evans, George 458
Esson, Louis 459
Essop, Ahmed 460
Evans, Hubert 461
Evasco, Marjorie 462
Expatriate Writers (India, West Africa, The Caribbean) 462
Experimental Theatre (New Zealand) 465
EXPLORATION LITERATURE 465
Exploration Literature (Overview) 465
Exploration Literature (Australia) 468
Exploration Literature (Canada) 470
Exploration Literature (New Zealand) 473
Exploration Literature (West Africa) 475
Ezekiel, Nissim 477

Facey, Albert 480
Fairburn, A. R. D. 480
Farah, Nuruddin 481
Farmer, Beverley 483
FEMINISM 484
Feminism (Overview) 484
Feminism (Australia) 486
Feminism (Canada) 487
Feminism (The Caribbean) 489
Feminism (India) 491
Feminism (New Zealand) 492
Feminism (Pakistan) 493
Feminism (The Philippines) 494
Feminism (South Africa) 495
Feminism (West Africa) 497
Fennario, David 498
Ferland, Barbara 499
Fernando, Gilda Cordero 500
Fernando, Lloyd 500
Fernando, Patrick 501
Field, Barron 502
Figueroa, John 503
FILM AND LITERATURE 504
Film and Literature (Australia) 504
Film and Literature (Canada) 505
Film and Literature (India) 506
Film and Literature (New Zealand) 508
Film and Literature (South Africa) 509
Film and Literature (West Africa) 511
Findley, Timothy 512
Finlayson, Roderick 514
FitzGerald, R. D. 515
Fitzpatrick, Sir James Percy 516
Florentino, Alberto 517
Fogarty, Lionel 517
FOLKLORE 518
Folklore (Australia) 518
Folklore (Canada) 519
Folklore (The Caribbean) 521
Folklore (East Africa) 523
Folklore (India) 525
Folklore (The Philippines) 526
Folklore (West Africa) 527
Folk Songs (The Caribbean) 529
Fonlon, Bernard Nsokika 529
Forbes, John 530
Forde, Alfred Nathaniel 531
FOREIGN WRITERS 532
Foreign Writers (Australia) 532
Foreign Writers (Canada) 537
Foreign Writers (Hong Kong) 541
Foreign Writers (India) 542
Foreign Writers (South Pacific) 546
Foreign Writers (Sri Lanka) 547
Foreign Writers (West Africa) 548
Foster, David 550
Frame, Janet 551
Franklin, Miles 552
Fraser, Keath 553
Frederick, Rawle 554
Freeman, David 554
French, Anne 555

French Caribbean Connections in Caribbean Literature 555
French, David 556
French, Stanley 557
Friggieri, Joe 558
Friggieri, Oliver 558
Frye, Northrop 559
Fugard, Athol 561
Furphy, Joseph 563
Furtado, Joseph 565

Gallant, Mavis 566
Galt, John 567
Gamalinda, Eric 568
Gandhi in Indian-English Literature 569
Gandhi, Mohandas Karamchand 570
Garner, Helen 571
Garner, Hugh 572
Geddes, Gary 573
Gee, Maurice 573
Ghana 574
Ghose, Aurobindo 577
Ghose, Manmohan 577
Ghose, Sudhindra Nath 578
Ghose, Zulfikar 580
Ghosh, Amitav 582
Gibbon, Reginald Perceval 584
Gibbs, May 584
Gibraltar 585
Gifkins, Michael 587
Gilbert, Kevin 587
Gilkes, Michael A. 588
Gilmore, Dame Mary 589
Gilroy, Beryl 590
Glen, Esther 590
Glover, Denis 591
Godfrey, Dave 592
Goh Poh Seng 593
Goldfields Literature (Australia) 593
Goldsmith, Oliver 595
Goldsworthy, Peter 596
Gonzalez, Anson John 597
Gonzalez, N. V. M. 597
Goodison, Lorna Gaye 599
Gooneratne, Yasmine 600
Goonewardene, James 602
Gordimer, Nadine 603
Gordon, Adam Lindsay 605
Gould, Alan 606
Gow, Michael 606
Grace, Patricia 607
Gray, Robert 608
Gray, Stephen Richard 609
Greer, Germaine 610
Grenville, Kate 610
Grey Owl 611
Grossmann, Edith Searle 612
Grove, Frederick Philip 612
Guerrero, Wilfrido Maria 614
Guerrero-Nakpil, Carmen 615
Gunn, Jeannie 615
Gustafson, Ralph 616
Guthrie-Smith, William Herbert 616
Gutteridge, Don 617
Guy, Rosa 617
Gwala, Mafika Pascal 618

Hagedorn, Jessica 620
Haggard, Henry Rider 620
Haley, Russell 621
Haliburton, Thomas Chandler 621
Hall, Rodney 623
Hall, Roger Leighton 624
Hamilton, Judith 625
Han Suyin 625
Hancock, Sir Keith 626
Hanrahan, Barbara 626
Haq, Kaiser 627
Harbourfront Centre 628
Hardy, Frank 628
Harlow, Robert 629
Harpur, Charles 630
Harris, Alexander 630
Harris, Claire 631
Harris, Max 632
Harris, Wilson 632
Harrison, Susie Frances 634
Harrower, Elizabeth 635

Hart, Julia Catherine 636
Hart, Kevin 636
Hart-Smith, William 637
Harwood, Gwen 637
Hashmi, (Aurangzeb) Alamgir 639
Hau'ofa, Epeli 640
Hay, William Gosse 641
Hazzard, Shirley 642
Head, Bessie 643
Hearne, John 644
Heath, Roy A. K. 645
Heavysege, Charles 646
Helu Thaman, Konai 647
Helwig, David 648
Hendriks, A. L. 648
Henning, Rachel 649
Henshaw, James Ene Ewa 650
Herbert, Cecil Lionel 650
Herbert, John 651
Herbert, Xavier 652
Hercules, Frank E. M. 653
Hereniko, Vilsoni Tausie 654
Hewett, Dorothy 655
Hibberd, Jack 656
Hicks, Bonny 656
Highway, Tomson 657
Hill, Barry 657
Hill, Errol 658
Hilliard, Noel 659
Hippolyte, Kendel 659
Historical Novel (India) 660
HISTORICAL WRITING 660
Historical Writing (Australia) 660
Historical Writing (Canada) 662
Historical Writing (The Caribbean) 665
Historical Writing (Gibraltar) 667
Historical Writing (Hong Kong) 668
Historical Writing (New Zealand) 669
Historical Writing (Pakistan) 671
Historical Writing (The Philippines) 672
Historical Writing (St Helena) 673
Historical Writing (West Africa) 674
HOAXES AND JOKES 675
Hoaxes and Jokes (Australia) 675
Hoaxes and Jokes (Canada) 676
Hodge, Merle 677
Hodgins, Jack 678
Holcroft, Montague Harry 679
Hong Kong 679
Honnalgere, Gopal R. 681
Hood, Hugh 682
Hope, A. D. 683
Hope, Christopher 684
Hopkinson, Slade 686
Horne, Donald 687
Horror Fiction (Singapore) 687
Hosain, Attia 687
Hosain, Shahid 688
Hosein, Clyde 689
Hospital, Janette Turner 689
Hove, Chenjerai 690
Howe, Joseph 690
Howes, Edith 691
Hudson, Flexmore 691
Hufana, Alejandrino G. 692
Hulme, Keri 693
Hume, Ferguson Wright 693
HUMOUR AND SATIRE 694
Humour (Australia) 694
Humour and Satire (Canada) 696
Humour and Satire (East Africa) 699
Humour and Satire (India) 700
Humour and Satire (Pakistan) 701
Humour (Singapore) 702
Humour and Satire (South Africa) 703
Humour and Satire (West Africa) 704
Humphries, Barry 704
Hunt, Sam 705
Hussein, Ebrahim 706
Hutchinson, Lionel 706
Huyghue, Douglas Smith 707
Hyatt, Charles 707
Hyde, Robin 708

Idriess, Ion 710
Ihimaera, Witi Tame 710
Ike, Vincent Chukwuemeka 712
Imbuga, Francis Davis 712

India 713
Ingamells, Rex 718
Ingram, Kenneth N. 719
Ireland and Irish Values in Australia 719
Ireland, David 721
Ireland, Kevin 722
Iroh, Eddie 722
Isvaran, Manjeri S. 723
Iyayi, Festus 724
Iyengar, K. R. S. 724

Jabavu, Noni 726
Jackman, Oliver 726
Jacobson, Dan 727
James, C. L. R. 728
Janes, Percy 729
Jekyll, Walter 730
Jenkins, Geoffrey (Ernest) 730
Jewish Writing (Australia) 731
Jeyaratnam, Philip 732
Jhabvala, Ruth Prawer 733
Jindyworobak Movement 734
Joaquin, Nick M. 735
John, Errol 736
Johnson, Colin 737
Johnson, Linton Kwesi 737
Johnson, Louis 738
Johnson, Pauline 738
Johnston, Basil H. 739
Johnston, George Henry 740
Jolley, Elizabeth 740
Jones, Douglas Gordon 742
Jones, Evan 742
Jones, Marion Patrick 743
Jordan, Archibald Campbell 744
José, Frankie Sionil 744
Joseph, Michael Kennedy 748
Joshi, Arun 748
Jurgensen, Manfred 750
Jussawalla, Adil 750

Kabir, Humayun 752
Kachingwe, Aubrey 753
Kadhani, Mudereri 753
Kahiga, Sam 753
Kailasam, Thyagaraja Paramasiva 754
Kalman, Yvonne 755
Kamal, Daud 755
Kannan, Lakshmi 756
Karaka, Dosabhai Framji 757
Karnad, Girish 757
Kasaipwalova, John 758
Kayira, Legson 759
Kearns, Lionel John 759
Kee Thuan Chye 760
Keens-Douglas, Paul 761
Keesing, Nancy 761
Kelly, Ned 762
Kempadoo, Peter 763
Kendall, Henry 763
Keneally, Thomas 764
Kenna, Peter 766
Kenya 767
Khan, Ismith 768
Khan, Razia 768
Kibera, Leonard N. 769
Kidman, Fiona 770
Kimenye, Barbara 771
Kincaid, Jamaica 771
King, Hugh 772
King, Michael 773
Kingsley, Henry 773
Kinsella, W. P. 774
Kirby, William 775
Kissoon, Freddie 775
Kiyooka, Roy Kenjiro 776
Klein, A. M. 776
Knister, Raymond 778
Koch, Christopher John 778
Kogawa, Joy Nozomi 780
Kolatkar, Arun Balakrishna 780
Kolia, John 781
Kon, Stella 782
Konadu, Asare 783
Kreisel, Henry 783
Kroetsch, Robert Paul 784
Kulyk Keefer, Janice 786
Kumar, Shiv K. 787

Kuo Pao Kun . . . 788
Kureishi, Hanif . . . 788
Kureishi, Maki . . . 789
Kuzwayo, Ellen Kate . . . 790

Lacambra Ayala, Tita . . . 791
Ladoo, Harold Sonny . . . 791
La Guma, Alex . . . 792
Lal, Purusottam . . . 794
Lambert, Betty . . . 795
Lamming, George . . . 795
Lampman, Archibald . . . 797
Lancaster, G. B. . . . 799
Lane, William . . . 799
Langley, Eve . . . 800
LANGUAGE . . . 800
Language (Australia) . . . 800
Language (Canadian English) . . . 805
Language (The Caribbean) . . . 808
Language (Indian English) . . . 811
Language (Pakistan) . . . 813
Language (The Philippines) . . . 813
Language (St Helena) . . . 815
Language (South Africa) . . . 815
Language (South Pacific English) . . . 818
Language (West African English) . . . 820
Lapido, Duro . . . 822
Laurence, Margaret . . . 822
Lawler, Ray . . . 824
Lawson, Henry . . . 825
Lawson, Louisa . . . 826
Laxman, Rasipuram Krishnaswamy . . . 827
Layton, Irving . . . 828
Leacock, Stephen . . . 829
Leakey, Caroline Woolmer . . . 830
Lee, Dennis Beynon . . . 831
Lee, Easton H. . . . 832
Lee, John Alexander . . . 832
Lee Kok Liang . . . 833
Lee, John Robert . . . 834
Lee, Russell . . . 835
Lee Tzu Pheng . . . 836
LEGENDS . . . 837
Legends (Australia) . . . 837
Legends (Canada) . . . 838
Legends and Myths (South Africa) . . . 839
Lehmann, Geoffrey . . . 842
Leprohon, Rosanna . . . 843
Leslie, Kenneth . . . 844
Lesotho . . . 845
Lessing, Doris . . . 846
LETTERS . . . 847
Letters (Australia) . . . 847
Letters (Canada) . . . 849
Letters (India) . . . 851
Letters (New Zealand) . . . 852
Levine, Norman . . . 853
Liberman, Serge . . . 854
LIFE WRITING . . . 855
Life Writing (Overview) . . . 855
Life Writing (Australia) . . . 856
Life Writing (Bangladesh) . . . 859
Life Writing (Canada) . . . 859
Life Writing (The Caribbean) . . . 865
Life Writing (India) . . . 867
Life Writing (Malaysia and Singapore) . . . 871
Life Writing (New Zealand) . . . 872
Life Writing (Pakistan) . . . 875
Life Writing (The Philippines) . . . 877
Life Writing (South Africa) . . . 878
Light Verse (India) . . . 884
Lim, Catherine . . . 884
Lim, Maria Fatima V. . . . 885
Lim, Shirley Geok-Lin . . . 886
Lim, Suchen Christine . . . 887
Lim Thean Soo . . . 887
Lindsay, Jack . . . 888
Lindsay, Joan . . . 889
Lindsay, Norman . . . 889
Lipenga, Ken . . . 891
LITERARY MAGAZINES . . . 891
Literary Magazines (Overview) . . . 891
Literary Magazines (Australia) . . . 893
Literary Magazines (Bangladesh) . . . 896
Literary Magazines (Canada) . . . 896
Literary Magazines (The Caribbean) . . . 899
Literary Magazines (India) . . . 901
Literary Magazines (New Zealand) . . . 902

Literary Magazines (The Philippines) 904
Literary Magazines (South Africa) 905
Literary Magazines (South Pacific) 906
Literary Magazines (Sri Lanka) 907
Literary Magazines (West Africa) 908
Literary Organizations (Australia) 909
Literary Organizations (New Zealand) 910
Literature Board (Australia) 911
Livesay, Dorothy 912
Livingstone, Douglas James 913
Liyong, Taban lo 916
Lochhead, Douglas 917
Locke, Elsie 917
Lopez Tiempo, Edith 918
Loukakis, Angelo 918
Lovelace, Earl 919
Lower, Lennie 920
Loyalists 921
Lumbera, Bienvenido 922
Lurie, Morris 923

McAlpine, Rachel 925
McAndrew, Wordsworth 925
McAuley, James 926
McCauley, Sue 927
McClung, Nellie 928
McCormick, Eric Hall 928
McCrae, Hugh 929
McCulloch, Thomas 930
McCullough, Colleen 930
Macdonald, Caroline 931
McDonald, Ian 932
McDonald, Roger 932
MacEwen, Gwendolyn 933
McFadden, David 935
McFarlane, John Ebenzer Clare 935
McGee, Gregory William 936
McGill Movement (Canada) 937
MacIntyre, Ernest Thalayasingam 937
McKay, Claude 939
Mackay, Jessie 941
Mackenzie, Kenneth 941
McLachlan, Alexander 942
MacLennan, Hugh 942
MacLeod, Alistair 944
McLuhan, Marshall 944
McNeill, Anthony 945
McNeish, James 946
Macpherson, Jay 946
McQueen, Cilla 947
McQueen, Humphrey 948
McQueen, James 948
McTair, Dionyse 949
McWatt, Mark 949
McWhirter, George 950
Maddy, Yulissa Amadu 950
Mahapatra, Jayanta 951
Mahy, Margaret 952
Maiden, Jennifer 954
Mair, Charles 954
Mais, Roger 955
Malaysia and Singapore 956
Malawi 960
Malgonkar, Manohar 962
Malik, Keshav 964
Malley, Ern 964
Malouf, David 965
Malta 966
Manalang Gloria, Angela 968
Mandel, Eli 969
Mander, (Mary) Jane 970
Mangua, Charles 971
Manhire, Bill 971
Maniam, K. S. (Subramaniam Krishnan) . . . 972
Manifold, John Streeter 973
Maning, Frederick 974
Manning, Frederic 974
Mansfield, Katherine 975
Maori Myths and Legends (New Zealand) . . 977
Maori Oral Culture and
Literature (New Zealand) 979
Maori Theatre (New Zealand) 982
Mapanje, Jack 982
Marachera, Dambudzo 983
Marath, S. Menon 984
Markandaya, Kamala 984
Marlatt, Daphne 986
Marley, Bob 987

Marquez Benitez, Paz 988
Marriott, Anne 989
Marsh, Dame Ngaio 989
Marshall, Alan 990
Marshall, Joyce 991
Marshall, Owen 991
Marshall, Paule 992
Marshall, Tom 994
Martin, David 994
Martin, Egbert 995
Mason, Bruce Edward George 995
Mason, R. A. K. 997
Massa, Daniel 997
Masters, Olga 998
Mateship (Australia) 999
Mathers, Peter 1000
Matshoba, Mtutuzeli 1000
Mattera, Don 1001
Matthews, James David 1002
Matthews, Marc 1003
Matura, Mustapha 1003
Mau Mau War 1004
Mayne, Seymour 1005
Mayuga, Sylvia 1005
Mbise, Ismael R. 1006
Mda, Zakes 1006
Mehrotra, Arvind Krishna 1007
Mehta, Ved 1008
Melwani, Murli Das 1009
MEMOIRS 1009
Memoirs (Overviews) 1009
Memoirs (Australia) 1011
Memoirs (Canada) 1013
Memoirs and Reminiscences (New Zealand) 1015
Memoirs (Pakistan) 1016
Memoirs (South Africa) 1018
Mendes, Alfred H. 1020
Menen, Aubrey 1021
Menezes, Luis Mathias Armando 1022
Metcalf, John 1022
Middleton, O. E. 1023
Migrant Writing (Australia) 1024
Miller, Ruth 1025
Millin, Sarah Gertrude 1026
Minor Poets (India) 1027
Mistry, Rohinton 1027
Mitchell, Ken 1027
Mitchell, W. O. 1028
Mittelholzer, Edgar 1029
Mnthali, Felix 1031
Mo, Timothy 1031
Modern Novel (India) 1033
Mofolo, Thomas Mokopu 1033
Mokashi-Punekar, Shankar 1033
Monar, Rooplall 1034
Montano, Severino M. 1034
Montgomery, Lucy Maud 1035
Moo, Joash 1036
Moodie, Susanna 1036
Moorhead, Finola 1037
Moorhouse, Frank 1038
Mopeli-Paulus, Atwell Sidwell 1039
Moraes, Dom 1040
Mordecai, Pamela Claire 1040
Moreno, Virginia R. 1041
Morgan, Sally 1042
Morrieson, Ronald Hugh 1042
Morris, Mervyn 1043
Morrison, John 1043
Mowat, Farley 1044
Mphahlele, Es'kia (Ezekiel) 1045
Mpina, Edison 1047
Mtshali, Oswald Mbuyiseni 1047
Muchemwa, Kizito Zhiradzago 1048
Mudie, Ian 1049
Muhammad Haji Salleh 1049
Mukerji, Dhan Gopal 1050
Mukherjee, Bharati 1051
Mulaisho, Dominic 1052
Mulgan, Alan Edward 1053
Mulgan, John Alan 1053
Multiculturalism (Canada) 1053
Munonye, John 1056
Munro, Alice 1056
Murnane, Gerald 1058
Murray, Les 1059
Mutabaruka 1061
Mwangi, Meja 1061

Mysticism in Indian-English Literature . . . 1062
Myth in Indian-English Literature 1064
Mzamane, Mbulelo Vizikhungo 1067

Nagarajan, K. 1069
Nahal, Chaman 1070
Naidu, Sarojini 1070
Naik, M. K. 1071
Naipaul, Seepersad 1072
Naipaul, Shiva 1072
Naipaul, Vidiadhar Surajprasad 1073
Nair, Chandran 1075
Namjoshi, Suniti 1076
Nandan, Satendra Pratap 1077
Nandy, Pritish 1078
Narain, Harry 1079
Narasimhaiah, C. D. 1079
Narayan, Rasipuram Krishnaswami 1080
Narlikar, Jayant V. 1083
Narogin, Mudrooroo 1084
Nazareth, Peter 1085
Nazombe, Anthony 1086
Ndebele, Njabulo Simakahle 1086
Ndu, Pol Nnamuzikam 1087
Nehru, Jawaharlal 1088
Neilson, John Shaw 1089
Newlove, John 1090
New Zealand 1091
New Zealand in Canadian Literature 1094
Ngugi wa Thiong'o 1095
Nichol, bp 1097
Nichols, Grace 1098
Nicol, Abioseh 1099
Nigeria 1100
Nigerian Civil War 1101
Niland, D'Arcy 1102
Nirodbaran 1102
Njau, Rebecca 1103
Nkosi, Lewis 1103
Noonuccal, Oodgeroo 1104
Nortje, Arthur Kenneth 1105
NOVEL 1106
Novel (Overview) 1106
Novel (Australia) 1108
Novel (Bangladesh) 1113
Novel (Canada) 1114
Novel (The Caribbean) 1119
Novel (East Africa) 1123
Novel (Hong Kong) 1125
Novel (India) 1126
Novel (Malaysia) 1135
Novel (New Zealand) 1136
Novel (Pakistan) 1141
Novel (The Philippines) 1142
Novel and Short Fiction (Singapore) 1145
Novel (South Africa) 1148
Novel (South Central Africa) 1153
Novel (South Pacific) 1154
Novel (Sri Lanka) 1155
Novel (West Africa) 1159
Nowlan, Alden 1164
Nowra, Louis 1165
Ntiru, Richard Carl 1165
Nwankwo, Nkem 1166
Nwapa, Flora 1166
Nzekwu, Onuora 1167

Oakley, Barry 1169
O'Connor, Mark 1169
Oculi, Okello 1170
Ogilvie, William George Graham 1171
Ogot, Grace Akinyi 1171
Ogunyemi, Wale 1172
O'Hagan, Howard 1172
Ojaide, Tanure 1173
Okai, Atukwei 1173
Okara, Gabriel 1174
Okigbo, Ifeanyichukwu Christopher 1175
Okpewho, Isidore 1176
Okri, Ben 1177
Omar, Kaleem 1179
Omotoso, Kole 1180
Ondaatje, Michael 1180
Onwueme, Tess 1181
Orality in Indian Literature in English 1182
Osadebay, Dennis Chukude 1183
Osofisan, Babafemi Adyemi 1183
Ostenso, Martha 1184

O'Sullivan, Vincent Gerard 1185
Osundare, Niyi 1186
Outram, Richard 1187

Page, Geoff 1188
Page, P. K. 1188
Pakistan 1189
Palangyo, Peter K. 1194
Palmer, Cyril Everard 1195
Palmer, Nettie 1195
Palmer, Vance 1196
Pan, Lynn 1197
Pantoja-Hidalgo, Cristina 1198
Park, Ruth 1199
Parker, Sir Gilbert 1199
Parker, K. Langloh 1200
Parthasarathy, Rajagopal 1201
Patel, Gieve 1202
Paterson, A. B. 1203
Paton, Alan Stewart 1204
Patronage 1207
Patterson, Orlando 1208
p'Bitek, Okot 1209
Peacocke, Isabel Maud 1210
Pearson, Bill 1211
Pedley, Ethel C. 1211
Penton, Brian 1212
Peters, Lenrie 1212
Philip, Marlene Nourbese 1213
Philippines 1214
Phillips, A. A. 1219
Phillips, Caryl 1220
Pilgrim, Frank 1221
Pillai, Raymond C. 1221
Plaatje, Solomon Tshekisho 1222
Plomer, William Charles Franklyn 1224
POETRY 1226
Poetry (Overview) 1226
Poetry (Australia) 1230
Poetry (Bangladesh) 1235
Poetry (Canada) 1236
Poetry (The Caribbean) 1241
Poetry (East Africa) 1245
Poetry (Hong Kong) 1247
Poetry (India) 1247
Poetry (Malaysia) 1256
Poetry (Malta) 1257
Poetry (New Zealand) 1259
Poetry (Pakistan) 1263
Poetry (The Philippines) 1265
Poetry (Singapore) 1267
Poetry (South Africa) 1269
Poetry (South Central Africa) 1275
Poetry (South Pacific) 1276
Poetry (Sri Lanka) 1278
Poetry (West Africa) 1281
Political Novel (India) 1285
Pollard, Velma 1285
Pollock, Sharon 1285
Pongweni, Alec J. C. 1286
Popular Fiction (South Africa) 1287
Popular Song (The Caribbean) 1287
POPULAR WRITING 1287
Popular Writing (Overview) 1287
Popular Writing (Australia) 1289
Popular Writing (Canada) 1291
Popular Writing (East Africa) 1294
Popular Writing (New Zealand) 1295
Popular Writing (St Helena) 1296
Popular Writing (South Africa) 1297
Popular Writing (West Africa) 1300
Porter, Hal 1301
Porter, Peter 1302
Post-Colonial Theorists 1303
Praed, Rosa Caroline 1306
Pratt, E. J. 1307
Prichard, Katharine Susannah 1309
Pringle, Thomas 1310
Prison Literature (South Africa) 1312
Proctor, Raja 1314
PUBLISHING 1315
Publishing (Australia) 1315
Publishing (Canada) 1318
Publishing (The Caribbean) 1321
Publishing (New Zealand) 1325
Publishing (The Philippines) 1327
Publishing (St Helena) 1328
Publishing (South Africa) 1330

Publishing (South Pacific) 1332
Purdy, A. W. 1333

Quayle, Ada 1335

Raddall, Thomas Head 1336
Rafat, Taufiq 1337
Rajan, Balachandra 1337
Rajendra, Cecil 1338
Ramanujan, Attipat Krishnaswami 1339
Ranasinghe, Anne 1340
Rao, Raja 1341
Rao, Ranga 1344
Rastafarianism 1344
Rau, Santha Rama 1345
Reaney, James 1346
Reckord, Barrington (Barry) 1347
Reckord, Michael 1348
Redcam, Tom 1348
Rees, Rosemary 1349
Reeves, William Pember 1349
Regionalism in Canadian Literature in English 1350
Reid, V. S. 1353
Religion and Caste (India) 1355
Renee 1357
Reviewing (India) 1358
Rhone, Trevor D. 1358
Rhys, Jean 1359
Richards, David Adams 1361
Richardson, Henry Handel 1362
Richardson, John 1364
Richler, Mordecai 1365
Richmond, Angus 1366
Riley, Joan 1367
Ringwood, Gwen Pharis 1368
Rive, Richard Moore 1369
Rivera-Ford, Aida 1370
Roach, Eric 1370
Roberts, Sir Charles G. D. 1371
Roberts, Sheila 1372
Roberts, Theodore Goodridge 1373
Roberts, Walter Adolphe 1374
Robinson, Michael Massey 1375
Robinson, Roland 1375
Rodriguez, Judith 1376
Rolls, Eric Charles 1376
Romeo-Mark, Althea 1377
Romeril, John 1378
Rooke, Daphne Marie 1378
Rooke, Leon 1379
Roopnaraine, Rupert 1380
Rosca, Ninotchka 1380
Ross, Sinclair 1381
Rotimi, Ola 1382
Rotor, Arturo B. 1383
Roughsey, Dick 1383
Rowbotham, David 1384
Roy, Lucinda 1384
Roy, Namba 1385
Roy, Rammohun 1385
Rubadiri, David 1386
Rudd, Steele 1387
Ruganda, John 1388
Ruhumbika, Gabriel 1388
Rule, Jane 1389
Rushdie, Salman 1390
Ryga, George 1392

Sahgal, Nayantara 1394
Sahita Akademi 1395
St Helena 1395
St John, Bruce 1397
St Omer, Garth 1397
Salanga, Alfrredo N. 1398
Salkey, Andrew 1399
Salleh Ben Joned 1400
Salom, Philip 1401
Salutin, Rick 1401
Salverson, Laura Goodman 1402
Sangster, Charles 1403
Sanskrit Literature (India) 1403
Santos, Bienvenido N. 1409
Sarachchandra, Ediriwira 1411
Sargeson, Frank 1413
Saro-Wiwa, Ken 1415
Satchell, William 1416
Savery, Henry 1416

Scanlan, Nelle 1417
Scholefield, Alan (Tweedie) 1418
Schreiner, Olive Emilie Albertina 1418
SCIENCE FICTION 1420
Science Fiction and Fantasy (Australia) . . . 1420
Science Fiction and Fantasy (Canada) 1422
Science Fiction and Fantasy (India) 1423
Science Fiction and Fantasy (New Zealand) 1424
Scobie, Stephen 1425
Scott, Dennis 1426
Scott, Duncan Campbell 1427
Scott, F. R. 1428
Scott, John A. 1429
Scott, Mary 1430
Scully, William Charles 1431
Seaforth, Sybil 1431
Sealy, I. Allan 1432
Segun, Mabel 1433
Selormey, Francis 1433
Selvon, Samuel Dickson 1434
Sen, Pradip 1435
Senior, Olive 1436
Sepamla, Sydney Sipho 1437
Serote, Mongane Wally 1438
Serumaga, Robert 1439
Service, Robert W. 1440
Seshadri, Pundi 1440
Seth, Vikram 1441
Sethna, Kaikhushru Dhunjibhoy 1441
Seton, Ernest Thompson 1442
Sewell, Stephen 1443
Seymour, A. J. 1444
Seymour, Alan 1444
Shadbolt, Maurice 1445
Shahane, Vasant Anant 1446
Shapcott, Thomas 1447
Sharma, Pratap 1448
Sharma, Vera 1449
Shaw, Helen Lilian 1450
Shields, Carol 1450
Shinebourne, Janice 1451
SHORT FICTION 1451
Short Fiction (Overview) 1451
Short Fiction (Australia) 1455
Short Fiction (Canada) 1459
Short Fiction (The Caribbean) 1463
Short Fiction (Hong Kong) 1468
Short Fiction (India) 1469
Short Fiction (New Zealand) 1471
Short Fiction (Pakistan) 1474
Short Fiction (The Philippines) 1476
Short Fiction (Singapore) 1479
Short Fiction (South Africa) 1479
Short Fiction (South Pacific) 1482
Short Fiction (Sri Lanka) 1484
Short Fiction (West Africa) 1485
Sibal, Nina 1488
Sidhwa, Bapsi 1489
Sierra Leone 1490
Simpson, Colin 1491
Simpson, Louis 1492
Sinclair, Keith 1493
Singapore 1493
Singh, Khushwant 1493
Singh, Kirpal 1495
Sinnett, Frederick 1496
Skelton, Robin 1496
Skrzynecki, Peter 1497
Škvorecký, Josef 1498
Slater, Francis Carey 1498
Slessor, Kenneth 1499
Smart, Elizabeth 1500
Smith, A. J. M. 1501
Smith, Goldwin 1502
Smith, Mikey 1502
Smith, Pauline Janet 1503
Smith, Vivian 1505
Smith, Wilbur (Addison) 1506
Smither, Elizabeth Edwina 1506
Smithyman, (William) Kendrick 1507
Soaba, Russell 1508
Sofola, 'Zulu 1509
Song Fishermen, The (Canada) 1510
SONGS AND BALLADS 1510
Songs and Ballads (Australia) 1510
Songs and Ballads (Canada) 1512
Songs and Ballads (The Caribbean) 1514
Souster, Raymond 1516

South Africa 1517
South Asia in Canadian Literature 1522
South Pacific 1525
Southall, Ivan 1527
Soyinka, Wole 1528
Spence, Catherine Helen 1530
Spinner, Alice 1531
Springer, Eintou Pearl 1532
Sri Lanka 1532
Srinivas, Krishna 1535
Stead, Christian Karlson 1536
Stead, Christina 1537
Stephens, Alfred George 1539
Stephensen, P. R. 1539
Stewart, Douglas 1540
Stewart, Harold 1541
Stewart, John 1542
Stivens, Dal 1543
Stone, Louis 1544
Stow, Randolph 1544
Subramani 1545
Suhrawardy, (Hasan) Shahid 1546
Summers, Essie 1547
Sutherland, Efua 1548
Sutton, Eve 1549

Tagore, Rabindranath 1550
Tanzania 1551
Tasma 1552
Tay, Simon 1552
Taylor, Andrew 1553
Taylor, William 1554
Telemaque, Harold Milton 1554
Tench, Watkin 1555
Tennant, Kylie 1555
Tharoor, Shashi 1556
Thelwell, Michael 1557
Themba, Can 1558
Thomas, Audrey 1559
Thomas, Elean 1559
Thompson, Judith 1560
Thompson, Mervyn 1561
Thompson, Ralph 1562
Thomson, Edward William 1563
Thumboo, Edwin 1563
Tiempo, Edilberto 1565
Tlali, Miriam Mesoli 1565
Tompson, Charles 1566
Torres, Eric 1567
Traill, Catharine Parr 1567
TRANSLATION 1569
Translation (Overview) 1569
Translation (Australia) 1570
Translation (Bangladesh) 1573
Translation (Canada) 1574
Translation (India) 1579
Translation (The Philippines) 1581
Translation (South Africa) 1582
Translation (South Pacific) 1584
Tranter, John 1585
TRAVEL LITERATURE 1586
Travel Literature (Overview) 1586
Travel Literature (Canada) 1589
Travel Literature (Hong Kong) 1591
Travel Literature (Malaysia and Singapore) 1592
Travel Literature (New Zealand) 1594
Travel Literature (South Africa) 1595
Tsaloumas, Dimitris 1598
Tsodzo, Thompson 1599
Tucker, James 1600
Turner, Brian Lindsay 1600
Turner, Ethel 1601
Turner, George 1601
Tutuola, Amos 1602
Tuvera, Putli Kerima Polotan 1604
Tuwhare, Hone 1604
Ty-Casper, Linda 1605

Uganda 1608
Unaipon, David 1609
Uys, Pieter-Dirk 1609

Valgardson, W. D. 1611
van der Post, Laurens 1611
van Herk, Aritha 1612
Vanderhaeghe, Guy 1613
Vassanji, Moyez G. 1613

Vaux, James Hardy 1614
Venkataramani, Kaveripattinam Siddhanatha 1615
Vijayaraghavachariar, S. V. 1616
Villa, Jose Garcia 1616
Viray, Manuel A. 1618
Virgo, Seán 1618
Virtue, Vivian Lancaster 1619
Vivekananda, Swami 1619
Voaden, Herman 1620

wa Kabika, Lyamba 1622
Wachira, Godwin 1622
Waciuma, Charity 1623
Waddington, Miriam 1623
Wah, Fred 1624
Walcott, Derek 1624
Walcott, Roderick 1626
Walker, George F. 1627
Walker, Kath 1628
Wallace, Bronwen 1628
Wallace-Crabbe, Chris 1629
Walrond, Eric 1629
Walwicz, Ania 1630
Wangusa, Timothy 1631
WAR LITERATURE 1631
War Literature (Overview) 1631
War Literature (Australia) 1633
War Literature (Canada) 1634
War Literature (East Africa) 1635
War Literature (Malaysia and Singapore) 1635
War Literature (New Zealand) 1637
War Literature (South Africa) 1638
War Literature (West Africa) 1640
Ward, Russel 1640
Warung, Price 1641
Waten, Judah 1642
Watson, Jean Catherine 1642
Watson, Sheila 1643
Webb, Francis Charles 1643
Webb, Phyllis 1645
Webber, Albert Raymond Forbes 1645
Wedde, Ian 1646
Weller, Archie 1647
Wendt, Albert 1648
Wentworth, William Charles 1649
West, Morris 1650
White, Patrick 1651
Wickham, John 1652
Wiebe, Rudy 1653
Wijenaike, Punyakante 1655
Wikkramasinha, Lakdasa 1656
Wilding, Michael 1657
Wilhelm, Peter 1657
Williams, Denis 1658
Williamson, David 1659
Wilson, Ethel 1659
Winton, Tim 1660
Wiseman, Adele 1661
Women Poets (India) 1662
Women's Drama and Theatre (New Zealand) 1662
Women's Writing (South Africa) 1662
Wong, David T. K. 1666
Wong Phui Nam 1666
Wongar, B. 1667
Woodcock, George 1668
Wright, Judith 1668
Wrightson, Patricia 1670
Wynter, Sylvia 1671

Yap, Arthur 1672
Yardan, Shana 1673
Yates, Alan Geoffrey 1673
Yeo, Robert 1674
Yu, Ovidia 1675
Yuson, Alfredo 1676

Zambia 1677
Zeleza, Paul 1678
Zimbabwe 1678
Zimunya, Musaemura B. 1680
Zulueta da Costa, R. 1681
Zwicky, Fay 1681

INDEX 1683

INTRODUCTION

In 1989, when we concluded our work on *The Oxford Companion to Canadian Theatre*, we wrote in the introduction that we were 'eyeing the rich literatures of the British Commonwealth, and expect to sally forth soon on an even longer voyage of editorial exploration than the one we have just concluded'. Now, in 1994, we have ended that voyage and these two volumes constituting the *Encyclopedia of Post-Colonial Literatures in English* are a record of our activities during this five-year odyssey.

This *Encyclopedia* represents the work of 574 contributors drawn from around the world, authorities in their fields who have written some 1,600 entries on a wide variety of topics in the area of post-colonial literatures in English. We are aware of the fact that the term 'post-colonial' is not as precise as one would like, but it has always proven difficult to find completely satisfactory nomenclature that would accommodate, for example, the literatures of such diverse countries as Canada, Nigeria, Sri Lanka, and New Zealand. Terms such as 'new literatures' or 'emergent literatures' do not adequately describe the literatures in English of Canada, Australia, and New Zealand, for example, which have a relatively long and established history.

We employ the term 'post-colonial' in the sense in which Bill Ashcroft, Gareth Griffith, and Helen Tiffin use it in *The Empire Writes Back: Theory and Practice in Post-Colonial Literatures* (1989): 'We use the term "post-colonial", however, to cover all the culture affected by the imperial process from the moment of colonization to the present day.' The entries 'Post-Colonial Theorists' and 'Criticism (Overview)' in the *Encyclopedia* are also useful in clarifying the term 'post-colonial'.

We have excluded the literatures of England, Scotland, Wales, and Ireland because they are already well documented in scholarly reference works and to have included them in these volumes would inevitably have reduced the coverage that we wished to extend to those literatures in English that have not been so extensively examined and documented. And while some of the finest writing in English in the twentieth century has come from the colonies of the former British Commonwealth and the Philippines, it has not generally been accorded due recognition and scholarly assessment.

The entries in the *Encyclopedia of Post-Colonial Literatures in English* encompass genres, major subjects, and critical biographies of writers. We also include entries on each country or region whose literatures are discussed in these volumes; these entries describe the countries or regions in terms of geography, history, religion(s), economy, politics, and culture. For a number of important genre entries and subject entries we have included '*overviews*', which offer a synoptic view of the field. In addition, we have included a number of entries specifically associated with particular countries: in the case of India, for example, there are major entries on *Sanskrit Literature* and on *Gandhi in Indian-English Literature*; in the case of Australia there are entries on *Ireland and Irish Values* (Australia) and *Jewish Writing* (Australia). The advice of our national and regional editors has been invaluable in this regard.

The Table of Contents shows the rich and varied nature of the genre entries, subject entries, and critical and biographical sketches representing the literatures in English of Australia, Bangladesh, Canada, the Caribbean, East Africa, Gibraltar, Hong Kong, India, Malaysia, Malta, New Zealand, Pakistan, the Philippines, Singapore, Sri Lanka, St Helena, South Africa, South

Central Africa, the South Pacific, and West Africa. We have encouraged our contributors to adopt, where appropriate, a comparative approach, comparing works with those by other writers in the same country or region and with those by writers in different countries or regions.

Entries are arranged alphabetically; readers should note that bolding throughout the text indicates that these authors or subjects have entries of their own. Dates in parentheses refer to first publication. We have given, where appropriate, cross references to relevant subject entries, genres, and authors. At the end of many entries suggestions for further reading are listed; although these works cited constitute an extensive research resource, it has not been the intention of the editors or contributors to provide exhaustive bibliographical information.

The entries that were chosen for brief treatment allowed mainly for factual information, but most entries were allotted sufficient space for contributors to supplement factual information with critical commentary. We have always believed it to be possible to combine information, evaluation, and interpretation in concisely written entries that can be interesting and insightful both to the specialist and the general reader. Genre entries have been allotted generous space — those on the novel, for example, run to some 30,000 words; the combined entries on the novel, drama, poetry, short fiction, and poetry constitute a significant work in themselves.

If we were to select a second principle governing our editorial work, it would be that we have sought to respect the individual voices of our many contributors from so many lands while maintaining a necessary sense of common purpose and editorial consistency.

We have benefited enormously from the generosity of many people who have assisted us with their advice and guided us with their expertise. Our first and primary debt is to our Board of Research Consultants — Professors Diana Brydon, Gwendolyn Davies, John P. Matthews, Govind Sharma, and Rowland Smith. Between 1987 and 1992 the Board met on six occasions at the University of Guelph where it offered invaluable help and guidance to the editors. Others who assisted greatly include Professor G. D. Killam, Canada, Professor Chris Tiffin, Australia, and Professor Bruce King, USA.

Because of the magnitude of our project and the many literatures we were documenting, we drew upon the expertise of a number of national and regional editors. They represent some of the most knowledgeable scholars in post-colonial literatures in English. We thank most sincerely Professor Stephen H. Arnold (Cameroon), Professor Diana Brydon (Canada), Professor Edward Baugh (The Caribbean), Professor Mimi Chan (Hong Kong), Professor Isagani R. Cruz (Philippines), Philip Dennis and Ann Taylor (Gibraltar), Professor Ken Goodwin (Australia), Professor D. C. R. A. Goonetilleke (Sri Lanka), Professor Alamgir Hashmi (Bangladesh and Pakistan), Professor G. D. Killam (East Africa and West Africa), Professor Daniel Massa (Malta), Professor C. D. Narasimhaiah, with Professor Shyamala Narayan (India), Professor Kirpal Singh (Malaysia and Singapore), Professor Terry Sturm (New Zealand), and Professor Chris Tiffin (South Pacific).

We were very fortunate in our staff. Olga Griffin joined us at the outset of the project and was responsible for all inputting, data collection, correspondence, and the maintenance of a complex web of electronic files. She was essential to the work. Ruth Happy, our efficient assistant editor in 1990–1, established many of our working procedures before going on to doctoral studies. She was succeeded by Jennifer Kelly, assistant editor and research co-ordinator, who worked tirelessly to bring the *Encyclopedia* to its conclusion before she too proceeded to take up doctoral studies in the area of post-colonial literatures in English. She proved to be an ideal colleague.

Les R. Dunn, President, Micro Management Systems, Guelph, Canada, prepared the Camera Ready Copy of these two volumes. In collaboration with Eugene Benson, he also designed the program that created the text-generated index, an unusual feature in so large a work as this encyclopedia. The index will help readers locate references to thousands of authors, books, publishing houses, theatre companies, individual short stories and poems, and other relevant literary materials to an extent that would be impossible otherwise. The program designed by Les Dunn and Eugene Benson was the subject of a paper, 'The "Routledge Encyclopaedia" Project: Indexing Tools and Management Techniques for Large Documents', published in *Literary and Linguistic Computing*, vol. 8, no. 2 (1993).

We are especially grateful to all our contributors who responded patiently and generously to our many queries. In a number of instances we had to cut entries that were too long; we thank these contributors for accepting our editorial surgery with such understanding. During our three-year correspondence with our contributors, we established many epistolary friendships that we have enjoyed greatly; the completion of this multi-authored encyclopedia represents international collegiality at its finest.

We are grateful to many other people who helped us: Dr John Black, Chief Librarian, the University of Guelph, and his staff, particularly Helen Salmon, Patricia Eaves, Pearl Milne (who cheerfully operated the library's optical scanner on our behalf), and Dr Moshie Dahms. We received generous clerical help from Janice Walker, Maria Walker, Gail McGinnis, Fran Keen, Betty King, and Lori Barnsley. To Carol Sherman, Dorothy Collins, Sybil Thorn, and Judy Grasmuck we owe special thanks. Walter McGregor spent many hours helping with all aspects of indexing. In her capacity as Chair of the Department of English, the University of Guelph, Professor Constance M. Rooke encouraged our work and provided generous office space and ancillary services. Dr Carole Stewart, Dean of the College of Arts, the University of Guelph, was also most helpful. Dr Renate Benson, the University of Guelph, helped with various editorial duties, as did Ormonde Benson, Shaun Benson, and Dione Holmes. Barbara Conolly read portions of the book at the proofing stage with an experienced editorial eye. For advice on various aspect of computing technology we thank Madge Brochet, Computing Services, the University of Guelph. Lise Rochon, Communication's Officer, the Canada Council, supplied us with useful statistics concerning the Council. Graduate students Danludi Bature, Heather Smythe, and Yong Huang did useful checking work as did undergraduate students Liana di Marco and Markus Kremer. We acknowledge gratefully the help of Alison Barr, formerly an editor at Routledge, who was of great assistance at the early stages of work. Since 1992 we have benefited greatly from the advice of Alex Clark, development editor at Routledge. Leonard Conolly expresses particular thanks to the Warden and Fellows of Robinson College, Cambridge, for electing him to a Bye Fellowship in 1991 to work on the *Encyclopedia.*

When we commenced planning the *Encyclopedia of Post-Colonial Literatures in English* in 1987, we received the enthusiastic support of Dr David Murray, then Dean of the College of Arts, the University of Guelph, who had also supported us throughout the preparation of *The Oxford Companion to Canadian Theatre.* In 1987 the Office of Research, the University of Guelph, awarded the editors a generous grant from the Research Excellence Fund in order to finance our preliminary planning sessions. In 1989 the Social Sciences and Humanities Research Council of Canada awarded the editors the generous grant that made this work possible, followed by a supplementary grant in 1992. Like so many Canadian scholars, we are deeply indebted to the Council, which we thank most sincerely. We are also indebted to the Alumni Association of the University of Guelph, which awarded us a grant in 1992 that helped us in the last stages of preparing the *Encyclopedia.* Trent University also generously assisted in the final preparation of the book.

And once again we thank Renate Benson and Barbara Conolly, who have tolerated the innumerable meetings and long working days associated with the complex task of editing this *Encyclopedia.* We hope that the final product meets with their approbation.

Guelph and Peterborough, Canada
April 1994

EUGENE BENSON
L.W. CONOLLY

ACKNOWLEDGMENTS

James C. Aboud: 'Pizza', from *The Stone Rose* (1986). Reprinted by permission of the author.

Fleur Adcock: 'Advice to a Discarded Lover', from *Tigers* (1967); 'Against Coupling', from *High Tide in the Garden* (1971). Reprinted by permission of Oxford University Press, New Zealand.

John Agard: 'Palm Tree King', from *Mangoes and Bullets: Selected and New Poems 1974–1982* (1985). Reprinted by permission of Serpent's Tail Publishers, England.

Jared Angira: 'Growing on', from *Cascades* (1979). Reprinted by permission of Longman Group UK.

bill bissett: Quotations reprinted by permission of Talonbooks, Canada.

George Bowering: 'My Father in New Zealand', from *Landfall* (1986). Reprinted by permission of The Caxton Press, New Zealand.

Charles Brasch: 'In your Presence', from *Ambulando* (1964). Reprinted by permission of The Caxton Press, New Zealand, and the author.

Charles Bruce: 'Fisherman's Son' and 'Words Are Never Enough'. Reprinted by permission of Harry Bruce, literary executor.

Alistair Campbell: 'The Return', from *Wild Honey* (1964). Reprinted by permission of the author.

Martin Carter: 'Letter 1' and 'Letter 2', from *Poems of Resistance* (1954); 'Shape and Motion Three', from *Poems of Shape and Motion* (1955); 'Being Always', from *Poems of Affinity* (1980). Reprinted by permission of Demerara Publishers Ltd., Guyana.

Sydney David Clouts: 'A Pool for the Image', 'Prince Henry the Navigator', 'Residuum', and 'Within', from *Collected Poems* (1984). Reprinted by permission of Marge Clouts, literary executor.

Christine Craig: 'All Things Bright and Beautiful', from *Quadrille for Tigers* (1984). Reprinted by permission of Mina Press, USA.

Eileen Duggan: 'And at the End', from *Poems* (1937); 'Admissions', from *More Poems* (1951). Reprinted by permission of Mark Horton, literary executor.

Lauris Edmond: Quotations reprinted by permission of Oxford University Press, New Zealand.

Nissim Ezekiel: 'The Patriot' and 'Night of the Scorpion', from *Latter-Day Psalms* (1982). Reprinted by permission of Oxford University Press, India.

Barbara Ferland: 'Le Petit Paysan (Modigliani)', from *Caribbean Voices* (1970). Reprinted by permission of the author.

Anne French: From *All Cretans Are Liars* (1987). Reprinted by permission of Auckland University Press, New Zealand, and the author.

Judy Hamilton: 'epitaph', from *Rain Carvers* (1990). Reprinted by permission of Sandberry Press, Jamaica.

Kaiser Haq: 'Moon', from *A Little Ado* (1978). Reprinted by permission of the author.

Alamgir Hashmi: 'My Second in Kentucky' and 'Ghazals', from *My Second in Kentucky* (1981); 'Poem in Pakistan', from *This Time in Lahore* (1983); from *America Is a Punjabi Word* (1979). Reprinted by permission of the author.

A. L. Hendriks: 'Jamaican Small Gal', from *To Speak Simply* (1986). Reprinted by permission of Agenda Magazine and Editions, England, and Diana Nelson Hendriks, literary executor.

Kevin Ireland: From *Literary Cartoons* (1977). Reprinted by permission of Oxford University Press, New Zealand.

D. G. Jones: 'A Problem of Space'. Reprinted by permission of the author.

Lakshmi Kannan: 'Fruits', from *The Glow and the Gray* (1976). Reprinted by permission of Writers Workshop, Calcutta, India.

Fatima Lim: 'Where I Am From', from *Wandering Roots 1978–1988* (1991). Reprinted by permission of Anvil Publishing, Inc., Philippines.

Shirley Geok-Lin Lim: 'Bukit China' and 'I Look for Women', from *Modern Secrets* (1989). Reprinted by permission of Dangaroo Press, Australia.

Bill Manhire: 'Children', from *Good Looks* (1982). Reprinted by permission of Auckland University Press, New Zealand, and the author.

Cilla McQueen: 'Vegetable Garden Poem IV', from *Anti Gravity* (1984). Reprinted by permission of the author.

Dionyse McTair: 'Song', from *Notes Towards an Escape from Death* (1987). Reprinted by permission of New Beacon Books Ltd., England.

Shankar Mokashi-Punekar: From *Parodigms* (1989). Reprinted by permission of Writers Workshop, Calcutta, India.

Dom Moraes: 'Babur', 'French Lesson', 'After Hours', and 'Letter to my Mother', from *The Collected Poems of Dom Moraes, 1957–1987* (1987). Reprinted by permission of Penguin Books India Pvt. Ltd., and the author.

M. K. Naik: From *Indian Clerihews* (1989); from *Indian Limericks* (1990). Reprinted by permission of Writers Workshop, Calcutta, India.

Anthony Nazombe: 'The Racket', from *The Haunting Wind* (1990). Reprinted by permission of the author.

Mark O'Connor: 'Fire-Stick Farming', from *Fire-Stick Farming: Selected Poems 1972–90* (1990). Reprinted by permission of the author.

Christopher Okigbo: 'Distances', from *Labyrinths, with Path of Thunder* (1971). Reprinted by permission of Heinemann Publishers (Oxford) Ltd., England.

Richard Outram: 'Epitaph for an Angler', from *The Promise of Light* (1979). Reprinted by permission of the author.

R. Parthasarathy: 'Delhi' was originally published in *New Letters* 48:2/3 (1982). Selections are reprinted with the permission of *New Letters* and the Curators of the University of Missouri-Kansas City, USA.

Alan Paton: 'I have approached', from *Knocking on the Door* (1975). Reprinted by permission of David Philip Publishers (Pty) Ltd., South Africa.

E. J. Pratt: *Towards the Last Spike* and 'Newfoundland Seamen', from *E.J Pratt: Complete Poems* (1989). Reprinted by permission of the University of Toronto Press, Canada.

Al Purdy: 'Trees at the Arctic Circle', from *The Collected Poems of Al Purdy* (1986). Reprinted by permission of McClelland and Stewart Inc., Canada.

Anne Ranasinghe: From *Not Even Shadows* (1989). Reprinted by permission of the author.

S. Santhi: From *Rhyme and Punnishment* (1975). Reprinted by permission of Arnold Publishers, India.

Stephen Scobie: From *Dunino*. Reprinted by permission of Véhicule Press, Canada; 'Mona Lisa', from *Ghosts: A Glossary of the Intertext* (1990). Reprinted by permission of Wolsak and Wynn Publishers Ltd., Canada.

Pradip Sen: 'In Each of Us', from *And Then the Sun* (1960). Reprinted by permission of the author.

Thomas Shapcott: 'Autumn', from *Shabbytown Calendar* (1975). Reprinted by permission of the University of Queensland Press, Australia.

Kirpal Singh: 'Old Age', from *Palm Readings* (1986). Reprinted by permission of Graham Brash (Pte) Ltd., Singapore.

Elizabeth Smither: 'A White Camellia', from *Shakespeare Virgins* (1983). Reprinted by permission of the author.

Talosaga Tolovae: 'To Albert', from *The Shadows Within* (1984). Reprinted by permission of Outrigger Publishers.

Eric Torres: From *The Smile on Smokey Mountain and Other Poems* (1992). Reprinted by permission of Ateneo de Manila University, Philippines.

John Tranter: 'Those Gods Made Permanent', from *Under Berlin* (1988). Reprinted by permission of the University of Queensland Press, Australia.

Brian Lindsay Turner: 'The Stopover', from *Ladders of Rain* (1978). Reprinted by permission of the author.

Manuel A. Viray: 'Eighteen Derivations', from *Morning Song* (1990). Reprinted by permission of De La Salle University Press, Philippines.

Miriam Waddington: 'Canadians', from *Collected Poems* (1986). Reprinted by permission of Oxford University Press, Canada.

Ania Walwicz: From 'Australia'. Reprinted by permission of the author.

K. S. Yadurajan: From *It Couldn't Be Verse — Or Worse Either* (1988). Reprinted by permission of Writers Workshop, Calcutta, India.

Contributors

P. A. Abraham
Gujarat University, India

Ian Adam
University of Calgary, Canada

Graham C. Adams
Acadia University, Canada

Olusegun Adekoya
Obafemi Awolowo University, Nigeria

Debra Adelaide
Australia

Funso Aiyejina
University of the West Indies, Jamaica

Ayo Akinwale
University of Ilorin, Nigeria

Adetayo Alabi
University of Saskatchewan, Canada

Peter F. Alexander
University of New South Wales, Australia

Carolyn Allen
University of the West Indies, Jamaica

Syed Ameeruddin
The New College, Madras, India

Sonia Nishat Amin
Bangladesh

G. S. Amur
Dharwad, India

Don Anderson
University of Sydney, Australia

Mia Anderson
Canada

Thelma E. Arambulo
University of the Philippines

John Arnold
Monash University, Australia

Stephen Arnold
University of Alberta, Canada

Yaw Asante
University of Calgary, Canada

Susan Ash
Edith Cowan University, Australia

Bill Ashcroft
University of New South Wales, Australia

David Attwell
University of Natal, South Africa

Margaret Atwood
Canada

Chris Kwame Awuyah
West Chester University, USA

E. A. Babalola
University of Lagos, Nigeria

Lynette Baer
University of Queensland, Australia

Nancy Bailey
University of Guelph, Canada

Abdul Majid B. Nabi Baksh
Malaysia

Douglas Barbour
University of Alberta, Canada

Jacqueline Bardolph
Université Nice-Sophia Antipolis, France

Harold Barratt
University College of Cape Breton, Canada

Angela Barry
Bermuda

Christine Barsby
University of Cape Town, South Africa

Judy L. Barton
Canada

Margaret Kent Bass
Vanderbilt University, USA

Edward Baugh
University of the West Indies, Jamaica

Julie Beddoes
University of Saskatchewan, Canada

Jameela Begum A.
University of Kerala, India

K. C. Belliappa
University of Mysore, India

Bruce Bennett
University of New South Wales, Australia

Wycliffe Bennett
Creative Production and Training Centre, Jamaica

Cliff Benson
University of the South Pacific, Fiji

Eugene Benson
University of Guelph, Canada

Neil Besner
University of Winnipeg, Canada

Curwen Best
University of the West Indies, Barbados

Frank Birbalsingh
York University, Canada

Delys Bird
University of Western Australia

Sebastian Black
University of Auckland, New Zealand

Gary Boire
Wilfrid Laurier University, Canada

Margriet Bonnin
Griffith University, Australia

Laurel Boone
Canada

Lawrence Bourke
Edith Cowan University, Australia

Anthony Boxill
University of New Brunswick, Canada

Veronica Brady
University of Western Australia

Laurence Breiner
Boston University, USA

Rachel Feldhay Brenner
University of Wisconsin-Madison, USA

Bridget Brereton
University of the West Indies, Trinidad and Tobago

Roger J. Bresnahan
Michigan State University, USA

Anne Brewster
Curtin University, Australia

Erna Brodber
Gettysburg College, USA

Stewart Brown
University of Birmingham, England

Patrick Bryan
University of the West Indies, Jamaica

Diana Brydon
University of Guelph, Canada

Patrick Buckridge
Griffith University, Australia

Elizabeth Caffin
Auckland University Press, New Zealand

Carole H. Carpenter
York University, Canada

Brenda Carr
University of Western Ontario, Canada

David Carter
Griffith University, Australia

Frederick Ivor Case
University of Toronto, Canada

Leonard Casper
USA

Mimi Chan
University of Hong Kong

Linley Chapman
University of Hawaii, USA

Michael Chapman
University of Natal, South Africa

Kalyan K. Chatterjee
University of Burdwan, India

P. S. Chauhan
Beaver College, USA

Vijay Lakshmi (Chauhan)
Community College of Philadelphia, USA

Colin Cheong
Singapore

Kabir Chowdhury
Pakistan

Helen Chukwuma
University of Cincinnati, USA

Laurie Clancy
La Trobe University, Australia

David Clandfield
University of Toronto, Canada

Cherry Clayton
University of Guelph, Canada

Stephen Clingman
University of Massachusetts, USA

Rhonda Cobham
Amherst College, USA

Dorothy Colmer
Australia

John Colmer
Australia

L. W. Conolly
Trent University, Canada

Geraldine D. E. Constance
South Africa

Carolyn Cooper
University of the West Indies, Jamaica

Vincent O. Cooper
University of the Virgin Islands, US Virgin Islands

Wayne F. Cooper
USA

Carlo Coppola
Oakland University, USA

Gareth Cornwell
Rhodes University, South Africa

Sheila Coulson
University of the West Indies, Jamaica

Tim Couzens
University of the Witwatersrand, South Africa

Terrence Craig
Mount Allison University, Canada

Ralph J. Crane
University of Waikato, New Zealand

C. A. Cranston
University of Tasmania, Australia

Al Creighton
University of Guyana

Terry Crowley
University of Waikato, New Zealand

Isagani R. Cruz
De La Salle University, Philippines

Selwyn R. Cudjoe
Wellesley College, USA

Lynda Curnoe
Canada

Cyril Dabydeen
Canada

J. Michael Dash
University of the West Indies, Jamaica

Barrie Davies
University of New Brunswick, Canada

Gwendolyn Davies
Acadia University, Canada

Richard A. Davies
Acadia University, Canada

Robertson Davies
University of Toronto, Canada

Kwame Dawes
University of South Carolina, USA

Douglas Daymond
University of Guelph, Canada

Margaret Daymond
University of Natal, South Africa

Jean D'Costa
Hamilton College, USA

Leon de Kock
University of South Africa

Ma. Teresa Luz De Manuel
Philippines

Lakshmi de Silva
University of Kelaniya, Sri Lanka

Dudley De Souza
Nanyang Technological University, Singapore

Misao Dean
University of Victoria, Canada

Dirk Den Hartog
Victoria University of Technology, Australia

Philip Dennis
England

Hubert Devonish
University of the West Indies, Jamaica

T. N. Dhar
Kashmir University, India

Robert Dixon
James Cook University, Australia

Stan Dragland
University of Western Ontario, Canada

Arthur Drayton
University of Kansas, USA

Ann Dry
National English Literary Museum, South Africa

Chris Dunton
National University of Lesotho

Jean-Pierre Durix
Université de Bourgogne, France

Len Early
York University, Canada

Afam Ebeogu
Abia State University, Nigeria

Murray Edmond
University of Auckland, New Zealand

Brian Edwards
Deakin University, Australia

Paul Edwards
Scotland

Ebele Eko
University of Calabar, Nigeria

Mohamed Elias
Calicut University, India

Isaac Elimimian
California Polytechnic State University, USA

David English
Victoria University of Technology, Australia

Damiana Eugenio
University of the Philippines

Patricia Excell
Australia

Margery Fee
University of British Columbia, Canada

Doreen G. Fernandez
Ateneo de Manila University, Philippines

Lloyd Fernando
Malaysia

Nihal Fernando
University of Peradeniya, Sri Lanka

Douglas Fetherling
Canada

Marya Fiamengo
University of British Columbia, Canada

Elaine Savory (Fido)
University of Maryland, USA

John J. Figueroa
England

Alan Filewod
University of Guelph, Canada

Timothy Findley
Canada

Howard Fink
Concordia University, Canada

Ross Fitzgerald
Griffith University, Australia

Peter Fitzpatrick
Monash University, Australia

Marcelino A. Foronda Jr.
Manila Bulletin Publishing Corp., Philippines

Richard Fotheringham
University of Queensland, Australia

Adrian Fowler
Memorial University of Newfoundland, Canada

Carol Franklin
Australia

Anne French
Oxford University Press, New Zealand

Alan Frost
La Trobe University, Australia

Anne Fuchs
Université de Nice-Sophia Antipolis, France

Joseph A. Galdon
Ateneo de Manila University, Philippines

Colin Gardner
University of Natal, South Africa

Lourdes Gatmaitan-Banez
USA

Allan J. Gedalof
University of Western Ontario, Canada

Carole Gerson
Simon Fraser University, Canada

Peter Gibbons
University of Waikato, New Zealand

Rawle Gibbons
University of the West Indies, Trinidad and Tobago

James Gibbs
Université de Liège, Belgium

Robert Gibbs
Canada

Betty Gilderdale
New Zealand

Susan Gingell
University of Saskatchewan, Canada

Gîtahi Gîtîtî
University of Rhode Island, USA

Michael Gnarowski
Carleton University Press, Canada

Barbara Godard
York University, Canada

Kevin Goddard
National English Literary Museum, South Africa

Goh Eck Keng
Malaysia

Terry Goldie
York University, Canada

Andrew Gonzalez
De La Salle University, Philippines

Anson Gonzalez
Trinidad and Tobago

Brian N. S. Gooch
University of Victoria, Canada

Ken Goodwin
University of Southern Queensland, Australia

Yasmine Gooneratne
Macquarie University, Australia

D. C. R. A. Goonetilleke
University of Kelaniya, Sri Lanka

Rebe Gostand
Australia

Barry Gough
Wilfrid Laurier University, Canada

Sherrill Grace
University of British Columbia, Canada

Stephen Gray
South Africa

Dorothy Green
Australia

Michael Green
University of Natal, South Africa

Glyne A. Griffith
University of the West Indies, Barbados

H. C. Groenewald
Rand Afrikaans University, South Africa

Estrellita V. Gruenberg
De La Salle University, Philippines

Naresh Guha
India

Sneja Gunew
University of Victoria, Canada

Kristjana Gunnars
University of Alberta, Canada

Liz Gunner
University of London, England

G. S. Balarama Gupta
Gulbarga University, India

Malcolm Hacksley
Rhodes University, South Africa

D. A. Hadfield
Canada

Rodney Hall
Australia

Patricia Handley
South Africa

Cliff Hanna
University of Newcastle, Australia

Kaiser Haq
University of Dhaka, Bangladesh

Bernie Harder
University of Windsor, Canada

Geoffrey Haresnape
University of Cape Town, South Africa

Syd Harrex
Flinders University of South Australia

James Harrison
University of Guelph, Canada

Kenneth W. Harrow
Michigan State University, USA

Shuaib bin Hasan
Pakistan

Alamgir Hashmi
Pakistan

Temple Hauptfleisch
University of Stellenbosch, South Africa

Jay Heale
Bookchat, South Africa

Trevor Hearl
England

Ajay Heble
University of Guelph, Canada

John Henningham
University of Queensland, Australia

Noel Henricksen
Australia

Laurie Hergenhan
University of Queensland, Australia

Kendel Hippolyte
Folk Research Centre, St Lucia

Paul Hjartarson
University of Alberta, Canada

Bruce W. Hodgins
Trent University, Canada

Patrick Holland
University of Guelph, Canada

Andrew Horn
University of the South Pacific, Western Samoa

Coral Ann Howells
University of Reading, England

Graham Huggan
Harvard University, USA

Eva Hunter
University of the Western Cape, South Africa

Geoffrey Hutchings
University of Zululand, South Africa

Van Ikin
University of Western Australia

Emilia V. Ilieva
Bulgaria

C. T. Indra
University of Madras, India

Patricia Ismond
University of the West Indies, Trinidad and Tobago

K. R. Srinivasa Iyengar
India

Roberta Jackson
University of Calgary, Canada

J. U. Jacobs
University of Natal, South Africa

S. Jagadisan
Presidency College, Madras, India

Jasbir Jain
University of Rajasthan, India

Adeola James
University of Guyana

Louis James
University of Kent, England

Karl Jirgens
University of Toronto, Canada

Kishen Jit
University of Malaya, Malaysia

Phil Joffe
University of Natal, South Africa

David Johnson
University of Sussex, England

Joyce Johnson
Delaware State College, USA

Joyce Jonas
Guyana

Adam Jones
J. W. Goethe-Universität, Germany

Bridget Jones
Roehampton Institute, England

Dorothy Jones
University of Wollongong, Australia

Lawrence Jones
University of Otago, New Zealand

Adil Jussawalla
India

Egara Kabaji
Kenyatta University, Kenya

Braj B. Kachru
University of Illinois, USA

Smaro Kamboureli
University of Victoria, Canada

Chelva Kanaganayakam
University of Toronto, Canada

Chetan Karnani
University of Jodhpur, India

R. K. Kaul
Delhi University, India

Nancy Keesing
Australia

Jennifer Kelly
University of Calgary, Canada

Veronica Kelly
University of Queensland, Australia

Douglas Kerr
University of Hong Kong

Khoo Sim Lyn
Nanyang Technological University, Singapore

G. D. Killam
University of Guelph, Canada

Bruce King
University of Guelph, Canada

Thelma B. Kintanar
University of the Philippines

Viney Kirpal
Indian Institute of Technology, India

Wallace Kirsop
Monash University, Australia

Dirk Klopper
Vista University, South Africa

Stephen Knight
University of Melbourne, Australia

R. P. Knowles
University of Guelph, Canada

Koh Buck Song
The Straits Times, Singapore

Koh Tai Ann
National University of Singapore

Devindra Kohli
Universities of Frankfurt and Essen, Germany

Katherine Koller
University of Alberta, Canada

Bala Kothandaraman
Osmania University, India

Mini Krishnan
Macmillan India Ltd., India

S. Krishnan
Indian Review of Books, India

Gita Krishnankutty
India

Janice Kulyk Keefer
University of Guelph, Canada

Joy Kuropatwa
University of Western Ontario, Canada

John Kwan-Terry
Nanyang Technological University, Singapore

Christopher Laird
Trinidad and Tobago

Ananda Lal
Jadavpur University, India

Karen Lamb
Australia

Linda Lamont-Stewart
York University, Canada

Marva Lashley
Barbados

Alan Lawson
University of Queensland, Australia

John LeBlanc
University of British Columbia, Canada

F. M. G. (Max) Le Blond
Nanyang Technological University, Singapore

Christopher Lee
University of Southern Queensland, Australia

John Robert Lee
St Lucia

Michele Leggott
University of Auckland, New Zealand

J. M. Leighton
South Africa

John Lennox
York University, Canada

Margaret Lenta
University of Natal, South Africa

Leong Liew Geok
National University of Singapore

Susan Lever
University of New South Wales, Australia

Marcia Leveson
University of the Witwatersrand, South Africa

Olive Lewin
Jamaica

Peter-John Lewis
Australia

Shirley Lim
University of California, USA

Walter S. H. Lim
National University of Singapore

Cedric Lindo
Jamaica

Jennifer Livett
University of Tasmania, Australia

Jacqueline Lo
University of Newcastle, Australia

Douglas G. Lochhead
Mount Allison University, Canada

Cecily Lockett
Rand Afrikaans University, South Africa

Rosario C. Lucero
Philippines

Gloria Lyn
University of the West Indies, Jamaica

Gerald Lynch
University of Ottawa, Canada

Doireann MacDermott
University of Barcelona, Spain

Ian McDonald
Guyana

Mary Lu MacDonald
Canada

Brian McDonnell
New Zealand

Dennis McEldowney
New Zealand

Robin McGrath
Memorial University of Newfoundland, Canada

Craig MacKenzie
Rand Afrikaans University, South Africa

John McLaren
Victoria University of Technology, Australia

Carrie MacMillan
Mount Allison University, Canada

Lorraine McMullen
University of Ottawa, Canada

Howard McNaughton
University of Canterbury, New Zealand

Jane McRae
University of Auckland, New Zealand

Mark McWatt
University of the West Indies, Barbados

George McWhirter
University of British Columbia, Canada

John Maddocks
Australia

Obi Maduakor
University of Nigeria

Hena Maes-Jelinek
Université de Liège, Belgium

Alberto Manguel
Canada

K. S. Maniam
University of Malaya, Malaysia

Edna Zapanta Manlapaz
Ateneo de Manila University, Philippines

Phillip Mann
Victoria University of Wellington, New Zealand

Carol P. Marsh-Lockett
Georgia State University, USA

John Stephen Martin
University of Calgary, Canada

Daniel Massa
University of Malta, Malta

Brian Matthews
University of London, England

John Matthews
Queen's University, Canada

Purnima Mehta
India

Patricia Merivale
University of British Columbia, Canada

Joan Meterlerkamp
University of Natal, South Africa

Marianne Micros
University of Guelph, Canada

Peter Midgley
National English Literary Museum, South Africa

Roy Miki
Simon Fraser University, Canada

Bernard Minol
University of Papua New Guinea

Sudesh Mishra
University of the South Pacific, Fiji

Vijay Mishra
Murdoch University, Australia

Ramesh Mohan
India

Shankar Mokashi-Punekar
Mysore University, India

Bruce Molloy
Queensland University of Technology, Australia

Patricia Monk
Dalhousie University, Canada

Leslie Monkman
Queen's University, Canada

Joash Moo
Singapore

Barbara Moore
University of the South Pacific, Fiji

Pamela C. Mordecai
Jamaica

Carol Morrell
University of Saskatchewan, Canada

Daphne Morris
Toronto Board of Education, Canada

Mervyn Morris
University of the West Indies, Jamaica

Alan Moss
University of the West Indies, Barbados

John Moss
University of Ottawa, Canada

Mpalive-Hangson Msiska
University of London, England

Arun P. Mukherjee
York University, Canada

Meenakshi Mukherjee
Jawaharlal Nehru University, India

Sujit Mukherjee
Orient Longman Limited, India

M. M. Mulokozi
University of Dar es Salaam, Tanzania

S. Murali
India

Mbulelo Mzamane
University of Vermont, USA

M. S. Nagarajan
University of Madras, India

S. Nagarajan
University of Hyderabad, India

M. K. Naik
India

N. Ramachandran Nair
Calicut University Centre, India

Prema Nandakumar
India

C. D. Narasimhaiah
Literary Criterion Centre, India

Shyamala A. Narayan
India

Susheila Nasta
University of London, England

Peter Nazareth
University of Iowa, USA

Philip Neilsen
Queensland University of Technology, Australia

W. H. New
University of British Columbia, Canada

David Newmarch
University of Natal, South Africa

Ng Wee Li
Murdoch University, Australia

Colin Nicholson
University of Edinburgh, Scotland

Alastair Niven
The Arts Council of Great Britain, England

Evelyn O'Callaghan
University of the West Indies, Barbados

Patrick O'Farrell
University of New South Wales, Australia

D. J. O'Hearn
University of Melbourne, Australia

Wale Okediran
Nigeria

Emilia Oko
University of Calabar, Nigeria

Chidi Okonkwo
University of Nigeria

Bernadette S. Oloroso
De La Salle University, Philippines

Elmer A. Ordonez
University of the Philippines

Femi Osofisan
University of Ibadan, Nigeria

Oyekan Owomoyela
University of Nebraska, USA

Malcolm Page
Simon Fraser University, Canada

Eustace Palmer
University of Sierra Leone

Daphne Pan
National University of Singapore

Sandra Pouchet Paquet
University of Miami, USA

Uma Parameswaran
University of Winnipeg, Canada

Makarand Paranjape
University of Hyderabad, India

Edward Parkinson
McMaster University, Canada

Rajeev Patke
National University of Singapore

Mary Paul
University of Auckland, New Zealand

Mari Peepre-Bordessa
University of Helsinki, Finland

Barbara Pell
Trinity Western University, Canada

Donna Palmateer Pennee
University of Guelph, Canada

Ernest Pereira
University of South Africa

Elizabeth Perkins
James Cook University of North Queensland, Australia

S. Penny Petrone
Lakehead University, Canada

Peter Pierce
Australia

David G. Pitt
Memorial University of Newfoundland, Canada

Velma Pollard
University of the West Indies, Jamaica

Jean-Marc Pottiez
France

H. Y. Sharada Prasad
India

Chris Prentice
University of Otago, New Zealand

D. V. K. Raghavacharyulu
Nagarjuna University, India

Lakshmi Raghunandan
Archarya Pathashala College, India

Jennifer Rahim
University of the West Indies, Trinidad and Tobago

Tariq Rahman
Quaid-i-Azam University, Pakistan

P. Raja
India

Ragini Ramachandra
Bangalore University, India

K. S. Ramamurti
Bharathidasan University, India

Vimala RamaRao
India

S. Ramaswamy
Bangalore University, India

Kenneth Ramchand
University of the West Indies, Trinidad and Tobago

Ruby S. Ramraj
University of Calgary, Canada

Sharon C. Ramraj
Canada

Victor Ramraj
University of Calgary, Canada

A. V. Krishna Rao
Indian Institute of Technology, India

K. Raghavendra Rao
Bangalore University, India

Beverly J. Rasporich
University of Calgary, Canada

Michael Reckord
Jamaica

Magdalene Redekop
University of Toronto, Canada

Carolyn Redl
Keyano College, Canada

John Reed
University of Zimbabwe

Polly Rewt
Open University, Scotland

Soledad S. Reyes
Ateneo de Manila University, Philippines

Jane Ricketts
University of the South Pacific, Fiji

Laurie Ricou
University of British Columbia, Canada

Robin Ridington
Canada

Dieter Riemenschneider
Der Johann Wolfgang Goethe Universität, Germany

Wendy Robbins
University of New Brunswick, Canada

Cherrell Shelley Robinson
University of the West Indies, Jamaica

Jeffrey Robinson
Canada

Judith Rodriquez
Australia

Constance Rooke
University of Guelph, Canada

Adrian Roscoe
University of the North, South Africa

Marilyn Rose
Brock University, Canada

Catherine Sheldrick Ross
University of Western Ontario, Canada

Graham Rowlands
Wakefield Press, Australia

Mary Rubio
University of Guelph, Canada

J. S. Ryan
University of New England, Australia

Yoni Ryan
Queensland University of Technology, Australia

Subhas Chandra Saha
Tripura University, India

Roydon Salick
University of the West Indies, Trinidad and Tobago

Reinhardt Sander
University of Pittsburgh, USA

Peter Sanger
Nova Scotia Agricultural College, Canada

Jayashree Sanjay
India

P. S. Sastri
University of Nagpur, India

L. S. R. Krishna Sastry
Andhra University, India

Victor R. Savage
National University of Singapore

Paul Scanlon
Sultan Qaboos University, Sultanate of Oman

Bill Schermbrucker
Capilano College, Canada

W. N. Scott
Australia

Graeme Seal
Curtin University, Australia

Andrew Seaman
Saint Mary's University, Canada

Mabel Segun
Children's Literature Documentation and Research Centre Nigeria

Ambika Sengupta
India

Aron Senkpiel
Yukon College, Canada

Peter Serracino-Inglott
University of Malta

Padma Seshadri
Stella Maris College, Madras, India

D. A. Shankar
University of Mysore, India

Ness Shannon
Australia

Thomas Shapcott
National Book Council, Australia

Michael Sharkey
University of New England, Australia

Govind Narain Sharma
Acadia University, Canada

Paul Sharrad
University of Wollongong, Australia

Susan Sheridan
Flinders University of South Australia

Anna Shnukal
National Library of Australia

Adam Shoemaker
Queensland University of Technology, Australia

Carol Sicherman
City University of New York, USA

Gillian Siebert
South Africa

Norman Simms
University of Waikato, New Zealand

Sherry Simon
Concordia University, Canada

Kirpal Singh
Nanyang Technological University, Singapore

Elizabeth Sinn
University of Hong Kong

S. S. Sirajuddin
University of the Punjab, Pakistan

Stephen Slemon
University of Alberta, Canada

Ian Smith
University of the West Indies, Jamaica

Donal Smith
University of Auckland, New Zealand

Donald B. Smith
University of Calgary, Canada

Rowland Smith
Dalhousie University, Canada

Donna E. Smyth
Acadia University, Canada

'Zulu Sofola
University of Ilorin, Nigeria

D. O. Spettigue
Queen's University, Canada

Consuelo López Springfield
Indiana University, USA

C. N. Srinath
Bangalore University, India

Dianne Stewart
Vista University, South Africa

Graham Stewart
University of Natal, South Africa

Robert J. Stewart
Trinity School, New York, USA

John A. Stotesbury
University of Joensuu, Finland

Glenys Stow
University of Guelph, Canada

Jennifer Strauss
Monash University, Australia

J. R. (Tim) Struthers
University of Guelph, Canada

Andrew Stubbs
Wilfrid Laurier University, Canada

Paul Stuewe
Books in Canada, Canada

Terry Sturm
University of Auckland, New Zealand

Subramani
University of Papua New Guinea

Rosemary Sullivan
University of Toronto, Canada

Padma Malini Sundararaghavan
Stella Maris College, Madras, India

Ciarunji Chesaina Swinimer
University of Nairobi, Kenya

Thomas E. Tausky
University of Western Ontario, Canada

Andrew Taylor
Edith Cowan University, Australia

Anne Taylor
England

Susan M. Taylor
University of Tampa, USA

Donald F. Theall
Trent University, Canada

John Thieme
University of Hull, England

Hilda L. Thomas
University of British Columbia, Canada

Lee Briscoe Thompson
University of Vermont, USA

Ralph Thompson
Jamaica

John Thomson
Victoria University, New Zealand

Michael Thorpe
Mount Allison University, Canada

Chris Tiffin
University of Queensland, Australia

Helen Tiffin
University of Queensland, Australia

Helen Pyne Timothy
University of the West Indies, Trinidad and Tobago

Nicanor G. Tiongson
Cultural Center of the Philippines, Philippines

K. V. Tirumalesh
Central Institute of English and Foreign Languages, India

Michael Tolley
University of Adelaide, Australia

Keyan G. Tomaselli
University of Natal, South Africa

Joanne Tompkins
La Trobe University, Australia

Brian Trehearne
McGill University, Canada

Harish Trivedi
University of Delhi, India

Martin Trump
University of South Africa

Alan Twigg
Canada

Alladi Uma
University of Hyderabad, India

T. G. Vaidyanathan
Bangalore University, India

Bruno van Dyk
Edgewood College of Education, South Africa

Aritha van Herk
University of Calgary, Canada

Kathryn Van Spanckeren
University of Tampa, USA

M. Van Wyk Smith
Rhodes University, South Africa

Ravi Veloo
Singapore

C. Vijayasree
India

John Henry Wadland
Trent University, Canada

Andrew Wainwright
Dalhousie University, Canada

David Walker
Deakin University, Australia

Shirley Walker
University of New England, Australia

Andrew Wallace
University College of Central Queensland, Australia

Martin Ware
Memorial University of Newfoundland, Canada

Maureen Warner-Lewis
University of the West Indies, Jamaica

Anne Warring
National English Literary Museum, South Africa

Jerry Wasserman
University of British Columbia, Canada

Cliff Watego
University of Queensland, Australia

Elizabeth Waterston
University of Guelph, Canada

Hugh Webb
Murdoch University, Australia

Elizabeth Webby
University of Sydney, Australia

Herb Weil
University of Manitoba, Canada

Julie Wells
Monash University, Australia

Lydia Wevers
New Zealand Mission, Switzerland

Terry Whalen
Saint Mary's University, Canada

Nicholas McCarthy Whistler
Canada

Kerry White
Australia

Bruce Whiteman
McGill University, Canada

Gillian Whitlock
Griffith University, Australia

James Wieland
University of Wollongong, Australia

Jenny Williams
Vista University, South Africa

Mark Williams
University of Canterbury, New Zealand

Catherine Woeber
National English Literary Museum, South Africa

Wong Phui Nam
Malaysia

Bruce Woodcock
University of Hull, England

George Woodcock
Canada

Silvana Woods
Media Productions, Belize

Brian Worsfold
University of Lleida, Spain

Chris Worth
Monash University, Australia

Derek Wright
Northern Territory University, Australia

Clement H. Wyke
University of Winnipeg, Canada

Dan Wylie
Rhodes University, South Africa

Paul Xuereb
University of Malta

Arthur Yap
National University of Singapore

Robert Yeo
Nanyang Technological University, Singapore

Margaret Yong
University of Malaya, Malaysia

Alan R. Young
Acadia University, Canada

Niaz Zaman
University of Dhaka, Bangladesh

A

ABAD, GEMINO HENSON (1939–)

Filipino poet, critic

Born in Manila, the Philippines, he was educated at the University of the Philippines (BA, 1963) and the University of Chicago, USA (MA, 1966; Ph.D., 1970). Abad is University Professor of English at the University of the Philippines. He was a Fellow at the 1988 Cambridge Seminar, England, and the 1991 International Writers Program at the University of Iowa, USA.

Abad's early poems in *Fugitive Emphasis* (1973), heavily influenced by Wallace Stevens, earned him an instant reputation as the country's leading academic poet. More dense, allusive poems followed in *In Another Light: Poems and Essays* (1976) and *The Space Between* (1985), before his association with the performance-oriented poets of the Philippine Literary Arts Council (of which he was co-founder in 1981) moved Abad to write more easily accessible poetry and poetic prose in *Poems and Parables* (1988) and *State of Play* (1990). The later texts also exhibit political discontent caused by the Marcos dictatorship. His poetry made Philippine poets aware of the need for control of voice, an issue sometimes neglected in the general rush to comment on political or psychological events.

Abad has also established himself as a literary scholar and critic of note. Starting out as a neo-Aristotelian in *In Another Light* and *A Formal Approach to Lyric Poetry* (1978), he discovered Saussure in *The Space Between*, leading him to problematize his earlier readings of Philippine poetry. His theoretically sophisticated rereading of earlier poetry in English bore fruit in two anthologies, *Man of Earth: An Anthology of Filipino Poetry and Verse from English, 1905 to the mid-50s* (1989, with Edna Zapanta Manlapaz) and *A Native Clearing: Filipino Poetry and Verse from English since the '50s to the Present from Edith L. Tiempo to Cirilo F. Bautista* (1993). Abad's phrase 'poetry from English' has gained currency among scholars to describe the way Philippine poets deconstruct the English language to make it suit local aesthetic needs. In *Man of Earth*, he writes:

> Nothing perhaps more dramatically *presents* — to show, to gift, to make ever present — the shaping power of language, its inherent way of thinking, than our verses in English; but conversely, paradoxically, nothing more dramatically *sub-verts* — to cultivate and plow under, as it were — the same power by its very means of shaping, of *in-forming* (forming us within), than our poems *from* English.

ISAGANI R. CRUZ

ABBAS, KHWAJA AHMAD (1914–87)

Indian novelist, short-story writer

Born at Panipat, Haryana State, India, he started his career as a journalist working for the *Bombay Chronicle*. He published more than seventy books in English, Urdu, and Hindi. Abbas was a committed writer, strongly influenced by Marxism. Of his longer narratives, most are popular film scripts, and even the serious novels do not altogether escape the impact of cinematic conventions. *Tomorrow is Ours: A Novel of the India of Today* (1943) deals with several issues, including leftism, fascism, nationalism, and social reform. Parvati, the protagonist, devotes her dancing talents to a leftist drama group, and her doctor-husband proceeds to China to tend the war-wounded. *Inquilab: A Novel of Indian Revolution* (1955) presents a panorama of early nineteenth-century Indian politics as viewed by Anwar, a Muslim youth. The plethora of characters and incidents, mostly from real life, allows for little more than reportage, while the ending, in which Anwar is discovered to be a Hindu's illegitimate son, smacks of film-script romanticism. The sequel, *The World Is My Village* (1984), offers the same mixture, though the setting here is international. Anwar, now a globe-trotting journalist, is finally killed in a communal riot in Bombay, stabbed by both Hindu and Muslim fanatics in separate encounters.

Abbas' short-story collections include *Rice and Other Stories* (1947), *Cages of Freedom and Other Stories* (1952), *One Thousand Nights on a Bed of Stones, and Other Stories* (1957), *The Black Sun and Other Stories* (1963), and *The Thirteenth Victim* (1986). Abbas' stories are well constructed and evince considerable narrative flair, but are generally overweighted with ideological import.

Abbas has also produced autobiographical writing, *I Write as I Feel* (1948) and *I Am Not an Island* (1977); travel books, *Outside India* (1939) and *An Indian Looks at America* (1943); a biography of Indira Gandhi, *That Woman — Her Seven Years of Power* (1973); and drama, *Barrister-at-Law: A Play about the Early Life of Mahatma Gandhi* (in collaboration with Pragji Dossa, 1977).

M. K. NAIK

Further reading: Elena J. Kalinnikova, 'The son of India: Khwaja Ahmed Abbas', in Elena J. Kalinnikova, *Indian-English Literature: A Perspective* (1982), trans. Virendra Pal Sharma.

ABORIGINAL LITERATURE

ABORIGINAL LITERATURE (Australia)

The emergence in the 1920s of indigenous black writing in Australia saw the publication of *Aboriginals: Their Traditions and Customs* (1924) by well-known Ngarrindjeri speaker and inventor, **David Unaipon.** Here the Aboriginal mission-born Unaipon emphasized the intricate system that had sustained his race for more than fifty thousand years prior to the British invasion and settlement in 1788. A firm believer that Aboriginal society contained oral literature to rival Homer's *Iliad* and *Odyssey*, Unaipon transformed Aboriginal spoken forms into Standard English written texts that culminated in the slim volume, *Native Legends* (1929). A far more extensive manuscript by Unaipon, which in 1925 had drawn the interest of publisher Angus and Robertson, appeared five years later as part of a larger work by a white anthropologist, W. R. Smith — *Myths and Legends of the Australian Aboriginals* (1930; repr. 1970). The discovery of this piracy has tended to project white (mis)appropriation of black literature into the broader sphere of white exploitation of black cultural material, reconfirming the political intensity characterizing the production of the black Australian text.

Impediments to Black Australians in having their work published lasted well into the 1960s when **Oodgeroo Noonuccal** (formerly Kath Walker) published the first volume of verse by an Aboriginal writer, *We Are Going* (1964). Meteoric sales of the book, unprecedented in the history of Australian poetry, are attributable as much to the political changes affecting the postwar conservatism of Australia as to the appearance of a first 'literary' volume by a black. Her representations of Aboriginal life dominated by discriminatory laws have their parallel particularly in the south-west Pacific basin in the poetic works a short time later by **John Kasaipwalova** (Papua New Guinea). The indigenous poet sought to explain the tensions, frustrations, and joys of his/her people extricating themselves from white colonial authority. Given the close proximity of these countries a common experience of white domination ensued, but historical and cultural differences assured a distinctiveness in how each colonized group would seek to determine its future. The major factor is that in all the former Commonwealth colonies *except* Australia indigenous sovereignty and right to ownership of the land (prior or present) had been formally ratified by the British invader.

The Aboriginal 'Tent Embassy' (a tent erected on Australia Day 1972), began as a peaceful demonstration by blacks against the denial of Aboriginal Land Rights and symbolized the political stand of blacks on a national basis. That most of the major figures responsible for creating a black literary movement in Australia identified with this political event is indicative of the crucial role the 'Embassy' would have upon Black Australian literature. Although several writer-activists, such as Gerald Bostock, Dobbi Eykoo, and Robert Merritt, remain largely unpublished in the field of literature, their involvement in the Embassy and its aftermath consolidated the realist underpinnings of Black Australian writing.

White Australian criticism tended to circumscribe the scope and influence of black writing by pointing to black writers' use of outdated forms and a preoccupation with confrontational topics. But the continual reworking of themes in later black works belies such criticism that was further repudiated by the rise of black drama. One of the authors targeted by this early criticism, **Jack Davis**, continues to write poetry and is recognised as one the foremost practising playwrights in Australia. More than any other Black writer, Davis epitomizes Bostock's statement that he saw drama as an extension of his poetry. It is further revealing that the first five plays performed, including Bostock's 'Here Comes the Nigger!' (premièred in 1976) and Davis' companion plays *Kullark* and *The Dreamers* (in *Kullark/The Dreamers*, 1982), provide an overview of the various forms of dependency upon white institutions that inhibited black advancement. The institutionalised stereotyping of blacks is evoked in the first of the five plays performed, **Kevin Gilbert**'s 'The Cherry Pickers' (premièred 1971), through the dependency of a community of a black itinerant fruit pickers upon a white orchard owner for their livelihood; Bostock's play 'Here Comes the Nigger!' features a blind black poet who must rely upon a white female tutor to help him qualify for his Higher School Certificate; without the benevolence of the white civilian in Merritt's *The Cake Man* (1978), the Aboriginal household will collapse; despite the continual efforts of the Nyoongahs in all phases of *Kullark* to meet white society on its own patronising terms, white justice operates to reaffirm their inferiority; in *The Dreamers*, social inertia fixes the Wallitch family in a cycle of dependency on alcohol and welfare benefits that serves to conceal their spiritual association with their Dreaming. Themes of Aboriginality (encompassing black identity and spiritual affinity with the land) and land rights are thus presented indirectly or implicitly, often with an ironic treatment of white superiority that serves to reinforce the dynamic communalism of the black family and the distinctiveness of black community values.

The group or family as central motif in black community social structures is naturally better facilitated by dramatic representation. Resistance to intrusive white elements upon Aboriginality none the less continues to be the major theme in novels with the broadening of individual consciousness representing the collective black response. Monica Clare's *Karobran: The Story of an Aboriginal Girl* (1979), until 1991 the only published novel by an Aboriginal woman, locates this representativeness in a story common to blacks throughout Australia; the forced separation of black children from their parents was so common and widespread that it has begun to surface as the subject of biographical writing particularly by black women, including Glenyse Ward's *Wandering Girl* (1987). Similar fragmentations of family and the debilitating effects of institutional racism are detailed in Marnie Kenenedy's *Born A Half-Caste* (1985) and **Sally Morgan**'s *My Place* (1986).

In *Karobran* the semi-autobiographical account about the break-up of Clare's family and her subsequent institutionalization by white authorities leads to a politicization of the main character that is indicative of both race and class sensitization. The leitmotif of coming to an understanding of the political realities for those who have been denied their freedom to determine their own future occurs coincidentally in the first published play by a Black Australian woman, Eva Johnson's *Murras* (1989). It is instructive that the first of Black Australia's female novelists and playwrights are determined to grapple with this phase. The expectation emerging from both texts is that the individual's struggle will empower the family to repel further assaults by an oppressive white society that seeks to hinder the social advancement of blacks in a subtle denigration of black political initiatives. Variations of resistance emanating from the community-based black perspective — a perspective that in its dynamics of a sharing and caring philosophy is compelled to engage in a reciprocality — are manifest in other works of prose fiction by blacks. **Archie Weller, Mudrooroo Narogin**, Sam Watson, and Eric Willmot probe black mentality as it has developed to invest Australia's black people with a sense of the necessity to struggle against the de-humanizing whiteman. Willmot's *Pemulwuy* (1987) traces the exploits of perhaps the prototype of black resistance fighters in the character of Pemulwuy, an Eora warrior who organized a successful thirteen-year campaign against British imperialism from 1788 onwards. Sam Watson's *The Kadaitcha Sung* (1990) explores the magico-mythical spectrum of Aboriginal spiritual power that operates to subordinate white authority in an unconquerable black landscape.

Narogin's critical work, *Writing From the Fringe* (1990), suggests that there will be more collaborative work between blacks and whites, especially in the area of biography. The novel's capacity for dealing with the intricacies of the magico-realist dichotomy of the Black Australian world-view — as evinced in Narogin's *Doctor Wooreddy's Prescription for Enduring the Ending of the World* (1983) and Watson's *The Kadaitcha Sung* — promises further revisioning of the Black experience by Black novelists.

CLIFF WATEGO

ABORIGINAL LITERATURE (Canada)

Native and Métis literature

Native Canadian literature begins with the ancient oral literatures that aboriginal peoples from different tribes across what is now Canada expressed in prose narratives, songs, chants, speeches, drama, and prayers, and utilized in tribal ceremony, ritual, and storytelling. Unique and linguistically specific, these oral literatures reflect a rich and complex diversity of culture and history.

Europeans who learned the Native languages marvelled that a people who had neither the wheel nor writing knew the power of the Word. They were amazed that the 'untrained savage mind' was capable of eloquence. But with their ethnocentric prejudices towards Native peoples and their antipathy towards oral literature, they dismissed it as 'primitive' or 'pagan', 'curious' or 'quaint', and betrayed its dynamics by infiltrating their translations of aboriginal literature with their own cultural and literary patterns. Traditional prose narratives were transformed into European fairy tales — their importance as repositories of religious beliefs, world concepts, tribal history, and communal wisdom was ignored, and their social functions minimized. Speeches of outstanding orators, many of whom remain anonymous, were recorded piecemeal, in the contexts of the fur trade, colonial warfare, and missionary activity, and were preserved merely as art objects to illustrate such 'surprising' literary qualities as 'pungent wit', 'metaphorical skill', or 'clever analogy'. It is only recently that scholars have begun to apply new and more appropriate techniques to the study of aboriginal oral literature.

By the mid-nineteenth century, some of Canada's Native peoples were writing and publishing in English — one result of the Christian missionary presence. Young Ojibwa converts in Ontario wrote their journals, life histories, reports, letters, travelogues, and sermons in English, many of which were published and circulated through missionary publications, newspapers, and in books. These included **George Copway**, the first Native Canadian to publish a book in English (*The Life, History and Travels of Kah-ge-ga-gah-bowh (George Copway)*, 1847); George Henry, who, as leader of an Ojibwa dance troupe, published a slim volume, *An Account of the Chippewa Indians, Who Have Been Travelling among the Whites, in the United States, England, Ireland, Scotland, France and Belgium* (1848); Peter Jacobs, the first Native Canadian to write a sketch of his Canadian travels, *Journal of the Reverend Peter Jacobs, Indian Wesleyan Missionary, from Rice Lake to the Hudson's Bay Territory, and Returning Commencing May, 1852 . . .* (1853); and Peter Jones, the first Native Methodist minister in Canada, whose *Life and Journals of Kah-ke-wa-quo-na-by (Rev. Peter Jones) Wesleyan Missionary* (1860) and *History of the Ojebway Indians, with Especial Reference to Their Conversion to Christianity* (1861) were published posthumously.

Because of great non-Native interest in Native Canadians at the time, personal histories, especially autobiography, were in demand. Autobiography was a new form, alien to an oral heritage in which the communal was sacrosanct. Consequently, autobiographical works retained many of the oral features of Native pre-literate cultures. Personal experiences were juxtaposed with communal narratives, with the anecdote and short essay, creating a distinctive literary form that combined history, traditions, beliefs, and personal experience.

Another new and enduring genre of Native literature emerged: a protest literature, official in nature, taking the forms of letters, petitions, and reports written to a variety of government agencies in Canada and England (including the British monarchy and the League of Nations). The predominant theme is indignation at the loss of land, of hunting and fishing rights, of self-sufficiency and dignity, of nationhood.

The literary accomplishment of this pioneering stage reveals the ability of Native writers to master the English language. It also gives a sense of their cultural identity and contributes something of value not only to social historians but also to early Canadian literature. Despite Christian and acculturated influence, their works are Native accounts. Aboriginal in origin, form, and inspiration, they comprise the first body of Native Canadian literature in English. Although they tend to be rhetorical and exhortatory, preoccupied largely with correcting the historical record of the past, they offer the first written evidence of the ideas, responses, and feelings of individual Native Canadians.

The last half of the nineteenth century produced a number of short-lived periodicals sponsored by local missionaries and Native interest groups that encouraged Native correspondents and subscribers, as well as two significant books: *Origin and Traditional History of the Wyandotts, and Sketches of Other Indian Tribes of North America* (1870) by Peter Dooyentate Clarke and *Our Caughnawagas in Egypt* (1885) by Louis Jackson, which gives a first-hand account of the famous Nile expedition to the Sudan in 1884–5. The period also produced the writings of Louis Riel (1844–85) and **Pauline Johnson**.

Literary output in the first half of the twentieth century was meagre. Government policies based on the assimilation and suppression of Native cultures, the commonly held belief that the Natives were a dying race, as well as lack of interest by publishers, a Depression, and two world wars made publication virtually impossible.

The 1960s, however, heralded considerable writing in English. The upsurge of Canadian nationalism that surrounded the 1967 centennial celebrations of Confederation focused peripheral attention on Native peoples. Native newspapers and periodicals funded by Native organizations or government agencies sprang up across Canada to provide a forum for energy and ideas. Native speakers emerged and Native oratory once again became a vigorous literary form. Journalistic reports and essays also became popular as a means of disseminating opinion and information. Whether in speech or in essay, Native voices were quintessentially political, addressing their persecution, betrayal, and aspirations in explicit terms. Several books of legends, published by Natives themselves, also appeared: *Legends of My People, the Great Ojibway* (1965), by the well-known artist Norval Morriseau, and *Son of Raven, Son of Deer* (1967) by the Tseshaht Indian George Clutesi, who also wrote *Potlatch* (1969), a detailed description of this important traditional rite. *I Am an Indian* (1969), the first anthology of Native Canadian literature, edited by the non-Native Kent Gooderham, included poems by the angry young political activist Duke Redbird and prose pieces by Chief Dan George, Alma Greene, Howard Adams, and Ethel Brant Monture.

During the late 1960s and early 1970s the influence of American civil-rights activists and the spectacular activities of the American Indian movement at Wounded Knee in 1973 drew the attention of the mass media to the plight of Native peoples. The *Statement of the Government of Canada on Indian Policy* (1969), the controversial white paper that recommended the abolition of special rights for Native peoples, mobilized Native leaders across the country. The support for Native causes made Canadian publishers eager to publish, and even to seek out, Native authors. A number of political activists published their works: Harold Cardinal, *The Unjust Society* (1969); William Wuttunee, *Ruffled Feathers* (1971); Howard Adams, *Prison of Grass* (1975). Although the 1970s began with books of protest and defence written from partisan motives, works of history with varying degrees of popular appeal also began to appear: *A Social History of the Manitoba Métis* (1974) by Emile Pelletier (Métis); *The Métis, Canada's Forgotten People* (1975) by D. Bruce Sealey (Métis) and Antoine S. Lussier (Métis); *The Fourth World* (1974) by George Manuel (Shuswap); and *These Mountains Are Our Sacred Places* (1977) by Chief John Snow (Stoney). The decade also produced traditional tales and legends retold by tribal elders: *Wild Drums* (1972) by Alex Grisdale; *Tales of Nokomis* (1970) by Patronella Johnston; *Tales of the Mohawks* (1975) by Alma Greene (Forbidden Voice); and *Medicine Boy and Other Cree Tales* (1976) by Eleanor Brass. Several books of poetry appeared: *My Heart Soars* (1974) by the coast Salish poet Chief Dan George (1899–1981); *Wisdom of Indian Poetry* (1976) and *Okanagan Indian* (1972) by Ben Abel; *Indians Don't Cry* (1977) by George Kenny; *Poems of Rita Joe* (1978) by the Micmac poet Rita Joe; and *Delicate Bodies* (1978) by Daniel David Moses.

Autobiography and its allied forms based on oral history, frequently written in the as-told-to tradition or with the help of a collaborator, dominated the 1970s. Many are 'one book' writers with a message to communicate to their predominantly white readership. Although their life stories are central, they tend not to be told sequentially, moving backwards and forwards in time recounting personal history along with communal stories, folklore, the wisdom of tribal elders, and short essays on how to acquire specialized hunting or fishing skills. Examples of these are *Recollections of an Assiniboine Chief* (1972) by Dan Kennedy (1877–1973); *Geniesh* (1973) by Jane Willis, a Cree from northern Quebec who recalls her childhood and adolescence in Anglican boarding schools; *Voices of the Plains Cree* (1973) by Edward Ahenakew (1885–1961); *First Among the Hurons* (1973), the autobiography of Max Gros-Louis, who played a prominent role in the James Bay hydro project; *Buffalo Days and Nights* (1976), the memoirs of Peter Erasmus (1833–1931), the last surviving member of the Palliser expedition of 1857–60, as told to Henry Thompson in 1920; *My Tribe the Crees* (1979) by Joseph F. Dion (1880–1960); *My People the Bloods* (1979) by Mike Mountain Horse (1888–1964); *Forty Years a Chief* (1977) by George Barker; *Visitors Who Never Left: The Origins of the People of Damelahamid* (1974) by Chief Kenneth B. Harris; and the decade's most popular autobiography, *Halfbreed* (1973), a disturbing reminder of the ugliness of the cultural conflict that is part of Canada's social history, by Métis writer Maria Campbell.

Since 1980 there has been a phenomenal burst of creative output in English by Native writers from different communities across Canada describing what it is like to live as a Native in today's society. Novelists such as Beatrice Culleton (Métis) in *In Search of April Raintree* (1983), Jeannette Armstrong (Okanagan) in *Slash* (1985), and Joan Crate (Métis) in *Breathing Water* (1989) depict the dilemma of Canada's Native peoples. In *Honour the Sun* (1987) Ruby Slipperjack portrays the joy and the pain of an isolated Native community in northwestern Ontario, and in *Medicine River* (1989) Thomas King focuses on a Métis protagonist in a Native community of a small prairie town. Fusing Native oral literary traditions and English literary forms, their novels reveal much humour and their structures are often episodic.

The short story is another favourite medium: *Achimoona* (1985), the first anthology of short fiction by Native Canadians, includes Jordan Wheeler (Métis), whose *Brothers in Arms* (1989) is a collection of three novellas. In 1990 Thomas King edited *All My Relations: An Anthology of Contemporary Native Fiction*, and Jeanne Perreault and Sylvia Vance *Writing the Circle: Native Women of Western Canada*. Autobiography is still a popular form: **Basil H. Johnston**, *Indian School Days* (1988); Eleanor Brass, *I Walk in Two Worlds* (1987); Lee Maracle (Métis) *I Am Woman* (1988); Beth Brant (Mohawk) *Mohawk Trail* (1985); Florence Davidson (Haida) *During My Time* (1982); and James Tyman (Métis) *Inside Out* (1989).

The didacticism integral to Native oral traditions remains a prominent element in recent history books by Native Canadians: *We Are Métis* (1980) by Duke Redbird; *Kipawa: Portrait of a People* (1982) by Kermot A. Moore (Métis); *The Ways of My Grandmothers* (1980) by Beverly Hungry Wolf (Blood); *In Our Own Words: Northern Saskatchewan Métis Women Speak Out* (1986), edited by Dolores T. Poelzer and Irene A. Poelzer; and *Ste. Madeleine Community without a Town: Métis Elders in Interview* (1987), edited by Ken Zeilig and Victoria Zeilig.

In poetry, *Loveshine and Red Wine* (1981) reveals a mellowed Duke Redbird who has moved from bitterness and anger to such new subjects as the beauty of nature and the love of family, home, and friends. In *First Person Plural* (1988), Daniel David Moses demonstrates a strikingly original sensibility and probing intelligence in his surreal images and subtle ironies. In *Pale as Real Ladies: Poems for Pauline Johnson* (1989), Joan Crate's sardonic wit and sharply pointed images wonderfully capture the tensions within a family troubled by divided loyalties and Victorian prudery. *Seventh Generation* (1989), edited by Heather Hodgson, includes work by such established poets as Jeannette Armstrong, Lenore Keeshig-Tobias, and A. Garnet Ruffo as well as a number of relatively new poets: Marie Annharte Baker, Kateri Damn, and Tracey Bonneau.

Although a formal body of literature specifically for children did not exist in traditional times, it has recently become a favourite with Native writers. Maria Campbell, Bernelda Wheeler, Jeannette Armstrong, Lenore Keeshig-Tobias, and Beatrice Culleton are creating their own tales for children.

Along with the new literary forms, traditional stories are being retold to keep alive the knowledge of the past: *Earth Elder Stories* (1988) by Alexander Wolfe (Saulteaux), *Kwakiutl Legends* (1981) by James Wallas as told to Pamela Whitaker, and *Tagish Tlaagu* ('Tagish stories', 1982), recorded by Julie Cruikshank and narrated by Angela Sidney. In *Write It on Your Heart: The Epic World of an Okanagan Storyteller* (1989), Wendy Wickwire has tried to preserve in print the oral storytelling art of Harry Robinson.

Considering the traditional inclination towards drama, the vitality of aboriginal theatre is not surprising. Young playwrights are drawing heavily on traditional cultures. Canada's most celebrated Native playwright is **Tomson Highway**. Others include Daniel David Moses — *Coyote City* (1990) and 'Big Buck City' (unpublished); John McLeod — 'Diary of a Crazy Boy' (unpublished); Val Dudoward — *Teach Me the Ways of the Sacred Circle*, published in *The Land Called Morning* (1986), edited by Caroline Heath; and Drew Taylor, who has written for the stage and other media.

Native Canadian writing in English is evolving. Young Native writers, influenced by the rich spiritual dimensions of aboriginal life, are exploring the reality of aboriginality in Canada. They are particularizing universals within Native sensibilities and are developing their uniqueness within a stronger, more diversified literary aesthetic.

S. PENNY PETRONE

Further reading: Thomas King, Cheryl Calver, and Helen Hoy, eds, *The Native in Literature: Canadian and Comparative Perspectives* (1987); W. H. New, ed., *Native Writers and Canadian Writing*, special issue of *Canadian Literature* (1990); Penny Petrone, *Native Literature in Canada* (1990).

Inuit Literature

Canadian Inuit, who inhabit the arctic coast of Canada from the Yukon border east to Labrador, share their aboriginal language with the Inuit of Alaska and Greenland. Pre-contact Inuit (the term 'Eskimo' being the pre-colonial Algonkian term for the Inuit that gained widespread currency) had a rich, strictly oral, literature. Song, drama, legends, and histories of both a religious and secular nature were part of the oral tradition, but none of these were recorded in print until writing was introduced by Europeans in the eighteenth and nineteenth centuries.

Traditional Inuit song is often magical or ritualistic, but it can also have a narrative or lineal structure. The Greenland ethnographer Knud Rasmussen identified four basic types of Inuit song: mood poems, which are reflective and involve no central action; hunting songs, which are narrative and full of incident; charms or incantations, which employ magical language or code; and songs of derision, which are usually satiric monologues or dialogues. Songs of derision can have a judicial function. Transcriptions of traditional Inuit songs can be found in the works of the ethnographers Rasmussen, Diamond Jenness, and Paul Emile Victor. A more recent work, *Poems of the Inuit* (1981), edited by John Robert Colombo, contains examples from all of these ethnographers' collections.

Traditional Inuit prose is generally considered more accessible to non-Inuit readers. Rasmussen divided the legends into five types: creation myths, which are religiously based; monster stories, which involve ghosts, trolls, and other odd creatures; epics, which are not political or nationalistic but which feature a heroic leader who has numerous adventures; tales of murder and revenge; and beast fables, involving animals that talk and act like humans. Inuit legends have been collected in the twentieth century; *Tales from the Igloo* (1972), translated and edited by Maurice Metayer, is an excellent representative collection.

Today, two primary orthographies are used to write Inuktitut — a standard Roman orthography and a system of syllabics that was first developed for mission use among the Cree Indians of northern Ontario. English is a second language for most young Inuit, and is the only language of a significant number of Inuit children. Publication by Inuit writers in both Inuktitut and English enjoyed an unusual flowering in the 1970s, and this bilingualism is now considered an accepted and desirable part of contemporary Inuit life.

Modern Inuit poetry still has ties to the oral tradition. The mood poems are much the same, presenting brief pictures of emotions such as loneliness or maternal love. Charms have disappeared or gone underground with the rise of Christianity, and there is now a blossoming of Christian songs and hymns similar to those found in English. Hunting songs are rarely written except out of nostalgia, but there is a significant body of songs and poems about politics and land-claim negotiations. Political songs tend to be derisive, and frequently take up ecological concerns. Songs and poems about romantic love are also popular. There are four basic categories of contemporary Inuit prose — autobiography, fiction, history of the material culture, and articles and essays on modern life. Like the poetry, the prose builds on the structures of the oral tradition while dealing with issues of contact life.

ROBIN McGRATH

Further reading: Robin Gedalof, ed., *Paper Stays Put: A Collection of Inuit Writing* (1980); Robin McGrath, *Canadian Inuit Literature: The Development of a Tradition* (1984); Penny Petrone, ed., *Northern Voices: Inuit Writing in English* (1988).

ABORIGINAL SONG AND NARRATIVE (Australia) Speaking more than two hundred languages and with a traditional culture reaching back thousands of years, the indigenous peoples of what came to be called 'Australia' faced a total invasion of their lands by a European group with nineteenth-century assumptions about the inferiority of 'primitive' peoples. This historical process links Aboriginal culture with that of the North American Indians and other invaded groups such as the Inuit people in Canada. The Europeans saw no writing, no value, no culture. Yet a sophisticated artistic life existed in Australia, with complex spiritual linkages among people, the land, and stories — a considerable oral and material culture.

Aboriginal cultural forms were (and continue to be) part of a holistic social response in which art is a social act and the artist is a communal value-creator whether speaking and singing in 'language' or in the more recent discourse of Aboriginal English. Songs and stories 'traded' across wide areas keep the land and its people alive and, in the process, map the continent with lines of culture and ceremony. The originating time, called (by Europeans) 'the Dreaming', is central: all song and narrative evoke this period to renew the land, to mark sites of importance, to 'tell the country'. The process of telling and singing is a vital, physical life force that is part of a ritual of living important to all. As Bill Neidjie puts it in *Story About Feeling* (1989),

> This story e can listen careful
> and how you want to feel on your feeling
> This story e coming through your body
> e go right down foot and head
> fingernail and blood . . . through the heart
> . . . White-European got to be listen this
> culture
> and this story
> because important one this.

Stories do not exist in isolation but are linked within a subtle matrix of art, ritual, oral performance, and physical location.

One of the major forms of Aboriginal culture

is the song cycle or series. Any one cycle, often performed as part of a corroboree, is an epic narrative journey. The *manikay* form, to which the 'Djambidj' series belongs, consists of a group of thematically associated songs about ancestral beings who inhabit the lands of the Djambidj-owning clans. The stories and songs, performed within a symbolic oral formulary with ritualized terms and traditionally established patterns, are in the hands of custodians who have the right and responsibility to perform them. Each text reiterates the world that it evokes and is multimedia in nature (combining story, music, and dance with material icons such as paint and flowers). Varied forms of any one songline exist with open and secret versions and with separate songs and narratives tied to women's or men's experience and authority.

The formal modes of the *manikay* and the corroboree can be contrasted with more individualized forms such as the *tabi* songs in which one singer creates a mix of poetry and music that tells of kinspeople, indiscretions, dream journeys, or the alien machines of the newcomer's culture. And there are chants, initiation songs, stories about food, the land, animals, the stars, and the post-contact narratives of murder and Aboriginal resistance. Nothing is outside the realm of song and story.

Paddy Roe says that his book *Gularabulu: Stories from the West Kimberley* (1983) is for everybody. 'See, this is the thing they used to tell us: Story, and we know.' To know the story is to be alive in a culture. Many contemporary Aboriginal writers in English find inspiration and identity in linking back with the long-standing traditions of their culture. This process is typified in **Mudrooroo Narogin**'s *Dalwurra* (1988). He writes his narrative poetry as a conscious re-enactment of *manikay* form 'attempting to reach towards the brevity and purity of Aboriginal expression'. His work, and that of **Oodgeroo Noonuccal** and others, continues a narrative and song tradition of major world importance.

HUGH WEBB

Further reading: Margaret Clunies Ross and Stephen Wild, *Djambidj: An Aboriginal Song Series from Northern Australia* (1982); Anna Rutherford, ed., *Aboriginal Culture Today* (1988); Peggy Brock, ed., *Women, Rites and Sites* (1989).

ABORIGINES IN LITERATURE (Australia)
The earliest written consideration of Aborigines stems from the journals of European exploration — both to and within Australia — in the second half of the eighteenth century. One example, *A Mother's Offering to Her Children* (1841), written by 'A Lady Long Resident in New South Wales', is an immature amalgam of naïvety and sententious moralizing. Until the 1840s Australian poetry and fiction said little about Aboriginal themes or characters. Even in the first novel that depicts extended interaction with Aboriginal people — **James Tucker**'s *Ralph Rashleigh* (1845?) — the protagonist's four-year sojourn as a 'white blackfellow' is less significant than the convict system from which he is attempting to escape.

Tucker, **Rolf Boldrewood** — especially in *Robbery Under Arms* (1882–3) — and **Rosa Praed** — particularly in *Australian Life: Black and White* (1985) and *My Australian Girlhood* (1902) — had strongly ambivalent views of Aborigines. There are interesting parallels between these attitudes and literary approaches to indigenous peoples in nineteenth-century Canadian novels such as **John Richardson**'s *Wacousta; or, The Prophecy* (1832).

The nineteenth century also saw the first serious attempts by Australian poets to engage Aborigines as subject matter. These attempts varied from uneven epics such as George Gordon McCrae's 'The Story of Balladeadro' (1867) and 'noble savage' lamentations such as **Henry Ken-**

dall's 'The Last of His Tribe' (first published in 1863 in the *Sydney Morning Herald* as 'Woonoona' and under the quoted title in Kendall's *Leaves from Australian Forests*, 1869) to more skilled and explicitly violent ballads such as **Charles Harpur**'s 'The Creek of the Four Graves' (1853). The push towards Australian Federation in 1901 suggested to authors of the Nationalist school that themes about Aborigines could be redeployed in support of Australian distinctiveness. However, this marginal use of 'the blackfellow' by such authors as **Joseph Furphy** was confined almost entirely to nonfiction writing (as in Furphy's 'Black Australia', an article published in the ***Bulletin*** on 30 October 1902). **Katharine Susannah Prichard**'s major novel, *Coonardoo* (1929), with its depiction of miscegenation, resituated Aborigines at the centre of fictional attention and moral controversy. From 1930 onwards, perspectives on the thematic use of Aborigines expanded dramatically. At the same time that populist 'settler' fiction of the type made famous by **Ion L. Idriess** was first being read — *Lasseter's Last Ride* (1931), for example — **Xavier Herbert**'s seminal novel, *Capricornia* (1938), examined the concept of Aboriginal culture as an alternative world view, a process taken even further in his mammoth epic, *Poor Fellow My Country* (1975).

The Moving Image (1946) by **Judith Wright** established the moral dimension of the Aboriginal theme as never before, involving Aboriginal characters and situations in a symbolic interrogation of white violence and dispossession. This metaphysical approach was later followed by **Randolph Stow** in *To the Islands* (1958) and by **Patrick White** in *Voss* (1957), *Riders in the Chariot* (1961), and *A Fringe of Leaves* (1976). White's novels on the indigenous theme have been productively compared to those of the Canadian **Rudy Wiebe**, author of *The Temptations of Big Bear* (1973) and *The Scorched-Wood People* (1977).

Sensitivity to Aboriginal concerns has increased in Australian literature written since 1960. Paradoxically — or perhaps logically — this has resulted in fewer titles dealing with Aborigines as subject matter. Significantly, too, despite selected examples of historical novels — **Thomas Keneally**'s *The Chant of Jimmie Blacksmith* (1972) — and contemporary treatments — **Peter Mathers**' *Trap* (1966) and Nene Gare's *The Fringe Dwellers* (1961) — it has been in the genres of drama and poetry that this theme has received far more emphasis since the mid-1970s. The one important exception to this trend is the idiosyncratic prose of **Banumbir Wongar** (Sreten Bozic), whose novels and short stories strike an Aboriginal chord that is in many ways more indebted to Kafka than to Katharine Susannah Prichard.

Les A. Murray's 'The Ballad of Jimmy Governor' (1972), 'The Buladelah-Taree Holiday Song Cycle' (1977), and *The Boys Who Stole the Funeral* (1980) utilize the rhythms and tones of traditional Aboriginal song cycles. Billy Marshall-Stoneking's poetry in *Singing the Snake* (1990) is so sensitive to collective Pintupi orality that it is difficult to determine the individual voice of some pieces.

On the stage, **David Ireland**'s *Image in the Clay* (1964), Jill Shearer's *The Foreman* (1977), Thomas Keneally's *Bullie's House* (1981), and Tony Strachan's *State of Shock* (1986) establish a dramatic universe that revolves around a majority black cast, is focused upon issues of cultural clash, and considers the possibilities for racial accommodation. Like Canadian playwright **George Ryga**'s *The Ecstasy of Rita Joe* (1970), these plays have provided a useful platform for indigenous actors, even though the works themselves are not written by Aboriginal authors.

ADAM SHOEMAKER

Further reading: Terry Goldie, *Fear and Temptation: The Image of the Indigene in Canadian, Austral-*

ian and New Zealand Literatures (1989).

ABOUD, JAMES C. (1956–)
Trinidadian poet
He was born in Woodbrook, a district of Port of Spain, the capital city of Trinidad and Tobago. Qualified in literature and law, he studied at the University of Western Ontario, Canada, the University of the West Indies, the Polytechnic of London, England, and the Middle Temple, London, England. Aboud has published one book of poems, *The Stone Rose* (1986), and a few poems in other publications. His writing deals with his heritage as part of the later group of arrivals in Trinidad and Tobago — those of Syrian-Lebanese ancestry — that is often perceived to be wealthy, clannish, and not integrated into the society. Aboud is the first member of his country's Syrian-Lebanese community to participate in the literary arts of the nation.

An attorney and political activist, Aboud is critical of contemporary Caribbean poets, whom he characterizes as being 'soft at the core'. He finds their poetry 'not fresh and newly created. It takes no risks or gambles'. While Aboud finds such work unmistakably Caribbean, he also states that 'it is derivation rather than true creativity', evolving 'by always looking backwards, plodding forward into its own same self'.

Uncommitted to any order or tradition of poetry, Aboud does not want to change the world through poetry; he wishes simply to write it, with any social or political changes being incidental. His poems in *The Stone Rose* are occasionally marked by strange juxtapositions and refreshing images that conform to his approach to the writing of poetry. He often speaks about the search for voice, as in 'Pizza': 'The man's voice / will find him / eventually / . . . Sooner or later / The man's voice / will find him — / Or mock him / from a distance.'

Although Aboud has not published since 1986, he retains his anti-neo-colonialist stance, viewing neo-colonialism as a crutch for facile attempts at creativity.

ANSON GONZALEZ

ABRAHAMS, LIONEL (1928–)
South African poet, short-story writer, editor
Born in Johannesburg, South Africa, he graduated from Witwatersrand University in 1955. His collections of poetry include *Thresholds of Tolerance* (1975), *Journal of a New Man* (1984), and *The Writer in Sand* (1988). The best poems combine a deeply philosophical approach with a controlled lyricism.

In 1977 Abrahams published *The Celibacy of Felix Greenspan: A Novel in 18 Stories*. Some of these stories are strongly Johannesburg-bound and, according to **Patrick Cullinan**, 'are rooted in the unique joy and suffering of an individual life'. As an occasional essayist Abrahams has had a considerable influence in intellectual circles and was at one time a regular columnist on literary matters in the *South African Literary Review*.

In 1956 Abrahams founded an occasional literary magazine in Johannesburg, *The Purple Renoster*. The magazine continued to espouse values of liberal tolerance throughout much of the repressive apartheid era and had accumulated twelve issues by 1972. It was eventually succeeded by Abrahams' *Sesame*, another occasional magazine. During the 1980s he was co-editor, with Walter Saunders, of a literary annual, *Quarry* (1976–83). He has also co-edited with **Nadine Gordimer** the well-regarded Penguin anthology, *South African Writing Today* (1967).

Abrahams has been respected for his encouragement of fellow writers through workshops and reading groups. He has also, through editing and publishing ventures, promoted the work of at least three widely regarded South African authors — **H. C. Bosman**, Mongane Serote, and **Oswald Mbuyiseni Mtshali**. Through the Renoster Press he proved himself to be a courageous publisher of alternative literature during the repressive apartheid regime.

Abrahams has come to be regarded as an elder statesman of South African letters. His diverse literary contributions were acknowledged in 1992 with the award of a medal by the English Academy of South Africa.

GEOFFREY HARESNAPE

Further reading: Lionel Abrahams, 'My face in my place', in M. J. Daymond, J. U. Jacobs, and Margaret Lenta (eds) *Momentum: On Recent South African Writing* (1984); Patrick Cullinan, 'Introduction', *Lionel Abrahams Reader* (1988).

ABRAHAMS, PETER (1919–)

South African novelist

Born to James Abrahams, an Ethiopian seaman, and his Coloured wife Angelina du Plessis, in Vrededorp, Johannesburg, South Africa, he began his schooling only in his tenth year, attending Grace Dieu, near Pietersburg, and St Peter's College, Rosettenville. The turning point in Abrahams' life was his encounter with the Bantu Men's Social Centre in Johannesburg, where he was exposed to black American literature. In 1939 he went into exile in order to pursue his desire to be a writer and to find his identity. After two years at sea as a ship's stoker, Abrahams married an English woman and worked in London with the Communist Party as an editor of the *Daily Worker*. After spending time in Paris, he returned to England, married his second wife Daphne Miller, and in 1952 was sent by the *Observer* to report on the colour question in South Africa and Kenya. In 1955 he visited Jamaica at the request of the Colonial Office that he write a book on the island. This issued in his documentary, *Jamaica: An Island Mosaic* (1957), and in his immigration to the hills above Kingston with his family in 1959. Abrahams has worked for the Jamaican radio service, and has been a contributor to *Holiday* magazine, and editor (1958–62) of the *West Indian Economist.*

Abrahams' lifelong preoccupation has been with the attempt of black people to find identity within a white world as a precondition for achieving true independence — as individuals and, collectively, as a race. Abrahams' early vision of a society in which colour played no part was gradually modified through his involvement with the Pan-African Movement to a position where he now advocates black people's withdrawal from western society and the discovery of their identity in a black world. His early novels place freedom of mind over political freedom; the emphasis shifts in the later novels as his life experience proved the importance of political power as a condition for racial liberation.

Following his only volume of poetry, *A Blackman Speaks of Freedom* (1941), and a collection of sketches, *Dark Testament* (1942), Abrahams published two novels with an overtly Marxist thrust — *Song of the City* (1945) and *Mine Boy* (1946). The novels were among the first in Africa to deal with tribal peoples' attempts to come to terms with industrialized society, one circumscribed, moreover, by racial discrimination. Taken together with *The Path of Thunder* (1948), which celebrates love across racial barriers in South Africa, these works constitute the early period of Abrahams' career and reflect his liberal conviction at the time that the freeing of the white mind from fear and prejudice would enable the black person to shed the burden of colour.

Some have seen *Wild Conquest* (1950) as the start of a new artistic creed by which Abrahams became particularly concerned with the history and future of the black race; he continued to wrestle with these issues in every subsequent book. *Wild Conquest* tries to find in the encounter between the Afrikaner and Matabele people during the Great Trek the seeds for the race conflict in South Africa and, like his earlier novels, still expresses the belief that individuals can transcend the colour consciousness of their society. However, the realization that such individuals will not have a significant impact on society led Abrahams to his later examination of political change as a prerequisite for a change of heart.

Abrahams returned to South Africa for six weeks in 1952 and his findings gave rise to the uncharacteristic bitterness of *Return to Goli* (1953). This documentary is crucial to an understanding of his art and beliefs and was the spur he needed to consolidate his life story in his autobiography, *Tell Freedom* (1954). The first autobiography by a black South African, it chronicles Abrahams' life under the oppressive system in South Africa before he went into exile. Influenced by the autobiography of American Richard Wright, *Tell Freedom* shows Abrahams' differentiation from his community, anticipating his increasing isolation from the masses in his life and writing. In his later novels it is the figure of the artist or writer who is empowered to comment on individual and society alike. (See **Life Writing**, South Africa.)

The publication of *A Wreath for Udomo* (1956) marks a third phase of Abrahams' career. In its indictment of colonialism and its prophetic insight into the problems that would beset the newly independent African countries of the next decade, the book has features in common with the post-colonial novel, anticipating those of **Ayi Kwei Armah** of Ghana. *A Wreath for Udomo*, however, bears out Abrahams' conviction that the writer must stand aside from direct political engagement in order to criticize those policies that threaten the autonomy of the individual or community. In the novel, the artist Paul Mabi has difficulty in accepting a portfolio in independent Panafrica and relinquishes it after realizing to what lengths Udomo is prepared to go to keep his country on the road to freedom.

This question of how to resist the inroads made into individual integrity during attempts to set a community free is central in Abrahams' *This Island Now* (1966), a novel set on an island modelled on Jamaica and Haiti. This critique of neocolonialism depicts how, some twenty-five years after independence, effective power remains in the hands of a minority of expatriates and is gradually transferred to a dictator. Through the reporter Martha Lee, Abrahams examines how colour consciousness and industrialization constitute the cruel legacy left to former colonies by the colonizer. Josiah, like Udomo, is finally alienated from his constituency because of his ruthless attempts to translate his noble ideals into political reality.

Abrahams' own sense of alienation is suggested in *A Night of Their Own* (1965), which marks a return to a South African setting, probably prompted by the Rivonia treason trial of 1963. The hero, Richard Nkosi, an artist working for an underground political movement, is elevated at the end to the status of a myth. This sense of remoteness from the masses is still evident in *The View from Coyaba* (1985), which begins and ends in the hills above Kingston, Jamaica. Abrahams uses crucial periods in 150 years of international black history, such as slavery on a Jamaican plantation, share-cropping in the American South, and the transition from colonialism to independence in Uganda, to show his belief that black people must withdraw from western society to free themselves from the centuries-long occupation of their minds. This saga is the culmination of Abrahams' life and writing and a view of his own place in the history of the black people.

The first prolific and widely read black writer from South Africa, Abrahams has exerted enormous inspirational influence on other black African writers in English, including **Cyprian Ekwensi** and **Ngugi wa Thiong'o**. Unlike the latter, however, Abrahams has tried to meet western literary demands in the form of his novels. The development of his thought, however, indicates how African writing has attempted to deal with power, race, and culture during the past fifty years. In both his life and his writings Abrahams has tried to reconcile the tensions between individual and social needs and he has embraced contradiction. Apart from his initial espousal of Marxism, he has never submitted to ideological constraints in his work, but neither does he deny the necessity of political commitment in a writer. Abrahams' politics have always determined his art; ultimately, it is his experiences as a black man that have shaped his artistic consciousness.

CATHERINE WOEBER

Further reading: Michael Wade, *Peter Abrahams* (1972); Kolawole Ogungbesan, *The Writing of Peter Abrahams* (1979).

ABRUQUAH, JOSEPH WILFRED (1921–)
Ghanaian novelist
Born in Saltpond, in the Central Region of Ghana, he was educated at Wesley College, Kumasi, Ghana, and at King's College, Cambridge University, England, and Westminster College, London, England. He taught at Keta Secondary School, Ghana, and later became headmaster of Mfantsipim School, Cape Coast. His importance as a novelist derives from *The Catechist* (1965) and *The Torrent* (1968).

At the beginning of *The Catechist* an omniscient narrator describes the death of the older Abruquah, whose *nom de plume* is Kobina Afram. This narrator then relinquishes the narrative thread to an internal narrator, the catechist, who recalls the story of his life from the late nineteenth to mid-twentieth centuries. The self-indulgent catechist, however, has a fuzzy memory and is paranoid about church officials. The novel reveals little about the tensions that marked the early history of the Christian church in Ghana; moreover, the narrative is strained by too much sermonizing and by the author's inability to mesh various episodes into imaginative art. However, Afram, self-righteous though ironically naïve, is an interesting, quixotic character whose self-delusion is balanced by his kind heart.

The Torrent is a *Bildungsroman* about Josiah Afful, a boy-hero who moves out of a traditional Nzimah village to attend a grammar school, modelled after Mfantsipim School. In this urban setting, Afful is confused by issues of sexuality and relationships and by the conflicts between Ghanaian and European cultures. Unfortunately, Abruquah crowds his canvas with details about boarding school and with episodes (Afful's final examination and visit to his village) that are residuals of a plot sustained too long. In contrast to a similar work, **George Lamming**'s *In The Castle of My Skin* (1953), which reveals the experience of Barbadian society through the consciousness of a child-narrator, *The Torrent* barely shows Afful's personal response to the socio-cultural transformation of his society. The apparent weaknesses of his two novels notwithstanding, Abruquah is one of the first Ghanaian writers to record the experience of the indigenous society in transition as western values gained ground.

CHRIS KWAME AWUYAH

Further reading: Danièle Stewart, 'Ghanaian writing in prose: a critical survey', *Présence Africaine* 91 (1974).

ACHEBE, CHINUA (1930–)
Nigerian novelist, short-story writer
He was born Albert Chinualumogo Achebe in the village of Ogidi, eastern Nigeria, to Janet Iloegbunam Achebe and Isaiah Okafo Achebe, a catechist for the Church Missionary Society. Chinua Achebe's primary education was in the society's school in Ogidi. He was eight years old when he began to learn English, and fourteen when he went, as one of the few boys selected, to the Government College at Umuahia, one of the best schools in West Africa. In 1948 he enrolled at University College, Ibadan, as a member of the first class to attend this new constituent college of

the University of London, England. He intended to study medicine, but soon switched to English literary studies and followed a syllabus that resembled the University of London honours degree programme. Achebe contributed stories, essays, and sketches to the *University Herald.*

After receiving his BA in 1953, he taught briefly at the Merchants of Light School in Oba, eastern Nigeria. In 1954 he joined the Nigeria Broadcasting Corporation (NBC) as a talks producer, advancing to the position of Comptroller of the Eastern Region of the NBC, a position he held from 1958 to 1961. In 1961 he became director of the external broadcasting programme for the corporation, 'The Voice of Nigeria', in Lagos and remained there until 1966, when the political crisis, which escalated into the **Nigerian Civil War** (1967–70), forced his return to eastern Nigeria. During the war Achebe went on many missions abroad in support of Biafra.

At the war's end Achebe resigned his post at NBC and entered university teaching, first as senior research fellow at the Institute of African Studies in the University of Nigeria at Nsukka and then in a variety of professorial positions in Canada and the USA.

Achebe is arguably the most widely read and discussed African writer of his generation. His first novel, *Things Fall Apart* (1958), has become a classic; it has been read throughout the anglophone world and has been translated into some forty languages. Sales are estimated to be in excess of three million copies. His other novels, *No Longer at Ease* (1960), *Arrow of God* (1964), *A Man of the People* (1966), and *Anthills of the Savannah* (1987), are equally respected.

Achebe's purpose has been to write about his people and for his people. His novels form a continuum over some one hundred years of Igbo (and latterly Nigerian) civilization. In *Things Fall Apart*, for example, Europe has not yet penetrated the village of Umuofia. When the novel ends, colonial rule has been established, and the character of the community — its values and freedoms — has been substantially and irrevocably altered. The process continues in *Arrow of God,* where the lives of the villagers have been completely circumscribed by European intervention. *No Longer at Ease* is set in pre-independence Nigeria. *A Man of the People* and *Anthills of the Savannah* are located in unspecified African countries (strongly resembling Nigeria), the former in the immediate post-independence period, the latter some twenty years later.

Achebe describes *Things Fall Apart* as 'an act of atonement with my past, the ritual return and homage of a prodigal son'. The novel tells the tragic stories of the rise and fall of Okonkwo and of the disintegration of Igbo culture, symbolized by the relentless encroachments of British Christian imperialism. Okonkwo embodies, if in an exaggerated form, the qualities most valued by his society — energy, a strong sense of purpose, a sense of communal co-operativeness — which, at the same time, are marked by a strong sense of individuality. There is also an inflexibility and rigidity in the social and psychological makeup of Okonkwo and his clan, however, that make it impossible for them to adapt to the inevitable change wrought by an imported and more powerful culture. *Things Fall Apart* is an apostrophe to and a lament for the past and a fictional evocation of the inevitability of historical change.

Arrow of God moves the historical examination forward to the firm establishment of colonial rule, as seen through the story of Ezeulu, chief priest of the god Ulu, the most powerful member of the people of Umuaro. The novel is a meditation on the nature and uses of power and on the responsibility of the person who possesses it. Ezeulu becomes engaged in a struggle with the people of his village and the officers of the British political service. He is forced to reconcile the conflicting impulses in his own nature — his wish to serve as the protecting deity of the people of Umuaro and his desire to gain greater personal power by pushing his authority to its limits. Out of the failure of this attempt his tragedy arises.

In *No Longer at Ease* Achebe presents, through its hero Obi Okonkwo, a tragic story of the modern African state. The novel balances an examination of Nigerian 'modernity' — the social, political, and economic implications of the accommodation to colonial rule — with an awareness of the price Nigerians have paid for their 'modernity'.

A Man of the People examines questions of power and leadership in the emergent nation state. The government of the country is nominally in the hands of the people, but there is no responsible leadership, merely self-interest. While Achebe's novels set in the past society show how a balance between collective religious observance and personal ambition provides social order, those set in contemporary society offer a vision of how a culture devoid of religious belief leads to unrestrained acquisitiveness and unchecked political corruption. The novel ends with military intervention seen as offering the only possible redemption for a society in which traditional and imported constitutional methods are both ineffective.

Anthills of the Savannah, published twenty years after *A Man of the People*, reveals the extent to which any political hope placed in the hands of the military is misplaced. Like its predecessors, the novel is an examination of power and of the responsibility of those who possess it. A novel about leadership, it is also an examination of the role of the writer in society. There are persistent references to 'story' and 'storyteller' that exemplify the claims for the function of art that Achebe makes in his various essays; for example, in 'The Truth of Fiction' and 'What Has Literature Got to Do With It?'. In the latter essay Achebe states that stories serve the purpose of consolidating whatever gains a people or their leaders have made, or imagine they have made, in their existential journey through the world; but, he argues, stories also serve to sanction change when it can no longer be denied. Selections of Achebe's essays include *Morning Yet on Creation Day: Essays* (1975) and *Hopes and Impediments: Selected Essays, 1965–1987* (1988).

Achebe's other writing includes a volume of poetry, *Beware, Soul Brother* (1971; rev. 1972, and published in the USA in 1973 as *Christmas in Biafra and Other Poems*), winner of the 1972 Commonwealth Poetry Prize. He has published the short-story collections *Girls at War* (1972) — some of the stories of which appeared in his 1962 collection *The Sacrificial Egg, and Other Stories* — and the children's books *Chike and the River* (1966), *How the Leopard Got His Claws* (1976), written in collaboration with the artist John Iroaganachi, *The Drum* (1977), and *The Flute* (1977). In 1971 Achebe founded the journal *Okike* (1971–), a forum for the presentation of new imaginative writing and the expression of critical opinions. He was also instrumental in reviving the **Association of Nigerian Authors** in 1981. The aims of the association are to create a forum in which young Nigerian and African writers can publish their writing, to foster the growth of local publishing, and to provide the conditions through which a genuine African literary tradition can be fostered.

Taken together, Achebe's imaginative and non-fictional writing reveals his wish to determine a just system of government for Nigerians and his advocacy of the role of literature in serving society's needs. In recognition of his concern and achievement, Achebe has twice been awarded the Nigerian National Merit Award, the only Nigerian to achieve this honour.

Achebe's achievement has been to set the record of Nigerian history straight, to restore his people's faith in themselves, and, in his own words, to provide a context in which they can 'articulate their values and define their goals in relation to the cold, alien world around them'. Achebe has a central place in African and contemporary literature because he has reflectively and unobtrusively modified the traditions of fiction. He has derived forms distinctively his own for the purpose of envisaging and convincingly conveying experience.

G. D. KILLAM

Further reading: Robert Wren, *Achebe's World: The Historical and Cultural Contexts of the Novels of Chinua Achebe* (1980); C. L. Innes, *Chinua Achebe* (1990); Simon Gikandi, *Reading Achebe* (1991).

ACORN, MILTON (1923–86)

Canadian poet

He returned to his birthplace, Charlottetown, Prince Edward Island, Canada, five years before his death, having previously lived in Montreal, Toronto, and Vancouver. Profoundly conservative in his love of the land and its dying ancestral traditions, contemptuous of the false gods of progress, Acorn was also a poet of revolutionary affirmation. With the possible exception of Pat Lowther, he is Canada's only genuinely political poet.

A political activist, Acorn never found a permanent home in any of the political factions he aligned himself with: the Communist Party (which he left after the Soviet invasion of Hungary in 1956), Socialist Forum in Montreal, and the Canadian Liberation Movement (which disintegrated in the mid-1970s). Throughout his life, however, he remained a committed socialist. Like **Archibald Lampman**, a poet with whom he strongly identified, he believed that 'the cause of Socialism is the cause of love and hope and humanity'. Like Lampman, too, Acorn is a master of his craft. He constantly experiments with form in both his overtly political poems and his compressed and often tender lyrics of love and nature.

Acorn's insistent 'I' — 'I've tasted my blood too much'; 'I shout love'; 'Knowing I live in a dark age before history' — distinguishes him from the revolutionary poets of Africa and the Caribbean. There is no 'we' in Canada, nor is there a well-defined strain of anti-colonialism in Canada (outside of Quebec). In the absence of such a tradition, Acorn's aggressively political persona may have deprived him of the critical recognition he deserved during his lifetime. His unmistakable integrity and his great gift as a poet did, however, win him the acclaim of fellow writers. When *I've Tasted My Blood* (1969) failed to win the Governor General's Award, the writers created the Canadian Poetry Award in his honour. Since his death, Acorn's reputation has grown with the publication of three volumes — *I Shout Love and Other Poems* (1987), *The Uncollected Acorn* (1987), and *Hundred Proof Earth* (1988) — lovingly edited by Acorn's fellow poet and collaborator, James Deahl.

HILDA L. THOMAS

Further reading: Hilda Thomas, 'History-making', *Canadian Literature* 78 (1978); Milton Acorn, 'My philosophy of poetry', in James Deahl (ed.) *Hundred Proof Earth* (1988).

ADAMS, ARTHUR H. (1872–1936)

New Zealand poet, novelist, dramatist

Born in Otago, New Zealand, he was a prominent editor and journalist who wrote poetry, novels, and a number of plays that were successfully produced in New Zealand and Australia. His career, in fact, epitomizes the period of unparalleled closeness between Australian and New Zealand literary culture. Adams went to China as a war correspondent (1900–1), during the Boxer rebellion, and was in England until 1905. In 1906, after a brief period in New Zealand, he was back in Australia, where he worked for the ***Bulletin***, *Lone Hand*, and the *Sun*.

Adams worked as a journalist in Sydney, Australia, and his first volume of poetry, *Maoriland, and Other Verses* (1899) was published there. Its intended audience was Australasian and it is among the first New Zealand literary productions to express a sense of exile *from* rather than exile *to* New Zealand. *The Nazarene: A Study of a Man*

(1902) contains Adams' most accomplished verse; the Christ of its title poem has strong affinities with **R. A. K. Mason**'s later explorations of the Arian heresy. *Collected Verses* (1913) marked the end of his poetry career, though he continued to publish prose and dramatic writing.

Adams wrote several novels, beginning with *Tussock Land: A Romance of New Zealand and the Commonwealth* (1904). His continued interest in drama is demonstrated in *Three Plays for the Australian Stage* (1914). The sketch called *A Man's Life* (1926) is a fictionalized autobiography.

MICHELE LEGGOTT

Further reading: Macdonald P. Jackson, 'Poetry: beginnings to 1945', in Terry Sturm (ed.) *The Oxford History of New Zealand Literature in English* (1991).

ADAMS, GLENDA (1939–)

Australian novelist, short-story writer

Born and educated in Sydney, Australia, she immigrated to the USA in 1964. Despite her long and continued absence, Adams characteristically uses Australia as her narrative impulse. It has been suggested that like other expatriate writers, Adams' 'bifocal vision' generates 'original and critical responses to Australia' in her work.

The ambiguous situation of the expatriate writer was illustrated when Adams won the prestigious New South Wales Premier's Literary Award for fiction in 1988 for her second novel, *Dancing on Coral* (1987) — which also won the Miles Franklin Award — but was not awarded the prize money because she was not resident in Australia.

The theme of separation and her usually female protagonists' search for identity are major elements in Adams' fiction. Her narratives are intricately structured, often comic, and always informed by her political concern with issues such as colonialism, imperialism, and oppression. In her first novel, the underrated *Games of the Story* (1982), the examination of totalitarian political structures and power relationships between human beings and the state recalls George Orwell's *Nineteen Eighty-Four*. This futuristic fiction, with its female narrator, is also reminiscent of work by **Margaret Atwood** and **Doris Lessing**.

Adams' first publication was a collection of short stories, *The Hottest Night of the Century* (1979); her short fiction has been widely published and anthologized. *Dancing on Coral* has been read as a wittily parodic reworking of **Christina Stead**'s *For Love Alone*. The novel also brings into question many of the conventions of masculinist narratives.

Adams says Luigi Pirandello taught her that truth and reality are not fixed. Increasingly, this notion and its narrative consequences are the subjects of her writing. In her 1990 novel, *Longleg*, the central character, William Badger, learns to inhabit, finally to construct, an uncertain and shifting 'reality' as he grows up and undertakes the archetypal Australian journey to the 'old world' and back. As Badger, who may be compared with **Patrick White**'s Sam Parker or Hurtle Duffield in some instances, loses his naïvety and consolidates his position as the individualistic outsider, he typifies the wayward, creative energy of contemporary Australian culture.

DELYS BIRD

ADAMSON, ROBERT (1944–)

Australian poet

Born in Sydney, Australia, he has lived all his life there or near the Hawkesbury River. He spent some of his adolescence and early adulthood in correctional institutions. In the late 1960s he was a major figure in changing the direction of the Poetry Society of Australia's *Poetry Magazine* to the modernist *New Poetry* (1970–), which he controlled until 1981 either as editor, associate editor, or through close involvement with the editor. He founded and co-edited Prism Poets and Prism Books, was co-editor/co-director of the poetry publisher Big Smoke Books, and is co-director of the poetry publisher Paper Bark Press.

Adamson's poetry volumes are *Canticles on the Skin* (1970), where he is an outlaw and surrealist, a drug-using visionary nevertheless attracted to the Hawkesbury; *The Rumour* (1971), where he creates a private, autonomous universe of language; *Swamp Riddles* (1974), where the Hawkesbury provides a way of searching for meaning in the universe and which contains 'Sonnets to be Written from Prison', in which he is reminded of Stéphane Mallarmé; *Theatre I–XIX* (1976) and *Cross the Border* (1977), where, under the influence of Mallarmé and the Hawkesbury, he creates a self-referential, imaginary world, including an exploration of the Arthurian legend; *Selected Poems* (1977); *Where I Come From* (1979), where he selects from childhood memories to create an impression of outrageous realism; *The Law at Heart's Desire* (1982), where he explores his adult self in conflict with a materialistic society; and the award-winning *The Clean Dark* (1989), where he returns to the Hawkesbury to re-explore themes from his earlier work, including conventional social criticism from the alienated artist's viewpoint. Adamson also co-authored *Zimmer's Essay* (1974), which analyses prison experience, and he co-edited with **M. Jurgensen** *Australian Writing Now* (1988).

Adamson's poetry combines romanticism with modernism. His obsession with writing poetry becomes a triumph of the will and a means of redemption, ironically facilitated by his violent adolescent experiences. Despite the lack of formal education, he read western poetry extensively and frequently alludes to other poets and poetry in his own work. His unresolved adolescent hero-worship continued, not just as hero-worship of poets but also as deliberate imitation of their poetry. (The American poet Robert Duncan told Adamson to stop imitating him.) Adamson's criminal convictions and imprisonment reinforced his detestation of society, his extremely relativist viewpoint, and his need to impose particular opinions on other people. His use of hard drugs reinforced his relativism, contributing to his view that literal and imaginative worlds are almost identical. While many critics see his Hawkesbury poetry as his best, Adamson sees his poetic survival as the sum total of perpetual changes of personae (as distinct from social role-playing). He regards the entire body of his poems as unfinished, revising published work and writing new poems to give new meanings to earlier work. No matter how impressive his descriptive ability in some Hawkesbury poems, his main drive is to convert riverscape into the paradoxical mirror maze of a modernist altar.

GRAHAM ROWLANDS

Further reading: Martin Duwell, ed., *A Possible Contemporary Poetry* (1982).

ADCOCK, FLEUR (1934–)
New Zealand poet

She was born in Papakura, New Zealand, but spent part of her childhood in England. She graduated in classics from Victoria University of Wellington, New Zealand, and taught briefly at Otago University. In 1963 she left New Zealand permanently to live in England. For many years she worked as a librarian, but has been a free-lance writer since 1979. Her poetry collections include *The Eye of the Hurricane: Poems* (1964), *Tigers* (1967), *High Tide in the Garden* (1971), *The Scenic Route* (1974), and *The Inner Harbour* (1979). Her *Selected Poems* (1983) was followed by two volumes of translations — *Orient Express: Poems by Grete Tartler* (1989) and *Letters from Dark-ness: Poems by Daniela Crăsnaru* (1991).

Whether or not Adcock is a New Zealand poet is a question that arises in the poems themselves — 'Please Identify Yourself' (*The Scenic Route*) and 'Instead of an Interview' (*The Inner Harbour*), for example. Adcock has managed to make the transition to the British literary mainstream while retaining close links with New Zealand. Her early poems, such as 'Ngauranga Gorge Hill' and 'Stewart Island' (*High Tide in the Garden*), deal explicitly with New Zealand and her decision to leave it; later poems record her perception of her homeland when she returns as a visitor 'ingrained; ingrown; incestuous'.

Adcock's poetry has always exhibited a classical economy of phrasing and a distinctive air of detachment. Decorum, precision, and control are the hallmarks of Adcock's poetic style. Her distinctive voice, with its characteristic mixture of candour and detachment, has given rise to a school of New Zealand imitators.

Adcock is an exact and unsentimental commentator on human relationships. 'Advice to a Discarded Lover' (*Tigers*) is an early example, providing a rebarbative, unforgettable final image: 'If I were to touch you I should feel, / Against my fingers fat, moist worm-skin. / Do not ask me for charity now: / Go away until your bones are clean.' The tone of these poems is wry, ironic, cool. 'Against Coupling' (*High Tide in the Garden*) wittily advises against the act of love — 'this no longer novel exercise'. Adcock's elegies are judicious, stoical, yet there is a sense — rare in her work — that they have barely controlled the underlying emotion. *Time-Zones* (1991) builds on the political poems of *The Incident Book* (1986), observing with Adcock's typical detachment the anxieties of the time — birth defects, AIDS, Alzheimer's disease, and World War Three.

Adcock has published translations of Roman and Greek poets, a collection of medieval Latin poems, *The Virgin and the Nightingale* (1983), and has also contributed translations to Peter Jay's *The Greek Anthology* (1973).

ANNE FRENCH

AFRICA IN CANADIAN LITERATURE

Africa features in Canadian literature as subject, setting, image, and idea. Several Canadian writers have lived in or visited Africa and adapted their experience into fiction or poetry. Some have written of an imaginary Africa. A number of African-born writers have also immigrated to Canada and written of or alluded to their homeland.

Among the earliest documentary allusions to Africa in Canadian writing are the comments of various nineteenth-century travellers and military personnel who recounted their African experiences autobiographically. J. W. Dunbar Moodie told in *Ten Years in South Africa* (1835) of his experiences as a magistrate in that colony and of his interest in Africa's 'wild sports'. Returning to his native England in 1829, two years before his marriage and immigration to Canada, Moodie met his future wife, Susanna Strickland (see **Moodie, Susanna**) at the London home of **Thomas Pringle**, the English-born author of *Narrative of a Residence in South Africa* (1834) who is now claimed as one of South Africa's most prominent colonial poets. As secretary of the Anti-Slavery League, Pringle encouraged the Moodies, as well as numerous other figures, to question institutional racism, but such questioning did not altogether eliminate conventional European literary and social stereotyping of non-European peoples and places.

Evidence of the British empire's ability to construct resistant images of Africa shows in the stereotypes of the 'dark continent' and the numerous colonial allusions to imperial heroes. European soldiers who ventured into Africa were frequently depicted as dauntless figures in conflict with 'savages' or 'rebels'; such images helped to justify, to the imperial mind, the European military, political, and missionary presence abroad. General Gordon's defence against the Mahdi's siege of Khartoum in 1885, and Lord Kitchener's efforts to retake the city in 1898 were both deemed subjects suitable for romantic poetry in Canada, as was the Anglo-Boer War of 1899–1902. **Wilfred Campbell**'s 'Show the Way, England' (1905) typifies how imperial conquests were read as signs of a manly heritage and adapted to local political conditions.

Selectively reading history, Campbell wrote: 'We, whose fathers were / Victors with Wellington, / Masters with Nelson, / Under the old flag / They flapped at the Nile, / . . . / Won you, with Wolfe, / Canada's glorious / Mile upon mile.' In 'Ahmet' (1905), Campbell also rewrote a North African folk tale, but early adaptations of this kind characteristically did not appreciate the sophistication of oral cultures; rather, they fostered an image of an Africa that remained 'primitive' until European contact. Many missionary hymns encouraged a similar image and hence constructed Eurocentric versions of power.

North Africa appears relatively infrequently in Canadian writing. One nineteenth-century writer who travelled to Egypt was Alice Jones, whose travel sketches were published in the Toronto *Week* as 'Nile Vignettes' from 19 July to 16 August 1895. Prominent among twentieth-century allusions is Scott Symons' 1986 novel *Helmet of Flesh,* a tale of homosexual desire set in Morocco, which aims primarily to attack blandness in Canadian society. South, East, and West African allusions recur more frequently in Canadian literature, perhaps because more immigrants to Canada from these areas have themselves been writers. Among these immigrants are the poets Jeni Couzyn and **Arthur Nortje**, the fiction writers William Schermbrucker, John Peter, Réshard Gool, **M. G. Vassanji**, and Ernst Havemann, and the critic Cecil Abrahams. Couzyn's books of poetry — among them *Monkey's Wedding* (1972), *Christmas in Africa* (1975), and *House of Changes* (1978) — include a variety of charms, memoirs, political comments, and glimpses of place and character. Nortje's residence in Canada was brief, and his dissatisfaction with the society is revealed in his sardonic 1967 poem 'Immigrant' (posthumously collected in *Dead Roots,* 1973), which contrasts Canadian materialism with his spiritual longing for home. Schermbrucker's fictions, *Chameleon and Other Stories* (1983) and *Mimosa* (1988), recall his childhood in Kenya and his quest for a lost family history in South Africa. Havemann's *Bloodsong and Other Stories of South Africa* (1987) tells of social violence under apartheid, as do Peter's *Along That Coast* (1964) and *Runaway* (1969), which juxtapose the political naïvety of visitors to South Africa with the racial realities of living in that country. Gool's realistic anti-apartheid novel, *Price*, appeared in 1973.

Among Canadian writers who have lived in Africa and written of it are **Margaret Laurence**, **Dave Godfrey**, **Audrey Thomas**, **Dorothy Livesay**, and Richard Stevenson. Godfrey went to Ghana with CUSO (Canadian University Students Overseas) in 1963 and was acting head of the department of English at Adisadel College until 1965. Thomas lived in Kumasi, Ghana, with her husband, an art teacher, between 1964 and 1966. Livesay worked with UNESCO in Northern Rhodesia between 1960 and 1963. Stevenson taught at teachers' college in Maiduguri, Nigeria, from 1980 to 1982. Livesay's poems about the Zambian religious figure Alice Lenchina, together with several celebrations of voice and sensuousness, were published as *The Colour of God's Face* (1964) and republished in *The Unquiet Bed* (1967) and as the 'Zambia' sequence in *Collected Poems: The Two Seasons* (1972). Godfrey's documentary *Man Deserves Man* (1968) details CUSO experiences and calls for international solutions to economic disparities; his novel *The New Ancestors* (1970) transforms Ghana and Mali into fictional political territory, a symbolic ground on which forces of power (and separate systems of language) compete for control but succeed only in hastening social fracture. In Thomas' fiction — some of the stories in *Ten Green Bottles* (1967) and *Ladies and Escorts* (1977) and especially the Isobel Cleary trilogy: *Mrs. Blood* (1970), *Songs My Mother Taught Me* (1973), and *Blown Figures* (1974) — Africa is more personal than political. Thomas' Africa is the setting for her central character's psychologically devastating miscarriage and is also the embodiment of her sense of estrangement, both from others and from herself. Stevenson's experience of West Africa in the early 1980s resulted in *Driving Offensively* (1985) and marked later poems as well. In the preface to *Driving Offensively*, Stevenson observes that he is less concerned with culture shock than with recognizing the depth of his own acculturation.

Margaret Laurence, who had accompanied her engineer husband to Somaliland in 1950 and lived there and in the Gold Coast until 1957, preceded all of these writers into print: with a translation of Somali folk tales, *A Tree for Poverty* (1954), which showed her interest in women's roles and rights, especially in male-dominated societies; a novel, *This Side Jordan* (1960); an autobiographical travel-journal, *The Prophet's Camel Bell* (1963; published in the USA the next year as *New Wind in a Dry Land*); several short stories, most collected in *The Tomorrow-Tamer* (1963), all concerned with a culture in transition; and a critical tribute to **Chinua Achebe** and other Nigerian writers, *Long Drums and Cannons* (1968). The autobiography reveals her indebtedness to the writings of O. Mannoni, demonstrates her growing appreciation of the power of oral cultures, and (like some of her subsequent essays, collected in *Heart of a Stranger*, 1976) reflects on the unthinking biases that travellers continue to take to Africa.

Some of the more conventional references to Africa show in works by Ralph Allen, **Hugh Hood**, Jacques Godbout, and Jacques Ferron, most of whom have imagined Africa without actually visiting it. Hood's *You Can't Get There from Here* (1972) uses Africa as an exotic setting for a satire of North American society. Ferron's *Le Saint-Elias* (1972) parallels an imaginary Africa with a real Quebec, emphasizing the marginality of both, and Hubert Aquin's *Trou de mémoire* (1968) adapts the conventional parallel between Quebec and Africa (in this case the Ivory Coast) to explore symbolically the nature of political separation. Godbout's *L'aquarium* (1962) only implies Africa as its setting, the idea of 'tropic' serving as an intellectual construct, a deliberate contrast with 'north'. Allen's *Ask the Name of the Lion* (1962) casts the Congolese 'rebellion' as the setting for a romantic narrative thriller. By contrast, David Knight's poems, in *The Army Does Not Go Away* (1969), tell realistically of social violence, and his 1971 novel *Farquharson's Physique and What It Did to His Mind* portrays a man being drawn into commitment and action as the horror of the **Nigerian Civil War** becomes clear to him.

Critics have generalized about Africa in Canadian literature. Some read 'Africa' in Jungian terms, treating it as an image of the psychological 'unknown' into which individuals must venture in their quest for 'wholeness'. Some stress the politics of Canadian-African relations, focusing on such issues as imperialism, race, economic disparities, and exoticism. The notion of 'otherness' — whether perceived as the characteristic of 'natural' distinctions or the product of socially engendered bias — has been extensively analysed. Critics also emphasize the differences between written and oral cultures and the degree to which contemporary Canadian writers have learned to read their own society more sensitively by becoming more familiar with alternative sophisticated versions of history, community, and civilization.

W. H. NEW

Further reading: Patricia Monk, 'Shadow continent: the image of Africa in three Canadian writers', *Ariel* 8 (1977); Micere Githae-Mugo, *Visions of Africa* (1978); W. H. New, 'The other and I: Laurence's African stories', in George Woodcock (ed.) *A Place to Stand On* (1983); Francis Barker, ed., *Europe and Its Others*, 2 vols (1985); James Clifford and George E. Marcus, eds, *Writing Culture: The Poetics and Politics of Ethnography* (1986); Michel de Certeau, *Heterologies: Discourse on the Other* (1986), trans. Brian Massumi.

AFRICAN CONNECTIONS (The Caribbean)
To date no African epic has surfaced in the Caribbean; this fact indicates the fragmentation of ethnic units in the region and the erosion of historicocultural memory as encompassed within that literary form. Rather, culture-specific and transcultural literary retentions emerge in genres such as Yoruba religious myths (in Cuba and Trinidad), folk tales, proverbs and riddles, abuse styles, and song types. In the search for greater authenticity in representing the culture of Caribbean people, scribal artists have increasingly turned to reproducing and refashioning such oral traditions.

Storytelling is conventionally a moonlit-night activity; as in Africa, its enactment during daylight (i.e., work-time) is taboo. Nevertheless, it also accompanies non-time-specific manual work such as corn- and pea-shelling. Although a declining art in contemporary rural environments because of expanding technology and mass media, storytelling is being revived by libraries, bookshops, mass education programmes, and audio-visual media.

Obviously of African tradition are the Caribbean trickster stories of Anansi the Spider and his brother/friend/adversary Takooma, those of Tortoise, and of Hare, also called Brer/Bra/*Bredda* ('Brother') Rabbit. These trickster heroes derive from various African culture groups. Their use of cunning for survival in certain famine-prone African subsistence economies translated well into the Caribbean's similar ecological and economic conditions, while their status as disrupters of the African communal ethos assumed positive value under conditions of plantation servitude and ethnic confrontation. There are also aetiological, cautionary, and wonder-child tales. Many tales feature animal characters, but some present humans and spirits. Structurally, many tales have lost the songs characteristic of African storytelling methodology, but others have retained refrains, some now cryptic. (See **Folklore**, The Caribbean.)

Attempts to incorporate this narrative tradition into scribal literature have met with varying success. Examples include **Neville Dawes**' cumulative folk-tale epilogue to *The Last Enchantment* (1960); **Derek Walcott**'s adaptation of performance technique and allegory in *Ti-Jean and His Brothers* (1970); **Andrew Salkey**'s parabolic satires, *Anancy's Score* (1973); **Erna Brodber**'s symbolist use of folk tale in *Jane and Louisa Will Soon Come Home* (1980); the storytelling narrator of **Trevor Rhone**'s *Old Story Time* (1981); **Earl Lovelace**'s *The Wine of Astonishment* (1982); **Vic Reid**'s *Nanny-Town* (1983), and some of the stories in **Olive Senior**'s collection *Summer Lightning* (1986).

In several Caribbean islands, as in Africa, riddle contests between storyteller and audience precede traditional storytelling sessions. (The interconnection of the two genres is so established that in Dominica riddles are called 'tim-tim', whereas in Grenada 'tim-tim' announces the start of the folk-tale session.) It appears, however, that the riddle has not yet been consciously reworked in the scribal literature, the nearest example of riddle technique being Brodber's novels *Jane and Louisa Will Soon Come Home* and *Myal* (1988).

Caribbean proverbs derive from African, European, Indian, as well as Biblical sources. African proverbs and riddles, for example, are characterized by their indirect and metaphoric allusion to images drawn largely from flora and fauna, some of which have been replaced with correspondingly familiar items in the Caribbean environment. For example, imagery of African lions and hyenas has yielded to that of cat and dog. Other resemblances between African and Caribbean proverbs in terms of structure, imagery, and philosophical content are striking and are further confirmed by proverb similarities among varying Caribbean island communities. Proverbs still exert great influence on the expression of ideas and enter the forms of popular songs, such as calypso and reggae, performance-oriented poetry, and the novel. **George Lamm-**

ing's *In the Castle of My Skin* (1953), Vic Reid's *Nanny-Town*, and **Louise Bennett**'s *Jamaica Labrish* (1966) draw on this tradition. The brevity and common sense of proverbs have no doubt been reasons for insufficient critical awareness of their function in Caribbean scribal literature. Also of note, however, is the relationship between education and the use of proverbs — the more educated the speaker, the less homely is proverb use; Shakespeare and Latin authors instead supply the anglophone speaker with parallel, succinct, philosophical comment.

In topic and in vocal and gestural behaviour, Caribbean abuse styles bear resemblance to various African modes. Abuse content focuses largely on the opponent's physical attributes, insisting on data — real, exaggerated, even fictive — regarding height, size, disabilities, uncleanliness, infertility, illness, sexual unattractiveness, and deviance. Caribbean creole languages are replete with ideophonic perjorative terms for physical appearance and action that are either African words or neologisms based on African-language sound symbolisms. (An ideophone is a word suggestive of a sound.) The abuse genre characterizes some calypsoes, much stage, radio, and audio-visual drama, **Claude McKay**'s 'A Midnight Woman to the Bobby' (in *Songs of Jamaica*, 1912, introduced by **Walter Jekyll**), and some of Louise Bennett's most memorable poems. **V. S. Naipaul**'s early works and **Merle Hodge**'s *Crick Crack, Monkey* (1970) also make creditable use of the genre.

The love-song tradition in the Caribbean is relatively weak when compared with the impulse to narrative and commentary, both satiric and protest. This may signal the comparative weakness of the ecstatic Arabic poetic traditions channelled through Islam (which passed from a caste to a popular religion in West Africa only in the nineteenth century) in relation to the vibrancy of pragmatic attitudes to sex and marriage in sub-Saharan traditional Africa, where less emphasis was placed on love and courtship than on procreation and the realization of socio-economic needs through clan and family alliances. Such pragmatism was reinforced under Caribbean slavery by unstable family-life conditions and the absence of familial imperatives and censure in the regulation of mating.

The dirge was fed by slavery, but this genre has weakened recently, leaving the popular song of news/gossip, celebration or censure of behaviour and event, and socio-political commentary and critique. Electronic recording and mass dissemination have made popular song the most overt oral literary form in the Caribbean. (See **Songs and Ballads**, The Caribbean.) Its musical idiom reflects African influence in its insistent rhythmic base and its marked rhythmic syncopation (in some territories), in cantor-chorus structural complementarity (whether responsorial or in simultaneous vocalization), in vocal imitations of musical instruments, and, whether for semantic punning or technical flamboyance, in intensive sound echo/rhyme (the European-language substitute for African tonal matching). These rhythmic and singing styles cross-fertilize **E. K. Brathwaite**'s poetry and are integral to dub/performance poetry.

MAUREEN WARNER-LEWIS

Further reading: Maureen Warner-Lewis, 'The African impact on language and literature in the English-speaking Caribbean', in Margaret Crahan and Franklin Knight (eds) *Africa and the Caribbean: Legacies of a Link* (1979).

AGARD, JOHN (1949–)

Guyanese/British poet

Born in Guyana, he published his first poetry collection, *Shoot Me with Flowers* (1973), in Guyana, but moved in 1977 to England, where he has published several books and established a considerable reputation as a poet-performer. His work has always challenged the conventional colonial norms of English poetry, not only in his broadly political concerns, but in his use of language and, most particularly, in the manner of delivery his poems demand. A self-styled 'poetsonian', Agard toured with the All-Ah-We theatre company before settling in the UK. *Shoot Me with Flowers* anticipates many of the concerns of Agard's later work and establishes his essential idealism. If these early poems read now as rather naïve in their politics, the collection is memorable for some striking love poems.

Agard's characteristic brand of witty, ironic satire owes much to the wry survivor humour of Caribbean oral traditions. Since he moved to England, one aim of his work has been to highlight and undercut the pervasive stereotypes of black people there. In 'Palm Tree King', for example, the persona turns the feigned interest in exotic trees shown by his patronizing English acquaintance into a pointed lesson in post-colonial economics: 'If 6 straw hat / and half a dozen bikini / multiply by the same number of coconut tree / equal one postcard / how many square miles of straw hat / you need to make a tourist industry?'

Underpinning Agard's wit is a core of lyrical anger that gives his work its distinctive bite. *Mangoes and Bullets* (1985) contains several impassioned poems lamenting the corruption and injustice that have maimed the dream of an independent Caribbean. Nowhere has that dream been more tarnished than in Guyana, and Agard's superbly measured poem 'Come from That Window Child', written in response to the assassination of Walter Rodney, exemplifies both Agard's rage against the cynicism of Guyanese politics and the despite-it-all optimism that is another hallmark of his work.

In many ways Agard's well-deserved reputation as a performer has distracted attention from the style and originality of his poetry. On the page his poems work well enough, but it is Agard's voice-print rather than the type's imprint that carries the force of his words. In performance he uses the full range and power of his voice to unleash the energy and resonance crafted into his poetry. This is particularly true of his Casa de las Americas Poetry Prize-winning sequence *Man to Pan* (1982), written in celebration of the steel pan as a metaphor for Caribbean creativity.

Lovelines for a Goat-Born Lady (1990) is a collection of raunchy, sensual love poems, typically wry and politically alert; these poems represent the inclination to praise-song that has always been a counterweight to Agard's satire.

Agard has also published several books for children, including *Quetzy de Saviour* (1976), *Letters for Lettie* (1979), *Dig Away Two-Hole Tim* (1981), *I Din Do Nuttin* (1983), *Say It Again Granny* (1985), and *Laughter Is an Egg* (1989).

STEWART BROWN

Further reading: Stewart Brown, 'Taster: recent Guyanese writing from the UK', *Kyk-over-al* 31 (1985); Matt Holland, 'Mango mischief', *Poetry Review* 4 (1990–1).

AHMAD, SAYEED (1931–)

Bangladeshi dramatist

He was born in Dhaka (Bangladesh), into an affluent family that owned the city's Lion Theatre and had a number of its members as practising thespians and painters. Ahmad had early training in music, attended university in Dhaka and at the London School of Economics, England, and followed a career in government bureaucracy, writing his dramas at night.

Ahmad's plays staged to date have placed him at the forefront of Bangladesh theatre. Like fellow playwrights Syed Shamsul Haq, Alauddin Al-Azad, Shaukat Osman, and Munier Chowdhury, he wrote his plays in Bengali, but, unlike them, he also created them in English. *The Thing*, first published in *Vision* (Karachi) in 1961, was premièred in 1962 by the Drama Circle in Dhaka and has since been staged in other parts of the world. It deals with the tug of force and circumstance between humanity and nature, a contest and a companionship so evident in the cyclonic Bangladeshi existence. A similar concern is the focus of *The Milepost* (first published in *Vision*, 1964), based on the horrendous 1943 famine in Bengal, in which the stunning forces of nature are contemplated and reconciled with human courage. *Survival* (first published in the weekly *Holiday* in 1967) dramatizes the legend of a mother crocodile who entrusts her seven children to a fox, who eats up six of them, keeping the seventh to show each time the mother visits. A powerful metaphor of the exploitation of the masses, *Survival* was first staged in 1967 in Punjabi, under the title *Jungul da rakha*, by Najm Hossain Syed, who translated and directed it. Performed under the auspices of Majlis Shah Hosain of Lahore without government licence, it was feared that it would arouse riots as the underclasses began to fill the stalls.

The Thing, *The Milepost*, and *Survival* were collected in *Three Plays by Sayeed Ahmad* (1979; 2nd ed., 1989) and were translated into Bengali by Ahmad and collected in *Sayeed Ahmad-er Tinti Natok* (1976).

Ahmad's later play, *The Last King* (published in Bengali as *Shesh Nawab*, 1989), is historical, interpreting and capturing a time of grand transition, the year 1757, when Bengal's last king, Sirajuddaula, was defeated at the Battle of Plassey by the British under Robert Clive. Ahmad combines elements of the realistic, legendary, and folk theatre in the style of Chinese opera and packs a power into his language that links him to the Indian tradition of Street Theatre.

ALAMGIR HASHMI

AIDOO, AMA ATA (1942–)

Ghanaian poet, dramatist, short-story writer

Born Christina Ama Ata Aidoo, near Saltpond, Ghana, she graduated with a BA from the University of Ghana in 1964. Much of her published work, all appearing under the name Ama Ata Aidoo, dates from the mid- and late-1960s. Unlike other west African women writers such as **Efua Sutherland**, **Tess Onwueme**, **Flora Nwapa**, and **'Zulu Sofola**, Aidoo has declined to concentrate on a single genre; she has published two novels, two plays, a book of short stories, and two poetry collections. She has worked in the USA (where she held a fellowship in creative writing at Stanford University), at the Institute of African Studies, University of Ghana, at the University of Nairobi, Kenya, and at Ahmadu Bello University, Nigeria.

Aidoo's first published play, *The Dilemma of a Ghost* (1965), deals with a conflict of values between a young western-educated couple and the village community. Husband and wife here share the same cultural preferences: the fact that he is Ghanaian, village-born, and she is Afro-American is not of central thematic importance (unlike in plays on mixed marriages by **Ola Rotimi** and **Joe de Graft**). However, in her novel *Our Sister Killjoy* (1977) Aidoo establishes a more complex conflict of principles: the central character, a Ghanaian woman, asserts her opposition both to white supremacy and to male compatriots who, despite their nationalist rhetoric, are unable to accept that her own more radical critique is legitimate and not a symptom of neurosis. Among African English-language novels of its time, *Our Sister Killjoy* is also boldly experimental in form and in the daring with which it characterizes lesbian affection to highlight the interrelationship between race and gender.

Aidoo's second play, *Anowa* (1969), moves from a relatively light treatment of parental/child conflict over marriage (the chief friction-point in *The Dilemma of a Ghost*) in its early scenes towards the heroine's articulation of a more profound vision of social freedom though her rejection of her husband's resort to slave-keeping. Technically a highly assured play, *Anowa* employs an increasingly formal *mise-en-scène* to mark the alienation between Anowa's values and her husband's. The image of false masculinity with which the play closes (wealth and slave-ownership identified with impotence) ensures its provocative impact, especially for a male audience.

In all these works and in her short stories (*No Sweetness Here*, 1970), Aidoo establishes how acutely individuals may feel themselves under the critical observation of the community and how identity and role are often the subject of fierce negotiation. Aidoo's work also shares an important source in orature. In the poetry collections *Someone Talking to Sometime* (1985) and *An Angry Letter in January* (1992) she writes on both the diaspora and external visions of Africa and on the continent's problems — poverty, ethnicity, and the abstractions of the élite revolutionary. The novel *Changes* (1991), winner of the 1992 Commonwealth Writers Prize for Best Book (Africa), deals again with conflict of value systems, but here, as with major novels by **Buchi Emecheta** and Mariama Bâ, Aidoo focuses on the husband-wife relationship.

CHRIS DUNTON

Further reading: Lloyd W. Brown, *Women Writers in Black Africa* (1981); Adeola James, *In Their Own Voices: African Women Writers Talk* (1990).

ALEXANDER, MEENA (1951–)

Indian poet, novelist, critic

Born in Allahabad, India, and educated in India, North Africa (BA, 1969, the University of Khartoum), and England (Ph.D., 1973, University of Nottingham), she worked for a short time as an English teacher in Hyderabad, India. In 1988 she was writer-in-residence at the Center for American Cultural Studies at Columbia University, USA, and she currently teaches writing at Columbia University, at Hunter College, and at the Graduate Center, City University of New York.

Alexander is noted for her sharp, post-colonial perception of India's colonial past and for her feminist focus. In *Nampally Road* (1991), Alexander's only novel, the central character, Mira, speaks of her mission, as a poet and as an individual, as one in which she could 'stitch it all together: my birth in India a few years after national independence, my colonial education, my rebellion against the arranged marriage my mother had in mind for me, my years of research in England'. Mira soon realizes that she must turn to the people and their basic problems (poverty, hunger, politics, resistance, and exploitation) to define her 'self'. The suffering of the Indian woman is Alexander's recurrent and feminist motif. She searches continually for the possible roles of women as mother, freedom fighter, social ameliorator, and feminist in the post-colonial milieu.

Alexander's poetry collections include *The Bird's Bright Ring: A Long Poem* (1976), *I Root My Name* (1977), and *Without Place* (1977); these poems are included in the volume *House of a Thousand Doors: Poems and Prose Pieces of Meena Alexander* (1988). In the latter collection Alexander projects the emerging self of a New Woman through a symbolically structured pilgrimage into the 'selves' of two grandmothers, Kanda, political grandmother, and Mariamma, her father's mother. *The Storm: A Poem in Five Parts* (1989) also highlights Alexander's feminist concerns.

Alexander's critical study *Women in Romanticism: Mary Wollstonecraft, Dorothy Wordsworth and Mary Shelley* (1989) further develops her concern for the feminine self. One of India's most vigorous post-colonial feminists, Alexander deserves profitable comparison with **Kamala Das** and the Canadians **Margaret Laurence** and **Margaret Atwood**.

N. RAMACHANDRAN NAIR

ALFON, ESTRELLA D. (1917–83)

Filipino short-story writer, dramatist, journalist

Born in Cebu City, the Philippines, she later set many of her stories in the fictional community of

Espeleta, a recognizable lower middle-class district of that city. Though she wrote mostly in English, she also wrote some stories in Cebuano. Of the women writers of the region, she is among the most prominent.

Unable to complete a pre-medical course at the University of the Philippines because of poor health, Alfon instead earned an Associate in Arts certificate. Her first short story, 'Grey Confetti' (1935), was quickly followed by many others. A regular contributor to Manila-based national magazines, she had several stories cited in **Jose Garcia Villa**'s annual honour rolls. Seventeen of her stories appear in *Magnificence and Other Stories* (1960), the only collection of her short fiction. Of these stories, **Francisco Arcellana** said, 'When I say that these stories are powerful as stories, I mean they are compelling. They are told with urgency. They make you think of the ancient mariner.'

While critics found cause to commend her, a conservative group of Catholics charged Alfon in court with obscenity over one of her short stories, 'Fairy Tale for the City', about a young man's initiation into sex. Fellow writers were quick to rally around her, claiming her as a martyr to the cause of artistic integrity. The present generation of readers, having dismissed obscenity as a legitimate issue in the critical discussion of literature, prefers to claim her as a writer for the feminist cause. By populating her fictional world largely with women and children, she calls attention to their marginalized roles in Philippine patriarchal society. Though most of her women characters are unable even to recognize themselves as victims, Alfon's sympathetic portrayals allow for readings subversive of the society that victimizes women.

Reportedly the most prolific Filipino woman writer before the war, Alfon was at times charged with sloppy writing and suspected of writing for money. Undeterred, she continued to write, not just more stories and journalistic pieces, but also plays. In the Arena Theater Play Writing Contest of 1961–2, four of her one-act plays won all the prizes.

EDNA ZAPANTA MANLAPAZ

ALI, AHMED (1910–)

Pakistani novelist, poet, critic

He was born in Delhi, India, and educated at Aligarh Muslim University and Lucknow University. Ali began a career in teaching in 1931 as a lecturer in English at Lucknow and, apart from an appointment as director of Listener Research for the British Broadcasting Corporation's New Delhi office during the Second World War, served as professor at Agra, Allahabad, and Calcutta, India, before leaving for China in 1947 as a British Council visiting professor. He was a founder of the Progressive Writers Movement in the 1930s. Following the Partition, he moved to Karachi and joined the Pakistan Foreign Service, retiring in 1960. Until the 1990s, Ali worked as a businessman and as a visiting professor at a number of universities.

Ali started his writing career as a poet and a playwright and soon found his forté in the short story and the novel, developing fast as a bilingual (English and Urdu) writer who wrote most of his short stories in Urdu but his plays, poems, and novels in English. In fact, it can be argued that some of the characterization and symbolism in his novels *Twilight in Delhi* (1940; repr. 1984) and *Ocean of Night* (1964) were drawn from the sociological and structural kernel of his plays and short stories of the 1930s, which ranged stylistically from the realistic and the allegorical to the autobiographical/psychological and the surrealistic.

Ali's other publications include the poetry collection *Purple Gold Mountain: Poems from China* (1960), selections in *First Voices: Six Poets from Pakistan* (1965), edited by **Shahid Hosain**, *Selected Poems* (1988), the plays 'Break the Chains' (premièred 1932) and *The Land of Twilight* (1937), and the novel *Rats and Diplomats* (1986; first published in India as *Of Rats and Diplomats,* 1985). His short-story collections, in Urdu and English, are *Sholay* (1934), *Hamar Gali* (1944), *Qaid Khana* (1944), *Maut Se Pahlay* (1945), and *The Prison House* (1985) and he contributed to *Angaray* (1932).

Twilight in Delhi and *Ocean of Night*, as well as much other fiction in Urdu, were written, Ali states, to 'depict a phase of our national life and the decay of a whole culture, a particular mode of thought and living, values now dead and gone . . . ' Accordingly, *Twilight in Delhi* is set in the great Indian centre of Muslim civilization, Delhi, and the plot revolves round a simple love story of a boy and a girl, of Mughal and noble Arabic extractions respectively, who experience cyclical joys and difficulties to have their love accepted, formalized, and renewed despite social barriers or death. Around it is built a whole way of life, customs, and ceremonies that sustain a colourful though declining feudal culture, including the father's pigeon-flying pastime, the zenana, and the wedding rituals. In the outer circle, around the old house in a by-lane of Old Delhi, *history* is seen at work in the Great Durbar held by the King-Emperor in 1911, the influenza epidemic of 1919, the Jallianwalla Bagh Massacre of 1919 in Amritsar, and the political turmoil of 1920 in Northern India — nearly everything to interest Bonamy Dobrée, Edwin Muir, and E. M. Forster, who commended the novel — and also in elements that could barely pass the British censor's examination of the manuscript during the Second World War.

Ocean of Night, dealing with life between the two world wars, explores the possibility of the modern spirit within a feudal structure, and whereas E. M. Forster finds, in *A Passage to India* (1924), the 'heart' to be undeveloped, Ali finds it here half atrophied, half searching in confusion. The novel is set in the other great Muslim centre, Lucknow. The mood is somewhat subdued, the atmosphere one of repose and contemplation amid a celebration dance and Muslim ideas of love, peace, and friendship. The Nawab's mistress is a fine courtesan, and the young lawyer in love with her cannot overcome the class barrier to find fulfilment. The intellectual and mystical elements in the Muslim tradition are related to the political degeneration of the Muslim civilization; both ordinary feelings and the more delicate emotions are seen as atrophied or sacrificed to the remaining oligarchy's reckless life-style and idle, indiscriminate social pursuits.

These early novels were concerned with the last of Muslim civilization in British India. Both are in the realistic-poetic tradition and use verse quotations as explicating, moralizing, and foreshadowing frames within the straightforward prose narrative. But Ali's more recent concerns in *Rats and Diplomats* are with a general decay in the world, in which representatives of the 'newly-freed fourth world' find analogues of decay and depravity matched to their own and prevalent on a universal scale. Consequently, the poetry disappears completely — so does realism.

In *Rats and Diplomats* a dismissed general is appointed ambassador of Bachusan and posted to Micea, the capital of Ratisan. He finds himself flung headlong into quasi-diplomacy in a country that he had earlier found difficult to locate on map or compass. His handling of actual life and affairs in the territory proves no better than his theoretical grasp of the place, and after a clumsy and rather public escapade he is peremptorily recalled by the president of Bachusan. There ends the novel, as well as our *hero*'s short and not-too-happy career in *diplomacy*. But what is more important is that, before the end, he wakes up one morning with a tail grown at his back and transformed into a rat. The ratty business has taken its moral toll, whose evident denomination, as in Oscar Wilde's novel *The Picture of Dorian Gray* (1891), is biological and (un)aesthetic. The historical imagination in the earlier works did not offer to subvert history so as to re-order the moral universe, and such verve and humour had never been to the forefront. *Rats and Diplomats* aspires to the moral status of a fable. The general relates all in his vigorous and sometimes self-parodic language, and what he relates is bleak though humorous, in a style now gravid, now brisk, and in a novel that takes Ali's fiction into the post-colonial era and into a post-colonial mode.

Ali's example in this respect is most instructive. From historical fictions of decay at a time when reconstructive urges were paramount in the writing in major Indian languages, including English, as in the work of **Mulk Raj Anand, R. K. Narayan, Raja Rao**, and **K. A. Abbas**, his long fictional silence and preparation only lead him to wielding what he calls the 'scalpel'.

While Lao She's (Shu Ch'ing-ch'un's) *Cat Country* (written in and serialized in 1932; first published in book form in 1949), a satirical novel of China in the 1930s, may have been a model for Ali's latest novel considering his Chinese interests, this development has not taken place in isolation from the South Asian and international literary milieu, wherein the non-realist work of Gabriel Garciá Marquéz, Grass, Borges, Fuentes, Fowles, and Kundera has held the attention of a large readership and even pepped up the vogue for magic realism. Evidently an ironic instrument of discourse, the 'scalpel' had to replace the realistic and reconstructive fictions of the colonial period, which insufficiently grasped the historical forces at work and the tremendous flux they had caused in the fundamental structure of colonial societies. **Salman Rushdie**'s Saleem Sinai (*Midnight's Children*, 1981) thus demolishes the distinctions between the internal and the external experience and between private and public history, both of which undergo an equally mythical 'perforation', 'chutnification', and 'pickling'. Rushdie's *Shame* (1983), likewise, uses the fairy-tale/nightmare technique to structure a fabulistic *roman à clef* that satirizes well-known referents picked from the contemporary common life that first pretend to a mock history. The choppy text is made to mimic the discontinuity of good sense and harmony in the subject itself.

The search for harmony and love is indeed the main concern in Ali's fiction as much as in his poetry. His poems reflect influences imbibed from the Chinese lyric, English Romantic, Urdu, and Persian traditions. Often written in a deliberately antiquated style — as if an English translation of old Chinese — these poems achieve a certain distance and impersonality while dealing with personal details or human, moral, and metaphysical themes; they also lend themselves both to personal and political allegories, to which most of Ali's work since the 1930s responds rather readily. Their main interest today is in the inventive and expressive aspects of form.

Non-fiction and translation are also among Ali's active interests. He has produced an important translation of the *Qur'an* entitled *Al-Qur'an: A Contemporary Translation* (1984) as well as a penetrating critical anthology of Urdu poetry, *The Golden Tradition* (1973). Considering his career, which spans the better part of the twentieth century, and his output, which closely concerns both Pakistani and Indian cultural contexts, it is necessary to see Ali's position as a man of letters in South Asia and not only in Pakistan.

Ali's other works include criticism (*Mr Eliot's Penny World of Dreams*, 1941, *The Problem of Style and Technique in Ghalib*, 1969, and *The Shadow and the Substance: The Principles of Reality, Art and Literature*, 1977); non-fiction (*Muslim China*, 1949); and numerous translations, including *The Flaming Earth: Poems from Indonesia (1949)*, *The Falcon and the Hunted Bird: An Anthology of Urdu Poetry* (1950), *The Bulbul and the Rose: An Anthology of Urdu Poetry* (1962), and *Ghalib:*

Selected Poems (1969).

ALAMGIR HASHMI

Further reading: Anita S. Kumar, '*Twilight in Delhi*: a study in lyricism', *Indian Literature* March-April (1976); Carlo Coppola, 'The short stories of Ahmed Ali', in Muhammad Umar Memon (ed.) *Studies in the Urdu Gazal and Prose Fiction* (1979); Alamgir Hashmi, 'Ahmed Ali: the transition to a post-colonial mode', *World Literature Written in English* 2 (1989).

ALKALI, ZAYNAB (1950–)
Nigerian novelist
Born in Biu, Nigeria, she attended Bayero University, Kano, where she obtained a BA in English (1973) and an MA (1979). She has taught English and African literature at various institutions in Nigeria, including Bayero University and the University of Maiduguri. Alkali won the **Association of Nigerian Authors**' award for prose fiction in 1985 with her first novel, *The Stillborn* (1984). *The Virtuous Woman* followed in 1985.

Alkali's arrival on the Nigerian male-dominated literary scene was highly acclaimed because she is one of the first female novelists from northern Nigeria and because of her examination of the position of the African woman in patriarchial Africa. Her concern with the position of African women in Africa, the challenges facing young African women, and African women's reactions to patriarchy can be situated within the sociological dialogue in which Nigerian and other African literatures have been involved.

Unlike those of colonial literatures (e.g., Joseph Conrad's *Heart of Darkness*) and some earlier Nigerian novels (such as **Chinua Achebe**'s *Things Fall Apart*, 1958), Alkali's protagonists are women who challenge their position in society, offering a corrective to the depiction of African women in previous works. Interestingly, these characters are still contained within the marital institution they set out to question. For example, Li, in *The Stillborn*, cannot sustain her initial subversion of patriarchy, especially after her marriage to Habu Adams, and Nana Ai, in *The Virtuous Woman*, accepts patriarchy unquestioningly. Although Li is unable to sustain her assault on patriarchy (she comes from a predominantly Islamic and patriarchal northern Nigeria), her struggle, like Alkali's efforts, is significant.

ADETEYO ALABI

Further reading: Seiyifa Koroye, 'The ascetic feminist vision of Zaynab Alkali', in Henrietta C. Otokunefor and Obiageli C. Nwodo (eds) *Nigerian Female Writers: A Critical Perspective* (1991).

ALLEY, REWI (1897–1987)
New Zealand poet
Born of European descent in Springfield, in a farming area outside Christchurch, New Zealand, he was named after a Maori chief prominent in the Land Wars of the 1860s. After war service in Europe, Alley travelled to Shanghai in 1927 and lived in close contact with Chinese workers until his death. He was involved in the wars of resistance and liberation, organizing Gung Ho industrial co-operatives, and schoolteaching.

From the 1940s Alley published in both New Zealand and China many volumes of poetry that he later described as 'Poetry to Deal with Life and People'; *Upsurge: Asia and the Pacific: Poems* (privately published in 1969) is a representative volume. The simplicity of his writing has deflected critical attention, but is consistent with its ideological motivation; clarity is essential to its acknowledged propagandist function; imagery and symbolism are extremely simple; and the immediacy of its purpose results in a lack of polishing and revision beyond the elimination of any obscurity. Alley's style was also determined by his extensive readership in developing countries, especially in Africa and India, where English was often a second language. His work also shows stylistic affinities with poets he respected: the Maori **Hone Tuwhare** and the Australian Aboriginal **Oodgeroo Noonuccal** (Kath Walker).

Alley's Communist commitment (from the early 1930s) co-existed with his high regard for traditional Chinese culture; during the Cultural Revolution his translations of Chinese classics were termed a 'poisonous weed'. Many of his English poems express a love for China's landscape and buildings. Alley's autobiographical writing — *At 90: Memoirs of My China Years* (1986), reprinted as *Rewi Alley: An Autobiography* (1987) — and other non-fiction have an unpretentiousness similar to that of his poetry.

HOWARD McNAUGHTON

Further reading: George Chapple, *Rewi Alley of China* (1980).

ALLFREY, PHYLLIS SHAND (1915–86)
Dominican novelist

Born Phyllis Byam Shand in Roseau, Dominica, the Caribbean, she never attended school, but was educated by a series of tutors. She travelled to England, where she met her husband. They moved to the USA and later returned to England, where Phyllis Allfrey became secretary to the novelist Naomi Mitchison and became involved in socialist politics. In London she wrote mostly poetry and began the novel *The Orchid House* (1953). The family returned to Dominica in 1954, where Allfrey co-founded the Dominica Labour Party. In 1958 she became minister of labour and social affairs in the Federal Government of the West Indies (based in Trinidad). She returned to Dominica in 1961 (when the Federation failed) and, with her husband, ran *The Dominica Herald*. In 1965 she founded the weekly *Star*. She wrote a second novel, 'In the Cabinet', which remains unpublished.

As most of her work (including *Palm and Oak I*, 1950, *Contrasts*, 1955, and *Palm and Oak II*, 1974, all privately published) is virtually inaccessible to the public, Allfrey's reputation rests on *The Orchid House*. The novel is divided into three parts, one devoted to each of three sisters, Stella, Joan, and Natalie, who precipitate the action in the almost torpid house and are a life-force in the moribund society. The central motif is the orchid, which has a symbiotic and epiphytic relationship with its host. Having no roots, it draws moisture from the air and not the earth. The image of the three-petalled flower suggests that the three sisters provide not only beauty but utility. The story is narrated by the ageing nurse Lally, who is dying of cancer.

Subtle image patterns, conspicuously Keatsian, evoke the hot-house atmosphere of disease, death, and drugs; the novel's major focus is the paradox of beauty and disease, represented, for example, in the Master, who has retreated into a drug-sustained pipe-dream, and in Andrew, a consumptive Knight-at-Arms straight out of 'La Belle Dame Sans Merci'. The possibilities for vital change lie with the three sisters, especially Joan. Stella murders the drug dispenser Lillipoulala, and Natalie flies her invalid father to his death, but Joan (like Allfrey) remains on the island to help the black radical Baptiste with political, social, and economic reconstruction. She cannot take direct action because she is blackmailed by the Roman Catholic priest (who suspects Stella's involvement in the murder of Lillipoulala), but she persuades her husband, fighting in the Spanish Civil War, to return to the island. As well as evoking the total society, Allfrey sharply criticizes the Roman Catholic Church, which is seen as rigid, conservative, and stifling.

The Orchid House succeeds in avoiding the promotion of a single group, the clichés of race, colour, class, and tourist landscapes, didacticism, bitter flourishes, and wooden allegorical characters.

BARRIE DAVIES

Further reading: Elaine Campbell, 'Phyllis Shand Allfrey', in Daryl C. Dance (ed.) *Fifty Caribbean*

Writers: A Bio-bibliographical Critical Sourcebook (1986).

ALUKO, TIMOTHY MOFOLORUNSO (1918–)
Nigerian novelist
Born in Ilesha, Western Nigeria, he studied civil engineering and town planning in Lagos, Nigeria, and in London, England. After leaving his position as director of public works for Western Nigeria in 1966, Aluko studied public health engineering at the University of Newcastle upon Tyne, England, and later at the University of Lagos, where he lectured and from which he retired as associate professor in 1979. He has since taken up a career as a consulting engineer and writer in Lagos.

Aluko has published seven novels, the subject matter of which falls into two broad phases: the colonial and the post-colonial. His first novel, *One Man, One Wife* (1959), satirizes African Christian converts who condemn all aspects of their cultural heritage. The image of the one-eyed pastor David recalls Kurtz's painting in Joseph Conrad's *Heart of Darkness* (1902) and expresses the idea of the blind leading the blind. *Kinsman and Foreman* (1966), like **Ayi Kwei Armah**'s *Fragments* (1970), highlights the encumbrances of the African extended family system in contemporary society. *Chief, the Honourable Minister* (1970) explores a recurrent theme in African and Caribbean literature — the betrayal of the neo-colonial politician and the disillusionment that follows political independence. The problem of adaptation often leads Aluko's protagonists to a sad ending.

Many stylistic elements from the Yoruba oral tradition give Aluko's fiction the flavour of local colour writing. He places his characters on different language levels; in *One Man, One Matchet* (1964) the range includes the meaningless bombast of Royanson, the oily grandiloquence of Benjamin Benjamin, and the educated, ornate style of Gorgeous Gregory. In the mouth of Alaiye in *His Worshipful Majesty* (1973), language still retains its poetic and magical power. Pidgin English is used profusely by slum dwellers in *Wrong Ones in the Dock* (1982).

A critical realist like **V. S. Naipaul**, Aluko practises the 'truth of fact' theory of literary representation. Unlike Naipaul, however, satire in Aluko's skilful hand does not degenerate into abuse, nor criticism into cynicism. Aluko imbues his characters — even the mischievous and the treacherous — with abundant ardour.

A powerful humanist-satirist, Aluko captures the different colours and shades of Nigerian life in transition from the indigenous mode of existence, with all its trammels of ignorance and superstition, to the modern. He places special emphasis on education; however, Western education fails to obliterate the primacy of indigeneity in his African élite. Some of these élite still patronize native medicine while others cherish chieftaincy titles. Like **Chinua Achebe**, Aluko depicts both positive and negative sides of both African culture(s) and Western civilization and strongly supports the preservation of ennobling African customs and traditions.

Simplicity of style, linearity of plot structure, topicality of theme — for example, agitation for creation of more states in *A State of Our Own* (1986) — humorous characters, and catchy titles characterize Aluko's prose fiction and possibly account for its great popularity in Nigeria among the general readership and high school students.

OLUSEGUN ADEKOYA

Further reading: Margaret Laurence, *Long Drums and Cannons* (1968); O. R. Dathorne, *The Black Mind* (1974).

AMADI, ELECHI (1934–)
Nigerian novelist, dramatist, essayist
Born in Aluu, near Port Harcourt, Nigeria, he attended University College, Ibadan, where he graduated in physics and mathematics (1959). This scientific education may account for Amadi's descrip-

tive precision and fidelity to schematized presentation of fictional materials. For many years he was also associated with the military, both as a soldier and civilian functionary in Nigeria's military administrations; this fraternity with military culture may explain why his fictional and non-fictional views are usually candidly expressed and why his major male characters are strikingly martial in temperament. Amadi's humanism, however, remains largely intact; his life and publications mark him as an educator and writer. His published works include four novels (*The Concubine*, 1966, *The Great Ponds*, 1969, *The Slave*, 1978, and *Estrangement*, 1986); four plays (*Isiburu*, 1973, *The Dancer of Johannesburg*, 1977, *Peppersoup*, 1977, and *The Road to Ibadan*, 1977); a memoir (*Sunset in Biafra*, 1973); and a book of essays (*Ethics in Nigerian Culture*, 1982).

One of the fictional legacies for which Amadi is known is his credible portrayal of closely knit post-colonial African communities. His first three novels deal with romance, religions, superstitions, family and intercommunal feuds, and communalist values that characterized most African communities before colonial contact. Even *Estrangement*, set in Nigeria during and immediately after the Nigerian Civil War, draws its greatest appeal from events set in a rural environment. Amadi's novels and plays also reveal him as a 'male feminist' of the traditional African society — he presents his female characters with penetrating insight and sympathy, bestowing them with a disarming zest for life, a touching concern for humane values, and an inclination towards an independent life resistant to the chauvinism of their male counterparts.

Amadi's major works evoke a strong feeling of the defencelessness of human beings in the face of the supernatural. Even though his male characters are usually valiant warriors, wrestlers, and strong-willed men, and his women characters are playful, loving, intelligent, and self-willed, there are always in these works invisible figures lurking in the shadows, ironic twists lying in wait, hopes bound to be thwarted, and inscrutable forces undermining humanity's determination to control its destiny. Even in the plays, all comedies in terms of mode and dénouement, life's journey does not always lead to freedom. Amadi's views in his memoir and essays confirm that he is a lover of humanity, but that he is disenchanted with humanity's antics and with forces to which great power and authority are entrusted.

Amadi acknowledges that he read much of Thomas Hardy, and some critics have argued that the latter's philosophic pessimism infected Amadi's work. It should be noted, however, that the rural worlds of Amadi's novels have similarities with those of his contemporaries **Chinua Achebe**, **Chukwuemeka Ike**, **Nkem Nwankwo**, **John Munonye**, **Onuora Nzekwu**, and **Flora Nwapa**, among others, with whom he shares a similar background. Perhaps they all draw from a common social anthropology, history, and literary sensibility.

AFAM EBEOGU

Further reading: Ebele Eko, *Elechi Amadi: The Man and His Work* (1991).

AMANUDDIN, SYED (1934–89)

Indian poet

Born in Mysore, India, he was educated at the University of Mysore and at Bowling Green State University, Ohio, USA. He taught English at Osmania University, Hyderabad, India, and later at Bowling Green and Morris College, South Carolina, USA. He was a long-time resident of South Carolina — he lived in the USA from 1967 until his death — and often appeared on South Carolina educational television as a writer and scholar. Although Amanuddin published two volumes of critical essays, various plays, and a novel, he was primarily a poet — the dozen volumes of poetry testify to his major quest, which, in the words of one critic, was for 'a perfect spiritual and human liberty with fewer prejudices, falsehoods, and sins of humanity'. His poetry includes: *The Forbidden Fruit* (1967); *The Children of Hiroshima* (1967); *Poems of Protest* (1972); *The Age of Female Eunuchs* (1974); *Adventures of Atman: An Epic of the Soul* (1977), which is included in his volume *Poems* (1984); and *Challenger Poems* (1988), containing three poem sequences — 'Challenger Poems', 'Bhopal Cantos', and 'Hiroshima and After' — and the epic 'The Master'. An intense mode of artistic inclusiveness ranging from mysticism to social protest and a ceaseless seeking for the essential human experience, even in the local and the immediate, inform his entire work.

Amanuddin's verse is remarkable for its daring and innovative diction. Living abroad helped him to look with greater objectivity upon his experience — as Indian and as poet. In his major poems *Adventures of Atman: An Epic of the Soul* and 'The Master', his struggle is to unlock the mysteries of humanity, nature, and the universe and their interrelationships with God (whom he terms the Ultimate Consciousness).

Amanuddin inherited the two dominant modes in the history of Indian poetry in English: the sublime, as in the poetry of **Sri Aurobindo** and **Rabindranath Tagore**, and the equivocal and post-independence mode, ironic and conversational, as in the poetry of **Nissim Ezekiel** and **P. Lal.** However, his poetry lacks the spiritual amplitude and the visionary depth of Aurobindo, and often fails to achieve the subtlety and conscious artistry of Ezekiel.

S. MURALI

Further reading: A. N. Dwivedi, *Syed Amanuddin: His Mind and Art* (1988).

AMERINDIANS IN CARIBBEAN LITERATURE

Since American Indians disappeared from most of the Caribbean islands long before a written indigenous literature began, the relevance of their culture to Caribbean writing is largely confined to works set in the mainland territory of Guyana. Amerindian characters in Caribbean writing appear mainly in historical fiction such as the Jamaican **H. G. De Lisser**'s *The Arawak Girl* (1958). The temptation for writers of such fiction is to make the Amerindian character a noble savage whose values contrast with the savagery of the European conquerors. However, in *Another Life* (1973), by the St Lucian **Derek Walcott**, a passage occurs that is functionally too complex to attract such criticism. Here, the Caribs' suicidal leap from a cliff at Sauteurs in Grenada to avoid enslavement by the French is seen as both heroic and wasteful, as an instance of universal heroism and tragedy (since the Caribs are identified with the Spartans at Thermopylae), rather than as an exotic basis for political criticism. Amerindian myth occasionally appears in the poetry of the Guyanese **Martin Carter**, notably in 'Weroon Weroon' (from *Poems of Succession*, 1977), where the poet imagines his death in the persona of an Amerindian paddling his canoe towards heaven.

Because most of the population of Guyana inhabits the coastal plain and has little contact with the Amerindians — most of whom live in the interior — there is more opportunity than usual for the formation of racial stereotypes. The stereotype of the Amerindian is made up of the qualities of silence or inscrutability, strength, and cunning. In *Children of Kaywana* (1952) by **Edgar Mittelholzer**, the half-Amerindian woman, Kaywana, is a figure of great strength who becomes the ancestress of the racially mixed van Groenwegels. The similarity between the names 'Kaywana' and 'Guiana' suggests that she symbolizes both the family's roots in the land and the aboriginal people and is thus much more symbol than woman. However, Mittelholzer is less interested in contrasting natural virtue with civilized vice than in tracing inherited strength and weakness through Kaywana's descendants.

In **Jan Carew**'s *The Wild Coast* (1958) and

Wilson Harris' *Palace of the Peacock* (1960) and *The Secret Ladder* (1963), Amerindian women again possess the stereotypical qualities of silence and inscrutability. A more recent novel, **Roy Heath**'s *Orealla* (1984), presents an Amerindian man in much the same way. While inscrutability is appropriate in *Palace of the Peacock* because the character is also a goddess, the realism of Carew's novel makes Dela, the 'child of silence', more obviously a racial stereotype. In *Palace of the Peacock* the search for the Amerindian 'folk' is very similar to the search for the Australian heartland in **Patrick White**'s *Voss* (1957) or the search for the heart of Africa in Joseph Conrad's *Heart of Darkness* (1902). In all these cases the aboriginal people have a special relationship with the land, which later immigrants must emulate. In Conrad's novella, however, this relationship is a source of horror while in both *Voss* and *Palace of the Peacock* it is a prelude to necessary renewal.

JEFFREY ROBINSON

Further reading: Jeffrey Robinson, 'The aboriginal enigma: *Heart of Darkness*, *Voss* and *Palace of the Peacock*', *The Journal of Commonwealth Literature* 20 (1985).

ANAND, MULK RAJ (1905–)

Indian novelist, short-story writer, art critic

Born in Peshawar (now in Pakistan) to a Hindu coppersmith family, he read philosophy at the University of Punjab, India, and at the University of London, England. Upon his return to India in 1932, he lived for some time in **Gandhi**'s Sabarmati Ashram, where he wrote the first draft of *Untouchable* (1935). While in London, Anand became interested in Indian art, avant-garde movements, and left-wing politics. Later, he joined the International Brigade during the Spanish Civil War. Returning permanently to India in 1945, he founded, in 1946, the art magazine *Marg*, which he edited for thirty years. After divorcing his first wife, Kathleen Van Gelder, an actress, in 1948, he suffered a nervous breakdown, which probably made him turn inward and resulted in the first of his ongoing series of autobiographical novels: *Seven Summers* (1951) and *The Private Life of an Indian Prince* (1953), in which the hero has a nervous breakdown. The rest of Anand's career has been marked by prolific writing and active association with numerous literary and cultural associations in India and abroad, including the World Peace Council, the Asian Writers' Conference, and the Afro-Asian Writers' Bureau. He has also worked as Tagore Professor of Art and Literature, Punjab University, as honorary president of Lalit Kala Akademi, New Delhi, and as visiting professor at the Indian Institute of Advanced Study, Simla. Among his distinctions are the International Peace Prize (1962), Padma Bhushan (1967), and the Sahitya Akademi Award (1971).

Anand's fiction has been shaped by what he calls 'the double burden on my shoulders, the Alps of European tradition and the Himalaya of my Indian past'. Though alive to the finer and enduring aspects of the Indian tradition, he is also a stern critic of its fossilization and obscurantism. His fervent socialist faith and his vision of a modern egalitarian society have been mainly derived from European thought. However, he owes as much to the Indian Muslim poet-philosopher Muhammad Iqbal and Bhai Vir Singh, 'the bard of Punjab', as to Tolstoy, Victor Hugo, and perhaps Dickens.

Anand's numerous novels and short-story collections form an extensive fictional chronicle marked by his eclectic humanism, his zeal for social reform, and his humanitarian compassion for the downtrodden. These themes receive perhaps their best fictional treatment in his first novel, *Untouchable*, which describes an eventful day in the life of Bakha, a young sweeper-outcaste. Unsparing in its realism but objective in approach and restrained in treatment, this compact novel is generally free from the sentimentality, verbosity, and looseness of some of his later works. *Coolie*

(1936) and *Two Leaves and a Bud* (1937) deal with another segment of the underprivileged: the landless peasant. The range and scope of Anand's fiction widened to include themes barely suggested in *Untouchable*: rural versus urban India and colonial race relations. *Coolie* is the pathetic odyssey of Munoo, a rustic orphan transplanted in an urban setting, with fatal consequences. The novel has an almost epic quality, but is marred by a crusading zeal that often distorts action and character. More disastrously affected by these flaws, *Two Leaves and a Bud* recounts the tragedy of Gangu, a Punjabi peasant lured to a tea plantation in Assam, where he is bullied, starved, and killed by a British official who tries to rape his daughter.

The Village (1939), *Across the Black Waters* (1940), and *The Sword and the Sickle* (1942), an ambitious trilogy dealing with Lal Singh, a young Punjabi peasant, is a qualified success. *The Village* is a triumph of realistic portraiture of rustic life, and *Across the Black Waters* is perhaps the only major war novel in Indian-English literature, inviting comparison on the grounds of honesty and compassion with E. M. Remarque's *All Quiet on the Western Front* and Stephen Crane's *The Red Badge of Courage*. But *The Sword and the Sickle*, a rather confused book about a confused hero, lacks a firm centre. It shows the hero returning home from a German prison, hob-nobbing with Communists, and ending up in prison again. The cheap irony with which both Communism and Gandhism are treated here deprives Lal Singh's quest of seriousness. *The Big Heart* (1945), Anand's last novel before Indian independence (1947), recounts the tragedy of a young coppersmith who unsuccessfully tries to champion modernity in a traditional society.

After independence, Anand began publishing a series of autobiographical novels. Of the proposed seven parts, the first, *Seven Summers*, is an engaging fictional account of his childhood, material from which was later reworked into the more directly autobiographical *Pilpali Sal* (1985). *Morning Face* (1968; 1971 Sahitya Akademi Award), *Confession of a Lover* (1976), *The Bubble* (1984), and *Little Plays of Mahatma Gandhi* (1991) — the first section of the fifth volume, *And So He Played His Part* — have appeared so far in the series, which closely follows the course of Anand's career from childhood onwards. Their rich autobiographical content has endowed the novels with immediacy and vividness, and the entire series, when completed, promises to be an impressive fictional chronicle about a crucial period in modern Indian life.

Notable among the remaining novels are *The Private Life of an Indian Prince*, Anand's only novel with an aristocratic protagonist and a work that has met with a mixed reception, and *The Old Woman and the Cow* (1960; also published as *Gauri*, 1976), a spirited study of the transformation of a docile rustic girl into a rebel. Far less successful are *The Road* (1961), a rehash of the *Untouchable* theme, *Death of a Hero* (1963), dealing rather superficially with a Kashmir freedom fighter, and the sentimental novella *Lament on the Death of a Master of Arts* (1939).

Anand's short-story collections include *The Lost Child and Other Stories* (1934), *The Barber's Trade Union and Other Stories* (1944), *The Tractor and the Corn Goddess and Other Stories* (1947), *Reflections on the Golden Bed and Other Stories* (1953), *The Power of Darkness and other Stories* (1959), *Lajwanti and Other Stories* (1966), and *Between Tears and Laughter* (1973). *Selected Short Stories of Mulk Raj Anand*, edited by **M. K. Naik** (1977), is a representative selection.

Anand's short stories are remarkable for their range and variety, not only in mood, tone, and spirit, but also in locale, characters, form, and style. The village and the city are almost equally represented, and the characters are drawn from all strata of society. The various forms drawn upon are the fable, the parable, the folk tale, the bardic narrative, and sometimes even the well-made story. Stories such as 'The Lost Child', in which the traumatic experience of a child separated from its parents at a country fair symbolizes a universal human plight, and 'Birth' which testifies to the extraordinary courage and strength a young peasant woman derives from her staunch religious faith in her hour of trial, are imaginative tales with a lyric awareness. Starkly realistic studies of men and women crushed by overwhelming forces include 'Lajwanti' and 'The Cobbler and the Machine'; Anand's acute awareness of the clash between tradition and modernity is revealed in stories such as 'The Power of Darkness' and 'The Tractor and the Corn Goddess'; feudalism and capitalism are pilloried in 'A Kashmir Idyll' and 'The Price of Bananas' respectively; 'The Tamarind Tree' and 'The Thief' offer subtle psychological studies, while uproarious farce enlivens 'The Barber's Trade Union' and 'The Liar'.

As novelist and short-story writer, Anand stands out among his contemporaries though the vast range of his work, his wealth of living characters, his ruthless realism, and his fervent championship of the underprivileged. His style at its best is redolent of the Indian soil and experimental in its bold importation into English of words, expletives, turns of expression, and proverbs drawn from his native Punjabi and Hindi. His chief limitations are sentimentality, a weakness for preaching, and a penchant for verbosity leading to occasionally slipshod expression. Although his work is uneven, he remains a major novelist and short-story writer.

Apart from the autobiographical *Apology for Heroism* (1946), which evocatively traces his mental development, and *Conversations in Bloomsbury* (1981), Anand has also written extensively on art in *Persian Painting* (1930), *The Hindu View of Art* (1933), *Lines Written to an Indian Air* (1949), and several other studies. As an art critic he has achieved more as a knowledgeable popularizer than an original thinker. His literary criticism, marked by gusto, includes *The Golden Breath: Studies in Five Poets of the New India* (1933), *Homage to Tagore* (1946), *The King-Emperor's English* (1948), *Roots and Flowers* (1972), and *Author to Critic: Letters of Mulk Raj Anand to Saros Cowasjee* (1973).

M. K. NAIK

Further reading: K. N. Sinha, *Mulk Raj Anand* (1972); M. K. Naik, *Mulk Raj Anand* (1973); Saros Cowasjee, *So Many Freedoms: A Study of the Major Fiction of Mulk Raj Anand* (1977); Alastair Niven, *The Yoke of Pity: A Study in the Fictional Writing of Mulk Raj Anand* (1978).

ANANTANARAYANAN, MADHAVAIAH (1907–)
Indian novelist

Born in Tirunelveli, Tamil Nadu, India, to an upper-middle-class Brahmin family, he entered the Indian civil service. His only novel, *The Silver Pilgrimage* (1961), is slender but hilariously erudite, a forerunner in the Indian subcontinent of the postmodern novel that has become popular since **Salman Rushdie**'s *Midnight's Children* (1981). It mixes pastiche, chronicle, parody, farce, and the picaresque. The novel is set in medieval India, as traversed by a Sri Lankan, Prince Jayasurya, and his intellectual companion Tilaka (the pilgrimage to Kashi undertaken on the advice of Sage Agastya, one of the many bearing that hallowed name); it re-creates the various facets of life on the Indian subcontinent with a tongue-in-cheek solemnity.

The theme of the resilience of the Hindu religion — its incredible range of manifestations, from superstition to metaphysics, the inclusive ideal of the Indian way of life — is explored through a chequered narrative mode that is a feat at once of realism and of refined farce. Wearing his scholarship gracefully and lightly, Anantanarayanan parodies a number of ancient and medieval Indian discourses such as the folk tale, folk and mystical poetry in Tamil, court language, philosophical and metaphysical debates between rival sects, spiritual initiation, and necromancer's seance.

The most marked feature of *The Silver Pilgrimage* is its nonchalant shifts from the sublime to the ridiculous and vice versa, which enable the author to hold up a postmodern mirror to Indian culture. Its technical virtuosity and sophisticated treatment of realistic narrative mark the novel as a pioneer in the genre of discontinuous, parodic fiction exploiting pastiche. It may be compared to Angus Wilson's adroit attempt in *No Laughing Matter* (1967) to structure his chronicle of British social history from Edwardian to post-colonial times in terms of several dramatic modes from naturalism to the absurd. In both, the critique of the author's own culture is offered through a brilliant and humane farce. Both Anantanarayanan and Wilson have a greater variety of narrative techniques and are less glaringly discontinuous in projecting reality than Rushdie in *Midnight's Children*.

C. T. INDRA

ANDERSEN, JOHANNES CARL (1873–1962)
New Zealand historian, ethnologist
Born in Jutland, Denmark, and taken to New Zealand before the age of two, he found his Danish heritage too attenuated for literary development and 'English' themes lacking cultural resonance in New Zealand. Like several of his 'native-born' contemporaries, Andersen turned to indigenous subjects. His first substantial work, *Maori Life in Ao-tea* (1907), a prose characterization of traditional Maori society, draws upon Maori materials in what J. O. C. Phillips has described as 'an effort to provide an instant history and mythology in a new and unlettered land'. Andersen maintained this approach during the next forty years with such works as *Myths & Legends of the Polynesians* (1928), *Maori Place-Names, Also Personal Names and Names of Colours, Weapons and Natural Objects* (1942), and *The Maori Tohunga and His Spirit World* (1948). His celebration of indigenous flora and fauna is exemplified by *Bird-Song and New Zealand Song Birds* (1926). Important writers of the next generation scorned these facile attempts to create an autochthonous literature. More significantly, apart from a handful of ethnographic studies that were authorized by Maori, Andersen's works, and many similar efforts by other writers, may now be seen as a form of colonization through cultural appropriation. Though this process took place in all settler societies, it appears to have been a more extensive practice in New Zealand than elsewhere.

PETER GIBBONS

Further reading: J. O. C. Phillips, 'Musings in Maoriland — or was there a *Bulletin* school in New Zealand?', *Historical Studies* 20 (1983).

ANDERSON, BALFOUR (1953–)
Jamaican dramatist
Born in Port Antonio, Jamaica, he attended high school and teachers' college there. He taught for several years before taking a three-year course at the Jamaica School of Drama. While a teacher, Anderson wrote, between 1976 and 1982, more than fifteen one-act plays (all unpublished). He produced and directed them for students at his school and for a community-based teenage drama group he formed. These early plays are serious considerations of problems affecting young people.

After graduation from drama school, Anderson worked with the Jamaica Cultural Development Commission to foster drama and to encourage the production of plays in the Commission's annual island drama competition. In 1986 he became seriously involved in commercial theatre and by 1991 he had written nine full-length plays (unpublished), all but one of which ('King Root', premièred 1987) he directed and produced himself. These include: 'Secret Lovers' (premièred 1986), with a reggae motif; the comedy 'Two to One' (premièred 1988); 'Rip Off' (premièred 1990), about a rapacious landlord and housing problems; 'Hustler' (premièred 1990), about street-side food vending; and 'Ragamuffin' (premièred 1991), about crooked reggae music promoters. 'King Root' is a musical — commissioned by Jamaica's most important theatrical production company, the Little Theatre Movement (founded 1941) — for which Anderson wrote the lyrics.

One of the few Jamaicans making a living from full-time work in theatre, Anderson is the manager of a theatre in Kingston that he keeps open all year with productions of his own works. This entails his writing two plays a year — all comedies and usually sex comedies — though such social issues as teenage pregnancy, housing problems, and educational concerns feature strongly in many. Anderson's comedy is broad, and as a director he emphasizes outrageous action for laughs.

MICHAEL RECKORD

ANDERSON, ETHEL (1883–1958)

Australian poet, novelist, short-story writer

Born in Leamington, England, she was a fifth-generation Australian. She lived with her husband in India and England, before returning to Australia in 1926. Her serious work came late in life. It includes essays: *Adventures in Appleshire* (1944), *Timeless Garden* (1945); short stories: *Indian Tales* (1948), *The Little Ghosts* (1959); an episodic novel: *At Parramatta* (1956); poetry: *Squatter's Luck and Other Poems* (1942), *Squatter's Luck and Other Bucolic Eclogues* (1954), *Sunday at Yarralumla: A Symphony* (1947); a libretto: *The Song of Hagar to the Patriarch Abraham* (1957); and biography: *The Joy of Youth: Letters of Patrick Hore-Ruthven* (1950).

Anderson's work is characterized by its pictorial quality, sensuousness, daring experimentation, formal variety, and breadth of cultural reference. A compilation of her writing — *The Best of Ethel Anderson* (1973), edited by John Pringle — and the Penguin reissue in 1985 of *At Parramatta*, her *roman à tiroir*, are hopeful signs of a deserved critical revival.

The magic-realist mode of *Indian Tales* and *At Parramatta*, where the historical element is suggestive and allegorical, licenses Anderson's interest in 'the dangerous edge of things' — here sexual love and the power relations between the sexes. In *At Parramatta*, ghost story, fairy tale, melodrama, and the darker folk tale are ironically combined to undercut Genesis, the Decalogue, the High Church of England, and St Paul. (Mrs McCree regrets that Horace did not write an epistle to St Paul.) Despite male pride, anger, envy, sloth, gluttony, avarice, and lust, airily displaced on to women, all ends well, with women ensuring the fecundity of the land and its denizens.

In her introduction to *Squatter's Luck* Anderson saw Australians as having 'attributes more Attic than English'. This sequence domesticates classical bucolics in Australia, where the man-on-the-land battles seasonal extremes to achieve a brief pastoral idyll before the advent of war.

The more ambitious *Sunday at Yarralumla*, in its excavation of the past and celebration of a particular significant place, deserves recognition as a precursor of such 'mapping' poems as **Geoffrey Lehmann**'s *Ross' Poems*, Laurie Duggan's *The Ash Range*, and poems of **Les Murray**. One poem, 'Afternoon in the Garden' — ' . . . let the sun stand still . . . / I, evoking pictures from the past, / Do again what lordly Joshua did' — sums up Anderson's characteristic resistance to transience.

CAROL FRANKLIN

Further reading: Bethia Foot, *Ethel and The Governors' General: A Biography of Ethel Anderson (1883–1958) and Brigadier-General A. T. Anderson (1868–1949)* (1992).

ANDERSON, JESSICA (1923–)

Australian novelist

Born and educated in Brisbane, Australia, she sailed for Europe when she was twenty-one years old. After two years there she returned to Sydney, where she has lived since, perhaps sharing with Nora, the protagonist of the novel *Tirra Lirra by the River* (1978), the conviction that Sydney is 'the only place where I've ever felt at home'.

Ambivalence about place and the journey motif recur throughout Anderson's work. Her preoccupation with place is often expressed in terms that characterize post-colonial writing more generally — for instance, the contrast between Europe and Australia and the significance of the house. Critic Alrene Sykes argues that in its exploration of these issues Anderson's work is similar to **Henry Handel Richardson**'s Richard Mahony trilogy. In *Tirra Lirra by the River* Nora makes the traditional voyage back to the motherland, a spiritual and geographic progression moving from the periphery to the metropolis: Brisbane/Sydney/London/Sydney and finally Brisbane, which, in old age, she sees with new eyes as 'home' rather than a place of exile. In *Tirra Lirra by the River*, Tennyson's poem 'The Lady of Shalott' is appropriated and rewritten. As in the poem, mirrors, the river, and the tower are important motifs, and the role of the artist and artistic creation a central concern.

In both *Tirra Lirra by the River* and *The Impersonators* (1980; published in the USA and England as *The Only Daughter*, 1985), expatriation is explored not only in character and action but also in open debate. Binary oppositions — centre and periphery, old and new, home and away — are resolved in both these novels as the Australian protagonists come to accept the country and culture to which they are born.

The short fictions of *Stories from the Warm Zone and Sydney Stories* (1987) are interesting for their explorations of the oppositions between different regions, the subtropical Brisbane remembered in a series of stories about girlhood, and the contemporary urban metropolis of Sydney. Anderson's contrast of these regions and her evocation of Brisbane bear comparison with recent writings by **Thea Astley** and **Janette Turner Hospital**. The Brisbane stories foreground the intersections of colonialism and gender apparent elsewhere in Anderson's writing; women are presented as being in a kind of double exile, outsiders to language and discourse. This is also taken up in the historical novel *The Commandant* (1975), a fiction about the penal settlement of Moreton Bay on the Brisbane River under the command of Patrick Logan in the 1830s. The brutality of the penal colony dominates the narrative, in which women, convicts, Aborigines, and ultimately the commander himself are incarcerated. This novel presents the process of colonization in one of its ugliest and most destructive manifestations.

GILLIAN WHITLOCK

Further reading: Elaine Barry, 'The expatriate vision of Jessica Anderson', *Meridian* 3 (1984); Roslynn D. Haynes, 'Art as reflection in Jessica Anderson's *Tirra Lirra by the River*', *Australian Literary Studies* 12 (1986); Alrene Sykes, 'Jessica Anderson: arrivals and places', *Southerly* 46 (1986).

ANDERSON, VERNON (1900–)

Jamaican novelist

Born in Guy's Hill, in the parish of St Ann, Jamaica, he was educated at Calabar High School, Jamaica, at the University of London, England, where he received his Doctor of Medicine (1934), and at various other English universities. Anderson had a long and distinguished career in medicine in several countries. His interest in medicine is matched by his strong commitment to literature and the arts. In 1947 he was named an officer of the Order of the British Empire. His sojourn in Belize, to which he was posted in 1928 as a doctor in Britain's colonial service, was the matrix from which his only published novel, *Sudden Glory* (1987), grew.

Sudden Glory is an elegantly written story of

the tension-ridden relationships of archaeologists, professional and mercenary soldiers, and earthy *chicleros* whose tough withers have been wrung through Guatemala's chicle trade. The novel's themes are not distinctively Caribbean. Anderson brings to his subject-matter a finely focused sensibility and the ability to delineate character with deft understatement. He has a perceptive understanding of the complexity and vicissitudes of human relationships and he can convey the essential quality of a character in one or two strong strokes.

Anderson's enthusiasm for too many characters, some of whom are given short shrift, however, is one of the novel's weaknesses. The central characters are more satisfactory. Harkness, the erudite botanist, experiences his own private hell and epiphany in Guatemala's jungle after he inadvertently kills his colleague. Karen Farr, the formidable intellectual, is a guilt-ridden Medea figure who callously burns her husband's *magnum opus* in a fit of anger and revenge. At the end of the novel, Karen searches for atonement.

The novel's strength is its powerful evocation of the menacing, yet compelling, Central American landscape, the symbolic resonances of which link it with the equally compelling Guyana jungle of **Wilson Harris**' fiction.

HAROLD BARRATT

ANGIRA, JARED (1947–)

Kenyan poet

He was born in the Siaya district of Kenya and was educated at Maseno and Shiwo la Tewa and at the University of Nairobi, where he earned a degree in commerce. Among the major poets in East Africa, Angira perhaps has followed an individual path; his poetry is distinct from the more committed or experimental poetry of his contemporaries. He is notable mainly for his simplicity; although he refers to poets such as **Christopher Okigbo** and Pablo Neruda and to thinkers who have influenced him, Angira writes in a clear idiom, using a medium range, somewhere between the lyrics of popular tunes and more academic texts. His first two volumes, *Juices* (1970) and *Silent Voices* (1972), offer a selection of brief poems, with very short lines, in his characteristic understated, elliptic mode. The rhythm is effortless, the singing voice easy on the ear. Angira's themes are pastoral, his imagery organic; his views are usually presented without sentimentality or clichés. *Soft Corals* (1973) attempts longer forms and lines, and social concerns give a new urgency to the tone of the poems. Poetic monologues create a variety of characters in shorter versions of the East African 'song' tradition.

Occasionally some poems are too didactic or too explicit, as is the case in the later, more political *The Years Go By* (1980). *Cascades* (1979) is a mature collection of dreamy poems about sea and harbour. The topic is well suited to the melancholy mood of the songs; musical and religious references are summoned by titles such as 'Cantata' and 'Canticle'. Perhaps best known for his topical polemic verse, Angira is particularly at ease in an intimate range, not yet very common in African poetry, exploring the uncertainties and dreams of an ordinary man who claims no privileged poetic vision, but, like Don Quixote, 'stumbles ahead / Into the unknown'.

J. BARDOLPH

ANTHOLOGIES

ANTHOLOGIES (Australia)

Innocent gatherings of literary blooms or powerful instruments of canon formation? Early examples of anthologies in Australia follow Isaac Nathan's *The Southern Euphrosyne and Australian Miscellany, Containing Oriental Moral Tales, Original Anecdote, Poetry and Music* (1848) in embracing the former model, though not all did so with the enthusiasm for colonial metaphoric variation of

Hash: A Mixed Dish for Christmas, with Ingredients by Various Australian Authors (1877), edited by Garnet Walch. Clearly addressed as entertainment to the 'common reader', these manifested early the financial incentive that anthologies offer serious writers: **Tasma** and **Marcus Clarke** were among contributors to *Hash*.

Douglas Sladen, the first serious anthologist of Australian poetry, published no fewer than three anthologies in London, England, in 1888, but the preface to his *A Century of Australian Song* (1888) is unprophetic in its preference for poets working from English models and in its respect for 'poetesses'. Sladen's recognition of the thematic importance of the bush did not comprehend the social radicalism already being defined by the ***Bulletin*** poets, whom he largely neglected, unaware that they were to dominate tradition for several decades. The strand of social radicalism, retrospectively emphasized in **Russel Ward**'s *The Penguin Book of Australian Ballads* (1964), probably had its last active manifestation in Marjorie Pizer's *Freedom on the Wallaby: Poems of the Australian People* (1953). One preoccupation, the problematic nature of cultural dependence on England, had already been taken up by the **Jindyworobak Movement. Rex Ingamells**' *New Song in an Old Land: Australian Verse* (1943; rev. 1954) reversed nationalist concepts of 'a new country'; Brian Elliott's preface to *The Jindyworobaks* (1979) presents the group as anticipating later positions on colonialism, environmentalism, and the spirituality of Aboriginal relationships with the land.

The overshadowing of the claims to innovation of *Applestealers* (1974), edited by Robert Kenny and Colin Talbot, and of **Thomas Shapcott**'s *Contemporary American and Australian Poetry* (1976) by **John Tranter**'s more tendentious *The New Australian Poetry* (1979) reflected a Sydney dominance matched in prose by the 'new' fiction of *The Most Beautiful Lies* (1977), edited by B. Keirnan. **Frank Moorhouse**, a major contributor to the theory and practice of that collection, had edited the 1973 *Coast to Coast*, last in the series of fiction anthologies produced by Angus and Robertson from 1941 onwards (with the influential annual volumes *Australian Poetry* as a matching series).

Increased critical interest in short fiction, reflecting its rise as a dominant form of the past two decades, has been responsible for recent survey collections that aim to be definitive in a manner more ambitious than past special purpose or general anthologies (the latter often intended primarily for school syllabuses). *Australian Short Stories* (1983), selected by Kerryn Goldsworthy, *The Australian Short Story: An Anthology from the 1890s to the 1980s* (1986), edited by Laurie Hergenhan and revised in 1992 as *The Australian Short Story: A Collection 1890s–1990s*, and *The Penguin Best Australian Short Stories* (1991), edited by Mary Lord, show little overlap of selections; the four taken together provide a comprehensive overview of the genre.

Among publishers claiming definitiveness in poetry anthologies, Angus and Robertson were early contenders, with Bertram Stevens' *Golden Treasury of Australian Verse* (1906, 1909, 1912) followed by George Mackaness' anthologies of 1934 and 1946, a two-volume *Poetry in Australia* (1964) — the first volume edited by T. Inglis Moore and the second by **Douglas Stewart** — and Stewart's *The Wide Brown Land* (1971). Oxford's *Book of Australian and New Zealand Verse* (1950), edited by Walter Murdoch and **Alan Mulgan**, exhibited a conflation of colonial cousins recurrent as late as 1989 in *Kiwi and Emu: An Anthology of Australian and New Zealand Women Poets*, edited by Barbara Petrie. **Judith Wright**'s 1956 Oxford *A Book of Australian Verse* was revised in 1968 and was followed by **James McAuley**'s *Map of Australian Verse: The Twentieth Century* (1975), **Les A. Murray**'s *The New Oxford Book of Australian Verse* (1986; rev. 1991), and **Mark O'-**

Connor's *Two Centuries of Australian Poetry* (1988).

Penguin, starting relatively late with their 1958 *Book of Australian Verse*, followed by Harry Heseltine's versions of 1972 and 1981, have been more active in responding to demands for specialist anthologies. *The Penguin Book of Modern Australian Poetry* (1991), edited by John Tranter and Philip Mead, is one of several recent anthologies reflecting a trend away from would-be comprehensiveness into period anthologies, while Philip Neilsen's *The Penguin Book of Australian Satirical Verse* (1986) is that rarity, a poetic genre anthology — equivalents in science and crime fiction being more common. In terms of canonization, certain groups, notably women, Aborigines, and non-British immigrants, complained vigorously of exclusion. Women noted that their inclusion in 'definitive' anthologies did not match their representation in journals and the less formal anthologies of poetry societies and competitions, for example. They also noted an actual decline from representations above twenty-five percent in early anthologies to fourteen percent in Stewart's *The Wide Brown Land* and sixteen percent in Wright (1968) and Heseltine (1972). Kate Jennings' *Mother I'm Rooted* (1975) heralded several alternative-press women's anthologies; *The Penguin Book of Australian Women Poets*, edited by Susan Hampton and Kate Llewellyn, followed in 1986, but exhausted neither such anthologies nor their prose counterparts, which have been particularly active in 'recovering' earlier women writers — for example, Lynne Spender's *Her Selection: Writing by Nineteenth Century Australian Women* (1988).

Penguin offered the first anthology of Aboriginal poetry, **Kevin Gilbert**'s *Inside Black Australia* (1988), although inclusion of Aboriginal poems, both traditional and contemporary, had marked anthologies of the 1980s. **Rodney Hall** claimed this as a radical departure for his *The Collins Book of Australian Poetry* (1981), but the first inclusion of Aboriginal poems (untranslated) had occurred in 1905 — surprisingly — in **A. B. Paterson**'s *The Old Bush Songs*.

Mixed anthologies of poetry and fiction still address general audiences. Convenient perpetuators of the output of literary journals, anthologies such as *On Native Grounds: Australian Writing in Meanjin Quarterly* (1968), selected by C. B. Christesen, or *Quadrant: Twenty-five Years* (1982), selected by Peter Coleman, Lee Shrubb, and **Vivian Smith**, are also popular for representing writing from literary associations or informal interest groups. Overtly political anthologies such as *We Took Their Orders and Are Dead*, the 1971 anti-Vietnam War anthology compiled by Shirley Cass, Ros Cheney, **David Malouf**, and **Michael Wilding**, are less common than the more ecumenical approach exemplified in the South Australian Friendly Street Readers or the regional anthologies of state branches of the Fellowship of Australian Writers (FAW) — *Island Authors* (1971, no editor) or *Sandgropers: A Western Australian Anthology* (1973), edited by **Dorothy Hewett**, for example. Canberra FAW anthologies, however, present a national image with titles such as *Australian Signpost* (1956), edited by T. A. Hungerford, and *Australia Writes* (1953), edited by T. Inglis Moore. The titular *Austral Garden* (1912), edited by D. McLachlan and M. P. Hansen, paired poetry and prose anthologies published in Melbourne by George Russell. George Mackaness and Joan Mackaness edited the poetry anthology *The Wide Brown Land* (1934; repr. 1959), the title also of Douglas Stewart's 1971 anthology. George Mackaness also edited *Poets of Australia* (1946). Short stories were gathered in **A. A. Phillips**' *An Australian Muster* (1946) and Colin Roderick's *Australian Round-Up: Stories from 1790 to 1950* (1953).

While the multicultural programmes of *Joseph's Coat* (1985), edited by **Peter K. Skrzynecki**, and Penguin's *Australian Writing Now* (1988), edited by **R. Adamson** and **M. Jurgensen**, included Aboriginal writing, women sought separate publication here too, as in *Beyond the Echo: Multicultural Women's Writing* (1988), edited by S. Gunew and J. Mahyuddin. Meanwhile, despite the presence of writers of Asian origin, systematic presentation of Australian writing as part of wider regional literature is rare. Publications include the FAW's *Span: An Adventure into Asian and Australian Writing* (1958), edited by Lionel Wigmore, *An Asian PEN Anthology* (1960), edited by F. J. Jose, and *South Pacific Stories* (1980), edited by Chris Tiffin and Helen Tiffin. In the apparently inexorable march of anthologizing, this may be the area of growth.

Canon definition seems clearly intended in one major recent attempt at a comprehensive anthology, *The Oxford Anthology of Australian Literature* (1985), edited by Leonie Kramer and A. Mitchell. Its chronological, genre, and author organization matches the literary traditionalism of its companion *The Oxford History of Australian Literature* (1981), edited by Leonie Kramer, while the different cultural attitudes of Ken Goodwin's *History of Australian Literature* (1986) are reflected in the thematically organized *Macmillan Anthology of Australian Literature* (1990), edited by Goodwin and Alan Lawson.

Anthologies of Australian drama appear much later than those of prose and poetry and share in the genre's general history of sporadic publishing. The best-known early collection is *Best Australian One-Act Plays* (1937), edited by William Moore and T. Inglis Moore. All four anthologies of the decade between 1934, when the Melbourne Dramatists' Club published *Eight Plays by Australians* (no editor), and 1944, when *Six Australian One-Act Plays* (no editor) was published by Mulga Productions, Sydney, were devoted to the one-act play. Some collections are of texts generated specifically for festivals, such as *Five Warana One Act Winners* (1985, no editor), and of radio plays, such as Leslie Rees' *Australian Radio Plays* (1946).

The series projected by Eunice Hanger's *Australian One-Act Plays: Book One* (1962) did not eventuate, but she went on to publish *Khaki, Bush, and Bigotry: Three Australian Plays* (1968). Anthologies published overseas include Penguin's *Three Australian Plays* (1963, no editor), *Plays by Buzo/Hibberd/Romeril* (1970, no editor), and *Australia Plays* (1989), edited by Katharine Brisbane. *Five Plays for Radio: Nightmares of the Old Obscenity Master and Other Plays* (1975) was edited by Alrene Sykes, who played a major editorial role in the Contemporary Australian Plays series produced during the 1970s by the University of Queensland Press — *Five Plays for Stage, Radio and Television* (1977) and *Three Political Plays* (1981), for example. Two anthologies from Currency Press show both continuity, with *Seven One-Act Plays* (1983), edited by Rodney Fisher, and change, with the emergence of Aboriginal dramatists in *Plays from Black Australia* (1989), edited by **Jack Davis**, Eva Johnson, Richard Walley, and Bob Maza.

JENNIFER STRAUSS

Further reading: E. Morris Miller, *Australian Literature from Its Beginnings to 1935* Vol. 2 (rev. 1975); Elizabeth Webby, 'Australian short stories from *While the Billy Boils* to *The Everlasting Secret Family*', *Australian Literary Studies* 2 (1981); Jennifer Strauss, 'Anthologies and orthodoxies', *Australian Literary Studies* 13 (1987).

ANTHOLOGIES (Canada)

In a country where monographic publication has often been difficult, expensive, and no guarantor of public recognition, anthologies have played a key role in identifying authors, maintaining their visibility, and establishing the dominant literary canon. An unpublished checklist of English-language Canadian literary anthologies, compiled in 1978, lists 550 separate titles; this number alone demonstrates the importance of this form of publication to English-Canadian literature. The majority of Canadian anthologies focus on specific regional, thematic, and/or generic concerns. These include predictable subjects such as Canadian poetry from each of the world wars, regional interests as represented in volumes such as *The Atlantic Anthology* (1959) and *Vancouver Short Stories* (1985), and less-expected titles such as *Best Mounted Police Stories* (1978). In a country as large and as sparsely populated as Canada it is not surprising that since the 1920s close to one-third of the anthologies have collected writing from a specific city, province, or geographical area. Many budding authors first appear in the various anthology series issued by literary societies or branches of the Canadian Authors' Association, such as the *Alberta Poetry Year Book* (1929–80) and the *Saskatchewan Poetry Book* (1950–).

The earlier Canadian anthologies, primarily of poetry, published from the middle of the nineteenth century until about 1935, are characterized by a principle of inclusiveness. Eager to demonstrate that there was indeed a viable Canadian literature, their editors cast a broad net. The arrangement of the poems in the first of these volumes, Revd E. H. Dewart's *Selections from Canadian Poets* (1864), reveals its editor's priorities, with 'Sacred and Reflective' verse preceding that identified as 'Descriptive and National'. Dewart's introductory essay, which proclaims that 'A national literature is an essential element in the formation of national character,' has itself been canonized as a classic plea to Canadians to recognize and value their local authors. Greater optimism was possible twenty-five years later when W. D. Lighthall's *Songs of the Great Dominion: Voices from the Forests and Waters, the Settlements and Cities of Canada* (1889) was published in London, England, as a companion volume to Douglas Sladen's *A Century of Australian Song* (1888). Lighthall's opening sections, 'The Imperial Spirit' and 'The New Nationality', reflect the growing alignment between nationalism and imperialism that characterized much Canadian writing around the turn of the century; his introduction declares, 'Australian rhyme is a poetry of the *horse*; Canadian, of the *canoe*.' A similar imperialist motive underscores **Wilfred Campbell**'s selections for the first *The Oxford Book of Canadian Verse* (1913).

During the opening decades of the twentieth century, most national literary anthologies, such as John Garvin's *Canadian Poets* (1916; rev. 1926) and Albert Durrant Watson's and Lorne Pierce's *Our Canadian Literature: Representative Prose and Verse* (1922), continued to offer a wide sampling of Canadian writing. Their projected audience was the general reader, and their effect was to develop what Alan C. Golding (following Alistair Fowler) calls an accessible canon. However, J. E. Wetherell's *Later Canadian Poems* (1893), which concentrates on seven currently prominent male poets (with six women added in the appendix as a brief afterthought), anticipated the shift in editorial practice that would become increasingly prevalent in literary anthologies compiled from the late 1920s onward. Generally speaking, editors showed less interest in identifying an accessible canon than in creating a selective canon, their anthologies now serving an ideological purpose more specific than the articulation of an aesthetically conservative cultural nationalism. In the hands of **Raymond Knister**, who edited *Canadian Short Stories* in 1928, and the six poets represented in *New Provinces* (1936) — **F. R. Scott**, **A. J. M. Smith**, **E. J. Pratt**, **A. M. Klein**, Robert Finch, and Leo Kennedy — the anthology functioned as a manifesto of modernism. The importance of *New Provinces*, edited by Smith and Scott, which sold just eighty-two copies within the first year of publication (ten to Scott), has been constructed retrospectively by the country's modernist critics.

The most influential figure to use anthologies to develop a selective canon based on modernist values has been **A. J. M. Smith**, whose three editions of the *Book of Canadian Poetry* (1943, 1948, 1957), followed by his 1960 edition of *The Oxford*

Book of Canadian Verse, established the pantheon of early and modern poets who would dominate the Canadian literature curriculum as the study of Canadian literature gained acceptability within the academy. In their application of modernist principles to Canadian authors, Smith and fellow anthologist **Ralph Gustafson** (in his five versions of *The Penguin Book of Canadian Verse*: 1942, 1958, 1967, 1975, 1984) favoured an austere virility and anti-romantic aesthetic (in Smith's well-known phrase, 'a contemporary and cosmopolitan literary consciousness'), one of whose effects was to devalue and decanonize many previously admired women writers, including Ethelwyn Wetherald, **Susie Frances Harrison** and Florence Randall Livesay, and to limit recognition of their own female contemporaries. So stable has been the canonic structure erected by Smith that **Margaret Atwood**'s *New Oxford Book of Canadian Verse in English* (1982) adds only one new poet, Robert Hayman (1575–1629), to the entire pre-1950 period.

The extent of Smith's influence can best be measured in the pedagogical anthologies that began with Carl F. Klinck's and R. E. Watters' *Canadian Anthology* (1955; rev. 1966, 1972) and continue to structure much of the post-secondary teaching of Canadian literature (Douglas Daymond and Leslie Monkman, *Literature in Canada*, 1978; Russell Brown and Donna Bennett, *An Anthology of Canadian Literature in English*, 1982, rev. and abridged 1990; Robert Lecker and Jack David, *The New Canadian Anthology*, 1988). Despite the efforts of a few scholars to reconstruct Canada's cultural past, these mainstream anthologies scarcely alter Smith's original selection of pre-modern and modernist Canadian poets. Rather, their selections reinforce **Northrop Frye**'s view that 'the central Canadian tragic theme' is 'the indifference of nature to human values', which is in turn based on the notion (as expressed in 1965 by Desmond Pacey) that 'The Canadian imagination thus far is mainly a function of a landscape and a climate, and only secondarily of a society.'

The modernist effort to counter the romantic nationalism of earlier Canadian anthologies resulted in an academic canonical rigidity that has in turn incited several waves of anthology editors to challenge the quest for unified cultural expression that marks most survey anthologies. This attack comes from many different directions. The explicitly left-wing vision of John Sutherland's original assault on Smith's privileging of 'cosmopolitan' over 'native' values was argued in his preface to his counter anthology, *Other Canadians* (1947); it was revived in the 1970s and 1980s in N. Brian Davis' two volumes, *Poetry of the Canadian People*, largely culled from old labour newspapers, and in the collections of workers' poetry edited by Tom Wayman. The proliferation of anthologies of women's writing that began during the mid-1970s attempts to rectify the historical suppression of women authors. Regional anthologies and a growing number of English-language anthologies of writers from specific ethnic groups, including blacks, Asian Canadians, and Native Canadians, challenge the notion of a centralized national literature. Anthologies of Native Canadian literature include *I Am an Indian* (1969), edited by Kent Gooderham; *Achimoona* (1985), a collection of short fiction; *All My Relations: An Anthology of Contemporary Native Fiction* (1990), edited by Thomas King; and *Writing the Circle: Native Women of Western Canada* (1990), edited by Jeanne Perreault and Sylvia Vance. Moreover, anthologies of avant-garde writing continue to assail the preferences of survey anthologists for familiar works and authors. During the heady publishing years of the 1970s and early 1980s, so disparate were the theoretical positions of modernist editors of short-story anthologies, who were rooted in the conventions of realism, and those of postmodernist editors proclaiming the uncertainty of language, that critic W. H. New described the literary scene as the battleground of the Wars of the Anthologies.

Just as anthologies served as the medium through which modernism came to dominate the criticism and canonization of Canadian writing during the middle years of the twentieth century, so is postmodernism gaining acceptability as the mode of the late 1980s and 1990s through anthologies, edited in some cases by the country's leading postmodernist authors. These include **George Bowering**'s *The Contemporary Canadian Poem Anthology* (1983), **Michael Ondaatje**'s *The Long Poem Anthology* (1979), **Dennis Lee**'s *The New Canadian Poets, 1970–1985* (1985), Geoff Hancock's collection of stories, *Magic Realism* (1980), and the annual anthologies of stories issued by Oberon Press and Coach House Press.

Anthologizing Canadian plays began only in the twentieth century. The best-known early collections are the two-volume *Canadian Plays from Hart House* (1926–7), edited by Vincent Massey, and *Six Canadian Plays* (1930), edited by **Herman Voaden**. Other significant anthologies include *A Collection of Canadian Plays*, 5 vols (1972–8), edited by Rolf Kalman; *Encounter: Canadian Drama in Four Media* (1973), edited by Eugene Benson; *West Coast Plays* (1975), edited by Connie Brissenden; *Popular Performance Plays of Canada*, 2 vols (1976), edited by Marian Wilson; *Prairie Performance: A Collection of Short Plays* (1980), edited by Diane Bessai; and *Twenty Years at Play: A New Play Centre Anthology* (1990), edited by Jerry Wasserman. *Canada's Lost Plays*, 4 vols (1978–82), edited by Anton Wagner, brings together representative English-Canadian and French-Canadian plays from the seventeenth to the twentieth century. Three anthologies of Canadian plays that seek to establish a canon are *Major Plays of the Canadian Theatre 1934–1984* (1984), edited by Richard Perkyns; *The Penguin Book of Modern Canadian Drama* (1984), edited by Richard Plant; and *Modern Canadian Plays* (1985), edited by Jerry Wasserman.

CAROLE GERSON

Further reading: A. J. M. Smith, 'The confessions of a compulsive anthologist', *Journal of Canadian Studies* 11 (1976); Carole Gerson, 'Anthologies and the canon of early Canadian women writers', in Lorraine McMullen (ed.) *Re(Dis)covering Our Foremothers* (1990).

ANTHOLOGIES (The Caribbean)

Anthologies have done much to give Caribbean literature a sense of itself. Early anthologies such as **Norman Cameron**'s *Guianese Poetry: 1831–1931* (1931) and **J. E. Clare McFarlane**'s *A Treasury of Jamaican Poetry* (1950) restricted their attention to the writing of particular territories. By 1950, however, although the various literatures were yet to see themselves as one, political developments were promoting the concept of interrelationship. The magazines *Bim* in Barbados and *Kyk-over-al* in Guyana published writers from Barbados and Guyana together with those from Trinidad, St Lucia, and Jamaica. The founding of the University of the West Indies (1948) began to break down insularity, and the movement towards a federation helped create a sense of Caribbean nationalism.

The Pioneer Press, which had promoted Jamaican nationalism by publishing such distinctly Jamaican books as *14 Jamaican Short Stories* (1950), also issued *Caribbean Anthology of Short Stories* (1953), embracing the whole region. In 1957 *Kyk-over-al* published an issue, *Anthology of West Indian Poetry*, to commemorate the new federation. Products of stirrings of nationalism, these collections in turn stimulated the nationalism that helped create them.

In the 1950s the idea of a Caribbean literature was reinforced by the dramatic explosion of Caribbean writing published in London. Anthologists lost no time in presenting the literature of the Caribbean as an entity to audiences in London and New York. Both G. R. Coulthard's *Caribbean Literature: An Anthology* (1966) and Barbara Howes' *From the Green Antilles: Writings of the Caribbean* (1966) include writing not only from the English territories, but also from the Spanish and French in translation, bridging language differences for thematic ends.

Caribbean anthologists then began to produce books meant for both foreign and local audiences. **Errol Hill** edited several collections of Caribbean plays such as *Caribbean Plays* (vol. 1, 1958; vol. 2, 1965), *Three Caribbean Plays* (1979), and *Plays for Today* (1985); **Andrew Salkey** edited *West Indian Stories* (1960) and *Breaklight: An Anthology of Caribbean Poetry* (1971); and **John Figueroa** published *Caribbean Voices: An Anthology of West Indian Poetry* (vol. 1, 1966; vol. 2, 1970). Figueroa has also edited *An Anthology of African and Caribbean Writing in English* (1986) to serve as a text for England's Open University. This volume encourages a comparative reading of Caribbean and African writing.

There are also children's anthologies of Caribbean literature. Since the 1960s these have secured a more substantial place in school syllabuses and include *The Sun's Eye: West Indian Writing for Young Readers* (1968), edited by Anne Walmsley, and *West Indian Poetry: An Anthology for Schools* (1971), edited by Kenneth Ramchand and Cecil Gray. These anthologies emphasize the work of a group of writers who were being canonized as major authors. **Edgar Mittelholzer**, **George Lamming**, **Samuel Selvon**, **Roger Mais**, **John Hearne**, **Wilson Harris**, **V. S. Naipaul**, **Derek Walcott**, and **E. K. Brathwaite** were names one could expect to find in any Caribbean collection. Some anthologists question this canon, including Sebastian Clarke, whose *New Planet: Anthology of Modern Caribbean Writing* (1978) omits the 'big' names in favour of such writers as Faustin Charles and Lindsay Barrett. Stewart Brown, in *Caribbean New Wave: Contemporary Short Stories* (1990), gives prominence to younger writers such as **Jamaica Kincaid** and **Olive Senior**.

Anthologies have also helped introduce Caribbean writing to different countries. In 1960 *The Tamarack Review*'s *The West Indies* brought names such as Walcott and Lamming to the attention of Canadian readers. In 1983 *Pacific Quarterly Moana* performed a similar service in New Zealand with its special issue, *One People's Grief: Recent Writing from the Caribbean.*

As anthologies proliferate, many have become more specialized. **Pamela Mordecai** and **Mervyn Morris** underline the important work of women writers in their *Jamaica Woman: An Anthology of Poems* (1980), while Frank Birbalsingh, in *Jahaji Bhai: An Anthology of Indo-Caribbean Literature* (1988), pays tribute to the Indian contribution to Caribbean life. Reinhard Sander's *From Trinidad: An Anthology of Early West Indian Writing* (1978) draws attention to a fascinating but little known period of literary ferment.

Cyril Dabydeen's *A Shapely Fire: Changing the Literary Landscape* (1987), which contains work of Caribbean writers in Canada, and **James Berry**'s *News for Babylon* (1984), a collection of writing by Caribbean poets in England, drive home such profoundly Caribbean themes as journeying and homelessness. They widen the scope of Caribbean literature while blurring the lines that separate Commonwealth nations.

The perception of Caribbean literature, both at home and abroad, has been significantly affected by anthologists who have endeavoured to suggest their individual visions in their collections.

ANTHONY BOXILL

ANTHOLOGIES (East Africa)

The large number of anthologies in English published in East Africa since 1965 bears proof of the region's creative activity and of the ability of East African writers to master the English language in articulating their African experience. A number of crucial themes developed and re-defined by later East African writers found expression with the publication of short stories, one-act plays, poetry, and essays in *Origin East Africa: A Makerere Anthology* (1965), edited by David Cook. (Most of its contributions are from Kenya, Malawi, Tanzania, and Uganda.) These themes explore questions about the kind of society to be built from the ruins of colonialism, about the role of the élite in society, and about urbanization and the problems that result from it. The selections in Cook's anthology suggest a Negritudinist outlook and the consequent nostalgic portrayal of the African past, but this is balanced by the sense of enthusiasm and hope that characterized East African writing following independence (Uganda in 1962, Kenya in 1963, Tanzania in 1964, and Mauritius in 1968).

Major East African writers established their careers in the anthologies of the 1960s and 1970s. The work of such writers as **Peter Nazareth**, **Ngugi wa Thiong'o**, Jonathan Kariara, Elvania Zirimu, **Austin Bukenya**, Richard Nitru, and Chris Wanjala appeared in the anthologies *Drum Beat: East African Poems* (1967), edited by Lennard Okola, and *Introduction to East African Poetry* (1976), edited by Jonathan Kariara and Helen Kitonga.

Anthologies of poetry, which comprise the majority of East African anthologies, include *Just a Moment, God! An Anthology of Prose and Verse from East Africa* (1970), edited by Robert Green, and *Poems from East Africa* (1971) and *Growing Up with Poetry: An Anthology for Secondary Schools* (1989), both edited by **David Rubadiri**. The poems of Rubadiri's second anthology are arranged to cover seven subjects: love, identity, death, village life, separation, power, and freedom. Everett Standa's 'I speak for the bush', for example, depicts the cultural alienation of Africans who attempt to appear 'modern' by aping western ways. Although some of the poems in this anthology are written by non-East Africans, they graphically depict African experience. Eric Ng'maryo of Tanzania and Stella Ngatho and Henry Barlow of Uganda are three of the poets represented whose creative use of language is remarkable.

Other poetry anthologies include *Attachments to the Sun* (1976), edited by Dougall Blackburn, Alfred Horsfall, and Chris Wanjala; *Boundless Voices: Poems from Kenya* (1988), edited by Arthur I. Luvai, which introduces such young East African poets as Loice Abukutsa and Z. Osore, whose writing is informed by African oral traditions; *An Anthology of East African Poetry* (1988), edited by A. D. Amateshe; and *Tender Memories: Poems and Short Stories* (1989), edited by Arthur I. Luvai, W. Kabira, and B. Bhuluka. *Our Secret Lives* (1990), edited by Wanjiku Mukabi *et al.*, is an anthology of poems and short stories by East African women.

Anthologies of East African oral literature include *The Heroic Recitations of the Bahima of Ankole* (1964), edited by Henry Morris — mainly praise poems from Uganda; *Akamba Stories* (1966), edited by John Mbiti — fables and tales from the Akamba people of Kenya; *Agikuyu Folk Tales* (1966), edited by Njumbo Njururi — stories and legends from the Agikuru (Kikuyu) people of Kenya; *Keep My Words: Luo Oral Literature* (1974), edited by Adrian Roscoe; *Kenyan Oral Narratives: A Selection* (1985), edited by Waryiku Mukabi Kabira and Kavetsa Adagala; and Bolo Odago's *Yesterdays Today* (1986). These materials are slowly influencing East African writers as they seek an authentic African form and subject-matter.

East African short stories have been collected in *An Anthology of East African Short Stories* (1987), edited by Valerie Kibera, in *Chameleon's Second Delivery*, (1987), edited by the Kenya Institute of Education, and in *The Coming of Power and Other Stories*, edited by Jonathan Kariara. East African drama has been collected in *Short East African Plays in English* (1968), edited by David Cook and Miles Lee, in *Short African Plays* (1972), edited by Cosmo Pieterse, containing plays by Kuldip Sondhi of Kenya (*The Magic Pool*) and Ngugi wa Thiong'o (*This Time Tomorrow*), in *Drama Festival Plays* (1986), edited by Dougall Blackburn and Wasambo Were Arnold, and in *An Anthology of East African Plays* (1991), edited by Kasigwa N. Barnabas.

EGARA KABAJI

ANTHOLOGIES (India)

P. Lal's *Modern Indian Poetry in English: An Anthology and a Credo* (1969; 2nd ed. 1971) set the tone for many of the anthologies of Indian literature in English that followed. The 'credo' of its subtitle refers to personal statements by the selected poets on why they wrote in English. Lal marshalled these statements together for his own war against those who attacked him, and other poets, for writing in English. His combative introduction and the poets' often pugnacious statements were meant to silence their critics.

The critics have fallen silent, but many of the anthologists that followed, even when very critical of Lal, have retained his combative stance. Saleem Peeradina's *Contemporary Indian Poetry in English: An Assessment and Selection* (1972; repr. 1977) whittles Lal's 132 poets down to fourteen, simultaneously attacking Lal for encouraging mediocrity. **R. Parthasarathy**'s *Ten Twentieth-Century Indian Poets* (1976; repr. 1978, 1988, 1989, 1992), **Keki N. Daruwalla**'s *Two Decades of Indian Poetry (1960–1980)* (1980), Vilas Sarang's *Indian English Poetry Since 1950* (1989), and **Arvind Krishna Mehrotra**'s *The Oxford India Anthology: Twelve Modern Indian Poets* (1992) all contain critical assessments of the poets included. The asperity of some of the assessments has led to a debate on whether anthologies are the proper place for them. Mehrotra's *Twenty Indian Poems* (1990), an anthology for school-leavers and first-year college students, includes a poem by **Sarojini Naidu** on the grounds that students should learn to recognize a bad poem.

Both Naidu and **Sri Aurobindo**, a revolutionary turned spiritual teacher and poet, came under fire from Lal, and practically every subsequent anthologist has dismissed them. But they have shown surprising resilience, cropping up in Makarand Paranjape's *Indian Poetry in English* (1993), an anthology that seeks to correct both the inclusiveness of Lal and the exclusiveness of most subsequent anthologists. **Gauri Deshpande**'s *An Anthology of Indo-English Poetry* (1974), **Pritish Nandy**'s *Indian Poetry in English: 1947–1972* (1972), *Indian Poetry in English Today* (1973), and *Strangertime; An Anthology of Indian Poetry in English* (1977) also have a certain catholicity in common, but unlike Paranjape's anthology they restrict themselves to the 'moderns' — those who did their best writing during and after the 1950s.

Paranjape goes so far as to question the very concept of modernity in Indian poetry written in English, implying that there is a link between the earliest known poets, such as **Henry Louis Vivian Derozio**, and the poets writing today. He stretches the point further in *An Anthology of New Indian English Poetry* (1993), categorically stating that modernism is dead. Paranjape's very concept of modernism is debatable and there is little to show that the new poets are free of it, but his original approach has at least led to **Shahid Suhrawardy**, a forgotten poet whom he has sought to reinstate in the canon.

Debates raised by the anthologists are naturally about the choice of poets and a poet's choice of poets, since practically all the anthologists are poets. (A notable exception is V. K. Gokak, whose *The Golden Treasury of Indo-Anglian Poetry, 1825–1965*, 1970, as its title suggests, suffers from a certain late Victorian Romanticism.) More significant are debates arising out of regional loyalty —

anthologists are accused of having a Bombay bias or a Calcutta bias, or, since a great deal of poetry is being written there, an Orissa bias. There certainly is some truth in the accusations.

Also, the omnipresent twenty poets (give or take a few) that feature in all the anthologies published since Peeradina's (except for the Paranjape anthology, which features young poets) have made readers feel that there is not very much new contemporary work of significance and that it is time to cease publication of so many anthologies. But with courses in Indian literature gaining ground in some universities, publishers have sensed a captive market for textbooks and it is unlikely the flow will stop.

K. Ayyapa Paniker's *Modern Indian Poetry in English* (1991) and **Kaiser Haq**'s *Contemporary Indian Poetry* (1990) are important for different reasons. The first, published by the Sahitya Akademi, the official Academy of Literature, signals official recognition of a poetry that was nationally derided thirty years ago. The second is the first substantial anthology of Indian poetry to be published in the west (by Ohio State University Press, USA).

Meenakshi Mukherjee's *Let's Go Home and Other Stories* (1975; repr. 1977, 1983, 1984, 1986, 1987, 1989, 1991, 1992), an anthology that features fourteen writers, appears to be the only anthology of Indian short stories written in English. Anthologies of plays, short or full-length, fare even worse — there are none. The clear lead that anthologies of poetry have over anthologies of short stories and plays, however, should not be taken to mean that poetry is the mode Indians prefer. Though this was once widely believed, the new wave of fiction following **Salman Rushdie**'s *Midnight's Children* (1981) has belied such a claim. On the evidence of the current crop of short stories and plays, anthologies in both areas will not be long in coming.

ADIL JUSSAWALLA

ANTHOLOGIES (Malaysia and Singapore)
Anthologies of Singaporean literature in English were published during the initial burst of creative writing of the 1950s, following the establishment of an English Department in what was then the University of Malaya in Singapore.

A collection of campus poetry entitled *Litmus One: Selected University Verse: 1949–1957* (1958) led the way. Edited by the Raffles Society of the University of Malaya, it attempted to provide a platform for local poetry in English. The Raffles Society followed this a year later with Herman Hochstadt's compilation of campus fiction, *The Compact: A Selection of University of Malaya Short Stories, 1953–1959*. Notable among the writers to emerge in the 1950s and whose work appeared in these university publications were the poets **Wong Phui Nam, Edwin Thumboo, Ee Tiang Hong,** and Tan Han Hoe. After a lull in the publication of anthologies, T. Wignesan edited *Bunga Emas: An Anthology of Contemporary Malaysian Literature (1930–1963)* (1964). The collection included the work of Chinese, Tamil, and Malay writers as well as that of writers in English. Among the more prominent contributions were poems by Wong Phui Nam, Oliver Seet, and Tan Han Hoe.

In the 1970s there was a spate of anthologies: *The Flowering Tree: Selected Writings from Singapore and Malaysia* (1970), *Seven Poets: Singapore and Malaysia* (1973), and *The Second Tongue: An Anthology of Poetry from Malaysia and Singapore* (1976), all edited by Edwin Thumboo. The work of established figures such as **Lim Thean Soo**, Wang Gungwu, and Thumboo were presented together with that of younger writers such as Wong May, **Cecil Rajendra, Chandran Nair, Goh Poh Seng, Muhammad Haji Salleh**, and **Lee Tzu Pheng**. Two years later, Chung Yee Chong, Geraldine Heng, and **Kirpal Singh** were represented in *Articulations: An Anthology of Poems*, edited by Kirpal Singh. Another poetry collection, *Five*

Takes, published in 1974, included pieces by **Arthur Yap**, Yeo Bock Cheng, **Robert Yeo**, Sng Boh Khim, and Chung Yee Chong.

A collection of women's fiction, *The Sun In Her Eyes: Stories by Singapore Women* (1976), edited by Geraldine Heng, launched the work of Nalla Tan, **Stella Kon**, Theresa Lim, Tan Lian Choo, Rebecca Chua, and others. A more wide-ranging anthology of local literature, *Singapore Writing* (1977), was edited by Chandran Nair. The collection brought together important new work by such Malay and Chinese writers as A. Ghani, S. N. Masuri, Meng Yi, Wong Yoon Wah, and Yu Mo-Mo, as well as pieces by such English-language writers as Chandran Nair, Dudley de Souza, and Angeline Yap. Robert Yeo edited *Singapore Short Stories* (1978) and *ASEAN Short Stories* (1981). Malaysian short fiction was collected in *Twenty-Two Malaysian Stories* (1968) and *Malaysian Short Stories* (1981), both edited by **Lloyd Fernando**.

Anthologies of the 1980s and early 1990s were dominated largely by the hitherto relatively under-represented genre of drama. A series entitled *Prize-winning Plays*, edited by Robert Yeo, was published in four volumes between 1980 and 1981. The best plays selected from a government-sponsored competition were published in each volume. Ronald Alcantra, Elizabeth Su, and Dorothy Jones were some of the playwrights included. A series of five volumes of *Prize-winning Plays* emerged between 1986 and 1991. Edited by different individuals (Max Le Blond, Arthur Lindley, and Thiru Kandiah), these volumes presented the playscripts of younger dramatists such as Tan Tarn How, Eleanor Wong, **Christine Lim**, **Ovidia Yu**, Daniel Koh, and Desmond Sim.

The *Asean* anthologies of poetry, fiction, and drama have been appearing since 1985. These volumes, edited by a committee of writers, are sponsored by inter-governmental cultural institutions and are for institutional distribution. Though comprehensive in terms of genres and communities represented, they are hampered by a lack of public availability.

Poetry and prose returned with a vengeance in the 1990s with two anthologies: *Words for the 25th: Readings by Singapore Writers* (1990), edited by Edwin Thumboo, an occasional collection celebrating Singapore's independence day; and *Voices of Singapore: Multi-Lingual Poetry and Prose* (1990), edited by Anne Pakir, a volume providing a multicultural perspective. The Tamil poet/dramatist Elangovan, the fictionist **Philip Jeyaratnam**, as well as a number of National University of Singapore writers are among those represented in these two collections.

Anthologies aimed at the school market and consisting of poetry, short fiction, or drama have made their appearance from time to time, edited by various hands. It is likely that with the burgeoning of new writers and with the increased emphasis on support for the arts in Singapore, more anthologies, of all categories, are likely to be published before the close of the 1990s.

DUDLEY De SOUZA

ANTHOLOGIES (New Zealand)

Despite the formal colonization of New Zealand by British settlers as early as the 1840s, nineteenth-century anthologies were few and unimportant. *New Zealand Verse* (1906), edited by W. F. Alexander and A. E. Currie, was the first significant collection of New Zealand poetry. While some poems in this collection deal with the experience of emigration, few reflect on the particular experience of life in the new colony. The distinction of the new land was found in its scenery and in Maori legends. (Very few of the poems have been found worthy of retention in recent anthologies.) Some early anthologies, such as *The Oxford Book of Australasian Verse* (1918), edited by Walter Murdoch, regarded New Zealand as an Australasian colony, and it was not until the volume's fourth edition, *A Book of Australian and New Zealand Verse* (1950), that New Zealand poems were separated from Australian poems. (This anthology contains a separate section of New Zealand verse, edited by **Alan Mulgan**.) Though partly the result of an English attitude to the Antipodes, this combination of the two countries did reflect the popularity in New Zealand of some Australian balladeers.

The long-held notion that 'New Zealand literature' began in the 1930s needs some qualification, but later anthologies lend it support. The chief of those published before 1945 were distinctly backward-looking and conscious of Britain. Quentin Pope's *Kowhai Gold* (1930) and C. A. Marris' *Lyric Poems 1928–1942* (1944) contain poems almost uniformly sentimental and shallow. *New Zealand Short Stories* (1930) was the first collection of stories. The editor, O. N. Gillespie, seems to have chosen stories to describe New Zealand for English readers, though most were written for local or at least antipodean publication, several coming from the Sydney weekly ***Bulletin***. The connection with Australia did not last much beyond this time. A recognition of contemporary New Zealand social conditions did occasionally appear in five collections of one-act plays edited by Victor Lloyd (1933–6).

The influential anthology that defined a new beginning in poetry was **Allen Curnow**'s *A Book of New Zealand Verse 1923–45* (1945). It introduced a new canon that has since been added to, but which otherwise has been only slightly modified, and it printed fuller selections from fewer poets. In a long and important introduction, Curnow pointed to the insecurity and rootlessness of New Zealanders. The most widely distributed of all anthologies, Curnow's later *The Penguin Book of New Zealand Verse* (1960) overshadowed the perhaps less-tendentious *An Anthology of New Zealand Verse* (1956), edited by Robert Chapman and Jonathan Bennett.

As its title suggests, **Frank Sargeson**'s collection of stories *Speaking for Ourselves* (1945) introduced a new attitude to the short story, but it was the inclusion in the World's Classics series of **Dan Davin**'s *New Zealand Short Stories* (1953) that ensured that volume's worldwide appeal. Oxford University Press was to add to *New Zealand Short Stories* each decade, bringing readers up to date with a second (1966), third (1975), and fourth (1984) series of stories, edited by **C. K. Stead**, **Vincent O'Sullivan**, and Lydia Wevers, respectively; all have thoughtful introductions.

Curnow's anthologies were superseded, but his judgements were not significantly revised, by O'Sullivan's *An Anthology of Twentieth Century New Zealand Poetry* (1970; 3rd rev. ed., 1987), which has held its place as the standard anthology. A new generation of poets scarcely represented in Curnow's 1945 collection is found in Charles Doyle's *Recent Poetry in New Zealand* (1965), and there is a still newer generation in Arthur Baysting's *The Young New Zealand Poets* (1973), which has no overlap, even with Doyle's collection. The very large but unfocused *The Oxford Book of New Zealand Writing since 1945* (1983), edited by MacDonald Jackson and Vincent O'Sullivan, also surveys the period following Curnow's and Sargeson's collections. There is still no successful anthology of New Zealand plays.

Since the 1970s anthologies of poems and, particularly, short stories have become numerous and often illustrate particular kinds of writing. There is work drawn from a single periodical — for example, *Landfall Country: Work from Landfall 1947–1961* (1962), edited by **Charles Brasch**, and *N. Z. Listener Short Stories* (1977), edited by **Bill Manhire**. There is the anthology for secondary schools, well exemplified by Helen Hogan's *Nowhere Far from the Sea* (1971), and for younger children there is Dorothy Butler's *The Magpies Said* (1980). *New Zealand Farm and Station Verse 1850–1950* (1950), edited by Airini Woodhouse, is regional in that it collects verse that describes rural and especially sheep-farming life from firsthand knowledge. Trudie McNaughton's *Countless Signs: The New Zealand Landscape in Literature* (1986) reflects a degree of conservation consciousness appropriate to its later date. Writing by Maori, however, is represented by only one substantial collection, **Witi Ihimaera**'s and D. S. Long's *Into the World of Light* (1982). *Te ao marama: Contemporary Maori Writing*, selected and edited by Ihimaera, is planned as an anthology of both imaginative and non-fiction writing in five volumes and a sound cassette. The first of the three volumes of fiction and verse is *Te Whakahuatanga o te ao: Reflections of Reality* (1992). This work will extensively sample writing mostly published since *Into the World of Light*.

The late 1970s and the 1980s were particularly marked by volumes devoted to women's writing. Verse was collected in *Private Gardens: An Anthology of New Zealand Women Poets* (1977), edited by Riemke Ensing, and short stories in *Shirley Temple Is a Wife and Mother: 34 Stories by 22 New Zealanders* (1977), edited by Christine Cole Catley. More recent work is represented in *Women's Work: Contemporary Short Stories by New Zealand Women* (1985), edited by Marion McLeod and Lydia Wevers (published in England as *One Whale Singing; and Other Stories from New Zealand*, 1986), and *Yellow Pencils: Contemporary Poetry by New Zealand Women* (1988), edited by Lydia Wevers.

Among recent general anthologies are three published by Penguin and marked by their considerable size and the large number of contributors. *The Penguin Book of New Zealand Verse* (1985), edited by **Ian Wedde** and Harvey McQueen, is characterized by a preference for the longer poem and is notable for its inclusion, in chronological position, of poems in Maori (with translations). Miriama Evans joined Wedde and McQueen to choose recent verse in Maori for similar inclusion in *The Penguin Book of Contemporary New Zealand Poetry* (1989). *The Penguin Book of Contemporary New Zealand Short Stories* (1989), edited by Susan Davis and **Russell Haley**, offers forty-five stories by almost as many writers from a period of ten years. The only anthologies of stories to survey the whole field historically are Marion McLeod's and Bill Manhire's *Some Other Country: New Zealand's Best Short Stories* (1984) and Vincent O'Sullivan's *The Oxford Book of New Zealand Short Stories* (1992).

Two recent anthologies have reintroduced a link with Australia, but they reflect editorial friendship as much as any widespread new interest in cross-Tasman links. However, books such as Elizabeth Webby's and Lydia Wevers' *Happy Endings: Stories by Australian and New Zealand Women 1850s–1930s* (1987) and their *Goodbye to Romance: Stories by Australian and New Zealand Women 1930s–1980s* (1989) offer the opportunity for interesting comparison.

JOHN THOMSON

ANTHOLOGIES (Pakistan)

Although random selections of Pakistani English literature have appeared from time to time in various journals and books, only five anthologies can be considered as serious attempts at selection of the work. Of these, four present only poetry and one is an anthology of prose and poetry.

First Voices: Six Poets from Pakistan (1965), edited by **Shahid Hosain**, includes poems written before and after 1947 by **Ahmed Ali**, **Zulfikar Ghose**, Hosain, Riaz Qadir, **Taufiq Rafat**, and **Shahid Suhrawardy**. In his introduction, Hosain denies that the anthology offers 'a Pakistani version of negritude', but claims the presence of 'a uniquely Pakistani flavour'. *Pieces of Eight: Eight Poets from Pakistan* (1971), edited by Yunus Said, contains poems by Zulfikar Ghose, M. K. Hameed, Shahid Hosain, Adrian Husain, Nadir Hussein, Salman Tariq Kureshi, **Kaleem Omar**, and Taufiq Rafat. In his introduction, Said finds 'the landscapes and responses' in the poems to be Pakistani. *Wordfall: Three Pakistani Poets* (1975), edited by Kaleem Omar, includes work by Taufiq Rafat, **Maki Kureishi**, and Kaleem Omar. There is no preface, but the back-cover blurb denies the poets were a 'school', while suggesting that they shared certain qualities and subjects. *Pieces of Eight* and *Wordfall* contain only poems written after 1947.

The Blue Wind: Poems in English from Pakistan (1984), edited by Peter Dent, is the only anthology of Pakistani work to have appeared in England. It includes poems by **Daud Kamal**, Adrian Husain, Mansoor Y. Sheikh, Salman Tarik[q] Kureshi, and **Alamgir Hashmi**. In his introduction Dent states: 'One commends these writers without reservation: they are no "backwater", but *mainstream* and affording us all valid and fruitful directions.'

The only anthology of literature to have been published to date, *Pakistani Literature: The Contemporary English Writers*, edited by Alamgir Hashmi, first appeared in 1978 and contains work by ten Pakistani writers. (The second edition, with corrections and additions, was published in 1987.) The poetry and prose selections (fictional and nonfictional) all date from the post-1947 period. The poets included are Zulfikar Ghose, Ahmed Ali, Daud Kamal, Athar Tahir, Maki Kureishi, Shahid Hosain, Taufiq Rafat, Alamgir Hashmi, and Kaleem Omar; the prose writers included are Ahmed Ali, Athar Tahir, Zulfikar Ghose, and Shuaib Bin Hasan. Carlo Coppola and Beatrice Stoerk contribute articles (on poetry and fiction respectively) to the criticism section. Pakistani writing since 1978 requires a further selection.

ALAMGIR HASHMI

ANTHOLOGIES (The Philippines)

Philippine Prose and Poetry (1927), edited by the Philippines' Bureau of Education, is an early anthology of essays, short stories, plays, and poems. *Dear Devices* (1933), edited by Antonio Estrada, Alfredo Litiatco, and Francisco Icasiano, is considered the first general anthology of Philippine essays in English.

Following the Second World War came a resurgence in creative writing in the Philippines. *Guerilla Flower* (1946), collected and edited by *guerillero* Juan L. Raso, gives vivid pictures of the trying experiences of those who did not surrender, but continued fighting the enemy until victory and liberation. *Heart of the Island: An Anthology of Philippine Poetry in English* (1947), edited by **Manuel Viray**, was followed by *Philippine Poetry Annual 1947–1949* (1950), also edited by Viray. Jean Edades edited two volumes of plays — *Short Plays of the Philippines* (1940) and *More Short Plays of the Philippines* (1947), the former appearing in several editions. The plays portray the life and struggles of the common people in towns and barrios.

Philippine Cross Section (1950), edited by Maximo Ramos and Florentino B. Valeros, contains twenty-five short stories (nine from before the Second World War and sixteen from the postwar period). As suggested by the title, the events and scenes represent a cross-section of Filipino life and places. *Philippine Writing* (1953), edited by T. D. Agcaoili, contains short stories and poetry by fifty outstanding Filipino writers in English. The book, intended for classroom teaching, is designed to strengthen love of country.

Philippine Contemporary Literature in English and Pilipino (1962), edited by Asuncion David-Maramba, devotes the larger portion to Philippine writing in English. It includes short stories, poems, essays, plays, speeches, literary criticism, and column writing. *Philippine Harvest* (1964), edited by Maximo Ramos and Florentino B. Valeros, is a collection of short stories, poems, essays, and biographical studies by well-known writers and is designed to make Filipino readers aware of their rich heritage. *Equinox I* (1965), edited by **F. Sionil José**, presents mainly the young writers in order to give them more exposure. *New Writing from the Philippines* (1966), edited by Leonard Casper, is a critical analysis and anthology of the works of outstanding Filipino creative writers in English.

Philippine Literature in English (1973) edited by Esperanza V. Manuel and Resil B. Mojares, contains short stories, poems, plays, and essays. It gives a brief history of Philippine literature and concludes with the view that 'the most dynamic writing fields are those in English and Tagalog'. *The Development of Philippine Literature in English Since 1900* (1975), edited by Richard V. Croghan, divides Filipino writing in English into three periods — the early period (1900–30), the middle period (1930–60), and the modern period (1960–75) — and provides an introduction for each.

A Survey of Filipino Literature in English (1987), by Josephine B. Serrano and Trinidad M. Ames, is a collection of short stories, poems, essays, and one contemporary play grouped into three periods, with introductions and suggested readings. The periods are the Apprenticeship Period (1910–35), the Emergence Period (1935–45), and the Contemporary Period (1945–).

Anthologies of the early 1990s show an increasing use of the national language, Filipino, as well as of the other Philippine vernaculars in Philippine literature.

ESTRELLITA V. GRUENBERG

ANTHOLOGIES (South Africa)

British forces occupied the Cape, South Africa, in 1795 and, after a brief interregnum, took permanent possession in 1806. The arrival of approximately 5,000 British settlers in the Eastern Cape in 1820 greatly increased the English-speaking population, with a concomitant increase in English cultural activities. In 1828 R. J. Stapleton produced the first slim anthology of South African literature in English, *Poetry of the Cape of Good Hope*, culled from local newspapers and journals. The first substantial collection, Alexander Wilmot's *The Poetry of South Africa* (1887), was largely derivative in style and colonial in sentiment. Promising new voices were included in E. H. Crouch's *Treasury of South African Poetry and Verse* (1907); however, it was **F. C. Slater**'s *The Centenary Book of South African Verse* (1925) that drew attention to an emerging indigenous tradition.

Slater's *The New Centenary Book of South African Verse* (1945) was superseded by an adventurous postwar selection edited by Roy Macnab and Charles Gulston: *South African Poetry: A New Anthology* (1948). The latter collection was also the first to feature the work of a black poet, **H. I. E. Dhlomo**. More selective, but covering developments over 150 years, was **Guy Butler**'s *A Book of South African Verse* (1959), which pointed towards a 'canon' of established poets. **Jack Cope** and Uys Krige covered a wider spectrum in *The Penguin Book of South African Verse* (1968), including Afrikaans as well as black poetry in translation. A similar holistic approach, though marred by imbalances, has been followed in *SA in Poësie/SA in Poetry* (1988), edited by Johan van Wyk *et al.*, and in **Stephen Gray**'s *Penguin Book of Southern African Verse* (1989).

Michael Chapman's *A Century of South African Poetry* (1981) had a major impact, reflecting both historical trends and the emergence of important new black poets. Black poets had been previously featured in selections such as Cosmo Pieterse's *Seven South African Poets* (1971) and **James Matthews**' *Black Voices Shout!* (1974); the 1980s saw a proliferation of locally published anthologies, including *The Return of the Amasi Bird: Black South African Poetry 1891–1981* (1982), edited by Tim Couzens and Essop Patel, and *Voices from Within: Black Poetry from Southern Africa* (1982), edited by Chapman and **Achmat Dangor**. Poetry anthologies have largely succeeded in escaping censorship, and volumes such as the bilingual *I Quabane Labantu: Poetry in the Emergency/Poësie in die Noodtoestand* (1989), edited by Ampie Coetzee and Hein Willemse, and Ari Sitas' *Black Mamba Rising* (1986), featuring 'South African Worker Poets in the Struggle', have given the disfranchised a local voice and audience. More narrowly focused are Stephen Gray's *Modern South African Poetry* (1984), Nohra Moerat's *Siren Songs: An Anthology of Poetry Written by Women* (1989), and Cecily Lockett's feminist collection *Breaking the Silence: A Century of South African Women's Poetry* (1990).

The focus in short-story anthologies shifted from pioneering tales of adventure and encounters with 'savage Africa' to the study of human relationships in an often-hostile environment; from the 1970s, however, anthologists began concentrating on the injustices of apartheid and on socio-political realities. An early, largely Eurocentric collection is E. C. Parnwell's *Stories of Africa* (1930). Most subsequent anthologies were aimed at the schools market; however, *Veld-Trails and Pavements; An Anthology of South African Short Stories* (1949), edited by **H. C. Bosman** and C. Bredell, and **Richard Rive**'s volume of stories by black writers, *Quartet: New Voices from South Africa* (1963), deserve mention. Jean Marquard's *A Century of South African Short Stories* (1978) provides a comprehensive overview, whereas Stephen Gray's *The Penguin Book of Southern African Stories* (1985) offers a more challenging survey. Narrower in scope are: Mothobi Mutloatse's *Forced Landing. Africa South: Contemporary Writings* (1980) and **Mbulelo Mzamane**'s *Hungry Flames and Other Black African Short Stories* (1986), both focusing on black writers; Gray's *Modern South African Stories* (1980); Norman Hodge's *To Kill a Man's Pride and Other Stories from Southern Africa* (1984); and Michael Chapman's *The 'Drum' Decade: Stories from the 1950s* (1989). Feminist selections have been compiled by Ann Oosthuizen (*Sometimes When It Rains: Writings by South African Women*, 1987), Lindiwe Mabuza (*One Never Knows: An Anthology of Black South African Women Writers in Exile*, 1989), and Annemarié van Niekerk (*Raising the Blinds: A Century of South African Women's Stories*, 1990). E. M. Macphail's *Hippogriff New Writing 1990* (1990) is among several recent publications offering a platform for new talent.

Until recently, few anthologies of South African plays had appeared (apart from collections of one-act plays intended for schools). One of the earliest, *Six One-Act Plays by South African Authors* (1949, no editor), remains of literary-historical interest; more recent selections reflecting a renaissance in South African theatre in the 1970s include Ernest Pereira's *Contemporary South African Plays* (1977), Gray's *Theatre One* (1978) and *Theatre Two* (1981), and Robert Kavanagh's *South African People's Plays* (1981). These were followed by Temple Hauptfleisch's and Ian Steadman's *South African Theatre: Four Plays and an Introduction* (1984), which juxtaposes Afrikaans, English, 'black', and 'alternative' dramas; *Market Plays* (1986), edited by Gray, containing contemporary works staged at Johannesburg's Market Theatre; and Duma Ndlovu's substantial volume *Woza Afrika!* (1986).

Anthologies covering several genres, including non-fiction, have been appearing since 1930; post-war selections include Roy Macnab's *Towards the Sun: A Miscellany of Southern Africa* (1950), *South African Writing Today* (1967), edited by **Nadine Gordimer** and **Lionel Abrahams**, and Gray's *Writers' Territory* (1973). Afrikaans writers in translation are included in **André Brink**'s and **J. M. Coetzee**'s *A Land Apart: A South African Reader* (1986), while David Bunn and Jane Taylor present South African art and writing 'in a state of emergency' in *From South Africa: New Writing, Photographs and Art* (a special issue of *Tri Quarterly*, 69, Spring/Summer 1987). More specialized miscellanies include Mothobi Mutloatse's *Reconstruction: 90 Years of Black Historical Literature* (1981) and, edited by Susan Brown *et al.*, the feminist publication *LIP from Southern African Women* (1983). Topics such as exploration, hunting, and folklore have supplied material for popular anthologies, and selections of critical essays are making a regular appearance.

Only a few of the anthologists listed have provided a sound theoretical basis for their selections: most have been guided by personal taste or socio-political considerations. It remains to be seen what impact recent political developments in South Africa will have on the nation's writers and, consequently, on the direction taken by future anthologists.

ERNEST PEREIRA

Further reading: 'Anthologies', in David Adey, Ridley Beeton, Michael Chapman, and Ernest Pereira (eds) *Companion to South African English Literature* (1986).

ANTHOLOGIES (South Pacific)

Lali: A Pacific Anthology (1980), edited by **Albert Wendt**, is the only exclusively regional anthology of the Papua New Guinea/Islands arena. All others are either national in orientation or uncomfortably straddle the 'boundaries' of the Commonwealth South Pacific by including, variously, the islands of Asia, Australia, New Zealand, or the USA-dominated islands of Micronesia.

The difficulties for editors are the extent to which indigeneity, 'islandness', black politics, or sense of place should govern selection procedures and the imperative of market considerations. For instance, *A Pacific Islands Collection* (1983), edited by R. Hamasaki and W. K. Westlake, emanating from Hawaii, includes Maori literature but not that of Aboriginal Australians; *South Pacific Stories* (1980), edited by Chris Tiffin and Helen Tiffin, contains works by visiting white Australians as well as local writers.

Those anthologies published in metropolitan countries by European editors — for example, *Five New Guinea Plays* (1971), *Black Writing from New Guinea* (1973), *The Eyes of God Does Not Grow Any Grass* (1978), and *Voices of Independence: New Black Writing from PNG* (1980), all edited by Ulli Beier — have generally aimed at the First-World market for Third-World literature, notwithstanding a dual intention to gain exposure for Pacific literature. Those published locally have aimed primarily at stimulating national (less often regional) cultural activity through the secondary-school and tertiary market. Many are anthologies of student writing, such as *Gong: Young Voices from Vanuatu* (1975), edited by B. Gadd, *The Floating Coconut* (1977), edited by I. Gerta, and *Our World: Poems by Young Pacific Poets* (1991), edited by C. Benson and G. Deverell. Pragmatic considerations heighten the popularity of such publications — they provide a useful, comprehensive textbook, whereas imported books are expensive; they are invaluable for whole class use; they display a variety of genres, styles and modes; and their educative value in encouraging literary expression (albeit in a second and hegemonic language) is not questioned.

Anthologies of the region's literature include: *Words of Paradise: Poetry of Papua New Guinea* (1972) and *The Night Warrior and Other Stories from Papua New Guinea* (1972), both edited by Albert Wendt; *Modern Poetry from Papua New Guinea Vol 1* (1972), edited by N. Krauth and E. Brash; *Niugini Stories* (1973), edited by M. Greicus and E. Brash; *Some Modern Poetry from Fiji* (1974), edited by Albert Wendt; *Some Modern Poetry from Western Samoa* (1974) and *The Mana Annual of Creative Writing* (1974), both edited by M. Crocombe; *In the Beginning* (undated; *c.*1975), edited by CWAMEL; *Some Modern Poetry from the New Hebrides/Vanuatu* (1975) and *Some Modern Poetry from the Solomon Islands*, both edited by A. Wendt; *The Mana Annual of Creative Writing 1975* (1976), edited by M. Crocombe; *Essays from the Pacific*, *Short Essays and Poems*, and *Laughter and Smile*, all edited by CWAMEL (and all undated; *c.*1976); *The Mana Annual of Creative Writing 1976* (1977), edited by M. Crocombe; *Pacific Voices: An Anthology of Writing by and about Pacific People* (1977), edited by B. Gadd; *Twenty-Four Poems of the Solomon Islands* (1977), edited by D. Lulei; *Waka: Roots* (1977), edited by F. Mangubhai; *The Indo-Fijian Experience*, (1979), edited by **Subramani**; *Melanesia: Thoughts and Words* (1981), edited by **John Kolia**; *Houra'a: Solomon Islands Short Stories* (1981), edited by J. Villia *et al.*; *Mi Mere: Poetry and Prose by Solomon Islands Women Writers* (1983), edited by A. Billy *et al.*; *Creative Writing from Fiji* (1986), edited by S. Atherton and **S. Nandan**; and *Pacific Voices: An Anthology of Maori and Pacific Writing* (1989), edited by B. Gadd.

YONI RYAN

ANTHOLOGIES (Sri Lanka)

Early anthologies aimed at introducing Sri Lankan writing in English, Sinhalese, and Tamil to overseas readers. Christopher Reynolds' *An Anthology of Sinhalese Literature up to 1815* (1970) is a UNESCO publication — as is his *An Anthology of Sinhalese Literature of the Twentieth Century* (1987); both present Sinhala literature in English translation. Michigan State University's Asian Studies Center published 'The Poetry of Sri Lanka' in the *Journal of South Asian Literature* 12 (1976) — a volume entirely devoted to Sri Lankan poetry — with an informative introductory essay by editor **Yasmine Gooneratne**. Of the seventy poems published, sixty-one are written in English. 'Sinhala and Tamil Writing' (from Sri Lanka) in the *Journal of South Asian Literature* 22 (1987), edited by Ranjini Obeyesekere, published English translations of Tamil and Sinhala prose and verse. Gooneratne also edited *Stories from Sri Lanka* (1979) — fourteen of the eighteen stories were written in English — and *Poems from India, Sri Lanka, Malaysia and Singapore* (1979) — the Sri Lankan poems are all by writers in English. *An Anthology of Modern Writing from Sri Lanka* (1981), edited by Ranjini Obeyesekere and Chitra Fernando, contains original fiction and poetry in English and translations from Sinhalese.

A comprehensive approach in terms of trends and themes is evident in anthologies compiled by D. C. R. A. Goonetilleke; his *Modern Sri Lankan Stories* (1986) and *Modern Sri Lankan Poetry: An Anthology* (1987) cover the work of three decades — from the 1950s to the 1980s — accurately reflecting not only individual achievements but a crucial era of writing in English. *An Anthology of Contemporary Sri Lankan Poetry in English* (1988) and a companion volume of short stories (1990), edited respectively by Rajiva Wijesinha and Ashley Halpé, followed.

Modern Sri Lankan Drama (1991), edited by Goonetilleke, is the only anthology to cover this particular area, while *Penguin New Writing in Sri Lanka* (1992) — also edited by Goonetilleke — is the only anthology to include fiction and poetry in all three major languages of the island — Sinhalese, Tamil, and English.

LAKSHMI DE SILVA

ANTHOLOGIES (West Africa)

Ethnological imperatives

Whether considered in terms of the inclusion of West African works in larger anthologies, or of the anthologizing of all-West African writing, the role of anthologies in West Africa began as ethnological scholarship serving political arguments. European colonizers needed ethnological profiles of conquered peoples for formulating colonial policies, while European philanthropists and African nationalists deployed them to counter racial myths created to justify slavery and colonialism. (See **Foreign Writers**, West Africa.) There is thus a direct progression from the Abbé Grégoire's influential 1808 anthology of black intellectuals — *De la littérature des nègres*, which included work by West African-born **Olaudah Equiano** and Ignatius Sancho (1729–80), 'who had distinguished themselves in science, arts or literature' — to the mid-twentieth century literary nationalism of **Chinua Achebe**, who initially employed fiction to demonstrate that Africans 'were not mindless but frequently had a philosophy . . . poetry [and] dignity' (in 'The Role of a Writer in a New Nation', *Nigeria Magazine* 81, 1964), and Cameroonian prince Dika Akwa. Akwa compiled an anthology of Cameroonian proverbs, *Bible de la sagesse bantou* (1955), to argue philosophical analogies between the proverbs and the thoughts of European philosophers such as Marx, Bergson, and Nietzsche. Such ethnological bias later contributed immensely to western treatment of post-colonial literatures as merely ethnological gateways into the black man's mind.

Early West African anthologies had predominantly ethnic focus and were loosely organized collections of all kinds of writing, including complete short works as well as extracts from longer works. Predictably, the two world wars encouraged outbursts of anthologizing fervour, with special attention to such cultures as the Ashanti, Yoruba, and Hausa-Fulani, who had offered large-scale military resistance to European conquest. Robert S. Rattray's *Hausa Folklore: Customs, Proverbs, etc.* appeared in 1913, *Ashanti Proverbs* in 1916, and *Akan-Ashanti Folk-Tales* in 1930. William Henry Barker's *West African Folk-Tales* appeared in 1917. By the 1950s, European ethnological interests converged with resurgent African nationalism. Seeking to demonstrate indigenous civilizations' glorious achievements, West Africans produced anthologies of their people's folklore with missionary zeal. However, Europeans remained active, and both sides often collaborated. Donald St John Parsons edited two volumes of North Ghanaian legends (*Legends of North Ghana*, 1958, and *More Legends of North Ghana*, 1960), while Ulli Beier produced anthologies of traditional Yoruba poetry (*Yoruba Poetry: An Anthology of Traditional Poems*, 1970, and, with Bakare Gbadomosi, *Yoruba Poetry*, 1959, and *Ijala: Animal Songs by Yoruba Hunters*, 1967). Alta Jablow's *An Anthology of West African Folklore* appeared in 1962, but Ruth Finnegan's *Limba Stories and Storytelling* (1967) represents the first sustained and consistent effort made by a major scholar to treat oral forms as serious literature in their own right. In francophone states, cultural nationalism was invigorated by the Négritude movement's effective integration of racial ideology, ethnology, and aesthetics. Traditional Senegalese narratives were anthologized by such writers as Bernard Dadié, Fily-Dabo Sissoko, Birago Diop, and Jean Copans throughout the 1960s. The decade closed with the publication of the first of Neil Skinner's three-volume *Hausa Tales and Traditions* (1969), a compendium of various literary forms as well as historical narratives, religious material, and official correspondence collected by Major Edgar, a British administrative officer in northern Nigeria between 1905 and 1927.

European-language Writings

Anthologies of European-language literatures emerged with the literature itself. Not surprisingly, the first of these, *African New Writing* (1947, no editor cited), presented the first products of the 'Scribblers' Club', founded in Nigeria by a British Council official. It is essentially an anthology of six West African writers, with a South African Zulu included to support fashionable western stereotypes, approvingly quoted in the foreword, contrasting the 'statuesque and simple Zulu' with 'the Negro brimming over with side-plots and character'. Conversely, the first major anthology in Négritude territories was Léopold Sédar Senghor's indigenous initiative, *Anthologie de la nouvelle poésie nègre et malgache* (1948), additionally famous for Jean-Paul Sartre's introductory essay, 'L'Orphée noir', which gave its title to the anglophone journal *Black Orpheus*. Another decade elapsed, however, before such anthologies became regular, with the publication of *An Anthology of West African Verse* (1957), edited by Donatus Ibe Nwoga.

The anthologies were generally national or even regional rather than ethnic, as in the case of Frances Ademola's *Reflections: Nigerian Prose and Verse* (1962; 2nd ed., 1965), with a foreword by frontline nationalist Dr Nnamdi Azikiwe; A. D. Banks-Henries' *Poems of Liberia (1836–1961)* (1966); A. C. Brench's *Writing in French from Senegal to Cameroon* (1967); Ime Ikiddeh's *Drum Beats: An Anthology of West African Writing* (1968); and Abiola Irele's *Lectures Africaines: A Prose Anthology of African Writing in French* (1969), with French texts and English commentary.

Various writers' associations, professional associations, cultural institutions, and government agencies also played major roles in the development of anthologies. Their activities often reflected mid-century West African realities in which governments' ideological positions affected the intellectual and cultural climate. This largely explains the prominent roles in Ghana of literary clubs, the Association of Writers, and the Association of Teachers of English, under Kwame Nkrumah's ideologically articulate leadership. These organizations encouraged budding writers through creative writing competitions and offered outlets through the publication of anthologies such as *Talent for Tomorrow: An Anthology of Creative Writing from the Training Colleges of Ghana* (1966), edited by E. C. Sangster and C. K. A. Quashire, and *The New Generation: Prose and Verse from the Secondary Schools and Training Colleges of Ghana* (1967), edited by Margaret E. Watts. A notable equivalent outside Ghana was Martin Banham's *Nigerian Student Verse, 1959* (1960), a selection of verse previously published in *The Horn* magazine, University College, Ibadan. Governments also promoted literary works on radio, some of which were later anthologized. *Voices of Ghana: Literary Contributions to the Ghana Broadcasting System, 1955–57*, edited by Henry Swanzy, was published in 1958.

Particularly important since the 1960s are the anthologies produced to counter foreign school anthologies — those compiled by non-Africans and whose contents oriented African pupils away from local realities and tended to reinforce Europeans negative myths about Africans. Students' aesthetic, cultural, and historical appreciation of such works was aided by the addition of pedagogical introductions, annotations, critical and explanatory notes, classroom-type questions, and biographical sketches. Representative examples are Donald St John Parsons' *Our Poets Speak: An Anthology of West African Verse* (1966), with an introduction by West Indian scholar **O. R. Dathorne**; Paul Edwards' *West African Narrative: An Anthology for Schools* (1966), comprising both stories written in English and translations from indigenous languages and French; and Donatus Nwoga's *West African Verse: An Annotated Anthology* (1967), still widely used in West African schools.

Anthologists since the 1970s have continued the tradition of making their works responsive to their societies' quest for self-definition. **Wole Soyinka**'s *Poems of Black Africa* (1975) accordingly abandons the customary sectional organization of anthology materials, preferring themes as the organizing principle. Journals such as *Okike: An African Journal of New Writing* (1971–) continue to promote creative writing and periodically anthologize such writing, notable successes being *African Creations* (1982), introduced by E. N. Obiechina, and *Rhythms of Creation* (1982), selected and introduced by D. I. Nwoga, anthologies of prose and poetry, respectively, celebrating the journal's tenth anniversary in the early 1980s.

Nevertheless, economic deterioration and control of publishing by western interests are transforming the West African literary scene by subjecting literary production to foreign patronage and coercion. Thus, after successfully publishing its poetry anthology *Voices from the Fringe* (1988), edited and introduced by Harry Garuba, the **Association of Nigerian Authors** needed a British Council subsidy to publish its drama anthology, *5 Plays* (no editor cited), in 1990. The 1980s and 1990s are witnessing an ominous trend for western publishers who, exploiting the current vogue for gendered literature, sponsor 'feminist' anthologies that may actually reflect not the contributor's autonomous inspirations but the interplay of the sponsor's commercial and ideological programmes. In so far as this trend, illustrated by Charlotte Bruner's *Heinemann Book of African Women's Writing* (1993), encourages creative diversity, it has its merits. However, given the socio-economic context of literary production in West Africa, such marriage of commerce and ideology represents subtle neo-colonialist interests packaging new myths as potentially enslaving as the racial myths the original anthologies sought to debunk.

CHIDI OKONKWO

Further reading: Claude Wauthier, *The Literature and Thought of Modern Africa: A Survey* (1966); Janheinz Jahn, *Neo African Literature and Culture: A History of Black Writing* (1969), trans. Oliver Coburn and Ursula Lehrburger; Hans M. Zell and Helene Silver, eds, *A Reader's Guide to African Literature* (1971); Donald E. Herdeck, ed., *African Authors: A Companion to Black African Writing Vol. I: 1300–1973* (1973).

ANTHONY, FRANK SHELDON (1891–1927)

New Zealand short-story writer, novelist

Born at Poverty Bay, New Zealand, he grew up on a South Taranaki farm and left home in 1909 to work as a deck hand on coastal steamers and international sailing ships. At the outbreak of the First World War, Anthony went to England and joined the Royal Navy as a gunner. Injured in the Battle of Jutland, he was invalided home, where he purchased a small farm in Central Taranaki. Most of Anthony's fiction is centred on his experience of struggling to make his farm viable. Before moving to England in 1924, he wrote at least three novels and sixteen 'Me and Gus' stories. Two novels, *Follow the Call* (1936) and *Windjammer Sailors*, were serialized in the *Weekly Press*, the latter during 1924; the 'Me and Gus' stories appeared in weekly papers during 1923 and 1924 and were collected as *Me and Gus* (1938) and *Gus Tomlins, together with the Original Stories of 'Me and Gus'* (1977).

Celebrated for their use of vernacular speech, rural setting, and comic realism, Anthony's sketches resemble those of **Steele Rudd** and **Henry Lawson** in Australia and the work of his favourite writer, Mark Twain. Anthony's Gus Tomlins is a comic inverse of a cultural stereotype, the capable do-it-yourselfer. The stories about Gus reflect the social and emotional patterns that characterize nationalist rural-centred writing in Australia and New Zealand. A minor writer, Anthony is nevertheless significant as a genre writer, his ironic sketches replicating many of the sexual ambiguities and cultural myths found in the work of major figures such as Lawson or **Frank Sargeson**.

LYDIA WEVERS

ANTHONY, MICHAEL (1930–)

Trinidadian novelist, historian

Born in Mayaro, in rural south-eastern Trinidad, he attended elementary school there and in San Fernando, Trinidad's southern city, where in 1944 he entered the Junior Technical School as a trainee mechanic. Two years later Anthony was apprenticed at the foundry in nearby Pointe-à-Pierre. In 1954 he immigrated to London, England, intent on developing his writing career, and there met and in 1958 married Yvette Phillip, a fellow Trinidadian. In 1968 the family moved to Rio de Janeiro, Brazil, where for two years he served as cultural officer in the Trinidad and Tobago Embassy. Returning to Trinidad, Anthony worked as a journalist for two years before spending sixteen years as cultural officer in the ministry of education. He was twice a resident member of the international writing programme at the University of Iowa, USA. His work, comprising six novels and several short-stories and historical works, draws substantially on his personal experiences. For his literary achievements Anthony was honoured in 1979 with the Hummingbird Gold Award, and in 1988 he received the City of Port of Spain Award for his contributions to history and literature.

The first phase of Anthony's work, embracing his major fiction, effectively ends with *Streets of Conflict* (1976), though *All That Glitters* (1981) also belongs to it. Characterized by disguised eclectic autobiography, these works focus the developing consciousness of young protagonists, setting them in the landscape, society, and ethos of rural Trinidad of the 1930s and 1940s. They offer period portraits that help reconstruct the neglected past, such as that of the selfless elementary schoolteachers so fundamental to the flowering of the country's first crop of intellectuals (projected through the motif of the portrait of the writer as a schoolboy) and the society's emerging ethnic pluriverse.

The second phase of Anthony's writing, beginning with *Profile Trinidad: A Historical Survey from the Discovery to 1900* (1975), consists mainly of historical and cultural writings, originating in but outlasting his work as cultural officer. Its range includes a re-focused history of country, city, towns, and villages, the reclamation of the land's unsung heroes, and a chronicle of carnival.

Both phases share the common objective of celebrating the physical, cultural, and historical landscape of Trinidad and Tobago. In Anthony's first three novels — *The Games Were Coming* (1963), *The Year in San Fernando* (1965), and *Green Days by the River* (1967) — and in the earlier short stories, a somewhat pointilistic proliferation of details of local colour, human and physical, consolidates this landscape. This enables the fiction to anticipate the later historical-cultural writings in engendering a potential for elevating national consciousness and pride; the integration of vernacular usages reinforces this. Being essential elements of the decolonization process, antecedent to and characteristic of the early stages of post-colonial experience, these features establish for Anthony a place in anti-colonial discourse. Its most explicit rendering is in stories such as 'Sandra Street' (in *Cricket in the Road,* 1973), somewhat critically in the uneven *Streets of Conflict*, and in *King of the Masquerade* (1974) and *All That Glitters*. Moreover, his major fiction highlights everyday, uneventful, marginalized, usually rural lives, clothed in the warmth, foibles, and venalities of their humanity, the muted criticism of the mores sustaining and sustained by them outweighed by their dignity of personhood.

If Anthony's work does not provide the social and political analysis typical of Caribbean anti-colonial and post-colonial literature, his tranquil prose and the limited perspective of the young protagonists do not conceal from the adult reader the disturbing relevance of those issues. Such larger concerns are indeed signified through an inescapable subtext, in which adult behaviour and relationships and society's mores provide the parameters of the major themes.

Male-female contestation is one example. Men stake out as inviolate male space what should be shared space. In 'The Village Shop' (*Cricket in the Road*) and *The Year in San Fernando* the female self is diminished by an ethos that enforces economic female dependency, and in *The Games Were Coming* the puritanical, exploited Sylvia must negotiate social survival by becoming the blasé exploiter. In *Streets of Conflict* callous and exploitative males are counterbalanced by a mutually accommodating relationship between a more refined, sensitive man and a strong, intelligent woman.

ARTHUR D. DRAYTON

Further reading: Daryl Cumber Dance, 'Michael Anthony', in Daryl Cumber Dance (ed.), *Fifty Caribbean Writers: A Bio-bibliographical Critical Sourcebook* (1986).

Anyidoho, Kofi (1947–)

Ghanaian poet, critic, translator

Born in Wheta, Volta region, Ghana, he attended Accra Teacher Training College (1968) and undertook advanced teacher training at Winneba (1972). Anyidoho studied English and linguistics at the University of Ghana, Legon (1977), and earned an MA (1980) in folklore at Indiana University, USA, and a Ph.D. (1983) in comparative literature at the University of Texas, Austin, USA. Following teaching in Nigeria's secondary schools he taught English at the University of Ghana.

Anyidoho's volumes of poetry are *Elegy for the Revolution* (1978), *A Harvest of Our Dreams* (1984), and *Earthchild, with Brain Surgery* (1985). Anyidoho was born into a family of traditional Ewe poets, and in his poetry he uses the Ewe dirge, with its integration of music, song, traditional rhythms, symbols, organization, and world view as a natural form of self-expression in English. Anyidoho modernizes the dirge tradition, blending the personal, the communal, and the philosophical. His volumes of poetry contain sequences in which sections are about himself, politics, the state, and the cosmos; individuals are seen within a larger, continuing, communal drama linked to the past and the future. The mood of a sequence varies from the depressive and celebratory to the speculative and prophetic. The traditions he uses can be found in his University of Texas dissertation, *Oral Poetics and Traditions of Verbal Art in Africa* (1983), and in his critical study, *The Pan African Ideal in Literatures of the Black World* (1989). In his essay 'Ewe Tradition of Songs of Abuse' (in *Towards Defining the African Aesthetic*, 1982, edited by Lemuel A. Johnson *et al.*), Anyidoho discusses the work of **Kofi Awoonor** in relation to song traditions; his essay in Kolawole Ogunbesan's *New West African Literature* (1979) discusses the poetry of **Atukwei Okai**.

Anyidoho regards himself as the voice of the post-Nkrumah generation, which, between 1972 and 1979, saw its dreams of revolution through Colonel Acheampong's National Redemption Council turn into political repression and economic incompetence. In the at times strident *Elegy for the Revolution*, written in Ghana, the metaphors, imagery, and diction create an analogy between Ewe poetry and his public discussion of post-colonial Ghanaian political history. *A Harvest of Our Dreams*, written in the USA, deepens the poet's displacement from home. The movement is antiphonal, with exchanges between a solo voice and the nation. The solo voice is both a communal self and the poet, a person with a strong sense of individuality, isolation, and introspection; there is a variety of moods ranging from the comic and satiric to the grave and strident. In 'Earthchild' and 'Brain Surgery' the introspective and hermetical tendencies predominate as the focus shifts to the metaphysical and the ritualistic.

Anyidoho co-edited an anthology of Ghanaian poetry, *Our Soul's Harvest* (1978, with Kojo Kankan), and the critical collections *Cross Rhythms: Occasional Papers in African Folklore* (1983, with Avorgbedor *et al.*) and *Interdisciplinary Dimensions of African Literature* (1985, with Abioseh M. Porter, *et al.*).

BRUCE KING

Further reading: Robert Fraser, *West African Poetry: A Critical History* (1986); Richard K. Priebe, ed., *Ghanaian Literatures* (1988); Jane Wilkinson, ed., *Talking with African Writers* (1990).

Arcellana, Francisco (1916–)

Filipino short-story writer

Born in Manila, the Philippines, and raised in the working-class district of Tondo, he wrote a moderate number of short stories between the mid-1930s and the mid-1960s. Never a highly prolific writer, he has preferred to revise and refine his stories. Critic Leonard Casper has observed in his *New Writing from the Philippines: A Critique and Anthology* (1966) that with Arcellana 'revision becomes genuine re-vision . . . so that through other stories with nearly identical themes and situations he writes more and more variations on the original'. Three collections of Arcellina's stories have been published: *Selected Stories* (1962), *15 Stories* (1973), and *The Francisco Arcellana Sampler* (1988). He also edited *PEN Short Stories* (1962). In recognition of lifetime achievement, the Philippine government has awarded him the title of National Artist.

Arcellana's recurrent themes involve deeply felt emotion. Most often pathos is the controlling emotion, but he is equally able to make bathos serve his larger purpose, which is to illuminate the human psyche. An example of the bathetic mode is 'Trilogy of the Turtles' (*15 Stories*), a story that recounts the intensity of a young man who is baffled by his inability to tell a young woman of his love for her.

The story 'The Mats' (*Selected Stories* and *15 Stories*), on the other hand, focuses on a father who, having come home from a business trip, unrolls sleeping mats that he has bought for each member of the family. After everyone has received a mat, he unrolls one for each of his three children who have died and calls out their names. To the rekindled grief of his wife, who begs him not to go on, he replies, 'Is it fair to forget them?' Seen from the point of view of the remaining children, this story exposes the unspoken wounds that divide people. More than a decade later, Arcellana returned to the depiction of this family in 'The Flowers of May' (*15 Stories*). Here it is the mother who wishes to remember her daughters with a simple gesture — three lilies for the family altar. And here it is the father who protests. For the children gathered around them, and for the reader, there is the realization that death is not a beautiful thing.

Much of Arcellana's fiction reveals a playful otherworldliness. In the middle section of 'Trilogy of the Turtles' (*15 Stories*), a child listens so intently to the silent laughter of a turtle that he fails to see the lights of an oncoming train. Afterward, the turtle silently weeps. In 'Thy Kingdom Come' (*15 Stories*), a writer yearns to meet Jesus, not for the conventional reasons but so that he can write his biography. 'A Marriage Was Made' (*15 Stories*) depicts a couple that has eloped with the unrealistic notion (in the Philippines) of living on the husband's meagre income as a writer.

Arcellana has influenced an entire generation of Filipino writers, both through his own fiction and his book reviews, and especially as a teacher of creative writing and founding director of the Creative Writing Center at the University of the Philippines.

ROGER BRESNAHAN

Further reading: Edilberto N. Alegre and Doreen G. Fernandez, *Writers and Their Mileu: An Oral History of Second Generation Writers in English* (1987); Roger J. Bresnahan, *Conversations with Filipino Writers* (1990); Leonard Casper, 'Lyrics for wind chime and prayer wheel: Arcellana', *Philippine Studies* 39 (1990).

ARCHIBALD, DOUGLAS RUPERT (1919–)
Trinidadian dramatist
Born in Port of Spain, Trinidad and Tobago, he was educated at Queen's Royal College (1928–35). He joined the Trinidad Light Infantry (1938–40), worked for the Trinidad Government railways (1935–41, 1946–8), studied civil engineering (bachelor of engineering, 1946) at McGill University, Montreal, Canada, and was a civil engineering consultant until 1983. Archibald was a founding member of the Readers and Writers Guild of Trinidad and Tobago (1948–54), president of the Historical Society of Trinidad, and tutor in creative

writing at the University of the West Indies, St Augustine (in 1971, 1973, and 1975).

The author of two series of radio plays, 'That Family Next Door' (broadcast 1973) and *Island Tide* (1972; broadcast 1973), and a novel, *Isidore and the Turtle* (1977), Archibald is one of the founders of modern Caribbean drama who moved beyond writing one-act to full-length plays. His plays for the theatre carefully delineate character and use relationships between men and women, adults and youth, to show how the degeneration, decay, and collapse of the society established by the white plantocracy were followed by disorder and poverty; youth, for example, lack direction and turn towards violence. *Junction Village* (1958), a folk comedy that was a success in London, England, in 1955, is set during a wake for the supposed death of the elderly Grannie Gumbo. It contrasts her energy, passion, and trickery with the loneliness of the old men and the foolishness and violence of the younger men. *Anne-Marie* (1967), produced at the West Indian Festival of the Arts in 1958, uses four white and three non-white characters to show the collapse of the traditional plantocracy at the end of the nineteenth century. In *The Bamboo Clump* (1967) the owner of a house is ignored while his children drift towards failure. *The Rose Slip* (1967), set in barrack yards of the urban poor, uses lonely old men and aimless, violent youths to show the hopeless life of an underclass unable to feed its children. *Old Maid's Tale* (1965), concerning the romantic fantasies of the last of the Macdougals (representative of the old white order), was followed by *Island Tide* (1972), *Defeat with Honour* (1977), and 'Back of Beyond' (premièred 1988).

BRUCE KING

ARGUILLA, MANUEL E. (1910–44)
Filipino short-story writer
Born in Nagrebcan, Bauang, La Union, the Philippines, to Ilocano peasants Crisanto Arguilla and Margarita Estabillo, he spent his childhood years in his birthplace. He moved to Manila, where he obtained his bachelor of science degree (1933) from the University of the Philippines. Arguilla became a teacher and later worked with the Bureau of Public Welfare. He married Lydia Villanueva — a short-story writer, poet, and essayist — whom he met at university. During the Pacific War, he joined the guerrilla movement, but was arrested by the Japanese in February 1944 and executed, probably in August of that year.

Arguilla collected the best of his short stories, which had previously appeared in magazines, in the volume *How My Brother Leon Brought Home a Wife and Other Stories* (1940); it won first prize in the Commonwealth Literary Contest.

In his anthology *The Development of Philippine Literature in English* (1975), Richard V. Croghan writes: 'It is the general opinion today that Arguilla wrote some of the finest Filipino short stories in English. His portrayal of the Ilocano peasant life is unsurpassed.' Edward J. O'Brien included Arguilla's 'Midsummer' in his 1936 *Yearbook of the American Short Story*, ranking it the best of the year's crop. A. V. H. Hartendorp, editor-publisher of the pre-war *Philippine Magazine*, wrote:

> Arguilla has remained among the most forthrightly Filipino, using English almost as if it were a Philippine dialect — so adequate he finds it for his purpose. His work affords new proof of the singular adaptability of that great world language, which the Filipino writers are further enriching by new human as well as philological elements . . . His work is as salty as the breezes that blow over the Ilocos, as human as the smell of the armpits of some of his characters, as deep as the

rumblings in the cavernous bellies of his
carabaos.

ESTRELLITA V. GRUENBERG

ARMAH, AYI KWEI (1939–)

Ghanaian novelist, essayist, short-story writer

Born to Fante-speaking parents in Takoradi, Ghana (formerly the British colony of the Gold Coast), he was educated at Achimota College and the University of Ghana, Accra, and, on an American scholarship, at Harvard University, USA. The first twenty years of Armah's life coincided with the growth of Ghana into Africa's first independent state, and at the time of his departure for the USA, two years after independence, the ideals of nationalism and Nkrumahist socialism were at their height; the betrayal of, and subsequent disillusionment with, these ideals in the 1960s was to colour all of his early fiction. Armah's desire to write from an African base has taken him, in the capacity of translator and teacher, to a number of African countries, including Algeria, Tanzania, Lesotho, and, most recently, Senegal. He has also worked as an editor in Paris, France, and as a university teacher in the USA.

Armah writes insistently, and often obsessively, about Africa's continuing oppression under the mystification of independence and its entrapment in a cycle of neo-colonial dependency. Influenced by Frantz Fanon's *The Wretched of the Earth* (1961), Armah's first two novels, *The Beautyful Ones Are Not Yet Born* (1968) and *Fragments* (1970), emphasize the sterility, corruption, and economic stagnation of an indolent ruling bourgeoisie. Armah's writing presents a country where little or no local wealth is created and where the craving for western commodities leads inevitably to embezzlement of government and municipal funds and to bribery and fraud on a national scale. These novels depict a modern urbanized Africa trapped in a materialist malaise and caught, culturally, in a trance of whiteness, in which everyone from the government politician to the lowliest clerk apes European manners, dress, and speech and aspires to western patterns of acquisitive consumerism and privilege. In *Fragments* the colonial dependency complexes, crises of confidence, and cultural cringe that are familiar features of Commonwealth writing — particularly of the 'white' Commonwealth of Canada and Australia — are given spectacular African expression in the form of a modern cargo-cult mentality. The indigenous artists in *Fragments* are racked by self-distrust and go overseas in search of foreign approval; even local folk-myths are perverted into insidious neo-colonial propaganda by television technocrats angling for foreign foundations. In Armah's third novel, *Why Are We So Blest?* (1972), western luxury, bourgeois class pyramids, and white mistresses infiltrate the fabric of African revolution.

In *The Beautyful Ones Are Not Yet Born* the legacy of decades of consumption without production issues, symbolically, in mountains of undisposed filth and waste piled in streets and latrines. In the lurid, surreal finale, set during the anti-Nkrumah coup of 1966, the corrupt, fallen politician Koomson is imaged as the nation's collected excrement, evacuated through the public latrine hole and carried off by the novel's anonymous hero in the role of communal latrine man. Koomson, by implication, is also both the collected ills of the moribund Nkrumah regime that must be expelled before a new era can be born and, by the novel's interior poetic logic, the accumulated, unexpurgated evils of Africa's colonial and precolonial history in which post-colonial corruption is rooted. There is a touch of Dickens in Armah's exuberant hyperbole and of Rabelais in his indefatigable scatology, but also a vividly poetic sense of history and heritage comparable with that of other black Commonwealth writers such as **Wilson Harris** and **George Lamming**. In *Why Are We So Blest?* the oppressive power of the past and the Commonwealth writer's penchant for allegory are once more in evidence, this time in the racial stereotypes of colonial history that penetrate even to the secret corners of private relationships. In this novel, Africa's molestation by western imperialism is telescoped into the fatal attraction of a naive Ghanaian student to a psychopathic white American girl, resulting in the metaphoric transposition of the west's devouring of Africa's material resources into a corresponding draining of black sexual energy by white women.

In *Two Thousand Seasons* (1973) and *The Healers* (1978), Armah experiments with strange and arresting new literary forms, bursting the bounds of historical realism and moving into the terrain of myth, legend, and racial memory. *Two Thousand Seasons* uses simulated oral narrative and a pluralized communal voice to present a thousand years of migratory Akan history, though this 'history' draws not upon specific tribal memories but on the hypothetical race consciousness of a fictitious pan-African brotherhood and on the dogma of a pristine, indigenous, pre-colonial African 'Way'. The group experience is now paramount and the novel's characterization implicitly reproves the alienated, individualistic perspectives of Armah's first three novels. The reader is addressed by an anonymous, timeless (and racially chauvinistic) 'We' that speaks for the whole social body during its wanderings across history in pursuit of its racial destiny. *The Healers* refracts some of the historical myths of *Two Thousand Seasons* through the specific episode of the fall of the Ashanti empire and ends with the enforced regathering of the world's black peoples in white captivity, ironically seen to portend their eventual reunification. The visionary mythologized history of *The Healers* and *Two Thousand Seasons* aims to cure an errant modern Africa of its distrust in its own indigenous forms and values.

The books have been compared by critic Robert Fraser to two francophone texts, Malian Yambo Ouologuem's *Le Devoir de violence* (1968), published in 1971 as *Bound to Violence*, translated by Ralph Manheim, and André Schwarz-Bart's *Le Dernier des justes* (1959), translated by Stephen Becker and published in 1961 as *The Last of the Just*. Fraser has also compared the exercises in racial retrieval in *The Healers* and *Two Thousand Seasons* to those in Negritude writing. These pursuits of racial heritages, black aesthetics, and authentic ethnic world views are common themes in Commonwealth writing of the black diaspora. They appear in such widely different contexts as the later fiction of George Lamming, the travelogues of **V. S. Naipaul**, the metaphysics of **Wole Soyinka**'s *Myth, Literature and the African World* (1976), and, on a more popular level, in black American writings such as Alex Haley's *Roots* (1976).

DEREK WRIGHT

Further reading: Robert Fraser, *The Novels of Ayi Kwei Armah: A Study in Polemical Fiction* (1980); Derek Wright, *Ayi Kwei Armah's Africa: The Sources of His Fiction* (1989); Derek Wright, ed., *Critical Perspectives on Ayi Kwei Armah* (1992).

ASARE, BEDIAKO (1930–)

Ghanaian novelist

Born in the Gold Coast (now Ghana), he trained and worked as a journalist with various newspapers in Ghana before moving to Tanzania in 1963. His fictional works are not well known in Ghana, partly because his subjects are not typically Ghanaian, and he is often mistaken for **Asare Konadu,** a writer of popular literature. However, Asare's novels, *Rebel* (1969) and *The Stubborn* (1976), which explore the theme of social change, follow a trend in Ghanaian writing of the mid-1960s.

Rebel vividly recalls **Ngugi wa Thiong'o**'s *The River Between* (1965). It contrasts Ngurumo, Asare's fictional protegé and champion of a new order and values, with the fetish priest Mzee Matata (much like Ngugi's thoroughly negative Kabonyi), who advocates a return to traditional ways. The strength of *Rebel* lies in its well-paced, suspenseful, descriptive narrative; however, it appears that the plot is ready-made as Asare seems eager to resolve issues in favour of Ngurumo.

The Stubborn deals specifically with conflict between youth and their elders and, generally, with the problems of modern living. The protagonist, Okello, rebels against parental authority and leaves for Nairobi with Sanga, a delinquent. The plot follows the course of popular literature that represents the city as a magnet that draws and frustrates young people. Okello, however, redeems himself and becomes a distinguished doctor. Artistically, the transformation of the protagonist is sudden and apparently designed to underscore the author's homily about the need to submit to parental control. The plot seems to come to a natural conclusion, but the novelist overextends it. When Okello, in defiance of his parents, marries the manipulative Emma (a relationship that immediately ends in a divorce court) the resolution seems *déjà vu*.

CHRIS KWAME AWUYAH

Further reading: Richard Priebe, 'The novel' in Albert Gérard (ed.) *European-Language Writing in Sub-Saharan Africa* vol. 1 (1986).

ASHTON-WARNER, SYLVIA (1908–84)
New Zealand novelist

Born in Stratford, Taranaki, New Zealand, she was educated there, and at teachers' colleges in Wellington and Auckland, New Zealand. With her husband, she taught in primary schools in remote areas of the Hawkes Bay, Bay of Plenty, and East Cape, as well as in Taranaki and Wanganui. Ashton-Warner was an educational innovator who taught predominantly Maori children in small rural communities and utilized her personal theory of a 'key vocabulary', which she saw as capable of unlocking the learning potential of her students. This encouragement of learning through creative individuality, attempted among the most underprivileged communities, is recounted in her first novel, *Spinster* (1958). Between 1960 and 1979 Ashton-Warner went on to produce a number of works of fiction as well as accounts of her work as a teacher. *Incense to Idols* (1960), *Bell Call* (1964), *Greenstone* (1966), and *Three* (1971) are novels, while her teaching experiences are recalled and explained in *Teacher* (1963), *Myself* (1967), and *Spearpoint: 'Teacher' in America* (1972). An autobiography, *I Passed This Way*, was published in 1979. Ashton-Warner won much attention for her work as an educator, particularly in the USA, where most of her books were published.

C. K. Stead's essay in his *In the Glass Case* (1981) provides an important assessment of Ashton-Warner's work, while the story of her struggle to be taken seriously as both writer and educator is documented in Lynley Hood's biography *Sylvia!* (1988).

MARY PAUL

Further reading: Dennis McEldowney, 'Sylvia Ashton-Warner: a problem of grounding', *Landfall 23* (1969); Carol Durix, 'Literary autobiography or autobiographical literature? The work of Sylvia Ashton-Warner', *Ariel* 2 (1987).

ASSOCIATION FOR COMMONWEALTH LITERATURE AND LANGUAGE STUDIES
Malaysia

Registered on 24 October 1979, the Association for Commonwealth Literature and Language Studies in Malaysia (MACLALS) has three recognizable categories of members: (i) those professionally interested in literature in English — principally but not exclusively from the University of Malaya; (ii) those professionally interested in the teaching of the English language, principally in the schools; and (iii) non-professional enthusiasts interested in cultural activities related but not confined to the study of literature in English and the teaching of the English language. To cater for the different categories of members, MACLALS organizes a broad spectrum of activities. It has held seminars on such themes as 'Identifying Problems of Teaching Literature in English in Schools', 'The Teaching of English in Upper Secondary Schools and Tertiary Institutions in Malaysia', and 'English Proficiency Targets for Malaysia'. It has financed productions of plays from Indonesia, Malaysia, England, and America and organized talks on Commonwealth language and literature by both local and foreign scholars and writers. It has also sponsored readings in Commonwealth language and literature, film shows, and Readers' Theatre Workshops and productions. For the literature professionals and creative writers, it has, since 1980, published the *Southeast Asian Review of English* (*SARE*). Like its parent, ACLALS, MACLALS is a private and entirely non-profit body. Its activities are funded by members' subscriptions, a modest grant from ACLALS, and donations.

ABDUL MAJID B NABI BAKSH

Singapore

The 1986 hosting of the Seventh Triennial Conference of the Association for Commonwealth Literature and Language Studies (ACLALS) was the high point of the Association's Singapore branch. For many years prior to the Triennial, the Branch Association had conducted numerous activities designed to promote the cause of Commonwealth literature. From the early 1970s, the membership has steadily increased to fifty-five in 1986, and the Association itself had begun to make an impact on the local literary scene. From the start it was headed by **Edwin Thumboo**, respected poet and latterly professor of English at the National University of Singapore, where the Association had its administrative office. Helping Thumboo were **Kirpal Singh** as vice-chair and Dudley De Souza as secretary. During the three years that the Singapore ACLALS was also the headquarters for the international body, several issues of the ACLALS *Bulletin* were published. The Seventh Triennial's theme — 'The Writer as Historical Witness: the Commonwealth Experience' — drew together more than two hundred writers and scholars, and a massive programme highlighted the week of the Conference itself.

The Singapore branch has also sponsored, either jointly or singly, readings and seminars by visiting writers and scholars from around the Commonwealth. In recent years the Association has weakened, but since both of Singapore's universities now emphasize Commonwealth literature, and since the prestigious Commonwealth Writers Prize is being hosted from Singapore in 1993 and 1994, there is a good chance that the Association can be restored to its full potential.

KIRPAL SINGH

South Pacific

The South Pacific Association for Commonwealth Literature and Language Studies (SPACLALS) was founded in 1975 as a result of the 1974 decision taken at Stirling, Scotland, to regionalize ACLALS. It commenced operating from Brisbane, Australia, with an interim executive chaired by Ken Goodwin, who went on to serve two further terms. SPACLALS operates with a rotating centralized executive advised by representatives from other parts of the South Pacific region. In 1982 the executive moved to Christchurch, New Zealand, under the chairmanship of Peter Simpson; then in 1987 to Wollongong (chaired by Bill McGaw), and in 1991 to Perth (chaired by Kateryna Longley).

SPACLALS holds triennial conferences (Brisbane, Australia, 1977; Christchurch, New Zealand, 1981; Sydney, Australia, 1984; Palmerston North, New Zealand, 1987; Wollongong, Australia, 1990; and Perth, Australia, 1992) and has also sponsored or supported smaller seminars, including one for high-school teachers — 'Commonwealth Literature in the Curriculum' (Brisbane, 1980). The proceedings of the inaugural conference were published as *South Pacific Images* (1978), edited by Chris Tiffin, and *Commonwealth Literature in the Curriculum* (1980), edited by Ken Goodwin. Other conference proceedings have formed special numbers of the association's journal, *SPAN* (1975–).

Initially, *SPAN* was edited by Laurie Hergenhan and Chris Tiffin as an informational bulletin with news and bibliographical coverage. Under subsequent editors, Peter Simpson (1982–6), Bill McGaw (1987–90), Gerry Turcotte (1991), and Kateryna Longley (1991–) it has been transformed into an important post-colonial critical journal.

SPACLALS has sponsored several short-story competitions, the best entries being published as *South Pacific Stories* (1980), edited by Chris and Helen Tiffin, and in *SPAN*.

Although numerically dominated by its Australian membership, SPACLALS is a truly regional association with a special focus on South Pacific writing. At the time of its inception, the major nationalist literary associations in Australia and New Zealand had not been founded; consequently it played a significant role in the curriculum struggle between nationalists and conservatives in the region's universities. It has responded to the discipline's change from 'Commonwealth' to 'post-colonial' by reasserting its commitment to comparative study and by maintaining a special focus on Pacific (including Papua New Guinea, Australian Aboriginal, and New Zealand Maori) writing.

SPACLALS has been a significant player on the wider ACLALS scene. It contributed the 1977–80 ACLALS executive and hosted the 1980 ACLALS conference in Fiji and the judging of the Commonwealth Writers Prize in 1990.

CHRIS TIFFIN

Association of Nigerian Authors

The Association of Nigerian Authors (ANA) was formed on 27 June 1980 under the leadership of Africa's foremost novelist, **Chinua Achebe**. A Society of Nigerian Authors had, under the leadership of **Cyprian Ekwensi**, existed from 1965 until its disruption by the political crisis of 1966 and the subsequent civil war.

The objectives of ANA include the encouragement and promotion of both Nigerian literature and the commitment of authors to the ideals of a humane and egalitarian society. Apart from its commitment to ensure the freedom and safety of writers in Nigeria, the ANA's aims are to provide guidance in dealing with contracts, copyright, and other business relating to writing. In view of these objectives the Association has assisted both young and established writers in the publication of their works, both individually and in anthologies. An important publishing outlet for ANA members exists in the form of *ANA Review* (1982–), the association's annual journal.

In conjunction with various sponsors, ANA has been able to establish eight national annual literary prizes and one African prize in all literary genres. Association membership totals approximately 200.

The Association, administered at the National Theatre, Iganmu, Lagos, has as its current president **Ken Saro-Wiwa**, while Bode Sowande is the general secretary.

WALE OKEDIRAN

Astley, Thea (1925–)

Australian novelist

Born in Brisbane, Australia, she grew up in Queensland, teaching English in Queensland country schools and, for a lengthy period, at Macquarie University in Sydney. Her experience of small country towns and their narrow-minded prejudice has provided material for many of her novels, including *Girl with a Monkey* (1958), *A Descant for Gossips* (1960), and *An Item from the Late News* (1982). In her more recent work Astley has moved to political spheres: in *Beachmasters* (1985), which is set during the struggle of a Pacific island for independence, and in *It's Raining in Mango* (1987), which debunks self-important family sagas by examining the lives of victimized people within the panorama of white history in Australia.

Astley's long career as a writer — twelve novels to date — offers a reflection of the great changes in Australian writing and social opinion since the 1950s. Her early works attack complacent Australian social attitudes in a relatively conventional way, but by the late 1960s she was influenced by **Patrick White** to experiment with structure and style. *The Acolyte* (1972), for example, has been compared to White's *The Vivisector* (1970), while her *The Slow Natives* (1965) has a structure similar to White's *Riders in the Chariot* (1961). In her later work, such as the short-story collection *Hunting the Wild Pineapple* (1979) and *It's Raining in Mango*, Astley has found an understated style that nevertheless allows full force to her wit and ironic vision. These works about north Queensland country towns form a kind of 'discontinuous narrative' by following the fortunes of a group of related people. They can be compared to the work of Canadian writer **Alice Munro** in collections such as *Lives of Girls and Women* (1971), though Astley's writing retains an impersonal quality, and even at her most sympathetic she maintains a distance from her characters — often through a virtuoso performance of verbal games.

Behind all of Astley's work, even at its most verbally complicated, is a sense of moral outrage at the way institutions and powerful men crush women, children, Aborigines, or outsiders. Critic Pam Gilbert has argued that Astley's frequent choice of male protagonists is the result of her experience in the male world of the university and her recognition of male power within both the community and literary circles. Margaret Smith suggests that this use of male characters, like **Doris Lessing**'s occasional choice of male protagonists, is a way of evading the prejudices and assumptions inevitably attached to the female character, and J. M. Couper posits the idea that in Astley's novel there is a third sex — the androgynous outsiders who gain her sympathy.

Astley's Catholic background is important in discussions of the sex of her characters; her preoccupation with the world of men and with their institutional power sometimes focuses specifically on the Catholic priest and the invisibility of women to the Catholic hierarchy. In this respect, her writing may be compared to that of Irish women writers, such as the early work of Edna O'Brien. Astley often takes an ambivalent attitude to Catholicism — some of her moral outrage seems to come from a Catholic tradition of social concern, yet this outrage is also directed at the self-centred and inhumane attitudes of some of her Catholic characters. Her attitude to homosexuality, too, fluctuates between a sympathy for the outsider and a wariness of unconventional sexuality.

Astley is a social satirist who manages to address both the power relations within the family group and the wider political sphere. However, her brilliant satire can rest on a simplification of social complexity and, paradoxically, on an apparent intolerance for unconventional behaviour, as in her unsympathetic depiction of the hippies in *Hunting the Wild Pineapple* and *It's Raining in Mango*. Her novels might be compared with **Margaret Atwood**'s witty attacks on social assumptions, and her anger at hypocrisy often creates a similar confusion about the author's attitude to reform and change. But though her novels bridle against injustice and selfishness, Astley keeps a suspicious distance from feminism and other seemingly radical solutions. Her novel *Reaching Tin River* (1990) renders the familiar first-person 'woman in search of herself' novel in Astley's cynical and ironic style.

SUSAN LEVER

Further reading: Ross Smith and Cheryl Frost, 'Thea Astley: a bibliography', *Literature in North*

Queensland 10 (1982); Pam Gilbert, *Coming Out from Under: Contemporary Australian Women Writers* (1988).

ATWOOD, MARGARET (1939–)

Canadian novelist, poet, short-story writer, critic

The second of three children born to Carl Atwood and his wife, Margaret Killam Atwood, she spent her childhood years in Ottawa, Canada, the city of her birth, and in the northern woods of Ontario and Quebec. Her father, an entomologist, often took his family on field trips, producing in Atwood an early and abiding interest in the wilderness — the setting of her second novel, *Surfacing* (1972). In 1946 the family settled in Leaside, a suburb of Toronto. The contrasts between its Christian, middle-class morality and its blatant materialism define the spiritual wasteland through which many of Atwood's characters pass on their way from childhood to maturity.

In 1957 Atwood entered Victoria College, University of Toronto, graduating with honours in 1961. In 1962 she received her MA in English from Radcliffe College, USA, going on to further graduate work at Harvard University, 1962–3 and 1965–7.

Since 1973 she has lived with Canadian novelist and cultural activist Graeme Gibson. They have one daughter, Eleanor Jess, born in 1976. They now reside in Toronto. Atwood has been writer-in-residence at universities in Canada, the USA, and Australia. In 1986 she occupied the Berg Chair at New York University and has taught at the University of British Columbia, the University of Alberta, Sir George Williams (now Concordia) University, Montreal, and at York University, Toronto. She was chair of the Writers' Union of Canada (of which she was a founding member), 1982–3, and president of the Canadian Centre of International PEN, 1984–6. She continues to be an effective spokesperson and energetic activist on behalf of Canadian writers and writing, and of women's rights, Native rights, and the environment.

Her first published work was *Double Persephone* (1961). Her second, *The Circle Game* (1966), won a Governor General's Award for Poetry. She has published more than a dozen collections of poetry and two volumes of *Selected Poems* (1976, 1986). *The Journals of Susanna Moodie* (1970) is an extrapolation in verse from *Roughing It in the Bush*, **Susanna Moodie**'s account of her years as a settler in Upper Canada during the 1830s. Moodie gave up her youth, her children, and her place in society to an implacable wilderness she ultimately came to love. Under Atwood's hand, Moodie's final thoughts — long after death — are vehement prayers against the ruinous civilization her sacrifice has spawned. This is quintessential Atwood — terse, evocative, intellectually unforgiving.

The title sequence in *Two-Headed Poems* (1978) was written at a time when it seemed Quebec might secede from Canada. It depicts the troubled nation as Siamese twins joined at the head, each twin desperate to be an individual, but each caught in the other's identity.

Atwood is properly vehement in her insistence that the narrative voice in her writing is not her own. It belongs, book by book, to the characters inside each work. Most are women who have lost their sense of self and of place. They look, but cannot find themselves in the reflecting surfaces around them. But the surfaces in Atwood's writing are more than mere reflectors. They are also shells and skins — potential hiding places for one's true identity. What you do not see in the mirror may be squirming beneath the glass.

What most of the characters in Atwood's novels are seeking is a fresh beginning. In *The Edible Woman* (1969), Marian McAlpin finds herself adrift in a consumer society that threatens to engulf her. Faced with the prospect of marriage, she begins to understand that, being a woman, she is the stuff upon which that society feeds and survives, and that marriage — in itself a staple of the consumerist society — is a kind of sexist cannibalism.

Suicide is contemplated by leading characters in several Atwood novels — including *Surfacing* and *Life Before Man* (1979). Although it is seldom the answer they ultimately accept, the ritual gestures — the running of baths, the flirting with knives — are symbolic of the various states of self-abnegation these women must pass through in order to be reborn. In *Lady Oracle* (1976), a novel of dazzling comic invention, the narrator is a novelist whose life has become intolerably complicated by fame and by the trap of sameness in her creative activity. She pretends to kill herself in order to be reborn without having to actually die. The ruse works, but her new life becomes almost as unbearable as her old.

In *Bodily Harm* (1981) and *The Handmaid's Tale* (1985), Atwood brings her themes of identity and survival together in stories that unfold in a context of politics and ideologies. In *The Handmaid's Tale*, the narrator is the victim of a society in which women are completely subjugated by the state. Here, Atwood has focused not only the best of her considerable talents as a writer, but the best also of her philosophical insights and political skills.

Cat's Eye (1988), while not in the absolute sense an autobiographical novel, is certainly the story of its author's time and place in twentieth-century history. It is the easiest of her books to read, which suggests it may also be her most skilled accomplishment. It draws a line beneath the first fifty years of Atwood's life and suggests, by doing so, that the next fifty years will be better — if that is possible — in the telling.

Atwood has published two books of literary and political criticism: *Survival: A Thematic Guide to Canadian Literature* (1972) and *Second Words* (1982). In these essays Atwood is deftly outspoken, often using humour to lead her readers down the garden path before pouncing on them with cold, hard truths. Her writings on women's issues and cultural integrity are particularly valuable, having much in common with the writings of Australian critic and essayist **Germaine Greer**. She shares Greer's sense of creative openness about feminist politics and cultural survival. Atwood also shares the thematic territory explored by the Caribbean-born **Jean Rhys**, whose stories and short novels centre on the sexual 'imperialism' of men. Atwood's poetry, however, has more in common with the work of her American rather than her Commonwealth contemporaries. This may have more to do with sharing a physical landscape than with a shared political stance. Atwood has much in common, too, with her Canadian contemporary **Marian Engel**, whose novels *The Honeyman Festival* (1970) and *Bear* (1976) are different reflections on themes and landscapes explored simultaneously in *Life Before Man* and *Surfacing*.

Whatever traditions are shared by Atwood's writings, they do not include the traditions that dominated Canadian writing prior to her own arrival on the scene. In that sense, her work remains unique. The intensity of its focus is its salient quality. Its greatest strength lies in its seductive but entirely deceptive subjectivity. Hooking her readers on the irresistible lure of the first person singular, she has managed to disseminate an objective view of modern life that is among the most challenging in present-day writing.

Her work has won a multitude of Canadian and international awards, and both *The Handmaid's Tale* and *Cat's Eye* were short-listed for the Booker Prize. She is a Companion of the Order of Canada (1981) and a Member of the Order of Ontario (1990). Her books have been translated into more than sixteen languages.

TIMOTHY FINDLEY

Further reading: Arnold Davidson and Cathy Davidson, eds, *The Art of Margaret Atwood: Essays in Criticism* (1981); Judith McCombs, ed., *Critical*

Essays on Margaret Atwood (1988).

AUROBINDO, SRI (1872–1950)
Indian philosopher, poet
He was born Aurobindo Ghose in Calcutta, India. The younger brother of **Manmohan Ghose**, he attended school at Darjeeling. His father, Dr Krishnadhan Ghose, an Anglophile, sent his son to England in 1879. Better known by his honorific title, Sri Aurobindo, Ghose had a brilliant academic career at St Paul's, London, and King's College, Cambridge, and won several prizes and a scholarship. Although he passed the Indian Civil Service examination with credit, he decided not to enter government service and returned to India in 1893, joining the Baroda State Service. While working in the Maharajah's College at Baroda, Sri Aurobindo quickly mastered Sanskrit and Bengali. He began writing for the journal *Indu Prakash* and became interested in yoga and politics. Sri Aurobindo entered active politics in 1906, taking charge of the National College at Calcutta and the daily *Bande Mataram*, the organ of the Nationalists in the Congress. His powerful journalism and outspoken speeches espousing freedom provoked the government; he was also believed to be behind the activities of those preaching open revolution against the British raj. Arrested in 1908 in connection with a bombing in Muzzaferpore, he was kept in solitary confinement for a year. A historic trial followed and he was acquitted and released in 1909.

In the solitary cell Sri Aurobindo had a vision of the all-pervading Divine. On his release he devoted himself to yoga; drawing his inspiration from the *sanatana dharma*, the religion of ancient India, and living for the next four decades as the head of a community of spiritual seekers in Pondicherry. He also edited the magazine *Arya* (1914–21) for six years and wrote extensively on philosophy, literature, and sociology. He composed plays, lyrics, and an epic in English, *Savitri* (1954).

On 24 November 1926 Sri Aurobindo experienced the descent of a new power of consciousness and went into seclusion, though he continued to write and correspond with his devotees until his death. His was a remarkable life of action and contemplation and today Aurobindo's devotees are found all over the world. He left behind a considerable mass of writing and is certainly the central pillar of Indian writing in English. Even his philosophical and political writings are redolent with literary allusions from the Occident and the Orient and are rich in metaphor and diction. He was an inspired translator from Sanskrit into English. Apart from numerous passages from the epics, he rendered into English selected hymns from the Vedas, several Upanishads, and Kalidasa's play *Vikramorvasiyam*.

Sri Aurobindo began writing poetry while an undergraduate; some of these early poems can be found in his first publication, *Songs to Myrtilla and Other Poems* (1895). *Urvasie* (1896) and *Love and Death* (1899) are narrative poems that bring back the legendary past of India, when gods walked on earth. *Baji Prabhou* (1910) immortalizes a heroic incident in Maratha history. To this early period belong such insightful poems as 'Who', 'The Mahatmas', and 'In the Moonlight', which seek to understand the mystery of creation.

Once established in Pondicherry, Sri Aurobindo began his extensive study of the Vedas and the Upanishads. His Vedantic outlook informs the sixty sonnets and other lyrics that he wrote in the 1930s and 1940s. He experimented with classical metres, and one of his poems in hendecasyllabics, 'Thought the Paraclete', has been widely admired. He sought to use the hexameter in English and wrote the spiritual narrative *Ahana* (1915) in rhymed hexameter. A more ambitious attempt was to write a whole epic in hexameter. Although *Ilion* (1957) was not completed, the existing nine books reveal his mastery of classical prosody, his imaginative use of the English language, and a pervasive

Greek atmosphere. *Ilion* covers the last day of the Trojan war, and the Indian Queen Penthesilea plays a key part in the developing tragedy.

The practice of yoga undoubtedly contributed to Sri Aurobindo's prolificness. A deeper mystic note is evident in such richly metaphoric poems as 'The Tiger and the Deer' and 'Rose of God'. Although Aurobindo seems to have been drawn deeply into spiritual worlds, he continued to keep in constant touch with current events all over the globe. When Hitler's armies were overrunning western Europe in 1940 and the future of civilization seemed bleak, he threw his force behind the Allies and wrote the powerfully articulated poem 'The Children of Wotan'. The dreadful possibilities of the splitting of the atom were recorded in a sonnet, 'A Dream of Surreal Science'. His *Collected Poems* (1972) contains more than 200 poems, short and long.

Sri Aurobindo's treatise, *The Life Divine* (2 vols, 1939–40), which, in his words, is 'the work of intuition and inspiration' based on his spiritual experience, posits his philosophy of evolution. He describes a phenomenal lapse from undivided to divided existence — a veil separates the Mind from Supermind. If humanity and earth-nature are to change decisively, he writes, the veil must be removed so that the supramental consciousness can act on earth-nature and replace ignorance with spiritual knowledge. Sri Aurobindo's other major philosophical works are *The Synthesis of Yoga* (1914–18, published in *Arya*) and *Essays on the Gita* (1922). His writings on sociology include *The Human Cycle* (1949) and *The Ideal of Human Unity* (1919). His *The Foundations of Indian Culture* (1953) gives a comprehensive view of India's literary, philosophical, cultural, and artistic heritage; it is a classic of compression.

Sri Aurobindo's poetic masterpiece is *Savitri.* Though it was published in its entirety only in 1954, it had been in the making for nearly half a century. Indian myths and legends held a great fascination for Aurobindo, and the secular legend of Savitri came closest to his heart. He returned to the legend from time to time, progressively setting out his philosophy of the divine life received from his practice of yoga. He realized that such mystic poetry would not be understood easily: '*Savitri* is the record of a seeing, of an experience which is not of the common kind . . . there must be a new extension of consciousness and aesthesis to appreciate a new kind of mystic poetry.'

The nucleus of this epic testament is the tale found in Vyasa's *Mahabharata.* Aswapathy, King of Madra, is childless and undergoes austerities for eighteen years. By the grace of the Goddess Savitri, he is gifted with a daughter whom he names Savitri. When she grows up into a wonderful young woman, she chooses as her husband Satyavan, the exiled prince of Shalwa. Despite Rishi Narad's prophecy that Satyavan has but one year to live, she marries him and goes to live with him in the forest. When four days remain before the prophesied end of Satyavan's life, Savitri vows to save him. On Satyavan's death, she follows the god of death and engages him in conversation. Pleased with her sweet, truthful, and sincere speech he grants her several boons, including the life of Satyavan.

One of Sri Aurobindo's early versions of *Savitri* has only two books, each better than 1,000 lines. However, the enlightenment Aurobindo gained in 1926 led to the introduction of many new elements, including yoga. For more than two decades he continued to revise the poem, and at the time of his death the epic was all but complete. Subtitled 'A Legend and a Symbol', *Savitri* is now a modern English epic in twelve books of forty-nine cantos, encompassing some 24,000 lines.

Sri Aurobindo's epic introduces three major expansions of the original theme. Aswapathy's eighteen-year austerities become his yoga. The fifteen cantos of the Book of the Traveller of the Worlds describe in vivid particularity Aswapathy's spiritual journey. He descends to the worlds below, which are mapped out in psychological terms, traverses the grim spaces of infernal night, and then ascends on the wings of will-power to the Heavens of the Ideal. Entering the Centre of Silence within, he meets the Divine Mother, who assures him that an incarnation would descend to the earth to help humanity ascend upward in evolution.

The second expansion occurs in the description of Savitri's vow preceding the fateful day of Satyavan's death. Aurobindo sought to uncoil the significances of the vow in terms of Savitri's yoga. Her aim is to change the decree of Fate, to break through to a new dispensation. Since the sorrow and darkness threatening her life with Satyavan are symptomatic of the present human destiny, she wishes to track them to their source and master them. In the spiritual and psychological realms within her she encounters several possibilities — the triple soul forces, for instance — but the chief need is the total power of the soul, which she gains by achieving a great calm, the 'Superconscient's high retreat'.

Sri Aurobindo presents the final movement in Vyasa's tale as the Book of Eternal Night, the Book of Double Twilight, and the Book of Everlasting Day. Savitri faces Death unflinchingly even as Death tries threats and appeasement to make her go away. Savitri is not deceived, and when her words are disregarded by Death's sophistry her inner light explodes in a glorious blaze and her cosmic vision destroys Death. In the final temptation the Supreme Divine offers the young couple paradisal felicity, but Savitri rejects the gift, for 'earth is the chosen place of mightiest souls; earth is the heroic spirit's battlefield'. She returns to earth with Satyavan and the epic concludes in an atmosphere of expectancy of the greater dawn of a divinized life.

Of the symbol behind the legend Sri Aurobindo said: 'Satyavan is the soul carrying the divine truth of being within itself but descended into the grip of death and ignorance; Savitri is the Divine Word, daughter of the Sun, goddess of the supreme Truth who comes down and is born to save.' The divine word (mantra) is crucial to Aurobindo's aesthetic. The canto 'The Kingdoms and Godheads of the Greater Mind' describes the planes above the mind in vivid detail and how they all — higher mind, illumined mind, intuition, and overmind — influence human activities at the mental and vital planes. The supermind gives rise to the mantric utterance. If one could practise the intense concentration of yoga, one could reach to these higher planes of consciousness and bring power to bear on the work in progress. Aurobindo himself seems to have succeeded in achieving this at different times, as *Savitri* contains some of the most superb passages in modern Indian poetry written in English.

Sri Aurobindo was not only a significant poet but also a fine critic of poetry. His *The Future Poetry* (1953) is a fascinating adventure in creative understanding; it tells readers of the 'poetic' view of life, which is a 'soul-view' as traced in the inner evolution of English poetry. Aurobindo felt that the poetry of the future would be sustained by five powers: truth, life, beauty, delight, and the spirit. His own heroine, Savitri, is an assurance of this possibility because, in her, earth and heaven meet, truth blazes forth to destroy ignorance, and life is enriched by beauty, delight, and the spirit's ways.

Sri Aurobindo wrote five full-length plays, most of which were published posthumously. The theme of *Perseus the Deliverer* (1907) is taken from Greek mythology, that of *Rodogune* (1958) from Syrian history. *Vasavadutta* (1957) is inspired by an Indian legend, *The Viziers of Bassora* (1957) is indebted to *The Arabian Nights*, and *Eric* (1960) draws on Scandinavian sagas. All of these are Elizabethan in cast and redolent with Shakespearean echoes. Aurobindo's own philosophy of human evolution provides the plays' basic strength.

PREMA NANDAKUMAR

Further reading: The Sri Aurobindo Ashram Trust, ed., *Sri Aurobindo: Birth Centenary Library* 30 vols (1972–6); K. R. Srinivasa Iyengar, *Sri Aurobindo: A Biography and a History* (4th ed., 1985).

AUSTRALIA

Geography

The Mercator projection, with its elongation of land near the poles and its normally lowered equator, diminishes the apparent relative size of Australia. The total Australian land mass consists of almost 7.7 million square kilometres, the vast majority of it constituted by a single island, almost four thousand kilometres across, straddling the Tropic of Capricorn. It is in land mass the sixth largest nation in the world.

It is also one of the driest: for seventy percent of its area the annual evaporation is greater than the rainfall. Ninety percent of the population is concentrated in two strips of coastline, where the rainfall is moderate: from north of Brisbane around to Adelaide and the much smaller strip around Perth. These strips are heavily populated with cities and medium to large towns, for Australia is a highly urbanized country.

Aboriginal population

The Australian Aborigines, apart from some of the Arnhem Land and island people, assume in their myths that the land is without beginning and that they are descended from spirit beings who roamed the land. White anthropologists believe that the first Aboriginals reached Australia forty or fifty thousand years ago, during the last ice age. The Aboriginal population at the beginning of white settlement consisted of several hundred clans, each with its own territory and its own language. The people lived on many sites during a yearly cycle, following game and the availability of nuts, roots, seed, and other food. Governor Arthur Phillip, extrapolating from the population around Botany Bay, estimated an Aboriginal population of one million, but he was unaware of the variability in climatic conditions across the continent. Twentieth-century estimates of the Aboriginal population in 1788 vary between three hundred thousand and seven hundred and fifty thousand. White settlers shot and poisoned Aborigines, and introduced deadly diseases to the population, reducing it to about three hundred thousand — but it is now rising in number.

White settlement

White settlement began in 1788 with the arrival of eleven ships under the command of Captain Arthur Phillip to establish a settlement at Botany Bay. He in fact established it at Sydney Cove in Port Jackson, a little to the north. Most of his company were convicts, sent to Australia to alleviate the overcrowding of English prisons. Other considerations may have been the British Navy's need for flax and timber, the protection of the tea trade with China, and a concern to exclude the French from colonizing the land.

Van Diemen's Land (Tasmania) was established as a subsidiary convict settlement in 1803, Moreton Bay (Brisbane, now the capital of Queensland) as another in 1824. The Swan River settlement (Perth, the capital of Western Australia) was a company scheme for immigrants who were offered free grants of land in 1829; convicts were brought in to increase numbers from 1850. The Port Phillip district (now Melbourne, the capital of Victoria) was occupied by free settlers, chiefly from Tasmania, in the 1830s. The site of Adelaide (South Australia) was settled by immigrants under the control of a company in 1836.

Since the beginnings of white settlement the constituency of the population has frequently been in a state of flux. The transport of convicts lasted for eighty years and totalled 162,000. Most convicts remained in the colonies; some were pardoned or given tickets-of-leave before the expiration of their sentences. By the end of transportation, however, the convicts and emancipated convicts had long been substantially outnumbered by free settlers, though an awareness of the convict origins of settlement, now regarded more with pride than with shame, persists to this day. Sympathy for those on the wrong side of the law is also evident in the mythification of bushrangers (see **Kelly, Ned**). Free or greatly subsidized migration schemes encouraged migration from Britain until the late 1960s. After the Second World War the national government scheme was extended to migrants from continental Europe, who were needed to supplement the labour force.

In 1850 the total white population was about four hundred thousand. The gold rushes in the second half of the century produced a startling increase in population, to four million in 1905. A corresponding increase occurred in the proportion of the population born in Australia. It reached just over fifty percent in 1871, sixty-nine percent twenty years later, seventy-seven percent at Federation in 1901.

The effects of the second major wave of migration, following the Second World War, can be understood from a few salient statistics. In 1947, after a period of negligible migration, ninety percent of the population had been born in Australia (though over a third of that number would have had at least one parent born outside Australia); this is the highest native-born figure ever achieved. The figure is now below eighty percent and is estimated to drop below seventy-five percent within another thirty years. Anglo-Celtic origin accounted for almost ninety percent of the population in 1947, less than seventy-five percent now, and a projected sixty-five percent within thirty years. Emigration from Europe after the Second World War pushed the percentage of the population born in continental Europe from under nine percent in 1947 to over eighteen percent in 1986; it is expected to fall slightly in the next thirty years. The proportion of the population born in Asia was less than one percent in 1947, 4.5 percent in 1986, and is likely to rise to over twelve percent in the next thirty years. The Middle Eastern component has remained steadier, though it is rising: from 1.5 percent in 1947, to over two percent now, and a projected nearly three percent in thirty years' time. The proportion and range of this immigration is paralleled by immigration during some of the boom decades of the nineteenth century, particularly those due to the gold rushes. The total non-Aboriginal population of Australia reached seven million in 1939; the total population (including Aborigines) reached seventeen million in 1990.

Until the late 1960s the commonest Australian attitude to immigration was akin to the USA's notion of the melting pot. Since then — and parallel to a change in the USA itself — the notion of multiculturalism, as in Canada, has become the official bipartisan government policy. The languages of migrant communities have been cultivated — in some cases as the medium of instruction in the initial years of primary school — and ethnic links with other countries have been encouraged. Correspondingly, Aboriginal Australians have increasingly asserted pride in their ancestry and derided the former assimilationist policies.

Constitution

The Australian Constitution united the six states (and territories) in the Commonwealth of Australia in 1901; the federal parliament consists of two houses, the House of Representatives, elected in single-member constituencies each with approximately the same number of voters, and the Senate, elected by proportional representation in multi-member state-wide constituencies, each state being allotted an equal number of elected representatives. Australia is still constitutionally a monarchy, with Elizabeth II as Queen of Australia; most real powers as head of state reside with the governor general, though holders of that office are appointed (and could be removed) by the Queen on the advice of the Australian government. The emotional and legal ties with Great Britain have gradually been eroded. In the early 1940s Australia turned to the USA for defence aid; in the last two decades it has turned increasingly to Asia as a trading partner. Australia may well become formally a republic before the twenty-first century is far advanced.

The two major political parties in federal politics (and in almost all the states) are the Australian Labor party (originally a union and workers' party formed in 1891) and the Liberal party (formed from a set of other conservative groups by Robert Gordon Menzies in 1945). The Liberal party often governs in coalition with a smaller conservative party, the National party, previously known as the Country party. More radical groups on the left (for example, the Communist Party of Australia and its various offshoots) or the right (the New Guard and the League of Rights) have had almost no electoral success. Women continue to be grossly under-represented in parliaments, governments, the judiciary, and the public service.

Governments influenced by the Labor party were instrumental in introducing (as in New Zealand) a substantial number of social programmes in the early years of the century. They included the old-age pension (1900 in New South Wales and Victoria, 1909 Commonwealth), invalid pensions (1910 Commonwealth), maternity allowance (1912 Commonwealth), widow's pension (New South Wales 1926, Commonwealth 1942), child endowment (New South Wales 1927, Commonwealth 1941), unemployment benefits (Queensland 1923, Commonwealth 1945). Health and hospital benefits were introduced in stages after the Second World War.

Economy

In 1890 Australians earned the highest per capita income in the world, chiefly as a result of exports of wool, wheat, mutton, beef, gold, silver, and copper. From early in the twentieth century, however, it was overtaken by other countries better placed to add value to raw materials; it now lies no higher than sixteenth. Agriculture has suffered during the twentieth century by over-reliance on irrigation with the consequent production of high levels of soil salinity. Minerals, particularly coal, remain a large contributor to export income.

Culture

Unlike the USA, Australia was not influenced in its settlement by the search for a religious or political New World. Its official white religion (Anglicanism) was resented from the beginning by many of the convicts, particularly Irish Roman Catholics (see **Ireland and Irish Values in Australia**). Sport in a multitude of national and local competitions undoubtedly provides a substitute for religious enthusiasm in contemporary Australia. Art galleries, theatres (for drama, opera, ballet, and light opera), 'entertainment centres' (large, barn-like buildings for popular music performers), and a great variety of community arts also attract very large attendances.

Like several other countries, Australia is reputed to have the largest per capita book-buying habits in the world. Since the 1960s even capital-city bookshops have followed the book-stocking habits previously confined to rural newsagents, in which cooking, gardening, do-it-yourself, coffee table, and sporting books outnumber fiction, and poetry is hard to find at all. (But see **Australia Council** and **Literature Board** for information about support for writers and other artists.)

Military Affairs

Although Australia has had almost no contact with enemy forces on its own soil, Australians have been ready to enlist in foreign wars. Sixteen thousand volunteered for the Boer War (compared with six thousand Canadians). In the First World War, the landing and evacuation at Gallipoli south of the Dardanelles in 1915 is still honoured as a courageous feat of arms in Australia and New Zealand (whose forces were combined as the ANZAC — Australian and New Zealand Army Corps — under British command). Out of a population of five million, 417,000 Australians enlisted; 59,000 were killed, and about 174,000 wounded, the casualty rate being substantially higher than for British forces. The Second World War, the Korean War, and the Vietnam War (during which a massive protest movement against conscription occurred) also drew major contributions from Australia. (See **War Literature**, Australia.)

Armed clashes on Australian soil have involved only small numbers. Many clashes were between Aborigines and white settlers, the best known probably being the Myall Creek massacre in northern New South Wales in 1838, when more than thirty Aborigines were brutally murdered. Gold-miners who barricaded themselves in a stockade at Eureka in Victoria in 1854 to protest against the licensing system and anomalies in land tenure and the franchise were rapidly overcome by a company of military and police. The incident of the Eureka stockade and the flag flown on that occasion have often subsequently been adopted by radicals and republicans, including strikers. Jail terms, punitive fines, and physical violence have been used against strikers during some of the major strikes in Australia, including the maritime strike of 1890, the shearers' strikes of the 1890s, the northern coalfields' lockout (1929), and the national coal strike (1949).

The article on **mateship** provides an explanation of Australian attitudes to comradeship in work, sport, war, and literature.

KEN GOODWIN

Further reading: Anne Summers, *Damned Whores and Gold's Police: The Colonization of Women in Australia* (1975); Geoffrey Sherington, *Australia's Immigrants 1788–1978* (1980); Richard White, *Inventing Australia: Images and Identity 1688–1980* (1981); Susan Dermody, John Docker, and Drusilla Modjeska, eds, *Nellie Melba, Ginger Meggs and Friends: Essays in Australian Cultural History* (1982); Geoffrey Bolton, Beverley Kingston, Stuart MacIntyre, et al., *The Oxford History of Australia*, 5 vols (1986).

AUSTRALIA COUNCIL

A statutory authority of the Australian government, it was established in 1975 to perform the following functions: to promote excellence in the arts; to provide and encourage opportunities for persons to practise the arts; to promote the appreciation, understanding, and enjoyment of the arts; to promote the general application of the arts in the community; to foster the expression of a national identity by means of the arts; to uphold and promote the rights of persons to freedom in the practice of the arts; to promote the knowledge and appreciation of Australian arts abroad; to promote incentives for, and recognition of, achievement in the practice of the arts; to encourage the support of the arts by the states, local governing bodies, and other persons and organizations; and, to furnish advice to the government of the Commonwealth either of its own motion or upon request made to it by the minister, on matters connected with the promotion of the arts or otherwise related to performance of its functions.

The Australia Council took over the structure and activities of the Australian Council for the Arts (founded in 1968 and expanded in 1973). In its consolidation process the Australia Council and its predecessor inherited the work of the Commonwealth Literary Fund (1908–72), which was the federal government's first arts support programme. With a yearly parliamentary appropriation of A$60 million (1989–90), the Council has become a crucial sponsor of arts activities.

The Australia Council consists of a governing council and five boards (Aboriginal arts, literature, performing arts, visual arts/crafts, and community cultural development). The share of funding for literature in 1989–90 was approximately A$4 million dollars; for Aboriginal arts, approximately A$3 million; for Community Cultural Development A$5 million; for visual arts/crafts A$6 million; and for performing arts A$31 million. The balance of funds was absorbed by Council programmes and administration. The Australian Opera has been the biggest single client; its funding, however, was separated from that of the Australia Council in 1990.

H. C. Coombs was the Council's first chair; his successors have been Peter Karmel, **Geoffrey Blainey**, Timothy Pascoe, and **Donald Horne**.

THOMAS SHAPCOTT

AUSTRALIA IN CANADIAN LITERATURE IN ENGLISH

Marian Engel's novel *No Clouds of Glory!* (1968) sets out the anxieties of the critic, Sarah, who probes the relations between Australia and Canadian literatures: 'Those of us who operate from bastard territory, disinherited countries and traditions, long always for our nonexistent mothers. For this reason, I deviled five years — six? when did I start? how many? — in the literature of Australians and Canadians, hoping to be the one to track her down.' To think about these two literatures in relation to each other sharpens the sense of exile and dispossession for Sarah. Neither traditional criticism, which directs her to 'transcendent' and 'universal' values and to the English canon, nor nationalist criticism can activate the kind of lateral thinking that makes the comparison possible. As an 'Austcan' critic Sarah is confronted by literary and critical traditions that 'fail' to accede to the comforting chronological and evolutionary metaphors. She is faced with the task of seeking a new language, a new myth of location. To speak her illegitimacy she needs to find a new way of being 'at home', which for her will involve a turning away from the lineal, the central, the authoritative concepts that initiate her discourse of despair. She pursues, then, what we would now refer to as a post-colonial imagination and discourse, a way of speaking out from illegitimate territories.

Engel's novel is a modern statement of what was for a long time a characteristic effect of bringing Australia into the Canadian frame of reference: an apparently central and original English tradition is invoked. The comparative sense of Australia and Canada as sharing what critic R. E. Watters called a kind of 'original relation' has a long but discontinuous history. In fact, the early colonists had a strong sense of a 'shared condition' among the settler colonies. The empire was administered by a highly mobile corps of officers and administrators who shared a familiar world of social privilege throughout the British colonies. Among the settlers the Australian-Canadian comparison usually worked to Canada's advantage. So, for instance, in *The Backwoods of Canada* (1836) **Catharine Parr Traill** consoles herself that, for all the difficulties of backwoods life, things must surely be worse at Botany Bay. (In fact, a relative of Traill's, W. H. Traill, was editor and proprietor of Australia's ***Bulletin*** from 1881 to 1886.) The moral hierarchy implied by Parr Traill (free settler, penal settlement, plantation economy) was the basis of an impression that lingered throughout the period of settlement of Canada as the appropriate location for the middle-class settler, leaving it to Australia to be 'the workingman's paradise'. No doubt impressions of the institutional nature of early Australian settlement were also reinforced when some of the 1837 Quebec rebels were transported to

Tasmania. Antoine Gérin-Lajoie's poem 'Un Canadien Errant' (1844) represents this exile.

In the literary sphere there was by the 1880s a marked sense of these two colonies as having comparable 'frontier' literatures. Douglas Sladen's *A Century of Australian Song* (1888) and William D. Lighthall's *Songs of the Great Dominion* (1889) were published as companion volumes in Great Britain. Australian and Canadian poetry, in this British series, were sibling rivals competing for the attention of the 'parent' culture. Lighthall characterizes these as literatures of a 'fresh world': 'The romantic life of each Colony has a special flavour — Australian rhyme is a poetry of the horse; Canadian of the canoe.' Both Lighthall and Sladen locate the two national literatures within the supranational culture of empire. Both editors deliberately selected poems that presented 'fresh' pictures of the unfamiliar rather than poems of formal or intellectual pretence. Other connections emerge in journalistic writings of this period. **Gilbert Parker** began his career in Australia in the 1880s while working for the *Morning Herald* in Sydney. His writings from this period were published as *Round the Compass in Australia* (1892). The editor of the *Bulletin*'s famed Red Page, **A. G. Stephens**, looked to Canada directly for a comparison for the national(ist) literature he had done so much to develop in Australia in the 1890s. Canadians, he discovered on his travels through Canada in 1892–3, found the verse of **Henry Lawson** 'disgustingly rough'. As John P. Matthews was later to argue in *Tradition in Exile* (1962) — the first sustained comparative study of Australian and Canadian literatures — the literary development in these two cultures has taken markedly different paths.

During the 1950s it was the bringing together of Australian and Canadian literatures in an institutional context that became a crucial precursor of Commonwealth literary studies. The Australian critic Brian Elliott was the first serious advocate of a comparative approach to the two literatures, although he located them as two dominion traditions in relation to Great Britain. The Humanities Research Council of Canada (HRCC), chaired by A. S. P. Woodhouse, set up the Dominions Project in 1950–1 to foster comparative cultural and literary studies of Canada and Australia. A number of academic exchanges were part of this program, which, through the participation of A. N. Jeffares, was a precursor of the Commonwealth Fellowship program, later set up at the University of Leeds. A number of leading Canadian critics — Claude Bissell, R. E. Watters, Desmond Pacey, R. L. McDougall, **Earle Birney** — who travelled to Australia as part of this project later went on to establish key centres for research in Canadian literature. It was under the auspices of this program that John Matthews, supervised by Claude Bissell, University of Toronto, wrote *Tradition in Exile*. By the time a 1964 University of Leeds Conference identified 'Commonwealth literature' as a literary entity, the Australian-Canadian comparison already had a significant critical history and a major book-length study to its credit. From this seed-bed came the hypothesis that one of the most fruitful ways of learning about colonial literatures is by comparing them with other literatures that have developmental factors in common. The particular contours of the Australian-Canadian comparison were explored at the Badlands conference convened by Australian Alan Lawson and Canadian Charles Steele at Calgary in 1986; in R. McDougall and G. Whitlock, *Australian/Canadian Literatures in English: Comparative Perspectives* (1987); and in Terry Goldie's book *Fear and Temptation* (1989), which considers images of the indigene in Canadian, Australian, and New Zealand writing.

Since 1976 the Canada-Australia Literary Prize has increased mutual literary awareness by a series of exchanges that have taken a number of Canadian writers to Australia, and vice versa. In 1981 Kevin Roberts edited a journal dedicated to the Australian-Canadian connection, *True North/ Down Under: A Journal of Australian and Canadian Literature*, published by Eletheria Press, British Columbia. The journal, which was short-lived, set out to promote, review, survey, and foster 'worthwhile writing' from the two nations. Roberts argued that Australians and Canadians should know each other's writings better than they do because the 'similarities in heritage and cultural background suggest a reciprocity of experience and a common language'. Along with courses that include Australian writing in the curriculum in Canada, and vice versa, the journal is further evidence of the strong sense of interrelationship that existed between these 'bastard territories'. Finally, the journal *Australian and New Zealand Studies in Canada*, established in 1989 at the University of Western Ontario, Canada, under the editorship of Thomas Tausky, promotes an ongoing connection between Australasian and Canadian critics and writers.

A thorough bibliography of references to Australia in Canadian literature is yet to be undertaken; however, what is significant is the increased frequency of these references along with the development of Commonwealth and post-colonial studies and the institutional initiatives — courses and visitors' programs for both critics and writers. Mutual awareness is stronger than ever before. Australia enters Canadian literary texts in a number of ways. Among the earliest examples is Benjamin Doane's travel journal, *Following the Sea* (1987), which includes a good description of a visit to Sydney in 1847. Even earlier is **Thomas McCulloch**'s *Letters of Mephibosheth Stepsure* (1821–3), which refers to immigrating to Botany Bay, Australia. In a more recent example **Hugh MacLennan** begins his novel *Two Solitudes* (1945) with an Australia-shaped cloud that hovers ominously over Montreal, symbolizing the kind of monolithic nationalist sentiment that must be avoided if the Canadian mosaic is to survive. **Robert Kroetsch**, Betsy Warland, **Daphne Marlatt**, Betsy Struthers, Douglas Barbour, and **P. K. Page** have all written about Australia in their poetry after visits there. In prose, Australia enters the Bragg and Minna stories in **Timothy Findley**'s *Stones* (1990) and **Alice Munro**'s short story 'Bardon Bus', in *Moons of Jupiter* (1982). Canadian **Jack Hodgins**' novel *Innocent Cities* (1990) is set partly in nineteenth-century Victoria, Australia. This novel is a landmark in other ways — it was recently published by an Australian publisher, the University of Queensland Press. Finally, Australia and Canada are both deeply implicated in the fiction of **Janette Turner Hospital**, a writer who inhabits and writes from both of these terrains.

GILLIAN WHITLOCK

AUTOBIOGRAPHY

See **LIFE WRITING**

AVISON, MARGARET (1918–)

Canadian poet

Born in Galt, Ontario, Canada, she was educated at the University of Toronto (BA, 1940). Employment as a social worker in Toronto kept her in touch with the city and its needy.

Avison's poetry includes *Winter Sun* (1960), *The Dumbfounding* (1966), *Sunblue* (1978), *No Time* (1989), and *Selected Poems* (1991). Both *Winter Sun* and *No Time* won Governor General Awards. *Winter Sun* is a highly wrought work with full reverberations of the English literary tradition. The title's image informs the 'outdoor chill, some stoney wonder' of the book's terrain with its pre-baptismal light — precious as far as it goes, though turning sunward in a well of 'dayshine' is the spring the poet waits for. Hope is what Avison writes about implicitly in the collection: the hope of regeneration, rescue, or restoration. Creation is exiled from the Garden; how shall it find its way back, or towards a new, the poet inquires. To 'persist in penetrating further' (than stone), or to 'dare the knowledge', she writes, is a daredevil business, but if eschewed, then 'the long years' march deadens ardour'.

For Avison, light is usually the touchstone of renewal. Stone is a recurring symbol for space, and space is shorthand for the scientific account of cosmology that leaves out God the actor and God's proscenium arch, the world. The salient image of *Winter Sun* is the earth as ludicrous ball, with its creatures, 'slung by the feet / in the universe'. The voice is generalizing, cosmic.

Much is made of Avison's 'the optic heart must venture: a jail-break / and re-creation': imagination, the poetic act, is supposed the redeemer of an otherwise wintry-forlorn world. But Avison is not so exclusive as this suggests. If the saving act does not include the 'clerk . . . in all his lustreless life', she will have none of it. The kind of act that in Avison's view will redeem is captured by the recurring image of someone plunking out a tune on a wonky piano: 'Don't you suppose / anything could start it? / music and all? / some time?' The 'it' is kingdom come, 'which to embrace / our world would have to stretch and swell with strangeness'. Avison identifies with the man (the dog, the pigeon) in the street, but while throughout *Winter Sun* she speaks for the cement-bound, she seldom speaks from the personal or lyric 'I'. Not until *The Dumbfounding* does she use an intimate voice.

Although Avison had been associated with the group of poets that included Charles Olson, Robert Duncan, Robert Creeley, and Denise Levertov, her content — Christian conversion and conviction — led in a different direction. She had grown up familiar with the Christian terrain, but familiarity did not preclude the sudden surrender of conversion. In the eponymous 'The Dumbfounding', she rehearses her discovery that the way leads, after all, not *to* the Garden but '*through* the garden to / trash, rubble, hill . . . ' She seeks to share her evangelical 'head over heels' experience of the face of Love. She often resorts to plonking quatrains — by hymn out of ballad — to tell her good news; this is particularly evident in *Sunblue*. She often uses conversation as a device. She continues her use of nature imagery, those slices of nature one can see between high-rises. Increasingly, her purpose is to unleash the godly metaphor in the natural phenomenon.

Hope now turns explicit: '"Hope is a dark place that does not refuse / fear?" True . . . ' 'Seal', a word from which one could unpack the whole of Avison, comes into its own in her post-conversion writing. liberation. Always there, hinting at ambivalences, it prefigured in *Winter Sun* its role in *The Dumbfounding* and *Sunblue* as the symbol of Christ's tomb and of Christian liberation. As with the theme and image of 'seal', so 'still': it has always been there, but it pervades *No Time*, where it intones an answer to the problem posed by the book's title. Hope enmeshed with fear clusters in poems near the book's end; yet the poem 'Nostrils' moves through comic anxiety to an untypically buoyant expectation of heaven. Finally, 'I see that I have used / the holy given as / my way of refuge' sums up Avison's relation to nature and neighbour, and her struggle always more perfectly to embody Christian hope and love.

MIA ANDERSON

Further reading: David Kent, *'Lighting up the terrain': The Poetry of Margaret Avison* (1987).

AWARDS

AWARDS (Australia)

Literary awards in Australia were made sporadically by both government and private patronage during the nineteenth century, but in 1908 the recently formed Commonwealth government inaugurated the Commonwealth Literary Fund, initially to provide 'literary pensions'; after the Second World War it was greatly expanded to include fellowships and publishing assistance. Since 1973 the **Literature Board** of the **Australia Council** has been the country's principal funding agency for awards: more than fifty per cent of its annual budget has gone to individual writers through three-year senior writing fellowships, Emeritus Fellowships — which provide a 'literary pension' to as many as twenty writers of substantial achievement for the remainder of their lives — and other awards. Occasional Churchill Fellowships are awarded by the Winston Churchill Memorial Trust, Anzac Fellowships by the New Zealand government, and grants to individual writers by the New South Wales state government annually and by the South Australian government biennially.

Literary prizes proliferated in Australia in the 1970s and 1980s. The National Book Council Annual Book Awards, called the Banjo awards after poet **A. B. Paterson**, are given for fiction and non-fiction; poetry was added as a separate award in 1990. The Children's Book Council's annual awards have also become well established and respected among educationalists and booksellers. The New South Wales Premier's Literary Awards were inaugurated in 1979, with generous cash prizes in several genres; the Victorian Premier's Literary Awards followed, with further substantial cash prizes, and Western Australia, Queensland, and South Australia governments have instituted their own award systems, all of which carry considerable prestige and attract wide publicity for authors short-listed or awarded prizes.

The oldest and most prestigious Australian award for fiction is the Miles Franklin Award for a published novel, first awarded in 1957 — to **Patrick White**'s *Voss*; this was preceded by the Australian Literature Society Gold Medal, first awarded in 1928 — to **Martin Boyd**'s *The Montforts* — and now administered by the Association for the Study of Australian Literature. The Grace Leven Poetry Prize, first awarded in 1947 — to Nan McDonald's *Pacific Sea* — retains its prestige but has no longer any significant cash value. The Melbourne *Age* Book of the Year Awards, begun in 1974, are awarded for fiction and non-fiction. The Fellowship of Australian Writers in Victoria administers a series of annual literary awards, the chief being the Christopher Brennan Award for poetry, the Australian Natives' Association Literature Award (mainly fiction), Local History Award, Anne Elder Trust Fund Award for a first book of poems, the Alan Marshall Award for short stories, the Barbara Ramsden Award for 'quality writing', and the Patricia Weickhardt Award for Aboriginal writers. The most original, and perhaps most revered, literary award in Australia is the Patrick White Award, begun in 1974 after White was awarded the Nobel Prize for Literature. It is for 'writers who have been highly creative over a long period, but have not received adequate recognition of their work'; distinguished recipients include **Christina Stead**, **David Campbell**, **Gwen Harwood**, **Randolph Stow**, **Bruce Dawe**, and **David Malouf**.

THOMAS SHAPCOTT

AWARDS (Canada)

Canada currently offers a variety of awards for writers working in virtually every genre. The most prestigious among them are the Governor General's Awards, which were established in 1937 by the Canadian Authors' Association but have been administered and funded since 1959 by Canada's principal funding agency for awards, the **Canada Council**. The 'GG's' are presented annually for outstanding achievement in the categories of drama, fiction, non-fiction, poetry, children's literature, translation, and book design. Two awards of $10,000 each are made in each of these seven categories, one for English-language and one for French-language works. The Council also administers the annual $50,000 Molson Prize, which recognizes outstanding achievement in the arts and in the humanities or social sciences. In addition, the Council offers specific prizes for books that promote cultural understanding between Canada and other countries.

The Canadian Authors' Association now administers its own Literary Awards, funded by Harlequin Enterprises. A silver medal and cash prize of $5,000 are awarded annually in each of the four categories of fiction, non-fiction, poetry, and drama. The Association also sponsors the annual Vicky Metcalf Short Story Award, a cash prize of $1,000 for the best short story for children published in an anthology or magazine.

Several Canadian booksellers and publishers sponsor their own literary awards. The Canadian Booksellers' Association prizes cover the range of the publishing industry from authorship to book sales. Their $2,000 Ruth Schwartz Children's Book Award is notable for its final jury composed entirely of children. The awards sponsored by the Coles bookstore chain also recognize achievement in authorship, sales, and publishing. Rather than presenting cash prizes to the winners, Coles makes donations on their behalf to agencies promoting writing and literacy in Canada. The largest Canadian award for a first novel is sponsored jointly by the bookstore chain of W. H. Smith and the literary magazine *Books in Canada.* Winners of this annual $5,000 prize include **Michael Ondaatje, Clark Blaise, Joy Kogawa**, and Heather Robertson. One of the most unusual sponsorship teams on the awards scene is the partnership of the *Financial Times* of Canada and the accounting firm of Coopers and Lybrand of Canada, who offer the National Business Book Award, valued at $10,000 for first prize and $5,000 for second prize.

Often, prizes are associated with the oeuvre of a particular author, such as the Stephen Leacock Award for humour ($2,500 and a silver medal) or the Journey Prize established by James Michener in 1988 for the best short fiction published in a Canadian literary journal. The $10,000 award for the author and $2,000 award for the publisher of the winning story are funded by Canadian royalties from Michener's novel *Journey*.

Canadian Broadcasting Corporation radio sponsors an annual literary competition, which awards a first prize of $3,000 and second prize of $2,500 in each of the categories of radio plays, poetry, and short stories.

In addition to these national awards, most of the provinces present their own literary prizes. Among the most notable of these are the QSPELL (Quebec Society for the Promotion of English Language Literature) Prize, the British Columbia Book Prizes, and Ontario's $10,000 Trillium Book Award and the Toronto Book Awards. Ontario also offers the Chalmers Canadian Play Awards for the most outstanding scripts written by Canadian playwrights and produced within the past year in the metropolitan Toronto area. The Chalmers Award, created in 1972 by an endowment from Toronto businessman Floyd S. Chalmers and administered by the Ontario Arts Council, is currently valued at $8,000, to be divided among a winner and up to four finalists. In 1982 the Ontario Arts Council added the Chalmers Canadian Children's Play Award, valued at $5,000, to be divided among the winning playwright and one or more runners-up.

D. A. HADFIELD
L.W. CONOLLY

AWARDS (India)

India's Sahitya Akademi, an autonomous organization established by the Government of India on 12 March 1954, functions as the national academy of letters. It sets high literary standards, fosters and co-ordinates literary activities in all Indian languages, and promotes through them all the cultural unity of the country. It is also responsible for administering the Akademi's prestigious literary awards.

Besides the fifteen languages enumerated in the Constitution of India — Assamese, Bengali, Gujarati, Hindi, Kannada, Kashmiri, Malayalam,

Marathi, Oriya, Punjabi, Sanskrit, Sindhi, Tamil, Telugu, and Urdu — Sahitya Akademi also recognizes Dogri, English, Konkani, Manipuri, Maithili, Nepali, and Rajasthani as languages in which its programmes may be implemented. These programmes include: literary seminars and conferences; publication of journals, bibliographies, dictionaries, and monographs related to Indian literature; translation of Indian and foreign classics; and annual awards to books of outstanding literary merit by Indian nationals, first published during the preceding three years in any of the twenty-two recognized languages. Translations, anthologies, abridgements, edited, or annotated works are not eligible for these awards. Since 1989, however, the Akademi has instituted a separate prize for translation of creative and critical works.

The first Akademi Award for a work in English was given in 1960. No Awards were given in the years 1955, 1964, 1966, 1968, and 1970. The award-winning books in English are:

1960 **R. K. Narayan**, *The Guide* (1958), a novel.
1963 **Raja Rao**, *The Serpent and the Rope* (1960), a novel.
1965 Verrier Elwin, *The Tribal World of Verrier Elwin* (1964), an autobiography.
1967 **Bhabani Bhattacharya**, *Shadow from Ladakh* (1966), a novel.
1969 Niharranjan Ray, *An Artist in Life* (1967), a study of **Rabindranath Tagore**.
1971 **Mulk Raj Anand**, *Morning Face* (1968), an autobiographical novel.
1975 **Nirad C. Chaudhuri**, *Scholar Extraordinary: The Life of Professor the Rt. Hon. Friedrich Max Müller* (1974).
1976 Sarvepalli Gopal, *Jawaharlal Nehru: 1889–1947* vol. 1 (1975), a biography.
1977 **Chaman Nahal**, *Azadi* (1975), a novel.
1978 **Anita Desai**, *Fire on the Mountain* (1977), a novel.
1979 Rama Mehta, *Inside the Haveli* (1977), a novel.
1980 **K. R. Srinivasa Iyengar**, *On the Mother: The Chronicle of a Manifestation and Ministry*, Vol. 1 and 2 (2nd rev. ed., 1978), a biography of Mira Alfassa, known as 'The Mother of Sri Aurobindo Ashram, Pondicherry'. (The first, much smaller edition was published in 1952.)
1981 **Jayanta Mahapatra**, *Relationship* (1980), poems.
1982 **Arun Joshi**, *The Last Labyrinth* (1981), a novel.
1983 **Nissim Ezekiel**, *Latter-Day Psalms* (1982), poems.
1984 **Keki N. Daruwalla**, *The Keeper of the Dead* (1982), poems.
1985 **Kamala Das**, *Collected Poems* (1984).
1986 **Nayantara Sahgal**, *Rich Like Us* (1985), a novel.
1987 **Shiv K. Kumar**, *Trapfalls in the Sky* (1986), poems.
1988 **Vikram Seth**, *The Golden Gate* (1986), a novel in verse.
1989 **Amitav Ghosh**, *The Shadow Lines* (1988), a novel.
1990 **Shashi Deshpande**, *That Long Silence* (1988), a novel.
1991 **I. Allan Sealy**, *The Trotter-Nama* (1988), a novel.
1992 **Ruskin Bond**, *Our Trees Still Grow in Dehra* (1992), a novel.

RAMESH MOHAN

AWARDS (New Zealand)

The longest-established New Zealand literary award is for children's literature. The Esther Glen Award, named after the pioneer New Zealand writer for children, **Esther Glen**, was established in 1945 by the New Zealand Library Association. From its foundation, a high standard was demanded and in its first twenty years it was awarded only five times; with the flowering of New Zealand children's literature in recent years it has now become an annual event. The Library Association also administers two parallel prizes, the Russell Clark Award for illustrations to children's books and an award for children's nonfiction. In 1991 the more recently established Children's Book Awards, administered by the Booksellers' Association and the Queen Elizabeth II Arts Council with commercial sponsorship, offered $4,000 NZ for a winning storybook and $2,000 NZ each to the author and illustrator of a winning picture storybook.

The Wattie Book of the Year award, sponsored by a food manufacturing company and administered by the Book Publishers' Association, has had the highest public profile of any New Zealand literary award since its establishment in 1968, the short list being heavily promoted by publishers and booksellers. The three judges appointed each year are expected to take into account literary merit, production, and 'public impact' — the latter to ensure that the award is not given to an esoteric work difficult to promote. There are no genre categories so that very disparate works compete. First, second, and third places in 1991 were worth $20,000 NZ, $10,000 NZ, and $5,000 NZ.

Literary merit is the sole criterion for three of the four categories in the New Zealand Book Awards, established in 1976 and funded and administered by the Literature Committee of the Queen Elizabeth II Arts Council. These are for poetry, fiction, and nonfiction. The fourth category, for book production, was introduced in 1980. Like the Wattie award, the New Zealand Book Awards are competitive and entries are required. The prize for each category in 1991 was $5,000 NZ. The Literature Committee also gives an annual Award for Achievement 'in recognition of the contribution to New Zealand literature of an individual writer, an editor, an anthology, or a book'.

Among privately sponsored awards are three biennial awards, offered by the Bank of New Zealand, for unpublished short stories: the BNZ Katherine Mansfield Award, the BNZ Novice Writers Award — for a writer who has had no previous work published — and the BNZ Young Writers Award for secondary school pupils. Several other awards for short stories are offered by commercial firms and newspapers with commercial sponsorship.

With funding from the Literature Committee, New Zealand PEN, the writers' organization, offers annual awards for the Best First Book of Fictional Prose, the Best First Book of Nonfiction, and the Best First Book of Poetry. There are special awards available for playwrights, travel writers, and historians, and literature is among the arts eligible for the largest of New Zealand's arts awards — the Turnovsky Prize, given by a privately funded endowment trust and worth $40,000 NZ in 1991. The first recipient of the prize, in 1984, was **Janet Frame**.

New Zealanders are eligible for several prizes awarded elsewhere. **Lauris Edmond** and **Allen Curnow** have both won the Commonwealth Prize for Poetry, and **Keri Hulme** the Booker Prize for her novel, *The Bone People* (1983). (See also **Patronage**, New Zealand.)

DENNIS McELDOWNEY

AWARDS (The Philippines)

Probably the earliest public recognition given to Philippine writers in English was the 'honor roll' of short stories that poet, fictionist, and critic **Jose Garcia Villa** began publishing in 1926. Villa encouraged literary experimentation and a departure from the classic form exemplified by the fiction of Guy de Maupassant, O. Henry, and Edgar Allan Poe. Villa's honour roll was modelled after that of Edward O'Brien, who published a list of 'Distinctive Short Stories in American Magazines' in his yearly anthology *The Best Short Stories.* In 1937, because the Philippines was still a USA Commonwealth nation, the stories of Philippine writers **Estrella Alfon, Manuel Arguilla,** Consorcio Borje, **N. V. M. Gonzalez**, and Daniel Fresnosa were included in this list.

Villa's honour roll was published in the *Philippines Free Press* magazine, which also published an anthology of Villa's selections. In 1929 the magazine itself began giving cash awards to the best stories it had published within the year. Jose Garcia Villa's 'Mir-i-nisa' was the first winner. The magazine has since tried to continue this competition, although it has been occasionally interrupted by political upheaval, such as the Second World War and the martial law period between 1972 and 1986, when most magazines and newspapers were closed down.

A counterpoint to Villa's stress on aestheticism was represented by the 1940 Commonwealth Literary Awards, which were cash prizes given for socially concious literature. The competition was divided into four categories: the novel, short story, poetry, and the essay. Characters in the fictional works were drawn from the peasant and working classes; poetry had a patriotic theme, with the hardwood molave as the central metaphor for the Philippine character of strength and resilience. Salvador P. Lopez's *Literature and Society* (1940) urged writers to infuse their works with a social consciousness; thus he defined a theory of literature that has since been a dominant influence in Philippine letters.

The most prestigious literary awards are the Don Palanca Memorial Awards, sponsored by a private foundation that provides the cash prizes. The awards began in 1950 with the short-story category. They have since increased to include seven other genres: the novel (held every three years), poetry, three-act play, one-act play, essay, children's story, and teleplay. Judges consist of literature professors, critics, and writers. During the 1950s and 1960s, the judging for the Palanca Awards was heavily influenced by the standards of American New Criticism. The first Palanca Award was given to the short story, 'Clay', by Juan Gatbonton, who used symbolic representation to characterize the colonial nature of the Philippine-American relationship.

Very similar to the Palanca Memorial Awards is the government-sponsored Cultural Center of the Philippines (CCP) literary competition. It began in 1969 with a playwriting contest and in subsequent years included other categories: epic narrative, short story, novel, essay, biography, criticism, and play adaptation. Under a new government administration in 1986, the contest became open only to works written in Filipino, the national language. The competition ended in 1992 for lack of funds.

The *Graphic* magazine's short-story contest was short-lived, beginning in 1970 and ending in 1972. However, the high political content of the winning entries was a portent of the cultural revolution that Ferdinand Marcos' martial law sought to abort. *Focus*, a magazine approved by the martial law administration, ran a yearly contest for the short story, essay, and poetry from 1973 to 1983. Craft was the primary concern, and an apolitical content characterized the works published in this magazine.

In the 1960s awards for lifetime achievement in literature were the Republic Heritage Award and the Pro-Patria Award for Literature. Since 1988 the Writers' Union of the Philippines has accorded the same recognition to writers, who receive a trophy called 'Ang Manunulat' ('The Writer'), sculpted by an established artist. The awardees are nominated by writers' and artists' organizations, academic institutions, and individual writers. Among the awardees in English are essayist **Carmen Guerrero-Nakpil**, fictionist **Francisco Arcellana**, fictionist **Edilberto Tiempo**, and poet and fictionist **Edith Lopez Tiempo**.

In 1981 the Manila Critics Circle established the National Book Awards for publishers and books. Winners, who receive a trophy, have included alleged former head of the Communist Party Jose Maria Sison (for his prison poems), Charlson L. Ong (for his short stories about the Chinese Filipinos, *Man of the East and Other Stories*, 1990), and **Gemino Abad** and Edna Z. Manlapaz (for editing the most extensive anthology of Philippine poetry in English, *Man of Earth: An Anthology of Filipino Poetry and Verse from English, 1905 to the mid-50s*, 1989).

Awards that Philippine writers share with those of other Southeast Asian Nations are the SEAWRITE Awards, which are given in Bangkok, Thailand, in the presence of the Thai royalty, and the Ramon Magsaysay Awards.

ROSARIO CRUZ LUCERO

AWARDS (Singapore)

The major literary awards in Singapore are the Book Awards, presented by the National Book Development Council of Singapore (NBDCS) every two years since 1976. These awards are for published works in English, Chinese, Tamil, and Malay written by Singaporeans and permanent residents in Singapore or abroad; there are awards for prose, poetry, drama, non-fiction, and children's books. Award-winners receive S$2,000; prizes of S$1,000 and S$500 are given for highly commended and commended works, respectively. The NBDCS awards had a relatively low profile until 1992, when **Gopal Baratham** rejected his prize for *A Candle or the Sun* (1991), alleging that the judging was unfair.

The most financially valuable award is the Singapore Literature Prize, which was first presented to **Suchen Christine Lim** for her novel *Fistful of Colours* (1992) in 1992. The first prize is worth S$10,000, and winners in each category receive S$5,000. The annual contest is co-sponsored by EPB Publishers and Singapore National Printers and is organized by the NBDCS. The contest for unpublished work only alternates between prose (short stories and novels) in one year and drama and poetry the next.

Singapore's former ministry of culture, in association with the national daily newspapers, first organized an annual short-story competition in 1982. Cancelled in 1988, it was revived in 1992 and renamed the Golden Point Award. Now a biennial contest, it is co-organized by the National Arts Council and Singapore Press Holdings. Prizes of S$5,000, S$3,000, and S$2,000 are awarded in each of the four language streams.

New dramatists had been identified since the 1980s through the Shell short play competition and the National University of Singapore, but the contest is no longer held.

Regionally, works by Singapore authors are eligible for the 35,000 baht (S$2,400) South-east Asian Write Award given by Thailand every year since 1979 to honour a body of work by one author chosen from each of the four language streams.

Singapore authors can also vie for the annual Commonwealth Writers Prize awarded in the south-east Asia and South Pacific region.

KOH BUCK SONG

AWARDS (South Africa)

The first literary award in South Africa, the Hertzog Prize, established in 1914, was intended to foster literary works in the relatively new language of Afrikaans. While this article focuses on literary awards for works written in English, the trend at present in South Africa, with its small reading public, is towards establishing awards that include works in indigenous languages, for example, the Skotaville Bertrams VO award (established in 1990), which is open to all South Africa's languages and was won by Gladys Thomas for *Avalon Court* (1992).

One of the richest literary prizes available in South Africa, the CNA Literary Award, established in 1961, is sponsored by a stationery and fancy goods chain-store, the Central News Agency. Superseded in monetary value in 1990 by the N-Net Book Prize, the CNA award is twelve years older than Britain's Booker McConnell award. Past winners of the CNA Prize include **Alan Paton** for *Apartheid and the Archbishop* (1973) and **Jack Cope** for *The Rain-Maker* (1971). **J. M. Coetzee** won in 1983 for *Life and Times of Michael K* (1983). One of the more successful literary periodicals, *New Contrast*, created the Arthur Nortje Memorial Award, which was won in 1991 by poets Lynne Dryer and John Eppel.

The N-Net Book Prize (1989), at present the largest prize, worth 50,000 SAR, is sponsored by the sole subscription-television service for works written in the two official languages, English and Afrikaans. *A Cageful of Butterflies* (1989), by children's author Lesley Beake, won in 1990. Another children's novel, a fantasy entitled *The Man Who Snarled at Flowers* (1991), by Tony Spencer-Smith, won in 1991. Eligible works must have a strong narrative content and some financial viability.

In the past, some local publishing houses have sponsored awards, but more recently it has been large business concerns that have provided the funds, with academics, writers, and members of the media acting as judges. Insurance giant SANLAM sponsors its own awards for works in both official languages by established or aspiring authors writing in the fields of biography, travel, nature conservation, or culture. Past winners include *The Mind of South Africa* (1990) by Allister Sparks, correspondent for the *Washington Post* and *The Observer*, and the poet Francis Faller, whose anthology *Verse-Over* (1991) 'constantly challenges the relationship between private life and public event'. Runner-up in 1992 was Shaun de Waal's short story 'Stalwart' (published in *Firetalk* 2 1993), in which he draws upon his experiences in exile as he 'examines the conflict of personal needs, and the sacrifices that have been made for the struggle against apartheid — and whether they were made for political or personal reasons'. John Conyngham's much translated novel *The Arrowing of the Cane* (1986) won in 1989.

Olive Schreiner lends her name to an English Academy of Southern Africa award. Among the winners are Sheila Fugard for *The Castaways* (1972), **Oswald Mtshali** for *Sounds of a Cowhide Drum* (1971), and **Lionel Abrahams** for *Journal of a New Man* (1984).

In 1964 the winner of the Thomas Pringle Prize was South Africa's 1991 Nobel Literature laureate **Nadine Gordimer**, for a short story. Gordimer pledged a part of her million-dollar (US) Nobel prize to the Congress of South African Writers, which has sponsored awards honouring, among others, **Alex La Guma**, **Bessie Head**, Gordimer, and Mankayi Sontonga.

ANNE WARRING

AWARDS (West Africa)

Literary awards in Ghana include the Ghana Book Award, instituted in 1977. It is worth ¢1,000 and is accompanied by a citation. The Ghana *Observer* short-story competition offers three awards for short stories ranging from 1,000 to 1,500 words. The awards are worth ¢1,000, ¢500, and ¢300. The Valco Fund Literary Award comprises five annual awards given for drama, fiction, and poetry. Ghana's journalists administer the Ghana Union of Journalists Poetry Award.

The Ivory Coast's Prix Litteraire Mobil was instituted in 1980 and is worth CFA 250,000. It is awarded for a novel or collection of short stories (published or unpublished) by an author from the Ivory Coast.

Nigeria offers a large number of literary awards. They include the **Association of Nigerian Authors** Award, instituted in 1983. The three awards for prose, drama, and poetry are worth $2,000 (Nigerian) each.

The Wole Soyinka Okigbo Prize, instituted in 1990, is worth $1,500 (US). It is given for the best work of poetry, prose, or drama. The Cadbury Poetry Prize, instituted in 1989, is worth $3,000 (Nigerian). The Jacaranda Prize for the best first work of fiction was instituted in 1990; it is worth $2,500 (Nigerian).

The Nigerian Newspaper Printing Corporation Prize, instituted in 1990, comprises four awards for prose, poetry, children's literature, and non-fiction. Each prize is worth $5,000 (Nigerian).

The Oyo State ANA Prize, instituted in 1991, comprises four awards for prose, poetry, Yoruba prose, and Yoruba poetry. Each award is worth $250 (Nigerian).

In Senegal, the Senghor Foundation International Literary Prize is an annual award for a work of fiction or poetry written or translated into French. It is worth CFA one million.

The Prix el Hadj Ahmadou Ahidyo is offered in Cameroon.

WALE OKEDIRAN

Further reading: James Gibbs, *A Handbook for African Writers* (1986).

AWOONOR, KOFI (1935–)

Ghanaian poet, dramatist, novelist, critic

Born at Wheta, in the Volta region of Ghana, to a Sierra Leonean father and a Togolese mother, he was formerly known as George Awoonor-Williams. He received his BA in English (1960) from the University College of Ghana, an MA (1968) from London University, England, and a Ph.D. (1972) from the State University of New York, Stony Brook, USA. Awoonor was editor (1961–4) of the literary magazine *Okyeame* and chair of the Ghana Film Corporation (1964–7). From 1968 to 1975 he taught at the State University of New York, Stony Brook. In 1976 he became professor at the University of Cape Coast, Ghana. Since 1983 Awoonor has been a diplomat in Brazil, Argentina, and Venezuela. He is currently Ghana's ambassador to the United Nations.

Awoonor's major poetic works are *Rediscovery and Other Poems* (1964, published under the name George Awoonor-Williams), *Night of My Blood* (1971), *Ride Me, Memory* (1973), *The House by the Sea* (1978), and *Guardians of the Sacred Word: Ewe Poetry* (1974), translations of the oral verse of his Ewe tribe. The theme of indigenous African culture is central to Awoonor's poetry, and he frequently draws on Ewe lore and folk songs in his work. Much in the satiric spirit of David Diop, Awoonor repudiates western civilization in such lyrics as 'The Cathedral' and 'Rediscovery' (in *Ride Me, Memory*).

Ancestral Power and Lament (1970) is a collection of two plays (*Ancestral Power* and *Lament*) articulating Awoonor's commitment to his cultural roots. The novel *This Earth, My Brother* (1971) details one man's struggle to adjust his western education within his corrupt indigenous culture.

Awoonor's critical study *The Breast of the Earth: A Survey of the History, Culture and Literature of Africa South of the Sahara* (1975) examines the contributions to African poetics of former and contemporary authors and discusses what he describes as cultural 'self-discovery'. For Awoonor, as poet, novelist, dramatist, and critic, the message is the same: he believes strongly in the culture of his people and articulates his commitment through irony, folklore, and satire.

ISAAC I. ELIMIMIAN

Further reading: Ken Goodwin, *Understanding African Poetry: A Study of Ten Poets* (1982); Kofi Anyidoho, 'Kofi Awoonor', in Bernth Lindfors and Reinhard Sander (eds) *Twentieth-Century Caribbean and Black African Writers*, vol. 117 of *Dictionary of Literary Biography* (1992); Isaac I. Elimimian, 'Kofi

Awoonor as a Poet', in Eldred Jones (ed.) *African Literature Today* 18 (1992).

AYYAR, AYILAM SUBRAMANIA PANCHAPAKESA (1899–1963)

Indian novelist, dramatist, short-story writer

Born near Palghat, India, he was educated in Trivandrum and Madras. He went to England in 1919 for higher studies at Oxford University and became a lawyer. Ayyar was elected a fellow of the Royal Society of Literature in 1933. Following an appointment in the Indian Civil Service, he became justice of the Madras High Court (1948–59). Ayyar's some twenty-seven published works include novels, plays, short stories, literary criticism, religious works, jurisprudence, travelogue, biography, and autobiography. He also translated classical drama and poetry from Sanskrit into English.

Ayyar's travelogue, *An Indian in Western Europe* (vol. 1, 1929; vol. 2, 1930), consists largely of humorous reflections on his youthful encounters abroad. His autobiography, *Twenty-Five Years a Civilian* (1962), is charged with considerable irony. In one anecdote, a proud Englishman is reminded of the comparative youth of Mother England — India, the colonial daughter, is senior by four thousand years. Ayyar was a Caliban who turned out to be more than a match for the Anglo-Indian Prospero. Ayyar's intellectual independence during the days of the raj proved costly, however, and he had to wait until after India's independence to be elevated to the High Court.

Ayyar is thus typical of the early post-colonial writer, who sees himself as an intruding disciple of the imperial paragon. There is something in him of the acolyte's anxiety to deserve and then excel the master. The insecure colonial maverick finds an opportune legacy in Sanskrit literature. In Ayyar's case, it was in the work of the ancient dramatist Bhasa. He translated two of Bhasa's plays and wrote a biography of this literary ancestor for the Indian Men of Letters series. These exercises in Indology also inspired three volumes of religious writing: *Brahma's Way* (1935), *A Layman's Bhagavad Gita* (1946), and *Sri Krishna, the Darling of Humanity* (1952).

As a follower of English writing on India, Ayyar was well aware of the need for social reform. This is evident in his first collection of plays, *The Slave of Ideas and Other Plays* (1941). The plays are a satire on his countrymen who are enslaved, not by foreign but by native ideas of expediency contingent on superficial modernity and insensitive traditionalism. In *Sita's Choice* (in *Sita's Choice and Other Plays*, 1935) Ayyar attacks the prejudice against the remarriage of widows. *A Mother's Sacrifice* (1937) is a protest against the exploitation of lower castes. *In the Clutch of the Devil* (1926) vehemently denounces the popular religious practice of offering human sacrifices to propitiate a bloodthirsty deity. *The Trial of Science for the Murder of Humanity* (2nd ed., 1942) is a naïve but passionate attempt to resolve the dilemma of the modern Indian faced with the prospect of abandoning traditional superstitions only to be decoyed into a scientific wasteland.

Ayyar's novels, written in the late 1940s and early 1950s, have historical settings and are his best-known works. *Baladitya: A Historical Romance of Ancient India* (1930) is about a Gupta king who resisted Hun invaders during the sixth century. *Three Men of Destiny* (1939) is the story of Alexander the Great, but gives equal importance to Alexander, Chandragupta, and Chanakya. *The Legions Thunder Past* (1947) fictionalizes Alexander the Great's campaigns. *Chanakya and Chandragupta* (1951) is a refined version, excluding Alexander's adventures. In all these novels, India appears to fall prey to foreign invaders when there is disunity among native rulers.

As in his plays, there is no attempt to experiment with technique in any of Ayyar's novels or in the numerous short stories collected in ten volumes. Ayyar has a weakness for indulging in tedious descriptions and superfluous details. The most unlikely characters in his fiction quote Shelley, Byron, and Browning. All his characters speak similarly and use Ayyar's version of the King's English. A collection of essays, *Rambles in Literature, Art, Law and Philosophy* (1958), and a monograph, *The Contribution of Hindu Law to World Jurisprudence* (1941), also appeared during the latter part of his life.

MOHAMED ELIAS

Further reading: K. P. K. Menon, *A. S. P. Ayyar* (1990).

B

BAIL, MURRAY (1941–)
Australian novelist, short-story writer
Born in Adelaide, Australia, he has lived in India (1968–70) and in Europe — especially England (1970–4). Aspects of this period are recorded in *Longhand: A Writer's Notebook* (1989). Since the mid-1970s he has lived in Sydney.

Contemporary Portraits and Other Stories (1975) was also published in London as *The Drover's Wife and Other Stories* (1986). In 'A, B, C . . . Z', Bail cites William James: 'the word "dog" does not bite.' Such linguistic reflexivity informs Bail's *ficciones.* One can say of his 'contemporary portraits' what William H. Gass claims Gertrude Stein perceived in Cézanne's portrait of his wife, that 'the reality of the composition had superseded the reality of the subject.'

In the story 'Zoellner's Definition', Zoellner is 'suddenly filled with profound melancholy and pointlessness'. Similarly, Bail's first novel, *Homesickness* (1980), which won a National Book Council Award and the Melbourne *Age* Book of the Year Award, is pervaded by melancholy. Although the major bias of Australian writing has until recently been realist, empiricist, and historicist, there is no such bias to *Homesickness.* The novel follows a group of middle-class Australian tourists visiting museums in Europe, Africa, and North and South America. It is pervaded by a sense of loss, absence, and sadness. How can these tourists ever come 'home', it asks, for they have been transformed in their consciousness. Like Baudelaire's soul, they may find that they are home nowhere.

Bail's reading is eclectic, principally American — North and South — and European — Flaubert, Proust, Herman Broch, George Steiner — and he is a passionate reader of dictionaries. But his fiction is essentially concerned with 'Australianness', as *Holden's Performance* (1987), with its 'hero' named after a well-known Australian car, bears out. Critic Helen Daniel characterizes this novel as 'a poignant meditation on an Australian geometry of place and consciousness, of time and space . . . a kind of psychogeometry of Holden which is also a measuring of an Australian identity, "This problem of emptiness in vast space"'. Bail has also written a study (1981) of the Australian painter Ian Fairweather and has edited *The Faber Book of Contemporary Australian Short Stories* (1988).

DON ANDERSON

BAIRD, IRENE (1901–81)
Canadian novelist
Born in Carlisle, England, she immigrated to Vancouver, Canada, in 1919. After moving to Victoria, British Columbia in 1937, she wrote her first novel 'with one hand on the typewriter and one hand in the kitchen sink'. A pastoral romance, *John* (1937) idealizes its British hero, John Dorey, closing with an elegiac tribute: 'to the name of Dorey; in obscurity . . . at home or abroad — *sound and clean and true!*' *Waste Heritage* (1939), Baird's most memorable work, is radically different from *John.* Based on personal observations of the unemployed sit-down in Victoria in 1938, the novel is aptly described in the words of one of its characters as 'a kind of social document . . . that will bring before the nation this whole problem of unemployment that is festering on its body like a bloody sore'. *Waste Heritage* captures the raging despair of its central character, Matt Striker. Like the hero in Steinbeck's *Of Mice and Men,* Striker is a victim bound by pity to his mentally confused comrade, Eddy. His girlfriend, however, is utterly

unlike Steinbeck's stereotypical female. Too little developed to be compared to **Christina Stead**'s heroines, Hazel is none the less a strong-minded, independent woman. In this portrayal, as in her sympathy for the plight of the unemployed, Baird was ahead of her time. Despite good reviews, *Waste Heritage* was out of print by 1942 and was largely ignored until its reissue in 1973.

With the outbreak of war, Baird turned to patriotic themes, writing columns for the Vancouver *Sun* and the *Daily Province*, a series of radio talks, published as *The North American Tradition* (1941), and a documentary novel, *He Rides the Sky* (1941), based on actual letters from a pilot killed in 1940.

In 1942 Baird began a five-year stint with the National Film Board in Ottawa. She then entered the federal civil service, rising to become senior information officer and chief of information services while continuing to write lectures, articles, and poems, chiefly on the North. She retired to England in 1967, where she published *The Climate of Power* (1971), a somewhat melodramatic study of the political backroom. She returned to Victoria in 1973.

HILDA L. THOMAS

BALLANTYNE, DAVID (1924–86)

New Zealand novelist, journalist

Born in Auckland, New Zealand, he was raised in Rotorua, Hicks Bay, and Gisborne. He worked as a journalist in Auckland and Wellington from 1943–1955, spent 1955–1966 in Fleet Street, London, England, and then returned to the *Auckland Star*, where he remained until his retirement in 1984.

Ballantyne's career as a novelist was a broken one, primarily because his fiction never received the critical recognition and financial reward that it deserved. His first novel, *The Cunninghams* (1948), modelled on the work of James T. Farrell, is perhaps the best New Zealand novel of the 1940s with its scrupulously realistic portrayal of a New Zealand family during the Depression. It was well received in the USA, but not in New Zealand. When his next three novels were all refused by publishers, Ballantyne put aside novel-writing and took up writing drama for television to supplement his journalism.

Ballantyne resumed the publication of fiction in 1963 with the first New Zealand printing of *The Cunninghams* and with the publication of a collection of short stories, *And the Glory*, and his second novel, *The Last Pioneer*. The third novel, *A Friend of the Family*, appeared in 1966, followed by his finest novel, *Sydney Bridge Upside Down* (1968). The story of 'all the terrible happenings up the coast that summer', told by a dangerously disturbed pre-adolescent protagonist, ranks with **Ian Cross**' *The God Boy* (1957) and **Janet Frame**'s *Owls Do Cry* (1957) as among the best New Zealand novels of growing up, although it has received almost no critical attention.

Discouraged, Ballantyne did not return to fiction until 1978 with *The Talkback Man*, followed by *The Penfriend* (1980). These final two novels mark a distinct change in direction in his work; they deal with contemporary New Zealand society (including such phenomena as racial tensions, talkback radio, and drug smuggling) and involve sophisticated narrative games.

Despite the efforts of **C. K. Stead** and Patrick Evans to call attention to Ballantyne's work, his fiction remains relatively unrecognized. However, his strong narrative gifts and his sharply drawn pictures of a changing New Zealand society may make his work last longer than that of some of his initially better-known contemporaries.

LAWRENCE JONES

Further reading: Patrick Evans, 'David Ballantyne and the art of writing in New Zealand', *Islands* 31–32 (1981).

BANDLER, FAITH (1918–)

Australian novelist

She was born at Tumbulgum, Murwillumbah, New South Wales, Australia. She is the daughter of Wacvie Mussingkon (Peter Mussing), a 'Kanak' (a Hebridean Islander who was kidnapped by slave traders in 1893 to work in the Queensland canefields). In *Wacvie* (1977), *Marani in Australia* (1980, with Len Fox), and *Welou, My Brother* (1984) Bandler re-creates her father's story and that of other South Pacific islanders pressed into slavery (technically indenture) in Australia in the last decades of the nineteenth century and in the early twentieth century.

Bandler has also been particularly active in Aboriginal and Islander political struggles. In 1956 she was co-founder of the Aboriginal Australian Fellowship, and in 1967 was New South Wales director of the referendum campaign that led to equal citizenship for Aborigines under the Australian Constitution. She was an executive member for many years of the Federal Council for the Advancement of Aboriginals and Torres Strait Islanders. Declining an MBE (Member of the British Empire) in 1976 she stated, 'I cannot accept an award from an empire that kidnapped my father and enslaved him in a "blackbirding" operation that was one of the most iniquitous blots in Australian colonial history', but she did accept membership in the Order of Australia in 1984. *The Time Was Ripe* (1983), edited with Len Fox, captures something of these political battles.

Wacvie, like Jamaican **Orlando Patterson**'s *Die the Long Day* (1972), is a historical novel of black slavery, but in this instance, in the Queensland canefields. Abducted from his Ambryn home, Wacvie is forced to labour in atrocious conditions. He eventually escapes but, like Bandler's father (who took up farming in northern New South Wales), he is permanently exiled in an alien country. In *Welou, My Brother* the classic colonial/post-colonial dilemma over white education is explored. Like **Ngugi wa Thiong'o**'s *Weep not, Child* and **Erna Brodber**'s *Myal* and **Jamaica Kincaid**'s *Lucy*, Bandler's novel 'debates' the contradictory impulses generated by the prospect of white education: the twin dangers of ideological interpellation and loss of community values against the possibilities of economic and political empowerment within a numerically dominant white community.

HELEN TIFFIN

Further reading: 'Faith Bandler', in Martin Duwell and Laurie Hergenhan (eds) *The ALS Guide to Australian Writers: A Bibliography 1963–1990* (1992).

BANGLADESH

Geography

The People's Republic of Bangladesh became a sovereign state on 16 December 1971; from 14 August 1947 to 15 December 1971 it was known as East Pakistan. A large South Asian nation with an area of 144,000 square kilometres and a population of more than 110 million, it exists in the largest delta in the world, formed by the Ganges-Brahmaputra-Meghna river system. The country is bounded by India to the west and north, by India and Burma to the east, and by the Bay of Bengal to the south. Eighty-five per cent of the land is a low, flat alluvial plain criss-crossed by some 230 large and small rivers with a total length of about 24,000 kilometres. The only significant uplands are in the north-east and south-east — on account of the Assam Range on the Shillong Plateau and the tertiary folds branching off the Himalayas — with average elevations of 244 metres and 610 metres respectively.

The average annual temperature ranges between 24.4 degrees Celsius and 26.7 degrees Celsius. Annual rainfall varies from 120 centimetres in the west to 250 centimetres in the south-east, and to 570 centimetres in the north-east. Winters are generally dry and pleasant, with temperatures around seventeen degrees Celsius. Summer temperatures rise to thirty-seven degrees Celsius. Humidity can be as high as ninety-eight per cent. Rain, cyclones, tidal waves, and sea storms occasionally come together, causing great havoc.

History

The earliest inhabitants are believed to have been Austro-Asians, who were joined later by the Dravidians, Aryans, Mongols, and Abbysinians, among others. Later, certainly, the Muslims of Arab, Turkish, Afghan, and Persian origins entered the region, first as religious preachers and traders, then as rulers. Whether independent or answerable to the imperial court at Delhi, Muslims held sway from the thirteenth to the eighteenth centuries. Bengali folk poetry flourished during this period and the earlier Sanskritized models were increasingly discarded. In the seventeenth and eighteenth centuries, Bengal, under the Mughals, moved towards Persian and Urdu as state languages and also began to develop, with poets such as Daulat Kazi and Sayyid Alaol, a syncretistic tradition that would later see further heights in the work of Kazi Nazrul Islam (1899–1976), Bangladesh's national poet. (In the same spirit, a poem by **Rabindranath Tagore** has become Bangladesh's national anthem.)

Extremely crucial to Bangladeshi national self-realization and identity through this entire process is the Bangladeshi people's love of their land and traditions, no less than their love for the Bengali language, which they began to see as being undermined by the state as early as 1952; the Bengali-versus-Urdu claims led to conflict on the streets of Dhaka on 21 February 1952. Ironically, it was in Dhaka that the All-India Muslim League, the political party that struggled for and won Pakistan, was founded in 1906. Bengali Muslims were also in the forefront of the Pakistan Movement in the 1940s. At the end of British rule in the subcontinent, the region became part of Pakistan. But following sharp political, economic, and administrative differences with the dominant West Pakistan, a mass revolt and armed struggle finally led to independence in 1971.

Language and Religion

Bengali resistance to domination by outsiders has a very long history, made possible by the unity of language and a culture largely ethnically homogeneous — no less that ninety-seven per cent of the population speaks Bengali (Bangla). About eighty-seven per cent of the population is Muslim, with 12.1 per cent Hindus, 0.6 per cent Buddhists, 0.3 per cent Christians, and 0.4 per cent others. Tribal ethnic populations are marginal in terms of political influence. English is used widely. In addition to eighteen daily newspapers in Bangla, there are seven that are published in English. English remains an essential skill among the upper strata of society and the professions, but it is no longer the strong cultural medium that it was during the country's Pakistan years (1947–71).

The Bangala artistic and cultural scene, however, is quite lively. Michael Madhusudan Dutt (1824–73), born in what is Bangladesh today, had given up poetry in despair because of the negative social incentives and literary discouragements that he had to face writing in English. His solution, like Bankim Chandra Chatterjee's (1834–94), was to turn to the mother tongue. Colonial East Bengal was not much different, in this respect, from Bangladesh, which relies substantially and rather single-mindedly on domestic cultural resources. A more open economy and relative stability and prosperity in the next decade will likely encourage even greater interaction with South Asian neighbours and the world at large.

Economy

The country's national resources include gas, limestone, and some coal and oil. The economy is planned and administered through five-year plans. The annual growth rate of the Gross Domestic Product (GDP) towards the end of the 1980s was about six per cent, but has been much lower in the 1990s. Agriculture accounts for forty-six per cent of GDP and seventy-three per cent of total employment. Raw jute, jute goods, tea, frozen foods, and ready-made garments are the main exports. Food, manufactured goods, machinery, and medicine are the main imports. The country has many jute, textile, fertilizer, and paper mills. More industry is being installed. At present (1993) the industrial sector contributes approximately 9.5 per cent of the GDP.

A good network of roads, railways, and waterways exists, but during the dry months alternative transportation must be found for the riverine routes. The country needs irrigation during the dry winter months, as it must drain the arable land (sixty-six per cent of the total area) during the monsoon.

Per capita income is very low. The incidence of poverty, unemployment, disease, and homelessness is high. Inflation is approximately ten per cent. But the country is grappling with some of its major problems in a planned approach and has set itself specific goals: to attain self-sufficiency in food; to increase the literary rate, which is twenty-four per cent at present; to increase the science and technology inputs in education; to reduce the rate of population increase, which is about 2.16 per cent per annum; to review nationalization policies, open the economy to foreign capital, and encourage industrialization; to provide universal vaccination, health coverage, and housing by the year 2000 (including the eighty-five per cent population currently living in villages); and generally to raise the standard of living through integrated social and economic development programmes.

Politics

Bangladesh's political system has gradually settled into the parliamentary form of government, and the idea of government accountability to the people has begun to take root. Such issues as human rights and women's rights are being addressed. Recent land and administrative reforms, rural development schemes, and the co-operative movement are likely to bear fruit. A grass-roots democracy may indeed be brought about by taking the government to the doorstep of the village communities and allowing them to take their own decisions.

Bangladesh is also active in the world community. The South Asian Association for Regional Cooperation (SAARC) was the result of Bangladesh's 1980s' initiative. The country is also a member of such international organizations as the United Nations, the Commonwealth of Nations, and the Group of 77. With her extensive experience of natural disasters, the country recently offered its expertise concerning flood control to the USA.

Bangladesh is a strikingly green, homogeneous, and tightly packed country with a very fertile land and impressive variety of fauna and flora. Folk traditions, music, dance, poetry, and drama flourish. Football is a favourite sport. Volleyball, kabadi, badminton, cricket, and hockey are also popular. The land of the Sundarbans and the Royal Bengal Tiger is full of natural colour; its energetic and spirited people are engaged in building themselves a secure and happy country.

ALAMGIR HASHMI

Further reading: *Poems from East Bengal: Selections from East Bengal Poetry of the Last Five Hundred Years: 1389–1954*, translated into English by Begum Yusuf Jamal (1954); M. E. Haq, *Muslim Bengali Literature* (1957); Syed Ali Ashraf, *Muslim Traditions in Bengali Literature* (1960); J. Tambimuttu, comp., *Poems from Bangla Desh: The Voice of a New Nation*, translated by P. Nandy (1972); D. Zbavitel, *Bengali Literature* (1976); Charles P. O'Donnell, *Bangladesh: Biography of a Nation* (1984).

BARATHAM, GOPAL (1935–)
Singaporean short-story writer
A neurosurgeon by profession, he was born in Singapore and received his early education at St Andrew's School. He graduated from the University of Singapore in 1960 and went on to specialize in neurosurgery in the UK. He lives and practises in Singapore.

Baratham began experimenting with short fiction in his school years, but his first collection, *Figments of Experience*, was not published until 1981. This was reissued in 1988 as *Love Letter and Other Stories*, the year in which *People Make You Cry and Other Stories* was published.

'Roses in December' (broadcast on the World Service of the British Broadcasting Corporation and published in *People Make You Cry*) is a wry, poignant rendering of the last days of an elderly man, crippled by a stroke and watched over by anxious relatives. The story focuses on his discovery, in familiar household smells and especially in the aromas of various objects in an old wooden family chest (for example, the fragrance of a sandalwood fan that belonged to his dead wife), of the still-vital correlatives of a life fully and sensuously lived. The story ends as the man drags himself to the chest; he dies as he inhales its odours, most alive and life-affirming at the moment of his passing.

'Roses in December' is a useful entry into Baratham's fictional world. His stories are characterized by an uncompromisingly secular and humanistic celebration of ordinary life in all its contrarieties. There is the awareness, as expressed by the narrative voice in 'Vocation', that 'suffering [is] the only constant feature of experience' and that death awaits us all; yet life is to be affirmed in all its experiential variety and concreteness, as the old man of 'Roses in December' so touchingly demonstrates.

Characters who represent a nexus with the supernatural are dubious, ineffectual — the Swami of 'People Make You Cry', Father Rodrigues of 'The Wafer' — or, like Father Noonan in 'Dutch Courage', sustained more by their sense of human solidarity with and responsibilities in the human world than by faith in the hereafter. The old man in 'Roses in December', for example, does not reach for religion as he nears death. In the words of Krishna, the central character in 'People Make You Cry', for all its vicissitudes the world is 'too beautiful to need the supernatural'. Moreover, the stories lovingly explore the ironies of love relationships or take delight in the adventures and misadventures of sexual liaison and sexual initiation (for example, 'The Gift of Sara Richardson'). In this connection, the stories are particularly noteworthy in the Singaporean context for the frankness, in dialogue and narratorial comment, of their treatment of sexual themes.

A number of the stories are particularly interesting in dealing with the human comedy of cross-cultural encounter. Events are usually refracted through the consciousness of an English-educated, and to some extent detribalized, Tamil Singaporean returning to confront relatives and the world he left behind. The results are hilarious and often trenchantly perceptive studies of human foibles ('Welcome' and 'Wedding Night', for example).

F. M. G. (MAX) LE BLOND

BARKER, LADY MARY ANN (1831–1911)
English/New Zealand children's writer, memoirist
She was born Mary Ann Stewart in Spanish Town, Jamaica, to Walter George Stewart, colonial secretary of Jamaica. She was educated in England, married Colonel Sir George Barker, and followed him to India after the Relief of Lucknow (1857). Colonel Barker died in the same year, and she returned to England, where she met and married Frederick Broome, a New Zealand sheep farmer. She was later Lady Broome.

Barker's writings record a feminine viewpoint on the growth of the British Empire. Largely autobiographical, her work is shaped with considerable artistry. In New Zealand she wrote *Station Life in New Zealand* (1870) and *Station Amusements in New Zealand* (1873), giving spirited accounts of the three years she and her husband spent on a Canterbury sheep station in the 1860s. The couple returned to England, where Barker edited a magazine, *Evening Hours*, and was appointed principal of the first national school of cooking. Her children's stories, *Stories About* (1871), which echo in their title the Peter Parley series, Stories About America, was the first children's book to relate non-fictional anecdotal animal stories.

Frederick Broome's appointment as colonial secretary in Natal, South Africa, resulted in Barker's *A Year's Housekeeping in South Africa* (1877), as much a classic in South Africa as *Station Life in New Zealand* has become in New Zealand. After a period in Mauritius, Broome was appointed governor of Western Australia, and Barker's *Letters to Guy* (1885) describes an interesting period of development in that state.

BETTY GILDERDALE

BARNARD, MARJORIE FAITH (1897–1987)

Australian short-story writer, novelist, historian, critic

She was born and educated in Sydney, Australia, and spent her life in New South Wales. While at the University of Sydney she became friends with fellow history student **Flora Eldershaw**, with whom she collaborated as M. Barnard Eldershaw; together they produced nine books between 1929 and 1947 — five works of fiction and four of non-fiction — culminating in the novel *Tomorrow and Tomorrow* (1947).

Barnard became a librarian, an occupation that she found lacking in stimulation; although her resources allowed her to resign in 1935 to live as a full-time writer, she resumed library work in 1942. In the last decade of her life she won numerous awards for her contribution to Australian literature, including the Order of Australia (1981), the Patrick White Award (1983), the New South Wales Premier's Special Award (1984), and an honorary Doctorate of Letters from the University of Sydney (1986).

A House is Built (1929), M. Barnard Eldershaw's prize-winning first novel, was followed by *Green Memory* (1931), *The Glasshouse* (1936), and *Plaque with Laurel* (1937), all concerned in some way with women's lives and their place in society. The 1930s were the most fruitful period for Barnard and Eldershaw; they not only published fiction but also a critical work, *Essays in Australian Fiction* (1938), dealing with the early history of Australia.

The collaboration virtually ended during the Second World War when Flora Eldershaw moved to Melbourne; *Tomorrow and Tomorrow*, the last M. Barnard Eldershaw book to appear, was written mainly by Marjorie Barnard. The novel, didactic in purpose, has two time frames; Knarf, an Australian of the twenty-fourth century, writes a novel in which he attempts to reconstruct life as it would have been in twentieth-century Australia. The book was intended to be 'an essay in perspective and a dramatization of the forces at work in our society'. Censored before publication in 1947, the original manuscript, with the full title restored, was published in 1983 as *Tomorrow and Tomorrow and Tomorrow*.

Barnard produced work under her own name — history, short stories, and *Miles Franklin: A Biography* (1967). *The Persimmon Tree and Other Stories* (1943) displays another facet of her writing; she called her short stories 'indulgences' and referred to them as 'the most private sector of my literary output'. Unlike the novels with their larger concerns, the stories focus on the solitary individual who experiences either a rare moment of illumination or, more often, painful revelation. In their emphasis on personal relations, the stories are reminiscent of E. M. Forster; Barnard's colours are muted, her brush strokes delicate, the overall feeling is one of desolation, as expressed in the last line of 'The Party': 'It was being alone that was so terrible.' *But Not for Love, Stories of Marjorie Barnard and M. Barnard Eldershaw*, edited by Robert Darby, was published in 1988.

The range of Barnard's work extends from an awareness of the way life is shaped by external events — evident in the novels and indicative of the historian's trained imagination — to the intensely intimate, symbolist nature of her stories.

PATRICIA EXCELL

Further reading: Drusilla Modjeska, *Exiles at Home: Australian Women Writers 1925–1945* (1981); Giulia Giuffre, ed., *A Writing Life: Interviews with Australian Women Writers* (1990).

BASCOM, HAROLD A. (1951–)
Guyanese dramatist, novelist
He was born at Vergenoegen, on the east bank of Guyana's Essequibo River. His first novel, *Apata* (1986), was short-listed for the Guyana Prize for Literature in 1987; two of his thirteen plays, 'Family Budget' (premièred 1989) and 'Philbert and Lorraine' (premièred 1992) were also short-listed for the same prize.

Apata, engaging and fast-paced, is developed from the true story of a fugitive hunted and killed by British Guiana colonial police and creates a sense of outrage against the fate of the underprivileged in a social order ruled by class and colour. The hero, a brilliant boy destroyed by these forces, is the folk hero/villain like the legendary Jamaican 'Rigin' reincarnated in the Perry Henzell-**Trevor Rhone** film *The Harder They Come* (1972); the novel recalls the styling of **John Hearne**.

Bascom's greatest national impact was in the theatre, as writer-director of his Ira Aldridge Workshop and Ambience Productions. He deals with local issues — the street life, language, and problems of the grass-roots — in the manner of the Jamaican popular topical-issue theatre of the 1970s and 1980s of Ed 'Bim' Lewis, Ginger Knight, Carmen Tipling, and Trevor Rhone. 'Philbert and Lorraine', Bascom's best theatrical achievement to date, sees him moving away from the popular writer of stagey melodrama and 'soap operas' in which crowd-pleasing gimmicks interfered with tragic statement and robbed him of much critical recognition. Bascom has grown into a more mature dramatist while still concentrating on domestic settings. His popular plays and their sequels helped to change local Guyanese theatre from a small post-colonial middle-class activity to a commercial theatre involving all classes.

After winning the National Academy of Performing Arts Award for Best New Guyanese Play in 1988 and the Theatre Arts Award for Best Guyanese Play in 1989, Bascom set about revising earlier scripts, including a 1992 restaging of two of his better dramas 'Tessa Real Girl' (premièred 1990; revised 1992) and 'The Barrel' (premièred 1987).

AL CREIGHTON

BASU, ROMEN (1923–)
Indian novelist, poet
Born in Calcutta, India, into a family of poets and creative writers, he is an accomplished man of letters. He moved to the USA in 1948, after his university education, at the age of twenty five. An economist by training and profession, Basu worked for the United Nations for nearly thirty-five years. Although his various official assignments kept him out of India for a long time, he has retained a deep concern for his country and people. His prolific literary output reveals his earnest commitment to the pressing social and political problems of contemporary India.

Basu's works include the short-story collection *Canvas and the Brush* (1971), the novels *A House Full of People* (1968), *Your Life to Live* (1972), *A Gift of Love* (1974), *The Tamarind Tree* (1975), *Candles and Roses* (1978), *Portrait on the Roof*

(1980), *Sands of Time* (1985), *Outcast* (1986), *Hours Before Time* (1988), *Blackstone* (1989), and *The Street Corner Boys* (1992) and the poetry collection *Wings at a Distance* (1988).

Basu's work must be read as a part of the resurgence of a strong current of social awareness in early twentieth-century India, when the Indian world view was being gradually qualified by a developing humanistic concern and social criticism. His work belongs to the tradition of the Indian social novel that developed through the writings of Bankim Chandra, **Rabindranath Tagore**, and Prem Chand, although it lacks the vigour and the emotional depth of the regional novel. Basu's novels constitute a sort of social history, tracing various socio-political movements that affected Indian life in the first half of the twentieth century — colonial rule, the collapse of Indian traditional family structures, the disappearance of subsistence economy, the **East-West encounter**, the Indian national movement, post-independence political upheavals, the spread of Communism, and the rise of radical revolutionary movements.

Basu's fictional work falls into two phases: in the early phase, his focus is on individual experience and he shows an almost obsessive preoccupation with the theme of marital and family strife. *Your Life to Live* and *A Gift of Love* probe the psychological conflicts that accompany a marriage outside one's caste and community. Basu unequivocally upholds the innate strength of a Hindu marriage in *Candles and Roses*, where he writes that a Hindu marriage 'is not for one life but eternity'. *Portrait on the Roof*, however, demonstrates that true love cuts across the barriers of caste, colour, and creed. The novelist has an ambiguous attitude to his subject and this results in a general confusion affecting his handling of plot and character. These novels are flawed by contradictions, inconsistency, improbabilities, and shallow characterization.

The second phase, a more fruitful one, marks the shift of focus to larger social and political issues, and Basu performs much better as he begins to fictionalize actual historical events to tell realistic tales of Bengali rural life. *Outcast*, artistically the most satisfying of Basu's novels, offers a vivid account of the strict caste structure in Hindu society, unfolding a tragic love tale against that background. This novel succeeds where others fail because its structure is tight and varied and the action is depicted vividly.

Blackstone and *The Street Corner Boys* mark a steady maturation in Basu's artistry and these may well come to be regarded as his most significant works. *Blackstone*, a powerful political novel dealing with the outbreak of the Naxal movement in the 1960s in Bengal, tells an unvarnished tale of human suffering in modern India. *The Street Corner Boys*, a novel of ideas, has for its theme the spread of Communism in eastern India. The text becomes the context for a critical analysis of the socio-political implications of Communism for the common individual. The author conclusively suggests apolitical humanism as a more desirable alternative. The historical perspective gives these novels greater credibility and dignity.

Basu's poetic work as evidenced in *Wings at a Distance* is rather slim and adds little to his literary reputation. But his short stories, many collected in *Canvas and the Brush*, show greater technical sophistication and subtler narratorial skill. He is at his best in stories such as 'Gun smoke in Phonexia', 'Schefflera', and 'Christmas Party', where he deals with the little ironies of life, choosing expatriate experience as his background. While elegant prose, analytical perception of socio-political reality, accuracy and detail of observation, and mature social vision are among Basu's strengths, inadequate attention to details of plot, failure to tap the resources of myth, and a lack of emotional depth in characterization constitute his weaknesses.

C. VIJAYASREE

BAUGH, EDWARD ALSTON CECIL (1936–)
Jamaican poet, critic
He was born in Port Antonio, Jamaica, and educated at the University of the West Indies when it was still a college of the University of London, England, located in Jamaica. He graduated with a BA in 1957 and completed an MA in English at Queen's University, Kingston, Canada, in 1959. His Ph.D. in English was obtained at the University of Manchester, England, in 1964. Since 1965 Baugh has taught in the English department of the University of the West Indies, first at the Cave Hill campus in Barbados and subsequently at the Mona campus in Jamaica. Baugh was promoted to professor in 1978, and has served in executive positions on several academic and literary bodies. He has been, for example, a member of the adjudicating panel for the Commonwealth Poetry Prize and the Commonwealth Writers Prize.

Baugh is also one of the foremost critics of Caribbean literature. *Critics on Caribbean Literature* (1978), which he edited, is a landmark anthology of criticism on major Caribbean writers, and his *Derek Walcott: Memory as Vision* (1978) confirms his insight in championing a future winner of the Nobel Prize for Literature. Further criticism by Baugh of Caribbean and post-colonial literature has appeared in many journals. He is also a poet whose work has appeared in periodicals and anthologies, such as *The Penguin Book of Caribbean Verse in English* (1986), edited by Paula Burnett, and the *Heinemann Book of Caribbean Poetry* (1992), edited by **Ian McDonald** and Stewart Brown. Baugh's volume of poems, *A Tale From the Rainforest*, appeared in 1988.

In language that is both urbane and demotic, his poems express an educated commentary on racial and political problems inherited from Caribbean and colonial history. In one poem, for instance, Baugh employs Standard English to discuss a sophisticated debate about political commitment in art, while in another he uses Jamaican Creole, just as deftly, to dramatize raw feelings of resentment.

FRANK M. BIRBALSINGH

BAUGHAN, BLANCHE EDITH (1870–1958)
New Zealand essayist, poet, travel writer
Born in England, she graduated from the University of London with a BA in classics. Baughan supported suffrage, did welfare work in London's East End, and published *Verses* (1898). She immigrated to Akaroa, New Zealand, in 1900 and worked as a housekeeper on a Banks Peninsula farm and published *Reuben and Other Poems* in 1903. With *Shingle-Short and Other Verses* (1908) she extended her repertoire of poems about backblocks pioneering narrated by characters ranging from a sharp-witted granny to a haunted murderer. Her verse narratives, particularly the dramatic monologues of *Shingle-Short and Other Verses*, offer a kind of *Winesburg, Ohio* of colonial experience that is eminently readable and reflects her preoccupation with pioneer voices. A long verse drama, 'The Paddock', is remarkable for its entirely female cast, one of whom is Maori. *Brown Bread from a Colonial Oven* (1912) presents sketches of settlement in prose format. *Poems from the Port Hills* (1923) is Baughan's last poetry collection and shows evidence of her interest in eastern religion. Illness in 1909–10 affected Baughan's impetus to verse; she turned successfully to writing books of scenic description that were collected as *Studies in New Zealand Scenery* (1916).

A long-standing commitment to prison reform led Baughan to found in 1924 the New Zealand branch of the Howard League for Penal Reform; under the pseudonym T. L. S. she co-authored

People in Prison (1936) with F. A. de la Mare.

MICHELE LEGGOTT

Bautista, Cirilo F. (1941–)

Filipino poet, short-story writer

Born in Luzon, the Philippines, and educated at the University of Santo Tomas, Manila, Saint Louis University Graduate School, Baguio, and the State University of Iowa, USA, he won early recognition for his poetry and prose written in English and Philipino. Currently professor of literature at De La Salle University, Manila, Bautista brought together some of his long-standing preoccupations with language and social meaning in *Breaking Signs: Lectures on Literature and Semiotics* (1990). A highly regarded and original writer and thinker with an international reputation, Bautista has published many articles on Philippine literature in English; in 1970 he declared: 'Philippine poetry in English is a bastard; it was begot in an instance of passion by an overzealous father and a mother who knew no better; it probably does not realize where it is going.'

Bautista's major work in English is an impressive and resonant epic trilogy, *The Trilogy of Saint Lazarus — The Archipelago* (1970), *Telex Moon* (1980), and 'Lotus Apocalypse'. The trilogy takes various forms and offers, in Bautista's words, 'a poetical-historical interpretation of the evolution of the Filipino Soul'. *The Trilogy of Saint Lazarus* engages with the spirit of Rizal as a central consciousness. *The Archipelago* is an overview of Spanish settlement in the Philippines up to the founding of Manila and reaching forward to the death of Rizal. *Telex Moon*, a densely written, sardonically playful poem, critiques the colonial past, but avoids the limitations of overt politicism for an intenser metaphysical focus. Published extracts from 'Lotus Apocalypse' indicate that it engages with the Marcos regime and later contemporary society in a philosophical perspective where the creative writer is a historian bringing to life the complex forces and motives of historical events and personages.

Bautista's short stories and poetry, which are experimental but also acutely aware of tradition, emerge from a passionate relationship with his country and its people and are shaped by a concern with universal ethical and aesthetic values. His first collection was *The Cave and Other Poems* (1963); later publications in English include *Charts: New Poems* (1973) and the prose *Stories* (1990).

ELIZABETH PERKINS

Baxter, James Keir (1926–72)

New Zealand poet, dramatist

Born in Dunedin, New Zealand, to a self-educated farmer and the daughter of a university professor, he established himself as the most precocious and promising figure in New Zealand poetry with his first collection, *Beyond the Palisade* (1944). Recovery from alcoholism and conversion to Roman Catholicism were in his view more important to his later development than his sporadic and undistinguished academic record. Returning to Dunedin from Wellington in 1966, Baxter held a university writers' fellowship for three years, leading to a highly prolific period in which most of his plays and an increasing volume of poetry were composed. Most of Baxter's last years were spent in an isolated community that he founded at Jerusalem, a village and former Maori mission station on the Wanganui River.

Baxter's early stylistic eclecticism reflects a young writer skilfully experimenting with forms ranging from the Tennysonian to the contemporary British, but with sufficient tonal and thematic consistency to present an individual voice speaking with considerable clarity. The mood surrounding the natural romantic subject matter has generally been interpreted as regretful, but there is also a prospective direction to many of the poems, a questioning of the land that would become a major focus of subsequent volumes. *Blow, Wind of Fruitfulness* (1948) and *The Fallen House* (1953) combine the enigma of a sense of colonial placelessness with the role of boy-as-discoverer; the recurrent theme is that of loss, which some critics have read as a search for a lost Eden. Technically, this period shows Baxter using much less Latinate diction and developing a trait that would continue throughout his poetry — the audacious use of heavy monosyllabic spondaic phrasing, often bound together with assonance.

The vicissitudes of Baxter's life in the 1950s accounted for the varying quantity of his literary output and its sporadic changes of tone. The 1947 'Songs of the Desert' — first published in *The Night Shift: Poems on Aspects of Love* (1957), co-authored with Charles Doyle, **Louis Johnson**, and **Kendrick Smithyman** — established a position of alienation that would recur in his work for two decades; images of living in a 'sunk land' or on a 'barbarian coast' beside a 'cannibal sea' or 'barren waves' reflect the 'menopause of the mind' that Baxter connected with both boyhood isolation and the struggle for sobriety. The perception of alienation is dominant in *Pig Island Letters* (1966), where the poet still shows little sense of social integration. In other poems of the 1960s, however, Baxter increasingly acknowledges not only a land, but also a society around him, and he becomes overtly a social critic. Though the Vietnam War would initiate Baxter's most directly polemical poetry, his earlier work on social themes reflects his religious conversion and also a gradual alignment with his father's pacifist stance in the First World War.

Semi-dramatized human subjects, such as urban bush-ranger figures exalted for their antisocial heroics, had appeared in Baxter's poetry since his period of heavy drinking, but these were used in an anecdotal or celebratory way. Such poems express a side of Baxter that was never subdued — the anti-establishment figure who constantly defied institutions, employers, universities, and officialdom, reflecting the influence of Scottish poet Robert Burns and Australian colonial writers. In the 1960s such defiance co-existed in Baxter's poetry with a more thoughtful criticism, but found an easy outlet in his numerous plays for stage and radio, eventually published as *Collected Plays* (1982). His demarcation of genres was emphatic: theatre was the domain of 'human stupidity', while more serious religious, social, and philosophical issues belonged to poetry. His single novel, *Horse* (1985), unequivocally evokes the world of human stupidity.

Some of Baxter's plays are largely the slapstick of the student revue. In most, however, the vicissitudes of human frailty are structured within a (sometimes modernized) version of Greek myth or within inverted New Testament archetypes populated by an alcoholic subculture, so that a group of drunks may be caught up in a contemporary passion and crucifixion situation. Several plays develop characters from Baxter's ballads or anecdotal verse.

Returning to Dunedin in 1966 meant renewed contact with the land Baxter had wrestled with in adolescence, populated not only by boyhood and student memories, but also by various remaining friends and relatives. This intensified a new kind of treatment of human material in his poetry — the poem as a re-animated family photograph or as a fractional section of legendary or historical time; in this Baxter acknowledged an affinity with American Robert Lowell's *Life Studies* (1959). For several years Baxter's Rimbaud imitations and imaginary re-creations of the pioneering circumstances of ancestors had anticipated this development, but it was his discovery of the potential of the unrhymed run-on couplet that gave him the perfect vehicle for the measured wryness of his later poems.

Baxter had used this form occasionally since 1958, but it was only in his final phase — and particularly within the sonnet structure — that it became predominant in his work. He was using the form extensively in 1968 when, after his university fellowship, he remained in Dunedin writing articles for a Catholic magazine; he wrote that he had accepted 'God's bribe' and had become 'His singing eunuch'. Such was the context of his sudden calling (in a dream, he alleged) to live at Jerusalem. Abandoning domesticity and embracing Franciscan austerity with a commitment to squalor that his verse celebrated, he immersed himself in Maori culture and wrote the remarkable sequences published as *Jerusalem Sonnets: Poems for Colin Durning* (1970), *Jerusalem Daybook* (1971), and *Autumn Testament* (1972). This isolation, very like that of his boyhood, provided a grounding for a revalidation of the themes of his earlier work, and the social, religious, and intellectual freedom allowed the questioning, diversity, and cultural hybridization reflected in the sonnets. These poems constitute Baxter's last major work before his death and, like all his best work, are generated out of paradox, displacement, or disorientation. Like the Franciscan rule that Baxter embraced with varying degrees of rigour, the sonnet is a form that he selected to fight against; the poems echo with the cries of the disciplined Baxter demanding answers from eternity.

HOWARD McNAUGHTON

Further reading: Vincent O'Sullivan, *James K. Baxter* (1976); Frank McKay, *The Life of James K. Baxter* (1990).

BAYNTON, BARBARA (1857–1929)

Australian novelist, short-story writer

Born in Scone, New South Wales, Australia, she set most of her fiction in the Upper Hunter River district of her younger life — **Henry Lawson** country. Baynton's writing, begun in the 1890s, displeased **A. G. Stephens** for not conforming to the ***Bulletin*** ethos, and only one of her stories ever appeared there, editorially bowdlerized. Baynton published verse, some journalism, and three incidental stories, but her reputation is based securely on the six stories that appeared first in *Bush Studies* (1902), and, increasingly, on *Human Toll* (1907), her only published novel.

Invariably compared with Lawson, Baynton said of him in *Home* (September 1920), 'I remember thinking, after reading *While the Billy Boils* that here for the first time a man had shown that the Bush was worth writing about.' The use of 'man' is significant, as her perspective on the bush differs markedly from his, her stories resisting underlying concepts in Lawson's. She uses such familiar motifs as the bush woman, **mateship**, alcohol, dogs, and the 'hatter'/misogynist in critically transformative ways that often carry gender-related reversals of value. The stories in *Bush Studies* involve archetypal bush experiences with sympathetic and unsympathetic bush characters of both sexes. Visually powerful, these ironic stories display a remarkable range of dialogue, humour, and literary complexity. Several stories illustrate that, in **Louisa Lawson**'s words, in the outback 'man is king and force is ruler.' *Bush Studies* can instructively be read beside **Katherine Mansfield**'s New Zealand 'bush woman' stories — 'The Woman at the Store' (1912), 'Millie' (1913) — for their shared questioning of the masculinist bush ethos.

The notion of the bush is conceptually important, but not monolithic. The township is equally important. Baynton explores unsentimentally what Henry Lawson, in 'The Star of Australasia' (1896), called 'the living death in the lonely bush, the greed of the selfish town'. But the problem is not the bush itself: extreme isolation merely licences whatever evil exists in people, what Lawson, in 'Crime in the Bush' (1898), called 'mental darkness' and 'monotony . . . which darkens the mind'.

Baynton is a modernist in style and outlook, using sophisticated narrative techniques. In contrast to Lawson's characteristic 'personal' narrative voice, Baynton's is authorially detached, at a transitional stage towards the full polyvocality of free indirect discourse. A feature of Baynton's modernism is the psychological intensity with which inner states are conveyed empathetically, yet through objective technique: in 'Scrammy 'And' two extremes of sensibility co-exist — the hatter and Scrammy; in 'Bush Church' the vulnerablity of the poor selectors, whose vulgar ignorance renders others vulnerable, is given equal status with the mental agony of their victims — the grazier couple and the clergyman. Outstanding as an example of prolonged dissection of mental states under physical stress — terror, thirst, increasing hallucination — is the final chapter in *Human Toll*. The handling of this as a psychological episode (Ursula lost in the bush) is original and unsurpassed until **Henry Handel Richardson**'s *The Fortunes of Richard Mahony* (1930).

Human Toll gains in literary value when read against William Satchell's *The Toll of the Bush* (1905), a romantic pioneering story with elements typical of contemporary New Zealand and Australian fiction. Both employ Victorian romance elements and the plot machinery of melodrama (withheld letters, lost inheritance, lecherous preachers, marriage to the wrong person), but, naturalizing them in a post-colonial context, Satchell endorses them, while Baynton deconstructs them as do both **Miles Franklin**'s *My Brilliant Career* (1901) and **Joseph Furphy**'s *Such is Life* (1903). Baynton satirizes morality, the church, mateship, virtue rewarded, while simultaneously revaluing stock Australian colonial literary motifs, giving readers a female *Bildung* variant in which 'true love' is tested in a colonial outback setting. It is the greed and lust of people that take the toll, not the bush.

Serious criticism dates mainly from the 1980s after the publication of *Barbara Baynton*, ed. S. Krimmer and A. Lawson (1980), which contains the first reprint of *Human Toll*. A further reissue of *Bush Studies* appeared in 1989. The first articles on *Human Toll* appeared in 1989.

CAROL FRANKLIN

Further reading: Penne Hackforth-Jones, *Barbara Baynton: Between Two Worlds* (1989).

BEAGLEHOLE, JOHN CAWTE (1901–71)
New Zealand historian
Born and educated in Wellington, New Zealand, he earned a Ph.D. in history at the University of London (1929). Returning home during the Depression years of the early 1930s, he was at first denied university posts because of his supposed radical opinions, but eventually became professor of Commonwealth history at Victoria University, Wellington. Beaglehole's interests were wide: his works include *New Zealand: A Short History* (1936) and two histories of university institutions — *The University of New Zealand* (1937) and *Victoria University College: An Essay Towards a History* (1949). He was a distinguished prose stylist and a writer of a volume of discursive philosophical poetry, *Words for Music* (1938). He was also a talented typographical designer. Increasingly, like several distinguished Australian and New Zealand contemporaries, Beaglehole's work focused on early European incursion into the Pacific, which he saw as a heroic enterprise rather than as the 'fatal impact' of Alan Moorehead's view. Work begun with *The Exploration of the Pacific* (1934) and *The Discovery of New Zealand* (1939) culminated in his massively authoritative edition for the Hakluyt Society of *The Journals of Captain James Cook on His Voyages of Discovery* (4 vols, 1955–74). Beaglehole rescued Cook's rough vigour and integrity from the gentility of his eighteenth-century editors and unravelled Cook's writings from those of his fellow voyagers, which had often been merged by editors. Beaglehole also edited *The 'Endeavour' Journals of Joseph Banks 1768–1771* (2 vols, 1962). The admirable (and wholly admiring) *The Life of Captain James Cook*

(1974), with its detailed knowledge of eighteenth-century seamanship, navigation, and the philosophical concerns of the time, was a fitting conclusion to his work. Beaglehole and the physicist Ernest Rutherford are the only New Zealanders to have been awarded the British Order of Merit.

DENNIS McELDOWNEY

Further Reading: Margery Walton, Julia Bergen, and Janet Paul, *John Cawte Beaglehole, a Bibliography* (1972).

BEAN, C. E. W. (1879–1968)
Australian historian
Born Charles Edwin Woodrow Bean at Bathurst, New South Wales, Australia, he was educated in England, where he was called to the bar in 1903. Returning to Australia, Bean's experiences on the country legal circuit led to his appreciation of western New South Wales as 'the real Australia', and of the wool industry as the creator of 'some of the outstanding national types'. Thus he foreshadowed his influential interpretation of Australian involvement in the First World War as leading directly to the birth of Australian nationhood.

On the recommendation of **A. B. Paterson** Bean joined the *Sydney Morning Herald* in 1908. His articles on the outback were published as *On the Wool Track* (1910). When war began, he was chosen by fellow journalists as official Australian war correspondent. Wounded at Gallipoli, he compiled and astutely promoted *The Anzac Book* (1916), from contributions by soldiers. Bean formulated the notion of an *Official History* — not completed until 1942 — as 'the only memorial which could be worthy' of these serving men. It was largely at his initiative that the Australian War Memorial in Canberra was begun.

As he had borne a legend of the Australian bush back to its urban citizens, so Bean's was the pivotal role in the definition of the martial and national legend of Anzac (Australian and New Zealand Army Corps). He returned to Turkey in 1919 to answer questions concerning the topography and enemy tactics. This expedition produced *Gallipoli Mission* (1948). The *Official History of the War of 1914–1918*, of which Bean wrote six volumes and edited eight more, is a massive achievement that has no parallel in other Commonwealth literatures. No official history was written for New Zealand, for example. G. W. L. Nicholson's *The Canadian Expeditionary Force* (1962) completed the work of Fortescue Duguid. John Buchan wrote *The History of the South African Forces in France* (1920) in addition to his multi-volume history of the war. But none had Bean's front-line experience nor his commitment to writing military history from accounts of men in the line. His enduring love of England did not hinder his career as a creator and celebrant of Australian patriotism.

PETER PIERCE

BEAVER, BRUCE (1928–)
Australian poet
He was born in Manly, New South Wales, Australia, and this area has become the background for much of his writing. Although he is acknowledged to be one of the most important and influential poets of his generation, his influence has been mainly upon younger contemporaries, most notably those writers who were jolted by the Vietnam War and who sought American rather than English or European models. From the age of seventeen Beaver suffered from a manic-depressive condition that was stabilized only in the late 1970s. After working as a proofreader on a Sydney newspaper for many years he received an invalid pension; he has lived in Manly since the 1970s.

Beaver's early publications include *Under the Bridge* (1961), *Seawall and Shoreline* (1964), and *Open at Random* (1967). But it was his book-length sequence *Letters to Live Poets* (1969) that thrust his work onto the central stage of contemporary Australian poetry. These *Letters* explore a broad range of poetic styles and references, and their wit, honesty, and anti-lyrical tenor combine with a wide-ranging intellectual curiosity to project Beaver as a forceful and energetic poet. Beaver's antecedents in Australian poetry are apparent — they range through **Christopher Brennan**, **R. D. FitzGerald**, **John Blight**, and **Francis Webb** to **Vincent Buckley** and **Peter Porter** — but his own consolidation in *Letters to Live Poets* of particular inheritances achieved the synthesis that made this book a landmark. It won the Grace Leven Poetry Prize, the Poetry Society of Australia Prize, and the Captain Cook Bicentennial Prize for Poetry (all in 1970).

Lauds and Plaints (1968–1972) (1974) is in many ways a more astonishing achievement. In scope and emotional risk-taking it stretches the boundaries already established, and it is in this work that Beaver's essentially religious or spiritual dimension is most ardently articulated, though by 'religious' one must understand a pluralist concept of being and a non-Christian ethos. The influence of eastern philosophies (perhaps through the writings of Jung) combines in Beaver's work with a powerful search for identification with fellow 'seekers', who may well be such European creative forces as Friedrich Hölderlin, Rainer Maria Rilke, or Gustav Mahler.

The succeeding books, *Odes and Days* (1975) and *Death's Directives* (1978), consolidate the language and the poetic world Beaver created for himself in *Lauds and Plaints*. In *As It Was* (1979) Beaver found a remarkably engaging yet rich way of approaching autobiographical material. This book, which won him the Patrick White Award, balances an existential hurt and gloom with the self-confidence of affirmative insight. Its very informality and seemingly digressive delight in small details is its great achievement.

Selected Poems appeared in 1979, followed by a curious book of prose pieces or prose-poems, *Headlands* (1986). These travel pieces pursue the anecdotal debate with the reader, but there is a disturbing subtext of old manic-depressive tension.

Charmed Lives (1988) is a triumphant and extraordinary book. It offers something of the surprise, energy, and discovery of the poet's earlier major collections. It is in four sections, the two inner ones being closer to the earlier work, though reinforcing the sense of a creative artist in full command of his material. But the external sequences are what make *Charmed Lives* extraordinary. The first of these, 'R. M. R. A Verse Biography of Rainer Maria Rilke', is a set of twelve poems, the most detailed and distinguished study in Beaver's output of a fellow creative artist. The final sequence, though, 'Tiresias Sees', is the book's triumph, and perhaps the triumph of Beaver's own poetic career. He subsumes himself within the androgynous character of the Greek sage in a wonderful, salacious, and irreverent set of eighteen virtuoso variations. If one had thought that T. S. Eliot exhausted the Tiresias theme, Beaver's sequence pushes that aside to strut, prance, lurch, slither, and coerce us into this ultimate dance, a defiance in the face of death, and a jig to the xylophone of one's own rib cage and other delectable parts. In 1990 Bruce Beaver was awarded the Special Prize from the New South Wales Premier's Literary Awards, a tribute to his sustained creative literary contribution.

THOMAS SHAPCOTT

Further reading: Thomas Shapcott, 'Bruce Beaver: a survey', *Biting the Bullet: A Literary Memoir* (1990).

BEKEDEREMO (1935–)

Nigerian poet, dramatist, critic

Widely known as J. P. Clark, he was born at Kiagbodo village near Warri in the Delta State of Nigeria, to Chief Clark Fuludu Bekederemo and his wife, Poro Amakashe Adoni Clark, an Urhobo princess. He has Ijo and Urhobo ancestry through his father and mother respectively and in the 1980s he adopted the name Bekederemo, which he describes as his 'family name'. Bekederemo earned his BA in English (1960) from University College, Ibadan.

While a research fellow at the Institute of African Studies, University of Ibadan, Bekederemo met Ebun Odutola, a Yoruba from Ijebu Ode, later a professor and the director of the Centre for Cultural Studies at the University of Lagos. Married in 1964, the couple collaborated to found in 1982 the PEC Repertory Theatre in Lagos, of which Bekederemo is the artistic director.

As an undergraduate, Bekederemo recorded several wide-ranging educational successes. He edited the student union journal *The Beacon* (1956–), and through the encouragement of his teacher, Martin Banham, founded the influential magazine *The Horn* (1957–). His colleagues who published in *The Horn*, or who were closely associated with it, included **Christopher Okigbo**, Aig Higo, **Wole Soyinka**, Abiola Irele, Mac Akpoyaware, and Pius Oleghe.

Bekederemo has held various appointments: he was features editor of the *Daily Express* (Lagos); held a fellowship at Princeton University, USA, as a Parvin scholar (from which came his satirical travelogue *America, Their America*, 1964); was a research fellow at the Institute of African Studies, University of Ibadan; and was appointed professor of English in 1972 by the University of Lagos at the age of thirty-eight, the first African of his generation to be thus recognized.

Bekederemo has generally enjoyed adulation from serious critics of African literature. Critic R. N. Egudu notes that Bekederemo's 'interest is in the problems of human beings everywhere'; Dan Izevbaye avers that he is 'interesting not only for the quality of his poetry, but for his historical importance as one of the first poets to begin writing the type of verse that should eventually lead to the foundation of a national tradition of Nigerian poetry'.

Bekederemo's major fortes are drama and poetry. His interest in the theatre began at the University of Ibadan, where in 1963 he first recorded Okabou Ojobolo's version of *The Ozidi Saga* — an epic poem in the Ijaw oral tradition — which Bekederemo translated and published in 1977. While his early but less-successful plays, *Song of a Goat* (1961), *The Masquerade* (1964), and *The Raft* (1964), are derivative of the Greek classics in which the protagonist is doomed by powerful forces over which he has little or no control, Bekederemo's later and more effective dramas, notably *Ozidi* (1966) and *The Boat* (1981), are cast in the indigenous African culture, particularly that of the Ijo region. Interestingly, much like his Nigerian contemporary Soyinka, Bekederemo's major strength as a playwright is his ability to explore the theme of Africanness.

Apart from its effective fusion of the political and the mythic, *Ozidi* is a typical African drama; it is rich in mime, musical composition, and dance, set against a background of rites and rituals, water spirits, the gods, and dead ancestors. Witty and ironic, the play has a poetic quality that enhances its theatricality.

The Boat is Bekederemo's first venture into prose drama. Although lacking the aura and dramatic intensity of *Ozidi*, it is also rooted in African cultural tradition. Like *Ozidi*, the tragic history of the hero is one of a rise and fall; here, too, the familiar myths of the interrelationship between god and humanity, humanity and fate, life and its vicissitudes are interwoven with amazing dexterity.

Bekederemo's poetry is even more successful than his drama, for here the entire universe is his topos where he records his emotions and experiences, grappling with the human condition in all its urgency. Compared to his African contemporaries who are often characterized as the 'conscious internationalists' — **Lenrie Peters**, **Gabriel Okara**,

Christopher Okigbo, and **Dennis Brutus** — Bekederemo is the most topical and expansive. In his major poetic works, *Poems* (1961), *A Reed in the Tide* (1965), *Casualties: Poems 1966–68* (1970), *State of the Union* (1985), and *Mandela and Other Poems* (1988), he draws his imagery from native and modernist traditions. He has stated that he sometimes wonders 'what in my make-up is "traditional" and "native" and what "derived" and "modern"'.

The success of Bekederemo's poetry can also be viewed in the way in which he harmonizes heterogeneous themes — art, love, politics, war and peace, culture, and tradition predominate. Among his most successful individual lyrics are 'Night Rain', 'Song', and 'Out of the Tower', which explore the eerie landscapes of water, wind, and land *vis-à-vis* private predicament. When read individually and against a backdrop of his entire verse, their effect is one of realism and contemporariness.

The future direction that Bekederemo's poetics may take is found in the general tenor of *State of the Union* and *Mandela and Other Poems*. In these works — unlike such earlier volumes as *Poems* and *A Reed in the Tide*, which are heavily influenced by the prosody of G. M. Hopkins, and by W. B. Yeats, T. S. Eliot, and Ezra Pound — the diction is remarkable for its earthiness and originality of form. Here, too, the poet primarily addresses public issues, empathizing with the downtrodden of society while effectively satirizing those who cause their misfortune. Bekederemo can be seen in these later works in light of what **Northrop Frye** characterizes as the 'Utopian writer' whose business, he says, is 'communicating a vision to his readers, not sharing a fantasy dream with them'.

Bekederemo continues to establish himself as one of Nigeria's most vocal and relevant artists and as a perceptive and sensitive critic; his *The Example of Shakespeare* (1970) expresses his views on the nature of poetry, drama, and contemporary society. Although he officially retired from academic life in 1980, he continues to articulate his commitment to African intellectualism. Recently he has held visiting professorial appointments at several institutions, including Yale and Wesleyan universities in the USA. He won the Nigerian National Merit Award, for excellence in the Arts and Sciences in Nigeria, in 1991.

ISAAC I. ELIMIMIAN

Further reading: Robert M. Wren, *J. P. Clark* (1984); Isaac I. Elimimian, *The Poetry of J. P. Clark Bekederemo* (1989).

BELGRAVE, VALERIE (1949–)
Trinidadian novelist
Born in San Juan, Trinidad, she graduated from Sir George Williams (now Concordia) University, Montreal, Canada, in 1971 with a BA in literature and art. Belgrave currently works as an artist and fabric designer in Trinidad.

Belgrave's novel, *Ti Marie* (1988), is set in sixteenth-century Trinidad — a time of great turmoil — when the island was passing from Spanish to British rule. The central story in the complex plot tells of the love affair between the beautiful mulatto woman Marie Hélène (the 'Ti Marie' of the title) and Barry, a dashing young Englishman. Earlier Caribbean novelists writing about the slave era, such as **Edgar Mittelholzer** in *Children of Kaywana* (1952), have sensationalized the violence of the period. As a 1989 review in *The Trinidad and Tobago Review* noted, Belgrave has written a story to be read as entertainment, 'in a spirit of romance . . . coming from a position of strength, of conviction of black equality, and victory of global humanism'.

The historical background has been well researched, and the interacting social, national, and racial groups on the island are portrayed with assurance. Although the characters themselves tend to be stereotypes and the island is used mainly as a decorative backcloth, the novel succeeds in its confessed intention to entertain. The first edition of *Ti Marie* was quickly reprinted.

LOUIS JAMES

Further reading: Madeline Coopsammy, '*Ti Marie* by Valerie Belgrave', *Caribe* August (1990); Lyn Innes, '*Ti Marie* by Valerie Belgrave', *Wasafiri* Spring (1990).

BENNETT, ALVIN GLADSTONE (1918–)
Jamaican novelist, poet
Born in Falmouth, Trelawney, Jamaica, he served as a ship's purser for several years before settling in England in 1954 and becoming a social worker. In 1982 he immigrated to Canada. Since the early 1950s Bennett has written regularly for *The Daily Gleaner* and other Jamaican newspapers. His feature columns and poetry are characterized by his mastery of irony, humour, and acerbic comments on the affairs of God and humanity. Several of his short stories were broadcast by the British Broadcasting Corporation during the 1960s and 1970s. Bennett's experience as a social worker is directly related to the themes of his first novel, *Because they Know Not* (1958).

The experiences of the novel's protagonist reflect the struggles and triumphs of Caribbean immigrants to Britain in the 1950s. Bennett's effectively ironic and searching analysis reveals the pitfalls of the colonial experience. Thematically, the work recalls **Sam Selvon**'s *The Lonely Londoners* (1956), though Bennett's prose, as a whole, can be best compared with that of his friend **Roger Mais**.

Bennett's mastery of irony as a structured aesthetic device is more clearly seen in his second novel, *God the Stonebreaker* (1964), whose character Granny B. (generally known as G. B.) is a classic figure of Caribbean literature. She is scheming, manipulative, and insensitive, but pathetic. As in *Because they Know Not*, Bennett uses satire to expose the ills of society while expressing a degree of humanism that is rarely evident in contemporary Caribbean fiction. Bennett's linguistic versatility is such that he fully exploits a wide range of semantic possibilities while exploring the ontological depths of his characters and their context.

Though Bennett's poetry collection *Out of Darkness* (undated) displays a degree of irreverence similar to that of his novels, the poems are conservative and traditional in structure.

F. I. CASE

BENNETT, LOUISE (1919–)
Jamaican poet, short-story writer
Born in Kingston, Jamaica, she attended St Simon's College and Excelsior High School, Kingston, and Friends' College in St Mary, Jamaica. Awarded a British Council scholarship in 1945, Bennett was trained in drama at the Royal Academy of Dramatic Art in London, England. From 1955 to 1959, as drama officer with the Jamaica Welfare Commission, she researched Jamaican folk culture.

Bennett began writing 'dialect verses' in the late 1930s. She recited at concerts, and her first collection of poems, *(Jamaica) Dialect Verses,* appeared in 1942. In 1943 Jamaica's leading newspaper, *The Daily Gleaner*, began to publish a weekly column of her poems. Though there were, and are, dissenting voices about the artistic merit of Bennett's poetry, the public in general has been supportive. Serious consideration of her work began only in the early 1960s and culminated with the publication of the collection *Jamaica Labrish* (1966), a comprehensive anthology of her work. Bennett has since published *Anancy and Miss Lou* (1979), a collection of her Anancy stories, and *Selected Poems* (1982), designed to encourage detailed literary study.

Although Bennett's work is often enhanced by her own expert performance, her writing offers the reader considerable rewards. Some critics argue, however, that only in performance are her talents truly realized. Her available recordings include *Yes, M'Dear: Miss Lou Live* (1984), *Bre' Anancy & Miss Lou* (1991), *Miss Lou's Views* (1991), and a video, *Miss Lou and Friends* (1991).

The Bennett poem is normally, almost invariably, a dramatic monologue in Jamaican Creole, employing a version of the ballad quatrain, but her verses are not constrained by the metrical restrictions of the model. They carry the rhythms and, in performance, the variations of tone and pitch of Jamaican speech. The dramatic monologue is a form that encourages irony — Bennett's work is pervasively ironic.

In a typical poem, 'No Lickle Twang', a Creole-speaking mother expresses disappointment that her son, after spending six months in the USA, has returned with none of the expected status symbols to show he has been away — he has no fashionable foreign clothes, no gold teeth, no gold chain, and, most disappointing of all, no American accent:

> Yuh mean yuh go dah Merica
> An spen six whole mont deh
> An come back not a piece better
> Dan how yuh did go weh?
>
> Bwoy, yuh no shame? Is so yuh come?
> After yuh tan so lang!
> Not even lickle language, bwoy?
> Not even lickle twang?

The persona of the poem deems it better to be impressive than to be intelligible. These stanzas suggest a comment not only on attitudes to language but also on colonial reverence for whatever comes from abroad.

Through the comedy, beyond the laughter, there is an ongoing social critique in Bennett's work. Her writings evaluate. They pillory pretension and self-contempt. They ridicule class and colour prejudice; they criticize people ashamed of being Jamaican or ashamed of being black. They respect, but sometimes criticize, the values and perceptions of the ordinary Jamaican, the 'small man' struggling in systems he does not yet control. What is implied in Bennett's Anancy stories and in her creative radio commentaries ('Miss Lou's Views') is consistent with the values in the poems. She celebrates Jamaican culture, often incorporating the metaphoric richness and wisdom of Jamaican proverbs.

Before Bennett, **Claude McKay** and others had attempted to write effectively in Creole; except perhaps for Edward Cordle of Barbados, no Caribbean poet prior to Bennett managed to seem authentic. Bennett's achievement has cleared the way for many other writers, especially performance poets such as **Paul Keens-Douglas**, **Mikey Smith**, and **Mutabaruka**, who have frequently acknowledged her influence.

MERVYN MORRIS

Further reading: Lloyd Brown, *West Indian Poetry* (rev. 1984).

BENSON, MARY (1919–)

South African biographer, novelist, autobiographer

She was born in Pretoria, South Africa, into a typical white, middle-class South African family. She left South Africa as a teenager, identifying fully with the colonial conception that 'true' civilization was to be found in Europe and North America. But while working in London, England, Benson read **Alan Paton**'s *Cry, the Beloved Country* (1948), which shattered her complacency and began her long career as a committed spokesperson for, and writer on, Southern African humanitarian and racial issues. During the 1950s she worked as secretary to the Treason Trial Defence Fund. In 1965 Benson reported for the London *Observer* on political trials in the Eastern Cape. The following year she was banned and placed under house arrest and, unable to publish her writings or to be quoted in South Africa, she went into exile in London.

Benson's achievement has been to document the history (both national and individual) of Southern Africa at a time when colonial control was at its most absolute. Her biography *Nelson Mandela* (1986; revised 1990) formed part of an ongoing exercise in reconstruction as Benson attempted to recover and reassert silenced voices. Her history of the African National Congress, *The African Patriots* (1962; reissued in 1966 and 1985 as *South Africa: The Struggle for a Birthright*), and her biographies *Albert Lutuli of South Africa* (1963) and *Tshekedi Khama* (1960) were published at a time when their subjects were banned, silenced, imprisoned, or banished.

Much of Benson's work records and reveals lives and histories that would otherwise have been lost. Thus, many of her projects focus on publicizing the violation of human rights inherent in the apartheid system: her radio plays for the British Broadcasting Corporation include 'Nelson Mandela and the Rivonia Trial' (broadcast 1972) and 'Robben Island — A Place of Martyrs' (broadcast 1976). She edited *The Sun Will Rise*: *Statements from the Dock* (1974; repr. 1981) — testimonies of prisoners in political trials — and she also adapted tapes of Winnie Mandela's life as *Part of My Soul* (1985; first published in German in 1984), edited by Anne Benjamin.

Benson's work reveals her essentially liberal-humanist stance, and her depictions of public figures tend to exemplify attitudes and ideals that she herself values rather than provide rigorous interrogations of character. Her biography of Mandela, for instance, concentrates on discrediting the demonized image of him favoured by the South African authorities by locating Mandela's story within the tradition of the 'Jim-comes-to-Jo'burg' fictive convention, thus making his story uncontentious and familiar.

Benson's autobiography, *A Far Cry: The Making of a South African* (1989), centres on an investigation of what it means to be South African. Like Helen Joseph in her autobiography *Side By Side* (1986), Benson defines herself primarily through her public activities. She relies heavily on her interaction with well-known public figures to give shape and purpose to her life. In contrast, her autobiographical novel *At the Still Point* (1969), while revealing a clear political agenda, gives space, behind the thinly veiled fictionality, for more intimate, personal concern.

DIANNE STEWART

Further reading: Michael Chapman, 'A certain responsibility: interview with Mary Benson,' *Current Writing: Text and Reception in Southern Africa* 1 (1991).

BERRY, JAMES (1924–)

Jamaican/British poet, short-story writer

He was born in Jamaica and grew up there, but left to work briefly in the USA before immigrating to the UK in 1948. The poems in his first collection, *Fractured Circles* (1979), chart the life of Caribbean immigrants in the London of the 1950s: the hustle for work and warmth, the petty and not-so-petty racism, and a sense of a betrayal by the 'mother country'. But his poems of that period also catch, uniquely, the spirit of adventure and elation that the 'country bwoy' making life in the big city retained, despite all the aggravation.

Even in the early poems, the persona's language establishes a distinctive 'way of saying' that is both Berry's individual voice and a whole culture's cadence. Berry has been at the forefront of the struggle to validate and honour the language that people of Caribbean origin in Britain actually speak, including its capacity to adapt and to accommodate new experience. In several poems in the wonderfully evocative 'Lucy's Letters' sequence — in which Lucy, a long-time exile from Jamaica, writes home to her friend Leela, who has never left the village — the creolized voice of West Indian London becomes both the medium and the message.

The Lucy poems — included in his second collection, *Lucy's Letters and Loving* (1982) — often move towards conclusions that take the form of Jamaican proverbs. Berry has since adapted other traditional Caribbean forms and has taken energy from the folk beliefs of the region, particularly the Anancy stories. Of his several Anancy poems, Berry's interest in that tradition is best focused in his collection of tall tales, *Anancy Spiderman* (1988).

Berry's respect for the region's folk culture has led him to investigate its roots in an African past still 'submerged' in Caribbean consciousness. Early poems such as 'Black Study Students' responded to the energy that the communal rediscovery of African history released, while others, such as the cathartic 'Reclamation', from the collection *Chain of Days* (1985), chart a personal rite of passage. A concern with Africa and a concomitant political awareness inform all Berry's later work and underpin his pivotal role as a cultural activist. His anthologies of poetry by 'Westindian-British' (his term) writers — *Bluefoot Traveller* (1976) and *News for Babylon* (1984) — provide important platforms for writers who might otherwise have remained unheard.

The various aspects of Berry's cultural work interrelate; his collection of stories *A Thief in the Village* (1989) largely emerges from memories of his own childhood in Jamaica, stirred, possibly, by his work in schools. The collection's widespread use within the mainstream British school system reinforced Berry's overall cultural project to the extent that, in the introduction to his collection of poems, *When I Dance* (1988), he could remark that 'the old excluding culture' was finally beginning to change, to accommodate and value a voice like his that could celebrate, without romanticizing, the experience of Caribbean people in Britain. The poems in *When I Dance* confidently assert, 'Nobody else makes the words / I shape with sound when I talk.'

STEWART BROWN

BEST, ELSDON (1856–1931)
New Zealand ethnologist
He was born at Porirua, near Wellington, New Zealand, and as a young man developed an interest in Maori people and their customs. From 1895 Best held a variety of minor government posts in the Urewera district and took the opportunity to collect ethnographic information about the local Tuhoe people. During fifteen years of intermittent field work among this tribe — he later spent shorter periods with other Maori communities — Best acquired fluency in the Maori language and access to a wealth of traditional lore, much of which he reported in articles in both learned journals and newspapers. Appointed ethnologist to the Dominion Museum in 1910, his primary concern thereafter was the publication of definitive ethnographic works to preserve in print the cultural residues of a 'dying race'. In addition to a substantial publication on Tuhoe tribal lore and genealogies, *Tuhoe: The Children of the Mist* (2 vols, 1925), Best compiled ten large monographs, including *The Stone Implements of the Maori* (1912), all written in an engagingly trenchant style; he summarized his researches in a standard ethnography, *The Maori* (2 vols, 1924).

If Best's work marks the finest achievement of those numerous autodidacts who found intellectual stimulation through contemplation of the indigenes, it also exhibits the more problematic characteristics of such discourse — esoteric knowledge desacralized through transmission in print; the paternalism of sympathetic portrayals of the 'primitive' culture; the projection of European intellectual fancies upon the data; and the concern with the 'ancient' Maori rather than with the contemporary people. What Best produced was not so much *The Maori As He Was* (1924), but the Maori as he wanted them to have been. As Ranginui Walker has observed, the 'expropriation of knowledge and its transformation from the spoken to the written word is just one of the many facets of colonization.'

PETER GIBBONS

Further reading: M. P. K. Sorrenson, *Maori Origins and Migrations: The Genesis of Some Pakeha Myths and Legends* (1979).

BETHELL, MARY URSULA (1874–1945)
New Zealand poet
Born at Horsell, Surrey, England, she immigrated with her parents to Rangiora, Canterbury, New Zealand, in 1881, then divided much of her life between the two countries before finally settling at 'Rise Cottage' on the Cashmere Hills, Christchurch, in 1924 — the setting of her first volume of poems, *From a Garden in the Antipodes* (1929). In the intervening years Bethell had been educated in Christchurch and England, studied painting and music in Switzerland, spent some time in an Anglican women's community in London (the 'Grey Ladies'), and devoted much of her life to social work among working-class families in London and Christchurch.

In her later life Bethell was a highly innovative New Zealand landscape poet who rejected exotic colonial pictorialism, turning instead to a plain (often ironically understated) language, in unrhymed lines of variable length, that conveyed deep personal feeling about the themes that mattered most to her: the transience of life, the insecurity of the colonists' tenure of land and history, the arrogance of much that passed as rational or scientific progress, and the difficulties and triumphs of religious faith and vision. In one of her best-known poems, 'Pause', she observes the elemental grandeur of the distant Southern Alps from her fragile garden enclosure on the Cashmere Hills, and typically concludes:

In a very little while, it may be,
When our impulsive limbs and our
  superior skulls
Have to the soil restored several ounces
  of fertiliser,

The Mother of all will take charge again,
And soon wipe away with her elements
Our small fond human enclosures.

In two later volumes, *Time and Place* (1936) and *Day and Night: Poems 1924–35* (1939), Bethell attempted a more complex, often elegiac mode of meditative utterance — more literary, perhaps, but always strongly rooted in observations of the Canterbury landscape and mountains. This mode was strongly influential on younger poets such as **Charles Brasch** and **James K. Baxter**. **Allen Curnow** saw Bethell as an important figure in the transition of New Zealand poetry from 'colonial' to 'modern' in the 1920s and 1930s. More recently, emphasis has fallen on the relevance of her personal and domestic perspectives, informed by 'alert irony', to a line of women's poetry that includes that by **Robin Hyde**, **Janet Frame**, **Fleur Adcock**, and **Elizabeth Smither**. Bethell's last, unfinished sequence, 'By the River Ashley', which returns to the landscape of her Rangiora childhood, shows this intimate, personal mode at its most accomplished.

TERRY STURM

Further reading: M. H. Holcroft, *Mary Ursula Bethell* (1975).

BHARATI, SARABHAI (1912–)
Indian dramatist
Born in Gujarat, India, she came under Mahatma **Gandhi**'s influence early in life and moved to Sabarmati Ashram, run by Gandhi in Ahmedabad, where she participated in daily chores such as sweeping, cooking, and cutting vegetables. At the Haripura session of the Indian Congress in 1930

she worked as a volunteer under **Jawaharlal Nehru**. Following the Congress she went to Kumbha Mela and while watching the masses of religious bathers in the Ganga at Haridwar, she saw a vision of Mother India.

At this time, in *Harijan* (1933–*c.*51) — a daily edited by Gandhi — Bharati read a story about an old Brahmin woman who, unable to visit Benares (one of India's holy places) due to financial hardship and physical debility, donated her savings for the digging of a well in her village from which even the untouchables would be allowed to draw water.

Inspired by her vision and this story, Bharati wrote the verse play *The Well of the People* (1943). **Rabindranath Tagore** termed it a 'rich cargo of poems'. The protagonist, the old woman whose life story is narrated by the chorus, is a representative of the 'dumb millions' of India. There is little action in the play; Bharati's style, however evocative and sometimes arresting, cannot make the play actable. However, in the pre-independence period when there was very little Indian drama in English being written or produced, *The Well of the People* was a pioneering venture. A portrait of the contemporary society, the play has undeniable historical significance.

Bharati's next play, *Two Women* (1952) — written in prose — was staged at the Excelsior Theatre, Bombay, in 1948. In contrast to the setting of poverty and the low-caste characters in the earlier play, *Two Women* is set in Saurashtra, in the lavish sitting room of a rich landowner and minister of state, Kanak Raya. The play projects 'the outer and inner life of India in transition' — the period between the launching of Gandhi's freedom movement and the achievement of Indian independence — through the tensions and conflicts arising out of the relationship between two characters, Darshan, a sculptor, and Urvashie, a singer. Darshan concludes with an observation on his sister Anuradha and her friend Urvashie who has declined to accept his offer of love: 'There are two women in each of you, one of stone and one of flesh and blood.'

Bharati's two plays in English were appreciated by contemporary intellectual and literary circles in India. The plays explore the traumatic emotional concerns of Indians in their march towards independence. But because the plays' language is stilted and stylized, they have not attracted producers or the reading public. Yet no account of Indian drama in English can overlook these early attempts in a dry period of indigenous dramatic activity in English in India.

SUBHAS CHANDRA SAHA

Further reading: S. Mokashi-Punekar, 'The plays of Bharati', in M. K. Naik and S. Mokashi-Punekar (eds) *Perspectives on Indian Drama in English* (1977).

BHATNAGAR, OM PRAKASH (1932–)

Indian poet, critic

Born in Agra, India, he was awarded an honorary Doctor of Literature degree from the World University, New York, USA, in 1979. He taught at Vidarbha Ayurved Mahavidyalaya College of Amriviti University, India, where he was head of the post-graduate department until 1992. Bhatnagar has published six volumes of poetry — *Thought Poems* (1976), *Feeling Fossils* (1977), *Angels of Retreat* (1979), *Oneiric Vision* (1980), *Shadows in Floodlights* (1984), and *The Audible Landscape* (1986). He has edited *Intercontinental Poetry* (1979), *New Dimensions in Indo-English Poetry* (1980), and *Rising Columns: Some Indian Poets in English* (1983).

The traditional themes and elevated thoughts so characteristic of Indian poets are not Bhatnagar's primary concern; he is more interested in humanity and the environment. Metaphorical issues do colour some poems, as in 'Of Self and True Self', and he also treats such themes as love and death. But his poetry's chief characteristic is its social concern.

In *Thought Poems* and *Feeling Fossils*, the darkness of Bhatnagar's vision is due to human sorrow, pain, pride, desire, hypocrisy, and moral depravity. But darkness, Bhatnagar suggests, will eventually give way to the dawn. His love poems are unusually intellectual and lacking in passion. Bhatnagar seems not to distinguish between love and sex; in this respect he differs from **Shiv K. Kumar** and **Kamala Das**, in whose work sexuality plays a prominent role.

Angels of Retreat and *The Audible Landscape* present a more optimistic view of life. Ironic in their treatment of modern intellectual trends, these two volumes offer qualified affirmation rather than denial. Birth and death are the predominant themes of *Oneiric Vision* and *Shadows in Floodlights*.

In spite of occasional excesses and repetitions, Bhatnagar's poetry merits careful reading and study.

PURNIMA MEHTA

BHATTACHARYA, BHABANI (1906–88)

Indian novelist

Born in the town of Bhagalpur, India, his mother tongue was Bengali, and his earliest writings were for a Bengali children's magazine, *Mouchak*. Bhattacharya studied at Patna College, Patna, for his BA Honours degree in English (1927), and at the University of London, England (1928–34), where he took another BA degree before proceeding to a Ph.D. in history. While a student in England, he translated into English some poems and allegorical tales of **Rabindranath Tagore** for publication in the *Spectator*; most of these were collected in his *The Golden Boat* (1932), a collection of translations from Tagore.

Bhattacharya returned to India in 1934 and settled in Nagpur with his wife Salila Mukherjee. He began writing a Sunday feature, 'This Week in Indian History', for the Madras-based newspaper the *Hindu*, and selections from this material went into his second book, *Some Memorable Yesterdays* (1941). He used the same source a few years later for *Indian Cavalcade* (1948).

The publication of Bhattacharya's first novel, *So Many Hungers!* (1947), launched him on an international career. Written in English, the novel was translated into several European languages within a few years and earned Bhattacharya recognition, somewhat inaccurately, as the representative novelist of the new India. He was appointed press attaché to the Indian embassy in Washington, USA, for a year (1949–50), and he subsequently worked briefly as assistant editor for the *Illustrated Weekly of India*. He was a member of the first Indian cultural delegation to the USSR and travelled extensively in the Soviet Union in 1951.

Bhattacharya's reputation abroad was strengthened by his extensive travels and lectures. After 1970 he and his wife lived almost continuously in the USA. Other than *So Many Hungers!*, Bhattacharya's novels were first published outside of India. During the better part of his career as a novelist, Bhattacharya was rated more highly by his foreign readers than by Indians. However, when the Sahitya Akademi, India's national academy of letters, was formed, he was nominated a member of the advisory board for Indian-English literature. In 1959 he was appointed executive secretary of the Tagore Commemorative Volume Society, a project sponsored by India's ministry of education; he was also invited by the ministry to assist in compiling a selection of English translations of Tagore's essays. The latter was published as *Towards Universal Man* in 1961, the poet's centenary year. The 1967 Sahitya Akademi award for English writing — for *Shadow from Ladakh* (1966) — capped Bhattacharya's most creative period as a writer.

Five of Bhattacharya's six novels are concerned directly or otherwise with India's emergence as a new nation. This preoccupation is presented in various situations and is tackled with different fictional strategies. In *So Many Hungers!* the British still rule India, but it is clear they cannot do so for much longer. Their failure to rule justly is represented by the terrible Bengali famine of 1942–3, a pervasive presence in the book. If at one level *So Many Hungers!* is a relentless indictment of colonial rule, *Music for Mohini* (1952) is light-hearted in comparison, handling almost allegorically the typical conflict in free India between modern progress and traditional values. Bhattacharya returns to the Bengali famine and to his more realistic mode in *He Who Rides a Tiger* (1954), but here the famine forms the background to a plot in which an underprivileged person avenges himself upon society. The critique in this work is not of foreign rule but of native inequities, such as caste discrimination, that must be removed before Indian society can support a modern nation. With *A Goddess Named Gold* (1960) the author retreats again to a less substantial world; the work is like an extended parable in which greed endangers individual freedom as a consequence of opportunities created by political independence.

In *Shadow from Ladakh* contemporary history is presented in order to pose the central dilemma in modern India's developmental efforts — whether to follow the path directed by Gandhian ideals or adopt the course traced by **Jawaharlal Nehru**'s dreams. Translated into human terms, the novel's Cambridge-educated, scholarly, and ascetic Satyajit is placed in charge of the ideal village community of Gandhigram; in nearby Steeltown the America-trained Bhashkar, chief engineer of a large modern factory, is planning expansion that threatens the future of the village. A clash becomes imminent when the government, chastened by the Chinese aggression of 1962, supports Bhashkar's plans, while Satyajit offers to organize non-violent resistance against the invaders. The crisis passes when the Chinese withdraw and Bhashkar falls in love with Satyajit's daughter and can visualize a future in which the simpler life of rural India can continue while industrial development takes place elsewhere in the country.

Bhattacharya's writing career passed its peak around 1966. He edited Sahitya Akademi's second volume of *Contemporary Indian Short Stories* (Series 2, 1967); the first volume (1959) included one of his stories, 'A Moment of Eternity'. His own collection, *Steel Hawk and Other Stories* (1968), draws upon earlier, and not very successful, efforts. Bhattacharya was given a grant by the Ford Foundation to write a volume for the **M. K. Gandhi** centennial; *Gandhi the Writer* was published in 1969. That year began his long association with Hawaii, USA, first as a specialist at the East-West Centre, then in several spells as visiting professor at the University of Hawaii. Out of his initial encounter with this Pacific retreat came his last novel, *A Dream in Hawaii* (1978), in which an Indian professor turned yogi aspires to heal certain sicknesses of American society before he himself gets caught up in its corruption. *Glimpses of Indian History* (1976) contains *Some Memorable Yesterdays* and *Indian Cavalcade; Socio-Political Currents in Bengal: A Nineteenth Century Perspective* (1980) is the doctoral dissertation he wrote in the 1930s for the University of London.

The social realism of his first and third novels brought Bhattacharya early fame. At one time critics often compared him with **Mulk Raj Anand** as an unflinching portrayer of contemporary India's flaws. In later estimation, however, he is regarded as a novelist with social purpose who has used the novel form as a vehicle for ideas and debate. Bhattacharya will always be respected as a writer of newly independent India for whom the future of his country was an abiding concern.

SUJIT MUKHERJEE

Further reading: K. K. Sharma, *Bhabani Bhatta-*

charya: His Vision and Themes (1979); R. K. Srivastava, ed., *Perspectives on Bhabani Bhattacharya* (1982); Malta Grover, *Bhabani Bhattacharya as a Novelist of Social Conscience* (1991).

BHUSHAN, V. N. (1909–51)

Indian poet, critic

Born in Machilipatnam, Andhra Pradesh, India, he studied at Benares Hindu University (MA, 1933) before becoming a professor in Maharashtra and Madhyapradesh. Bhushan's English poetical works include *Silhouettes* (1928), *Moonbeams* (1929), *Flute Tunes* (1931), *Star Fires* (1932), *Enchantments* (1934), *Horizons* (1937), *Footfalls* (1938), and *The Far Ascent* (1948). Writing at the peak of the 'Bhavakavitva' movement in Telugu poetry and profoundly influenced by **Rabindranath Tagore**, Bhushan found his authentic lyric voice in English, a voice distinguished by a lively imagination, exuberant feeling, and a keen sense of expressive form. His poetry marks the activization of the romantic impulse in its characteristic mutations of the Indian sensibility: idealism, mysticism, naturalism, and nationalism. Bhushan regarded poetry as a hieratic realm 'full of treasures — dreams, hopes, visions, ecstasies, a devotion to something afar, winged words and wizard phrases'. He also published two plays, *Samyukta* (1933) and *Mortal Coils* (1934), besides editing Shakespeare and writing a critical study of comedy and tragedy, *Hawk over Heron* (1944), which contains interesting comparativist crosslights from western and oriental drama.

With **K. R. S. Iyengar**, Bhushan promoted and established Indian-English literature as a serious and relevant area of critical attention and academic pursuit. His *The Peacock Lute* (1945, poetry), *The Moving Finger* (1945, criticism), *The Blaring Shrine* (1946, one-act plays), and *The Earthen Bowl* (1945, short stories) were pioneering anthologies of Indian creative writing in English. Bhushan viewed Indian-English poetry as a product of the east-west synthesis, reflecting the mainstream Indian literary tradition as it is mediated by the modern cultural dynamic and characterized by 'a Virgilian sadness' and a sense of 'intense brooding reflection . . . combining the metaphysical symbolism of the Upanishads, the contemplative passivity of Buddhism, the luscious eroticism of Sanskrit poetry, the subtle symbolism of the singer saints of South India and the sensuous Court Poetry of Medieval India'. He also formulated the well-known paradigm of imitation-Indianization-individualization in plotting the growth of Indian-English poetry.

Although Bhushan's creative work and his critical idiom are no longer fashionable, his historical contribution to Indian-English literary studies remains undisputed.

D. V. K. RAGHAVACHARYULU

Further reading: V. N. Bhushan, 'Behold the blossoms', introduction to *The Peacock Lute* (1945).

BIOGRAPHY

See **LIFE WRITING**

BIRNEY, EARLE (1904–)

Canadian poet, novelist, dramatist

Born of a Scottish father and an English mother in Calgary, Canada, in what was then Canada's Northwest Territories, he spent his early childhood on the family homestead near Morningside, Alberta, before the family moved to Banff. He enrolled at the University of British Columbia in 1922, originally in engineering, later in honours English. Doctoral studies in medieval literature at Berkeley, USA, and Toronto, Canada, were not completed until 1936, much of his energy in this period going to the radical political activity of the 1930s. Birney served in the Canadian army as a personnel officer during the Second World War. After earlier pedagogic wanderings he taught full-time at the University of British Columbia from 1946 to 1965, heading a newly created department of creative writing in 1963.

Best known as a poet, Birney is also the author of two novels, *Turvey* (1949) and *Down the Long Table* (1955), and of fourteen radio plays, some of them adaptations. While he wrote through much of his youth, his first book, *David and Other Poems*, did not appear until 1942. Two further volumes were published in the 1940s — *Now Is Time* (1945) and *The Strait of Anian* (1948), which includes some poems from the previous volumes. *Trial of a City and Other Verse* (1952) contains thirteen poems and the titular verse drama (given its manuscript title *The Damnation of Vancouver* in all other printings). From the 1960s on appeared *Ice, Cod, Bell or Stone* (1962), *Near False Creek Mouth* (1964), *Rag and Bone Shop* (1971), *What's So Big About Green?* (1973), *The Rugging and the Moving Times* (1976), *Fall by Fury*, and the stories and sketches of *Big Bird in the Bush* (both 1978), along with non-fiction, six volumes of selected poems, and the *Collected Poems* (1975). A final volume of new and selected poems, *Last Makings*, appeared in 1991. Birney has twice won a Governor General's Award for Poetry, for *David and Other Poems* in 1942 and for *Now Is Time* in 1945.

After a slow start Birney's writing career has been long and varied, with significant production sustained with accelerating pace over forty years. Until the 1960s it moved restlessly through a multifaceted modernism. Always, however, the modernism was Canadian, touched by political issues inherent in the post-colonial condition (elements seen also in the works of **F. R. Scott** and **Dorothy Livesay**). For this reason, satire, that mode exemplary of commitment, is a frequent feature of this poetry as well as the later. From this period come such frequently anthologized pieces as the Joycean 'Mammorial Stunzas to Aimee Simple McFarcin', 'Bushed', 'Slug in Woods', and 'Anglosaxon Street'. Ingenious and closely wrought structures, concentrated effects, and a studied impersonality link such works with the international movement, which in Birney's work must be seen as reactive to a prevalent nineteenth-century manner associated with colonialism. The now-classic narrative poem 'David' in many ways exemplifies the affiliations that dominated his work for nearly two decades. Set in the Rocky Mountains, the poem recounts a young man's discovery of self and place through the friendship of and shared experiences with David, a slightly older 'mountain man' who teaches him climbing and the lore of the mountains. Its tight structure and vivid imagery provide formal strength and signal its affiliation with Canadian modernism; its celebration of a majestic but unromantically alien nature form its distinctively post-colonial base, and its narrative of euthanasian murder continues to appeal to a major receptive audience of young readers.

From the late 1950s through the 1960s, sponsored by the newly formed **Canada Council** and other agencies, Birney travelled and read widely and internationally. While it is impossible to date its beginnings precisely, the later poetic manner — more playful, personal, and informal — becomes evident in this period. Its ground is both in medium (the extension of language beyond the poetic 'standard') and in place (the use of the 'language of the tribe'). There is much experimentation with concrete verse. Spacing largely replaces conventional punctuation, and earlier poems are so revised even if retaining most other original features. A comparison of early and later versions of a poem such as 'The Bear on the Delhi Road' makes the gain clear. The linguistic zest is also extended orally, the modernist formality of the earlier poems abandoned for a more flexible and idiomatic voice. Poems frequently incorporate the dialect of others — Australian, Fijian, American — orthographically captured. 'To Swindon from London by BritRail Aloud/Bagatelle' is a stunning oral mimesis of the journey described in the title. Anecdote, a particularly Canadian post-colonial mode, frequently provides narrative structure, as in 'ARRIVALS Wolfville/Locals . . .', and meditative modes of the earlier period recur ('El Greco: Espolio'). In the late 1970s some tender and moving love poems emerge. In both early and later writings Birney's social, political, and ecological commitments frequently surface, always distinguishing his writing from the artistic detachment of modernism and the relativism of postmodernism.

It is difficult to find exact parallels to Birney in other post-colonial writers. Like **V. S. Naipaul,** he travels widely, but unlike him retains his native roots and commitments. Like **A. D. Hope,** he comes to terms with modernism, but his departure from it is not into classicism but rather to the poetic experimentation of young Canadian writers less than half his age — **bp Nichol,** Judith Copithorne, Andy Suknaski. Like **Wilson Harris,** he tries to speak on behalf of an entire nation/region, but where Harris is a moral visionary Birney focuses more pessimistically on the contradictions, disorders, and failings of the times. The redemptions of his poems are distinctively his: of dancing in the Caribbean at **George Lamming**'s, of finding the mouse celebrated in **Al Purdy**'s poems, of a boy flying a kite in Japan. They are, like Birney, of the margin, and powerfully so.

IAN ADAM

Further reading: Peter Aichinger, *Earle Birney* (1979); Peter Noel-Bentley, 'Earle Birney: an annotated bibliography', in Robert Lecker and Jack David (eds) *The Annotated Bibliography of Canada's Major Authors* 4 (1983).

BISSETT, BILL (1939–)

Canadian poet

Born in Halifax, Canada, and a proud university drop-out, he has lived principally in Vancouver and London, Canada. Among the most substantial of his more than fifty books are *nobody owns th earth* (1971), *MEDICINE my mouths on fire* (1974), *canada gees mate for life* (1985), and *what we have* (1989), which won the Milton Acorn People's Poetry Award. Several of these books incorporate visionary cover art by the poet, who is also a prolific painter. Unusually, bissett makes poetry by *narrowing* his vocabulary and linguistic resources. He attempts to democratize poetry by honouring a vernacular far removed from the Canadian Broadcasting Corporation ideal and more readily appreciated in performance, or in his many recordings, than in print. His chanting, accompanied by rattles (shamanistic and child's toy), is hypnotic yet sensitive to the meanings of intonation. His stubbornly naïve radicalism gives him a prominence in international sound poetry often unappreciated within Canada.

bissett's typical poem features repeated colloquial tags, graphic play with type, and quasi-phonetic spelling. His lower-case, anti-power-structure politics is distantly allied with the simpler poems of Australian **Michael Dransfield** and the concrete poetry of Australian Peter Murphy. But in his emphasis on the integrity and freedom of restricted codes, bissett comes closer to the black street English of Jamaican poet **E. K. Brathwaite**.

In divesting language of its hierarchical principles, bissett attempts to be 'the voice uv ths things speaking thru us'. Insistent repetition of a few general, monosyllabic nouns — sky, wind, grass, fire, clouds, sun — and the verbs 'dew' and 'cum' mark a primitivism that 'dreem[s] / we are all / whun / creature'. Through cheeky anecdotes burlesquing establishment norms, a proclivity for the forms of indigenous peoples, ecological themes, and privately eccentric notation, bissett manages to be both at the edge of contemporary movements in language art and at the centre of the democratization of poetry.

LAURIE RICOU

Further reading: Len Early, 'Introduction', *Selected Poems: Beyond Even Faithful Legends* by bill bissett (1980); Steve McCaffery, 'bill bissett: a writing outside writing', *Open Letter* 3 (1978).

Bissoondath, Neil (1955–)
Trinidadian/Canadian novelist, short-story writer
Born in Arima, Trinidad, he spent his childhood in Sangre Grande before immigrating to Canada in 1973 on the advice of his uncle, **V. S. Naipaul.** After graduating from York University, Toronto (BA, 1977), he taught French and English as second languages. In 1984 he received a Banff School of Fine Arts writing scholarship, which led to the publication of *Digging Up the Mountains* (1985), a collection of stories. The novels *A Casual Brutality* (1988) and *The Innocence of Age* (1992) and another volume of stories, *On the Eve of Uncertain Tomorrows* (1990), followed. These works and several published essays have established Bissoondath as a vibrant new writer on the Canadian, Caribbean, and post-colonial scene.

Bissoondath's fiction focuses on the individual's sense of placelessness and alienation in a new society. As *Digging Up the Mountains* shows, the lives of immigrants are fraught with insecurity and disillusionment. Bissoondath attempts, with varying success, to portray protagonists of different ethnic backgrounds and of both genders — for example, an East Indian father in 'Insecurity', a young Japanese woman in 'The Cage', and a female Guatemalan in 'In the Kingdom of the Golden Dust'. *On the Eve of Uncertain Tomorrows* foregrounds even more darkly the loneliness and distress of immigrants and refugees. In the title story, two Latin American refugees dread their appearance at a hearing that decides their refugee status. They are as helpless as the women in 'Kira and Anna' who, marginalized as immigrants, become pawns of unscrupulous men. Bissoondath's depiction of his immigrant protagonists lacks **Sam Selvon**'s comic affirmation in *The Lonely Londoners* (1956). Pessimistic and at times depressing, his stories are closer to V. S. Naipaul's 'Tell Me Who to Kill', in his *In a Free State* (1971).

A Casual Brutality emphasizes the East Indian immigrant's rootlessness and instability. A medical doctor from the Caribbean who has been studying and living in Toronto returns home with his white Canadian wife and their son. The violent deaths of the wife and son in a political uprising send him back to Canada, which for him is simply a haven, not a home. Like his ancestors, whose journey from India to the Caribbean left them adrift, he is now the perpetual itinerant.

In *The Innocence of Age* Bissoondath's protagonist is a white Canadian whose alienation from family members parallels that of the novel's many secondary immigrant characters. Bissoondath's appropriation of the voice of a white Canadian, like **George Ryga**'s of a Native Canadian in *The Ecstasy of Rita Joe* (1970), enables him to propose that beneath overt differences and stereotypes all alienated individuals need to be loved and understood. As in his stories, Bissoondath captures well the feel of place, using the setting as a metaphor for estrangement. The protagonist watches helplessly as Toronto changes from a friendly, peaceful city to a fast-paced metropolis with skin-heads, drug pushers, immigrants, and defensive police reeling under charges of brutality and racism.

RUBY RAMRAJ

Further reading: Victor J. Ramraj, 'Still arriving', in Emmanuel Nelson (ed.) *Reworlding: Essays on the Literature of the Indian Diaspora* (1992).

Black, Stephen (1880–1931)
South African dramatist, novelist
He was born in poor circumstances in Cape Town, South Africa, to an alcoholic British bookkeeper and his Capetonian wife. By 1903 Black was known as a featherweight boxer; in 1904 he first went to school at Diocesan College, Cape Town, on an athletic scholarship. As sporting correspondent for *The Cape Argus Weekly* he also wrote sketches in the vernacular on low life in the magistrate's courts. In 1908 Rudyard Kipling 'discovered' Black, commending his use of local colour.

Edwardian theatre in South Africa was on the typical circuit of British companies 'playing the Empire' from Cape Town to Sydney. (See **Drama**, South Africa.) In 1908 Black scratched together from stranded music-hall performers the first substantial South African production, *Love and the Hyphen* (1984). Like Australian George Darrell's *The Sunny South* (premièred 1883; first published in 1975), Black's play includes representative spectacles of colonial life, but his mode was not melodrama: he mixed drawing-room social comedy with ribald farce. *Love and the Hyphen* praises the spirit of the National Convention of that year, which attempted to reconstruct the post-Second Anglo-Boer War world by bringing the four British colonies into Union in 1910. The departure of the colonial power's garrison and the rise of local politicians is celebrated in the play as both whites and Coloureds foresee opportunities for self-expressive nation-building and more equal, responsible status. Between 1909 and 1929 *Love and the Hyphen* was revived for six distinct seasons.

In his second play, *Helena's Hope, Ltd.* (1984; premièred 1909), which is named after a gold-mine and which still holds the record for most performances (approximately 600) of any South African play, Black formed the nucleus of his repertory company with himself as playwright, manager, and leading man. He wrote another dozen scripts over the years, which the company toured as far as Victoria Falls (in modern Zimbabwe). *Helena's Hope, Ltd.* outlines the penetration of the imperial cash economy in the rural Transvaal, and the lure of the industrial city for poor settlers and dispossessed indigenes alike. The hero is an independent English pressman who lives by exposing extortion and corruption, siding with the locals in their struggle. For himself Black wrote the role of Zachariah, an 'Uncle Tom' who learns to survive as a swindler.

During the First World War, Black moved to London, England, and worked as the *Daily Mail*'s theatre critic before immigrating with his French wife to Nice, France, in order to farm. There he wrote the satirical novel *The Dorp* ('The Village', 1920), a comedy that pits 'Boer' against 'Brit' over a young mixed couple's intended marriage. Another novel, *The Golden Calf* (1925), deals with illicit diamond buying.

On his return to South Africa in 1925, Black rewrote and revived his many shows. Beaten, however, by talking films, he turned to running a satirical weekly paper, *The Sjambok* (1929–31). The paper strongly resisted the control of the entertainment industry by London and Hollywood, and first published the work of many South Africans such as **Herman Charles Bosman**. Crippled by libel suits, Black died bankrupt. Today he is known as the 'father' of South African English-language drama.

STEPHEN GRAY

Further reading: M. F. Cartwright, 'Stephen Black: a chronology', *English in Africa* 2 (1981); Stephen Gray, ed., *Stephen Black: Three Plays* (1984).

BLACK WRITERS IN BRITAIN

There is evidence of small numbers of black people in Britain since at least the second century AD; they worked as soldiers with the Roman imperial army and as entertainers, musicians, and servants in royal households. As a result of Britain's role in the Atlantic slave trade from the sixteenth through the eighteenth centuries, their numbers steadily increased. Royal proclamations, parish register entries, and documents relating to the slave trade testify to their silent presence and to prevailing social prejudices about dark-skinned people. By the mid-eighteenth century, the 15,000-strong London black community found its voice and began to give accounts of life among pale-skinned people. Acquiring and using a new language and literacy skills were fundamental rites of passage in the process of assimilation to, and commentary on, British society. Emerging from the silent status of the observed to seize the word, the early black writers mastered language in their oral accounts, speeches, letters, and written texts.

The earliest accounts — Briton Hammon's *A Narrative of the Uncommon Sufferings, and Surprizing Deliverance of Briton Hammon, A Negro Man* (1760) and Ukawsaw Gronniosaw's (*c*.1710) *A Narrative of the Most Remarkable Particulars in the Life of James Albert Ukawsaw Gronniosaw, An African Prince, as Related by Himself* (*c*.1770) — treat a variety of subjects: adventurous sea travel, cultural adjustment, precarious survival, and religious conversion. Complex personal, familial, and social relationships emerge in most of the early writing. Gronniosaw's moving scenes of family life, often in extreme poverty, may be compared with details of relatively comfortable family life given by the erudite African Ignatius Sancho (1729–80) in his *Letters of the Late Ignatius Sancho* (1782). Sancho's witty correspondence with famous and ordinary men and women conveys his skilled use of the English language, his knowledge of the arts, literature, and politics and the ups and downs of trade in his Westminster grocery shop. A number of the eighteenth-century slave narrators — Gronniosaw, **Olaudah Equiano**, and Ottobah Cugoano (*c*.1757) — include memories of African childhood in their autobiographical accounts of the journey from slavery to freedom. Mary Prince (*c*.1788) broke the silence of the female slave in the first substantial account by a female slave narrator, *The History of Mary Prince, A West Indian Slave* (1831). Like Hammon and Gronniosaw, Prince dictated her account to a white amanuensis; Prince's account was then edited by a second hand. Equiano is thought to be the 'invisible hand' shaping Cugoano's narrative for publication. The multiple 'voices' in these accounts are fundamental to the slave narrative tradition, foregrounding complex relationships and issues of authorial control and self-representation.

Black people who spoke and wrote their experiences implicitly refuted prevailing myths and ideologies that denied all black people full human status and dignity. Since such myths and ideologies helped justify the slave trade, their words were essential in the Anti-Slavery movement. In Equiano's two-volume autobiography, *The Interesting Narrative of the Life of Olaudah Equiano, or Gustavus Vassa, the African, written by Himself* (1789), the skilled use of irony and foregrounding of African identity result in a subtle and complex analysis of slavery personally experienced. His public speaking and letter writing against the slave trade also established him as the principal black spokesman in the British Anti-Slavery movement. Cugoano's *Thoughts and Sentiments on the Evil and Wicked Traffic of the Slavery and Commerce of the Human Species* (1787) is overt and strident in condemning slavery; as such it may be compared with the autobiographical account of the radical Jamaican-Scots preacher Robert Wedderburn (*c*.1761–*c*.1835), *The Horrors of Slavery* (1824).

Unwilling travellers of the African diaspora were pioneers of African, Caribbean, Black-British and African-American literary traditions. Common patterns and themes are repeated and revised from the earliest oral accounts through the creative work of contemporary black writers. Mary Prince is important in relation to contemporary Caribbean women's writing and nineteenth-century African-American women's writing, especially Harriet Jacobs' (*c*.1815–97) *Incidents in the Life of a Slave Girl, Written by Herself* (1861). Toni Morrison's (1931–) novel *Beloved* (1987) is the finest example of a number of neo-slave narratives by African-American authors. The symbolic importance of the African woman figured in Negritude poetry and in African literature emerging at the time of nationhood is anticipated in Equiano's placement of his own mother in his memories of 'Mother Africa'. West African writers resident in Britain can be linked to the early writers: **Buchi Emecheta**'s novels revise and challenge stereotypes of 'Mother Africa'; **Ben Okri**'s stunning novels, including *The Famished Road* (1991), celebrate the life-affirming power of storytelling. **Sam Selvon**'s early life in Trinidad, followed by residence in England and Canada, traces a geography of cross-cultural experience common in early black and post-colonial writing. Selvon's brilliant use of dialect in novels sharing a Caribbean focus testifies to the continued importance of the spoken word to inscribe unique individual and cultural identity. **Caryl Phillips** directly engages eighteenth-century accounts as source and inspiration for the diasporan setting, characters, and complex relationships in his novel *Cambridge* (1991). Phillips' earliest novels move between the Caribbean, his birthplace, and the U.K., where he grew up and was educated. In Equiano's words, the reader may 'look back with pleasure' to an unbroken arch of continuity from the early black writers in Britain to the flourishing traditions of black creativity today.

POLLY REWT

Further reading: Peter Fryer, *Staying Power: A History of Black People in Britain* (1984); Prabhu Guptara, *Black British Literature: An Annotated Bibliography* (1986); Keith A. Sandiford, *Measuring the Moment: Strategies of Protest in Eighteenth-Century Afro-English Writing* (1988); Paul Edwards and David Dabydeen, eds, *Black Writers in Britain: 1760–1890* (1991).

BLAINEY, GEOFFREY (1930–)

Australian historian

Born in Victoria, Australia, he has pursued his career both independently and at the University of Melbourne. His historical interests have ranged exceptionally widely, from mining — *The Peaks of Lyell* (1954), *The Rush That Never Ended* (1963) — to banking and other institutions — *Gold and Paper: A History of the National Bank of Australasia* (1958) — to Aborigines, to the growth of colonial Australian society — *Our Side of the Country* (1984) — to human conflict — *The Causes of War* (1973) — to the long-term oscillations between optimism and pessimism in the Western world — *The Great Seesaw: A New View of the Western World, 1750–2000* (1988). Between these major works Blainey has published a number of iconoclastic ones — *Across a Red World* (1968), a reflective account of a railway journey across China, Siberia, and Russia, and *All for Australia* (1984), which, by questioning the government's immigration policy, embroiled him in considerable public controversy. His television series *The Blainey View* (1982) brought together many of his interests in economics, war, and world events. He has been an active member of the **Literature Board** of the **Australia Council**, the Australia-China Council, and the Australian Heritage Commission.

Of all his works, Blainey is likely to be most remembered for *The Triumph of the Nomads: A History of Ancient Australia* (1975), which presents traditional Aboriginal society in an exceptionally sympathetic light and which remains valuable, despite subsequent very rapid advances in knowledge of Aboriginal prehistory and ethnography, and especially for *The Tyranny of Distance: How Distance Shaped Australia's History* (1966), whose title has become a signifier of national experience.

Blainey's great strengths as a writer lie in his ability to present the results of specialist studies in a way intelligible to general audiences and to convey the nature of past circumstance by way of a striking analogy with the present. Together with **Manning Clark**, Blainey largely created the post-Second World War audience for Australian history, and has been instrumental in taking a society becoming conscious of itself past its colonial cringe.

ALAN FROST

Blaise, Clark (1940–)

Canadian novelist, short-story writer

Professing to be the 'only Canadian writer to come from Fargo, North Dakota', he has lived in Cincinnati, Pittsburgh, Jacksonville (Florida), Springfield (Missouri), Montreal, New York, and Iowa City. Blaise's work is similarly diffuse, with numerous locations in the United States, Canada, and India — this last being the birthplace of his wife, **Bharati Mukherjee**, also a writer and the co-author of two of his works, *Days and Nights in Calcutta* (1977) and *The Sorrow and the Terror* (1987). Blaise is better known for his short stories — *A North American Education* (1973), *Tribal Justice* (1974), *Resident Alien* (1986) — than for his novels — *Lunar Attractions* (1979), and *Lusts* (1983). Both the shorter and the longer fiction, however, provide variations on a theme: himself. Obsessively self-conscious, unashamedly self-indulgent, Blaise's fictions are perhaps best seen as autobiographical explorations of 'the whereness of who and what I am'. The quest is continuous, for out of the traversal of a series of different environments emerges a succession of different selves, each as accidental, as impermanent, and finally as inadequate as the last. For Blaise, autobiography is a continual process of self-invention. But as the selves multiply and scatter, the writer becomes alienated from his own creations; the writing self contemplates the written self and finds it 'other'.

Alternately exhibitionist and paranoid, Blaise's wilfully eccentric narrator-protagonists draw the reader into complicity with their voyeuristic activities. The delight of seeing is offset by the fear of being seen: to read Blaise (reading himself) is to collaborate in an ambivalent process of self-creation in which much is revealed but more concealed, and the writer is as likely to deceive the reader as he is to confide in him. Blaise's prose style is no less duplicitous, making frequent use of paradox and oxymoron. Self-parody is a prevalent mode: Blaise sizes up his first-person narrators, his child and adolescent characters, and his neurotic obsessions with the past, then declares himself to be 'wedded like a reborn Wordsworth to the epic of my own becoming'.

Yet if, in his serio-comic quest for 'identity' — as a man, as a writer, as a born-again Canadian — Blaise is haunted by a fear of failure, he is also struck by the advantages of indeterminacy. For Blaise, autobiography is less a process of self-discovery than one of self-estrangement; but like several other contemporary writers from Canada and different parts of the Commonwealth, Blaise is as much given to celebrating his own sense of displacement as he is to lamenting it. Blaise is understandably wary of the 'Commonwealth' label, believing that Commonwealth literature, 'a category without conscious (or admitted) practitioners, claiming participants from every race, religion and national background, from six continents and Oceania . . . either points to a spontaneous fertility that is humbling or a loose Platonism that is embarrassing.' Blaise does recognize his affinity, however, with other Commonwealth writers whose material, like his own, 'has been tractlessness, [a] grasping for compasses, [an] envy of those who were born knowing what they were, or never having to ask.' Unsurprisingly, Blaise cites his admiration for **V. S. Naipaul**, but his work probably has more in common with that of an Australian, **David Malouf**, another writer of mixed background and wandering habits whose autobiographical fictions chart the uncertain movements of a self that both seeks and resists definition. Like Blaise's, Malouf's stories radiate outwards from an undefined centre, co-ordinating the 'otherness' of a self that remains elusive, multiform, dynamic. In their challenge to the notion of fixed identity — personal, cultural or national — Blaise and Malouf align themselves with a new generation of Commonwealth writers whose work is less concerned with describing a (colonial) condition of exile than with exploring the heterogeneity of (post-colonial) societies such as Canada's or Australia's that thrive on the capacity to locate — and invent — themselves anew.

GRAHAM HUGGAN

Further reading: Robert Lecker, *An Other I: The Fiction of Clark Blaise* (1988).

BLAND, PETER (1934–)

New Zealand poet

Born in Yorkshire, England, he immigrated to New Zealand in 1954 and became prominent in the Wellington group of poets and as co-founder of Downstage Theatre. Returning to the UK in 1968, he was immediately successful as a professional actor; a film role led him to resume residence in New Zealand in 1985.

As an immigrant, Bland lived in a state house and was obliged to work in the public service, a life that defines the parameters of most of his early poems and plays. As an actor, his early reputation rested on comic inventiveness, and satire of suburbia was prominent in his early writing. But Bland's state house was not merely an arena for domestic absurdity or trivialization; *Fathers' Day* (first published in *Landfall* 21, 1967) is a full-length stage analysis of the tensions between three women in a mind-destroying social environment.

Bland's immigrant perspective, especially in *My Side of the Story* (1964), brought an immediacy to New Zealand poetry, some of which had been preoccupied with origins, ancestry, and national identity. His rootlessness meant that his scrutiny was of surfaces, devoid of mystery and myth, but nevertheless often loaded with enigma. Here, Bland found an affinity with other Wellington poets of the 1950s, notably **James K. Baxter** and **Louis Johnson**.

In England, Bland's poet's eye searched through fifteen years of absence for residues of childhood. That it was also a New Zealand gaze is wryly acknowledged in the personae of *The Crusoe Factor* (1985), *Mr Maui* (1976) — which alludes to the mythical Polynesian discoverer — and the edged Auckland nostalgias of *Paper Boats* (1991).

HOWARD McNAUGHTON

BLIGHT, JOHN (1913–)

Australian poet

Born in Unley, South Australia, he has spent most of his life in Queensland. His substantial contribution to Australian poetry is based largely on his obsessive preoccupation with what he has called his 'sea sonnets', short poems of precise observation and speculation using as first reference the myriad life-forms (nonhuman and human) of the ocean, the littoral, and specifically the coastal areas of Queensland: reef life, bay life, and holiday makers. Although these sonnets are substantially collected in three individual volumes that almost cover Blight's full writing career — *A Beachcomber's Diary* (1963), *My Beachcombing Days* (1968), and *Holiday Sea Sonnets* (1985) — his *Selected Poems* (1976), which received both the National Book Council and Patrick White awards, also reveals a more urban, if not urbane, imagination. Blight's concern with contemporary social issues is highlighted in the opening section of his *Selected Poems* under the heading 'Poems 1969–1975'. This was the period of the Vietnam conflict and Blight's responsiveness was reflected not only in an opening up of subject matter but also in technical innovation stimulated by a new contact with Canadian poetry following the migration of one of his daughters to Canada.

Blight's poetic career was consolidated with the publication of *Selected Poems*. His stature was further enhanced by his three subsequent volumes, which placed the compulsive observer of quiddities and oddities (including his own) within the raucous high-rise development world of 'the new city' in the technological decades: *Hart* (1975), *Pageantry for a Lost Empire* (1977), and *The New City Poems* (1980).

Blight stands outside the mainstream of Australian poetry not so much because the subject material of much of his writing ostentatiously isolates itself through its restriction of form and content, but because of his pursuit of the determinedly nonlyrical mode, staccato and clustered, and often with quite complex thought structures compressed into tight phrases. It was not until the appearance of the later 'new city' poems that a truer appreciation of Blight's rugged individuality of mind and his strikingly idiosyncratic cadence became widespread. It was a period when a review of poetic forms and processes was being undertaken and Blight was hailed as a precursor to the work of **Bruce Beaver** and the new ironists.

Despite a certain 'fashionableness' attributed to his work in the 1970s, Blight's poetry retains a remarkable consistency of tone and voice, though within this individuality there has certainly been technical development, especially regarding not only the use of rhyme but also the placement of it. Nevertheless, what is apparent is how early the poetic compression and the rasping, quirky tone established themselves to distinguish an original poetic identity. Blight is a substantial contributor to what might be termed the 'anti-lyric' line of Australian poetry that makes an uneasy linking through **Christopher Brennan, R. D. FitzGerald**, and Blight down to Bruce Beaver and **Philip Salom**.

Blight was awarded the Dame Mary Gilmore Medal in 1965, the Grace Leven Poetry Prize in 1977, and the Christopher Brennan Award in 1980.

THOMAS SHAPCOTT

Further reading: Graeme Kinross Smith, *Australia's Writers* (1980).

BOEY KIM CHENG (1965–)

Singaporean poet

He was born in Singapore and graduated with honours in English from the National University of Singapore in 1988. His poetic inclinations were noted early in his university career, and the poet **Lee Tzu Pheng** took him under her wings from the start. In 1989 his first collection, *Somewhere Bound*, was published and received very favourable reviews. There is a strength in the volume that definitely makes Boey one of the best young poets writing in Singapore today. In 1992 his second volume, *Another Place*, was published.

As the titles of the collections indicate, Boey's poems deal with displacement and the human cost involved. There is an impressive maturity about the poems as he ponders in *Another Place* on his experience during a sojourn 'into a land which looks like the past'. Boey's travels in India helped to extend the dimensions of his well-crafted poems and provide the basis for significant reflections verging on the interconnectedness of reality. The voice is quiet, the tone serious, and the language terse. It is a remarkably mature achievement for a young poet.

DUDLEY De SOUZA

BOLDREWOOD, ROLF (1826–1915)

Australian novelist

Born Thomas A. Browne in London, England, the eldest son of a merchant and sea captain, he went to Australia at the age of five, was educated in the classics at Sydney College, and developed a profound admiration for Sir Walter Scott, whose *Marmion* supplied his pen name. Boldrewood commenced running cattle in Western Victoria, changed to sheep, and fell victim to drought. In 1870 he abandoned grazing and sought an alternative income through the political patronage of a brother-in-law and through writing. In 1871 he was appointed police magistrate and clerk of petty sessions in Gulgong, New South Wales, and in 1872 he became gold commissioner. Subsequently he held positions at Dubbo, Armidale, and Albury until he retired from government services and settled in Melbourne, where he died.

Boldrewood published a kangaroo-hunting

sketch as early as 1866 in the *Cornhill Magazine*, but the real impetus and opportunity to write came with the failure of his farming career in 1870. With a substantial family to support and a wealth of pastoral, goldmining, and judicial experience on which to draw, Boldrewood plunged into a twenty-five year career during which he produced some twenty works of fiction.

Boldrewood's plots range from the pastoral apologia of a successful Kentish immigrant (*A Sydney-Side Saxon*, 1891) to a historical romance of the Maori wars in New Zealand (*War to the Knife*, 1899). His realism, which is most convincing when he writes directly from his own experience, is tempered by a romantic cult of the aristocratic: characters intuit the true status of the dishevelled remittance man and feel a *paysannerie obligé* need to assist him.

Boldrewood's masterpiece is *Robbery Under Arms* (serialized in the *Sydney Mail* in 1882–3), a vernacular repentance novel that recounts the exploits of a gang of Australian bushrangers led by a charming, courteous, and superhuman English gentleman, Captain Starlight. Boldrewood sets the exciting but illicit adventures and exotic locations within the frame of Dick Marston's 'what-a-fool-I've-been' thoughts in the condemned cell. The commitment to racy vernacular narration alongside the casting of the English gentry as the exemplum of ability, manners, and style is typical of a phase of colonial ambivalence.

CHRIS TIFFIN

Further reading: Alan Brissenden, ed., *Rolf Boldrewood* (1979).

BOLT, CAROL (1941–)
Canadian dramatist
She was born in Winnipeg, Canada, and educated at the University of British Columbia (BA, 1961). She lives in Toronto, Canada.

Known best for *Buffalo Jump* (1972), *Gabe* (1973), and *Red Emma: Queen of the Anarchists* (1974), Bolt blends a variety of styles with fact and fiction. She has written some seventeen plays, including children's plays, plus radio and television work.

Most often compared to that of the Canadian playwright **Sharon Pollock**, Bolt's work is more akin to that of the Australian writer **Dorothy Hewett** and the New Zealand playwright **Renee**. The comparison to Pollock seems to derive from their both being Canadian women playwrights in the 1970s and from their interest in history. Bolt's use of history is more closely associated with a desire to re-create moments of forgotten history than to document the past: these re-creations establish mythical figures for today, including 'Red Evans' (a combination of two marchers who protested the Depression government's treatment of the jobless) in *Buffalo Jump*; the anarchist, Emma Goldman, in *Red Emma*; Métis leaders Gabriel Dumont and Louis Riel in *Gabe*; and **Pauline Johnson** in 'Pauline' (premièred 1973).

Like Hewett, Bolt uses short scenes, shifting time sequences, music, satire, myth-making, and puppets or 'fake' people to swell the numbers of 'actors' (particularly in *Buffalo Jump*). Her work relies on quick pacing and wide-ranging action. The influence of the theatre collective (from which Bolt came) is often apparent in, among other things, her montage style scenes and multiple roles for many actors.

Bolt shares with Renee an interest in social equity. Maintaining more than one political agenda, Bolt's plays convince audiences to think issues through: *Shelter* (1975), for instance, uses the experiences of five women at a bridal shower to debunk many contemporary institutions.

Bolt's nationalist stance is also obvious in her satirical film industry plays ('Desperadoes', premièred 1977, and *Escape Entertainment*, 1982). With the very successful thriller *One Night Stand* (1977) — the filmed script won three Canada Film Awards in 1978) — these later plays demonstrate

Bolt's ability to write theatrically exciting and socially relevant plays in a variety of genres.

JOANNE TOMPKINS

Further reading: Sandra Souchotte, *Playwrights in Profile: Carol Bolt* (1976).

BOND, RUSKIN (1934–)

Indian novelist, short-story writer, children's writer

He was born in Kasauli, India, and attended Bishop Cotton School, Simla. Bond's first novel, *The Room on the Roof* (1956), which received the John Llewellyn-Rhys Memorial Prize in 1957, is a sensitive treatment of friendship in a cold and inconstant world. He has since written more than a hundred short stories, essays, novels, poetry collections, and more than thirty books for children (including *Grandfather's Private Zoo*, 1969, and *Adventures of Rusty*, 1986). His short-story collections include, among others, *The Neighbour's Wife and Other Stories* (1967) and *My First Love and Other Stories* (1968); his poetry collections include *It Isn't Time that's Passing; Poems 1970–71* (1972) and *Lone Fox Dancing: Lyric Poems* (1975). Bond's reputation as writer, however, rests on the fictional works *The Room on the Roof*, *The Night Train at Deoli* (1988), *Time Stops at Shamli* (1989), and *Our Trees Still Grow in Dehra* (1992), winner of the Sahitya Akademi Award in 1992.

Bond excels at writing 'mood' pieces about his own life and the lives of those whose paths have crossed his. His recurring motifs are 'the longings after something lost' and 'the striving after better hopes', as he states (quoting poet Sarah Doudney), in his introduction to *The Night Train at Deoli*. Not political history but the history of places and ordinary people engages Bond. *A Flight of Pigeons* (1980) is a detailed story of an Anglo-Indian mother and her daughter during the Sepoy uprising of 1857. *Strange Men, Strange Places* (1969) is a vivid introduction to some of the chief actors, mostly European, who dominated the North Indian scene of colonial India, but are now almost wholly forgotten.

Landscape dominates Bond's writing, his favourite settings being the slow-to-change villages or small towns of the Himalayan foothills, where the British once set up hill stations (Dehra Dun, Pipalnagar, Deoli, Shamli). Kasauli and Mussoorie feature regularly. An empathy for all forms of life and an instinctive openness to the unglamorous in life make his panther, tiger, and leopard stories, such as 'Panther's Moon', 'Tiger, Tiger, Burning Bright', 'The Leopard', and 'The Tunnel', comparable to the masterly suspense tales of Jim Corbett.

Bond's stories spring from his instinctive enjoyment of the variegated Indian life; his evocation of it is reminiscent of Rudyard Kipling. The bazaar is a metaphor for easy acceptance among individuals; railway trains mark, like the flow of time itself, meetings and partings, changing destinations, possibilities to which one can never return. 'The Woman on Platform 8', 'The Eyes Have It', 'The Night Train at Deoli', and 'Time Stops at Shamli' all capture a mood of yearning for what might have been.

The child protagonists of some of Bond's powerful stories, such as 'Most Beautiful', 'Panther's Moon', 'Bus Stop, Pipalnagar', and 'Sita and the River', though deprived and capable of sadness, stand out for their individualism and their instinctive enjoyment of life. In this they are like Lila and Hari in **Anita Desai**'s *The Village by the Sea* (1982). To Bond's achievement must be added his revival, in the manner of Lafcadio Hearn, of the ghost story, not as a tale of evil and horror but as the more cosy narrative with which people entertain each other.

DEVINDRA KOHLI

Further reading: Meena Khorana, 'Ruskin Bond', in Tracy Chevalier (ed.) *Twentieth-Century Children's Writers* (3rd ed., 1989).

BOSMAN, HERMAN CHARLES (1905–51)

South African short-story writer, novelist, poet

He was born in Kuils River, near Cape Town, South Africa. Although Afrikaans was his home language, Bosman was educated at English-language institutions: Jeppe Boys' High School, Houghton College, the University of the Witwatersrand, and the Johannesburg Normal College. In 1926, two days after an impulsive secret marriage to Vera Sawyer, he left Johannesburg without her to take up a teaching post in the Groot Marico District of the Western Transvaal. He spent only six months in the small rural Afrikaner community from which he would derive the characters and setting for most of his short fiction. While at home for the school holidays, he killed his stepbrother during an altercation and was sentenced to death for murder.

Subsequently reprieved and his sentence commuted, Bosman was released from prison in 1930 and joined Aegidius Jean Blignaut in writing for journalistic enterprises ranging from *The Touleier*, a pioneering South African literary endeavour, to gutter-press periodicals such as *The New LSD*. In 1932, having obtained a divorce, he married Ellaleen Manson, and in 1934 they left for London, England. There Bosman worked as literary editor of the short-lived *Sunday Critic*, published short stories, articles, and poems in *The SA Opinion*, and with his wife started an unsuccessful publishing venture. They returned to South Africa in 1940.

During the next decade Bosman's occupations included the literary editorship of *The SA Opinion* and its successor, *Trek*. He also taught poetry and gave private lessons in short-story writing to **Lionel Abrahams**. His eight months in Pietersburg as editor of *The Zoutpansberg Review and Mining Journal* in 1943 provided him with material and a setting that he would use in his two novels. Following his second divorce, Bosman married Helena Stegmann in 1944. He left *Trek* in 1950 and worked as a proofreader for *The Sunday Express* to allow himself more time to write.

Publications of Bosman's work include the story collections *Mafeking Road* (1947) and *Unto Dust* (1963); *A Bekkersdal Marathon* (1971) and *Jurie Steyn's Post Office* (1971), which comprise selections from his voorkamer conversation pieces published in *The Forum*; the novels *Jacaranda in the Night* (1947) and *Willemsdorp* (1977); his prison memoir, *Cold Stone Jug* (1949); *A Cask of Jerepigo* (1964) and *Uncollected Essays* (1981), comprising selected essays, articles, and literary criticism; *The Earth is Waiting* (1974) and *Death Hath Eloquence* (1981), which include poems from *The Blue Princess* (1931), *Mara* (1932), *Rust* (1932), and *Jesus: an Ode* (1933). His 1951 play *Street-woman* appears in *Theatre One: New South African Drama* (1978), edited by **Stephen Gray**. *Collected Works* (two volumes) was published in 1981. His major works were reissued in 1992.

The literary scene Bosman entered in 1931 was still largely colonial, and most writers looked to England for publishers and readers. Bosman, however, was from the first committed to the development of an indigenous South African literature. Central to his work are certain themes: he saw the heart as supreme, human nature as eternally and everywhere the same, poetic truth as superior to historical and scientific fact, humour as residing in contrast and incongruity, and Africa as symbol of and setting for man's oldest, truest impulses. Drawing largely on his own experience, he used the same themes, character types, and human situations in all his fiction, but with modifications that reflect the changes he saw in his people, his country, and himself over some two decades.

The early phase of Bosman's adult writing career took impetus from his partnership with Blignaut, whose Hottentot Ruiter stories inspired 'The Rooinek', his first Marico story. (At this time Bosman used the pen-name Herman Malan). The nine Marico stories from this period are by no means free from the youthful arrogance and desire to shock displayed in his esoterically romantic poetry and three stories set in Johannesburg, but it is clear that the Marico afforded Bosman the ironic distance he needed to give both a national and universal dimension to his personal preoccupations. In this period he portrays the Marico as he had seen it in 1926: an isolated, backward, conservative community whose people viewed blacks as an inferior race.

Features typical of Bosman's work appear in these early Marico stories: his awareness of life's victims and the bond of common humanity, his audacious use of humour and irony to expose hypocrisy and prejudice, his flair for the telling realistic or historical detail, and his technique of statement by implication. These stories also introduce characters and elements that form part of Bosman's fictional stock-in-trade, among them Oom Schalk Lourens, the typical old backveld Afrikaner who narrates most of the stories Bosman wrote before 1950, the central character who is a misfit, loser, or outsider, and violent deaths, love affairs, inferiority complexes, racial tension, droughts, and the voorkamer post office.

The nineteen Marico stories Bosman wrote in England mark a development from the previous group in that he uses the Marico as the setting for an ironically humanized version of the romantic visions he had earlier confined to his poetry. With frequent comic effect and no loss of realism, several of these stories feature the world of chivalric romance in Marico guise, replacing wizards, love potions, and princesses with witch-doctors, juba berries, and Bushveld girls.

Bosman's literary activities after 1944 show him taking stock of South Africa and himself. Depicting a community irrevocably linked to the outside world and contemporary realities, the Marico stories of this period capture the humorous, ironic, and painful aspects of change and progress in South Africa at the time. Many of his essays and articles evaluate the present against the past; they are also increasingly concerned with the question of an authentic South African literary culture. *Jacaranda in the Night*, based on his relationship with Helena Stegmann, uses Pietersburg (renamed Kalvyn) as setting for the emergent phase in the evolution of the Afrikaner; describing Hannah Theron's love affairs, Bosman looks at the people of his own generation, whose occupations have removed them from the soil to an urban milieu where their basic needs and impulses, still in step with the veld, conflict with the imperatives of progress, Calvinism, and Afrikaner middle-class respectability. The semi-autobiographical *Cold Stone Jug* reviews his prison experience.

Bosman's experiments with form and the statement of his work in the eighteen months before his death mark this period as a separate creative phase. Taken together, the voorkamer conversation pieces, *Willemsdorp*, and the play *Street-woman* amount to a personal overview of South Africa at mid-century: the voorkamer series focuses on the rural poor white Afrikaner, *Willemsdorp* on the entire South African community, though more particularly the middle-class Afrikaner, and *Street-woman* on the English-speaking outcasts of urban society.

In the voorkamer series Bosman expands the voorkamer post office conversations sometimes occurring in Oom Schalk Lourens' stories from a narrative device into a versatile literary form suited both to wide-ranging social satire and to suggesting the displacement of the rural Afrikaner in South Africa's post-war development.

Willemsdorp, in which a white newspaper editor has an affair with an coloured prostitute, focuses on the recently enacted extension to the Immorality Act of 1927, which outlawed sexual intercourse between people of different races. Here Bosman portrays characters alienated from their African heritage, each other, and themselves.

Influences on Bosman's writing include Edgar

Allan Poe, other nineteenth-century American short-story writers, and a local tradition of fireside tales such as those he had heard in the Marico. Its irony, psychological insight, literary resonances, and inclusion of South African terms without explanation distinguish Bosman's fiction from much similar contemporaneous work. He may be compared with Frank Brownlee and **Pauline Smith**, South African regional writers of roughly the same period who wrote English with the cadence of the language spoken by the community they described, but unlike them, he belonged to his characters' language group, wrote specifically for South Africans, and published his work locally. In the people he depicts and in his awareness of their vulnerability in the face of social change, he bears similarities to William Faulkner and John Steinbeck.

Except in a handful of short lyrics, Bosman's poetic persona is incapable of achieving the ironic and humanizing objectivity of his Marico stories and voorkamer conversations. He is similarly handicapped by his closeness to the central characters in his novels. His short fiction, however, includes some of the early masterpieces of South African post-colonial fiction.

GILLIAN SIEBERT

Further reading: Stephen Gray, ed., *Herman Charles Bosman* (1986).

BOTSWANA

The Republic of Botswana (formerly Bechuanaland) is a vast and sparsely populated country in South Africa, bordered by Namibia and the Caprivi Strip to the west and north, Zimbabwe to the north-east, and South Africa to the south and south-east. Although much of the country is dominated by the Kalahari Desert, with its arid climate, the lush waterways of the Okavango Delta in the north-west produce tropical conditions, while in the eastern area rainfall is moderate and the soil arable.

It is largely in this eastern region that the Tswana came to settle. Little is known of Botswana's history before their arrival, but by the early nineteenth century these Bantu peoples were already firmly established. Displacing the indigenous Khoi-San groups ('Hottentot-Bushmen'), they introduced sophisticated political structures and enjoyed successful economies based on cattle and grain farming.

During this period the first contact with Europeans was made through Christian missionaries, notably Robert Moffat and Mary Moffat and David Livingstone. But it was only later in the nineteenth century, primarily over land and gold, that tensions developed with the Boer trekkers from the Transvaal (now in the Republic of South Africa). One of the most able of Tswana leaders, Khama III, chief of the Bamangwato, skilfully negotiated with the Europeans and won the protection of the British government (1885), which led to the formal establishment of the Bechuanaland Protectorate in 1891. Using British support, Khama was not only able to defend his eastern borders against incursions of the Boers but he secured his northern borders from attack by the traditional enemy, the Ndebele of Matabeleland (now in Zimbabwe).

From this time until 1960 Bechuanaland remained under the protection of the British crown, its powers exercised by the high commissioner in South Africa. The South African Act of Union of 1909, which created the Union (now the Republic) of South Africa, provided for eventual transfer to South Africa of Bechuanaland and the two other High Commission Territories, Basutoland and Swaziland, despite their resistance to it. The provision was dropped in 1961, however, after the withdrawal of South Africa from the Commonwealth.

A major step was taken towards independence in 1965 with the implementation of Bechuanaland's self-government constitution under Seretse Khama, hereditary chief of the Bamangwato, who had become prime minister in recent general elections. As a grandson of Khama III, he enjoyed substantial rural and traditional support in the country. He had also emerged as a cautious and conservative politician, generally acceptable to Britain on both domestic and foreign grounds. In early 1966 final constitutional talks were held in London, and a number of months later, on 30 September, under the leadership of President Khama, the Republic of Botswana was created.

At independence Botswana was one of Africa's poorest states, with minimal infrastructural development and a predominantly subsistence economy. Despite a series of devastating droughts, however, drastically reducing the national livestock and crop output, Botswana has become one of the continent's richest states in terms of GDP per capita. This has been achieved largely through its mining operations, with abundant mineral deposits — especially diamonds — having been discovered since 1966. Some of this wealth has been used for rural development, in an attempt to check the increasing unemployment. Yet agricultural production remains relatively low, and migration continues from the farms to the mines and towns.

With the death of Sir Seretse in 1980, his vice-president and chosen successor Quett Ketumile Masire (later Sir Ketumile) became president in his stead. While less conservative than his predecessor, he has continued with much the same political and economic policies, which led to his renewal as president in the general elections of 1984 and 1989. (He comes from the smaller Bangwaketse group and so does not have as strong a personal power base. But tribalism has not proved to be a serious problem in Botswana's politics.)

The roots of the country's multi-party democracy date back to Tswana traditions, particularly the 'Kgotla' or village council, in which the powers of traditional leaders were limited by custom and law. This has resulted in one of the most open political systems in Africa, in which the various ethnic minorities participate freely. Although a government-owned newspaper and broadcasting operation dominate the media, there is an independent press, and foreign publications are readily available.

Also contributing to the country's stability and progress is the recent emphasis placed on education. Until 1961, primary schooling was completely financed by tribal treasuries, with some groups spending up to seventy per cent of their budget on education. After independence primary schooling became free, although not compulsory. Out of a population approaching one and a half million, virtually all primary-aged children are now enrolled at schools, and the adult literacy rate has been officially estimated to be more than seventy-five per cent. As well as vocational, technical, and teacher-training institutions, there is an agricultural college and a national university, located near the capital city of Gaborone.

Although the official language of Botswana is English, Setswana (the language of the eight Batswana tribes) is spoken by the majority of people and is predominant. *Dikgang Tsa Gompieno* (Botswana Daily News) is published in Setswana and English by the Department of Information and Broadcasting. Moreover, Radio Botswana, the sole broadcasting service, transmits a variety of news, educational, cultural, and entertainment programmes in both languages. The TV Association of Botswana is presently limited to a relay service from South Africa, but plans are under consideration for a national television system.

The boundaries of Botswana literature have yet to be clearly determined. There were three figures of note whose works largely appeared in the decades leading up to independence: Lettle Disang Raditladi (1910–71), Michael Ontepetse Seboni (1912–), and Moliri Silas Molema (1892–1965). The first two, who were educated in South Africa, preferred to write in Tswana while the bulk of Molema's literary efforts was in English. In keeping with the social conditions and publishing practices of the times, these pieces were generally formal in style and biographical-historical in subject-matter.

Only one contemporary writer has succeeded in breaking through these limitations and achieving international recognition. **Bessie Head** was born in South Africa, but took up a teaching position in Botswana in 1964. In such works as *When Rain Clouds Gather* (1969), *Maru* (1971), and *A Question of Power* (1974), she explores the recurrent themes of racism, women's oppression, exile/expatriation, and the tyranny of chieftaincy.

PAUL SCANLON

Further reading: R. Renee Hitchcock and Mary Smith, *Settlement in Botswana* (1982); L. A. Picard, ed., *The Evolution of Modern Botswana* (1988).

BOWERING, GEORGE (1935–)

Canadian poet, novelist

He was born in Penticton, British Columbia, Canada, and grew up in nearby Oliver. He served in the Royal Canadian Air Force (1954–7) and then studied at the University of British Columbia for his BA (1960) and MA (1963). At university he met such writers as **Frank Davey** and **Fred Wah** and became part of the notorious poetry magazine *Tish*. Influenced by the open form poetics of Charles Olson and other New American poets, the Canadian group valued process, voice, and form in the poetic act, and the local as the ground of poetry. Such qualities shaped Bowering's first collections of lyric poems, *Sticks and Stones* (1962; rev. 1989), *Points on the Grid* (1964), and *The Man in Yellow Boots* (1965).

Bowering taught at the University of Calgary (1963–6), enrolled in the Ph.D. program at the University of Western Ontario (1966–7), then withdrew to become writer-in-residence and, later, lecturer at Sir George Williams University (now Concordia University) in Montreal (1967–71). In 1972 he began teaching at Simon Fraser University where he remains on faculty.

Bowering has published more than fifty books and pamphlets in a range of genres: poetry, short stories, fiction, essays, reviews, plays, and works that combine genres. The localism of his upbringing in British Columbia is evident in such works as *George Vancouver* (1970), *Autobiology* (1972), *Flycatcher and Other Stories* (1974), and *A Short Sad Book* (1977).

Bowering has challenged literary forms that assert control and that, to him, characterize the 'centralist' bias (or the Ontario bias) of mainstream Canadian literary thought, with its humanist preoccupation with national unity and identity. For Bowering, such attempts to establish order restrict the freedom of the writer and repress the power of the writing act itself; he was drawn to literary forms in which the materiality of language takes precedence. Bowering's early lyrics soon gave way to his interest in the 'suite' of poems, as in *Rocky Mountain Foot* (1969). This extended form, arising from the localism of the writing moment, developed into what is perhaps Bowering's unique contribution: 'serial' texts (adapting the term from the American poets Jack Spicer and Robin Blaser), his version of the long poem form so prevalent in modern Canadian poetry. His breakthrough serial poem, *Baseball* (1967), dedicated to Spicer, was followed by a succession of distinguished titles: *Genève* (1971), *Autobiology*, *Curious* (1973), *Allophanes* (1976), *A Short Sad Book*, and *Kerrisdale Elegies* (1984).

Serial writing combines a faith in the moment of composition with formal limits or 'rules' (as in a game) that prevent the writer from predetermining the writing; the assurance of the latter enables a writing act in which chance and indeterminacy become operative. Continuity, or aesthetic order, is not governed by the writer's memory of what preceded, but by connections that emerge in the process of writing each successive piece. *Genève*, for instance, was composed using the Tarot's Higher Arcana, which were shuffled, turned over, and left in a desk drawer. For each writing occasion, the top card was revealed and a poem written through immediate attention to the card's details, the length of the series governed by the number of cards.

Many years after his first novel, *Mirror on the Floor* (1967) — still in the 'realist' mode that he would abandon — Bowering published three radically self-reflexive fictional works also written in a 'serial' mode of composition: *Burning Water* (1980), *Caprice* (1987), and *Harry's Fragments* (1990). In these Bowering adopts a parodic strategy to expose the formal and perceptual expectations of genre, using as types histories, westerns, and mysteries, respectively. The writer-narrator openly participates in the construction of the novel as it proceeds, making readers aware of fiction as artifice or, in Bowering's terms, as a 'stained-glass window' that reveals consciousness both in the process of creating form and of apprehending its own mortality.

Bowering has advanced his postmodernist sense of writing as integral to the creation of self and history through numerous critical essays and editorial projects, including his magazine *Imago* (1964–74). He has won two Governor General's Awards: for poetry in 1969, for *Rocky Mountain Foot* and *The Gangs of Kosmos* (1969), and for fiction in 1980, for *Burning Water*.

ROY MIKI

Further reading: Ken Norris, ed., *Essays in Canadian Writing* 38 (1989), special issue on George Bowering; Roy Miki, *A Record of Writing: An Annotated and Illustrated Bibliography of George Bowering* (1990).

BOYD, MARTIN (1893–1972)

Australian novelist

Born in Lucerne, Switzerland, he was a child of delicate health. His family, long established in Australia, was pedigreed and predisposed to artistic accomplishment; it provided the background to Boyd's more celebrated fiction. He attended St John's Theological College, Melbourne, but withdrew before taking orders, realizing that his 'desire was no longer set exclusively on the Kingdom of Heaven'; he was articled to an architectural firm in Melbourne until the outbreak of the First World War. As a commissioned officer in the British Army in France, and subsequently in the Flying Corps, he found 'male comradeship' the 'redeeming feature of the war', and was imbued with that detestation of belligerence and militarism — his 'most important negative preoccupation' — that reverberates through his writing and finds as symbols the war-shattered Hugo Brayford; his son Stephen, 'crucified' for his pacifist ideals; and the Marazion hospital for the shell-shocked. The year 1914, Boyd believed, marked the conclusion of aristocratic pre-eminence and consequently the inception of his 'geographical schizophrenia': 'I have suffered through being considered an Englishman in Australia and an Australian in England.' He restlessly spent the remainder of his life in both countries and in Italy.

In 1920 Boyd privately published *Retrospect*, a volume of poems 'in the style of Rupert Brooke'. His career as a novelist began five years later. Boyd's early books were pseudonymously written (as Martin Mills) and poorly received in England, although *The Montforts* (1928), a cluttered 'pseudo-Galsworthian account of [his] mother's family over five generations', achieved an enthusiastic Australian audience and the first gold medal of the Australian Literature Society. *Lucinda Brayford* (1946) adhered to this formula: Boyd chronicled the family history of the Brayfords, leaves imbibing failing sap from the 'fallen tree' of aristocracy. In the Langton tetralogy — *The Cardboard Crown* (1952), *A Difficult Young Man* (1955), *Outbreak of Love* (1957), and *When Blackbirds Sing* (1962) — tentatively entitled 'The Past Within Us', Boyd was surpassingly comfortable with the theme of the dying aristocratic system, and in the society he described elegantly, meticulously, and empathetically.

Contemporary trends, the demands that fiction should be 'violent, outspoken and crudely sexual', prematurely 'killed the Langton sequence' and diverted Boyd's interest from literature to art, save for an insubstantial entertainment, and a second autobiography, *Day of My Delight* (1965) — the first was *A Single Flame* (1939). His 'Australian' fiction, therefore, entered neither the post-aristocratic era, nor post-colonial Australia. Doubtlessly Boyd aligned himself and his fiction with the traditional trinity of aristocracy, art, and Platonism embattled with the modern forces of commerce, science, and materialism. As long as the old order survived, Australia was culturally dependent upon England. Unlike Henry James, however, Boyd viewed the land of his youth not as culturally anaemic but as possessing a 'far more living creative culture' than the motherland. In *The Picnic* (1937), for example, he proffered as examples of a vital Australian art paintings by Sir Hans Heysen, Sir A. E. Streeton, and his own brother Penleigh Boyd. The images of natural Australia in his writing are vibrant and lovingly executed. Differences between colony and motherland he recognized, but 'both [were] Anglo-Saxon countries', and Boyd created his 'characters as people, not as nationals'. 'I was not patriotic in the nationalistic sense,' he argued, 'but I was patriotic in that I wished my country to be a land of justice, human wellbeing, and creative achievement.' Boyd concerned himself more with a 'spiritual home, built over two thousand years with marble from Athens and rock from Galilee.' In the materialistic, postwar world, he could find 'no abiding city'; during these years, the tone of the author (or narrator) was pervasively threnodic. Boyd's diplopia was not, in a Jamesian sense, geographical so much as chronological.

As Boyd's sentiments were conservative, so was his style. He described his technique as akin to the painter Alfred Sisley's *pointillisme*. Like pointillist art, Boyd's writing lacks dynamic passion: sentiment and lyrical love are abundant, but his fiction, teeming with trysts, elopements, and adulteries, is never convincingly libidinous. More fruitfully, Boyd conveys mystical emotions — awe inspired by Palestrina's masses sung in Dijon's cathedral, for example; epiphanies wrought by great art; incorporation into the 'myth' that spiritual Christian truth mediated artistically through a less important 'factual truth'.

NOEL HENRICKSEN

Further reading: Brenda Niall, *Martin Boyd* (1977).

BRAINARD, CECELIA MANGUERRA (1947?–)
Filipino novelist, short story-writer, essayist
Born in Cebu City, the Philippines, she grew up in the old aristocracy of Cebu, studying in an exclusive girls' school run by nuns, with whom she studied Anglo-American literature. An outsider-spectator to the tumultuous events of the Marcos years, which culminated in the People Power Revolution of 1986, Brainard was, by her own admission in her collection of essays, *Philippine Woman in America* (1991), neither 'just Filipino' nor completely American, but one who had 'evolved into another creature — a Filipino American'. She left the Philippines in 1969 and has since lived with her family in California, USA, where she is a board member of the USA West PEN Centre.

Brainard draws heavily on memories of childhood and youth for much of her fiction. These memories include a wealth of stories, both fictive and historical, such as folk-tales, quasi-legends, superstitions, quaint customs and traditions, and notorious or famous personages who fuelled gossip in Cebuano high society.

This historical Cebu becomes the fictive 'Ubec' in her stories, collected in *Woman with Horns and Other Stories* (1987). Inspired by Latin American writers as well as Filipino writers such as **Nick Joaquin**, she weaves romantic fantasies of Ubec during different periods of an imagined past. In the stories set in the 1960s, however, Brainard shifts to a more realistic mode as she culls more directly from her memories of adolescence — close kinship ties, extended families with innumerable aunts and cousins, young girls agonizing over their first stirrings of sexual passion.

In her novel *The Song of Yvonne* (1991), Brainard grapples with 'the ghost of that War ever present' during her childhood, as she grew up with 'endless war stories [which] were there, always there'. Set in Ubec during the Japanese occupation, the novel is her earnest attempt to understand 'the collective wounding that Filipinos experienced in that War'.

THELMA E. ARAMBULO

BRAITHWAITE, E. R. (1922–)
Guyanese novelist
Born and educated in Georgetown, Guyana, he studied in England and served in the Royal Air Force during the Second World War. After demobilization he worked as a schoolteacher in a poor neighbourhood of London, England, and used his experience of racial prejudice there in his best-selling novel *To Sir, With Love* (1959). The book was made into a popular film starring Sidney Poitier. Braithwaite was also a social worker in London before he became head of the Guyanese Mission at the United Nations. He later became Guyana's ambassador to Venezuela, and educational consultant to UNESCO in Paris.

In *To Sir, With Love* Braithwaite's account of his experience is interwoven with commentary and analysis. This is his standard method and is seen again in *Paid Servant* (1962), describing his experience as a social worker in London. His third book, *A Kind of Homecoming* (1962), concerns Braithwaite's travels in west Africa, his ancestral homeland (his ancestors were taken as slaves from west Africa to Guyana). *A Choice of Straws* (1965) departs from his standard method: it is a novel dealing with interracial love in London. *Reluctant Neighbours* (1972) gives Braithwaite's impressions of racial discrimination in the USA, and *Honorary White* (1975) describes a visit to South Africa, where he was regarded as an honorary white under apartheid laws.

Whether based on his experience in England, the USA, or Africa, Braithwaite's books provide documented reports of discrimination suffered by black people. Braithwaite deserves credit for bringing the subject of racial discrimination to a wider audience, but to the extent that he suggests that racial discrimination may be removed by education alone, thereby ignoring possible political and economic motives, his commentary is well-meaning though somewhat outdated. Only in the final pages of *Honorary White* does Braithwaite show some awareness of the complex human motives through which racial prejudice is generated and sustained.

FRANK M. BIRBALSINGH

BRAND, DIONNE (1953–)
Canadian/Trinidadian poet, short-story writer
Born in Guayguayare, Trinidad, she attended a private girls' school in Trinidad before studying at the University of Toronto (BA, 1975) and the Ontario Institute for Studies in Education (MA, 1988). Her work includes children's poems (*Earth Magic*, 1980) and a collection of essays and interviews (*Rivers Have Sources, Trees Have Roots: Speaking of Racism*, 1986), co-authored with K. Sri Bhaggiyadatta.

Complaining of a 'Past / always on yuh arse', Brand shares many post-colonial writers' obsession with history and a determination to appropriate imperial languages to serve formerly colonized peoples. The liminal state Brand records in the title of her book of poems *'Fore Day Morning* (1978) and elsewhere reflects in themes, puns, oxymoronic syntax, and ironic lineation is a counterpart to the twilight condition between two cultures that **Derek Walcott** recurrently constructs. Whereas, however, Walcott seeks to reconcile himself with imperial 'civilization', Brand takes issue with imperial barbarities. She often offers feminist correctives to male texts, a practice exemplified in *Winter Epigrams and Epigrams to Ernesto Cardenal in Defense of Claudia* (1983) and *No Language Is Neutral* (1990), a lesbian feminist response to Walcott's volume of poetry *Midsummer* (1984). The surrealistic poetry collection *Primitive Offensive* (1982) parallels parts of **Edward Brathwaite**'s *The Arrivants* (1973) as the protean, ancestral, naked, dismembered, and contemporary warrior/woman protagonist journeys to recover her African roots and the names lost in the middle passage (the sea route used to transport slaves from Africa), documenting the racism that those in the black diaspora endure and fight.

In 1970 Brand moved to Toronto and a condition of double exile represented in the witty 'Winter Epigrams' and in many narratives of *Sans Souci and Other Stories* (1988). Frequently parallel workings of experiences recorded in her poetry, some of these stories have Caribbean settings, while others bear comparison to **Samuel Selvon**'s accounts of Caribbean emigrants' experiences of racism in northern climes. Brand's more isolated protagonists, however, additionally encounter misogynistic behaviours. The poetry collection *Chronicles of the Hostile Sun* (1984) represents Brand's angry response to the 1983 American invasion of Grenada.

SUSAN GINGELL

Further reading: Himani Bannerji, 'Dionne Brand', in Daryl Cumber Dance (ed.) *Fifty Caribbean Writers* (1986); Claire Harris, 'Poets in limbo', in Shirley Neuman and Smaro Kamboureli (eds) *A Mazing Space: Writing Canadian Women Writing* (1986).

BRASCH, CHARLES ORWELL (1909–73)
New Zealand poet, editor
He was born and raised in Dunedin, New Zealand, of Jewish descent on both sides; members of his mother's family were well-established merchants with many European connections and interests in scholarship and the arts. Between 1927 and 1945 Brasch lived mostly abroad, as student, teacher, and civil servant in England, as amateur archaeologist in Egypt, and as eager traveller in Italy and Russia, years described in his memoir, *Indirections* (1980). Gradually becoming more determined to be a poet, he was initially enthused by Shelley and Yeats, and subsequently admired Rilke, Auden, and Eliot.

In his first two collections, *The Land and the People and Other Poems* (1939) and *Disputed Ground: Poems 1939–45* (1948), Brasch recalled New Zealand landscapes with clarity and nostalgia, in a conscious, but never crude, attempt to define the New Zealand condition. Repeated images of sea, hill, bird, and tree evoke the power and emptiness of nature and the insecurity of human settlement on the land; restless and rootless, like Brasch himself, New Zealanders seem in Brasch's poetry to be a pattern of modern humanity, 'creatures of the shore, disputed ground'. This sense of the public and pioneering function of the poet was also personal; the poems of his return to New Zealand in the 1957 collection *The Estate* show a rediscovery of familiar places and a dedicated struggle to find a foothold for the spirit, a community truly responsive to the natural world it inhabits. This is the theme — of universal, not merely nationalistic, significance — of Brasch's long meditative poem 'The Estate'. Written in blank verse with variations, it moves characteristically between vivid, natural image and solemn, abstract reflection in celebration of a friendship and of brief epiphanies of harmony and beauty.

Ambulando (1964) and *Not Far Off* (1969)

show a marked change in style, the shades of Shelley yielding to a more direct, spare, informal manner, capable of wry humour and self-irony. The short, tight lines of 'In Your Presence' (*Ambulando*), for example, define with clarity and without extravagance the ambiguities of love. In these books landscape is a less prominent motif and the focus is more frequently on identity, the self, and its search for meaning: 'Poems are questions put to you / At pistol point. They ask your life.' Many poems repeat the idea of the extinction of personality, the dispersal of self in the natural cycle of life and death, 'sieved and sea-changed through / The calendar of roles'. Others are graceful tributes to friends and fellow artists.

Home Ground (1974), published posthumously, is often considered to contain Brasch's finest work. In this collection, disputed ground has become 'Home Ground'; in the title poem, alienation and isolation are succeeded by a reconciliation with place and process, and varied fragments link the poet's personal journey and approaching death with the city, his home town of Dunedin, but also with the wider human community, past and present.

As he developed as a poet, Brasch was also engaged in a remarkable career as an editor, making *Landfall* (1947–), which he founded, the single most important journal in New Zealand literary history. (See **Literary Magazines**, New Zealand.) His aims, first awakened by his early association with the student journal the *Phoenix* (1932–3), were ambitious; primarily a literary journal, *Landfall* would also attend to other arts and to the society from which they emerged. Brasch's search was for an 'imaginative order' by which New Zealand, this offshoot of Europe, as he saw it, could begin to know itself. Poetry, short stories, reviews, commentary on theatre and art, social and political analysis — all could be found in a typical issue, introduced by an elegantly expressed and seriously considered 'Note' from the editor. Brasch insisted always on the highest quality in the contributions, attending scrupulously to every detail and actively suggesting changes or improvements. During the 'twenty years hard' in which Brasch edited *Landfall*, his standards of excellence and his taste pervaded it. An apostle of high culture and of European traditions, he had his blind spots; *Landfall*, it could be said, was lacking in robustness, in humour, and in irreverence. However, most contemporary writers of distinction appeared in its pages, and the existence of a stable and regular journal, with a responsive and dedicated editor, played a major part in the growing confidence of New Zealand writing in those years. Tireless in his encouragement of the arts, Brasch was also a significant collector, connoisseur, and patron. His *Collected Poems* appeared in 1984.

ELIZABETH CAFFIN

Further reading: James Bertram, *Charles Brasch* (1976).

BRATA, SASTHI (1939–)

Indian novelist, short-story writer, autobiographer

He was born Sasthibrata Chakravarti in Calcutta, India, and took his degree from Presidency College, Calcutta. He writes under the name Sasthi Brata. He left India in 1961 and worked at a variety of jobs in England, as described in the first volume of his somewhat fictionalized autobiography, *My God Died Young* (1968). Brata is now a free-lance journalist. He has published three novels — *Confessions of an Indian Woman Eater* (1971), *She and He* (1973), and *The Sensuous Guru: The Making of a Mystic President* (1980) — the more fictionalized autobiography, *A Search for Home* (1975) and *Astride Two Worlds: Traitor to India* (1976, published in the UK as *Traitor to India*), two books on India (including *India: The Perpetual Paradise*, 1985), and the short-story collection *Encounter* (1978). Brata's *Astride Two Worlds: Traitor to India* is much more balanced than *My God Died Young*, perhaps because of the device of presenting some chapters in the third person.

Brata's heroes seem to be modelled on the novelist. *Confessions of an Indian Woman Eater*, written in the first person, begins where *My God Died Young* leaves off. Amit Ray, like Brata, runs away from home; he recounts his sexual experiences in New Delhi, Rome, London, Paris, and Copenhagen. His success with women is unlimited; described in explicit detail, it verges on pornography. In *He and She* the first-person account of the hero Zamir alternates with the third-person narrative of his ex-girlfriend. But one gets bored with the hero's mindless drifting from bed to bed. *The Sensuous Guru*, a satire on modern American life, is very funny in parts. The hero is an Indian journalist who sets himself up as a guru in New York and eventually becomes president of the USA.

'Smiles Among the Bric-a-Brac', the longest of Brata's stories (more than 16,000 words), is his best; using the autobiographical mode, Brata shows up the racism and hypocrisy of the narrator, Robert Lomax, a young Oxford graduate, born of a rich English family, who happily accepts the girl and the job his parents have chosen for him, though he loves a girl of mixed parentage. Brata is capable of writing very good fiction, but needs to temper his autobiographical obsession and concentrate on satire.

SHYAMALA A. NARAYAN

BRATHWAITE, EDWARD KAMAU (1930–)

Caribbean poet, historian, essayist

Born Lawson Edward Brathwaite in Bridgetown, Barbados, he studied history at Cambridge University, England, after being educated at Harrison College. His Ph.D. from Sussex University, England, was based on a study of creole society in Jamaica. After teaching in Ghana for a number of years, Brathwaite returned to the Caribbean in 1962 to take up a post as extra-mural tutor in St Lucia. In 1963 he became a lecturer in the department of History at the University of the West Indies, Jamaica. At this point his reputation as a major Caribbean poet and historian was established. He was a founding member of the Caribbean Artists Movement (CAM) and launched, with Kenneth Ramchand, the journal and publishing house *Savacou*. Brathwaite resigned from the University of the West Indies in 1991 and took up a position as Professor of Comparative Literature at New York University, USA.

Brathwaite's creative and theoretical work is best understood as epitomizing the ideals of the CAM. In his first major work, the trilogy *The Arrivants* (1973) — comprising *Rights of Passage* (1967), *Masks* (1968), and *Islands* (1969) — his preoccupations are made apparent: a sense of the spiritual dispossession of the Caribbean, the importance of recognizing the 'Great Tradition' of Africa, and the healing and hallowing of the creative imagination. These ideas are first evident in early poems published in *Other Exiles* (1975). Brathwaite's almost religious sense of the world's fallen state (because of materialism) and of the redemptive force of poetry is later woven into the dialectic and epic structure of *The Arrivants*, which invites comparison with Aimé Césaire's *Notebook of a Return to the Native Land* (1939).

Rights of Passage evokes a Caribbean that is anything but the exotic tropics. Images of desolation and sterility are inscribed in the landscape. These features echo a larger picture of racial dispossession as Brathwaite the historian traces in verse the journeys of dispossession of the black diaspora. The second cycle of the trilogy, *Masks*, is built around the poetic quest for spirituality in African culture. African, or more precisely Ghanaian, rituals provide the poet with the masks for visualizing the possibility of wholeness in the desecrated Caribbean. Africa is not an end in itself, but a significant stop on Brathwaite's journey back to the Caribbean. *Islands* is a kind of homecoming, as the poet celebrates a retrieval of a sense of the numinous, a community's fragile sense of belonging, and the creative power of the folk despite the Caribbean's history of exploitation and injustice.

The Arrivants is important to Caribbean literature in English both thematically and technically. Given Brathwaite's early interest in creole culture and the objective of the Caribbean Artists Movement to recognize the Caribbean as a cultural entity, the poet explores the artistic possibilities of dialect and indigenous musical forms. His early essay, 'Jazz and the West Indian novel' (in *Bim*, 1967), shows his concern with the spontaneous and improvisatory qualities of local speech. In *The Arrivants* there are not only poems in dialect but explorations of religious ritual and forms of folk music. For instance, Haitian vodoun is as evident as the calypso of Trinidad and Jamaican reggae. Implicit in all this is an attempt to establish affinities between the literary artist and the folk artist, and between the Great Tradition and the Little Tradition.

In the early 1970s Brathwaite focused on the vision of an original creole culture emerging in the Caribbean. The publication of *The Development of Creole Society in Jamaica (1770–1820)* (1971) and *Contradictory Omens: Cultural Diversity and Integration in the Caribbean* (1974) indicates a theoretical concern with the issue of creolization. It is in the latter that Brathwaite, in theorizing about the possibility of a Caribbean culture, produced the often-quoted line, 'Unity is submarine.' In the 1970s he also began another trilogy, less panoramic than *The Arrivants* and located in his own island home of Barbados — *Mother Poem* (1977), *Sun Poem* (1982), and *X/Self* (1987).

Mother Poem concentrates on the Barbadian landscape of harsh limestone and dried-up watercourses. In these poems, Brathwaite gives free rein to his considerable dramatic skills in the multiple female voices heard throughout the collection. The poet sees in many of these victimized females the capacity to reach back to an ancestral past and find solace. In *Sun Poem* Brathwaite focuses on the male figure. Here, the poet longs for an elusive ideal of male rebellion. Childhood is evoked in passages of lyrical prose, but this fragile bubble is burst as the world intrudes. In the pathetic parade of eclipsed masculinity, the poet laments the need for a revitalized life force. If Caliban lives at all, it is in the dim memory of the rebellious slave Bussa and in the racial self-affirmation of **Rastafarianism**. The rainbow image of the closing poem is not one of reconciliation but of revived potency.

X/Self is characteristic of an increasing sense of frustration and impatience in Brathwaite's later poetry. These poems are as much passionate indictments of imperialism as despairing accounts of failed Caribbean revolutions, from Haiti to Grenada. The celebration of the apocalyptic vision of Xango is an invocation of black rebellion. Nevertheless, a growing sense of the artist and revolutionary as sacrificial figures to the philistine and uncaring world dominates the later poems. Two collections in 1986, *The Visibility Trigger* and *Jah Music*, contain a number of poems dedicated to murdered artists and activists. The murders of the Jamaican poet **Mikey Smith** and the Guyanese historian George Rodney in particular, as well as Brathwaite's personal misfortunes, dominate his work of this decade. It is not surprising that a sense of cosmic catastrophe pervades his 'hurricane poem', *Shar* (1990). His *The Zea/Mexican Diary* (1993) uses a new and eccentric graphic presentation to explore his private grief at his wife's death.

Brathwaite may be among the last in the Caribbean to believe with such fervour in the ideal of the poet as divine interpreter, favoured by the gods but a victim of mammon. His entire poetic career is devoted to articulating this ideal. The problematic nature of his latter verse indicates how precarious such a posture has become, given the ideological and political changes in the Caribbean.

J. MICHAEL DASH

Further reading: Pat Ismond, 'Walcott versus Brathwaite' *Caribbean Quarterly* Vol. 17 (1971); Kenneth Ramchand, 'Edward Brathwaite', in *An Introduction to the Study of West Indian Literature* by Kenneth Ramchand (1976); Mervyn Morris, 'This broken ground: Edward Brathwaite's trilogy of poems', *New World Quarterly* Vol. 23 (1977); Maureen Warner-Lewis, *Notes to Masks* (1977); J. Michael Dash, 'Edward Brathwaite', in Bruce King (ed.) *West Indian Literature* (1979); Gordon Rohlehr, *Pathfinder* (1981); Mark McWatt, 'Edward Kamau Brathwaite', in Daryl C. Dance (ed.) *Fifty Caribbean Writers: A Bio-bibliographical Critical Sourcebook* (1986).

BREEZE, JEAN BINTA (1956–)

Jamaican poet

She was born Jean Lumsden in Patty Hill, Hanover, Jamaica, and she attended Rusea's High School. She taught there in 1973, and in 1974 met her first husband, Brian Breese, whose name she adapted to Breeze. She was appointed cultural organizer (Westmoreland) by the Jamaica Cultural Development Commission (1976–8), before enrolling in the drama school of the Cultural Training Centre, Kingston (1978–9). Breeze worked as national co-ordinator for the literary arts in the Jamaica Cultural Development Commission (1983–5), and for the first time dub poetry was included in the national syllabus. Breeze earned a certificate in education (1987) at Garnett College, London, England, and taught at Brixton College.

Having been introduced to Rastafari, Breeze retreated to the hills of Clarendon, Jamaica, for the period from 1979 to 1981, but became disillusioned with the dissembling gender politics of **Rastafarianism**. In 1981 she met **Mutabaruka**, who produced the album *Word Sound Ave Power* on which she performs 'Aid Travels with a Bomb' and 'To Plant or Not to Plant'.

Breeze's major publications include *Answers* (1983), works in the anthology *Riddym Ravings* (1988), edited by **Mervyn Morris**, and the album *Tracks* (1988), on the LKJ records label of **Linton Kwesi Johnson**. Kwesi Johnson has been influential in Breeze's career; they performed on the British Broadcasting Corporation's (BBC) programme 'Poetry in Dub and Otherwise', in 1982. She co-authored with Matthew Jacobs the film script 'Hallelujah Anyhow' (broadcast 1991), and her second film script, 'All Saints Road', was commissioned by the BBC. A number of her poems appear in *The Virago Book of Love Poetry* (1990), edited by Wendy Mulford. *Spring Cleaning*, a volume of poetry, was published in 1992.

Breeze, who chooses to write and perform largely in Jamaican English, rather than in Standard English, usually in a public, oral 'dub' mode rather than a private, scribal vein, can create difficulties of categorization. The semantic subtlety of her work has not always been detected or appreciated by reviewers and critics; in the poem 'Dubbed Out' Breeze anticipates the response of those critics who might be tempted to hear in some of her work the substitution of beat for (in)significant word.

CAROLYN COOPER

Further reading: Carolyn Cooper, 'Words unbroken by the beat: the performance poetry of Jean Binta Breeze and Mikey Smith', *Wasafiri* 11 (1990).

BRENNAN, CHRISTOPHER JOHN (1870–1932)

Australian poet

Born in Sydney, New South Wales, Australia, he was the eldest child of Irish Catholic immigrants. A sickly, self-absorbed, but highly intelligent child who enjoyed the favouritism of his mother and his teachers, Brennan was set apart from his peers from an early age. This, together with his Irish background and Catholic upbringing, helped to foster the cherished sense of personal isolation that became a distinctive feature of his life and work.

Brennan was educated by the Jesuits at St Ignatius' College, Riverview, before entering the

University of Sydney to study classics and philosophy. His university results suffered because of his pursuit of private intellectual interests at the expense of the curriculum. Despite this he completed his degree with first-class honours in philosophy in 1890. After brief unsatisfactory teaching appointments he returned to the university, completing his MA in 1892. Soon after he was awarded the James King of Irrawang Travelling Scholarship to Berlin, Germany. Brennan spent the next two years in Germany studying philosophy. During this period he again spent much of his time pursuing personal interests in music, European literature, and, more particularly on this occasion, Anna Elisabeth Werth, the beautiful daughter of his German landlady. Brennan returned to Sydney in 1894 with a sound knowledge of contemporary European philosophy and literature, a passionate love of the work of the French symbolist poet Mallarmé, and a promise of marriage, but with no degree.

It was around this time that Brennan began to direct his attention to poetry as a compensation for the spiritual gap left by his lapsed Catholicism. He published four volumes of poetry in his lifetime: *XVIII Poems* (privately published run of eight copies in 1897), *XXI Poems (1893–1897): Towards the Source* (1897), *Poems [1913]* (1914), and *A Chant of Doom and Other Verses* (1918). A collection of Brennan's anti-Boer War poetry, *The Burden of Tyre*, was published in 1953.

Poems [1913] reprints a revised selection from Brennan's earlier work together with new material. The collection is divided into three chronological sections: 'Towards the Source (1894–97)'; 'The Forest of Night (1898–1902)'; and 'The Wanderer (1902–)'. The collection is organized according to the principles of the Symbolist *livre composé* and chronicles Brennan's romantic search for a paradisal state, Eden. 'Towards the Source' was written in the years that separated his return from Berlin and the arrival of his fiancée. Brennan used his separation from Anna during this period to elevate an expressionist form of heroic love as a means to Eden. He abandons this theme soon after his marriage, and in 'The Forest of the Night' he supersedes it with the heroic individual's introspective search for the transcendent self. This phase of Brennan's verse is notoriously difficult and reflects the poet's view that the artist writes for himself alone and not the public. The final section, 'The Wanderer', retains an interest in the heroic self but abandons the possibility of an Eden. The poet's verse style becomes more accessible as he relinquishes the struggle to find in language and image an absolute symbol. The abandonment of the quest for Eden is met by a corresponding sense of resignation to what seems inevitable defeat. It is here that Brennan's poetry comes closest to establishing thematic connections with his Australian contemporaries.

Brennan's lifelong friendship with John Le Gay Brereton introduced him to Sydney's important literary figures, and he shared his (anti-English) love of French literary culture with the Sydney ***Bulletin***'s noted Francophiles, J. F. Archibald and **A. G. Stephens**. His work, however, bears little resemblance to that of the Bush nationalists. His poetry is characterized by an uneasy technical dependence upon Victorian verse forms and diction (Patmore, Swinburne, Tennyson), which is often incompatible with the metaphysical aims he drew from European romanticism in general and from French symbolism in particular (Baudelaire, Rimbaud, Mallarmé). He was a talented classicist and an interesting critic, and his breadth of learning is demonstrated in his many critical essays — a number of them published in the *Bulletin*.

After waiting fourteen years for a permanent appointment, Brennan was finally hired by the University of Sydney as a lecturer in modern literature in 1909. He was promoted to associate professor of German and comparative literature in 1920, but dismissed in 1925 when newspapers reported his admission of infidelity in divorce proceedings with his wife. Always a heavy drinker and frequenter of Sydney's bohemian haunts, Brennan's later life saw him decline into poverty and alcoholism.

CHRISTOPHER LEE

Further reading: Axel Clark, *Christopher Brennan: A Critical Biography* (1980).

BRETT, LILY (1946–)
Australian poet
Born in Germany of Jewish parents, she immigrated to Australia in 1948 and was educated in Melbourne. Her poem 'Poland' won the Mattara poetry prize, and her collection *The Auschwitz Poems* (1986) won the C. J. Dennis prize for poetry in the 1987 Victorian Premier's Literary Awards. Other poetry collections are *Poland and Other Poems* (1987) and *After the War* (1990). She has also produced a collection of linked short stories, *Things Could Be Worse* (1990). She now lives in New York, USA.

Brett represents an illuminating example of the second generation of post-Holocaust Jewish writers, removed from the direct historical traumas of their parents' lives and arguably better able imaginatively to reconstruct those experiences in literature. Although she was born after the Second World War, her work draws upon the experience of her parents' generation of Holocaust survivors. Her terse, short poems elliptically re-create that period in a style whose minimalism accentuates the horrors of what is being depicted.

Brett's stories are characterized by their extremely adept movements between horror and humour. 'It is important to be normal!' is the injunction offered by an earlier generation of Australian Jews when they encounter the interlopers, the survivors of the Holocaust who have been deposited in the antipodes. By the end of the collection 'normal' has become re-defined to harmonize with the idiosyncratic worlds created by this constellation of recurrent characters. The minutiae of daily life usually encompassed by 'normal' here comprise extravaganzas precipitated by the aftershocks, which are also the legacy of the second and third generations. Brett's ferocious humour documents the excesses, the exaggerated behaviour that is the bedrock of what is reductively known as Jewish humour, but a sudden word will plunge the reader into and through the dark mirrors of the past. Caught in two paragraphs, for example, is the saga of the boy who sustained his family in the Warsaw ghetto by growing vegetables in a pram he guarded day and night. The stories comprise miniature epics that attempt to reach across the abyss of human evil yoked to the impossible optimism and humour of human survival. (See **Jewish Writing**, Australia.)

SNEJA GUNEW

BREW, KWESI (1928–)
Ghanaian poet
Born at Cape Coast, Ghana, he lost both of his parents at an early age, but came under the tutelage of a British colonial educational officer, K. J. Dickens, who educated and helped him to cultivate a love of books. Brew played leading roles in student dramas at Legon, and he later featured in films produced by the Gold Coast (Ghana) Film Unit, but it was in poetry that he showed great promise, winning a poetry prize in a British Council competition. Brew's poetry has subsequently appeared in major collections of African poetry, though he has published only one volume, *The Shadows of Laughter* (1969). Like many Ghanaian writers of the independence era, Brew combined the role of writer and public servant. After serving as a district administrator, he joined the diplomatic service and was posted to the UK, France, India, Germany, and the USSR. He became the chief of protocol at the ministry of foreign affairs and, later, ambassador to Mexico and Senegal.

Unlike **Michael Dei-Anang**, who is forthright

in his treatment of political subjects, Brew exercises a guarded reticence that nevertheless gives a quiet resonance. In much of his poetry, meaning is rendered in a subtle and suggestive way, ensuring a disquieting effect. The majestic rhythm of 'The Heart Anchor', for example, is undermined in the last two lines, where it is revealed that the poet is denied blessing; in 'A Plea for Mercy' the insensitivity of authority is contrasted with the desperation, the 'tattered penury', of the suppliants. Brew's poetry always shows a careful rhythm and control.

The subject of 'The Sea Eats Our Land' is the erosion of both the landscape and the moral fabric of Keta, an isthmus perilously lodged between a raging sea and a lagoon. Brew's depiction of the tragedy of this once-thriving trading centre strongly echoes **Kofi Awoonor**'s famous poem, 'The Sea Eats the Land at Home', about the same phenomenon. In 'The Woods Decay', set against a background of seasonal harmattan wind, Brew represents the dry wind as a metaphor for internal frustration and unrequited love.

In 'Ancestral Voices' (in *Op'on If'a*, 2, 1980) Brew notes the centrality of continuity between the past and present, the dead and the living, between 'they' (ancestors) and 'us' (the living). This continuum is sustained through regular performance of rites, but, as Brew's poem 'Compunction' suggests, it is often broken by the living, who violate sacred traditions.

Western cultural hegemony is shown to have reduced the indigenous society to 'decades of night' ('The Dirge'). In advocating return to the African tradition, Brew, like **Christopher Okigbo**, uses archetypal images of journey ('The Lonely Traveller') and river ('Wild Oats'). However, Brew's homecoming poems lack the intricate internal structure that progressively enhances meaning in Okigbo's poetry.

Brew's occasional pedestrian poems and trite language ('The Middle River' and 'Nickname') are uncharacteristic; he is without doubt a brilliant artist. It is regrettable that he is not a more prolific poet.

CHRIS KWAME AWUYAH

BREWSTER, ELIZABETH (1922–)
Canadian poet

Born at Chipman, New Brunswick, Canada, she has moved often, pursuing her education and career as librarian, university professor, and writer. Brewster was a founding member of *The Fiddlehead*, a literary journal, and maintains membership in various writers' associations, reflecting her belief in the importance of creative writing to the individual and to Canadian culture.

Brewster's extensive oeuvre is varied and eludes attempts at categorization, either by mode or chronology. A conveniently broad rubric is autobiographical/exploratory, as her work arises largely from her own experience and poses more questions than it answers. While the novels *The Sisters* (1974) and *Junction* (1982), as well as many poems and stories, begin as recollections, the prose tends to realism and irony, the poetry more to meditation and romance. Voice is most often ironic; meaning, accommodative.

One consistent subject in Brewster's writing — her personal loss of place, tradition, family, and lovers — is a local version of the great Commonwealth theme of exile, deracination, and rebuilding. Here, personal anguish is balanced by Brewster's vision of its universality. *Lilloet* (1954), a volume of poetry, and *Junction* re-create the history and ambience of an earlier way of life in New Brunswick. Poems about personal loneliness are contemporaneous with poems about Canada's isolated setting — 'East Coast-Canada' (1951) and 'Train Journey' (1972), for example. *The Way Home* (1982) and *Spring Again* (1990) reveal that travel to Europe and the Antipodes has prompted identification with the experience of displacement and adjustment common to many groups. Later poems and stories stress that ideas of regeneration and cyclicity are consolatory, that memory unites past and present, near and far, as in 'The Hoop' (1982), 'Collage' (1987), 'The Story' (1990), and 'Spring Again' (1990). Brewster's writing responds overtly to many literary influences, technical and philosophical; through them, she assesses experience and affirms her own basic religious reading of it.

CAROL MORRELL

Further reading: Desmond Pacey, 'The poetry of Elizabeth Brewster', *Ariel* 4 (1973); Robert Gibbs, 'Next time from a different country', *Canadian Literature* 62 (1974); Diana M. A. Relke, 'In/tense reconciliation', *NeWest Review* 14 (1989).

BRINGHURST, ROBERT (1946–)

Canadian poet

Born in Los Angeles, USA, he has lived and studied in the USA and Canada and has a BA and a Master of Fine Arts (1975) from the universities of Indiana, USA, and British Columbia, Canada, respectively. He has worked as a journalist in Beirut, Lebanon, and Boston, USA, as a tourist guide in Israel and Palestine, and as a teacher or writer-in-residence at the Banff School of Fine Arts and universities in British Columbia and Manitoba (all in Canada). Bringhurst has published poems in numerous small chapbooks, subsequently collected in *Bergschrund* (1975), *The Beauty of the Weapons: Selected Poems 1972–82* (1982), and *Pieces of Map, Pieces of Music* (1986). The latter includes 'The Blue Roofs of Japan', winner of the Canadian Broadcasting Corporation Poetry Competition in 1985.

Bringhurst is a widely travelled, multilingual polymath. He refers self-deprecatingly to his 'little Greek and less Chinese', quotes with ease from French writers, and spent ten years mastering Arabic. More recently he has turned his attention to such indigenous North American languages and cultures as Navajo, Haida, Ojibwa, and Cree, whose pre-industrial, anti-imperial thinkers (together with those from the Aboriginal Australian, Buddhist, and early Chinese and Greek cultures) form an intellectual Third World from which, in Bringhurst's view, we have more to learn than they have from us. He reads 'European and even colonial North American poets', but finds more real poetry in the work of biologists and anthropologists.

Bringhurst's work is dauntingly yet refreshingly intellectual, whether through its use of early Greek and Buddhist philosophy, its reworking of Old Testament material, or its intertextual fencing matches, as with Wallace Stevens in 'Hachadura'. Yet he is always insistent on the primacy of speech in the composition and the experiencing of poetry. His prize-winning 'The Blue Roofs of Japan' is subtitled 'A Score for Interpenetrating [i.e., overlapping] Voices'. Such emphasis on the spoken word derives equally, moreover, from his early admiration of Ezra Pound and his sympathy with cultures that are still primarily oral.

JAMES HARRISON

Further reading: Robert Bringhurst, 'Breathing through the feet: an autobiographical meditation', *Pieces of Map, Pieces of Music* (1986).

BRINK, ANDRÉ (1935–)

South African novelist, dramatist, essayist

Born in Vrede, Orange Free State, South Africa, and educated at Lydenburg High School, he obtained an MA in English (1958) and another in Afrikaans (1959) from Potchefstroom University, South Africa. After research in comparative literature (1959–61) at the Sorbonne in Paris, France, Brink lectured in Afrikaans at Rhodes University, South Africa, where he was awarded a Doctor of Literature degree in 1975. During his thirty years at Rhodes, Brink became professor and head of department. In 1991 he joined the English Department of the University of Cape Town, South Africa. Afrikaans-speaking, Brink felt that this move was a reflection of his situation: 'Because more and more of my writing is in English it is a natural shift rather than a dramatic break.'

Brink's interest in world literature can be dated from his student days in Paris and resulted through the years in his approximately seventy translations into Afrikaans of works in English, French, German, and Spanish. He published his first novel (also the first of more than forty works of fiction, travel, and literary criticism in Afrikaans), *Die Meul Teen Die Hang* in 1958. (This work has not been translated into English.) It was his fourth novel, *Lobola Vir Die Lewe* ('Dowry for Life', 1962), that became a key work in the renewal of Afrikaans writing by the 'Sestigers' or new young writers in the 1960s. This novel was written after Brink's return from Paris, where in 1960, so he proclaimed in his collection of essays, *Mapmakers* (1983), he was born again politically on a park bench.

If the Sharpeville massacre seen from Paris was Brink's first awakening to the horrors of apartheid, his determination to dedicate his work to fighting it was strengthened by the political upheavals in Europe in 1968. Brink's first book to be banned in South Africa was *Kennis van die Aand* (1973, translated into English by Brink as *Looking on Darkness*, 1974) and from then on he began to write in English so that he could be published in England and reach a new readership. With works often written and published in Afrikaans and English, such as *An Instant in the Wind* (1976) and *Rumours of Rain* (1978), he rapidly became an internationally known novelist. His work has been translated into twenty-three languages and he is the recipient of numerous literary awards both in South Africa and overseas; these awards include the Martin Luther King Memorial Prize in the UK (where he has twice been runner-up for the Booker Prize) and the Prix Médicis Etranger in France for *A Dry White Season* (1979), first published in Afrikaans in 1978 as *'n Droë wit Seisoen*. Brink has been nominated several times for the Nobel Prize for Literature and in South Africa has received the CNA (Central News Agency) Award three times. When the French government decorated Brink with the *Légion d'Honneur* in 1983, it was essentially to reward his contributions to French culture, but it was also to recognize his concern for social justice.

Particularly interesting is the way in which Brink translates this support of racial equality into the very structure of a novel such as *Houd-den-Bek* (1982), translated and published as *A Chain of Voices* (1982), in which no voice is privileged above the other. In comparisons with fellow white South African novelists **Nadine Gordimer** and **J. M. Coetzee**, with whom he shares similar themes and an interest in modern and postmodern narrative forms (Brink's obsession with the perspectives of time dates back to *Lobola Vir Die Lewe*), Brink's English style has sometimes been criticized for being 'pedestrian'. This may even have increased his popularity with the general public, which appreciates his dramatic sagas of what Brink himself calls 'human solitude' face-to-face with the apartheid regime, as, for example, in *An Act of Terror* (1991). If Brink is also well known in South Africa for his work both as a dramatist and director in Afrikaans theatre, he will perhaps be remembered best for being one of the writers who have contributed most to making the South African situation known worldwide; he has accomplished this through the universal appeal of his novels in English.

ANNE FUCHS

Further reading: Jacques Berthoud, 'Deconstructing André Brink', *Southern African Review of Books* Summer (1988); Jack Cope, 'A driving ferment', *The Adversary Within: Dissident Writers in Afrikaans* (1982).

British Influences on Caribbean Literature

The pervasive influence of Britain on Caribbean literature is not surprising, the nations of the Caribbean having been associated with Britain for over three hundred years, first as slave societies, then as colonies, and now as members of the Commonwealth. All Caribbean writers were subjected to some form of colonial education. Even at the primary levels, many students learned 'Memory Gems', uplifting epigrams by famous and not-so-famous English writers. These passages inculcated respect for 'fair play' and 'a stiff upper lip' — attitudes that were reinforced on the playing field at soccer and cricket. **C. L. R. James**, in *Beyond a Boundary* (1963), outlines how thoroughly the Caribbean attitude was conditioned by this colonial education. But this education also taught colonials that England was their source of guidance and excellence.

Important examples of this excellence were the works of literature taught in the schools. Students studied not 'literature' but 'English literature'; Shakespeare and English nineteenth-century poets and novelists dominated the syllabuses. Early Caribbean writers were convinced that to achieve excellence they had to emulate English models. In the eighteenth century, Francis Williams, a black Jamaican protégé of the Duke of Montagu, wrote Latin odes full of Miltonic classical allusions. Eighteenth- and nineteenth-century poems such as *The Sugar Cane* (1764) by James Grainger and *Barbadoes and Other Poems* (1833) by M. J. Chapman use heroic couplets and classical allusion to describe slave and plantation life. In the first half of the twentieth century, a group of poets in Jamaica, centred around **Tom Redcam**, produced slim volume after slim volume of sentimental verse, slavishly imitating the mannerisms of English poets such as Keats, Shelley, and Tennyson. English landscapes were merely exchanged for Jamaican ones. The only distinctly Caribbean aspect of their voice was its colonial imitativeness.

After 1950, with the coming of suffrage and political independence, Caribbean writers, although continuing to refer to works of English literature, began to question their relationship with Britain. The career of **Derek Walcott**, the greatest Caribbean poet and dramatist, can serve as an example of the evolution of the influence of English literature on Caribbean writing. In his first book, *25 Poems* (1948), it is difficult to separate the voice of Walcott from those of Dylan Thomas and W. H. Auden, his British mentors. Walcott's early play, *Henri Christophe* (1950), is patterned on Shakespearean tragedy, and its blank verse sometimes sounds more Elizabethan than Caribbean. As he has matured as a poet, Walcott has absorbed his English influences and made them part of his own voice. His *Another Life* (1973) has drawn comparison with Wordsworth's *The Prelude*. An understanding of the devil in Walcott's *Ti-Jean and His Brothers* (1970) is enhanced by a familiarity with Milton's Satan, and of Chantal in his *Malcochon or, The Six in the Rain* (1970) by a knowledge of Blake's 'The Tyger'. Walcott's play *Pantomime* (in the collection *Remembrance and Pantomime*, 1980) would not mean much without some knowledge of Daniel Defoe's *Robinson Crusoe*. However, in Walcott's mature works one does not hear echoes of Wordsworth, Milton, Blake, or Defoe, but Walcott's own distinctive Caribbean voice.

Other distinguished Caribbean writers use sources in English literature to modify the tradition from which they draw. Many of them allude subversively to English 'classics'. Some of the most provocative of recent Caribbean works are indeed attempts to rewrite from a different centre famous English works. **Jean Rhys**' *Wide Sargasso Sea* (1966) makes one perceive Charlotte Brontë's *Jane Eyre* in a new way, as does **George Lamming**'s *Water with Berries* (1971) for Shakespeare's *The Tempest*. **V. S. Naipaul**'s *A House for Mr. Biswas* (1961) offers a new perspective on H. G. Wells' *The History of Mr Polly*, as does

Naipaul's *Guerrillas* (1975) on Emily Brontë's *Wuthering Heights* and Samuel Richardson's *Clarissa.* Joseph Conrad's *Heart of Darkness* is used ironically in novels such as **Wilson Harris**' *Palace of the Peacock* (1960) and Naipaul's *A Bend in the River* (1979).

While the relationship of Caribbean writing and English literature remains intense, it is no longer slavish. A Caribbean literature is emerging with its own voice, confident enough to make use of English writing to help it articulate a distinctly Caribbean vision. (See **Criticism**, The Caribbean.)

ANTHONY BOXILL

BROADCASTING

BROADCASTING (Australia)

Radio

Radio broadcasting commenced in Australia in a systematic way in the 1920s. The governing legislation delineates the pattern of delivery: national, commercial, or public. National and commercial systems came from the initial system of 'A' and 'B' class stations. 'A' stations were funded from licence fees, while 'B' class stations supported themselves. 'B' class stations soon became 'commercial', raising revenue from advertising. The government nationalized 'A' class stations in 1932 with the formation of the Australian Broadcasting Commission (ABC). In 1974 licence fees were abolished and the ABC was funded from general taxation. In 1983 the ABC was restructured as the Australian Broadcasting Corporation. Public broadcasting, funded by subscriptions, began in the mid-1970s, along with the multicultural Special Broadcasting Service.

Ideological debates about its function occurred early in radio development, but stations established by governments and political or religious groups were soon exhibiting the characteristics of other stations. News services began as the preserve of the ABC. Readings from newspapers gave way by 1938 to a special radio news style and format, and recorded voices were introduced to lend actuality. Commercial stations broadcast dramatized documentaries such as 'Time Marches On'. The war changed the attitude of audiences to radio news since radio had an immediacy that newspapers lacked.

New import regulations forced Australian stations to rely on their own resources to produce serials and drama instead of using American transcriptions. First produced in 1925, serials by the mid-1930s had developed a successful formula of family situation comedy and drama. The American-derived series 'One Man's Family' (1936–8) reshaped Australian serials, and was followed by 'Dad and Dave' (1937–51), 'When a Girl Marries' (1939), and the ABC's 'The Lawsons' (1944). In 1949 'The Lawsons' became 'Blue Hills', continuing to 1976. Frequency and family verisimilitude led to 'listening in' becoming a family ritual.

In the postwar period, adventure serials became more common, with 'Superman' and 'The Air Adventures of Biggles' taking over from 'The Search for the Golden Boomerang'. These led in the later 1950s to the more Americanized 'Night Beat'. Serious radio drama developed on the ABC, where Leslie Rees used such talents as **Vance Palmer**, **Katharine Susannah Prichard**, and **Ruth Park**. Commercial stations replied with the 'Lux Radio Theatre' and the 'General Motors Hour'.

Music programmes also evolved over time. At first the ABC concentrated on serious music, establishing symphony orchestras in the late 1940s. 'The Mobil Quest' identified new talent, while Hector Crawford produced such programmes as 'The Melba Story'. The coming of rock music coincided with the revolution in listening patterns made possible by the transistor. This pattern of mobile individual listening accelerated with the arrival of FM radio in the 1970s. By 1975 the ABC had established its own rock station, 2JJ.

Talkback radio experiments had occurred in 1925, but regular talkback programs started in 1967 and were soon a feature of commercial and ABC networks.

Television

Regular experimental television broadcasting in Australia commenced in 1934, with transmissions sent from Brisbane to Ipswich, Queensland. Progressive improvement occurred until the experiments ceased with the onset of the Second World War. Initial plans for introducing public television broadcasting were deferred when the Menzies-led Conservatives defeated the Chifley Labor government in 1949. A Royal Commission in 1953 recommended gradual introduction of a dual television broadcasting system, comprising government-sponsored stations of the Australian Broadcasting Corporation (ABC) and commercial stations. The first broadcasts occurred in 1956 in Sydney, when the commercial Channel 9 commenced, followed shortly by ABC Channel 2; then came Melbourne in 1957, with all state capitals having two television channels by 1960. These services were expanded by a second commercial channel, so that all capitals had Channels 2, 7, and 9. A third commercial channel (0/10) was added in all mainland capitals in 1965. Extension of television channels to regional areas continued until the 1970s, while satellite delivery expanded this coverage in the 1980s.

Initially, the system was controlled by the Broadcasting Control Board (BCB), established in 1948, which conducted licence application hearings and made recommendations to government on awards. The issue of cross-media ownership was contentious from the outset. A BCB enquiry into colour television selected the PAL (phase alternation line) 625-line screen system for introduction in 1975, and penetration by colour was almost complete within the decade. In 1980 the government-sponsored Special Broadcasting Service (SBS) began in Sydney and Melbourne, and by 1986 had extended to other capitals and was strong enough to resist pressure for an ABC take-over of its services. SBS is aimed primarily at ethnic audience segments and includes much foreign language programming.

In 1977 the Australian Broadcasting Tribunal (ABT) replaced the BCB. The ABT was given power to award licences at renewal hearings and to enforce standards. It revised BCB provisions about Australian content, refining the 'points system' requiring licence-holders to provide a proportion of approved Australian drama and children's programming. ABT provisions did not apply to ABC or SBS, but government-sponsored and commercial channels discovered that high quality Australian programmes, including soap operas and drama, usually out-rated imported programmes, and often achieved export sales. 'Neighbours' is one internationally successful example.

During the 1980s a series of enquiries into television services led to revised cross-media ownership provisions, aggregation of metropolitan and regional commercial channels into national networks, and widespread ownership changes. Ill-considered speculation in television ownership, coupled with the post-1987 economic downturn, led some commercial networks into financial crisis and ownership by financial institutions and constrained investment in quality programming and local production. In the 1980s ownership of video recorders in Australian homes exceeded seventy per cent, allowing time-shifting and 'zapping' of commercials.

In 1992, under a new Broadcasting Services Bill, the Australian Broadcasting Authority (ABA), covering ABC and SBS as well, replaced the ABT as regulator of television broadcasting. The ABA will preside over radical change as satellite-delivered pay channels to domestic consumers are introduced to supplement existing Sky Channel services to clubs and hotels.

Despite recent turbulence, Australian television, by drawing programmes from the USA and the UK for its major channels and from foreign distributors for SBS, and through requirements for quality local production, offers viewers an extremely varied and high standard of cosmopolitan programming in drama, news, current affairs, and sport.

BRUCE MOLLOY

Further reading: R. R. Walker, *The Magic Spark* (1973); Sandra Hall, *Supertoy: 20 Years of Australian Television* (1976); Sandra Hall, *Turning On, Turning Off: Australian Television in the Eighties* (1981); Yolanda Allen and Susan Spencer, *The Broadcasting Chronology* (1983); Leslie Johnson, *The Unseen Voice* (1988).

BROADCASTING (Bangladesh)

Radio

Radio Bangladesh, which in 1939 began broadcasting from Dhaka (now in Bangladesh) with a single five-kilowatt transmitter, had, by 1992, fourteen medium-wave, five short-wave, and fourteen FM transmitters covering the entire country. The ninety-two hours of daily broadcasting comprise news and news commentaries and commercial, farm, population, and External Service programmes. All broadcasts are in Bengali except certain news bulletins, special programmes, and the External Service programmes, which are given six-and-a-half hours daily and are mostly in English; the other languages used are Urdu, Hindi, Nepali, and Arabic.

The bulk of the domestic services is taken up by music (sixty per cent), programmes on socio-economic development (twelve per cent), news and news commentaries (five per cent), and the rest by drama, children's programmes, interviews, and so on. The External Service, aside from providing news and commentaries, carries talks on various aspects of Bangladesh life, literature, and culture as well as short plays and music.

Television

Television broadcasting began in Dhaka in 1964. Eleven transmitters have been added since 1971, and Bangladesh Television (BTV) switched to colour in 1980. Of an average of seven-and-a-half hours of daily television broadcasting, nearly eighty per cent of the time is taken up by programmes produced locally, while approximately twenty per cent is imported fare (films and videotapes). Except for certain news bulletins and special programmes in English, virtually all locally produced programmes are in Bengali.

News and current affairs programmes constitute approximately sixty per cent of the broadcasting day, while music, drama, and dance make up approximately sixteen per cent. Other areas covered are sports, development, health, education, children's issues, religion, and science and technology. BTV subscribes to satellite daily news services of Eurovision and Asiavision and provides Asiavision with two news stories daily. Both Radio Bangladesh and BTV are fully government controlled and show bias for the ruling regime.

KABIR CHOWDHURY

BROADCASTING (Canada)

Broadcasting (in both English and French) has played a crucial role in Canada since its beginnings in the 1920s. That role has been social and economic, but also cultural. Canada's successive national public broadcasting institutions have been the CNR Radio Network (1925–32), which was nationalized on the British model in 1932 as the Canadian Radio Broadcasting Commission (CRBC), and changed administratively in 1936 into the Canadian Broadcasting Corporation (CBC). The CRBC and CBC were intended — by government mandate and general expectation — to bind the country together by providing for Canadians a common cultural experience and to help develop a Canadian identity.

Since Canada, like Australia, has chosen to

follow the British practice of a nationalized broadcasting service, both the government and the people have determined to maintain national control over the airwaves, to maintain the CBC as a non-profit (though not completely non-commercial) institution, and to accept that government subsidies must continue to help underwrite Canadian programming. As a result, Canadian broadcasting, both radio and television (like its British and Australian counterparts), has produced a significantly larger proportion of serious, non-commercial, cultural programmes than the USA, particularly in literature and drama.

Radio drama has perhaps been the most important artistic and cultural contribution of Canadian radio. When radio plays began to be broadcast in the late 1920s, there was no indigenous Canadian national theatre, and very few established theatre institutions that could give continuing full-time employment to theatre professionals. The earliest national radio-drama series — 'The Romance of Canada' — was broadcast over the CN network from Montreal in 1931–2; it comprised serious historical documentary-dramas written by Merrill Denison and produced and directed by Tyrone Guthrie. By the early 1930s the CRBC was broadcasting regionally and nationally a number of dramatic and documentary-drama series. By the early 1940s, spurred on by its new wartime prominence, the CBC had created major radio-drama series in Toronto and in most of the regional production centres. In January 1944 Andrew Allan, the new CBC national drama supervisor, created the 'Stage' series, the senior sustaining national radio-drama series, which proclaimed that it was reporting 'the state of drama in Canada'. During its long run (to 1979), 'CBC Stage' became Canada's first national theatre. 'Wednesday Night', founded in 1947, also continued into the late 1970s, offering the best in classical and modern drama of the western world. These two were the most ambitious of a group of hundreds of radio-drama series in English. The role of radio drama gradually became less central in the decade after the creation of the CBC television networks and with the growth of Canadian stage companies. To date the CBC drama department has produced some twelve thousand radio plays, of which about one-half are original dramas.

While CBC Radio had a clear field after 1947, when the USA abandoned its radio networks for television, CBC Television, beginning some six years after the American TV networks started broadcasting, had to respond to the expectations of Canadians who had been exposed to American popular commercial programmes.

There were, according to critic Mary Jane Miller, some thirty-five major Canadian television series and serials in the period from 1952 to 1990, ranging from serious and experimental plays, through mystery and western series, to popular comedy shows and family situation dramas. Among the best-known of the serious drama series were 'CBC Television Theatre' (1953–4), 'Scope' (1954–5), 'First Performance' (1954–8), 'Folio' (1955–60), 'On Camera' (1955–7), and 'Festival' (1959–69). The experimental series included 'Q for Quest' (1960–4), 'The Eyeopener' (1965), 'Program X' (1970–3), and 'Peepshow' (1975–6).

Contemporary Canadian fiction and poetry have been broadcast mainly on CBC Radio, particularly on the long-running weekly series 'Anthology', a magazine of original contemporary Canadian poetry and fiction founded by Robert Weaver in 1954. Nearly every modern Canadian poet and fiction writer of any talent has been on the programme, which was retired only in the 1980s.

HOWARD FINK

Further reading: Frank W. Peers, *The Politics of Canadian Broadcasting 1920–51* (1969); N. Alice Frick, *Image in the Mind: CBC Radio Drama*

1944–55 (1985); Howard Fink and John Jackson, eds, *All the Bright Company: Radio Drama Produced by Andrew Allan* (1987); Mary Jane Miller, *Turn Up the Contrast: CBC Television Drama Since 1952* (1987).

BROADCASTING (India)

Radio

Radio broadcasting began in India in the closing decades of British rule. After the desultory efforts of some private groups in the late 1920s, the government established an Indian Broadcasting Service in 1930. Six years later it was renamed All India Radio and became widely known by its acronym, AIR.

AIR took many lessons from the British Broadcasting Corporation (BBC), but not that of organizational autonomy. AIR's senior personnel were either drawn from the BBC or sent to England for training. When AIR started a journal of its own, it was named *The Indian Listener* (1935–58, succeeded by *Akashvani*, 1958–87), recalling the BBC's *The Listener*.

For many years the Indian radio audience was confined to the upper classes, for only they could afford the cost of radio sets. A high proportion of the programmes were in English, although AIR endeavoured to offer Indian classical music and news in the mother-tongues. The main news bulletins were spoken in BBC English, but Indian drawls kept breaking cheerfully into the announcements. Radio enabled a large number of Indians who had not been educated in upper-class, private schools to make the acquaintance of spoken English.

Although broadcasting was an agency of the foreign British government, professionalism within the system was strong enough for AIR station directors to seek to record and broadcast the voices of India's national leaders. The novelty of the medium and its potential as a nation-wide university of the air also attracted scholars and scientists. Speaking on the radio became a sign of distinction for the more literate civil servants.

Most of these broadcasts were in English, the language that then, as now, was an indispensable medium of pan-Indian communication and discourse. AIR had many able and gifted writers of English on its staff, such as **Nirad C. Chaudhuri**. Several AIR journalists later became editors of leading English-language newspapers in India.

Even after the achievement of Indian independence in 1947, broadcasting continued to be a state monopoly. However, it did respond to local conditions. In 1957 AIR acquired an additional name, Akashvani (a Sanskrit word meaning 'voice of the sky'). A vigorous plan was undertaken to promote the mother-tongues and Indian classical and folk music through radio. Great musicians were able to reach mass audiences, and aspiring artists came to regard their inclusion on AIR's poster as a mark of success. Many front-rank authors in the Indian languages worked as radio producers; poets' conferences on radio became an institution; and radio plays prospered. The commentaries broadcast in Hindi and in English during important national occasions and cricket matches maintain a wide following.

The English language continues to hold sway in broadcasting news bulletins; the master copy is still compiled in English before being translated into the various mother-tongues. As a result of this 'translationitis', the various language bulletins suffer from stilted vocabulary and syntax. Less familiar proper names are pronounced as they are spelled in English, and English usage is adopted even for familiar place names; for example, Mumbai and Chennai are referred to by their English names, Bombay and Madras.

All India Radio has 104 stations that reach ninety-five per cent of the population (which in 1991 was estimated at some 844 million). News bulletins are broadcast from New Delhi in nineteen languages; they are broadcast from regional stations in seventy-two languages and dialects. The external services division broadcasts news in twenty-five languages.

Television

Television broadcasting in India began on an experimental basis in 1959. It has since grown vastly to rival the cinema as the dominant medium of culture. It is a friendly rivalry, however, for the two media are mutually supportive. From the outset the state-owned television service has had an Indian title, Doordarshan (the Sanskrit equivalent of the word television). Doordarshan theoreticians proclaim the educational role of television and its utility in fostering regional cultural forms. What has happened in practice is that television is seen as a portable provider of entertainment whose content and manner are strongly influenced by advertisements. Satellite television and its concomitants, cable television and videotapes, have tended to obliterate the old regional and national constraints and inhibitions. They accentuate what the processes of industrialization and urbanization began and are bringing about changes in dress, hair styles, and eating habits. New jargon and dialectal forms of mother tongues, teeming with American words, have come into being. In turn, many Indian slang expressions and words of endearment have made their way into Indian English. This process is likely to accelerate when the government relaxes its hold over television and radio, as it promises.

H. Y. SHARADA PRASAD

Further reading: H. R. Luthra, *Indian Broadcasting* (1986); P. C. Chatterji, *Broadcasting in India* (1987; rev. 1991).

BROADCASTING (Pakistan)

Radio

Radio Pakistan began broadcasting on 14 August 1947 with one five-kilowatt transmitter at Lahore and another ten-kilowatt transmitter at Peshawar. It has expanded and was renamed Pakistan Broadcasting Corporation (PBC) in 1972, but it retains its old call-sign, 'Radio Pakistan'. Currently its sixteen stations reach ninety-five per cent of the population and seventy-five per cent of the area on medium wave. Short-wave coverage within the country is one hundred per cent for both area and population.

Daily transmission consists of 393 hours and eleven minutes on both short wave and medium wave, with the following division: Home Service Programmes in Urdu, English, and eighteen other languages — 270 hours; External Services Programmes in fifteen foreign languages directed to sixty-four countries — eighteen hours; and World Service Programmes in Urdu and English — twelve hours. The programmes cover a wide variety of interests and there are featured programmes for and about religion, students, women, children, rural and farm matters, sports, armed forces, music, drama, literature, and so on. A small percentage of the literary programmes are in English. There has also been a late-night western music programme. News and current affairs programmes are the responsibility of the Central News Organization and take up eleven per cent of broadcasting time, involving eighty-two Home Service bulletins, seventeen External Services bulletins, ten World Service bulletins, three General Overseas Slow-Speed bulletins, and five Current Affairs programmes a day. A dozen of these are broadcast in Urdu and English, and no less than twenty-five in regional languages and dialects. Additionally, each of the radio stations broadcasts local news bulletins. The broadcasts begin early in the morning and continue until eleven p.m. Sports are given twenty-one per cent of the time, and running commentaries on matches and interviews with sportsmen and women are very popular, as are the music programmes and the features.

The Central Monitoring Unit currently monitors more than 120 foreign broadcasts in eight languages from about twenty stations, for thirty hours daily. These numbers vary from time to time. PBC also possesses extensive archival material. The Central Production Unit, established in 1960, is based at Lahore, Karachi, and Islamabad. The National Sound Library is located at its Islamabad office. The records pertain to every aspect of life in Pakistan and these are lent to media in Pakistan and around the world. The Pakistan Broadcasting Academy trains radio personnel. Its engineering wing has recently begun to manufacture high-power transmitters.

Television

Pakistan Television began with two pilot stations, the first of which went on air in Lahore on 26 November 1964; the other went on air in Dhaka a month later. The Pakistan Television Corporation came into being in 1967 and took over from the private limited company that had operated television since 1965. The five main production and transmission centres are at Lahore, Karachi, Islamabad, Quetta, and Peshawar. A microwave link connects these centres with twenty-eight rebroadcast stations to form the National Network. Transmission via satellite commenced in 1972. Colour came to the television screen in 1976. PTV productions began to enter international competitions in 1971 and several have won awards.

Daily telecast is about seven hours. A second channel was added in 1990 to the Islamabad centre, where Educational Television was also introduced in 1992. PTV Academy trains its own personnel, and has co-operation agreements with agencies abroad. Coverage now extends to about eighty-six per cent of the total population — in all four provinces of the country and parts of Azad Jammu and Kashmir. The area covered has risen steadily from 8,029 square kilometres in 1964 to approximately 295,906 square kilometres by 1989. There are about 1.5 million television sets in the country, with an average of eight viewers to a set.

There are several daily news bulletins in Urdu and one in English. Normal fare includes music, soap operas, films (Urdu and English), drama, and serious discussion programmes (Urdu and English). About twenty per cent of the programmes are imported from western sources; many are re-runs. Time is not apportioned according to popularity ratings, though advertising has increased. Cable News Network (CNN) and the British Broadcasting Corporation (BBC) have also become available in the 1990s, via satellite, but they are spot-censored in Pakistan. Electronic media in general are less free than print media, and television tends to be more subservient to government than radio. The fact that both have been made into corporations from government departments has not actually released the grip of the Ministry of Information or afforded respite from blatant government propaganda.

ALAMGIR HASHMI

BROADCASTING (St Helena)

A medium-wave station on St Helena, provided by Commonwealth development funds in 1967, was placed under the Education Department, but without staff. By 1970 the main studio was derelict, but some thirty volunteers provided a weekly twenty-hour service (including school programmes) as well as technical maintenance. It was later transferred to an information office and, with a broadcasting officer appointed in April 1973, output had risen to thirty-two hours weekly by 1990. There is still much reliance on recorded material and voluntary contributions, but it is a popular medium, especially for live interviews on local affairs. Original material is devised mainly for schools, local news, and religious programmes, some of which, notably short stories on local themes, may find permanence in print. On St Helena Day (21 May) 1989, education officer Lilian Crowie gave an address over the British Broadcasting Corporation World Service, the first by a St Helenian.

A weekly bulletin of St Helena news is carried by Ascension Island Radio. Tristan da Cunha has a video-cable system laid to homes and public buildings.

TREVOR W. HEARL

BROADCASTING (South Pacific)

Until the 1960s, broadcasting in the South Pacific exclusively meant radio, which was introduced to most of the region's island states shortly after the Second World War.

Most radio drama offered to Pacific listeners has been produced overseas — by the British Broadcasting Corporation, the Australian Broadcasting Corporation, France's Radio-Television Française d'Outre-Mer, Radio New Zealand, and All-India Radio. But several broadcast services, particularly in Melanesia, have taken an active, if intermittent, interest in drama production.

Papua New Guinea's National Broadcasting Commission is the only radio service in the region with a dedicated drama department. It commissions new plays in both English and Tok Pisin (pidgin) for its national service, although rarely plays in Melanesian languages for the local services.

The Solomon Islands Broadcasting Corporation had a period of popular radio drama in the 1970s that drew large audiences. Aedo was a weekly series of episodes in the life of the eponymous civil servant. Production was largely impromptu and few effects were employed, putting emphasis upon the often-satirical dialogue. One of the programme's prominent contributors was Solomon Mamaloni, later to become his country's prime minister.

Radio Vanuatu has broadcast several series of Bislama-language plays in co-operation with the Wan Smolbag Theatre. (See **Drama**, South Pacific.) In Polynesia, only Radio Tonga has a regular schedule of storytelling and dramatizations of traditional tales and translated western novels, usually presented during school holiday periods.

In an effort to stimulate the production of local radio drama, the Pacific Broadcasting Development Project (PacBroad) began a series of workshops on improvised radio theatre techniques in 1986. This has led to several multicultural productions and has encouraged new approaches to playmaking, especially in the western Pacific.

Television services in the region began during the 1960s in the American and French territories, spread to Papua New Guinea, the Cook Islands, and Niue in the 1980s, and arrived in Fiji, Vanuatu, and Western Samoa in the early 1990s. An overwhelming proportion of the broadcast schedule is imported programming, already familiar to Pacific audiences through the ubiquitous video cassette recorder. This firmly established domination by western situation comedies and adventure series, as well as high television production costs (especially as compared with radio drama), has impeded the emergence of a local television drama tradition.

ANDREW HORN

BRODBER, ERNA (1940–)

Jamaican novelist

Born in Woodside, St Mary, Jamaica, and schooled in Jamaica, Canada, and the USA, she is both historian and sociologist by training and has published widely in these fields. She has been lecturer and research fellow in sociology at the University of the West Indies and is a free-lance writer and scholar, based in Jamaica but with frequent lecture tours abroad. Although Brodber had published poetry and short stories in Caribbean journals, it was her first novel, *Jane and Louisa Will Soon Come Home* (1980), that brought her local and international acclaim. Her second, *Myal* (1988), won the 1989 Commonwealth Writers Prize (Canada/Caribbean region).

Brodber asserts that both her academic and fictional work have 'activist intentions', and her concern with recording the oral history and traditional wisdom of Afro-Jamaicans testifies to an underlying commitment to the recovery and preservation of what has been invalidated or undervalued in her colonized culture. Both her novels describe a strongly rooted peasant community, connected with, and sanctioned by, ancestors. However, alienating pressures towards class- and colour-conscious education and upward mobility stress and fragment her village-born protagonists. Nellie (*Jane and Louisa*) suffers psychic collapse; Ella (*Myal*), already ostracized locally for her light complexion, ventures further afield (the USA) in search of belonging, but with the same results. In both texts, communication with, and reconstruction by, the original community effects healing; racial and cultural alienation ('spirit thievery') are overcome by revitalizing severed links with a nurturing folk tradition. As in **Keri Hulme**'s *The Bone People* (1983), reconnection with ancestors becomes a matter of life and death.

Brodber's sociology and fiction focus also on black Caribbean women. For Nellie, contradictory images and models of womanhood and the shameful nature of sexuality (womb as scrap-heap) result in temporary withdrawal into a self-defensive *kumbla* ('cocoon'). In *Myal*, Brodber links male appropriation and rewriting of female with empire's insidious 'othering' of native. Black solidarity operates on a spiritual as well as political level for Brodber, perhaps because of her Rastafarian beliefs. Thus the novels detail a reconstruction of female subjectivity through the predominantly black collective largely by means of non-physical forces.

Exploration of states of psychic fragmentation — *Jane and Louisa* originated as a case study in abnormal psychology — appears often in literature by anglophone and francophone Caribbean women writers and, in Brodber's case, is facilitated by exciting stylistic experimentation. Like **Wilson Harris**, she eschews linear time, blurs the boundaries between reality and illusion, and favours convoluted structures. Individual characters merge with collective personality, and Brodber wittily exploits a range of narrative voices and languages (mannered English to basilectal Creole, with influences from the Bible, English literature, popular song, and folk tale). The effect is a 'diffusion' of omniscient narrator and a 'consolidated' fiction, in favour of a musically textured communal voice and a creole epistemology that negotiates between realities outside the cosmology of the master narrative that wrote indigenous women as absence and lack.

EVELYN O'CALLAGHAN

Further reading: Carolyn Cooper, 'Afro-Jamaican folk elements in Brodber's *Jane and Louisa Will Soon Come Home*', in Carole Davies and Elaine Savory Fido (eds) *Out of the Kumbla: Caribbean Women and Literature* (1990); Evelyn O'Callaghan, 'Engineering the female subject: Erna Brodber's *Myal*', *Kunapipi* 12 (1990).

BROOKE, FRANCES (1724–89)

Canadian/English novelist, dramatist

Born Frances Moore in England, by the 1750s she was writing poetry and plays and moving in London's literary circles. Her weekly periodical *The Old Maid* (1755–6) included letters and essays on religion, politics, society, and theatre, written in lively, entertaining style. In 1756 she published a number of poems along with a play, *Virginia*. Her *Letters from Juliet, Lady Catesby, to Her Friend, Lady Henrietta Campley* (1760), a translation of Marie-Jeanne Riccoboni's novel of sensibility, was highly popular, and was followed by her own novel of sensibility, the even more successful *The History of Lady Julia Mandeville* (1763).

In 1763 Brooke joined her husband, John, chaplain to the British forces in Quebec. There she wrote her still-popular novel of Canada, *The History of Emily Montague* (1769). With her husband and son she returned permanently to England in 1768. She continued to write, publishing two translations from the French and a novel, *The Excursion* (1777). Despite her pronounced success as a novelist, Brooke was primarily interested in theatre; she had three plays produced in London: a tragedy, *The Siege of Sinope* (1781), and two comic operas, *Rosina* (1783) and *Marian* (1788), with music by William Shield. *Rosina* proved the most popular short piece of its time.

Brooke contributed to the novel of sensibility and to the movement towards realism in the novel. All of her novels are characterized by natural, witty dialogue and dramatic irony. Because of its detailed observations on the society, religion, and politics of Quebec, and because of its descriptions of landscape and climate, *Emily Montague* continues to be of interest as the first Canadian, indeed the first North American, novel. Less popular, *The Excursion*, with its sophisticated, witty narrative voice counterpointing that of the naïve protagonist, may be Brooke's best novel.

Frances Brooke's feminist stance is indicated in the wit and independence of central women in *Julia Mandeville* and *Emily Montague*, and in the voices of *The Excursion*'s narrator and 'Mary Singleton', the pseudonymous editor of *The Old Maid*.

LORRAINE McMULLEN

Further reading: Lorraine McMullen, *An Odd Attempt in a Woman: The Literary Life of Frances Brooke* (1983).

BROWN, WAYNE VINCENT (1944–)

Trinidadian poet, short-story writer, critic

Born in Woodbrook, Trinidad, he graduated from the University of the West Indies, Jamaica (BA, 1968). Brown won the Commonwealth Prize for Poetry in 1973 for his collection *On the Coast* (1972). *Edna Manley: The Private Years, 1900–1938* (1976), a highly respected biography of the Jamaican sculptor, revealed his ease in another genre and prepared the way for his short fiction, book reviews, criticism, and newspaper journalism. With Tom Whorton, Brown co-edited an anthology of major British poets, *Twenty-One Years of 'Poetry and Audience'* (1975), and edited a selection of poetry by **Derek Walcott** — *Derek Walcott: Selected Poetry* (1981). In 1989 Brown published a volume of poetry, *Voyages*, and the prose collection *Child of the Sea: Stories and Remembrances.* He lectures in English poetry and creative writing at the University of the West Indies, Trinidad, and has, since 1984, published a distinguished social commentary column, 'In Our Time', in the daily newspaper *Trinidad Express.*

Critic Kenneth Ramchand considers Brown's a 'distinctive voice' among those of the 'new generation' poets, including **Anthony McNeill**, **Mervyn Morris**, and **Dennis Scott**. Notable, however, is Brown's use of the sea as archetype and metaphor in the inquiry into the personal and the communal Caribbean experience. In this aspect his work is linked with that of his mentors Derek Walcott and fellow Trinidadian **Eric Roach**.

Brown's concern with place does not overshadow the search for style, which is predominantly lyrical; he concedes the influence of Wordsworth, T. S. Eliot, Robert Lowell, and Ted Hughes. He employs the extended conceit and the reticulated metaphor, but forges an individual style as he parallels the search for national identity and independence with that of the internal struggle for self-affirmation.

Brown's prose further displays his rich descriptive and metaphoric gifts and his keen perception of the ambiguous link between inner and outer spaces in the lives of intelligent and sensitive Trinidadians. Love and its passing and the uses of memory provide themes through which experience is reflected and contemplated. Brown's vision is based on the self as subject; text and author are inseparable. The writer explores the complexity of his own existence and the psychological scapes encountered as he deciphers the motivations of those around him. Characteristically, however, these perceptions are hedged by delicacy, elusiveness, ambiguity, and irresolution, thus conveying the open-endedness and unfathomability of human connectedness. Brown's work has received relatively little critical attention.

HELEN PYNE TIMOTHY

Further reading: Basil McFarlane, '"The century of exile": Basil McFarlane speaks to Wayne Brown', *Jamaica Journal* 7 (1975); Lloyd Brown, 'West Indian poetry since 1960: Wayne Brown', in *West Indian Poetry* (1978) by Lloyd Brown; Kenneth Ramchand, 'Wayne Vincent Brown', in Daryl C. Dance (ed.) *Fifty Caribbean Writers: A Bio-bibliographical Critical Sourcebook* (1986).

BRUCE, CHARLES (1906–71)

Canadian poet, novelist, short-story writer

Born in the farming and fishing community of Port Shoreham, Nova Scotia, Canada, he attended Mount Allison University in New Brunswick from 1923 to 1927. For seven months after graduation Bruce was a reporter for the Halifax *Chronicle-Herald*. At the beginning of 1928 he joined the Canadian Press news agency, where he was to work for the next thirty-five years. Based mostly in Toronto, he was a war correspondent for Canadian Press from 1944 to 1945; from 1945 to 1963 he was the agency's general superintendent and one of the most respected newspapermen in Canada.

Bruce's major poetry and fiction are based deeply in his Port Shoreham heritage. His early verse at Mount Allison was strongly influenced by the Georgian poets, and his first book, *Wild Apples* (1927), is replete with vague pantheism and references to Truth and Beauty. However, in several poems in *Tomorrow's Tide* (1932) he effectively employs simple, concrete imagery to convey the shoreline and fields of his youth. When he left Nova Scotia in 1933, Bruce began to look back at the lived experience of the farmer-fishermen. While he produced a eulogy to Britain's war effort, *Personal Note* (1941), and his book *Grey Ship Moving* (1945) contains a long narrative poem about a Canadian troopship, the most memorable pieces of this period are drawn from his early experience of kinship 'More eloquent than blood' and of the tide that 'Must always wash the land's remotest heart'. *The Flowing Summer* (1947) is a celebration of the meeting ground between generations, represented by a boy and his grandfather, but the height of his poetic expression occurs in *The Mulgrave Road* (1951), in which the strengths and limitations of rural life are encountered and a sense of place is conveyed through the deceptively simple use of detail.

Bruce's exploration of his roots led him to write short stories in the late 1940s that were published in a variety of North American magazines and journals. He also began his novel, *The Channel Shore* (1954), into which he poured his vision of the balance of 'yesterday, today, and tomorrow' that is provided by individual and communal heritage. The triumph of individual life occurs within an inherited pattern of time and place, and Bruce emphasizes the contribution of regional threads to the national fabric in a growing country. In his collection of linked short stories, *The Township of Time* (1959), he chronicles history and hearsay on the shore from Loyalist times to the 1950s, reflecting the collective Commonwealth movement from colony to independence.

After his retirement from Canadian Press, Bruce wrote *News and the Southams* (1968), a history of the influential Canadian newspaper family. His fiction and poetry, considered too local and even nostalgic, faded from mainstream consideration in the 1960s and 1970s. However, his work has been recently reprinted, and *The Channel Shore* is now recognized as a Canadian classic.

ANDREW WAINWRIGHT

Further reading: Andrew Wainwright, *World Enough and Time: Charles Bruce, A Literary Biography* (1988).

BRUCE, MARY (MINNIE) GRANT (1878–1958)
Australian children's writer, journalist
Born Minnie Grant Bruce, in Sale, Australia, she worked in Melbourne as a journalist and in 1913 travelled to England, where she met her future husband, George Evans Bruce, thereafter living variously in Australia, Ireland, and England. Bruce wrote thirty-seven novels, a collection of retold Aboriginal legends, articles, short stories, and journalism. Her popularity rests on her fifteen 'Billabong' books — the first, *A Little Bush Maid*, was serialized in the *Leader* from October 1905 to August 1907 and published in book form by Ward, Lock in 1910. Her last work, *Billabong Riders*, appeared in 1942.

The 'bush maid' is Norah, who lives with her widower father David Linton and brother Jim on Billabong, a Gippsland cattle station. In this Australian utopia the faithful servants remain the same, the landscape does not alter (except for the occasional bushfire), and Norah, Jim, and their friend Wally Meadows never really grow up. In their relationships with each other (even after Wally and Norah marry) and in the eyes of everyone else on the station, they remain perpetual adolescents. World war and economic depression trouble the Lintons, but through all setbacks Billabong remains a haven for them and for the many people they help and befriend.

Comparisons with other children's works serve mostly to show Bruce's originality, particularly in her portrayal of Norah. Norah is motherless, but this does not leave her the household drudge or lacking in moral direction. She is adventurous and sturdy but not a tomboy and, unlike so many other outgoing heroines, she has no writing ambitions nor does she desire fame. Bruce's characters live by a moral code reminiscent of British boys' adventure stories, but a major feature of behaviour is the distinctly Australian concept of **mateship**, together with the notion that bush life is morally superior to an urban existence. As contemporary rivals and as popular writers who helped shape Australian self image, Bruce is often compared with **Ethel Turner**, but there are very few points of similarity in their writing, and of the two, Bruce's is the more conservative Australian vision.

KERRY WHITE

Further reading: Brenda Niall, *Seven Little Billabongs. The World of Ethel Turner and Mary Grant Bruce* (1979); Alison Alexander, *Billabong's Author: the Life of Mary Grant Bruce* (1979).

BRUTUS, DENNIS VINCENT (1924–)
South African poet
Born in Salisbury, Rhodesia (now Zimbabwe), he studied at the University of Fort Hare (BA, 1947) and the University of the Witwatersrand and taught in schools for fourteen years before becoming deeply involved in the struggle against apartheid. Banned in 1961 from taking part in political activity, Brutus was arrested in 1963 and shot while trying to escape; he spent eighteen months in the notorious prison on Robben Island. In 1966 he went on a one-way 'exit permit' to London, England, and then travelled extensively, campaigning against apartheid. He moved to the USA in 1970, becoming a professor at Northwestern University, Illinois, and later at the University of Pittsburgh. Brutus' first volume of poems, *Sirens, Knuckles, Boots*, was published in Nigeria in 1963, while he was in prison. His second collection, *Letters to Martha*, appeared in 1968.

Brutus' verse is profoundly political, but it is very different from most of the protest and resistance poetry that has been so significant in South Africa since about 1970. Brutus' voice is intensely personal and his mode is lyrical. In his first volume, which pictures vividly the suffering caused by the South African regime, the themes of human love and love of one's country are subtly intertwined; one is conscious that the poet is steeped in a lyrical tradition that stretches from Donne to Wallace Stevens. Many of the poems in the second volume, which uses a more obviously contemporary style of heightened and rhythmical everyday speech, record with rare imaginativeness and honesty the experience of being a political prisoner.

Brutus' poems about the complex emotions of an activist and a prisoner have been widely influential, particularly in other parts of Africa. These poems have also provided a poetic definition of central aspects of the apartheid phenomenon: apartheid has been above all an imprisoning of the human spirit. In a broader perspective Brutus' poetry can be seen as articulating a passionate but mature rejection of one of the more ferocious manifestations of colonialism; at times one is reminded of **Edward Kamau Brathwaite** and **Derek Walcott**, who are Brutus' near contemporaries.

In South Africa, Brutus' work was almost entirely unknown because until 1990 his writing was banned by the regime. Although almost all prohibitions on literature in South Africa were lifted some years before that date, Brutus seems to have been singled out for special treatment, not because his poetry is unusually 'subversive' — it isn't — but because he, more than anyone else, was responsible for the exclusion of South Africa from the Olympic Games in the 1960s.

In exile Brutus has continued to write and to publish — *A Simple Lust* (1973) and *Stubborn Hope* (1978) — though he calls himself an 'occasional' poet. All of his poetry is sensitive, probing, in a manner that is both shaped and colloquial; not many of the poems written in exile, however, achieve the memorable impact of his earlier work.

COLIN GARDNER

Further reading: R. N. Egudu, 'Pictures of pain: the poetry of Dennis Brutus', in Christopher Heywood (ed) *Aspects of South African Literature* (1976); K. L. Goodwin, *Understanding African Poetry* (1982).

BUCKLER, ERNEST (1908–84)

Canadian novelist, short-story writer

Born near Annapolis Royal, Nova Scotia, Canada, he spent all but nine years of his life (during which he studied, with great distinction, at Dalhousie University and the University of Toronto and worked briefly as an actuary in Toronto) as a farmer in the Annapolis Valley, the setting for all of his writings. After more than a decade of writing short stories and articles for American and Canadian magazines on the themes of human relationships in an idealized natural setting, he drew these materials into his first novel.

The Mountain and the Valley (1952) is Buckler's only real claim to a place in the Canadian literary canon. It is often compared to **W. O. Mitchell**'s *Who Has Seen the Wind* (1947) and **Sinclair Ross**' *As For Me and My House* (1941) on the bases of their regional settings, their sensitive protagonists in conflict with the 'garrison culture', and their contribution to their authors' 'one Canadian classic' status. The novel tells the story of David Canaan, ironically named because this frustrated, self-indulgent, and unfulfilled artist can neither liberate himself from his idyllic but stifling rural environment nor articulate the mythology of his generous but inarticulate people. His final escape from the valley and his achievement of aesthetic perspective on it result only in his death on the mountain. The book's larger themes of nostalgia and transience, the structural patterns of symbolism and cyclical time, and Buckler's (critically underrated) ironic characterization of the protagonist achieve a textual complexity and ambiguity that qualify **Margaret Atwood**'s assessment of the book as yet another portrait of 'the failed artist' in Canadian literature. The point of view and language are, however, problematic. David's 'phallogocentricity' (as **Janice Kulyk Keefer** terms it), can easily be confused with Buckler's because of an inconsistent ironic distancing and a style so poetically lush and metaphysically dense as to be obscurantist.

These problems are exacerbated in *The Cruelest Month* (1963), a didactic 'novel of ideas' that gathers a group of intellectual urbanites in a rustic retreat called Endlaw (a pretentious anagram of Walden that typifies the novel). Here they indulge in long psychoanalytical debates and pastoral revisionings and regroupings under the guidance of a mysterious terminally-ill mentor. Although the Arcadian descriptions are compelling, the sophisticated characters and dialogue are tedious and unconvincing, and the self-consciously literary text founders on the contradiction that the one vibrant, admirable character is aggressively illiterate.

In *Ox Bells and Fireflies* (1968) Buckler writes the book David Canaan hoped to write. This 'fictional memoir' is a roughly chronological collection of sketches and anecdotes, the reminiscences of a nostalgic narrator who balances pastoral perfection and comic mores with intimations of mortality. Again, the author typically re-creates the lost harmonies of pre-Second World War Nova Scotia in exuberantly, sometimes exhaustingly, metaphoric prose. However, Buckler's 'Paradise Regained' is both created and subverted by his language, which seems to represent a desperate attempt to repossess Eden through naming it. Ultimately, as Janice Kulyk Keefer has argued, the idyll is deconstructed by a subtext of anxiety and isolation.

Nova Scotia: Window on the Sea (1973) celebrates, with counterpointing photographs by Hans Weber, the rural countryside and pioneer values Buckler idealized, often with the elegiac tone that marks the passage of time, and always in his distinctive style — a litany of similes, metaphors, and descriptive catalogues. *Whirligig* (1977) is an unfortunate collection of light verse, trivial essays, and often crude comedy that won the Stephen Leacock Medal for Humour but did not enhance Buckler's artistic reputation. Many of his earlier short stories were collected by Robert Chambers in *The Rebellion of Young David and Other Stories* (1975).

Buckler's regional idylls are distinctively indebted to his Annapolis Valley childhood experience. He had little knowledge of the rest of his province, let alone his country. In all his works he enshrines traditional, humanistic ideals and laments encroaching urban technology. Generally, his is not the 'Maritime realism' of contemporary social problems portrayed in the books of **Alistair MacLeod**, **Alden Nowlan**, and **David Adams Richards**.

BARBARA PELL

Further reading: John Orange, 'Ernest Buckler: an annotated bibliography', in Robert Lecker and Jack David (eds) *The Annotated Bibliography of Canada's Major Authors* 3 (1981).

BUCKLEY, VINCENT (1925–88)

Australian poet, critic, editor

Born in Romsey, Victoria, Australia, he was educated at the University of Melbourne, Australia, and at Cambridge University, England. Associated with the University of Melbourne, where he became professor in 1968, Buckley was construed as a Leavisite/Arnoldian conservative by hostile Sydney writers and critics such as John Docker and **John Tranter**, although as ***Bulletin*** poetry editor (1961–3) his policy encouraged new poets and broke the dominance of figures such as **Douglas Stewart** and **R. D. FitzGerald**. Buckley's *Book of Modern Australian Verse* (1991) completes editorial work that included anthologies and the magazine *Prospect* (1958–74). While titles such as *Poetry and Morality* (1959) and *Poetry and the Sacred* (1968) indicate the general concerns of his poetics, *Essays in Poetry: Mainly Australian* (1957) opened up new local critical dimensions, challenging prevailing emphases on nationalism, radicalism, and the vitalism of the group associated with **Norman Lindsay**.

Buckley's Irish Catholic heritage was crucial. Explored in the poems of *The Pattern* (1979), his attachment to Ireland — where he spent considerable time — and to Irish poets such as Thomas Kinsella and Seamus Heaney was less problematic than relationships with his immediate forebears, powerfully treated in several 'life studies' poems, notably 'Stroke', the sequence on his father's death that opens his third collection, *Arcady and Other Places* (1966). The same volume contains satirical pieces that reveal disenchantment with the political atmosphere generated by attempts to pose the Catholic church as a counterforce to communism. However, just as his memoir *Cutting Green Hay* (1983) speaks simultaneously of such disillusionments and of the strength drawn from friendships with fellow poets such as **Francis Webb** or **A. D. Hope**, so 'Golden Builders', the long, technically adventurous title poem of his 1976 collection, is as much celebration as critique of the human spirit and those literal and symbolic cities it creates.

Selected Poems (1982) displays something of the range of Buckley's public and personal themes and of his technical development from highly rhetorical lyricism to a style combining 'hardness of phrasing', specificity of naming, and the rhythmic impulse he considered poetically vital. Final assessment of his work will have to take into account the impressive *Last Poems* (1991), a posthumous collection edited by Penelope Buckley from recent journal publications and unpublished manuscripts; meanwhile, his outstanding contributions to literature were recognized in the University of Melbourne's Dublin Prize (1977) and the Fellowship of Australian Writers Christopher Brennan Award (1982).

JENNIFER STRAUSS

Further reading: Vincent O'Sullivan, 'Singing mastery: the poetics of Vincent Buckley', *Westerly* 43 (1989).

BUKENYA, AUSTIN (1944–)

Ugandan poet, novelist, dramatist

Born in Masaka, Uganda, he was educated in Entebbe and Kampala before proceeding to the University of Dar es Salaam, Tanzania, for undergraduate studies. Bukenya studied further in Madagascar, at York University, England, and at the University of Stirling, Scotland. He currently teaches at the University of Kenyatta, Kenya.

Bukenya's novel *The People's Bachelor* (1972) is critical of the waste of resources in African universities, where apparently no serious work is done. It suggests a complete restructuring of the universities so that they do not become places for sloganeering and cheap talk. This kind of radical and critical assessment is also discernible in Bukenya's play *The Bride: A Play in Four Movements* (1984). It breaks from what the author himself describes in the introduction as 'the false simplistic representation of African folk prevalent in African writings in the 1960s and early 1970s', and from the work of **Chinua Achebe** and **Okot p'Bitek**. The play dramatizes the cultural conflicts inherent in East African society in a language akin to that of Nigerian **Wole Soyinka**, although Bukenya's images are drawn from his East African environment.

Bukenya maintains that he is first and foremost a teacher. His enthusiasm is evident in such publications as *Notes on East African Poetry* (1978), *Note on the Floods* (1986), and in texts he has written for use in Kenyan schools. These texts reflect the critical sense that characterizes Bukenya's other works. Bukenya's research in the oral literature of the peoples of East Africa culminated in his *Oral Literature for Schools* (1983).

EGARA KABAJI

BULLETIN

A weekly newspaper established in 1880 in Sydney, Australia, by John Haynes and J. F. Archibald, it had by 1890 become the most significant literary and political journal in the Australian colonies. Its early years were marked by precarious finances, frequent libel suits, and a rambunctious and populist style of journalism in keeping with the style of colonial politics but more like USA models than its serious and respectable Australian contemporaries. Its style was shared with the Sydney *Truth*, the republican and egalitarian overtones of its nationalism by the *Queensland Boomerang* and *Worker*, and its contributors by all three.

Although editorially the early *Bulletin* was sympathetic to Aborigines and outraged by their treatment, its contributors reflected the prejudices of their time. The journal's contempt for Chinese immigrants, maintained to the 1960s, helped to establish and maintain the white Australia immigration policy. Although its nationalism paralleled that of Canadian literary periodicals established in the Confederation period after the 1860s, it lacked their sententiousness and sectarianism. It was highly suspicious of Britain and imperialism, it was sympathetic to Louis Riel's 1885 rebellion against the Canadian government, and it opposed Australia's involvement in both the Sudan War and the Boer War. Its nationalism became more conservative after Archibald's departure in 1907, it became more sympathetic to imperialism during the First World War, and by the 1950s it had become the voice of rural conservatism. Sold to a new owner in 1961, it was resurrected as a journal of business and affairs, gradually shedding its literary interests and its rural basis and gathering support instead from the urban business and professional classes.

The first editors, Archibald (1880–1 and 1886–1903) and W. H. Traill (1881–6), gave the *Bulletin* its distinctive mixture of malice, mischief, and high seriousness. They filled it with black-and-white art, news, denunciatory editorials, and readers' contributions of gossip or comment, ballads, poems, and yarns. Dubbed the Bushman's Bible, it created a community that extended to all the Australian colonies and New Zealand and provided a basis of nationalist sentiment for the colloquial literature that grew from it. Archibald encouraged writers such as **Henry Lawson** and **A. B. Paterson**, who established bush egalitarianism as a dominant theme in Australian literature, and he fostered the short story and ballad as the *Bulletin*'s major forms.

This literary interest was extended by **A. G. Stephens**, who in 1896 established the Red Page, which published poems, reviews, and articles on Australian and European literature and until 1961 remained a major forum for the discussion of Australian literature. Between the wars the *Bulletin* continued its tradition of light verse with such writers as **C. J. Dennis** and Ronald McCuaig, and provided a first opportunity for the publication of Australian fiction, which it further encouraged through annual prizes and the publication of Australian novels through the Endeavour Press. Its last Red Page editor, **Douglas Stewart**, presided over the postwar flourishing of a school of Australian poetry that included **Judith Wright**, **Rosemary Dobson**, **Francis Webb**, and **Vincent Buckley**.

JOHN McLAREN

Further reading: Patricia Rolfe, *The Journalistic Javelin: An Illustrated History of the Bulletin* (1970); Sylvia Lawson, *The Archibald Paradox* (1983).

BULOSAN, CARLOS (1913–56)

Filipino novelist, poet, short-story writer

He was born in Binalonan, Pangasinan, the Philippines, to a peasant family of five brothers and two sisters. When one of his older brothers went to the USA, young Carlos, with only a few years of secondary schooling, joined him. At the age of eighteen, Bulosan was a migrant worker in Seattle, Washington, USA, and became a union activist like his brother. While confined in hospital with tuberculosis, he taught himself to write, making up for lost time by extensive reading.

In 1942 Bulosan published a collection of poetry entitled *Chorus for America: Six Philippine Poets*; one of the poets represented was **Jose Garcia Villa**. That same year Bulosan published *Letter from America*; in 1943 he published his first book of poems, *The Voice of Bataan*.

Bulosan's first real success came with the publication of his short-story collection *The Laughter of My Father* (1944). Many of these stories had been previously published in *The New Yorker*; the book was so well received that it went through several printings, one in paperback.

P. G. Morantte, a close friend of Bulosan, wrote of him as an imaginative and entertaining storyteller endowed with charming wit and extravagant humour. Bulosan, however, wanted his stories to be taken seriously; he said that *The Laughter of My Father* was not merely lightweight humour but 'satire, indictment against an economic system that stifled the primitive'.

Seriousness is more evident in his quasi-autobiographical *America is in the Heart* (1946), a novel one critic describes as 'a painful record of the experiences of a Filipino who did not find his American dream'. Another critic calls it 'a living testimony, almost a legacy to those shamed and silenced and maimed by injustice and hatred and persecution'. There is anger, sorrow, fear, and bitterness in this 'personal history', but the feeling at the end is one of optimism and idealism, for Bulosan had also discovered the paradoxically compassionate, humane, and beautiful side of America. He died in Seattle.

MA. TERESA LUZ DE MANUEL

BUNTING, JOHN REGINALD (1916–)

English/Jamaican poet, short-story writer

He was born in Mansfield, England. An Oxford graduate, he went to Jamaica in 1939 to teach English at Munro College. In 1943 he replaced the progressive and controversial Dr Lewis Davidson as headmaster of Wolmer's Boys' School, Kingston. A keen cricketer and footballer, Bunting was manager of Jamaica's 1948 Olympic team. He helped to broadcast Jamaican sporting events for the BBC Overseas Service while the BBC's **'Caribbean Voices'** programme was broadcasting his poetry. Bunting left Wolmer's in 1949 to enter the Colonial Education Service in Nigeria, where he eventually became Chief Federal Advisor on Education and where he continued to write. After leaving Nigeria, Bunting joined the publishers Evans Brothers, London, England, where he was primarily concerned with books for the Caribbean market. His poetry appears in the first volume of *Caribbean Voices: An Anthology of West Indian Poetry* (1966), edited by **John Figueroa**, in the journal *Focus* (1948 issue), edited by Edna Manley, and in *John O'London*'s.

A traditionalist in both education and literature, Bunting has spoken of the influence on his verse of contemporary American poetry. Much of his poetry is of a Romantic bent, showing a concern with Jamaica and its natural beauty. Although mainly a writer of verse, he has also written short stories, mainly for 'Caribbean Voices', under the pseudonym John Mansfield. Bunting was a founding member of Jamaica's Columbus Circle, which encouraged a voyage of discovery into the arts and which at one time expressed concern that programmes such as 'Caribbean Voices' were siphoning off good Caribbean writing.

Bunting contributed, as if from the inside, to Jamaica's educational and cultural growth. In literature he was perhaps more of an enabler than an outstanding performer, but that was an important role in Jamaica in the 1940s.

JOHN J. FIGUEROA

BURKE, EDDIE (1909–)

Jamaican educator

Born in the rural township of Chapelton, Clarendon, Jamaica, he grew up shifting between the homes of his parents, who lived apart. His father, a shopkeeper, and his mother, a college-trained teacher who ran a dame school between daily household chores, afforded him access in this way to two different service-oriented styles of behaviour. Burke chose his mother's profession, but what distinguished him from his colleagues was his application of a pedagogy that was to be copied by teachers throughout Jamaica.

In 1931 Burke graduated from the Caribbean's major male teacher-training institution, Mico Training College, Kingston, Jamaica. There he learned a zealous nationalism from Marcus Garvey and others who wanted to build a new Jamaica. Armed with his teacher-training certificate and the heritage of his parents, Burke joined them. He became the sole teacher in a rural village in the west of the island. He doubled as assistant cleric, filling simultaneously two high-status positions within the community; this was not unusual.

When old methodologies failed to inspire his students to complete the syllabus set by the educational authorities, Burke decided to motivate individuals through community action: he treated the school as a community sensitive to its own needs and able to say what it wanted to learn. He saw teachers as following this lead, injecting into the learning process, as the opportunity arose, what they wished to transmit. This, the 'project approach' to teaching, was the beginning of Burke's career as a community organizer.

In 1938, when Jamaica's first national social welfare programme began, Burke extended his practice of community organization into the wider Jamaican community and became one of the country's first community development officers. While serving in this capacity he became aware of the potential danger of a new import — the comic book. He was particularly upset by one comic book's denigrating portrayal of men. To correct this bias he designed and published himself in the late 1940s and 1950s his Newsy Wapps series, an amusing depiction of the life of a Jamaican boy of the 1920s. Burke sold the books so cheaply — the cost of one bottle of beer — that its message could reach all Jamaicans. The Newsy Wapps series was a further expression of Burke's commitment to serve the Jamaican people.

Retired from a career in community development that took him to England and Ethiopia as the agent of the Jamaican government and of the United Nations, he continues to serve: he is an Anglican priest ministering to a rural Jamaican community.

ERNA BRODBER

Further reading: 'A life of service; Rev. E. N. Burke', interview with Erna Brodber, *Jamaica Journal* 2 (1984).

BURN, DAVID (1798/9?–1875)

Australian dramatist

Born in Edinburgh, Scotland, he arrived in Tasmania, Australia, as a free settler in 1826. Like many emigrants with a literary bent, he bombarded the press with accounts of the new colony — more than 300 by 1842 — laying the basis for his later success as editor and newspaper proprietor in New Zealand.

Burn's literary reputation has rested on his plays and their claims to precedence. His melodrama *The Bushrangers* (1971) was performed in Edinburgh in 1829, the first staged representation of Australian scenes by an Australian inhabitant. *Plays and Fugitive Pieces in Verse* (1842) was offered as 'the first series of Dramatic Compositions which as yet have issued from an Antipodean Press'. The volume included the twice-produced naval farce *Our First Lieutenant*, stories and poems, as well as four historical tragedies in verse; sentimental and fustian, these plays do not live up to H. M. Green's assertion that they contain 'really tragic feeling'. Burn seems much more at ease with the rambunctious burlesque *Sydney Delivered* (1845), its francophobic patriotism demonstrating vividly how European antagonisms were echoed in the furthest-flung corners of colonialism.

The Bushrangers has attracted attention for its use of several motifs characteristic of early nineteenth-century Australian writing: unfair, brutal treatment of convicts; incompetent, self-seeking authorities; childish but dangerous Aborigines; and mistreated, honourable bushrangers brought to a morally satisfactory death. This is romantic melodrama, with the mythic figures of popular imagination adapted to Tasmania's exotic *mise-en-scène*.

Burn's work is also part of a politically potent search for colonial identity (like that **Margaret Atwood** identifies as intrinsic to Canadian literature). The penal origins of Australia weigh on writers, encouraging formal homage to the conventions of 'home' (as in Burn's verse plays), but the colonies' ambivalent status also generates a defence of the immigrants, in opposition to the whims of corrupt governors and the claims of pre-existing inhabitants. Freedom and liberty may be among Burn's favourite topics, but they are concepts framed in colonial terms, invoking Enlightenment laws of property not only against arbitrary government and lawlessness, but also, implicitly, against any threat to 'settlement' of the supposed *terra nullius*.

CHRIS WORTH

BUTLER, FREDERICK GUY (1918–)

South African poet, playwright, critic

Born in Cradock, a town in the semi-desert Karoo region of the Eastern Cape, South Africa, he was educated at Rhodes University, Grahamstown. After serving in the Second World War, Butler was awarded a scholarship to study at Oxford University, England. On his return to South Africa, he took up a lectureship at the University of the Witwatersrand. He was appointed head of the Department of English at Rhodes University in the early 1950s, retiring from this position in 1983.

Butler's chief contribution to South African literature has been as poet and as critic. His *Selected Poems* (1975) was awarded the CNA (Central News Agency) Literary Prize. He has also received acclaim for his two-part autobiography, *Karoo Morning: An Autobiography 1918–35* (1977) and *Bursting World: An Autobiography 1936–45* (1983), and is author of several plays on settler themes, including *Take Root or Die* (1970) and *Richard Gush of Salem* (1982). Butler has published two historical works, *When Boys Were Men* (1969) and *The 1820 Settlers* (1974).

The central feature of Butler's poetry is its preoccupation with the encounter of Europe and Africa. He brings to a new level of self-consciousness the attempt by the European poet to enter into dialogue with a continent that continues, despite more than a century of occupation, to be largely unresponsive to the importunities of the European settler-poet. By entering into dialogue with Africa, European poets wish to discover the authentic voice of the land. In striving to make this voice their own, they seek to translate physical appropriation of the land into cultural appropriation of its means of expression.

In his seminal poem 'Home Thoughts' (1960), Butler employs Nietzsche's conception of a conflict between Apollonian rationality and Dionysian irrationality to represent the struggle between, and eventual reconciliation of, an intellectual Europe and an instinctual Africa. Although the poem is evocative, Butler's use of the Nietzschean myth is flawed, since the reconciliation is at the initiative, and under the effective control, of the skilful Apollo. Consequently, the paternalism and the prejudice that Butler seeks to overthrow are simply perpetuated, albeit in a more sophisticated register.

The difference between Butler and earlier South African poets such as **Thomas Pringle** and **Francis Carey Slater**, whose poetry is also preoccupied with the encounter of Europe and Africa, is that Butler is conscious of the difficulties raised by the European poet who speaks on behalf of Africa.

Butler's poetry evinces an ironic double perspective, a simultaneous affirmation and denial of its own adequacy as an effective means of expression, sharing with the work of his contemporary Anthony Delius an acute sense of alienation and doubt.

Butler's imagination turns readily to myth, and some of his most significant poetry, such as 'Myths' (first published in *Poets in South Africa: An Anthology*, 1950, edited by Roy Macnab), explores the possibility of finding an African equivalent for the archetypal situations he had discovered in European literature. His interest in myth derives in large measure from the work of Carl Jung, whose notion of the shadow personality, the renounced but also desirable *other*, forms the basis of his own conception of the relation between Europe and Africa. Butler's Africa is really an Africa within, a psychical construct. Thus, when he speaks of integrating himself with Africa, he is referring also, perhaps even primarily, to an integration with what is hidden and unknown in himself, with his own instinctual being.

Butler's preoccupation with the encounter of Europe and Africa features most prominently in his early volumes, *Stranger to Europe: Poems 1939–1949* (1952, enlarged 1960) and *South of the Zambezi: Poems from South Africa* (1966). Although this preoccupation is sustained in *24 Songs and Ballads* (1978), the emphasis shifts from mythic encounter to actual historical encounter and draws substantially on Butler's knowledge of settler history.

In *Pilgrimage to Dias Cross: A Narrative Poem* (1987) the historical dimension is retained, but is fused with an overall mythic structure, that of the quest. In his imaginary journey to Kwaaihoek — where Bartolomeu Diaz planted a cross to mark his furthest point of navigation and thereby signalled the opening of southern Africa to colonial occupation — the persona is accompanied by the ghosts of various historical figures, European and African. By evoking a diversity of voices and giving each voice a historical context, the poem offers a more complex conception of the encounter between Europe and Africa than that provided by the bold but abstract depiction of an Apollonian Europe and a Dionysian Africa.

As critic and lecturer, and through his work on many cultural bodies, Butler promoted South African literature at a time when it was regarded as inferior to the 'Great Tradition' and excluded from serious study. In his critical writings he took up such issues as the criteria appropriate to a study of South African literature and the recognition of a regional South African English. In this Butler anticipated a debate that surfaced in the 1970s, when the necessity for new ways of reading and evaluating South African literature made itself felt.

It may be true, as the critic Mike Kirkwood has argued, that the colonial tradition culminates in the work of Butler, but it is equally true that it finds here the conditions of its transformation.

DIRK KLOPPER

Further reading: Muriel Bradbrook, 'A dome of many-coloured glass: the lyric poetry of Guy Butler', in Malvern van Wyk Smith and Don Maclennan (eds) *Olive Schreiner and After: Essays on Southern African Literature in Honour of Guy Butler* (1983); J. M. Coetzee, 'Reading the South African landscape', in his *White Writing: On the Culture of Letters in South Africa* (1988).

BUZO, ALEXANDER (1944–)

Australian dramatist

Born in Sydney, Australia, he began writing plays soon after graduating in English from the University of New South Wales, Australia, in 1965. His early plays, such as *Norm and Ahmed* (1969) and *Rooted* (1973), offer jaundiced views of the social restraints on individual expression, particularly in Australia of the 1960s. *Tom* (1975) and *Coralie Lansdowne Says No* (1974) explore the possibility of retaining human qualities in a social world where individuals must become tough or break down completely; *Martello Towers* (1976) and *Makassar Reef* (1979) seem to offer sexual love as something to hang on to (however tenuously) amid the confusion and shallowness of modern life. Buzo's plays *Big River* and *The Marginal Farm* — published together in 1985 — focus on periods of social and political change as Buzo watches his tough and questing central characters adapt and become changed in turn by their decisions.

Though Buzo's plays have been seen as studies of Australian middle-class social mores (*Rooted*, *Tom*, *Coralie Lansdowne Says No*, *Martello Towers*), or Australian racism (*Norm and Ahmed*), or Australian attitudes to Asia and the Pacific (*Makassar Reef*, *The Marginal Farm*), they all examine the problems of the liberal humanist in a world of crumbling values. His historical play *Macquarie* (1971) overtly expresses the dilemma of the liberal caught between reactionary and revolutionary forces. Buzo's satirical detective novel, *The Search for Harry Allway* (1985), and his commentaries on Australian language, *Tautology* (1981) and *Meet the New Class* (1981), suggest that his liberalism is taking an increasingly conservative turn.

Buzo's achievements as a playwright are difficult to compare with those of his contemporaries. Certainly, many influences, including Hollywood film, can be discerned in his plays. He has been compared to Anton Chekhov for his ability to mix tragedy and comedy, to Ben Jonson for his characterization, to G. B. Shaw for his verbal brilliance, and to Neil Simon for his depiction of contemporary suburban dilemmas, but the mixture of styles in his work offers grounds for comparison with almost any playwright with an interest in language and social change.

SUSAN LEVER

Further reading: John McCallum, *Buzo* (1987).

C

CALLAGHAN, MORLEY (1903–90)

Canadian novelist, short-story writer

Born in Toronto, Canada, he attended Riverdale Collegiate and St Michael's College, University of Toronto. In 1925 he entered Osgoode Hall and was called to the bar in 1928. (Though he was never to practise law, his works often explore natural justice versus mere legality.) During this period Callaghan worked part-time for the Toronto *Daily Star*, where he met Ernest Hemingway, his first major literary contact, and honed his characteristic reportorial style. In 1929–30 he visited Paris, France, and lived briefly in the USA. He also worked as a sports and public affairs columnist for *New World Illustrated* (1940–8) and as a radio and television host for the Canadian Broadcasting Corporation (intermittently from 1943). In 1930 Callaghan settled permanently in Toronto, the locale in most of his fiction. He was made a Companion of the Order of Canada in 1982 and received numerous literary awards both in Canada and abroad.

Callaghan's long career is distinguished by a paradox. On the one hand he displays an iconoclastic resistance to colonial and neo-colonial influences in his attempts to develop non-Eurocentric styles and forms. As early as 1938, in a review of C. R. Allen's *Tales of New Zealanders*, he remarked:

> From a Canadian point of view this collection of New Zealand stories has a special interest . . . are [New Zealanders] still writing colonial literature, or have they got something of their own? . . . what are they doing with the language? Does there seem to be any kind of native sensibility of imagination?

On the other hand, his refusal to support nationalist movements, his sustained interest in American writing, and his resistance to regionalism define him unequivocally as an 'internationalist'. Until his death he maintained that 'Canada is part of the British North American pattern.'

Callaghan's first phase, from 1928 to 1937, was his most prolific and constitutes an oeuvre similar to that of New Zealand's **Frank Sargeson**. Both examine stifling neo-puritan social pressures; both often return to stock situations: a marginalized outsider frustrating a homogeneous conservative state; the limitations of totalizing ideologies (especially Christianity, scientific determinism, Freudianism, and Marxism); the possibility of anarchic vitalism; and the 'sacramental' nature of the individual. At this time Callaghan self-consciously withstood the colonial mainstream of Canadian and, he argues, American and European language practice (though his latter claim has met with much critical dubiety). Against the romanticism of the early century he, like Sargeson, countered with a crisp neo-imagism: simple characterizations, parable-like structures, and an almost skeletal, pared-down language. In this first phase he published two collections of short stories dealing mostly with day-to-day situations, *A Native Argosy* (1929) and *Now That April's Here* (1936); *An Autumn Penitent* (1929, containing two novellas); three deterministic novels, *Strange Fugitive* (1928), *It's Never Over* (1930), and *A Broken Journey* (1932); and the biblically entitled triad *Such Is My Beloved* (1934), *They Shall Inherit the Earth* (1935), and *More Joy in Heaven* (1937). These last remain Callaghan's most distinctive, for here he distances himself from American naturalist influences (like Sherwood Anderson and Theodore Dreiser), digests the influential Christian teachings of Jacques Maritain, and evolves his novelistic idiom of simplicity and sustained ambiguity.

After a fallow period from 1938 to 1945, Callaghan initiated his second phase with a fictionalized account of the University of Toronto, *The Varsity Story* (1948), and the juvenile novel *Luke Baldwin's Vow* (1948). Though limited, both signpost crucial features in the developing oeuvre. Like the spiritual novels of the 1930s, they foreground his continued interest in marginalized individuals and social ideologies. Callaghan's 'solution' is here a privileged sense of imaginative selfhood — a theme that dominates the self-conscious novels of the 1950s and 1960s. Like many post-colonial writers of his generation, Callaghan saw parody as one means of reclaiming literary authority for himself. Accordingly, *The Loved and the Lost* (1951), winner of a Governor General's Award for Fiction, is a deceptively simple subversion of the conventional murder mystery; *The Many Colored Coat* (1960), an expansion of the 1955 novella *The Man with the Coat*, ironically resurrects the latter's dead hero; *A Passion in Rome* (1961) wittily incorporates Callaghan's own previous journalistic writing.

Intriguingly, this literary game-playing coincides with his growing interest in autobiographical revision and readerly entrapment. Following *That Summer in Paris: Memoirs of Tangled Friendships with Hemingway, Fitzgerald, and Some Others* (1963), the works become overtly metafictional, as Callaghan recycles past novels, interviews, and non-fictional essays. In a paradoxical post-colonial gesture, Callaghan confidently writes *Canadian* autobiography, while seeking valorization from European contexts and American fellow writers. The result is a sophisticated (albeit narcissistic) meditation upon his own art, as well as a fascinating confidence game for readers 'in the know'. *A Fine and Private Place* (1975), *A Time for Judas* (1983), and *A Wild Old Man on the Road* (1988) all revise Callaghan's earlier literary and philosophical themes (i.e., the criminal saint, the artist as individualist). Similarly, his play *Season of the Witch* (1976) revises an earlier play, 'Going Home' (premièred 1950), which in turn was adapted from *They Shall Inherit the Earth*. This compulsive revision underpins *Close to the Sun Again* (1977), *The Enchanted Pimp* (1978), and *Our Lady of the Snows* (1985), not to mention *The Lost and Found Stories of Morley Callaghan* (1985), which reprints twenty-six stories omitted from the earlier collection, *Morley Callaghan's Stories* (1959).

Callaghan has had a turbulent critical reputation. Whereas American critics of the 1920s and 1930s praised his compassion, psychological insights, and hard-boiled plots, later critics have focused on his occasionally derivative style, crude dialogue, pedestrian prose, and awkward characterization. But like Frank Sargeson — and to a lesser degree, **Katherine Mansfield**, whom Callaghan admired — his detailed prose and neo-imagistic theorizing (language should be as 'clear as glass', 'tell the truth cleanly') mark one of Canadian literature's early major steps away from colonial repetition. As critic Malcolm Ross rightly remarked in 1960, whatever the limitations of his style, it was Callaghan who first 'broke open for [Canada] the egg-shell of our cultural colonialism'.

GARY BOIRE

Further reading: David Staines, ed., *The Callaghan Symposium* (1981); Judith Kendle, 'Morley Callaghan: an annotated bibliography', in Robert Lecker and Jack David (eds) *The Annotated Bibliography of Canada's Major Authors* 5 (1985).

CALLENDER, TIMOTHY (1946–89)

Barbadian short-story writer, novelist

Born in Hindsbury, in the parish of St Michael, Barbados, he began writing stories at the age of sixteen, encouraged by **Frank Collymore**, founder of the literary magazine *Bim*. Callender attended St Giles Boys' School, Combermere, the University of the West Indies, and the University of London, England, where he gained an MA in art and design in education. An artist and sculptor, he taught for several years at training colleges and secondary schools in Jamaica, St Kitts, and Barbados. He won numerous awards in the National Independence Festival of Creative Arts for his short stories, plays, poems, and essays.

Callender's publications include: *It So Happen* (1975), a short-story collection; *How Music Came to the Ainchan People* (1979), a novel; and *The Elements of Art* (1977), a critical study. Callender published numerous essays, poems, and short stories in *Bim* and other literary journals and some of his stories were broadcast on radio in Barbados and serialized in *The Nation* newspaper.

Callender's literary ability is best manifested in his short stories. His use of dialect in 'Peace and Love' and 'The Course of True Love' aids the naturalism of his fiction. Many of his short stories re-create early Barbadian village life and folk culture; in effect, Callender captures a bygone era of Barbadian life on his literary canvas. *How Music Came to the Ainchan People* is an imaginative exploration of the power of art to overcome oppression and human degradation; although it is technically less compelling than Callender's short stories, its theme best represents the essence of his artistic vision.

Callender's paintings, such as *Fisherman In Sunset*, echo the brightly etched beauty and spirituality of a Kapo on one hand and a Beckettian sparseness and futility on the other.

GLYNE A. GRIFFITH

CAMBRIDGE, ADA (1844–1926)

Australian novelist, poet, short-story writer

Born in Norfolk, England, she immigrated to Melbourne, Australia, with her husband, an Anglican clergyman, in 1870. She steadily built up a reputation that was consolidated with her first novel, *A Marked Man* (1890). Between 1856 and 1914 Cambridge published twenty-eight novels and five volumes of poetry, plus stories, essays, articles, and autobiographical works. Her life was crowded with duties as a mother and clergyman's wife, marked cruelly by tragedy, hampered by financial worries, and confined by ill health. Yet she was a natural writer, thoroughly professional, and maintained both independence and immense popularity.

Cambridge portrays the typical anxieties of the Anglo-Australian middle classes, and, while often endorsing British, imperialist, and masculine viewpoints, she is not beyond incisive criticism of her own class. Her exquisite skill at irony is seen at its height in the satirical monologue of *Materfamilias* (1898) and in the dryly amusing *A Woman's Friendship* (1889), which has been likened to Henry James' *The Bostonians* (1886).

Always uneasy in Australia, Cambridge was self-consciously colonial, although a visit to England surprised her by confirming how Australian she had become in the years away from 'Home'. Her autobiography, *Thirty Years in Australia* (1903), explains the personal sense of exile that features strongly in her fiction. The universal 'woman question' (about which Cambridge was ambivalent) adds further complexities: Cambridge's modern woman — in *A Happy Marriage* (1906) or *The Eternal Feminine* (1907), for example — is on the verge of escaping both nineteenth-century and colonial constraints.

Cambridge was a social humanitarian, but abhorred socialism; she wanted to see the lives of individuals improve, but rejected revolution; she criticized Australian unionism, but supported British strikers: thus the odd mixture of radicalism and conservatism throughout her work.

Even more than her novels, Cambridge's poetry, particularly *Unspoken Thoughts* (1887) and *The Hand in the Dark* (1913), reveals a keen engagement with contemporary social issues. Her unorthodox religious and social opinions are here given fuller dramatic expression. Arguably, her novels were more mindful of popular acceptance.

DEBRA ADELAIDE

Further reading: Margaret Bradstock and Louise Wakeling, *Rattling the Orthodoxies: A Life of Ada Cambridge* (1990).

CAMERON, NORMAN EUSTACE (1903–83)
Guyanese dramatist
He was born in New Amsterdam, British Guiana (now Guyana), when access to the best education for poor black youth was limited to a bright few. Cameron won a scholarship to Queens College and, as a winner of a Guyana Scholarship, earned an MA in mathematics at Cambridge University, England. After returning home he taught at Queens College, worked in theatre, founded the British Guiana Literary Society, lectured in mathematics at the University of Guyana (retiring as professor emeritus in 1968), contributed radio 'Viewpoints', and was named a Member of the Order of the British Empire.

The full significance of Cameron to Guyanese letters is not adequately recognized. He is not placed among the major writers; the import of his three books, eight plays, four mathematical texts, and approximately fourteen essays, self-published between 1929 and 1970, lie in their timing and concerns.

Cameron stated that he began a literary career because of his inability to answer questions about Guyanese literature while at Cambridge. This interest developed alongside the increase in cultural awareness and nationalism in the colony in the 1930s and the growth in black consciousness, the Garvey movement, and the Negro Progress Convention. Cameron became determined to counter the low image and comic stature given blacks in much of the literature and drama of the time.

However, his drama on black heroism was often set in mythical and biblical North Africa, as in *Adoniya* ('Wife of Moses'), *Sabaco*, *Ebedmelech* (all three published together in *Three Immortals*, 1953), and *Balthasar* (1931). Others touching Guyana more closely are 'Kayssa or Hear the Other Side' (premièred 1959), *Price of Victory* (1965) and *The Trumpet* (1969), while *Jamaica Joe* (1962) depicts Jamaican seasonal farm workers in the USA.

Cameron's most important non-fiction, the two-volume *The Evolution of the Negro* (vol. 1, 1929; vol. 2, Books 1 and 2, 1934; repr. 1970), traces African medieval civilization, slavery, and development among blacks since emancipation. He edited *Guianese Poetry* (1931; repr. 1970), a valuable anthology covering the period from 1831 to 1931, which is his best contribution to Caribbean literature. *Thoughts on Life and Literature* (1950) surveys Guyanese literature and culture, and his 'Drama in British Guiana' first appeared in *Kyk-over-al* (1, 1945). Cameron published *Additional Mathematics* (1942) in four books, a collection of poems, *Interlude* (1944), and several local histories and political commentaries.

AL CREIGHTON

Further reading: Joycelynne Loncke, *Norman E. Cameron: The Man and his Work* (1981).

CAMEROON

Anglophone Cameroonian literature is unique in English letters. Fostered by the League of Nations instead of formally re-colonized after the First World War, fostered again instead of freed by the United Nations after the Second World War, orphaned by the Commonwealth since independence, and isolated from the rest of anglophone Africa since the early 1960s, anglophone Cameroon has a distinct literary culture.

History

From 1884 to the early stages of the First World War, Kamerun was a German colony. During the war, the western part of the colony went to Britain; the north, south, and east were taken over by

France. From 1916 to 1960, Britain administered British Northern Cameroons and British Southern Cameroons from Lagos, as a non-colonized, trusteeship part of Nigeria. Following the war, the League of Nations mandated these territories as protectorates to Britain. Because they no longer had the status of colonies, Britain put substantially fewer resources into infrastructure than into other territories that were fully colonized. The areas of the former Kamerun controlled by the French, on the contrary, were understood by their guardians to be a colony, with no concern for the administrative subtleties of the League of Nation's designation. When the United Nations was born, it renewed the legal status of 'trusteeships', in counter-distinction to colonies, with regard to the British and French Cameroons.

On 1 January 1960, 'East Cameroon' (the French 'colony') received independence from France. On 11 February 1961 a plebiscite was held in the British territories, with British Northern Cameroon opting to join Nigeria, and British Southern Cameroon voting for 'reunification' with the French zone. Formal reunification occurred on 1 October 1961, with the establishment of a federated state. The anglophone capital became Buea, the former capital of German Kamerun, and a quasi-anglophone national identity was recognized. The road to independence in the two Cameroons had been more violent than in most of the rest of Africa. To further quell militancy after armed interventions by France against guerrilla insurgencies in the 1950s, many repressive laws were passed in the two federated Cameroonian parliaments in 1962, putting an end to the right of free association and ensuring an enduring era of exiles and of political murders by the state. In a rigged election in 1972, the anglophone state was dissolved and a 'unified' republic was declared, ushering in a period that until today anglophone Cameroonians have denounced as a protracted effort at cultural genocide of them by the French and francophones. Only the fate of neighbouring Biafra has kept the anglophone provinces from declaring outright independence.

In 1982 Paul Biya took over as president of the Republic of Cameroon, declaring a 'New Deal' that was to bring limited democracy to the country and greater anglophone participation in the nation's affairs. This brought some exiles home, among them such anglophones as Bate Besong, who gave new verve to anglophone militancy. Although Biya's 'New Deal' turned out to be as repressive as the 'Old Deal' of the first president, Ahidjo, pressures by democratic forces in the country have been relentless, and anglophones have been among the strongest leaders. By the late 1980s, censorship laws were relaxed and political and cultural activity in the anglophone community resurfaced, giving vent to vigorous literary and para-literary forces that proclaimed the need for a truly new deal. In May 1990, John Fru Ndi, an anglophone bookseller, formed the SDS, Cameroon's first opposition party since a uni-party state had been declared in 1966. In 1992 Fru Ndi led the opposition forces of Cameroon's 'limping democracy' to an electoral defeat of President Biya, who — according to international observers — subsequently 'stole' the election and remains in power (1993).

The aborted victory of Fru Ndi and his SDS in 1992 was a stunning event in Cameroonian and African history, owing much to literary activity and promising to be a watershed in the country's political and cultural evolution. The leader of a marginalized, 'distinct society' within the larger society had formed a coalition that transcended the imputed divisions of many African states along ethnic and linguistic lines. The role of literature in Cameroon's movement toward democracy has been decisive.

Geography, Language, and Culture

Anglophone Cameroon covers approximately one

eighth of the surface of the country and includes between one fifth and one quarter of the population (approximately 2.5 to three million of ten to twelve million), roughly the inverse proportion to that of anglophone to francophone Canada. (The Canadian comparison is not casual, for Cameroonian and Canadian biculturalism and bilingualism policies and structures were profoundly influenced by each other through the friendship of Canadian Prime Minister Pierre Trudeau and Cameroon's **Bernard Nsokika Fonlon** in the 1960s and 1970s.) Two of Cameroon's ten provinces — the North West and South West Provinces — are anglophone. They are home to more than 230 ethnic groups with separate languages. Pidgin is the region's *lingua franca*, with English being the preserve of the educated.

As a result of being a remote appendage of Empire under the British, schools in Cameroon from 1916 to 1960 received far fewer resources and attention than in other colonized societies. In 1961 only one anglophone, Bernard Nsokika Fonlon, had a Ph.D. By 1983 there were only about 100, most of them exiled. In 1961 only about fifty had baccalaureate degrees, and by 1983 only about 2,000. The literacy rate was officially (over-) estimated at seventy-five per cent. With no major urban centres, no publishing houses, few — and very poorly stocked — bookshops, with only one radio station (broadcasting in thirty languages), and with no university, anglophone Cameroon had a totally insufficient infrastructure for a literary culture at the beginning of the 1980s. Yet, paradoxically, such a culture was blooming unseen in the rainforests and the grasslands.

Literature

In 1977 Patrick Sam-Kubam gave a speech titled 'The Paucity of Literary Creativity in Anglophone Cameroon' at a Yaoundé Colloquium on Cameroon Literature and Literary Criticism. Buma Kor, another anglophone speaking at the same symposium on 'The Rough Edges of Cameroon Writing', referred to 'burgeoning literary activity in anglophone West Cameroon'. The debate was on. If in the 1970s any literate anglophone Cameroonian or even any Cameroonian author was asked to name anglophone writers, probably only two could be cited: Fonlon and Dipoko. Subsequent research revealed that the work of many dozens of Cameroonian anglophone writers had already been published, and today the work of hundreds of writers has been published and dozens are widely known among their compatriots, though few are known outside Cameroon. Organized English-language literary activity had begun around 1970 and included radio shows and workshops, and in 1973 Buma Kor organized the first anglophone Cameroonian book exhibit, complete with a small pamphlet on the subject at the Buea Agricultural Fair.

There is much that is special and unique about Cameroonian literary culture. Instead of discussing Cameroon as a post-colonial society, we must clearly apply the term neo-colonial. In anglophone Cameroon the tropes and tendencies of literary culture are not susceptible to such reductionist simplifications as centre and periphery, North versus South, and other such formulations. Cameroon society's personality is probably less revealed by print culture than is any other developing state's personality, and even its print culture is little concerned with the influence of external forces on Cameroon when compared with other national, 'post-colonial' literary profiles. Non-urban, yet sophisticated, hardly influenced at all by cinema and television, yet highly imagistic, significantly intertextual, and close to its streams of orature, anglophone Cameroonian literature is more centred on the local and historical than any other contemporary African literature. To an outsider, Cameroonian literature is curiously anchored in the past, but to Cameroonians, who know their own peculiar codes, it is obvious in almost every case that when the past is the ostensible topic, the present is being addressed. Yet the past still means something, and is neither remote nor pure pretext.

It is also evident that Cameroon's anglophone literature is wilfully old-fashioned in its insistence on moral, didactic messages and in its focus on positive, uplifting themes. The colonial capital at which it fires volleys from the cannons of all the literary forms in its arsenal is Yaoundé, in the same country, not London or New York. This locally oriented literature has famous, exciting literary artists unknown outside Cameroon's borders, such as Linus Asong. Asong practises genres never identified elsewhere, as when he launches regularly into Pidgin and English pseudo-recitations of 'tomorrow's news today' to end evenings in Bamenda palm-wine bars, where he delivers impromptu, hilarious, artful satires on government-controlled newscasts and on sycophantic, pseudo-criticism issued by intellectual supporters of the status quo in politics and culture. In reflecting on such unique, dynamic literary riches as those found in this orphan of the Commonwealth, we are brought to question just how useful our western, text-oriented, academic lenses are in helping us see literature as it is lived in the anglophone world.

Autobiography and biography have not flourished in Cameroon. This is likely due to political reasons and certainly not to lack of fascinating political and literary personalities. Jedida Asheri's (pseudonym) *Promise* (1969) is a delightfully written account of growing up in the colonial era; Asheri has written a sequel to be published after her death so that there is less embarrassment for her family. Albert Mukong's *Prisoner without a Crime* (1985) is fully autobiographical as an account of life in detention. Bernard Fonlon's death in 1986 occasioned publication of two biographical/memorial volumes, *Dr. Bernard Nsokika Fonlon (1924–1986) is Now a Legend (Funeral Addresses, Tributes and Eulogies)* (1988), edited by D. N. Lantum, and *A Tribute to Professor Bernard Nsokika Fonlon* (1988). A fully researched biography is inevitable. (See **Essays**, West Africa.)

STEPHEN H. ARNOLD

CAMPBELL, ALISTAIR TE ARIKI (1925–)

New Zealand/Polynesian poet, novelist

He was born in Rarotonga, the Cook Islands, to a Scottish father and a Polynesian mother. Orphaned as a child, he was sent to New Zealand where he grew up. Best known as a poet, Campbell has published a play — *When the Bough Breaks* (1970); a book for children — *The Happy Summer* (1961); a memoir — *Island to Island* (1984); and two novels of a projected trilogy — *The Frigate Bird* (1989) and *Sidewinder* (1991). His early poetry, in the spectacularly successful collection *Mine Eyes Dazzle* (1950), is in a neo-romantic mode, haunting, melancholy, and mysterious in its evocation of landscape and love and much indebted to earlier European traditions. It introduces themes of isolation, death, and the beautiful but unattainable woman that recur throughout his work. 'The Return' (in his collection *Wild Honey*, 1964), with its strange and compelling image of 'The drowned Dionysus, sand in his eyes and mouth, / In the dim tide lolling . . . ', is the most famous of these poems. A breakdown in 1960 seems to have forced a confrontation with a painful childhood and provoked a more direct, informal, and personal verse, seen at its best in a group of 'Personal Sonnets'.

Much of Campbell's subsequent work explores aspects of those early years, and especially his Polynesian background, often seen in the context of mental disturbance. For the powerful central figure of a poetic sequence for radio, *Sanctuary of Spirits: Poems* (1963), he took the great Maori chief Te Rauparaha, who had many associations with the place where Campbell then lived. In *Sanctuary of Spirits* and in a number of subsequent plays, primarily for radio, he explores his personal turmoil. Two brief sequences of poems, *The Dark Lord of Savaiki* (1980) and *Soul Traps: A Lyric Sequence* (1985), followed Campbell's rediscovery of his Cook Islands relations and several trips to his ancestral islands of Tongareva. Brief, simple lyrics, they make use of figures and stories of Tongarevan legend, as well as memories and anecdotes of his own family, and range in mood from a characteristic melancholy through an irreverent earthy humour to a moving acceptance of death. The journey from New Zealand to Polynesia is the subject of *The Frigate Bird*, a complex and anguished work in which bitter and zany comedy offers some relief from the painful dislocation of cultural patterns experienced by the central character.

ELIZABETH CAFFIN

Further reading: Peter Smart, *Introducing Alistair Campbell* (1982).

CAMPBELL, DAVID (1915–79)

Australian poet

Born in Adelong, New South Wales, Australia, he served with distinction in the Royal Australian Air Force during the Second World War and lived until his death on various properties in the Canberra district, Australia, farming and writing poetry. His first collection, *Speak with the Sun* (1949), is notable for its celebration of the Outback in poems such as 'The Stockman' and 'Harry Pearce'. Campbell, like **John Manifold**, established a new type of Australian 'pastoral' poem in which wry humour, characteristic of **A. B. Paterson** and the 'bush ballad' writers of the 1890s, was stripped of its loping Alexandrine rhythms and compressed into tighter lyric forms. It has some thematic and stylistic points in common with **Les A. Murray**'s early pastoral poetry and New Zealander **Denis Glover**'s wry pastoral observations.

During **Douglas Stewart**'s editorship of the ***Bulletin***, Campbell published 138 poems and established an audience for sophisticated lyrics that could be fierce or sardonic as well as festive and mellifluous. 'Men in Green', one of Campbell's outstanding war poems, borrows from Coleridge's 'The Rhyme of the Ancient Mariner' to describe sick men in a powerfully detached manner. Tall tales, legendary 'types', and appreciations of landscape characterize much of the early verse. In his love poems Campbell excels in taut meditations on rapture, folly, and friendship.

The Miracle of Mullion Hill (1956) and *Poems* (1962) continue Campbell's interest in ballad experiments and tall stories, but they move from local concerns to philosophical meditations. The sequence 'Cocky's Calendar' combines classical meditations on the seasons with song forms. *The Branch of Dodona and Other Poems 1969–1970* (1970) reworks the Jason and Medea legend in a satire on contemporary manners. 'Works and Days', in the same collection, employs brilliant vernacular in sonnet form. A biographical sequence in *Devil's Rock and Other Poems, 1970–1972* (1974) takes stock of friendship with Douglas Stewart and **Kenneth Slessor**, while other works explore personal significances seen in Aboriginal carvings at Devil's Rock. Dramatic and narrative explorations in *Deaths and Pretty Cousins* (1975) were followed by lyrical vignettes and humoresques in *Words with a Black Orpington* (1978). Campbell's last collection, *The Man in the Honeysuckle* (1979), pares away language to consider poetry and science.

MICHAEL SHARKEY

CAMPBELL, GEORGE (1916–)

Jamaican poet, journalist

Though he was born in Panama and spent much of his life in the USA, he is assured a place in Jamaican literature as the voice of a movement and of a crucial moment in the nation's history. Formative for Campbell was his friendship, from boyhood, with the Manley family: Edna Manley, a sculptor and generous patron of many artists, her husband

Norman Manley, leader of the People's National Party who was to become Jamaica's first prime minister, and their son Michael Manley, who later twice succeeded his father in that office. Edna Manley encouraged Campbell to write — much of his work appeared in her literary journal *Focus*. The family's political vision shaped Campbell's, and the extraordinary circle the Manleys gathered around them provided the young poet with a challenging but supportive audience.

When *First Poems* was published in 1945, a line such as 'sing to me after the elections' constituted a gesture of originality and poetic independence. While Campbell's work was not so much an influence as an inspiration, it is fair to say that *First Poems*' directness, vigour, and innocence indicated a new direction for West Indian poets of that turbulent period. **Martin Carter** in Guyana and **Eric Roach** in Trinidad produced poetry of greater subtlety and more sustained attention to politics, but in the anglophone Caribbean only Campbell comes close to the accessible public poetry of a Latin American writer such as Roque Dalton. At his concise best, Campbell's political poems have the force of William Blake's. Poems such as 'Holy', 'Litany', and 'History Makers' — still memorized by Jamaican schoolchildren — established Campbell as a national figure.

Campbell immigrated to the USA in the late 1940s; his return to Jamaica in the 1980s was marked by the publication, after long silence, of a second volume, *Earth's Testament* (1983), illustrated by Edna Manley. These poems of love and faith are not unlike the earlier work, but without the sustaining political fire their affirmations seem unfocused. Campbell's reputation rests, securely, on *First Poems*.

LAURENCE A. BREINER

Further reading: S. O. Asein, 'The protest tradition in West Indian poetry from George Campbell to Martin Carter', *Jamaica Journal* 2 (1972).

CAMPBELL, HAZEL DOROTHY (1940–)
Jamaican short-story writer
Born and educated in Kingston, Jamaica, she graduated from the University of the West Indies in 1967. Campbell has worked as a public relations officer, taught English language and literature to secondary-school students, and is currently a private creative production consultant. In addition to her two major collections of short stories — *The Rag Doll and Other Stories* (1978) and *Woman's Tongue* (1985) — she has written a series of educational stories for UNESCO.

The passive, suffering woman trapped in exploitative male/female relationships is a recurrent motif in Campbell's writing. Some of these women survive, but there is no suggestion of any of them transcending or transforming her situation. In *The Rag Doll and Other Stories* the women are mostly victims. In one story, for example, a woman seeks meaning and solace in religion, but the result is increased domestic brutality that eventually ends in a miscarriage and sterility. *Woman's Tongue* focuses on women who are forced to confront their multi-faceted, but always oppressive, reality. The stories suggest the inescapable suffering that seems to be women's fate, but they also demonstrate an indomitable will to survive.

Campbell's work also reflects a wider socio-political concern that is occasionally interwoven with more intimate gender politics. She utilizes the folk culture both as theme and technique and although the longer stories tend to be more finely crafted, she achieves in all the stories a comfortable synthesis of Standard English and local dialect. Paucity of critical analysis notwithstanding, Campbell's work is a significant contribution to the growing body of Caribbean women's writing.

SHEILA COULSON

Further reading: Evelyn O'Callaghan, 'Feminist consciousness: European/American theory, Jamaican stories', in Lowell Fiet (ed.) *Sargasso* (1988), special issue, Proceedings of the Seventh Annual Conference on West Indian Literature 1977.

CAMPBELL, MARIA (1940–)

Canadian autobiographer, children's writer, dramatist

Born in Park Valley, Saskatchewan, Canada, she gives voice to Métis pride, anger, and suffering and celebrates the capacity of the Métis people to survive near cultural genocide. In *Halfbreed* (1973) Campbell documents her life in a terse, sometimes-humorous style that avoids self-pity and sentimentality. When her family falls apart, the fifteen-year-old Maria deliberately turns her back on Métis culture. She wants to 'make it' in the white world. Instead, she sinks into a self-destructive hell of prostitution, drugs, and alcohol. Her lifeline is her memory of 'Cheechum', her great-grandmother, and her own children. Healing begins when she accepts who she is and starts to work with some of her own people.

In her writing for children Campbell informs a new generation of their heritage. *People of the Buffalo* (1976), *Little Badger and the Fire Spirit* (1977), and *Riel's People* (1978) teach Native cultures through the storytelling traditions of the tribe.

In theatre, Campbell collaborated with Linda Griffiths and Paul Thompson, both of Toronto's Theatre Passe Muraille, to produce a play, 'Jessica' (premièred 1986), based on her life. The play's success inspired *The Book of Jessica: A Theatrical Transformation* (1989), which Campbell co-authored with Griffiths. Dialectical in structure, incorporating fragments of taped conversation, it documents the conflicts between the women and includes the final version of the play. The complexity of this cross-cultural relationship, the love and pain involved, and the commitment of both women to reach 'truths' about what happened to them create a dynamic text. In the process, Campbell articulates her aesthetic of the artist as the healer of the community. The sacred nature of this task belongs to aboriginal traditions in Canada, Australia, and New Zealand.

DONNA E. SMYTH

Further reading: Agnes Grant, 'Contemporary Native women's voices', *Canadian Literature* 124–5 (1990).

CAMPBELL, MARION (1948–)

Australian novelist, short-story writer

Born in Sydney, Australia, she was educated in France and Australia; her dissertation for a master's degree in modern literature (1973) at the University of Provence, France, was on the semiotics of poetry, emphasizing the work of Stéphane Mallarmé. She teaches French and English language and literature at Murdoch University, Perth, Western Australia.

First published in *Westerly*, later in *Meanjin*, Campbell's short fiction has been reprinted in anthologies and in special issues of literary journals, particularly those devoted to experimental writing. Her essays include 'Remembering Remembering' (1989) and 'Spectacular Motherhood' (1990). She has also written scripts for theatrical production.

Campbell's first novel, *Lines of Flight* (1985), attracted critical responses ranging from irritation (by reviewers convinced that a certain 'restraint' would have made for better writing) through confused incomprehension ('Who is she writing for?') and awed respect for the author's originality and inventiveness ('Hail, Marion Campbell') to pleasure at encountering 'a major literary accomplishment' likely 'to bring literate Australia, screaming if necessary, into the last quarter of the Twentieth Century'.

Possessing a cosmopolitan flavour rare in the Australian novel, heavily influenced by the French symbolists and by contemporary feminist critical theory, Campbell's writing can be compared with that of Australian writer Mark Henshaw, who places his novel *Out of the Line of Fire* (1988) in a context that combines German philosophical ideas and European response theory. Campbell's second novel, *Not Being Miriam* (1988), won the Western Australia Week Literary Award for fiction in 1989.

YASMINE GOONERATNE

CAMPBELL, ROY (1901–57)

South African poet, autobiographer, critic

Born Royston Dunnachie Campbell in Durban, Natal, South Africa, the third son of a wealthy doctor, he attributed to his fortunate childhood his adult enthusiasm for physical pursuits, his love of energy, violence, and colour (in writing as in life), and his dislike of mechanization and urban living. Campbell's Zulu nurse taught him to speak Zulu. This is significant, for his upbringing divided him between the cultural heritage of Britain and the African reality in which he was growing up; this division shows in even his earliest writing. Campbell's juvenile verse, written before 1919, shows the influence of Scott, Burns, Shelley, and early Yeats; it also indicates the strong influence of the Canadian **Robert W. Service**, whose celebration of natural beauty and the men who conquered the Yukon seemed to offer Campbell an alternative and non-British model to follow.

Campbell completed his schooling at the Durban Boys' High School in 1917, and after a year at Natal University College, Pietermaritzburg, he sailed for England. Failing to gain entry to Oxford University, he travelled in France and the Mediterranean in 1920. His search for non-British models in literature is accentuated from this period onwards. He married Mary Garman, a talented painter, in 1922. While living in west Wales, Campbell completed a long poem, *The Flaming Terrapin* (1924). An immediate success, its energy, prodigality of imagery, and strangeness of setting seemed a breath of fresh air to critics and readers grown accustomed to the genteel tones of the Georgian verse fashionable at the time. Critics attributed the colour and passion of Campbell's writing to his African background, though, in fact, his literary antecedents in poems such as *The Flaming Terrapin* were Elizabethan and Jacobean poets. The poem's central metaphor, however, of an escape from a decadent Europe to renewal in the southern hemisphere is the direct result of Campbell's African upbringing.

Campbell returned to Natal and in 1926, in company with **William Plomer** and **Laurens van der Post**, edited a bilingual literary magazine, *Voorslag* ('Whiplash', 1926–7). His contact with van der Post and Plomer opened Campbell's eyes to the existence in South Africa of groups other than the English-speakers dominant in Natal. *Voorslag* printed articles in Afrikaans, and Campbell also planned to include Zulu contributions. A quarrel with the financial backers of the journal caused Campbell to resign after the second issue and to return to Europe. Shortly before leaving South Africa he wrote several of the poems in which his sympathy for Africans is most clearly shown, among them 'The Zulu Girl' and 'The Serf' (published in his 1930 collection *Adamastor*). In other poems of this period, among them 'Tristan da Cunha' and 'To a Pet Cobra' (first published in *The New Statesman* in 1927), he identifies himself with the marginalized elements in South African society. In such poems one clearly sees the affinity of his work with Plomer's similar concerns in *Turbott Wolfe* (1926) and *Sado* (1931), and with those of van der Post's *In a Province* (1934).

Campbell's African poems mark the beginning of the mature work he produced until the mid-1930s. To this period belong also his two major satires, *The Wayzgoose* (1928) and *The Georgiad* (1931), a sense of persecution having been awakened in Campbell by his set-backs in South Africa and by the lesbian love affair that his wife Mary had in 1927 with Vita Sackville-West, whose guests the Campbells were for some months in Kent. Campbell associated Sackville-West and her diplomat husband Harold Nicolson with the ruling class of Britain and came to see in them everything he most disliked.

Campbell's model for an alternative society was provided by his own African upbringing and by the camaraderie that he found among the tough horsemen and fishermen he encountered in southern Europe between 1928 and 1936. He idealized these models in his writings, notably in his autobiographies, *Broken Record* (1934) and *Light on a Dark Horse* (1951), and in such prose works as *Taurine Provence* (1932). Ernest Hemingway, for all his political differences from Campbell, shows similar ideals — similarly arrived at — in much of his writing.

Campbell lived in southern France between 1928 and 1931 and in Spain from 1931 to 1936; his love of southern Europe is evident everywhere in his poetry of this period, notably in the finest of his collections of verse, *Adamastor*. His friendship with the vorticist Wyndham Lewis brought him into contact with many of the central movements of modernism, and some of his work of the early 1930s shows the influence of futurism — paradoxically, for Campbell disliked machines and 'progress' as much as the Italian futurist Marinetti exulted in them. 'Choosing a Mast' (1931), *Pomegranates* (1932), and *Flowering Reeds* (1933) exemplify his preoccupations at this time.

Campbell's conversion to Roman Catholicism between 1933 and 1935 marks another change in his writing; this change is reflected in the obscurity of the 'Mithraic Emblems' sequence from *Mithraic Emblems* (1936), in the religious commitment of many of the lyrics, and in the increasing shrillness of the satirical pieces. (He was baptized a Roman Catholic at the age of thirty-three and adopted the name Ignatius.)

Campbell's emotional involvement in the Spanish Civil War is evident in many of the poems written after 1936; several reflect his direct experience of the fighting in Toledo, where he was living when the war broke out. His sympathies were for the Nationalists (the result chiefly of his Catholicism), though he never fought for them as he claimed to have done. The most striking of his Spanish Civil War poems are the fine lyrics of *Mithraic Emblems* and the long and partisan poem *Flowering Rifle* (1939), which glorified Franco and which did Campbell's reputation great harm.

Campbell joined the British Army in 1942 and served in east Africa, though he was by then over forty years old and in poor health. His wartime experiences gave rise to the poems he published in *Talking Bronco* (1946), where he continues to depict himself as struggling single-handedly against a hostile social and literary establishment in Britain. In his close and often humorous depiction of wartime experience, Campbell shares some affinity with his fellow South African poet **Guy Butler**.

After the war Campbell worked as a clerk for the War Damage Commission in London before joining the British Broadcasting Corporation as a Talks producer. For a short period he edited an unsuccessful magazine, *The Catacomb* (1949–52), which espoused a right-wing position in British politics. Campbell's most important postwar publications are translations: *The Poems of St John of the Cross* (1951), *Poems: A Translation of Les Fleurs du Mal* (1952), two novels by Eça de Queirós, six Spanish plays, and the poems of Paco d'Arcos. His translations, particularly of St John of the Cross, are masterful works of art in their own right. Campbell also showed himself to be a sensitive critic in *Lorca: An Appreciation of His Poetry* (1952), which is interspersed with his fine translations of Lorca's poems, and in *Wyndham Lewis*, written in 1931, published posthumously in 1985. From 1952 Campbell lived in Portugal, where he was killed in a car accident in 1957.

Campbell's writing shows his painful sense of being culturally divided and of being an outsider always longing to form part of some powerful and respected group at the centre. These preoccupations, shared by such American poets as Ezra

Pound and by the Australian **Christina Stead**, help to explain his search for commitment in the army and in the Catholic Church. They also explain Campell's angry attacks on the 'imperial centre', symbolized for him by Vita Sackville-West and her friends, and by such later 'enemies' as those poets to whom he gave the composite name 'Macspaunday' (Louis MacNeice, Stephen Spender, W. H. Auden, and C. Day Lewis). Campbell is a peculiarly modernist figure in his sense of belonging nowhere and in his lifelong search for some group or belief to which to give his allegiance.

PETER F. ALEXANDER

Further reading: Rowland Smith, *Lyric and Polemic: The Literary Personality of Roy Campbell* (1972); Peter F. Alexander, *Roy Campbell: A Critical Biography* (1982).

CAMPBELL, WILLIAM WILFRED (1860–1918)
Canadian poet

Born in Newmarket, Canada West (not, as commonly supposed, in 1858 in Berlin, Canada West), he studied at University College (1880–2) and Wycliffe College (1882–3), Toronto, and Episcopal Theological School, Cambridge, Massachusetts, USA (1883–5). In 1891 he left the priesthood to make his career as a civil-service clerk in Ottawa. Campbell is best known as a nature poet, but patriotism and imperialism were central to his life and works. He felt called to be a poet laureate: to record events, inspire his countrymen, and even advise Queen Victoria and King Edward VII about the empire in 'Victoria (Jubilee Ode)' and 'Crowning of Empire'.

Campbell's imperialist poetry is found in *The Collected Poems of Wilfred Campbell* (1905), *Sagas of Vaster Britain* (1914, edited by Theodore Watts-Dunton), and the pamphlets *War Lyrics* (1915), *Lyrics of Iron and Mist* (1916), *Lyrics of the Dread Redoubt* (1917), and *Langemarck and Other Poems* (1918). Imperialist principles guided his choices for *Poems of Loyalty by British and Canadian Authors* (1913) and *The Oxford Book of Canadian Verse* (1913), and he spread his ideals in lectures such as 'Literature and the National Life' (1900), 'Imperialism in Canada' (1904), and 'Canada's Duty to the Empire and to the Race' (1915). Campbell thought Kipling's work vulgar, but he worshipped Shakespeare's as the highest achievement of the British race. In his treatise 'The Tragedy of Man' he argues that the British race represents the pinnacle of evolution; this theory informs the two-volume *The Scotsman in Canada* (1911), of which he wrote the first volume and George Bryce the second. Campbell believed his maternal grandfather to be the son of King George III of England and Hannah Lightfoot; consequently his strongest personal ties were with men such as his clan chieftain the ninth Duke of Argyll (governor general of Canada, 1878–83) and Earl Grey (governor general, 1904–11), to whom he was related by his daughter's marriage. His philosophy coincided with that of Prime Minister William Lyon Mackenzie King, whose diaries document Campbell's influence upon him. His only literary disciple was John Masefield, who decided to become a poet when, at the age of twelve, he read Campbell's *Lake Lyrics* (1889). Campbell also wrote novels, short stories, plays, magazine articles, and three series of newspaper columns.

LAUREL BOONE

Further reading: Laurel Boone, ed., *William Wilfred Campbell: Selected Poetry and Essays* (1987).

CANADA
Geography

In the mid-Depression year of 1936 William Lyon Mackenzie King, the durable Liberal prime minister of Canada, remarked that 'if some countries have too much history, we have too much geography'. Canada, with its some 9,977,000 square kilometres over seven time zones, is the largest country in the world. Its natural boundaries are the shores of three oceans, the Atlantic, the Pacific, and the Arctic. One artificial boundary divides Canada from the USA; it loops through the middle of the Great Lakes until it reaches the edge of the Prairies, then follows a straight line on the forty-ninth parallel of latitude across the Prairies and Western Cordillera to the Pacific coast.

The Prairies and the Western Cordillera are part of the geographical systems of the North American continent — the Prairies stretch uninterrupted from the American plains to the tundra or the barren ground of the Northwest Territories, and the British Columbian mountain ranges extend the North American Western Cordillera northwestward into the volcanic mountains of Alaska. The highest British Columbian — and Canadian — mountain is Mount Robson in the Rockies at 3,954 metres. The western slopes of the Cordillera descend to a coastline of deep fjords and small archipelagos clothed in dense rainforest. East of the Prairies and north of the Great Lakes stretches the vast and lake-dotted deposit of ancient rocks, two and a half billion years old, known as the Canadian or Precambrian shield, and east of that the extension of the Appalachian mountain system extends northeast in a broken pattern into the Maritime provinces and Newfoundland.

First Peoples

The first peoples of Canada were not true aboriginals, for there is no evidence that any part of the early evolution of humankind occurred on the American continent. The first peoples were races of *homo sapiens*, themselves immigrants and not particularly early ones. The first waves of hunters penetrated, either by boat or by a vanished land bridge, over the Bering Strait. They appear to have come, following the great animals of the period such as the mastodon, the mammoth, and the giant bison, as the last great ice age began to relax its grip; they wandered at first in the ice-free enclave of northwestern Alaska and then pushed southward as the ice retreated along the corridor between the cordilleran ice field and the great Laurentian ice field that covered most of Canada. The first peoples came in two waves. The earliest, who began to appear about twelve millennia ago, were ancestors of the many peoples who, because of an error by Christopher Columbus, became generally known as Indians; now they prefer to be known by individual tribal names or as First Nations or Native peoples. The second wave, appearing about the fourth millennia BC, was the succession of related peoples originally called by others 'the Eskimo', but now known by their preferred name of Inuit — 'the people'.

Most of the first peoples continued the occupations of the earliest comers, living as nomadic hunters in small wandering family groups with little political organization. In special circumstances, four groups more culturally specialized than the rest emerged. A relatively fertile area in the St Lawrence River valley and around the Great Lakes allowed Canada's only agrarian culture to emerge and give rise to an original and democratic political structure, the Iroquois League of the Five (later Six) Nations. On the Prairies the abundance of the bison fostered a hunting culture more secure and advanced than elsewhere, out of which developed the warrior democracy of the Blackfoot Confederation. On the Pacific coast the abundance of natural resources, including ample seafood and the easily workable wood of the cedar, allowed the emergence of a ceremonially and artistically complex life-style that is often regarded as the world's most sophisticated primitive culture. In the North the Inuit developed a technologically complex way of life to feed and clothe themselves in a hostile environment.

Late Comers

The first Europeans to arrive in North America were the Icelanders who came with Lief Ericson to Greenland around AD 1000 and established at least one short-lived settlement at L'Anse aux Meadow, Newfoundland. They had encounters, hostile and perhaps otherwise, with the Inuit and with people — possibly the Beothuk of Newfoundland or the Micmac of Nova Scotia — whom they called Skraelings. After the sighting of Newfoundland by John Cabot in 1497, the Europeans were as nomadic a presence in North America and its waters as the first peoples had been. They were mainly Basque whalers and Breton fishermen, but they started the fur trade and began the acculturation of the Native peoples that led eventually to their dependence on a life of trapping to gain the metal tools, weapons and utensils, and the woven cloth that quickly rendered obsolete their laboriously made native equivalents. English mariners by the late sixteenth century were venturing into Arctic waters in search of the Northwest Passage, and in 1576 Martin Frobisher reached Baffin Island, where he was hit in the rump by an Inuit arrow and departed with a cargo of iron pyrites under the illusion he had struck gold on a large scale. But apart from Jacques Cartier's wintering in 1535–6 at Stadacona (later Quebec) and an even earlier but badly documented venture of Bristol merchants called the Company of Adventurers to the New Found Land, which received a royal patent in 1502 and may have attempted a settlement on Newfoundland in 1503, it was not until the early seventeenth century that French and English settlements followed closely on each other. In 1605 the Sieur de Monts founded Port Royal on the Bay of Fundy in Acadia (now Nova Scotia) and in 1608 Samuel de Champlain founded the *habitation* at Quebec, the first permanent French settlement on the St Lawrence River. In 1610 another group of English merchants founded the first authenticated settlement on Newfoundland at Cupers Cove (now known as Cupids), and other groups followed later in the decade.

The English focus of settlement soon moved southward to the softer climate of Virginia. The French settlements remained, increased because of immigration, and were formed into a royal domain, La Nouvelle France. Soldiers to defend the territory and priests intent on converting the 'heathen' arrived, as well as the peasant *habitants* who laid out their farms in long strips going inland from the St Lawrence River. The soldiers' forts and the priests' churches were among the important nuclei of settlement. Since maritime connections were mainly with Channel ports, the people who came to settle as *habitants* were largely Norman and Breton. Their origins determined the peculiarities of the language now known in Quebec as French.

By the time of the English conquest of Quebec in 1760, the French-speaking population of Quebec had risen to 65,000. There were a few hundred people, mainly Irish and Devon people, in the settlements and fishing stations of Newfoundland. Nova Scotia (the former Acadia) had been ceded to Britain in 1713, its French-speaking Acadians had largely been expelled, and New England farmers and some Scots, mostly displaced crofters, had been settled there. After the conquest English and Scottish merchants moved north to make Montreal a cosmopolitan town and to take over the fur trade established by the French, expanding it westward until it reached the Pacific. American independence created by 1783 the first major wave of immigration, sending north tens of thousands of Loyalists who refused to live under the American flag. They were mostly English but included some Dutch from New York and German Mennonites from Pennsylvania, as well as the first Native people following European settlement to immigrate to Canada — the Iroquois who had fought beside the British in the recent war.

Two new colonies, New Brunswick and Upper Canada (later Ontario), were founded to accommodate the overflow of immigrants into the forest around the St Lawrence River and the Great Lakes. Later, non-Loyalist Americans came, attracted by the cheap land, but their inflow was halted by the war of 1812–14, in which the Americans attacked the British North American colonies and were repulsed. After 1814 the flow of European immigration came from the Napoleonic wars and from the driving out of Scots and Irish peasants by enclosures and general pressure on the land. During the 1840s a further flood of Irish came as a result of the potato famine that began in 1845. It left its special mark on Canadian nineteenth-century social and political life in the bitter rivalry that continued for several generations between Ulster Protestants (Orangemen) and Catholics from southern Ireland.

The fur trade, spreading its trade routes and posts as far as the Pacific coast, created out of relationships between Québécois voyageurs and Cree women the 'New Nation' of the Métis. Largely nomadic hunters, these people nevertheless started — with Scottish immigrants — the Red River Colony, the first settlement in the Canadian West. The discovery of gold beyond the mountains in the 1850s led to a rush from California and to the appearance of a number of settlements, most of which ended as ghost towns. When the gold rush ebbed, what is now British Columbia had a largely British population of approximately ten thousand.

By the time Canada had become a confederation of former colonies (1867) and Rupert's Land and British Columbia had been absorbed into Canada (1870–1), the populating of the West as a market for an industrialized central Canada became a major plank in Prime Minister John A. Macdonald's National Program, but it could not be fulfilled until the Canadian Pacific Railway was completed in 1885. Then, to attract immigrants, the old preference for British stock had to be abandoned; large numbers from northern and eastern Europe came to dominate the Prairies with Slavic and Germanic strains, though the British were still encouraged, and in all no fewer then 400,870 people came to Canada in 1913, the peak year. Two world wars and the Depression of the 1930s slowed down the pace of immigration, which did not begin to pick up until 1946; the postwar newcomers were at first mainly British, with Dutch and German quickly gathering numbers, followed in the 1960s by the Mediterranean peoples, notably Italians, Greeks and Portuguese, and in the 1970s by a steadily growing number of Asians — from India and China via Hong Kong especially — and of people of ultimately African origin via the Caribbean. Immigration continues to be an important element in Canadian population increase; in 1990 about one in six of Canada's estimated 26,440,000 people were foreign-born.

In the 1986 census 6.3 million people claimed French as their mother tongue, almost a hundredfold increase since 1760, the result of large Québécois families during the nineteenth and twentieth centuries. Until the mid-1930s Canada's was mainly a rural population; now more than three-quarters of Canadians live in communities of more than 5,000 people, mainly concentrated in a corridor no more than 320 kilometres broad north of the border with the USA. Vast areas remain virtually uninhabited. In the Yukon and Northwest Territories approximately 75,000 people inhabit 2.4 million square kilometres of tundra and northern forest.

The First Peoples Today

In recent years a resurgence of population and pride has taken place among the first peoples. Robbed of their land and living on scanty reserves, voteless and turned into wards of the state by various Indian Acts, decimated by whites' diseases against which they had no immunity, deprived of their ceremonial heritage by laws forbidding sacred feasts, they declined in numbers and morale until by the 1930s even responsible ethnologists believed they were doomed as peoples. In recent years, however, they have increased and now there are probably more of them than at the time of contact with white intruders in the sixteenth century, their cultures are reviving, and they have become politically active. The total of people claiming Native descent in the 1986 census was approximately 756,725, about three percent of the Canadian population.

Confederation Unattained

New France was a royal domain ruled by a governor and council, and similar colonial governments existed afterwards in various British North American colonies, sometimes with assemblies that had limited suffrage and restricted powers. In practice a kind of oligarchical government developed, with a few magnates sharing power. By the 1830s discontent had developed in all colonies; in 1837 rebellions broke out in Upper Canada, led by William Lyon Mackenzie, and in Lower Canada, led by Louis-Joseph Papineau. They were easily defeated, but the rebellions led to the despatch of 'Radical Jack', earl of Durham, from London as a one-man commission. In his 1839 report, one of the great documents of imperial history, Durham stressed the importance of the cultural division between French and English, of 'two nations warring in the bosom of a single state'. In an attempt to swamp 'the French fact', as it quickly became known, Durham recommended the melding into a single state of the Canadas and the Maritime colonies, with a full parliamentary system and responsible government. Westminster went part way by uniting the two Canadas into a single province. Responsible government followed by administrative fiat during the 1840s and for a quarter of a century French- and English-speaking politicians sustained shifting alliances that grew steadily more unworkable. In 1864 the leaders of the Maritime provinces met to discuss a local confederation; the Canadian leaders asked to be invited, and out of meetings in Charlottetown and Quebec emerged proposals for a confederation that were accepted by the imperial government and enshrined in the British North America Act of 1867.

It was a constitution that never developed a true confederal structure, like that of Switzerland, because its terms were too uncertain and could be interpreted by centralizing politicians such as John A. Macdonald in one way and by provincial leaders anxious for more power in another. Nor did the Anglo-French conflict recede; it was merely strengthened by the struggle between centralist and decentralist interests with the result that — though the federal government in Ottawa has generally retained control of matters such as foreign policy, defence, banking and currency, and communications — the ten provinces have remained in firm control of such areas as education, property, civil rights, and policing. As government concerns itself in more areas, the borderline skirmishes between provinces and Ottawa, the federal capital, over their respective areas of authority have increased.

As a constitution, the British North America Act became repugnant to growing Canadian nationalism as early as the 1920s, since it could be amended only by the imperial parliament and the final court of appeal on constitutional and other matters was the Judicial Committee of the Privy Council in London, England. During half a century frequent conferences of federal and provincial politicians tried to reach agreement on terms of a new and independent constitution acceptable to all regions and both language groups (the First Nations were mostly ignored). But when a wide measure of agreement was reached and the constitution was 'patriated' in 1981 (making Canada at last a formally independent country) it happened without Quebec's agreement. In 1990 that final touch to the constitution seemed complete with the Meech Lake Accord, but the accord was aborted by the parliamentary manoeuvres of Native leaders, who were discontented by the lack of provision for aboriginal rights. The result was a sharp increase in Quebec separatist sentiment and continued peril for the Canadian constitution.

Two major political parties, the Progressive

Conservative and the Liberals, have shared power in Canada. A third, the social-democratic New Democratic Party, has wielded influence at times of minority government and is largely responsible for Canada's widespread social assistance programs. Local discontent tends to find expression in provincial politics, where voters often return minority parties; thus Social Credit ruled many years in British Columbia and Alberta as did the Cooperative Commonwealth Federation (precursor of the New Democratic Party) in Saskatchewan, while nationalist groups (including the separatist Parti Québécois) have at times held power in Quebec.

In Canada economic problems are closely related to political discontent. They arise from the fact that Canada is so largely dependent on an export trade based on its great primary industries — farming, forestry, fishing, and mining. Manufacturing tends to be concentrated in the central and most populous provinces of Ontario and Quebec, and because the votes are there successive governments have kept it so. The result is abiding discontent in the western provinces, whose people see themselves treated as mere 'hewers of wood', and also in the Maritime provinces, where old, established industries such as shipbuilding and a healthy merchant marine were allowed to decay for lack of federal support. These factors too contribute to the difficulty in gaining constitutional accord. Less and less do Canadians trust their political leaders.

Cultural Upsurge

Before the 1950s a readily distinguishable Canadian tradition of literature or painting hardly existed. Artists and writers tended to be derivative even in their rebellion, so that there were good Canadian impressionists (such as James Wilson Morrice) and imagists (such as W. W. E. Ross) without a Canadian equivalent to imagism or to impressionism, with the possible exception of the work of the famous Group of Seven painters, now seen as less innovative than it once appeared. During the 1950s a considerable literary and artistic movement emerged, with new publishers and magazines and galleries, along with a rising public interest, both unofficial and official. (See **Canada Council**.) Writers and painters, it became evident, were breaking free of their British, French, and American mentors. A sound tradition of criticism, that sure sign of a maturing literature, began to emerge. Quantitatively, as **Northrop Frye** put it, there was an 'explosion' of exhibitions held and of plays performed as drama emerged from the radio studios where it had survived the long winter of war and Depression and on to the open stage again. (See **Broadcasting**, Canada, and **Drama**, Canada.) Qualitatively there was a remarkable progression as literature and the other arts went through stages of domination by a few leading figures, followed by the fervent nationalism of the 1960s, into the stages of individuation and variegation that also characterize a maturing tradition. Artists and writers in Canada no longer feel the need to show they are Canadian.

French and English cultures in Canada remain sharply distinct; translation between them is rare, and bilingual magazines are even rarer. (See **Translation**, Canada.) Literatures other than English and French have continued in Canada; some of the most distinguished recent European, Asian, and Caribbean writers have lived and worked there. The cultures of the Canadian Native groups were entirely oral, but a literature in English is now emerging parallel to the political reawakening of these first peoples and to the emergence of artists intent of presenting ancestral motifs in new settings; some, such as the Haida sculptor Bill Reid and the Ojibwa painter Norval Morriseau, have achieved international reputations. (See **Aboriginal Literature**, Canada.)

GEORGE WOODCOCK

Further Reading: George Woodcock, *The Canadians* (1979).

CANADA COUNCIL, THE

In its 1951 report to the government of Canada, the Royal Commission on National Development in the Arts, Letters and Sciences (the Massey Commission), recommended that 'a body be created to be known as the Canada Council for the Encouragement of the Arts, Letters, Humanities and Social Sciences'. In 1956 the government received death duties in the amount of $100 million from the estates of Sir James Dunn and Izaak Walton Killam, and in 1957 established the Canada Council, endowed with half of these funds. In 1966 the Council began receiving an annual Parliamentary appropriation, which grew to represent ninety per cent of the Council's budget. In 1957–8 the Canada Council awarded forty-two grants totalling some $660,000; in 1992–3 it awarded more than 4,000 grants (on the basis of a process of peer assessment) totalling about 95.4 million dollars. These were distributed as follows: Music and Opera ($16,668,000); Theatre ($17,237,000); Visual Arts ($5,905,000); Writing and Publishing ($14,076,000); Arts Awards — grants to individual artists in all disciplines ($10,595,000); Explorations Program — for innovative artistic projects ($3,110,000); Dance ($10,776,000); Media Arts ($4,705,000); Art Bank — for the purchase of contemporary Canadian works of art (paintings, sculpture, etc.) for rental to government departments and non-profit organizations ($909,000); Public Lending Right Commission — payment to writers for the public's use of their books in libraries ($6,925,000); and the Touring Office, which assists Canadian performing artists touring in Canada ($4,444,000). Research in the humanities and social sciences was funded by the Council until 1978, when a separate organization, the Social Sciences and Humanities Research Council of Canada, was established.

The Canada Council also maintains the secretariat of the Canadian Commission for UNESCO and administers a number of prestigious prizes and awards. (See **Awards**, Canada.)

EUGENE BENSON

CANADIAN CONNECTIONS WITH CARIBBEAN LITERATURE

Canada has enjoyed a special relationship with the Caribbean for many years. Possibly because they are the only two Commonwealth territories in the western Hemisphere, trade between the islands and Atlantic Canada flourished in the great days of shipping. Numerous Caribbean students have chosen to study at Canadian universities. Today, thousands of tourists annually seek out the Caribbean sun while an opposite flow of Caribbean immigrants searches in the big cities for the Canadian El Dorado.

These patterns of connection have been explored in the literatures of the two areas. **Thomas Raddall** wrote about trade between Nova Scotia and Haiti in *Pride's Fancy* (1946), and **Bliss Carman** commemorated a visit to the Bahamas in *A Winter Holiday* (1898). **Margaret Atwood** in *Bodily Harm* (1981) and Philip Kreiner in *Heartlands* (1984) describe their Canadian heroines' attempts to find themselves in the Caribbean. From the other direction, Lorris Elliott in *Coming for to Carry: A Novel in Five Parts* (1982) examines the problems faced by a Caribbean student in Vancouver. **Austin Clarke** in *The Bigger Light* (1975) and **Neil Bissoondath** in *Digging Up the Mountains* (1985) describe with varying degrees of irony and compassion the frantic attempts of Caribbean immigrants to adjust to the foreignness of Toronto.

Because of these tangible links, Canadians, especially in universities, have shown an increasing interest in Caribbean literature, which is taught in several departments of English across the country. Numerous post-graduate dissertations on Caribbean authors have been completed in Canada and a major academic journal, *Canadian Literature*, published a special issue in Winter 1982,

Caribbean Connections. As early as 1960, *The Tamarack Review* devoted an issue to an anthology of Caribbean writing. More recently the *Toronto South Asian Review* published *Jahaji Bhai: An Anthology of Indo-Caribbean Literature* (1988), edited by Frank Birbalsingh, to mark East Indian contributions to Caribbean life. **Sam Selvon**, the distinguished Trinidadian comic novelist who now lives in Calgary, and the Jamaican novelist, **John Hearne**, among others, have served as writers-in-residence at several Canadian universities. Williams Wallace, a small Toronto publishing house, has reissued some of Selvon's early novels, thus introducing him to a Canadian audience.

A group of writers from the Caribbean who now live in Canada, including Austin Clarke, **Sonny Ladoo**, Neil Bissoondath, **Cyril Dabydeen**, **Dionne Brand**, **Claire Harris**, Arnold Itwaru, **Marlene Nourbese Philip** and Lillian Allen, has produced a substantial and vigorous body of writing about their experiences in their strange land of adoption. In Canada, they are perceived as part of a mosaic and their work is labelled 'New Canadian'. In the Caribbean, the literature of which includes an appreciable amount of expatriate writing, they are still considered Caribbean authors. These writers, then, whose work straddles two territories, are physical symbols of the connections between Caribbean and Canadian literatures.

ANTHONY BOXILL

Canadian North, The

Canada is the most northerly country in the Commonwealth, and the coldest. These simple facts have profoundly influenced the country's economic, political, and social development and, consequently, its literature.

The North has been variously defined during the five hundred years of Canada's development. The early French spoke of *le pays en haut* — the vast area lying north and west of the St Lawrence River. With the founding of the Hudson's Bay Company in 1670, the English referred to it as 'Rupert's Land'. Shortly after Confederation (1867), the new country consolidated its northern holdings as the Northwest Territories, out of which it then carved, during the next four decades, the three provinces of Manitoba, Alberta, and Saskatchewan, and the Yukon Territory. Today, when francophones speak of *le nord* and anglophones speak of 'the North', they usually mean the provinces' northern hinterlands and the Yukon and Northwest Territories. While this area represents about seventy per cent — almost seven million square kilometres — of the country, only about two per cent of the country's population resides there. Not even Australia has had, in the words of **Northrop Frye**, 'so large an amount of the unknown, the unrealized, the humanly undigested, so built into it'. To say, therefore, that Canada is 'northern' is to state more than a geographical fact; it is to acknowledge the central place of the North in the Canadian ethos. As recently as 1988 Thomas Berger asserted, 'In the North lies the future of Canada.'

Like the American West and the Australian Outback, the Canadian North is often viewed as a 'last frontier', a land where adventurous individuals can realize their private dreams free of the constraints imposed by conventional society. This frontier vision of the North is usually expressed in one of two forms. Some see the northern frontier as a place of unlimited resources — furs, whales, oil, and forests — waiting to be exploited. The popular balladeer **Robert W. Service** captures the essence of this in his famous lines 'I wanted the gold, and I sought it . . . I wanted the gold, and I got it.' Others see it as a last refuge from over-populated and polluted southern Canada.

The exploration of the North, both physically and psychologically, has been a dominant theme in Canadian literature since its beginnings. Early accounts fed an almost insatiable appetite, first in Europe and then in southern Canada and the USA, for stories of discovery and adventure in the northern reaches of the 'new world'. Some of these accounts — for example, those written by Samuel Hearne, Alexander Mackenzie, and **John Richardson** — are now considered classics. (See **Exploration Literature**, Canada.)

Following the discovery of gold in the Klondike River area of the Yukon in the late nineteenth century, the Canadian North again caught the world's attention. Even after the gold rush collapsed, a huge popular literature continued to flourish right up until the Second World War. It was, like the rush itself, more international than Canadian. So powerful were the romantic images put forward by writers such as Jack London, Robert Service, and Rex Beach that the Yukon is still trying to shake itself free of them.

In the 1960s many of the country's writers followed the lead set by painters such as Tom Thomson, Lawren Harris, and A. Y. Jackson and went north looking for a new, distinctively Canadian aesthetic and technique. One of the earliest and most successful results is **Al Purdy**'s *North of Summer: Poems from Baffin Island* (1967), which is based on a summer Purdy spent on Baffin Island. In the last two decades dozens of other Canadian writers have made the journey north. Many contemporary classics have resulted, including **Robert Kroetsch**'s *But We Are Exiles* (1965), James Houston's *The White Dawn: An Eskimo Saga* (1971), Harold Horwood's *White Eskimo* (1972), and **Margaret Atwood**'s *Surfacing* (1972). These works record the northern imaginings of a largely 'southern' and urban group of artists, most of whom have limited first-hand experience of the North.

A new regional literature is now beginning to emerge in the North. Paralleling recent efforts to move towards political, social, and economic self-determination in the Yukon and Northwest Territories, this literature is challenging many of the established notions of the North held elsewhere in the country. Firmly rooted in the oral traditions of the Inuit and Indians, it argues a radically old view of the North, one that sees it not as frontier, but as homeland. (See **Aboriginal Literature**, Canada.)

ARON E. SENKPIEL

Further reading: Louis-Edmond Hamelin, *Canadian Nordicity: It's Your North, Too* (1979); Allison Mitcham, *The Northern Imagination: A Study of Northern Canadian Literature* (1983); Penny Petrone, ed., *Northern Voices: Inuit Writing in English* (1988).

CAPPIELLO, ROSA (1942–)

Australian novelist, poet, short-story writer

Born in Naples, Italy, she immigrated to Australia in 1971. She came to national attention when her novel *Paese Fortunato* (1981), translated by Gaetano Rando as *Oh Lucky Country* (1984), was awarded a New South Wales Premier's Literary Award in 1985. It had previously won the Premio Calabria in Italy. Since then she has published poetry and short stories in a range of Australian magazines. Cappiello perceives herself as an iconoclast who does not fit into her current environment. Her work has been seen as following in the tradition of the worker or proletarian novel established by writers such as Pier Paolo Pasolini, although she herself derives her literary inspiration from American writers of the 1940s and 1950s such as Ernest Hemingway and Henry Miller.

Based loosely on her own life, Cappiello's novel created controversy within both the Italo-Australian and the general Australian community. Dealing with the experiences of a working-class Italian woman's attempts to survive in Australia, it paints a less-than-complimentary picture of both new and old Australians. Characterized by its earthy language and Rabelaisian humour, it subverts the genres of the migrant life story as well as expectations concerning women's narratives. The narrator, Rosa, does not suffer fools lightly, and her barbed comments expose the pretensions within her own circles, as well as those within the ocker culture:

> Together with the migrant masses I am contributing to the process of your civilization, to widening your horizon which doesn't extend any further than the point of your great ugly nose. I tear the weeds out of your ears. I give you a certain style. I teach you to eat, to dress, to behave and above all not to belch in restaurants, trains, buses, cinemas, schools.

Cappiello is as ferocious concerning migrant groups as she is when exposing the vulnerabilities and faults of the older Australians. (See **Migrant Writing**, Australia.)

SNEJA GUNEW

Further reading: S. Gunew, 'Rosa Cappiello's *Oh Lucky Country*: multicultural reading strategies', *Meanjin* 44 (1985).

CAREW, JAN (1925–)

Guyanese novelist, critic

Born in Agricola, Guyana, he was educated at Berbice High School, Guyana, and at several universities in Europe and the USA. For most of his writing life he has lived outside of the Caribbean; he now lives in the USA, where he taught African-American studies at Northwestern University, Illinois. He is married to the novelist **Sylvia Wynter**. Widely travelled, Carew has written about places other than his homeland and as a result is perceived as a cosmopolitan rather than a Caribbean author. His novels are set in Harlem, New York, USA (*The Last Barbarian*, 1960), London, England (*Save the Last Dance for Me*, 1976), and Russia (*Moscow Is Not My Mecca*, 1964) and are not always peopled by Caribbean characters. He has also published several children's books, poems, plays, and non-fictional political books, articles, and essays.

Carew's works, both fiction and non-fiction, indicate an evolving ideological position regarding the politics and history of post-colonial societies. His Frantz Fanon-inspired Marxist interpretation of racially charged Guyanese society in *Black Midas* (1958) and *The Wild Coast* (1958) extends to a direct attack on the politics of racism in the USA in *The Last Barbarian*. In *Moscow Is Not My Mecca* Carew uncovers racism in the Soviet Union. His suspicions of the imperialistic interests of both the USSR and the USA are comparable to the rigorous examination of the relationship between post-colonial societies and First World nations in the works of writers such as **George Lamming** and **Wole Soyinka**. Like them, Carew discovers that the polemics of colonial society are rooted in race issues that have their antecedents in slavery and exploitation. Marxism and capitalist ideologies cannot be applied in post-colonial societies without a close examination of the racialist stance of their purveyors.

KWAME DAWES

CAREY, PETER (1943–)

Australian novelist, short-story writer

Born in Bacchus Marsh, Victoria, Australia, he attended the local township primary school, but completed his senior years at Geelong Grammar School, alongside sons of the wealthy and powerful. Carey sometimes refers to this abrupt elevation of his social status as a trauma, though he was popular and successful within the school. His keenest interests at this time were chemistry and comic strips, not literature. However, his study of science at the university level disillusioned him, and he strayed, without real intention, into work in advertising.

Carey's interest in writing developed during his first years in an advertising agency, where he wrote copy with other writers and would-be writers. He became fascinated by literary experiment and French writer Alain Robbe-Grillet's *nouveau roman* movement of the late 1960s. This enthusiasm and the influence of writers Carey had begun to read and admire — William Faulkner, Jack Kerouac, James Joyce, Vladimir Nabokov, Franz Kafka — are reflected in his unpublished novel manuscripts.

It was the publication of the short stories Carey had begun writing in the late 1960s and early 1970s, with their exotic content and fabulistic nature, that immediately identified him as an original talent. His first collection, *The Fat Man in History* (1974), is one of the great critical and sales success stories of Australian publishing. A second collection, *War Crimes* (1979), and his three subsequent novels, *Bliss* (1981), *Illywhacker* (1985), and *Oscar and Lucinda* (1988), have all won major awards in Australia and overseas, including the 1988 Booker Prize for *Oscar and Lucinda*. Two successful feature films, *Bliss* and *Dead-End Drive-In* (1986), the latter based on the story 'Crabs', have further extended Carey's popular readership.

Carey's stories are usually futuristic fables or surrealist fantasies that, like those of Jorge Luis Borges, manage to convey an uncanny and convincing reality. The value of individual will and its place within institutionalized, often corrupt, systems of control is a recurring theme in Carey's fiction. Yet these allegorical fantasy worlds often expose the seductiveness of totalitarianism as well as its destructiveness. Critics don't usually compare the stories with the novels, yet Carey's short studies in the nature and persistence of domination and power, in small groups and between individuals, seem a natural precursor to his preoccupation in the novels with aspects of cultural colonization and domination.

His satirical view of the advertising world in *Bliss* is a sharp comment on the Americanization of Australian culture and is continued in *Illywhacker* at a powerful allegorical level. It is an American, Nathan Schick, who plans the 'best pet shop in the world', a place where American tourists can find Australian culture, conveniently reduced and packaged to satisfy their passing interest.

Illywhacker and *Oscar and Lucinda* are written in the style of picaresque historical fantasy. In these rapid and ebullient narratives Carey has produced some of the most quixotic, unlikely, and memorable characters in Australian fiction. As in the work of Colombian writer Gabriel García Márquez, the chief effect of this mythic realism is that it demythologizes factual history by suggesting the fictionality of all representations of the past. The focus is on the value of storytelling, as it is in *Bliss*, and the energy of individual invention as a means of sustaining a culture in the face of national, political, and economic expediency and lingering colonial patronage.

KAREN LAMB

Further reading: Teresa Dovey, 'An infinite onion: narrative structure in Peter Carey's fiction', *Australian Literary Studies* 11 (1983); Graeme Turner, 'American dreaming: the fictions of Peter Carey', *Australian Literary Studies* 12 (1986); Helen Daniel, *Liars: Australian New Novelists* (1988).

CARGILL, MORRIS (1914–)
Jamaican journalist, novelist
Born into a family whose white ancestry dates back to the first English settlers, he was educated at Munro College, Jamaica, and later at the English public school, Stowe, where he became a close friend of such writers as Ian Fleming, Noël Coward, and Lawrence Durrell. He trained as a solicitor but never practised. In 1942 he returned to England and worked in the Ministry of Information, producing documentaries and broadcasting for the British Broadcasting Corporation. Cargill returned to Jamaica after the Second World War and has since run banana plantations and has served as a Member of Parliament in the West Indian Federation and on many boards of directors. He knows Jamaican life — rural and urban, high and low —

as few others do. Such insight underpins the satiric style of his print and radio journalism. His polished prose expresses an endemic absurdist Caribbean vision shared by writers such as **Louise Bennett** and **Wilson Harris**. In 1983 the government of Jamaica awarded Cargill the Order of Distinction for his work as a journalist.

Cargill's reputation and influence as a journalist span four decades. He has helped to shape social and political attitudes in Jamaica and is widely enjoyed for his characteristically biting exposure of public idiocy and corruption. *Jamaica Farewell* (1978), a memoir written during his short-lived stay in the USA in 1977–8, revels in the absurdities of Jamaican society: the sanity of the mad woman, Miss Mumma, stands in contrast to the insanity of bureaucracy. This interplay of lunacy and sanity appears to a lesser extent in three thrillers Cargill co-authored with **John Hearne**, under the joint pen-name John Morris — *Fever Grass* (1969), *The Candywine Development* (1970), and *The Checkerboard Caper* (1975). Cargill's work includes the anthology *Ian Fleming Introduces Jamaica* (1965), *A Gallery of Nazis* (1978), and *Morris Cargill: A Selection of His Writings in The Gleaner 1952–1985* (1987).

JEAN D'COSTA

CARIBBEAN, THE

The term 'West Indies' superseded 'British West Indies' when, beginning with Jamaica and Trinidad and Tobago in 1962, most of the Caribbean colonies of Great Britain, which the earlier term had denoted, gained their political independence. The concept of the West Indies had itself resulted from Christopher Columbus' mistake in thinking that he had reached India. One rather bizarre consequence of this misnomer is that West Indians whose place of ethnic origin is India are sometimes differentiated, in the West Indies, as East Indians.

Strictly speaking, 'West Indies' refers to the Anglophone islands, but for all practical purposes, except that of postal addresses, it has been used more widely and conveniently to include as well the former British mainland territories, more or less adjacent to the Caribbean, of Belize (formerly British Honduras) in Central America, and Guyana (formerly British Guiana) in South America. Hence the West Indies may be seen as curving up from Guyana, through the Caribbean archipelago, to Belize.

In some circumstances the term West Indies has also been conveniently used to include the Bahamas, which most certainly lie outside the Caribbean (in the Atlantic) and, by association as it were, the yet more distant Bermuda. West Indian literature, then, is Anglophone Caribbean literature, also now sometimes called Commonwealth Caribbean literature — 'Caribbean' being understood with a sensible flexibility. Furthermore, given the large twentieth-century migration of West Indian peoples to the UK and North America, and the emergence of Britain and Canada as important centres of West Indian writing, the term West Indian literature has broken out of its traditional geographic boundaries, flexible enough as they were. (See **The Caribbean in Canadian Literature**.)

The defining linguistic provenance of the West Indies reminds us of their ambiguous position in relation to their non-Anglophone neighbouring islands and adjacent Central and South American nations. (See **Language**, The Caribbean.) The accidents of history and conquest, reinforced by the coinciding power of language, imposed artificial separations between islands that otherwise, by virtue of history and geography, belong together. These partitions have had obvious implications for West Indian literature, one of which is that it has come to be seen largely in the Commonwealth/post-colonial context. However, there has recently been a markedly increasing awareness among West Indians of the imperative of the Pan-Caribbean context of West Indian literature. This heightening consciousness is no doubt one factor that accounts for the increasing frequency with which 'Caribbean literature' is used instead of 'West Indian literature'.

Even among the Anglophone islands and countries, and despite such similarities of topography, history, ethnicity, and culture as they share and such movement of people as has occurred among them, there persist insular jealousies and prejudices that have militated against vibrant, sustained regional co-operation. These have been the result not only of physical separation, but also of a British colonial influence that caused each of the colonies to look more towards the 'mother country' than towards its neighbours.

A political Federation of the West Indies came into being in 1958, but within four years it collapsed, when Jamaica, the largest of the islands and the one most isolated physically from the rest, withdrew. Subsequently, through Caricom (the Caribbean Community), there has been a half-hearted institutionalizing of a structure to promote regional co-operation. The most successful regional institutions remain the West Indies cricket team, the University of the West Indies (with campuses in Barbados, Jamaica, and Trinidad), and, the most spontaneously emerging one of all, West Indian literature.

History

When Christopher Columbus first arrived in the Caribbean, in the last decade of the fifteenth century, the region was inhabited by Taino peoples — Arawaks and Caribs — to whom the Europeans applied the misnomer Indian, or Amerindian. It did not take long for the Spaniards, in the name of the Bible, of the king of Spain, and of elusive gold, to all but eliminate these original islanders, whether through forced labour or by the sword. Apart from one or two diminishing or diluted remnants, nothing survives of these cultures except a few shards and middens and burial sites, some place names, a few rock carvings and pieces of sculpture, one or two food crops (cassava, maize), and a few words added to English, such as hammock and hurricane.

Other European nations — English, French, Dutch — followed the Spaniards into the Caribbean and in many places supplanted them. The socio-cultural character of West Indian countries varies today partly as a function of the mix of European colonizing influences to which each was subjected. For instance, Barbados was colonized only by the British, Jamaica first by the Spanish and then by the British, whereas St Lucia changed hands between the British and the French thirteen times.

The Europeans instituted slavery in the West Indies, beginning with the Spanish, who brought Africans to replace the decimated Amerindians whom they had enslaved. The Africans survived, and the plantation system that they sustained by their sweat and suffering was the machinery of a purely exploitative economic adventure on the part of the Europeans that drained the productive capacity of the 'sugar isles' to enrich absentee landlords and kings. The foundations of modern West Indian society were laid by this enforced and purely expedient encounter of Africa and Europe in the Caribbean.

After the British abolished slavery in the 1830s, the ex-slaves were reluctant to continue working on the estates; in the nineteenth century, a large number of Asiatics, mostly from India but also including some Chinese, were imported to form the labour force and consequently to add to the ethnic and cultural mix of the Caribbean. The Indian presence became particularly strong in Guyana and Trinidad and Tobago, where today they make up more than half of the population and complicate attempts at general ethnicity-based theories of West Indian society and culture. Other smaller migrations, in some cases occasioned by religious persecution — from Portugal, Spain, and the Middle East — have also been appreciable, however small the numbers, in the making of West

Indian society.

When slavery was abolished, West Indian sugar had already begun to lose its hold on the European market, the plantations were declining, and the small white population became even smaller; but Britain held on to these colonies for more than a hundred years. Local agitation led to the granting of some internal self-government in the 1940s and then, inevitably, to independence, except for one or two of the smallest islands. The West Indies have remained part of the British Commonwealth, and West Indians inherited from the British the Westminster model of parliamentary democracy, but, given the relatively poor economic health of many of the countries and the competition for insufficient benefits, the two-party system has tended, most markedly in Jamaica, to deteriorate into violent and wasteful political tribalism. Not surprisingly, there have been experiments with Marxism, not without some unfortunate results, most evident in Grenada and Guyana.

Economy

Sugar, which once was 'king' in the Caribbean, continues to be a major export, though sometimes of questionable profitability, but other crops, especially bananas, subsequently claimed a large share of the export market. Petroleum in Trinidad and Tobago, and bauxite in Jamaica and Guyana are crucial to the economies of these countries. Guyana also has other valuable mineral reserves — gold and diamonds — that are yet to be fully tapped. For some islands, however, tourism has come to be a major economic lifeline, and this situation is likely to be increasingly true for the region as a whole. The pressure of unemployment and low wages has also during the years been eased by a steady stream of immigration into North America and the UK.

Religion and Culture

The church was a crucial instrument of European colonization, and today the traditional mainstream denominations, whether Roman Catholic or Protestant, still enjoy high status and visibility. However, some African religious cults have survived, and revivalist churches that incorporate aspects of African rituals have always had strong support at the grass-roots and lower-middle class levels. The emergence and rise of **Rastafarianism** in the twentieth century also attest to the strength and creative, mythopoeic efficacy of the African connection. (See **African Connections**, The Caribbean.) Hinduism and Islam are also alive, in certain instances somewhat creolized, among the Indian communities.

Out of the matrix of Rastafarianism, Jamaica has given to the world the popular musical form reggae and its relation, dub poetry, and has provided icons and inspiration for counter-cultures of youth throughout the world. The other great original artistic contributions of the Caribbean have also been in the field of popular music — Trinidadian calypso and steel pan. (See **Songs and Ballads**, The Caribbean.) The rich artistic potential of the region has no doubt been a function of its diverse cultural heritage and, more particularly, of the capacity of the strong African base to adapt, adjust, and accommodate.

EDWARD BAUGH

Further reading: Eric Williams, *From Columbus to Castro* (1971); P. M. Sherlock, *West Indian Nations* (1973); Paul Sutton, ed., *Europe and the Caribbean* (1991); Irving Rouse, *The Tainos: Rise and Decline of the People Who Greeted Columbus* (1992).

CARIBBEAN IN CANADIAN LITERATURE, THE

The Caribbean is depicted in Canadian literature from almost opposite perspectives. On the one hand, there are the accounts of white Canadian visitors to the Caribbean, and, on the other, those of new immigrants, mostly black and East Indian, from the islands to Canada.

Although trade between Canada — especially Maritime Canada — and the Caribbean flourished for centuries, the Caribbean is not a significant presence in early Canadian writing. Critic Gwendolyn Davies suggests that few Maritime traders in the eighteenth and nineteenth centuries 'had either the time or the inclination to give imaginative expression to the experience in fiction, poetry, or drama'. The most substantial eighteenth-century account of Caribbean life by a Nova Scotian exists in a collection of letters (in the public archives of Nova Scotia, Halifax) that Mather Byles III wrote home to Halifax from Grenada, in the Windward Islands, where he was stationed from 1790 to 1802.

In 1898 **Bliss Carman**, the poet, visited the Bahamas to write a series of articles to promote tourism there. The poetic result of his brief stay was *A Winter Holiday* (1898), which contains five poems set in the Bahamas. Carman was invigorated by the colour and romance of the islands, as the following lines from 'Bahaman' indicate: 'In a world all glad with color, / gladdest of all things was I.' However, his vision was that of a tourist to whom the Bahamian people were exotics: 'Under burdens finely poised, / and with freedom unsurpassed, / Move the naked-footed bearers / in the blue day deep and vast.'

Charles G. D. Roberts, Carman's cousin, also visited the Caribbean, and he wrote two short stories, 'The Peril of the Green Pool' (1907) and 'The Lord of the Glass House' (1909), which deal with the marine life of the area. Roberts' younger brother, **Theodore Goodridge Roberts**, knew the Caribbean much more intimately than his brother and his cousin, having lived for two years, 1904–5, in 'a pinkwalled house between the cane-fields and the surf' of Barbados, but his vision of the islands did not differ markedly from theirs. His collection of poems, *The Leather Bottle* (1934), contains a section called 'Stuff of Neptune's Brewing', twenty-four poems about the sea and the islands. Poems such as 'Night Wind of Barbados' and 'Christmas in Alurio' describe sensitively the seascapes and landscape of Barbados. Other poems express a fascination with the area's history of piracy. The people of Barbados, however, remain picturesque parts of the landscape: 'The lithe brown children have gone to rest — / Shell-hunting over for one more day. / Purple the east and purple the west, / And white stars over Martin's Bay.' Roberts also wrote ten stories of love and adventure, seafaring, and piracy in the region. He was attracted to the sensational in Caribbean history — 'Everything Came High' (1950) is about a hurricane in Barbados, and 'In New Atmosphere' (1913) features the eruption of Mt Pelé in Martinique. Like the stories, some of Roberts' novels exploit the history and landscape of the Caribbean for romantic effect. *The 'Wasp'* (1914), set in England and the Caribbean, is concerned with the naval struggle between France and England at the end of the seventeenth century.

Thomas Raddall, another Maritime Canadian novelist, shares Roberts' fascination with the sea and the adventurous history of the Caribbean. His *Pride's Fancy* (1946) is about privateering off the coast of Haiti at the time of the 1791 revolution. In the novel, Amos Pride, a Nova Scotian, capitalizes on the turmoil in the area to enrich himself. His stepson, Nathan Cain, however, rejects the Pride fortune to marry a Haitian woman. *Pride's Fancy* contains a brief but sympathetic sketch of Toussaint L'Ouverture, the black leader of the revolution. Although Raddall is a more complex and accomplished novelist than Roberts, and his attitude to the Caribbean more ambiguous, the islands remain for him places of adventure and excitement with which he can compare the austere climate and temperament of Nova Scotia.

Although more contemporary Canadian fictions set in the Caribbean are less romantic, the adventure story has not disappeared. Lew Anthony's thriller *Dreadlock* (1981), set in Jamaica, competes with the earlier novels in violence and sensationalism. The majority of novels, however, seem to question the sentimentality of the earlier vision. The romantic atmosphere of Diane Giguère's *L'Eau est profonde* (1965), translated as *Whirlpool* (1966), is undercut by the narrator's sense of the dangers of the landscape. Other novels that counteract the island paradise images meant for tourists are *Canadian Healing Oil* (1974) by Juan Butler, *Famous Last Words* (1981) by **Timothy Findley**, and *Bodily Harm* (1981) by **Margaret Atwood**. Rennie, Atwood's protagonist, wants to go to the Caribbean because her life in Toronto is 'the pits right now. I need a tan'. She finds that society on St Antoine does not play by the rules that apply in Canada, and she ends up trapped in a Caribbean prison from which she may never escape. Atwood's novel resists the neat closure of the conventional political thriller.

Ten of the stories in Harold Horwood's *Only the Gods Speak* (1979) are set in the Caribbean, and as the author himself says, 'they are freighted with many of my deepest concerns, from the need for closer communion between people to the fear that white civilization has shot its bolt'. Similarly, Philip Kreiner's novel *Heartlands* (1984) explores the failure of a Canadian woman, Vikki, to make contact with the people of Jamaica, which she is visiting because, like Atwood's Rennie, her life in Canada is in a tailspin.

Contemporary works of fiction by native-born Canadian writers use the Caribbean as an unknown, dangerous place to which their characters go to escape from themselves and/or to find themselves. Although they do not sentimentalize the islands and present them as paradises, most of them are not primarily concerned with, nor are they particularly knowledgeable about, life in the Caribbean.

In *El Dorado and Paradise: Canada and the Caribbean in Austin Clarke's Fiction* (1989), Lloyd Brown identifies the dilemma of **Austin Clarke**'s Caribbean immigrants as resulting from their conviction that they are leaving island paradises behind to come to Canada, an El Dorado of opportunity. The fiction of Clarke and of other new Canadian writers from the Caribbean struggles to dispel these myths. Clarke's *Survivors of the Crossing* (1964) and *Amongst Thistles and Thorns* (1965) and the novels of **Harold Sonny Ladoo**, *No Pain Like This Body* (1972) and *Yesterdays* (1974), present Caribbean societies as poor and brutal rather than as paradisiacal. In his trilogy of West Indian life in Toronto — *The Meeting Point* (1967), *Storm of Fortune* (1971), and *The Bigger Light* (1975) — Clarke explores the difficulties and bigotry that non-white immigrants to Canada encounter. Other works of fiction that underline the point that Canada is no El Dorado are such novels as Lorris Elliott's *Coming for to Carry* (1982) and **Marlene Nourbese Philip**'s *Harriet's Daughter* (1988), and collections of short stories such as **Cyril Dabydeen**'s *Still Close to the Island* (1980), **Neil Bissoondath**'s *Digging Up the Mountains* (1985), **Dionne Brand**'s *Sans Souci and Other Stories* (1988), and Clarke's three volumes of short stories.

Two novels by new Canadian writers from the Caribbean that, like Atwood's *Bodily Harm* and Kreiner's *Heartlands*, send their protagonists on quests to the Caribbean are Clarke's *The Prime Minister* (1977) and Bissoondath's *A Casual Brutality* (1988). They contain a complication that Atwood's book does not because they are about Caribbean immigrants who, having become Canadian citizens, discover that they cannot go home again.

Among the most vehement and enterprising of the voices of these new Canadian writers are those of poets such as Lillian Allen, Ayanna Black, Dionne Brand, Afua Cooper, Cyril Dabydeen, **Claire Harris**, Arnold Itwaru, Marlene Nourbese Philip, and Charles Roach. Recognizing their rights as Canadians, they have set about possessing their new country by contributing their own language and rhythms of life to the culture that they found in Canada.

That the new Canadian writers have complicated and enriched the literary perception of the Caribbean in Canadian literature is suggested by the titles of the following three anthologies of their work: *Canada in Us Now: The First Anthology of Black Poetry and Prose in Canada* (1976), edited by Harold Head, *Other Voices: Writings by Blacks in Canada* (1985), edited by Lorris Elliott, and *A Shapely Fire: Changing the Literary Landscape* (1987), edited by Cyril Dabydeen. A full account of the Caribbean in Canadian literature must, therefore, now include not only the romantic enthusiasms of Carman and Roberts and the bleaker, less sentimental fictions of Atwood and Findley, but also the explosion of writing by Canadians of Caribbean origin that demands to have a say about how Canada perceives the Caribbean.

ANTHONY BOXILL

Further reading: *Canadian Literature* 95 (1982), special issue on 'Caribbean Connections'.

'CARIBBEAN VOICES'

The British Broadcasting Corporation's (BBC's) overseas programme 'Caribbean Voices' was the first serious acknowledgement, in a metropolitan country, of the existence and importance of a corpus of anglophone writing in the Caribbean and of a group of writers, many unknown to each other, seriously working in that area. It also represented one of the few 'publishing' opportunities for Caribbean writers and put the important stamp of payment for literary work on their often lonely efforts. Further, the BBC's high reputation, won during the Second World War, was probably at its highest during the programme's run, and Caribbean writers, hardly known in their own countries, had the satisfaction of hearing their works broadcast from London, England.

'Caribbean Voices' was begun in 1945 by the distinguished Jamaican Una Marson. When she became ill, she was succeeded in 1946 by Henry Swanzy, who directed this programme with vigour and imagination until 1954. In those years he carried on a correspondence with such Caribbean writers as **Frank Collymore**, **Wilson Harris**, **Edgar Mittelholzer**, **Harold Telemaque**, and **E. K. Brathwaite**. On 22 January 1949, for example, Collymore wrote to Swanzy about **Derek Walcott**'s *25 Poems* (1948): 'Walcott who is nineteen years old tomorrow writes with a remarkable fervour . . . his work is obviously sincere and wonderfully mature.'

Swanzy was the first in England to 'publish' Walcott and other writers such as **Gloria Escoffery**, **George Lamming**, and Willy Richardson. The first Swanzy production was a short story by **John Figueroa** called 'Do You Appreciate Music?' (From 1946 until 1953 Figueroa was associated with Swanzy's work mainly as verse reader on the programme, but also as critic and author. Lamming and Pauline Henriques were also readers in the early years.) By early 1952 the programme had broadcast the work of one hundred and fifty Caribbean writers.

While the programme enjoyed esteem in the Caribbean, it was not without its critics. Some disliked the reading of scripts and the catholic taste shown in the programme's selection of short stories and poems. Some wanted only 'proper' middle-class stories, and some, in those colonial days, preferred to hear English voices rather than Caribbean voices reading the programme's selections. Caribbean critics and readers with independent views were mistrusted, *au principe*, at home: for some Jamaicans, the BBC was wrong to encourage such critics instead of holding to the tastes and views of those who had accepted the British as arbiters of taste.

There were also some Caribbean critics who genuinely feared that through the programme London might siphon off all good Caribbean writing. When Caribbean producers tried to develop local literary radio programmes, they were not successful. (It is a difficult problem not yet solved, despite the existence now of indigenous publishing in the Caribbean.)

But despite criticism — and it is unlikely that such an imaginative programme was without fault — in its first years 'Caribbean Voices' provided exactly the kind of stimulus and opportunity that Caribbean writers and readers needed.

'Caribbean Voices' ended in September 1958. By then it had been produced by Ken Ablack, Willy Edmett, Willy Richardson, Ulric Cross, and Billy Pilgrim, among others. **V. S. Naipaul** had done extensive editing. **Andrew Salkey** edited the final programme. Copies of the programme's scripts are in the library of the University of the West Indies, Mona, Jamaica.

John Figueroa's anthology, *Caribbean Voices: An Anthology of West Indian Poetry* (vol. 1, 1966; vol. 2, 1970), especially Volume One, presents many of the verse contributions to the programme. The short stories and critical pieces have not been collected.

JOHN J. FIGUEROA

CARMAN, BLISS (1861–1929)

Canadian poet, essayist

Born in Fredericton, New Brunswick, Canada, he obtained his MA from the University of New Brunswick before entering Harvard University, USA, in 1886. There he met Josiah Royce, George Santayana, Francis Child, and Richard Hovey, who profoundly influenced his writing. A mystic and bachelor poet of the open road who published more than fifty volumes of verse during his lifetime, Carman travelled widely, but he spent much of his writing life in New England. He participated as a poet, editor, and critical commentator in the literary life of the USA to such an extent that when his first book of poems, *Low Tide on Grand Pré* (1893), appeared, he was celebrated as a new American as well as a new Canadian voice. He returned to Canada frequently during the 1920s and became the recipient of many Canadian literary honours and awards.

Like other Canadian **Confederation Poets**, Carman was early and often viewed as a derivative, colonial poetaster whose work seldom transcended the Romantic and Victorian models by which he was inspired during his early years studying the works of dead masters who had written from the imperial centre of England. In truth, however, his thinking and his accomplishment were wider than this — his canon embodies a plurality of impulses, including those of sea balladist, mystic, elegist, poet of nostalgia, poet of horror, and philosopher (he was greatly influenced by François Delsarte's theories of education). Recent criticism is quick to point out that it was and is the unfortunate timidity of his more colonial critics that accounts for the imprecise view of him as derivative and second rate.

Reassessment shows that Carman was, at his best, an intense poet of witness and a significant advocate of the new British, American, and Canadian literature of his time. He wrote four books of prose — *The Poetry of Life* (1905) is his best known — in which he attempted to remedy the spiritual crises of modernity with prescriptions for imaginative renewal.

TERRY WHALEN

Further reading: Terry Whalen, *Bliss Carman and His Works* (1983); Gerald Lynch, ed., *Bliss Carman: A Reappraisal* (1990).

CARMAN, DULCE (1883–1970)

New Zealand novelist, children's writer

Born at Horsham St Faiths, Norfolk, England, she immigrated to New Zealand in 1892. She married a farmer in Hawkes Bay and turned, in 1948, from writing children's fiction to writing adult novels. She published under the name Dulce Carman, but is sometimes referred to as Dulce Carman Drummond. During the next two decades Carman wrote twenty-five 'romances of Maoriland' with such titles as *Neath the Maori Moon* (1948), *The Tapu Tree* (1954), and *The Miracle of Tane* (1962).

Carman developed a reputation in her time for writing sympathetically about Maori-Pakeha relations. However, her novels unconsciously reveal social attitudes underlying official integrationist policies in the 1950s and 1960s. Her convoluted plots, crammed with bizarre incidents and coincidences, provide a precise metaphor of integration in action, with the destinies of Maori characters almost invariably subservient to those of Pakeha characters, and Maori legendary material, lavishly adding romantic mystery, also invariably appropriated to the destinies of Pakeha characters.

Carman's Maori characters tend to be of two types: highly idealized older chiefly figures, and a shiftless, younger generation urgently in need of saving from itself. Beneath their transparent surfaces, Carman's novels reveal precisely why the integrationist philosophy of race relations was soon to collapse, under the pressure of a renascent Maori drive for self-determination in the 1970s.

TERRY STURM

CARR, EMILY (1871–1945)

Canadian painter, writer

Born in Victoria, Canada, she was the youngest daughter of Richard Carr, a well-to-do merchant, and his wife Emily, and by her own account grew up in a traditional, religious household that looked towards England for its standard of culture. Educated at private institutions in Victoria, Carr studied painting for short periods at the California School of Design in San Francisco, USA (1891–3), the Westminster School of Art in London, England (1899–1901), and with several private teachers, including the New Zealander Frances Hodgkins, during a trip to Europe in 1910–11. Carr's paintings and sketches, inspired by the art of the Canadian west-coast Native tribes and by the coastal rain forest of British Columbia, express her sense of the spiritual in nature and draw on her experience of French post-impressionism and her admiration for the Canadian nationalist Group of Seven painters (especially Lawren Harris).

When age and ill health curtailed her strength, Carr began to rewrite and further develop the stories she had been writing for some years. She produced several volumes of autobiographical sketches including *Klee Wyck* (1941), which won a Governor General's Award, *The Book of Small* (1942), and *The House of All Sorts* (1944). An autobiography, *Growing Pains* (1946), *Hundreds and Thousands: The Journals of an Artist* (1966), as well as two further volumes of sketches, *Pause* (1953) and *The Heart of a Peacock* (1953), and two addresses on modernist art, published together as *Fresh Seeing* (1972), appeared posthumously.

Carr's autobiographical sketches typically present her as a young and powerless innocent whose deepest feelings are for animals and the natural world. In *The Book of Small* her alter ego, Small (distinguished from her older sisters Middle and Bigger), delights in the company of the birds and animals of the family cow yard and rejects the civilized (and English) conventions of dainty clothes and polite deference to adults. This plot is reiterated in collections of sketches that represent Carr's adolescence and maturity, emphasizing her isolation in Victoria, her identification with the Canadian landscape and the Canadian Native peoples, and her antipathy to metropolitan centres, especially those of Europe. In these stories, as in *Growing Pains*, Carr often departs from strict fact to heighten the sense of her protagonist's victimization, shearing as much as ten years off her age and dramatically describing such childhood punishments as whippings, which most biographers agree probably never took place. Simple, direct diction, repetitive noun-verb sentence structure, and abrupt shifts in narrative chronology give her writing a sense of immediacy and unconventionality.

For Carr, the metropolitan centres of London, Paris, and New York were the source of artistic companionship and instruction; yet, in *Growing Pains* and *Pause* these cities are depicted as literally causing the combination of physical and mental illness that resulted in Carr's repeated breakdowns (including a fifteen-month stay in an English sanatorium in 1903–4). Aggressively colonial, resentful of British condescension, Carr retreated into her identity as Klee Wyck, 'the laughing one', in order to defend herself against negative pronouncements on her appearance and manners. She found spiritual sustenance, companionship, and artistic inspiration in nature, doing her best paintings in outdoor sketch classes and fleeing her London schoolroom for afternoon visits with the familiar specimen trees from home kept at Kew Gardens. Like Monica Gall, the aspiring Canadian opera singer in **Robertson Davies'** *A Mixture of Frailties*, Carr was ambivalent towards what she learned of social customs in London and, later, in Paris and was uncertain whether the artistic training she received was appropriate to express Canada. A pioneer of Canadian modernism, Carr rejected attempts to theorize her work or identify her influences and proudly claimed that she expressed the spirit of the place instinctively and reverentially in her paintings and her writing.

MISAO DEAN

Further reading: Paula Blanchard, *The Life of Emily Carr* (1987); Doris Shadbolt, *Emily Carr* (1989).

CARTER, MARTIN WYLDE (1927–)

Guyanese poet

Born in Georgetown, British Guiana (now Guyana), he received his secondary-school education at Queen's College, Georgetown. By his early twenties Carter was a part of the political movement for independence and a contributor to **A. J. Seymour**'s literary magazine *Kyk-over-al*. In his earliest poetry his voice is that of the radical faction of British Guiana's anti-colonial movement. Because of his prominence and his publications, Carter became an obvious target for the British colonial administration, which arrested and imprisoned him in 1953, at the time of the suspension of the colony's constitution. His poetry, forged in the heat of struggle, or, as in the case of *Poems of Resistance* (1954), written in the forced calm of the prison cell, has survived the cause that inspired it to become the finest — some would say the only — example of revolutionary literature in the anglophone Caribbean.

Upon release from prison, where he wrote several of his most famous poems, Carter continued to be involved in the independence movement and worked in several civil-service posts. In 1965 he travelled to London, England, as a member of the colony's delegation to the Constitutional Conference that would make the final decisions concerning independence. After independence in 1966 he served in the Guyanese government in various capacities, including those of delegate to the United Nations (1966–7) and minister of information and culture (1967–70). Since leaving the government in 1971 he has been writer/artist-in-residence at a number of universities and, from 1981, he has been a senior research fellow at the University of Guyana. Writing poetry has been the deep, unchanging aspect of Carter's life, anchoring his various activities to a constant commitment and vision.

From his earliest collections, such as *The Hill of Fire Glows Red* (1951) and *The Kind Eagle* (1952), Carter's distinctive voice of protest and his major theme of revolution are in evidence: 'No! / I will not still my voice . . . ' ('Looking at your Hands'); 'This is my hand / for the revolution . . . ' ('A Banner for the Revolution'). His poetry and vision are carefully located in a particular context and landscape: the bridges, the canefields, the river, and 'the sea behind the wall' all identify the coastland of Guyana, while the mention of 'the blood of Quamina' and the 'tongueless whisperings' of the land invoke in the struggle for independence the memory of a buried slave.

Carter's best-known poems are in *Poems of Resistance*. These are not poems of shrill defiance, imprisoned in a historical moment; rather, they transcend the moment through the use of a perspective that includes ancestors, 'my dead ancestor Accabreh' ('I Clench My Fist'), and the unborn: 'If I do not live to see that day / My son will see it. / If he does not see that day / His son will see it' ('Letter 1'). Carter's concern in his letters from prison is not just with those he calls 'my people', but with his own 'dear wife whose voice I cannot hear' ('Letter 2') and with his son, fatherless at home. This personal element tends to focus sharply the sense of injustice and helps account for the fact that the poems have remained powerful and fresh long after the struggle for independence has ended.

Carter's poetry extends beyond the specific moment through an expansion of the sensation of space. Although the language of the poem 'Till I Collect' is tainted with 'blood' and 'anguish', it is set in an entire universe, where the poet is navigating 'the islands of the stars' rather than a narrow prison. In 'The University of Hunger' the simple statement of the people's misery is expanded within the immense dimensions of the traditional elements of earth, air, and water, in a poetic universe rather than in a specific political context.

This dual reference, seen in all of Carter's major poems, may be intended to convey the dual focus of consciousness itself — consciousness of the world and of the self as subject. The relationship between the self and the world is at the centre of his concern, both as a revolutionary poet and, simply, as a poet. Thus, Carter often examines a situation and consciousness at the same time and in the light of each other. For this reason many of his later poems — in *Poems of Affinity* (1980), for example — have a dense, philosophical texture, the origin of which is traceable nevertheless to the complex nature of the voice in the poems of resistance. In the first lines of 'Being Always', Carter plays in an abstract way with this duality of consciousness: 'Being, always to arrange / myself in the world, and the world / in myself, I try to do both . . . '. In poems such as 'Till I Collect' and 'The Kind Eagle', however, the self and the world are rendered in terms of the vastness of space outside the imprisoned or oppressed self.

The tension between the infinities of air, earth, water, and fire, on the one hand, and the restricted self, on the other, is what generates meaning in Carter's poetry. For this reason, his most typical collection, it might be argued, is *Poems of Shape and Motion* (1955). In the collection generally and in 'Shape and Motion Three' in particular, a vision of the oppressed ('houses tight with sickness . . . the loneliness of a child') combines perfectly with the philosophical ('the challenge of space in my soul') and with the familiar features of the Guyana littoral ('the long river', 'the sweeping ocean of water', 'the sky blue like silk'). With whatever perspective one approaches the poems, however, they resonate with the power of voice and vision, thought and action, body and mind.

MARK McWATT

Further reading: Mark McWatt, 'The challenge of space: being and consciousness in the poetry of Martin Carter', in Jennifer Jackson and Jeanette B. Allis (eds) *West Indian Poetry* (1985); Jeffrey Robinson, 'The root and the stone: the rhetoric of Martin Carter's *Poems of Resistance*', *Journal of West Indian Literature* 1 (1986).

CARTEY, WILFRED (1931–92)

Trinidadian poet, novelist, critic

Born Wilfred George Onslow Cartey at Clifton Hill, Laventille, Trinidad, he attended Queen's Royal College, Port of Spain, Trinidad. He earned his BA (1955) at the University of the West Indies, Jamaica, and, as the recipient of a Fulbright-Hays award, travelled to the USA, where he earned his MA and Ph.D. (1964) at Columbia University. Cartey taught Spanish at Columbia from 1957 to 1977, then became distinguished professor, department of Black Studies, City College of New York.

Cartey's critical works include *The West Indies: Islands in the Sun* (1967), the acclaimed study *Whispers from a Continent: The Literature of Contemporary Black Africa* (1969), *Black Images* (1970), *Palaver: A Critical Anthology of African Literature* (1970), and *Whispers from the Caribbean* (1991). From 1973 to 1976 he edited *Communities: A Journal of Black Studies* (1970–8), and in 1984 he edited *Afro-Hispanic Review* (1982–). From 1987 to his death Cartey was editor of *Cimarron: Journal of Caribbean Culture* (1967–).

Cartey produced twelve volumes of poetry: *The House of Blue Lightning* (1973), *Waters of My Soul* (1975), *Red Rain* (1977), *Suns and Shadows* (1978), *Fires in the Wind* (1980), *The Dawn, the Desert, the Sands, Kundija* (1982), *Embryos* (1982), *Black Velvet Time* (1984), *Children of Lalibela* (1985), *Potentialities* (1987), *Spirit Time* (1988), and *Choreographers of the Dawn* (1989). *Oakman*, a novel, appeared in 1989.

Cartey's writings reflect his concern for the liberation of African, African Caribbean, and 'New World' peoples. His poetry is notable for its political concerns, its depth of understanding of post-colonial African-descended peoples, and its geographic sweep. The use of African rhythms and repetition recalls the African nation language poets of the 1960s and 1970s, but their work lacks the musicality and measured flow of the Cartey line.

Despite its sometimes angry and forceful protest and the pained lamentation evident in such works as *Fires in the Wind*, Cartey's themes are enriched by a view that is ultimately universal in scope and that envisions the interconnectedness of black people, humanity, and nature.

HELEN PYNE TIMOTHY

CASEY, GAVIN (1907–64)

Australian novelist, short-story writer

Born in Kalgoorlie, Western Australia, he was employed as a miner and as a journalist. He worked for the Australian News and Information Service in New York, USA, between 1945 and 1947, then as a journalist in Sydney, Australia. Casey's fiction continued to be set in Western Australia, and much of it draws on the particular conditions of social and working life on the goldfields.

As with other Australian writers in the period between the 1930s and the 1950s, work is a major subject. The male world of labour, unemployment, pubs, gambling, **mateship**, and violence figures in some of Casey's most powerful writing: stories such as 'Short Shift Saturday' and 'Back for Good' from his first short-story collection, *It's Harder for Girls* (1942) and the novel *Downhill Is Easier* (1945). He adapted realist 'tough-guy' prose to represent inarticulate male characters coming to terms with the disillusion and bewilderments of their lives in work, friendship, and marriage.

Two novels are based on the lives of 'ordinary' working-class families in the suburbs: *The Wits Are Out* (1947) and *Amid the Plenty* (1962). The optimistic accounts of decent, even irrepressible characters are tempered by a sense of their limited options and inevitable disappointments. *Snowball* (1958), an important novel although not widely known, is a convincing study of an Aboriginal family and the white township on whose fringe they live. It deserves comparison with **Xavier Herbert**'s fiction. *City of Men* (1950), set on the goldfields, is one of a number of Australian 'sagas' written between the 1930s and the 1950s, including work by **Vance Palmer**, **Brian Penton**,

Miles Franklin, and **Katharine Susannah Prichard**. Sharing something of the saga form, though also a study of personal emotions, *The Man Whose Name Was Mud* (1963) draws together many of the themes of Casey's fiction: the male ethos (which it shares, but not uncritically), an unsentimental view of sexual relations, comparisons between city/coast and goldfields/bush, an emphasis on circumstance (even luck), and a central focus on manual and 'managerial' work. (See also **Goldfields Literature**.)

It's Harder for Girls was republished as *Short Shift Saturday and Other Stories* (1973).

DAVID CARTER

CATO, NANCY (1917–)

Australian novelist, poet

Born in Adelaide, Australia, she first worked as a journalist and art critic; since 1958 she has been a full-time writer, mainly of historical novels. Two early volumes of poetry, *The Darkened Window* (1950) and *The Dancing Bough* (1957), demonstrate a fondness for short lyrics capturing the brief moment in time, finding significance in the trivial.

Greatly contrasting are the lengthy family sagas that comprise Cato's fiction. A trilogy published between 1958 and 1962 was republished as the one-volume *All the Rivers Run* (1978) and achieved significant international success. While often packaged for the commercially popular market, the historical epics are far more subtle and serious than most fiction of this genre, explaining the present by demonstrating the effects of time upon family and national character and exploring crucial aspects of white Australia's morally impoverished past.

Historical accuracy in Cato's fiction lies not so much in faithful re-creation of events and time — although her research is extensive and, indeed, in the novel *Forefathers* (1983), most of the important incidents in Australian history are covered — as in capturing the mood and flavour of colonial Australia and the preoccupations of the present generation towards its history. The treatment of the Aborigines is one example. Cato's interest in Aboriginal life may be traced to the influence of **Rex Ingamells** and the **Jindyworobak Movement**, although she was never fully committed to it. Both *Forefathers* and *Queen Trucanini* (1976), with Vivienne Rae Ellis — a fictionalized account of the last survivor of the tribal Tasmanian Aborigines — consciously protest at the injustices dealt to the Aborigines. *Brown Sugar* (1974) extends this to the Kanakas, Pacific islanders who were 'blackbirded' into slavery on the Queensland canefields.

Cato has claimed the influence on her style of Henry James, but, apart from the slow and careful revelation of character, influences and similarities might be better found closer to home: her characters are pushed and manipulated by a universal force, often malignant, at best indifferent, in a manner suggesting **Xavier Herbert**'s novels, and even, more recently, the Queensland novels of **Thea Astley**.

DEBRA ADELAIDE

Further reading: Giulia Giuffrè, *A Writing Life: Interviews with Australian Women Writers* (1990).

CENSORSHIP

CENSORSHIP (Overview)

Censorship is as old as organized government; it existed in ancient Greece — Athens as well as Sparta — and in ancient China. It is also as old as religious fanaticism, and one can say fairly that there are no countries in the Commonwealth that have wholly avoided it, either at the hands of the colonizers or those of successor administrations.

There are really two main forms of official censorship — political and moral — with two different sources, as well as the less direct forms, such as libel actions, which are embodied in civil rather than criminal codes. Every government, it can be taken as axiomatic, is afraid of its own subjects, and of their minds being turned against it, which is why every country has anti-sedition laws and official secrets legislation with varying degrees of intensity. To expect to live without censorship is to expect to live without government. Moral censorship, which protects religious beliefs and institutions from attack and criminalizes writing about sex, is perhaps more dangerous because it springs largely from popular feeling, often operating extra-legally. There was, for example, no legal condemnation of the novels of the Canadian **Margaret Laurence**, but private citizens succeeded in getting them excluded from some school libraries.

Political censorship is more rational and predictable than moral censorship. According to the nature of the government, the writer knows just how far he or she can go without risk in attacking it (the object of attack in the case of South Africa, for example, being the ruling race). Moral censorship is less predictable, because the collective morality of a group changes more rapidly than its political form; in that battle the writer gains in some places while he or she loses in others. The worst cases are those in which there is close identification between the government and a prevailing puritanical religion, as in South Africa, Ireland, and fundamentalist Islamic states. But in most of the settlement colonies — Canada, Australia, New Zealand — there has been a steady decline in the censorship of books on moral grounds, although the situation is more doubtful in the case of films and theatre, where the issue of visuality complicates the situation, but often complicates it in curious ways. In the UK, in the 1940s and 1950s, *tableaux vivants* featured women in various states of undress, including nudity, who posed as 'living statues'; if they moved in any way, they could be prosecuted by the police!

Peculiar to the colonies that received democracy and independence late and slowly, such as India and other Asian and also African countries, is the fact that much of their law is inherited from the former imperial rulers. Hindu society, for example, is by its nature absorptive and tolerant. It fights the unorthodox by trying to contain it, while much of the imagery and symbolic practices of, say, Tantric Hinduism, might seem highly immoral to an adherent of the Dutch Reformed Church or a Plymouth Brother. Something alien to the culture has to be invoked, and the consequence is that when the operation of the modern state requires restrictive laws, the laws often tend to be those already established by the imperial rulers; for example, when Indira Gandhi suspended civil liberties, arrested her rivals, and imposed strict censorship in India in 1975, she did so under a viceregal decree dating from the 1930s, which had been used to imprison her father, **Jawaharlal Nehru**.

In the larger and predominantly English-speaking former colonies, when all is said about the intricacies of legal censorship, including the extraordinary powers accorded to customs officers in seizing 'undesirable' books and magazines, the greatest perils to authors probably lie in the civil code which is, at times, outside legality of any kind. The libel law in Canada, for example, is much more likely to favour the plaintiff even more than in the USA, since the mere telling of truth is not automatically accepted as evidence for the defendant, and the very threat of a libel action can ruin a writer or a small publisher with legal costs, even if all is eventually settled out of court.

The rise of political correctness as a criterion, especially on the left, has introduced a new and paradoxical factor. Groups aiming at liberty for themselves try to impose restrictions on expression by others in areas they wish to control; for example, militant feminist groups seek to impose censorship on books or art or films that include women, and militant native groups seek to prevent non-aboriginals from writing about them, their traditions, or their customs. The unrestrained activity of special-interest pressure groups, whether fundamentalist Christian or Islamic on the right, or feminist and nativist on the left, can be as inhibitive to the creative artist as the actions of any customs officer tipsy with a little authority.

GEORGE WOODCOCK

CENSORSHIP (Australia)

In pre-colonial Aboriginal Australia, censorship seems hardly to have been an issue. The collective nature of decision-making within Aboriginal societies meant that the issue of individual declaration was irrelevant. There is no oral literature of protest or dissent. In *The Speaking Land: Myth and Story in Aboriginal Australia* (1989), by Ronald Berndt and Catherine Berndt, there is no index reference for such subjects. If there were 'curse poems' or incantations, these were taboo outside their specific context, which puts them outside the concept of 'censorship'.

With the arrival of white settlement in 1788 came censorship as part of its baggage. The influx of free settlers stimulated the emergence of newspapers. Economic pressures and licence control were as important in establishing censorship procedures as was any specific legislation, although the Laws of Sedition, Libel, Blasphemy, and Inciting Civil Unrest were there to be called upon — and they were.

It was not until well into the second half of the twentieth century that the right of censorship of sexual or moral issues was seriously challenged. Before the Australian legal test case over D. H. Lawrence's *Lady Chatterley's Lover* (which followed closely on the English precursor), the power of Church or 'family' groups was as influential as that of legislation or of the customs department.

The crucial local demonstration against published sexual content, though, was in the University of Sydney student magazine *Thorunka* in 1970, which, under the editorship of **Frank Moorhouse** and Wendy Bacon (among others), invited prosecution by publishing what at the time seemed provocative material. There were court cases, and Bacon was imprisoned. The end result proved, however, that existing censorship laws were out of touch with a changing society, a society in which the Vietnam War had provoked debate on wider issues of freedom and moral alignment and in which the musical *Hair* had provided an entire generation with a sense of unshackled affirmation of hedonistic exploration of the senses, 'as long as you don't hurt anyone'.

It should be borne in mind that Australia remained, until well into the mid-1980s, conspicuously dependent upon imported books rather than local publication. This meant that even through the 1960s and 1970s the influence of overseas models and exemplars remained more than formidable; they remained dominant. (See **Publishing**, Australia.) The list of prohibited customs imports includes all the recognized classics from Boccaccio to James Joyce. As Judith Brett has pointed out in 'Publishing, Censorship and Writers' Incomes', in *The Penguin New Literary History of Australia*, 1988, edited by Laurie Hergenhan, 'In 1969 the following books were banned in Australia: Gore Vidal's *Myra Breckenridge*, Stephen Vizinczey's *In Praise of Older Women*, Philip Roth's *Portnoy's Complaint*, Stephen Marcus' *The Other Victorians*, **Barry Humphries**' *The Wonderful World of Barry McKenzie* . . . ' Individual customs inspectors had startingly wide powers of seizure, though it is possibly an apocryphal story that one Western Australian public servant confiscated *The Autobiography of A. Trollope* and *Fun in Bed with Enid Blyton.*

Within Australian publishing, the laws of defamation have acted, and continue to act, as a medium of censorship. Defamation, as legally defined, is subject to separate legislation and interpretation in each Australian state, so that it is possible for a book to be banned in one state but not in another. An example is **Dorothy Hewett**'s play *The Chapel Perilous* (1972), banned in Western Australia, but widely used as a teaching text elsewhere.

New South Wales provided the most stringent defamation laws, especially in relation to deceased persons as well as the living. (There was for a long time great sensitivity in some quarters concerning convict ancestry.) Defamation proceedings as a form of censorship have worked effectively in Australia, as recently as in 1988, when Amanda Lohrey's novel *The Reading Group* (1988) was the subject of a case (in Tasmania) that was settled out of court. Perhaps the most famous example is **Frank Hardy**'s novel *Power Without Glory* (1950), the subject of a protracted libel suit. This was eventually lost. At around the same time Robert Close was taken to court for alleged obscenity in his novel *Love Me Sailor* (1945). While Hardy survived his ordeal, Close was effectively destroyed as a writer when he was found guilty of obscene libel.

In the late 1980s the Queensland state government was responsible for an extraordinary and virulent series of book bannings: a booklet on the Australian High Court, a booklet on the Red Cross that appeared to support South Africa's black population, two social studies courses developed by federal and state education departments that acknowledged alternative family structures, and the anti-racism novel *Black Like Me* (1965), by John Howard Griffin. Censorship through selective vetting of school library holdings has been commonly reported in all Australian states and still continues.

The extremes in Queensland, however, under the government of Sir Johannes Bjelke-Peterson, were the most blatant and most discriminatory. Succeeding state governments appear to have modified that position, though as yet there has not been agreement on uniform libel and defamation law reform throughout Australia. In recent years the Australian Society of Authors has taken an active position in lobbying for such reforms.

The Victorian and Western Australian Chapters of International PEN have been active in drawing attention to another form of censorship — attempted suppression of information, as in the case of Avon Lovell, Western Australian author of The *Mickelberg Stitch* (1985), which sets out to expose police corruption.

Although the libertarian movements of the late 1960s and 1970s secured a much greater freedom of expression of individual rights on the matter of censorship of sexual material, there has been in the 1990s something of a backlash — from feminist groups against perceived exploitation, from those concerned with the rise of violence and child abuse, and from fundamentalist religious sects both Christian and Islamic. The **Salman Rushdie** case, which generated threats of violence against booksellers of *The Satanic Verses* (1988), provoked much discussion and also a general affirmation of Australia as a pluralist democratic society where individual rights and freedoms must be defended. To reconcile that affirmation with the continued calling into question of particular 'excesses' or 'transgressions' will remain the challenge. This makes even more important the pressure towards uniform laws within the Australian federal structure.

The Australian Author has featured articles, letters, and editorial comment on censorship and free speech issues, most notably while Robert Pullan was editor (in the 1980s until 1990). This tradition continues, with pressure on the state attorneys general for uniform legislation on defamation and free speech issues.

THOMAS SHAPCOTT

CENSORSHIP (Canada)

Although Canadian writers and creative artists enjoy considerable freedom of expression relative to those in most other countries of the world, there remain significant restraints imposed by law and by society's values and conventions.

Film-makers must contend with classification

systems mandated by provincial governments that define, by age, who may or may not see their films, and under the terms of the Criminal Code of Canada successful prosecutions have been launched against distributors of 'obscene' videotapes. The mere threat of prosecution is sometimes equally effective, as was the case in 1992 when sexually explicit photographs by Toronto artist Ron Giii were removed from an exhibition after cautions by a police officer. Senate investigations of a 1992 television documentary on Canadian participation in the Second World War (*The Valour and the Horror*), judged by some war veterans to be unpatriotic, have caused producers of documentaries to think twice before tackling sensitive subjects. *The Boys of St. Vincent* (1992), a television docudrama on sexual and physical abuse in a Roman Catholic orphanage, was suppressed by the courts in some areas of Ontario and Quebec while trials of accused priests were taking place. Concerns about influencing juries also led courts in Newfoundland and Alberta in 1992 to impose temporary bans, respectively, on an autobiographical account of childhood sexual abuse in an orphanage (*Suffer Little Children*, 1991, by Dereck O'Brien) and on a musical comedy about an individual charged with publishing hate literature about Jews (Blake Brooker's 'Ilsa, Queen of the Nazi Love Camp', premièred 1987). It is an indictable offence under the Criminal Code to promote hatred against any identifiable group, a proscription that prompted a federal Member of Parliament to call for proceedings against **Mordecai Richler**'s long essay *Oh Canada! Oh Quebec! Requiem for a Divided Country* (1992) for promoting hatred against the francophone people of Quebec. The call went unheeded.

Canadian customs officials are legally empowered to prevent books from entering the country and have long exercised this power. In 1949 more than 500 books were on the Canada Customs' banned list, including Joyce's *Ulysses* and Lawrence's *Lady Chatterley's Lover*. The ban on *Ulysses* was lifted in 1950, but *Lady Chatterley's Lover* suffered further setbacks in 1960 when it was judged obscene by a Montreal court. The case eventually went to the Supreme Court of Canada, which concluded in 1962 that the novel was not obscene. In 1989, **Salman Rushdie**'s *The Satanic Verses* (1988) temporarily suffered a customs embargo, though the more usual target is gay literature. According to the owners of Canada's gay book stores, some seventy-five per cent of books and magazines they order from abroad are routinely held at the border for review. If in the judgement of customs officials the publications are obscene, they are either destroyed or returned to the shipper. Works of fiction — **Jane Rule**'s *The Young in One Another's Arms* (1977), for example — as well as non-fiction and run-of-the-mill pornography have been detained by customs.

School officials also exercise considerable powers of control over literature admitted into school curricula and libraries. *Giant, or Waiting for the Thursday Boat* (1989), by children's author Robert Munsch, has been banned from some primary schools for — in the words of one school board — 'depicting violence towards God'. The giant in the story — he's Irish — threatens to pound God 'until he looks like apple sauce'. The issue is further complicated by the depiction of God as a little girl. In Newfoundland, works by Ernest Hemingway, **Margaret Atwood**, Jules Verne, Isaac Asimov, and **Alice Munro** have been removed from a school anthology because some of the language ('damn', 'hell', 'for Christ's sake') was judged to be offensive to some religious groups. There is a long history in Canada of school boards' removal of literature on moral grounds from curricula and school libraries — J. D. Salinger's *Catcher in the Rye*, William Golding's *Lord of the Flies*, **Hugh MacLennan**'s *Barometer Rising*, and **Margaret Laurence**'s *The Diviners* are some prominent examples.

The lexicon of censorship has been increased in recent years by concepts such as 'political correctness' and 'libel chill'. Major Canadian publishers declined to publish a book by journalist Wendy Smith, on the 1987 collapse of an Alberta financial company, for fear of libel suits by the company's founder, while the debate about the 'political correctness' of 'voice appropriation' (i.e., an author writing about a culture, a people, a race different from his or her own) has led at least one Canadian publisher (Women's Press) to adopt a policy against 'publishing manuscripts in which the protagonist's experience in the world, by virtue of race or ethnicity, is substantially removed from that of the writer'.

Under the Criminal Code, any publication of which 'a dominant characteristic' is 'the undue exploitation of sex, or of sex and any one or more of the following subjects, namely, crime, horror, cruelty and violence, shall be deemed to be obscene'. In addition, it is an offence, punishable by imprisonment of up to two years, to be the lessee, manager, agent, or person in charge of a theatre that presents or allows to be presented therein 'an immoral, indecent or obscene performance, entertainment or representation'. Although no Canadian playwrights have been convicted under the Criminal Code, there is a long history in Canada of government control of theatre, stretching from the suppression by church authorities of Molière's *Tartuffe* in 1694 in Quebec City to the banning of 'Ilsa, Queen of the Nazi Love Camp'.

In the nineteenth and early twentieth centuries, the Methodist Church in English Canada took a leading role against the theatre; the 1898 edition of *The Doctrine and the Discipline of the Methodist Church of Canada* forbade attending plays, and prominent Methodists such as John Coburn successfully agitated for the suppression on moral grounds (i.e., sympathetic portrayal of an unmarried mother) of American playwright Legrand Howland's *Deborah* in Toronto in 1913. In the following year a production of Bernard Shaw's *The Shewing-up of Blanco Posnet* was banned by Toronto censor William Banks, owing to 'irreverent references and remarks regarding the Deity'.

One of the most celebrated cases of theatrical censorship in Canada occurred in Toronto in 1933 when a play called *Eight Men Speak*, collectively written by Oscar Ryan, Frank Love, Edward Cecil-Smith, and Mildred Goldberg and produced by the Workers' Experimental Theatre of Toronto, attracted the attention of Toronto 'Red Squad' officers. *Eight Men Speak* (published in *Eight Men Speak and other Plays from the Canadian Workers' Theatre*, 1976, edited by Richard Wright and Robin Endres) is a protest against the imprisonment of eight members of the Communist Party of Canada and against the alleged attempted murder in prison of Party leader Tim Buck. The play was performed once in 1933, but all subsequent performances were suppressed. (The play was not seen again in its entirety until a 1982 production in Halifax, Nova Scotia.)

Canadian police authorities have always shown a special interest in theatre. In 1953 police arrested five actors on the stage of Vancouver's Everyman Theatre during a performance of Frank Kirkland's sexually frank *Tobacco Road* (1934, adapted from Erskine Caldwell's 1940 novel of the same title), and it was sexual explicitness that again attracted Vancouver police to Michael McClure's *The Beard* (1967) in 1969. The play was closed by the morality squad, as was (temporarily) Theatre Passe Muraille's collective production of *I Love You, Baby Blue* (1977) — a spoof on 'blue' movies — in Toronto in 1975.

L. W. CONOLLY

Further reading: Peter Birdsall and Delores Broten, *Mind War: Book Censorship in English Canada* (1978).

CENSORSHIP (St Helena)

A recurring issue in St Helena since the arrival of

printing in 1806, censorship put Saul Solomon's press under government control in 1808, prompted the importation of a 'free press' in 1851, and instigated testy accusations of scurrility by government or of suppressing free speech by victims. Since the 1960s censorship has provoked some protest publications, including *The Voice of the Union* (1961–2) and St Helena Association *Newsletters*, both occasional typescript foolscaps of caustic comment by St Helenian Fred Ward; and *St. Helena News and Comment* (1971–2), edited and printed monthly by W. C. Beauchamp, an expatriate resident, and 'given free to the people of St Helena so that they can know more about the things that are happening on the Island'.

In April 1990 another frustrated settler, Julian Cairns-Wicks, began issuing a desk-top eight-page fortnightly, *The New Wirebird*, to give Islanders a voice. But few seem to want a public voice. Dependent on government employment, most see free speech as risky. Journalists are more resented than censorship; therefore, elected councillors do not make censorship or poor information a political issue, and free news-sheets have brief lives. But the ship RMS *St. Helena* now brings from London, England, an independent *St. Helena News Review*, a two-monthly sixteen-page colour magazine launched in November 1989 by Allan Bannister, a journalist married to a St Helenian, which provides an attractive illustrated paper linking Islanders at home and overseas. To this extent St Helena now has a professionally produced periodical free of government control.

TREVOR W. HEARL

CENSORSHIP (Singapore)

Censorship is strict in Singapore and is exercised in a variety of ways. All pornographic publications are automatically banned — there is no *Penthouse* or *Playboy* available — and a vigilant watch is kept on all possible avenues for the distribution of pornographic materials. For writers, there are other less obvious forms of censorship: because Singaporean society is a fragile mix of different races, religions, and languages, the authorities view seriously any attempt to undermine the *status quo* by reference to matters of race, language, or religion.

Political censorship in the more obvious sense — as in blocking all that is not considered ideologically correct — is on the decline, as is the censorship of plays, movies, and imported books. No book in Singapore is censored prior to publication, though books have been withdrawn or detained after publication. A recent instance was the withdrawal of a book called *Harlots*, which had sold more than 7,000 copies before it was withdrawn. The issue here was sexual exploitation without the necessary redeeming virtue of literary excellence, and the author apologized publicly for his book.

The crucial Censorship Review Committee, set up in 1991 to review all censorship policies, issued its report — which the government accepted — in 1993. Its main point is that censorship should be relaxed in order to allow for the development of a more mature and sophisticated society, but one in which obvious crudity and violence will have no place. Several different committees and panels, made up of vastly different individuals from all walks of life and from the different ethnic/religious/language groups, ensure that a balanced sense of values prevails. On the whole it is rare in Singapore for a book to be censored, though censorship of magazines, videotapes, laser-discs, and films is quite stringent. The situation is now markedly different from a few years ago, when censorship was rife.

KIRPAL SINGH

CENSORSHIP (South Africa)

Justice C. J. Rumpff, summing up a 1965 South African censorship case (the Publications Control Board versus William Heinemann *et al.*), attributed the determination of the powerful to exact obedience to their ideologies to 'a primitive urge to prohibit that with which one does not agree'. This urge is most noticeable where rulers protect and promote obedience at the expense of the common good. It has regulated South African politics and publications since 1948, when the National Party came into power, although the Party's most significant publications control act was not passed until 1963, when Act Number 26 became a pillar of National Party authority. The chair, vice-chair, and three permanent members of the Publications Control Board (PCB) shared the Afrikaans language, Calvinist religion, and National Party affiliation. Of the seven part-time members, four were Afrikaans and three English-speaking. Voting, however, was not always on party lines, the part-time (mainly academic) members maintaining a strong independence. None the less, the permanent members could and did overrule any decision by a team of three scrutinizing a book.

Sections five and six of the Act defined the areas of undesirability in six categories: sexual ('indecent or obscene or . . . offensive, or harmful to public morals'); religious ('blasphemous or . . . offensive to the religious convictions of any section of the inhabitants of the Republic'); contempt for any individual or group ('brings any section of the inhabitants . . . into ridicule or contempt'); group harmony ('harmful to the relations between any sections'); public safety ('prejudicial to the safety of the state, the general welfare or the peace and good order'); and judicial ('libel, contempt of court, etc.'). The terms, especially of the first two categories, are vague if not indefinable. Seen in the light of 'apartheid' policy, anomaly is added to obscurity; for example, nudity of white women is 'indecent', but nudity of the indigenous population is acceptable as it is 'their custom'. Black Africans, seemingly, are no threat to public morals as they are unenfranchized, and so unrecognized as members of the 'public'. Only those sensibilities regarded by the PCB as Christian need protection from blasphemy — Hindu, Muslim, and others being excluded from this Christian society. Because of the lack of definition of such terms as 'indecent', 'obscene', 'offensive', or 'harmful', it was easy (and became easier with subsequent amendments) for the restrictions to be administered. Furthermore, because the PCB operated in secrecy, no public debate of any decision was possible. Use of the clause regarding contempt for individuals or groups was largely for self-protection of the hegemony; satire was put on trial.

In 1974 the law was amended (Act 42). The categories of undesirability remained unchanged. However, where it had previously been possible to appeal against a decision in the Supreme Court, now an administrative Publications Appeal Board (PAB) was established to hear appeals. The PAB's decision was final. Only where clear malicious intent was identified could the courts be asked to intervene, and then only to require that the matter be referred back to the PAB for reconsideration. Intentionality being almost impossible to establish, this proviso has never been used. In his *Censorship in South Africa* (1987), J. C. W. van Rooyen, former chair of the PAB, states that this amendment was 'more effective in administering the law — less slow'.

The courts, van Rooyen reports, had indicated that the matters referred to the PCB 'were foreign to the judicial process, that they could bring the courts into controversy, and they also indicated they [the courts] would rather not perform this function'. Instead of interpreting this as a clear signal that the law itself was undesirable, the government took it as an invitation to bypass the courts altogether. Yvonne Burns states in her *Media Law* (1990) that this amendment 'drastically affected individual freedom of speech, as well as media freedom in general'.

Censorship between 1963 and 1990, after which many acts were repealed to allow for a 'normalization' of political activity, was not provided for solely in the publications control acts, but in countless others, allowing the government and its state officials to act in secret, protected from criticism. Such acts as the Suppression of Communism Act (1950, later termed the Internal Security Act, and frequently amended), the Radio Act (1952), the Police Act (1958), the Prisons Act (1959), the Public Safety Act (1963), the Broadcasting Act (1967), the Indecent or Obscene Photographic Act (1967), the Armaments Development and Production Act (1968), the National Supplies Procurement Act (1970), the Newspaper Registration Act (1971), the Petroleum Products Act (1977), the Demonstrations in or near Court Buildings Prohibition Act (1982), and the Protection of Information Act (1982) indicate how far parliament was used to give dictatorial powers to a ruling minority that perceived itself to be under siege.

The September 1992 list of books banned in South Africa contained some 36,000 entries; the list of unbanned books in December of that year totalled roughly one tenth of that amount. Thus, while a more liberal system seems to prevail, the effects of forty years of authoritarian protection remain. Literature, seemingly less urgent than political writing, suffers noticeably.

Cleland's *Fanny Hill*, Nabokov's *Ada*, and Lawrence's *Lady Chatterley's Lover* have been unbanned recently, but works by Anthony Burgess, Brigid Brophy, **Mordecai Richler**, Norman Mailer, the Marquis de Sade, J. P. Donleavy, Robert Penn Warren, Jack Kerouac, D. M. Thomas, John Fowles, Françoise Sagan, Guy de Maupassant, Karl Shapiro, and Herman Wouk, to name but a few of the better-known names, remain prohibited, as does Calder Willingham's *Rambling Rose* (1974), despite the release of its film adaptation. Works by South African writers of the calibre of **Nadine Gordimer** and **Es'kia Mphahlele** are off the banned list, but those of such overseas civil rights authors as James Baldwin, Onyeama, and Stokely Carmichael remain banned.

The recent unbanning of the standard works on Communism by Marx, Engels, Trotsky, Lenin, and Mao Tse-tung and of such pioneering works on sexology as Peter Tarnesby's *Abortion*, Havelock Ellis' *Female Auto-erotic Practices*, David Reuben's *Any Woman Can*, *The Kinsey Report*, works by Masters and Johnson, and treatises on homosexuality, lesbianism, and various sexual pathologies has not instantly cured the ills of a deprived society, since generations of young people have had to rely on secondary sources, with their inevitable biases, for their basic education, unless they have the rare advantage of overseas study.

J. M. LEIGHTON

Further reading: L. H. Hugo, *Authority, Literature and Freedom* (1970).

CENSORSHIP (South Pacific)

The South Pacific was the last major region to be decolonized. Most of the island nations in the area have been self-governing for less than twenty years. Since independence, domestic unrest has been fuelled by dissatisfaction with low living standards, caused, at least in part, by isolation. The population of these islands is very small, and each island group is dispersed over a wide area with great cultural and linguistic differences among the islands. As with Australia, in pre-colonial days censorship was not an issue since literacy arrived with the colonizers.

Censorship has been an issue in Fiji, however, since the military coups of 1987. Following these coups, the authorities closed two daily newspapers and charged a New Zealand reporter who tried to interview a member of the former government. The publishers of the *Fiji Sun* and the *Pacific Island News* were arrested and held for four days. The military government then suspended the right to freedom of expression and the right to freedom of assembly and association. In November 1988, the Internal Security Decree, which had given the police the power to arrest, search, and detain suspects, was suspended. More than 100 people were detained without charges. **Subramani** and **Raymond Pillai**, two well-known Indo-Fijian writers, have been in exile since the coup (Subramani in Australia and Pillai in New Zealand).

In Western Samoa, the editor of the *Samoa Times* was arrested on 29 January 1990, after he published an article alleging corruption in the judiciary. Legislation has been introduced that would compel journalists to reveal their sources in the event of a defamation case.

In Tonga, a suit brought against a pro-democracy member of Parliament and newspaper publisher Akilisi Pohiva for publishing confidential government materials was dismissed in October 1993. In Papua New Guinea, two journalists from the Australian Broadcasting Corporation who interviewed an Irian Jaya rebel leader were banned from working in the country in May 1984. And late in 1993, Papua New Guinea's censor banned a local rock group's video from being shown on television, believing that it would encourage people to tease crocodiles! (It showed musicians from Banditz trying to kiss a crocodile.)

Censorship in the South Pacific will undoubtedly become more prevalent as literacy rates move towards western standards and as South Pacific readers are exposed to imported materials that breach South Pacific standards related to freedom of expression.

ROBERTA JACKSON

CENSORSHIP (West Africa)

The earliest form of censorship in West Africa was the linguistic taboo of the pre-colonial period that forbade the use of certain expressions about royalty, who at that time were believed to possess divine attributes. In colonial times, sedition laws were enacted, but were rarely invoked, and nationalism was able to flourish and grow into independence. Today, independent West African states, except The Gambia, practise various forms of censorship whether they are ruled by military juntas, are one-party states, or multi-party democracies.

Interestingly, books, especially literary works, rarely come under government censorship. Exceptions include Kwame Nkrumah's books, which were not allowed into Ghana for a long time after his overthrow as president. Writers of books are generally free from the official harassment suffered by newspaper, magazine, and electronic journalists because, in a subregion with a poor book-reading culture, books are not considered a threat by governments. (A Nigerian exception, however, is Arthur Nwankwo, who was prosecuted for sedition in 1983 for his *How Jim Nwobodo Rules Anambra State*, 1982.) Nevertheless, literary supplements are adversely affected when newspapers and magazines are proscribed.

Official harassment and intimidation are directed mostly at journalists because their criticism is considered by governments to be more damaging because of their media's wider circulation, especially the electronic media, which have considerable impact in a subregion with a high rate of illiteracy. This was especially the case in Nigeria following media criticism of the federal government's annulment of the presidential election in June 1993. Electronic media establishments are usually government-owned and controlled.

Many journalists have been detained without trial and sometimes physically assaulted. Notable detainees include Sierra Leonian Paul Kamara, Ghanaian John Kugblenu, who died a month after his release in 1984, and Nigeria's Minere Amakiri, whose head was shaved and who was flogged in 1973 because of his injudicious timing — on the governor's birthday — of an article criticizing the governor.

Some journalists have been murdered, including Charles Gbenyon, editor-in-chief of Liberian Television, who was bayoneted to death in President Samuel Doe's executive mansion in 1984, and Nigerian Dele Giwa, founding editor-in-chief of *Newswatch*, who was killed by a parcel bomb in

1986. Deportation of foreign journalists, such as the 1991 ousting of British journalist William Keeling by the Nigerian government, is a regular occurrence in West Africa.

More systematic action to suppress the press takes the form of media-regulating laws, such as Ghana's licensing laws of 1963, 1973, and 1989; Nigeria's Official Secrets Act (1962) and Decree Number 4 of 1984; and Liberia's Decree 88A of 1984. Ghana's licensing law of 1989, for example, states that no newspaper may be published without a licence from the secretary of the government; further, the secretary may revoke or suspend licences if licensing conditions are not met, or 'for any other reason . . . as he deems fit'. Liberia's Decree 88A is more openly restrictive, stating that any person who 'accuses any authority or individual of a crime, by word-of-mouth, writing, or public broadcast, may be arrested and detained, without bail, by the security force'. Under these laws, the offices of the various media have been closed down or denied operating licences, newspapers and magazines have been proscribed, and journalists imprisoned.

Decree Number 4, promulgated in Nigeria during the Buhari regime, was abrogated soon after General Ibrahim Babangida came to power in August 1985. Immediately, repression of the press was resumed under Decree 2, which allows for the detention of perons who are considered security risks. The Nigerian press' criticism of the annulment of the June 1993 presidential election gave rise to new press laws and to the proscription of several media outlets.

Attempts at direct censorship of copy have failed. In 1978 Nigeria's Bendel State set up a panel to censor all news and features 'inimical to government interest' in the media which it controlled. The times of day given for submitting copy, however, were unrealistic and the panel lasted only three days. A similar regulation by Ogun State, Nigeria, was again short-lived; so also were the federal government of Nigeria's censorship directives to the *Daily Times*, in which it owned the majority shares.

MABEL SEGUN

Further reading: Arthur Nwankwo, *Justice: Sedition, Change, Conviction and Acquittal of Arthur Nwankwo, Enugu* (1982); Adewale Jama-pearse, 'The press in West Africa: The Gambia, Liberia, Sierra Leone, Ghana', *Index on Censorship* 6 (1990).

CHANDLER, A. BERTRAM (1912–84)
Australian novelist, short-story writer
Born and educated in England, he became Australia's best known and most prolific science fiction writer, though he did not settle in Australia until 1956. A merchant mariner, he was apprenticed in London, England, in 1928 and was a ship's master upon retirement in 1975. He won the Australian Ditmar Award in 1969, 1971, 1974, and 1976, the Japanese Seiun Sho Award and the USA Invisible Little Man Award in 1975, and held a **Literature Board** fellowship in 1980.

Though Chandler wrote for an international audience and set most of his stories in outer space, some of his best works are those with an Australian locus. *The Bitter Pill* (1914) envisages an Australian society that enforces euthanasia at age forty-five, the alternative being passage to Mars as convict labour. When the Martian convicts rebel and take their freedom, they declare Mars the sovereign state of Botany Bay. (See **Science Fiction and Fantasy**, Australia.)

Pursuing this interest in permutations of history, *Kelly Country* (1983) traces the history Australia might have had if **Ned Kelly** had won the siege at Glenrowan. In the Chandler scenario Kelly founds a republican dynasty, becomes ever more despotic, and is ultimately responsible for dropping an Australian nuclear bomb on Hanoi in the closing stages of the Vietnam War, an act of aggression that prompts the atomic-bombing of Glenrowan.

Despite their controversial subject matter, these Chandler novels seem curiously lacking in moral passion when compared with the work of, say, Ursula K. Le Guin or Jack Womack. Chandler's main interest is action and dovetailed plotting and his philosophical stance is surprisingly fatalistic. The best-known Chandler works are those stories and novels involving the series character John Grimes, an ensign (later promoted to commodore) in the merchant navy of the outer galactic rim worlds. A decent and well-intentioned (but rather flat) character, Grimes is enlivened by his sense of humour and by his (moderately) libertarian attitudes to sex and nudity. Chandler frankly admitted that his SF stories are 'essentially sea stories' based upon the monosexual society of merchant ships and that Commodore John Grimes is descended from C. S. Forester's Horatio Hornblower.

VAN IKIN

CHATTERJEE, UPAMANYU (1959–)
Indian novelist
Born in Patna, in the state of Bihar, India, he became an officer in India's premier bureaucratic service, the Indian Administrative Service (IAS). He is one of a trio (the other members being **Amitav Ghosh** and **Bharati Mukherjee**) sounding on a high note the recent return of Bengalis to writing English fiction. Chatterjee's critically acclaimed first novel, *English, August* (1988), reads like a satire on the bureaucracy the author serves. It is, however, a story of renunciation and self-knowledge, that of the eponymous hero Agastya Sen (his name anglicized to August), who smokes marijuana, thinks 'dirty', and reads the *Bhagavadgita* and Marcus Aurelius in the secrecy of his mess room. On the eve of his departure for Madna in southern India, where he is posted as an IAS trainee, Sen is warned by his insightful Yale-returned friend Dhrubo that he is not the type to succeed as a bureaucrat. In hot and dirty Madna, Sen 'felt as though he was living someone else's life'. In *English, August* Chatterjee employs the familiar literary motif of a journey to the other world; the main character's name is also a play on that of the mythical Indian sage who crossed the Vindhyas never to return.

But even that myth is ironic in the context of *English, August*. Sen is lionized by his senior and junior colleagues alike — he is, in addition, the son of a governor, the ultimate reach of an IAS employee — and, after struggling with a double life, outwardly quiet and inwardly cynical (he makes his colleagues look like fools), he leaves Madna, apparently on home leave, but in reality never to return again. He makes, thereby, an *Agasta Yatra* (a journey from which one does not return on purpose). Sen resigns, despite a promotion to assistant collector of a district. The motivation for Sen's resignation is left ambiguous — is it because of boredom, a Hamlet-like *ennui*, or contempt for bureaucracy? Chatterjee does not sermonize, but utilizes a comic irony that cannot be missed; as Sen quits, believing that he would be happy with a job like Dhrubo's — an executive position in a Delhi-based private company — Dhrubo prepares to take the IAS examination.

KALYAN K. CHATTERJEE

CHATTOPADHYAYA, HARINDRANATH (1898–1990)
Indian poet, dramatist
Born in Hyderabad, India, to a Brahmo Bengali family, and younger brother to the poet-politician **Sarojini Naidu**, he grew up immersed in English poetry and culture in the heyday of the Indian renaissance. Both brother and sister wrote sentimental verse that followed Victorian notions of 'the poetical', as may be seen in Chattopadhyaya's 1939 poem 'Cloudland': 'Gold-breasted lightning mates dark-bosomed thunder/ Cloud trumpets flare, and foaming spaces neigh/ In the divine procession.' Their poetry was already frozen into

forms relatively untouched by the modern sensibility by then present in Indian poetry in English.

Chattopadhyaya's first published volume of poetry, *The Feast of Youth* (1918), was followed by numerous other volumes of verse and drama. During his long career, he tried many voices — romantic, Theosophical, Tagorean, even propagandistic, as in his play *Sidharta*: *The Man of Peace* (1956), which eulogizes India's political leaders. In such early collections of poetry as *The Coloured Garden* (1919), *The Magic Tree* (1922), and *Out of the Deep Dark Mould* (1924), he speaks from a world of dreamy languor about the moon, music, and the stars. His poems are characterized by rhyming verse and conventional diction. Tagore-like, Chattopadhyaya tried to create a poetic picture of life and to go on to live it, but **Rabindranath Tagore** wrote in his native tongue, while Chattopadhyaya floundered on a sea of imitation. Unable to find his own voice, he copied those of his contemporaries — AE (George Russell), Laurence Binyon, **Sri Aurobindo**, Alice Meynell, Harold Child, and James Cousins.

In *Edgeways and the Saint* (1946), a new zest and straightforwardness is occasionally perceptible: 'I, poet, dip my pen / In mine own blood to write my songs for men / Since every song is but a keen self-giving.' But it was only rhetoric: he did not follow up. It should be remembered, however, that few among his contemporaries worked out an Indian-English idiom such as that associated with younger Indian poets writing in English.

By the time Chattopadhyaya published *What I Saw*: *A Collection of Nonsense Rhymes* (1971), his published collections of verse and verse plays numbered well beyond a score, but the old habit remained with him: an incurable passion for rhyming verse and decorative imagery that characterizes such volumes as *Masts and Farewells* (1961), *Virgins and Vagabonds* (1967), and *Roses of Eternal Life* (1978). He wrote without any sense of an audience, a fact that was also responsible for the failure of his plays: *Abu Hasan* (1918), *Tukaram* (1927), and *Sidharta* (1956). Chattopadhyaya was for a long time a member of the Indian parliament, to which he was wont to play the role of court poet. He took part in many cultural missions of the Indian government. Late in his life he acted in Satyajit Ray's films for children.

KALYAN K. CHATTERJEE

Further reading: G. S. Balarma Gupta, 'The plays of Harindranath Chattopadhyaya', in M. K. Naik and S. Mokashi-Punekar (eds) *Perspectives on Indian Drama in English* (1977); K. Venkata Reddy, 'An atheist turned mystic', *Triveni* April/June (1982).

CHAUDHURI, NIRAD C. (1897–)

Indian autobiographer, historian

Born in Kishorganj, east Bengal, India, to a lawyer father and a religious but enlightened mother, he was raised in a home in which religious and political ideas were moulded by European liberal thought and humanism. Chaudhuri came under the twin influences of the Indian Renaissance and the Indian Nationalist movement, but it was the conservative revival of Hinduism, spearheaded by Bankim Chandra Chatterjee, that appealed to him much more than Raja **Rammohun Roy**'s Brahmo Samaj movement, with its pseudo-scientifism. Chaudhuri owed his intellectual development to western education and European thought, which, far from destroying or disrupting Indian culture, brought about its revival and resuscitation. Like most other distinguished writers of the Indian Renaissance, such as Roy, **Sri Aurobindo**, and **Rabindranath Tagore**, Chaudhuri used the English language to help him discover and define himself, both as an Indian and in terms of the history and culture of his country. He is perhaps one of the few Indian exponents of English prose who do not come under the class of orators and political leaders and who have used the language for non-fictional purposes alone.

Chaudhuri rose to fame with his first publication, *The Autobiography of an Unknown Indian* (1951); his second book, *A Passage to England* (1959), was the outcome of his 'short visit of five weeks to England' at the age of fifty-seven. His most controversial book, *The Continent of Circe*: *An Essay on the Peoples of India*, appeared in 1966, and was followed by *The Intellectual in India* (1967) and *To Live or Not to Live* (1970), in addition to a few provocative articles published in *The Times of India* and *London Magazine*.

The Autobiography, in Chaudhuri's words, is 'more of a national than personal history'; Chaudhuri's stated intention was to make it a 'contribution to contemporary history'. Dedicated to 'the memory of the British Empire in India', the book seeks to 'tell the story of the struggle of a civilization with a hostile environment in which the destiny of the British rule in India became necessarily involved'. *The Autobiography*, addressed to the English-speaking world, carries certain attitudes and intentions that prevent it from being as objective in its survey of Indian history as are the autobiographies of **M. K. Gandhi** and **Jawaharlal Nehru**. The principal merit of the book, however, lies in its balance of theories, judgements, and observations.

A Passage to England is a travelogue like **V. S. Naipaul**'s *An Area of Darkness* (1964), and its title is inspired by E. M. Forster's *A Passage to India* (1924) or perhaps by Malabari Behramji's *The Indian Eye on English Life* (1893). *A Passage to England* attempts to grasp the reality of 'Timeless England' set against that of 'Timeless India' and to present a perception of England as something *not* India. Visiting England with many preconceptions, Chaudhuri is indeed surprised by the differences between his earlier perceptions and the country's realities, but he maintains that the 'historical personality' of the people and 'the permanent form and spirit of society' have remained unchanged. Both India and England have their permanent faces; the former's is 'stark, chastened and sad', the latter's is 'smiling'. Chaudhuri's book seems to draw attention to these two contrasting faces. However, many of the book's views and impressions are somewhat prejudiced, especially those on the unattractiveness of English women and on the differences between western and Indian concepts of beauty, and between Hinduism and Christianity. Most of his views have an unmistakable slant in favour of the west and its religion and culture. *A Passage to England* strikes one as an unreliable commentary on England and India by a confirmed Anglophile who has alienated himself from his country.

In *The Continent of Circe*, which he calls 'a trial in exposition', Chaudhuri develops the controversial thesis that Hindus are actually a race alien to India and are arrivals from Europe. In his view they are the victims of Circe, fair European-Aryans turned brown, who, with the same pride and sense of racial superiority, suffered a similar plight to that of westerners in India. While rationalizing and giving a historical colouring to all his prejudices against his own people, Chaudhuri tries to invoke a new theory of knowledge, 'a full-fledged epistemology', in his attempt to understand India and its people. He comes to perceive India according to the categories of the western intellectual tradition and he rejects most of the books on Indian history as prejudiced and unreliable, written mostly by westerners and Anglicized Indians out of touch with the life of the people. He condemns the Aryan Hindu as a victim of Circe with the principal attributes of 'insanity' and 'inertia'. *The Continent of Circe* reveals Chaudhuri's pathological detestation of everything Indian. His views and theories do not make for a disinterested assessment of the Hindu character nor is the sympathy he shows for Muslims and Christians as suffering minorities well founded.

Chaudhuri's later books, such as *The Intellectual in India* and *To Live or Not to Live*, principally intended for Indian readers, are more objective in their analyses of the Indian mind and character.

The mood of Chaudhuri's books on India is similar to that of Naipaul's books on India — anger and disgust being the principal determinants of that mood. Naipaul's diatribe against India in *An Area of Darkness* arose from his disappointment and disillusionment with the land of his ancestors, which he visited as an outsider, while Chaudhuri, an insider, takes an anti-Indian stance although he is a historian and scholar who knows his country and its people intimately. Nevertheless, his books have value in exemplifying the success with which an Indian intellectual handled English as a medium of creative expression capable of accommodating Indian thought and sensibility and for creating a very individual Indian-English idiom.

K. S. RAMAMURTI

Further reading: C. Paul Verghese, *Nirad C. Chaudhuri* (1973); D. S. Philip, *Perceiving India through the Works of Nirad C. Chaudhuri, R. K. Narayan and Ved Mehta* (1986).

CHEN, WILLI (1934–)

Trinidadian short-story writer, dramatist

Born in Couva, Trinidad, to Iris and John Chen, Chinese immigrants from the Guandang Province, China, he was educated at St Mary's College, Port of Spain. Chen was a successful businessman before he pursued his interest in writing in the 1980s. His stories have appeared in the *Trinidad Guardian, The Trinidad and Tobago Review, The Nantucket Review, Callaloo*, and in his *King of the Carnival and Other Stories* (1988) — the first collection of stories published by a Caribbean writer of Chinese extraction, as Kenneth Ramchand notes in a foreword to the volume.

Chen's stories, almost all of which are set in Trinidad, depend for their effect on faithfully re-created settings and situations and on externally (rather than internally or psychologically) observed characters. He engages readers with stark depictions of primary passions and elemental emotions. Unabashedly traditional, he indulges in no formal experimentation or novelty, though he is capable of subtle variations of style and technique, as shown in his effortless shifts from pared prose to lyrical cadence.

Chen emphasizes the multiracial nature of Trinidad, evoking the meetings of cultures, often sadly, occasionally comically. Many of his stories are about the rural East Indian community of the 1940s and the 1950s; and in focussing on relationships that lead to brutal, violent deaths, they provide a perspective on Trinidadian rural life not found in such other recorders of the East Indian experience as **Ismith Khan**, **Harold Ladoo**, **V. S. Naipaul**, and **Samuel Selvon**. What surprises in Chen's stories is the absence of extended portrayals of major Chinese characters. There is the occasional Chinese shopkeeper, but no exploration of the Chinese community or of its experiences in a new land, as **Timothy Mo** offers in his *Sour Sweet* (1982).

Chen has dramatized some of his stories for the Trinidadian theatre. His plays include 'Freedom Road' (premièred 1985), 'Tainted Blood' (premièred 1987), 'One Love' (premièred 1989), 'Joke is Joke' (premièred 1993), and 'Stickman' (premièred 1993). Also a painter and sculptor, Chen has had his works exhibited in Trinidad. Active in the cultural life of Trinidad, he was awarded the National Humming Bird Medal for Art and Culture in 1989.

VICTOR J. RAMRAJ

Further reading: Victor J. Ramraj, Review of *King of the Carnival and Other Stories, Third World Quarterly* 1 (1990).

CHENEY-COKER, SYL (1945–)

Sierra Leonean poet, novelist

He was born Syl Cheney Coker in Freetown, Sierra Leone. He had his primary and secondary schooling in Freetown and then attended various universities in the USA — the University of Oregon (1967–70), the University of California, Los Angeles (1970), and the University of Wisconsin, Madison (1971–2). He legally changed his surname to Cheney-Coker in 1970. He has worked as a journalist, a broadcaster, a free-lance writer, a drummer, a dock worker, and factory hand and he has been a visiting professor of English in the Philippines and in Nigeria.

Cheney-Coker's published volumes of poetry include *Concerto for an Exile*: *Poems* (1973), *The Graveyard Also Has Teeth* (1974; rev. 1979), and *The Blood in the Desert's Eye* (1990). These reflect his left-wing political views and his assertion that his poetry 'comes from the wellspring of a country, a world continually brutalized, and from the depths of my own suffering I am trying to reach that man, brother of grief, and his mother, who chews a thousand pieces of cocaine to fill her stomach's void.'

Cheney-Coker's first novel, *The Last Harmattan of Alusine Dunbar* (1990), won the 1991 Commonwealth Writers Prize (Africa region). In reviewing the novel, **Peter Nazareth** stated,

> There has not, in my reading, been a novel quite like this before in African literature . . . *The Last Harmattan of Alusine Dunbar* deals with the African, the English, the Americans, the Canadians, the American Indians, the returning Africans, syncretism, the role of the artist.

G. D. KILLAM

Further reading: Peter Nazareth, 'Something new is happening in African literature', *The Toronto South Asian Review* 2 (1991).

CHEONG, COLIN (1965–)

Singaporean novelist

He was born in Singapore and educated at the National University of Singapore, where he earned a BA (1988) in English and language. He worked as a writer and sub-editor with *The Straits Times* newspaper and shot to fame with his first novel, *The Stolen Child* (1989), a powerful and moving work that won a Book Development Council of Singapore award.

The Stolen Child traces the growth of Wings, the protagonist, from childhood to adulthood and charts his quest for meaning in a hard and pragmatic world. *Poets, Priests and Prostitutes* (1990) depicts the journey of Puck into the shadowy underworld of motorcycle cults, where he falls into deluded love. As in *The Stolen Child*, the characters expound a disenchantment with life, a cosmopolitan dilemma representative of twentieth-century writing.

Cheong's writing displays a succinct clarity and exudes a poignancy unique to Singapore. He utilizes local linguistic idiosyncrasies and 'Singlish' (Singapore slang) in his creation of character and place. His prose is semi-autobiographical — his art, photography, and Christian religion mould the essential form of his works. Through motifs such as the airplane and the motorcycle — icons of the lone individual's dream to fly and to be free — Cheong draws on the tradition of the introspective hero coping with the trials and tribulations of a mundane existence.

JOASH MOO

CHETTUR, G. K. (1898–1936)

Indian poet, memoirist, short-story writer

The older brother of **S. K. Chettur**, he published five slender volumes of verse, a collection of stories, and a book of memoirs in addition to editing a massive anthology, *Altars of Silence* (1935), containing more than three hundred prose passages intended for constant reading and meditation.

Heavily weighed down with such words as 'sorrow', 'shadow', 'moon', 'mountain', 'love', 'passion', 'death', and 'despair', and with phrases such as 'whispering winds', 'trembling stars', and 'pearl-lit caves', the poems in Chettur's *Sounds and Images* (1921) are so deeply dream-drenched that they appear as pale imitations of British Romantic poetry and establish Chettur as an adolescent poet lost in reverie and contemplation of nature. They fail to startle the reader who may be impressed by the poet's technical competence. In *The Temple Tank* (1932), Chettur is still in the grip of his passion for rhyme. Though he achieves some pleasing conversational ease and haunting melody, most of these poems seem to be concoctions and fabrications rather than imaginative creations. In *Gumataraya* (1932), however, cloying thematic monotony yields to variety. *The Shadow of God: A Sonnet Sequence* (1935) remains Chettur's best-wrought poetry; cast in an elegiac mould, the verse, less laboured and more impassioned, runs smoothly. Most of these sonnets reveal the poet's obsession with death and his attempt to face it squarely.

One of the characters in 'Pacheco's Story', in the short-story collection *The Ghost City* (1932), says: 'I am afraid that I do not get along fast enough with my story.' This is true of most of Chettur's stories. Another major defect of *Ghost Stories*, which deals mostly with supernatural themes, is its ponderous and pompous language.

Chettur deserves to be best remembered as the writer of one of the most pleasing memoirs in Indian English literature, *The Last Enchantment* (1934). It narrates Chettur's experiences during his three-year stay at Oxford University, England, with authors such as W. B. Yeats, John Masefield, Arthur Symons, **Rabindranath Tagore**, and **Sarojini Naidu** and his association with the Oxford Majlis ('parliament') and the Oxford Union Society.

G. S. BALARAMA GUPTA

CHETTUR, S. K. (1905–72)

Indian poet, short-story writer, memoirist

The younger brother of **G. K. Chettur** and an Oxford-educated Indian Civil Service officer who retired as secretary to the government of Madras, he was a passionate lover of hockey, tennis, and swimming who cultivated literature as an avocation. He wrote one volume of poetry, *The Golden Stair* (1967); four collections of stories — *Muffled Drums* (1927), *The Cobras of Dharmashevi* (1937), *The Spell of Aphrodite* (1957), and *Mango Seed* (1974); a murder-mystery novel, *Bombay Murder* (1940); and three books of memoirs.

Chettur started writing verse in his early teens, though he did not achieve much in this sphere, quantitatively or qualitatively. However, some of his poems — such as 'Cigarette', 'Koni: The Auspicious Vision', 'Loneliness', and 'The Coldest Thing' — show that he could write good poems the moment he stopped hunting for pairs of rhyming words. He was more prolific as a short-story writer. Spoiled by wearisome beginnings or inept endings, frequent authorial intrusions or inane asides, and ostentatious language, most of his stories fail because they lack restraint and economy, suspense and suggestion. He wrote humorous stories like those of **R. K. Narayan** — 'The Gift of Peacock', 'The Alarm Clock', 'Love in a Sack', 'Her Finest Hour', and 'Shulai Takes the Plunge', all in *Mango Seed*, are among his best — but less writing and more revision would have improved his work.

Curiously, Chettur furnished examples both of how to and how not to write memoirs. Whereas *The Steel Frame and I* (1962) and *The Crystal Years* (1965) are conspicuous failures because of their insistent egotism, *The Malayan Adventure* (1948) is a singular triumph. A happy amalgam of autobiography, travelogue, and diary, it succeeds, despite some repetition of factual details, because it is minimally egotistical. Interspersed with brief but lively vignettes of nature, the narrative is continually enlivened by scintillating flashes of humour.

G. S. BALARAMA GUPTA

CHIANG, MICHAEL (1954–)

Singaporean novelist, dramatist

Born in Muar, Jahore, West Malaysia, he graduated from the University of Singapore (BA, 1977). Chiang worked in media-related fields before establishing his reputation as the founder of *8 Days Magazine* (1990), a weekly arts periodical. He is a senior member of the Singapore Broadcasting Corporation.

Chiang is best known in Singapore for his book *Army Daze* (1985), which humorously recounts the experiences (linguistic and otherwise) of men in the Singapore National Service. Chiang's bold use of 'Singlish', a variety of English spoken in Singapore, established him on Singapore's literary map. The popularity of *Army Daze* is attested by its sequel, *The New Army Daze* (1992), as well as by its appearance in cartoon-form comic-strip.

Chiang's entry into drama started with a small playlet, 'Beauty Box' (premièred 1984), a satire on beauty pageants. Chiang projected himself as a writer who could, cleverly and wittily, plumb the average Singaporean's world of campaigns (Singapore is well-known for its never-ending campaigns) and middle-class comforts. Together with Singapore's Dick Lee, a music composer, Chiang wrote 'Beauty World' for the 1988 Singapore Arts Festival. This highly successful musical play looked at the world of the 1960s, with its complex network of characters seeking a new life in a large modern city. Combining nostalgia with contemporary comment, 'Beauty World' appealed to the young and the old and cut across barriers of ethnicity, class, and religious affiliation.

Chiang's comedy, 'Private Parts' (premièred 1992), written for the 1992 Arts Festival, deals sympathetically with the problems of transsexuals. It was the subject of much critical comment in conservative Singapore.

KIRPAL SINGH

CHIFUNYISE, STEPHEN (1948–)

Zambian dramatist

He took his BA in education from the University of Zambia, where he majored in literature and theatre and worked at Chikwakwa Theatre, the university open-air theatre, which for several years produced a great number of topical plays that often subsequently toured the country. On his return to Zimbabwe after Independence, Chifunyise worked in the Ministry of Youth, Sports and Culture, where he was responsible for initiating much crucial work in youth and community theatre. He is now in the Ministry of Education and Culture.

Between 1974 and 1980, a number of Chifunyise's television dramas were broadcast on Zambian television; they included 'Because of Principles', 'Organized Disorganization', and 'Thorn in Our Flesh'. The latter, written in the early 1970s and still performed in Zambia, focuses on the relationship between middle-class and working-class Zambians. Others, which speak directly to the present because of the relevance of their social themes, are still often performed; they are 'The Returned Ones', about miners; 'Mr. Polera', about cholera; 'The District Government Goes to a Village', a political satire; 'Blood', which deals with traditional beliefs centring on blood; and 'Vultures', which focuses on issues of inheritance.

Many of Chifunyise's plays have never been published, but this has not affected either his standing in the region or the frequency with which his plays are performed. A published collection of his plays, *Medicine for Love and Other Plays* (1984), is now a text at the University of Zimbabwe. In Zimbabwe, his television serial drama 'Solo and Mutsiai' ran for more than thirteen weeks in 1988.

Chifunyise has written several plays used in theatre for development work. He has also written 'Temporary Market' (premièred 1993) for the Glen Norah Women's Theatre; it is an environmental play that deals with unemployment and its consequences. 'May Day, May Day' was performed by the Dzivare Sekwa Theatre Group, Harare, in 1993.

LIZ GUNNER

CHILDREN'S LITERATURE

CHILDREN'S LITERATURE (Overview)

Countries that were at one time part of the British Empire share a common influence in the field of children's literature; this is true of Africa (East, South, and West), Australia, Canada, India, New Zealand, the South Pacific, and Singapore. Initially, the British colonial settlers brought books for their children from the 'old country', generally ignoring the rich oral literatures of the indigenous peoples. Once a local children's book production began, generally in the second half of the nineteenth century, the countries of the white diaspora (Australia, Canada, New Zealand) showed strong parallels in the development of their respective children's literatures. Initially, their first locally produced reading for children was in the nature of religious tracts or texts. Next, English-born settlers such as **Catharine Parr Traill** in Canada supported their families by writing books such as *The Canadian Crusoes* (1852), about enterprising children in the bush. Although these books were published in England, they found their way back to the colonies and were read by settlers' children along with other imported texts and local periodical literature during the second half of the nineteenth century. Around the turn of the century, the domestic story arose, adding girls' stories to the already popular boys' adventure stories, particularly those of Empire. Tales about the different animals in the new lands also started about this time (the realistic animal story in Canada, for instance) and have continued in popularity. Generally, the long stretch from the beginnings of the First World War to reconstruction after the Second World War was a fallow publishing period in children's literature everywhere. Also, at the same time, a combination of forces (including increasing literacy, the increasing sophistication of readers due to the media explosion, and, most important, the movement from realism to modernism in adult literature) resulted in books that had formerly been in the category of 'popular literature' for a general adult readership (e.g., the works of F. H. Burnett and **Lucy Maud Montgomery**, both writers of bestsellers with young protagonists) being shifted into the category of children's literature.

In the second half of the twentieth century there has been a veritable explosion in children's literature in all developed nations. In those countries that had been part of the British Empire, this was specifically fostered by literary nationalism, and some countries witnessed the phenomenon of writers of adult literature also writing children's books. This period also has seen an outburst of diverse production (picture-books for young children and many kinds of books for older children: regional poetry, drama, and fiction; social realism, problem novels about cultural transition and gender politics, fantasies, and science fiction, etc.). Another interesting phenomenon throughout the post-colonial countries has been a greatly revived interest in the oral literatures of the first indigenous peoples of the land (Maori, Inuit, First Nations). These stories, which stress such values as the necessity of humanity living in harmony with nature rather than despoiling it, fit in with late twentieth-century concerns about conservation and ecology. Interest in the tales from indigenous cultures is accompanied by shame over the earlier portrayals of these peoples in children's literature written by non-native writers.

Children's literature from the countries not part of the white diaspora shows slower development. Factors responsible for this reflect various economic, political, and educational conditions. A healthy children's literature does not develop until there is a large and stable middle class to become consumers. Only when the conditions for market capitalism exist does business enterprise develop around the production of children's books. There must be widespread literacy and political stability, a large populace that regards the education of children as important, and, most important, a public and school library system to buy the books produced in that country in quantity. Children's literature from South and East Africa, India, the South Pacific, and to a lesser extent West Africa, all testify to handicaps related to these conditions.

Nationalistic phases of political development are always accompanied by great attention in that country to the development of books that socialize children in accepted ways. During periods of nationalistic pride and expansion, there also occurs the establishment of prizes to recognize quality in that country's book production. (See **Awards**.) In addition, there is a growth of a secondary critical literature surrounding children's books. However, in order for all of this development to take place, each country must have a large enough pool of consumers, a mechanism to protect national book production if imported English-language children's books from another country provide a threat, and, finally, an outlook that sees children's books as an integral part of overall cultural enterprise.

One distinctive feature of children's literature today is the widespread sale of international rights at international book fairs. This will ultimately shrink the global village, making children more aware of children's lives in other countries: the pictures of children from different races and environments carry a visual impact that adult books do not. One unfortunate effect of this globalization of children's books is that it will be harder for countries without a strong native children's literature already in place ever to develop one: a business in Singapore, for instance, that prints children's books from countries such as Canada, Australia, and the UK may find it cheaper to distribute these locally than to develop native authors. There is no question that children's book production is entering a transnational stage: the best writers of English-language children's books (and others that are translated into English) are purchased and read worldwide — a factor that will only increase the power of the English language in its already established position as the language of commerce and business. As part of the decolonizing process, some African children's writers are now producing children's books in their native languages. But this attempt to resist cultural assimilation has working against it the knowledge that these books will reach a greatly reduced readership.

It is now recognized that a country's children's literature provides an x-ray vision into the perceptual frameworks held by those who produce it. Publishers, of course, cater to the values of the book-buying hegemony, although the development of desk-top publishing in the last decade of the twentieth century may alter this. Because children's literature naturalizes constructed values (such as attitudes towards gender and marginalized peoples, standards of truth, decency, order, and authenticity), it encodes the hierarchical power structures of society, which are then internalized by children readers. A child's reading is part of what constructs the child who becomes the adult. Thus, children's literature in highly developed countries is now the energetic site of sharp critical practice; curiously there have been stronger attacks on ideologically inappropriate literature (e.g., stories that reinforce the 'inferiority' of women and other marginalized groups) than on the equally important but more transient media images. Contemporary critical practices, particularly those of Marxism, feminism, and some postmodernist approaches, have assisted in opening the whole field of cultural studies, and children's literature is now seen as an integral part of this broader view. In fact, one of the observations of post-colonial theory is that the imperialistic cognitive process has often constructed the 'mother-country/colony' relationship in the 'parent/child' paradigm in children's literature.

MARY RUBIO

Children's Literature (Australia)

Australian writing for children is a rich and diverse aspect of the country's culture. From tales of Pacific explorers' voyages published in Europe in the eighteenth century to the present day, when hundreds of titles representing many genres are published annually, Australian children's books reflect and have even perhaps helped shape concepts of Australia and what it means to be Australian.

Even prior to European settlement in 1788, the great southern continent was a topic of interest in children's books, particularly in French and British compilations about great voyages. This interest increased with colonization, with the 'exotic' location and unusual animals spawning many tales of adventure, often by writers as unfamiliar with the country as their readers. Despite the struggle for existence in the new colony, there was, early in the nineteenth century, some indigenous publishing of hymns and tracts for children, crudely produced. The first children's book published in Australia was *A Mother's Offering to Her Children* (1841) by Charlotte Barton (mother of Louisa Atkinson, Australia's first woman novelist). It is a collection of facts and anecdotes in the form of a catechism with four children asking their mother questions related to her stories of shipwrecks, local flora and fauna, pioneer life, and brutal accounts of Aboriginals murdering their own children.

Until the 1890s, pioneering endeavours, an outback setting, and tales of immigration predominated in books for Australian children, or at least for their British counterparts, because these tales of 'new chums' struggling against the vicissitudes of a tough new land are addressed to outsiders. This was the feature of books such as William Howitt's *A Boy's Adventures in the Wilds of Australia: or, Herbert's Notebook* (1854) and Richard Rowe's *The Boy in the Bush* (1869). The latter opens with Wonga-Wonga station beset by bushrangers. Shots are fired and people abducted in the first few pages and the hectic pace continues through to the conclusion when 'the boy' Harry announces to the family's English governess, 'Miss Smith . . . I no longer consider myself a *Boy* in the Bush!'

There is more diversity towards the end of the century, when from the 1870s a small number of illustrated books were produced, including an Australian version of 'Who killed Cock Robin?' — *Who Killed Cockatoo?* (1860) by William Cawthorne — the eccentric *Cole's Funny Picture Book* (1876), compiled by E. W. Cole, **Ethel Pedley**'s animal fantasy *Dot and the Kangaroo* (1899), and an innovative collection of Aboriginal stories, **K. Langloh Parker**'s *Australian Legendary Tales: Folklore of the Noongahburrahs as Told to the Piccaninnies* (1896). All of these books, with the exception of the first two London editions of *Dot and the Kangaroo*, were published in Australia and are still in print in various forms.

The publication of **Ethel Turner**'s *Seven Little Australians* (1894) initiated a major change in the emphasis of the Australian children's books market from boys' adventure stories to family stories. These featured major female characters, with larrikins and 'pickles' of both sexes preferred to empire-building boyish heroes, and there is a switch from country to city and suburban settings. Turner's story of seven children, none of whom 'is really good', was an immediate success. The work of her sister, Lilian Turner, and eventually that of her daughter, Jean Curlewis, was published by the English firm Ward, Lock, as was the work of Turner's rival **Mary Grant Bruce**, who is best known for her family adventure stories set on a country station, 'Billabong'.

Until the 1940s the majority of Australian children's books were still produced overseas, but the Sydney firm Angus and Robertson established a fine children's list with Louise Mack's *Teens: A*

Story of Australian Schoolgirls (1897), the first of several outstanding children's books published by the firm. Its publication of **May Gibbs'** *Snugglepot and Cuddlepie* (1918), **Norman Lindsay**'s *The Magic Pudding* (1918), and Dorothy Wall's *Blinky Bill* (1933), together with the Melbourne publication of Ida Rentoul Outhwaite's beautiful fairyland images, constitutes a 'golden age' in Australian fantasy illustration and story. An Australian icon, cartoon character Ginger Meggs, a freckle-faced boy always in strife but one step ahead of the police or his other enemies, was created by James C. Bancks in 1921 and continues the Australian preference for the sturdy 'naughty' child. Also in 1921, **C. J. Dennis**' *A Book for Kids* introduced verse, like the nonsense rhyme 'Triantiwontigongelope', that has amused generations of Australian children.

A Children's Book Council was formed in New South Wales in 1945, and in 1946 the Australian Children's Book of the Year Award was established. This movement, and a growing interest in children's libraries, seems to have been the stimulus for the development of a core of outstanding children's novelists who quickly moved from conservative beginnings to become major innovators in the field. Nan Chauncy, **Patricia Wrightson,** Joan Phipson, **Ivan Southall,** Eleanor Spence, Colin Thiele, **Ruth Park,** Reginald Ottley, and Hesba Brinsmead, who first published in the 1950s and 1960s, have achieved both Australian and international recognition. Of the period 1945 to 1985 the British critic John Rowe Townsend writes, in his *Written for Children* (3rd rev. ed., 1987), 'proportionally to population, the Australian achievement has probably been more notable than the American or British'.

The rise of the picture-book is a notable feature of contemporary publishing. Outstanding examples from an impressive range include the illustrated version of **A. B. Paterson**'s lyric *Waltzing Matilda* (1970) by Desmond Digby, Ted Greenwood's quirky creations, the three-book partnership of Jenny Wagner and Ron Brooks, of which the best-known title is *John Brown, Rose and the Midnight Cat* (1977), and **Dick Roughsey**'s striking Aboriginal stories and histories. Recently, the extraordinary success of the animal fantasy *Possum Magic* (1983) by Mem Fox and Julie Vivas has led to a burgeoning of Australiana products. Graeme Base's intricate alphabet book, *Animalia* (1986), and the works of Bob Graham, Pamela Allen, and Alison Lester are favourites at home and overseas.

As recently as the mid-1980s it was possible to make generalized comments about the trends and the themes of Australian children's books, but the chief feature now is diversity. Poetry for children and books for middle readers are gaining in quality where once there was a lack. Bestselling authors Robin Klein, Paul Jennings, and Morris Gleitzman write humorous books with serious themes, while writers such as Nadia Wheatley and Gillian Rubinstein confront adolescents with challenging topics but turn with equal skill to the writing of picture-books for the young reader. Authors and illustrators no longer feel tied to representing local images, and although much that is published is mediocre, the best shows a richness and quality that appear unlikely to diminish.

KERRY WHITE

Further reading: Brenda Niall, *Australia Through the Looking-Glass, Children's Fiction 1830–1980* (1984); Marcie Muir, comp., *Australian Children's Books: a Bibliography, vol. 1 1774–1972* (rev. 1992); Kerry White, comp, *Australian Children's Books: a Bibliography, vol. 2 1973–1988* (1992); Stella Lees and Pam Macintyre, *The Oxford Companion to Australian Children's Literature* (1993); Maurice Saxby, *The Proof of the Puddin': Australian Children's Literature: 1970–1990* (1993).

CHILDREN'S LITERATURE (Canada)

Myths and misconceptions about Canada, as well

as matters of fact, have been spread by children's literature. Just as Rudyard Kipling's *Kim* (1901) kindled a dream of India, stories of the **Canadian North**, such as R. M. Ballantyne's *The Young Fur Traders* (1856), created a dream of Canadian adventure for boys all over the world, and an idyll such as **L. M. Montgomery**'s *Anne of Green Gables* (1908) and its sequels gave all girls a magic Canadian island of domesticity, friendship, and self-discovery.

Unlike such Australians as Nan Chauncy, who early highlighted the problems of aboriginal people — in *Tangara* (1960), for example — many Canadian writers have presented Native and Inuit characters as heroes or supportive comrades, from W. F. Butler's *Red Cloud, the Solitary Sioux* (1882) to **Farley Mowat**'s *Lost in the Barrens* (1956) and James Houston's *Tikta'liktak: An Eskimo Legend* (1965). (See **Children's Literature**, Australia.) More realistic portrayals of Native people, and presentations of Native central characters, appear in Jan Andrews' *Very Last First Time* (1985), illustrated by Ian Wallace, in Markoosie's *Harpoon of the Hunter* (1970), and in Jan Hudson's *Sweet Grass* (1984). As in most parts of the Commonwealth, Native Canadian legends have been retold both by non-Natives (William Toye's *The Loon's Necklace*, 1977, illustrated by Elizabeth Cleaver, for example) and by Native and Métis writers (for instance, **Maria Campbell**'s *Little Badger and the Fire Spirit*, 1977). It would be interesting to compare the latter legend, in which a small being confronts the great gods, with a similar legend in Shirley Arora's book from India, *What Then, Raman?* (1960). Raman's quest is for books and learning; Little Badger's needs are more basic — for fire, warmth, and survival. Raman must defy his parents, and he emerges as a teacher of younger children; Little Badger learns to depend on his peers and his elders. The Canadian legend perhaps reflects the harsher realities of a northern land.

Uniquely, publication of children's literature in Canada began in two languages, French and English, with the religious text *Le Petit Livre de vie*, printed in Montreal in 1777, and the pamphlet *An Hymn*, printed in Halifax in 1788. Recently, official bilingualism has fostered the development of alphabet books and easy-to-translate picture books; works from francophone writers of children's literature include Ginette Anfousse's *Mon Ami Pichou* (1976), which the author translated as *My Friend Pichou* (1978); Marie-Louise Gay's *Voyage au claire de lune* (1986), published simultaneously with her own translation, *Moonbeam on a Cat's Ear* (1986); and Stéphane Poulin's *Peux-tu attraper Josephine?* (1987), which Poulin translated as *Can You Catch Josephine?* (1987). The works of anglophone writers include Ann Blades' *Mary of Mile 18* (1971, untranslated); Kathy Stinson's *Red is Best* (1982), adapted by Paule Daveluy as *Le Rouge c'est bien mieux* (1986); Tim Wynne-Jones' *Zoom at Sea* (1983), translated by Françoise Marois as *Le Matou marin* (1984); and Jo-Ellen Bogart's *Sarah Saw a Blue Macaw* (1991, untranslated).

As in notable picture-books from other nations — the Australian *John Brown, Rose and the Midnight Cat* (1977), by Jenny Wagner and Ron Brooks, for example — many of these Canadian early-reader books feature friendship between a human and a pet. Earlier Canadian writers had made a specialty of stories of wilderness animals, such as **Charles G. D. Roberts'** *The Kindred of the Wild* (1902), **Ernest Thompson Seton**'s *Wild Animals I have Known* (1898), and Roderick Haig-Brown's *Ki-yu, A Story of Panthers* (1934). Canadians remain tied to real animals — no Australian Aboriginal bunyips here, only genuine wild animals naturalistically treated, as are the jungle animals in **Dhan Gopal Mukerji**'s stories of India. In this tradition, Canadian writers read and were influenced by British books, such as Anna Sewell's *Black Beauty* (1877), that grew out of crusades for humane treatment of animals — Margaret Marshall Saunders' 1894 bestseller *Beautiful Joe* swung reader concern towards domestic pets, as did later books such as **Morley Callaghan**'s *Luke Baldwin's Vow* (1948), Mowat's *The Dog Who Wouldn't Be* (1957), Sheila Burnford's *The Incredible Journey* (1961), and Gabrielle Roy's *Cliptail* (1980, first published as *Courte-Queue*, 1979, translated by Alan Brown).

After a period of intense Canadian nationalism in the 1960s, many other Canadian writers began to produce careful work for young audiences, including **Margaret Atwood** (*Up in the Tree*, 1978), **Mordecai Richler** (*Jacob Two-Two Meets the Hooded Fang*, 1975), and **Margaret Laurence** (*The Olden Days Coat*, 1979). Their children's books represent poetry, fantasy, and time-shift fiction respectively. In all three genres of children's literature, other Canadian writers, troubled by a long period of dependency on British traditions, have tried to locate themselves in their own geographical space by drawing on regional detail: **Dennis Lee** uses Canadian place names such as Kamloops, Winnipeg, and Kitimat in the poems in *Alligator Pie* (1974); Ruth Nichols invokes Muskoka lake country in her fantasy *A Walk out of the World* (1969); Janet Lunn moves from an Ontario farmhouse into the 1860s in her time-shift novel *The Root Cellar* (1981).

Lunn's book bears interesting similarities to Australian **Ruth Park**'s *Playing Beatie Bow* (1980); this time-slip fantasy also involves a bad-tempered, unhappy girl: a common worldwide debt to Frances Hodgson Burnett's *The Secret Garden* (1911) can be postulated. Following the work of British writers Philippa Pearce and Alison Uttley, the 1980s saw a burst of time-shift stories from Canadians such as Karleen Bradford (*The Other Elizabeth*, 1982), Margaret Buffie (*Who is Frances Rain?*, 1983), and Kit Pearson (*A Handful of Time*, 1987).

A serious tone combined with sharp regional detail also marks the realistic problem novels that deal with the psychological and social development of children — Jean Little's *Mama's Going to Buy You a Mockingbird* (1984) and Sarah Ellis' *Pick-up Sticks* (1991) are notable examples. Cultural integration has become a theme in many realistic stories that emphasize difficulties of accommodation, as in Little's *From Anna* (1972), Myra Paperny's *The Wooden People* (1976), Ian Wallace's *Chin Chiang and the Dragon's Dance* (1984), and **Joy Kogawa**'s *Naomi's Road* (1986).

Recent boys' books also present youths caught in social or psychological dilemmas, as in John Craig's *Zach* (1972), Claire Mackay's *Exit Barney McGee* (1979), Kevin Major's *Far from Shore* (1980), Brian Doyle's *Up to Low* (1982), and Marilyn Halvorson's *Let It Go* (1985). These books have an honesty, vigour, and dramatic plotting comparable to the boys' stories of Australians **Ivan Southall** and **Patricia Wrightson**; like Southall, Major, particularly in his Newfoundland stories, delineates a harsh and isolated life. In the transition from works dominated by British imagery and situations, post-colonial writers for boys seem to swing to extremes of deprivation and alienation.

For girls, L. M. Montgomery's many novels set a world standard of wit and charm, but they also suggest that young people face an indifferent or repressive adult world. Nevertheless, all Montgomery's young heroines are essentially buoyant in disposition and have sweet, but independent, natures. The difference between these characters, for instance, and the mean, self-absorbed Australian girl in H. F. Brinsmead's *Pastures of the Blue Crane* (1964) perhaps reflects the essentially more open world of Canadian girls. **Nellie McClung**'s *Sowing Seeds in Danny* (1908), Dora Olive Thompson's *That Girl Ginger* (1932), Lyn Cook's *Samantha's Secret Room* (1963), Suzanne Martel's *The King's Daughter* (1982, originally published as *Jeanne, fille du roy*, 1974, translated by David

Homel and Margaret Rose), and Jan Truss' *Jasmin* (1982), create a succession of capable, imaginative, and lovable protagonists, good evidence of the opportunities open to girls both in city and country settings.

Historical fiction, a favourite genre in the early days of the Dominion, is dwindling; tales of the conquest and the United Empire Loyalists have been replaced by stories of rebellion (**James Reaney**'s *The Boy with an R in His Hand*, 1965, for example), of slavery (Barbara Smucker's *Underground to Canada*, 1977), and of labour troubles (Bill Freeman's *Shantymen of Cache Lake*, 1975, Marsha Hewitt's and Claire Mackay's *One Proud Summer*, 1981, and Geoffrey Bilson's *Goodbye Sarah*, 1982).

Escaping from time and place, young Canadians can read science fiction such as Monica Hughes' *The Keeper of the Isis Light* (1980) and Welwyn Katz's *The Third Magic* (1988), or fantasy such as Donn Kushner's *A Book Dragon* (1987). (See **Science Fiction and Fantasy**, Canada.) For younger readers, fantasies include Robert Munsch's *The Paper Bag Princess* (1980). To enjoy these books fully, the young reader needs some awareness of earlier fictions — fairy tales, medieval legend, or Crusoe stories — the traditional roots from which much Commonwealth literature grows. Besides sharing roots, many Commonwealth writers now also read each others' work. We might guess that a pair of books such as New Zealand's **Margaret Mahy**'s *The Haunting* (1982) and Canadian Janet Lunn's *The Double Spell* (1968) adumbrates some mutual knowledge. Generally speaking, however, Canadians are much more influenced by American and British children's books than by those from former British colonies such as Kenya, India, Jamaica, or South Africa. The amazing growth in publication of children's books in Canada, from about thirty-five a year in the 1940s to about 450 a year in the 1990s, can be explained partly by the amalgam of educational influences and the availability of publishing outlets in the UK, the USA, and France, by the successful example of earlier world best-sellers such as Roberts and Montgomery, by the rise of Canadian nationalism and government support of the arts, by the opening of the Children's Book Centre in Toronto and of many specialist children's bookstores across the country, and by the existence of a journal of criticism, *Canadian Children's Literature: A Journal of Criticism and Review* (1975–).

MARY RUBIO
ELIZABETH WATERSTON

Further reading: Judith Saltman, *Modern Canadian Children's Books* (1987); Jon C. Stott and Raymond E. Jones, *Canadian Books for Children: A Guide to Authors and Illustrators* (1989); Sheila Egoff and Judith Saltman, *The NEW Republic of Childhood: A Critical Guide to Canadian Children's Literature in English* (1990); Elizabeth Waterston, *Children's Literature in Canada* (1992).

CHILDREN'S LITERATURE (The Caribbean)
Books written specifically about the life experiences of children from the English-speaking Caribbean did not appear in any substantial quantity until the late 1960s. This is because the colonial government's control of the educational system provided little incentive for local production of books, since books were imported directly from the home country, England. Although the upsurge of nationalism in the 1930s produced a cadre of writers, they concentrated almost exclusively on adult books, most likely because of the low prestige and meagre financial returns associated with writing for children. **Vic Reid** stated that he decided to write some books for his children only after discovering the absence of works that positively presented Caribbean history.

Some other factors that militate against indigenous children's book production in the Caribbean are the small size of the market, the heavy capital investments required, and the lack of trained personnel. (See **Publishing**, The Caribbean.) Consequently, most titles appear under British or American imprints with the focus mainly on educational materials. However, more books for curricular and recreational reading have been produced over the years as a result of changing educational needs, the introduction of Caribbean-based examinations, and the emergence of a core of writers at home and abroad. A handful of local publishing houses, including Kingston Publishers, Jamaica Publishing House, and Children's Writing Circle, has also been established.

As with the development of children's literature elsewhere, books of folk tales were among the first children's books to appear in the Caribbean. Of the numerous collections available the best known is *West Indian Folk-Tales* (1966), by the master storyteller Phillip Sherlock. Other notable writers of this genre include Trinidad's Grace Hallworth (*The Carnival Kite*, 1980, and *Cric Crac: A Collection of West Indian Stories*, 1990) and Guyana's David Makhanlall (*The Further Adventures of Brer Anansi*, 1980, and *Brer Anansi and the Boat Race: A Folktale from the Caribbean*, 1988, among others). However, realistic stories soon outnumbered all others and quickly moved away from the patronizing tales of island life, written by well-intentioned foreigners, to the more authentic realism of local authors. Much-needed incentive came from the increasing demand for indigenous material that led education authorities to adopt already existing stories for classroom use or to commission Caribbean nationals to write new ones.

A sampling of these realistic stories — historical and contemporary — includes Vic Reid's well-crafted historical novels, **C. Everard Palmer**'s exuberant celebration of village life (*Big Doc Bitteroot*, 1968), **Jean D'Costa**'s realistic slices of Jamaican society (*Escape to Last Man Peak*, 1976, *Voice in the Wind*, 1978), and **Andrew Salkey**'s harrowing depiction of natural and man-made disasters (*Hurricane*, 1964, *Earthquake*, 1965, *Drought*, 1966, and *Riot*, 1967). Mention must also be made of **Rosa Guy** and **Marlene Nourbese Philip**, outstanding writers resident abroad who have successfully written about Caribbean adolescents facing the challenges of immigrants in a new country, as in Guy's *The Friends* (1973) and Philip's *Harriet's Daughter* (1988).

As part of schools' literature programmes, several anthologies of regional short stories and poetry of varying quality have been compiled, but individual volumes of well-written poetry for children are few. The gentle rhythm of **Pamela Mordecai**'s *Story Poems* (1987) teases the young child's imagination, while **John Agard**, in his zesty humorous verses, makes deft use of the Caribbean dialect (*I Din Do Nuttin*, 1983, *Say It Again Granny*, 1985) in much the same way as **James Berry** in describing childhood experiences.

Because picture-book production is costly, few are published in the Caribbean. Notable examples include Karl Craig's lavishly illustrated books about Emmanuel and his parrot (*Emmanuel and his Parrot*, 1970, *Emmanuel Goes to Market*, 1971), while Dennis Ranston contributed the energetic tale of the kite and the petchary. The combination of art and simple text in Franc Lessac's books suggests a world of childhood innocence, and the illustrations do not do justice to most of Diane Browne's stories, for example, *Debonair and the Donkey* (1986).

Caribbean expatriates abroad have also contributed some good picture-books, such as the Sean series written by Petronella Breinburg and illustrated by Errol Lloyd. (*My Brother Sean*, 1973, was a runner-up for the prestigious Greenway medal in 1974.) **Jan Carew**'s mythical picture-books are richly illustrated, and Vyanne Samuel's family stories accompanied by bold vibrant pictures are a delight.

Informational works are confined mainly to

the geography/travel kind, many of which are written by foreigners and read like expanded tourist brochures. A miscellany of other subjects touched upon are marine life, folk songs, and a handful of biographies by Undine Giuseppi, Therese Mills, and others.

Despite the present unfavourable economic climate, there are still some positive developments in Caribbean children's literature. Heinemann released seven new titles in 1990 and there are plans to establish a regional council for children's books to promote indigenous writing and publishing.

CHERRELL SHELLEY ROBINSON

CHILDREN'S LITERATURE (East Africa)

East African children's literature in English written after the attainment of independence has attracted male and female creative writers from diverse walks of life. For example, Miriam Were of Kenya, author of *The Boy in Between* (1969), is a medical doctor, and Taaitta Toweett, author of *Tears over a Dead Cow* (1970), has a Ph.D. in linguistics and is a renowned Kenyan politician.

Uganda, Kenya, and Tanzania adventure stories populated by young characters have dominated East African creative literature for children. The leading writers of these adventure stories are **Barbara Kimenye** of Uganda and Asenath Odaga of Kenya, Kimenye's Moses series of novellas for older children being popular throughout the region. The series follows the adventures of a schoolboy named Moses and includes *Moses* (1966), *Moses and Mildred* (1967), and *Moses and the Kidnappers* (1968).

Where Kimenye writes mainly adventure stories targeted for teenagers, Odaga writes for both very young readers and older children. She also writes in a number of genres. In addition to her adventure stories, she has recorded folklore, such as *Thu Thinda: Stories from Kenya* (1980), and she has also written a play, *Simbi Nyaima* (1982). Odaga's interest in the problems girls have to face to succeed in a male-dominated world is apparent in her realistic story for older children, *Jande's Ambition* (1966).

Contemporary problems have provided the social background for East African prose fiction for older children. In *Groping in the Dark* (1974), B. A. Katigula of Tanzania examines the problems confronting children growing up in a world of cultural transition, where traditional values have lost their significance and the formal school does not provide clear-cut guidelines. Similar sensitivity to contemporary problems is shown by G. Kalimugogo of Uganda in *Pilgrimage to Nowhere* (1974), in which he narrates the futile efforts of an old villager in retrieving his son who deserts the moral village environment and becomes an urban social misfit.

Stories re-created from folklore have interested East African writers since the 1960s. (See **Folklore**, East Africa.) A leading writer of such stories is Pamela Kola of Kenya. In *East African When Stories* (1968) Kola has reworked popular East African myths to suit pre-teenage readers. In the story 'When Death Began', for example, she re-creates a myth about the origin of death to help young readers come to terms with the phenomenon of death without getting emotionally upset. In 'The Origin of Lake Bogaria' (in *Give the Devil his Due*, 1969), William Kibiegon Boruet has given young readers a creative explanation about the origin of the strange, hot Lake Bogoria in Kenya.

Conservation of wildlife is an area that has received the attention of contemporary East African writers of children's literature. In *Ogilo and the Hippo* (1991, translated from a Luo story published in 1983), Asenath Odaga educates young readers on the importance of discouraging wildlife poaching. An interesting work on the subject of wildlife conservation is Tanzanian J. P. Mbonde's *Hugo and the Hippo* (1972, translated from a Swahili work published in 1968). Mbonde considers various points of view in wildlife conservation by blending narrative with drama, using both human and animal characters.

Young readers in East Africa are now being exposed to the subjects of gender relations and the role of women in society. Female writers especially have shown interest in this area in such works as Ugandan Sala Nagenda's *Mother of Twins* (1971) and Kenyan Ciarunji Chesaina's 'Little Fishes and Crocodiles' (in *Little Amu and the Kobole*, 1989, edited by W. Mwotia *et al.*). Prior to independence, drama and poetry in English received negligible attention in East Africa. Contemporary literature for children in the area is beginning to fill this gap. Sam Mbure of Kenya has given young readers a collection of easy and interesting poetry in *Lots of Wonders* (1989). *World of Enchantment* (1991) is the product of collaborative efforts between the Kenya ministry of education and the British Council and contains prize-winning poems by high-school students. Kasigwa N. Barnabas, a high-school teacher from Uganda, has recently published *An Anthology of East African Plays* (1991), a collection of plays he wrote and produced for the annual Kenya School Drama Festival during the 1980s.

A development in East African children's literature that is worth noting is the fact that established writers for adults are now showing interest in young readers. **Austin Bukenya**, an established Ugandan critic and poet, has written a play for children, *A Test of Strength* (in *The River Without Frogs*, 1990, edited by Muthoni Karega *et al.*). David Maillu, East Africa's leading writer of popular literature, is now writing stories for children based on contemporary issues, such as *The Poor Child* (1988). **Meja Mwangi**, an established Kenyan novelist, has also published an adventure story for children, *Little White Man* (1990).

The focus on literature for children by established East African artists of adult literature is an indication that these writers recognize that literature is a tool for education and that in order to be effective in stirring the conscience of society their work must interest children, who are the society of the future.

CIARUNJI CHESAINA SWINIMER

CHILDREN'S LITERATURE (India)

Children's literature in English is relatively young in India, in contrast to that written in the other major languages, whose traditions date back to their own regional versions of the Indian epics, Vyasa's *Mahabharata* (Sanskrit, 900–500 BC) and Valmiki's *Ramayana* (Sanskrit, 600–300 BC), and to the didactic *Jataka Tales* (Pali, 400 BC) and the animal stories of *Panchatantra* (Sanskrit, 200 BC). English translations of these works began to appear only in the early twentieth century, but were not meant primarily for children. The earliest standard translation of *Jataka Tales* is dated 1916; that of *Panchatantra*, 1924.

Early fiction for children written in English and set in India was written by India-born Rudyard Kipling (1865–1936), whose two *Jungle Books* (1894 and 1895) and *Kim* (1901) evoke the colonial experience, and by Rumer Godden (1907–). Godden wrote juvenile fiction that does not adequately reflect her Indian childhood. In British India, few Indians wrote for children in English. A notable exception was **Jawaharlal Nehru**'s *Letters From a Father to His Daughter* (1930). With its child hero and leisured storytelling, **R. K. Narayan**'s *Swami and Friends* (1935), the first in his Malgudi series, could well qualify as literature for children. Some prose writings of **M. K. Gandhi** and a number of poems by **Sarojini Naidu** now find a place in school textbooks.

In post-independence India, sporadically published children's books imitated the school and adventure stories of the Enid Blyton variety until the establishment in 1957 of the Children's Book Trust. The Trust holds an annual competition for both fiction and non-fiction work for different age groups and has published more than 250 titles in

English. It sponsored the establishment in 1981 of an active Association of Writers and Illustrators for Children. The government-sponsored National Book Trust, also established in 1957, produces a few books annually. Most publishers, however, find it profitable to publish mainly textbooks; they publish little fiction and no poetry. This situation is now changing with the recent entry of foreign publishers such as Puffin and Harper Collins into India.

Encouragement for Indian writers of children's literature in English has come from newspapers that reserve a Sunday page for children and from magazines. The better-known periodicals are *Children's World* (1968–), *Chandamama* (1969–), and *Target* (1979–). *Chandamama*, published in twelve languages, confines itself to myth and folk tales; the others have a wider range of theme and content and a readership that is largely urban and pre-teen. *Children's World* publishes possibly the world's longest-running humour column for children, 'A Letter to You', begun in 1969, detailing the escapades of a ten-year-old schoolboy.

Writing for children in India is not yet given the recognition it deserves. Children's books are seldom acclaimed, or even reviewed. But a new generation of writers has begun to emerge: **Ruskin Bond** — *The Adventures of Rusty* (1981); Geeta Dharmarajan (1948–) — *Superbrat and Other Stories* (1989); Arup Kumar Dutta (1946–) — *The Kaziranga Trail* (1979) and *Smack* (1990); Subhadra Sen Gupta (1952–) — *Good Times at Islamgunj* (1982); Poile Sengupta (1948–) — *The Exquisite Balance* (1987); and Sigrun Srivastava (1943–) — *Ghost Rider of Darbhanga and Other Stories* (1989), among others. This group writes for children who have made an alien language their own and whose experiences of loneliness, fear, and joy are not unlike those of children elsewhere in the world.

AMBIKA SENGUPTA

CHILDREN'S LITERATURE (New Zealand)
While in many aspects the development of New Zealand children's literature is analogous to that of Australia, four specifically indigenous themes can be distinguished — the settlers' reactions to their new environment, relationships between Maori and Europeans, the idiosyncratic elderly, and the conservation of New Zealand's unique flora and fauna.

The earliest writers were absorbed with the strangeness of the land, its uncompromising bush-covered mountains, its rushing waterways, and its indigenous inhabitants, the Maori. But while the 'settler' stories were concerned with the difficulties of adapting to the land and to the vast distances from 'civilization', the 'adventure' stories by overseas writers such as G. A. Henty, R. E. Horsley, and Jules Verne made considerable capital from the disputes between Maori and settlers.

Many of the 'settler' books were the result of diaries or letters 'home' to England and were predominantly written by well-educated women such as **Lady Mary Ann Barker** (later Lady Broome). The first book about the Land Wars by a New Zealand-born author, **William Satchell**'s *The Greenstone Door* (1914), poignantly depicts the conflict of loyalties inherent in any civil war. It is a dilemma frequently articulated in New Zealand children's literature, particularly in the writing of contemporary author **Anne de Roo**.

By the 1890s a generation of European children had been born in New Zealand, but there were few indigenous books catering to younger readers. This resulted in a flurry of activity to write fantasy stories that either retold Maori legends or used the 'flower fairy' theme, so popular overseas, to instruct children about New Zealand flora and fauna. These books were predominantly didactic and of little literary worth, but one author who developed the genre to its maximum potential was **Edith Howes**, whose children's books outshone their predecessors.

The works of **Isabel Maud Peacocke** dominated the post-First World War period in New Zealand children's literature. Her novels give a good picture of daily New Zealand life between the world wars, and in a number of her books crises are the direct or indirect result of the First World War. New Zealand writers of the period were undoubtedly influenced by such overseas writers of girls' stories as American L. M. Alcott, Canada's **Lucy Maud Montgomery**, and Australia's **Mary Grant Bruce** and **Ethel Turner**. It was in direct response to Turner's *Seven Little Australians* (1894) that **Esther Glen**, a Christchurch journalist, wrote *Six Little New Zealanders* (1917), a lively and readable account of six children who visit their uncles' farm in Canterbury.

The school story, which became so popular overseas in the wake of authors such as Angela Brazil, never achieved the same popularity among New Zealand authors. Only two series of New Zealand school stories were written at this time. The first, the Hilda at School stories by Phillis Garrard, is set in a North Island day school and includes *Hilda at School: A New Zealand Story* (1929), *The Doings of Hilda* (1932), *Hilda's Adventures* (1938), and *Hilda Fifteen* (1944). The second, the Merry stories of Claire Mallory (pseudonym of Winifred Hall), is set in a South Island girls' boarding school and includes *Merry Beings* (1947), *Merry Again* (1947), *Merry Marches On* (1947), *Leith and Friends* (1950), and *The Pen and Pencil Girls* (1950).

Although the 1930s and 1940s were lean years for New Zealand publishing, constructive measures were taken to address the scarcity of indigenous books for children. These included the establishment of the School Library Service in 1942 and of the New Zealand Library School in 1946, which provided books and trained children's librarians. By the 1940s, The School Journal, a series first published in 1907 as school readers, had become a major source of fiction and poetry for children. The work of some of New Zealand's finest children's writers, including **Margaret Mahy**, **Elsie Locke**, and **Ruth Dallas**, was first published in The School Journal.

The institutional market promoted more overtly nationalistic stories for children, and the 1950s saw a large number of books with titles such as *On a Farm in New Zealand*, *The New Zealand Twins*, or *Verena Visits New Zealand*. By the 1960s, however, the scope of local junior fiction had widened. Authors such as Phyl Wardell, whose works are set in the remote South Island, and Joyce West, whose stories are set in rural agricultural North Island districts, appeared, while Elsie Locke and Ruth Dallas revived an interest in the early settlers.

With the 1960s came an increasing awareness of the condescending and inappropriate literary depiction of the Maori. Lesley Cameron Powell's *Turi, The Story of a Little Boy* (1963) is a landmark in its sensitive treatment of a small Maori boy who lives with his grandmother. Its sympathetic depiction of the elderly is a recurrent theme in New Zealand junior fiction. R. L. Bacon has done much to heighten awareness of Maori legends. His *Rua and the Sea People* (1968) uses the device of a grandmother passing on legendary material to her grandchild. Bacon was the first to encourage a Maori artist, the well-known Para Matchitt, to illustrate a children's book. This practice has continued, resulting in fine decorative books by Maori artists Robyn Kahukiwa, Robert Jahnke, and Katerina Mataira. Another book about a grandmother, *Crayfishing with Grandmother* (1973), by Jill Bagnall, was not only the first full-colour picture-book to be produced locally but also the first to have dual Maori/English texts — a practice increasingly common in picture-books.

Unfortunately, the worthy motives behind institutional pressures to produce books with overtly New Zealand subject-matter worked against the writing of good fantasy stories, which are more likely to be universal than regional. For example, the stories of Margaret Mahy, New Zealand's most celebrated author for children, were initially rejected by the local market because it was deemed that her archetypal wizards, dragons, and pirates were too 'English'. (Her work was published in The School Journal.) It was only when her stories appeared in the USA that Mahy was 'discovered'; she has since published her major books in the USA or the UK and has used overseas illustrators. Mahy's success has undoubtedly inspired other New Zealand writers of fantasy; although their works are very different in mood and treatment, both Anthony Holcroft and Judy Corbalis write stories that have their roots, like Mahy's, in traditional fantasy.

The work of three other fantasy writers, **Maurice Gee**, Barry Faville, and **Caroline Macdonald**, could legitimately be placed in the genre of 'science fiction'. (See **Science Fiction**, New Zealand.) Gee explores the misuse of power (as does Australia's Victor Kelleher) in his imaginary world of 'O', while Faville and Macdonald set their novels in the future or use visitants from other worlds. These and such adventure writers as Phyl Wardell and Joan De Hamel express concern for the environment and anxiety to preserve New Zealand's natural heritage.

New Zealand children's literature has increasingly utilized social realism, although New Zealand has largely escaped the huge increase in 'problem novels' so prevalent overseas, particularly in the USA. Only **William Taylor** (*Possum Perkins*, 1987), Jack Lasenby (*The Lake*, 1987), and Ruth Corrin (*Secrets*, 1990) have depicted the darker side of reality, including incest. The most authentic novel in the social realism genre is **Tessa Duder**'s *Alex* (1987), which draws upon Duder's girlhood experiences as a New Zealand champion swimmer and shows considerable insight into the psychological and physical stresses experienced by a young woman.

The flowering of New Zealand literature for children in the 1980s was undoubtedly assisted by previous developments: the formation in 1969 of the Children's Literature Association of New Zealand, which drew together parents, authors, teachers, and librarians; the founding of New Zealand Literary Fund Grants to assist children's writers; and the establishment of multinational publishing firms in Auckland that offered incentives to authors to publish locally. Today almost all of the major metropolitan papers review junior fiction on a regular basis.

An enormous increase in picture-book publishing for children has been heightened by educational researchers Marie Clay, of Auckland University, and Dorothy Butler, a specialist bookseller and author, whose research has shown that children learn to read more readily when given high-interest stories rather than 'graded readers'. One result of this theory has been a growing number of lively, well-illustrated stories for beginner readers written by authors of the calibre of **Joy Cowley** and Margaret Mahy.

One of the most popular New Zealand picture-book authors, Lynley Dodd, has created in *Hairy Maclary of Donaldson's Dairy* (1983) and its sequels a gallery of canine and feline characters who are never treated anthropomorphically but develop distinctive characteristics as they feature in everyday but amusing circumstances. The skilful writing is complemented by Dodd's own jaunty illustrations. Expatriate New Zealand picture-book authors include Ronda Armitage and David Armitage (who live in England), creators of *The Lighthouse Keeper's Lunch* (1977) and its sequels, and Pamela Allen, who lives in Australia and whose energetic creations include *Bertie and the Bear* (1983) and *A Lion in the Night* (1985).

In this upsurge of quality and diversity of

New Zealand children's writing, however, the discerning reader may still identify the distinctive, but now unself-conscious, characteristics of New Zealand writing for children.

BETTY GILDERDALE

Further reading: J. B. Ringer, *Young Emigrants: New Zealand Juvenile Fiction 1833–1919* (1980); Betty Gilderdale, *A Sea Change: 145 Years of New Zealand Junior Fiction* (1982); Betty Gilderdale, 'Children's literature', in Terry Sturm (ed.) *The Oxford History of New Zealand Literature in English* (1991); Betty Gilderdale, *Introducing Twenty-One New Zealand Children's Writers* (1991).

CHILDREN'S LITERATURE (The Philippines)
The origins of Philippine children's literature dates to orally transmitted myths, legends, and folk tales in the different languages and ethnic communities. In the Spanish colonial era, reading material was imported from Europe, and national hero Jose Rizal was among the first to retell European stories and Philippine legends in Tagalog.

The textbooks used in the American regime soon came to be written especially for Filipino children, among them the *Pepe and Pilar* beginning readers, which began publication in 1930 and came into widespread use in the 1940s. Many of the books for children published prior to the 1960s were simply collections of retold Philippine folklore — for example, *Tales of Long Ago in the Philippines* (1953), by Maximo Ramos, and *Philippine Tales and Fables* (1957), by **Manuel Arguilla** and Lyd Arguilla.

Literature with a wider range resulted when the publishing firm PAMANA ran contests for children's books and published the winning entries. Among the titles were Ceres Alabado's *The Little Lizard and Other Stories* (1960); Gemma Cruz's *Makisig, the Little Hero of Mactan* (1964); **Gilda Cordero Fernando**'s *Horgle and the King's Soup* (1965), about a flying horse; and Isabel Taylor Escoda's *Once Upon a Hilltop* (1968), based on archaeological diggings and about a friendship between a child and a dog that lasts until death.

The nationalist movement of the 1970s encouraged Philacor, a business corporation, to publish a Young People's Library, including *Filipino Myths and Rituals* (1973), *Filipino Myths and Legends*, and *Filipino Arts and Crafts* (1980); no author is identified for these works. Soon other writers were writing fiction and retelling more tales, and in 1983 the Philippine Board of Books for Young People was established. It sponsors an annual competition for writers and illustrators of children's books, with such winners as Wystan Dimalanta's *The Adventures of Pilandok* (1985) and Maria Elena Paterno's *Sampaguita* (1986).

Since then, writing workshops (at the University of the Philippines' Creative Writing Center), prizes (the Palanca Memorial Award for Children's Stories), and interested publishers (New Day, Bookmark, Cacho, Goethe Institut) have reaped a harvest of books mostly for children under ten years of age. Few books are being written for preteens or early teens.

More recent publications include the Cacho Publishing House Trampoline series, bilingual (English-Filipino) texts such as *Two Friends, One World* (1991), by Ramon Sunico, *The Boy Who Ate Stars* (1991), by **Alfredo Yuson**, and Rene Villanueva's *Kung Bakit Umuulan* ('Why it Rains', 1991) and *Ang Unang Baboy sa Langit* ('The First Pig to Go to Heaven', 1991). Bookmark has published a series of folk tales (retold by Marla Yotoko Chorengel) including *Why the Sky is High* (1990) and *Philippine Wild Life* (1992), and two books for pre-adolescents by Marvivi Soliven, *The Unicorn* (1992, about growing up) and *Chun* (1992, about racial discrimination). The Tahanan Books for Young People include a series on Philippine heroes — *Gabriela Silang* (1992) by Neni Santa Romana-Cruz and *Jose Rizal* (1992) by Sylvia Mendez-Ventura — and nature books such as *Volcanoes* (1993) and *Typhoons* (1993) by

Maria Elena Paterno. Cacho's We Love the Earth Books are on ecology.

The advance in the quantity and the quality of children's literature comes from growth in the book publishing industry itself, but especially in the operative consciousness among writers, publishers, and readers.

DOREEN G. FERNANDEZ

Further reading: Maria Elena Paterno, 'Children's literature', *The Encyclopedia of Philippine Arts and Culture* (1993).

CHILDREN'S LITERATURE (Singapore)
Despite Singapore's high literacy rate of ninety-four per cent, the value of reading, especially of imaginative literature, is not fully appreciated. Instead, there is general emphasis on 'reading's usefulness in schoolwork and the garnering of information' (*Report of the Committee on Literary Arts*, 1988). Given the smallness of the local market in Singapore, publishing for children is not seen as a profitable venture, except for nonfiction. Writing for children is too often seen as a puerile task that any reasonably educated person could do; nor are good illustrators attracted to the field.

This uninspiring situation accounts for the slow development of Singaporean children's fiction. A commendable effort was made by Chia Hearn Chek with the Moongate Collection series (1972) of folk tales from around the world. While the illustrations by Dwan Sham Mei are impressive, the stories themselves tend to be rather tedious. Although the collection was well received and generated considerable publicity, it did not manage to give children's book publishing the impetus it badly needed.

The 1980s continued to see the market dominated by 'useful' reading material, such as stories to teach children moral values, retellings of folk tales (often unimaginative) to teach cultural values, and school readers. The unsatisfactory illustrations and the inclusion of comprehension exercises give these readers an uninviting appearance, which is regrettable because some of the stories are well told — for example, *The Smugglers* (1981) by Chuah Ai Meem, a story highlighting the social problems created by the influx of Vietnamese boat refugees to Malaysia. And although the storylines in *Stories from Singapore* (2 vols, 1981) by Wong Wai Chow are not exceptional, the author manages to portray a convincing Singaporeanness in her characterization and settings.

Other writers, however, have been more imaginative. Jessie Wee's *The Adventures of Mooty* (1980) comprises ten picturebooks about a lovable mouse; its popularity established Wee as a significant Singaporean children's writer. She has continued to write books with which Singaporean children can clearly identify. Her other works include *Animal Friends* (1982), *Grandpa's Remedy* (1989), a collection of autobiographical stories depicting life in an extended family in Singapore in the 1950s, and several works published in 1990 as Heinemann Asia supplementary readers — *When Owls Hoot*, *Night of the Pontianak*, *Match of the Year*, *Gorilla on the Loose*, and *The Tail of a Tale*. Sylvia Sherry, a well-known British children's author, successfully depicted a Singaporean setting in her fastmoving and enjoyable story *Street of the Small Night Market* (1966; reprinted 1985), based on her experiences as an expatriate in Singapore for a number of years. A schoolgirl, Ivy Koh, wrote an interesting mystery, *The Tiger's Treasure: A Murder Thriller for Younger Readers* (1989); although readers can easily identify the murderer, Koh creates credible child characters and avoids using them as moralistic mouthpieces. Cecile Parrish's *Charles Kitten and the Story of Beaufort the Supreme Champion* (1989) is a highly readable and well-illustrated picturebook, and *One Big Problem* (1989) by Anthea Gupta and *The Daredevils of Lagoon View* (1990) by Ophelia Ooi are also worth reading.

In 1989 and 1990 numerous books by overseas writers, commissioned by local publishers, were published in Singapore. This worrying trend militates against efforts to move towards the creation of a viable Singaporean children's literature. For this to become a reality, the concerted support of all concerned is needed: authors, illustrators, publishers, teachers, librarians, and, ultimately, the reading public.

KHOO SIM LYN

CHILDREN'S LITERATURE (South Africa)
South African children's literature has developed from three main sources: the indigenous African tradition (mainly an oral tradition until recent years); the Dutch-European tradition (because of the local need for books in the Afrikaans language); and the English tradition.

Until the second half of the twentieth century, English-speaking families in South Africa relied on books from 'home'. Children read books published (and usually written) in England, after the writers' briefest of acquaintances (if any) with Africa. Such titles as *In the Land of the Lion and the Ostrich* (undated), by Gordon Stables, and *The Settler and the Savage* (1877), by R. M. Ballantyne, are typical of the colonial view of South Africa. Books of this period stem from either a hunting, exploration theme or a war theme. **Henry Rider Haggard**'s *King Solomon's Mines* (1885) was spurred by the author's visit to the Sudwala Caves in the eastern Transvaal and is a typical mixture of inventive adventure and snippets of local lore. The various excursions of the British army to South Africa led to a number of pseudo-historical novels, such as *Perils in the Transvaal; A Tale of the Zulu and Boer War* (1888), by the Revd Henry Cadwallader Adams. In all of these books the British explorer or soldier is portrayed as a total gentleman, the Boer as a gallant but undisciplined foe, and the black African as either a 'noble savage' or a dutiful servant, in much the same way Rudyard Kipling viewed the British army and 'the natives' in India.

The first South African children's book to achieve any significantly authentic local detail was *Jock of the Bushveld* (1907) by **Percy Fitzpatrick**. Though the book can be rightly regarded as the beginning of South African indigenous children's literature, it is also firmly colonial in its attitudes. Black wagon drivers are referred to as 'boys' and 'kaffirs', and whites are presented as inherently superior. In the years after the two world wars, South African publishers did not attempt to compete with the quantity of children's books, by such writers as Enid Blyton, that poured out of Britain. African folklore had been recorded (and so preserved) by zealous missionaries, but hardly anything was published locally for children. Indigenous authors of quality, such as Norman Hunter, **Pauline Smith**, and Noel Langley, sent their work to Britain for publication. Jenny Seed used a South African setting for her historical novels, including *The Voice of the Great Elephant* (1968), about Shaka, the Zulu king, and *The Red Dust Soldiers* (1972), about the Anglo-Boer War.

The few indigenous publications of this period are mainly animal or hunting stories: *Kana and his Dog* (1946) by Jessie Hertslet, *Munya the Lion* (1946) by Dorothy Martin, and *Okara the Hunter* (1955) by F. Denver, in which a sort of South African white Tarzan proves himself superior to the natives. South Africa's first picture-book in colour was probably Penny Miller's *The Story of Rory* (1963). The 1960s saw a new interest in African folklore. Phyllis Savory collected voraciously from her oral sources and retold the stories faithfully. The few other children's books published were mostly pale copies of the English colonial tradition: adventure stories of clean-limbed white children, animal tales, showing as yet no thought of conservation, and historical yarns based on the achievements of the Afrikaner and English settlers (or invaders, depending on one's point of view). No stories had a black central character.

Even today, books, and certainly not those of fiction or for relaxation reading, are not a part of the African cultural upbringing.

Dogged by a reputation for poor quality, local books have been slow to improve. The Percy Fitzpatrick Award (for an outstanding South African children's book in English) has only been awarded five times since its inception in 1974: twice to Marguerite Poland for *The Mantis and the Moon* (1979) and *The Wood-Ash Stars* (1983), twice to Lesley Beake for *The Strollers* (1988) and *A Cageful of Butterflies* (1989), and to Dianne Case for *92 Queens Road* (1991).

Probably as a result of an economic upswing, together with interest roused by the first national symposium on children's literature, 1987 saw a sudden surge of new indigenous youth literature. Readers and writers became aware that *all* South Africa's children needed books — not those about cute, furry, European animals, dainty fairies, or white-dominated upper-middle-class households, but books to which South African children could relate and in which white children might meet the black, Coloured, and Indian children from whom they were separated by apartheid laws.

In the 1990s South African children have seen a steady supply of indigenous books portraying a world to which they can relate. The main publishers in this field have been Human and Rousseau, Tafelberg, De Jager-Haum, Daan Retief, Maskew Miller Longman, and David Philip. The most prominent children's authors writing in English are Marguerite Poland, Lesley Beake, Peter Slingsby, Brenda Munitich, Cicely van Straten, and Dianne Hofmeyr, while the best illustrators include Niki Daly, Joan Rankin, Cora Coetzee, Marjorie van Heerden, Alida Bothma, and Ian Lusted.

Although book selectors (for public and school libraries) and educationalists still tend to choose many old 'classics' from the UK, South Africa is at last creating an indigenous children's literature worth considering. There are plenty of stories of friendships across the 'colour bar', such as *The Scar* (1987) by Brenda Munitich, and stories about the squatter camps and the underprivileged urban blacks, such as *Sidwell's Seeds* (1985) by Maretha Maartens and *Serena's Story* (1990) by Lesley Beake. There is constant attention to pollution and the preservation of the environment, as in *Encounters with Wildlife* (1987) by Lynn Hurry. Interest in youth literature is growing: the magazine *Bookchat* (about children's books) enjoys increased support.

The first children's books by black Africans are now appearing and include: *Our Village Bus* (1986) by Maria Mabetoa; *Spotty Dog* (1988) by Gladys Thomas; and *The Boy Who Could Fly* (1991) by Mothobi Mutloatse. In the 'new South Africa' education for all is promised as a high priority. That can only mean more books.

JAY HEALE

Further reading: Isabel Cilliers, ed., *Towards Understanding Children's Literature for Southern Africa* (1988).

CHILDREN'S LITERATURE (South Pacific)
English is a second language for most Pacific children, who have limited access to books, and libraries are poor and confined to urban centres. Despite these difficulties, a group of dedicated writers and illustrators formed during the 1980s to create books in English for local children. While this literature may be modest in quantity and appearance, it is comparable in vigour and originality to the literature being published for children elsewhere in the Commonwealth. The foundations for this writing are the Pacific people's oral traditions and their knowledge of the Bible, together with the work of several generations of expatriate teachers. The catalyst for this literature was a series of creative writing workshops beginning in 1984 and organized by Barbara Moore of the Uni-

versity of the South Pacific, to which established Pacific writers of adult fiction — **Albert Wendt**, **Subramani**, **Satendra Nandan**, Pio Manoa, and **Vilsoni Hereniko** — gave support.

The current interest in recording and dramatizing traditional stories has also led to a desire to see these stories in print and made available to children. *The Wicked Cat* (1991), by Hereniko, is an amusing story for younger children. Traditional stories from Tuvalu have been retold by Maseiga Ionatana and Salilo F. Enele, and from Fiji by Bessie Kingdon. Also from Fiji is Joseph C. Veramu's *The Shark* (1983), an original story for older children reminiscent of Ernest Hemingway's *The Old Man and the Sea* (1952).

Other writers from Fiji include Vanessa Griffen, Sendar Pillay, Sereima Lumelume, and Gwen Deverell, who have written simple, lively stories for younger children, some illustrated by Josefa Uluinaceva and John Robinson. New Zealand Schools' Publications has published a fantasy by Susana Tuisawau and realistic stories about Samoa by Peggy Dunlop and Emma Kruse Va'ai. Aukusitino Tualusea is also writing for children in Samoa, as are Siu Cocker in Tonga and Luhiano Perez in Tokelau.

In Papua New Guinea, writers' workshops have resulted in a number of successful books, although it is difficult to identify any one Papua New Guinean as a children's author. Meanwhile, the work of expatriates Dianne McInnes and Kevin D'Arcy provides inspiration as well as opportunities for such illustrators as Kiri Mimi and Jodam Lambagase.

The production of children's books will probably never be economically viable in the small countries of Oceania. However, by working in English, creative writers are enabling Pacific children to be part of a larger world.

BARBARA MOORE
JANE RICKETTS

Further reading: Institute of Education, The University of the South Pacific, *Tukuni Mada Mai! Towards Children's Literature for the South Pacific* (1987).

CHILDREN'S LITERATURE (West Africa)
The Gambia, Ghana, Nigeria, Sierra Leone
Oral literature in West Africa has existed for centuries in the form of folk tales, myths, legends, proverbs, and riddles. The tales feature animals and human beings, monsters, ogres, ghosts, spirits, and even inanimate objects, usually personified. Frequently, the protagonists in the animal stories are two cunning animals — Ijapa the Tortoise and Anansi the Spider. In traditional societies folk tales were used for socialization, hence each tale has a moral; proverbs were ready-made tools for resolving difficult situations.

West African written children's literature dates from the nineteenth century, when European adventurers who had little knowledge of African culture wrote sensational and highly prejudiced books about Africa for their home audience. These books, which were full of stereotypes and unflattering generalizations about the African bush, were eventually exported to Africa as part of the tools of western education. These included Hugh Lofting's Dr Dolittle series, in which Africans were described as 'coons' and 'savages'.

During the colonial era, from about 1920, a few books written by West African authors, such as **Cyprian Ekwensi**'s *Ikolo the Wrestler* (1947), were published in Europe and by local literature bureaux or missionary presses. Political independence (Ghana, 1957; Nigeria, 1960; Sierra Leone, 1961; Cameroon, 1961; The Gambia, 1965) brought educational expansion, curriculum changes, and an increase in locally produced books, including school supplementary readers, many of which were published by British multinationals such as Oxford University Press, Longman Ltd., Macmillan Ltd., and two local publishers — Pilgrim Books Ltd (Lagos) and Onibonoje Press and Book Industries (Ibadan) which specialized in children's books. More children's books were produced in the 1970s and 1980s, when a number of local children's publishing houses, some of which published both in English and in West African languages, sprang up in the subregion. Such houses include Flora Nwapa and Co (Enugu), Obobo Books (Lagos), West African Book Publishers Limited (Lagos), and Fourth Dimension (Enugu). The bulk of today's written children's literature comes from Nigeria and Ghana, since there is little local publishing in other countries of the subregion (The Gambia, Liberia, and Sierra Leone), because of their small populations and weak economic base.

The cultural alienation experienced by West African children during the colonial era is today being countered by children's writing by such indigenous writers as **Chinua Achebe** (*Chike and the River*, 1966, *How the Leopard Got His Claws*, 1976, with J. Iroaganachi), Peggy Appiah (*The Children of Ananse*, 1968), Meshack Asare (*The Brassman's Secret*, 1981, *Chipo and the Bird on the Hill*, 1984), **Flora Nwapa** (*Mammywater*, 1979, *The Miracle Kittens*, 1980), and Ada Onwu (*Ifeanyi and Obi*, 1984, *Our Granny's Tales*, 1988). Folk-tale collections, of which there are many (Onwu's *Our Granny's Tales* is a representative example), now indicate their ethnic sources, while the presentation tries to capture the liveliness of the traditional oral form, which encourages audience participation.

Folk tales and myths are preponderant in West African children's literature, followed by fiction. There is very little published poetry for children, even though poetry has permeated traditional African life in the form of work and play songs, dirges, praise poems, incantations, and ceremonial chants. However, there is a notable two-volume anthology in English edited by **Mabel Segun** and Neville Grant (*Under the Mango Tree*, 1980) that features poems from all over Africa and the diaspora. Drama fares worse than poetry, with hardly any suitable plays published for children. Works of non-fiction are low on publishers' publishing programmes, although some autobiographies have been published.

Modern West African children's fiction consists largely of adventure stories, many of which have school settings. The influence of European-style treasure hunting and the melodramatic writing of **H. Rider Haggard** and R. L. Stevenson can be discerned in Ekwensi's early works, particularly in *The Passport of Mallam Ilia* (1960), *Juju Rock* (1966), and *Samankwe and the Highway Robbers* (1979). Similarly, school stories are generally patterned after British stories about boarding-school life. The 'X goes to school' stories, such as C. Ade-Ajayi's and M. Crowder's *Akin Goes to School* (1978) and Crowder's and U. Landan's *Sani Goes to School* (1979), have a local slant that shows the premium placed by West Africans on the acquisition of western education as a passport to higher status. Realistic fiction is concerned primarily with character-building; its civic themes and insistence on implicit obedience, respect for elders, honesty, industry, and helpfulness are an indication that many authors attempt to preserve oral traditions and their attendant didacticism.

Unlike Southern and East Africa, where authors write about liberation wars and politics, West African children's writers avoid these topics, even though, for example, a civil war was fought in Nigeria and there have been mini-wars and political and religious riots in various countries of the subregion. Colonialism in West African children's literature is not portrayed in negative terms. Instead, there are nostalgic reminiscences about Empire Day celebrations and other symbols of colonialism. This may be attributed to the fact that no liberation war was ever fought in the subregion, where independence was achieved peacefully.

West African children's stories emphasize action and contain little description. Psychological elements are almost totally absent from the literature, perhaps because Africa is still tradition-directed rather than inner-directed. Nor did authors pay much attention to fantasy until the publication of Cyprian Ekwensi's *Samankwe in the Strange Forest* (1975), Meshack Asare's Noma Award-winning picture-book *The Brassman's Secret*, and James Ebo Whyte's *The Dancing Joromi* (1985).

Cultural heritage is the theme of Asare's picture-book, in which a brass figure comes alive and leads a boy in a search for the meaning of his past. Indeed, the search for identity and the preservation of cultural heritage are the themes of a number of books in English by authors such as J. O. de Graft Hanson, Naiwu Osahon, and Mabel Segun. African beliefs such as taboos, beliefs in spirits and charms, witchcraft, reincarnation, and life after death are featured in a number of children's books. Some authors reaffirm their convictions about African belief systems, while others jettison such beliefs in favour of western views.

Concern for the environment is only just beginning to feature in West African children's books; it may be seen in such picture-books as Segun's *The Twins and the Tree Spirits* (1990). In contrast, tourism-oriented East and Southern Africa, with their game parks, already have many children's stories about the environment.

The 1970s and 1980s witnessed the gradual indigenization of West African children's literature, which is now largely authored, illustrated, edited, and published by West Africans. The quality of illustration has not yet matched that of text, but efforts are being made to improve this. Illustrators' workshops, co-ordinated by voluntary children's book organizations such as the Ghana and Sierra Leone Library boards, Ghana's Children's Literature Foundation, and the Children's Literature Association of Nigeria, are beginning to yield results. The *Journal of African Children's and Youth Literature* (formerly *Journal of African Children's Literature*) is an important publication in the field, as is *African Youth Literature Today and Tomorrow* (1986), the report of an international symposium organized by the International Youth Library.

MABEL SEGUN

Further reading: Nancy Schmidt, *Children's Books on Africa and Their Authors: An Annotated Bibliography* (1975); Nancy Schmidt, *Supplement to Children's Books on Africa and Their Authors: An Annotated Bibliography* (1979); Nancy Schmidt, *Children's Fiction About Africa in English* (1981); Osayinwense Osa, *Foundation Essays on Children's and Youth Literature* (1987).

Cameroon

The earliest known children's story published by a Cameroonian is Sankie Maimo's *Adventuring with Jaja* (1962; reprinted several times), a tale of adolescent individualism and romantic dreams. Some of the most significant work in this genre has been done by Kenjo Jumbam, whose *Children's Verse and Stories* (1979) was designed to supplant imported fare for schoolchildren with indigenously inspired rhymes and stories, using forms and aesthetic elements and mythology transported into English from artistic traditions native to Grasslands people in the North West of Cameroon. Jonas N. Ndah's *Around the Fire* (1988) supplies schoolchildren with other artfully cast traditional materials new to English rendition. Another source of unusual stories in English is the Bamenda and Buea based Association for Creative Teaching's ('ACT') series of experiments, in which children gather stories in their home languages and villages for translation, gestetner publication, and dissemination throughout the entire anglophone zone.

STEPHEN H. ARNOLD

CHIMOMBO, STEVE (1945–)

Malawian dramatist, short-story writer

He was born in the old colonial capital of Zomba, Malawi, and after attending Zomba Catholic Secondary School earned a BA from the University of Malawi, a postgraduate diploma in English as a second language at the University of Wales, and an MA and his doctorate in education from Columbia University, USA. Currently professor of English at Chancellor College, Malawi, he has written poetry, plays, short stories, and criticism. One of Malawi's most productive and versatile writers, Chimombo strenuously promotes the development of a modern local literary tradition. He is founding editor of *Wasi Writer*, a journal for local authors.

Chimombo's first full-length play, *The Rainmaker* (1978), became a local classic virtually overnight and was followed by *Wachiona Ndani?* (1983). He is best known, however, for his verse, which has won British Broadcasting Corporation and Penguin publisher's awards; his *Napolo Poems* (1987), containing his finest work, was nominated for the Commonwealth Poetry Prize. *Python Python* (1992) is an epic poem. Chimombo has also published a short novel, *The Basket Girl* (1990).

Chimombo's verse displays two broad lines of growth — one consciously modernist (he frankly acknowledges a debt to T. S. Eliot), the other imaginatively traditionalist, using the semantic fluidity, symbolic resonance, and ready-made structures of oral texts. His creation of a poetic-symbolic world fashioned from narratives about the legendary figure Napolo has been especially fruitful, a tapping of oral tradition not unlike **Wole Soyinka**'s exploration of Yoruba texts about the god Ogun. At his best, Chimombo is a poet of marked intensity and subtlety, whose work seems designed to help him and his society come to grips with life in an oppressive political dispensation.

Chimombo's critical work includes *A Bibliography of Oral Literature in Malawi: 1860–1986* (1987) and *Malawian Oral Literature: The Aesthetics of Indigenous Arts* (1988).

ADRIAN ROSCOE

Further reading: Adrian Roscoe and Mpalive-Hangson Msiska, 'Steve Chimombo and the voice of irony', *The Quiet Chameleon: Modern Poetry from Central Africa* by Adrian Roscoe and Mpalive-Hangson Msiska (1992).

CHING, FRANK (1940–)

Hong Kong journalist, historical writer

Born in Hong Kong, he received his secondary education in Catholic missionary schools there. Ching left for university studies in the USA at the age of nineteen, obtaining a BA in English from Fordham University, an MA in philosophy from New York University, and, with a Ford Foundation Fellowship, a certificate in advanced international reporting from Columbia University, New York. Ching has specialized in the coverage of China for almost two decades, first with *The New York Times* and later with *The Wall Street Journal.*

In 1979, in the wake of the establishment of diplomatic relations between the USA and the People's Republic of China, Ching was named Beijing correspondent of *The Wall Street Journal* and became one of only four American newspaper reporters to be based in China since 1949. He remained in Beijing until 1983, when he left the newspaper to devote himself to writing. Based in Hong Kong, Ching writes a weekly political column for *The South China Morning Post.*

Ching has published four books and numerous articles on Chinese and Hong Kong history and politics. For general readers, his most interesting book is the fascinating and lucid *Ancestors: 900 Years in the Life of a Chinese Family* (1988). In this book Ching meticulously traces his family history, going back thirty-three generations on his father's side and thirty-four on his mother's. His parents are distantly related, their ancestors descended from Qin Guan, a prominent poet of the Sang Dynasty (AD 960–1279).

MIMI CHAN

CHINODYA, SHIMMER (1957–)

Zimbabwean poet, novelist

He was born in Zimbabwe and educated at Goromonzi High School and the University of Zimbabwe. He now works in the ministry of education in Harare. Chinodya has published three novels — *Dew in the Morning* (1982), *Farai's Girls* (1984), and *Harvest of Thorns* (1989). His poetry has appeared in several local magazines and anthologies; for example, 'An Old Man at his Death', 'Recollection', and 'Wild Mushroom' appear in *New Writing in Rhodesia* (1976), edited by T. O. McLoughlin.

Chinodya's work reveals a recurrent interest in rural life, the process of growing up, and the relationship between the past and present. *Dew in the Morning* depicts the rural physical and cultural landscape in a manner reminiscent of Camara Laye's *The African Child* (1959, translated by James Kirkup; Laye's original work was entitled *L'enfant noir*). Chinodya's interest in the country is also evident in poems such as 'African Grass', in which the poet invests the savanna grassland with Edenic attributes without giving in, however, to the temptation to romanticize: the poem ends with a meditation on the ephemeral nature of all beauty.

In *Farai's Girls* Chinodya addresses the issue of personal development. Through his relationships, some successful and others less so, with various women, the protagonist achieves insight into the nature of love. The interest in the psychology of personal development is continued in *Harvest of Thorns*, which explores the effect of the Zimbabwe war of liberation on teenage combatants who, while contributing to something of great social magnitude and requiring the resources of adult experience, must undergo typical teenage experiences. As a family saga, the novel exemplifies how the past can shape an individual's consciousness.

In his technical competence, in his ability to tell a story well, and in his conceptual breadth, Chinodya exhibits a mastery that has not yet received sufficient international critical attention.

MPALIVE-HANGSON MSISKA

Further reading: Adrian Roscoe and Mpalive-Hangson Msiska, *The Quiet Chameleon: Modern Poetry from Central Africa* (1992); Flora Veit-Wild, *Teachers, Preachers, Non-Believers* (1992).

CHINWEIZU (1943–)

Nigerian poet, critic

Born in Eluama Isuikwuato, eastern Nigeria, he attended Government College, Afikpo, Nigeria, studied mathematics and philosophy at the Massachusetts Institute of Technology (MIT) in the USA, and received his MA (1975) and Ph.D. (1976) at the State University of New York at Buffalo, USA. He was a Rockefeller Research Fellow in Environmental Economics at MIT and an associate professor (1978–9) at San Jose State University, USA.

Chinweizu came to prominence with the publication of *The West and the Rest of Us* (1975), a book reminiscent of Frantz Fanon's *The Wretched of the Earth* (1961) and Walter Rodney's *How Europe Underdeveloped Africa* (1972) but written in a more visceral and polemical language. *Toward the Decolonization of African Literature* (1980), co-authored with Onwuchekwa Jemie and Ihechukwu Madubuike, further established his reputation as a controversial polemicist and sets out to chastise the bulk of modern African writers, especially poets, for technical obscurity and ideological subservience to the west.

Chinweizu's poetry collections include *Energy Crisis and Other Poems* (1978) and *Invocations and Admonitions* (1986), the manuscript for which won the **Association of Nigerian Authors**' poetry prize in 1985. Although his poetry focuses on themes as diverse as the moral corruption of western societies, the horrors of the Nigerian Civil War, and the often-tragic fate of the visionary in Africa, Chinweizu has always been preoccupied with pan-Africanism and the need to popularize the African contribution to civilization. In his uncompromising indictment of Caucasian and Arab plunderers of Africa, he recalls the vision of **Ayi Kwei Armah**. Stylistically, his poetry is reminiscent of **Okot p'Bitek**'s neo-traditional directness and is consistent with the literary prescriptions proffered in *Toward the Decolonization of African Literature*.

FUNSO AIYEJINA

CHIPASULA, FRANK (1949–)

Malawian poet

He was born in northern Malawi and received his secondary education at Malosa Anglican Mission School. He began studies for a BA in English at the University of Malawi, completing the degree in exile at the University of Zambia. After receiving an MA from Yale University, USA, and a Ph.D. from Brown University, USA, Chipasula became associate professor of Black Studies at the University of Nebraska, USA.

With *Visions and Reflections* (1972), Chipasula was the first Malawian to have a book of verse published. His poetry collection *O Earth, Wait for Me* (1984) received an honourable mention in the 1985 Noma Awards for publishing in Africa. Other volumes include the long poem *Nightwatcher, Nightsong* (1986), *When My Brothers Come Home: Poems from Central and Southern Africa* (1985), which he edited, and *Whispers in the Wings* (1991).

The most outspoken of Malawi's modern poets, Chipasula grew swiftly to intellectual and poetic maturity in the hothouse atmosphere of front-line Zambia during the height of the freedom struggles in Zimbabwe and South Africa. The resulting changes between his first book of verse and *Nightwatcher, Nightsong* are remarkable. His development, in part, is a change in tone — from reticence to screaming outrage, for, as he puts it: 'I had almost choked on a silence that is familiar to our people.' Chipasula's later work has been influenced by the example of Black American and South American writers. He stresses the alerting power of literature in an age of tyranny, and the poet's priestly task of bearing witness when good and evil do battle. His verse carries some of the most powerful attacks on the Banda regime, often using imagery of nightmarish intensity. It is significant that Chipasula's central figure in *Nightwatcher, Nightsong*, to whom the poems are addressed, is, in Chipasula's words, 'a composite metaphorical figure of vigilance through a dark season'.

Chipasula has written radio plays and some fiction. His most mature verse appears in *Whispers in the Wings*.

ADRIAN ROSCOE

Further reading: Adrian Roscoe and Mpalive-Hangson Msiska, 'Frank Chipasula and the voice of exile', *The Quiet Chameleon: Modern Poetry from Central Africa* by Adrian Roscoe and Mpalive-Hangson Msiska (1992).

CLARK, J. P. See **BEKEDEREMO**

CLARK, MANNING (1915–91)

Australian historian

Born in Sydney, Australia, he was educated at the University of Melbourne, Australia, and at Oxford University, England. Appointed professor of history at Canberra University College (later merged with the Australian National University) in 1949, he fostered a school of historians who have followed him in elaborating the many facets of Australia's European past. With **Geoffrey Blainey**, he can be said to have largely created the contemporary audience for Australian history. (See **Historical Writing**, Australia.)

Clark's work includes essays, short stories, and a sociological travel narrative, *Meeting Soviet Man* (1960). His documentary collections and his *A Short History of Australia* (1963) have been influential in shaping the perceptions of generations of teachers and students. Together with A. G. L. Shaw and Lloyd Robson, Clark was of the first generation of Australian historians to confront squarely the fact of the nation's convict beginning. This focus, which gave a particular emphasis to his instinctive sympathy for the downtrodden, was a strong influence in much of his subsequent work — *In Search of Henry Lawson* (1987), for example.

However, it is for his massive six-volume *A History of Australia* (1962–87) that Clark is most renowned. Showing some affinities with such nineteenth-century nationalist historians as Thomas Macaulay and George Bancroft, he traces in this work the transference of European civilization to Australia and the development in the new continent of a distinctive variety thereof. With its central subject being the interplay of the three great European streams of Catholicism, Protestantism, and Enlightenment rationality and liberalism, Clark's *History* is also notable for the sense of bleak failure it conveys, whether of individual lives, of the European treatment of the Aborigines, of the struggle to come to grips with an alien environment, or, especially, of the efforts in the second half of the nineteenth century to forge a new society free of the entrenched privilege and class divisions of the old one. In the end, for Clark, the darkness in the human heart involves, as much as any innate depravity, the mind's inability to know fully the nature of the past, a failure on which he meditates much in his autobiographical volumes *The Puzzles of Childhood* (1989) and *The Quest for Grace* (1990).

ALAN FROST

CLARKE, A. M. (1912–)

Trinidadian poet, novelist, short-story writer, dramatist

Born in Port of Spain, Trinidad, his work first appeared in the 1930s during the radical 'awakening' of the country's literary movement. Although he pursued careers in teaching and law, he has remained an active and prolific writer. **Derek Walcott** has called him 'one of the industrious survivors of the Trinidad literary movement'.

Also a biographer and essayist, Clarke published his first collection of short stories — *Ma Mamba and Other Stories*, co-authored with E. A. Carr — in 1939. His other publications include: the short-story collections *Revolution at the Grassroots* (1976) and *Collected Short Stories* (with R. C. Brown, 1938); poetry — *Burnt Bush* (with **H. M. Telemaque**, 1947), *Wheels Within Wheels* (1975), *Ballads of Haile Selassie and the Rastafarians and Other Verses* (1983), *Verses for Emancipation: a Tribute to Dr. Eric Williams* (1986), and *Little Flames of Freedom* (1990) — and his only novel, *Caribbean Coup* (1979).

Clarke belongs to the early twentieth-century search for an 'authentic' Caribbean literature. His recognition that 'it was not enough' for local writers to settle for a romantic engagement with the '*poui* and *immortelle*' or to replicate foreign cultures, landscapes, and forms of English literary traditions echoes the dissatisfaction of writers such as **C. L. R. James**, Albert Gomes, and **Alfred Mendes** who were in the vanguard of the nationalistic Caribbean literary movement.

Clarke's writing, like that of Telemaque, is characterized by patriotic celebration of local life, landscape, folklore, and people. However, his contemplation of life tends always to the universal, as in his verse dramas, including 'Road to Glory' (premièred 1964), *Green Magic: A Folktale in Verse* (privately published in 1963, premièred in 1978), and *House of Love* (produced and privately published in 1967). Clarke's recurrent concern is with the condition of humanity in an elusive world where the passage of time seldom brings the desired understanding and security.

JENNIFER RAHIM

Further reading: Jennifer Rahim, 'A. M. Clarke: the contribution of a literary pioneer', *The New Voices* 17 (1989).

CLARKE, AUSTIN (1934–)

Canadian/Barbadian novelist, short-story writer

Born in Barbados, the West Indies, he attended two of the best schools on the island — Combermere and Harrison College — before proceeding to the University of Toronto, Canada. Clarke later settled in Canada where, after seven novels, three collections of short stories, a volume of autobiography, and varied work as a journalist, critic, and broadcaster, he is regarded as the country's leading black writer. Two novels, *Survivors of the Crossing* (1964) and *Amongst Thistles and Thorns* (1965), and the autobiographical *Growing Up Stupid under the Union Jack* (1980) record the author's early memories of colonial Barbados, while his novel *The Prime Minister* (1977) exposes corruption and chaos in his homeland after independence from Britain. But the bulk of Clarke's writing considers black experience in Canada through such collections of stories as *When He Was Free and Young and He Used to Wear Silks* (1971), *When Women Rule* (1985), *Nine Men Who Laughed* (1986), and an ambitious trilogy of novels — *The Meeting Point* (1967), *Storm of Fortune* (1971), and *The Bigger Light* (1975) — set in Toronto.

Clarke's black immigrants from the Caribbean encounter unemployment, racial discrimination, and police brutality, not to mention the more inward effects of alienation and exile in an urban, industrial environment whose culture, habits, and customs are dominated by inhibition, calculation, selfishness, and exploitation. Yet their less inhibited ways promote tolerance and resilience in Clarke's immigrants and help them to survive cultural conflict.

Clarke reveals profound insight into the character, manners, and aspirations of his Caribbean countrymen, and remarkable skill in reproducing the pungent, ribald, idiomatic richness of their speech. These features enable him to produce comic writing that entertains while it brandishes a critical but not satirical edge on contemporary social, cultural, and ethnic issues.

Clarke has also achieved some popularity, not to say notoriety, as an outspoken public commentator and lecturer. But the peak of his achievement remains his Toronto trilogy, which offers a comprehensive portrait of blacks, not only in Toronto but in Canada as a whole.

FRANK M. BIRBALSINGH

CLARKE, GEORGE ELLIOTT (1960–)

Canadian poet

He was born in the black community of Windsor, Nova Scotia, Canada, and is a descendant of black Loyalists who immigrated to Canada from the USA in the late eighteenth century. Clarke grew up in Halifax, Nova Scotia, and earned an Honours English degree (1984) at the University of Waterloo, Ontario, where he was involved in forming the Creative Writing Collective. Returning to Nova Scotia in 1985, he became a social worker in the Annapolis Valley, an experience that brought him into contact with rural blacks, whose stories and voices became incorporated in his writing. Clarke received his MA (1989) from Dalhousie University, writing his thesis on **Michael Ondaatje**, whose experiments with multiple media for storytelling and whose fusion of visual and acoustic elements of language he admires. His Ph.D. thesis (Queen's University, Canada) is a comparative study of modern and contemporary English Canadian and African-American poetry and poetics.

A self-consciously political writer, with extensive knowledge of black literature and history,

Clarke is fascinated by the possibilities of vernacular. He is influenced by various writers of the long poem form and, notably, by Jean Toomer's *Cane* (1923), which revealed to him the opportunities of interweaving genres, and by the contemporary black American writer Rita Dove.

Clarke's first collection, *Saltwater Spirituals and Deeper Blues* (1983), gives primacy to the lyric. His second volume, *Whylah Falls* (1990), which won the 1991 Ottawa Independent Writers' Archibald Lampman Award, mixes verse forms, narrative, drama, and photographs to explore the relation of language to popular and personal memory and to desire. The writing act has its signature in the text via 'X', the poet, and is thus implicated in the duplicity of the 'erotic and morbid'.

Clarke has edited the two-volume *Fire on Water: An Anthology of Black Nova Scotian Writing* (vol. 1, 1991; vol. 2, 1992).

ANDREW STUBBS

Further reading: Dan Bortolotti, 'The vernacular muse of George Elliott Clarke', *Books in Canada* 7 (1991); George Elliott Clarke, 'Discovering *Whylah Falls*', *Quarry* 4 (1991); M. Travis Lane, 'Maximalist poetry', *The Fiddlehead* 72 (1992).

CLARKE, MARCUS (1846–81)

Australian novelist, short-story writer, essayist, editor

An only child, he was born in Kensington, London, England, and raised by his widowed father. He was educated at Highgate, where he developed a close friendship with Cyril Hopkins and Gerard Manley Hopkins. After the collapse of his father's health and finances Clarke immigrated to Australia in 1863. In Melbourne he worked in the Bank of Australasia before taking up station work in Victoria's Wimmera district. It was at this time that he began writing regularly for the Melbourne press.

Clarke was the pre-eminent man of letters of his day. He serialized most of his novels in the colonial press prior to their publication in book form. His novels are *Long Odds* (1868–9, 1869), in collaboration with G. A. Walstab, *His Natural Life* (1870–2, 1874), *'Twixt Shadow and Shine* (1875), and *Chidiock Tichbourne or the Catholic Conspiracy* (1874–5, 1893). Clark also published three collections of short stories, *Holiday Peak and Other Tales* (1873), *Four Stories High* (1877), and *The Mystery of Major Mollineux and Human Repetends* (1881, published posthumously); a collection of historical essays, *Old Tales of a Young Country* (1871); a group of essays, *Civilisation Without Delusion* (1880); and a collection of his journalism, *The Peripatetic Philosopher* (1886). He edited the *Colonial Monthly* (1868–9), *Humbug* (1869–70), and the *Australian Journal* (1870–1) and wrote plays, sketches, pantomimes, and the text of an opera for the Melbourne theatre.

Despite the phenomenal variety of Clarke's literary activity, he is most famous for the convict melodrama *His Natural Life*. The novel represents a 200,000-word condensation of the 370,000-word serial published in the *Australian Journal* from March 1870 to June 1872. A number of versions of *His Natural Life* have been printed and reprinted in a variety of countries, and there have been numerous stage, film, and television versions produced in Australia and overseas. The novel follows the fortunes of Richard Devine, the disinherited heir to a vast shipping fortune who changes his name to Rufus Dawes when he is wrongly convicted and transported for the murder of Lord Bellasis, his mother's lover and his biological father. Clarke meticulously details the worst features of the convict system and incorporates into his novel much of the historical research that went in to *Old Tales of a Young Country*. *His Natural Life* has often been criticized for its concentration upon an extreme case and for its melodramatic form; however, **Michael Wilding** has argued for the psychological depth of its study of the effects of the penal system on character. *His Natural Life* can be compared to other nineteenth-century convict novels such as Balzac's *Splendour and Misery of Courtesans* (1839–47), Dumas' *The Count of Monte Cristo* (1844–5), Reade's *It is Never too Late to Mend* (1856), Dostoevsky's *The House of the Dead* (1860), and Hugo's *Les Misérables* (1862). Clarke's historical-literary work in *Old Tales of a Young Country* and *His Natural Life*, like the work of Cooper, Hawthorne, and Harte in America, was important in demonstrating that the colonies possessed the historical background required to produce and sustain a literature of merit.

Despite Clarke's talent and energy, he was continually under financial pressure. When antagonistic political interests thwarted his attempt to become public librarian in 1881, he was bankrupted for the second time. Clarke collapsed with pleurisy and died soon after.

CHRISTOPHER LEE

Further reading: Michael Wilding, ed., *Marcus Clarke* (1976).

CLEARY, JON (1917–)

Australian novelist, short-story writer

Born in Sydney, Australia, he left school at the age of fifteen and served from 1940 to 1945 with the Australian Army in the Middle East and Papua New Guinea. Cleary started writing short stories during the war, and when his first novel, *You Can't See Round Corners* (1947), won a major award, he became a full-time writer. His thirty-nine novels and two collections of short stories have a wide overseas readership, and several have been filmed or televised. He has written plays and screenplays and in 1944 was co-winner of the first prize for the Australian Broadcasting Commission's National Play Award. In 1977 Cleary was expected to sell 110,000 paperbacks every year in Australia alone, and in 1984 he could reasonably expect a run of 20,000 hardback issues of each novel, followed by 50,000 paperbacks, translated into eleven languages. He describes himself as 'an Irish Australian Catholic with a Protestant work ethic' and writes about fifteen hundred words a day. He may read and travel for two months to research a book and spend six months writing it.

Cleary's output is varied, but he is best known as a writer of crime fiction, particularly for the series of seven novels featuring Sydney police detective Scobie Malone, which appeared in two bursts: 1966 to 1973 — *The High Commissioner* (1966), *Helga's Web* (1970), *Ransom* (1973); and 1987 onwards — *Dragons at the Party* (1987), *Now and Then, Amen* (1988), *Babylon South* (1989), *Murder Song* (1990). (See also **Crime and Mystery Fiction**, Australia.) All except the first and third of these are set principally in Sydney and feature sharp but humorous satire directed at politicians and silvertails. Earlier, Cleary's reputation rested mainly on *The Sundowners* (1952), which features an itinerant outback family and was made into a popular 'Australian' film (it was an American production); the film of Cleary's adventure novel *High Road to China* (1977) also boosted his sales. Cleary can be compared with Australian novelist **Morris West**: both often feature Roman Catholics and Catholic themes — Cleary's *Peter's Pence* (1974) won the Edgar Allan Poe Award for best crime novel — but where West favours the blockbuster, Cleary favours the crime and adventure novel with occasional forays into the mainstream.

MICHAEL J. TOLLEY

CLIFF, MICHELLE (1946–)

Jamaican novelist, poet

Born in Kingston, Jamaica, she spent her early years in Jamaica and the USA, and was educated there and in England. She has taught and lectured at many colleges and universities and has worked as editor, publisher, and researcher. She resides in

California.

Little critical and scholarly attention has been paid to Cliff's work. Her novels, *Abeng* (1984) and *No Telephone to Heaven* (1987), are widely read, but her prose and poetry in *Claiming an Identity They Taught Me to Despise* (1980), *The Land of Look Behind* (1985), and *Bodies of Water* (1990) represent some of Cliff's best and most powerful writing.

Although Cliff has spent most of her adult life outside Jamaica, she writes from a Jamaican consciousness and sensibility. Her work addresses the personal, social, and political realities associated with growing up under colonial domination. A preoccupation with the question of identity is the central focus of all her work. She cites 'colourism' or colour prejudice among Jamaicans of African descent as one of the primary legacies of colonialism. One of Cliff's recurring characters is the 'tragic mulatto', or the light-skinned black woman who has difficulty finding her place in a predominantly black culture where white skin is viewed as both blessing and curse.

Most of Cliff's work is autobiographical. *Abeng* and *No Telephone to Heaven* trace the development of Clare Savage, a character with whom Cliff strongly identifies. She has said that Clare's life represents her own in experience rather than fact. Sexual identity is an understated theme in Cliff's work; she seems only to suggest that her homosexuality has been yet another source of her alienation from her community. Cliff offers a unique perspective on racism, sexism, and colonialism; hers is a voice worth hearing.

MARGARET KENT BASS

CLIFT, CHARMIAN (1923–69)

Australian novelist, short-story writer, essayist

Born in Kiama, New South Wales, Australia, she began her journalistic career on the Melbourne *Argus* and subsequently wrote novels, short stories, and newspaper columns and features. She collaborated with her husband **George Johnston** on three novels — *High Valley* (1949), *The Big Chariot* (1953), and *The Sponge Divers* (1955) — and some of her short fiction was posthumously collected with Johnston's in *Strong Man from Piraeus and Other Stories* (1984).

Clift's individual novels are *Walk to the Paradise Gardens* (1960) and *Honour's Mimic* (1964). *Mermaid Singing* (1956) and *Peel Me a Lotus* (1959) are accounts of life on the Greek islands; they were called 'subtly, romantically, acerbically beautiful' by her son, Martin Johnston. *Images in Aspic* (1965) and *The World of Charmian Clift* (1970) are collections of newspaper essays. Johnston commented on her 'curious learning' (including Shakespeare, Donne, Burton, Aubrey, Browne, and Sterne) and her 'love of the long, complicated yet ringing sentence'. She appears as Cressida in her husband's David Meredith trilogy, but she is not characterized as a writer. In the trilogy as in life she seems often to have been regarded as the Zelda to Johnston's Scott Fitzgerald. She adapted Johnston's *My Brother Jack* for television.

Clift's two novels, both with long gestations, deal with passion that longs for an outlet before it is able to express itself in love or in violence, and with the taunting jealousy and self-regarding lechery of husbands. *Walk to the Paradise Gardens*, which is the more understated and witty, is set in an Australian beachside holiday resort; one of its themes is an architect's querulousness at not being at the top of his profession; another is concern for style and intimations of vulgarity. *Honour's Mimic*, more journalistic in its impressionism, is set on a Greek island.

Troubled, like her husband, by heavy drinking (and the fierce domestic fights resulting from it), by a career, interrupted as it had been by childbearing, that seemed to have brought her back to journalism, and concerned for the fading of her remarkable beauty, Clift committed suicide at the height of her journalistic career.

NESS SHANNON

CLOETE, STUART (1897–1976)

South African novelist, short-story writer

Born in Paris, France, of South African parents, he was educated in the UK and served in the British Army during and after the First World War. Cloete first visited South Africa in the mid-1920s and there attempted to establish himself as a rancher and farmer; thereafter he lived intermittently in South Africa and Britain. He died in Cape Town, South Africa.

Cloete's first novel, *Turning Wheels* (1937), coinciding with the centennial celebrations of the Great Trek, raised a furore that reached government levels because of its racy treatment of the Boer pioneers. Its banning — it was the first of several of Cloete's works to be so treated — ensured large sales worldwide. (The ban was not withdrawn until 1974.)

Most of Cloete's historical novels contain a now-familiar amalgam of imaginary and 'real' characters acting in emotionally charged situations of conflict, whether racial or sexual. *The Mask* (1957), a novel of maturity, is representative of Cloete's 'African' fiction (a minority of his works are set elsewhere) in its focus on a young, heroic Cape Afrikaner protagonist tested in love and war on the ever-advancing Transvaal frontier: 'This was Africa, where one thing preyed on another. Where the law was eat or be eaten, where only the fit and strong survived whether they were men or beasts.' Other conflicts treated by Cloete involve British and Boers in *The Hill of Doves* (1941), the early nineteenth-century Karoo frontier in *Watch for the Dawn* (1939), and the voortrekkers again in *The Fiercest Heart* (1960).

Cloete's short stories appeared in journals such as *The Saturday Evening Post*, *Esquire*, and *Cosmopolitan*. His collections of short stories include *The Soldiers' Peaches* (1959), *The Silver Trumpet* (1961), *The Looking Glass* (1963), *The Honey Bird* (1964), *The Writing on the Wall* (1968), and *The Company with the Heart of Gold* (1973). He also campaigned for international acceptance of 'the South African solution', which, in 'The Conspiracy' (in *White Africans Are Also People*, 1966, edited by **Sarah Gertrude Millin**), Cloete claimed 'is so far merely a step in the specific direction of separate development for which the white man is prepared to make great sacrifices'. (See also **Popular Writing**, South Africa.)

JOHN A. STOTESBURY

CLOUTS, SYDNEY DAVID (1926–82)

South African poet

Born in Cape Town, South Africa, the first of four children of Philip and Feodora Clouts, he matriculated from the South African College School, then volunteered for military service (1944–5). He obtained a BA in law and philosophy from the University of Cape Town and in 1952 married Marjorie Leftwich, with whom he had three sons. Clouts' poetry began to appear in South African magazines during the 1950s, and in 1961 he departed for the UK to become a literary agent. Some of his poems were broadcast by the British Broadcasting Corporation in 1965, and in 1966 his collection *One Life* was published in South Africa. Clouts returned there in 1969 to take up a research fellowship at Rhodes University, Grahamstown, and was later awarded an MA. He became a librarian on his return to London, England, and worked as such until his death. A *Collected Poems*, edited by Clouts' wife and brother, was published posthumously in 1984.

Clouts' prominence in South African poetry is assured, but controversial. Critical commentary has ranged from **J. M. Coetzee**'s description of him as South Africa's 'purest poetic talent' to both Ian

Glenn's reading of Clouts' poetry as 'blinkered' because it tends to ignore social issues and the argument of Glenn, Stephen Watson, and Susan Joubert that it deals with such concerns from a position of naïve romanticism. These ideological difficulties are compounded by what for many is an occasional, unnecessary impenetrability in Clouts' poetry, often the result of the poet's attempt to reduce language to the barest minimum. Clouts himself did not deny this impenetrability, but, as with those who admire his work, felt that linguistic and ideational compression are among its strong points. Clouts' work facilitates a multivalency, a sense of dramatic immediacy, and a philosophical depth seldom encountered in South African poetry. The poems are often prosodically experimental and to some may at times seem ostentatious; however, they avoid flamboyancy by the weight of ideas offered and by the emotional control exercised.

Romantic and metaphysical concerns play a large part in Clouts' aesthetic. His effort is to encounter what in the poem 'Intimate Lighting' (in *Collected Poems*) he calls the 'obstinate dusks and rains' of ontology, epistemology, and their correlative, language. The influence, among others, of the pre-Socratic philosophers inspires an attempt to bridge the gap between subject and object and to jettison the Platonism and Cartesianism that in western thought have led to the dichotomy between the two. Unity of being is an important, even quasi-religious, goal and Clouts, for the most part, seeks a oneness between the self and nature. 'A Pool for the Image', the opening poem in *Collected Poems*, is suggestive of much of his later writing:

A pool for the image,
a cool image of sun.
Desiring more than reflection,
What shall I take?
Flowerstem, clod, or a bouncing stone?
A plain round pebble is best.
The rings glance backward to their rest.

Round, round, round.
Bright heaven, lap the ground.

The rejection of Platonic 'reflection' in favour of the ordinary tangible pebble is a valorization, in the manner of the phenomenologists, of the thing in itself. The pool is required to give meaning to the image, not vice versa. With this goes a scepticism about the ultimate value of those rational processes ('reflection') that deny the Blakean possibility of the eternal inhabiting the temporal. The pebble assumes a symbolic force that is Coleridgean, embodying rather than depicting. The elaborate conceit developed from 'rings' seems to insist on the possibility of language containing metaphysical realities and facilitating something of the unity sought.

To many this is a naïve romanticism, and some have suggested that Clouts himself became disillusioned with it during his career, to the extent of abandoning writing altogether. Some of the later poems emphasize sound and rhythm over image and use personae other than the poet, as if Clouts were becoming more tentative. The oeuvre as a whole does not support such a reading, however. Fundamentally, the poet wants the world to speak for itself and he wants to participate in that speech. The difficulty of achieving this generates an ongoing theme in the poems, depicted most often through the idea of darkness, blackness, or the motif of the journey into darkness. This darkness relates, among other things, to the epistemological, the spiritual, the psychological, and the existential.

Clouts is modernist in his concern with these issues; he leans towards the postmodern in his awareness of language's opacity, but is romantic in his insistence (like a Keatsian 'negative capability') on the value of existing *in* darkness. Perception is fraught with darkness — 'At the summit of perception / a blackness starts to rise' ('Prince Henry the Navigator', *Collected Poems*); so too is language — 'One word is too many; many, too few' ('Residuum', *Collected Poems*), and even inner being — '[the eye] must not look within, / . . . / flat is the world [it would] find: / a row of wooden rooftops / that can easily topple / and bring the heart down / and bring down the mind' ('Within', *Collected Poems*). True discovery demands the recognition of these difficulties and even the willingness to reject rational, largely subjective frames of knowledge in favour of an encounter with 'thingbedded' reality. From this perspective one can begin to 'listen amongst the particles' and 'enter the quick grain' to find that 'everything is first' ('Residuum'). The pre-Socratic and romantic ideal of unity can be attained, but only with the realization that the journey towards attainment will never cease.

KEVIN GODDARD

Further reading: *English in Africa 2* (1984), special issue on Sydney Clouts; Susan Joubert, 'The unresolved shibboleth: Sydney Clouts and the problems of an African poetry', *Theoria* 75 (1990); Stephen Watson, 'Sydney Clouts and the limits of romanticism', *Selected Essays 1980–1990* (1990).

COETZEE, JOHN MAXWELL (1940–)

South African novelist, critic

He was born in Cape Town, South Africa, and while the name 'Coetzee' dates from the Dutch *vryburgers* of the late seventeenth century, his parents were not model nationalists. Although a Protestant, Coetzee attended an English-medium Catholic high school in Cape Town. After taking higher degrees in English and mathematics at the University of Cape Town (MA, 1963), he moved in the 1960s to England, where he worked as a computer programmer. In 1965 he moved to the USA as a Fulbright scholar, earning a Ph.D. in linguistics (1969) at the University of Texas at Austin. Turning down jobs in Hong Kong and Canada, Coetzee taught for two years at the State University of New York in Buffalo, USA. Unable to extend his visa any further, he returned to his native country in 1971, taking up a position in the English department at the University of Cape Town, where he has remained and is now Arderne Professor of English. Coetzee has won several major local and international awards, including the Booker-McConnell and Jerusalem prizes, the Prix Femina Etranger, and the *Sunday Express* Book of the Year Award.

Coetzee began writing novels after a varied apprenticeship. His literary scholarship, especially, is close to the surface of his fiction. His early critical studies include dissertations on Ford Madox Ford and Samuel Beckett, essays on stylistics, Barthesian forays into popular culture, and studies in translation. *White Writing: On the Culture of Letters in South Africa* (1988) is a collection of his essays on the ideological and discursive frames in colonial discourse about Southern Africa; in several of these essays the guiding spirit is Michel Foucault. Later criticism is on metropolitan writers, on the postmodernist Dutch poet Gerrit Achterberg, on the semantics of time in Kafka, and on confession in Rousseau, Tolstoy, and Dostoevsky. The intellectual and biographical links between this scholarly activity and his novels are explored in *Doubling the Point: Essays and Interviews* (1992), edited by David Attwell.

Coetzee's first novel, *Dusklands* (1974), is an aggressive parody of colonial discourses, signalling his ethical revulsion from colonial power and its failure to imagine reciprocal relations with the colonized. The reaction is fuelled by a sense of complicity in this history, for Coetzee is responding to forces shaping his own situation and identity: the novel links two narratives, one by a Dutch adventurer on a fruitless ivory expedition who encounters the indigenous Namaqua of the Western Cape, the other by a late twentieth-century military strategist who is trying to improve the USA's propaganda effort in Vietnam. Beckettian in style, but structurally indebted to Vladimir Nabokov's *Pale Fire*, *Dusklands* is both angry and avante-garde; on publication it made a deep impression on the common-sense world of English-language liberal humanism in South Africa.

Coetzee's experimentalism is also expressed in his second novel, *In the Heart of the Country* (1977). Written as a series of numbered paragraphs, it represents the stream of consciousness of the lonely and passionate Magda, a colonial spinster on a Karoo farm nursing her father into the grave while unsuccessfully seeking some affinity with the servants. There are signs in the narration of an interest in psychoanalysis, but Coetzee had also read Sartre's *Being and Nothingness*. The existentialist gaze (Sartre's Look) that proved useful to Frantz Fanon and Albert Memmi in their studies of colonial relations is reinforced at a formal level in Coetzee by echoes of the *nouveau roman* and of films by directors such as Chris Marker, Andrzej Munk, and Jean-Luc Godard. A memorable aspect of *In the Heart of the Country* is the intensity with which it brings elements of late European modernism into an uncompromising analysis of the pathologies of the master-servant relationship.

In *Waiting for the Barbarians* (1980) Coetzee writes as a fabulist (prompting critical comparison with **Wilson Harris**), setting this novel in the remote western provinces of an empire of no particular historical period or locale. Coetzee has always been an 'anti-realist' — as he puts it, an 'anti-illusionist' — and in this novel he removes himself to an entirely fictional milieu. The relative freedom provided by this move enables Coetzee to focus on the binary structures of discourse informing the imperial impulse and to explore their effects on subjectivity. The liberal-minded magistrate-narrator experiences a crisis of conscience and identity as the agents of the imperial secret police descend on his placid domain and begin torturing captive barbarians for information about an imaginary attack. Despite the oblique quality of the work's reference to South Africa, there are suggestions of the government's security-driven policy of 'total strategy' in the late 1970s and of the death by torture of Stephen Biko in 1977.

In *Life and Times of Michael K* (1983) and especially in *Foe* (1986), Coetzee turns his attention to questions of agency and authority in fiction. The former, with a nod to Kafka, explores the elusiveness of a man without social connections whose harelip marks him as different. K lives outside of the prevailing terms of discourse: Coetzee develops a scenario of full-scale civil war, but K miraculously slips through it all, untouched. Coetzee is testing the capacities of fiction to hold its own against the (apparently) overwhelming appetites of history. *Foe*, a work even more conscious of literary antecedents than *Life and Times of Michael K*, weaves together the plots of Daniel Defoe's *Robinson Crusoe* and *Roxana*. Susan Barton is put ashore on Crusoe's island (Crusoe is spelled 'Cruso' in the novel) after a mutiny aboard the vessel taking her to find a lost daughter. She, Cruso, and Friday are rescued; Cruso dies on the return journey to England; and Susan, with Friday in tow, seeks out the author, Foe, to write her story. Friday's tongue has been severed in an act of mutilation, although no one knows by whom. The novel turns on Susan's desire to have her story told and on Friday's power to withhold meaning through silence. Coetzee's identification is clearly with Susan, who writes from the margins of the institution of letters provided by the metropolis, but whose truth is subject to the power and presence of Friday. The allegory encapsulates the dilemmas of the relocated white writer who experiences himself or herself as an outsider, but cannot draw on or reconstruct an alternative, autochthonous identity and tradition.

Age of Iron (1990) reveals Coetzee's continuing concern with the question of writing from a position of disablement or lack of authority. Elizabeth Curren is a retired lecturer in classics — a hopeless vocation in a revolution — writing a memoir for a daughter exiled in the USA. Elizabeth is dying of cancer in a society torn apart by the malignancy of apartheid, which is now in its final stages. She enters a liaison with a tramp, Vercueil, who takes up residence in her garden on the day she learns of her disease and whom she creates as her 'angel of death'. Events take Elizabeth into the townships around Cape Town in midwinter; there, a conflict is staged over the right to speak about life and death, loyalty, childhood, the future, and the nation. Elizabeth's precarious voice is counter-balanced by Coetzee's rigorous insight into the conflicting ethical imperatives of living with and speaking about South Africa in the declining years of white nationalist rule.

Coetzee's novels, with their metafictional strategies, are postmodern in ethos, which marks them as different from much South African writing, including **Nadine Gordimer**'s, in which the dominant (though not exclusive) narrative mode is realist. Coetzee's work openly declares its European heritage. These tendencies have to be seen alongside Coetzee's trenchant critique of colonialism and its effects and his careful delineation of the historical and ethical constraints acting on authorship, particularly of white writers. The dilemmas Coetzee addresses are representative of their time. They include conflicts over ethical and political rationality, and the inescapability of thinking historically despite the linguistic self-consciousness of contemporary culture. These factors give Coetzee's novels their current international appeal and importance.

DAVID ATTWELL

Further reading: Teresa Dovey, *The Novels of J. M. Coetzee: Lacanian Allegories* (1988); Dick Penner, *Countries of the Mind: The Fiction of J. M. Coetzee* (1989); Susan Van Zanten Gallagher, *A Story of South Africa: J. M. Coetzee's Fiction in Context* (1991); David Attwell, *J. M. Coetzee: South Africa and the Politics of Writing* (1993).

COGSWELL, FREDERICK WILLIAM (1917–)
Canadian poet, editor
Born in East Centreville, New Brunswick, Canada, he was educated at the Provincial Normal School and, after service overseas in the Canadian Army, at the University of New Brunswick and Edinburgh University, Scotland (Ph.D., 1952). In 1952 Cogswell returned to teach English at UNB. As an undergraduate, he began publishing poems in *The Fiddlehead*, a local magazine begun in 1945 that, under his editorship (1952–67), became an international literary journal. (See **Literary Magazines**, Canada.) Between 1954 and 1981 he published more than three hundred titles as Fiddlehead Poetry Books. Cogswell's own poetry has appeared in twenty collections, including *A Long Apprenticeship: The Collected Poems of Fred Cogswell* (1980), *Selected Poems* (1983), and *Meditations: 50 Sestinas* (1986). He has published four books of translations from Quebec poets, including *The Complete Poems of Émile Nelligan* (1983), and numerous critical articles, chapters of literary history, and reviews.

Growing up in Atlantic Canada between the wars, Cogswell shared with writers from other parts of the Commonwealth a strongly colonial heritage, lodged in a school curriculum whose literary content emphasized British writing of the nineteenth century, including such turn-of-the-century figures as Rudyard Kipling and W. E. Henley. Like others of his generation, Cogswell has seen the craft of making poems as exercising maximum freedom within formal controls. When he encountered modernism in the 1940s he began to experiment with more open verse, but like **A. D. Hope** of Australia, a poet he knows and admires, he retained his love for formal verse. He claims to feel a closer affinity with British, particularly Scottish, writers than with North American writers.

The main themes of his early sonnets, collected in *The Stunted Strong* (1954), are truancies against the constricting norms of a rural society. Later work enlarges and complicates this preoccupation, but still contains it formally.

ROBERT GIBBS

COHEN, LEONARD NORMAN (1934–)

Canadian poet, novelist, singer/song-writer

Born in Montreal, Canada, he attended McGill University, Montreal. By the age of thirty Cohen had published three volumes of poetry (*Let Us Compare Mythologies*, 1956, *The Spice-Box of Earth*, 1961, and *Flowers for Hitler*, 1964), and a novel (*The Favourite Game*, 1963). In 1965 he was the subject of a National Film Board of Canada documentary, *Ladies and Gentlemen: Mr. Leonard Cohen*. His second novel, the controversial *Beautiful Losers* (1966), is a religious meditation and sexual fantasy centred around the life and death of Catherine Tekakwitha, the seventeenth-century Iroquois saint. Cohen's poetry includes *Parasites of Heaven* (1966), *Selected Poems: 1956–1968* (1968), *The Energy of Slaves* (1972), *Death of a Lady's Man* (1978), and *Book of Mercy* (1984).

Cohen's first record album, *Songs of Leonard Cohen* (1968), marked a shift in his career from poet/novelist to singer/song-writer. In the several albums that have followed, Cohen has earned respect and praise worldwide as a poet-singer whose style encompasses Bob Dylan, Georges Moustaki, and such Québécois *chanteurs* as Giles Vigneault and Félix Leclerc. Although his published writing after 1968 is not without interest, Cohen's creative energies have since then been absorbed in his singing and song-writing. His albums include *Songs from a Room* (1969), *Songs of Love and Hate* (1971), *Leonard Cohen: Live Songs* (1973), *New Skin for the Old Ceremony* (1974), *Death of a Ladies' Man* (1977), *Recent Songs* (1979), *Various Positions* (1985), *I'm Your Man* (1988), and *The Future* (1992). Indeed, Cohen's early work as a poet and novelist may be regarded as an apprenticeship; his enduring achievement is likely to be a small number of finely crafted songs.

Cohen's preoccupations are erotic, spiritual, and political. The song 'First We Take Manhattan' demonstrates his ambivalence towards revolutionary politics, which are presented in terms of romance ('the beauty of our weapons'), caprice ('guided by the birthmark on my skin'), and apocalypse. The revolutionary theme often seems limited, however, to an ironic exploitation of metaphorical possibilities. The erotic and the spiritual are Cohen's truer concerns. They are bound together in a religious quest characterized by a cycle of Dionysian experience and ritualistic purification. Cohen's eroticism, though modern in its explicit sexuality, is in other respects romantic and traditional. Technically his work is remarkable for its lyric grace, and thematically for its depiction of the life of an artist.

ADRIAN FOWLER

Further reading: Linda Hutcheon, '*Caveat lector*: the early postmodernism of Leonard Cohen', in her *The Canadian Postmodern* (1988).

COHEN, MATT (1942–)

Canadian novelist, short-story writer

Born in Kingston, Canada, he grew up in Ottawa, graduated from the University of Toronto (BA, 1964), and, following graduate studies in philosophy and religion, he lectured in religion at McMaster University for a year. Since the publication of his first novel, *Korsoniloff* (1969), Cohen has devoted himself virtually full time to writing. *Emotional Arithmetic* (1990) was his tenth novel. He has also published five books of short stories, various translations from French, and numerous articles, essays, and reviews on Canadian literature and culture.

Cohen's work divides into a series of distinct

phases. His early work was quite radically avant-garde. His second novel, *Johnny Crackle Sings* (1971), and the stories in *Columbus and the Fat Lady* (1972), as well as several other experimental texts, marked Cohen as one of the most interesting young writers in the Toronto-based group that also included **Margaret Atwood, Dennis Lee**, Graeme Gibson, and Peter Such.

Following his own move to rural southeastern Ontario, Cohen's fiction took a sharp turn towards realism and conventional form. *The Disinherited* (1974) was the first in a series of four novels, ranging in mode from comic through romantic to speculative and Gothic, centred around the fictional town of Salem, north of Kingston, a series known collectively as 'The Salem Novels'. None of his odd and sometimes elliptical vision of reality was lost in these novels or the related short stories, but emphasis clearly shifted from innovative pyrotechnics to perception, insight, and compassion.

In 1984 Cohen published *The Spanish Doctor*, a sweeping historical novel beginning in Toledo and ending in Kiev, which chronicles the life of a Jewish prophet-hero during the Renaissance. This novel marks Cohen's transition into another phase in which modern Jewish and European experience become central in terms of both plot and world view. *Nadine* (1986) and *Emotional Arithmetic*, as well as a number of his shorter fictions, reflect this turning towards more cosmopolitan interests associated with his return to Toronto.

JOHN MOSS

COLLINS, MERLE (1950–)

Grenadian poet, novelist

Born in Aruba and brought up in Grenada, she attended St Joseph's Convent before entering the University of the West Indies, Jamaica, in 1969. After graduating in 1972, Collins held various teaching positions in Grenada and St Lucia and between 1978 and 1981 completed an MA in Latin American studies at Georgetown University, USA. In 1981 she returned to Grenada to work as a research officer for Latin America with Maurice Bishop's People's Revolutionary government. She first established her reputation as a poet during this period. Some of her best-known early pieces were collected in Chris Searle's *Callaloo: Four Writers from Grenada* (1984).

After Bishop's assassination, Collins moved to London, England, where she performed her poetry with the group New Dawn. Her volume *Because The Dawn Breaks!: Poems Dedicated to the Grenadian People* (1985) contains an introduction by **Ngugi wa Thiong'o**, who notes the commonalities between Collins' work and that of politically committed poets and dramatists in Africa. Other poems by Collins from this period appear in *Watchers and Seekers: Creative Writing by Black Women in Britain* (1987), which Collins co-edited with Rhonda Cobham.

Many of Collins' best-known early poems were written for performance to music or drumming, but Collins' repertoire extends far beyond the range of 'Dub' poetry. Her novel *Angel* (1987) is a coming-of-age chronicle framed by historical events in Grenada from the 1930s to the demise of the revolutionary government. It recalls **George Lamming**'s *In The Castle of My Skin* (1953) in its intertwining of personal and political themes. It is also the first Caribbean novel to make extensive use of the French Creole spoken in Grenada. *Rain Darling and Other Stories* (1990) is a haunting series of vignettes about lonely and displaced Caribbean women. Collins' most recent poetry collection, *Rotten Pomerack* (1992), explores the nuances, insights, and uncertainties of life in London.

RHONDA COBHAM

COLLYMORE, FRANK (1893–1980)

Barbadian poet, short-story writer

Born in Woodville, Barbados, he was at the centre

of the Caribbean literary renaissance of the 1940s and 1950s. As a teacher at Barbados' famous Combermere School for boys, where he himself had been a student, Collymore had a profound influence on the development of several notable Caribbean writers, including **George Lamming** and **Austin Clarke**. Collymore also worked strenuously to ensure the survival of *Bim*, Barbados' literary journal, which he edited and offered as a forum for young writers. In addition to his short stories, all first published in *Bim*, Collymore's publications include the poetry collections *Thirty Poems* (1944), *Beneath the Casuarinas* (1945), *Flotsam: Poems 1942–8* (1948), *Collected Poems* (1959), *Rhymed Ruminations on the Fauna of Barbados* (1968), and *Selected Poems* (1971).

Collymore was also a painter, accomplished actor, and man of letters. Scholars, unfortunately, have neglected his poetry and short fiction, concentrating instead on his role as editor and teacher. Several of Collymore's poems, 'Hymn to the Sea' (1971) and 'Triptych' (1948), for instance (both in his *Collected Poems*), deserve more attention. In the latter, the heterogeneity of Caribbean ancestry, together with its concomitant violence and suffering, is treated as an important source of Caribbean identity. In 'Hymn to the Sea' the encircling sea has symbolic and metaphorical resonances; Collymore's sea is a chthonic, embracing womb to which man is drawn by the pull of his evolutionary memory.

Collymore's treatment of the sea and of the symbiotic relationship between man and sea suggests parallels with the mystique of the sea in the work of Canadian writer **Alistair Macleod**. Some of Macleod's characters in his story collection *The Lost Salt Gift of Blood* (1976) are indelibly marked by the implacably cold and indifferent Atlantic; the 'patterning' of the sea's rhythms, which, Collymore asserts, 'finds echoes within the musing mind', reminds one of the Atlantic's shifting nuances to which Macleod's characters are particularly sensitive.

In his short stories Collymore achieves an admirable intensity through effective use of language and narrative sparseness. Although his characters and settings are Caribbean, his themes are universal. Some stories explore the dark underside of humanity, while others examine such issues as alienation and loneliness. 'Shadows' (1942) and 'Rewards and Chrysanthemums' (1961) show Collymore's fascination with the mind's dark side. The latter is a symbolically resonant story of two middle-aged, incompatible Barbadian sisters of fragile sensibilities living together after years of separation. 'Shadows' creates compelling tension out of the narrator's terrifying realization that he is going insane. Other stories, such as 'R. S. V. P. to Mrs. Bush-Hall' (1962), show Collymore's sharply honed satirical skills. Although he is a transparent con-man, Lucas, the mediocre English expatriate poet, thrives in the colonial society of sham respectability depicted in the story.

Dramatic contrast is a noticeable feature of Collymore's fiction. In 'Some People Are Meant to Live Alone' (1944), the recluse's 'gaunt and cockeyed house' matches its owner's distorted personality. In 'To Meet her Mother' (1967) a youngster's discovery of sober reality is placed within the context of a universal archetype: the dreaming boy, who is driven by his antiseptic vision of ideal womanhood, pays a high price when dream is contaminated by reality.

'The Diaries' (1966) shows Collymore's skill in characterization. The narrator's circumspect and wry personality is subtly revealed through his astute and ironic comments. The old man of 'There's Always the Angels' (1945) is also carefully drawn. He is crushed, it seems, by his painful recognition of the Virgilian *lacrimae rerum*, as well as by the loss of the Edenic dream. Collymore's skill is also evident in his characterization of children. Mark, an imaginative and sensitive youngster, appears in three stories. In each case, he undergoes a rite of passage, and his observations and reflections spring from his developing sensibilities rather than from Colllymore's adult perceptions.

Collymore's work as editor of *Bim* and his influence on such writers as George Lamming and Austin Clarke assure him a permanent place in the history of Caribbean literature. But his poetry and short stories are also important contributions to the development of these genres in Caribbean literature.

HAROLD BARRATT

Further reading: John Wickham, 'Colly: a profile', *The Bajan and South Caribbean* January (1973); Edward Baugh, 'Frank Collymore', in Daryl C. Dance (ed.) *Fifty Caribbean Writers: A Bio-bibliographical Critical Sourcebook* (1986); Harold Barratt, 'The short stories of Frank Collymore', *Bim* 73, June (1990).

CONFEDERATION POETS (Canada)

This term now refers to four English-Canadian poets born shortly before the Canadian Confederation of 1867. **Charles G. D. Roberts,** his cousin, **Bliss Carman, Archibald Lampman,** and **Duncan Campbell Scott** published their first poetry during the 1880s or 1890s, when Canada was beginning to achieve self-definition as a nation. Together, they are credited with having forged an authentic, internationally recognized Canadian poetic voice that presented Canadian experience in accomplished lyrics and sonnets that now form the cornerstone of the Canadian poetic canon.

Although convenient, the term 'Confederation poets' is misleading, especially when extrapolated to a 'Confederation school'. It first entered the Canadian critical vocabulary as a definitive phrase in 1960, when Malcolm Ross edited *Poets of the Confederation* in the New Canadian Library series published by McClelland and Stewart. Ross' decision to limit the canon of early Canadian poets to four names has ill served other poets of the same generation also active during the late nineteenth century, principally **Wilfred Campbell,** a close associate of Lampman and Scott during the early 1890s, and the many women who contributed significantly to the development of Canadian literature: **Isabella Valancy Crawford, Susie Frances Harrison**, Ethelwyn Wetherald, and **Pauline Johnson**. (See **Anthologies**, Canada.)

The 'Confederation Poets' were not a self-defined quartet (in contrast to the Group of Seven in Canadian painting). The signifier 'Confederation' overemphasizes the degree to which the four shared an articulated political or nationalist agenda. Roberts and Carman, both from New Brunswick, spent most of their adult lives outside Canada. Indeed Carman, the most popular of the four, was not regarded as a Canadian by his American fans. Lampman and Scott, both career civil servants, were close literary friends in Ottawa. While Lampman and Scott praised Roberts' *Orion and Other Poems* (1880) for setting a new direction for Canadian poetry, Scott in 1901 dismissed the notion of a 'School of Canadian Poetry' as 'too pretentious', regarding its only value to be a means of distinguishing Canadian literature from that of the United States.

CAROLE GERSON

Further reading: Duncan Campbell Scott, 'A decade of Canadian poetry', *Twentieth-Century Essays on Confederation Literature*, ed. Lorraine McMullen (1976).

CONNOR, RALPH (1860–1937)

Canadian novelist, short-story writer

Born Charles William Gordon in Glengarry County, in what was then Canada West, he became a Presbyterian minister and a notable figure in church and national affairs. As Ralph Connor, he published twenty-six works of fiction between 1898 and 1936, achieving widespread Canadian and international popularity.

Connor combines formulaic didactic plots with

a keen awareness of landscape detail and local dialect. His technique resembles that of American local colourists, and also of the Scottish kailyard school, where plots are typically set in the rural past and stress patriarchal moral values.

While Connor fares badly by literary standards, he can be striking as a social historian and myth-maker. His most lasting works, *The Man from Glengarry* (1901) and *Glengarry Schooldays* (1902), are based on childhood memories of pioneer life. Critic Roy Daniells has noted the magical quality of Connor's Ontario settings, where larger-than-life Highlanders battle for survival in a primeval forest. In many other novels, Connor transports this conflict between humanity and nature to the new territory of the Canadian West, creating a myth of national destiny. Here muscular Christian heroes labour to bring the rule of secular and sacred law to an unredeemed populace and landscape.

Connor's love of the anarchic western scene conflicts with his imperialistic desire to turn the wilderness into a garden. Similarly, his relish for violence contrasts oddly with his Christian values. His Glengarry origins explain these ambiguities, since they taught him a simultaneous love of wild forest and cultivated farm, as well as an admiration for physical courage along with a determination to fight evil.

While Connor created an idealized concept of Canada based on Anglo-Saxon principles, he promoted the cultural assimilation of non-English-speaking inhabitants. His patriotism and spiritual imperialism, along with his romantic sentimentality, contributed to his immediate success as well as to his ultimate decline. Limited in his political vision, he survives as a recorder of the past and as a maker of myths.

GLENYS STOW

Further reading: John Lennox, 'Charles W. Gordon [Ralph Connor] (1860–1937)', in Robert Lecker, Jack David, and Ellen Quigley (eds) *Canadian Writers and Their Works*, Fiction Series 3 (1988).

CONTON, WILLIAM (1925–)
Gambian/Sierra Leonean novelist
Born in Bathurst, The Gambia, he was educated partly in Sierra Leone, now his adopted country, and in the UK. A distinguished educationalist and international civil servant, Conton's interest in education is reflected in both his novels, *The African* (1960), in which the protagonist's process of education is nostalgically described, and *The Flights* (1987), in which the hero's successful attempt at self-education is sympathetically presented.

Equally at home in both western and African culture, Conton's works reflect his cosmopolitanism and lifelong interest in music, drama, art, and literature. Some critics deplore the numerous western references to be found in his novels, such as those to the music of Bach and to the poetry of Wordsworth and Byron. Conton, however, is also capable of presenting genuine pictures of African life, such as the touching accounts in *The African* of a young boy in a rural community experiencing the rites of passage, even though these are not as detailed as presentations of similar aspects of traditional African life in the works of **Chinua Achebe** and **Ngugi wa Thiong'o**. Unlike Achebe, Conton does little to Africanize the English language. Critics often mention Conton's Churchillian vocabulary, which they feel is quite out of character with everyday language in both Africa and England.

The African traces the hero's development from boyhood in rural Songhai, through his education in Songhai and England, to his return to lead his country to independence. As some critics have noted, the early scenes in Songhai and England are tellingly presented, but the novel seems to fall apart once the hero returns to his native country. Most disturbing is the anticlimactic conclusion, in which the hero irrationally abandons national and international obligations to travel incognito to South Africa to support the struggle there.

The suggestion of the hero's disorientation in *The African* is more explicitly drawn in the protagonist of *The Flights*, but it is still not convincingly demonstrated. However, in its adoption of a shifting narrative focus, *The Flights* is technically an advance on *The African*, which adopts a linear and chronological structure.

EUSTACE PALMER

CONVICT LITERATURE (Australia)
From the beginnings of European settlement in Australia, literature about convicts and the convict system has loomed large and has included various historical writings, popular ballads, and oral literature as well as fiction, poetry, and drama. Because convictism was inevitably linked with the origins of white settlement, and at times seemed synonymous with settlement, the impulse to investigate, question, protest about, and rewrite origins has always been strong. This impulse was heightened by the inferiority/superiority feelings aroused by colonialism. Attempts were made to use convictism to construct a national ethos, to turn, for instance, a shameful past into a stick to beat British imperialism as seen, for example, in **Price Warung**'s numerous stories in the ***Bulletin*** of the pre-Federation 1890s, or in **Brian Penton**'s iconoclastic exposé of pioneering in *Landtakers* (1934). An alternative was to see in convictism the seeds of such cherished national virtues as egalitarianism and social protest in favour of the underdog, as in **Russel Ward**'s *The Australian Legend* (1958).

The myth of convicts as social victims, as more sinned against than sinning, sustains some of Australia's earliest literature, including **Marcus Clarke**'s classic *His Natural Life* (1870–72). This view was reinforced by sociological and leftist analysis in the early twentieth century, only to be later questioned by historian **Manning Clark**, who argued that the convicts were mainly confirmed criminals, not trivial offenders. Today, questions about who the convicts were — in both the sociological and 'human' sense (how would they have thought, felt, behaved?) — continue to be asked by historians and creative writers alike and by their reading public, which, as Robert Hughes' popular *The Fatal Shore* (1987) shows, can be vast and international. The fate of women convicts has been brought under scrutiny along with that of the majority of convicts who were not confined to special prisons and subjected to their particularly cruel punishment, and who were able to 'earn' their freedom.

The symbolic richness of convictism as a theme was heightened for writers because it lends itself to some of the deep-rooted metaphors and the metaphoric language expressive of antipodean dislocation and alienation. This sense of alienation enters all colonial experience of settler societies, and its expression achieves extra resonance through links with the disintegration of Western society under the influence of industrial and political oppression. The prison and the madhouse, often conjoined, emerged as master literary symbols in Victorian times, and a later work such as **Jean Rhys**' *Wide Sargasso Sea* (1966), in its rewriting of *Jane Eyre*, has affinities with Australian convict literature, as does the work of West Indian novelist **George Lamming**. So too do American slave narratives and modern novels such as William Styron's *The Confessions of Nat Turner* (1967).

Clarke's *His Natural Life* indicates the network of influences, literary and social, that fed into convict fiction; consequently colonialism, rather than being muffled, was given a more expressive voice through links with analogous worldwide and recurrent experiences. Influences on this novel included Henry Mayhew's documentary *London Labour and the London Poor* (1851), Charles Reade's *It is Never Too Late to Mend* (1856), an exposé of English prisons, Victor Hugo's *Les*

Misérables (1862), Nathaniel Hawthorne's *The Scarlet Letter* (1850), and even perhaps Dostoevsky's *The House of the Dead* (1862), one of the earliest works about gulags. There were also local influences, notably **Caroline Leakey**'s widely read story of a woman prisoner, *The Broad Arrow* (1859). Out of such materials, as well as local stories and documentation, Clarke, like later novelists, was able to weave a work that was resolutely and resonantly literary and at the same time deeply moving and humane in its appeal. **Hal Porter**'s *The Tilted Cross* (1961), **Thomas Keneally**'s *Bring Larks and Heroes* (1967), **Patrick White**'s *A Fringe of Leaves* (1976), and **Jessica Anderson**'s *The Commandant* (1975), for example, develop this tradition, all using an interpretation of the convict system as a parable for the changing times in which they were written. Some works, notably convict **James Tucker**'s *Ralph Rashleigh* (1952, written *c.* 1845) and **Eleanor Dark**'s *The Timeless Land* (1941), link convictism with exploitation of the Aborigines.

LAURIE HERGENHAN

Further reading: John F. Bayliss, 'Slave and convict narratives: a discussion of American and Australian writing', *Journal of Commonwealth Literature* 8 (1969); Laurie Hergenhan, *Unnatural Lives: Studies in Australian Fiction about the Convicts from James Tucker to Patrick White* (1983).

COOK, MICHAEL (1933–)

Canadian dramatist

Born in London, England, he joined the British Army in 1949 and served in Germany and the Far East for twelve years. Following teacher training at Nottingham University College of Education, England, Cook immigrated in 1965 to Newfoundland, Canada, where he worked part-time as a journalist before becoming a full-time teacher in the department of English, Memorial University, St John's.

Cook has written extensively for radio (some fifty plays) and for the stage. The best of the published radio plays is *Tiln* (1973, in *Encounter: Canadian Drama in Four Media*, edited by Eugene Benson), a short Absurdist drama about two lighthouse-keepers. When one dies, the other (Tiln) pickles him in brine as he awaits the relief ship that will only come after the winter has passed. The play dramatizes the impact of a Newfoundland Atlantic environment that evokes individual defiance in the face of the chaos represented by Nature.

Three of Cook's stage plays are historical in character, revealing in their form the influence of Brechtian epic theatre. The seventeenth-century struggle of France and England to establish political and military hegemony on the eastern seaboard of North America (here, St John's, Newfoundland) is the setting for the first of these plays, *Colour the Flesh the Colour of Dust* (1972). The struggle, in which possession of St John's passes from the English to the French and back to the English, is seen as irrelevant to the needs of the common people; the flag of the colonizing power represents only oppression. *The Gayden Chronicles* (1977) and *On the Rim of the Curve* (1977) are also attempts to recuperate and interrogate Canada's colonial past. The latter play dramatizes the encounter between the British colonizers and the Native People of Newfoundland, the Beothuks, in which the Beothuks were annihilated.

The Head, Guts and Sound Bone Dance (1974) and *Jacob's Wake* (1975) are full-length plays with a contemporary Newfoundland setting. The subtitle of the former play, 'a controversial play that deals with Newfoundland's future', suggests ironically that Newfoundland has no future. The play's black humour and its carefully detailed and choreographed presentation of Newfoundland fishing mores are complemented by an elegiac note that portends the passing of a way of life that was once heroic in character.

Jacob's Wake is an even more pessimistic work. As the corruption of the various members of a family is revealed in powerful scenes of confrontation, a storm grows in intensity, finally sweeping away the family home and, it is suggested, a decayed Newfoundland culture. The final scene echoes the apocalyptic conclusion to G. B. Shaw's *Heartbreak House*.

Cook's entire work is noteworthy for its strong emotional impact and for its engagement with large cultural issues; it is weakened, however, by a delight in language that too often tends to the rhetorical and by an attraction to the melodramatic. Following a highly productive period of writing in the 1970s, Cook has produced little significant work.

EUGENE BENSON

Further reading: Brian Parker, 'On the edge: Michael Cook's Newfoundland trilogy', *Canadian Literature* 85 (1980).

COOMARASWAMY, ANANDA K. (1877–1947)
Sri Lankan art historian, cultural critic
Born in Colombo, Ceylon (now Sri Lanka), to a Tamil father, Sir Muttu Coomaraswamy, and an English mother, Elizabeth Clay Beeby, he was educated in England, at Wycliffe public school (Gloucestershire) and at the University of London, where he earned a bachelor of science degree (1900) and a Ph.D. (1906) in geology. Between 1903 and 1906, when Coomaraswamy was director of the Mineralogical Survey of Ceylon, he became interested in Ceylonese crafts and culture, an interest that resulted in his *Medieval Sinhalese Art* (1908). Following research into the art, culture, and religion of India, he returned to England, where he created a collection of Indian arts and crafts. This collection became part of the Indian and Muhammadan Art exhibit at the Museum of Fine Arts, Boston, USA, of which he became keeper in 1917 and with which he was associated for the rest of his life.

Rajput Art (1916) is an important publication in which Coomaraswamy clearly distinguished the Hindu art of Rajputana (a state in India's north west) from the Moghul art with which it had long been mistakenly linked. *Myths of the Hindus and Buddhists* (1913), *Buddha and the Gospel of Buddhism* (1916), and *The Dance of Shiva* (1918) reveal Coomaraswamy's deep and enduring interest in religion; his later publications were primarily concerned with art history and aesthetics and with comparative studies of religious cultures. He read intensively in the philosophical tradition of the west (Platonism and Christianity, and especially in the philosophy of St Thomas Aquinas) and in the spiritual traditions of Hinduism, Buddhism, and Islam. Representative works include *History of Indian and Indonesian Art* (1927), *The Transformation of Nature in Art* (1934), *Elements of Buddhist Iconography* (1935), *Hinduism and Buddhism* (1943), *Why Exhibit Works of Art?* (1943), and *Time and Eternity* (1947).

Coomaraswamy developed an influential philosophy of art based on traditional Indian aesthetics but placed within the context of contemporary Asian and European art and art criticism. He rejected the concept of art for art's sake and the distinctions between fine and useful art and between sacred and profane art, and argued that the secularization of art in the contemporary world, like the rationalization of religion, is destructive. Coomaraswamy nevertheless pleaded for an art expressive of social experience; art, he claimed, must make life significant, and this it does when it is inspired by a love of life. He sought to relate works of art to historical factors, religious ideas, mystical tendencies, and social and personal conditions; in doing so he drew heavily on such traditional Indian works of aesthetics as *Sahitya Darpana*, *Agni Purana*, *Vyakti Viveka*, *Dasa Pupaka*, and *Sukra Niti Sara*. In emphasizing the impersonality of art he noted that Hindu artists, following ceremonial purification and prayer, meditate on the emptiness or non-existence of all things in order to be released from ego-consciousness. The freedom that follows, Coomaraswamy stated, has two characteristics: it arises from *Yoga* ('contemplation') and it is determined by the traditional discipline from which the artist should not or would not escape. Coomaraswamy also drew on traditional Indian aesthetics in his discussion of the nature of beauty, relating it to the concept of *Rasa* ('aesthetic experience'), which includes not only pleasure and instruction but a detachment in which, Coomaraswamy argued, the aesthetic and the mystical experiences are alike.

An example of Coomaraswamy's theory in practice is his consideration of Indian painting, which he views first from the standpoint of Indian theories, attitudes and ideals, then within the broader framework of Asian and European art. Without the recognition that the meaning of a work of art transcends the mere visual form, he felt, one will not be able to grasp the significance of the yogi cat at the famous temples of Mamallapuram or of the talking geese of the caves of Ajanta.

P. S. SASTRI

Further reading: P. S. Sastri, *Ananda K. Coomaraswamy* (1974); A. Moore and R. P. Coomaraswamy, eds, *Selected Letters of Ananda K. Coomaraswamy* (1988).

COPE, JACK (1913–91)

South African novelist, short-story writer, poet, editor

Born Robert Knox Cope on a farm near the community of Mooi River, Natal, South Africa, he began his writing career as a journalist in Durban and in London, England. Upon returning to his father's farm in 1940, and after taking various jobs, he concentrated on creative writing.

Cope published eight novels, more than one hundred short stories (including four collections — *The Tame Ox*, 1960, *The Man Who Doubted and Other Stories*, 1967, *Alley Cat and Other Stories*, 1973, and *Selected Stories*, 1986), and three volumes of poetry (*Lyrics and Diatribes*, 1948, *Marie: A South African Satire*, 1948, and *Recorded in the Sun*, 1979). From 1960 to 1979 he edited *Contrast* (1960–90; renamed *New Contrast*), a literary magazine in English and Afrikaans, which kept him in close contact with the country's leading writers. In 1980 he moved to England, where he published the commentary *The Adversary Within: Dissident Writers in Afrikaans* (1982) and other prose and verse works.

Central to Cope's novels is the destruction of the black culture in South Africa by the white man, and the attempts of the blacks to regain their sense of identity. Many of Cope's novels, particularly *The Golden Oriole* (1958) and *Albino* (1964), not only provide keen insights into Zulu life, making abundant use of traditional phrases and customs, but explore the collective psyche of black people through individual characterization. This is accomplished most effectively in *The Rain-Maker* (1971), winner of the Argus Prize for Literature, the Veld Trust, and the CNA Prize, which is reminiscent of **Chinua Achebe**'s *Things Fall Apart* (1958) in its reconstruction of tribal ways.

It is Cope's short stories, however, that are generally regarded as displaying his finest talent. They are more descriptive and narrative in character than those of **Alan Paton**, who noted that in *The Man Who Doubted and Other Stories* 'Cope is able to evoke with a few words the scents and sounds and colours of our country'.

Cope powerfully influenced South African writing during the 1960s and 1970s by giving encouragement to young talent of different races and helping to popularize local literature through anthologies, translations, lectures, and criticism. His was the voice of common sense, firmly spoken, insisting upon literary standards while denouncing censorship.

PAUL SCANLON

Further reading: *New Contrast*, nos. 74–75.

COPWAY, GEORGE (1818–69)

Canadian autobiographer, journalist

Born in Ontario, Canada, he belonged to the Mississauga band of the aboriginal Ojibwa people. When the first native Christian missionaries reached Rice Lake, where he lived, Kahgegagahbowh ('Standing Firm'), or George Copway, as the missionaries called him, briefly attended mission school before leaving, in 1834, as a Methodist mission worker to the Lake Superior Ojibwa. Following his graduation in 1839, Copway met his future bride in Upper Canada; Elizabeth Howell was the daughter of Captain Henry Howell, an English gentleman who farmed east of Toronto.

After two years at Ojibwa mission stations in the USA, the Copways returned to Upper Canada in late 1842. Copway proved a successful missionary until he was accused in 1845 of embezzlement of band funds. The Canadian Methodists expelled him, and he moved to the USA. Taking advantage of his Christianized Indian identity, he wrote his life story for a white audience, *The Life, History and Travels of Kah-ge-ga-gah-bowh (George Copway), a Young Indian Chief of the Ojebwa Nation, a Convert to the Christian Faith, and a Missionary to His People for Twelve Years* (1847). By the end of 1848 the autobiography had gone through seven printings. Copway became a good friend of American historian Francis Parkman and American poet Henry Wadsworth Longfellow. In 1855 Longfellow published *The Song of Hiawatha*; apparently Copway was the only Ojibwa Longfellow met before he wrote his famous poem, which he based on the Lake Superior Ojibwa.

In 1850 Copway published *The Traditional History and Characteristic Sketches of the Ojibway Nation*, the first tribal history in English by a North American Indian; an epic poem, *The Ojibway Conquest: A Tale of the Northwest*, was also published in 1850; and a travelogue, *Running Sketches of Men and Places in England, France, Germany, Belgium, and Scotland*, followed in 1851. *Copway's American Indian*, a weekly that he founded in New York City in 1851, folded after three months.

In the 1850s Copway descended into poverty and obscurity. In 1868 he returned to Canada, where he was baptized a Roman Catholic under the name Joseph-Antoine on 17 January 1869. Several days later he died suddenly.

DONALD SMITH

CORRIS, PETER (1942–)

Australian novelist, short-story writer

Born in Stawell, Victoria, Australia, he was educated in Melbourne and at the Australian National University. After a short period as an academic historian he turned to journalism and fiction, adapting to Sydney, Australia, the Californian private-eye novel in the Cliff Hardy series.

The Dying Trade (1980), Corris' first novel, and *The Marvellous Boy* (1982), his third, reflect the psychological influence of Ross Macdonald, but among the family dramas there are clear signs of an interest in social and political crimes. Corris' second novel, *White Meat* (1981), still thought by many to be his best, takes those interpersonal concerns further, into Aboriginal-white tensions. From then on the novels emphasize civil corruption: criminal extortion in *The Empty Beach* (1984), which has also been filmed; CIA activities in *Make Me Rich* (1985); political dishonesty in *The Greenwich Apartments* (1986); and drug involvement in *Deal Me Out* (1986).

Heroin Annie (1984), a successful book of stories, was followed by *The Big Drop* (1985). The flow of Hardy material slackened in the later 1980s as Corris stressed other genres: spy novels — the Crawley series — and a novel of recent history, *The Gulliver Fortune* (1989).

Cliff Hardy's tide did not ebb for long; Corris changed publishers, refocused his concentration, and produced a strong private-eye novel, *O'Fear* (1990), followed quickly by *Wet Graves* (1991), at once crisply historical and criminal, and *Aftershock* (1991), based on the Newcastle earthquake. Corris' prolific output and energetic variety have established him as the first widely known and strong-selling Australian thriller-writer since Arthur Upfield.

STEPHEN KNIGHT

COUANI, ANNA (1948–)

Australian short-story writer

Born in Sydney, Australia, of Greek and Polish background, she publishes in English. Trained as an architect, she has taught art in secondary schools for some years. A third generation Australian writer, Couani can hardly be classified as 'migrant' in the usual way, but partly because of her name and also because of the anti-assimilationist stance of the narrators and implied readers in her work, she is often bracketed with the so-called migrant writers. (See **Migrant Writing**, Australia.) She combines writing and editing with being the publisher of the independent Sea Cruise Books and is a member of the women writers' group, No Regrets.

Couani has published several collections of prose poems and has been anthologized as an experimental writer. Her collections of prose poems include *Italy* (1977), *Were All Women Sex-Mad?* (1982), and *The Train* (1983). Recently her work with the photomontage artist Peter Lyssiotis, *The Harbour Breathes* (1990), was short-listed in the New Writing category of the Victorian Premier's Literary Awards.

Couani's short fiction is innovative, often characterized by fragments of reportage and collage pervaded by the voices of disembodied, degendered outsiders who often express left-wing views. Her writing always includes the threat of some unnamed element that will re-position and re-name the traditional narrative conventions and the subject positions that accompany them. Her first collection, somewhat arbitrarily named *Italy*, explores domestic and private alienation in which the routine and the predictable are in constant danger of being shattered; images of sudden accidents, to people and objects, abound. In the other collections the narrator functions as sleuth, pursuing and cataloguing the minutiae of everyday life as though this enterprise in itself might precipitate an unambiguous meaning, a resolution in which the guilty and innocent are clearly exposed. Familiar themes in Australian writing function as the terrain of the Other re-read by an alien interpreter. The results are that Couani's writing accentuates gender, political adherences, and cultural difference.

SNEJA GUNEW

COULTER, JOHN (1888–1980)

Canadian/Irish dramatist

Born in Belfast, Ireland, he was a teacher between 1912 and 1919, when he began writing radio scripts for the British Broadcasting Corporation. He became editor of *The Ulster Review* in 1924 and managing editor in 1927 of J. M. Murry's journal, *The New Adelphi*. In 1936 Coulter immigrated to Canada, settling in Toronto, where he married a Canadian, Olive Clare Primrose.

Coulter's early plays are strongly influenced by those dramatists associated with Dublin's Abbey Theatre, especially J. M. Synge and W. B. Yeats, as may be seen in his *Conochar* (1917) and in the libretto *Deirdre of the Sorrows* (1944, music by Healey Willan), which are based on Celtic legends. Other plays by Coulter with an Irish theme include *The House in the Quiet Glen* (1937), *Family Portrait* (1937), and *The Drums Are Out* (1971). The best of the Irish plays is *The Drums Are Out*, which dramatizes the conflict in an Irish family in Belfast in the troubled political period of 1920–1. Enthusiastically reviewed when it was first produced by the Abbey Theatre in 1948, it bears comparison with Sean O'Casey's *Juno and the Paycock* (1925).

Coulter is best known for his Riel trilogy,

which dramatizes events in the life of the Canadian Métis leader Louis Riel. The trilogy comprises *Riel* (1962; premièred 1950), *The Trial of Louis Riel* (1968; premièred 1967), and *The Crime of Louis Riel* (1976; premièred 1966). Coulter's *In My Day: Memoirs* (1980) records his search in the 1940s for a Canadian myth that might afford him the material for a major Canadian work, just as legendary Irish figures such as Cuchulain, Conochar, and Deirdre had afforded Yeats and Synge (and Coulter) material for major plays. Sensitized by his Irish background to religious bigotry and the evils of colonization, Coulter felt he had discovered his Canadian myth in the person of Riel, the founder of the province of Manitoba who, responding to the threat of British annexation of Métis land, led rebellions against the Canadian government in 1869–70 and in 1885. He was tried for high treason, found guilty, and hanged in 1885.

In *Riel*, the most ambitious play of the trilogy, Coulter's stage directions emphasize the 'Elizabethan' manner and the epic scope of the play, which fuses myth, legend, and history in free-flowing pageantry. The play's episodic nature is given coherence by Riel, who is at once leader and victim/martyr. Coulter draws heavily on the New Testament to suggest affinities between Christ's trial, passion, and death and Riel's. Coulter also portrays Riel as representative of Canada's marginalized Native Peoples (the Métis are of Native and French descent) and of French Canadian Catholics oppressed by the colonizing Protestant English. *The Crime of Louis Riel* was written for small theatre companies unable to mount the full-scale *Riel*. It simplifies the historical action and calls for substantially fewer characters than are needed for *Riel*. *The Trial of Louis Riel*, a one-act documentary, is based on the transcripts of Riel's trial. Staged annually in a Regina courthouse/theatre built as a facsimile of the courthouse where Riel was tried and condemned to death, it makes a powerful theatrical statement. Following the play/trial, the audience/jury is asked to deliver its verdict on the guilt or innocence of Riel, thereby rendering a verdict on the truth or untruth of the colonizer's history. The play suggests that the Riel trilogy should be read as a historiographic metadrama in which issues of cultural denigration, appropriation of land, and an imperial, official history are interrogated at the bar of contemporary justice.

Coulter's importance for Canadian drama lies in the fact that he showed other Canadian dramatists that significant work could be created from indigenous materials. The Riel trilogy influenced both dramatists of the next generation, including **George Ryga** (*The Ecstasy of Rita Joe*, 1970), **James Reaney** (the Donnelly trilogy), and **Sharon Pollock** (*Walsh*, 1973), and such collectively written plays as *1837: The Farmers' Revolt* (1976).

Coulter's radical revision of the Riel story can also be compared profitably with that afforded **Ned Kelly** by Australian writers; both outlaws, Kelly and Riel were later mythologized as representatives of the marginalized and as martyrs to a colonial system that had no tolerance for diversity or difference.

EUGENE BENSON

Further reading: *Riel and Canadian Drama*, special issue of *Canadian Drama, L'Art dramatique canadien* 11 (1985).

COURAGE, JAMES FRANCIS (1903–63)
New Zealand novelist
Born in Christchurch, New Zealand, he grew up in North Canterbury and went to England in 1923 to read English at Oxford University. Except for return visits to New Zealand in 1927 and in 1934, he spent the rest of his life in England. Although his novel *One House* was published in 1933, his career as a writer effectively began with the novel *The Fifth Child* (1948). There, and in the four novels that followed — *Desire without Content* (1950), *Fires in the Distance* (1952), *The Young*

Have Secrets (1954), and *The Call Home* (1956) — as well as in many of his short stories, Courage established the world for which he will be remembered: the genteel Canterbury of sheep stations and private schools between 1914 and 1936. All of these well-made and somewhat artificial novels turn on sexual tensions within a family context, bringing a painful conflict from which the characters must learn to accept the competing demands and restraints of their own natures, the natures of others, the needs of their families, and the forces of heredity and sexuality.

Two later novels, *A Way of Love* (1959) and *The Visit to Penmorten* (1961), are set in England and bring to the forefront the homosexual theme that is secondary in the earlier novels. *Such Separate Creatures*, a posthumous selection of short stories edited by **Charles Brasch**, appeared in 1973.

LAWRENCE JONES

Further reading: R. A. Copland, 'The New Zealand novels of James Courage', *Landfall* 71 (1964).

COUVREUR, JESSIE
See **TASMA**

COWAN, JAMES (1870–1943)
New Zealand historian, journalist
Born at Pakuranga, near Auckland, New Zealand, he grew up on the 'frontier' of the King Country — in his boyhood still patrolled by the colonial Armed Constabulary — where he developed not only an admiration for the pioneers, but also sympathetic respect for Maori people. Initially a journalist (for a period with the Government's Tourist Department), Cowan compiled enthusiastic, promotional works such as *New Zealand, or, Aotea-roa (the Long Bright World)* (1907). Later a free-lance writer, he produced numerous articles and some forty books, mostly nonfiction — including popular ethnographic surveys (*The Maoris of New Zealand*, 1910; *The Maori of Yesterday and To-Day*, 1930), retellings of Maori lore and legends (*Fairy Folk Tales of the Maori*, 1925, for example), history, and 'tales' with a historical basis.

Cowan attempted to cultivate a 'spirit of nationhood' among Pakeha New Zealanders, particularly by recounting in colourful fashion the interaction between settlers and Maori, depicted in romantic rather than tragic terms. *Hero Stories of New Zealand* (1935), characterizations of various incidents during conflicts of the 1860s with both Maori and Pakeha cast as heroes, exemplifies Cowan's methods, rhetoric, and subject matter. Recognizing the parallels between settler societies, he sought his literary models in the USA, and as early as 1901 he drew the attention of other New Zealand writers to the achievements of James Fenimore Cooper and Henry Wadsworth Longfellow. Cowan's greatest work, *The New Zealand Wars: A History of the Maori Campaigns and the Pioneering Period* (2 vols, 1922–3; 3rd ed., 1983), begins by invoking Francis Parkman and other historians of the American frontier. Cowan relished oral reminiscence and, since he had acquired facility in the Maori language, his writings were invigorated by the testimony of Maori people as well as that of settlers. Later scholars preferred to use documentary evidence and plainer prose, but Cowan's works had much influence in arousing an interest in the New Zealand past, and his florid style has been imitated by writers of local histories.

PETER GIBBONS

Further reading: Michael King, 'Introduction', in James Cowan, *The New Zealand Wars: A History of the Maori Campaigns and the Pioneering Period* 2 vols (3rd ed., 1983).

COWAN, PETER (1914–)
Australian novelist, short-story writer
He was born in Perth, Western Australia, and after the early death of his father when he was ten years old, he was educated at Wesley College and Perth Technical College. Resigning from his first job as

an insurance clerk, Cowan spent most of the 1930s working as an itinerant farm labourer in country districts of Western Australia before taking up university studies and becoming a teacher. From 1964 to 1979 he taught in the English department at the University of Western Australia, where he still co-edits the quarterly literary magazine *Westerly*.

Cowan's published work includes six volumes of stories — *Drift* (1944), *The Unploughed Land* (1958), *The Empty Street* (1965), *The Tins* (1973), *Mobiles* (1979), and *Voices* (1988). *A Window in Mrs Xs Place: Selected Stories* appeared in 1986. His four novels are *Summer* (1964), *Seed* (1966), *The Color of the Sky* (1986), and *The Hills of Apollo Bay* (1989). In addition, Cowan has published several biographical studies of his pioneer forebears in Western Australia, including one of his grandmother, Edith Dircksey Cowan, the first woman member of an Australian parliament.

Best known as a short-story writer, Cowan published stories in *Angry Penguins* in the early 1940s and in *Ern Malley's Journal* in the 1950s. Always interested in experimenting with the forms of prose fiction, he has been described as a post-modernist in his later novels, *The Color of the Sky* and *The Hills of Apollo Bay*. A self-confessed regionalist, Cowan has commented on the importance of the physical landscapes of Western Australia in his writing. Humans are often diminished against Cowan's flat landscapes and the vast bowl of the sky. In this, they sometimes resemble the characters created by Canadian prairie writers **Sinclair Ross** and **Frederick Philip Grove** or the American Willa Cather. Where other white Australians tend to see ugliness or emptiness, Cowan finds a hard and enduring beauty in such Australian landscapes. Against such settings, his confused or tortured suburbanites discover, in aloneness and silence, the fragility of human life and relationships.

BRUCE BENNETT

COWASJEE, SAROS (1931–)

Indian/Canadian novelist, short-story writer, critic

Born in Secunderabad, India, and educated at St John's College, Agra (BA, 1951; MA, 1955), and Leeds University, England (Ph.D., 1960), he worked as an assistant editor (1961–3) with the Times of India Press, and since 1963 has been a member of the Department of English, the University of Regina, Canada. His publications include *Sean O'Casey: The Man Behind the Plays* (1963); *O'Casey* (1966); *Stories and Sketches* (1970); a novel, *Goodbye to Elsa* (1974); *'Coolie': An Assessment* (1976); *So Many Freedoms: A Study of the Major Fiction of Mulk Raj Anand* (1977); a second volume of short stories, *Nude Therapy* (1978); a screenplay, *The Last of the Maharajas* (1980), based on a **Mulk Raj Anand** novel (*The Private Life of an Indian Prince*, 1953); and a second novel, *Suffer Little Children* (1982). He has edited five novels by Anand as well as *Author to Critic: The Letters of Mulk Raj Anand to Saros Cowasjee* (1973), *Modern Indian Fiction* (1980, with Vasant Shahane), *Modern Indian Short Stories* (1982, with **Shiv K. Kumar**), *Stories from the Raj* (1982), *More Stories from the Raj* (1986), *The Raj and After* (1987), *When the British Left* (1987, with K. S. Duggal), and *Women Writers of the Raj: Short Fiction* (1990). Cowasjee is also general editor of the Literature of the Raj series, which, since 1984, has republished books by J. R. Ackerley, Philip Mason, Captain Meadows Taylor, and others.

Besides his scholarship on Irish and Indian literature and his rediscovery of neglected older Indian and foreign writing about India, Cowasjee is an interesting, amusing writer of fiction. He has a strong sense of being different; the unexpected directions his novels take reflect a sense of life as comically absurd. His ten days of training as an officer cadet in the Indian army before he fled is the basis for the story 'Tristan reads Marie in Section 25', from *Goodbye to Elsa*, a novel written with *Gulliver's Travels* in mind. Tristan's search for love, and his loneliness when in the presence of others, is associated with his divided Anglo-Indianness. Tristan, in *Suffer Little Children*, falls in love with Maura at a nude-therapy session and comes to believe that in an era of women's liberation her year-old daughter is a Messiah whom he attempts to kidnap after being rejected by the mother.

BRUCE KING

COWLEY, JOY (1936–)

New Zealand children's writer, novelist

She was born in Levin, New Zealand, and educated at Palmerston North Girls' High School. Cowley's writing career can be divided sharply between that of a successful author for adults from 1967 to 1979 and that of a highly acclaimed writer for children from 1981 to the present (apart from one collection of adult short stories, *Heart Attack and Other Stories*, 1985).

Cowley's adult novels and short stories are firmly realistic, frequently focusing upon the unintentional destruction of one human being by another. The main protagonist in *Nest in a Falling Tree* (1967) exacts revenge upon a puritanical mother by embarking upon a doomed love affair. *Man of Straw* (1970) chronicles the oppression of a thirteen-year-old girl by the indifference and selfishness of her family. In *The Mandrake Root* (1975) the central character is not only victimized by dominating parents but is subject to the incest of her drug-dealing brother. Cowley's characters, however, triumph over the competing self-interests of their families and take control of their own lives. In her short stories Cowley compresses emotions that seem too large for the narrow containment of their settings. In 'Heart Attack', for example, she writes, 'There was no room in the house for his grief. It was a pain too big to be contained within walls and yet there was nowhere else to go.'

Apart from one full-length novel for children, *The Silent One* (1981), Cowley's children's writing comprises short fantasy stories that have been published as picture-books, frequently featuring traditional characters such as pirates, giants, soldiers, or monsters. Although written with sparkling humour, her stories nevertheless explore serious issues and offer alternatives to conflict. In *The Duck in the Gun* (1969), illustrated by Edward Sorel, war is delayed and finally averted when a gun cannot be used because a duck has made a nest in it. In *Brith the Terrible* (1986) a giant is prevailed upon to stop bullying a city when tickled by butterflies. Only in *Salmagundi* (1985) is a darker picture drawn of an arms race that temporarily ceases but is later re-activated by the wicked protagonists.

The Silent One is set in the Pacific islands and movingly recounts how a deaf and mute boy is blamed for every natural disaster until finally he leaves the island and resumes his turtle shape. Emotional depth and mythic resonance combine with stylistic elegance in this work, which will assuredly become a classic of New Zealand children's literature.

BETTY GILDERDALE

Further reading: Betty Gilderdale, *Introducing Twenty-One New Zealand Children's Writers* (1991).

CRAIG, CHRISTINE (1943–)

Jamaican poet, short-story writer, children's writer

Born in Kingston, Jamaica, she spent her early childhood in the country, in St Elizabeth. She states that both the flatlands and the hills importantly influenced her imagination. She has written three children's books: *Emmanuel and His Parrot* (1970), *Emmanuel Goes to Market* (1971), and *The Bird Gang* (1990). She began publishing poetry in the late 1970s and published her first volume,

Quadrille for Tigers, in 1984. Her story 'In The Hills' appeared in the anthology *Her True-True Name* (1989), edited by **Pamela Mordecai** and Betty Wilson.

Craig's poetry portrays social tensions, especially those caused by poverty and the condition of women. She has said that when the work is at its most obscure, it is at its most realistic and that simplicity cannot always do justice to complex feeling and thought. Her observations on the ordinary are often remarkably striking — 'Her freckled plumpness wedged / in school' ('All Things Bright and Beautiful') — and frequently reflect the intersection of gender, race, and class consciousness. One of her best-known poems is 'Crow Poem', in which a woman's consciousness is imaged as that of a crow — awkward, outside the stereotypes of conventional beauty, trying to love. There is a strong awareness of shape, line, and colour in the poems, which, in theme and form, are declarations of the survival of love and a sense of moral order in an often-cruel and divided environment. In her newer poems, in *Sweet Fruit, Hard Life* (1991), many of the concerns of her earlier work are present: an emphasis on women in society, a sensuous awareness of the world, a clear, precisely articulated morality of caring, in a conflicted and divided social context. Craig's linguistic register varies from Jamaican accented international English to Creole and demonstrates a strong, if often-pained, commitment to Jamaica.

ELAINE SAVORY (FIDO)

CRAIG, DENNIS ROY (1929–)

Guyanese poet, educator

Born in Georgetown, Guyana, he earned a BA in English and French (1952) from the University of the West Indies and an MA in education and language education (1963) and a Ph.D. in sociolinguistics (1971) from the University of London, England. He began teaching at the University of the West Indies, Jamaica, in 1964, becoming department head and dean of the faculty of education. In 1991 he was appointed vice-chancellor of the University of Guyana. Craig has been a pioneer in the analytic study of English-based Creoles in the Caribbean and their socio-linguistic effect on teacher-learner relations in the classroom. He has authored and co-authored several textbooks on the teaching of English as a second language.

Although Craig has not published a full volume of poetry, his poems have been published in journals since 1961, when 'Tribute' and 'Flowers' were published in *Bim*. 'Empty Lot (near Kingston)' and 'To a Country Girl' were published in *Caribbean Quarterly* in 1969. These poems speak of the harshness and squalor of the urban environment and constitute an elegiac lament for the loss of youth and beauty. 'Age' and 'Waiting' were both recorded in *Savacou* (1970–1), while *Caribbean Voices* (1970) published 'The Day the Nation Mourned' and 'Interlude for Native Pride'. *The Greenfield Review*, in its 1985 edition, 'New Poetry from the West Indies', edited by **Edward Baugh**, included Craig's 'By the Hudson, New York' and 'Roots revisited from Jamaica (with apologies to Alex Haley)'. *Kyk-over-al* published 'Trader' in 1991.

Each poem or group of poems seems to encapsulate a vision of each Caribbean decade from the 1960s to the 1990s, and the poetry as a whole reveals a serious engagement with aspects of the political and social movements in the Caribbean and is marked by a firm control of structure and line.

HELEN PYNE TIMOTHY

CRAWFORD, ISABELLA VALANCY (1850–87)

Canadian poet, short-story writer

Born in Dublin, Ireland, into an educated, genteel family, Crawford, her younger sister Emma Naomi, and her brother Stephen Walter were the only survivors of the twelve or thirteen children of Dr Stephen Dennis Crawford and his wife Sidney

Scott Crawford. About 1857 the family settled in the newly surveyed village of Paisley, Ontario, Canada, where Dr Crawford was disgraced over his embezzlement of public funds. The family moved frequently and acquired a reputation for being reclusive, proud, and very poor. After Dr Crawford's death in 1875, Crawford and her mother moved from Peterborough to Toronto. One of the very few nineteenth-century colonial writers able to survive on income from writing, Crawford sold short lyric poems to Toronto newspapers, and short stories and serialized novels to American magazines such as *Frank Leslie's*.

Crawford published only one book, *Old Spookses' Pass, Malcolm's Katie, and Other Poems* (1884), which was printed at the author's expense in a run of a thousand and sold only fifty copies, despite favourable reviews. Almost unknown in her lifetime, Crawford is now celebrated as an early and influential figure in developing the long narrative poem in Canada. She fused eclectic influences — Dante and Tennyson, and Norse, Greek, and Amerindian mythology — into a style authentically her own, a style at once mythopoeic and energized by highly charged and often-erotic imagery. Her poetry gives striking expression to subjects familiar from her own experience: life in a pioneer colonial settlement; Native culture and mythology; Canadian wilderness landscape as it contrasts with civilization; life as a battleground of love and violence, creation and destruction; the dialogue of hope and despair.

CATHERINE SHELDRICK ROSS

Further reading: John Garvin, ed., *The Collected Poems of Isabella Valancy Crawford* (1905; repr. in facsimile 1972); Glenn Clever, ed., *Hugh and Ion* (1977); Frank M. Tierney, ed., *The Isabella Valancy Crawford Symposium* (1977); D. M. R. Bentley, ed., *Malcolm's Katie: A Love Story* (1987).

CRIME AND MYSTERY FICTION (Australia)
The first bestselling crime novel of all was written, set, and published in Melbourne, Australia, in 1886. **Fergus Hume**'s *The Mystery of a Hansom Cab* sold out in Australia, and in London sold perhaps half a million copies. This is not as surprising as it might seem. Crime fiction is a product of the new world of cities, changeable identity, portable money, and elusive crime: after the great gold rushes of the 1850s Melbourne was a roaring boom town, rich in mystery and temptation.

Crime stories appeared in nineteenth-century magazines. The world's first female thriller writer may have been Mary Fortune, whose 'Detective's Album' began in 1868 in the *Australian Journal*. Others followed the genre: some, like Guy Boothby (of Dr Nikola fame), made their name overseas; others, such as A. E. Hornung, the creator of 'Raffles', started writing in Australia and then returned to England. Much of the local material, however, was unknown elsewhere and until comparatively recently never reprinted in Australia, including such items as Randolph Bedford's *Billy Pagan, Mining Engineer* (1911), tales about a robust bush detective, or the relatively nonracist stories in *The Black Police* (1890), by Arthur Vogan.

London eventually came to dominate the crime publishing world. Helen Simpson and J. M. Walsh were only two of many Australians who made their names in the golden age of crime writing in London. From the 1930s to the 1950s Australians such as Max Afford, Paul McGuire, and (as Shane Martin) **George Johnston** wrote for the European market, sometimes with local settings. The best-known Australian contributor to the crime genre was Arthur Upfield, a British immigrant turned Outback-lover who crossed the English procedural mystery with the bush romance and centred it on an improbable Aboriginal detective, Napoleon Bonaparte. Sound sellers at home and in England, the stories took off internationally in 1942 when a New York publisher made a link between Upfield's setting and the American war effort in the South Pacific. Books by Upfield include *The Barakee Mystery* (1929), *Death of a Lake* (1954), *Man of Two Tribes* (1956), and *Bony Buys a Woman* (1967).

The American connection and the coming of television attenuated the British lifeline of Australian crime writing, though some good work still emerged — the clue-puzzles of Margot Neville (the Goyder sisters, Margaret and Anne), for example. Sidney Courtier, a Victorian headmaster, wrote mildly realist, Buchan-like adventures; Pat Flower produced psycho-thrillers capable of comparison with those of Patricia Highsmith and Ruth Rendell; and the evergreen **Jon Cleary** handled crime of various kinds in his series about Scobie Malone, a rough-hewn honest cop.

A new wave of writing and a new consciousness of local thrillers came with the redevelopment of local publishing. **Peter Corris** was a leader, though others had written about Sydney private eyes — Ian Hamilton and Otto Beeby, for example. Corris' steady success attracted others; Jennifer Rowe, a publishing editor, produced *Grim Pickings* (1987), a sharply observed, mildly feminist classic mystery, and its success started something of a flood. Robert Wallace (Robin Wallace-Crabbe, a well-known painter) writes spirited crime adventures, set mostly in Europe, and others of note are Martin Long — whose trademark is historical Sydney settings — and Marele Day, who writes Sydney-based feminist thrillers.

The short story also revived, especially with a monthly competition in the *Australian Way* (an airline in-flight magazine), which attracted hundreds of entries, the best being published as *The Golden Dagger Mysteries* in 1988 and 1989. Retrospective collections were edited by Dave Latta (*Sand on the Gumshoe*, 1989) and Stephen Knight (*Dead Witness*, 1989), and an annual of new stories, *Crimes for a Summer Christmas*, edited by Knight, first appeared in 1990.

Like police procedurals, spy fiction is under-represented in Australian publishing — a notable exception is Corris' Crawley series. Although the country may be too isolated for international threats to mean much, it has its own related genre of Asian adventure from writers such as Louis Becke and Beatrice Grimshaw in the past (not forgetting Errol Flynn's not contemptible novel, *Showdown*, 1946); contemporary novelists Ian Moffitt, Margaret Jones, and Bob Brissenden have all written spy fiction.

More writers are emerging all the time, and some may stay the distance. Crime writing was always structural to the culture of a country whose first settlement as a penal colony itself depended on crime, and it is a significant part of the healthy resurgence in publishing in Australia.

STEPHEN KNIGHT

Further reading: Stephen Knight, 'The case of the missing genre', *Southerly* 48 (1988).

CRIME AND MYSTERY FICTION (Canada)
While mysteries have been written by Canadian-born writers since the late nineteenth century and, more rarely, set in Canada, an identifiably Canadian tradition has emerged only since the 1960s. Unlike early Australian mystery writers, who characteristically used remote settings and the common British motif of hiding and hidden identities, or writers of stories set in India or Africa that seem as much travelogue as mystery and are usually concerned with the colonial experience, Canadian mystery writers were drawn to the urban and cultural centres of the UK and the USA, and their stories are thematically very diverse.

Although most mysteries written during the first fifty years of the genre's history in Canada are indistinguishable from their American or British counterparts, several make important contributions to the development of the genre and its stock of conventions and stereotypes. Grant Allen (1848–99) was born in Kingston, Canada; his picaresque swindler and thief, Colonel Clay, who made his début in *An African Millionaire* (1897), anticipates Ernest Hornung's Raffles by two years. Robert Barr (1850–1912), who lived in Canada between the ages of four and thirty-one, wrote the first Sherlock Holmes parody and created Eugène Valmont, a comic French detective working in London, England, who prefigures Agatha Christie's Poirot. Montreal-born Frank L. Packard (1877–1942) created New York socialite and safecracker Jimmy Dale, who, like Allen's Colonel Clay, is a type of Robin Hood figure. Arthur Stringer (1874–1950) of Chatham, Ontario, moved to the USA in 1898 and wrote a series of mysteries, some set in New York and some in the Canadian North, and introduced a woman detective who relies heavily on intuition. Harvey O'Higgins (1876–1929) of London, Canada, moved to New York with Stringer and introduced two staple American figures, boy detective Barney Cook and Inspector John Duff, the first serious psychoanalytic detective.

The careers of these early Canadian mystery writers are remarkably similar: education and early successes at home were followed by immigration to the USA or the UK. Margaret Millar, whose work marks an important transition period for the Canadian mystery, also follows this pattern. In the early 1940s she introduced Paul Pyne, an American psychiatrist who solves mysteries near his Canadian summer home, and Toronto police Inspector Sands, who appeared in two novels. Sands looked as if he might become a Canadian original: lonely, non-descript, and unromantic, made in the national self-image. Millar moved to California, USA, however, with her husband Ross Macdonald, and earned a Mystery Writers of America Edgar Allan Poe Award for her classic American west coast mysteries. Ann Cardwell's superb *Crazy to Kill* (1941), narrated by a patient in an exclusive asylum, was the basis for what might be a first in the genre, the highly acclaimed *Crazy to Kill: A Detective Opera* (1989) with libretto by **James Reaney** and music by John Beckwith.

In the 1960s growing self-consciousness and nationalism prompted the beginings of a recognizable Canadian tradition. Ellen Godfrey and **Hugh Garner** made historically important but generically negligible attempts to patriate the mystery. John Norman Harris published the more influential *The Weird World of Wes Beattie* (1963), in which eccentric Toronto lawyer Sidney Grant sets out to clear the title character of a murder charge. Unashamedly making use of and gently satirizing its Toronto-and-environs setting and atmosphere, this characteristically Canadian story teams the lawyer with the accused's sister to form a mixed-gender detecting duo, which became a dominant feature of later Canadian mysteries. This pairing seems to originate with the myths and practices of colonial Canada. Where the British mystery typically uses a pair or group of class-conscious males to detect, and the proto-story seems to be that of Robin Hood and his band, and the Americans have played on the tradition of the cowboy hero imposing his internalized code on the chaos without, the Canadian story images a woman and a man bravely facing the threatening wilderness together. This pattern is evident during the flowering of the Canadian mystery in the 1980s in some or all of the the works of Eric Wright, L. R. Wright, Medora Sale, William Deverell, Laurence Gough, Alison Gordon, Elisabeth Bowers, David Laing Dawson, and E. X. Giroux.

Colonial experience is hardly the sole determinant of the nature of contemporary Canadian mysteries. There is great diversity among even the very selective group listed above, so that while Gough's Vancouver police detective team of Parker and Willows fits the mutually supportive female-male pattern, the explosions of violent action in Gough's climaxes are more characteristic of American style than Canadian. Eric Wright appears on the list not because Toronto police inspector Charlie Salter has a female 'partner in crime detecting' but because his home life is as much a part of the story as his professional life. This conforms to the Canadian norm, but could also be said of the Pascoe/Dalziel novels of Britain's Reginald Hill. Elisabeth Bowers' *Ladies' Night* (1988) presents a single mother fledgling private eye who works with a police detective to solve a child-pornography-cum-drug case, offering a realistic antidote to the US model of the female supersleuth as presented in the works of American Sarah Paretsky or Canadian Maurice Gagnon. Howard Engel plays off his deeply Canadian hero of limited competence — the short, overweight, and insecure Benny Cooperman — against British and American stereotypes and conventions.

In the 1980s two other developments accompanied the flowering of Canadian mystery fiction. Where once Canadians uniformly emigrated to further their careers, writers including Czechoslovakia's **Josef Škvorecký**, England's Peter Robinson, and Ireland's John Brady have moved to Canada, although for the most part they continue to set their stories in their native environments. The Canadian tradition has also been enriched by writers established in mainstream fiction exploiting the narrative energy of and fascination with the mystery. This group includes **Timothy Findley** in *The Telling of Lies* (1986), **Carol Shields** in *Swann* (1987), Škvorecký in his Boruvka novels and stories, **David Helwig** in *Old Wars* (1989), and **George Bowering** in *Harry's Fragments* (1990). Even these last two groups participate in the Canadian mystery writers' desire to respond to international genre conventions and topical issues in accord with Canada's contemporary self-image, resulting in mysteries that highlight gender and class politics, the environment, and national differences themselves and tend towards the gentler, kinder styles of murder, mayhem, and detection.

ALLAN J. GEDALOF

Further reading: Michael Richardson, *A Casebook of Canadian Detective Fiction* (1982).

CRIME AND MYSTERY FICTION (India)

Crime fiction made a late entry into Indian-English literature, appearing only in the 1970s; only four novelists have written more than one thriller each. **Ruskin Bond**, winner of the Sahitya Akademi Award in 1992, published *An Axe for the Rani* in 1972. In the work the identity of the murderer of the Rani is rather obvious, but the book is notable for its sympathetic portrayal of Keemat Lall, the police officer investigating the case. E. N. Mangat Rai, who was in the Indian Civil Service, is the author of such scholarly books as *Patterns of Administrative Development in Independent India* (1974); he has written one interesting detective book, *The Lalru Murders* (1973), set in the Punjab. Aamir Ali, author of the novels *Conflict* (1947) and *Via Geneva* (1967), has his young hero taking on a gang of gun-runners in *Assignment in Kashmir* (1973). Shakuntala Devi, the mathematical genius (she is known as the 'Human Computer') has written *Perfect Murder* (1976), a thriller in which the narrator, a clever lawyer, plans what he thinks is the perfect murder. K. Ramayya Rai's *The Tell Tale Teeth* (1982) is a 'true detective story' based on a case he handled when he was a deputy superintendent of police. Ramesh Menon's first novel, *The Hunt for K* (1992), begins as a thriller with detective inspector Partha as hero, but drifts into satire and metaphysics with most of the people in the book named after characters from the *Mahabharata*.

Manohar Malgonkar has written one spy thriller, *Bandicoot Run* (1982), in which Pakistan gets vital military secrets from India by blackmailing a powerful Indian general who has a dark secret in his past. As in his first novel, *Distant Drum* (1960), Malgonkar makes good use of his experience as an officer in the Indian army. The hero, a retired army officer, helps Kiran Garud (the protagonist of *Distant Drum*, who has now risen to the rank of general) to clear his name. *Bandicoot Run* is readable, but lacks the power of Malgonkar's earlier novels *The Princes* (1963) and *A Bend in the Ganges* (1964).

Amarjit Kullar, a squadron leader in the Indian Air Force, wrote two thrillers with a fighter pilot as protagonist — *Shadow of the Dragon* (1975) and *The Alpertol Affair* (1976). Set in southern France and the Persian Gulf respectively, these have plenty of action, complete with beautiful girls. Hugh Gantzer, an officer in the Indian navy, has written five thrillers, the last being *Flashpoint!* (1978); he has since turned to writing travelogues. Netto, the secret agent in *Operation Overkill* (1975) and *The President's Ransom* (1976), owes more to John le Carré than to Ian Fleming. The ageing Netto longs to return to his home in South India. (Gantzer is a Jew from Malabar, which has a very old Jewish community.) The novels present an authentic picture of life in India. Gantzer's earlier thrillers, *The Kumbh Docket* (1972) and *Ballot for Violence* (1974), written under the name of Shyam Dave, have active young heroes.

Another novelist who has written thrillers is Timeri Murari. Like Graham Greene, he divides his fiction into two categories: 'novels', such as *The Marriage* (1973), *Lovers Are Not People* (1978), and *Taj* (1985), and 'entertainments', such as *The Oblivion Tapes* (1978) and *The Shooter* (1984). There is nothing Indian about the characters or the settings of Murari's thrillers, but they are well written. In *The Oblivion Tapes*, a New York journalist discovers that a mysterious and deadly epidemic in a South American country is man-made; *The Shooter* is set in affluent Manhattan. Murari's sequels to Rudyard Kipling's *Kim* — *The Imperial Agent* (1987) and *The Last Victory* (1988) — are 'novels' with elements of the thriller.

There are no outstanding Indian writers of detective fiction. Indian-English literature has no one to compare with Satyajit Ray in Bengali, for instance: Ray has written eighteen detective stories, meant primarily for younger readers, though adults also enjoy them. Recently, Rupa and Company (Calcutta) has launched a Crime series of slickly produced run-of-the mill thrillers, which can serve to pass the time on a tedious journey.

SHYAMALA A. NARAYAN

CRIME AND MYSTERY FICTION (New Zealand) Crime fiction in New Zealand is virtually synonymous with the name of **Ngaio Marsh**, and mystery with the name of **Dorothy Eden**, both of whose international careers span the middle decades of the twentieth century. There was no significant New Zealand crime fiction in the nineteenth century, by contrast with Australia, whose origins as a penal colony and subsequent history of bushranging produced a vigorous local tradition. (See **Crime and Mystery Fiction**, Australia.) **Fergus Hume**, a barrister educated in Otago, New Zealand, published *The Mystery of a Hansom Cab* (1886) in Melbourne, and in the wake of its huge success immigrated to England, where he wrote a further 140 mysteries. **G. B. Lancaster** (Edith Lyttleton) touched on issues of law and lawlessness in 'frontier' novels set, not in New Zealand, but in Australia (*Jim of the Ranges*, 1910) and in Canada (*The Law-Bringers*, 1913).

However, a number of Lancaster's early short stories were mystery stories of a type relatively common in New Zealand colonial short fiction — especially where representation of Maori 'otherness' was anxiously at issue. **F. E. Maning**'s chapters on the *tohunga*'s mysterious powers of *tapu* in *Old New Zealand* (1863), framed within the anxious, Eurocentric rationality of the story's mocking narrator, perhaps provided the model for this local variant of the mystery genre, whose racial stereotypes survived in many different kinds of fiction after 1900 — from **William Satchell**'s *The Greenstone Door* (1914) to **Dulce Carman**'s popular 'Maoriland' romances in the 1950s.

Marsh's four New Zealand detective novels

represented a very different kind of adaptation of a British model, an attempt to graft an exploration of issues of national identity onto the whodunit formula. Both *Colour Scheme* (1943) and *Died in the Wool* (1944), with their multiple punning titles, are especially skilled in exploring a New Zealand context that, in the words of critic Carol Acheson, is 'no mere travelogue but a significant and well-integrated element of the story', representing New Zealand as a society still in the making, troubled by unresolved racial issues, rejecting the older colonial connection but unsure what to put in place of it. Eden's New Zealand romantic mysteries lack the exploratory quality of Marsh's novels, but are equally skilled at integrating local settings with suspense actions, in order to intensify the general atmosphere of male menace and intimidation.

Since the 1960s no individual authors have matched the professional achievements of Marsh and Eden. In the 1950s and 1960s Elizabeth Messenger was the first author to use wholly localized (tourist) settings, and Valerie Grayland attempted to establish a Maori detective. Simon Jay, Terence Journet, George Joseph, and Colin Peel produced a variety of thrillers with local and international settings in the 1960s and 1970s, and in the 1980s Laurie Mantell had some success with a local detective-hero, in contexts that emphasized crimes of violence against women. At least as significant as the growing diversity of popular writing, however, has been the utilization of the genres for serious purposes, as New Zealand fiction moved beyond several decades of realism. Novels as diverse as **Maurice Gee**'s *In My Father's Den* (1972) and **C. K. Stead**'s *The Death of the Body* (1986) draw strongly on the conventions of crime fiction, and varieties of Gothic convention are prominent in the fiction of **R. H. Morrieson** and **Marilyn Duckworth**, as well as in **Fiona Kidman**'s *Mandarin Summer* (1981) and *The Book of Secrets* (1987).

TERRY STURM

CRITICISM

CRITICISM (Overview)

Criticism of post-colonial literatures in English refers to three distinct but often overlapping activities: the individual nation-based literary histories and criticism produced in formerly colonized countries; the comparative study of these literatures and their contexts; and the theorizing of their study under the rubric of post-colonialism. As a currently contested terrain of literary study, the post-colonial field is variously used to refer to a period (either that following the attainment of nominal independence from imperial control or to the entire range of colonial, neo-colonial, and post-colonial participations since the eighteenth century); a subject-matter (usually focusing on either the cultural productions of colonies and ex-colonies or of writers from ex-colonies now living in the metropolis); and a variety of interrelated reading strategies designed, in **Ngugi Wa Thiong'o**'s phrase, to 'decolonise the mind'.

Far from being the sum of the national and regional criticisms described elsewhere in this volume, post-colonial criticism involves an alternative approach to understanding imperialism and its impact as a global rather than primarily a local phenomenon. The post-colonial approach offers an interrogation of the relations between culture and imperialism, identifying that relation as the central global context for understanding politics and culture in the present age of decolonization. Self-interrogation remains a central concern for the discipline, because it questions the very disciplinary structures of knowledge (particularly anthropology, geography, and English literary studies) developed during the imperial period. Like feminism, post-colonial critique has usually been a theory of engagement, concerned with creating agency for the marginalized and oppressed, with recovering lost histories and voices, and with opening up the academy to the world. (See **Femin-**

ism.) Increasingly, however, post-colonial critics have expressed doubts about the growing institutionalization of the discipline and the possible co-option of its earlier message of resistance, removing it from the terrain of material encounters into a totally textualized field.

One account of the history and methodology of post-colonial criticism may be found in Bill Ashcroft's, Gareth Griffiths', and Helen Tiffin's *The Empire Writes Back* (1989), which traces the development of post-colonial criticism from Commonwealth literature and its formation through the influential theories of the Caribbean writers Frantz Fanon, **Wilson Harris**, and **Edward Kamau Brathwaite** and of the African writer **Chinua Achebe**. This study has been criticized for underestimating the importance of some African theorists, particularly Ngugi, for privileging the English language, and for presenting what is in effect a homogenizing discourse, despite its insistence on hybridity and difference. It remains, however, an exhaustive and challenging introduction to the field; it is particularly strong in its analyses of the settler-invader cultures and the Caribbean and in its critique of postmodernism.

An alternative genealogy may be found in Robert Young's *White Mytholgies: Writing History and the West* (1990), which traces the origins of post-colonial critique to European philosophy, articulating a line of development from Hegel through Jean-Paul Sartre and on to Edward Said, Gayatri Spivak, and Homi K. Bhabha. Certainly Said can be credited with bringing post-colonial issues to centre stage in the Anglo-American arena, with the publication most notably of *Orientalism* (1978), *After the Last Sky* (1986), and *Culture and Imperialism* (1993). Spivak and Bhabha have been most influential through their articles, although Spivak's book *In Other Worlds* (1987) and a collection of her interviews, *The Post-Colonial Critic* (1990), as well as Bhabha's edited collection, *Nation and Narration* (1990), are much cited. The work of these theorists, all cosmopolitan intellectuals located in metropolitan centres, derives its methodology from different strands in European poststructuralism and deconstruction. (See **Post-Colonial Theorists.**)

This methodology has led to important breakthroughs in our understanding of specific colonial formations. Gauri Viswanathan in *Masks of Conquest: Literary Study and British Rule in India* (1989) illuminates the colonial origins of English studies. Sara Suleri advances colonial discourse analysis in *The Rhetoric of English India* (1992). Kwame Anthony Appiah rethinks contemporary African culture in *In My Father's House*: *Africa in the Philosophy of Culture* (1992). Barbara Harlow develops the transcultural term 'resistance literature' (in her *Resistance Literature*, 1987) to focus attention away from colonial discourse back to the literary productions of the colonized. Yet although such ground-breaking studies may be assimilated under the banner of 'post-colonial' criticism, the term 'post-colonial' has not yet gained general acceptance, particularly among critics working outside the metropolis. 'Post-colonial' is a term either ignored or disparaged in large parts of Africa, in the Caribbean, in India, or among indigenous First Nations groups and African-Americans in North America. Cultural and economic nationalism still seems to be the more important priority for these groups, which do not wish to sacrifice the specificity of their concerns to the more general term 'post-colonial'. In this spirit, Arun Mukherjee argues for an engaged oppositional stance in combating residual imperialist ideologies within contemporary capitalist culture in *Towards an Aesthetic of Opposition: Essays on Literature, Criticism and Cultural Imperialism* (1988).

Literary criticism throughout the post-colonial world has necessarily been attentive to its own historical and local contexts in working through its most pressing preoccupations with questions of definition and evaluation. Each region has grappled with the problem of formulating a methodology appropriate to the kinds of writing produced locally. Certain unresolved issues recur: determining the relation of English to indigenous languages; the importance of translation; cross-cultural influences within and from outside a culture; the roles of orality and literacy; appropriate standards of value; the status of literary representation; the central role of institutional sites for literary and critical production; and the imagining of competing identities (national, regional, racial, gendered, class).

Yet in addition to its self-conscious scrutiny of its own complicities, post-colonial criticism, in all its variety, has been largely concerned with documenting, preserving, and celebrating the literature produced by peoples who were denigrated by imperialism, but who often maintained their own alternative sources of cultural strength. The challenge for critics is to recognize the distortions produced by imperialism and maintained under the current capitalist world system, without over-privileging them. Local literary debates were never determined exclusively by colonial conditions alone; other material conditions have contributed to their production and reception.

DIANA BRYDON

Further Reading: Aijaz Ahmad, *In Theory: Classes, Nations, Literatures* (1992); Diana Brydon and Helen Tiffin, *Decolonising Fictions* (1993).

CRITICISM (Australia)

Criticism has been a problematic activity in Australia. Initially the concern was to come to terms with the cultural void that seemed to yawn before the first settlers: the Aboriginal people and culture were beyond consideration for numerous reasons, both economic and ideological. Anticipating Nathaniel Hawthorne in the USA, **Frederick Sinnett**, for instance, complained in 1856 in his *The Fiction Fields of Australia* (published in two instalments in the *Journal of Australasia*) that the cultural soil was far too thin to support a worthwhile literature: 'Debarred from all the interest to be extracted from any kind of archaeological accessories . . . storied windows, richly dight [which would] cast a dim, religious light over any Australian premises', Australian writers were therefore suffering (he suggested) from imaginative malnutrition.

The point is not a minor one. Henry James was expressing the common view when he wrote that it takes hundreds of years of culture to produce even a little literature. Nor was this lack merely a matter of 'archaeological accessories' or even familiarity with contemporary writing and critical thought. However, improved communications, the prosperity that flooded in with the discovery of gold in the 1850s, and subsequent commercial as well as pastoral expansion led to the establishment of libraries as well as good bookshops. In Sydney, the literary circle that gathered at the home of patron and lawyer Nicholas Stenhouse from the 1850s until into the 1870s became a clearing-house for ideas. Elsewhere, too, literary clubs and discussion circles appeared: in Melbourne the Yorick Club, founded in 1868, in Hobart the Macquarie Debating Society (1855–80), and in Brisbane the Johnsonian Club, founded in 1879. As for Adelaide and Perth, the smallness of the settlement and the genteel nature of the settlers made talk about books and ideas from 'home' a way of life. The question remained, however, of how to come to terms with the environment itself, not merely so distant geographically from England, the centre and guarantee of value for the educated and genteel, but physically so different. As **Marcus Clarke** wrote in his preface to the new edition of **Adam Lindsay Gordon**'s *Sea Spray and Smoke Drift* (1867), the problem was ontological and epistemological. Here, the Book of Nature from which writers in England drew their sustenance seemed, if not entirely closed, at least indecipherable. Here he could discern only 'the scribblings of Nature learning to write', the 'phantasmagoria of that wild dreamland the Bush'.

Among the first to respond to this problem were the native-born writers **Charles Harpur** and his admirer **Henry Kendall.** Harpur in particular argued strenuously that Australian subjects were worthwhile for their own sake and would create their own style. In practice, however, neither he nor Kendall was able to develop this style, relying heavily on English models. But Harpur stands also at the beginning of another strain in Australia's literary criticism, its preoccupation with the political. For him poetry was 'not only religious in spirit but moral in influence' and therefore bound up with the struggle for freedom from imperial domination, which he saw as crucial to the establishment of national identity.

While it is clear with hindsight that this tradition was in part at least the self-conscious creation of writers such as **Vance Palmer** (*The Legend of the Nineties*, 1954), **Russel Ward** (*The Australian Legend*, 1958), and **A. A. Phillips** (*The Australian Tradition*, 1958), it established and sustained links between literary criticism and social concern that inspired most of the significant writers of the 1920s and 1930s, such as Vance Palmer and **Nettie Palmer, Katharine Susannah Prichard, Louis Esson**, Frank Wilmot, **Kylie Tennant**, and Dymphna Cusack. Largely a result of their work, 'Australian' writing was until recently identified with the Left, and in this sense was politically significant. The Australian Labour party, for instance, has traditionally seen itself as heir to the 'Legend of the 90s' and as therefore more 'Australian' than the conservative parties; note the nationalism promoted by the legendary Whitlam government (1972–5). It is perhaps no coincidence that courses in Australian literature were introduced into most Australian universities at this time and that the Association for the Study of Australian Literature was formed in 1978.

None the less, criticism has also kept up the international connections. At the turn of the century, **A. G. Stephens**, the literary editor of the ***Bulletin*** who encouraged the development of a national literature, also wrote essays on the French and English avant garde of his day, and **Christopher Brennan**, poet and polymath, lectured on the poetry of William Blake, theories of symbolism, and the aesthetics of art. In Sydney in the 1920s the Vision group, even as it proclaimed its independence, drew on the ideas of Nietzsche as well as on those of Alfred Orage, Havelock Ellis, and P. D. Ouspensky. Similarly, nationalists and populists like Prichard, Esson, and the Palmers owed a great deal to the Irish literary revival as well as to this European vitalist tradition. So, too, with **P. R. Stephensen**'s passionately polemical *The Foundations of Culture In Australia* (1936), said to have inspired **Xavier Herbert**'s *Capricornia* (1938) and the **Jindyworobak Movement,** which attempted to create an 'Australian' literature by drawing on Aboriginal culture. Outraged by the charge made by the professor of English at Melbourne that Australian writing was unworthy of the name 'literature', Stephensen's argument was grounded on Nietzsche's contempt for values imposed from outside.

The Second World War stimulated patriotism and an explosion of creativity that led to the foundation of a number of new literary journals, including *Meanjin* (1940–), *Southerly* (1939–), *Overland* (1954–), *Quadrant* (1956–), and *Westerly* (1956–). (See **Literary Magazines**, Australia.) But it also led to a new sense of Australia's involvement with the rest of the world, and these journals drew attention to current intellectual debates. Even more significant was the expansion of the university system in the 1960s. Until then most academics were either English or had been educated in England, usually at Oxford or Cambridge. But many of those appointed in the 1960s, especially to the new universities, had been trained in the USA and were interested in continental as well as Anglocentric ideas. Thus prevailing new critical approaches began to give way to new interest in semiotics, structuralism and poststructuralism, Marxism, deconstruction, and the new historicism, though not without lively and usually fruitful discussion.

Perhaps because of its traditional links with 'the common reader', discussion of Australian literature itself was at first least affected. A change was signalled, however, by Graeme Turner and Delys Bird, whose paper at the 1982 Conference of the Association for the Study of Australian Literature discussed the general lack of theoretical reflection they discerned in Australia. Significantly, the most notable developments in this direction have been in the study of popular culture, in writing about Australian films, sports, popular music, and life-style generally. This has had some effect on popular journalism, while at the more scholarly level journals such as *Art* and *Text* have opened up connections between literary criticism and the other arts as well as between popular and 'high' culture. Literary theory has also begun to have some influence on historical studies. Paul Carter's *The Road to Botany Bay* (1987), for instance, offers a theoretical reading of the history of exploration and settlement.

To look at more specific instances, feminist criticism has been notably receptive to theory: journals such as *Hecate* (1975–) and *Australian Feminist Studies* (1987–) and critics such as Carole Ferrier and Kay Iseman have linked literary criticism with the discussion of social, economic, and ideological issues. (See **Feminism**, Australia.) Although little work has been done in this area, it is apparent also that the growing interest in Aboriginal issues, in both writing by Aborigines and the representation of Aborigines, demands a critical methodology that, if not able to cut entirely across cultural, social, and historical preconceptions, at least takes them into account. (See also **Aboriginal Literature**, **Aborigines in Literature**, and **Aboriginal Song and Narrative**, Australia.) In *Reading the Country* (1985), which he wrote with the help of Krim Benterrak and the Aboriginal leader Paddy Roe, Stephen Muecke, for instance, draws on current French theory. More conventionally, Adam Shoemaker's *Black Words, White Page* (1989) gives the first historical overview of Aboriginal writing, and J. J. Healy's *Literature and the Aborigine in Australian Literature* (1979; 2nd ed., 1989) does the same for the representation of Aboriginal people.

Along more conventional lines there is growing interest in questions of regionalism in literature, especially in states such as Queensland and Western Australia or in particular areas such as Gippsland and the Hunter Valley. *Windows Onto Worlds* (1987), the report of the federal government committee appointed to study the condition of Australian studies in education, witnesses to a continuing sense of the political importance of Australian literature, as does the interest of government in teaching and research in this area overseas.

On the whole, criticism in Australia reflects the nature of Australian culture: it is lively, even combative, uneasily suspended between belonging and alienation, the national and the international, the aesthetic and the civic, suspicious of metaphysics and expressing its ethical concerns in terms of social commitment. If the man or woman of letters has not flourished there, largely perhaps for economic reasons, criticism has nevertheless made a significant contribution to Australian culture.

VERONICA BRADY

Further reading: John Docker, *In a Critical Condition* (1984); Laurie Hergenhan, ed., *Penguin New Literary History of Australia* (1988).

CRITICISM (Canada)

In the terms of Benedict Anderson's *Imagined Communities: Reflections on the Origin and Spread of Nationalism* (1983), Canada is an 'imagined community', and its citizens are, as Tony Wilden puts it in *The Imaginary Canadian: An*

Examination for Discovery (1980), 'imaginary Canadians'. Ideas about what it means to be Canadian have been constructed within a discourse of nationalism originating in Europe during the Romantic period. Just as the discourse of nationalism constructs nations, so the discourse of literary criticism and theory, in Barry Cameron's words, 'systematically forms the objects of which it speaks', including the works that are held up as the national literary canon. Literary criticism is one of the many cultural institutions that develop and rationalize a selective definition of Canada.

The discourse of nationalism naturalized the idea that a nation's right to exist was founded, not on its constitution as a state, but on its production of great art. This belief is still commonplace in Europe and its former colonies. **Goldwin Smith** manifests an anxiety especially widespread in the colonies in *Canada and the Canadian Question* (1891), where he writes that 'to expect a national literature' from thinly populated, culturally divided Canada is 'unfair'. He concluded that Canada would inevitably join the USA. More optimistic and more nationalistic voices persisted in arguing that a great national literature was imminent, or like Sir John George Bourinot, writing in *Our Intellectual Strength and Weakness: A Short Historical and Critical Review of Literature, Art and Education in Canada* (1893), that it already existed. As the writing from 1823 to 1928 collected in Carl Ballstadt's *The Search for English-Canadian Literature: An Anthology of Critical Articles from the Nineteenth and Early Twentieth Centuries* (1975) and that from 1752 to 1983 in Douglas M. Daymond and Leslie G. Monkman's *Towards a Canadian Literature: Essays, Editorials, and Manifestos* (1984–5) make clear, a belief in the connection between national worth — even national survival — and a unified and great national culture has lent urgency to most discussions of Canadian literature.

Since English literature replaced classics at the centre of the arts curriculum only in the late nineteenth century, criticism of Canadian literature until the 1920s was usually both fugitive and polemic. After the First World War, courses in Canadian literature were introduced in universities, and anthologies and books such as Edmund Kemper Broadus' and Eleanor Hammond Broadus' *A Book of Canadian Prose and Verse* (1923) and Archibald MacMechan's *Head-waters of Canadian Literature* (1924) were produced as textbooks. Their authors' belief in the nationalist function of literature is exemplified in MacMechan's words: 'Literature . . . is the voice of a people. Through its literature, the life, the soul of a people may be known.'

During the 1920s realism in fiction and modernism in poetry began to displace romanticism. Outlets for literary publication in Canada were underdeveloped, however, and the Depression prolonged the struggle between the romantics and the modernists. In 1943 E. K. Brown's *On Canadian Poetry* set **Archibald Lampman**, who wrote in the romantic tradition, at the centre of the Canadian poetic tradition; in the same year **A. J. M. Smith**'s modernist revision of the national poetic canon, *The Book of Canadian Poetry*, appeared. Even more influential than either of these canon-making books was **Northrop Frye**'s 1943 positive review of Smith's anthology, reprinted in *The Bush Garden: Essays on the Canadian Imagination* (1971). Here Frye begins to work on his construct of the 'garrison mentality' as the Canadian literary response to a 'sinister and menacing' nature, which he fully develops in his conclusion to the *Literary History of Canada* (1965). Frye continued the romantic nationalist critical tradition in connecting Canada as a national whole with literature, but he left behind the romantic taste of his predecessors. His perspective influenced a large number of critical books, including **D. G. Jones**' *Butterfly on Rock: A Study of Themes and Images in Canadian Literature* (1970), **Margaret Atwood**'s *Survival:*

A Thematic Guide to Canadian Literature (1972), which has sold seventy thousand copies, John Moss' *Patterns of Isolation in English Canadian Fiction* (1974), **Tom Marshall**'s *Harsh and Lovely Land: The Major Canadian Poets and the Making of a Canadian Tradition* (1979), and Gaile McGregor's *The Wacousta Syndrome: Explorations in the Canadian Langscape* (1985). These critics not only focus on Canadian literature as a unity that can be explained by a single image, mentality, or model, but, as Frye put it of his model, also maintain that 'this inner unity . . . is really there'. As their titles reveal, most also assume that this uniformity is connected to Canada's harsh climate and rugged landscape.

Almost as soon as Frye had finished formulating his position, **Eli Mandel** began to undermine it, pointing out in the introduction to *Contexts of Canadian Criticism* (1971) Frye's omission of the social and historical context in favour of what Mandel called 'geographical determinism'. The critics influenced by Frye place their emphasis on literature as determined either by nature or by some generalized feature of Canadian social life, diminishing the importance of the counter-influence of language or literature in constructing how Canadians understand nature and society. On the other side, Mandel stresses that 'far from being a determinism, an environment may be a human creation'. **Frank Davey**'s 'Surviving the Paraphrase' (1976) — reprinted in *Surviving the Paraphrase: Eleven Essays on Canadian Literature* (1983) — labels the critics influenced by Frye 'thematic critics' because of their propensity to reduce complex works to examples of large themes, and calls for alternative approaches. In 1988, in *Reading Canadian Reading*, Davey argues that the most important assumptions of thematic criticism are 'that Canada is a monolithic nation, that literature is best read as a body of sociological indicators, that language is linked to phenomena in a stable, decodable, and passively consumable system of referents' and notes that most of this criticism privileges central Canada over the regions. Thematic generalizations became highly problematic almost as soon as they were formulated, destabilized by changing demographic, economic, social, and political trends and by new theoretical frameworks imported from France and the USA.

In 1965 Frye characterized Canada as an inward-looking garrison. Only six years later, shortly after the kidnappings by the FLQ (Front de libération du Québec) of two prominent officials and the imposition of the War Measures Act, he wrote that 'the question of Canadian identity, so far as it affects the creative imagination, is not a "Canadian" question at all, but a regional question' and concluded that 'most of the imaginative factors common to the country as a whole are negative influences'. Ronald Sutherland's *Second Image: Comparative Studies in Quebec/Canadian Literature* (1971), devoted to finding similarities between the two literatures, was succeeded a decade later by *Configuration: Essays on the Canadian Literatures* (1982), by E. D. Blodgett, who resists 'any position that unifies the Canadian literatures through a metaphor by which their plurality is subsumed by a singularity'. Quebec separatist demands for political independence had forced a reaction from English-Canadian critics, who began to see that political disintegration was too high a price to pay for insisting on the cultural homogeneity required by romantic nationalism.

The 1970s radically changed Canada, Canadian literature, and English-Canadian literary criticism as both the university population and cultural nationalism soared in English Canada and Quebec. Canadian literature, rationalized by the thematic critics, became a field of academic study. Reference works, inexpensive paperback editions of novels, academic associations, conferences, graduate programmes — all flourished. Journals devoted solely to academic literary criticism joined

Canadian Literature (1959–), including the *Journal of Canadian Fiction* (1972–), *Essays on Canadian Writing* (1974–), *Studies in Canadian Literature* (1976–), and *Canadian Poetry* (1977–). Davey moved *Open Letter* (1965–) from Vancouver to Toronto in 1971, where it became known for its innovative theoretical articles. Three national journals — *Canadian Theatre Review* (1974–), *Canadian Drama, L'Art dramatique canadien* (1975–90), and *Theatre History in Canada/Histoire du théâtre au Canada* (1980–) — were founded to study a previously neglected field. (See **Literary Magazines**, Canada.) The Association for Canadian and Quebec Literatures was founded in 1973, and, subsidized by the Canadian government, Canadian Studies associations began to appear abroad. The Association of Universities and Colleges in Canada commissioned T. H. B. Symons to examine the status of Canadian studies in Canadian universities, and his report, *To Know Ourselves* (1975), had the 'effect of doubling the number of undergraduate Canadian literature courses taught' in Canada.

Despite the speed at which both events and theoretical innovation overtook the thematic critics, they have had a lasting impact on the formation of the discipline of Canadian literature. Their ideas generally hold sway in the classroom, as does their canon. In fact, as T. D. MacLulich points out, if some of the generalizations of the thematic critics are not upheld, Canadian literature as a subject disappears altogether: 'Whatever the literary purists among us may like to think, the justification for isolating Canadian literature as a separate field of study is linked with the conviction of our cultural divergence from the United States.'

A focus on regional literature signalled the first split in the critical insistence that literary Canada invariably be viewed from sea to sea. Edward A. McCourt's *The Canadian West in Fiction* (1949), L. Ricou's *Vertical Man/Horizontal World: Man and Landscape in Canadian Prairie Fiction* (1973), Dick Harrison's *Unnamed Country: The Struggle for a Canadian Prairie Fiction* (1977), Patrick O'Flaherty's *The Rock Observed: Studies in the Literature of Newfoundland* (1979), **Janice Kulyk Keefer**'s *Under Eastern Eyes: A Critical Reading of Maritime Fiction* (1987), and Kenneth G. Probert's *Writing Saskatchewan: Twenty Critical Essays* (1989) guide readers through regional writing that often is either ignored or assimilated by national overviews. Some of these regional critics simply adapted thematic criticism to a smaller territory. Others countered more than the Canada and the Canadian canon constructed by the central Canadian critics by adapting new theoretical approaches to their needs, notably western Canadian poet-critics **George Bowering**, Frank Davey, **Robert Kroetsch**, Eli Mandel, and **Stephen Scobie**.

Feminist critical activity also became visible in the 1970s as women began to consolidate their position in the academy. Here the focus was not so much on formulating generalizations about Canadian literature as about exploding approaches that had favoured a patriarchal criticism and a male-dominated canon. *Room of One's Own* (1975–) and *Atlantis* (1975–) both publish literary criticism on Canadian women writers. The proceedings of the Dialogue Conference (1981), edited by Barbara Godard, appeared in *Gynocritics/La Gynocritique: Feminist Approaches to Writing by Canadian and Québécoise Women* (1987), with the addition of a comprehensive 'Bibliography of Feminist Criticism in Canada and Quebec'. The proceedings of the Women and Words Conference (1983) were edited by Ann Dybikowski and others as *In the Feminine: Women and Words/Les Femmes et les mots* (1985). Important feminist collections followed, including: *A Mazing Space: Writing Canadian Women Writing*, edited by Shirley Neuman and Smaro Kamboureli (1986); Gail Scott's *Spaces like Stairs* (1989); *Language in Her Eye: Writing and Gender: Views by Canadian Women Writing in Eng-*

lish, edited by Libby Scheier and others (1990); and *Telling It: Women and Language across Cultures*, edited by the Telling It Book Collective (1990). The Tessera Collective (Barbara Godard, **Daphne Marlatt**, Kathy Mezei, and Gail Scott) began publishing theoretical and experimental feminist writing in annual special issues of different journals in 1984, finally moving to the founding of *Tessera* in 1988. Interestingly, the first book-length studies of contemporary fiction by Canadian women, Lorna Irvine's *Sub/Version: Canadian Fictions by Women* (1986) and Coral Ann Howells' *Private and Fictional Words: Canadian Women Novelists of the 1970s and 1980s* (1987), were written by scholars who teach in the USA and the UK respectively. (See **Feminism**, Canada.)

The same demographic and political pressures that led to the Canadian Multiculturalism Act (1988) also led to increased visibility for writers from a variety of cultural backgrounds as well as for the critics constructing their place in the canon. *Identifications: Ethnicity and the Writer in Canada* (1982), edited by Jars Balan; *The Old World and the New: Literary Perspectives of German-Speaking Canadians* (1984), edited by Walter Riedel; *A Meeting of Streams: South Asian Canadian Literature*, edited by **M. G. Vassanji** (1985); Joseph Pivato's *Contrasts: Comparative Essays on Italian-Canadian Writing* (1985); George Bisztray's *Hungarian-Canadian Literature* (1987); Arun Mukherjee's *Towards an Aesthetic of Opposition: Essays on Literature, Criticism and Cultural Imperialism* (1988); Michael Greenstein's *Third Solitudes: Tradition and Discontinuity in Jewish-Canadian Literature* (1989); and Arnold Harrichand Itwaru's *The Invention of Canada: Literary Text and the Immigrant Imagination* (1991), for example, generally promote writers excluded from, or forced to fit, the national canon. (See **Multiculturalism**, Canada.)

Growing interest in the image of, and writing by, Native people is marked by the publication of such works as Leslie Monkman's *A Native Heritage: Images of the Indian in English-Canadian Literature* (1981), *The Native in Literature: Canadian and Comparative Perspectives* (1987), edited by Thomas King, Cheryl Calver, and Helen Hoy, and Terry Goldie's *Fear and Temptation: The Image of the Indigene in Canadian, Australian, and New Zealand Literatures* (1989). Literature by Native writers has been collected in several anthologies and is the subject of a collection of critical articles that make up a special issue of *Canadian Literature, Native Writers and Canadian Writing* (1990), edited by W. H. New. (See **Aboriginal Literature**, Canada.)

A sign, perhaps, of the waning power in the academy of the modernist-realist canon and of the thematic approach is an increasing focus on literary theory. The proceedings of a conference on literary theory and Canadian literature held at the University of Ottawa in 1986 were published as *Future Indicative: Literary Theory and Canadian Literature* (1987), edited by John Moss; *Signature: A Journal of Theory and Canadian Literature* was founded in 1989; and a variety of structuralist, poststructuralist, Marxist, psychoanalytic, and feminist theoretical approaches have become common not only in Canadian literary criticism but also in the classroom. Stephen Scobie's *Signature/Event/Can-Text* (1989) and Rosmarin Heidenreich's *The Postwar Novel in Canada: Narrative Patterns and Reader Response* (1989) are two examples of general studies that apply particular theoretical approaches to Canadian literature.

Clearly, the metaphor of the garrison is deservedly beseiged, and yet, however often its walls are stormed and demolished by those bearing the banners of a new literary style or a new theory, something suspiciously like a garrison is built over and over again. Although any myth of Canada or of its literature that requires a belief in harmonious unity is clearly doomed, nationalism is not on the wane. And however fragmented Canada or the

Canadian literary institution becomes, positions of power for those who construct the most appealing versions of Canadian literature do remain to be struggled over. As excluded minority members point out, the supply of grants, publication contracts, literary prizes, and tenured positions is limited, and usually flows to those who occupy the literary garrison.

Because of the power of nationalism, each new literary style has ultimately found itself embedded in a nationalist framework. As new works become accepted, the established canonical hierarchy is challenged; some critics work to revise the canon as others decry any change as the end of the nation. Linda Hutcheon, for example, in *The Canadian Postmodern: A Study of Contemporary English-Canadian Fiction* (1988) and *Splitting Images: Contemporary Canadian Ironies* (1991) is writing into the national canon postmodern works previously seen as marginal or even opposed to it. Just as E. K. Brown placed Lampman at the pinnacle of the Canadian literary tradition, and Frye elevated **E. J. Pratt**, Hutcheon calls Robert Kroetsch 'Mr Canadian Postmodern'.

Canadian literary criticism has generally limited itself to particular literary movements, valorizing one set of writers and obliterating another. The goal of this criticism is to promote a particular style and to train readers to enjoy it. Recent Canadian critical battles have been fought between those critics who account for everything distinctive in Canadian literature by stressing the implicitly uniform responses to one monolithic landscape or political situation (colonialism) and those who argue for a closer examination of form and language. Both moves usually avoid that difficult terrain where critics contend with critics for authority, where institutions slug it out for prestige, and where publishers, bureaucrats, literary agents, and booksellers profit from the sale of literature. Everything between the landscape and the writer, or between the text and the reader, is elided; this elision is easily accomplished because the influence of historical, sociological, Marxist, and feminist approaches to literature in Canada has been slight. Considerable scholarly work, however, is represented by the *Literary History of Canada* (2nd ed. 1976; vol. 4, 1990), *The Oxford Companion to Canadian Literature* (1983), edited by William Toye, *Studies on Canadian Literature* (1990), edited by Arnold E. Davidson, and the ongoing *Dictionary of Canadian Biography* (12 vols. 1966–). The Centre for Editing Early Canadian Texts was founded in 1979 at Carleton University. Major collaborative projects include complete scholarly editions of the works of E. J. Pratt and **A. M. Klein**. The scholarly group, 'Toward a History of the Literary Institution in Canada', began holding conferences in 1986 at the Research Institute for Comparative Literature, University of Alberta. ECW Press publishes annotated bibliographies and reference works. Such work supports scholarly publications elucidating the institutional aspects of literature, including W. H. New's *A History of Canadian Literature* (1989), *The Oxford Companion to Canadian Theatre* (1989), edited by Eugene Benson and L. W. Conolly, and *Canadian Canons: Essays in Literary Value* (1991), edited by Robert Lecker. The continuing development of a metacriticism that looks self-consciously at how critics construct a nation, a canon, a literary institution, and a discipline in a nexus of economic, political, and social discourses provides a helpful perspective on other criticisms.

Those critics working in Commonwealth/post-colonial literatures have been in the forefront of the development of such a metacriticism, because it is difficult for them to ignore how many of the supposedly 'distinctive' national features of one post-colonial literature can be found in others. And since they are 'outside' at least one of the cultures they are examining, they are less likely to overlook how such factors as the intervention of the state, educational policies, internal cultural struggles, and the domination by external cultures affect literary and critical strategies. Post-colonial critics, already used to stressing the subversive anti-imperialism implicit in the construction of an independent national literature out of a subservient colonial one, are ready to see how all cultural constructs have the potential to oppress as well as to liberate. John Matthews, author of *Tradition in Exile: A Comparative Study of Social Influences on the Development of Australian and Canadian Poetry in the Nineteenth Century* (1962), has trained several generations of students in the importance of a comparative approach. The introduction to *Australian/Canadian Literatures in English: Comparative Perspectives* (1987), edited by Russell McDougall and Gillian Whitlock (former students of Matthews), outlines in detail the history of the Australian-Canadian literary connection. W. H. New has produced major reference and critical works not only in Canadian but also in post-colonial literatures, notably *Among Worlds: An Introduction to Modern Commonwealth and South African Fiction* (1975) and *Dreams of Speech and Violence: The Art of the Short Story in Canada and New Zealand* (1987). Two Canadian journals that specialize in post-colonial literary studies are *Ariel* (*A Review of International Literature in English*) (1970–) and *WLWE* (*World Literature Written in English*, 1962–); *Australian and New Zealand Studies in Canada* (1989–) devotes much of its attention to literature.

To adhere to a comparative metacritical approach requires a major shift of perspective. Australian critic Alan Lawson sees 'national literature as an *institution* discursively constructed rather than a "body" of texts having attained a measurable standard, or having certain themes, preoccupations, or content'. Thus national literatures become sites of ideological conflict rather than mausoleums of canonical texts, and criticism participates in a partisan struggle rather than simply guiding tours around the monuments.

MARGERY FEE

CRITICISM (The Caribbean)
Caribbean literary criticism in English may be said to reflect two general approaches to the literary text — one tending towards the formalist school, the other displaying a socio-historical inclination. Although such a generalization risks obscuring the particular subtleties and nuances of critical emphasis that can distinguish one critical practice from another, this fictive binarism may facilitate an understanding of the critical cross-currents agitating among what Louis James referred to as 'the islands in between' (in his *The Islands in Between*, 1968).

Perhaps some of the ambiguity and paradox that inform so much Caribbean criticism — not necessarily as a scrupulously hermetic New Critical enterprise — may be gleaned from the example of the British Broadcasting Corporation's (BBC's) '**Caribbean Voices**' programme (1945–58). The weekly radio broadcasts from England to the Caribbean nurtured such Caribbean writers and critics as **George Lamming**, **V. S. Naipaul**, and **Edward Kamau Brathwaite** and provided an oral link between 'exiled' Caribbean critics and their counterparts at home. Caribbean orature (in a manner of speaking) from the metropole engaged the literature of the Caribbean as it developed and sought its own distinctive voice in what, for many, was still a predominantly oral culture. At the same time, it was impossible to ignore the political and historical symbolism of a BBC broadcast radiating from the metropole, albeit with Caribbean inflection, and reaching out to the Empire's periphery.

Caribbean criticism may be seen in one sense as an exploration of the aesthetic and existential paradoxes resonant in colonial and post-colonial societies. It is not insignificant that Kenneth Ramchand's seminal work, *The West Indian Novel and its Background* (1970), examines the socio-historical background of prose fiction in the Caribbean as a necessary preface to textual analysis, or that E. K. Brathwaite's *History of the Voice: The Development of Nation Language in Anglophone Caribbean Poetry* (1984) examines the complex dialectic between creole voice and Euro-text, synthesized in Nation language. Nor is it idiosyncratic, in the context of the Caribbean, that **Wilson Harris**' *Tradition, The Writer and Society* (1967) explores a poetics of the novel within the compass of the Haitian Revolution and the political and epistemological radicalism of **C. L. R. James**' study *The Black Jacobins: Toussaint L'Ouverture and the San Domingo Revolution* (1938). The aesthetic and the ontological often represent two sides of the same coin in Caribbean criticism. Caribbean critical praxis can often be understood as a simultaneous *engagement* with the text and with a canonical history that would seek to overwhelm alternative texts and critiques. However, despite the generally shared intent among Caribbean critical approaches to 'write' the Caribbean out of the prison-house of colonial and post-colonial otherness, there is wonderful heterogeneity within this body of criticism.

Brathwaite, for example, interrogates the structure of the Caribbean novel using the motif of African-American jazz in 'Jazz and the West Indian Novel', serialized in *Bim* (11 and 12, 1967 and 1968). C. L. R. James deconstructs (even before Derrida's work popularized the term) McCarthyism through an analysis of Herman Melville's *Moby-Dick* in *Mariners, Renegades, and Castaways: The Story of Herman Melville and The World We Live In* (1953), and **Derek Walcott**, self-styled 'mulatto of style', creolizes Eurocentric history in 'The Muse of History', in *Is Massa Day Dead?* (1974), edited by Orde Coombs.

Caribbean criticism can sometimes display a dualism that mimics equivocation or even a kind of aesthetic schizophrenia, but often this is a mark of the creole sensibility at work. Walcott can recognize the heroic epic in the lives of St Lucian fishermen and the 'Shabeen' in Odysseus; James visions the reality of the totalitarian mind in Captain Ahab and characterizes the fiction of a sustainable humanity, founded upon technological progress, in his critique of Melville's novel. Wilson Harris foregrounds the inter-connectedness of the corporeal and metaphysical rather than a dichotomized experience; indeed, his fiction promotes his theory as his theory, in turn, categorizes his fiction — as in *Palace of the Peacock* (1960) and *The Far Journey of Oudin* (1961), for example.

The criticism of **Michael Gilkes**, **Edward Baugh**, **Sylvia Wynter**, **Mervyn Morris**, and Gordon Rohlehr is no less literary for being engaged in what the rigid structuralist would construe as the extra-textual world. Perhaps in a world such as the Caribbean, where word and speech, scribal and oral, absence and presence are often already marks of ontological crisis, the Caribbean critic is unlikely to suffer the Rousseauist fallacy that Derrida exposes in *Of Grammatology* (1974). Somewhat akin to Edward Said's argument in relation to some modern novels in his *The World, The Text, and The Critic* (1983), Caribbean existence (and by extrapolation Caribbean criticism) can hardly be deconstructed to reveal its unconscious contradictions and *aporias*; these contradictions often function as conscious strategies of identity construction and survival. The Caribbean writer and critic may be understood to have always consciously begun the deconstruction of canonical western texts. Such an unravelling was necessary not only to clear a space for Caribbean literature and criticism, but was indeed a necessary strategy of Caribbean survival. Caribbean criticism was born out of the need to indicate the presence in what had been construed as absence, and the absence in what had been represented as full presence. Thus, what might be called a deconstructive practice in some Caribbean literature and criticism is not the kind of hermeneutic impasse which characterizes, for example, the Yale School of deconstructionists. It is rather a dismantling in order to reassemble more equitably, even in the knowledge that dismantling is a continuing process that threatens any new assemblage.

James disassembles the stereotype of European superiority in *The Black Jacobins* to demonstrate the dignity and resolve of Toussaint and the Haitian ex-slaves; **Jean Rhys**, in *Wide Sargasso Sea* (1966), dismantles the myth of the mad woman in Rochester's attic in Charlotte Brontë's *Jane Eyre* (1847) to reveal Antoinette as a victim of patriarchy and colonialism; Maureen Warner-Lewis, in *Guinea's Other Suns: The African Dynamic in Trinidad Culture* (1991), locates the African oral tradition informing Creole in Afro-Trinidad culture. These are but a few of the wide-ranging yet similarly motivated analyses and critiques that represent Caribbean criticism and ontology.

GLYNE A. GRIFFITH

Further reading: Jeanette B. Allis, *West Indian Literature: An Index to Criticism, 1930–1975* (1981).

CRITICISM (India)

Indian literary criticism in Sanskrit has a long and venerable tradition stretching back to the pre-Christian era. This is worth mentioning since, with the notable exceptions of Aristotle and Longinus, there was a virtual cessation of critical activity in the west, and literary criticism in the English-speaking world is of relatively recent origin. The Dark Ages of Europe were the most creative period in India, a claim scholar **C. D. Narasimhaiah** substantiates by citing a long list of illustrious Indian critics such as Bharata, Bhamaha, Dandin, Vamana, Anandavardhana, Kuntaka, Mammata, Abhinavagupta, and Kshemendra. (See **Sanskrit Literature**.) Their critical theories are astonishingly modern in character, and the extent of their contribution to Sanskrit poetics may be seen in such concepts as *rasa* ('emotion'), *alankara* ('imagery'), *riti* ('style'), *dhvani* ('inner resonance'), *vakrokti* ('obliqueness'), and *auchitya* ('propriety'). They anticipated American New Critics in their use of irony, paradox, texture, and ambiguity as critical terms, but unlike the New Critics they never forgot that the end of a work of art is *rasa*, its soul. While the poet and the critic were esteemed as the 'two eyes' of the Muse of Poetry, it was claimed that a good critic was even rarer than a poet.

Indian literary criticism is metaphysical in character rather than empirical, as in the west. The values and ideals that have nourished Indian life have also sustained its literature. The concepts of *shantha* ('serenity'), *auchitya* ('propriety'), *nishkama karma* ('disinterested action'), *pramana* ('criterion'), *prayojana* ('immediate end'), and *purushartha* ('ultimate end') are common to both. This explains why critics bracket *rasanubhava* ('aesthetic experience') with *brahmananda* ('the bliss of Brahman').

Interest in traditional Indian criticism (especially that associated with the great Sanskrit rhetoricians) was aroused in the twentieth century by such critics writing in English as M. Hiriyanna, **Sri Aurobindo**, and **Ananda K. Coomaraswamy**, mediators between past and present, east and west.

Hiriyanna (1871–1950), distinguished scholar, teacher, and art historian and author of works on aesthetics, Sanskrit studies, and philosophy, upholds the transcendental character of Indian art while subjecting it to rigorous aesthetic criteria. His *Art Experience* (1954) and *The Quest after Perfection* (1952) are regarded as classics. In view of India's meagre literature in English on aesthetics, Hiriyanna's contribution assumes additional importance.

Aurobindo — poet, mystic, and critic — defined poetry with unprecedented originality, investing it with a profoundly spiritual import. His writings on the Vedas, the Upanishads, Gita, Vyasa, Valmiki, and Kalidasa and his letters on art and literature establish him as a major critical force. His seminal work of criticism, *The Future Poetry and Letters on Literature and Art* (1953), not only attempts for the first time in India a breathtaking survey of the whole of English poetry but envisions a future poetry of 'overhead' planes (higher levels of consciousness) and mantric verse. In several ways he anticipates the English critic F. R. Leavis in his work on Milton, the Augustans, and Wordsworth.

Coomaraswamy, a geologist by training, distinguished art critic, and exponent of the *philosophia perennis*, revolutionized entire fields of art and helped India take her 'due rank as a first class artistic power'. His *The Dance of Shiva* (1918), *The Transformation of Nature in Art* (1934), and *Christian and Oriental Philosophy of Art* (1956) recover ancient values and establish art as a way of life.

Ironically, all three critics have suffered neglect in India. Aurobindo's example in particular might have been emulated to advantage by subsequent Indian critics, who have instead begun to lean heavily on the west. This is true of those critics writing in both English and India's regional languages except, to some extent, in Hindi, where *rasa-sidhanta* (philosophy of rasa) is still current. Having lost the initiative for originality, recent Indian critics — **B. Rajan** (*The Lofty Rhyme: A Study of Milton's Major Poetry*, 1970), Brijraj Singh (*Development of a Critical Tradition from Pater to Yeats*, 1978), and R. N. Srivastava (*W. H. Auden the Poet*, 1979), for example — have been content to import western values, criteria, and even their quarrels, without relating them to the Indian context. Their continued deference to Aristotle, the New Critics, the Chicago critics, F. R. Leavis, T. S. Eliot, and I. A. Richards and their obsession with such western concepts as original sin, evil, and tragedy as the ultimate in literary experience, despite their irrelevance in Indian analyses of works of art, smacks of cultural colonization and suggest a loss of national identity.

There have been many books and articles by Indian critics in the field of Shakespearean studies; these include S. C. Sen Gupta's *Shakespearean Comedy* (1950) and *Aspects of Shakespearean Tragedy* (1972), P. C. Ghosh's *Shakespeare's Mingled Drama* (1960), Alur Janakiram's *Reason and Love in Shakespeare: A Selective Study* (1977), and V. Y. Kantak's 'Shakespeare's Dramatic Design', in *The Hero as Critic* (1982), edited by T. S. Prabhakar, M. S. Nagarajan, and **K. S. Nagarajan**. But their chief drawback is their over-emphasis on plot and characterization (an Aristotelian legacy) and their failure to bring an Indian critical sensibility to bear on their subject. The application of key concepts drawn from Indian aesthetic theory or a comparison of Shakespearean drama with representative Sanskrit plays might have proven useful and distinctive.

The Indian critics' special fondness for the English Romantic period (because of the poets' emphasis on idealism) has made for a spate of books in the area. But when writing on Wordsworth and Coleridge, for example, such critics as **Shiv K. Kumar** in *British Romantic Poets* (1966), which he edited, and P. S. Sastri in *The Vision of Coleridge* (1966) extol the poet's treatment of Man and Nature, ignoring the connections that could be made with the magnificent Nature poetry of the Vedas and the *Ramayana* and the *Mahabharata*. Shelley's immense popularity with Indian critics has too often resulted in studies such as P. G. Rama Rao's *Poetic Rapture* (1960), the central point of which is to emphasize Shelley's lyricism, a point already sufficiently demonstrated by western critics; these Indian critics could have benefited from Sri Aurobindo's acute observation on Shelley's lack of the virtue of asceticism. Despite the obvious interest of W. B. Yeats in Indian philosophy and literature, few Indian critics, including Vinod Sena in his *Yeats: The Poet as Critic* (1980), have studied his work in terms of Indian traditional aesthetics. They might, for example, have challenged Yeats' assertion that the Indian mind lacked a 'tragic sense' by relating that remark to the Indian position that the value of a work consists in realized response or equanimity.

Indian critical response to American literature has been no different. When the critic H. Bruce Franklin wrote of Melville's 'The Confidence Man' as 'a kind of Indian Holi festival', and James Baird attempted to identify Moby Dick with Vishnu, there was no informed Indian response despite the profound Indian parallels in Melville's intellectual make-up. When, occasionally, an Indian critic makes a connection between Walt Whitman and Indian concepts, as does O. K. Nambiar in *Walt Whitman and Yoga* (1966), the accent is placed on the poet's mysticism, not on his poetry. When F. R. Leavis wrote that the line 'Shantih Shantih Shantih' from T. S. Eliot's *The Waste Land* was ironic, Indian scholars unquestioningly endorsed his view, forgetting that the words are a time-honoured benediction wholly without any irony so cherished in modern western criticism. The response of Indian critics even to Indian writing in English has suffered from two extremes — uncritical adulation, as in the case of **Sarojini Naidu**'s poetry, or unwarranted denigration, as in the case of **Raja Rao**'s fiction.

Some Indian intellectuals have, however, rebelled against uncritical and wholesale western borrowings. The pioneering work of **K. R. Srinivasa Iyengar** and C. D. Narasimhaiah has created awareness of the urgency of going back to India's vital past. Iyengar, scholar, teacher, and critic, achieved a breakthrough with the publication of his *Indian Writing in English* (1962; rev. 1973, 1982, and 1987), a comprehensive assessment of the achievement of Indian writers in English from the early nineteenth century to the present. An ambitious undertaking, still regarded as the standard reference work, Iyengar's book has the distinction of being the first to win attention and respect for Indian-English literature.

Narasimhaiah — scholar, teacher, critic, and author of several important critical works reflecting his total commitment to the Indian critical scene — achieves a fine synthesis of Indian and western traditions. He has played an important role in creating a critical climate in India by training the reader's sensibility in his crusade against imitativeness and derivativeness and by pleading for an Indian context. A student of Leavis, responsible for promoting American and Commonwealth literatures and intellectually nurtured in the Indian literary tradition, Narasimhaiah founded *The Literary Criterion* in 1952 to promote his views. His works include *Literary Criticism: European and Indian Traditions* (1965), *The Swan and the Eagle* (1969), *Moving Frontiers of English Studies in India* (1977), *A Common Poetic for Indian Literatures* (1984), which he edited, *The Function of Criticism in India* (1986), and *Indian Critical Scene* (1990). His emphasis on Indianness and his attempts to demonstrate the relevance of Indian concepts to international literature mark the beginning of a potentially important movement in Indian criticism. However, the actual application of Indian theories and criteria to specific works is not yet widely practised.

M. K. Naik has also contributed greatly to an understanding of Indian writing in English; he is, perhaps, the only Indian critic who has used relevant biographical material in his studies *Raja Rao* (1972) and *Mulk Raj Anand* (1973). Other notable critics are R. K. Kaul (*Augustans*, 1982), Naresh Guha (*W. B. Yeats: An Indian Approach*, 1968), Sishirkumar Ghosh (*Mine Oyster*, 1968), G. S. Amur (*Images and Impressions: Essays Mainly on Contemporary Indian Literature*, 1979), S. K. Desai (*Critical Essays on Indian Writing in English Presented to Armando Menezes*, 1968, 2nd rev. ed., 1972, co-edited with M. K. Naik and G. S. Amur), and Meenakshi Mukherjee (*The Twice Born Fiction: Theme and Techniques of the Indian Novel in English*, 1971). They have not, however, always applied rigorous Indian standards in their critical approaches.

Although there is an increasing awareness on the part of Indian critics writing in English that they should cultivate their own critical traditions — this is a common reaction in such post-colonial societies as those of the Caribbean, Africa, and Australasia, for example — contemporary critical movements such as feminism, structuralism, post-structuralism, deconstruction, and semiotics are manifesting themselves in Indian criticism, as may be seen in such works as Krishna Sharma's *Imagery in the Plays of Christopher Fry* (1972), Satyan Kaur's *Graham Greene: An Existentialist Interpretation* (1990), and *Gender and Literature* (1992), edited by Iqbal Kaur.

Sanskrit scholars S. K. De (*History of Sanskrit Poetics*, 1960), P. V. Kane (*History of Sanskrit Poetics*, 1923, third revised edition, 1961, first published as *Introduction to Vishwanatha's Sahityadarpana*, 1910), V. Raghavan (co-editor with Nagendra, *An Introduction to Indian Poetics*, 1970), R. C. Dwivedi (editor, *Principles of Literary Criticism in Sanskrit*, 1969), K. Krishnamoorthy (*Essays in Sanskrit Criticism*, 1964), and Krishna Chaitanya (*Sanskrit Poetics*, 1965) have also played a significant role in making the Sanskrit critical and literary heritage available to non-Sanskrit readers and through translations of ancient Sanskrit critical texts.

RAGINI RAMACHANDRA

Further reading: Ragini Ramachandra, *Indian Literary Criticism* (1989); *Indian Poetics in Application*, special issue of *The Literary Criterion* 1 (1991).

Reviewing (India)

The reviewing of newly published books in India began with the introduction of English-language journals. The launching of J. A. Hicky's *Bengal Gazette* (1780–2) marked the formal beginning, and reviewing soon made astonishing progress. Indian reviewers brought to their writing a knowledge of western critical criteria and Indian concepts such as *rasa* ('emotion') and *dhwani* ('inner resonance'). Magazines such as *Indu Prakash* (1862–), *Modern Review* (1907–65), *Arya* (1914–21), and *Commonweal* (1924–) encouraged long reviews since both writers and readers took serious interest in the written word. Often a review spilled over into several issues of the magazine. For instance, the bulk of **Sri Aurobindo**'s *The Future Poetry* (1953) was inspired by his congratulatory review of James Cousins' *New Ways in English Literature* (2nd rev. ed. 1919). But when occasion demanded it, reviewers could also wield an incisive scalpel.

Since independence there has been a veritable explosion of English journals in India; however, there has not been a corresponding increase in the elbow room allotted to the reviewer of books. Sensing readers' preference for the glamour of action photos, political comment, and catchy exposures of public and private scandals, editors rarely encourage reviews that exceed 500 words. Lack of scope has induced a kind of listlessness in reviewers; not surprisingly, a few reviewers have become altogether careless. However, select journals such as the *Indian Book Chronicle* and *Triveni* do encourage serious reviewers. The reviewers are not paid, but the satisfaction of a job well done is evidently a reward in itself.

Recently some self-analysis has been attempted in this field. Writing in *Publishing in India*, B. N. Banerjee has criticized the servility of the Indian press, which is more hospitable to Indian writers whose books have been published abroad. Additionally, the author who has managed to win an award has a better chance with the review editor. More often, bad and fraudulent books are not criticized, and even the most obvious plagiarism remains undetected. There is also too long a time lapse between the publication of a book and the appearance of the reviews.

In spite of these limitations, book reviewing in India remains a healthy enterprise. Undeterred by limitations of space, some reviewers crystallize their opinions very well, projecting the contents of a book, and exhibiting an exemplary sense of responsibility. Hence, the reviewers of the leading papers of India — *Hindu* (1878–), *Deccan Herald* (1948–), *Indian Express* (1932–), *Hindustan Times* (1923–), among others — are read with care. Reviews in magazines such as *Gentleman* (1980–), *Debonair* (1972–), and *Aside* are read particularly by the younger generation. Journals such as the *Journal of Indian Writing in English* (1973–), the *Literary Criterion* (1952–), and the *Bhubhaneshwar Review* do publish a number of reviews, but they appear very late. *Indian Literature* (1957–), published by the nation's central academy of literature, Sahitya Akademi, has a satisfactory review section and symbolizes the state of book reviewing in India: a respected art that yet needs massive state patronage for survival as a serious pursuit of letters. (See **Literary Magazines**, India.)

PREMA NANDAKUMAR

CRITICISM (Malaysia)

Lloyd Fernando, introducing the anthology, *Malaysian Short Stories* (1981), wrote of the contributors: 'It looks as if these writers, like short story writers elsewhere, seek to break the bounds of the short story.' The remark contains the ambivalence with which critics have approached Malaysian literature in English. Most of the criticism appears in MA and Ph.D. dissertations (barely accessible to the general reader) on poetry, fiction, and drama; the rest is found in journals meant for academic readers.

The criticism has been mainly textual; there has been no attempt to see the works of Malaysian writers using English within a larger context. If any attitudes could be discerned, they are ephemeral and unsubstantive. In the 1960s, for instance, Malaysian writing in English was seen as one of the offshoots of the British literary tradition. The attitude changed slightly in the 1970s, after the 13 May 1969 racial riots in the country, to become more parochial. The new viewing was an attempt to integrate Malaysian literature in English into the National literary paradigm. While literature in Malay was accepted as the national literature, literatures in English, Mandarin, and Tamil were slotted in as sectional literatures.

But Malaysian literature in English, besides the initial difficulties of cutting itself adrift from the British tradition, has produced forms and styles that need to be viewed in a more encompassing and innovative manner. Malaysians have developed forms of perceptions that are not so much a conscious discarding of the colonialist approach as they are visions that manifest a genuinely felt desire to explore an individual's place in a multicultural society just released from the colonial yoke.

Consequently, writers in English have had to work out for themselves a literary destiny not quite as safe as the one to be found in a homogeneous society. Released from the colonialist's divide-and-rule political system, writers have had to confront another, less provenant political structure. Their works are, therefore, grounded on the conflicts an immigrant society faces when a protective — because it wants to safeguard its own political and material interests — governing body removes itself from the scene.

In the process of rediscovering their identity, writers also discovered, in poetry, fiction and drama, specific sets of imagery and allegories that are typically Malaysian. There seems to be here not just alienation but a double alienation, first, from the life-style they accepted under the British regime and, second, from their need to be truly Malaysian. It seems, therefore, that they not only seek to break the bounds of the short story and of the other genres as well but also to discover a particular perceptual standpoint from which to justify living in their adopted country, Malaysia.

The question that arises here is whether critics can enclose (closure or openness?) their works within canons that will add to more than emergent theories about post-colonial literature.

K. S. MANIAM

CRITICISM (New Zealand)

Literary criticism in New Zealand has a short history. Beginning as the domain of journalists, and then for some time essentially academic, there is now a good range of critical work available. The audience, however, is not large, and this, by inhibiting the development of overly esoteric critical writing, has ensured that literary criticism has retained a public face. Even today critical work of book length is published infrequently.

Very little critical writing of any kind was printed before 1960. Newspapers avoided book reviewing until recently, with a few notable exceptions — the Christchurch *Press* (1861–) has since the 1920s offered thoughtful and full reviews and occasional essays. Literary reviews, though at first brief, have always been a feature of the weekly *Listener* (1939–) and have also been a particularly valuable part of the quarterly *Landfall* (1947–); both have made a point of covering New Zealand literary publications. (See **Literary Magazines**, New Zealand.) In the 1960s the four colleges of the University of New Zealand split into four (now seven) autonomous universities, but even with their ensuing expansion the study of New Zealand literature was slow to establish a place. Most critical articles and much important reviewing, however, have since come from university staff.

The first major work was **E. H. McCormick**'s *Letters and Art in New Zealand* (1940), a survey of literary (and artistic) endeavour; it was revised as *New Zealand Literature: A Survey* (1959) and remained until 1990 the only full-length study. It included (otherwise it would have been very short) nonfiction — early journals, letters, histories, and descriptive studies — an area much neglected until *The Oxford History of New Zealand Literature in English* (1991), edited by Terry Sturm, was published.

Students as well as writers (chiefly of poetry) in the 1930s and 1940s were interested in the nature of what a New Zealand literature would or perhaps should be as well as its defining qualities and its limiting conditions. A series of essays developed by critic **M. H. Holcroft**, first published in three volumes beginning with *The Deepening Stream: Cultural Influences in New Zealand* (1940) and later as a single trilogy, *Discovered Isles* (1950), though ranging well beyond purely literary matters, focused on the New Zealand artist's geographical and cultural isolation.

Isolation, alienation, and an insistence on response to a personally experienced environment underlie **Allen Curnow**'s extensive introductions to his *A Book of New Zealand Verse 1923–45* (1945) and his *The Penguin Book of New Zealand Verse* (1960). It is notable that introductions to anthologies were the vehicle for the wide dissemination of these essays. Curnow and Holcroft may have been influenced by their own experience of life in the emptier and more mountainous South Island, a point made later by some North Island critics, but between them they set the agenda for critical discussion of poetry for many years to come. Important later contributions came from **C. K. Stead** (*In the Glass Case*, 1981), **Bill Pearson** (*Fretful Sleepers and Other Essays*, 1974), and from Curnow himself (*Look Back Harder*, 1987).

A fruitful debate arose over a distinction, sometimes excessively stated, between the poets who began in the 1930s and those who began in the 1950s. **Kendrick Smithyman**, in *A Way of Saying* (1965), a densely packed and idiosyncratic book that remains the only full-length study of

New Zealand poetry, distinguished the two groups using the terms 'romantic' and 'provincial' for the earlier poets and 'academic' and 'regional' for the later poets. In *Aspects of Poetry in New Zealand* (1967), **James K. Baxter** also commented on the distinction. That there was a distinction seemed clear, but the newer poets were less homogeneous and less susceptible to classification. There was to be more agreement about the pervasive influence of American poetry on the later generations. In the major statement, 'From Wystan to Carlos: Modern and Modernism in Recent New Zealand Poetry' (*In the Glass Case*), C. K. Stead argued that earlier poetry had derived from the Georgians and W. H. Auden and that T. S. Eliot and Ezra Pound had influenced New Zealand poets' consciousnesses and technique only through American poetry in the 1960s. Younger critics, however, noted Stead's failure to engage with the concepts of postmodernism. Discussion of recent critical inquiry found space in periodicals such as *And* (1983–5), covering cultural matters generally and established for that purpose.

Criticism of poetry, from 1945 at least, has had the advantage of a history and structure, as is seen in Elizabeth Caffin's essay 'Poetry 1945–90', in *The Oxford History of New Zealand Literature in English*, an essay that largely, but still productively, adopts the binary pattern outlined above. And in much other criticism and reviewing there is an implicit recognition of that groundwork.

Fiction has not enjoyed critical debate at such a general level. Although in recent years more criticism of individual works of fiction and their authors has been published than of poetry and poets, serious attention was slow to evolve. The most extended line of inquiry has been into the relationship between fiction and society, which explains in part the relative lack of critical interest in one of New Zealand's greatest writers, **Katherine Mansfield**. The foundation essay, 'Fiction and the Social Pattern', by Robert Chapman (*Landfall* 25, 1953), established a way of looking at a critical realist tradition. The most thoughtful and persistent analyst of this tradition has been Lawrence Jones, whose series of articles, though mostly devoted to particular authors, is collected in *Barbed Wire and Mirrors* (1987) to form a coherent criticism of the country's fiction. The Canadian critic William New attends to the short story in *Dreams of Speech and Violence* (1987) and earlier included consideration of longer fiction in 'Escape into Distance', a chapter in his *Among Worlds* (1975), in which he contrasts the depiction of an ideal new land and an uncultured conventional society. Patrick Evans, in a number of articles, notably in *Landfall* between 1976 and 1977, argues that a provincial preoccupation with the failure of the dream of an ideal society offered no opportunity for novelists to report on wider concerns. That there is space for book-length studies is shown in Mark Williams' *Leaving the Highway* (1990), which, in discussing the innovations of recent novelists, stresses the presence of a forceful fictional tradition.

A common but little investigated distinction between an impressionist Mansfield and a critical realist **Frank Sargeson** tradition in fiction has been revived recently, with greater justification, to handle the growth of a more clearly nonrealist fiction. It is accounted for in the term 'mirrors' in the title of Jones' *Barbed Wire and Mirrors*. Jones' chapter in *The Oxford History of New Zealand Literature in English* covers both traditions and is the most up-to-date and thorough analysis of thematic and technical aspects of the New Zealand novel.

The fairly recent publication of fiction by Maori writers has prompted articles on individual writers, but there has been little general response to Maori literature in English.

Other literary genres have been attended to rarely in New Zealand and although there are significant articles and even a few books, critical work on drama, nonfiction (including biography and autobiography), and popular fiction is best approached through the relevant chapters of *The Oxford History of New Zealand Literature in English*. Children's literature, also covered there, is surveyed in greater detail by Betty Gilderdale in *A Sea Change* (1982). Feminist criticism has appeared mostly in journals not limited to literary work, such as *And*, *Antic* (1986–), and *Women's Studies Journal* (1984–).

The most fully developed line of critical inquiry in New Zealand has been directed to individual authors. On occasion one might doubt whether an author's oeuvre deserved, or at least was ready for, such extensive discussion, and, indicating the partly nonacademic audience of such work, some books of criticism have been as much biographical as critical. In the Twayne's World Author series have appeared studies of James K. Baxter (1976), D'Arcy Cresswell (1972), **Janet Frame** (1977), **Jane Mander** (1972), **R. A. K. Mason** (1970), **John Mulgan** (1968), **William Satchell** (1968), and, in a notable work by Winston Rhodes, Frank Sargeson (1969). Slightly shorter studies have appeared in the New Zealand Writers and Their Work series edited by James Bertram. Authors examined are James K. Baxter (1976), **Ursula Bethell** (1975), **Charles Brasch** (1976), Allen Curnow (1980), **Dan Davin** (1983), Janet Frame (1980), **Maurice Gee** (1986), **Denis Glover** (1977), R. A. K. Mason (1977), John Mulgan (1977), and Frank Sargeson (1976).

Another form of critical publication, a little surprising in its relative abundance, is the book of collected essays and reviews. There is criticism available by James K. Baxter (edited by Frank Mackay, 1978), James Bertram (1985), Charles Brasch (edited by John Watson, 1981), Allen Curnow (edited by Peter Simpson, 1987), **A. R. D. Fairburn** (edited by Denis Glover, 1967), Lawrence Jones (1987), Bill Pearson (1974), Frank Sargeson (edited by Kevin Cunningham, 1983), and C. K. Stead (1981 and 1989).

The viability of the book of literary criticism of a more general kind is signalled by the appearance of Patrick Evans' *Penguin History of New Zealand Literature* (1990), which sets the historical story in a wider cultural setting, and the 750-page *The Oxford History of New Zealand Literature in English*, which, though more traditional in its general approach, is innovative in its inclusion on an equal basis of areas such as children's writing and popular fiction.

JOHN THOMSON

CRITICISM (Pakistan)

As British literature has been the cornerstone of literary studies in the educational curriculum in English in Pakistan and remains a major reference even for the study of national literatures, a strong scholarly tradition exists in British literature. Throughout the twentieth century there has been a constant stream of books and articles by Pakistani scholars and critics on British literary subjects. There is also a relatively new interest in American literature, but critical writing about it has been sparse. Any criticism about South Asian literatures is generally published abroad.

Pakistani literature in English began to draw serious attention in the 1960s. S. Sajjad Husain, Syed Ali Ashraf, and Maya Jamil contributed articles to journals and collections on topics in Pakistani literature. The approaches then prevalent were mostly biographical, with some formal analysis. The critics treated the subject in the national and regional categories, or studied (the mostly British) influences. The Commonwealth context was well understood, but its critical bases had not emerged fully. The comparisons and linkages stopped at India or pre-war England.

Recently, the literature in other Pakistani languages has been studied by English-based critics and it is now an increasingly important area, along with the literatures of other Commonwealth countries. Article-length studies of fiction, poetry, and prose now proliferate in journals. The variety of critical methods being practised — from the biographical to the Cambridge school to structuralism and post-structuralism — has given the discipline a new vigour. S. S. Sirajuddin has published short studies of Pakistani poetry from the perspective of language and communication theory. Tariq Rahman has published studies on 'deviation' as a stylistic device in fiction. Foreign critics such as Laurence Brander, David Anderson, C. Kanaganayakam, Carlo Coppola, Alastair Niven, and Bruce King have participated in this process from their distinctive perspectives, and published studies of individual authors. Analyses of colonial and postcolonial discourses have been made in the frameworks of cultural criticism and theory as well. In such works as *Commonwealth Literature: An Essay towards the Redefinition of a Popular/Counter Culture* (1983) and *The Commonwealth, Comparative Literature and the World* (1988), **Alamgir Hashmi** discusses the strategies of resistance and liberation, through self-definition and the development of a counter-discourse, while Sara Suleri, in *The Rhetoric of English India* (1992), offers an exposition of the idioms of collusion. **Zulfikar Ghose**'s creative criticism ranges over numerous works of western literature; detailed analyses of certain works largely serve to announce and underpin his aesthetic manifesto. Ghose's critical works include *Hamlet, Prufrock, and Language* (1978), *The Fiction of Reality* (1983), and *The Art of Creating Fiction* (1991).

Academic criticism has flourished. Cultural criticism and interdisciplinary approaches, as practised in the best of African criticism, or feminist critique, as practised in India, are rare, as the Pakistani academy and political structure deny room for a broader cultural discourse.

There are useful 'Introduction' and 'Criticism' sections in *The Journal of Commonwealth Literature*'s annual bibliography; the annual 'The Year That Was' section of the journal *Kunapipi* (1979–), which began coverage of Pakistani literature in 1981, also contains useful material.

S. S. SIRAJUDDIN

CRITICISM (The Philippines)

Criticism as a specific mode of discourse began in the Philippines in the postwar years with the publication of a number of critical texts focused on Philippine literature in English. What existed pervious to this period were essays and articles in magazines and newspapers, forewords, and prefaces in anthologies characterized by a great deal of impressionism and subjectivity. Even the much publicized controversy between Salvador Lopez, a proponent of committed literature, and **Jose Garcia Villa**, a disciple of the art for art's sake movement, had little theoretical foregrounding. Lopez's *Literature and Society* (1940), influenced by Marxist critics in the USA, fired the initial salvo against literature that failed to grapple with societal realities, best represented by the Philippines' leading poet Jose Garcia Villa. This debate between two schools of thought would shape the development of theory and criticism in the postwar years.

By the 1950s Philippine literature had achieved its privileged status as object of formal critical inquiries. This was the period that witnessed the return of Filipino scholars who studied either in the USA or in local universities such as the University of the Philippines. This was also the period when New Criticism, the most powerful programmatic in the west, shaped the critical perspective of critics who turned their attention to Philippine Literature. Cleanth Brooks, Robert Penn Warren, T. S. Eliot, Mark Schorer, Percy Lubbock, and F. R. Leavis, among Anglo-American critics, were cited with much familiarity by Filipino critics.

The 1960s gave rise to a number of critical texts that dealt exclusively with writings in English. Among these works were Miguel Bernad's

Bamboo and the Greenwood Tree (1961), the earliest study of indigenous fiction from **Manuel Arguilla**, who wrote before the Pacific War, to Gregorio Brillantes, a postwar short-story writer. **Ricaredo Demetillo**'s *The Authentic Voice of Poetry* (1962), on the other hand, inquired into the nature and function of poetry, both local and foreign. Hewing close to formalist categories, Demetillo's work gave emphasis to craft as a means to discovery.

Formalist criticism received an added impetus when Leonard Casper, an American critic, decided to pay attention to the works of Filipino writers in English. In two collections of essays — *The Wayward Horizon* (1961) and *The Wounded Diamond* (1964) — Casper analyzed almost all the major writers in the different genres. Among the authors included in his studies were those who wrote before the Pacific War, including Jose Garcia Villa, **Arturo Rotor**, and Manuel Arguilla, and those writing in the 1950s and 1960s such as **Nick Joaquin, N. V. M. Gonzalez, Bienvenido Santos, F. Sionil José, Edilberto Tiempo**, and **Edith Lopez Tiempo.**

Although Casper attempted to contextualize the texts against societal and historical contexts, Formalist orientation held sway as the primary mode of understanding and interpreting literature. The same orientation was evident in two other collections edited by Joseph Galdon — *Philippine Fiction: Essays from Philippine Studies (1953–1972)* (1972) and *Essays on the Philippine Novel in English* (1979). These were notable for their detailed illustrations of the manner in which Filipino critics employed formalist categories in analyzing the short stories and novels of the postwar period. In the works of Casper and Galdon, the pre-eminence of Philippine fiction as most reflective of the almost obsessive search for identity was affirmed.

There were, however, other critical texts that chose a less narrow path concerned with problematics linked to self-identity. In a number of more historically oriented studies, literature's social and historical contexts became important issues. Lucila Hosillos' *Philippine-American Literary Relations* (1960), for example, employed a comparative perspective to study twentieth-century Philippine literature in English *vis-à-vis* literary and socio-historical currents in the USA.

In *Brown Heritage: Essays on Philippine Cultural Tradition and Literature* (1967), edited by A. Manuud, the major Philippine literary writings from the colonial to the post-colonial periods were examined by various Filipino scholars and critics. The publication of this book was significant because, for the first time, an attempt was made to arrive at an overview of the development of Philippine literature from the Spanish period until the postwar years. More significantly, the much neglected vernacular writing, which in *Brown Heritage* meant primarily Tagalog texts, occupied a key section. The approaches varied: where the home-grown critics dealt with literature from the traditional historical/sociological approaches, those trained in the USA viewed the texts from the canonized formalist position.

Bienvenido Lumbera's pioneering study of Tagalog poetry, *Tagalog Poetry (1570–1898): Tradition and Influences in its Development*, which was published in book form only in 1986, exemplified the tendency of a number of Filipino critics to combine the categories culled from Formalism with a more historical consciousness. Thus, *Tagalog Poetry* paved the way for an approach that concentrated not only on the formal qualities of texts but on the historical specificities that determined the texts' production and even their consumption.

Certain historical events shaped the direction that literary criticism took in the late 1960s and early 1970s. With the rise of activism in this period, literature as an institution became a site for the struggle between Formalism and Marxism, largely influenced by the teachings of Lenin and Mao Tse-tung, whose writings figured prominently in the critical repertoire of a number of Filipino critics. By the early 1970s, such critics as Lumbera, Petronilo Bn. Daroy, Virgilio Almario, and Epifanio San Juan, Jr. had openly come out for a more politicized literature that objectively reflected the turmoil Philippine society was undergoing at this historical juncture. In the process, Marxist criticism pitted itself against the Formalist school as represented by Leonard Casper.

A major consequence of this confrontation was the denigration of the achievements of the writers in English, championed by the likes of Casper, by critics espousing Marxism. Philippine literature in English was viewed, rather simplistically, as the by-product of a pervasive colonial mentality that compelled the writers to deal with themes and to employ techniques that were largely drawn from western literature.

On the other hand, vernacular literature was perceived as having been the site where various writers in the vernacular manifested their rejection of the colonial rule. In some cases, notably in drama and in the novel, vernacular writing emerged as an instrument of subversion. Thus, the interest in vernacular texts deepened even as the critics of the 1970s examined the works of major writers who wrote in the different vernaculars and were largely ignored by the critics in English.

Of these Marxist critics, the most prolific was Epifanio San Juan, Jr., who studied at Harvard University, USA, and who early in the 1960s decided to turn his critical attention to Tagalog literature. His critical texts include *Balagtas: Art and Revolution* (1969), a study of the leading poet of the nineteenth century, and *The Radical Tradition in Philippine Literature* (1971), which was an attempt to examine the continuity of the tradition begun by the novels of Jose Rizal in the nineteenth century and affirmed in the major writers of the twentieth century such as Lope K. Santos, **Carlos Bulosan**, and Amado V. Hernandez.

In the succeeding years, San Juan published a number of scholarly works that demonstrated his attempt to view literature not from the orthodox Marxist position articulated by older Marxist critics such as the Hungarian Georg Lukacs, but from a position where Marxist critical theory had undergone changes because of the influence of various contemporary thinkers such as Louis Althusser, Pierre Macherey, Michel Foucault, Jacques Lacan, and other European thinkers. His *Toward A People's Literature* (1984) and *Subversions of Desire: Prolegomena to Nick Joaquin* (1988) bore witness to this effort at studying Philippine literature from this new interdisciplinary perspective.

Other critical texts written in the 1970s and 1980s must be perceived as parts of the continuing debate between the proponents of literature for its own sake and literature *engagé*. Included in the first category were a number of books by **Gemino Abad**, whose formal training was in neo-Aristotelian criticism as defined and elaborated by the Chicago School led by R. S. Crane and Elder Olson. Abad's *In Another Light: Poems and Essays* (1976) and *A Formal Approach to Lyric Poetry* (1978) are noted for the rigour with which the critic proceeded to examine poetry from a definite critical perspective.

Other books that attempt to theorize Philippine writing are **Ophelia Alcantara Dimalanta**'s *Philippine Poetics* (1976) and Alfeo Nudas' *Telic Contemplation* (1981), both dealing with literature in English. Critical texts that focus their attention on vernacular texts included Lucila Hosillos' *Originality as Vengeance in Philippine Literature* (1984), where the critic insists on the importance of a methodology she terms concentric comparaticism. Resil Mojares' *Origins and Rise of the Filipino Novel* (1982) and *Theatre in Society/ Society in Theatre* (1985), on the other hand, focus their attention on two specific genres from a multidisciplinary perspective. Bienvenido Lumbera's *Revaluation* (1984) is a collection of his essays on Philippine literature and popular culture. His studies demonstrate a pervasive Marxist perspective, which by this time had grown in strength in criticism and theory.

Two significant works were published in the 1980s. Isagani R. Cruz's *Beyond Futility* (1984) directly confronts the problems of literary criticism plaguing Filipino critics. This collection of essays also provided the first indication of the manner in which literary criticism and theory in the Philippines had begun to absorb certain categories from contemporary currents in Europe. The other text is Gemino Abad's *The Space Between* (1985), which introduced certain categories from structuralist and post-structuralist thought as defined and elaborated and/or deconstructed by such critics as Ferdinand de Saussure, Roland Barthes, Althusser, and Jacques Derrida. Certain developments in criticism and theory suggest a widening of the critical horizon. The rather simplistic views that shaped earlier critical works — for example, the one-dimensional and causal view of the relationship between text and context, the emphasis on purely formal structures, and the dissolution of the text's literariness — are giving way to more rigorous perspectives and modes of analysis.

Although still powerful movements, both Formalism and Marxism are currently undergoing some revisions in the works of younger critics in the process of coming to terms with the theories of such critics as Foucault and Derrida. In the 1980s, significant questions on the nature of literature, language, the author, ideology, and gender were raised. Although theirs is the voice of a minority, the works of Gemino Abad, Isagani R. Cruz, Soledad S. Reyes, Priscelina Legasto, and Edna Z. Manlapaz, among others, constitute a substantial body of critical texts that can no longer be ignored.

Formalism and Marxism, which shaped much of literary theory and criticism in the Philippines for a number of decades, are no longer viewed as monolithic movements. Their basic assumptions have been challenged by a new generation of critics now more exposed not only to Anglo-American literary movements but, as importantly, to European currents of thought. It is hoped that after the ferment has settled down, critics can turn their attention to primary texts viewed from a more holistic perspective that encompasses the notion of text as shaped by both politics and aesthetics.

SOLEDAD S. REYES

CRITICISM (Singapore)
Reviews and critical appraisals of Singapore literature in English are found in various publications, including: *Singapore Book World* and *NBDCS News*, both published by the National Book Development Council of Singapore; *Commentary* and *Focus*, journals associated with the National University of Singapore; and *The Straits Times*, a daily newspaper. (See **Cultural Journalism**, Singapore.) *Critical Engagements: Singapore Poems in Focus* (1986), edited by **Kirpal Singh**, contains assessments of poems by Singapore writers. **Arthur Yap**'s 'A Survey of the Criticisms on Singapore Poetry in English', in *Singapore Studies* (edited by B. K. Kapur, 1986), examines the range of critical writings on the genre.

Many of the critics were, and are, creative writers. One strand of evaluation encompassing and underpinning their various concerns focuses on the problems of cultural and linguistic identity. In the early 1950s Singapore poetry in English had its teething problems, attended to by discussions on the resources available from which both content and form could draw, including, in the pre-independence context, a 'new Malayan consciousness' and its relationship with the bigger, outer world, as well as Engmalchin (a fusion of English, Malay, and Chinese) and emerging forms of international Englishes. As poetry in English gains a surer footing in Singapore, the more parochial aspects of these experiential and formal roots no longer seem so contentious. (See **Poetry**, Singapore.)

Much of Singaporean criticism of poetry in English falls into the category of exposition. This includes general surveys, checklists, and bibliographies. The surveys sometimes carry the writers' own predispositions and viewpoints concerning the directions poetry should take and what the poet's role should be. Personal viewpoints are more succinctly expressed in journals such as *Commentary*, which focus on language and socio-cultural issues. The bibliographies include those published by the National Library and the National University of Singapore Library. *The Journal of Commonwealth Literature* carries annual bibliographies of Singaporean creative writing.

Of the various forms of critical appraisal, reviews — not always evaluative — of individual collections are the most numerous. These reviews are sometimes complemented by the forewords and introductions in the individual collections and anthologies. There are also a few studies of the writings of individual poets, notably those on **Edwin Thumboo**. Published interviews have been featured in some journals, but these are few.

ARTHUR YAP

CRITICISM (South Africa)

The first South African literary criticism appeared in the small literary magazines of the Cape in the first half of the nineteenth century, including the *South African Journal* (1824), the *Cape of Good Hope Literary Gazette* (1830–5), the *South African Quarterly Journal* (1829–31; 1833–6), the *Cape Town Mirror* (1848–9), and the *Cape Monthly Magazine* (1857–62; 1870–81). The criticism in these journals generally took the form of book reviews and biographical sketches of English poets and was identical in nature to that by critics writing in London, England. For example, the disagreements within English culture as to the function of imaginative literature (identified as something of limited value in the emergent capitalist social order, as a proselytizing aid and occasional substitute for the Scriptures, or as the ultimate repository of spiritual truth) are reproduced in the pages of the Cape's literary journals. A. J. Jardine's *Cape of Good Hope Literary Gazette* declared itself to be 'Devoted Exclusively to Literature, Criticism, Science, and the Advancement of Useful Knowledge', yet included articles condemning novel-reading as contrary to the teachings of the New Testament (November 1832) and some celebrating poetry as a 'chief instrument of civilisation' (July 1830).

Besides appearing in these short-lived magazines, South African literary criticism also emerged in public lectures and in college classrooms. The earliest English lecturers at the South African College, such as Edward Conduitt Judge and James Constantine Adamson, combined missionary work with the teaching of English literature, and this was reflected in their criticism. In his *Modern Literature: An Address at the Fifteenth Annual Meeting of the Subscribers to the Public Library* (1844), for example, Adamson combines the thoughts of the German Romantics with his own evangelical fervour in describing what were for him the appropriate methods of literary criticism. The first glimmer of an attempt to relate the study of English literature to its South African context is to be found during this period in Nathaniel James Merriman's lecture to the General Institute in Grahamstown, entitled *On the Study of Shakespeare* (1857). Establishing at the outset Shakespeare's pre-eminence as moral instructor, Merriman reads the relationship among Caliban and Stephano and Trinculo in *The Tempest* as a parable warning the white man of the temptations offered by the colonial experience. Merriman insists that there are counterparts to these three characters in South Africa and adds that they abound in even greater number in Western Australia.

In the second half of the nineteenth century,

South African literary criticism continued as a minority activity in the lecture halls and periodicals of the settler populace. The forms of literary criticism at the South African College were increasingly determined by the invention and rapid expansion at this stage of English literature as an examination subject for entry into the civil service and the professions in England. The examination system required the reduction of 'Great Works' to a finite number of examinable facts that could then be memorized by students. Since the majority of the teachers at the South African College were from London University, England — an institution central in presiding over this fusion of culture and utility — commentaries on English literature appearing in such periodicals as the *South African Magazine* (1867–9) and the *Cape Monthly Magazine* were limited to factual descriptions of the lives of poets and to short reviews. This is not to suggest, however, that the Cape's leading literary intellectuals entirely shunned questions regarding the meaning and social function of literature; indeed, Langham Dale, second superintendent general of education for the Cape and frequent contributor to the *Cape Monthly Magazine*, argued in his *The Philosophy of Method* (1877) for the pursuit of enlightenment via the contemplation of poetry. To the arduous intellectual task of 'piling fact upon fact, and thus adding to the edifice of universal knowledge', Dale adds the uplifting element of culture, which for him resides in books, in nature, and 'in the philanthropic atmosphere of Christian practice'. Similarly, James Cameron, lecturer at the South African College and the University of the Cape of Good Hope, provided for Roderick Noble's anthology *The Cape and its People, and Other Essays by South African Writers* (1869) an essay first summarizing the main arguments about the place of a classical education in a 'modern' curriculum and then arguing that for the Cape, where 'the moral and intellectual tone among us is not high', the application of classical literature to young minds would insure against further degeneration.

The first criticism by a black South African was **Solomon Plaatje**'s 'A South African's Homage', a tribute to Shakespeare in *A Book of Homage to Shakespeare* (1916), edited by Israel Gollancz (commemorating the tercentenary of Shakespeare's death), and his collection of 732 Tswana proverbs in *Sechuana Proverbs with Literal Translations and their European Equivalents* (1916). These two pieces, like the criticism of Plaatje's contemporary in India, **Sri Aurobindo,** deserve prominence because they remain in many ways paradigmatic of how the colonized negotiates the relationship to the literature and culture of the colonizer. In 'A South African's Homage', Plaatje accepts the western construction of Shakespeare as universal genius, while at the same time reading Shakespeare as an opponent of racism: 'Shakespeare's dramas . . . show that nobility and valour, like depravity and cowardice, are not the monopoly of any colour.'

Plaatje's contribution, however, was in no way the forerunner to any substantial change in the personnel of the South African critical establishment, which continued in the first decades of the twentieth century to be controlled by a small élite of white middle-class men. Periodicals publishing literary criticism included *The Cape Illustrated Magazine* (1890–1900), *African Monthly* (1906–10), *The State* (1909–12), and the *South African College Magazine* (1900–17), and full-length books of literary criticism started appearing during this period. Most dealt with conventional fare, such as John Clark's *Aristotle's Poetics and Shakespeare's Tragedies* (1912), Arnold Wynne's well received *The Growth of English Drama* (1914), and F. C. Kolbe's innovative *Shakespeare's Way: A Psychological Study* (1930). But for the first time there were also studies of South African writing, with the publication of Sidney Mendelssohn's *South African Bibliography* (1910), which covered all varieties of literary activity, and Manfred Nathan's *South African Literature: A General Survey* (1925), which discussed English, Afrikaans, and Dutch literature. These two books — like H. G. Turner's and A. Sutherland's *The Development of Australian Literature* (1898) and Archibald MacMurchy's *Handbook of Canadian Literature* (1906) — reflect the gradual emergence of a national identity independent of England.

In the 1930s the South African critical industry expanded further. The total dominance of South African literary criticism by white middle-class men moderated slightly, with women writing about English literature as well as political and social issues in *The Bluestocking* (1930–), the journal for South African university women, and with such black critics as **H. I. E. Dhlomo** and B. W. Vilikazi writing and disagreeing in *The South African Outlook* (1870–) about literary and aesthetic questions relating to primarily African, but also to western, literature. The best known South African journal, however, was the Cape Town-based *The Critic* (1932–9), which carried a greater number of articles on literature than any of its predecessors. Whereas in Canada and Australia in the 1930s there were certain critics proclaiming the value of their respective national literatures, in South Africa the gaze towards England and its literature was unwavering. The first edition of *The Critic* set out to nurture 'the development and maintenance of a sound literary and critical tradition', and in succeeding issues never included an article on South African literature. Towards the end of the decade, however, following the major changes in English literary culture, it started carrying articles reflecting the influence of both the English Marxists published in *The New Statesman* and of the Cambridge critics associated with *Scrutiny*.

After the Second World War, following the pattern in England, the critical practices associated with the latter tendency were taken up in South Africa. At two conferences of university English teachers in 1948 and 1949, and with only token dissent from older lecturers, South Africa's committed disciples of F. R. Leavis, including G. H. Durrant, Christina van Heyningen, and W. H. Gardner, argued successfully for the institutionalization of practical criticism at South African universities. The total hegemony of this critical method, and its near-exclusive application to English writers, is reflected both in the literary journals of the time, including *Theoria* (1947–), *English Studies in Africa* (1958–), and *Unisa English Studies* (1963–), and in the books of criticism published, such as Philip Segal's *Philip Segal: Essays and Lectures* (1973), D. R. C. Marsh's *The Recurring Miracle: A Study of Cymbeline and the Last Plays* (1962), D. G. Gillham's *Blake's Contrary States: The 'Songs of Innocence and Experience' as Dramatic Poems* (1966), and Geoffrey Durrant's *William Wordsworth* (1969). Although there were individual critics from this tradition who participated in anti-apartheid politics — Marsh, for example, completed his book on Elizabethan drama while in prison — in general there was little attempt to move intellectually or institutionally beyond the Arnold-Leavis tradition. A. C. Partridge distils the dominant view in the first edition of *English Studies in Africa* (1958), where he quotes with approval James Cameron's commitment to educating 'the higher nature' and describes the critic's function 'as torch-bearer of a stable morality and acknowledged aesthetic values'.

Criticism seeking to connect literature to its political context was thus banished from university English departments, but it did appear in book reviews by critics such as Sam Kahn and Michael Harmel, in such anti-apartheid magazines as *Advance* (1952–4), *New Age* (1954–62), the *Guardian* (1937–52), and *The Torch* (1946–63), and in occasional articles in the Non-European Unity Movement journal *Discussion* (1951–2). **Es'kia Mphahlele**, in *The African Image* (1962) and in a similar spirit to other African writers such as **Chinua Achebe**, challenged the racist stereotypes inscribed in the literature of the west and of white South Africa particularly, demonstrating the different real and imaginative worlds inhabited by white and black members of South Africa's literary intelligentsia.

The breakup of the liberal practical criticism consensus in the university English departments of South Africa took place in the 1970s, with pressure for change coming from a new generation of critics frustrated with the political myopia of the critical establishment. The issues at stake were best summarized in Mike Kirkwood's essay 'The Colonizer: A Critique of the English South African Culture Theory', published in James Polley's and **Peter Wilhelm**'s collection of essays, *Poetry South Africa* (1976). Focusing on **Guy Butler** as the pre-eminent representative of South African English literary culture, Kirkwood demonstrates the hypocrisy of the economically powerful English community representing itself as embattled interlocutor between African and Afrikaner nationalism and argues for the development of a literary culture rooted in Africa. These issues have been contested since at the annual conferences of the Association of University English Teachers and in the expanded number of literary journals, which now include *English in Africa* (1974–), *The Journal of Literary Studies* (1985–), *Critical Arts* (1980–), *Current Writing* (1989–), and *Pretexts* (1989–). Gradually, and in different ways, a number of South African critics — Eve Bertelsen, **J. M. Coetzee**, Tim Couzens, Vernon February, **Stephen Gray**, Robert Kavanagh, David Maugham Brown, **Njabulo Ndebele**, Martin Orkin, Kelwyn Sole, and others — have since the late 1970s met Kirkwood's plea, writing criticism that conceives the relation between political context and literary text as central. The earlier preoccupation with the English canon has been replaced by a rediscovery and reinterpretation of South African writers, and the displacement of practical criticism has been accompanied by an uneven adoption of post-1968 European critical discourses, with critics relying variously on Marxism, feminism, social history, structuralism and post-structuralism, and psychoanalysis to forge their arguments.

With the dramatic expansion of Commonwealth literature as an independent area of research, South African literature has become an increasingly popular focus for critics in England and North America. Journals in the USA particularly, such as *Cultural Critique*, *Boundary 2*, and *Critical Inquiry*, have carried articles about South African literature, and several metropolitan-based critics, including Ursula Barnett, Kenneth Parker, and Christopher Heywood, have produced collections of essays or full-length studies of South African literature.

DAVID JOHNSON

Further reading: *English Studies in Transition*, special issue of *Critical Arts* 2 (1984); 'Criticism', 'English and education', and 'Periodicals', in David Adey *et al.* (eds) *Companion to South African English Literature* (1986).

CRITICISM (South Pacific)

Historically, criticism in the Pacific by Pacific writers and/or those associated with the region has been hampered by colonial methodologies that kept the domain of literature separate from that of culture. Consequently, significant ethnographic studies of the Pacific by Bronislaw Malinowski, Margaret Mead, and others were not considered acceptable resources when it came to literary criticism. Since the curricula of the colonizers (Britain, Australia, New Zealand, France) invoked an absent European standard of the written text as the defining feature of literariness, Pacific criticism could not draw upon its own rich and complex oral traditions. The recent growth in critical consciousness is directly attributable to an urgent need in the universities of the region to formulate a critical discourse more meaningful to the real conditions of life in the Pacific. Taking their cue from Ken Arvidson's seminal essay, 'Aspects of Writing in the South Pacific' (in *The Mana Annual of Creative Writing*, 1973), post-colonial indigenous critics now tell a different story in their criticism, foregrounding much more relevant cross-cultural readings of literature. Defined as any cultural object that requires aesthetic judgement and emotional response, literature is now once again a living artefact inseparable from culture.

The most complete account of Pacific writing (excluding that of Papua New Guinea) is **Subramani**'s *South Pacific Literature: From Myth to Fabulation* (1985), in which he traces a continuous, though relatively unproblematic, tradition of literature from its genesis in myths and legends to the world of **Albert Wendt**, the 'magnificent fabulator'. Samoan *fagogo* (legendary tales or fables) and Fijian *talanoa* (anecdotal conversational narratives) are seen as legitimate literary antecedents of the written narratives of the Pacific. In 'Towards a New Oceana' (in *Mana Review* 1, 1976), Wendt, the Pacific's foremost writer, sees writers as creating a new oceania; he uses metaphors of the mystical concept of *mana* (a supernatural force, an inherent power in individuals) and of the politically more resonating 'stone castle in the Pacific' to theorize about Pacific literature. Another critical view is that of Marjorie Crocombe (in 'Mana and Creative Regional Co-operation' in *Third Mana Annual of Creative Writing*, 1977) and Ron Crocombe (in *The Pacific Way; An Emerging Identity*, 1976), who offer the 'Pacific Way' (an extension of the *faa-Samoa*, 'the Samoan Way') as a descriptive term that explains both political and cultural discourses of the Pacific. The social theorist **Epeli Hau'ofa**, further, questions western positivism and, in his own short stories (in the collections *Tales of the Tikongs*, 1983, and *Kisses in the Nederends*, 1987), gestures towards a more cynical, though socially oriented, reading of Pacific literature.

Vijay Mishra, in 'Indo-Fijian Fiction: Towards an Interpretation' (in *World Literature Written in English* 2, 1977) and in 'Rama's Banishment: A Theoretical Footnote to Indo-Fijian Writing' (*World Literature Written in English* 2, 1980), has theorized Fiji Indian writing in terms of the *girmit* ideology, an imaginary indenture consciousness locked into prior narratives of millenarianism. In *Margaret Mead and Samoa* (1983), Derek Freeman critiques the paradigm of cultural determinism as advanced by Mead and is wary of all *grands récits*. Ron Blaber, in 'The Short Story in the Pacific' (*SPAN* 21, 1985), uses the post-structuralist concept of 'writing' to explain the appropriation of western genres by Pacific writers, notably Subramani.

The genesis of Papua New Guinea post-colonial literature has been located by Ulli Beier, in his *Five New Guinea Plays* (1971), in vernacular plays modelled on European morality plays and Biblical narratives. He discovers Papua New Guinea's most vibrant writing in the period of self-government (1973–5), when a heightened sense of political awareness and national consciousness informed its literature at every level. Beier's reading of Papua New Guinea literature as a political weapon (in *Voices of Independence: New Black Writing of Papua New Guinea*, 1980, which he edited) is echoed in **John Kolia**'s interpretation of the literature as 'culturally re-integrative' (in his *Victims of Independence*, 1980) and in Lynette Baer's 'Cultural Syncretism in John Kolia's Papua New Guinea Novels' (in *World Literature Written in English* 2, 1986). Nigel Krauth and Norman Simms have also advanced political strategies of reading. B. S. Minol, further, has alluded to the complex relationship between fiction and history through the Papua New Guinea concept of *maus wara* (literally 'mouth water'), which refers to overdetermined lies or inversions of truth, similar to the Sanskrit *sandhya bhasha* ('twilight language').

VIJAY MISHRA

Further reading: *Imagining the Pacific*, special issue of *Meanjin* 4 (1990); Norman Simms, *Writers from the South Pacific* (1991).

CRITICISM (Sri Lanka)

In the 1930s, when F. R. Leavis was establishing 'close reading' as a critical technique, and I. A. Richards 'practical criticism' as a teaching and examining method in English universities, E. F. C. Ludowyk, the first Sri Lankan to be appointed professor of English (in 1936) at the University of Ceylon, was introducing these innovations to Sri Lanka. Supported by H. A. Passé and Doric de Souza, Ludowyk made 'Cambridge English' the dominant critical school in the island.

The school's focus was British literature, and it produced some notable results, usually after its members emigrated: Ludowyk's *Understanding Shakespeare* (1962), Upali Amerasinghe's *Dryden and Pope in the Nineteenth Century* (1962), and Dennis Bartholomeusz's *Macbeth and the Players* (1969) and *The Winter's Tale in Performance* (1982), for example. The most successful was Gamini Salgado, who spent his entire professional life in England, becoming professor of English at the University of Exeter. He published extensively, mainly on Shakespeare and D. H. Lawrence.

When Commonwealth literature secured a place as a field of study in the late 1960s, literary interests in Sri Lanka widened to include it, though recognition of Sri Lanka's literature in English came late in the day. **Yasmine Gooneratne** worked in this area, especially after immigrating to Australia. In *English Literature in Ceylon 1815–1878* (1968), Gooneratne documented the origins of Sri Lankan literature in English, and the journal she launched — *New Ceylon Writing* (1970–) — has been influential in developing criticism. (See **Literary Magazines**, Sri Lanka.) D. C. R. A. Goonetilleke, University of Kelaniya, has made three major contributions to Commonwealth studies: *Developing Countries in British Fiction* (1977); *Images of the Raj: South Asia in the Literature of Empire* (1988); and *Joseph Conrad: Beyond Culture and Background* (1990). Goonetilleke departs from the purely literary analysis characteristic of most Sri Lankan critics; while he sees literature in the context of relevant historical, political, and biographical facts, he sees it primarily as art, unlike the ideological and radical critics of Nigeria. He succeeded Gooneratne as regional representative for the *Journal of Commonwealth Literature*.

The most senior scholars in Sri Lanka, Reggie Siriwardena and M. I. Kuruvilla, have played an important role locally in stimulating thought, maintaining critical standards, and educating taste. Noteworthy is Kuruvilla's *Studies in World Literature* (1984).

D. C. R. A. GOONETILLEKE

CRITICISM (West Africa)

The Gambia, Ghana, Nigeria, Sierra Leone

Since West African literature in English is one of the direct consequences of British colonialism, its criticism has also tended to be linked to the critical traditions associated with English literature, in particular, and with western literature in general. The first critical problem associated with West African literature in English is that of definition: what is African literature? Is it an appendage to English literature or an independent literature in its own right? Although the issue has never been formally resolved, **Chinua Achebe**, in his essay 'Thoughts on the African Novel', suggested that the issue of definition be deferred until there was enough African literature for it to define itself in action. With the magnitude and quality of works by Africans now available, critical attention has shifted from the problem of definition to practical evaluation and to the articulation of theoretical positions.

The first critics of West African literature in English were foreigners who naturally brought to their criticism their western critical consciousness — although the more perceptive among them were quick to realize that, for their criticism to be relevant to Africa, they must take the African writers' primary cultures into consideration. Ulli Beier, Janheinz Jahn, G. D. Killam, **Margaret Laurence**, Charles Larsen, Bernth Lindfors, M. M. Mahood, Gerald Moore, Adrian A. Roscoe, and W. Walsh are some of the critics from the west who have contributed, through articles, monographs, and full-length books, to the criticism of West African literature in English. Achebe divides such critics into three groups: 'the peevishly hostile', 'those that are amazed that we [Africans] should be able to write at all', and the 'universalists', who insist on a wholesale application of western critical standards to African literature. While accepting the fact that African writers must remember that they cannot write in a world language without expecting international comment, Achebe is impatient with those western critics who are unwilling to accept the validity of sensibilities other than their own. In spite of the reservation of a good number of Africans about foreign criticism of African literature, however, it must be acknowledged that a number of these critics have been well meaning and have contributed very positively to the development of an African critical tradition.

The origin and development of an indigenous West African critical tradition may be traced to the regional institutions of higher learning established in the 1940s at Fourah Bay College, Sierra Leone, at University College of Legon, Ghana, and at University College of Ibadan, Nigeria. From these institutions emerged some of the most perceptive literary critics and creative writers of the region, who, in turn have been either partially or completely responsible for the training of subsequent generations of West African critics. Prominent West African critics such as Eldred Jones (as the editor of the influential *African Literature Today* and author of *The Writing of Wole Soyinka*, 1973), Abiola Irele (comparative critic of English and French literature, theorist, editor, publisher, and author of *The African Experience in Literature and Ideology*, 1981), Dan Izevbaye (a perceptive and regular contributor to journals of African literature), Donatus Nwoga (anthologist, critic, and translator), Emmanuel Obiechina (*Culture, Tradition and Society in the West African Novel*, 1975), Oyin Ogunba (*The Movement of Transition: A Study of the Plays of Wole Soyinka*, 1975), Kolawole Ogungbesan (editor, *New West African Literature*, 1979), and Eustace Palmer (*Introduction to African Literature*, 1972, and *The Growth of the African Novel*, 1979), to name a few, have been at the forefront of literary criticism in West Africa.

Similarly, the first generation of contemporary West African writers such as Achebe and **Wole Soyinka** has been active in moulding an African literary canon. The temper of this group's criticism is generally sociological, humanist, and cultural. While still basically faithful to the formalist criticism enunciated in I. A. Richards' *Practical Criticism* (1929), which served as the bible of criticism in colonial West African institutions of higher learning, this group of African critics introduced the examination of African culture, history, and contemporary conditions in an effort to relate African literature to its source. Although the impact of this group of critics still holds sway in West Africa, by the 1970s there emerged a number of critical movements, such as Marxism, championed by a new generation of Ibadan scholars including Omafume Onoge (a sociologist with literary interests) and Biodun Jeyifo (a member of the editorial collective of the radical/Marxist *Posi-*

tive Review). In a manner similar to the impact of **Ngugi wa Thiong'o**'s ideological crusade in East Africa, their emphasis on class conflicts and labour relations as an alternative tradition for the criticism of West African literature caused intense debates across many West African campuses, contributed to the emergence of a crop of ideologically committed writers such as **Femi Osofisan**, **Kole Omotoso**, **Festus Iyayi**, Odia Ofeimun, and **Niyi Osundare** and significantly altered the landscape of African literary criticism.

While some West African critics embraced Marxism, others turned to such contemporary theories as structuralism, semiotics, feminism, and stylistic criticism. However, their exponents attempt to domesticate the borrowed canons.

Against the background of the continued influence of western literary and critical traditions on African letters, the trio of **Chinweizu**, Onwuchekwa Jemie, and Ihechukwu Madubuike has made a strident call for a new critical approach in *Toward the Decolonization of African Literature* (1980). The future of West African criticism would seem to include the application of the logic of Africa's oral literature to its contemporary literature and criticism. One West African critic who has been in the forefront of the attempt to derive such a critical consciousness has been **Isidore Okpewho**, who has undertaken the study of oral African literature with particular emphasis on myth and the epic. Other similar efforts include those of Kwabena Nketia on Akan poetry, of **Kofi Awoonor** on Ewe poetry, of Egudu and Nwoga on Igbo poetic heritage, and of Wande Abimbola on Ifa. For the criticism of African literature to come of age, its practitioners must be ready to combine their acquired western critical canons with their inherited African consciousness of art.

While the pages of African literary journals such as *Black Orpheus*, *Nigeria Magazine*, *Transition/Ch'indaba*, *Asemka*, *Okike*, and *African Literature Today* and of such western periodicals as *World Literature Written in English* and *Ariel* have continued to play important roles in the development of an African critical tradition, literary conferences, at home and abroad, have also become avenues for raising, sharing, and developing critical opinion. The annual Ibadan conference on African literature, for example, was instrumental in the shaping of the Marxist literary parameters that subsequently influenced radical readings of African literature. Similarly, the annual Calabar conference on African literature and its publication of conference proceedings (under the editorship of E. Emenyonu) have helped to keep vibrant the debate on West African literature.

FUNSO AIYEJINA

Cameroon

As recently as 1977, educated anglophone Cameroonians were sceptical about the existence of a literature of their own, and the intervening decade and a half of plentiful scholarly mapping has not brought them to a detailed chronicle, let alone a deep, historical understanding of their own literary heritage. *Anglophone Cameroon Writing* (1993), edited by Nalova Lyonga, Echkard Breitinger, and Bole Butake, gathers some marvellous articles on the topic, but its lack of thoroughness is glaringly evident in its bibliography. The country's university-based scholars have yet to realize the distinctiveness of the country's traditional, historical, linguistic, and formal subject-matter. The state's watchful eye over cultural workers accounts for this syndrome of literary lacunae. Much academic Cameroonian literary scholarship resembles Soviet criticism. Pages of platitudes dissuade any but the most dogged readers from finding their way to deeply buried dissidence, where shallow criticism suddenly turns toward political discussion.

Universities are not the only locus of literary criticism. In magazines and newspapers read by the educated classes, lively cultural debates swirl around literary works. It is in the popular press as much as in the literature that Richard Bjornson's monumental *The African Quest For Freedom and Identity: Cameroonian Writing and the National Experience* (1991) found 'shared references' and 'a universe of discourse that is distinctly Cameroonian [that] has emerged through all these trials'. But perhaps it is only a comparatist such as Bjornson, who knows the inside intimately yet comes from the outside, who can capture what is so special about a vibrant, oppressed people that has few ties with the rest of the world. (See **Cameroon.**)

STEPHEN H. ARNOLD

Further reading: Stephen H. Arnold, 'Preface to a history of Cameroonian literature in English', *Research in African Literatures* 4 (1983).

CROSS, IAN (1925–)

New Zealand novelist

Born in Wanganui, New Zealand, he was educated at Wanganui Technical College and worked as a journalist in Wellington. Cross began writing fiction seriously in 1954 while he was Nieman Fellow at Harvard University, USA, and on his return to New Zealand he finished the novel *The God Boy* (1957). It received some acclaim and was followed by *The Backward Sex* (1960) and *After Anzac Day* (1961), after which Cross gave up fiction-writing. He moved into public relations work and became editor of the *N. Z. Listener*, 1973–7, then was chair of the New Zealand Broadcasting Corporation until 1985. Although he has written some short stories and television plays as well as a book of memoirs (*The Unlikely Bureaucrat: My Years in Broadcasting,* 1988), Cross is known chiefly for his three novels.

The God Boy deals with a terrible year in the life of an eleven-year-old boy as his unhappy family breaks up violently; it is told from the boy's naïve point of view, a method borrowed from Sherwood Anderson. *The Backward Sex* similarly tells of the painful sexual initiation of its seventeen-year-old narrator. *After Anzac Day*, which Cross considered his 'best sustained piece of writing', is more ambitious, using the occasion of a 1951 waterfront strike to present both a critical picture of New Zealand society, and, through the memories of the four main characters, the historical forces that had formed it.

LAWRENCE JONES

Further reading: Patrick Evans, 'The provincial dilemma', *Landfall* 30–1 (1976–7).

CRUMP, BARRY (1935–)

New Zealand novelist

Born in South Auckland, New Zealand, he became a professional pig-hunter and deer-stalker in New Zealand's rugged back-country before publishing his first two books, *A Good Keen Man* (1960) and *Hang On a Minute Mate* (1961), based on his experiences. These and fifteen later books written to the same formula sold more than a million copies in New Zealand alone by 1991. An entertaining autobiography, *The Life and Times of A Good Keen Man* (1992), recounts Crump's life drifting throughout New Zealand, with interludes in northern Australia (crocodile-hunting) and Kashmir.

New Zealand's bestselling male author, Crump writes in a racy, vernacular, yarn-spinning style, describing comic or adventurous incidents in the lives of a variety of often-eccentric male characters, all, like himself, on the run from urban bureaucracy, domesticity, and conformism. At its best the writing is crisp and economic, and numerous phrases (like the titles of Crump's first two books) have become part of the New Zealand vernacular.

Crump's work celebrates the New Zealand male icon of the Man Alone — the tough, resourceful, do-it-yourself Kiwi able to survive independently in rugged physical environments and always on the move, avoiding any lasting social ties such as **mateship** or marriage. Its roots lie deep in the popular journalism of pioneering days that became the subject of more serious fictional treatment in the work of **Frank Anthony**, **John Mulgan**, **Frank Sargeson**, and others. In Crump's contemporary male populist mode, however, the moral or social implications of the Man Alone icon are rarely questioned.

TERRY STURM

CULLINAN, PATRICK ROLAND (1932–)
South African poet
Born in Pretoria, South Africa, he attended Charterhouse School and read modern languages at Oxford University, England. After returning to South Africa he ran a sawmill in the Eastern Transvaal; his poems of this period appeared in South African, British, and American magazines. He founded, with **Lionel Abrahams**, the Bataleur Press and established the journal *the bloody horse: writing & the arts* (1980–1). In taking his journal's name from a quatrain by **Roy Campbell**, Cullinan challenged his readers to evaluate the quality, relevance, and continuity of South African writing; his first editorial declared: 'even in the atmosphere of a squalid, unresolved civil war it is not corrupt to be involved with the structures of words, with art or even artifice. It can be heroic.' Cullinan taught at the University of the Western Cape, South Africa, from 1983 to 1992.

Cullinan's poetry collections include *The Horizon Forty Miles Away* (1973), *Today Is Not Different* (1978), *The White Hail in the Orchard* (1984), and *Selected Poems, 1961–1991* (1992). *White Hail in the Orchard* contains 'Versions' (or translations) from the poetry of Eugenio Montale; Cullinan has also made 'Versions' — *I Sing Where I Stand* (1985) — from the Afrikaans poet Phil du Plessis.

Cullinan's writing arises from his western heritage and from his life in Africa: a cultural interaction is explicitly present in poems about his colonial heritage (for example, 'The Billiard Room' and 'The Garden'); it pervades poems such as '1818. M Francois Le Vaillant Recalls His Travels to the Interior Parts of Africa; 1780–1785' as well as those set in Europe ('Venice', 'September at the Tuilleries') and it echoes in his personal lyrics and meditations ('To Have Love', 'Mimesis'). While Cullinan has asserted his belief that writers 'should demonstrate visibly their loathing of racism [and] . . . apartheid', he has also said that he cannot write a 'successful, overtly political poem'. But, he continues, 'I believe that the verse I have published could only have been written by someone with a South African commitment, with my beliefs and background.'

Cullinan has also published a study of the Dutch soldier-traveller Robert Jacob Gordon, *Robert Jacob Gordon 1743–1795: The Man and His Travels at the Cape* (1992).

M. J. DAYMOND

Further reading: M. J. Daymond, J. U. Jacobs, and M. Lenta, eds, *Momentum: On Recent South African Writing* (1984).

CULTURAL JOURNALISM

CULTURAL JOURNALISM (Australia)
As a relative newcomer to literary forms (the first independent newspaper did not emerge until 1824), Australian journalism inherited a fully developed tradition of English literary journalism. Colonial and post-colonial newspapers in Australia resembled those in other English-speaking countries in readily combining news and opinion with criticism and literary writings, including, for example, serializations of novels by such authors as Charles Dickens. (See also **Publishing**, Australia.) Home-grown literature was belatedly serialized: **Rolf Boldrewood**'s *Robbery Under Arms* was serialized in the *Sydney Mail* in 1882–3 over the objections of director James Fairfax (who thought it would encourage criminal behaviour). Indeed, nineteenth-century journalism was often seen as a somewhat bohemian and seedy occupation. It is of more than passing interest that Australia's first novelist,

Henry Savery, author of *Quintus Servinton* (1831), was a journalist and a convict who was transported to Van Diemen's Land for forgery in 1825.

The ***Bulletin*** is the exemplary magazine combining literature and journalism. Founded in 1880, it provided the springboard for many of Australia's writers for half a century or more. It is Australia's only nineteenth-century magazine well known to the general public (in contrast with such titles as the *Heads of the People*, *Illustrated Melbourne Post*, *Sydney Times*, the *Lone Hand*, and *Melbourne Punch*), not only because it launched such popular literary figures as **Henry Lawson**, **A. B. Paterson**, and **Steele Rudd** but because of its survival as a successful news magazine. Yet the modern *Bulletin* has almost nothing in common with its forebear, having largely marginalized literary concerns. (See also **Literary Magazines**, Australia.) The lore of 'the bush' was a recurring theme in the *Bulletin*, reflected in other colonial publications. Critic Ken Stewart has pointed out that country newspapers were a particularly fertile field for the development of leading colonial writers, including J. F. Archibald, **William Lane**, **A. G. Stephens**, and **Catharine Parr Traill**, which may explain the strong 'bush' orientation of much journalism and literature written in cities.

The sub-editors' table has in Australia, as elsewhere, attracted people of literary interests who work anonymously behind the scenes to tidy up reporters' prose. According to **Thea Astley**, the journal *Meanjin* 'had its birthpangs on the sub-editor's table of the [Brisbane] *Courier-Mail* where Clem Christesen was working'. The best-known Australian pre-Second World War poet to have earned his living from journalism was **Kenneth Slessor**, a sub-editor whose journalistic achievements included being leader-writer of the Sydney *Daily Telegraph* and editor from 1935 to 1939 of *Smith's Weekly*.

Although much book reviewing in daily and weekly newspapers is undertaken (for extra dollars) by subs, computerization of newspapers has put an end to the traditional, rather urbane and scholarly sub-editors' tables: contemporary subs tend to be young and technical. It would be quite inconceivable for a literary journal to emerge from the subs' table of the contemporary *Courier-Mail*.

Literary journalism is no longer, as it has not been for more than a generation, a route to such responsibilities as being a political correspondent, a foreign correspondent, or the editor of a daily newspaper. Margaret Gee's *Media Guide* lists only eighteen literary editors, writers, or critics employed by mainstream metropolitan Australian newspapers. By contrast, Gee lists nineteen specialists in motoring, thirty-five in football, and fifty-six in politics. Some contemporary Australians keeping a foot in both camps are Peter Coleman, who edited the *Bulletin* and who keeps literary and journalistic interests alive in *Quadrant*; **Max Harris**, who thunders from his regular Saturday column in the *Australian*; **Donald Horne**, an established journalist and author before becoming an academic social scientist and subsequently the country's leading cultural bureaucrat; and **Barry Oakley**, editor of the *Australian*'s book section, who has successfully combined his own creative writing interests with the function of newspaper literary criticism. (In general, the review pages of Australian newspapers are but a shadow of their past impressive contribution to literary appreciation.)

Many who have made their mark in literature are unknown in their former or parallel careers as journalists — from nineteenth-century poet **Henry Kendall** and novelist **Marcus Clarke** to modern novelists **Olga Masters** and **Nancy Cato**. The journalistic narrative style of other contemporary journalists-turned-authors, such as **Robert Drewe** and **Blanche d'Alpuget**, makes their origins as journalists more evident.

JOHN HENNINGHAM

Further reading: J. P. Henningham, 'Two hundred years of Australian journalism: a history waiting to be written', *Australian Cultural History* 7 (1988); Ken Stewart, 'Journalism and the world of the writer: the production of Australian literature, 1855–1915', Laurie Hergenhan (ed.) *The Penguin New Literary History of Australia* (1988).

CULTURAL JOURNALISM (Canada)

The prevalence in Canada as early as the late eighteenth century of American journals and newspapers is the principal reason that cultural journalism in Canada has not reached the level it occupies in, for example, Australia. The closest Canadian equivalent to the *Argus* or the *Age* of Melbourne, with their intellectual as well as material support of reviewers and writers in the arts, has been the Toronto *Globe* (1844; since 1936, the *Globe and Mail*) which, in its best-remembered show of *noblesse oblige*, ran a rotating arts column from 1892 to 1894 by three poets, **Wilfred Campbell**, **Archibald Lampman**, and **Duncan Campbell Scott**. Significantly, though, all three depended for their livelihoods on civil service appointments. While the Roman Catholic church in Quebec offered another option, a few examples of church-supported authors can be cited even in Ontario, as with Thomas O'Hagan (1855–1939), author of works such as *Intimacies in Canadian Life and Letters* (1927). In English Canada, however, the tradition of Protestant literary life, typified by the critic, compiler, and publisher Lorne Pierce (1890–1961) and reaching its highest expression in the critic **Northrop Frye**, has always been more conspicuous.

Even amid the profusion of journals that characterized the late Victorian period, it was apparent that the thin market for cultural commentary conduced towards a nation of part-time critics to explain and celebrate the part-time creative writers. Many journalists were cultural reporters *ex officio* and some attained a high level of accomplishment as stylists, as with Kathleen Blake Coleman (1864–1915), known as 'Kit of the *Mail*', and **Sara Jeannette Duncan**, who would graduate to writing novels and plays. At the time, such primitive polymaths could be found even in academic life, as instanced by George Monro Grant, the senatorial man of letters and principal of Queen's University, Kingston. In more recent times, however, the private-sector generalists and the academic specialists have usually run along parallel (though not always mutually agreed upon) lines. The resulting tension was prefigured by **Goldwin Smith**, the wealthy former Oxford don who settled in Canada where he devoted himself to political mischief and a long shelf of books. He used his fortune to help found newspapers and journals. One of them, *The Week* (1883–96), which is justly remembered for its arts quotient, was edited briefly by **Charles G. D. Roberts**, the poet and writer of nature stories, whose long career was a hymn to the need for literary dexterity. A different combination of aesthetic and political instincts found expression in J. W. Bengough (1851–1923), caricaturist, radical reformer, and jack of all writing trades, who edited and published the magazine *Grip* (1873–94).

In the last quarter of the nineteenth century, commentary in the establishment press was led by John Reade (1837–1919) of the Montreal *Star*, its literary editor for forty years. Yet the distinction of being Canada's first full-time professional reviewer of books is accorded William Arthur Deacon (1890–1977), whose work at its highest, as reflected in *Pens and Pirates* (1923) and *Poteen: A Pot-Pourri of Canadian Essays* (1926), aspires to the level of J. C. Squire in the UK. Fittingly, Deacon began his career on the *Manitoba Free Press* (since 1931 the *Winnipeg Free Press*) whose *Manchester Guardian* brand of liberalism included certain presumptions about the cultural interests of its constituency. Other figures respected in their day include Augustus Bridle (1869–1952) and B. K. Sandwell (1876–1954), journalists dissimilar in most ways except the ease with which they wrote about music and drama as easily as about politics. Another of the same sort was Hector Charlesworth (1872–1945), a critic of all the arts, who is now, sadly, recalled only for his hysterical opposition to the Group of Seven painters. Before joining the *Globe*, Deacon was literary editor of the magazine *Saturday Night* (1887–), the same position held a generation later by **Robertson Davies**. It was with *Saturday Night* that first Charlesworth and then Sandwell were associated for the greater portions of their careers.

The early twentieth century saw numerous attempts to publish national periodicals that would give expression to Canadian culture. The two hardiest proved to be the left-wing monthly *The Canadian Forum* (1920–) and the mass-market magazine *Maclean's* (1905–). The latter was actually considered a component of the culture itself until the 1970s when, like the ***Bulletin*** in Australia, it was remade as a news weekly on the American model. Since the 1950s, opportunities for serious arts journalism have widened, thanks largely to the **Canada Council** and its provincial equivalents, the Canadian Broadcasting Corporation, and the maturing Canadian book-publishing industry (see **Publishing**, Canada). One sees in Canada now what was obvious in other cultures earlier: the disappearance of those who feel the need to write convincingly in almost any area even though their hearts lie with the arts, and their replacement by full-time arts specialists, some of whom later choose politics and economics instead. An example of the latter is Robert Fulford (1932–), himself a long-serving former editor of *Saturday Night* who was also a regular critic of literature, film, fine art, and jazz. Yet the new spectrum of opportunity, with its tempting diversions, has also produced a few people who rise to take advantage of all its possibilities, illustrating the role of culture in the society that they themselves make their own by such acts of participation. **George Woodcock**, the author of approximately one hundred books of poetry, criticism, history, biography, travel, and politics, can be compared to few others in Commonwealth writing except Australian **Jack Lindsay**. In general, however, the reinvigoration of the tradition of the man and woman of letters, so obvious in the UK since the 1970s in figures ranging from Maureen Duffy to Peter Ackroyd to A. N. Wilson, has not manifested itself in Canada in quite the same way. A number of the better-known writers still in mid-career, such as **Margaret Atwood** and **Michael Ondaatje**, give a hint of this approach at times. But the suggestion stems from abilities that cannot be contained within any one form, nor allegiance to the old convention.

DOUGLAS FETHERLING

Further reading: Douglas Fetherling, *The Rise of the Canadian Newspaper* (1990).

Cultural Journalism (India)

The first printing presses in India were set up by the Portuguese to propagate the Christian faith. Other Europeans emulated them. In 1780, after the British had established themselves as rulers, the first newspaper was published in India — it was in English. The credit for this goes to the rather discreditable James Augustus Hicky, who used his *Bengal Gazette* (1780–2) — also known as the *Calcutta General Advertiser* — to attack Warren Hastings and his colleagues of the East India Company. The government founded the *Calcutta Gazette* in 1784 to defend itself. Several other periodicals made their appearance in quick succession in Calcutta, Serampore, Bombay, and Madras. All these were of, for, and by the British community, and they lived on controversy and personal attack.

The power of the press was not lost on educated groups among Indians, who brought out their own journals to protect their interests and propagate their views. The great reformer, Raja **Rammohun Roy**, for example, was associated with *Sambad Kaumudi* (in Bengali, established 1821),

Brahmunical Magazine (in English), and *Mirat-ul-Akhbar* (in Persian, established 1822).

At this time the people of India viewed the English language as a means of intellectual enrichment rather than as an instrument of enslavement. Bal Shastri Jambhekar, who in 1832 brought out the first Marathi periodical, *Bombay Durpan*, wrote in his prospectus:

> Stimulated by a desire to encourage amongst their countrymen the pursuit of English literature, and to open a field for free and public discussion on points connected with the prosperity of the country and the happiness of its inhabitants, a few natives, resident in Bombay, intend to publish a newspaper entitled the *Bombay Durpan* . . . The publication is undertaken chiefly with the object of promoting European literature and the diffusion of European knowledge; the sphere of its usefulness will be extended by having two columns in each place, one English and the other Muratee.

This passage throws light on the deep impression that English and European literature had made on Indian minds as a vehicle of intellectual freedom. Edmund Burke's prose and the heady ideas of the American and French revolutions had taken root in India.

The journals published by the British community proved so irksome to the government that in 1823 it promulgated a regulation to control them. Raja Rammohun Roy was quick to raise his voice in protest:

> Every good Ruler who is convinced of the imperfections of human nature, and reverences the Eternal Governor of the world, must be conscious of the great liability to error in managing the affairs of a vast empire; and therefore he will be anxious to afford every individual the readiest means of bringing to his notice whatever may require his interference. To secure this important objective, the unrestricted liberty of publication is the only effectual means that can be employed.

The need of the expatriate British community to keep in touch with developments in politics, the arts, and trade in the mother country grew. To meet this need, many new English journals appeared, the more prominent being the *Spectator* (Madras, established 1836), the *Bombay Times* (1839) — later to become the *Times of India* (1880–) — the *Lahore Chronicle* (1846), the *Pioneer* (Allahabad, 1865), the *Madras Mail* (1868), the *Civil and Military Gazette* (Lahore, 1872), and the *Statesman* (Calcutta, 1875). They had to get their editors, sometimes even their compositors, from the UK. Rudyard Kipling, still in his teens, came to work for the *Civil and Military Gazette*. His 'Departmental Ditties' and earliest short stories were published in it; he later moved to the *Pioneer*.

Besides publishing 'hard' news, the English and vernacular journals also published accounts of the work of orientalists, archaeologists, and natural historians who were making important findings. But the Indian-language press also published political commentary, and what they wrote at the time of the Great Mutiny (or Sepoy Mutiny), between 1857 and 1859, unnerved the government. The 'mutiny' and its aftermath and their own increasing prosperity made the Anglo-Indian papers side wholly with the government, bitterly attacking the 'vernacular press'. The government finally attempted to curb Indian-language newspapers with 'An Act for the Better Control of Publications in Oriental Languages, 1878', which included provision for confiscating the printing presses of offending newspapers. To evade its clutches, the Bengali

Amrita Bazar Patrika of Calcutta converted itself overnight into an English newspaper, thereby providing the press with a legend. The growing Indian intellectual and professional classes brought out new journals in English. The *Hindu* (1878–) of Madras remains one of India's most influential newspapers to this day.

A milestone in the political life of India was the establishment of the Indian National Congress in 1885. According to critic Pat Lovatt, 'The real development of the art and business of journalism, as understood in the West, dates from the birth of the Indian National Congress.' The leaders of the Congress had an all-India vision; their political outlook was liberal, and their ethical values and eloquence very Victorian.

The next major influence on Indian journalism was the work of **Mohandas Karamchand Gandhi**, who brought to India the politics of open confrontation and non-violent defiance of British power. Petitioning, however well-documented, and oratory, however impassioned, would no longer do; they gave way to mass action. Gandhi's close associates founded newspapers to mobilize the people. Gandhi, who had founded *Indian Opinion* in 1904 in South Africa, was perhaps the greatest of Indian editors. He ran journals in English, Hindi, and Gujarati for the benefit of adherents and adversaries. These journals looked more like the creations of a cottage industry (which in fact they were) than the products of modern manufacture. The English journals were *Young India* (1919–30) and its successor *Harijan* (1933–*c.*51).

Independence signalled the Indianization of British-owned newspapers and news agencies. Free India, however, has also witnessed an acceleration of the westernization process. For many segments of the middle class, English has virtually become the mother tongue. The number of newspapers in India in all languages stood at 30,153 on 1 January 1990; of them, 4,627 were in English. This ratio, however, does not reflect the influence and dominance of the English publications. Not only does the English press attract the lion's share of advertising, it also serves as a role model for journals in the other languages. The reports and editorials of the leading English dailies — the *Statesman*, the *Hindu*, the *Times of India*, the *Hindustan Times* (1923–), the *Indian Express* (1932–), the *Economic Times* (1961–), and the *Telegraph* (1982–), to name the leaders in the field — and the investigative stories and gossip in such periodicals as *Blitz* (1941–), *Sunday* (1973–), *India Today* (1975–), and *Frontline* (1983–) are widely discussed. In films, sport, fashion, and commerce, the English journals are the trend-setters. Because information sources and reference books are mostly in English, Indian-language newspapers are afflicted with 'translationitis'. The English journals, for their part, have their own journalese, compounded in varying parts of Indianisms, Fleet Street jargon, and, increasingly, Americanisms. Sub-editors and editorial writers are no longer afraid of Fowler and Gowers if they have discovered a different usage in *Time* magazine. However, British spelling still persists.

Journalism is not only news and public affairs, it is also an important part of education and general culture. The press has made a particularly significant contribution to the literary renaissance in Indian literature written in English, and some of the greatest literary and intellectual figures of modern India — such as Bankim Chandra Chatterjee, **Sri Aurobindo**, Prem Chand, and Subramania Bharati, for example — have managed or worked for journals. English publications have done much to enable regional art and literature to acquire national recognition. Even a brief account of the Indian press cannot fail to mention the great work in this direction of the *Modern Review* (1907–65). English newspapers regularly publish translations of stories, essays, and poems from the mother tongues as well as original writings in English. It was the *Hindu* of Madras that discovered **R. K.**

Narayan's literary gifts, and the *Illustrated Weekly of India* (1880–) has a long record of hospitality towards young poets. Most scientific and professional journals are in English.

Because English came to India as the language of a foreign colonizer, there are many Indians who view it as the language of internal colonialists exploiting the large masses of 'have-nots'. From time to time *Angrezi Hatao* ('off with English') movements have erupted, but there is little likelihood of its going.

H. Y. SHARADA PRASAD

Further reading: Margarita Barns, *The Indian Press* (1940); S. Natarajan, *A History of the Press in India* (1962).

CULTURAL JOURNALISM (Singapore)

Singapore's main outlet for cultural journalism in English is probably 'Life!', the features section of the main English daily, *The Straits Times* (1845–). Containing more than twenty pages of articles on the arts and entertainment, it covers literature, the visual arts, music, film, television, and trends in social and intellectual life, both national and international. Lively debates about the arts are often generated by arts reviews in *The Straits Times*.

The paper also features a daily section on the arts and cultural activities of the other communities, namely Malay, Indian, and Chinese. Arts coverage in the paper's weekend edition is more broadly based. *Arts on Campus* (1990–), a magazine published by the university theatre group NUS Theatre, offers coverage of the arts. Coverage of arts and culture also takes place regularly in the features section of the financial daily, *Business Times* (1976–), and *Trends* (1990–), the monthly supplement of the Institute of South-east Asian Studies.

Commissioned articles, usually surveys of the state of the various arts, appear in *Singa* (1980–), Singapore's main literary journal, published twice yearly by the National University of Singapore and sponsored by the National Arts Council. *Singa* publishes mainly original literary works. Other arts coverage appears in entertainment magazines and occasionally in the pages of some women's and society magazines.

There is no commercially sustained periodical devoted to the arts in Singapore, mainly because the experience has been that a select readership cannot draw enough advertising revenue. The writers and reviewers of the flagship *The Straits Times* shoulder a heavier responsibility regarding discussion of the arts than would otherwise be the case.

KOH BUCK SONG

CUMPER, PATRICIA (1954–)

Jamaican dramatist

Born in Kingston, Jamaica, she earned a BA from the University of the West Indies. Cumper is one of many Caribbean dramatists whose works, while significant, have not been published. Since 1977, at least ten of her plays have had major stagings and she has written a number of highly popular radio serials, including 'Mortimer Simmons' (broadcast 1980–2), 'Malvina's Revenge' (1990–2), and 'Legacy' (1992–). Cumper has taught playwriting at the Jamaica School of Drama and is now a freelance writer, researcher, and video producer in Jamaica.

Cumper's plays are compelling and controversial explorations of insanity and alienation as they relate to the female experience. Her earliest play, 'The Rapist' (premièred 1977), explores the dynamics of sexual violence in a politically volatile society. Cumper's picture of Jamaican society, however, is at once bleak and resilient; she undercuts tension with wit and humour. Cumper has had a fruitful relationship with an outstanding director, Barbadian Earl Warner, who directed her 'Checkers' (premièred 1992), a two-hander that explores the realities of post-independence and post-socialist Jamaica.

For Cumper, it is important to 'make people uncomfortable'. She shares both **Trevor Rhone**'s insight into the folk experience and his capacity to discover beauty and humour in the narratives of working-class Jamaicans; at the same time, however, her work displays a propensity towards a harsher poetics that is reminiscent of the work of **Dennis Scott**. Her play 'Fallen Angel and The Devil Concubine' (premièred 1987), co-written with Honor Ford Smith, reflects this paradoxical quality.

Cumper has adapted for stage the work of several Caribbean authors, including **Erna Brodber**'s *Jane and Louisa Will Soon Come Home* (1980) under the same title (premièred 1992); **Claude McKay**'s short story 'Crazy Jane' (1932) — about a young Mulatto woman's psychological destruction by the sexual repression in her village — as 'Crazy Mary' (premièred 1991); and Shakespeare's *Romeo and Juliet* as 'Benny's Song' (premièred 1991).

KWAME DAWES

CURNOW, ALLEN (1911–)

New Zealand poet, editor

Born in Timaru, New Zealand, he studied for the Anglican ministry and contributed topical light verse to a Dunedin newspaper. In 1934, in 'a fit of young poet's idealism and egotism', he abandoned his studies and returned to writing for newspapers. The beginnings of religious doubt can be seen in his first collection of poems, *Valley of Decision* (1933), and doubt in one form or another has been a constant in Curnow's work. He has published more than twenty volumes of poetry and plays in verse and edited two influential anthologies of New Zealand literature — *A Book of New Zealand Verse 1923–45* (1945; rev. 1951) and *The Penguin Book of New Zealand Verse* (1960).

'Aspects of Monism', in *Three Poems* (1935), hints at an interest in philosophy, while history and nationalism, the great themes that were to preoccupy Curnow for more than a decade, announce themselves in a minor way in *Enemies: Poems 1934–36* (1937) and find full expression in *Not in Narrow Seas* (1939). Like **A. R. D. Fairburn**'s long poem *Dominion* (1938), *Not in Narrow Seas* is a 'study of the birth, life, and growth' of New Zealand: 'Small trade and no triumph, men of strength / Proved at football and in wars not their own'. The language varies in tone from high formalism to an easy vernacular, sometimes within the same line. 'Statement' is an Audenesque sestina, a form Curnow found especially useful for worrying away at a single large idea.

New Zealand's centenary was celebrated in 1940, and 'The Unhistoric Story' (in *Island and Time*, 1941) sums it up: New Zealand's discovery was not peaceful, its settlement scarcely a success ('the pilgrim dream pricked by a cold dawn'), and its consequences, in a memorable phrase, were 'something different, something / Nobody counted on'. The inheritors of the colonial dream feel an unease, expressed in 'House and Land' as the 'great gloom' of 'a land of settlers / With never a soul at home'.

Sailing or Drowning (1943) broadens Curnow's range to include personal poems (an elegy, a verse letter to **Denis Glover**) and a public commission, 'Landfall in Unknown Seas', to commemorate the tercentenary of Abel Tasman's discovery — 'The stain of blood that writes an island story'. During this period Curnow began working on his anthology of New Zealand poetry, *A Book of New Zealand Verse 1923–45*, which was to establish the canon so firmly that anything done since has seemed to challenge only the details. 'Attitudes for a New Zealand Poet' (in *Sailing or Drowning*) noted the temporary failure of art, but predicted a future in which the poet might flourish: 'Not I, some child, born in a marvellous year, / Will learn the trick of standing upright here.'

Curnow's public themes give way to more personal concerns in *Jack Without Magic* (1946), which contains a major work, the long poem 'At Dead Low Water'; it provides a rich lode of material Curnow was to mine again and again. The poem recalls a childhood visit to the beach at low tide; the child is both actual and emblematic, the imagery is biblical ('When the word alone was, and the waters'), but the valency has changed: now the Bible is exploited as a rich repository of myth.

Curnow's interest in epistemology is apparent in a group of poems published in the 1950s (in *Poems 1949–1957*, 1957). 'To Forget Self and All' both questions what the subject of the poem is to be and demonstrates its answer: the mind of the poet must be 'capable to detect where reality was not / And scrupulous what to put in place of it'. In 'A Small Room with Large Windows', Curnow is clear that 'the imagination takes flight from the ground of fact', but he is not above positing an alternative geometry to suit a nation capable of one point of view and then detonating his own poem with a series of particular, precisely observed images that 'Explode a dozen diverse dullnesses / Like a burst of accurate fire'.

These poems are difficult: the thought is often dense and the syntax knotty, ambiguous, and punning. 'Spectacular Blossom' (in *Poems 1949–1957*) evokes suburban Auckland, with pohutukawa trees growing along the beaches, and introduces the idea of blood sacrifice that was to be taken up in the late poems, especially in 'An Incorrigible Music': 'An old man's blood spills bright as a girl's / On beaches where the knees of light crash down. / These dying ejaculate their bloom.'

Curnow's late maturity began with *Trees Effigies Moving Objects* (1972), in which the concern with problems of knowledge has intensified, and the phenomenal world begins to seem downright menacing ('Look hard at nature. It is in the nature / of things to look, and look back, harder.'). God may have been disposed of forty years earlier, but in His absence the sun becomes a 'bloodshot cornea'; a 'dead lamb on the beach' may be no less than the Agnus Dei.

Three later collections — *An Incorrigible Music* (1979), *You Will Know When You Get There* (1982), and *The Loop in Lone Kauri Road* (1986) — equal anything Curnow has written. The title poem of *An Incorrigible Music* takes up the theme of violence compressed in 'Spectacular Blossom', giving the political and contemporary (the kidnapping and assassination of the Italian politician Aldo Moro) a mythic and historical dimension as well as a local correlative — fishing off the rocks on the west coast of Auckland for kahawai. The latter two collections are concerned with memory and death.

Curnow's *Collected Poems: 1933–1973* was published in 1974, *Selected Poems* in 1982, and *Continuum: New and Later Poems 1972–1988* in 1988. *Selected Poems, 1940–1989* (1990) makes a new selection from his entire oeuvre. An incomplete selection from his light verse has been gathered together as *The Best of Whim-Wham* (1959), published under Curnow's pseudonym Whim-Wham. Much of his criticism has been published in *Look Back Harder* (1987), edited by Peter Simpson, including the introductions to his influential anthologies of New Zealand poetry. All but two of his plays appear in *Four Plays* (1972).

ANNE FRENCH

Further reading: Terry L. Sturm, 'Allen Curnow: forty years of poems', *Islands* 1 (1975); Alan Roddick, *Allen Curnow* (1980).

CURRIMBHOY, ASIF (1928–)
Indian dramatist
The scion of a distinguished Muslim Indian family of Khoja baronets, he was born in Bombay, India, where he studied in a Jesuit mission school. Graduating from the University of California, USA, he joined India's Burmah-Shell as an executive; his business travel across India supplied him with diverse locales for his unusually topical dramas. Thus his début, *The Tourist Mecca* (in *The Tourist*

Mecca and The Clock: Two Plays, 1961), was an Indo-American romance set against the Taj Mahal. But his name first gained currency when government censors in Bombay banned *The Doldrummers* (1961) from public performance, a ban revoked after a year following protests by many celebrities and artists.

The Doldrummers offended conservative sensibilities with its frank depiction of promiscuity in the *demi-monde* living in shanties along Bombay's Juhu Beach; it also looked realistically at alienated youth in urban India. *The Dumb Dancer* (1962) is an innovative, psychological, Kathakali dance-drama-within-a-drama. *'OM'* (1962), a daring attempt to dramatize Hindu mysticism, occasionally recalls **Rabindranath Tagore**. (The mantra 'ōm' is used in contemplating ultimate reality.) *Thorns on a Canvas* (1963) — a satire on institutionalized patronage — is a surreal farce about the nature of true art. *The Captives* (1963) examines Indian political decisions in the light of the Sino-Indian war, as well as the loyalties of the Muslim minority (the protagonist, a Muslim in the army, has a Hindu wife). In 1964 Currimbhoy allegorized India's invasion of the Portuguese colony of Goa into a lyrical, passionate love story, *Goa* (1966), that suggests India's political rape of that enclave.

Currimbhoy's second peak period started with *Inquilab* ('Revolution', 1971), on the contemporary Maoist Naxalite movement in Bengal and its appeal to the young. The seriocomic *Darjeeling Tea?* (1971) paints the mixed emotions of the last pukka Englishmen in India — the tea planters. The epic *Sonar Bangla* ('Golden Bengal', 1972) encompasses the entire liberation of Bangladesh in its cinematic, sometimes almost-unstageable historical sweep; the production of 'Om Mane Padme Hum!' ('Hail to the Jewel in the Lotus!', 1972) required multimedia treatment involving slide projection, newsreel clips, and filmed scenes while retelling the Dalai Lama's escape from Tibet in 1959. *This Alien . . . Native Land* (1975) portrays a Jewish Indian family in Bombay, exploring in the manner of Eugene O'Neill the complexities of familial ties and the relation between fantasy and reality.

Currimbhoy has written seventeen other plays, movie scenarios (*Valley of the Assassins*, privately printed, 1965), television scripts, and several one-act plays, of which *The Hungry Ones* (1966), juxtaposing famine victims with American beatniks, caused a stir off-off-Broadway in 1966. (*The Dumb Dancer* had played there before proceeding to the British Drama League festival of 1969.) In 1965 Paul Baker of the Dallas Theater Center, USA, presented Currimbhoy's disturbing exploration of abnormal psychology, *Monsoon* (1992), and Michigan State University, USA, premièred *Goa*, which reached Broadway in 1968 and was termed 'a beautifully acted tone poem' by critic Brooks Atkinson. Although Currimbhoy's work is the most challenging of any living Indo-English dramatist, his plays have won greater recognition outside India.

ANANDA LAL

Further reading: P. Bayapa Reddy, *The Plays of Asif Currimbhoy* (1985).

D

DABYDEEN, CYRIL (1945–)

Guyanese/Canadian poet, short-story writer, novelist

Born in Berbice, Guyana, he worked as a schoolteacher before immigrating to Canada in 1970. He graduated from Lakehead University, Thunder Bay, Ontario, then earned two MA degrees — in English and public administration — from Queen's University, Kingston, Ontario. He has taught creative writing in universities and colleges and lives in Ottawa, Canada, where he is involved in human rights issues and race relations in Canadian municipalities.

Dabydeen has compiled two anthologies: *A Shapely Fire: Changing the Literary Landscape* (1987) and *Another Way to Dance: An Anthology of Asian Canadian Poetry* (1990). His first volume of poems, *Poems in Recession*, was published in Guyana in 1972. Other collections published in Canada are *Distances* (1977), *Goatsong* (1977), *Heart's Frame* (1979), *This Planet Earth* (1980), *Elephants Make Good Stepladders* (1982), *Islands Lovelier than a Vision* (1986), and *Coastland: New and Selected Poems 1973–1987* (1989). He has also published two collections of stories, *Still Close to the Island* (1980) and *To Monkey Jungle* (1988), and two novels, *The Wizard Swami* (1985) and *Dark Swirl* (1989).

Dabydeen's writing embraces many subjects (politics, travel, immigration, the Caribbean, and Canada) and many themes (exile, alienation, injustice, displacement, and death). His first novel gives a Naipaulian view of religious charlatanism, corruption, and mimicry in Guyana, while *Dark Swirl* blends Guyanese folklore with what he calls 'the bottomless pool of origins'. His stories are set in both Canada and Guyana.

Dabydeen's writing betrays no obviously ideological assumptions and has gradually shifted away from Caribbean pungency and assertiveness towards a cosmopolitan approach that is urbane, tolerant, and catholic. At a literal level, Dabydeen may be regarded as a reliable interpreter not only of visible minorities but of all immigrants in Canada. At a more abstract level, his writing dramatizes the psychic displacement and alienation that are so characteristic of modern living. Thus, while it is correct to regard him as both Canadian and Caribbean, his writing reaches beyond national boundaries. Dabydeen has won prizes for his poetry, and between 1984 and 1987 served as poet laureate of the city of Ottawa.

FRANK M. BIRBALSINGH

DABYDEEN, DAVID (1956–)

Guyanese poet, novelist

Born in Berbice, Guyana, into the East Indian community of Guyana's Corentyne coast, he was a precocious and brilliant child; he won a government scholarship to Queen's College, Georgetown, Guyana. At the age of thirteen Dabydeen was sent to London, England, to live with his father, who had been divorced from his mother for several years. Dabydeen's writing bears the marks of this double experience, providing a vivid and sensuous evocation of the rural Guyana of his childhood and the knowledge and cunning gained from an unhappy adolescence as an immigrant in London.

Dabydeen's university career at Cambridge, England, also influences his writing; there he acquired a deeply informed scholarly perspective on his own experience. This influence is clear in *Slave Song* (1984), his first volume of poetry and winner of a Commonwealth Writers Prize for Poetry. In *Slave Song* an elaborate scholarly apparatus of translations and notes is appended to the poems to counteract the powerful, often-violent emotional content expressed in raw Guyanese Creole. This device separates the persona of the work into two distinct personalities: that of the 'slave' raging against his oppression or crudely recounting his dreams of sexual conquest and that of the detached, scholarly commentator, detoxifying the material for metropolitan consumption.

In the collection *Coolie Odyssey* (1988) the imaginative voyaging between homeland ('Coolie Mother') and the immigrant experience ('Coolie Son') is calmer; the poetry is more reflective and assured. The title poem compresses and personalizes Indo-Caribbean history in a manner similar to **Edward Kamau Brathwaite**'s use of Afro-Caribbean history and suggests the recovery of ancestors from oblivion: 'The ancestors . . . lie like texts . . . / Waiting to be written like children . . .'

Dabydeen's first novel, *The Intended* (1991), evokes the experience of an Indian immigrant at the heart of London's darkness. Making use of such themes as childhood memories of home, sexual initiation, money, and corruption, this is a clever, almost slick novel, cunningly aware of the shibboleths of contemporary critical theory and following the lead provided by **Hanif Kureishi**'s *The Buddha of Suburbia* (1990). *The Intended* confirms the impression of Dabydeen as a brilliant and versatile artist who has augmented the street-wise immigrant's instinct for opportunity with a thoughtful, muted professionalism.

MARK McWATT

D'AGUIAR, FRED (1960–)

Guyanese/English poet

Born in London, England, he spent his childhood in Guyana, his family's home, returning to England in 1972. D'Aguiar trained as a psychiatric nurse, but his literary interests led him to read African and Caribbean studies at the University of Kent, Canterbury. In 1985 his first volume of poems, *Mama Dot* (1985), won a Poetry Society Recommendation, and in 1988 he received the Guyana Prize for Poetry. A series of writing positions followed, including the Judith E. Wilson Fellowship at Cambridge, England, 1989–90, and a Northern Arts Literary Fellowship, 1990–1. He edited the Black British Poetry section of *The New British Poetry* (1988), edited by Gillian Allnutt; in 1989 he published his second volume of verse, *Airy Hall*. Perhaps because D'Aguiar is a member of the second generation of Caribbean immigrants to Britain, his poetry moves beyond the search for identity that marked the work of earlier immigrant writers.

D'Aguiar's fine 'Mama Dot' poems established his reputation. Mama Dot is part embodiment of Guyanese history as seen in its women and part embodiment of D'Aguiar's own imaginative impulse — part African, part Caribbean, part European. Technically innovative, these poems show D'Aguiar at ease in both dialect and in Standard English forms. His childhood experience in Guyana underlies the 'Mama Dot' poems and much of his best verse, including the 'Airy Hall' sequence in his second volume, about which D'Aguiar writes, 'Some of these poems arrived singly in odd lines that resonated for me because tied to a childhood memory, lines with built-in images which burnt with a beacon's clarity in my mind's eye . . . I mean the lines felt as much as meant something: meaning and feeling occupied the same space.' His less personal pieces, such as the experimental sequence 'The Kitchen Bitch' (also in *Airy Hall*), lack assurance and give the impression of a writer still searching for his poetic voice.

D'Aguiar's play 'High Life' was produced at the Albany Empire in 1987, and in 1991 'A Jamaican Airman Foresees His Death' was staged successfully at the Royal Court Theatre Upstairs, London.

LOUIS JAMES

Further reading: Fred D'Aguiar, 'Zigzag paths',

in Archie Markham (ed.) *Hinterland* (1989).

DALISAY, JOSE YAP (1954–)

Filipino novelist, short-story writer, dramatist

He was born in Romblon island, the Philippines. Shortly after President Marcos declared martial law in 1973, Dalisay was arrested for his political activities and imprisoned for seven months.

Dalisay was educated at the University of the Philippines, (AB, English, *cum laude*, 1984), the University of Michigan, USA (master of fine arts in creative writing, 1988), and the University of Wisconsin, USA (Ph.D., English, 1991). After spending five years in the USA on a Fulbright grant, he returned to the Philippines, where he teaches English and creative writing at the University of the Philippines.

Dalisay has been cited by Filipino critics as one of 'the masters of Filipino short fiction in English'. He has published two collections of short stories, *Oldtimer and Other Stories* (1984) and *Sarcophagus and Other Stories* (1992), a novel, *Killing Time in a Warm Place* (1992), and a book of plays in Filipino. He has also written the screenplays in Filipino for twenty full-length films. His poems have been anthologized in several books.

Dalisay's work, while preponderantly cosmopolitan in its outlook and concerns, retains a strong pastoral influence. His stories deal mostly with death, guilt, and the difficulties of finding personal happiness in the post-colonial condition. His book of plays, *Madilim ang Gabi sa Laot at iba Pang Dula ng Ligaw na Pag-Ibig* ('Dark is the Night at Midsea and Other Plays of Vagrant Love', 1993) is focused on the impact of the political on the personal.

Killing Time in a Warm Place traces the growth of its protagonist, Noel Ilustre Bulaong, from country to city to the outside world during the two decades of Marcos rule. In giving it the National Book Award for fiction in 1993, the Manila Critics Circle took notice of 'its consummate craftsmanship characterized by clear and firm language, an absorbing narrative, and loving insights into the Filipino psyche'.

Dalisay's work has been published in the USA, Japan, Germany, Malaysia, Singapore, and Taiwan. His short story 'Heartland' is included in *The Colors of Heaven: Stories from the Pacific Rim* (1992).

ELMER A. ORDONEZ

DALLAS, RUTH (1919–)

New Zealand children's writer, poet

She was born Ruth Mumford in Invercargill, New Zealand, and has lived most of her life in Dunedin; she took her grandmother's name (Dallas) as her pen name. Her work was first published when she was twelve years old, and her poetry soon attracted the attention of **Charles Brasch**, who encouraged and published her work.

Dallas writes firmly within the Wordsworthian Romantic tradition. She has a strong sense of place, and her poems evoke images of southern New Zealand landscapes and seascapes to create contrasts between the timeless and the temporal and between youth and age. Her collections include *Country Road and Other Poems* (1953), *The Turning Wheel* (1961), *Experiment in Form* (1964), *Day Book: Poems of a Year* (1966), *Shadow Show* (1968), *Song for a Guitar and Other Songs* (1976), edited by Charles Brasch, *Walking on the Snow* (1976), and *Collected Poems* (1987).

The same economy of style and similar preoccupations of subject-matter are evident in Dallas' novels for children. In *The House on the Cliffs* (1975), the central character, old Biddy Bristow, is reminiscent of the 'quiet old lady' in the poem 'Grandmother and Child' (in *Country Road and Other Poems*), as she walks alone on the beaches searching for 'a bell to ring when the wind blows'. In the novel, children believe that the old woman is a witch until two girls befriend her and begin to understand something of the delicate balance between loneliness and the desire for independence. Friendship between young and old is also the focus of the novel *Shining Rivers* (1979), in which a young, nineteenth-century boy goes to the gold diggings and is helped to survive by an indomitable old miner.

Dallas' books for younger readers include *The Children in the Bush* (1969), *Ragamuffin Scarecrow* (1969), *A Dog Called Wig* (1970), *The Wild Boy in the Bush* (1971), *The Big Flood in the Bush* (1972), *Shining Rivers* (1979), and *Holiday Time in the Bush* (1983). These recount the day-to-day events of a family of lively nineteenth-century children. Their widowed mother is the district nurse, and her frequent and necessary absences mean that the children must often fend for themselves.

Dallas' main concern in writing for children has been to recount something of their pioneer forebears' life; she was also one of the first contemporary New Zealand writers to revive the genre of the 'settler story'.

BETTY GILDERDALE

D'ALPUGET, BLANCHE (1944–)

Australian novelist, biographer

She was born and educated in Sydney, Australia. She has worked as a journalist in Australia, England, Indonesia, and Malaysia. Her *Turtle Beach* (1981) won the *Age* Book of the Year Award, the South Australian Government's Biennial Award, and the Sydney PEN Golden Jubilee Award for Fiction. *Mediator* (1977) is a biography of Richard Kirby, with whom d'Alpuget shared an interest in South East Asia, particularly Indonesia. Her first novel, *Monkeys in the Dark* (1980), is set in Indonesia, and her second, *Turtle Beach*, in Malaysia. Her biography of a former Australian prime minister, *Robert I. Hawke* (1982), won the New South Wales' Premier's award for non-fiction. *Winter in Jerusalem* (1986), a novel set in Israel, grew out of her research for the Hawke biography.

The protagonist of *Monkeys in the Dark* is a young Australian journalist attached to the embassy in Djakarta, Indonesia, which is seen almost exclusively from the perspective of the Australian outsiders whose attitudes and assumptions are constantly disturbed by those they encounter in local people such as Maruli Hutabarat. Similarly, in the climactic scene of *Turtle Beach*, the beliefs and actions of Chinese-Malaysian Minou and Hindu Kanan combine to challenge the self-referring and self-seeking attitudes of the uncomprehending Australian journalist Judith Wilkes. *Turtle Beach*, like **Margaret Atwood**'s *Bodily Harm*, faces colonized western settler-invader populations with radical differences in life-style and ideology. Caribbean and Indonesian characters and situations thus comment directly on and/or implicitly interrogate Canadian and Australian assumptions. Dr Minnow in *Bodily Harm* tells Rennie, 'Everyone is in politics here . . . all the time. Not like the sweet Canadians'; Minou in *Turtle Beach* demonstrates how, from her perspective, Judith's life lacks 'purpose' and has only 'function'. Both d'Alpuget's novels, then, are part of that significant trend in the post-colonial settler-invader novel, whereby 'second-hand colonials' operating in their regions though economic 'spheres of influence' have their western-derived ways interrogated and disturbed by contact with other cultures.

Winter in Jerusalem offers an incisive account of debates within Israel over the 1980s invasion of Lebanon, and though it once again focuses on a female figure ('an authentic example of late twentieth-century western women reared in prosperity at a forced pace' and thus 'undeveloped within', as one character in the novel puts it), it is less 'fiction' than 'faction' and its protagonist is really the divided city itself, Jerusalem. In *Winter in Jerusalem*, however, as in her earlier novels, d'Alpuget is engaged by cultural difference and by the excitement of differing perspectives. As she has noted, 'My sense of place is a sense of *displace*.

Not displacelessness. Displace.'

HELEN TIFFIN

Further reading: 'Blanche D'Alpuget', in Martin Duwell and Laurie Hergenhan (eds) *The ALS Guide to Australian Writers: A Bibliography 1963–1990* (1992).

DANGAREMBGA, TSITSI (1960–)

Zimbabwean novelist, dramatist

In a number of ways, Dangarembga's novel *Nervous Conditions* (1988) breaks new ground in writing from southern Africa. It addresses the question of colonialism and its psychological effects, primarily on the élite. Dangarembga shows the coalescence of the double patriarchy of colonizer and colonized in her devastating yet sympathetic portrait of the schoolmaster father and uncle, Babamukuru (Senior Uncle), who is instrumental in causing his daughter Nyasha's nervous breakdown. The at-times extremely painful struggle of the younger generation to knit together diverse and contradictory patterns of social behaviour and thinking is shown in the lives of the doomed Nyasha and her cousin Tambudzai, the calm, ironic, narrative voice of the novel. In another bold step in the southern African novel, Dangarembga peoples her text predominantly with women of different generations. Both the younger and older generations of women struggle to create a space for themselves as women in the new social order. It is above all, a story of women. As the narrator says on the final page, 'It is my own story; the story of four women whom I have loved, and our men.'

Dangarembga's play *She No Longer Weeps* (1987) shows a similar primary focus on the woman's voice. As in *Nervous Conditions* the play interrogates notions of macho maleness, suggesting instead a realm of social and psychological independence for women. The play is set in the city and focuses on the experience of a young woman who discovers she is pregnant and has to face the resulting problems. The presentation contrasts with the numerous stereotypical depictions in African writing of the city woman as prostitute and has been a forerunner in a new wave of women's theatre in Zimbabwe, which looks at unemployment, prostitution, AIDS, and sexuality from the point of view of women.

LIZ GUNNER

DANGOR, ACHMAT (1948–)

South African poet, short-story writer, novelist

Born Achmed Dangor in Newclare, Johannesburg, South Africa, he has worked in business and various development organizations. Banned for five years from 1973, Dangor abandoned his first language, Afrikaans, after the 1976 Soweto uprising. He has for many years been active on various cultural bodies, including, in the 1970s, the group Black Thoughts and, in the 1980s, the Writers' Forum and the Congress of South African Writers (COSAW), on which he has served as vice-president.

Dangor's early writing centres on the iniquitous effects of racial segregation and forced removals, and these themes bulk large in his award-winning prose collection *Waiting for Leila* (1981) and many of the poems in *Bulldozer* (1983). One of Dangor's major achievements is the title piece of *Waiting for Leila*. This novella focuses on the internal anguish of the degenerate drop-out Samad as he drunkenly reels through a series of personal mishaps and disasters that take place against the backdrop of the demolition of District Six and the momentous events of 1976.

A master of juxtaposing different linguistic registers — demotic *skollietaal* (Afrikaans slang meaning 'hooligan-language') exists alongside elevated English and a wealth of classical allusions — Dangor's distinction is to plumb the depths of his characters' private lives while taking cognizance of the weight of public events that falls upon them. The story 'Jobman' (later developed into a film) reveals his preoccupation with characters who have been marginalized by society. In this case, Jobman, a mute Karoo farm worker, comes back to reclaim his wife, but falls foul of the farm foreman and its owner. He is then hunted and eventually shot to death on the veld.

Dangor has also published a play, *Majiet* (1986), a novel, *The Z-Town Trilogy* (1989), and a second collection of poetry, *Private Voices* (1992), winner of the Book Award of the British Broadcasting Prize for African poetry. It reveals a poet unafraid of voicing the intensely personal while addressing the contradictory demands of political commitment with a wry and sardonic wit. Dangor has also collaborated with Michael Chapman in compiling *Voices from Within* (1982), an anthology of southern African poetry.

CRAIG MacKENZIE

Further reading: Andries Walter Oliphant, 'Achmat Dangor: writing and change', *Staffrider* 2 (1990).

DARK, ELEANOR (1901–85)

Australian novelist

She was born in Sydney, Australia, and grew up there. The only daughter of the Australian writer Dowell O'Reilly, she married a doctor in 1922 and in the following year moved to the Blue Mountains town of Katoomba, on the outskirts of Sydney. She began writing at an early age and produced ten books of fiction between 1923 and 1959, of which the best known are those that comprise her historical trilogy: *The Timeless Land* (1941), *Storm of Time* (1948), and *No Barrier* (1953). These novels cover the settlement of white Australia from its inception until the crossing of the Blue Mountains in 1813 and form the first, and still one of the most thoughtful and comprehensive, attempts to examine the origins of the society that eventually formed in Australia.

Dark's early novels, such as *Slow Dawning* (1932), *Prelude to Christopher* (1934), *Return to Coolami* (1936), *Sun across the Sky* (1937), and *Waterway* (1938), hardly seem preparation for the trilogy's immense undertaking. These are slow, subdued, meditative works; their relative lack of action, compression of time scale — often to a single day — and long passages of exposition suggest the influence of such writers as Virginia Woolf. Critic Drusilla Madjeska describes the novels as 'a delicate balancing act, in which Eleanor Dark was responding to the formal demands of a European modernism that was only just beginning to touch Australian writers, while also attempting to make a political challenge to the dominant meanings served up in a mass culture, without on either count relinquishing a novel-reading audience'.

Dark's trilogy is a massive and extraordinarily conscientious piece of historical reconstruction. There is an almost Brechtian quality in the large perspective and the detachment with which she views the processes of history and the muddled attempts of the protagonists to master and control them. She works often by intelligent juxtaposition, contrasting portraits of characters, for example: Governor Phillips as leader of the whites with Bennilong, the most notable black figure; Johnny Prentice, a youth of privilege, and Patrick Mannion, a youth without privilege; Arabanoo, the Aboriginal man thrust into an alien white environment, and Andrew Prentice, a white man who lives among the Aboriginal people. Dark's overt sympathy for the Aborigines and her respect for their attitudes towards the land emerges in her uncompromising statement that 'The Australian Aboriginal had great virtues; in a fairly extensive reading I have been able to discover no vices save those which they learned from the white invaders of their land.'

If the trilogy sometimes seems stylized, this is compensated for by the broad sweep of the narrative and its governing and organizing ideas — the land as the real hero, resisting the invasion and subjugation of the white men, humanity's irresistible urge towards freedom in even the most horrendous of circumstances, and the breakdown of false and artificial social constrictions in a new society.

LAURIE CLANCY

Further reading: A. Grove Day, *Eleanor Dark* (1976).

DAROY, ESTER V. (1928–)

Filipino short-story writer

Born in Fort Mills, Corregidor Island, the Philippines, where her father served in the American military forces, she grew up in a Filipino-American community. DaRoy went to Manila to study at the Philippine Women's University (PWU) and the University of the Philippines. She began teaching in 1963 and worked at the Press and Publications Office of the PWU until 1973. She now teaches at De La Salle University, where she received the 1990 Writers' Fellowship grant to write the novella 'Ecclesisastica', an account of a young woman's experiences with the Communist Movement in the rice plantations of Pampanga.

Bidasari (1980), DaRoy's first book, is an adaptation of a Maranao legend she chanced upon while on a research grant. Her first short-story collection, *Nobody Gathers Seashells and Gun Shells Anymore* (1981), is unified by the child-narrator, Lolet, through whom is seen the life of Filipinos in Corregidor during the Commonwealth period, when the mood was a mixture of hope for national independence and foreboding at the imminence of the Second World War. In these stories, American racism is presented against a backdrop of ocean and coconut trees.

DaRoy's second short-story collection, *The Drumbeater and Other Stories* (1982), is wider in scope and reveals a cross-section of society: the peasants of the northern region, the upper crust of Manila, older and younger generations, husbands and wives. Critic Leonard Casper has remarked that in these stories one divines a 'sense of endurance, hardship without real hope: a sense of dispossession, not just of loss'. The short stories in *Genesis of the Poison Tree* (1992) are studies in the psyche of a variety of people and reveal the similarities, more than the differences, between polarities: the self-sacrificing woman and the feminist, the pedant and the bohemian artist, the normal and the psychotic, the childish and the senile. The novella *The Hazards of Memory* (1993) explores the sense of alienation and ambivalence experienced by Filipino expatriates in the USA.

ROSARIO CRUZ LUCERO

DARUWALLA, KEKI NASSERWANJI (1937–)

Indian poet

Born into a Parsi Zoroastrian family in Lahore, India (now in Pakistan) and educated at Government College, Ludhiana, Punjab, he published his first collection of poems, *Under Orion*, in 1970. Daruwalla's other works include *Apparition in April* (1971), for which he won the Uttar Pradesh State Award in 1972, *Crossing of Rivers* (1976), *Winter Poems* (1980), *The Keeper of the Dead* (1982), for which he won the Sahitya Akademi Award in 1984, and *Landscapes* (1987). He has also published *Sword and Abyss* (1979), a collection of short stories, and edited *Two Decades of Indian Poetry (1960–1980)* (1980), one of the most significant anthologies of Indian-English poetry.

Daruwalla's poems are noted for their maturity, intellectual strength, social awareness, concern for the environment, and for their economy of language. Daruwalla's irony and his concrete and exact images often transcend barriers of the local and the regional in their expression of themes of love, death, self-betrayal, lack of harmony, and individual identity.

Images of death pervade many of Daruwalla's poems, as in 'Pestilence'. In 'The Ghaghra in Spate' the river floods the villages, bringing destruction. However, there is a greater sense of acceptance and awareness of death in 'With Vultures', 'Fire-Hymn', 'Apparition in April', and 'The Snowman' (from *Apparition in April*).

Daruwalla's view of Hindu India as a land of contradictions and disappointments is developed in 'The Waterfront', a long, thirteen-poem sequence from *Crossing of Rivers*. The poet shudders at the apparent grotesqueness of Varanasi (a Hindu pilgrim centre), where sewage emptying into the river is overlooked by those who consider its water holy. Interestingly, in 'River Silt' the poet claims that the 'collective layers' of his psyche sleep in Varanasi. He seems to seek reconciliation with a tradition about which he is sceptical and from which he feels alienated.

The poetry of Daruwalla is a testimony to the poet's complete involvement in the environment in which he was raised. He is a self-conscious artist who has developed a personal idiom that is fresh and genuinely Indian.

P. A. ABRAHAM

Further reading: Bruce King, *Modern Indian Poetry in English* (1987; rev. 1989).

Das, Gurcharan (1943–)

Indian dramatist

Born in Lyallpur, India (now in Pakistan), Das moved to India with his family at the time of India's partition (1947) and later received an American education, which culminated in the study of philosophy at Harvard University (1960–3). On returning to India he became a trainee at the company he eventually headed as chairman and managing director, Procter and Gamble (India).

Das' favourite hobby, reading history, led him to write his first play, *Larins Sahib* (1970), documenting a year (1846–7) in the career of Sir Henry Lawrence, first British Resident in the Punjab, who became a legend in the region for his sympathetic treatment of Indians. Although Das romanticizes Lawrence's life, particularly his liaison with the Sikh regent Rani Jindan, and the play develops to a conventional denouement as Lawrence megalomaniacally believes himself a reincarnated Ranjit Singh, Maharaja of the Sikhs, its production in Bombay (1970) and publication in England drew considerable enthusiasm and attention.

His second play, 'Mira' (unpublished), deals with the medieval Hindu mystic poet-princess Mirabai in a much more adventurous style. Subtitled 'A rite of Krishna for five actor-dancers' (Mira worshipped Krishna), it was performed off-off-Broadway at New York's La Mama Experimental Theatre Club in 1970. Set to music and dance — the cast had training under Martha Graham — it charmed viewers, dance/drama critic Clive Barnes praising its timeless flavour as having 'the quality of a dream ritual'. The dialogue revealed a rather modern heroine battling tradition, an interpretation of the subject that raised orthodox eyebrows when Alyque Padamsee staged it in Bombay in 1972; Das says, 'I showed a woman becoming a saint; they held that she was born a saint.'

Das' autobiographical novel, *A Fine Family* (1990) — relating the story of the Das family's migration to and resettling in India — sold very well but gathered only lukewarm reviews.

ANANDA LAL

Das, Kamala (1934–)

Indian poet

Born into a leading literary family in a Nair community in Malabar, Kerala, India, where she now lives, she was educated mostly at home and did not attend university. Das writes poetry in English, and fiction both in English and Malayalam, her mother tongue. 'It's my poems that are my life,' she has remarked, 'and not my prose.' She was awarded the Sahitya Akademi prize for *Collected Poems Vol. 1* (1984).

Summer in Calcutta (1965), Das' first volume of poems, made an immediate impact. The strength of her style lies in its closeness to the rhythms of intimate speech, its freedom from western literary influences, and in its imagery, which is drawn from immediate contexts of experience. Her fiction in English is limited and uneven and includes the poignant stories 'Doll for the Child Prostitute', 'The Young Man with the Pitted Face', and the humorous 'Santan Choudhuri's Wife' (all collected in her *A Doll for the Child Prostitute*, 1977). A critic may point to Das' lack of consciousness of technique and an impulsion against conforming to the traditional norms of grammar and syntax; these, arguably, can also be seen as attempts to forge another variety of English.

Das' themes cover the gamut of her experience as a woman, traumatized at the age of fifteen into a loveless (though not childless) marriage, from which there seemed no escape. 'A broken marriage was as distasteful, as horrifying as an attack of leprosy', she stated in her autobiography *My Story* (1976, first serialized in *The Current Weekly*, Bombay, in 1976). The connection between frustration in marriage and the act of writing poetry, which seems in *My Story* to be obscured by the onrush of a seemingly 'sensational' narrative, manifests itself in a variety of ways in her poems. While on one hand she states, 'I must let my mind striptease' and 'flaunt a grand, flamboyant lust', on the other, her assertion that 'every middle class bed is a cross on which the woman is crucified' is part of a larger sense of alienation of a post-colonial woman writer. (See **Feminism**, India.)

Das writes in her poem 'An Introduction', in *Summer in Calcutta*, that her friends and critics admonish her, 'Don't write in English', just as the social and cultural categorizers urge her to 'Fit in' and 'Belong', for 'It is time / Choose a name, a role . . .' In poems such as 'An Introduction', 'Someone Else's Song', 'Loud Posters', 'Ferns', 'Sepia', 'The Descendants', 'The Flag', 'The Child in the Factory', 'Visitors to the City', 'The Sunshine Cat', 'The House Builders', 'The Dance of the Eunuchs', 'A Hot Noon at Malabar', 'The Lunatic Asylum', and 'Nani', the confessional need is contained by empathy with those who in one way or another are victims of the same system against which she rebels: she is 'every woman who seeks love', a participant in all human experience. Although not primarily a political writer, Das has written poems with awareness of the ethnic crisis in Sri Lanka — for example, 'The Sea At Galle Face Green', 'Smoke in Columbo', 'After July', and 'The Return of Hitler'.

In telling, in the manner of the Ancient Mariner, so to speak, the tale of failure in love, Das' love poems are a critique of the patriarchal culture at odds with women's psychological needs. While she empathizes with the rebel, she also recognizes, and celebrates, her own feminity and her rootedness in her tradition and landscape (for example, 'In Love', 'Summer in Calcutta', 'The Freaks', 'A Relationship', 'An Apology to Goutama', 'Winter', 'Spoiling the Name', and 'With Its Quiet Tongue', from *Summer in Calcutta*). The complex articulation in 'Jaisurya' (*The Descendants*, 1967) is an interplay of the kind of lyrical intensity one finds in **Judith Wright**'s treatment of the relationship of man, woman, and child (in 'Woman to Man' and 'Woman to Child'), on the one hand, and, on the other, the subversive questioning of Margaret Drabble's novel *The Millstone*, in which the woman's discovery of her identity through the experience of motherhood is seen as marginally dependent on the male presence.

Most of the poems in *The Descendants* and the thirteen new poems included in *The Old Playhouse and Other Poems* (1973) revolve around images of illness, decay, and fragmentation, but the focus is on women's need for space and on married women's identity. In its suggestion of being trapped in the ultimate failure of love (images of snares, prison, prisoner, prisoners' clothes, convicts, bondage, containers, and traps recur in her poems), Das' image of the lover as 'a pale-green pond glimmering in the sun' in whom to 'swim all broken with longing' is comparable to 'Nude Swim' by Anne Sexton.

In 'I Shall Some Day' (from *Summer in Calcutta* and reprinted in *The Old Playhouse and Other Poems*), the speaker visualizes herself as returning to 'your nest of familiar scorn' built around her 'with morning tea' and 'tired lust' by the men (presumably her husband) — 'just a sad remnant of a root'. The return is his threatened punishment as well as her own confession of failure. In 'Composition' (first published in *The Descendants* and reprinted in *The Old Playhouse* and *Collected Poems*), this freedom has also given her a sense of guilt because it is a 'freedom I never once asked for'.

It is perhaps consistent with the matrilineal tradition to which Das traces her ancestry that she contrasts 'the warmth that her [great-grandmother] took away' with the 'arsonist's fire' of her 'thieving' lovers since 'Warmth was not their aim . . . ' According to Barbara Segnitz and Carol Rainey, editors of *Psyche: The Feminine Consciousness* (1973), western women poets find their mythic ancestresses in such figures as Leda, Cassandra, and Lot's wife — 'all victims of the gods or society' — instead of Aphrodite, Helen, and Eve, who are glorified by the male imagination. Das, however, identifies herself with Radha, whose love for Lord Krishna — the ideal lover and the epitome of the fullest consciousness that a human being can contemplate — is both physical and devotional, as in 'Vrindavan': 'Vrindavan lives on in every woman's mind, / and the flute luring her / From home and her husband . . . '

DEVINDRA KOHLI

Further reading: Devindra Kohli, *Kamala Das* (1975); S. C. Harrex and Vincent O'Sullivan, eds, *Kamala Das: A Selection with Essays on Her Work*, CRNLE Writers Series 1 (1986).

DAS, MAHADAI (1954–)

Guyanese poet

Born in Eccles, East Bank Demerara, Guyana, she was educated at Bishops' High School, Georgetown; when the Guyana National Service was formed she joined as a volunteer. Her talents as dancer, poet, and actress were much in demand and in 1976 she represented Guyana at Carifesta. Das holds an MA in philosophy from Columbia University, New York, USA. Ill health prevented her from completing the doctoral programme at the University of Chicago, and she returned to Guyana, where she currently lives.

Das' poetry covers three distinct phases. The first collection, *I Want to be a Poetess of My People* (1977), rings with buoyant, almost naïve patriotic optimism. Tracing the history of the Indo-Guyanese people from indentureship to independence, she urges pride, dignity, and hope in those tilling the land — no longer for the colonizer, but for themselves and their children.

Fervent nationalism is replaced by bitter disillusionment in Das' second volume, *My Finer Steel Will Grow* (1982), in which she recalls the death in 1980 of political dissident Walter Rodney. She proposes a military coup as the only way to deal with what she considers a corrupt regime. The images of fertility abounding in her first collection give way to a surreal scene of disease and decay, with the recurrent image of sharpened steel threatening revolution.

In *Bones* (1988) Das writes as a Third World woman in urban USA and about the act of writing itself. Entering upon a rite of passage, the poet, within an alien, materialist culture, seeks to rediscover her Indian-woman self and to trace the beauty of her racial heritage. Resurrection is the theme, as stripped bones of suffering become a flute of expressivity that affords release into authentic being.

JOYCE JONAS

DAS, MANOJ (1934–)

Indian short-story writer

Born in the seashore village of Sankhari, Orissa, India, he began writing in his mother tongue,

Oriya, early enough for his first book of poetry to be published when he was fourteen. He began contributing to English periodicals in 1955. A Marxist youth leader in his student days, Das spent a term in jail in 1955 and took an active part in the Afro-Asian students' conference at Bandung in 1956. His quest, however, led him to **Sri Aurobindo**, whose visualization of humanity as evolving and whose proposition that humanity can transcend its present mental stage and rise to a higher phase of evolution brought him a new awakening and optimism. After a short stint as an English lecturer in Orissa, he joined the Sri Aurobindo Ashram, Pondicherry, in 1963, where he continues to live and teach English literature.

Das has stated that he was motivated to write in English in order to present typical Indian characters and situations to a wider readership. No doubt it is because of their Indianness that his stories have won for him a discriminating world audience. Martha Foley's list of outstanding stories published in the USA and Canada in 1975 included all five short stories Das had published during that year in prestigious magazines and anthologies in North America. One of his stories has been included in volume 18 (1972) of the 'Winter's Tales' series of short-story yearbooks, edited by A. D. Maclean, published in the UK and the USA. Das' genuine Indianness is observed not only in his realistic stories but also in the many fantasies he has written.

Das' first collection of stories, *A Song for Sunday and Other Stories* (1967), was followed by eight more — *Short Stories by Manoj Das* (1969), *The Crocodile's Lady: A Collection of Stories* (1975), *Fables and Fantasies for Adults* (1978), *Man Who Lifted the Mountain and Other Fantasies* (1979), *The Vengeance and Other Stories* (1980), *The Submerged Valley and Other Stories* (1986), *The Dusky Horizon and Other Stories* (1989), *Bulldozers and Fables and Fantasies for Adults* (1990) — and the novels *Cyclones* (1987) and *A Tiger at Twilight* (1991).

Das' canvas is wide, embracing a variety of themes and changing techniques to suit them. He is adept at combining the old art of storytelling with modern ideas and forms. The largest part of his writing is realistic fiction, in which a spontaneous exposition of intricate psychology as well as a mystic undertone dominate. Marked more by internal than external action and interaction — though often there is a judicious combination of the two — his stories sparkle with rare simplicity and implicit humour. Along with a certain timelessness, critics find Das' social criticism of a high order. His targets are often pompous politicians and pretentious pundits who must grin and bear his barbs. What is inimitable in his writing is the ease with which he inspires tears and laughter in the reader.

Acknowledged as an authentic interpreter of India's cultural and spiritual heritage, Das has also written several books for children.

P. RAJA

Further reading: P. Raja, 'The short stories of Manoj Das', *Indian Literature* Sept./Oct. (1982).

DATHORNE, OSCAR RONALD (1934–)

Guyanese novelist, poet, critic

Born in Georgetown, Guyana (then British Guiana), he earned a BA in English (1958) from the University of Sheffield, England, a graduate certificate in education (1959) from the University of London, England, and an MA (1960) from Sheffield. Dathorne taught at Ahmadu Bello University, Nigeria (1959–63), and at the University of Ibadan (1963–6), where he was an editor of the journal *Black Orpheus*. A Ph.D. (1966) from Sheffield and a diploma in education with emphasis on teaching English as a foreign language (1967) from London were followed by professorships and work as a UNESCO consultant in English and education in Sierra Leone. Dathorne has held professorships in English and Black Studies in the USA, at the universities of Wisconsin, Ohio State, Miami, and Kentucky. He has been influential in establishing the scholarly study of African and Caribbean literatures.

Dathorne returned to Africa in search of his cultural origins, and his novels are about his discovery that he was as much British and 'new world' as African. His first novels amusingly examine contemporary fashions in black literature and thought; his protagonist is a puzzled West Indian expatriate surrounded by con men, hustlers, and black and white snobs who pretend to be authentic. *Dumplings in the Soup* (1963), concerning a black immigrant student in a London tenement during the 1950s, was followed by *The Scholar-Man* (1964), a satiric view of northern Nigeria after national independence. The African university at which Adam Questus lectures is an enclave of snobbery and corruption, having little to do with Africa, while Africa itself seems bewilderingly irrational.

Dathorne edited the African section of *Young Commonwealth Poetry '65* (1965), edited by Peter Brent, *Caribbean Narrative: An Anthology of West Indian Writing* (1965), *Caribbean Verse* (1967), and *African Poetry* (1968) and co-edited with Willfried Feuser the influential Penguin *African Prose* (1969). He also contributed to the *Penguin Companion to Literature IV*, edited by D. R. Dudley and D. M. Lang. Dathorne's *The Black Mind: A History of African Literature* (1974) was abridged as *African Literature in the Twentieth Century* (1976). A limited edition, *Kelly Poems* (1977), contains his early love poetry. *Dark Ancestor: Black Literature in the New World* (1981) examines the relationship between African-American and African writing.

After editing *The Afro-World: Adventures in Ideas* (1984), Dathorne published his third novel, *Dele's Child* (1987), and a volume of poems, *Songs of a New World* (1989). Later writings commemorate family and black history.

BRUCE KING

Further reading: Leota S. Lawrence, 'O. R. Dathorne', in Daryl C. Dance (ed.) *Fifty Caribbean Writers: A Bio-bibliographical Critical Sourcebook* (1986).

DAVEY, FRANK (1940–)

Canadian poet, critic, editor

Born in Vancouver, Canada, he attended the University of British Columbia, where he helped to found and edit *Tish* (1961–9), a poetry newsletter influenced by the poetics of Charles Olson, Robert Duncan, and other postmodern American writers. After taking his Ph.D. in 1968, he taught English at various Canadian universities, most notably York University, Toronto. He founded *Open Letter* (1965–), an important journal of avant-garde writing and theory, and *Swift Current*, a literary journal in database form published between 1984 and 1990. Davey emphasizes a phenomenological view of Canadian literature in *From There to Here: A Guide to English-Canadian Literature Since 1960* (1974). More recently his criticism has shown an intense interest in critical theory, following a seminal essay against thematic criticism that gave the title to his collection *Surviving the Paraphrase* (1983). *Reading Canadian Reading* (1988) collects some recent critical essays as well as containing a series of reflective (and corrective) pieces on his own critical books.

Davey's early poetry bespeaks the crucial importance to him during the 1960s of Olson's theory of projective verse. However, Davey's own commitment to the local and the personal kept him from being a simple Black Mountain myrmidon. This early work was brought together in *L'An Trentiesme: Selected Poems 1961–70* (1972). The work of the 1970s constellated around mythological and historical subjects, reinterpreted from a personal context, and evolving gradually towards a stubborn concern with personal relationships. This period is best represented in *Selected Poems: The Arches* (1980), which also contains a fine essay on Davey by **bp Nichol**. Since that book, Davey has published several collections that continue to explore historical and autobiographical material from a postmodernist sensibility not unsullied by a sense of humour. *The Abbotsford Guide to India* (1986), which combines travelogue with prose poems and views India through Davey's home town, is the most ambitious of these books.

BRUCE WHITEMAN

Further reading: D. Barbour, 'Frank Davey: finding your voice: to say what must be said: the recent poetry', in Jack David (ed.) *Brave New Wave* (1978); George Bowering, 'The early poetry of Frank Davey', *A Way With Words* (1982).

DAVIES, ROBERTSON (1913–)

Canadian novelist, dramatist, essayist

Born in Thamesville, Ontario, Canada, to William Rupert Davies and his wife, Florence Sheppard McKay Davies, he attended Upper Canada College in Toronto, Canada (the model for Colborne College in his fiction), Queen's University, Kingston, Canada, and Oxford University, England. While working with the Old Vic Company after graduation, he met Brenda Matthews, the company's Australian-born stage manager. Married in 1940, they returned to Canada, where Davies became literary editor of the weekly review *Saturday Night*. In 1946 he was appointed vice-president and publisher of the *Peterborough Examiner*, and in 1960 visiting professor of English, Trinity College, University of Toronto. In 1963 he became first master of Massey College and professor of English at University College (University of Toronto); he retired in 1981.

Davies' remarkable career as a man of letters reveals a lifelong compulsion to probe the comic and painful Canadian dimensions of the colonial mentality. The dead hand of the past, the tyranny of the family, the revenge of the unlived life, the barbarity and suffocation of cultural life on the fringes, and the pull towards the fulfilment promised by the metropolis have frequently been noted as recurrent themes in Davies' work. But it has seldom been remarked that these preoccupations are part of the imperialist legacy.

Despite his three collections of cultural commentary (*A Voice from the Attic*, 1960; *One Half of Robertson Davies: Provocative Pronouncements on a Wide Range of Topics*, 1977; *The Enthusiasms of Robertson Davies*, 1979), Davies' research into first Freudian and then Jungian psychological theories of the individual self has received more attention than his equally strong interest in a national Canadian identity. His writing asks what it means to be human, but that question is always couched within the context of what it means to be Canadian: that is, to be born within a highly contradictory society, both smugly self-satisfied yet insecure, outwardly bland and inwardly seething.

Davies' Marchbanks trilogy, begun in 1943 as a weekly column and published in separate volumes — *The Diary of Samuel Marchbanks* (1947), *The Table Talk of Samuel Marchbanks* (1949), *Marchbanks' Almanack* (1967) — was collected with revisions as *The Papers of Samuel Marchbanks* (1985). In the introduction Davies writes: 'Marchbanks is one of the last of a breed of Canadians whose racial strains and mental habits derive from those Loyalists who came north to this country after the American Revolution of 1776.' Marchbanks turns his satiric eye on everything Canadian; Davies' satire includes Marchbanks himself.

The Salterton novels embed Davies' satire more firmly in a fully articulated social context, described by Davies as 'a sort of delayed cultural tradition' reminiscent of Chekhov. *Tempest-Tost* (1951) reinscribes one of the canonical texts of cross-cultural encounter, Shakespeare's *Tempest*, within the Canadian context. Davies' provincial backwater inevitably courts failure when it attempts to mimic metropolitan standards; but pulling against the novel's explicit measuring of Canadian production against English text is the implicit shift in focus from Prospero as imperialist father to Miranda as Canadian daughter. Although Davies' use of *The Tempest* differs substantially from that of other post-colonial writers such as **George Lamming** or Aimé Césaire and even from that of his compatriot **Margaret Laurence**, it too illuminates the colonial mentality of mid-twentieth-century Canada. *Leaven of Malice* (1954) and *A Mixture of Frailties* (1958) trace the slow growth of dependent Canadian adolescence into adulthood through the story of Solly Bridgetower and Pearl Vambrace. The parallel story of Monica Gall in the latter novel, however, suggests that full spiritual and artistic growth may only be reached in England. As the colonial heroine who journeys to England to perfect her artistic and emotional education, Monica takes her place within an established tradition that may have begun with Henry James but that post-colonial writers continue to find useful.

Like Monica, the Canadian-born protagonists of the Deptford trilogy find their identities in Europe. True spiritual adventures, as Liesl claims in *Fifth Business* (1970), do not seem possible in Davies' Canada. Davies told interviewer Donald Cameron that *Fifth Business* records 'the bizarre and passionate life of the Canadian people'. In *Fifth Business* that life is filtered through the guilty conscience of Dunstan Ramsay facing his God. In *The Manticore* (1972), it is told through David Staunton's encounters with his analyst, and in *World of Wonders* (1975) it is enacted through Magnus Eisingrim's performance for his audience. These characters must shed their original names and the selves they defined to create themselves anew. This theme of symbolic death and rebirth recurs throughout colonial and post-colonial fiction. Davies, however, uses them to reassert European connections rather than to affirm the necessity of forging a new literature for Canada.

Increasingly, Davies' novels stress the European roots of the Canadian cultural heritage. *The Rebel Angels* (1981), *What's Bred in the Bone* (1985), and *The Lyre of Orpheus* (1988) comprise a trilogy centred on the Cornish family in which Canadian life is presented as absolutely brutish without the leaven of European wisdom. *The Rebel Angels*, set in the modern university, explores its roots in the medieval past. Painting focuses Davies' interest in the art of representation in *What's Bred in the Bone*, as does music in *The Lyre of Orpheus*, and film in *Murther and Walking Spirits* (1991), in which the dead narrator-protagonist watches his ancestral past unfold as a series of films set in the revolutionary USA, nineteenth-century Wales, and Ontario. In these books ideas take precedence over character.

Similar patterns and problems may be traced in Davies' plays. In *Overlaid* and *Hope Deferred* (1949) he examines the barrenness of the cultural life to which Canada seemed condemned as a colony. Full-length plays such as *Fortune, My Foe* (1949) and *At My Heart's Core* (1950) explore this dilemma more thoroughly and are cautiously optimistic for Canada's future. *Question Time* (1975) probes the links between place and soul in the psyche of the nation. *A Jig for the Gypsy* (1954) and *Hunting Stuart* (1972, written in 1955), like *What's Bred in the Bone* and *Murther and Walking Spirits*, demonstrate an interest in breeding that links Davies to other Commonwealth writers of a conservative, aristocratic bent. (See **Drama**, Canada.)

Like the Australians **Martin Boyd** and **Patrick White**, Davies represents a genteel tradition that abhors the materialism and bad taste associated with a rising middle class. But Davies does not share White's and Boyd's ambivalence about native home and imperial home. His autocratic world view, with its unquestioning acceptance of hierarchical values, continues to promote the imperial legacy. While it might appear that Davies' didacticism links him to the Commonwealth tradition of Nigerian **Chinua Achebe**'s 'novelist as teacher', Davies' teachings reaffirm rather than question established wisdom. Yet his powerful sense of history places him squarely within Canadian as well as Commonwealth traditions.

Although Davies' international reputation still derives from the achievement of the Deptford novels, he continues to win awards that recognize his stature as Canada's foremost man of letters. Much of his work may eventually be seen within the larger context of British nostalgia for the raj. Like **V. S. Naipaul**'s travelogues and recent fiction, Davies' latest work reconfirms the metropolitan dismissal of whatever lies beyond its reaches. The Cornish trilogy offers the illusion of a return to the stable values of a past where everything has its place and rebellion is punished by fate. Although thematically conservative, Davies writes witty, stylish prose and compelling stories. He has a wide comic and romantic range. His novels are complex enough to accommodate contradictory readings.

Davies was appointed a Companion of the Order of Canada in 1972, he won a Governor General's Award for Fiction in 1972 (for *The Manticore*), and in 1980 he became the first Canadian Honourable Member of the American Academy and Institute of Arts and Letters.

DIANA BRYDON

Further reading: John Ryrie, *Robertson Davies: An Annotated Bibliography* (1981); Michael Peterman, *Robertson Davies* (1986).

DAVIN, DAN(IEL) (1913–90)

New Zealand novelist

Born in Invercargill, New Zealand, he was educated at Marist Brothers School in Invercargill, Sacred Heart College in Auckland, the University of Otago, Dunedin, and Balliol College, Oxford, England, which he attended on a Rhodes scholarship. After 1936 he returned to New Zealand only for occasional visits. He served in the British Army, 1939–40, and in the New Zealand Division, 1940–5, as an intelligence officer. He worked with the Oxford University Press, becoming director of the academic division in 1974, retiring in 1978. His work in nonfiction includes the official New Zealand history of the Crete campaign, *Crete* (1953), and a book of memoirs of friends, *Closing Times* (1975), as well as miscellaneous literary criticism. In addition, he edited several short-story anthologies.

However, it is primarily for his fiction that Davin will be remembered. His seven novels include four on New Zealand life — *Cliffs of Fall* (1945), *Roads from Home* (1949), *No Remittance* (1959), and *Not Here, Not Now* (1970) — one on the war, *For the Rest of Our Lives* (1947), and two on New Zealand expatriates — *The Sullen Bell* (1956) and *Brides of Price* (1972). There are also two volumes of short stories, *The Gorse Blooms Pale* (1947) and *Breathing Spaces* (1975), with *Selected Stories* (1981) drawing from both. *The Salamander and the Fire: Collected War Stories* (1986) brings together the war stories from all of these and adds those previously uncollected. The New Zealand novels and stories present full pictures of an Irish Catholic childhood and adolescence in Southland and of university life in Dunedin. This provincial life provides a realistic backdrop for psychological dramas focusing on the struggle between ambition and obligation in the young protagonists. The novels and stories of war and expatriation deal more with the attempts of mature characters to make a successful accommodation with a complex world.

In the 1940s Davin seemed likely to rank with **Frank Sargeson** as the leading New Zealand writer of fiction, but that promise was never fully realized. His writing was relegated to the margins of a busy professional life and he discovered that expatriation left him drawing too much on the 'diminishing capital' of his experiences in New Zealand and with the New Zealand Division. Nevertheless, no other New Zealand writer of fiction of his generation has left as substantial a body of work.

LAWRENCE JONES

Further reading: James Bertram, *Dan Davin* (1983).

DAVIS, A. H.

See **RUDD, STEELE**

DAVIS, JACK (1917–)

Australian dramatist, poet

Born in Perth, Australia, into a family of eleven, he spent most of his childhood in the south-west timber and dairying town of Yarloop. At the age of fourteen he and an older brother were sent by their father to Moore River Native settlement to acquire farming skills. Here Davis witnessed first-hand white oppression of Aborigines. Although deprived of the promised job training, Davis did benefit from an education in the Nyoongah (Aboriginal) way of things, facilitated by his contact with a number of tribal men who would figure later in his best-known dramatic character, Worru. Often using a dictionary as his only text while doing station-work in remote areas of Western Australia during the 1930s and 1940s, Davis 'flirted with verse', occasionally sending the products to his sister. His poetry collections include *The First-Born and Other Poems* (1970), *Jagardoo: Poems from Aboriginal Australia* (1978), and *John Pat and Other Poems* (1988). His plays include *Kullark* and *The Dreamers* (in *Kullark/The Dreamers*, 1982), *No Sugar* (1986), and *Barungin (Smell the Wind)* (1988).

As with **Oodgeroo Noonuccal**, the political fermentation of the 1960s was the catalyst for Davis to publish his verse. However, it is in his plays that he has maintained dialogue with the white community in examining the distinctive mores and values of Nyoongahs and the need for both cultures to negotiate just solutions to mutual problems. Perhaps the most striking tenor in Davis' work that seems to attract to him the epithet of 'gentle' is the tone of regret and misgiving that relations between the two races had been thwarted at first contact through mutual misunderstanding. But as Davis' historical play *Kullark* points out, there is never any doubt as to the white intruders' duplicitous intentions. The motif of corruptibility is repeated in *The Dreamers* by the Dancer who manifests Worru's spiritual association with the Dreaming. Following Worru's death the Dancer states firmly:

Nitja Wetjala, warrah, warrah!
Gnullarah dumbart noychwa.
Noychwa, noychwa, noychwa.
Wetjala kie-e-ny gnullarah dumbart.
['The white man is evil, evil!
My people are dead.
Dead, dead, dead.
The white man kill my people.']

Davis' belief that without a language there is no culture encouraged him to assist in the restoration of the Nyoongah language of south-west Western Australia, a composite of the remnants of the fourteen Bibbulumun dialects spoken by the original tribes of the area; he features it widely in all of his plays except the children's piece, *Honey Spot*. For Davis, who works on the principle that there is an indelible difference between Aborigines and whites, the necessity to bridge the cultural gaps provides a panoply of themes.

Davis' plays, especially *Kullark* and the trilogy *The Dreamers*, *No Sugar*, and *Barungin (Smell the Wind)*, approximate the extensive re-inscriptions of indigenous language encountered in

Ngugi wa Thiong'o's play *I Will Marry When I Want* (1982). Given that white law and Christianity until recently prohibited Aborigines from using their tribal languages, Davis' reinvestment of the Nyoongah language strikes a profound political chord rivalling that of Ngugi. Davis' fellow Aboriginal Australian poet and playwright Gerald Bostock has also insisted that the basis for a vibrant and enduring Aboriginal theatre lies in the ordinary or 'grass-roots' Aborigines.

The tensions that emerge from the often naturalistic scenes in Davis' drama appear to be more directed in his verse. Davis' poetry can be divided into two distinct categories — poetry in which the social semiotics of Aboriginality must be wrenched from the European terms threatening to subsume it and that dealing with overtly Aboriginal issues and motifs. The latter poetry offers the greatest potential for experimentation, where the poet attempts to resolve the tensions between his commitment to portray faithfully the Nyoongah reality and the search for common ground with the *Wetjala* ('white man; white fella'). This is suggested in the manner in which a contemplative mood changes, without warning, from stridency to hopelessness and capitulation to a defiance of the stigmatized roles of Aborigines designated by a white society eager to rid itself of its racial guilt.

In *John Pat and Other Poems* the impact resulting from the author's skilful handling of the story of the murder of an Aboriginal youth (John Pat) while in custody of white authorities elevates the verse above more prosaic panderings to white conscience.

CLIFF WATEGO

DAWE, BRUCE (1930–)

Australian poet

Born in Geelong, Victoria, Australia, he left high school at the age of sixteen. He began studies at the University of Melbourne in 1954 and although he dropped out after a year, he was greatly influenced by the literary environment, especially that associated with the poets **Vincent Buckley** and **Chris Wallace-Crabbe**. He joined the Royal Australian Air Force (1959–68), during which time he served in Malaysia (one of his few overseas experiences). Following marriage, he settled in Toowoomba, Queensland, and completed an arts degree at the University of Queensland. He subsequently obtained a Ph.D. Since 1972 he has been a lecturer in English at Darling Downs Institute of Advanced Education in Queensland.

Dawe's awards include the Myer Award for Poetry (1966), the Sidney Myer Charity Trust Award for Poetry (1969), the Grace Leven Poetry Prize (1978), the Dame Mary Gilmore Medal (1973), and the Patrick White Award (1980). His published books of poetry are: *No Fixed Address* (1962), *A Need of Similar Name* (1965), *An Eye for a Tooth* (1968), *Beyond the Subdivisions* (1969), *Heat-Wave* (1970), *Condolences of the Season* (1971), *Just a Dugong at Twilight: Mainly Light Verse* (1975), *Sometimes Gladness: Collected Poems 1954–1978* (1978; enlarged edition 1983), *Towards Sunrise: Poems 1979–1986* (1986), *Sometimes Gladness: Collected Poems 1954–1987* (3rd ed., 1988), and *This Side of Silence* (1990). He has published one collection of short stories, *Over Here, Harv! and Other Stories* (1983), and a volume of essays, *Essays and Opinions* (1990, edited by Ken Goodwin).

From the publication of his first book of poems in 1962, Dawe created an extraordinary impact, initially among his contemporaries, but quickly also among a much more broadly based general readership. Because of the momentum in Australian education in the 1960s towards an awareness of Australian writing, Dawe became the most accessible and the most admired Australian poet — possibly Australian writer. His work has sold more copies than any other contemporary Australian poet.

The reason for this success is in itself significant: Dawe, almost from the outset of his writing career, found a tone and a voice that were strikingly attuned to what might be termed a backyard pith of ordinariness, making them not unaccessible and rarefied but memorable and potent. More than a decade before producers of Australian television commercials realized the recognition power of the broad Aussie accent dialect, Dawe had honed it in his poetry in a way that leapt like grassfire over the paddocks of the literary and non-literary landscape.

There had been some tentative feelers and precedents. The bush ballad tradition and the popular slang poems of **C. J. Dennis** in the early part of the century, and later attempts by Ian Mudie and even **Douglas Stewart** (especially in his early *Sonnets to the Unknown Soldier*, 1941), might be seen to foreshadow the tone and the tenor Dawe was to make central, not only in his own work but in Australian poetry in general. The very impulse of his poetry, the vision that thrust to define such inflection, was based on the underlying social energy behind language. Dawe's suburban 'man' (or person, though the quintessential Dawe persona is usually drenched in masculinist traditions) is a product of the hard gift of survival that spans most of the middle years of the twentieth century, just as he is a product of the larger and smaller political tides that sweep him, like dross, every which way.

The galvanizing force of Dawe's early poems was the 1956 Hungarian uprising against Communism. In seeking a voice of ordinary anguish at the west's failure to support this movement, Dawe found energies that were to be whiplash sharp by the time the Vietnam War ended. By the late 1960s a generation of Australian poets was able to step off from a groundwork Dawe had laid out; for the first time a high lyric *tessitura* could rise from a firmly held backyard ground bass. Dawe developed his satiric talents, especially in his directly political poems, around current happenings, through skilful borrowing or parody of a range of oral and written traditions, and from both popular songs and biblical texts. His work represents one of the key turning points in Australian poetry. His most recent writing shows him a master of wit and style, turning current political affairs into memorable occasions of insight. The pith is still in the vine.

THOMAS SHAPCOTT

Further reading: Basil Shaw, *Times and Seasons: An Introduction to Bruce Dawe* (1974); Ken Goodwin, *Adjacent Worlds: A Literary Life of Bruce Dawe* (1990).

DAWES, NEVILLE (1926–84)
Jamaican novelist, poet

He was born in Warri, Nigeria, to Jamaican parents. The family returned to Sturge Town, Jamaica, when he was three years old. In 1938 Dawes won a scholarship to Jamaica College. He taught at Calabar High School before entering Oriel College, Oxford, England, in 1948, where he earned a BA (1951) in English. In 1951 he returned to Calabar. In 1955 Dawes began teaching at Kumasi Institute of Technology, Ghana; from 1960 to 1970 he was senior lecturer in English at the University of Ghana, Legon. He was a leading light in the African Liberation Movement as an editor of *Okyeame*, a journal of the Ghana Society of Writers. From 1963 to 1964 Dawes was visiting professor of English and dean of arts at the University of Guyana. In 1970 he became deputy director of the Institute of Jamaica, serving as executive director from 1973 to 1974. He was teaching at Mandeville High School at the time of his death.

Dawes' first published book, the poetry collection *In Sepia* (1958), includes the experience of the West Indian intellectual in England, rural Jamaica, and Africa. His novels *The Last Enchantment* (1960) and *Interim* (1978) are concerned with politics in Jamaica (both are set in the hill country surrounding Sturge Town), the former on the eve of independence and the latter after independence. Both explore issues of race, class, and colour and the possibility of a revolutionary solution. In each the protagonist is a black peasant boy who is exposed to an élitist education; this education is rejected in favour of socialism and nationalism.

In the picaresque and satirical *The Last Enchantment* Dawes traces the fortunes of Ramsay Tull and paints a pessimistic picture of Jamaica in the late 1940s as a society still deeply committed to English values. The protagonist's sympathies lie with the radical socialist party, the People's Progressive League (PPL), which is committed to the working class. Ramsay travels to England for a typical colonial education at Oxford, where he studies English literature. At Oxford he feels alienated, has an affair with a white woman, and writes a story in which he exorcizes her by strangling her. Ramsay returns to Jamaica and becomes disillusioned by the People's Democratic Party, which has won the election but introduces no new changes. While his personal sense of failure is mirrored by the cancerous death of the founder and leader of the PPL, there is final affirmation in Ramsay's return to his roots in the rural black community. This affirmation is a separate peace, but not a political and social solution.

The antagonism between the urban and rural worlds is continued in *Interim*. This novel follows the career of a protagonist similar to Ramsay. Here, a revolution occurs, but is crushed by American military intervention, and much attention is devoted to the concept of the revolutionary mind and character. At the end of the novel the presence of revolutionary forces regrouping in the mountains suggests the possibility of achieving a just society.

BARRIE DAVIES

Further reading: Gerald Moore, *The Chosen Tongue* (1969); David Williams, 'The artist as revolutionary', in Mark McWatt (ed.) *West Indian Literature and its Social Context* (1985).

D'COSTA, JEAN CONSTANCE (1937–)
Jamaican critic, children's writer
Born in St Andrew, Jamaica, where she received her early education, she later studied at Oxford University, England, before teaching at the University of the West Indies. She now she teaches at Hamilton College, New York, USA. D'Costa is a professional linguist and literary scholar whose creative output has been primarily in the area of children's fiction. She has written three novels for children and, with **Velma Pollard**, has edited a book of short stories, *Over Our Way* (1980), to which she contributed stories. Her poetry has appeared in the anthologies *Jamaica Woman* (1980), edited by **Pamela Mordecai** and **Mervyn Morris**, and *Waltzing on Water* (1987), edited by Norma Mazer and Dorothy Lewis. D'Costa's experience as a linguist has directly influenced her fiction, which emphasizes problems of children's language development in an increasingly multilingual situation.

In reflecting the range of local language registers, D'Costa's fiction conveys the variety and complexity of Jamaica's cultural heritage. Having grown up in the waning days of colonialism, she is concerned with transition. Her fiction records important aspects of the material culture of rural Jamaica — which is being constantly eroded — and directs attention to the local landscape. *Sprat Morrison* (1972), her first novel, focuses on an important transitional stage for children in the formal educational process. *Escape to Last Man Peak* (1976), her second novel, is an adventure story exploring the anxieties of adolescents forced to rely on their own judgement and initiative. D'Costa's third novel, *Voice in the Wind* (1978), is set in Jamaica of the early 1940s and relates the formal educational process to the world of folk belief.

D'Costa's quest for authenticity in re-creating the details of her characters' existence gives her work a historical dimension. Her novels show how wider social issues impinge on a child's consciousness, balancing the claims of a material existence with the claims of the imaginative life.

D'Costa's other published works include *Roger Mais: 'The Hills Were Joyful Together' and 'Brother Man'* (1979), a critical study of Jamaican author **Roger Mais**, and, in collaboration with Barbara Lalla, *Voices in Exile* (1989) and *Language in Exile* (1990), companion handbooks on the linguistic and cultural history of Jamaicans.

JOYCE JOHNSON

DE BOISSIÈRE, RALPH (1907–)
Trinidadian novelist

He was born in Trinidad. His father, a solicitor, was a descendant of the unofficial coloured line of a well-known French Creole family. In the course of his education, at Tranquillity Boys Intermediate School and Queen's Royal College, Ralph de Boissière encountered the typical colonial syllabus. Music, particularly the piano, was his first passion and he dreamed of a career as a performer. When this failed to materialize, he turned to creative writing, but to secure a livelihood he trained as a typist/bookkeeper, working for various English and American firms until he left Trinidad in 1947. In 1947 he took a six-month course in motor mechanics in Chicago, USA, then immigrated to Australia, where his family joined him. His first job was on the assembly line at General Motors in Melbourne, an experience that deepened his understanding of the working class.

In the mid-1920s de Boissière was introduced to a group of young Trinidadian intellectuals and expatriates who were to spearhead the island's literary awakening. Among them were the editors of the literary magazine *Trinidad* (1929–30), **Alfred H. Mendes** and **C. L. R. James**, as well as Albert Gomes, who launched the first monthly cultural magazine, *The Beacon* (1931–3, 1939). Within the group de Boissière was encouraged to write. His first short stories exploring the island's pervasive race and class prejudices were published in these magazines. He became an ardent admirer of the work of such nineteenth-century Russian writers as Turgenev and Tolstoy and he emulated the Russians' realistic style and social vision in his Caribbean novels *Crown Jewel* (1952; rev. 1981) and its sequel, *Rum and Coca-Cola* (1956; rev. 1984). It was his first-hand experience of everyday life at all levels of Trinidad society, however, that provided de Boissière with his raw material. He was not only a keen observer, but a writer who subsequently became involved in radical trade unionism.

Crown Jewel and *Rum and Coca-Cola* dramatize ten crucial years (1935–45) in Trinidad's history. The two central events during this decade were the uprising in Trinidad's oil fields in 1937 and the American military presence on the island during the Second World War. What makes de Boissière's treatment of this period unique is his radical social perspective and his commitment to militant working-class politics. In order to achieve a vast social and historical canvas and to suggest the continuous sweep of political events, he builds a series of interlocking life histories that develop and repeat central motifs. Thus the patterns of exploitation during the war, for example, are given a personal dimension within the patterns of experiences of the major and minor characters, and each personal choice provides a further permutation of the types of alternatives open to the individual. Attention is constantly shifted from one character to another and from political crisis to individual crisis.

de Boissière's Australian experience provided the subject-matter for his third novel, *No Saddles for Kangaroos* (1964). Set in the early 1950s, when the Australian labour movement was seriously debilitated by widespread anti-Communist hysteria, the novel tells the story of an Australian working-class family that becomes involved in a series of industrial actions in an American-owned automobile factory and in the peace movement to end Australian involvement in the Korean War.

In Australia de Boissière moved more and more to the left. He began to study Marxist literature and literary criticism, became a member of the Realist Writers Group, and finally joined the Communist Party in 1951, remaining a member until 1967. It was a left-wing publishing house, the Australasian Book Society, that published his novels (in fact, *Crown Jewel* was its first title), and both *Crown Jewel* and *Rum and Coca-Cola* appeared in translation in several eastern-bloc countries.

The 1981 republication of *Crown Jewel* and the 1984 edition of *Rum and Coca-Cola*, both of which differ significantly from the original 1950s editions, were well received in the Caribbean, the UK, and the USA, where until then these two major Caribbean novels had been virtually unknown.

REINHARD SANDER

Further reading: Reinhard Sander, *The Trinidad Awakening: West Indian Literature of the Nineteen-Thirties* (1988).

DE GRAFT, JOE COLEMAN (1924–78)

Ghanaian dramatist, novelist, poet

Born in Cape Coast, Ghana, and educated at Mfantsipim and Achimota Schools and at the University College of the Gold Coast, he taught at Mfantsipim, founded drama studies at the University of Science and Technology, Ghana, directed the Ghana Dance Studio, Accra (1961), and founded theatre studies at the University of Ghana, Legon (1963). From 1969 until his death, de Graft was a UNESCO teacher of English as a second language in Nairobi, Kenya, and a drama instructor in the Faculty of Education at Nairobi.

de Graft's writing evolved from being imitative of British models to being consciously African. Although he wrote about the ritual sources of African drama, his earlier plays often are concerned with the psychology of his main characters and their conflicting perspectives on life. *Sons and Daughters* (1964) hinges on conflicts between a father's plans for his children to have respectable, financially secure careers and their desire to become artists. *Through a Film Darkly* (1970, titled 'Visitors from the Past' when first produced in 1962) concerns an upper-class Ghanaian haunted by earlier failures in love and by his memories of racial prejudice in England; both tragically continue to influence his relationships with women.

Muntu (1977), an epic drama based on a Balozi myth of Zamiba, retells the history of Africa, from its origins to the present, in an attempt to analyse the causes of contemporary African distress. The play follows current African dramatic practice by using folk, mythic, and historical materials. de Graft was an anti-Nkrumahist; like his poem 'Two Views From a Window', *Muntu* warns against allowing Africa to be ruled by charismatic absolutist leaders and their tyrannical political parties. de Graft's other plays include 'Ananse and the Glue Man' (premièred 1961) and 'Old Kweku' (premièred 1965). His poetry is collected in *Beneath the Jazz and Brass* (1975).

While de Graft's early poetry is sensitive in its language and form, much of his verse consists of fluent but insufficiently revised thoughts about life, Ghana, and personal relationships. His two novels, *The Success Story of the Girl with a Big State Secret* (1967) and *Visitors from the Past* (1968), have received little notice.

BRUCE KING

DE GROEN, ALMA (1941–)

Australian dramatist

Born in New Zealand, she became involved with the alternative theatre movement soon after immigrating to Australia in 1964. Early pieces such as the brief but very potent *The Joss Adams Show* (1977) — about the pressures that might create the battered baby syndrome — reflect the influence of agitprop. *Going Home* (1977), with its concern for consistency of illusion and its plot made up of lounge-room conversation, deals much more conventionally with the interactions of Australian expatriates in Canada. De Groen's major later works, *Vocations* (1983) and *The Rivers of China* (1988), represent a line of progress that might in one sense be defined as a regression to self-conscious theatricalism. But in both of these plays the radical form is a way of registering the complexity and ambiguity of their subjects, not merely as a problem of judgement, but also as a primary perceptual challenge to the ways in which reality might be known and named.

The issue of expatriatism in *Going Home* is something of a red herring. The play is certainly concerned with ideas of belonging and displacement, but at a more fundamental level that introduces the two central preoccupations of De Groen's subsequent work: the artist's attempt to reconcile the competing claims of vocation and other people, and the sources and processes of the social construction of gender.

Occasionally, *Vocations*, with its premise that the issues are mostly insoluble and with its fondness for amusing anecdote, risks softening or blurring its analysis. *The Rivers of China* is quite uncompromising, and its juxtaposition of fragments of the life of **Katherine Mansfield** with a present-day dystopia works powerfully. It leads to overwhelming questions, some of them not quite formulated; the processes of gender transformation on which the play turns are fascinating, but their relation to their historical subject is left at possibilities. The play confirms De Groen's importance in contemporary Australian theatre. Having demonstrated how engagingly she can adapt the dominant mainstream mode — the comedy of middle-class manners — she has shown an increasing readiness to challenge and reshape the ways in which relationships between the sexes are dramatized.

PETER FITZPATRICK

DEI-ANANG, MICHAEL FRANCIS (1909–78)
Ghanaian poet
Born at Mampong-Akwapim, Gold Coast (now Ghana), and educated at Mfantsipim, Achimota College, Ghana, and at the University of London, England, Dei-Anang belongs to the first generation of modern Ghanaian writers. He joined the civil service in 1938, becoming principal secretary in the ministry of foreign affairs in Nkrumah's government, and secretary for African affairs in the post-Nkrumah era. Dei-Anang's published works include poetry (*Wayward Lines from Africa*, 1946, and *Ghana Semi-Tones*, 1962), a historical sketch (*Cocoa Comes to Mampong and Some Occasional Verses*, 1949), and a play (*Okomfo Anokye's Golden Stool*, 1960). His writing marks a departure from missionary-influenced and proselytizing literature and from the market-oriented popular Ghanaian literature of the 1940s and 1950s. His style is too obviously pedantic, didactic, and populist, but his writing is important not only for interpreting Ghana's struggle for independence but also for prefiguring major concerns in modern Ghanaian imaginative writing.

In *Wayward Lines from Africa* Dei-Anang writes about an Africa that has been partitioned and pawned ('I Know A World'). Nevertheless, he is optimistic that a new Africa will rise from the ruins. Dei-Anang's beatification of an idyllic Africa is faintly reminiscent of Negritudinists, although he fails to demonstrate the technical excellence of much of early francophone African poetry. Dei-Anang's ambivalent sentiments about western values recall the writings of **Dennis Chukude Osadebay**.

In the 'Some Occasional Verses' section of *Cocoa Comes to Mampong and Some Occasional Verses*, Dei-Anang warns against the centrifugal forces of tribalism that threaten Ghana's unity. 'When I Die' is an imitation of **Claude McKay**'s 'If We Must Die', but without the passion of the Harlem Renaissance poet. The volume's 'Cocoa Comes to Mampong' section dramatizes the historical feat of Tetteh Quarshie, who brought cocoa beans from Fernan do Po and successfully cultivated them, making cocoa the mainstay of Ghana's economy. The language of the work, however, is largely high-flown and antiquated. At times Dei-Anang becomes a poet for political expediency ('Ghana Will Never Die', for example, first published in *Two Faces of Africa*, 1965, by Dei-Anang and his son Kofi Dei-Anang), but he fails to use language in an effective manner. The poet never really emerges in either 'God Walked the Dusty Streets of Life' (in *Wayward Lines*) or in *Ghana Semi-Tones*. Dei-Anang's fine poem 'Ka-ya, Ka-ya, Zambramma' (*Two Faces of Africa*) is a rhythmic dramatization of the daily chores of labourers in cities. Although 'Akosombo' (*Ghana Semi-Tones*) may lack the vitality of 'Ibadan' by J. P. Clark (**Bekederemo**), it succeeds in projecting a vision of Akosombo as a symbol of modernity rooted in the Ghanaian heritage.

Okomfo Anokye's Golden Stool carefully, even craftily, knits a pageant of traditional lore centring on Osei Tutu and Okomfo Anokye, legendary figures who consecrated the Golden Stool as the symbol of unity of the Ashanti people. Dei-Anang has not achieved the same level of artistic sophistication in any other work, but he is recognized for his writing dealing with key events in the history of Ghana. CHRIS KWAME AWUYAH

Further reading: Michael F. Dei-Anang, 'A writer's outlook', *Okyeame* 1 (1961).

DE LA ROCHE, MAZO (1879–1961)

Canadian novelist, short-story writer, dramatist

Among Canada's most popular and prolific writers during the first half of this century, she was born near Toronto, Canada, and adopted the French prefix to her family name as a child. By 1927, when she was awarded the *Atlantic Monthly* prize for *Jalna* (1927), she had published several plays, a collection of linked stories, and two novels, *Possession* (1923) and *Delight* (1926). The author of twenty-three novels, de la Roche characteristically presents a blend of realism and romance, sentimentalism and melodrama, and the combination of these elements is attuned to the preoccupation of post-colonial fiction with freedom and tradition. Although obviously sympathetic towards vital and unrestrained behaviour, de la Roche seldom failed to acknowledge the destructive effects of uncontrolled individualism, and her work emphasizes the importance of continuity, hierarchy, and what she described as the 'persistence of the past into the future', a past usually associated with England.

The remarkable popularity of *Jalna* and the fifteen sequels that comprise the Whiteoak chronicles was the chief source of de la Roche's international reputation. The Jalna novels describe the history of the Whiteoak family from 1852 until 1952. The principal setting for the series is Jalna, a southern Ontario estate named after the military station in India where the original Whiteoaks served in the British army. Jalna is an English outpost, an enclave of 'sturdy British stock' determined to 'honour the Queen, fight for her if necessary'. The imaginative history of the Whiteoak family records de la Roche's sceptical reaction to the modern world, her conviction that technology and materialism would threaten individualism and erode traditional sources of order, and her deeply felt regret at the steady reduction of English influence in Canada. Although often compared to John Galsworthy's Forsyte novels, de la Roche's family chronicle also invites comparison with works as diverse as the early novels of **Chinua Achebe** and the Plumb trilogy of **Maurice Gee**.

DOUGLAS DAYMOND

Further reading: Ronald Hambleton, *Mazo de la Roche of Jalna* (1966); Dennis Duffy, *Gardens, Covenants, Exiles: Loyalism in the Literature of Upper Canada/Ontario* (1982).

DE LISSER, HERBERT GEORGE (1878–1944)
Jamaican novelist, journalist
Born in Falmouth, Jamaica, his parent were of Afro-Jewish descent. When de Lisser was fourteen years old, his father, editor of an unsuccessful local newspaper in Trelawney, died, and Herbert was forced to leave school and find a job. After working in low-paying clerical positions, de Lisser went to work at the Institute of Jamaica, where he read voraciously, taught himself French and Spanish, and discovered Caribbean social and political history. In 1889, he began his first job as a journalist at the weekly *Jamaica Times*. In 1903 he moved to *The Gleaner*, where he became editor-in-chief, a position he held for the following four decades.

de Lisser married Ellen Gunther, from a well-established white Jamaican family, in 1909, the same year in which he published a collection of essays, *In Cuba and Jamaica*. His second book, *Twentieth Century Jamaica*, was published in 1912, the same year in which his novel *Jane, A Story of Jamaica*, was partially serialized in *The Gleaner*. (It was published locally in book form in 1913, and reissued in 1914, under the title *Jane's Career*.) Thereafter de Lisser published a new novel practically every other year, some in book form, others as novellas in *Planters' Punch* (1920–44), an annual magazine that de Lisser established in 1920. He received the Musgrave Silver Medal for Literary Work in 1919 and the C. M. G. of the British Empire for Journalistic and Literary Achievement in 1920. Despite his political conservatism, de Lisser was in many respects an astute and accurate observer of his society. His urbane satirical style and facility with closely observed detail anticipate **V. S. Naipaul**'s later achievement in his Trinidad novels. With *Planters' Punch* de Lisser was one of the first Caribbean writers to try to attract a popular readership for locally produced fiction. Of his twenty-odd full-length works of fiction, about half are historical romances. Most of the rest may be classified either as social realism or political satire.

de Lisser's best-known early novels, *Jane's Career* (1914) and *Susan Proudleigh* (1915), fall into the category of social realism, but it would be inaccurate to claim, as critic Kenneth Ramchand has, that de Lisser's interest in social realms waned as his conservationism gradually isolated him from the mainstream of his society. *Myrtle and Money* (first serialized in *Planters' Punch* in 1941–2), conceived as a sequel to *Jane's Career*, is one of de Lisser's best-written works, and *Under the Sun* (first serialized in *Planters' Punch* in 1936–6, and published in book form in 1937) and *The Rivals* (serialized in *Planters' Punch* in 1921) are both entertaining comic pieces on the near-white Jamaican middle class to which de Lisser belonged. *The Jamaica Nobility* (serialized in *Planters' Punch* in 1926–6) is a harsh satire on Marcus Garvey's Negro Improvement Association, which flourished in Jamaica in the 1920s. *The Jamaica Bandits* (serialized in *Planters' Punch* in 1929–30) is built around a series of robberies that took place in Kingston in 1929, while *The Sins of the Children* (serialized in *Planters' Punch* in 1928) and *The Crocodiles* (serialized in *Planters' Punch* in 1932–3) explore a recurrent theme in all de Lisser's novels — the problem of miscegenation.

Jane's Career follows the story of a young rural girl who goes to Kingston to work as a domestic for a mulatto woman. After several years of exploitation and sexual harassment Jane abandons the family for life in a Kingston tenement yard and finds a factory job. She is rescued from further debauchery and near homelessness when she contracts an alliance with a promising young typesetter. The birth of their first child is followed by an ostentatious white wedding, and the work ends with the couple on the road to middle-class respectability.

Many of de Lisser's historical romances portray coloured women involved in doomed love affairs with white men. *Morgan's Daughter* (serialized in *Planters' Punch* in 1930–1 and first published in book form in 1953) recounts how a pirate-governor's mulatto daughter allows her love for an English renegade to draw her into his crimes. *The Cup and the Lip* (serialized in *Planters' Punch* in 1931–2 and first published in book form in 1953) explores the ill-fated relationship between an East Indian indentured laborer and her white overseer in the late nineteenth century. *Anacanoa* (serialized in *Planters' Punch* in 1936 and 1937 and first published in book form as *The Arawak Girl*, 1958) is the name of the Arawak mistress of one of Christopher Columbus' officers shipwrecked on Jamaica's north coast in the sixteenth century.

In de Lisser's best-known historical novel, *The White Witch of Rosehall* (1929), the theme of miscegenation is relegated to subplot. However, its position remains pivotal as it is the rivalry between Rose Hall's mistress and a black girl for the attentions of a visiting Englishman that makes the white woman turn to the voodoo arts she had learned from her slave nanny in Haiti before the revolution there and her family's flight to Jamaica.

RHONDA COBHAM

Further reading: Kenneth Ramchand, *The West Indian Novel and Its Background* (2nd ed., 1983); Rhonda Cobham, 'Herbert George de Lisser', in Daryl C. Dance (ed.) *Fifty Caribbean Writers: A Bio-bibliographical Critical Sourcebook* (1986).

DEMETILLO, RICAREDO (1919–)

Filipino poet, dramatist, critic

Born in Dumangas, Iloilo, in the central Philippine region of the Visayas, he attended school in Iloilo before studying at Silliman University, on the neighboring island of Negros. His life as a Baptist seminarian in the Protestant College of Central Philippine College was interrupted by the Second World War. Demetillo received a Rockefeller grant in 1950 to study for a master of fine arts degree at the state University of Iowa, USA, where he was also a fellow at the Iowa Creative Writing Center. He has received many awards, including the Palanca Memorial Award for Literature, the Republic Cultural Heritage Award, and the Jose Rizal Centennial Award (for the essay). He taught at the University of the Philippines and is presently an associate of the university's Creative Writing Center.

Demetillo's poetry is marked by a Protestant's existential struggle to define his own concept of sin and morality against that defined by social and religious institutions. Themes of rebellion and individualism, the rise and fall of civilizations, the artist's self-exile and role as the proclaimer of truth and values run through his poetry. His collections include *No Certain Weather* (1956), *La Via: A Spiritual Journey* (1958), *Daedalus and Other Poems* (1961), *Masks and Signature* (1968), *The City and the Thread of Light and Other Poems* (1973), *Lazarus Troubadour* (1974), and *The Scare-Crow Christ* (1978). Demetillo's existentialism, however, is tempered by imagery and symbolism deriving from Philippine culture, society, and history.

Barter in Panay (1961), an epic poem based on folk history recounting the settling of ten groups of Borneans, led by *datus* (chiefs), on a Visayas island, and its sequel in drama form, *The Heart of Emptiness is Black: A Tragedy in Verse* (1975), reveal a move toward a native poetic vision, which is also the thesis of his monograph *My Sumakwelan Works in the Context of Philippine Culture* (1976). *Genesis of a Troubled Vision* (1976) is an autobiographical novel, focusing on a young man's involvement with two women at the outbreak of the Second World War.

Two collections of critical essays, *The Authentic Voice of Poetry* (1962) and *Major and Minor Keys: Critical Essays on Philippine Fiction and Poetry* (1986), reveal the strong influence of American New Criticism in his close reading of the works of both Philippine and non-Philippine authors.

ROSARIO CRUZ LUCERO

Further reading: Edilberto Alegre and Doreen G. Fernandez, *Writers and Their Milieu: A History of Second Generation Writers of English* (1987).

De Mille, James (1833–80)
Canadian novelist
The third son of Nathan Smith De Mill [*sic*] and Elizabeth Tongue (Budd) De Mill, he was born in Saint John, New Brunswick, Canada, and educated first at Horton Academy and Acadia College in Wolfville, Nova Scotia, and then, after a year spent travelling with his brother in Europe, at Brown University, Rhode Island, USA. Returning to Saint John after graduating from Brown, he made several attempts to establish a career, including opening a bookstore. In 1859 he married Elizabeth Anne Pryor. In 1861 he accepted an appointment as professor of classics at Acadia College; four years later, he left to take up an appointment as professor of history and rhetoric at Dalhousie University in Halifax, Nova Scotia, where he remained until his death.

While still a student at Brown, De Mille began publishing short stories and occasional verse in popular magazines such as *Godey's Lady's Book* and *Flag of Our Union*. After graduation, he began writing longer works during his years in Saint John. He wrote some extremely successful books for boys, including a series based on his own schooldays at Horton Academy, and a historical story of the early days of the Acadians. Apart from *Helena's Household* (1867), a historical novel about the early Christians that is set mostly in Rome, his novels for adults were designedly light romantic comedies or novels of sensation set, for the most part, in Italy as he remembered it from his travels, although *The Lady of the Ice* (1870), one of the romantic comedies, is set in Quebec City of the early years of the nineteenth century. They appeared as serials in magazines and were subsequently published in popular library format. His only scholarly publication of any note was *The Elements of Rhetoric* (1878), a textbook for university and college students.

De Mille is best known, however, for his posthumously published satire, *A Strange Manuscript Found in a Copper Cylinder* (1888). The narrative details the finding by four bookish and argumentative yachtsmen of a manuscript containing an account by a marooned sailor, Adam More, of his adventures in a lost civilization at the South Pole, whose inhabitants, the Kosekin, prefer death to life, darkness to light, poverty to wealth. In describing More's response to these reversals, and the response of the yachtsmen to More's account, De Mille achieves an intricate commentary on western society that attracted a considerable amount of critical attention.

De Mille's literary career illustrates precisely the difficulties and dilemma of the writer at the time in the Maritime provinces of Canada. The established literary community of the day, such as it was, was located in Toronto, from which he was separated by distance and lack of an established transport system. The company of other writers from which to draw support and encouragement might have enabled him to develop beyond the popular works with which he was successful and perhaps to assert a non-American perspective in his work. In the absence of markets for his work both locally and elsewhere in Canada, he was forced to publish in the USA with established firms in New York, such as Harper's, for his adult fiction, and in Boston, for his books for boys. Publishing in the USA demanded that he conform to established popular taste and ignore, by and large, anything that drew attention to the Canadian context out of which he was writing (*The Lady of the Ice*, the exception, was also among his least successful works). As a popular writer, however, De Mille appears to have responded pragmatically to his situation, and not to have theorized about it in terms of the effects of colonial status.

PATRICIA MONK

Further reading: Patricia Monk, *The Gilded Beaver: An Introduction to the Life and Work of James De Mille* (1991).

DENNIS, C. J. (1876–1936)

Australian poet, journalist

Born in Auburn, South Australia, to Irish immigrant parents, and for several years a knockabout and drinker, he eventually took up journalism, finally securing, in 1922, a unique appointment as staff poet on the Melbourne *Herald*, which enabled him, after years of wandering, to settle at Toolangi, northwest of Melbourne, and spend his time between city and bush.

Dennis' major work, *The Songs of a Sentimental Bloke* (1915), ran to fifteen editions within two years. This success has puzzled some critics who have failed to recognize in the language of the poems the first sustained celebration of the Australian idiom — its slang, vitality, and wit. Dennis captured the speech rhythms and humour of ordinary Australians, their gift of 'chiack', and their deflection of adversity with a ready joke. The Bloke's eventual discovery, within himself and his society, of fundamental moral values makes the poem an *éducation sentimentale*. The city larrikin who falls in love, marries, has a son, and finds the beauty of work on the land represents the idealized Australian Dream. His story is one of growth without any loss of self and owes nothing to the demands of a borrowed culture. For most Australians, it was a sustaining dream, written in their own language by a recognizable 'mate'. (See **Mateship.**)

A sequel, *The Moods of Ginger Mick* (1916), was also an immediate success, all the more appealing because it spoke directly to and for Australian troops overseas. Dennis' favourite work, the political satire *The Glugs of Gosh* (1917), was not as popular, being at once more complex and less immediate to the lives of his readers.

Dennis wrote thousands of pieces for the *Herald*, inventing the mythical character Ben Bowyang the Bushie, with his singular comments on city life and his individual orthography. Although Dennis' many lyrical pieces have not received the attention they deserve, his works celebrate and embody the best of Australia's myths and traditions.

D. J. O'HEARN

Further reading: A. H. Chisholm, *The Making of a Sentimental Bloke* (1946); I. F. McLaren, *C. J. Dennis: A Comprehensive Bibliography* (1979); G. Hutchinson, ed., *The C. J. Dennis Collection* (1987).

DE ROO, ANNE (1931–)

New Zealand children's writer

Born in Gore, New Zealand, she earned a BA (1952) from the University of Canterbury. She worked as a librarian, secretary, governess, and gardener before becoming a full-time writer.

Few New Zealand children's writers have explored as many genres or themes as de Roo. Her works include adventure, animal, fantasy, and historical stories: *The Gold Dog* (1969), *Moa Valley* (1969), *Boy and the Sea Beast* (1971), *Cinnamon and Nutmeg* (1972), *Mick's Country Cousins* (1974), *Scrub Fire* (1977), *Traveller* (1979), *Because of Rosie* (1980), *Jack Nobody* (1983), *The Bat's Nest* (1986), and *Friend Troll Friend Taniwha* (1986). Despite the diversity of her work, there are certain constants. Often, animals act as catalyst to the action, frequently providing consolation to a lonely or unhappy child. Indeed, de Roo's main protagonists are frequently outsiders — an academic, non-sporting boy, a homesick immigrant, or the only boy in a family of girls.

Several of de Roo's books explore the problems of the half-caste. In *Mick's Country Cousins*, set on a contemporary farm, Mick resents the fact that he feels European yet looks Maori. The protagonist of *Jack Nobody*, living during the nineteenth-century Land Wars, believes himself to be a European orphan and is shocked to discover that his mother was Maori. Even the amusing fantasy *Friend Troll Friend Taniwha* light-heartedly presents a clash between native and immigrant. While de Roo constantly develops the psychological depth of her novels, she also explores aspects of her native country, its landscape, fauna, and history. Like Australia's Nan Chauncy, de Roo has made a considerable contribution to establishing an indigenous literary identity for children.

BETTY GILDERDALE

DEROZIO, HENRY LOUIS VIVIAN (1809–31)
Indian poet

He was born in Calcutta, India, of Eurasian ancestry, educated at Drummond's Academy, and worked on an indigo plantation at Bhagalpur while still in his teens. Probably the first Indian poet to write in English, Derozio gained a reputation writing poems and articles that soon enabled him to return to Calcutta as the sub-editor of the *Indian Gazette*. He also joined the Hindu College as professor of history and English literature; the students were fascinated by his bold views on social reform.

Derozio made his mark as a prolific journalist, contributing to such magazines as the *Calcutta Literary Gazette* and the *Enquirer* and editing *Kaleidoscope* for a year. His uncompromising criticism of Hindu superstitions, including the custom of suttee, drew the ire of orthodox Hindus, who thought he was undermining their ancient religion and was misleading the young men of Calcutta by preaching atheism. When in 1831 a few of his followers rescued a young widow, Saraswati, from her husband's funeral pyre, Derozio was forced to resign his professorship. He tried to make a new beginning, launching the daily *East-Indian*. He died of cholera.

A romantic to the core, Derozio noted with melancholy the intellectual paralysis that had overtaken his motherland. He felt that India was worse than a tomb and that it was 'the priest's, the tyrant's den'. A decisive move away from the emasculating past is projected in his powerful *The Fakir of Jungheera; A Metrical Tale and Other Poems* (1828). In the title poem the Brahmin widow Nuleeni is saved by her former lover, the Fakir of the outlaws, from the funeral pyre of her husband. But Nuleeni's father, blinded by tradition, vows revenge and does not rest until the Fakir is killed; Nuleeni dies with her lover. In the luxurious despair of Derozio's poetry the social reformer is definitely subsumed by the poet. Derozio's lyrics and sonnets also prove that he could write memorable poetry while expertly handling philosophical speculation and sterling patriotism.

PREMA NANDAKUMAR

Further reading: Jasbir Jain, *The Colonial Encounter: Henry Derozio* (1981).

DESAI, ANITA (1937–)
Indian novelist

She was born in Mussoorie, India, to a Bengali father and a German mother. She graduated with a BA (1957) from Delhi University, India, and in 1958 married Ashvin Desai, a business executive. They settled in Bombay.

Anita Desai has served as a visiting fellow (1986) at Girton College, Cambridge University, England, and, in the USA, as a visiting professor (1987) at Smith College, Massachusetts, and as the Purington Professor of English (1988) at Mt Holyoke College, Massachusetts. She has won several awards including, in 1977, The Royal Society of Literature's Winifred Holtby Memorial Prize for *Fire on the Mountain* (1977), and, in India, the 1978 Sahitya Akademi Award for literature in English.

Coloured as Desai's fiction is by her personal views, the influence of her parental heritage — an important key to the social biases of her fiction — can be ignored only at the peril of a misreading of her work. Her father, D. N. Mazumdar, a product of Bengal's élitist culture, was a student in Germany, where he met and married Toni Nime. In the late 1920s the couple went to India, which, in passing through the heyday of British colonialism, was witnessing a resurgence of old philosophic traditions, vernacular literatures, and a new political nationalism, powered mostly by the educated middle class.

It is not an accident that Desai's first three novels (*Cry, the Peacock*, 1963; *Voices in the City*, 1965; and *Bye-Bye, Blackbird*, 1968) deal with such educated Bengali men and women — all intense, artistic, and witty — as the young author, growing up in an intellectual family, would have known closely. But running through her writing is another, European, vein — supplied by her mother's immersion in German folklore and history. Although she was too young to understand the Second World War, Desai experienced the war through her mother and paid three visits to Germany, where her mother's family was destroyed.

The western disdain for Indian social customs that one encounters in Desai's work can be understood, then, only as part of the outlook of the daughter of a woman who, in an interview with Corrine Demas Bliss ('Against the Current: An Interview with Anita Desai', in *Massachusetts Review*, Fall, 1988), Desai describes as carrying 'a European core in her which protested against certain Indian things, which always maintained its independence and its separateness'. And if in Desai's fiction one misses the warmth and compassion for the Indian humanity that one finds in, for example, **Kamala Markandaya**'s work, it is because while Desai 'feels about India as an Indian', she thinks about it, she confesses in the Bliss interview, 'as an outsider'. Her view of India, consequently, is no less Eurocentric than that of another German migrant to India, **Ruth Prawer Jhabvala**, whom Desai has described as 'the first writer I came to know as a college student', and as one whom she 'wanted to emulate'.

Desai has published eight novels, a collection of stories (*Games at Twilight*, 1978), and three juvenile books (*The Peacock Garden*, 1974; *Cat on a Houseboat*, 1976; and *The Village by the Sea: An Indian Family Story*, 1982). Her essays, some on Indian culture, others on politics, have appeared in *Daedalus*, *The New Republic*, and *The New York Review of Books*. She has for many years served as a channel between India and the west, interpreting to the west, in terms familiar to it, the Indian scene.

Desai's earlier fiction — with the exception of *Bye-Bye, Blackbird*, which touches upon the metropolitan-colonial tensions of the post-colonial psyche — deals exclusively with the furies that haunt women trapped in matrimony. The wind begins to shift only with *Fire on the Mountain* — the setting of which, Kasauli, is reminiscent of the Mussoorie of her youth — in which other social and political concerns begin to glimmer.

Desai's most powerful works are her novels *Cry, the Peacock*, a story of the psychological disintegration of a young wife who murders her husband; *Clear Light of Day* (1980), a tale of the fragmentation of a family among warring communities in a crumbling nation, a piece that contains several autobiographical elements; *In Custody* (1984), a narrative mapping the disillusionment of a professor of Hindi on the discovery that the Urdu poet he deified was all too human; and *Baumgartner's Bombay* (1988), recounting the life of a Jew who escapes Nazi Germany only to be murdered in his later years in Bombay by a German drifter whom he seeks to rescue from drug addiction. Desai's work, the later novels confirm, manifests a sombre (one could hardly call it a tragic) view of life in which no one ever comes out a winner.

Desai's fictional world is not bathed in the clear light of day, but in the murk of despair. Her narratives emanate from neurotic protagonists and invariably cast a distorting gloom upon the world where they act out their sick designs. Nothing redeems either their lives or their world: neither hope, nor delusion, and certainly never love, courage, or passion. **R. K. Narayan** writes of similarly vulnerable creatures, but seldom with such a sense of doom.

Desai's fiction covers most of the relations and phases of a woman's life cycle: woman as granddaughter, in *Fire on the Mountain*; as daughter, in *Cry, the Peacock*; as wife, in *Where Shall We Go this Summer?* (1975); as mother, in *Clear Light of Day*; and as grandmother, in *Fire on the Mountain*. In *Bye-Bye, Blackbird* the woman is involved in a mixed marriage; in *Baumgartner's Bombay* a woman's several interracial liaisons are explored. Yet, Desai's fiction commands a rather limited range, if only because hers is mainly a domestic world, and her focus the interior of a mind teetering at the brink.

There is plenty here to please the reader, though, if one is sensitive to lyrical expressions of transient emotions or to delicate hues of an inner landscape. Desai is undoubtedly one of the most intelligent and widely read authors writing fiction about India. It is not unusual to run into echoes of T. S. Eliot and William Faulkner, of Dostoevsky and Camus, or to discover in her work the resonance of a mature Virginia Woolf.

P. S. CHAUHAN

Further reading: R. S. Sharma, ed., *Anita Desai* (1981); Jasbir Jain, *Stairs to the Attic: The Novels of Anita Desai* (1987); Usha Bande, *The Novels Of Anita Desai* (1988).

DESAI, BOMAN (1950–)
Indian novelist
Born in Bombay, India, he travelled to Chicago, USA, in 1969 to study architecture at the Illinois Institute of Technology. During his freshman year he won the Lewis Prize for Creative Writing, and a chance reading of Plato's *Apology* altered his career. He next studied philosophy for a year in Pennsylvania before returning to Chicago (where he has lived since) to graduate from the University of Illinois with a BA in psychology and, much later (1990), an MA in English. He received an Illinois Arts Council award for a short story, 'Under the Moon', and a *Stand Magazine* award for another story, 'A Fine Madness', which is the basis for an unpublished novel of the same title. J. R. Salamanca (author of *Lilith*, 1961) is his greatest single inspiration, and the English novelist John Fowles his most important structural model. Desai was married briefly, sang and recorded with a rock band in the 1970s, and is currently combining writing with a secretarial career.

Desai's novel *The Memory of Elephants* (1988) is the story of Homi Seervai, a brilliant Parsi scientist who invents a machine that enables him to relive his memories. Homi falls in love, and when the object of his affection does not reciprocate, uses the machine on himself to relive *ad infinitum* the memory of their time together. Unfortunately the 'memoscan', not yet fully operational, slips into his collective unconsciousness instead and presents him with nightmare images of his ancestors in seventh-century Iran at war with their Arab conquerors. This strategy enables Desai to collapse vast stretches of time and space into the confines of his novel.

The narrative finally settles on a Parsi family in twentieth-century India and spans three generations, from grandmothers who have lived without electricity, through their offspring, who, despite familiarity with the attractions of the west, choose to remain in India, to Homi, who leaves India for the USA. The Parsis (from the province of Pars in Iran) form a small but very visible, affluent, educated, and westernized community in India, and Desai vividly evokes their lives through sharply defined, memorable characters and deft touches that are both comic and moving. (See **Science Fiction**, India.)

MEENAKSHI MUKHERJEE

DESANI, GOVINDAS VISHNOODAS (1909–)
Indian novelist, dramatist, essayist
He was born in Nairobi, Kenya, to Vishnoodas Manghinmal and Rukmani (Chabria) Desani. Educated privately, Desani left home at the age of eighteen. He settled in England where, until his departure for India in 1952, he worked in journalism (mainly as a correspondent) and broadcasting (for the British Broadcasting Corporation) and as a popular lecturer on Indian affairs (for the British Government, 1940–6, and freelance). His *All About Mr. Hatterr, A Gesture* (1948) was republished in 1951 under its better-known title, *All About H. Hatterr*. According to information supplied in the novel's pseudo-preface ('London, October 23, 1945'), it 'was written entirely during the war years, *and* in London, *and* during the bombing!' 'Though I was attending a world war, the first row, I worked.'

In India and the far East, Desani studied Buddhism, philosophy, and mysticism; he practised *raja* and *mantra* yogas, engaging in meditation during his long periods of seclusion, which included, he once said privately, a ten-year vow of silence in a Tibetan monastery. From 1960 to 1967 he was a special contributor to the *Illustrated Weekly of India*, and in 1968 was appointed professor of Philosophy at the University of Texas, Austin, USA.

Desani's contributions to Indian English literature include *All About H. Hatterr*, an extraordinary and influential work of fiction that has undergone revision and expansion since it was first published; the poetic drama *Hali* (1951); and miscellaneous sketches, parodies, short fictions, and essays. The publication history of *All About H. Hatterr* in England and the USA (1948, 1950, 1951, 1970, 1972, 1986) and India (1985) indicates the novel's durability as an avant-garde text. This may be attributed to several factors: its versatile humour and crazy comedy; its anti-static style; the prevalence of Absurdism since the Second World War; the work's affinity with, and influence on, popular culture (for example, *The Goon Show*, the Indian sources of Milliganese, and Peter-Sellers-style parodies of Indian English); and the flexibility of the text, which works as both written and oral narrative and may be better read and laughed at aloud than absorbed silently. Postmodernist in advance of postmodernism, *All About H. Hatterr* is a scintillating, original mix of forms and idioms. The question of its generic status, in fact, is addressed epigrammatically in both the frontice — 'Warning!': 'Melodramatic *gestures* against public security are a common form of self-expression in the East . . .' — and in the 'Indian middle-man's' address to the author: 'Sir, if you do not identify your composition a novel, how then do we itemise it? . . . Author . . . : Sir, I identify it a gesture.'

Novel as gesture, *All About H. Hatterr* is in the episodic, picaresque tradition of *Tristram Shandy* (1760–7), in which joking, gesturing, and expressing appear in numerous narrative permutations on every page. Desani has turned prose fiction into a performing art that, while recounting 'Hindustaniwalla' Hatterr's hilarious misadventures, illuminates through enactment, dialogue, and unreliable commentary the greatest of themes — illusion versus reality. This theme, communicated in operatic polyglot, is manifested in the quest for an east-west synthesis of literary and philosophical values and principles: *maya* ('illusion') as play, game; Shakespeare's 'All the world's a stage' metaphor; and the cast of players — Eurasian Hatterr, Indians, British — who are 'such stuff as dreams are made on'. The apotheosis of English culture, Shakespeare is as big, complicated, and incongruous a presence in the novel as the British were in post-Mogul India. Shakespeare is incorporated into the colonial matrix of cultural hybridization, which involves the production of complex stereotypes such as Hatterr's fanatical friend Banerrji, who has been aptly described by the critic **M. K. Naik** as 'the most memorable portrait of the "Babu" in Indian English fiction'. Shakespeare is here a cause of mirth, particularly through Banerrji's misappropriation of the Bard's famous phrases, as, for example, in his exclamation, 'A horse! My kingdom for a horse! I am myself entirely devoted to the turf!'

In keeping with Desani's pervasive comic irony, moreover, the preposterous Yati Rambeli, in a piece of accidental wisdom, writes that 'misunderstanding is universally rampant'; the insight can be meaningfully decontextualized from his portentous nonsense. Whether or not it is possible to discover sense in nonsense is one of the major mad-Hatterr questions, but it is posed with an intuition of paradox (mock serious? serious?), in the alluring guises of comic fantasy and existential chaos, in ways that make it difficult for the alert reader to distinguish Desani's leg-pulling from his arm-twisting.

Desani's literary trickery, abounding in a Nabokovian plethora of learned and pedantic allusions, produces much more complicated posturing by and between Desani and the putative autobiographer (Hatterr) than is found in the original English model (Daniel Defoe's *Moll Flanders*, 1722). Desani's preface to Hatterr's 'Autobiographical' . . . 'H. Hatterr by H. Hatterr' comically compounds both the issue of who begot what and whom (author or character?) and the claim that 'What follows is wholly H. Hatterr, his work, do believe' because it begins and ends with the confession that telling lies is his 'major fault'. In return, Hatterr, in 'his' text, denounces 'the pharisee G. V. Desani' for 'priestcraft obscurantisms and subtlety', his 'top-holy trumpeting', and his assertion that '*by confessing I lie, yoiks! I tell the truth*'. Given this confident display of self-consciousness, critics have not been slow to appreciate what Naik calls Desani's 'astonishing exhibition of a seemingly unlimited stylistic virtuosity' and what Anthony Burgess refers to as Desani's mastery of 'Whole Language . . . like the English of Shakespeare, Joyce and Kipling, gloriously impure'. These technical accomplishments are matched by Desani's intellectual gymnastics, as evident in the design of the climax of the 'Autobiographical', which presents a witty, audacious synthesis of the Christian paradox of the Fortunate Fall and the Hindu doctrine of *maya* in relation to the illusoriness of Evil.

The complex humour, technical resourcefulness, and picaresque energy of *All About H. Hatterr* have a special relevance for all the new literatures in English, inviting comparison with the works of **Steele Rudd**, **Joseph Furphy**'s *Such is Life* (1903), the novels of **Barry Oakley**, and **Peter Carey**'s *Illywhacker* (1985).

While Desani's other work does not have the appeal of his novel, *Hali* is a notable achievement, creating in English an illusion of the sensibility, mythos, mystical poetry, and transcendental symbolism that are of the essence of classical Indian literature.

SYD HARREX

Further reading: S. C. Harrex, *The Fire and the Offering* Vol. 2 (1978); M. K. Naik, *A History of Indian English Literature* (1982); Ron Blaber and Marvin Gilman, *Roguery* (1990).

DESHPANDE, GAURI (1942–)
Indian poet
Born and educated in Poona, India, she began writing at an early age. She is one of the new genera-

tion of Indian poets who has used poetry as a medium to analyze the complexities of human existence and relationships.

Between Births (1968), Deshpande's first collection of poems, sensitively explores the frustration and alienation that result from her incapacity to make meaningful relationships. In poems such as 'A Change of Seasons', 'Migraine', and 'The Female of the Species', an immediacy of experience is expressed through a tightly webbed series of images. In 'Family Portraits' she graphically portrays an entire lineage.

In her next collection, *Lost Love* (1970), Deshpande breaks away, as she had in *Between Births*, from the sensuous and mellifluous treatment of conventional love to a bold encounter with sexuality. However, her treatment of sex is more spiritual than carnal, and sexuality is usually seen as an entry point towards spiritual fulfilment. Her major preoccupation with man-woman relationships finds expression in a series of poems that range from the treatment of sexual love and abortion to barrenness and old age. Through poems such as 'The Eclipse', where she is forced to accept her alienation, and 'December', where she accepts love but 'hesitates because it chains her', Deshpande projects the dilemma of a lost love.

In *Beyond the Slaughter House* (1972) there is a clear progression towards the acceptance of poetry as a social outgrowth. She writes with rare insight about employed women in the busy city of Bombay. The sense of loss of selfhood amidst the crowds of Bombay becomes equated with the incapacity to create a meaningful nexus within the experience of human love. 'Workaday Women' explores the predicament of a woman who has lost her responsiveness to love, and 'Where Do the Lonely People Live' becomes a reiteration of the loss even of gender roles within a changing society.

Deshpande's poetry at its best involves a passionate involvement with the existential *Angst* of the modern woman confronted with her inability to find meaningful relationships in society.

JAMEELA BEGUM A.

DESHPANDE, SHASHI (1938–)

Indian novelist, short-story writer

Born in Dharwad, south India, she began to write in 1970 and has published more than seventy short stories, five novels, and four books for children. Deshpande's fiction is often spoken of as feminist, but she is not comfortable with the label. Most of her protagonists are well-educated, sensitive, and culturally rooted women who face a conflict when the demands of post-independence Indian society are at odds with emotional and ethical values that go back to Vedic times. The total surrender of the self for the good of one's husband and children — a duty traditionally enjoined upon women — is no longer meaningful to contemporary Indian women who have their own ambitions, careers, and dreams. In *That Long Silence* (1988) the narrator, Jaya, at a critical juncture in her married life, recalls the words of her aunt: 'A husband is like a sheltering tree.' Her own image for the marriage relationship is that of a pair of bullocks yoked together, which reflects the blurring of roles and the greater burden that women now have to shoulder along with men. Sarita and Indu, the central characters of *The Dark Holds No Terrors* (1980) and *Roots and Shadows* (1983) respectively, are both women who fought to break out of what they regarded as the stranglehold of the family. Having succeeded in that effort, with careers and marriages of their own choice, they feel the inexplicable need to return to their roots. Their children, brought up very differently, are an enigma, discontented and uncommunicative. These women are not sentimental, but they feel the tug of the past, the old network of relationships no longer seen as confining but as supportive. Sarita, a successful doctor, flees from marital rape to her parental home after the death of her mother, who had never accepted her. She finds no solution, but the skeletal routine of the household with her father and a young boy who lives there strengthens her.

Several of Deshpande's short stories explore themes related to those of her novels. In 'Why a Robin' a mother whose young daughter shuts her out of her life finds an unexpected bridge between them when the girl attains puberty. 'It Was The Nightingale' concerns a parting between lovers who are married to each other. The woman has chosen to go abroad for two years, but her marriage, in spite of its limitations, tugs at her. 'A Wall Is Safer' is about a woman who has shelved her own legal career to go with her researcher husband to a remote village. When a former colleague remonstrates with her she replies, 'Don't make me out to be one of your exploited women. I know all my legal rights.' But she has a fierce longing to be one of those women who can carry their work about with them — a writer, painter, or musician.

Deshpande's characters speak in an educated voice very much at home in western literature and psychically attuned to the archetypes of Indian mythology. Several of her stories, such as 'The Last Enemy' and 'The Inner Room', retell episodes from the epics with stress on the interior landscape of a character's mind, a mode popular in other contemporary Indian writing, for example, the work of Lalithambika Antarjanam in Malayalam. Deshpande's fiction is resonant with the echoes of earlier literatures ranging over several countries and ages. This is more clearly seen in the longer fiction than in such stories as 'My Beloved Charioteer', with the allusion to Krishna speaking to Arjuna on the battlefield, and 'It Was The Nightingale', with its echo of Juliet's words to Romeo. This allusiveness lends an authenticity and a depth to Deshpande's characterization that is lacking in the work of writers such as **Kamala Markandaya, Nayantara Sahgal,** Muriel Wasi, and Nergis Dalal, whose colourless 'convent' idiom inhibits their characters from speaking with a distinctive voice. Another writer whose language, like Deshpande's, reflects a similar identification with Indian experience is Tara Ali Baig in her novel *The Moon in Rahu* (1970).

VIMALA RAMARAO

Further reading: S. K. Sandhu, *The Novels of Shashi Deshpande* (1991).

DE SOUZA, EUNICE (1940–)
Indian poet, literary critic
Born in Poona, India, into a Roman Catholic Goan family, she obtained a BA (1960) from Sophia College, Bombay, India, an MA (1963) from Marquette University, USA, and a Ph.D. (1988) from the University of Bombay. de Souza is currently a teacher of English at St Xavier College, Bombay. Her published works include the poetry collections *Fix* (1979), *Women in Dutch Painting* (1988), and *Ways of Belonging* (1990) as well as several books of children's stories, including *All About Birbal* (1969), *More About Birbal* (1973), *Folktales from the Himalayas* (1973), and *Folk Tales from the Gujarat*. She has co-edited textbooks, including *Statements: An Anthology of Indian Prose in English* (1977, with **Adil Jussawalla**).

Influenced by **Nissim Ezekiel**'s anti-Romantic poetics of precise expression, intellectual clarity, and concise, clear images, de Souza's early verse has similarities with Robert Browning's dramatic monologues; her characterization is often like that found in novels. *Fix* offers a combination of irony, satire, and compassion in its recollections of de Souza's Goan Catholic family. 'Conversation Piece', for example, tells of a Portuguese-bred aunt who mistakes a clay *shivalingam* ('phallic god') for an ashtray. Although offered as a series of verse photographs, the poems have a feminist and

Indian nationalist perspective. And while her scenes of ordinary life tend towards the grotesque, de Souza has brought to the often-sentimental, self-dramatic conventions of Indian women's poetry an understated, witty, judgemental surface calmness and a more colloquial, direct, contemporary language. There is an immediacy to her memories. The woman in 'Miss Louise', for example, has romantic dreams of descending curving staircases while fluttering an ivory fan and of being surrounded by children — while inside she is physically and mentally rotting. Using representative, self-revealing scenes, characters, speech, and dialogue, de Souza reveals Goan Poona as a society of prudery, ignorance, injustice, and repression, especially in its treatment of women. Other poems indicate the psychic damage caused by colonialism and patriarchy. In 'My Students' the class members are surprised that the speaker, and others without Anglo-Saxon names, write poetry, as the students associate literature with England, and especially with men.

Women in Dutch Painting expresses low-key, well-crafted reflections on contemporary social experiences. The subject-matter includes the literary scene of London, England, off-centred love poetry, and a continuation of an argument with a friend who wants a consciously politicized literature. The title poem, with its praise of feminine quiet and seeming assurance, contrasts with the speaker's personal world, where ordinary experiences are charged with disquiet. The speaker, standing before her bank manager, feels ironically like the goddess Kali with her 'necklace of skulls'. In such poems the personal is political, offering glimpses of the wounds, insecurities, and humiliations that are behind a woman's smiles and conversations.

BRUCE KING

Further reading: Adil Jussawalla, 'One woman's poetry', *Journal of South Asian Literature* 1 (1983); Bruce King, *Modern Indian Poetry in English* (1987; rev. 1989).

DE UNGRIA, RICARDO (1951–)

Filipino poet

Born and raised in Manila, the Philippines, he studied fine art at the Philippine Women's University and graduated with a BA from De La Salle University. De Ungria teaches English at the University of the Philippines College, Manila. A founding member of the Philippines Literary Arts Council (PLAC), he is the managing director of its poetry journal, *Caracoa*. His poems protesting the assassination of Benigno Aquino in 1983 were issued by PLAC in the pamphlet *In Memoriam: A Tribute to Benigno S. Aquino*. In 1989, while on a Fulbright Fellowship at Washington University, USA (where he earned a master of fine arts degree), De Ungria won prizes in two categories in the St Louis Poetry Centre Annual Contest. In 1990 he won first prize in the Palanca Memorial Award for Literature.

De Ungria's first book, the award-winning *Radio* (1984), consists of experimental, avant-garde, and surrealistic poems. In his second collection, *Decimal Places: Poems* (1991), written for his master of fine arts degree, the voice of the expatriate poet is heard.

In many of the poems, the USA weaves in and out of the Filipino psyche, as in 'Room for Time Passing'. The poet's visit to a St Louis museum triggers memory of an exhibit in this same museum in 1904, when Philippine natives were displayed against a backdrop of scaled-down replicas of their mountain villages. Since then, the poet notes, the colonial mentality has not really disappeared.

In the final poem, 'Angel Radio', scenes that the poet encounters in his interstate travels remind him of those from his own country: Mayon Volcano, the white beaches of Vigan, and the Pasig

River. He notes the places where Filipino expatriate writers of the older generation once lived: poet **Jose Garcia Villa** in Greenwich Village, New York, and **Carlos Bulosan** travelling in a boxcar to Bakersfield, California. Other poems in this collection are about the Philippine-American War, the expatriate's sense of dislocation and homesickness, the misery and despair in certain pockets of the USA, and American expansionist policy.

ROSARIO CRUZ LUCERO

Further reading: Elmer A. Ordonez, 'Recent Philippine poetry in English', *Tenggra 29: Journal of Southeast Asian Literature, 1990* (1990).

DEVANNY, JEAN (1894–1962)
Australian novelist
Born Jane Crook in Ferntown, New Zealand, she immigrated to Australia with her husband and children in 1929. The daughter of a coal-miner, Devanny had been active in the New Zealand labour movement and joined the Communist Party of Australia (CPA) in 1930. She was also a passionate advocate of the rights of women; her first novel, *The Butcher Shop* (1926), is a critique of the economic and sexual subordination of women in marriage.

Feminism and socialism inform Devanny's subsequent fiction. One of her best-known novels, *Sugar Heaven* (1936), is an account of a canecutters' strike in North Queensland, Australia, in 1935, largely from the perspective of the cutters' wives. Like other Communist writers, most notably **Katharine Susannah Prichard**, Devanny was inspired by the example of European and American socialist realists who sought to make their fiction a tool for educating and inspiring workers in the class struggle. She found it difficult, however, to integrate her literary and political concerns. Her efforts to promote the value and work of writers in the Communist Party met with suspicion and sometimes hostility from party leaders, while readers outside the CPA denigrated her fiction for its 'propagandist' functions. She never abandoned her commitment to Communism and literature, despite expulsion from the CPA in 1941 on grounds that were never made clear to her. In later life, however, she retired from political activity to concentrate on writing fiction, autobiography, and reportage, much of which is set in North Queensland, where she settled after the Second World War.

Devanny's autobiography, *Point of Departure* (1986), edited by Carole Ferrier, reflects her passionate nature and eclectic interests, which included eugenics, natural history, the rights of Australian Aborigines, and the professional status of writers. Her life and work reveal some of the complexities and contradictions facing the politically committed writer in Australia, but at the same time she was to be an inspiration to other aspiring Communist writers, such as **Frank Hardy**.

JULIE WELLS

Further reading: Carole Ferrier, 'Jean Devanny: a bibliography', *Hecate* 13 (1987).

DEWDNEY, CHRISTOPHER (1951–)
Canadian poet
Born in London, Canada, he moved to Toronto in 1980, but his writing still dwells on the landscape of southwestern Ontario. His most important book, *Predators of the Adoration: Selected Poems 1972–82* (1983), claims to be 'the voice of the land and the creatures themselves, speaking from the inviolate fortress of a primeval history uncorrupted by humans'. Like most of Dewdney's nine other books, *Predators* is a mixed-form long poem involving not only poetry but prose and visuals of his own creation.

Dewdney is perhaps the ultimate post-colonial writer, confidently undercutting the foundation of all imperialisms — the evolution of human creatures into assumed superiority over all forms of life. He has elaborated the concept of remote control into an imaginary secret society that mysteriously subverts logical language and the sense-making universe that depends on it. As a writer, Dewdney is an undeclared or outlaw member of that society. The most compact expressions of his universe, a dreamlike, mutated collapse of all time and space, is the verbally synaesthetic, structurally non-sequential *Spring Trances in the Control Emerald Night and The Cenozoic Asylum* (1982). Two 'pataphysical' texts — a term borrowed by critic Steve McCaffery from dramatist Alfred Jarry to approximate Dewdney's parodic use of the language and taxonomies of science — supply a theoretical foundation for his experiments in writing out of Control. These texts are 'Parasite Maintenance', the essay on the neurology of the poet in Dewdney's *Alter Sublime* (1980), and its expansion into *The Immaculate Perception* (1986). Both Dewdney's theory and practice play upon the edge between seriousness and fantasy.

Predators, nominated for a 1983 Governor General's Award, was a turning point in a career nurtured by Coach House Press, where Dewdney designed and printed his own books, independently evolving his completely original vision. Dewdney's work lends itself to such different approaches as that of Steve McCaffery, who stresses its non-referentialist nature, and Stan Dragland, who recognizes in it a futuristic, satirical mimesis of fragmented contemporary reality.

STAN DRAGLAND

Further reading: Steve McCaffery, 'Strategy and strategy: pataphysics in the poetry of Christopher Dewdney', *Open Letter* Winter (1976); Stan Dragland, 'Afterword', *Predators of the Adoration* by Christopher Dewdney (1983).

DHLOMO, HERBERT ISAAC ERNEST

(1903–56)

South African dramatist, poet, essayist, journalist

He was born in Edendale, a black township outside Pietermaritzburg, Natal, South Africa, to Christian, educated, and 'progressive' parents who provided as thorough an education as was available at Adams Teachers' Training College in Amanzimtoti. Unlike his older brother, **Rolfes Dhlomo**, who wrote mainly in Zulu, Herbert worked primarily in English. Herbert Dhlomo found his first creative outlets in black newspapers, and the Dhlomo brothers, as journalists and editors, were part of a small élite band with considerable political influence. Herbert Dhlomo was one of the founders of the African National Congress (ANC) Youth League in 1944.

Dhlomo is regarded as the father of modern black drama in South Africa. He was a prolific, if uneven, writer, and much of his work has survived. Produced in the 1930s and 1940s it forms a vital bridge in South African literary history between early writers such as **Solomon Plaatje** and **Thomas Mofolo** and the ***Drum*** writers of the 1950s. (See **Drama**, South Africa.)

Dhlomo's plays are both historical and contemporary. His most ambitious project was a trilogy on the lives of the Zulu kings Shaka, Dingane, and Cetshwayo (only the last two of the three plays — *Dingane*, 1985, and *Cetshwayo*, 1985 — survive). Although much of his language is stilted and the final products flawed, Dhlomo's importance lies not merely in the bulk of his output but also in his theoretical writings and his attempt to structure his plays according to his theories. His play *Moshoeshoe* (premièred in 1939 and first published in his *Collected Works*, 1985, edited by Nick Visser and Tim Couzens) is a pioneering attempt to incorporate traditional forms of public ceremony into a western style of drama. Dhlomo's other plays include *The Girl who Killed to Save: Nongquase the Liberator* (1935) and 'Ruby and Frank' (premièred 1939). Dhlomo did stage *Moshoeshoe* and 'Ruby and Frank' in Johannesburg, but a lack of experience and the non-existence of professional black actors resulted in marginal success. Dhlomo lacked access to constructive criticism, and while his ideas were interesting, their proper execution stood little chance.

Dhlomo's poetry was heavily influenced by the English Romantics. His longest and most important poem is *Valley of a Thousand Hills* (1941). While Plaatje's novel *Mhudi* (1930) is an epic representing the ideals of the early ANC, Dhlomo's poetic epic represents the more radical aspirations of the Youth League.

Particularly in *Valley of a Thousand Hills*, Dhlomo struggled with the contradictions between Zulu nationalism and a greater nationalism. This tension manifested itself in his support for Albert Luthuli (whom he saw as a reborn Shaka) and his behind-the-scenes manoeuvring that helped Luthuli gain the presidency of the ANC. Later, Dhlomo developed an increasing bitterness in response to political and social frustration.

TIM COUZENS

Further reading: Tim Couzens, *The New African: A Study of the Life and Work of H. I. E. Dhlomo* (1985); N. W. Visser, 'Literary theory and criticism of H. I. E. Dhlomo', *English in Africa* 2 (1977).

Dhlomo, Rolfes Robert Reginald (1901–71)
South African novelist, journalist
Born at Siyamu, Edendale, a black township outside of Pietermaritzburg, Natal, South Africa, brother of **Herbert Dhlomo**, he was educated at Ohlange Institute and at Adams Teachers' Training College. Rolfes Dhlomo gained some experience in journalism writing for **Stephen Black**'s satirical magazine *The Sjambok* (1929–31). *The Sjambok* also published several of Dhlomo's short stories in English.

When Dhlomo moved to the newspaper *Bantu World* in 1932, he continued to publish stories. He also wrote regular educational and comic columns under such pseudonyms as 'R. Roamer Esq.', 'Rollie Reggie', and 'Rolling Stone'. His most extended piece of English prose was the novella *An African Tragedy* (1928), a moralistic fable on the dangers of a countryman coming to the evil city. The short stories have been collected in an edition of the journal *English in Africa* (1, 1975).

In 1935 Dhlomo embarked on a different course, publishing his first book in Zulu, *Izikhali Zanamuhla* ('The Weapons of Today'). His didactic purpose is made clear in the introduction: 'The war of today is fought with three weapons only: education, money and religion.' *Izikhali Zanamuhla* was followed by a series of novels on the Zulu kings: *UDingane* (1936), *UShaka* (1937), *UMpande* (1949), *UCetshwayo* (1952), and *UDinizulu* (1968) — none have been translated into English. Written Zulu developed late, compared with writing in the Xhosa or Setswana languages, and Dhlomo consequently benefited from being a pioneer in the field. Many editions of his works have been published and have been taught in schools for more than half a century, although Dhlomo himself did not reap a great financial harvest.

As editor of the influential newspaper *Ilanga Lase Natal* (1903–, now titled *Ilanga*) between 1943 and 1962, Dhlomo played a significant role in local Natal politics, but, like so many of his literary and political contemporaries, alcohol and ill health sapped his energies towards the end of his life.

Many of the complexities and contradictions of South African society are represented in the contrasting lives of Rolfes and his brother Herbert; Herbert wrote mainly in English, Rolfes, excepting his earlier work, wrote in Zulu. Herbert was politically radical while Rolfes was conservative.

TIM COUZENS

Dhondy, Farrukh (1944–)
Indian short-story writer, novelist, dramatist, children's writer
Born in Poona, India, of Parsi background, he received a bachelor of science degree in engineering (1964) from the University of Bombay, India,

a BA in English literature (1967) from the University of Cambridge, England, and an MA in literature from the University of Leicester, England. After teaching English at various schools in London, England, until 1982, Dhondy became a full-time writer. (In 1990–1 he worked as the commissioning editor of ethnic programmes for the British Broadcasting Corporation.)

Dhondy's experiences in London, England, inspired his award-winning children's books, *East End at Your Feet* (1976) and *Come to Mecca and Other Stories* (1978). His other writings include several collections of short stories for adolescents: *The Siege of Babylon* (1978), *Poona Company* (1980), and *Trip Trap* (1982). Dhondy has also written plays — 'Mama Dragon' (premièred 1980), 'Trojans' (premièred 1983), 'Kipling Sahib' (premièred 1982), and the television play 'Maids in the Mad Show' (broadcast 1981). His other publications include *Romance, Romance (and) the Bride* (1985) and *Vigilantes* (1988). In the 1980s Dhondy scripted 'King of the Ghetto', a series of television plays focusing on the poverty and desperate living conditions of the Bangladeshi immigrants in east London; he co-authored, with **Mustapha Matura**, the television series 'No Problem' (broadcast 1983). In 1990 he published his first novel, *Bombay Duck.*

Poona Company, though addressed to 'young adults', appeals to readers of all ages and cultures. It promotes cross-cultural understanding while providing Asian readers with intra-cultural perceptions of their heritage. If *Poona Company* is reminiscent of Dhondy's adolescent experiences in Poona without being nostalgic or pretentiously wise in its insights into human nature, *Trip Trap* is seemingly sophisticated in style without being sentimental about racial adjustment problems in the UK. Such stories as 'Lost Soul', 'Homework', and 'Batty and Winifred' reveal Dhondy's compassion and concern for adolescents.

Bombay Duck is about luck mixed with pluck; structured with shifting points of view, it is an amusing mixture of myth, fantasy, tragicomic situations, realistic descriptions, stylistic innovation, entertaining frivolity, and an apocalyptic vision of 'an avenging angel'. Dhondy's work bears resemblance to that of **Salman Rushdie, Bharati Mukherjee**, and **Ruth Prawer Jhabvala.**

A. V. KRISHNA RAO

DIKOBE, MODIKWE (1913–)

South African novelist, poet

He was born Marks Rammitloa in Seabe, near Settlers, the Northern Transvaal, South Africa. He writes under the pen-name Modikwe Dikobe — he got the name Dikobe from his mother. An illegitimate child, he had to struggle for an elementary education. During his first years in Johannesburg, he eked out a living as a newspaper-seller, then as a hawker. In the 1940s he was involved in bus boycotts, and after the Second World War he became a leader of the Alexandra squatters' movement. He joined the Communist Party, and his involvement in trade unions ultimately led to his being banned by the South African government. Despite these varied activities, he managed to produce a gem of a short novel, *The Marabi Dance* (1973).

The Marabi Dance is set in Johannesburg in the 1930s and 1940s and is partly and indirectly autobiographical. For anyone seeking knowledge of the life of the city at that time, *The Marabi Dance* offers a unique insight. It is a genuine working-class novel, written by a member of the working class. Its impact has been far greater than much of the more strident South African protest literature, in part because its message is understated. *The Marabi Dance* also has the immediacy of some Nigerian market literature, but its ultimate effect is far deeper and more devastating.

Dikobe has published a second, less well-known work, the poetry collection *Dispossessed* (1983). The title poem, in a few pages, gives as good a sense of the tragic changes that have occurred during the twentieth century in South Africa as one will find anywhere. Dikobe's is a clear, individual, and genuine voice, but generally it has not found favour in academic circles. Nevertheless, *The Marabi Dance* has had a subtle and unacknowledged influence on modern South African drama and sociological writings.

Dikobe retired in 1977 from his time-keeping job with the Johannesburg municipality to a small plot at Seabe. He lives on a pittance, continues to write prolifically, but has yet to publish anything further.

TIM COUZENS

DIMALANTA, OPHELIA ALCANTARA (1934–)
Filipino poet, short-story writer, critic
Born in San Juan, Rizal, the Philippines, she obtained her bachelor of science, MA, and Ph.D. (in literature) at the pontifical University of Santo Tomas. She has also occupied several administrative posts at that institution, currently serving as dean of the Faculty of Arts and Letters. Dimalanta has been the recipient of many awards, including, in 1990, the Gawad Pambansang Alagad ni Balagtas, a national award given by the Writers Union of the Philippines. A professor of literature and literary critic, she is a founding member of the Manila Critics Circle and an honorary fellow of the Philippine Literary Arts Council.

Hailed by poet-critic **Cirilo F. Bautista** as 'not only our foremost woman poet but also one of the best poets writing now, regardless of gender', Dimalanta learned her craft from intensive study of such poets as T. S. Eliot and Wallace Stevens, whose influences are strongly evident in her early poems. Her later poetry draws from a wider range of influences, among them poets such as Sylvia Plath, Anne Sexton, and Denise Levertov.

Reviewing her own growth as a poet through four decades and four volumes of poetry, Dimalanta believes that 'the older you become and the more mature your art becomes, the more you realize that you have your own identity'. Though her first collection of poems, *Montage* (1974), was greeted with praise, she now thinks that the poems there 'smelled of rooms, too indoor, too closeted — my kind of life then'. She claims that her second collection, *The Time Factor and Other Poems* (1983), is 'a liberation from the smothering confines of academe'. As its title indicates, *Flowing On* (1988) opens up to wider horizons and includes some political and feminist poems. *Lady Polyester* (1993), whose title is taken from a prize-winning short story Dimalanta wrote in 1981, is an implicit celebration of her mature identity as both woman and poet. In his foreword to this volume, poet-critic **Gemino H. Abad** affirms that 'fictive flesh' is the theme that runs through all Dimalanta's poems: 'Ophelia in fact is the poem still to write: to find, to invent, where words do not break.'

EDNA ZAPANTA MANLAPAZ

DIXON, MCDONALD ERNEST (1945–)
St Lucian poet, dramatist
Born in Castries, St Lucia, the Caribbean, his father was an East Indian from Trinidad and his mother a St Lucian of African ancestry. Dixon was educated at St Mary's College, St Lucia, before he entered the banking profession, where he has remained.

The first St Lucian poet to achieve prominence after **Derek Walcott**, Dixon has published two poetry collections, *Pebbles* (1973) and *The Poet Speaks* (1986). His poems are inspired by the St Lucian landscape, its history, and its folk figures. A poet of the 'grand gesture', his poems often seem as intoxicated by the sheer power of the sound of words as the poems of Dylan Thomas, one of his heroes. Growing up when his country was making its transition from colony to associated state to independence, Dixon reflects in his work the changes of allegiance. Also influenced strongly by the old core curricula of British literature, Dixon often adopts a tone of melodramatic romanticism. Yet, in form, his free-verse stylings early reached for the independence that is so much a mark of contemporary Caribbean and Commonwealth writing. His later, unpublished poetry reveals a more lyrical, less stentorian style.

Dixon's friendship with **Roderick Walcott** and his involvement with the work of the St Lucia Arts Guild have influenced the folk subjects of his drama, which includes 'Diablotin: A One-Act Play' (premièred 1970) and 'Tinday' (premièred 1992). With Derek Walcott, Roderick Walcott, and **Stanley French**, Dixon is part of the first generation of Caribbean writers to give a central place to St Lucian folk culture. Younger playwrights such as **Kendel Hippolyte** and Gandolph St Clair have built on these foundations and are now more concerned with the wider Caribbean. Dixon may be compared with many of the local, isolated writers throughout the Commonwealth from whose indigenous knowledge and experience have grown rooted literatures.

JOHN ROBERT LEE

DJOLETO, AMU (1929–)

Ghanaian novelist, poet

Born at Bana Hill (Manya Krobo), Ghana, he was educated at Accra Academy, St Augustine's College, Cape Coast, Legon, and the University of London, England. He edited *Teacher's Journal* and contributed to several handbooks on education in Ghana. He is the executive director of the Ghana Book Development Council, charged with promoting Ghana's book industry. In addition to his novels, *The Strange Man* (1967) and *Money Galore* (1975), Djoleto has published a few poems: 'The Lone Horse' (*Voices of Ghana: Literary Contributions to the Ghana Broadcasting Corporation*, 1958, edited by Henry Swanzy) and 'A Passing Thought', 'The Good Old Motto', 'Why is it?', 'The Quest', and 'The Search' (in *Messages: Poems From Ghana*, 1970, edited by **Kofi Awoonor** and G. Adali-Mortty).

The Strange Man traces the story of Old Mensah, from his boyhood in the colonial era to his successful career in the civil service and in business in independent Ghana. The novel opens and ends with death scenes, recalling **Joseph Abruquah**'s *The Catechist* (1965), and its theme, the horrors of colonial education, is much like that of **Francis Selormey**'s *The Narrow Path* (1966). Overall, however, *The Strange Man* is a weak novel, as its narrative and characterization are seriously flawed. The author constantly intervenes through an omniscient narrator who speculates and sermonizes. An episode such as the castration of a goat by Menash and his friends, which displays Djoleto's literary skills, is rare.

Money Galore, like **Ayi Kwei Armah**'s *The Beautyful Ones Are Not Yet Born* (1968), deals with corruption in post-independence Ghana, with underpinnings of such recent political acts as the dismissal of Ghanian civil servants without due process. In this light satirical novel, in a style reminiscent of **T. M. Aluko**'s, Djoleto exposes corrupt politicians and businessmen, cynical civil servants, and gregarious illiterate Makola (central Accra) market women. The recklessness of the élites makes it predictable that the army would join the mêlée of misrule, as in **Chinua Achebe**'s *A Man of the People* (1966), in which soldiers overthrow the corrupt politicians.

Djoleto has serious concerns about the moral atrophy in Ghana, but his story is weakened by his lack of attention to narrative pace, by his sudden leaps into episodes, and by ill-fitting language.

CHRIS KWAME AWUYAH

Further reading: Gerarld Moore, 'Ghanaian childhood', *The Journal of Commonwealth Literature* 6 (1969).

DOBSON, ROSEMARY (1920–)

Australian poet

Born in Sydney, Australia, she early acquired an

enthusiasm for poetry, Renaissance painting and typography, and a feeling for their affinities. Her first volume of poetry, *In a Convex Mirror*, appeared in 1944; she joined the Sydney publishers Angus and Robertson and befriended poets such as **A. D. Hope**, **James McAuley**, and **David Campbell**, with whom she later collaborated on imitations of Russian poems.

Always lucid, Dobson's poetry is usually quiet and contemplative, with feeling subordinate to deft formal control, cool intelligence, and gentle wit. Since *Over the Frontier* (1978) she has relinquished conventional prosody in favour of disciplined free verse, but she continues to write in stanzas. The poetry is not conspicuously Australian: an austere vision is sometimes embodied in images of ice and snow; her referents involve European art and mythology; and her spare, emblematic modes gesture towards the universal. Nevertheless, Dobson values her Australian roots; she found herself unable to write while living abroad between 1966 and 1971 and believes that isolation has allowed Australian writers to develop individual voices.

Dobson's poetry is a sustained meditation on time, which is related to the stages of life, motherhood, and especially the paradox of art. From 'The Ship of Ice' (1948) to 'The Three Fates' (1984) she acknowledges that we are grounded in time. Art preserves by abstracting; it cannot embrace the flux of actuality. Although she has repudiated early objections that her many poems about painting represented vicarious rather than lived experience, critics have been slow to appreciate the relevance to her themes of Dobson's detachment. The painting poems, often dramatic monologues, imaginatively revive the temporal actuality in which some artefact was created; yet in doing so they reconstitute life as art in the formality of a poem. But this affirms the 'continuance of poetry', an ongoing human participation in creative processes that transcends static abstraction. Later, Dobson uses mythology and the travel writings of Pausanias in a similar way, operating at one remove in order to establish an implicit dialectic between art and experience. Recent assessments correctly discern a modernist strain in her work. A revised *Selected Poems* (1980) was followed by *The Three Fates* (1984).

ANDREW WALLACE

DOMETT, ALFRED (1811–87)
New Zealand poet
Born in Surrey, England, he was educated at Cambridge University, but did not take a degree. He travelled extensively as a young man, especially in Canada, the USA, and the Caribbean. Domett's published works include *Poems* (1833); *Venice* (1839), a long poem; *Ranolf and Amohia: A South-Sea Day-Dream* (1872), an epic; *Flotsam and Jetsam: Rhymes Old and New* (1877); and two diaries — his lively *The Canadian Journal of Alfred Domett Being an Extract from a Journal of a Tour in Canada, the United States and Jamaica 1833–1835* (1955), edited by E. A. Horsman and Lillian Rea Benson, and *The Diary of Alfred Domett, 1872–1885* (1953). Domett's poem 'A Christmas Hymn' first appeared in *Blackwood's Edinburgh Magazine* in 1837 and was later much anthologized.

A friend of Robert Browning, with whom he toured in Europe, Domett immigrated in 1842 to the raw new settlement of Nelson, New Zealand. Browning lamented Domett's departure in affectionate verse: 'What's become of Waring / Since he gave us all the slip[?].' In New Zealand, Domett occupied himself with farming, journalism, the public service, and eventually politics, becoming premier in 1862–3 at the height of the settlers' war against the Maori.

After thirty years in New Zealand, Domett returned to London, England, with the manuscript of *Ranolf and Amohia*. On the frail scaffolding of a romance between a shipwrecked sailor and a mistreated Maori woman, Domett hangs metaphysical and philosophical reflections, Maori legends, landscape descriptions, and scientific treatises. His handling of verse forms is competent. In the late nineteenth century, in the absence of much else, *Ranolf and Amohia* stood for 'New Zealand literature'; nowadays it is seldom read.

DENNIS McELDOWNEY

Further reading: E. A. Horsman, 'Introduction', *The Diary of Alfred Domett 1872–1885* (1953).

DRAMA

DRAMA (Overview)

As a tool of cultural colonization, drama has an obvious efficacy. In some countries, such as Canada, South Africa, and New Zealand, a colonizing military presence brought drama as troop entertainment, thus very literally establishing it as a discourse of dominance. Wherever English was imposed on native peoples in the name of 'literacy programmes', drama found a prominent place in school textbooks as an effective instrument of language acquisition among people with an oral cultural orientation. At the same time, the texts that were thus advanced as 'drama' veiled or radically devalued native performance traditions, which might also be embedded in practices of warfare, religion, or even education and became in their various ways counter-discursive. The broader project of post-colonial drama may be seen as the gradual erosion of such cultural polarization in the name of hybridity, but the demographic, historical, and political profiles of the sites of British imperialism vary enormously, as does the composition of their various dramatic hybrids.

It has often been noted that in white settler societies local playwriting develops much more slowly than other literary forms: although pioneer playwrights occasionally found their way on to the colonial stage, in most cases a strong and continuing tradition of playwriting dates only from the 1950s. Partly, this must reflect the degree of social organization and population density that play production requires: one person can write, hand-print, and distribute a book of poems, one newspaper can serialize a colonial novel, but many people must be brought together for even a modestly successful production of a one-act play. Conversely, the complexity of the machinery of theatrical representation had an inherent conservatizing effect: simply on an institutional level, the nineteenth-century touring company from Britain was a structure of such vastness that the cultural values it enshrined were monumentalized, stunting anything that got in its way.

The death of the touring company in the face of film and radio simply meant that cultural imperialism was now technologized. Radio meant that drama — sometimes even locally-written drama — infiltrated the remotest settlements from the 1930s, and in low-density or isolated population areas such as Canada and Malta its importance has been considerable. In rare cases such as the Australian Dad and Dave series (adapted from the works of **Steele Rudd**) this was flamboyantly home-grown, but largely because of technical sophistication the British Broadcasting Corporation emerged as a standard not just for dramatic production but also for the 'right kind of language' to use in drama. Although it gave employment to actors and production to dramatists in the period following the Second World War, when professional theatre was weak, radio was also a conservatizing force, suppressing regional Englishes and indigenous languages. It was the stage rather than radio in the 1960s that explored the dramatic potential of the Okker, West African pidgins, even Sri Lankan English, just as it is the stage that gives audiences their first records of Afrikaans. (See **Broadcasting**.)

The stage, however, maintained its own colonizing mission, most overtly through the British Drama League (BDL), founded in 1919, set up as a global network a decade later, and in some countries surviving (although generally with name changes) into the 1990s. The ambiguity inherent in the BDL project lay in that while it encouraged local playwriting at its competitive dramatic festivals, the judging of those festivals and scripts was often by visiting experts or 'staff tutors' from the UK (sometimes also elocution examiners with Royal or Trinity College affiliations); even when judging became local the same standards were generally perpetrated. That not all adjudicators were narrowly Eurocentric is shown by a BDL judge's report from South Africa in 1940, insisting on the richness of Bantu drama compared with English.

The aura of nationalism surrounding independence inevitably found reflections in drama, although the tentative and variable nature of that 'independence' meant that the stage offered a platform for numerous agendas. In white settler societies, there was a quest for an artistically respectable 'high' local drama, a quest reinforced by the international 'Little Theatre' movement and conscious of the decolonizing programme of Irish theatre. In Australia, this generated the understated naturalism of **Louis Esson**, but the most innovative product was the 'symphonic theatre' of the Canadian **Herman Voaden**. More commonly, though, the search for respectability and classic self-sufficiency resulted in cumbersome verse dramas modelled on Shakespeare or T. S. Eliot. In countries where independence was politically synonymous with decolonization, however, the consequent revalorization of indigenous languages brought the downplaying of English as a vehicle for drama and — in some cases — for education. If the most famous practice of this is in the later work of **Ngugi wa Thiong'o** in Kenya, it is also reflected in the refusal of some French-Canadian playwrights to allow their work to be translated into English, and — less overtly politically — in the relative paucity of English writing in contemporary Indian and Philippine drama. Such a politics of language use — proclaimed by **Wole Soyinka**, theorized by Ngugi, and given an antecedent in the Irish theatre's occasional use of Gaelic — has led to the exploration of theatre as a means of resistance or separatist celebration, in countries as diverse as South Africa, New Zealand, and Kenya.

While it is often lamented that it is very difficult to achieve book publication for plays in post-colonial societies, the very ephemerality of drama can make it politically effective in contexts where censorship governs the printing press. In post-coup Fiji, drama has served precisely such a guerrilla function, as — more famously — it has done in South Africa. In more changeable contexts, such as Uganda, Singapore, Malaysia, and Nigeria, drama, because it is unpublished, can be subversive to an extent that tests the edges of political tolerance and audience receptivity, its very impermanence allowing it to straddle the boundaries of permissibility.

The 'founding' acts of invasion to which many colonial cultures look back construct a simplistic sense of dualism, the collision of two cultural orders. This overlooks the many other colonizations that network any society, as well as the diasporic penetrations and population drifts that continually reconstitute the cultural amalgam. Canada, South Africa, and Australia, which only a few decades ago articulated themselves in severely bicultural terms, can now only see themselves as multicultural, and this is inevitably reflected not just in their playwriting but also in their theatregoing practices. In countries such as Singapore, the Philippines, and South Africa, which have been subject to waves of colonizations rather than single founding events, cultural stratification has always been obvious, but this has rarely, if ever, been reflected in the composition of theatre audiences. Townships theatre, for example, has been anything but multicultural; it is, rather, a theatre of consolidation seeking for a homogeneity within a movement of resistance.

The alternative theatre movement, often addressing marginalized audiences, emerged in most countries only in the late 1960s, by which time metropolitan audiences were sufficiently large and heterogeneous enough to support them. But the progenitor of the alternative theatre was the Socialist or Unity theatre movement of the 1930s, most famous through its Canadian instances, but in fact promulgated throughout the anglophone world through the drama branches of the Gollancz Left Book Club. Although Unity was stridently left-wing, it was also in effect a coalition theatre offering a platform to many oppressed social groups; the feminist theatre movement, which in most countries would grow into a powerful and discrete entity in the 1970s, had antecedents in the women's groups of Unity, which contained obvious elements of social feminism and which in some cases gained strength during the Second World War when male actors and writers were mostly overseas. This work is little known today because it was generally neither published or reviewed in newspapers.

The idea of alternative theatre itself destabilized monolithic motions of nationhood, and with that authorized versions of 'history'. The Australian bicentennial of 1988 brought a wave of oppositional black writing, including an assertion of suppressed histories of Australia, such as those written by the Noongar playwright **Jack Davis**. The centenary of women's suffrage in New Zealand in 1993 brought a host of feminist revisions of history by playwrights such as **Renee**. For both Davis and Renee, this was the continuation of a dramatic project that had continued for more than a decade. A more extensive deployment of the stage to interrogate historical material has existed in Canada since the 1940s and has taken forms ranging from the annalistic to the reconstitutive amalgam of myth and history such as has more recently found popularity in Caribbean theatre. Indian drama in English, by contrast, has preferred a more linear search for historical 'truth', strangely at odds with Michel De Certeau's insistence on Indian tolerance of polyvalence in historiography.

Hybridity as the bedrock of post-colonial theatre was first theorized by the South African **H. I. E. Dhlomo** in 1936, who acknowledged the impossibility of a recapitulationist retrieval of pre-colonial cultural 'purity' and argued that the past can only exist inasmuch as it is 'grafted' on to the [westernized] present. Dhlomo's belief was little advanced by his own practice, largely because of an unreceptive social environment, and it has been left to contemporary playwrights such as **Derek Walcott** and Wole Soyinka to produce complex and sophisticated dramatizations of the hybrid moment. Heavy filaments of hybridity are central to Soyinka's backhanded tribute to Nigerian independence, *A Dance of the Forests* (1963), where a totemic retrieval of the past is trenchantly satirized, and such elements pervade his work of the 1960s, culminating in his *The Bacchae of Euripides* (1973). But Soyinka's *Bacchae* also shows that the dynamic of hybridity exists not just on the stage but also in the theatre, in the cultural exchange between play and audience. Any production of an 'old-world' classic on a third-world stage brings hybridity into the theatre, as is particularly shown in the frequently documented efforts of white educationalists to bring 'authentic' Shakespeare productions to native peoples. A 1992 Samoan production of *Romeo and Juliet* illustrated the elaborate negotiations necessary to accommodate a play that violates many facets of Samoan protocol and is thus paradigmatic of the moment of hybrid fracture. The testing of discursive authority is obvious in such a situation, but is carried to a confrontational extreme by the Noongar writer **Mudrooroo Narogin** in *The Aboriginal Protesters Confront the Declaration of the Australian Republic on 26 January 2001 with the Production of 'The Commission' by Heiner Müller* (1993), where his central strategy is to 'aboriginalize' Müller's text. But the text thus appropriated is both *by* Germany's best-known postmodernist and *about* Toussaint L'Ouverture, already the subject of **C. L. R. James'** famous play. That Narogin chose to express not direct solidarity with James (and thus the Caribbean/African nexus) but an aboriginalized takeover of European postmodernism problematizes the question of what is properly the 'graft' and what is the 'stock' in hybrid drama, at the same time fulfilling Dhlomo's argument that the past is only energized by tapping into the present.

By a further extension, dramatic hybridity may be observed in the relationship between theatre and its circumjacent society. The very idea of a theatre building, a solid construction with a managed environment of lighting and heating in which a privileged fraction of a population is segregated or quarantined from the rest of society, derives from northern Europe and is diametrically opposed to the performance practices of native peoples throughout the British colonial world. Similarly, the notion that certain areas of behaviour are inherently more dramatic than others rests on European exclusiveness, and as post-colonial drama acknowledges indigenous practice so does the spread of behaviours articulated through performance escalate. The quantity of post-colonial plays about sport reflects a dissolving of the boundaries of drama to merge with more elastic notions of recreation. The post-colonial prison play, prominent in Canada, Australia, New Zealand, and especially South Africa, confronts audiences with sordid realities they have traditionally come to the theatre to ignore. Health is often a more urgent priority than hubris in native drama, and the health play is typical of the new genres that post-coloniality has recognized, found in Western Desert drama in Australia (petrol sniffing), Raun Raun in Papua New Guinea (malnutrition), and Sistren in Jamaica (public health). Significantly, urban manifestations of the health play have been predominantly in women's theatre, where alienation from and by patriarchal tradition has facilitated receptivity to indigenous motifs and 'undramatic' subjects. (See **Feminism**.)

HOWARD McNAUGHTON

DRAMA (Australia)

A number of explanations have been proposed for the stalled, or at best stop-start, development of Australian drama in the twentieth century. Some of those factors have been sociological, such as the 'cultural cringe', which in Australia has conspicuously extended beyond the deference paid by colonial or post-colonial society to its colonizing parent into a sense that deference is due to any culture possessing the distinction of age: major theatrical 'occasions' have characteristically involved imported shows and performers. Some have been geographical — what **Geoffrey Blainey** called 'the tyranny of distance' — as the location of half a dozen urban centres dotted around the fringe of a huge continent ensured the isolation of those intellectual élites that might have provided the impetus and the audiences for a national theatre. And, of course, it is always possible to see the problem as a product of political neglect.

There were other difficulties to be overcome, though, of a more directly theatrical nature. Some kinds of indigenous theatre, some of the time, survived very well: Australian melodrama, in the last two decades of the nineteenth century, modestly adapted the inherited form to admit aspects of local experience that were usually comically quaint and found an enthusiastic audience. The folksy comedies that Bert Bailey adapted from the **Steele Rudd** *On Our Selection* stories played with great success in the early 1900s. In the serious theatre, though, nationalism was a particularly serious business. Although every vision for the indigenous drama paid homage to the notion of a theatre for the people, the avoidance of popular forms and familiar cultural realities could hardly have been more marked.

It is a truth universally acknowledged that an emergent national culture must be in want of images of its own distinctiveness. In Australia those images were initially located in the Outback, and the bush mythology proved problematic as a theatrical subject. **Louis Esson**, with unconscious irony borrowing from Ireland his model for an independent nationalist theatre, epitomizes the difficulty in potent vignettes such as *The Drovers* (1920; premièred 1923) and *Dead Timber* (1911). The problem lay not in defining the experience of the harsh interior, but in its potential for dramatic development; not only were the conventions of the naturalistic proscenium stage inhospitable to the elemental conflicts of flood, fire, and famine that were the natural subjects of that mythology, but the laconic stoicism that was an essential aspect of the bushman-hero made it inconceivable that the emotional meanings of those experiences could be expressed in any way other than reflex understatement.

In the brevity of those tragic instances of the inevitable victory of the land over all human aspiration, and in the uncertainty of focus in plays of urban low-life such as the powerful but sprawling *The Bride of Gospel Place* (1946), Esson reflects the difficulties of adapting received dramatic forms to new areas of experience. His chronicle play *Southern Cross* (1946), which remained unperformed in his lifetime, founders partly because it is too reverential about the Eureka myth, but also because it cries out for the formal liberation that Bertolt Brecht was about to bequeath to all theatrical narratives.

Not all Australian playwrights were preoccupied with cultural definition, of course; writers such as Haddon Chambers and Arthur Adams happily followed in the footsteps of Pinero, and Esson himself, in *The Time Is Not Yet Ripe* (1912), showed a genuine talent for the Shavian blend of thesis-play and comedy of manners. There were distinguished later exceptions, too, such as **Patrick White**'s *The Ham Funeral* (1947; premièred 1961), avant-garde even then, which very clearly asserts from the outset its non-parochialism. But on the whole, until very recently, the construction of myths of national identity in social realist form has remained the major preoccupation of Australian playwrights, and finding the appropriate stages and audience has remained their major problem.

The left-wing New Theatre movement and the range of suburban 'little theatres' were supportive of local products, but the consequent association of Australian plays with amateurism did little to challenge the 'cringe'. **Ray Lawler**'s *Summer of the Seventeenth Doll* (1957) represented a significant breakthrough, both in the immediate popularity it enjoyed in the mainstream theatre and in a travestied film version, and in the symbolic status it rapidly acquired as a kind of national monument. The success of the play was no doubt in part attributable to changes in the cultural environment; increased funding for the arts and a publicly expressed determination to establish a vigorous national theatre made it not only more likely but quite essential that a discovery should be made. But the play's richness and durability also reflect Lawler's resolution of some of those perennial problems. Like the Canadian playwright **David French** in *Leaving Home* (1972), he gives a retrospective frontier mythology an analytical and stageable frame by relocating it. Here the bushman myth comes south to the recognizable suburbs, and the avoidance of self-disclosure that is synonymous with manliness in that value system is juxtaposed with a range of emotional responses represented by the women who live there. The play offers both a critique of that ethos and an affectionate farewell to it.

Plays such as Richard Beynon's *The Shifting Heart* (1960), **Peter Kenna**'s *The Slaughter of St. Teresa's Day* (1972), and **Alan Seymour**'s *The One Day of the Year* (1962) also generated a good deal of power in their realist depictions of images of the culture, but, in general, *Summer of the Seventeenth Doll* left a disappointing bequest. The reassessment of the past is inevitably an important element in dramatizing cultural identity, but in Australian theatre of the middle decades of the twentieth century — as in Australian cinema of the 1970s — the retrospective mood left the contemporary reality looking decidedly undernourished.

Two important elements coincided in the late 1960s to create the revolution that began at the alternative seasons at Jane Street Theatre in Sydney, and especially at the La Mama Theatre and the Pram Factory in Melbourne, and soon came to be known as the 'New Wave' in Australian drama. One factor was the opportunity to work closely with a performance company, which the playwrights of previous decades had mostly lacked; in the case of Melbourne's Australian Performing Group, the collaborative model was underpinned by the radical political commitment that has been characteristic of innovative companies throughout the world and that might have sustained earlier swimmers against the tide, such as the Pioneer Players. The other new factor was the very noisy arrival of the 'ocker'.

The ocker rode in on the back of the breakthroughs in censorship that occurred in Australia and elsewhere in the late 1960s. He was brash, crude, and a violater of all decorums, big in his talk and his drinking, and — by his own graphic but questionable account — an accomplished sexual performer as well. He was mostly young and middle class, and he was, always, self-advertisingly male. His particular attraction for the 'New Wave' theatre lay not only in his uncouthness and comic vigour, but in his complexity as a speaker. For the first time, Australian theatre presented a style of talk that reflected the shifts in conversational register so striking in a culture in which idiom has very little to do with regional variations and a great deal to do with the class to which one belongs, or to which one aspires. Even Kenny Carter, the motor mechanic in **David Williamson**'s *The Removalists* (1972) who defines himself as 'just a beer-swilling slob', makes it clear that he is crude by choice and not by necessity. The affluent graduates of Williamson's *Don's Party* (1973) are even more sophisticated players of the game of verbal affront. But there were other distinguished variants on the theme: **Barry Oakley** and **Alexander Buzo** took the ocker to new heights of self-protective irony, and **John Romeril** in *The Floating World* (1975) dramatized Les Harding's almost successful suppression of the atrocities of war and imprisonment beneath his mask of comic assertiveness; even the octogenarian Monk O'Neill in **Jack Hibberd**'s *A Stretch of the Imagination* (1973) can be seen in the vulgarity and virtuosity of his talk as a very senior affiliate of the ocker tribe.

More recent Australian writing for the stage has attempted to redress the imbalance created by the ocker's peculiar ability to silence other voices, and to retrieve areas of feeling and forms of expression that were largely excluded by the dominant mode of satiric observation and the models of social realism to which it referred. It is virtually axiomatic that the articulation of previously marginalized experience requires the abandonment of those artistic structures that have expressed the perceptions that marginalized them. Certainly in contemporary feminist theatre in Australia, and even more strikingly in the dramatization of Aboriginal experience, the audience is consistently made aware of a radical revision of form. **Jack Davis**, the most widely performed of Australia's Aboriginal playwrights, handles naturalistic domestic interplay very comfortably, but challenges it continually with the perceptions that can only be communicated in verse, music, and dance. His plays formally enact the intersection of different cultures and different ways of knowing.

Patrick White and **Dorothy Hewett** have never had much time for the mainstream conventions, and both writers have focused primarily on female experience and on cultural myths that reflect the dark and irrational underside of social experience. Among the younger playwrights, **Louis Nowra** shows a similar disdain for the exploration of surfaces, and his charting of the human capacity to inflict and suffer cruelty has been very distinctively organized in terms of a series of indelible visual images. Ron Elisha has also pursued some of those larger, presocial subjects, though his frankly philosophical interests place a larger emphasis on talk as the means of analysis; like Nowra's, though, Elisha's kind of conversation is never centred on locally recognizable sliding registers.

David Williamson and **Stephen Sewell**, in very different ways, are the dominant figures in contemporary Australian theatre. Williamson has enjoyed an astonishing popularity, but while he remains concerned with satiric observation and with manipulative strategies in familiar social situations, he is certainly not a playwright who is standing still. The increasing readiness to experiment with episodic structures is one sign of a more obtrusive interest in dramatic form, which has also, in plays such as *Top Silk* (1989) and *Siren* (1990), produced particularly shaped plots. More interesting, though, are Williamson's use of music to broaden the emotional range of his fine and compassionate comedy about death and decay, as in *Travelling North* (1980), and his reference to the wonderful world of Oz in tightening the mythic framework of *Emerald City* (1986). **Michael Gow**'s *Away* (1986) similarly achieves a moving reconciliation with the grimmer facts of life with the help of Shakespearean parallels and Mendelssohn's music. Rather than finding the materials for distinctive cultural emblems wholly within the culture itself, this tactic locates Australianness within a larger story and a wider humanity.

Sewell's Marxism has always insisted on that broader context, and in early plays set outside Australia such as *Traitors* (1983) and *Welcome the Bright World* (1983) there is a historical framework as well to channel the lives of the participants. *The Blind Giant is Dancing* (1983) and *Dreams in an Empty City* (1986) do more than place their Australian actions within an international network of influence; both plays draw on received mythologies, the stories of Faust and Christ respectively, to shape and substantiate their passionate moral concerns. Even in the more intimate world of *Hate* (1989), the archetypal symbolism of the land as maternal principle and the invocation of familial tragedies from Sophocles to Shakespeare give a deeper resonance to the plot.

Almost as soon the 'New Wave' became a cliché, it began to be fashionable to speak of Australian theatre as though it were drowning, not waving. But there has been much to wave about. The preoccupation with language as culturally self-defining at once shaped Australian drama and placed constraints on it; it was, for a while, a rich if narrow vein, and it was almost certainly, in retrospect, a necessary line of interest in a culture preoccupied with establishing its difference. The move to a dramatic mythology on a larger scale and of a more analytical kind has provided some ways in which that difference can be questioned, measured, and redefined. That, too, is probably a necessary stage on the path of post-colonialism, and it might well reflect the passage from nationalist assertiveness or defensiveness to a proud if sceptical maturity.

PETER FITZPATRICK

Futher reading: Peter Fitzpatrick, *After 'The Doll': Australian Drama Since 1955* (1979); Harold Love, ed., *The Australian Stage* (1984); Leslie Rees, *A History of Australian Drama* (1978; rev. 1987).

DRAMA (Canada)

Before the colonization of North America by Europeans, an indigenous drama of great complexity and variety flourished, whether cultivated by the Inuit or by such Amerindians as the Iroquois, the Salish, and the Kwakutl. (See **Aboriginal Literature**, Canada.) Their performance traditions, which can be parallelled in the indigenous traditions of Australia, south-east Asia, Siberia, and the Kalahari region of Africa, relate primarily to initiation ceremonies and to public performances, ritualistic in character, designed to benefit the community. No written texts of this drama exist, and scholars are only now beginning to reconstruct the full character of this indigenous theatre from such artefacts as masks and stage props and from traditional dances and songs; this theatre, however, had no influence on the development in Canada of a dramatic tradition indebted almost entirely to European theatrical models.

The first recorded performance of a play in North America took place on Canada's east coast, at Port Royal, Nova Scotia, on 16 November 1606, when Marc Lescarbot's *Le Théâtre de Neptune en la Nouvelle-France* was performed. A masque, it celebrates French imperial power and lays claim to the 'new world' and the allegiance of its Native peoples. In the course of the seventeenth and eighteenth centuries, Britain challenged France for hegemony in North America and consequently much of the theatrical and dramatic activity of that period (especially in the case of English-language drama) is associated with military garrisons, where the officer class mounted plays drawn usually from Shakespeare, Sheridan, and Goldsmith. Such theatricals were complemented by touring companies, principally from the USA and Britain, which began in the late eighteenth century and dominated the Canadian theatrical scene until the First World War (when travelling costs and the rise of film and radio brought an end to what was essentially a foreign annexation of Canada's stage).

Little English-language drama by Canadians appeared before the middle of the nineteenth century, when a number of poetic closet dramas were published. The main practitioners in this genre were **Charles Heavysege** (*Saul*, 1857, and *Count Filippo*, 1860), **Charles Mair** (*Tecumseh*, 1886), Sarah Anne Curzon (*Laura Secord*, 1887), and **Wilfred Campbell** (*Poetical Tragedies*, 1908). **Northrop Frye**'s trenchant characterization of *Saul* as being 'in the tradition of the Victorian leviathan, the discursive poem combining a Biblical subject with middle-class morality' may be applied to most nineteenth-century Canadian plays in English.

There are, however, a few plays that draw energy from their source in local and national issues. These include *The Female Consistory of Brockville* (1856), by the pseudonymous Caroli Candidus; *Dolorsolatio* (1865), published under the pen-name Sam Scribble, which advocates the confederation of Canada's provinces; and N. F. Davin's *The Fair Grit* (1876) and W. H. Fuller's *H. M. S. Parliament* (1880), both satires on Canadian politics. F. A. Dixon's masque *Canada's Welcome* (1879) celebrates British imperialism in Canada as Lescarbot's masque of 1606 had celebrated French hegemony in New France. If a common theme can be found in such diverse plays as *Tecumseh*, *Laura Secord*, and *Dolorsolatio*, it is an affirmation of the values of the British Empire as opposed to American mobocracy. It is a paradox such that critic B. K. Sandwell, writing in 1911, could condemn the 'annexation' of the Canadian stage by American theatrical interests, while seeking to liberate it by promoting British drama, 'the drama of our people'. The history of theatre and drama in Canada thus resembles that of other post-colonial nations such as India, New Zealand, and Australia in the degree to which it is a record of the imposition of a foreign and imperial culture on a colonized people.

The gradual decolonization of the Canadian stage in the twentieth century was brought about by the rise of film and radio, which financially undercut the foreign touring companies. Radio was especially important. The Canadian Broadcasting Corporation, formed in 1936, became, in effect, Canada's 'National Repertory Theatre of the Air';

between 1939 and 1960 it employed some 1,300 playwrights who created some 8,000 drama broadcasts, including approximately 3,500 original Canadian plays. (See **Broadcasting**, Canada.) Europe's little theatre movement — especially the example of Dublin's Abbey Theatre — helped foster attempts to create an indigenous Canadian theatre. Toronto's Hart House Theatre, a semi-professional company, was founded in 1919 with a pronounced nationalist, cultural agenda; its leading dramatist, Merrill Denison (1893–1975), wrote a body of plays superior to any previously written in Canada. His *The Unheroic North: Four Canadian Plays* (1923), a seminal volume, contains three short plays — good-humoured satires on the mores of rural Canadians — and *Marsh Hay*, a full-length tragedy of great power. The volume's title reflected Denison's scepticism about the viability of a Canadian theatre and his view that Canadian culture was either 'colonial or American'. 'Until the national intentions of Canada are greatly clarified,' he wrote, 'the theatre would at best be an artificial graft.' In his plays and dramatic criticism **Herman Voaden** attempted to clarify the 'natural intentions' of Canada by postulating as its essence a heroic North idealized in its purity and mystical transcendence, a concept he expressed in such plays as *Wilderness: A Play of the North* (1978; premièred 1931), *Earth Song* (1976; premièred 1932), and *Murder Pattern* (1975; premièred 1936).

The Workers' Experimental Theatre movement of the 1930s offered a radically different clarification of Canadian identity by drawing on Marxism, which, because of its emphasis on the political, historic, and economic construction of culture, allowed for a new proletarian art. The best-known play of this movement is the multi-authored *Eight Men Speak* (1976; premièred 1933), about the imprisonment of members of the Canadian Communist Party and the attempted murder of its leader in a federal prison. Like so many Canadian plays — **John Coulter**'s Riel trilogy and **George Ryga**'s *The Ecstasy of Rita Joe* (1970), for example — it is a courtroom or prison play in which national values are interrogated and the audience is conscripted as jury. In *Riel* (1962; premièred 1950), *The Crime of Louis Riel* (1976; premièred 1966), and *The Trial of Louis Riel* (1968; premièred 1967), Coulter presents a revisionist account of the Métis leader who was hanged by the British for treason in 1885.

Robertson Davies' plays may be viewed as the dramatization of a search for cultural roots and as an attempt to 'place' Canada in relation to the UK and the USA. In *Fortune, My Foe* (1949), for example, a young university lecturer in Canada is tempted to immigrate to the USA, but is finally prevented from doing so by the possibility that European culture (represented by a European emigré, a puppet-maker) will leaven Canadian backwardness. The debate in *At My Heart's Core* (1950), set in 1830s Upper Canada, is a variation on the same theme. In the significantly titled *Question Time* (1975), the prime minister of Canada undergoes an internal journey of discovery as he struggles to survive following a plane crash in the Arctic. In the play's Jungian search he discovers a mystical affinity with the Great Bear, the incarnation of the North, seen as the true and essential Canada.

The number of plays dealing with Canada's Native Peoples increased significantly after 1967, the centennial of the founding of the Dominion of Canada. Post-colonial settler societies such as Canada, New Zealand, and Australia attempt to establish their indigeneity — that which makes them 'authentic' — and in doing so often turn to the native Other — whether Maori, Aboriginal, or First Nations peoples. Such plays as **Gwen Pharis Ringwood**'s trilogy *Drum Song* (1982), Ryga's *The Ecstasy of Rita Joe*, **Sharon Pollock**'s *Walsh* (1973), and Linda Griffiths' and **Maria Campbell**'s *The Book of Jessica: A Theatrical Trans-*

formation (1989) identify with Canada's Native Peoples as victim and expose a systematic and institutionalized discrimination.

In his best-known work, the Donnelly trilogy, **James Reaney** also celebrates the victim or underdog, in this case an Irish-Catholic family of nineteenth-century immigrants. Perhaps the most interesting feature of the trilogy is its regional character; from the circumstances of local (Ontario) history Reaney attempts to create a theatre that is radically opposed to Ontario's Stratford Festival and Shaw Festival, whose mandate has been to celebrate canonical figures of the European theatre. The underdog is also the subject of **John Herbert**'s *Fortune and Men's Eyes* (1967), a fine, brutal play about homosexuality and prison life that makes Australian Jim McNeil's play on the same theme, *How Does Your Garden Grow* (1974), seem sentimental.

David French first gained attention with his full-length play *Leaving Home* (1972), which dramatizes the conflict of a father and son and pits the father's Newfoundland against central Canada (Ontario) and supposed older heroic values against urban alienation represented by the city (Toronto). (Critics have found useful comparisons with Australian **Ray Lawler**'s *Summer of the Seventeenth Doll*, 1957.) In the light of three further plays that deal with the same Mercer family — *Of the Fields, Lately* (1973), *Salt-Water Moon* (1985), and *1949* (1989) — French's tetralogy may be seen not only as a family history but as a historical saga about the growth of nationhood (*1949* is about the entry of Newfoundland, then a British colony, into Canada). If the subtext of the tetralogy is covertly political, the ideological dimensions of French's classic comedy *Jitters* (1980) is overt — as its group of actors rehearses a Canadian play, French pokes fun at the 'colonial cringe' that afflicts so many post-colonial literatures.

Michael Cook also takes Newfoundland as subject-matter, notably in *Colour the Flesh the Colour of Dust* (1972), *The Head, Guts and Sound Bone Dance* (1974), and *Jacob's Wake* (1975). But his vision is darker than French's, as his plays suggest that the old, primitive (and heroic) ways of Newfoundland have passed or have been corrupted.

George Walker's early plays — *The Prince of Naples* (1972), *Beyond Mozambique* (1975), and *Zastrozzi* (1977), for example — offered in their exoticism a total contrast to the realism and rural nostalgia that pervaded so many Canadian plays in the 1970s and especially in such collectively written plays as *1837: The Farmers' Revolt* (1975), *The Farm Show* (1976), and *Paper Wheat* (1987). (The prevalence of docudrama and an undue reliance on the historical would seem to be characteristics differentiating Canadian drama in English from the drama in English of other post-colonial nations.) Walker's plays are irreverent and loosely structured, drawing their inspiration from B-grade movies, the electronic media, surrealism, and from the Theatre of the Absurd. In the 1980s Walker's theme seemed to become more Canadian as he located his plays in Toronto's east end. But, in fact, his 'East End' plays — *Criminals in Love* (1984), *Better Living* (1988), *Beautiful City* (1988), and *Love and Anger* (1990) — merely provide a more accessible locale (for audiences) that enables Walker to parade the same paranoias that possess the flamboyant characters of his early plays. Walker is a post-colonial writer, not a nationalist writer.

Montreal is **David Fennario**'s chosen locale. His bilingual *Balconville* (1980) — about one third of the dialogue is in French, the rest in English — exposes the exploitation of the poor in a Montreal suburb. The Marxist dimensions of the play are complemented by a Brechtian alienation device when the final lines of the play are addressed directly to the audience: 'Qu'est-ce qu'on va faire?' 'What are we going to do?' A similar, though non-Marxist, political commitment can be found in the plays of **Ken Mitchell**: *The Medicine Line* (1976), which treats the same historical material as Sharon Pollock's *Walsh*; *Davin: The Politician* (1979); and *Gone the Burning Sun* (1985), a re-creation of the life and times of Canadian Norman Bethune, a left-wing medical doctor who worked in Spain and China in the 1930s and 1940s. John Murrell is also interested in historical figures and historical subject-matter, but without a strong ideological bent. His best-known play, *Memoir* (1978), which has been translated into more than twenty languages, is a beautifully crafted two-hander about the last months in the life of the actress Sarah Bernhardt. The most Canadian of Murrell's plays is *Waiting for the Parade* (1980), a nostalgic look at the lives of five Canadian women who remember their loved ones overseas during the Second World War.

Until the 1970s, Canada had defined itself largely in terms of its British colonial traditions and, less so, in terms of its francophone legacy. But gradually the concept of biculturalism (with its suggestion of centuries-old, imperialistic baggage) gave way to an official policy of **multiculturalism** by which, paradoxically, nationhood and Canadianness are defined largely in terms of the principle that Canada has no 'official culture'. Critic **Frank Davey** argues that Canada is a post-nationalist state that lacks a nationalist discourse. Certainly the concerns of contemporary Canadian drama seem less related to the nationalist debate of the 1960s and 1970s than to such ideological issues as feminism, regionalism, the gay and lesbian agenda, and Native peoples' claims.

Important feminist dramatists include Sharon Pollock (*Blood Relations*, 1981), **Carol Bolt** (*Red Emma: Queen of the Anarchists*, 1974), Erika Ritter (*Automatic Pilot*, 1980), **Betty Lambert** (*Jennie's Story*, 1982), Wendy Lill (*The Fighting Days*, 1985), Ann-Marie MacDonald (*Goodnight Desdemona/Good Morning Juliet*, 1990), and **Judith Thompson** (*White Biting Dog*, 1984; *I Am Yours*, 1987). The key outlet for gay and lesbian drama in Canada is Sky Gilbert's Buddies in Bad Times company of Toronto. Although there was a significant number of Native Canadian writers prior to the 1980s, there had not been a significant dramatist. But **Tomson Highway**'s *The Rez Sisters* (1988) and *Dry Lips Oughta Move to Kapuskasing* (1990) represent a substantial achievement. In these plays he turns from Eurocentric (and Christian) theatrical models to write plays based on Native culture and mythology that complement his own non-Aristotelian dramatic form.

Children's drama and theatre in Canada have developed enormously in the 1970s and 1980s — some fifty professional theatres direct much of their work to this area; dramatists who have written for young audiences include James Reaney, Betty Lambert, Carol Bolt, Rex Deverell, and Tom Walmsley.

The study of Canadian drama and theatre is slowly winning a place in the curriculum of most Canadian universities, and it is now commonplace to find post-graduate students writing MA and Ph.D. theses in this area. A number of journals cater to the field, and anthologies document the rich and varied offerings of twentieth-century Canadian drama. (See **Criticism**, Canada, and **Anthologies**, Canada.)

EUGENE BENSON

Further reading: Anton Wagner, ed., *Contemporary Canadian Theatre* (1985); Eugene Benson and L. W. Conolly, *English-Canadian Theatre* (1987); Alan Filewod, *Collective Encounters: Documentary Theatre in English Canada* (1987); Eugene Benson and L. W. Conolly, eds, *The Oxford Companion to Canadian Theatre* (1989).

DRAMA (The Caribbean)

The governing factor in the development and nature of drama in the Caribbean is that it is created and performed by people who within recent history were all arrivants to that part of the world. This, and the assumed dominance of European cultural forms/norms within these artificially created societies, has stamped on Caribbean drama in English certain fundamental characteristics.

Historically, written drama has been separate from the concerns, images, and forms of expression of the black peoples who form the majority of the population in the Caribbean. Given that the people whom the Europeans met there and destroyed, or brought and tried to destroy, came from largely oral cultures, it follows that the first plays written about the Caribbean were by Europeans. While the record of theatre activity starts quite early — Jamaica had a public theatre as early as 1682; plays have been performed in Barbados since 1729; Antigua and St Lucia built theatres in 1788 and 1832 respectively — the drama presented was for what critic Richardson Wright describes as 'the very thin upper crust' of society. As with the practice of absentee ownership of sugar plantations, the writers may not necessarily have even visited the Caribbean, but often chose its landscape or some romanticized feature of local life to suit their purposes. Thus, the 'West Indian' of Richard Cumberland's play *The West Indian* (1771) is a rich planter on a visit to London, England, where the action is set. *Inkle and Yarico* (1787), by George Colman the Younger, is set in Barbados and is based on the apparently true story of an Indian girl who was betrayed and sold into slavery by her British lover. That Colman contrives a comedy of this story indicates sufficiently the European perspective on the lives of native peoples.

Of the dramas written in Trinidad during the nineteenth century, three satires are regarded as noteworthy by theatre historian **Errol Hill**: 'Martial Law' by Edward L. Joseph, a Scotsman resident in Trinidad, and two other short anti-British pieces published anonymously in local newspapers, *Proverbe Creole: ca qui pas bon pour z'eis pas bon pour canard* ('Creole Proverb: What's Good for the Goose is Good for the Gander', 1847) and *The Old Regime vs. The New, or Colonial Prejudice* (1881). The latter was a burlesque on certain prominent public officials. However, these local dramas were the exception since British and American touring companies provided most of the fare as late as the 1920s.

For the most part, early locally written dramas were testimonies to the beneficence of colonialism. *Carmelita, the Belle of San Jose* was written by Osborn Lewis Inniss in 1897 to celebrate the centenary of the British capture of Trinidad from the Spanish. *San Gloria* (1920), by **Tom Redcam** (T. H. MacDermot), Jamaica's Poet Laureate, muses on Columbus' sojourn in Jamaica and is unabashedly Shakespearean in style.

The lives of black Caribbean people did not enter written drama seriously until the wave of race, class, and national consciousness swept the region in the 1930s. In August 1930, following his return from the USA, Marcus Garvey began a series of pageants mounted at Edelweiss Park, Jamaica, that celebrated the achievements of the African race. Entitled 'The Coronation of an African King', 'Roaming Jamaicans', and 'Slavery: From Hut to Mansion', these performances drew Jamaicans to the park by the thousands.

While no script of the Garvey dramas seems to exist, the most revolutionary literary treatment of the African in the Caribbean was **C. L. R. James'** *Toussaint L'ouverture* (published as *The Black Jacobins* in *A Time and A Season: Eight Caribbean Plays*, 1976, edited by Errol Hill). Trinidad-born James, an intellectual, writer, political activist, and sportsman, attracted sufficient attention to have his play produced in 1936 at the Westminster Theatre, London, England, with Paul Robeson in the title role. The play celebrates the Haitian people's triumphs over the world powers of the day — Spain, England, and Bonaparte's France — and the proclamation of Haitian Independence in 1804.

Not only does James' play boldly thrust the African centre-stage, it insists he bring along his cultural baggage. The rhythms and practices of Haitian Vodun religion inspire rebellion and serve as a barometer of popular sentiment. Retracing the middle passage, the play's second production was in Nigeria in 1967 and its third in Jamaica in 1975. *Toussaint L'ouverture* also anticipates the anti-colonial outburst that ignited the Caribbean the following year. The social ferment of the 1930s, the fact that the population throughout the Caribbean was prepared to take action against economic and race discrimination and did so, the simmering discontent caused by the fact that a century after Emancipation there had been little discernible change for black people, and deteriorating living conditions aggravated by the Depression brought the demands of the masses and the weapons of the authorities to the front line in 1937 and 1938. In Jamaica, Frank Hill's 'Upheaval', produced in 1939, was written in direct response to these events. In Trinidad, where theatre was never regarded as a medium of mass expression, popular sentiment was channelled, as it had always been, through the vibrant, irrepressible ballads of the calypso. One dramatic text, **Freddie Kissoon**'s 'God and Uriah Butler', about one of the most fiery and powerful labour leaders of the period, was not written until 1967, and then only under commission.

In the decade following these political changes in the Caribbean, a number of drama groups were formed, from which the first wave of black West Indian theatre talents emerged. These groups included the Little Theatre Movement (Jamaica, 1941), the Whitehall Players (Trinidad, 1946), the Little Carib Theatre (Trinidad, 1948), the Georgetown Dramatic Group (Guyana, 1948), and the St Lucia Arts Guild (1950). The playwrights/directors of these groups and those responsible for the foundations of Caribbean theatre were Trinidad's Errol Hill, **Errol John**, and **Douglas Archibald**, the St Lucian twins **Derek Walcott** and **Roderick Walcott**, and Jamaica's **Louise Bennett** and Sam Hilary, among others.

Evident in the work of these playwrights is the struggle and affirmation of a new identity. It was neither possible nor desirable following the Second World War for Britain to retain colonies in the Caribbean. Adult suffrage, the growth of nationalist parties, the founding of the regional University of the West Indies, and the movement towards a political Federation (1958–62) brought the promises and problems of being West Indian to the stage. Derek Walcott (Nobel Laureate, 1992), even then the region's leading poet/playwright, was commissioned to write *Drums and Colours* (published in *Caribbean Quarterly* 1 and 2, 1961), a historical drama of West Indian struggle and achievement, to celebrate the opening of the Federal Parliament in April 1958. In Jamaica, the strong colonial legacy and stronger native performance traditions had been shaping since the 1940s the famous Jamaica Pantomime, a theatrical event as expressive of Jamaican identity as its music.

The finest work of the 1950s confronted the question of a Caribbean identity. In *Ti-Jean and His Brothers* (in *Dream on Monkey Mountain and Other Plays*, 1970) Walcott shows how the achievement of a Caribbean civilization is won with weapons of native wit, creativity, and courage. Ephraim, in Errol John's *Moon on a Rainbow Shawl* (1958), chooses, like many writers of the period (including John), to escape from the cramped, stifling conditions of working-class Caribbean society. While the play is frankly realist in its portrayal of the squalor and denial of possibilities inherent in slum life, his very vividness, vibrancy, and achievement have made it a work as affirmative of the Caribbean spirit as *Ti-Jean and His Brothers*. The 1957 winner of the London *Observer*'s prize for best new play, *Moon on a Rainbow Shawl* is one of the most acclaimed plays in the Caribbean repertoire.

From the 1960s, following political independence, to the 1970s, the work of Derek Walcott and his Trinidad Theatre Workshop commanded centre-stage. *Dream on Monkey Mountain* (premièred 1967), *The Joker of Seville* (1978; premièred 1974), *Remembrance* (premièred 1977), and *Pantomime* (premièred 1978) — the latter two plays published in *Remembrance and Pantomime* (1980) — are some of the outstanding Walcott productions. In his erudition, mastery of western literary forms, and hybrid aesthetics, Walcott is akin to Nigeria's **Wole Soyinka**.

The unsolved issues of Caribbean existence (race/povery/place), disturbed in the late 1960s by the American Black Power Movement, produced a decade of plays on altered forms, images, and states of consciousness. **Michael Gilkes'** *Couvade* (1974), 'a dream-play of Guyana', draws on Amerindian ritual in presenting the need to reach, and the impossibility of reaching, beyond history and beyond race into myth. Walcott's partly expressionistic *Dream on Monkey Mountain* offers perhaps resignation rather than resolution to the question of the black man's arrival at total self-acceptance. History and ritual were also the vehicle for the region's boldest playwright, Jamaica's **Dennis Scott**. His *An Echo in the Bone* (1985) painfully re-enacts the traumatization of Africans in the 'new world'. This story of the race is interfused through possession ritual with that of a family bereft of its head and is resolved only in the sacrifice of blood. **Trevor Rhone**, Jamaica's other major playwright, chooses the storytelling form to reflect in *Old Story Time* (1981) on stereotyping by colour. The work of **Kendel Hippolyte** (St Lucia), David Edgecombe (Montserrat), Alwyn Bully (Dominica), and Dobrene O'Marde (Antigua) to varying degrees questioned political arrangements in their territories during the 1970s.

If Caribbean drama of the 1970s was dominated by themes of race and politics, these were undercurrents in the 1980s when social issues gained prominence. *The Ritual or Friday Morning First Period* (1985) by Zeno Obi Constance of Trinidad deals with the causes of pregnancy among schoolgirls. Unwanted pregnancy and male/female relationships are also the subject of 'Belly Woman Bangarang' (premièred 1978), by the Jamaican women's group Sistren Theatre Collective. The work of this group focuses on issues such as domestic violence, sexual harassment, and the exploitation of women's labour. It has played a particularly important role in that, as the first professional theatre group from the English-speaking Caribbean, it has worked in the Spanish and Dutch-speaking islands.

At the same time, the quest to find a form reflective of the Caribbean experience leads much of the significant contemporary writing away from the obviously realistic. It is clear that written drama in the Caribbean has a rich and powerful reserve of oral traditions on which to draw, and some of the most characteristically Caribbean work has been based on these traditions. Aligned with Errol Hill's thesis, as developed in his *The Trinidad Carnival: Mandate for a National Theatre* (1972), on the use of Carnival, there exists a body of plays making use of Carnival as material or vehicle. *Devil Mas* by Lennox Brown (in *Kuntu Drama*, 1974, edited by Paul Carter Harrison), *Maskarade* (1979) by **Sylvia Wynter** (in the Jamaica Publishing House's *West Indian Plays for Schools, Vol. II*, 1979, edited by Jeanne Wilson), and *The Tramping Man* (1976) by **Ian McDonald** are all directly related to the festival.

Other folk traditions that appear in the drama of the region include stickfighting (as in Errol Hill's *Man Better Man*, 1964), St Lucia's Flower Festival (as in Roderick Walcott's *Banjo Man*, 1976), religious ritual (as in Edgar White's 'Nine Night', premièred 1983), and calypso (as in Rawle Gibbons' calypso trilogy — 'Sing de Chorus', premièred 1991, 'Ah Wanna Fall', premièred 1992, and 'Ten to One', premièred 1993).

The historical transplanting of the majority of the peoples who inhabit the region, traditional patterns of migration, and the overshadowing fact/phantom of the USA make the Caribbean a theatre of place and placelessness, assertion and dependence, starkness and fantasy. It is a theatre that has generated a drama of hope, a drama in which past and present travails are transcended and transformed into a new region of possibilities.

RAWLE GIBBONS

Further reading: R. Wright, *Revels in Jamaica* (1937); E. Hill, 'The emergence of a national drama in the West Indies', *Caribbean Quarterly* 4 (1972); E. Hill, *The Jamaican Stage, 1655–1900: Profile of a Colonial Theatre* (1992).

DRAMA (East Africa)

East African drama in the last twenty-five years has developed out of the historical and political experiences of the three countries of the region — Kenya, Uganda, and Tanzania. The playwrights have shown great concern for the human relations that have developed among their fellow citizens in the post-independence era. Many plays are scathing attacks on the East African societies for their tendency towards the erosion of traditional cultural values, which encouraged unity and concern for one's fellows.

East African playwrights use drama to propagate political ideas and to influence social change. This explains the predominance of serious political plays and the almost total absence of pure comedies or farces. The theatrical techniques are varied and include influences from the socialist realist theatre, Theatre of the Absurd, and satirical drama. Playwrights also tap African oral traditions.

Ngugi wa Thiong'o's and Micere Mugo's *The Trial of Dedan Kimathi* (1976) falls within the socialist realist theatre tradition. It was written with the aim of educating the Kenyan masses about the discrepancies among their contributions to the country's struggle for political independence. The dramatists used myths and facts surrounding Kimathi, the renowned Mau Mau freedom fighter, to link the war against colonial powers with what they view as an inevitable struggle against neo-colonial forces. Ngugi staged rehearsals of the play for FESTAC (Black Arts Festival), held in Nigeria in 1977, to reach various mass audiences by having the performances in non-conventional theatres in the slums of Nairobi. The playwrights later had the play translated into Kiswahili in order to reach a larger audience.

Kenya's second FESTAC entry, *Betrayal in the City* (1976), by **Francis Imbuga**, the nation's leading playwright, is another example of serious political drama. It dramatizes the disillusionment with independence of the masses and committed intellectuals. Imbuga further develops the theme of disillusionment in the satirical *Man of Kafira* (1984), which attacks the devaluation of human life that East African creative writers see as characterizing their post-independence political culture.

A relatively new subject in East African drama that is steadily gaining prominence concerns the place of women in society. Isaac Waweru's 'The End of the Road' (premièred 1982) and Imbuga's *Aminata* (1988) represent two opposite positions taken in relation to women in contemporary East Africa — the former opposes women's leadership while the latter supports women's progress. 'The End of the Road' uses a popular Kenyan myth about a woman ruler, Wangu wa Makeri, whose reign is said to have coincided with the chaotic end of matriarchy and the beginning of patrilineal rule among the Gikuyu of Kenya. In *Aminata* Imbuga presents a case for the elimination of those traditional patriarchal attitudes that have hindered women's progress and development.

Ugandan drama falls within two categories. Early works criticize the cultural alienation of Ugandans resulting from the experience of colonial domination and address post-independence *malaise*. The later drama is an outcry against the inhumanity experienced by Ugandans during and immediately after the period of military dictatorship between 1971 and 1979.

Robert Serumaga's drama falls within the first category. In *The Elephants* (1971) he adopts techniques of the Theatre of the Absurd to dramatize the abnormal human relations that have developed in independent Africa. Serumaga criticizes the social and economic dwarfing of the common individual by the powerful and rich. He sees a distortion of the role of African countries as motherlands of their people; Serumaga represents African countries devouring their citizens instead of protecting them. In *Manjangwa* (1974) he criticizes the sterility of the urban life that Africa is adopting in place of the traditional mores. Here, the playwright uses myth, a prevailing technique in East African drama.

In *The Floods* (1980), **John Ruganda**, Uganda's leading playwright, uses symbolism to comment on the grotesque human waste experienced in Uganda during the period of military dictatorship. Like Serumaga in *Majangwa*, Ruganda taps the creative potential of African myth. Ugandan playwrights' response to the post-military dictatorship period is represented by Lubwa P'Chong's *The Minister's Wife* (1983), in which the wife, Pearl Adnagu (Pearl Uganda), is a symbolic representation of Uganda. Her name is a play on Uganda's pet name, 'the Pearl of Africa', associated with the country's long-gone prosperous days. P'Chong uses irony to criticize Uganda during and immediately after the deposition of the military dictator in 1979, a period seen as one of chaos and total anarchy.

Drama from Tanzania is predominantly in Kiswahili. Following the socialist political orientation of Tanzania, Tanzanian playwrights have tried to bridge the gap between the educated élite and the masses. Serious playwrights such as **Ebrahim Hussein**, Penina Muhando, and Emmanuel Mbogo write in Kiswahili, which, unlike English, is understood by the majority. The only serious play that has been translated into English is Hussein's *Kinjeketile* (published in Kiswahili in 1969 and in English in 1970); it is based on Tanzania's resistance (popularly known as the 'Maji Maji Rebellion') against the Germans at the turn of the twentieth century. Mukotani Rugyendo's *The Contest*, in *The Barbed Wire and Other Plays* (1977), is a creative expression of the ideals of Tanzania's socialism. It upholds unity among human beings under socialism and condemns the selfishness inherent in capitalist systems.

The development of drama in East Africa has lagged behind that of prose. The publication of plays is difficult since the few publishing firms in the region are often reluctant to invest in the publication of plays whose readership is largely limited to schools. The future of drama in this region will depend on the commitment of playwrights, directors, and actors to present plays in terms of performance rather than in terms of publication.

CIARUNJI CHESAINA SWINIMER

Further reading: A. Gurr and A. Calder, eds, *Writers in East Africa* (1974); J. C. Chesaina (Swinimer), 'Who is on trial in *The Trial of Dedan Kimathi?*: a critical essay on Ngugi wa Thiong'o and Micere Githae Mugo's *The Trial of Dedan Kimathi*', *Busara* 2 (1976); G.D. Killam, ed., *The Writing of East and Central Africa* (1984).

DRAMA (Hong Kong)

Hong Kong has not produced any significant dramatists writing in English. Since the 1970s, in spite of the continued activities of English-speaking amateur and semi-professional drama companies, the vast majority of the population, including those who are bilingual, has favoured drama performed in Cantonese. Plays in English ranging from those by Shakespeare to those of Eugene O'Neill, Arthur Miller, Joe Orton, and Tom Stoppard, as well as those by such Europeans as Henrik Ibsen and Bertolt Brecht, for example, have been translated for performance in the Cantonese dialect.

In the 1950s, 1960s, and 1970s an amateur troupe, The Wah Yan Dramatic Society, led by Father Terence Sheridan, a Jesuit priest, made traditional Cantonese opera — originating in southern China and dealing generally with legends, myths, and old stories of court life — accessible to younger bilingual and English-speaking audiences. The troupe adapted well-known operas, using English lyrics, anachronisms, and topical allusions, for entertainment purposes. One such adaptation, 'A Lizard is No Dragon', based loosely on the structure of traditional Cantonese operas, enjoys an occasional revival.

Two expatriate Hong Kong University teachers, Rodney Davy and Piers Gray, both long-time residents of Hong Kong, have written for the local semi-professional theatre. Davy's 'Quire's Complaint' (premièrèd 1982) was an effort at baroque black comedy; Gray wrote, and in 1990 staged, adaptations of Anton Chekhov's *The Bear* and *The Proposal*. No attempt was made to adapt for a 'local' audience.

Original plays in standard Chinese or vernacular Cantonese, written and produced locally, are rarely translated. For example, a Chinese play by Leung Ping Kwan, itself an adaptation of a 1943 Chinese story by Eileen Chang (the title of which means 'Jasmin Tea'), was never published in its original form. It was translated into English as *Jasmin* by Jane Lai, not for performance but as a 'representative' work to be included in the *Renditions* special issue on Hong Kong literature (29 and 30, 1988). *Jasmin* is interesting for the light it throws on Hong Kong culture and mores.

MIMI CHAN

DRAMA (India)

Although the first theatre offering English-language drama in India was built in Bombay in 1776, Indian drama in English has never achieved the same stature as Indian fiction and poetry in English. As in other colonies, such as Canada, the Indian theatrical scene was dominated by foreign companies touring plays drawn mainly from Britain. Notable among the few examples of Indian plays written in English in the nineteenth century are *The First Parsi Baronet* (1866), by C. S. Nazir, probably the earliest Indian English play in verse, and *Is This Civilization?* (1871) by M. M. Dutt.

K. R. S. Iyengar, in his essay 'Drama in Modern India' (in *Drama in Modern India and the Writer's Responsibility in a Rapidly Changing World*, 1961, which he edited), points out that theatre implies not only a building but a cultivated audience. The production of Indian drama in English, however, continues to reveal an abyss between the producer and playwright and the audience. Indo-English drama, in the main, is a purely literary activity divorced from the realities of the theatre. While some Indian plays in English have been staged in the UK and the USA and have received laudatory notices, Indian playwrights in general seem to neglect conditioning their writing to meet the demands of a theatrical audience. Urban areas in India have responded well to experiments in local language drama, but theatre in English gets little ready response.

The Bengali plays of bilingual playwright **Rabindranath Tagore** are produced in Indian theatres; however, he intended the published English translations of these verse plays for a reading audience only, although critics are generally agreed that the power of the Bengali originals is lost in translation. At the turn of the century **Sri Aurobindo** wrote verse plays of remarkable sophistication — *Perseus the Deliverer* (1907) and *Rodogune* (1958), for example — but he was a literary dramatist largely uninterested in drama as theatre. **Harindranath Chattopadhyaya**, a prolific dramatist in English, wrote a number of plays on social themes (published in his *Five Plays*, 1937). *Siddhartha, the Man of Peace* (1956) is the best of a group of plays he devoted to dramatizing the lives of Indian saints. **T. P. Kailasam** was unable to get his plays that dealt with Indian myths produced; these plays include *The Burden* (1933), *Fulfilment* (1933), *The Purpose* (1944), *Karna: The Brahmin's Curse* (1946), and *Keechaka* (1949), the latter four based on episodes from the *Mahabharata*. **Sarabhai Bharati** wrote the verse play *The Well of the People* (1943) — about an old woman who builds a well for the 'untouchables' of her village — without any practical experience of writing for the theatre. An altogether different case is that of **Gieve Patel**, a dramatist whose plays have been staged, but not published. His remarkable 'Princes' (premièred 1970) depicts with great dynamism the disintegration of a Parsi middle-class family. Even the English dialogue is conditioned to reflect an Indian Parsi environment, and the claustrophobic climate of family life among Parsis is re-created with remarkable success, as it is in his later plays 'Savaksa' (premièred 1982) and *Mister Behram* (1988).

Shree Devi's *The Purple-Braided People* (1970) — an eight-scene tragedy depicting the decline and fall of India's aristocracy after independence — is a superbly stageworthy play, but there is no evidence that it has been produced. Although Devi calls it a 'poem-play', *The Purple-Braided People* is dramatic in character, with brilliant and witty dialogue. Other exceptional Indian plays in English are **Gurcharan Das'** *Larins Sahib* (1970) and Dilip Hiro's *To Anchor a Cloud* (1972) — both historical plays — and **Manohar Malgonkar**'s *Line of Mars* (1978), which presents an acceptable idiomatic *via media* between Indian expressive speech habit and Standard English.

Confrontation of cultures is apparent in *Larins Sahib*, which deals with the life of Henry Lawrence during the period 1846–7, following the death of the Maharajah Ranjit Singh and the accession to the throne of his weakling son, Maharajah Dalip Singh. Sent as British Resident of Lahore by the East India Company, Lawrence succeeded in placating the Punjab with his sympathetic attitude to Indian patriotic elements. He became a legend (Laurins Sahib) described by commoners as 'Angrez Badshah'. In *Larins Sahib*, the Queen Mother, valuing Lawrence's friendship, gives him the Kohinoor diamond. These events initiate Lawrence's transformation from a good officer to one ruined by hubris. At the play's close, Lawrence's enemies bring about his downfall and disgrace. The episodes of *Laurins Sahib* are well-knit and dynamic and convey a vivid picture of high politics in nineteenth-century India.

Dilip Hiro's romantic *To Anchor a Cloud* dramatizes events in the life of Shah Jahan, the ruler of the Mogul empire between 1627 and 1658 who built the Taj Mahal as a mausoleum for his favourite wife Mumtaz Mahal. In Hiro's treatment Jahan is a dreamer who remains unaware of how skilfully his beautiful wife had worked to make him emperor.

While astrology and palmistry are referred to in the plays of Devi and Hiro, these belief systems occupy a central role in Malgonkar's two-act *Line of Mars*. Because Nanasaheb is born under the evil star of Mars, he is destined for defeat in battle; this awareness of the star, of his 'line of Mars', shapes Nanasaheb's actions. The art of Malgonkar, both in handling language and manoeuvring episodes, objectifies Nanasaheb's doom and makes it appear inevitable.

Asif Currimbhoy is a prolific playwright with some thirty plays to his credit. His work often responds to topical events such as India's annexation of the Portuguese colony of Goa (*Goa*, 1966), the Dalai Lama's escape from Tibet ('Om Mane Padme Hum!', 'Hail to the Jewel in the Lotus!', 1972), and the Bangladesh/Pakistan War (*Sonar Bangla*, 1972). East-west relations are the subject of *The Tourist Mecca* (1961) — about an Indian gigolo who serves foreign tourists — and *Darjeeling Tea?* (1971) — concerning English tea planters in India at the time of Independence.

Better known as a poet, **Nissim Ezekiel** has written a number of plays, some published in *Three Plays* (1969). The three-act satirical comedy *Nalini* exposes the superficiality and mediocrity of two advertising executives fantasizing about the beauty of the women they seek to seduce. Nalini, a painter and their client, proves tougher and more insightful than her fantasized image as she exposes the lack of values in the executives' westernized life-style. In *Marriage Poem* the husband flirts with another woman while making a show of affection for his wife. The play ends with husband and wife making love, the wife still unaware of her husband's infidelity. Both plays are marred by nudity on stage. The one-act farce *The Sleepwalkers* is a satire on American-Indian relations in which the satire embraces both Americans and Indians. While *Three Plays* presents a limited view of Indian bourgeois life, the plays show some experimentation with technique, but little experimentation with language. *Don't Call It Suicide* (1989) is a two-act tragedy that has not been staged.

Pritish Nandy's verse play *Rites for a Plebeian Statue* (1969) celebrates mystical love in its modern recasting of Indian myths. Folk elements are exploited in **Girish Karnad**'s *Hayavadana* (1971; English version, 1975), which draws on a Sanskrit tale in which the heads and bodies of two friends are intertwined. More stageworthy is Karnad's historical play *Tughlaq* (1972), about the life of the fourteenth-century emperor Tughlaq. Both plays have been translated from Kannada by Karnad.

Pratap Sharma has written two controversial plays: *A Touch of Brightness* (1968), about Bombay's red-light district and how its inhabitants survive in inhuman conditions, and *The Professor Has a Warcry* (1970), in which the protagonist Virendra discovers that he is a child of rape. Garish episodes in both plays make them unpalatable for Indians, but they had long runs abroad. The action of Husenali Chagla's *The Director-General* (1968) takes place in an industrial setting and deals with mismanagement and poor production; the previously absent owner returns and sets things right. Satya Dev Jaggi's two one-act plays, *The Point of Light* (1967) and *End of Hunger* (1967), explore the nature of romantic love. *The Point of Light* examines the psychological nature of a teacher/artist whose wife attempts to save their marriage. In *End of Hunger* the flirtatious protagonist Surinder causes the suicide of a woman he abandons when he marries another; he learns nothing from the tragedy. Dina Mehta's three-act play *The Myth-Makers* (1969) deals with both the contemporary fanaticism surrounding language differences in India and the exploitation of those differences by unscrupulous politicians. **Murli Das Melwani**'s three-act *Deep Roots* (1970) has as its theme the paradigms of love and marriage in India; marriage entered into on the basis of mutual love is treated as a revolutionary concept. Rajinder Paul's *Ashes Above the Fire* (1970) treats the theme of love in four self-contained episodes. In the preface to the play, Paul writes, 'To offer love is to offer something of a suicide of some part of yourself, and to deny love to another person is to murder some part of the partner.' **Shiv K. Kumar**'s *The Last Wedding Anniversary* (1975) depicts the disintegration of a marriage, hastened by the arrival of a former lover. Incompatibilities are skilfully suggested through oblique dialogue.

The absence in the 1980s of new major Indian dramatists writing in English is indicative of the fact that while there is a vibrant theatre in the indigenous languages of India, there is little professional activity in English-language theatre. A flourishing theatrical and dramatic tradition is synonymous with performance; lacking close contact with the practical aspects of theatrical performance, Indian dramatists writing in English face a less optimistic future than their colleagues writing poetry and fiction in English.

SHANKAR MOKASHI-PUNEKAR

Further reading: M. K. Naik and S. Mokashi-Punekar, eds, *Perspectives on Indian Drama in English* (1977); K. R. S. Iyengar, *Indian Writing in English* (1984); S. Krishna Bhatta, *Indian English Drama: A Critical Study* (1987).

DRAMA (Malaysia)

The vagaries of the short history of indigenous English-language drama in Malaysia are linked to the archetypal politics of language and culture in a post-colonial society. Upon gaining independence from the British in 1957, Malay (or Bahasa Malaysia) became the official language, and English was abruptly relegated to a secondary position. In actual practice, however, English continued to be the most powerful economic and cultural medium, particularly in the urban areas. It was an optimistic political and linguistic atmosphere that precipitated the emergence of a spate of original English plays in the 1960s. Staged mostly in the capital city of Kuala Lumpur by young nationalist-minded and university-educated middle-class Malaysians, these plays were aimed at challenging the predominantly colonial theatre culture of metropolitan Malaysia. All of these western-educated dramatists were amateurs, and what distinguishes them, then and now, from playwrights working in Malay, Mandarin, and Tamil, is their multi-ethnic composition.

One of the earliest steps toward decolonization involved the take-over in 1967 of the Malaysian Arts Theatre Group (MATG), the most influential of the British-expatriate controlled drama groups in the country. Leading the nationalist *coup* was playwright-director and broadcaster Syed Alwi, who replaced the ubiquitous Shakespeare and G. B. Shaw of the MATG stage with original local plays in English, both his own and those written by K. Das and Patrick Yeoh. No major or resonating themes were generated by the new MATG group, although Syed's best play in English, *Going North* (1968), evoked a magical existentialist vision of the politically turbulent 1950s. At about the same time, Edward Dorall inspired his students at the Victoria Institution, long the bastion of Shakespeare-in-schools theatre, to perform his effervescent youth-oriented dramas. Dorall's most mature play, *The Hour of the Dog* (1975), is also the first drama to wrestle with the personal and public contradictions and ironies of political detention in post-independence Malaysia. The expressionist theatre of Lee Joo For, a respected visual artist turned dramatist, and particularly his wily exploitation of Asian dramatic strategies and resources, added substance to, and developed audiences for, the hitherto modestly received decolonization enterprise. Lee consciously invited controversy with his prankish and facile topicality and, initially at least, his sensational modes of presentation confounded a conservative theatrical culture wedded to mainstream, western dramaturgies. His first and best-known play, *The Son of Zen* (1968), an extravagantly absurd swipe at the imperialist psyche, is also the only Malaysian play to have been performed in New York's off-off Broadway.

So severe was the linguistic polarization in the nascent Malaysian theatre that few of these pioneering dramatists were aware that in their midst a western-influenced modern Malay theatre tradition was on the rise. Modern Malay drama mirrored the pathways of Malay nationalism that began in the 1930s as influential figures in the Malay literary vanguard, including its leading playwrights, spearheaded the growing movement to place Bahasa Malaysia in a genuinely hegemonic position, replacing English. Since the ethnic riots of 1969 there has been a virtual drought in English playwriting in Malaysia.

During the 1980s officially supported Malay literary and performing media increasingly dominated national cultural perceptions. Images of Chinese and Indians in these media were infrequent and often took the dubious form of tokenism. In theatre, efforts to fill this vacuum in the national consciousness were initiated by the Five Arts Centre, Pentas, and later Kamikasih, which staged original and/or devised plays in English. The Five Arts Centre produced a relatively new crop of English-educated playwrights led by **K. S. Maniam, Kee Thuan Chye**, Leow Puay Tin, and Chin San Sooi. Their total output is small, but their plays, in keeping with the times, are dramaturgically adventurous and probe deeply into the non-Malay condition in the new political order. Some of the linguistic experiments of Maniam and Leow are creating a viable Malaysian English voice on stage.

Maniam's *The Card* (1984) and *The Sandpit* (first published in the *South Asian Review of English* in 1987 and 1989) hammer concrete Indian icons out of quotidian experience and unveil a state of uneasy juxtaposition between tradition and modernity in contemporary Malaysian society. The strong survivalist instincts of the Chinese working class trapped in backwater Melaka are drawn on in Leow Puay Tin's dream play *Three Children* (1992); it has been performed in Kuala Lumpur and subsequently in Singapore and Japan. By far the most controversial political play of the 1980s was Kee Thuan Chye's *1984 — Here and Now* (1985), an Orwellian vision of Malaysia's future. The play, which attracted packed houses, brought official repercussions for the playwright and Five Arts Centre. Pentas, which staged naïve ensemble dramas that satirized social and political mores, faced disastrous consequences when one of its leaders was detained in 1987 during the government's massive sweep of political and social dissidents.

The indigenous English theatre of the 1980s in Malaysia seemed to foreshadow the rising status of English following Malaysia's imminent entry into the international economic order as a newly industrialized nation. Nevertheless, the future of English as a creative language remains uncertain if only because during the last two decades generations of locally educated Malaysians have passed through their formal learning to the university level, mainly in Bahasa Malaysia. Because of this profound change most of the prizes of a 1993 national playwriting competition in English were won by veteran playwrights, and not by those of the new generation.

KISHEN JIT

DRAMA (Malta)

Until the Second World War, the Maltese theatre was dominated by opera, typically performed by visiting professional artists, most of them Italian. The entry of Italy into the war in 1940, the bombardment of Malta by Italian planes, and the destruction of its magnificent opera house by German bombs in 1942 marked the end of an epoch in Malta's cultural history. Gradually, Maltese artists realized that it was not only respectable but necessary that their work be Maltese rather than merely imitative of English or Italian models.

The verse drama *Il-Fidwa tal-Bdiewa* (1936), by A. Cremona (1880–1972) — written in 1913 but not performed in its entirety until 1970 — became a text for university students of Maltese. (It was translated into English by May Butcher and published as *The Ransom of the Peasants*, 1960.) Although it did not create a school, it made a generation of writers see that a dignified theatre in the Maltese language was possible. The only other important Maltese writer to produce verse drama was Erin Serracino Inglott (1904–83), whose purist vocabulary produces an effect of austerity. His Maltese-language *Ir-Raheb* ('The Monk' 1971), although first performed in 1972, was written in 1941. It comes closer to a true tragedy than any other work yet produced by the Maltese theatre and shows a fine theatrical sense; it remains untranslated.

The wide diffusion of cable radio in the post-war years made radio drama popular in Malta during the 1940s and 1950s. Radio drama provided Maltese playwrights, directors, and actors with their first frequent, though very modest, source of income. It also gave an incentive for authors to experiment with dramatic forms. **Francis Ebejer**, the most important Maltese dramatist to date, wrote solely for this medium, in Maltese and English, before writing for the stage.

Between 1945 and 1951 the development of Maltese drama was also encouraged by several drama festivals and competitions organized by such bodies as the Malta Drama League, founded in 1944. Also influential in the 1940s was a university students' drama society inspired by Guze Aquilina, professor of Maltese at the University of Malta between 1937 and 1976. The society's productions, in Maltese, of Henrik Ibsen's *A Doll's House* and Bjornstjerne Bjornson's *The Bankrupt* introduced realistic social drama to a Maltese audience.

Maltese drama in the 1960s and 1970s was dominated by Francis Ebejer, whose first three-act play, *Vaganzi tas-Sajf* (1970), now translated into a number of European languages (including English, as *Summer Holidays*, 1980), established him as Malta's leading dramatist. (His plays in English have been published in *Francis Ebejer: Collected English Plays*, 3 vols, 1980.) Though Ebejer denied conscious influence, that of the European Absurdist theatre can be detected in his early stage plays, and Harold Pinter's Theatre of Menace has left its mark on the brooding atmosphere of *Summer Holidays*. Like Ebejer's Maltese-language radio plays, the dramas *Menz* (1980, first published in Maltese under the same title in 1970) and *The Cliff Hangers* (1980, first published in Maltese in 1973 as *L- Imwarrbin*) are satisfying amalgams of realism and expressionism that explore the individual's enslavement to the past and society's pressures on the individual to conform.

Boulevard (1980, first published in Maltese under the same title in 1970), the most Absurdist of Ebejer's plays, is poetic; it eschews all realism and utilizes an elegantly mannered style. Egoism is again a main theme: the characters' inability to transcend their individual problems makes them easy prey of Blonk, the artist/deicide, and Gregorex, the Christ-like leader, neither of whom can bring them happiness. The regretful scepticism of *Boulevard* became disrespectful in a later Maltese-language play, *Vum-Barala-Zungare* (1977, untranslated); Ebejer later recovered his religious beliefs. Of his English-language plays, the most successful are shorter pieces, such as the one-acter *Golden Tut* (1980).

Ebejer's example encouraged others to experiment, either as directors or as dramatists. The Xsenuru productions at Malta University Theatre, followed by those of such workshop groups as Theatre Workshop and Teatru Henri Dogg, were important for introducing two young dramatists, Oreste Calleja and Alfred Sant. Calleja's satirical and absurdist bent, with occasional outcrops of pathos, shows some kinship with Ionesco, but Pirandellian preoccupations with identity are never far in Calleja's drama.

The number of Maltese playwrights is small; even fewer work in English. For a long time Maltese women were not very active in the literary field, although they have been active as stage actors since the turn of the century.

PAUL XUEREB

Further reading: Joe Friggieri, 'Theatre in Malta', *The Malta Year Book 1978* (1978); Paul Xuereb, 'The theatre in Malta', *Civilization* 26 and 27 (1986).

DRAMA (New Zealand)

Settlement to the First World War

Few plays were written in New Zealand in the nineteenth century; often these were never performed, and the texts of most have not survived. During a brief burst of activity in Auckland in 1870–1, eight plays were staged and a ninth was promised, but only twenty-two performances in all were given. In the same years the city's two principal theatres gave 1,401 performances of some 440 different plays ranging from Dion Boucicault to Shakespeare. Recent research has uncovered a handful of scripts deposited in the archives of the Justice Department to protect their authors' rights under the Fine Arts Copyright Amendment Act of 1879. With the exception of G. H. Goodall's 'The Relief of Ladysmith' (premièred in 1900), the collection has little historical interest and is far removed from the theatrical gold found in Australian archives. Even the best-known New Zealand melodrama and the only one currently in print, George Leitch's *The Land of the Moa* — first performed in 1895 and first published in 1990 — was written with the author's eye on Australian performance and his heart set on London success.

To focus on New Zealand written plays of the period — be they by a future premier, in the case of Julius Vogel's version of *Lady Audley's Secret* (staged in 1863, unpublished), or by Mr Griffen of Wanganui, whose casually racist *Kainga of the Ladye Birds* (published in 1879 under the pseudonym 'Grif') is the first published New Zealand play — is curiously to distort the theatrical vitality in the country and the uses to which drama was put. There were arguments as to whether the 'immoral' theatre should exist at all, although these arguments were without the urgency that Australia's foundation as a penal settlement brought to that topic there. Theatres had to be rapidly removed from the hotel taprooms in which a 'professor of elocution' gave the first 'Entertainments' in Auckland in 1841. The Royal Victoria Theatre opened in Wellington in 1843, boasting that it was the city's first gaslit building. By 1853 Auckland's Theatre Royal was sufficiently respectable to be a church on Sundays. The need to justify theatre on the grounds of educational and moral uplift can be seen from the popularity of dioramas on biblical and historical subjects, where well-known actors became public lecturers. Henry Irving's leading lady, Ellen Terry, was to be found lecturing in the main centres as late as 1914.

In a country with different patterns of settlement for its isolated communities, social changes and tensions revealed themselves most in the South Island. The opening up of the Otago goldfields led to such a rush of entertainers from America and Australia that the Pacific Ocean became a theatrically navigable lake, while the Tasman Sea was only a stormy pond. At a time when a journey north to Auckland was called the equal to a trip from England to the Caribbean, peripatetic theatre companies traversed the land regularly, but first they had to conquer the most aristocratic centre, Christchurch. It was here that the gentry's hostility to theatre was the most entrenched, particularly when the stage spoke for the emerging middle class through the irreverent songs of Charles Thatcher.

Thatcher 'the inimitable', with his outrageous flights of song, toured the country three times in the 1860s, preparing the way for his successors who interpolated songs, more topical than any local play, into both theatrical interludes and plays. Tuneful representations of the country went hand in hand with scenic ones in familiarizing and taming the world in which the increasingly middle-class audience lived. When the bush setting of David Murray's 'Chums' (first performed in 1890) was applauded, 'the scene-painter walked in front and bowed as if he had been responsible for its beauties.' The ground had been prepared for Alfred Hill's Maori pageant *Hinemoa* (1896). When New Zealand theatre began, it was a fringe activity within a white enclave embedded in a Maori world, but by 1900 Maori had been theatrically 'Fenimore Cooperized', and the theatre had become part of the international entertainment industry dominated by 'The Firm' of J. C. Williamson.

Depression and War

Although some visiting companies had previously toured the plays of Henrik Ibsen, Oscar Wilde, and J. M. Barrie, the 1920s were to be 'a wonderful decade' for imported light theatrical fare. Local drama began to question, with **Alan Mulgan** in his *Three Plays of New Zealand* (1920), whether it was possible to love 'this fat prosperous New Zealand of ours'. Mulgan's mixture of social analysis and theatrical realism, echoing the spirit of the Australian **Louis Esson**, led to successors who answered him with a sharp 'no'. A popular theatrical base was lost and has never been consistently regained. This was the period of the rise in New Zealand of the serious amateur dramatic movement, often working within the confines of one-act plays for British Drama League competitions. The best were by women, most notably Violet Targuse, a 'domestic', who, spurred by the Depression, questioned what they had gained in the isolation of a largely agricultural new land. The titles of Targuse's most convincing work, *Fear* and *Rabbits* — both first published in *Seven One Act-Plays* (1933), edited by Victor S. Lloyd — reveal her response.

It has been noted that the 1930s saw the awakening of a nationalist literary spirit in the work of some New Zealand poets (see **Poetry**, New Zealand), but the writers of drama — always the most international literary medium — turned their eyes further afield. Eric Bradwell's *Clay* (first published in *'Clay' and Other New Zealand One-Act Plays*, 1936, edited by Victor S. Lloyd) is an expressionistic experiment centring on a woman whose 'whole attitude is one of despair'. J. A. S. Coppard placed individual pain in a broader social context. His *Machine Song* (first published in *Twelve One-Act Plays from the International One-Act Play Theatre*, 1939, edited by Elizabeth Everard) capitalizes on the stock expressionistic theme of dehumanizing mechanization, but hints at the fear of larger totalitarianisms. The prospect of war, as elsewhere, had encouraged the tendency of left-wing New Zealand writers to join 'organizations that paid no heed to national boundaries'. **R. A. K. Mason** put aside poetry to become a founder of the Auckland People's Theatre in 1936. Left-wing theatre groups, committed to agitprop sketches and scripts, spread to small towns, although the most important was Wellington's Unity Theatre. Plays created out of this ferment were impeccable in theme, although the playwrights' sense of the people they were writing for was shaky. Ian Hamilton's socialist, anti-violence play *Falls the Shadow* (1939) is as overwhelmed by its English manor house setting as the country would be by the Second World War.

Theatrical Starting Points

The great majority of New Zealand plays written before the Second World War were verbally stilted and theatrically unadventurous. As they dated, there was a need for new beginnings. Howard Wadman in *Life Sentence* (1949), carefully defined as 'A New Zealand Play', asserted that theatre must spring from 'the middle-class intelligentsia . . . because this stratum of society varies least throughout the English-speaking world'. The country was still at home in England. Wadman's play drifted into verse, which made his social complacency ever more pretentious, but his attitudes hint at the new élite that was coming into the theatre. Serious writers, of whom the most notable were **Allen Curnow** and **Frank Sargeson**, turned to drama. They showed their hostility to all forms of Anglophile theatre by searching their country's past for subjects. Curnow's verse drama *The Axe* (1949) is an allegorical account of New Zealand's beginnings reflected in the mirror of the Christianizing of Mangaia in the Cook Islands. In *A Time for Sowing* (first published in a collection of two Sargeson plays, *Wrestling with the Angel*, 1964),

Sargeson dramatizes an early missionary's encounters with Maori and the resulting 'legacy of guilt' that was bequeathed to the awkward puritans who inhabit his short stories. Both writers' stagework was finally frustrated by the lack of a viable theatre. Here their successor, poet **James K. Baxter**, was luckier. In the 1960s, for the most concentrated period of his theatrical career, Baxter worked out of a private, forty-seat theatre in Dunedin. However, for all his gifts as a playwright, he never quite wrote a play. His *Collected Plays* (1982), edited by Howard McNaughton, are lengthy notes towards what might have been and what almost was.

Interest in less narrowly focused drama was still widespread and, with fewer touring companies, the need for a national professional theatre was acknowledged. In 1953 the touring New Zealand Players Company was privately funded. The demand for local plays was less evident. Wellington's Unity Theatre, less political than in the past, encouraged Kathleen Ross' *The Trap* (1952), a powerful study of women from three generations locked in a male world; but although the play won prizes, few groups performed it. The Players, more overwhelmed than their nineteenth-century predecessors by the problems of transporting casts throughout the country, were as cautious in their approach to local plays. They toured Stella Jones' domestic drama *The Tree* (1960) only after it had been endorsed by overseas approval through production in England. The same might have happened to **Bruce Mason**'s *The Pohutukawa Tree* (1960), which was only given workshop performances by the Players before it was performed on British Broadcasting Corporation television in 1959. By then the Players were virtually defunct.

The remarkably similar stage careers of Bruce Mason and **Mervyn Thompson** dominated New Zealand theatre between the mid-1950s and the early 1980s. Mason, the older man, enunciated the creed they found themselves following: 'If I wanted to be a professional theatre man in New Zealand, I would have to do the whole job myself, Kiwi-style.' Mason and Thompson helped to found theatres in which they did everything from acting to directing. They both wrote a wide variety of plays and they spent several years, without a theatre to support them, writing and performing solo works. Their careers overlap — Thompson directed Mason's *Awatea* (1969) for the Commonwealth Games Arts Festival in 1974. They differ, however, in their visions of the country for whose theatre they worked so fervently. Mason was an élitist who lived in a 'green indifferent land' that could not offer as much as he was prepared to give. His early plays rage against narrowly constricted, puritanical, suburban lives. He turned to writing plays on Maori themes, finding in the Maori world shards of emotional grandeur and generosity in the midst of what he, the product of his time, took to be a dying culture whose only prospect was assimilation. Mason ended by retreating to internal exile, sometimes imaged in the imaginative freedom of the child, always an attempt to escape the brutality of a male world. All of Thompson's work is an attempt to create a history and a home he can celebrate. He is determined to shatter the myth of working-class philistinism as he peoples his stage with the large majority of those who live in the country: the workers, the housewives, the rugby players, and the racegoers. As Thompson has attempted to recapture buried aspects of the past, he has also — in his one-man performances — brought his own history more to the fore. As economic depression came around again, so his own hopes became more muted, but he is still asking for a Brechtian 'happy ending'.

Between 1964 and 1974 professional theatres were established in New Zealand's main cities under the auspices of the Queen Elizabeth II Arts Council. (See **Patronage**, New Zealand.) At last the theatre had a secure foundation, as touring was jettisoned and community development became the way to the future. This new structure came too late for Mason, while Thompson's radical populism sat uneasily in what were largely middlebrow theatres. Despite this growth and the founding of Playmarket as a playwrights' agency promoting local writing, there was still a diffidence about indigenous plays. The fear remained that self-exposure on a public stage would advertise the country as tiresomely provincial, cut off from the wider world where meaning resided. The major achievement of **Roger Hall**'s plays was to overcome this form of 'cultural cringe'. When *Glide Time* (1977) took the country by storm, managements saw that there was a national audience for an affectionate satire of bureaucratic folly. The next major breakthrough was engineered by Playmarket. In 1980, taking as a model the Australian National Playwrights' Conference, it launched a series of Playwrights' Workshops that were to run throughout the decade. The original director was Mervyn Thompson, who himself workshopped **Greg McGee**'s *Foreskin's Lament* (1981). This controversial and exhilarating theatrical examination of the 'state of the nation' changed New Zealand's attitude to the theatre. The play became a household name and, as in England after John Osborne's *Look Back in Anger* (1957), young New Zealand writers started to consider writing for the stage.

A Theatrical Theatre

Many of the most interesting New Zealand plays of the 1980s came out of the Playwrights' Workshops. Their performances were supported by the policy developed by Wellington's Victoria University Press of consistently publishing new plays. Initially the theatres, now staffed more by New Zealanders than overseas experts and drawing for their workers on graduates of a national drama school, encouraged new writing. Their staging at times failed to do justice to the works. This was largely because such was the excitement at the nation being described on stage that there was a tendency to present the plays in the realist mode in which the profession and its audience were trained — even while the playwrights themselves were writing ever more theatrically. This drove some dramatists out of the theatre, but along with an expanding youthful profession it also led to the creation of smaller experimental theatres and theatrical co-operatives. At the same time, the larger Arts Council theatres, in the increasingly stringent 'user-pays' economic climate, were retreating once again to an overseas repertoire whose goal was to guarantee box-office success. Auckland became the centre for alternative theatre — a form of performance theatre that had had a lively underground history since the 1960s — while Wellington became the theatrical capital of the country. In the latter city, plays — interesting in their own right — were able to attract audiences searching for more specialized theatrical fare. Maori theatre and women's theatre grew dramatically at the end of the decade.

The two most talented individual playwrights of this time cannot be so easily categorized. The large-cast, ambitious works of both **Vincent O'Sullivan** and Stuart Hoar need all the resources of the theatrical profession to be adequately staged. Both writers use the past, to differing ends, to reflect the country's present. O'Sullivan's cold comedy of manners, *Billy* (1990), is set in Sydney, Australia, in the 1820s. It examines how any society's encounter with the 'Other' — in this case a deaf mute Aboriginal — reveals the darker, hidden aspects of the dominant culture. New Zealand audiences are forced to meditate on what this theatrical encounter with early Australia exposes of themselves. Hoar has followed *Squatter* (1988) — a disconcerting mixture of murder and muddle, cast in the form of a southern western and describing the urgent need for change in society — with 'Exile' (premièred 1990), which mocks the narrow obsessions of recent local literati who continue trying to define a national identity at a time of worldwide crisis. New Zealand theatre has come of age as it has started to address problems that are larger than those of the world in which it is staged.

SEBASTIAN BLACK

Further reading: *Australasian Drama Studies: New Zealand Issue* 1 (1984), special issue on New Zealand theatre; *Australasian Drama Studies: Theatre and Drama in New Zealand* 18 (1991); Howard McNaughton, 'Drama', in Terry Sturm (ed.) *The Oxford History of New Zealand Literature in English* (1991).

Maori Theatre

Pre-colonial Maori culture in what is now New Zealand had a rich variety of ritualized performance that colonization did not suppress; critic and actor Roma Potiki has even shown (in her introduction to *He Reo Hou: Five Plays by Maori Playwrights*, 1991) that the 1975 Land March constituted a theatrical form defying European dramatic models as well as a protest against land injustice. Such performance did not include impersonation or role-creation, nor did it contain the animal plays or hunting games commonly used for tribal entertainment in Melanesia and Australia.

Although Maori performance was often crudely introduced into commercial entertainment throughout the colonial period, it retained its integrity in tribal situations. In the 1950s the Pakeha playwright Bruce Mason worked towards a Maori English-language theatre by writing on Maori themes, and in the 1960s **Alistair Campbell** wrote radio and stage plays exploring in part his own mixed-race Polynesian identity. In the same period, James Ritchie wrote for both media such works as *He Mana Toa* (privately published, 1966), *He Matakite* (privately published, 1967), and 'He Tohu O Waharoa — The Mark of a Chief' (premièred on radio in 1969), and Harry Dansey wrote *Te Raukura* (1974) for performance in a cathedral. Enthusiasm for more such works was reflected in the establishment of the Maori Theatre Trust in 1966.

The relative tolerance of diversity in post-colonial New Zealand culture has led to a rapid growth of interest in the extension and preservation of traditional performance and, encouraged by state subsidy, to many examples of cultural syncretism on the public stage. Rore Hapipi's (Rowley Habib's) *Death of the Land* (1991) was performed by the touring Te Ika A Maui players in 1976 and later by Radio New Zealand, and as the Maori language revival developed, many plays used both languages. Riwia Brown's English-language *Roimata* (1991) premièred during Maori Language Week in 1988, a coincidence that drew criticism. Brown's second play, 'Te Hokinga' ('The Return', premièred 1990), uses the same central characters to explore further the complexities of urban Maori life. Established writers were also drawn to the theatre: the poet **Hone Tuwhare** wrote *In the Wilderness without a Hat (On Ilkla Moor B'aht'at)* (1991) in 1977, while the novelist **Witi Ihimaera** wrote the libretto for the opera 'Waituhi' (premièred 1984).

In periods of acute controversy, during South Africa's Springbok rugby tour of 1981 or during various land disputes, for example, Maori theatre has been used as an instrument of resistance or aggression, most notably in the collectively written touring agitprop 'Maranga Mai' ('Wake Up!', premièred 1981). Paul Maunder, director of Amamus (a touring group theatre) and the bilingual Theatre of the Eighth Day, has become committed to 'the penetration of the confused and contradictory cultural experience of the people of Aotearoa [New Zealand] since colonization'. Both collectively written under the direction of Maunder, 'Electra (Thoughts during the Tour)' (premièred 1982) attacks apartheid and its supporting culture, while 'Encounter at Te Puna (Te Tutakitanga I Te Puna)' (premièred 1984) presents a modern Maori woman groping through early colonial history to find her cultural identity. Another collectively written and bilingual play, 'Ngati Pakeha' (premièred 1985), also uses a present-day perspective on material from the Hauhau period.

'Maranga Mai' was short-lived, but it introduced a tone of anger that was not overt in 1970s plays; the development is clear in Hapipi's television play *The Protesters* (1982). Selwyn Muru's 'Get the Hell Home Boy' (premièred 1982) was termed an *utu* ('revenge') play; like Rawhiti Paratene's 'Saturday Morning' (premièred 1980), it is set in police cells with European justice exposed as institutionalized oppression. In 'The Gospel According to Taane' (premièred 1983), Muru worked with the most lasting and influential Maori company, Te Ohu Whakaari ('Young Maori in Performance'), which also developed a touring theatre-in-education company; directed by Rangimoana Taylor, it has done innovative work including plays on health themes similar to those developed by the Raun Raun Theatre of Papua New Guinea. Other important companies include Don Selwyn's Tamaki Creative Arts Group and Taotahi ma Uo, performing Polynesian work developed by Stephen Sinclair and Samson Samasoni, notably 'Le Matau' ('The Fish Hook', premièred 1984), the first full-length Samoan play.

Wellington's Depot Theatre, where *Ngati Pakeha* premièred and which served as a base for Te Ohu Whakaari, was renamed Taki Rua ('weaving two threads', i.e., biculturalism) in 1991 and became the venue for Maori Theatre with the 1991 opening of 'Daddy's Girl' by Rena Owen. Though not publicized in New Zealand, Owen emerged in 1987 as the first Maori woman writer to achieve professional production with *Te Awa I Tahuti* ('The River that Ran Away', 1991). It was performed on the London pub theatre circuit, with Owen playing the part of a woman imprisoned for drug dealing. The play's action consists of interviews with a female prison psychiatrist, with the gradual emergence of a family history of conflict and abuse, focusing on the young woman, the fifth of nine children of a violent alcoholic Maori father and a European mother. Owen's programme note to 'Daddy's Girl' concerns the exploration of 'the consequences of denial of culture'; here the stark simplicity of the interview is replaced by a more complex family study as a girl talks to her dying Maori father and memory figures — the absent European mother and the dead Maori grandmother — appear.

As Paul Maunder has observed, the dynamics of place in Maori culture have meant resistance to the architecture of European theatres. One new playwright, John Broughton, has written specifically of the atmosphere of Maori buildings. 'Te Hokinga Mai' ('The Return Home', premièred 1988), referring to the Te Maori exhibition, was written to be performed in the porch of Mataatua, the famous Otago meeting house, and deals with a Vietnam veteran's attempts to adjust his shattered mind to a family context. In the solo work 'Michael James Manaia' (premièred 1991), Broughton again depicts the effects of war, particularly in its emotionally reductive capacity. The New Zealand theatre's receptivity to such material was shown when Downstage, the country's oldest professional theatre, took 'Michael James Manaia' to the 1991 Edinburgh Festival.

HOWARD McNAUGHTON

Further reading: Anne Salmond, *Hui: A Study of Maori Ceremonial Gatherings* (1975); Christopher Balme, 'New Maori theatre in New Zealand', *Australasian Drama Studies* 15–16 (1989–90); Roma Potiki, 'A Maori point of view: the journey from anxiety to confidence', *Australasian Drama Studies* 18 (1991); Roma Potiki, 'Introduction', *He Reo Hou: Five Plays by Maori Playwrights* (1991).

Women's Drama and Theatre

The category 'Women's Drama and Theatre (New Zealand)' here assumes an ideological cohesion and includes works written (collaboratively or individually) by women and those based on issues of gender.

'Women's theatre' began in New Zealand in the 1970s as a vital part of the women's movement of the period. Performances in student unions and at United Women's Conventions came out of collectives that were often student-based and formed around specific political issues concerning women. For example, the need for liberalization of the abortion laws was the subject of the collectively written 'The Back Street Women's Theatre Show' (premièred 1976), which toured small rural communities in the North Island. The spirit was often iconoclastic and humorous, and the style agitprop, not unlike the performances elsewhere during the period, for example, those of The Pram Factory (Australia) and Red Ladder (UK).

Many of these productions were conceived of, and performed as, signature tunes for women. However, collective creation was problematized as the range of what women considered 'women's issues' or even 'feminist' widened. (Separatist audiences were a feature of the period. The Broadsheet Women's Shows — supported and partially organized by the collective that produced *Broadsheet Magazine*, 1972 — toured annually from the late 1970s and featured the lesbian, twin-sister singing duo The Topp Twins, as well as many other significant women artists.)

New Zealand theatre inherited a tradition from British repertory and in the early 1970s much of the impulse in women's theatre was to redefine and expand an audience away from these colonial flagship theatres by using innovative and accessible styles of performance. A later, consciously defined intention was more nationalistic and centred around the Playwrights Workshops (begun in 1980) and the need for better roles for women actors as well as for more women playwrights. Individual women playwrights emerged out of both these movements; some had already worked in collaborative theatre, while others had plays 'workshopped' at the Playwrights Workshops. Of these only **Renee** has produced a substantial number of plays; others are now better known as fiction or television writers.

It was Renee, too, who began creating historical plays. Interest in New Zealand's colonial past was also taken up by Fiona Farrell Poole in her 'Passengers' (premièred 1985), about government-assisted immigration of single women in the 1850s, and in 'Waihi 1912' (premièred 1987), about a mining strike in a small town. Other plays of the 1980s were built around the ordinary and uncelebrated aspects of women's lives. Thus, Sarah Delahunty's musical drama 'Stretchmarks' (premièred 1986) puts motherhood on stage, while **Rachel McAlpine**'s plays address the phobias of female adolescence, and Lorae Parry's 'Strip' (premièred 1986) portrays a day in the life of a stripper. (Parry's later play 'Frontwomen', premièred 1989, also fits into this category; a naturalistic drama about a passionate lesbian love affair, it foregrounds lesbian visibility.)

Issues of gender oppression are also the subject of several New Zealand plays. Hilary Beaton's *Outside In* (1984) is set in a women's prison and shows how power roles determined by a patriarchal society persist within a women's institution. Norelle Scott looks at rape within the family in her 'Promise Not to Tell' (premièred 1984). *Objection Overruled* (1985), by Carolyn Burns, also uncovers violence. Presented as a cross between a television 'this-is-your-life' show and a courtroom drama, the play exposes the hidden truths of a suburban middle-class family. The play succeeds because it questions rather than perpetuates the notion of fixed gender characteristics — taking away the culpability from individuals and uncovering the social construction of gender. Stephanie Johnson's 'Accidental Fantasies' (premièred 1985) also achieves this level of awareness.

In the 1990s women's theatre in New Zealand continues to take the form of comedy and cabaret performances, most recently, for example, in the Wellington show *Hen's Teeth* (1991). However, the important new phenomenon is the rise of Maori women's theatre. The major names are Rena Owen, Riwia Brown, and the theatre company He Ara Hou, directed by writer Roma Potiki.

MARY PAUL

Further reading: Priscilla Pitt, 'Theatre of the unheard', *Broadsheet* 98 (1982); Helen White, 'Path for a flightless bird', *Australasian Drama Studies* 2 (1985); Judith Dale, 'Women's theatre and why', *Australasian Drama Studies* 18 (1991).

Experimental Theatre

In New Zealand a serious, self-conscious, professional theatre and its experimental opposition, also serious, self-conscious, and professional, grew up almost simultaneously. Downstage began in 1964 as a theatrical complement to Wellington's tiny bohemian-beatnik world of night clubs, coffee bars, and blues and rock venues, but by 1968 its radical inclinations had been tamed. The first production of Auckland's professional Mercury Theatre in 1968, J. M. Barrie's *The Admirable Crichton* (1914), was a clear statement about where it stood in relation to anything experimental. By the time the next flagship venue, Christchurch's The Court, was established in 1971, New Zealand had three quite different, genuinely experimental companies.

Amamus was founded in Wellington by Denise Maunder and Paul Maunder in 1971. They began by creating intense, home-grown, improvised dramas, notably on historical themes: 'The Wall Street Banks in London Have Closed' (premièred 1971), for example, dealt with New Zealand in the Depression; '51' (premièred 1972) was a laconic, left-wing docudrama about the waterfront lockout of 1951. Following these productions Amamus went through a major stylistic upheaval — the documentary approach seceded to wholesale ingestion of Grotowski. After Amamus closed in 1978, Paul Maunder moved on to write programmatically Marxist plays.

The Living Theatre Troupe, founded by Ken Rea and Sally Rodwell in Auckland in 1971, began as a political street-theatre group working in a *commedia dell'arte* style and moved on to indoor spectacles. Poet **Murray Edmond** and prose writer **Russell Haley** wrote 'Progress in the Dark' (premièred 1971) for the troupe as a lampoon of the Mercury Theatre's mealy-mouthed 'Prospect in the Park', written by Shirley Maddock, which marked Auckland's centenary in 1971. The Living Theatre Troupe folded in 1975.

Theatre Action was founded in 1971, when Francis Batten and other students graduating from Jacques Lecoq's school in Paris, France, sought New Zealand as fertile ground to test Lecoq's theory and practice. They brought life to the experimental tradition, creating two notable large-scale works: 'Once Upon a Planet' (premièred 1972) and 'The Best of All Possible Worlds' (premièred 1973). Their work also ranged from avant-garde electronic music to populist entertainment at local agricultural shows. In 1977 Batten and Bridget Brandon left for Sydney, where they founded a theatre school, The Drama Action Centre; with their departure Theatre Action ceased to exist.

Red Mole (1974–) embraced a similar spread from populist to avant-garde in its comedic visions of 'a small country in the South Pacific'. Started by poet Alan Brunton and ex-Living Theatre's Sally Rodwell, Red Mole worked in several modes: it turned a Wellington strip club into an art cabaret in 1977; it performed at beaches and motor camps; it created extravagant phantasmagorias such as 'Ace Follies' (premièred 1976) and 'Lord Galaxy's Travelling Players' (premièred 1980). Red Mole left New Zealand in 1978, seeking its fortune in New York's art cabaret scene and performing community theatre in New Mexico, USA; the company returned to New Zealand in 1988.

Brunton and Rodwell continue to write for Red Mole — 'Comrade Savage' (premièred 1990), for example.

Experimental literary writers (Brunton, Edmond, Haley, and poet **Ian Wedde**) were attracted to the experimental theatre companies. The experimental theatres were entry points for internationalist ideas as well as advocates of nationalist themes and images, while the establishment theatres remained regionalist and provincial in their tendencies.

In the 1980s, as the whole of New Zealand theatre became more pluralistic, so did the experimental wing. In Maori theatre, hard-hitting agit-prop companies such as Maranga Mai (1978) and He Ara Hou (1989) attracted attention. Feminist experimental theatre has flourished most successfully in the realm of cabaret, the collectively written *Hen's Teeth* (1991) being an outstanding example. Warwick Broadhead has consistently staged community events since the late 1970s. He has always worked with large groups of amateurs and in a highly visual mode to produce one-off, outrageous spectaculars, often in unusual or outdoor settings. Choreographer Douglas Wright has created major experimental dance works such as 'How on Earth' (premièred 1989) and 'As It Is' (premièred 1991). Other significant companies from the 1980s include the 'more-kiwi-than-kiwi' Front Lawn, the bizarre Inside Out, the acrobatic Dramadillo, and Theatre at Large. James Beaumont is a playwright whose writing ('Wild Cabbage', premièred 1985, and 'Black Halo', premièred 1989, for example) shows a genuinely experimental interest. His work of the mid-1980s was an anarchic post-punk collage of absurd and frightening images, ranging from low buffoonery and high camp to great delicacy and poignancy.

While experimental theatre in New Zealand has not been as well supported by government funding as establishment theatre (there was no government funding for non-establishment companies prior to 1984; it now receives approximately twelve per cent of all theatre funding from the Theatre Initiatives fund), it has none the less succeeded in creating a profile that stands out in contrast to establishment theatres.

MURRAY EDMOND

Further reading: Alan Brunton, *A Red Mole Sketch Book* (1989); Murray Edmond, 'Lighting out for paradise: New Zealand Theatre and the "other" tradition', *Australasian Drama Studies* 18 (1991).

DRAMA (Pakistan)

When compared to the traditions of poetry and narrative in subcontinental Muslim literature, the dramatic genre in Pakistan has not been greatly developed. This can be explained partly by the fact that Muslim religion and culture, unlike Hindu or some indigenous African cultures, incorporate few elements of festive, dramatic enactment; in Pakistan, religious and political obscurantism has further inhibited the growth of this medium.

There does exist in Pakistan, however, a small body of dramatic work in English that extends back to Muslim writing in pre-partition India. This early work includes the anti-imperialist, stylized poetic dramas of **Ahmed Ali** — *The Land of Twilight* (1937) and 'Break the Chains' (premièred 1932) — and of Atiya Begum Fyzee Rahamin — *Daughter of Ind* (1937). Post-partition drama is best represented by Nasir Farooki's *The Naked Night* (1965) and by **Taufiq Rafat**'s 'Foothold' (premièred 1967). Farooki and Rafat share a concern with the individual's existential and spiritual quest and their plays revolve around the romantic-ascetic or angry-nihilistic idealism of characters drawn mainly from an intellectual élite. Farooki experiments with certain modernist techniques of slide projection, a fragmented time scale, and hallucinatory interludes. Rafat combines verse and prose; his aphoristic, poetic drama is strongly reminiscent of T. S. Eliot's verse plays, while the psychological and symbolic elements in their plays evoke comparison with the plays of Indian **Nissim Ezekiel**, including his *Don't Call It Suicide* (1989).

Ikram Azam and Gulzar Khan write what may be termed 'cause and country' drama. Azam's *The Martyr* (first published in 1966 in the collection *The Martyr and Other Plays*) and Khan's *The Slaves of Time* (1986) draw on nationalist and patriotic themes such as war, the Kashmiri struggle, and partition and emphasize viewpoint and fervour rather than dramatic form.

More recent plays — Tariq Ali's *Iranian Nights* (1989) and *Mowcow Gold* (1990) and Rukhsana Ahmad's 'Song for a Sancturary' (premièred 1990) — focus on current political and feminist issues. The work of England-born **Hanif Kureishi** — including *My Beautiful Laundrette* (1986) — is particularly distinctive in the Pakistani context, yet belongs more to the tradition of contemporary British working-class drama. In its perspective of a multiracial and multilingual society, however, *My Beautiful Laundrette* spotlights elements of friction and social melding (found also in Indo-Canadian Uma Parameswaran's *Rootless but Green Are Boulevard Trees*, 1988).

While Nigerian **Wole Soyinka** and Indian **Girish Karnad** create dramas of larger forms that incorporate realistic, poetic, and folkloric elements, Pakistani dramatists, excepting Kureishi, Tariq Ali, and Rukhsana Ahmad, engage in ideas and rhetoric in the tradition of G. B. Shaw.

S. S. SIRAJUDDIN

DRAMA (The Philippines)

Philippine drama before western contact consisted of such mimetic forms as rituals, verbal jousts, songs, and dances. The Spanish colonial period introduced religious drama (i.e., the passion play), the *komedya* (a verse play about love and war between *Moros* and *Cristianos*), the *sarswela* (a musical comedy), and the *drama* (the prose play).

With the American Insular Government came a new culture. Theatre in English resulted from the educational system established in 1901, which used 'textbook plays' to teach the English language. Although not linked to life outside the classroom as were community-based folk plays, these were for many a first experience of theatre, since education had cut them off from the native theatre. Stories such as W. W. Jacobs' 'The Monkey's Paw', and poems such as H. W. Longfellow's *Evangeline* (1847) were dramatized, alongside such plays as G. B. Shaw's *Arms and the Man* (1898).

Ease in the new language eventually produced the first play written in English by a Filipino: 'The Modern Filipina' (premièred 1915) by Jesusa Araullo and Lino Castillejo. With mastery of language came playwrights such as Jorge Bocobo, Carlos Romulo, Vidal Tan (all later presidents of the University of the Philippines), who progressed from writing plays for school and civic occasions to commenting on local mores (i.e., marriage, election promises).

By the 1940s, drama had moved on to school and 'legitimate' stages, with Shakespeare and Greek tragedies performed in public by Ateneo and University of the Philippines theatre groups. Playwrights such as **Severino Montano, Wilfrido Maria Guerrero**, and **Alberto Florentino** developed, for whom theatre was no classroom exercise, but an earnest art.

Montano established the Arena Theater at the Philippine Normal School, fielding his plays (*Parting at Calamba*, 1953, *The Love of Leonor Rivera*, 1954) and teacher-actors throughout the country to bring modern drama to communities, in auditoriums and open spaces. At the university Guerrero wrote about the Philippine middle class, educated in English and adapting American mores (*Forever*, 1947, and *Three Rats*, 1948). The University Mobile Theater took his plays around the country, while his University Dramatic Club trained the actors, directors, and audiences of the next decades. Florentino brought onstage the slum world outside the English-speaking universe, in plays such as *The World Is an Apple* (1959) and *Cadaver* (1959). These playwrights also introduced realism, a new element and only nascent in the *sarswela*.

By the 1950s an active Philippines theatre flourished, with semi-professional groups (the Barangay Theater Guild, the Manila Theater Guild) presenting legitimate theatre. Through the educational system came as well the idea of modern theatre: Ibsen, Strindberg, Miller, and Williams, as well as Stanislavsky and Brecht. This was reinforced by movies, television, and especially by education in the USA. Scholarships (plus lectures, workshops, books) produced theatre specialists who knew American theatre as model and ideal.

In the late 1960s the nationalist movement brought about a resurgence of theatre in the native languages, and also a linking of indigenous, Hispanic, and American-influenced theatres. An awareness of the inordinate westernization of the Filipino impelled a conscious search for Filipino identity and culture.

Philippine theatre today has been shaped by this historical process. There is now little English-language theatre, except in some schools and in Repertory Philippines, which stages Broadway and London plays. Most plays are in local languages, but show the effects of an American education, reflecting such trends as psychological realism, social realism, Theatre of the Absurd, and expressionism. They deal with Philippine reality and have an urgency fired by such historical events as the imposition of martial law and the Marcos regime and its end, in which protest theatre played a vital role.

DOREEN G. FERNANDEZ

Further reading: Doreen G. Fernandez, 'From ritual to realism: a brief historical survey of Philippine theater', *Philippine Studies* 28 (1981); Nicanor G. Tiongson, *Dulaan: An Essay on Philippine Theater* (1989); Nicanor G. Tiongson, *Dulaan: An Essay on the Spanish Influence on Philippine Theater* (1992); Nicanor G. Tiongson and Ramon M. Obusan, *Dulaan: An Essay on Philippine Ethnic Theater* (1992).

DRAMA (Singapore)

Theatrical activity has taken place throughout Singapore's history in each of the four main languages of the dominant cultural groupings — Chinese (Mandarin), Malay, Tamil, and English — as well as in several subsidiary languages and dialects. English-language drama and theatre in Singapore, from the immediate postwar period to the early 1960s, refers primarily to the amateur theatrical activities of British colonial residents and members of the British Armed Forces Service drama clubs. The particularities of indigenous experience, character, language, and reality had little place.

The foundations of an indigenous English-language theatre by and for Singaporeans can be traced to the early 1950s. The Singapore Teachers' Union and a related organization, the Teachers' Repertory (founded in 1947), were responsible for initiating and nurturing the growth of drama in Singapore schools. The union sponsored the first Youth Drama and Music Festival in 1950, and out of this grew the Singapore Youth Festival, incorporating a drama component, now a significant part of the theatrical calendar. Teachers' Repertory provided students with training in production, stage management, and acting. Prominent members included Tung Muh Shih (Francis Thomas), H. Hochstadt, Leslie Woodford, C. V. Devan Nair, and Philip Liau.

Founded in 1950, the Raffles Society of the University of Malaya (in Singapore) worked energetically to indigenize the English-language theatre. In 1952 it organized a Festival of Drama that gave centrestage, both literally and metaphorically, to work in Asian traditions but performed in English, such as **Rabindranath Tagore**'s *Sacrifice*. The student-based University of Malaya Dramatic

Society, later known as the University of Singapore Drama Society, took up similar challenges. In 1955 the society presented the earliest example on record in Singapore of the adaptation of a foreign text to indigenous settings — 'Medicine without Effort', described as a 'Malayanized version of Molière's *Physician in Spite of Himself*'.

The 1960s and 1970s were crucial years for the Singapore theatre in English. In 1961 the Experimental Theatre Club was formed with an express commitment to new and experimental work and in particular to the presentation of modern Asian theatre and the nurturing of Singaporean work in English. Its first production, *Thunderstorm* (1934), by the Chinese playwright Cao Yu, was followed by two works by Singaporean Lim Chor Pee: 'Mimi Fan' (premièred 1962) and 'A White Rose at Midnight' (premièred 1964). The work of a second pioneering figure of the Singapore stage, **Goh Poh Seng**, was introduced when Centre '65 (taking its name from the year of its inauguration) performed Goh's 'When Smiles Are Done' in 1965, followed by his 'The Elder Brother' (premièred 1966). These works signalled a more aggressive ideological challenge, directed against a dominating Anglocentricity.

In the 1970s the challenge was complemented by the work of the University of Singapore Society, the organization for graduates of the university. In the 1960s it had concentrated on experimental work in the Anglo-American repertoire, but in 1974 it introduced to Singapore audiences the third of Singapore's pioneering dramatists, **Robert Yeo**. Yeo's 'Are You There, Singapore?' (premièred 1974), directed by Prem Kumar, broke all box-office records for a theatre performance in Singapore.

The 1980s witnessed encouraging growth, while at the same time attesting to the durability, in some areas of theatrical enterprise, of old colonial dispensations. In 1990–1, for example, the ministry of education theatre syllabus for schools was entirely Anglocentric in its fundamental orientation. Centre '65 is defunct; the drama committee of the University of Singapore Society is currently devoting its energies to lavish productions of European operetti; and while audiences are increasing, theatre remains to a significant extent the preserve of a middle-class English-educated intelligentsia, whose values tend towards the West End and Broadway.

However, while both Lim Chor Pee and Goh Poh Seng have remained silent in theatrical terms for more than two decades, the 1980s opened with Robert Yeo's 'One Year Back Home' playing to packed houses. The play's energetic dialogue and canny harnessing of topical political material served notice once again that the Singaporean playwright had things to say that could not be said by anybody else. A crucial artistic presence for the 1980s was provided by **Kuo Pao Kun**. As director, playwright, drama critic, and teacher, Kuo has worked tirelessly across the linguistic and cultural barriers that have traditionally compartmentalized Singaporean theatrical activity. In his own works, such as *Mama Looking for Her Cat* (1990) and *The Silly Little Girl and the Funny Old Tree* (Mandarin performance 1987, English version 1989), he has demonstrated brilliantly the theatrical potential residing in a fusion of eastern and western theatrical idioms.

Work by Singaporean dramatists has also begun to travel. In 1986 Yeo's second play was performed as a staged reading in New York at La Mama Experimental Theatre Club; in the same year Kuo Pao Kun's satiric-dramatic monologue, *No Parking on Odd Days*, was performed and enthusiastically received at the Hong Kong Festival of Arts. **Stella Kon**'s *Emily of Emerald Hill* (1990), first-prize winner in a ministry of culture drama-writing competition in 1983, became the hit of Singapore's 1985 Drama Festival and went on to represent Singapore at the Commonwealth Arts Festival in Edinburgh, Scotland, in 1986.

With the emergence of a fledgeling professional theatre in the mid-1980s, three groups deserve special mention. Act Three specializes in children's theatre, performing regularly in schools and private homes as part of its concept of 'living-room theatre'. Theatreworks, established in 1985 with the express aims of mounting 'fully fledged as well as financially self-sustaining productions' and of sowing the seeds 'for truly relevant and meaningful English-language drama', has had, under artistic director Ong Kong Sen, the most extensive commercial success. Finally, Kuo Pao Kun's Practice Theatre Ensemble continues to do important experimental work in breaking down the English-language theatre's traditionally exclusive dependence on western theatrical convention. A healthy sign for the Singapore theatre is that much of the new writing is produced expressly for performance. Wilson Wong, **Ovidia Yu**, Haresh Sharma, Teresa Tan, and Eleanor Wong are younger voices, now learning their trade.

F. M. G. (MAX) LE BLOND

Further reading: Seet Khiam Keong, 'Waiting in the wings: a critical look at Singapore's playscripts from the 1960s to 1980, part 1', *Commentary* 3-4 (1982); Robert Yeo, 'Towards an English language Singaporean theatre', *Southeast Asian Review of English* 4 (1982); David Birch, 'The life and times of Singapore English drama: loosening the chains, 1958–63', *Performing Arts* (Singapore) 1 (1986); M. Le Blond, 'Drama in Singapore: towards an English language theatre', in Peter Hyland (ed.) *Discharging the Canon: Cross-Cultural Readings in Literature* (1986).

DRAMA (South Africa)

The Pre-Colonial Period

Theatre in Africa is part of an ancient performance culture; rock paintings, depicting shamanistic dances among the San, date back 25,000 years (though others are less than two hundred years old) and versions of these dances still occur among the San. The arrival of the Nguni, Sotho, and other peoples brought a further set of social, religious, and military performance to the region. Their formally structured events had a strong mimetic content and included wedding ceremonies, initiation ceremonies, and harvest festivals.

The oral narrative tradition is equally old and widespread. The praise-poet (*izibongo* in Nguni, *liboko* in Sotho) is both poet and social critic for his patron and community, while the storyteller (*intsomi* in Xhosa, *inganekwane* in Zulu) is an oral historian, narrating and enacting stories from the life of the clan. These performance forms still exist in South Africa, though often in adapted form, and the traditions have also changed and extended the theatre through assimilation, syncretism, and imitation.

The Dutch Outpost (1652–1795)

In 1652 the Dutch East India Company established a station at the Cape of Good Hope. For many years the community remained small with little formal entertainment. Theatre in the European sense only appeared when the French Huguenot settlers (1688–1700) gradually altered concepts of cultural life, preparing the way for the British cultural invasion.

Another tradition established at the time concerned private performances by slaves, dealing with the social conditions of the times and performed for the amusement and 'conscientization' of their fellows.

Imperial Entertainments (1795–1880)

The British occupation of the Cape in 1795 brought formal European theatre to the subcontinent, but attitudes about theatre differed. The Dutch cultural clubs, organized along the lines of the *Rederykerskamers* ('cultural societies') of the Netherlands, held that the primary aim of theatre was to educate. To the British amateurs and the soldiers from the garrison, who preferred melodramas, farces, and the occasional classic (*Othello* and *Twelfth Night* were popular), the primary aim of theatre was to entertain. Gradually, West-End successes and a variety of other, less strictly dramatic entertainments touring the world — 'playing the Empire' as it became known — also reached the Cape. Among them were 'indigenous' spectacles such as the 'new Ballet Dance' entitled 'Jack at the Cape, or All Alive among the Hottentots' (premièred 1832, no author known) and a 'Grand Pantomime' called 'The Kafir War, or The Burnt Farm' (premièred 1850). Visitors to the colony were entertained with 'native dancing' and certain troupes were exported for the edification and pleasure of the inhabitants of the empire.

Local playwriting initially consisted of comic prologues and epilogues to the plays performed in the garrison, but the first complete text is a satirical farce by George Rex and Andrew Bain, performed in Grahamstown. Entitled *Kaatjie Kekkelbek, or Life among the Hottentots* (first published in 1846 in *Sam Sly's African Journal*, with a full version appearing in F. L. C. Bosman's *Drama en Toneel in Suid-Africa*, 1928), it is the first written example of 'kitchen Dutch', or what became Afrikaans.

A plethora of similar skits, satires, and farces followed, though few were published. However, the Dutch amateur tradition soon evolved into a serious Afrikaans one, with C. E. Boniface, J. Suasso de Lima, Melt Brink, and others providing numerous one-act plays and translations for amateur companies; many were printed, though they are of little literary merit.

Nationalism and Cultural Imperialism (1880–1939)

In this period a basic theatre structure involving three traditions was developed. A professional English theatre evolved from the touring companies, a local variant of colonial theatre elsewhere in the empire. Actor/managers who contributed to this were Sefton Parry (1857–62), Disney Roebuck (1873–85), the brothers Ben Wheeler and Frank Wheeler (1886–1910), Luscombe Searelle (1887–96), and Leonard Rayne (1905–25). There were few markets for local playwrights, given the competition with plays from abroad, though Bertha Goudvis (*A Husband for Rachel*, premièred 1906, first published in 1925) was a successful amateur, and actor/manager **Stephen Black** made a profitable career writing and producing many popular and incisive social satires between 1906 and 1930.

Afrikaans cultural nationalism initially found expression in the amateur theatre movement. Then, in 1925, the first professional Afrikaans touring companies prepared the way for serious playwrights who sought to emulate the European theatre. Among them were C. Louis Leipoldt (*Die Heks*, 'The Witch', 1923), J. F. W. Grosskopff (*Oorlog is Oorlog*, 1941), and H. A. Fagan (*Opdrifsels*, 'Flotsam', 1947). Western theatre inevitably affected many of the traditional performance forms in South Africa. Black urban culture flowered, producing vibrant music and glimmerings of a popular indigenous drama. There was a conscious attempt at promoting a formal theatrical culture among educated blacks, leading to the publication of plays in African languages (for example, *Imfene ka Debeza*, 'Debeza's Baboon', 1925, by Guybon Sinxo), and a lucrative but tightly controlled industry of writing plays for schools. The same process also saw the founding of western-style amateur theatrical societies in the 1930s (the Bantu People's Players and the Bantu Dramatic Society, for example) and the publication of English plays by black authors, including **H. I. E. Dhlomo**, whose *The Girl Who Killed to Save* (1935) was the first to be published. Dhlomo was to become the first real theorist of South African theatre.

Towards a Separate Development (1940–55)

The Depression and changing entertainment patterns slowed the growth of South African drama in the late 1930s. Professional theatre virtually died as theatres were turned into bioscopes (movie houses) by the African Consolidated Theatres and other entrepreneurs, and for almost fifteen years theatre became again the province of the amateur.

During the Second World War, theatre was largely maintained by women, including Muriel Alexander, Marda Vanne, Gwen ffrangcon-Davies, Leontine Sagan, Anna Neethling-Pohl, and Hermien Dommisse. The peace of 1945 brought the revival of full professional theatre, as experienced performers rejoined the industry. By the 1950s the primary focus was on commercial work from Britain and America, as Brian Brook, Taubie Kushlick, Leon Gluckman, Leonard Schach, and others presented West End and Broadway hits. Shakespeare and the classics survived largely because of the efforts of amateurs, the schools, and, eventually, because of state intervention.

In 1947 the National Theatre Organization (NTO) was established. It was the first state-supported theatrical organization in the Commonwealth, mandated to care for the cultural needs of South African citizens, to provide work for local performers, and to encourage indigenous writing. Managed by P. P. B. Breytenbach, the organization's companies toured the country and performed more than one hundred plays. Among the works premièred by the organization were the Afrikaans *Die Jaar van die Vuuros* ('The Year of the Fire-ox', *c.*1952) by W. A. de Klerk; *The Dam* (1952) by **Guy Butler**; the Afrikaans *Periandros van Korinthe* (1954) by D. J. Opperman; the Afrikaans *Germanicus* (1956) by N. P. van Wyk Louse; *Seven Against the Sun* (1962) by James Ambrose Brown; and the Afrikaans *Moeder Hanna* (1958) by Bartho Smit.

Despite its extensive influence the NTO was not a truly 'national' theatre, being colonialistic in its mandate and attitudes and basically serving the interests of whites. In 1961 it was replaced by a larger, more ostentatious governmental scheme comprising four regional Performing Arts Councils (PACs) with the same fundamental philosophy.

Meanwhile, the urban townships were further developing their own cultural style and industry. It was the time of ***Drum*** magazine and the shebeen culture, when authors, artists, musicians, poets, and performers all became cult figures. A number of jazzmen, hired to entertain the black units of the Allied troops, had returned and formed variety companies aimed at commercializing township music and performance. 'Zonk', a precursor of many such shows over the years, was performed between 1945 and 1947, was an enormous hit with both white and black audiences throughout the country, and popularized the new performance style.

Rising Consciousness and New Theatrical Forms (1956–1975)

Some writers had begun to rebel against the political regime and its policies, and theatre was seen as a powerful tool for expressing their opposition. Between 1956 and 1962 came the first significant break with the received tradition of colonial theatre and the beginnings of a long-term rift between the artist and the state. In rapid succession came Bartho Smit's *Putsonderwater* (1962, translated as *Well-without-Water, or The Virgin and the Vultures*, 1968), **Athol Fugard**'s *No-Good Friday* (premièred 1958 and first published in *Dimetos and Two Early Plays*, 1977), and the so-called 'try for white' plays such as Lewis Sowden's *The Kimberley Train* (premièred 1958, first published in 1977), Basil Warner's 'Try for White' (premièred 1959), Bartho Smit's *Die Verminktes* ('The Maimed', 1960), and Fugard's *The Blood Knot* (1963). There was a flowering of serious, non-institutionalized theatre and organizations, including Leonard Schach's Cockpit Players, Leon Gluckman's productions, the Serpent Players, the Union of Southern African Artists, and the Natal

Theatre Council.

In 1959 these innovative influences came together in the production of the musical *King Kong* (1961). A collaborative effort by black and white artists (including author Harry Bloom, composer Todd Matshikiza, and director Leon Gluckman), its success gave the local play legitimacy in the world of fashionable show business. Despite accusations of exploitation of black artists, the production stimulated theatre in the townships. Besides efforts at copying the success formula (for example, **Alan Paton**'s and Krishna Shah's *Sponono*, 1963), Sam Manghwane, Gibson Kente, and their imitators made a commercial success of the unique musical comedy style known as the 'township musical'. Kente later wrote plays of more substance such as 'How Long' (premièred 1973), 'I Believe' (premièred 1974), and *Too Late* (the latter published in *South African People's Plays*, 1981, edited by Robert Mshengu Kavanagh). Unfortunately, this success tended towards a voluntary submission to apartheid, since it became a theatre by blacks for blacks, while NTO was providing for whites. The Group Areas and Separate Amenities Acts of 1965 merely entrenched the virtual status quo: no racially mixed casts and no racially mixed audiences.

In the 1960s the theatre community began to feel the pinch of international censure — a playwrights' boycott in 1963 and an Equity ban on performers working in South Africa in 1966, for example — and had to rely on its own resources. Initially, this caused a surge of creative energy in mainstream indigenous (white) theatre. This renaissance was dominated by the PACs and Afrikaans playwrights such as Bartho Smit (*Christine*, 1971; English version, *Christine*, 1984), Chris Barnard (*Pa, maak vir my 'n vlieër Pa*, 1964; English version, *Tomorrow and Tomorrow and Tomorrow*, 1970), Adam Small (*Kanna hy kô hystoe*, 'Kanna Comes Home', 1965), and P. G. du Plessis (*Siener in die Suburbs*, 'Seër in the Suburbs', 1971). There were also performances of the works of a few prominent English playwrights, including H. W. D. Manson (*The Festival*, 1959, *The Magnolia Tree*, 1963) and Athol Fugard (*Hello and Goodbye*, 1971, *People Are Living There*, 1969).

Many other plays were produced, but few reached a wider public. Black writers, in particular, did not have the institutional backing provided by the PACs or the commercial theatres, and often fell foul of the censorship system created by the 1963 Publications and Entertainments Act. **Lewis Nkosi**'s *The Rhythm of Violence* (1964), for example, remained banned for almost twenty-five years. (See also **Censorship**, South Africa.)

Though significant avant-garde and political drama was produced by PAC workshop-theatres (The Presidency in Bloemfontein, the Arena in Johannesburg, and the Theatre Laboratory in Cape Town), it was the growing number of 'alternative' theatres that pushed theatre beyond its European roots between 1972 and 1976. Major factors were the growth of the Black Consciousness movement, the cumulative effect of boycotts, the increasing frustration of working along segregated lines, and disillusionment with the PACs as a force for change. These theatres provided both an outlet for the pent-up frustration and anger and training for many of the performers and directors of the post-Soweto period — particularly black performers, for whom the university system did not provide.

The most influential theatre was Cape Town's Space, founded in 1972 by Brian Astbury. It presented a multitude of new plays and launched many playwrights, including Fatima Dike (*The Sacrifice of Kreli*, in **Stephen Gray**'s *Theatre One*, 1978), **Pieter-Dirk Uys** (*God's Forgotten*, in Gray's *Theatre Two*, 1981), and Geraldine Aron (*Bar and Ger*, 1975). Other groups include Theatre Workshop '71 (1971), MDALI (1972), The People's Experimental Theatre (PET, 1973), The Company

(1974), and Junction Avenue Theatre (1976). The Company, run by Mannie Manim and Barney Simon, founded the Market Theatre complex in 1976, which also launched numerous new plays and playwrights as it dominated the 1980s.

Theatre as a Weapon (1976–1989)

By 1976 the political, economic, and cultural isolation of South Africa was increasing, television was introduced, and theatres were gradually being desegregated. The 1970s also signalled a marked swing towards playwriting in English as a viable means of public protest and discussion in the 'formal' theatres (such as the Market Theatre in Johannesburg and the People's Space and the Baxter Theatre in Cape Town), in certain university theatres, and in the much more radical and innovative theatre of the townships.

As the state clamped down on all 'subversive' publication and media presentations, spontaneous public protests, marches, dances, impromptu speeches, poems, and presentations became part of the mass struggle. Utilizing techniques from older indigenous forms — dances, songs, and narratives — performers rediscovered the power of performance. Township theatre, and 'city' versions of it, began to flourish, while fringe forms (cabaret, musicals, one-person shows, dance-drama, and so on) became legitimized in the 1980s — as the successes of Robert Kirby, Pieter-Dirk Uys, Ian Fraser, Gcina Mhlope, Casper de Vries, and 'people's poet' Mzwake Mbuli show. Similarly, the so-called workers' plays, evolved within the trade unions, became a very potent form of protest in their own right — even transferring to more formal venues on occasion.

The PACs constantly fought for more freedom, re-creating theatre workshops in the 1980s to present productions such as Sandra Kotze's and Elsa Joubert's *Poppie Nongena* (1984, based on Joubert's 1978 Afrikaans novel, *Die Swerfjare van Poppie Nongena*), Mitzi Booysen's 'The Time of the Hyena' (premièred 1986), and the controversial cabaret 'Piekniek by Dingaan' ('Picnic with Dingaan', premièred 1989). There was also an expanding body of student work, showcased at such events as the Grahamstown Arts Festival and the ATKV Kampustoneel. Festivals provided venues for the multilingual plays pouring from workshops and theatre groups. The township theatre, less accessible and based on open and changeable texts, became increasingly prominent as more and more of the productions crossed over into the city theatres and appeared at the festivals.

In this prolific period the dominant playwright was Athol Fugard and the dominant theatre the Market Theatre. Yet it was a time that turned South African playwriting into something unique, a blend of the many traditions inherited from Africa, Europe, and America. Significant workshop productions are Workshop '71's *Survival* (1981); Athol Fugard's, John Kani's, and Winston Ntshona's *The Island* (1973) and *Sizwe Bansi Is Dead* (1972); Barney Simon's and cast's *Cincinatti* (1984) and *Born in the RSA* (1986); Barney Simon's, Mbogeni Ngema's, and Percy Mtwa's *Woza Albert* (1984); Ngema's *Asinamali!* (1986) and 'Sarafina!' (premièred 1987); Phyllis Klotz's and cast's 'You Strike the Woman, You Strike the Rock' (premièred 1986); Junction Avenue Theatre's *Sophiatown* (1988); David Kramer's and Taliep Petersen's *'District Six — The Musical'* (premièred 1987); and Theatre for Africa's 'Horn of Sorrow' (premièred 1988).

Besides Fugard, the more notable playwrights of the period include Paul Slabolepszy (*Saturday Night at the Palace*, 1985), Pieter-Dirk Uys (*Paradise Is Closing Down*, 1978), Maishe Maponya (*The Hungry Earth*, 1984), Matsemela Manaka (*Egoli*, 1979), Pieter Fourie (*Die Koggelaar*, 'The Teaser', 1988), **Zakes Mda** (*We Shall Sing for the Fatherland*, 1980), Deon Opperman (*Môre is 'n* *lang dag*, 'Tomorrow Is a Long Day', 1987), Reza de Wet (*Diepe Grond*, 'Deep Ground', 1986), Gcina Mhlope (*Have You Seen Zandile?*, 1988), and Charles Fourie ('Diesel and Dust', premièred 1990).

In 1990 F. W. de Klerk and Nelson Mandela set in motion forces that would seek to dismantle apartheid. It is perhaps significant therefore that a popular show of this period was David Kramer's and Taliep Petersen's 'Fairyland' (premièred 1990) — a simple, effervescent, cross-cultural, and healing musical revue about living in South Africa.

TEMPLE HAUPTFLEISCH

Further reading: Temple Hauptfleisch and Ian Steadman, eds, *South African Theatre: Four Plays and an Introduction* (1984); Robert Kavanagh, *Theatre and Cultural Struggle in South Africa* (1985); Martin Orkin, *Drama and the South African State* (1991).

DRAMA (South Pacific)

Few, if any, reliable written accounts of the South Pacific's pre-colonial performance cultures survive. The gross distortions and ethnocentric judgments of early reports by European travellers, merchants, and missionaries and the firm Christianization of the islands during the mid-nineteenth century, which has shaped the transmission of oral narratives, leave the modern scholar with only scattered hints of the largely religious performances that must have been central to many of the region's societies.

In Tahiti, the travelling actor-dancer-initiates of the *arioi* seem to have supported themselves by touring plotted plays, perhaps simultaneously sacred and erotic. In Samoa, the *fale aitu* ('spirit house') enactments formed part of worship and today survive as comic entertainment. In the highlands of Papua New Guinea, what is now called a 'singsing' involved the whole community and appears to have included largely mimed mini-dramas, accompanied by song and dance. Such performances were closely related to the various forms of storytelling (e.g., the informal *fagogo* in Samoa), satirical clowning (e.g., the *han maneak su* on the Fiji island of Rotuma, the *koniseti* in Tonga), and mimetic dance (the frigate-bird dances of Kiribati and the animal imitations of the Solomon Islands).

Western theatre arrived in the Pacific through the colonial churches and schools. Small concentrations of population, except in Papua New Guinea, have meant that theatre production has been somewhat sporadic across the region.

The first major development in South Pacific drama in English was in Papua New Guinea in the period surrounding the attainment of independence in 1975. Highly politicized and nationalistic young playwright-producers such as Leo Hannet (*Em Rod Bilong Kago*, late 1960s; *The Ungrateful Daughter*, 1971), **John Kasaipwalova** (*Rooster in the Confessional*, 1973; *The Naked Jazz*, 1978), and Arthur Jawodimbari (*Cargo*, 1971; *The Old Man's Reward*, 1973; *The Sun*, 1980) not only anatomized the often troubled interface of local and colonial cultures, but also adapted mythic and folkloric material to the stage. What became the National Theatre was founded in Port Moresby, as was the Raun Raun Theatre, now based in the highlands. Both have continued as travelling theatre movements, bringing largely development-oriented plays to rural and urban audiences. The Papua New Guinea Literature Bureau began in 1971 to publish creative texts, including several plays.

In Fiji, two innovative playwrights emerged in the 1980s, **Vilsoni Hereniko** and Larry Thomas. Thomas' world is that of working-class urban Fiji, and his characters employ a closely observed Suva dialect. The uncompromising social realism of *Just Another Day* (1988), *Outcasts* (1989), and two one-act plays — *Yours Dearly* (1990) and *Men, Women and Insanity* (1990) — often centralizes women's sensibilities and interrogates the relationships between personality and environment.

Indo-Fijian writers have been more attracted to poetry and short fiction. But the community, especially before the traumatic 1987 coup, has occasionally staged elaborate dramatizations of episodes from the Indian epics the *Ramayana* and the *Mahabharata*.

Vanuatu's Wan Smolbag Theatre ('One Small Bag' Theatre), which was formed in the late 1980s, travels throughout the country with community development entertainments in English and Bislama, often commissioned by government ministries and international organizations. *The Old Stories* (1990) is an often-chilling episodic history of Vanuatu, celebrating the surviving culture and animating the more harrowing experiences of contact with Europe.

In the francophone Pacific, the Tahitian actor-playwright John Mairai, working at the Tefare Tauhiti Nui in Papeete, has mounted a number of spectacular productions, including his 'Maro Putoto' (premièred 1988), a Polynesian transposition of *Macbeth*. In New Caledonia, Jean-Marie Tjibaou, the popular nationalistic political leader who was assassinated in 1989, produced his epic *Kanaké* as part of the First Festival of Kanaka Arts in 1975. It was published as *Kanaké: The Melanesian Way* (1978), translated by Christopher Plant.

ANDREW HORN

DRAMA (Sri Lanka)

The picture of Sri Lankan drama in English in the last sixty years is complex. Several trends, discernible from the 1930s, took place concurrently, whereas in Australia, for example, similar trends tended to succeed one another. British touring companies to Sri Lanka staged British and American plays; expatriate groups staged British and American plays — usually light entertainment — for a mixed audience of fellow expatriates and Sri Lankans; local Sri Lankan groups staged British, American, and other foreign plays. The heyday of this trend was in the 1930s, 1940s, and early 1950s, when the Ceylon University Dramatic Society under the guidance of Professor E. F. C. Ludowyk dominated the theatrical scene. The most important trend, however, from the point of view of the development of local drama in English, was that Sri Lankan playwrights began writing original plays in English and had them performed by resident companies.

Sri Lankan playwrights have stuck firmly to two genres — the dramatization of history and legend, and farce and mild social comedy. The first tradition begins with Sri Nissanka's *Our Lanka* (1939), which celebrates a hero-king, Dutugemunu, who vanquished a foreign invader; while the theme was relevant to Sri Lanka's colonial situation, the play has little literary value. Even less effective are V. Ariyaratnam's completely abortive attempts in this vein — *Christopher Columbus* (1969) and *The Sigirian King* (1973). Lucien de Zoysa's experience in acting and directing plays gives his own works in this genre a certain effectiveness in stage craft and characterization. His works include *Fortress in the Sky* (his best play, first performed in 1956), *Princess of the Lonely Days* (1957), and *Put Out the Light* (1964).

Sri Nissanka and Lucien de Zoysa were probably inspired by the grandeur of Sri Lanka's history and legend and by a wish to promote national pride in the face of British dominance. Gamini Gunawardena's motivation in writing *Rama and Sita* (1964) is different; he wished to place the legend in 'proper perspective' and as universally relevant, and not merely to write a historical play in the accepted sense. He bases his play on the most interesting section of the *Ramayana*; Sita's immolation signifies Rama placing his public role, even political expedience, above personal considerations, including love. Influenced by T. S. Eliot's *Four Quartets*, *Rama and Sita* is couched in an idiom that is poetic but not dramatic; it tends to be abstract and lacks substance.

Sri Lankan audiences are much fonder of the

second dramatic genre — farce and social comedy. Its main exponents were H. C. N. Lanerolle and E. M. W. Joseph, who wrote a clutch of such plays in the 1930s and 1940s: *The Dictator*, *Well, Mudaliyar*, *The Senator*, *Fifty-Fifty*, *The Return of Ralahamy*, *Ralahamy Rides Again*. While these plays, then highly topical, now dated, demand a knowledge of the Sri Lankan context at that time to be appreciated, some of the character-types are universal.

Although **Ernest MacIntyre** wrote in this tradition of social satire, his departure from it is more important. In the Lanerolle-Joseph plays, Sri Lankan English was a target of ridicule; by the 1960s it was taken seriously. It is important to emphasize that in MacIntyre's plays language is not an issue and does not draw attention to itself; the language is a medium, as it is more recently in Nedra Vittachchi's plays. MacIntyre's use of language draws attention to itself only in his last published play, *Let's Give Them Curry* (1985), in which the situation of immigrants in Australia is defined by their speech. Influenced by the Theatre of the Absurd in the west, MacIntyre adopted this then-innovative form. In *The Loneliness of the Short-Distance Traveller* (1971) he dramatizes the theme of loneliness, a tragic aspect of the condition of modern humanity, with characters who are representative of the average, rather than individuals. *A Somewhat Mad and Grotesque Comedy* (1973) is both more local and more universal in what it says on the theme of violence — seen as something eternal and evil — while providing insights into family structures and priorities in life.

The satirical trend in Sri Lankan drama persists. It is evident in Nedra Vittachchi's flair for sophisticated comedy. She is MacIntyre's successor in that she is equally fond of experimental theatre. *Cave Walk* (1986) is a symbolic dramatization of how romantic love breaks up in the face of the demands and pressures of life. Her more ambitious efforts in this vein — *The Smart Ass* (1978) and *Pasteboard Crown* (1980) — do not quite succeed as literary texts, though they are piquant and entertaining in performance.

Reggie Siriwardena has enriched Sri Lankan drama with plays of a different nature. *The Long Day's Task* (1988) is more a political tract than literature, but *Prometheus* (1989) represents an advance in both form and meaning. It is an argumentative, intellectual, futuristic play on the permissible limits of technological development and its danger to human society. This issue, not Sri Lankan as such but one important for the whole of modern civilization, is orchestrated through a symbolic use of chess and a computer. **Ediriwira Sarachchandra**'s *The Golden Swan, or Beyond the Curtain* (1989) is based on a *Jataka* story, a story of one of the many births of the Buddha before Enlightenment. It suggests a tragic view — that acquisitiveness and the commercialization of art are not only sins of individuals but are social evils.

Drama in English in Sri Lanka has lagged behind poetry and fiction in English and behind drama in Sinhala, a situation like that in India, where there is a highly developed drama in Marathi, Hindi, and Bengali, but comparatively little in English. (See **Drama**, India.)

D. C. R. A. GOONETILLEKE

DRAMA (West Africa)

The Gambia, Ghana, Nigeria, Sierra Leone

The phenomenon of drama in English in West Africa is a relatively recent one. Although it is still very much an activity on the margin of the continent's cultural life, it would be an error to equate this marginality with insignificance. As with West African poetry and fiction in English, drama and theatre in English occupy a vital and dynamic space in the total cultural expression of the region and have garnered international acclaim.

The main reason for the marginality of West African drama in English is that English, for the most part, is still a second language in West Africa and is acquired only with difficulty through an imperfect educational system (itself not available to every citizen). As a result, the bulk of cultural activity continues to take place in the indigenous languages and in the inherited traditional formats. Nevertheless, artistic creativity continues in the medium of English because English continues to enjoy a privileged status as the national lingua franca and as the language in which most of Africa's official business is conducted. (See **Language**, West Africa.)

English is also the language that has been adopted by a substantial number of writers in Africa and particularly by writers who have been products of the school system. The real flowering of West African drama in English began in the 1960s, when many African countries won their freedom from colonial rule. While the origins of this theatrical activity predate the 1960s, the initial catalyst seems to have come, for a number of reasons, during the years of the nationalist struggle for independence in the years immediately following the Second World War. In that struggle, cultural activities played a considerable part both in mobilizing opinion against colonialism and in shoring up the self-awareness and the revolutionary spirit of the activists themselves. Certainly it was helpful to the nationalists to be able to challenge the colonial rulers directly in their own language. Coming as they did from various countries and ethnic backgrounds, Africans found the use of English to be essential in building solidarity.

After independence, greater attention was paid to education in West Africa, with the result that within a short time there was a proliferation of institutions of higher learning. This led to a tremendous increase in both audiences for theatre in English and in the number of dramatists writing for the theatre. Thus **Wole Soyinka** and John Pepper Clark (**Bekederemo**), for example, the pioneers of modern African drama in English, were both products of the University College of Ibadan, Nigeria.

Increasing literacy was complemented by the multiplication of the numbers of journals and newspapers and of publishing houses — operating mostly in English, though local languages were not neglected. These gave additional support to budding playwrights, by providing publication outlets or publicity in the form of advertisements, reviews, and interviews. In the subsequent growth of theatre in West Africa, politics continue to play a determining role, to such an extent indeed that all the movements that can be identified within Africa's dramatic repertory were shaped primarily by political factors. West African theatre in English, developing as part of nationalist struggles for independence, could not but be conscious of the paradox and the obstacles to its credibility evoked by its chosen linguistic medium. Instead of helping to resolve the problems of identity and difference, the plays only further foregrounded and heightened these problems, making the linguistic dilemma more obvious, as when illiterate African peasant farmers were shown dialoguing away in fine and grammatically correct English! Because the plays, for the most part, dealt with realistic events, located in familiar, historical contexts, such anachronistic scenarios vitiated the nationalist intent to rediscover African authenticity.

The problem arising from the use of a foreign language (English) for a native African theatre has merely been suspended, not resolved. The suspension has been made possible only through the adoption of specific theatrical conventions, that is, of stage mannerisms and dramatic sleights-of-hand unique to the region that have come to be generally accepted by both actor and audience. One such convention is the acceptance that the dialogue should remain in English, whatever the background of the speakers, but that this English should be localized in both syntax and lexicon as well as in its semiotic implications. This means that the diction has to be distinctly African and that the dialogue must be infused with local idioms and proverbs and with metaphors drawn from African flora and fauna. Also, in certain instances, the register is expanded to include regional pidgins of English.

Furthermore, the very form of dramaturgy itself has had to be reconceived in such a way that it mirrors and echoes African indigenous, pre-colonial forms of theatre. This means that the emphasis on rhetorical strategies in western drama that depend heavily on speech has been jettisoned, in the main, for a theatre in which song and music, dance and movement, mask and ritual, spectacle and procession are effectively integrated.

In this respect, perhaps the most notable example is to be found in the form of theatre developed by the Ghanaian playwright and director **Efua Sutherland** — *anansegoro*. *Anansegoro* is a storytelling theatre developed from the *anansesem* (tortoise stories) of traditional Ghanaian culture. The most famous example of such theatre is undoubtedly Sutherland's own *The Marriage of Anansewa* (1975). The Nigerian **Wale Ogunyemi** also offers a good example of *anansegoro* in his *Langbodo* (1979), but it is Wole Soyinka who has provided the most successful examples of this hybrid form of theatre in such plays as *Kongi's Harvest* (1967) and especially *Death and The King's Horseman* (1975), in which the medium of dance is fused effectively with the dialogue to carry the burden of the dramatic conflict. The point, however, is that today the convention has been accepted, and while most African plays from the English-speaking countries have their dialogue in English, albeit localized English, they integrate music, dance, and other paralinguistic resources in their form.

The earliest known, significant West African play in English is the Ghanaian Kobina Sekyi's *The Blinkards* (written and premièred in 1915, but not published, nor widely known, until 1974). It is a play that could well have been a precursor of West Africa's struggle for independence, since it attacks European cultural influences. This was the main theme of most plays written between 1940 and 1960, although their plea for African cultural authenticity takes diverse forms — aggressive, as in Herbert Ogunde's *Strike and Hunger* (1946) and *Bread and Bullet* (1950), and philosophical, as in the plays of F. K. Fiawoo (*The Fifth Landing Stage*, 1943) and of J. B. Danquah (*The Third Woman*, 1943).

After 1960, with the achievement of independence and political power by African states, the themes of African drama inevitably changed. Playwrights focused on the achievements or failures of the politicians, and, later, when the era of military *coups d'état* began, on those of the military. Thus, the broad thematic outline of the theatre in English-speaking West Africa since independence can be mapped as follows: plays that support civilian politicians; plays that indict them; plays that criticize military rule (none approve it); and plays that attempt to examine, through psychological or metaphysical explorations, the individual's predicament during these political avatars.

The Gambia and Sierra Leone are small countries, with, understandably, few plays in English in their repertoires. The English-language drama of Ghana and Nigeria, however, is certainly representative of the tendency in dramaturgy in West Africa to reflect the political issues of the times. In Ghana, for example, writers have always been intimately involved with the government, beginning with the rule of President Kwame Nkrumah, who patronized artists and supported the work of a playwright-scholar like Efua Sutherland, to the regime of Prime Minister Jerry Rawlings, who has given ministerial posts to such poets and playwrights as **Atukwei Okai, Ama Ata Aidoo,** Asiedu Yirenkyi, and Mohammed ben Abdallah. Even though many of these artists later left their posts in disillusionment and went into exile, they were able to devote their most active creative years to the goals of nation-building. As a consequence, Ghana has been one of the nations in which the arts have enjoyed official support and in which the state has committed a significant proportion of its resources to its artists and to artistic projects.

Perhaps because of this, and because they have been allowed to lend their dreams and their visions to the process of nation-building, the playwrights of Ghana have created works that are in the main devoid of existential anguish and are notably positive in their attitudes towards history and towards government. Sutherland's famous play *Foriwa* (1964) is one such instance, where the tensions between the modern and the traditional are resolved, and opposing ideologies blend into one ultimate humanizing ideal.

In Nigeria, however, perhaps because no visionary figure like Nkrumah has come to power since the 1960s, the rulers have always kept their distance from writers, whom they view at best with suspicion and disdain. Bitter mistrust has characterized relations between artists and the various Nigerian governments, and the artists, not surprisingly, are among the loudest and the most consistent critics of government. Consequently, the tradition of playwriting that has developed in Nigeria has been one of political commitment different from that of Ghana. Whereas the latter tends to be optimistic and reformist, that of Nigeria is mostly strident, radicalist, and iconoclastic. These two tendencies seen in Ghana and Nigeria represent the major differences in West African drama in English.

It is not surprising, therefore, that domestic problems have tended to dominate the concerns of playwrights in Ghana. Apart from a few plays that try to focus on the individual psyche (such as **Joe de Graft**'s *Through a Film Darkly*, 1970, Ama Ata Aidoo's brilliant *Anowa*, 1969, and Owusu's *The Mightier Sword*, 1973, in *The Sudden Return and Other Plays*), or on history and mythology (de Graft's *Muntu*, 1977), most plays in the Ghanaian repertory deal with crises in domestic relationships caused by changes in the social and economic order. The titles are self-explicit: Aidoo's *The Dilemma of a Ghost* (1965), de Graft's *Sons and Daughters* (1964), Kwesi Kay's 'Laughter and Hubbub in the House' (premièred 1972), and Asiedu Yirenkyi's 'Blood and Tears' (premièred 1973).

Such domestic dramas also exist, of course, in the repertory of other countries. In Nigeria, **James Ene Ewa Henshaw**'s *Dinner for Promotion* (1967) and Wale Ogunyemi's *The Divorce* (1977) are recognizably within the tradition, as is the Sierra Leonean **Sarif Easmon**'s *Dear Parent and Ogre* (1964).

When the atmosphere of these plays becomes more sombre, it is usually not because of political crises but because of individual failings and the resort to secret and occult agencies for material wealth. This is what makes for the extraordinary tension in such plays as Efua Sutherland's *Edufa* (1967), Yirenkyi's 'Kivuli' (premièred 1972), Owusu's *The Sudden Return* (1973), and Jacob Hevi's 'Amari' (premièred 1975).

In Nigeria, however, politics is more immediately the subject of drama in English, and the national leadership is almost always its target. The distinction will be obvious, for instance, in comparing a play such as Sutherland's *The Marriage of Anansewa* (1975) with **Ola Rotimi**'s *Our Husband Has Gone Mad Again* (first performed in 1966 in the USA and published in 1974) or with **Femi Osofisan**'s *Farewell to a Cannibal Rage* (1986), an adaptation of the Romeo and Juliet story.

Thus, the Nigerian repertory, which is undisputably the largest in Africa, for understandable reasons — population, educational institutions — covers the broadest and the most representative spectrum of the socio-political themes that preoccupy playwrights of the region. The plays range from mordant political satires (Fred Agbeyegbe's *Budiso*, 1985, and Osofisan's *Midnight Hotel*, 1986, for example), through historical epics and melodramas (most of the plays of Ola Rotimi) and radical, left-leaning agitprop dramas (Segun Oyekunle's *Katakata for Sofahead*, 1983, Olu Obafemi's *Nights of a Mystical Beast*, 1986, Tunde Fatunde's *Water No Get Enemy*, 1989) to more frankly experimental plays (**Kole Omotoso**'s *Shadows on the Horizon*, 1977, and Ola Rotimi's *Holding Talks*, 1979).

Women playwrights have followed in the tradition of Sutherland and Aidoo. This means that, quite apart from the general political issues, female concerns have received more emphasis in recent years. (See **Feminism**, West Africa.) Nevertheless, although there is now an increasing challenge to the traditional male hegemony and the prevailing sexism, feminist dramatists in West Africa tend to shun the stridently aggressive tones of plays by their western counterparts. The most prominent among these female playwrights — all of whom place great value on the positive virtues of motherhood, even while pleading for balanced relationship in marital affairs — are **'Zulu Sofola** (*Wedlock of the Gods*, 1972, *The Sweet Trap*, 1977, *Memories in the Moonlight*, 1986), **Tess Onwueme** (*The Broken Calabash*, 1984, *A Hen Too Soon*, 1983), and Stella Oyedepo ('The Rebellion of the Bumpy Chested', premièred 1990).

West Africa can boast of the presence of three of the most outstanding dramatists on the African continent. Wole Soyinka, who in 1986 became the first black person to win the Nobel Prize for Literature, has gained an international reputation. Since the early 1960s, there has hardly been a year in which this extraordinarily prolific dramatist has not provided a new play on the human condition. It is not surprising that his work spans the entire range of subjects discussed above. Among his most successful works are such plays as *The Lion and the Jewel* (1963), *The Road* (1965), *Madmen and Specialists* (1971), and *The Bacchae of Euripides* (1973).

Deserving of special mention are two playwrights from the same Yoruba community as Soyinka: Ola Rotimi and Femi Osofisan. Rotimi has distinguished himself in the area of historical drama; his mastery of stage and space, of spectacle and movement, helps account for the astounding impact of his plays *The Gods Are Not to Blame* (1971), *Kurunmi* (1971), and *Ovonramwen Nogbaise* (1974). Osofisan has achieved prominence with such plays as *The Chattering and the Song* (1976), *Once Upon Four Robbers* (1980), and *Morountodun and Other Plays* (1982), among others. He is now regarded as the leading dramatist of the generation immediately following Soyinka's.

Other playwrights worthy of attention are **Yulissa Amadu Maddy** of Sierra Leone (*Obasai and Other Plays*, 1971), Mohammed ben Abdallah of Ghana (*The Fall of Kumbi and Other Plays*, 1989), and, from Nigeria, Bode Osanyin (*The Flying Elephant* and *Waiting for the Ferry*, in *The Flying Elephant and Other Plays*, 1988), **Ken Saro-Wiwa** (*Four Farcical Plays*, 1989), and Bode Sowande (*Farewell to Babylon*, 1979, *Flamingo*, 1986, *Circus of Freedom Square*, 1986).

FEMI OSOFISAN

Further reading: Anthony Graham-White, *The Drama of Black Africa* (1974); Oyin Ogunba and Abioloa Irele, eds, *Theatre in Africa* (1978); E. Clark, *Hubert Ogunde: The Making of Nigerian Theatre* (1979); O. Ogunbiyi, ed., *Drama and Theatre in Nigeria: A Critical Sourcebook* (1981); Michael Etherton, *The Development of African Drama* (1982); B. Jeyifo, *The Yoruba Popular Travelling Theatre of Nigeria* (1984); B. Jeyifo, *The Truthful Lie: Essays in a Sociology of African Drama* (1985); Chidi Amuta, *The Theory of African Literature* (1989); Chris Dunton, *Make Man Talk True: Nigerian Drama in English Since 1970* (1992).

Cameroon

By far the most exciting literary art in Cameroon is found in the theatre, a realm closed to those not fortunate enough to travel there. The earliest known play in English was Charles Low's 'Westward Flows the Latex, Ho!' (premièred 1942), but the leader of the first generation of dramatists is Sankie Maimo. His *I am Vindicated* (1958) concerns the opposition of traditional and modern 'scientific' medicine. In *Sov Mbang the Soothsayer* (1968) Christianity is in conflict with traditional, indigenous religion. *The Mask* (1978?; repr. 1980) attacks the hypocrisies of modern society and its suppression of freedom. His more recent *Succession in Sarkov* (undated) stresses the necessity of maintaining continuity with traditional sources of wisdom.

Another generation of playwrights found its leader in Victor Elame Musinga (1943–), author, director, producer, and actor, with at least thirty plays to his credit, beginning with *The Tragedy of Mr. No Balance* (1976). Very close to the ordinary Cameroonians in his world view, Musinga creates blood-and-thunder thrillers and melodramas whose structural simplicity resembles folk tales. His themes are many: the evils of drink ('The Cup', premièred *c.*1974), corruption and bribery (*The Tragedy of Mr. No Balance*), abortion ('Njema', premièred *c.*1980), parental severity ('The Trials of Ngowo', premièred *c.*1981), and witchcraft and secret societies ('Colofonco', premièred 1982). In 1978 his Musinga Drama Group was the first anglophone troupe ever to win the coveted National Drama Competition. He continues to create and please large audiences, but the crown of leading dramatist has been passed among others in recent years.

Bole Butake (1947–) is the most widely known Cameroonian dramatist outside his homeland and a powerful successor to Sankie Maimo's strain of traditional realism. At the beginning of the 1980s, Butake's *Betrothal without Libation* (1981) and *The Rape of Michelle* (1984) presented positive views of modern individualistic concerns. His plays since then are far more complex. *Lake God* (1986) uses the Lake Nyos volcanic catastrophe of 1986 as a pretext for metaphoric examination of moral bankruptcy brought to a traditional society by the worship of western values. *The Survivors* (1989) is a moral play on the aftermath of the Nyos disaster, in which international aid is taken over by the powerful and greedy. *And Palm-wine Will Flow* (1990) presents a conflict between a Fon (traditional chief) and his Chief Priest, simultaneously commenting on the strengths and shortcomings within traditional society and delivering a thinly veiled revolutionary message in the context of the popular fervour for democracy in contemporary Cameroon. People power is led by women, a direct affront to prevailing prejudices. Butake's central themes are political, but they are built around obscure myths and symbols that refer indirectly to historical fact. His subversive side is obvious to many, yet authorities find it difficult to detect.

The most overtly political Cameroonian dramatist is Bate Besong (1954–), also a poet. (See **Poetry**, West Africa.) His plays virulently attack dictatorship and centre primarily on the anglophone problem and the lack of leaders. *The Most Cruel Death of a Talkative Zombie* (1986) is a plotless, absurdist, political drama in which two lepers denounce Cameroon's first president, Ahidjo. *Beasts of No Nation* (1990) has been hailed by some as a cry for freedom by a nation of workers reduced metaphorically to night soil gatherers. To others, this historically based drama may be provocative and propagandistic, but it is so avant garde in style that is borders on the incomprehensible, thus undercutting its main points. Nevertheless, when Bole Butake directed it in Yaoundé in 1991, Besong was detained and the state tried to intimidate the director. *Requiem for the Last Kaiser* (1991) assaults the continuation of dictatorship in Cameroon and its direction by a foreign mafia headed by the French ambassador. This play won the 1992 Drama Award from the **Association of Nigerian Authors**, Africa's most important literary association, an unusual endorsement of non-Nigerian art from a country whose art is barely accessible, even to its neighbours.

Other dramatists in the Besong school are Ba'bila Mutia and Victor Epie Ngome. Mutia's 'Before This Time Yesterday' (premièred *c.*1990) examines the destruction of the pre-independence radical movement, practising subversive dramatic hypnosis to overcome national amnesia imposed by the government. Ngome's 'Not the Name' (premièred 1985) and 'What God Has Put Asunder' (premièred 1992) are witty satires, the latter being an allegory about the fate of anglophone Cameroon, symbolized by the heroine Weca (an acronym for West Cameroon) in the wake of the 1972 referendum that forced the anglophone minority into a unified state with the francophones.

The latest sensations on Cameroon's stages are plays by Hansel Ndumbe-Eyoh, playwright, director, critic, teacher, and one of the most important animators of the African popular theatre for development movement. Less political than his militant colleagues, he writes plays that are close to the predominant paradigm of mainstream Cameroonian art, focusing on generation and gender conflicts, matters that lend themselves to allegorical interpretations, commonly generated by audiences in a repressive society where indirection is the artistic norm. In 'Munyenge' (premièred 1990) the heroine challenges the patriarchal establishment. 'The Magic Fruit' (premièred 1990) ends with the banishment of an avaricious chief. *The Inheritance* (1993) was an aesthetic triumph, whose meaning has critics divided. Some proclaim it to be apolitical, concerned only with family matters; others see it as a subtle challenge to specific reactionary social and political trends.

Ndumbe-Eyoh has been one of anglophone Cameroon's most astute theatre historians and critics. In various articles he has mapped the radical and historical currents that have dominated his people's dramatic culture, calling its artists' revolutionary preoccupations and aesthetics

> far removed from the molièresque influences in much of [francophone theatre] . . . Even in francophone centres these anglophones have become known in the last decade as the conscience of Cameroon society calling for social justice when most of the francophones avoid controversy.

STEPHEN H. ARNOLD

Further reading: Stephen H. Arnold, 'Preface to a history of Cameroon literature in English', *Research in African Literatures* 4 (1983); Richard Bjornson, *The African Quest for Freedom and Identity: Cameroonian Writing and the National Experience* (1991); Nalova Lyonga *et al.*, eds, *Anglophone Cameroon Writing, Weka* 1 (1993).

DRANSFIELD, MICHAEL (1948–73)
Australian poet

Born in Sydney, Australia, he wrote, between the ages of sixteen and twenty-four, a prodigious six hundred poems. He published three volumes of poetry — *Streets of the Long Voyage* (1970), *The Inspector of Tides* (1972), and *Drug Poems* (1972). Four other volumes of Dransfield's work have been published posthumously — *Memoirs of a Velvet Urinal* (1975), *Voyage into Solitude* (1978), *The Second Month of Spring* (1980), and *Collected Poems* (1987), the last three volumes edited by **Rodney Hall**. Dransfield died in hospital in circumstances that gave rise to sensational speculations about his well-known addiction to drugs.

Dransfield was a poet whose profession in life was to live as he believed a poet should: perpetually open to surprise and revelation, seldom passing more than a few days at a time without coming upon some pure moment of insight worthy of celebration.

After Dransfield had written a poem, he often re-explored it by seeking related illuminations of his own processes in writing it. Yet this had little in common with postmodernist practice. He was a romantic. His self-conscious celebration of his talent as it developed, along with the tragedy of a life often on the verge of being out of control, generated confidence in his romantic vision. He saw himself and the harsh realities of the twentieth century in relation to Keats and Shelley.

Dransfield's early poems are rich in colourful imagery and medieval allusions. Though not always avoiding the trap of whimsy, the best are astonishingly strong and true. For example, 'Bums' Rush' (in *Streets of the Long Voyage*), a poem of hallucinatory loneliness, despairs at public indifference to the plight of the homeless young, including a dead friend to whose memory it is dedicated. This mood modulates into anger in 'That which we call a rose', carrying the postscript 'Writ out of ashes, out of twenty years of ashes' and pivoting on the following lines: 'back in the world Rick and George on the morgue lists of morning / one dead of hunger the other of overdose their ideals precluded them / from the Great Society.' Such directness came as a palpable shock in the affluent Australia of 1969.

Dransfield had no lack of recognition. His poems were taken up — and not just as a cult statement. He was gifted with a fine ear. His musical lines showed a confident flexibility. The literary establishment welcomed him, especially for his love poems and such rhapsodic flights as 'Loft' (in *The Inspector of Tides*) — 'lightning is a bruise of pale / havoc around my eye's coast, and my arm, or / hers, draws in under a blanket from / the first morning of winter.'

While being treated for drug addiction at 'the House of Torment' (Canberra Hospital), Dransfield wrote the harrowing series of poems published as *The Second Month of Spring*. In notebooks crammed with an ever-deteriorating scrawl, the poems cry out with naked desperation — 'i do it / so my hands / at least will work / to keep my head alive.' These were the last poems Dransfield wrote.

RODNEY HALL

Further reading: Livio Dobrez, *Parnassus Mad Ward* (1990).

DRAYTON, GEOFFREY (1924–)

Barbadian novelist, poet

Born and educated in the parish of Christchurch, Barbados, he took a degree in economics at Cambridge University, England, and worked and lived for many years in Canada and England. He is retired and lives in Madrid.

Drayton's two novels — *Christopher* (1959) and *Zohara* (1961) — focus primarily on the impact of the adult world on the fragile world of childhood. The male adult world, in particular, is depicted as a negative force that taints and restricts the joys and liberties of the child. *Christopher* is quasi-autobiographical; it paints the experience of a white boy of the planter class growing up in Barbados and explores his relationships with his mother and father, with his surroundings, with death and sexuality and, especially, with Gip, his black nanny. Theirs is a meaningful and pleasurable relationship as Gip becomes like a mother to Christopher. When Gip dies, Christopher experiences an unprecedented emptiness and his childhood comes to an end. From the outset, Drayton places death markers and shows his protagonist confronting the twin experiences of death and sexuality so crucial in the Caribbean novel of adolescence.

Zohara is set in a southern Spanish rural community, ossified by ignorance, primitive conditions, and superstition. *Zohara* is not so much the story of its fourteen-year-old protagonist, Manrique, but of a community locked in the vice of medieval superstition. In this moral fable, Maria represents the voice of tradition in Zohara; Don Celeste, the feckless Roman Catholic church; and Manrique, the victim of nature, father, and community. Belief in the presence of witches and of Satan finally leads to the murder of the innocent boy. Medicine, the church, education, and even charity appear to be powerless against rampant vampire beliefs that suck the life-blood of the hapless young.

ROYDON SALICK

DREWE, ROBERT (1943–)

Australian novelist, short-story writer

Born in Melbourne, Australia, he worked as a journalist before publishing his first novel, *The Savage Crows* (1976). In his fiction Drewe explores the criminal possibilities and corruption beneath the banalities of suburban Australian life. In *The Savage Crows*, the story of George Augustus Robinson's attempts to 'save' the last of the Tasmanian Aborigines in the mid-nineteenth century erupts into the life of Drewe's 1970s journalist protagonist. The journalist's guilt for his failings as a father, husband, and son is linked to white Australian guilt for the dispossession of the Aborigines. **Randolph Stow** has compared the technique to that in **Leonard Cohen**'s *Beautiful Losers* and suggested debts to John Updike, **Mordecai Richler**, and to a 'North American empire' of white male writing.

Drewe's *A Cry in the Jungle Bar* (1979) follows the obsessions of an Australian agricultural consultant against a backdrop of the Philippines and Asia. Once again the 'ugly' white Australian confronts a racial guilt that is allied to personal failure and a guilty sexuality. These two novels are reminiscent of some of Graham Greene's fiction, in which a white male confronts a complex and exotic foreign society, with its associated problems of colonialism. However, Drewe consistently reflects on the nature of contemporary Australian society and, particularly in *The Savage Crows*, develops a strong satirical view of its complacency, racism, and affluence. His *Fortune* (1986) offers a slightly more experimental approach by reworking some well-known recent criminal activities into fiction in such a way that the line between fiction and journalism is constantly being called into question, and *Our Sunshine* (1991) explores the criminal through the imagination of **Ned Kelly**. In his two books of short stories — *The Bodysurfers* (1983) and *The Bay of Contented Men* (1989) — Drewe also reworks in fiction some notorious contemporary criminal cases. His work might be compared to Tom Wolfe's 'new journalism', in which the line between real events and their fictional counterparts is constantly blurred.

SUSAN LEVER

Further reading: Randolph Stow, 'Transfigured histories: recent novels of Patrick White and Robert Drewe', *Australian Literary Studies* 9 (1979); Bruce Bennett, 'Literature and journalism: the fiction of Robert Drewe', *Ariel* 20 (1989).

DRUM

In March 1951 the *African Drum* was produced in Cape Town and published throughout (the Union of) South Africa. The proprietor, Jim Bailey, had a pan-African vision for the magazine, hoping, as the first editorial stated, 'to reach the 150 million Bantu and Negro inhabitants of Africa'. However, these ambitions were initially not realized. Sensing that Johannesburg might prove to be a better informing locus, Bailey relocated the magazine in that city and, with the October 1951 issue, renamed it *Drum*. There Bailey hired Anthony Sampson as editor and a group of talented black journalists, which included at various times Ezekiel Mphahlele (now **Es'kia Mphahlele**), **Can Themba**, Bloke Modisane, Arthur Maimane, Nat Nakasa, **Lewis Nkosi**, Henry Nxumalo, Todd Matshikiza, and Casey Motsisi. This strategy was to prove successful, and *Drum* soon became the largest-selling magazine in Africa; by the middle 1950s, in addition to the Johannesburg edition, local editions were published in Nigeria, Ghana, east Africa, and central Africa.

Drum's significance for literary studies is confined to the years 1951–8. During this period it functioned as a medium of urban popular entertainment and as a vehicle for black social, political, and literary aspirations. The *Drum* of the 1950s poses a problem for analysis — although it demonstrated a keen understanding of the new urban mood of the black proletariat, featuring huckster advertising and busty pin-ups, celebrity pieces on local and international stars, and features that focused on the allure of the American style of life, it also ran a series of exposés that investigated life for people of colour under apartheid, covered the political manoeuvring of the period, and acted as a literary publishing medium for black writers at a time when no white venture would publish a story by blacks. *Drum* went on to publish more than ninety stories by blacks during the 1950s, including (in addition to those writers mentioned above) stories by **Richard Rive**, **Alex La Guma**, Peter Clarke, and **James Matthews**. *Drum* effectively established the black short story in South Africa. (See **Short Fiction**, South Africa.)

In April 1951 *African Drum* invited entries to the Great African International Short Story Contest, offering fifty pounds to the winning entry and four pounds for each story worthy of publication. The winner of this first contest was Can Themba. In its peak year (1957) the short-story contest drew manuscripts from 1,683 contestants. The stories represented the various shadings of black urban life in the 1950s, conveyed in the urban-rural hesitations of *Drum*'s early years (1951–2), the confident, peppy detective and true-love stories of the middle years (1952–5), and the broadly humanist portrayals of the final years (1955–7).

The first stories to appear in *Drum* were translations of folk tales, but these were soon shoved aside by the unmistakably urban evocation of William 'Bloke' Modisane's 'The Dignity of Begging' (September 1952). In relation to previous short stories by black South Africans such as **R. R. R. Dhlomo** and **Peter Abrahams**, Modisane's story was innovative, using a township argot and a detached, 'impertinent' tone that featured in many of the later Drum stories. The style of Modisane's work distinguished it, and much of the other writing that appeared in *Drum*, from the measured tones of a previous generation of missionary-educated writers and represented *Drum*'s singularity. Modisane signified the break with the past by making a quasi-*tsotsi* the protagonist of 'The Dignity of Begging', reflecting the swing of the urban mood away from characters such as the Reverend Stephen Kumalo in **Alan Paton**'s *Cry, the Beloved Country* (1948) towards those such as Nick 'Pretty Boy' Romano in black American writer Willard Motley's *Knock on Any Door* (1947). Motley's young gangster protagonist's motto, 'Live fast, die young, and have a good-looking corpse', became *de rigueur* for any young gangster aspirant on the Reef at the time.

Consequently, in a manner reminiscent of Charlie Parker's advice to jazzmen ('It's not what you play, but how you play'), most, but not all, of the *Drum* writers set out to produce fiction (and non-fiction — much of the journalism would blur the edges between imaginative fiction and reportage) with idiosyncratic turns-of-phrase, neologisms, paratactic structures, and unorthodox punctuation. The most regular purveyor of what Mphahlele refers to as that 'racy, concrete, impressionistic idiom, often incorporating the grand Shakespearean image' was Todd Matshikiza in his celebrity pieces; the style was dubbed 'matshikeze'.

In the context of the 1950s, the new idiom was provocatively ideological in its mockery of civilized English and in its refusal to conform to the colonial desire for the replication of English gentlemen abroad. The idiom also cocked a snook at the racist notion of the cheeky kaffir, as the writers announced their individualism and eschewed the ghettos — cultural, social, and political — that the newly fledged apartheid government had prepared for them. Two attitudes were implicit in the response to the *Drum* style: one is that the stories need not be judged on 'literary' terms alone (obviously they were not written for a highbrow audience), but in fact are better understood as avatars of the processes that constituted the 1950s; the other is that the stories, although apparently otiose, have a definite ideological function if relocated in their informing context.

In this regard it is necessary to mention that the generative literary frame of reference for most of the stories that appeared in *Drum* was the freehold township of Sophiatown, which lay to the west of Johannesburg. Instead of being an apartheid 'location', Sophiatown was really a multiracial suburb of Johannesburg, a vibrant community that attracted people of varying social gradations and rejected the values of traditional African society, as well as those apartheid legislated it should have, in favour of a progressive internationalism and an embracing humanism. In comparative terms Sophiatown is to the *Drum* writers what the Marico is to **H. C. Bosman** or the Little Karoo is to **Pauline Smith**: a quasi-real, quasi-mythical 'fiction' of a particularized era.

Drum was banned between April 1965 and 1968, when it appeared as a supplement to *Post*. The owner, Jim Bailey, sold *Drum* to the Afrikaner publishing house Nationale Pers in 1984. Today it has a competent editorial committee and produces worthwhile articles, but is only one of many magazines aimed at the black market.

BRUNO VAN DYK

Further reading: Michael Chapman, ed., *The 'Drum' Decade* (1989); Bruno van Dyk, 'Short story writing in *Drum*: an overview', *HSRC Bulletin* International Edition, 7 (1989).

DUCKWORTH, MARILYN (1935–)

New Zealand novelist, short-story writer

Born in South Auckland, New Zealand, the younger sister of the poet **Fleur Adcock**, she spent the war years in England, returning to New Zealand in 1947. Duckworth's first novel, *A Gap in the Spectrum*, was published in 1959. Two others followed, *The Matchbox House* (1960) and *A Barbarous Tongue* (1963), but during the next two decades Duckworth published only one novel (*Over the Fence Is Out*, 1969) and a few stories. In 1980 (by then the mother of four children and three step-children) she was awarded the Katherine Mansfield Memorial Fellowship and wrote *Rest for the Wicked*, published in 1986. A Fulbright fellowship and the Scholarship in Letters, which she has held twice, have enabled Duckworth to resume a steady output. In 1987 Duckworth was awarded the Order of the British Empire for her services to literature.

Although Duckworth is primarily a realist, her plots sometimes include elements of science fiction. In *A Gap in the Spectrum* the protagonist wakes up in a London bed-sit with no memory of who she is, convinced that in her country, Micald, the colour red is missing from the spectrum. The novel's sense of dislocation could be a symbol for the experiences of expatriate New Zealanders in England; significantly it provides a compelling reason for the heroine's passivity. *The Matchbox House* is a study of what has come to be called suburban neurosis, although it was drawn from Duckworth's experiences as an evacuee during the Second World War.

The protagonist of *Disorderly Conduct* (1984), perhaps her most successful novel, could stand for many Duckworth heroines — charming but feckless, beset by children and complications, including several ex-husbands and ex- or current lovers — while in the background looms the greater disorder of the 1981 Springbok Rugby Tour and the associated protests: 'It is as if the country is stained too.

A lost virginity almost. The rest of the world will never look at New Zealand in quite the same way again.' *Married Alive* (1985) is a mordant view of marriage, set in the near future, when a fifth of the population has been rendered insane from a contaminated flu vaccine. *Disorderly Conduct* won the New Zealand Book Award for Fiction. Duckworth's short stories have been collected in *Explosions on the Sun* (1989), and her poems in *Other Lovers' Children: Poems 1958–74* (1975).

ANNE FRENCH

DUDEK, LOUIS (1918–)

Canadian poet, critic

Born in Montreal, Canada, to Polish emigré parents, he attended McGill University, Montreal, later working for a time as an advertising copywriter. Following his marriage in 1944, he moved to New York, USA, where he earned MA and Ph.D. degrees at Columbia University. He returned to Montreal in 1951 to take up a teaching post at McGill, from which he retired in 1983.

During the 1940s Dudek was closely associated with John Sutherland, **Irving Layton**, and other writers who published in *First Statement* magazine. The aesthetic concreteness and social concerns of the *First Statement* poets are highly evident in Dudek's early poetry as collected in *East of the City* (1946), his first solo collection. A friendship, mainly epistolary, with Ezra Pound (whom Dudek visited at St Elizabeth's Hospital, Washington, during his New York years) helped to cement his work into the modernist line represented by Pound and William Carlos Williams. Several collections issued during the 1950s bear a strong Poundian cast, particularly the long poem *Europe* (1954; new edition 1991), and Dudek's lifelong devotion to the long poem reflects strong modernist affiliations. His other works in the form include *Atlantis* (1967), *Continuation I* (1981), and *Continuation II* (1990). Dudek's selected poems were published in 1988 as *Infinite Worlds*.

Dudek has been an important force in Canadian poetry as a critic, editor, and publisher. He co-founded Contact Press with **Raymond Souster** and Irving Layton in 1952, and later ran Delta (Canada) and DC Books, and *Delta* magazine (1957–66). His reviews and essays have appeared widely and always argue from the point of view of a ratiocinative modernist. Dudek's distaste for systematic criticism and his disdain for intellectual fashion led to well-known and longstanding arguments with the work of **Northrop Frye** and **Marshall McLuhan**. His essay collections include, among others, *Selected Essays and Criticism* (1978) and *In Defence of Art* (1988).

BRUCE WHITEMAN

Further reading: Frank Davey, *Louis Dudek and Raymond Souster* (1980); Susan Stromberg-Stein, *Louis Dudek: A Biographical Introduction to His Poetry* (1983); Terry Goldie, 'Louis Dudek', in Robert Lecker, Jack David, and Ellen Quigley (eds) *Canadian Writers and Their Works*, Poetry Series 5 (1985).

DUDER, TESSA (1940–)

New Zealand children's writer

She was born in Auckland, New Zealand, and educated at Auckland's Diocesan School and at the University of Auckland. Duder's novels reflect her interest in the dynamics of family life and in the pressures and prejudices facing girls in contemporary society.

Duder draws upon her own experiences as a musical schoolgirl growing up in Auckland, as the wife of a keen amateur sailor, and as a mother. Her first novel, *Night Race to Kawau* (1982), explores a situation in which the father is knocked unconscious on a yacht, and his inexperienced wife and children take over racing in rough seas and difficult conditions. It was followed by *Jellybean* (1985), which tells the story of Geraldine, the daughter of a professional musician mother, who decides that she wants to become a conductor.

Ambition is central to two highly acclaimed novels for older readers — *Alex* (1987) and its sequel, *Alex in Winter* (1989). In both, Duder draws upon her own experiences as a New Zealand swimming champion and traces the fortunes of the enthusiastic, exuberant Alex, who aims to swim for New Zealand in the 1960 Olympic Games. What is inevitably a demanding challenge becomes a nightmare, however, when Alex's boyfriend is killed. Although Alex does earn her place on the team, *Alex in Winter* is a bleak novel in which the protagonist battles with her own emotional crisis against a background of administrative incompetence and social hypocrisy.

BETTY GILDERDALE

DU FRESNE, YVONNE (1929–)

New Zealand short-story, writer, novelist

She was born and raised in a Danish-French Huguenot community on the Manawatu Plains, New Zealand. She trained as a teacher and has taught in primary schools, where much of her fiction is set, working as a music specialist and music lecturer in Wellington. Most of du Fresne's writing centres around her extended Huguenot family.

du Fresne published occasional stories in the 1970s, and in 1980 her first collection, *Farvel and Other Stories*, which records the experience of a child growing up on a Danish farming settlement in New Zealand in the 1930s. Her stories reflect the questions of identity and assimilation that characterize immigrant writing, with a distinct emphasis on the rituals of domestic and public life. du Fresne's fiction is distinguished by its fascination with storytelling as a context for knowledge and selfhood: in the preface to her novel *The Book of Ester* (1982), she comments on the 'two kinds of stories told to me in my beginnings': the first, stories of Hans Christian Andersen, of Danish families, legends, and folk tales and the second, those of French Huguenots — stories of battle, flight, and belief.

Like that of such immigrant writers in Australia as **Rosa Cappiello**, Antigone Kefala, and **Ania Walwicz**, du Fresne's fiction focuses on cultural difference through the medium of women's lives and stories. (See **Migrant Writing**, Australia.) Lively, engaging, and ironic, du Fresne's stories are more successful than her novels (her second novel is *Frederique*, 1987) and present a form of discontinuous narrative as a medium for exploring the discontinuities of history and culture. She has also published the story collection *The Growing of Astrid Westergaard and Other Stories* (1985) and the selection *The Bear from the North: Tales of a New Zealand Childhood* (1989).

LYDIA WEVERS

DUGGAN, EILEEN (1894–1972)

New Zealand poet

Born near Blenheim, New Zealand, her earliest poems, on religious and Irish themes, were published mainly in the Catholic press. Her first book, *Poems* (1922), is a selection of these; the title of her second collection, *New Zealand Bird Songs* (1929), reflects a growing nationalism towards her own country, whose history as well as wildlife she celebrated. In the 1920s and 1930s Duggan became by far the most widely known New Zealand poet. Her last three volumes, *Poems* (1937), *New Zealand Poems* (1940), and *More Poems* (1951) were published in England and the USA, and she had a considerable following in both countries, largely but by no means entirely among her co-religionists. She was gifted from the first with a genuine lyrical impulse and limpid style: 'I, made surer by sorrow, / Beg what seems more to me, / The faith of a willow in winter, / Or a blind hound nosing the knee.' When this impulse and style were united with genuine feeling and experience, memorable poetry resulted, though it was often frittered away in romantic rhetoric or pedestrian reflections on current events. A greater austerity and discipline appears in her later poetry:

'Although I fear the stone will rasp clean through, / Pumice my sheepskin into parchment, Lord!'

In recent years there has been renewed interest in Duggan's work, especially among feminist critics who believe that in her lifetime she was undervalued by a largely male literary establishment. There has not yet been a collected edition of her poetry.

DENNIS McELDOWNEY

Further reading: F. M. McKay, *Eileen Duggan* (1977).

DUGGAN, MAURICE (1922–74)

New Zealand short-story writer

Born in Auckland, New Zealand, he suffered from osteomyelitis as a child and subsequently had a leg amputated. Duggan left school at the age of thirteen, but attended the University of Auckland in 1947, passing some BA courses. He began writing at the age of nineteen, which, critic **C. K. Stead** conjectures, may have been partly in compensation for the life of action he was denied.

Duggan's first published story, 'Faith of Our Fathers', appeared in 1945. A story about a young man and Catholicism, it is an attempt at Joycean prose. 'Conversation Piece' (1947) parodies Hemingway, and 'Machinery' (1945) uses a Sargesonian idiom. In 1947 Duggan wrote for *Kiwi*, the literary annual of Auckland University College, where he published a number of stories and began to be recognized as a promising writer. In September 1950 Duggan left New Zealand and spent two years in England and Europe, returning in December 1952 following a tubercular haemorrhage in Spain. During these two years and after his return, he began to publish (starting with 'Six Place Names and a Girl' in *Landfall*, 1949) the stories that were collected in *Immanuel's Land* (1956), the volume that made his reputation as a writer. (He later worked in advertising.) For much of the 1950s Duggan recovered from tuberculosis, a recovery marked by his year as Burns Fellow in Otago in 1960. Most of the last eight years of his life were spent fighting first alcoholism and then cancer.

Duggan is considered to be one of three major writers of short fiction in New Zealand literature — the others are **Katherine Mansfield** and **Frank Sargeson**. His fiction moves from modernism to postmodernism, and although the quantity of his work is relatively small (thirty stories in thirty years according to C. K. Stead's edition of *Collected Stories*, 1981), it establishes Duggan as the writer who was able to take a different direction from Sargeson, whose realist stories dominated New Zealand fiction for twenty years. Intertextuality is also a feature of Duggan's work, and his stories show a willingness to explore distinctive styles of language. For his anthology *Speaking for Ourselves* (1945), Sargeson chose Duggan's story, 'Notes on an Abstract Arachnid', which Duggan later disliked for what he called its 'habit of rhetoric' and which is far removed from the undecorated idiom established by Sargeson as 'New Zealand' speech.

Although Duggan made various attempts to write a novel, he always returned to short fiction as his most successful medium. Like Mansfield, Duggan's best-known stories use a child's point of view and cluster around a particular family, in Duggan's case the Lenihans. 'Race Day', 'A Small Story', 'The Killer', 'Now is the Hour', and 'Chapter', all from *Immanuel's Land*, chart the development of Harry from child to young man and imply a discontinuous narrative, focused in a modernist style on particular events or moments of perception of the Lenihan family. Like Mansfield's, too, Duggan's stories do not focus on narrative or plot, but on the momentary significance in which meaning is glimpsed. As Duggan's writing changed, the emphasis in his fiction became focused on the rich surface of language — with its complex references to other texts and its 'enfolding' of culture — and moved further away from narrative.

Duggan wrote 'Blues for Miss Laverty' in 1960, following a talk to the Literary Society about the difficulties of writing fiction in which he imagined an author writing about a music teacher who drank too much. Widely celebrated, 'Blues for Miss Laverty', together with 'Along Rideout Road That Summer', formed the basis for Duggan's second collection, *Summer in the Gravel Pit* (1965). The intertextuality of Duggan's work is most widely recognized in 'Along Rideout Road That Summer', which describes Buster O'Leary's summer romance with the daughter of his employer. The story, like Duggan's article 'Only Connect' (in the Auckland Teachers College magazine *Manuka*, 1960) — on establishing 'the relationship between life and art' — suggests the difficulty of making connections between age and youth, Maori and European, memory and desire, life and art and offers New Zealand writing everything in the way of metaphor and textuality that Sargeson's early stories did not.

Duggan's third collection, *O'Leary's Orchard*, was published in 1970. From 'Along Rideout Road' to 'The Magsman's Miscellany' (Duggan's last story, which was published posthumously in *Islands*, 12, 1975), there is a submerged narrative connection in the recurrent references to O'Leary and his orchard. Duggan's writing, which began in modernism, is here moved along the road to postmodernism. The stories in *O'Leary's Orchard* recognize that narrative takes place in language and insist that connections, journeys, and fictions make and remake themselves in the attempt to connect life with art. It is their complex dialogues, the effort of connection, that characterize Duggan's stories.

LYDIA WEVERS

Further reading: Maurice Duggan, 'Beginnings', *Landfall* 80 (1966).

DUNCAN, SARA JEANNETTE (1861–1922)
Canadian novelist

Born in Brantford, Ontario, Canada, to Charles Duncan, an immigrant from Scotland, and Jane Bell Duncan, an Ulster immigrant, she attended local schools and a teacher training course, but soon turned to journalism instead of teaching. In 1884–5 she reported on the New Orleans Cotton Centennial for several newspapers, and subsequently worked for the Washington *Post*. She wrote frequent columns for the Toronto *Globe* and the Montreal *Star*, along with more formal essays for the literary journal *The Week*. A round-the-world trip commissioned by the *Star* took her to India, where she met her future husband, Everard Cotes, to whom she was married in Calcutta in 1890. Duncan's one child died at birth in 1900. She remained in India for more than two decades, and then took up residence in England where she died of bronchitis, a disease common among Anglo-Indians.

Duncan is an important figure in Canadian writing both as a journalist and as a novelist. Though her career in Canada as a journalist was relatively brief, her spirited and independent views are an excellent commentary on the political, social, and cultural climate of late Victorian Canada. Duncan felt that the 1880s were a 'golden age for girls, full of new interests and new opportunities', and she identified with the aspirations of the new class of professional women. Like Anna Jameson before her and **Robertson Davies** after, she strongly criticized Canadians for their cultural subservience: 'in our character as colonists', Duncan wrote, 'we find the root of all our sins of omission in letters.'

Duncan's reading of leading writers in the 1880s helped her to become a novelist in the 1890s. She greatly admired William Dean Howells and Henry James, and their presence can be seen in her early fiction, much concerned as it is with the 'international theme' they had pioneered. Both of Duncan's first two books, *A Social Departure: How Orthodocia and I Went Round the World by Ourselves* (1890) and *An American Girl in London* (1891), were popular successes much admired by critics for their witty lightness of touch. *A Daughter of To-day* (1894) is a much more sombre work, taking a very serious American Girl to Paris and London, and also initiating Duncan's repeated concern with the figure of the artistic creator. *Those Delightful Americans* (1902) interestingly reverses the usual formula by taking English country gentry to the USA.

Duncan's extended stay in India led her to write many books that, unlike the frontier romances of her best selling contemporaries Flora Annie Steel and Maud Diver, dealt with the difficulties urban Anglo-Indians faced in encountering an alien culture. In such works as the brilliantly written *The Simple Adventures of a Memsahib* (1893) Duncan seems to be testing the validity of the cultural myths Anglo-Indians created for themselves, among them the legend of the Simla *femme fatale* that Rudyard Kipling created in his early stories. In her Indian novels, Duncan closely scrutinizes both political issues and social practices: *His Honour, and a Lady* (1896) is an indictment of political expediency that also mercilessly satirizes Anglo-Indian nonconformity, while *The Path of a Star* (1899; American title *Hilda*) examines a wide spectrum of Anglo-Indian society in relation to marginalized outsiders — two missionaries and an actress. Duncan returns to the theme of the alienated artist in 'An Impossible Ideal', an excellent novella in her collection of short fiction *The Pool in the Desert* (1903). Her last two Indian novels, *Set in Authority* (1906) and *The Burnt Offering* (1909), are notable for the wider imaginative sympathy Duncan displays towards Indians and for their portrayal of the increased political and racial tensions of that historical moment.

A close relationship to actual events is also evident in *The Imperialist* (1904), Duncan's best, and best-known, novel. She consciously sets out to record 'the making of a nation' by having her title character, Lorne Murchison, passionately espouse the imperialist cause in a by-election held in Elgin, a community closely modelled on Brantford. A romance between Lorne's sister Advena and a Scottish minister provides another variation on the international theme. Duncan then takes two Canadian siblings to England in *Cousin Cinderella* (1908). The narrator and her brother are at first dazzled by London, 'the very citadel of the imagination', but whereas Graham Trent remains eager to make the colonial sacrifice by devoting himself through marriage to the restoration of a Tudor manor house, Mary increasingly feels she and Graham are 'aliens' in London and rebels against the indifference and condescension with which they are treated. Both these Canadian works explore the transition from a colonial to a nationalist sensibility.

Duncan wrote two autobiographical works that contain many interesting passages of personal reflection. *On the Other Side of the Latch* (1901; American title *The Crow's Nest*) records an alternation between melancholy and determination as she struggles with a bout of tuberculosis. *Two in a Flat* (1908) describes life with a servant in Kensington. Duncan's last thirteen years, which yielded four books — most of them inferior versions of the international romance, and several unsuccessful plays — were anti-climactic in relation to the productive previous two decades.

Like **Lucy Maud Montgomery** and **Stephen Leacock**, Duncan described small town Canadian life with a mixture of sympathy and irony. She also deserves comparison with **Henry Handel Richardson** and **Miles Franklin**, two Australian contemporaries who, like Duncan, wrote about creative young women who have to struggle to preserve their independence in the face of strong pressures to conform to the restrictive standards of a community. Duncan's talent for precise social observation and analysis gives her work distinction. She was a very self-conscious stylist, sometimes mannered but at other times very effective in communicating shades of meaning. *The Imperialist* has been very thoroughly analyzed in recent years by numerous critics, but her other work needs further study, particularly from a feminist or comparative perspective.

THOMAS E. TAUSKY

Further reading: Thomas E. Tausky, *Sara Jeannette Duncan: Novelist of Empire* (1983); Marian Fowler, *Redney: A Life of Sara Jeannette Duncan* (1983).

DUODO, CAMERON (1937–)

Ghanaian novelist

He was born in Asiakwa (Akim-Abuakwa district), Ghana, and after a basic education in his home town became a writer for *New Nation*, a Christian magazine in Accra. His short story, 'Tough Guy in Town' (in *Voices of Ghana*, 1958, edited by Henry Swanzy), about the experience of urban life by rural migrants, was broadcast by the Ghana Broadcasting Corporation, where he was news editor between 1956 and 1960. As chief editor (1960–5) of the Accra magazine *Drum* and of the *Daily Graphic* (Ghana's largest paper) between 1970 and 1971, Duodo defied on principle both Nkrumah's and Busia's governments. In the late 1960s he led a protest against the Nigerian Federal Government, which had jailed **Wole Soyinka** without trial. Duodo's reputation as a novelist rests on *The Gab Boys* (1967), which shows, however, that he has yet to make a successful transition from journalistic to creative writing.

Duodu's story 'The Tax Dodger' (in *Okyeame*, January 1961) has been incorporated in *The Gab Boys*. His poems 'Return to Eden' and 'The Stranded' have been published in *Messages: Poems from Ghana* (1970), edited by **Kofi Awoonor** and G. Adali-Mortty. *The Gab Boys* is named after the gabardine pants worn by delinquents from Pusupusu village whose imaginations are 'fuelled to combustion point by . . . action-packed American films'. By exploring the experience of these young people who fled to urban centres for work, adventure, and glamour, Duodu attempts to highlight the malaise in post-independence Ghana. However, he lacks the serious artistry and fertile imagination behind **Ayi Kwei Armah**'s treatment of the same phenomenon in *The Beautyful Ones Are Not Yet Born* (1968).

Duodu's penchant for sensationalism, extravagant expression, and cliché, which compares with W. K. Ansah's style in *The Denizens of the Street* (1971), grows out of Ghanaian popular literature. Like Benibengor Blay in *Coconut Boy* (1970), Duodo gives a cursory treatment of the themes of racism and cultural conflict. The narrative strands of *The Gab Boys* are anecdotal, episodic, and not fully meshed into the narrative form. The authorial indiscretions seem limitless.

CHRIS KWAME AWUYAH

Further reading: 'Gab Boys' (no author cited), *West Africa* 16 Sept. 1967.

DU PLESSIS, MENÁN (1952–)

South African novelist

Born in Cape Town, South Africa, she earned a BA (1981) from the University of Cape Town, where she began post-graduate studies in linguistics. Her two novels, *A State of Fear* (1983), winner of the Olive Schreiner Prize in 1985, and *Longlive!* (1989), have been translated into Dutch and German; her poetry has featured in various literary publications.

du Plessis' novels made her one of the most promising of a generation of writers surer of their South Africanness (others include poets Ingrid de Kok and Kelwyn Sole) than were earlier writers in English. (du Plessis' antecedents on her father's side were Afrikaner.) While her protagonists do not question whether or not they belong in South Africa, they are painfully aware of their marginalization from the white, especially Afrikaner, culture and society that was responsible for apartheid. Both novels trace an intense struggle with the Afrikaner father as patriarch, possessor of the land and language, and oppressor of women as well as blacks. (du Plessis, however, disclaims the label 'feminist' and specifically feminist goals.)

du Plessis' novels also reflect her activism, depicting what it was like in the streets, in schools, in offices, and at mass meetings for (some of) the small people who 'worked for change' in the early 1980s, when schoolchildren had placed themselves in the vanguard of open resistance. The setting is Cape Town, a city du Plessis evokes sometimes through lyrical and delicate celebration of its natural beauty, but more frequently through its voices — the local patois cries of hawkers in the streets, the chants in different languages at political rallies. The novels, however, are directed inward: these voices impinge on the consciousness of narrating characters intent on scrupulous examination (which can be over-detailed) of their ethical dilemmas about politics, work, and love.

EVA HUNTER

DURACK, MARY (1913–)

Australian biographer, novelist, children's writer

Born in Adelaide, Australia, into the pastoralist Durack family, she spent her early childhood and post-school years in the Kimberley region of Western Australia, her 'spirit country', to which she returns regularly from Perth. With her younger sister, the artist Elizabeth Durack, she helped to run the Durack cattle properties during the 1930s. Most of Mary Durack's non-fiction and fiction refers to the hot, rugged, and isolated Kimberley region.

Durack's major literary work is her Durack family saga *Kings in Grass Castles* (1959) and *Sons in the Saddle* (1983). The nineteenth-century landholders and ancestors are depicted as 'kings in grass castles' because 'this was a precarious livelihood, dependent on the drought-breaking storms, the goodwill of the Aborigines, the movement of the gold seekers, the booms and depressions of the developing continent'. Durack has likened her grandfather and his generation to the heroes of the Wild West in the USA.

Durack's only novel, *Keep Him My Country* (1955), was well received at first, but was later criticized for its 'romantic' treatment of the central relationship between an Aboriginal girl and a white station-owner. Durack's non-fiction books, *The Rock and the Sand* (1969), a study of Christian missionaries in northwestern Australia, and *To Be Heirs Forever* (1976), the story of Eliza Shaw, an early settler in the Swan River colony, continue the 'pioneer' theme in her work, for which she will be chiefly remembered.

BRUCE BENNETT

DUTT, NARENDRENATH

See **VIVEKANANDA, SWAMI**

DUTT, ROMESH CHUNDER (1848–1909)

Indian novelist, translator

Born in India, the cousin of **Toru Dutt**, he graduated from the Presidency College, Calcutta, and passed the Indian Civil Service examination in 1869. The first Indian to occupy the position of divisional commissioner, he was known as a farsighted administrator. For some time he was a member of the legislative council of the Bengal lieutenant governor and was honoured with the Companionship of the Indian Empire. He retired in 1897, but later took up service as the Dewan of Baroda.

Dutt's scholarly and literary work is both varied and valuable. Influenced by his contemporaries, Michael Madhusudan Dutt and Bankim Chandra Chatterjee, he wrote his novels in Bengali, two of which he translated into English as

The Lake of Palms (1902), a story of nineteenth-century Bengali domestic life, and *The Slave Girl of Agra* (1909), a romance set in seventeenth-century Agra. His son, Ajoy Dutt, translated into English three more of his Bengali novels including *Todar Mull, the Conqueror of Bengal* (1947). Though not satisfying as works of art, these are of considerable historical interest. Dutt's scholarly works include *The Peasantry of Bengal* (1874), *A History of Civilization in Ancient India* (3 vols, 1889–90), *A Brief History of Ancient and Modern India* (1891), *England and India: A Record of Progress During a Hundred Years, 1785–1885* (1897), *The Economic History of British India* (1902), *India in the Victorian Age* (1904), *Cultural Heritage of Bengal* (3rd rev. ed., 1962), and *Later Hindu Civilization* (4th ed., 1965).

Dutt's *Lays of Ancient India* (1894) presents in verse a representative selection from the *Rig Veda*, the Upanishads, the *Dhammapada*, Kalidasa's *Kumarasambhava*, and Bharavi's *Kiratarjuneeya*. Dutt's *The Ramayana: The Epic of Rama Rendered into English Verse* (1899) and *Mahabharata: The Epic of India Rendered into English Verse* (1898), however, constitute his major contributions as a translator. Passages narrating the main incidents are selected for translation and are connected by short notes. Dutt adopted the 'Locksley Hall' metre of Tennyson, in his view, a close equivalent to the Sanskrit Anushtup metre.

L. S. R. KRISHNA SASTRY

Further reading: M. K. Naik, *A History of Indian English Literature* (1982).

DUTT, TORU (1856–77)

Indian poet, novelist

She was born in Calcutta, India, into the aristocratic Dutt family of Rambagan, and was cousin of **Romesh Chunder Dutt**. She received the education of her time, completely western, eschewing everything 'native'. By the age of fourteen Dutt had read Shakespeare and Milton without learning to write her name in Bengali. She schooled in Nice, France, and attended lectures in Cambridge, England.

The story of Dutt's short life is one of promise rather than fulfilment. While her youth was packed with lessons in English, French, music, and painting, followed by heroic attempts to master Sanskrit, there were also upheaval and change — the family's conversion to Christianity, a grand European tour, meetings with eminent personalities, the early deaths of her brother and sister, and her own prolonged ill health. Yet Dutt was among the first Indians to publish poetry in English, and she made India known to the English- and French-speaking worlds.

A Sheaf Gleaned in French Fields (1876), Dutt's translation of French poetry, was received favourably by André Theuriet and Edmund Gosse, among others. Characteristically, the themes Dutt chose were 'separation and loneliness . . . loss and bereavement, declining seasons and untimely death', in the words of critic H. P. Dwivedi.

Bianca, or the Young Spanish Maiden (1878) is an unfinished romance full of pathos — melodrama according to one view — with autobiographical elements in the portrayal of the heroine, her strong love for her father, and the death of her sister.

Le Journal de Mlle. D'Arvers (1879) is a novel, in French, in the form of a diary written by a young French girl, Marguerite. Two brothers fight for her hand; there is fratricide, madness, and suicide. Marguerite finally finds true love, marriage, and motherhood, but falls ill and dies an early death (like all the Dutt children). Dutt's mastery of French is a tribute to her linguistic capability. (Gosse felt she wrote better French than English.)

If Dutt had written no more, her work would have remained imitative and derivative and her importance no more than historical. But in turning to her Indian roots and to stories from Indian epics and the Puranas for her *Ancient Ballads and Legends of Hindustan* (1882) she displayed her genius. She used the ballad form for tales, of which only 'Jogadhya Uma' is of folk origin. There are nine poems, not all of equal merit. The best-known are 'Savitri', a poem of sombre grandeur in its recital of Savitri's face-to-face meeting with Death to win back her husband, and 'Lakshman', a dialogue between Sita and her brother-in-law, where Sita's uncharacteristic behaviour under stress is effectively demonstrated. Dutt's adopted Christian faith does not generally colour her rendering of Hindu legends, possibly because she had absorbed them in childhood; the exception is 'The Royal Ascetic and the Hind'. 'Sita' is a nostalgic recollection of the days when all the Dutt children gathered in the evening to listen to tales and to shed tears as they heard the sufferings of Sita narrated.

The personal element marks many of Dutt's miscellaneous poems — recollections of childhood in 'Our Casuarina Tree', gratitude for the kindness of a stranger in 'Near Hastings', love for her father and a premonition of death in 'Tree of Life'. There are also echoes of the Romantics and of Victorian sentimentality, but sentimentality is also a characteristic of Indian poetry.

Dutt wrote critical essays on Le Comte de Lisle and **Henry Derozio** and translated the speeches of Victor Hugo and A. Thiers. Her letters to Mary Martin and Clarisse Bader were published by Harihar Das as *Life and Letters of Toru Dutt* (1921).

Dutt was the product of three languages, three cultures, and two religions. In her poem 'Lotus' she achieves a characteristic synthesis of symbols. She would have progressed to greater maturity and depth if time had been on her side.

PADMA SESHADRI
PADMA MALINI SUNDARARAGHAVAN

Further reading: Padmini Sen Gupta, *Toru Dutt* (1968); A. N. Dwivedi, *Toru Dutt* (1977).

DUTTON, GEOFFREY (1922–)
Australian poet, novelist, critic
Born near Kapunda, South Australia, he grew up on the sheep stud founded by his great-grandfather. He served as a wartime pilot, studied at Magdalen College, Oxford, England, travelled widely, and lectured in English at Adelaide University before embarking on a career in publishing in 1962.

As a member of the *Angry Penguins* movement in the 1940s, Dutton, frustrated by Australian philistinism, looked to the UK and Europe for his literary models. His first novel, *The Mortal and the Marble* (1950), reflects his cultural ambivalence. The 1967 poem 'A Finished Gentleman' mocks the Anglocentrism of his privileged upbringing, yet the neglect of ideas in 'this innocent country' qualifies the endorsement of its demotic vigour. Although he has become a republican and champion of the national literary heritage, in his own poetry Australia is important primarily as a source of natural imagery. Such social comment as there is mostly involves disdain for consumerism and puritanism and approval of the earthy integrity of country life. His dominant interest has always been love: the concerns of the self are usually those that dissolve in its sensual self-sufficiency or those provoked by separation. Love is the measure of all things; Dutton invokes the natural world to illumine love and vice versa. The derivative modernism of his first book of poetry, *Night Flight and Sunrise* (1944), is replaced in subsequent volumes by a relaxed lyricism. His use of form is conventional, sometimes complacently so. Nature is well observed in diverse settings, ranging from desert to ocean. *Selective Affinities* (1985) has his best work.

As well as novels based on wartime experience (*Andy*, 1968), Soviet travel (*Tamara*, 1970), and Pacific history (*Queen Emma of the South*

Seas, 1976), Dutton has written serious and popular works on aspects of Australian history, art, literature, and society. He edited *The Literature of Australia* (1964), a useful literary history. His study of Australian literary culture, *Snow on the Saltbush* (1984), manifests respect for popular opinion combined with a commitment to modernity.

ANDREW WALLACE

E

Early Novel (India). See **Novel** (India)

Easmon, Raymond Sarif (1913–)

Sierra Leonean novelist, dramatist, short-story writer

Born in Freetown, Sierra Leone, he received his primary education partly in Freetown, partly in Guinea, before proceeding to Newcastle University, England, where he qualified as a doctor. Easmon's part-creole, part-Susu ancestry is reflected in his affirmation of the values of Susu-creole aristocracy. The sense of integrity and hatred of corruption, incompetence, and injustice that led to Easmon's resignation from the government medical service and his entry into private practice are reflected in his plays, particularly *The New Patriots* (1965), a scathing denunciation of the ineptitude and corruption characterizing the government in post-independence Sierra Leone.

Easmon's plays, including *Dear Parent and Ogre* (1964) and 'Dilys Dear Dilys' (premièred *c.*1970), deal with tribalism, class snobbery, corruption, and incompetence. They have been denounced by critics such as **Ama Ata Aidoo** and Gerald Moore as racist, un-African, and old-fashioned. Although the charge of racism is difficult to sustain, the plays do exude an un-African atmosphere arising mainly from their characters' western life-style. Unlike such writers as **Chinua Achebe,** Easmon makes no attempt to impart an African flavour to the rather stylized version of English his characters use. In his novel *The Burnt-Out Marriage* (1967) there is little sympathy for traditional African life. However, in the collection *The Feud and Other Stories* (1981) there is greater responsiveness to traditional values.

Although Easmon has been faulted for weak characterization and melodrama, *The New Patriots* offers surer characterization, a tighter plot, and compelling drama.

EUSTACE PALMER

East-West Encounter (India)

Although British colonization of India, which was responsible for India's exposure to the west, formally ended in 1947, western domination in terms of ideas, attitudes, modes, and structures has continued unabated. From its beginning, the east-west encounter in India has been a source of tension — tension that also marks Indian writing in English. The nineteenth-century Marathi writer V. K. Chiplunkar, for example, was alarmed by the domination of British literary culture in India and declared that 'crushed by English poetry our freedom has been destroyed'. **M. K. Gandhi,** whose rejection of modern industrial civilization was total, offered an alternative goal in his conception of Swaraj (self-rule) for India. **A. K. Coomaraswamy** similarly warned Indians against cultural subjugation by the west. The philosopher K. C. Battacharya supported cultural assimilation, but insisted that this should be a conscious and selective process and pleaded for the recovery of the 'vernacular mind'. Even **Nirad C. Chaudhuri,** an ardent admirer of the British, regretted the fact that the British Empire 'conferred subjecthood on us but withheld citizenship'. While the source of tension preceding Indian independence was the awareness of both colonial exploitation and the benefits of British rule, the tension in the post-independence era results from the conflict between the growing intellectual dependence on the west in nearly all fields and the urgent need to re-establish the supremacy of the native mind and culture.

The encounter of the west and India has been addressed directly in some literary works in English, such as E. M. Forster's *A Passage to India* (1924) and **Raja Rao**'s *The Serpent and the Rope* (1960); however, it has also manifested itself more subtly, as critic A. N. Kaul has argued, as a shaping force and as a pervasive presence. In Indian writing in English, the meeting of east and west is articulated at various levels: the psychological, in terms of individual encounters; the socio-political, in terms of cultural, political, and economic conflicts; the philosophical, in terms of the clash of world views and value systems; and the literary, in terms of interactions between languages and modes of expression. These levels are not isolated, but interrelated, and are often simultaneously present in a given work, though the form of expression may vary from text to text.

Fiction, which constitutes the strongest and the most extensive area of Indian writing in English, illustrates such generalizations. Sarat Kumar Ghosh's *The Prince of Destiny* (1909), for example, is one of the earliest Indian novels in English to treat seriously the east-west theme. The protagonist, the Indian prince Barat, is believed by his people to be an incarnation of Krishna. His relationship with an English woman, Nora, whom he meets in England, is successful on the level of passion. Although in the end the couple must separate, east and west in this novel are conceived to be complementary, and Barat's return to his own people and his parting from Nora are not seen as a rejection of the west. Romain Rolland's metaphor of the 'archway' for the union of east and west aptly describes the theme of *The Prince of Destiny*.

The basic plot of *The Prince of Destiny* appears again in **Kamala Markandaya**'s *Some Inner Fury* (1955), but this post-independence novel is vitally different from Ghosh's work. Here again there is a passionate relationship — between Mira and Richard — that transcends all cultural barriers, but it flounders against the rock of political conflict; the archway collapses. Novels such as **Ruth Prawer Jhabvala**'s *Esmond in India* (1957), **Balachandra Rajan**'s *The Dark Dancer* (1958), and **Anita Desai**'s *Bye-Bye, Blackbird* (1968) are further illustrations of a cultural determinism that seals the fate of individual relationships. In *Esmond in India*, for example, Esmond and Gulab are not conscious representatives of their respective societies, and yet the conflict between them is represented as a clash of cultures. Esmond's conception of one's wife as an equal and a companion (though rarely translated into action) and his distaste for the Indian way of life, particularly in the area of family relationships, turn him into a bully and a sadist and cause his degradation as an individual. Yet it is not Esmond's cruelty that finally drives Gulab to leave him, but his failure as a protector of her honour as prescribed by the Indian marriage code. **Mulk Raj Anand**'s *Two Leaves and a Bud* (1937) and **Manohar Malgonkar**'s *Combat of Shadows* (1962) dramatize economic and sexual exploitation of the colonized, but lack the complexity of the novels of cross-cultural encounter.

Although Rao's *The Serpent and the Rope* also employs the structure of a marriage to explore issues of cross-cultural encounter, it is unique among Indian novels in English because of the multiplicity of levels on which the encounter takes place. Rama and Madeleine ultimately seek divorce on grounds of temperamental incompatibility, but what separates them is a basic metaphysical difference in their conceptions of self and reality, a difference rooted in their separate cultures. The distinction of *The Serpent and the Rope* is that both characters are fully immersed in their cultures and are able to articulate honestly and intelligently the values of these societies. Also distinctive is **G. V. Desani**'s *All About H. Hatterr* (1951, first published as *All About Mr. Hatterr, A Gesture*, 1948), which demonstrates the comedy implicit in the east-west encounter. Hatterr, a Eurasian who belongs nowhere, is a cultural Don Quixote involving himself in a series of misadventures; in Banerrji, the servile Anglophile, Hatterr finds a strange Sancho Panza. *All About H. Hatterr* and *The Serpent and the Rope* are daring and highly original experimentations with the English language.

In Anand's *Untouchable* (1935), Narayan's *The English Teacher* (1945), and **Attia Hosain**'s *Sunlight on a Broken Column* (1961) the focus is on the impact of the west, ideological and material, on the Indian reality. Anand presents his hero, Bakha, as 'a child of modern India'; Bakha's estrangement from Hindu society is a consequence of his brief exposure to the life of the white man in the British barracks. His awareness of a different life-style and new possibilities makes him critical of the caste-based Hindu society and transforms him into a problematic hero. In *The English Teacher* and *Sunlight on a Broken Column* the focus is on education. Both novels are set in colonial India, but they arrive at opposite conclusions. Narayan's hero, a university-educated teacher of English, finds himself totally frustrated by the system of colonial education and gives up a secure job to join an eccentric experiment in creative education. Conversely, the individualism that Laila, the protagonist of *Sunlight on a Broken Column*, upholds uncompromisingly is a result of her western education and leads to her alienation from her feudal and aristocratic Muslim family. Hosain's attitude to western education, then, is closer to that of the African writer **Ngugi wa Thiong'o** than to that of Narayan.

The east-west encounter did not pose serious problems for such early Indian poets writing in English as **Toru Dutt** and **Sarojini Naidu**, who freely borrowed western poetic forms from the British Romantics in order to express their Indian experience. For poets of the later generations, particularly of the post-independence era, however, the choices have been more difficult. The attitudes to the west of these poets can be categorized as assimilationist, ambivalent, and indifferent. An extreme example of an assimilationist perspective is that of the early **Dom Moraes**, who had reached the point of no return when he wrote to his mother from England: 'You know I will not return/ Forgive me my trespasses.' Unlike Moraes, **Nissim Ezekiel** has always remained committed to India; but he, too, has had no difficulty in assimilating the influence of such poets as T. S. Eliot and W. B. Yeats or in evolving his own individual idiom — ironic, meditative, and intellectual. **A. K. Ramanujan**, who writes original verse in Kannada and translates from Tamil, has approached the problem of living simultaneously in two worlds by borrowing his 'outer form' — 'linguistic, metrical and logical' — from the west, and his 'inner form' — 'substance, images, symbol' — from his Indian roots. In the collection *Rough Passage* (1977), **R. Parthasarathy** writes of his ambivalent response to the east-west encounter of his youth, spent 'whoring / after English Gods'; in 'Home Coming' he notes how the limits of the English language sent him back to his Tamil culture — 'My tongue in English chains / I return, after a generation, to you.' He subsequently wrote little poetry in English. **Jayanta Mahapatra**, perhaps the most important Indian poet writing in English today, has been comparatively free from alien influences. He is committed to his immediate environment and has been unconcerned with the west. He is the poet most likely to be absorbed into the indigenous poetic tradition.

Indian drama in English has never been of much consequence, and except for a few plays, such as **Asif Currimbhoy**'s *The Tourist Mecca and The Clock: Two Plays* (1961), it does not have much bearing on the theme of cross-cultural encounter.

G. S. AMUR

Further reading: Meenakshi Mukherjee, *The Twice Born Fiction* (1971); Meenakshi Mukherjee, ed., *Considerations* (1977).

EBEJER, FRANCIS (1925–93)
Maltese dramatist, novelist
Born in Dingli, Malta, he grew up near Malta's southern cliffs and terraced fields 'admiring the women who worked harder than the men'. In 1943 he served in the Second World War with the British Eighth Army in Tripolitania, subsequently becoming a teacher. During the 1980s Ebejer made writing his sole occupation. Somerset Maugham and Gabriel García Márquez were the most important foreign influences on his work.

Ebejer was the leading Maltese dramatist, but he also wrote seven novels and eleven plays in English, many of which were published in the UK and the USA and broadcast over French, Italian, and German television. (See **Drama**, Malta.) His novels have been translated into several languages. A recurrent theme in his work has been the past as it encroaches on the present and as it shapes the future. Ebejer carefully explored interpersonal conflicts as they affect wider relationships in communities and society. His creative work epitomizes 'the microcosm that is Malta' — its society, history, folk myth, culture, and way of life, particularly as it relates to the Mediterranean, which, in turn, has its insidious effect on the small island community. Ebejer wrote with love and dedication of the extended family system and of the exuberance of village neighbourhoods without shutting his eyes to the petty hate and infighting that he considered to be a Phoenician residue.

Following his first novel, *A Wreath for the Innocents* (1958, later published in Malta as *A Wreath of Maltese Innocents*, 1981), a central feature of Ebejer's writing is his 'search for Oneness', between the sexes and within and between communities, without negating the positive aspects of diversity. Ebejer's most successful novels are *In the Eye of the Sun* (1969), *Requiem for a Maltese Fascist* (1980), and *A Leap of Malta Dolphins* (1982). His best plays, almost all of which were first written in his native Maltese language and later translated into English, are *Summer Holidays* (1980, premièred 1962), *Boulevard* (1980; premièred 1964), and *Menz* (1980; premièred 1967). Most of these works are concerned with a search for identity placed within a broader search for a Mediterranean cultural identity, which is linked, in turn, to the ancient pagan ethos of the 'mother-goddess' and to modern Catholic concerns. Ebejer's persistent use of symbol, especially in *In the Eye of the Sun*, encourages the reader/audience to read events within a larger allegorical framework without reducing the realist bedrock on which his characters stand. Seven of Ebejer's plays, including *Boulevard*, *Menz*, and *Hour of the Sun* were published in *Francis Ebejer: Collected English Plays* (3 vols, 1980).

DANIEL MASSA

Further reading: Arthur Pollard, 'Francis Ebejer, novelist of Malta', *ACLALS Bulletin* 2 (1979); Daniel Massa, 'Individual and community: the hero in contemporary Maltese fiction', *ACLALS Bulletin* 3 (1980); Peter Nazareth, 'Ebejer's metaphoric writing', *Afriscope* 7 (1982).

EDEN, DOROTHY (1912–82)
New Zealand novelist
Born near Ashburton, Canterbury, New Zealand, she worked as a legal secretary before turning to writing romantic mystery fiction in 1940. In 1954 she settled in London, England, becoming a prolific contributor to the magazine market and publishing forty novels. Eden and **Ngaio Marsh** were New Zealand's most successful professional novelists, internationally, between the 1940s and the 1970s.

Until 1960 Eden used New Zealand regularly as a setting for contemporary 'Gothic' romances such as *Bride by Candlelight* (1954), in which the heroine is terrorized in a remote Canterbury mansion, and as a subject for historical romances such as *Sleep in the Woods* (1960), set in Taranaki at the time of the Land Wars. After this, except for her last novel, *An Important Family* (1982), a New Zealand colonial romantic mystery, Eden ranged widely in the Anglo-European past and present for most of her subjects.

Eden was a skilled exponent of Gothic tricks of the trade, producing expertly contrived, suspenseful narratives that gradually detached her heroines (and readers) from normality and plunged them into a paranoid, nightmare world of menace and violence. There is often also a sense of fairy-tale events and atmosphere in her novels, influenced, perhaps, by one of her favourite authors, Hans Christian Andersen. Like all Gothic novels, Eden's imply a great deal about the politics of gender relations, presenting their vulnerable heroines as struggling to survive in an unstable and deeply threatening world where males are generally predatory, often violent, and always unpredictable. The least plausible aspect of her novels is their happy endings.

TERRY STURM

EDGELL, ZEE (1940–)
Belizean novelist
Born in Belize City, Belize, and educated in Belize, she trained in journalism in London, England, and in Jamaica. She travelled widely — she worked with UNICEF in Somalia — but now lives in Belize. *Beka Lamb* (1982) — the first Belizean novel and winner of the 1982 Fawcett Society Prize — has been praised for its literary exploitation of Belizean Creole. Set in the early 1950s, *Beka Lamb* shares with other first novels by Caribbean women its semi-autobiographical form and its link between a maturing protagonist and an emerging sense of national identity; **Merle Collins**' *Angel* (1987) and **Janice Shinebourne**'s *Timepiece* (1986) provide useful comparisons. A fictionalized account of early anti-colonial stirrings in Belize, *Beka Lamb* focuses on women's experience and implicitly equates economic underdevelopment under colonial rule with the devaluation of black working-class women under an educational system run by American nuns.

A complex of binary oppositions underlies this apparently straightforward and limpid account of female adolescence: oral folk culture versus imposed western schooling; black proletariat versus white and brown middle class; a mutually supportive community of sexually active women versus a chaste, socially conscious convent of nuns. Beka's friend Toycie, for whom the novel is a mental 'wake', is a casualty of these conflicting social and moral codes, as is Tee in **Merle Hodge**'s *Crick Crack, Monkey* (1970).

Edgell's writing shares with the work of **Michael Anthony** a delicate, unsentimental evocation of childhood; in her use of Toycie's predicament to explore darker themes such as madness and death, Edgell's work is similar to that of other Caribbean women writers, including **Jean Rhys**, **Erna Brodber**, and **Marion Patrick Jones**. In Toycie's story, Beka's Caribbean counter-discourse exposes received colonial idealizations of womanhood as complicit in such destruction.

Edgell's second novel, *In Times Like These* (1991), explores the personal and political struggles of a Belizean woman who returns to pre-independence Belize after studying in England.

EVELYN O'CALLAGHAN

Further reading: Evelyn O'Callaghan, 'Driving women mad', *Jamaica Journal* 16 (1983); Bev Brown, 'Mansong and matrix: a radical experiment', *Kunapipi* 7 (1985).

EDMOND, LAURIS DOROTHY (1924–)
New Zealand poet, autobiographer
Born in Hawkes Bay, New Zealand, she attended university in Wellington and until her forties led a conventional married life. Her three volumes of autobiography, *Hot October: An Autobiographical Story* (1989), *Bonfires in the Rain* (1991), and *The Quick World* (1992), give an attractive record of Edmond's deliberate passage from housewife and

mother to serious writer. Widely read, especially by women, Edmond did not publish her first book of poems, *In Middle Air*, until 1975, but she has since been prolific, writing nine further poetry collections, including a *Selected Poems* (1984), which won the Commonwealth Poetry Prize in 1985. She has also published a novel, *High Country Weather* (1984).

The voice of Edmond's poems is self-aware, intimate, poised, and relaxed. The poem itself is usually the traditional discursive lyric — a vivid account of an experience, impression, or memory, leading towards a generalized conclusion. Though her themes are often sombre, the impulse is celebratory, seeking and finding solutions. Edmond's language and syntax are likewise simple, rhythmically sensitive, working towards harmony.

Much of the attraction of Edmond's work lies in its compassion, vitality, and generosity. Her favourite subjects include her family, especially her children and grandchildren, her friends and lovers, and gardens, trees, flowers, animals, and the seasons.

Edmond's notion of what constitutes a poem has changed little, the subject-matter alone adjusting to a wider range of acquaintances and places and later including an ironic awareness of her public role. Love, death, and the cycle of existence are persistent and interconnected concerns. Her best collections are responses to the death of a daughter, *The Pear Tree* (1977) and *Wellington Letter* (1980) — mature and moving treatments of a difficult subject. Much of *Catching It* (1983) derives from her period in Menton, France, as a Katherine Mansfield Memorial Fellow and shows a refreshing wit and liveliness.

Though she has never claimed to be a 'feminist' writer, the assertion of independence out of which Edmond's early poems grew is implicit in her work: 'What is a woman that she / should wake and sleep in other people's lives?' is a much-quoted early line; 'Latterday Lysistrata' contrasts the male drive to destruction with the 'mysterious rhythms of seeds and / seasons'. Edmond prefers a poetry that is instinctive, emotional, and in harmony with nature; she has frequently criticized such New Zealand poets as **Allen Curnow, Kendrick Smithyman**, and **Ian Wedde** for writing a detached, intellectual verse.

ELIZABETH CAFFIN

Further reading: Joseph Swann, 'The "separate self": wholeness and continuity in Lauris Edmond's poetry', *Journal of New Zealand Literature* 8 (1990).

EDMOND, MURRAY (1949–)

New Zealand poet, editor

Born in Hamilton, New Zealand, he is a poet, actor, and critic with strong links to a local tradition of alternative theatre.

In the late 1960s and early 1970s Edmond, along with Alan Brunton and **Russell Haley**, published articles in the influential magazine *The Word is Freed* (1969–72). The rowdy irreverence of Brunton and Haley was congenial to Edmond's own Creeley-inspired poetics. He edited the third and fourth of *Freed*'s five issues. His first book, *Entering the Eye* (1973), is an exuberant assortment of antic voices and typographies in the style of the journal.

Edmond's theatrical interests took him to London, England (1974–6), and to Europe, then to Wellington, New Zealand, where he worked in experimental and educational theatre until 1982. In 1984 he moved to Auckland, becoming a teacher of practical drama at the University of Auckland. His full-length musical, 'A New South Pacific', was first performed in 1987.

Alongside these activities Edmond continued to produce poetry. *Patchwork* (1978) is focused on the birth of a first child. *End Wall* (1981) includes long pieces or sequences, establishing Edmond as a poet whose interest in the sharp end of literary experimentalism is well served by dramatic and narrative skills carried over from his theatre experience. *Letters and Paragraphs* (1987) combines an acute sense of linguistic strategy with an appealing mode of personal address to a range of friends and writers, while *From the Word Go* (1992) extends this blend of the personal, political, and literary by means of an increasingly ambivalent, witty positioning of the authorial voice. In 1987 Edmond co-edited with Mary Paul a well-received anthology, *The New Poets: Initiatives in New Zealand Poetry.*

MICHELE LEGGOTT

EE TIANG HONG (1933–90)
Malaysian poet
Born in the old Portuguese-Dutch-English-Malay town of Malacca, he was a *Baba-Chinese* (Peranakan), inheriting a rich and cosmopolitan history. Ee worked primarily as a college and university teacher, and this contributed in no small way to his sense of poetry being socially and educationally purposeful. He did not believe in didacticism, but always underlined the significance of every poem and believed with utter conviction in the influence that poetry (and literature generally) extends over its readers. Ee was perhaps the most accomplished poet writing in English from the Singapore-Malaysia region. His poetry includes *I of the Many Faces* (1960), *Myths for a Wilderness* (1976), *Lines Written in Hawaii* (1973), and *Tranquerah* (1985).

The racial riots in Malaysia in May 1969 left Ee shattered by the realization that interracial harmony had been destroyed by narrow, tunnel-visioned politics and that he, like many of the other non-Bhumiputra, would henceforth always occupy a secondary position in national affairs. This eventually led to his adoption of Australian citizenship. He lived in Perth, Australia, for the last fifteen years of his life.

From the publication of his earliest poems in various literary periodicals, Ee maintained a standard of excellence. His poetry contains a rare combination of clarity and evocation and a strong moral voice; though subtly disguised, the poems became more and more openly political regarding the status of individuals not blessed with an automatic sense of belonging by virtue of race, language, and religion. Although his family had been in Malacca for seven generations, he often wondered why he was not regarded as a Bhumiputra, 'son of the soil'. Feeling exiled even at home, this dislocation left Ee disillusioned and sometimes bitter. Many of his later poems betray strong emotions of protest at the injustice suffered by those like him.

Ee wrote scathingly of what he saw as political hypocrisy, criticizing those who touted polemicisms but did not possess the courage to act. His writing argues for a definite stand against oppression and tyranny, reminding his readers that generations depend on present decisions and actions, as in the poem 'Statement' (in *Tranquerah*).

A deep obligation to uphold that which is felt and thought to be true, and which does not diminish human worth and respect, finds a pervasive voice in Ee's poetry. A sense of self imbued with a sense of place characterizes the poet's awareness of history and circumstance. Though much of the earlier poetry displays a reserve that Ee himself acknowledged, the later poems do not eschew candour and direct statement. In his later poems, especially those written in Australia and which appear in *Tranquerah*, Ee is more than willing to confront those issues that dominated his lifelong poetic pursuits, including his own departure from his homeland, which is seen as an exile.

Ee was concerned about the role and status of the writer — especially the poet — in society. He persisted in the conviction that any society that wanted to mature had to attend to its writers. In a very early poem, 'Dead End' in (*I of the Many Faces*), he raises the question of how a non-native speaker of the English language could avoid becoming merely a mimic and could strike a truly original note. It was Ee's pride in the local that made him, in later years, despair over political events, especially the manner in which the Malays and the Malay language gained constitutional hegemony.

Published posthumously, *Nearing a Horizon* (1990) contains poems that are in the main reflections of life led in Australia and of his own outlook given the passage of time. Ee had now obtained a quieter, gentler voice, fusing his personality with his poetry. He had suffered long from an illness, and these poems represent his farewell.

While most of his poetry deals with socio-political issues, Ee, retiring, reticent, and shy, occasionally wrote very good love poems, as in *Lines Written in Hawaii*.

Southeast Asia's most powerful poetic voice, Ee articulated the anxieties and the sorrows of his fellow Malaysians in a manner befitting the times. His acute insights into history and character will ensure the posterity of his poetry.

KIRPAL SINGH

Further reading: Edwin Thumboo, 'Foreword' to *Myths for a Wilderness* (1976) by Ee Tiang Hong; Leong Liew Geok, 'Place and identity in the poetry of Ee Tiang Hong', *SPAN* 27 (1988); Kirpal Singh, 'The only way out: the sense of exile in the poetry of Ee Tiang Hong', in Bruce Bennett (ed.) *A Sense of Exile* (1988).

EKWENSI, CYPRIAN O. D. (1921–)
Nigerian novelist, short-story writer
Born in Minna, northern Nigeria, he received his primary education in Minna and his secondary-school education in Ibadan. Trained in forestry and pharmacy in Nigeria, he took further studies in pharmacy at London University, England, and received broadcasting training with the British Broadcasting Corporation. Ekwensi has written film scripts and has published novels, novellas, and collections of short stories and folk tales.

Embracing the neo-classical ideal of 'holding a mirror up to nature', Ekwensi combines entertainment with pedagogy. His first novella, *When Love Whispers* (1948), treats inter-generational conflict through a love plot, predating **Chinua Achebe**'s 'Marriage is a Private Affair' first published in 1952 as 'The Beginning of the End' and included under this title in Achebe's *Girls at War and Other Stories* (1972). The novella inaugurated the tradition later dubbed the Onitsha Market Literature (the chapbook tradition of popular writing that flourished in the city of Onitsha from the late 1940s to the 1960s). *Yaba Roundabout Murder* (1962), *Samankwe and the Highway Robbers* (1979), and *Masquerade Time* (1991) are adventure thrillers. Serious social criticism, as in *People of the City* (1954) and *Jagua Nana* (1961), highlights emerging problems of urbanization, corruption, and political violence, foreshadowing post-colonial themes of disillusionment. Ekwensi's other novels include the pan-Africanist *Beautiful Feathers* (1963); the visionary *Iska* (1966), which, exploring ethnic tensions, forecast the **Nigerian Civil War**; *Survive the Peace* (1976), which explores the ravages of war; and *Divided We Stand* (1980), documenting the war's historical background. *King For Ever!* (1992) is a political allegory on misrule.

Ekwensi's style, easily accessible and aimed at a mass readership, characteristically embodies penetrating social criticism in cinematic thriller and romance plots, sometimes with elements of the marvellous (as in *Burning Grass*, 1962), all presented with a keen eye for sensational details. Technically conservative, he was among the first to employ pidgin English for cultural-linguistic realism. However, his considerable achievements often suffer from inconsistent characterization, random switches between speech registers, and alternations between tightly woven and loosely episodic sequences. *Jagua Nana's Daughter* (1986), a sequel to *Jagua Nana*, suffers from careless attributions of speech. Ekwensi's shorter fiction, with little scope for superfluous episodes, shows greater formal control.

Critics generally attribute these flaws to influences from eighteenth- and nineteenth-century western fiction and European novels of Africa. Yet Ekwensi's weakness is essentially the default expression of a storytelling impulse ungoverned by conscious art, compounded by adventure films such as the Sinbad stories, which he occasionally invokes, and his journalistic love of snapshots, topicality, and sensationalism.

Aiming, by his own confession (in his article 'Random Thoughts on Clocking Sixty-Five', in *The Essential Ekwensi: A Literary Celebration of Cyprian Ekwensi's Sixty-Fifth Birthday*, 1987, edited by Ernest Emenyonu), to be a populist writer, Ekwensi unhesitatingly adopts artistic short-cuts such as stretching short stories into novels ('Fashion Girl' into *Jagua Nana*), quilting a novel from several short stories (as in *People of the City*), and recycling decades-old material into *For a Roll of Parchment* (1986). *Jagua Nana's Daughter* introduces details incompatible with the *Jagua Nana*, even misnaming as 'Jagua Nana' the child who only acquired that nickname some thirty years later!

In 1991 Ekwensi published *Gone to Mecca*, a children's book, and *Masquerade Time*.

CHIDI OKONKWO

Further reading: Adrian Roscoe, *Mother Is Gold* (1971); Ernest Emenyonou, *Cyprian Ekwensi* (1974); Eustace Palmer, *The Growth of the African Novel* (1979).

ELDERSHAW, FLORA (1897–1956)

Australian historian, critic

Born in Sydney, Australia, and educated in New South Wales, she read history at the University of Sydney under the eminent historian Arnold Wood. At the university she formed an enduring friendship with fellow student **Marjorie Barnard**, an association that led to their long literary collaboration as M. Barnard Eldershaw. Under that name they produced nine works of fiction and non-fiction. Eldershaw was a teacher for many years before she joined the Commonwealth Government's Department of Labour and National Service during the Second World War, when she was able to exercise to the full her considerable administrative skills.

Throughout her life Eldershaw took an active part in writers' affairs, being the first woman president of the Sydney branch of the Fellowship of Australian Writers in 1935; she made her most important contribution to public life as a member of the Advisory Board of the Commonwealth Literary Fund from its inception in 1939 and for the fourteen following years. When Eldershaw died, **Vance Palmer** wrote of those years that she was 'the most valuable member of the Board', and T. Inglis Moore stated that writers 'were fortunate to be served so devotedly by someone of such calibre'.

Contemporary Australian Women Writers (1931) and *The Peaceful Army: A Memorial to the Pioneer Women of Australia 1788–1938* (1938) are Eldershaw's best-known works. The latter, an anthology, which she edited, is 'a tribute from the women of today to the women of yesterday', and includes poems by contemporary writers and articles on the achievements of earlier generations of women.

Eldershaw's cool, balanced style can be seen to advantage in her article 'The Landscape Writers', *Meanjin* 3 (1952), where, with a historian's eye, she sketches the development of landscape writing in Australia and celebrates the country and the men and women who have striven to identify themselves with 'the unique Australian world that is the possession and kingdom of our imagination'.

Eldershaw places herself firmly in the tradition that regards the bush as the most important element in the growth of the national culture. Her interest in social conditions is explored in the fiction of M. Barnard Eldershaw.

PATRICIA EXCELL

ELLIOTT, SUMNER LOCKE (1917–91)

Australian dramatist, novelist

He was born in Sydney, Australia; his mother, the novelist Sumner Locke, died the day after his birth. He joined Sydney's Independent Theatre, where between 1939 and 1948 seven of his plays were performed. The seventh, *Rusty Bugles* (1968), first produced in 1948, established his distinctive place in Australian theatre.

Rusty Bugles, based directly on the playwright's wartime experience at an army ordnance depot in the Northern Territory, is, in a sense, Australia's *Waiting for Godot*. The looseness of its episodic structure, the indeterminateness of its plot, and the rhythms of anticipation and disappointment reflect the tedium of the days of an oddly assorted group of men living together in a place far from anywhere, where it seems there is nothing to be done. The action consists of the rather desperate resourcefulness of their collaborative, mostly comic, attempts to kill time. But Elliott's play treats the experience of panic and emptiness very affectionately, and its mode is thoroughly naturalistic in a way that anticipates the dramatizations of male mythologies in **Ray Lawler**'s *Summer of the Seventeenth Doll* (1957) and **Alan Seymour**'s *The One Day of the Year* (1962). Its notoriety was secured by the much-modified crudity of its language, which led to the play being (briefly) banned. The playwright, however, missed most of the controversy, having already set out in 1948 to seek his writing fortune in the USA; he remained there after becoming an American citizen in 1955, and had relatively little to do with writing for the theatre, despite a prolific output for American television.

Elliott's more recent work included the novels *Careful, He Might Hear You* (1963), which won the Miles Franklin Award, *Edens Lost* (1969), and *Water under the Bridge* (1977). Despite his long absence from the country of his birth, however, a concern with authentic memories of Australian culture continued to dominate his writing. The citation for the Patrick White Award, which Elliott received in 1977, drew attention particularly to the extraordinary evocation of Sydney in his fiction.

PETER FITZPATRICK

ELLIS, ZOILA MARIA (1957–)

Belizean poet, short-story writer

Born in Dangriga, Belize, the Caribbean, she holds a law degree from the University of the West Indies and an MA in developmental studies from the University of Sussex, England. Ellis was the first director of the Belize Legal Aid Center and has been directly involved in several cultural organizations that support women's issues. She has worked in the Dominican Republic as subregional director of OXFAM UK, a development funding agency.

Ellis' work with women and with underprivileged people is reflected in her writing. In *Belizean Poets Part 3*, the third volume of the Government of Belize's 'Belizean Poets Series' (3 vols, undated), Ellis' 'Catalyst' is a tribute to women, while her poems 'Birthright' and 'Luwani Dangriga' ('The Soul of Dangriga') reveal Ellis as a cultural activist. In *Creation Fire: A CAFRA Anthology of Caribbean Women's Poetry* (1990), edited by Ramabai Espinet, Ellis' contributions are 'Requiem of Sorrow' and 'Snatches'. The latter deftly uses the local lingua franca, Belize Creole, to bemoan situations in which Belizeans display a lack of pride in the African heritage of a colonial past.

In her short-story collection *On Heroes, Lizards and Passion* (1988), Ellis' characters are instantly recognizable as Belizeans. In 'The Waiting Room' and 'And the Subway Takes Me Home' the recurrent theme of migration and 'escape' overseas is one that is all too familiar in Caribbean literature. Ellis' Belizean characters transplanted in the USA experience the same identity crisis and cultural deprivation that **Samuel Selvon**'s Jamaicans go through in the UK, the result of a shared history of slavery and colonialism. Ellis' main protagonists are such people as the village schoolteacher, the domestic worker, the ageing uncle; her settings are frequently rural. Ellis' interpretation of the often-subtle prejudice and discrimination that exist between and within ethnic groups in Belize provides a realistic portrayal of cultural conflicts in Belizean society today.

SILVANA WOODS

EMECHETA, BUCHI (1944–)
Nigerian novelist
Born in Lagos, Nigeria, to Ibusa parents, she was educated in Lagos before moving to London, England, in 1962. With a BA in sociology from London University, Emecheta has worked variously as librarian, teacher, social worker, and writer. From 1980 to 1981 she was a senior research fellow at the University of Calabar. Although she travels widely, Emecheta, a mother of five, resides in London. A novelist, she also writes children's books, scripts for radio, television plays, and articles for *The New Statesman* (West Africa), *The Times Educational Supplement*, and various periodicals. She is the recipient of many literary awards. Emecheta's novels include *The Bride Price* (1976), *Second Class Citizen* (1974), *The Slave Girl* (1977), *The Joys of Motherhood* (1979), *Destination Biafra* (1982), *Double Yoke* (1982), *Naira Power* (1982), *The Rape of Shavi* (1983), *A Kind of Marriage* (1986), and *The Family* (1990, also published as *Gwendolen*, 1990).

Emecheta's deep commitment to roots and orature places her among such African literary giants as **Chinua Achebe**, **Wole Soyinka**, **Ngugi wa Thiong'o**, and **Ayi Kwei Armah**. Her strength lies in her authentic feminist perspective, her focus on the exploitation of women and their tenacious struggle for freedom. Her novels highlight similarities and peculiar differences in the feminist ideologies of Africa, the diaspora, and the Commonwealth at large. (See **Feminism**, West Africa.)

Critics have praised and vilified Emecheta for her characterization. Her female protagonists are generally well-poised, hard-working, and dynamic, while their male counterparts are lazy, selfish, and irresponsible. Ogbanje Ojebeta, the heroine of *The Slave Girl*, fights her way doggedly to eventual freedom from the slavery into which her brother sold her. Akunna in *The Bride Price* successfully plots her escape from obnoxious suitors. Adah in *Second Class Citizen*, despite her lazy husband and five young children, struggles to improve her situation through education. Nnu-Ego, the love child of Agbadi and his concubine Ona, is 'posted' to a husband who is a washerman in Lagos after enduring torrents of abuse from her first husband. Emecheta's works condemn laziness and male exploitation while upholding female self-assertion.

Emecheta's style is vivid, highly descriptive, and occasionally poetic, as in her portrayal of Pa Noble in *Second Class Citizen*: 'A face that had been battered by gallons of African rain, burned almost to scorching point by years and years of direct wintry winds of England, a face crisis-crossed like a jute mat by bottled-up sorrows, disappointments and maybe occasional joy'.

Emecheta's work can be divided into three major phases. Her traditional novels are best represented by *The Joys of Motherhood*, which exposes the many abuses facing African women and explodes the many myths about motherhood. *Double Yoke*, set in the University of Calabar, captures the experiences of youth on African campuses and emphasizes options that education provides for modern women. *Naira Power* is a serious social indictment of Nigeria's craze for materialism and its worship of money.

Despite Emecheta's occasional stylistic incongruities, such as awkward imagery, which may be the result of her double culture (Nigerian and English), she has remained one of the strongest African voices for change. As an African woman of letters residing in the UK, she is keenly involved in the exposure of traditional and modern social problems facing women in Africa, the UK, and the world at large.

EBELE O EKO

Further reading: Carole Boyce Davies and Anne Adams Graves, *Ngambika: Studies of Women in African Literature* (1986); Henrietta Otunkunefor and Obiageli Nwodo, eds, *Nigerian Female Writers: A Critical Perspective* (1989).

ENGEL, MARIAN (1933–85)

Canadian novelist, short-story writer

Born Marian Passmore in Toronto, Canada, she completed a degree in French and German at McMaster University in 1955 and an MA at McGill in 1957. Between 1957 and 1963 she lived and worked in Canada, the USA, the UK, and Europe. The founding chair of The Writers' Union of Canada (1975), she was appointed an Officer of the Order of Canada in 1982.

Engel wrote a number of unpublished novels before *No Clouds of Glory!* (later reissued as *Sarah Bastard's Notebook*) was published in 1968. *The Honeyman Festival* appeared in 1970, and *Monodromos* (reissued as *One-Way Street*) in 1973. *Joanne: The Last Days of a Modern Marriage*, commissioned for the Canadian Broadcasting Corporation, appeared in 1975, the same year as her first collection of short stories, *Inside the Easter Egg*. *Bear* (1976), the infamous novel/fable about a love affair between a woman and a bear, brought her international attention and a Governor General's Award for fiction. *The Glassy Sea* was published in 1978 and *Lunatic Villas* in 1981. Her second collection of short fiction, *The Tattooed Woman* (1985), was published posthumously. Engel also wrote two children's books, *Adventure at Moon Bay Towers* (1974) and *My Name Is Not Odessa Yarker* (1977). With J. A. Kraulis she wrote the text to a picture-book, *The Islands of Canada* (1981).

Engel's studies steeped her in modern Canadian literature, and she cites **Doris Lessing** and especially Lawrence Durrell, as well as the explosion of the *nouveau roman* writers in France, as strong influences. Her background in French and German offered her a comparative range and instilled in her an early scepticism of realism, as well as a biting sense of irony and an elegantly spare style.

Out of a presbyterian sense of discipline and a futile search for perfection, her characters repeatedly struggle to define themselves against a Gothic Ontario background, through the presumed sophistication of European civilization. A search for excitement and cultural validation in Europe informs her characters' often lugubrious sense that, as Canadians, they are 'nowhere', perpetually waiting to arrive at a different colonial moment. *Monodromos* explores the intricate displacements of an expatriate living in Cyprus; the dramatic situation in *Bear* arises out of the essential transportation of nineteenth-century England to northern Ontario.

Engel's work addresses the double colonization of women, the imperialism of relationships, and the extent to which women are dominated by men and by children. Maternity, marriage, divorce, and sexual conflict pervade her fiction. Relationships are territories constantly threatened or invaded, and the frequent presence of untidy extended families gestures towards a splintered cultural mosaic. Her fiction shows affinities with the work of such Australian women writers as **Thea Astley**, **Elizabeth Jolley**, **Barbara Hanrahan**, and **Kate Grenville**. And like many post-colonial writers, Engel and her work travelled far afield in order to return to 'nowhere' and discover it spectacular.

ARITHA VAN HERK

Further reading: Graeme Gibson, *Eleven Canadian Novelists* (1973); *Room of One's Own* (1984), special issue on Marian Engel; Coral Ann Howells, *Private and Fictional Words* (1987).

ENRIQUEZ, EMIGDIO ALVAREZ (1925–)
Filipino novelist, short-story writer, dramatist
Born in Zamboanga City, the southern Philippines, he moved to Manila, where he earned a degree in journalism from Adamson University in 1951. He began publishing his fiction in national magazines in 1939. He earned a master of fine arts degree in creative writing, with a minor in theatre, from the State University of Iowa, USA, in 1957, on a Fulbright grant. Enriquez won a Guggenheim fellowship for his first novel, *The Devil Flower* (1959). In 1984 he joined the faculty of De La Salle University, Manila. In 1988 he was presented with the Patnubay ng Kalinangan (Guardian of Culture) Award for Literature for 'helping to propagate Philippine culture and literature in English abroad'.

The Devil Flower is a novel set in the Philippine southern region of Mindanao, where precolonial indigenous and Moslem traditions have been preserved more than in the Christianized areas of the country. Enriquez draws upon these sources to create an exotic nation undergoing the transition from its Hispanic past to its Americanized present. The main character is Ercelia, who embodies the various, and tragically conflicting, archetypes of Filipino womanhood: the pure, chaste, ideal Filipino maiden, Maria Clara; the legendary Princess Kulin Tangan; the nun who falls under the spell of the village rake; the tubercular spinster who, in white dress, lives out her days in self-imposed penitence.

House of Images (1983) uses the period of the Second World War to show the blurring of boundaries between nobility and self-interest, hypocrisy and gentility, sacrifice and betrayal, heroism and vengeance. Threading through these paradoxes are the conflicting loyalties that beset the Filipino: the Japanese as fellow Asian, the American as liberator, the Hispanic past as romanticized memory, the self as survivor.

In his short-story collection *The White Horse of Alih and Other Stories* (1985) and in *Two Liberation Plays: A Tale of Two Houses and The Fourth of July* (1990) Enriquez expresses similar concerns and uses his characteristic technique of drawing upon folklore to give his stories an exotic flavour. *Three Philippine Epic Plays* (1983) are dramatized re-tellings of the exploits and triumphs of Filipino historical figures and legendary heroes.

ROSARIO CRUZ LUCERO

EQUIANO, OLAUDAH (*c.*1745–97)
Nigerian autobiographer
He was born in an Igbo village that he referred to in his writing as Essaka (recently identified as Isseke), in the Benin region, now eastern Nigeria. He was kidnapped by local African raiders when he was approximately twelve years old and sold to British slave traders on the Niger Delta. He was 'named' twice — as Michael and as Jacob — before being dubbed Gustavus Vassa by Captain Michael Henry Pascal. Equiano reluctantly took the name. His autobiography, *The Interesting Narrative of the Life of Olaudah Equiano, or Gustavus Vassa, the African, written by Himself* (1789), is considered by many to be the greatest of the slave narrative genre.

Equiano received sporadic schooling. He was sold into American slavery in 1763 to a Philadelphia Quaker, on whose merchant ships he served as a seaman. Permitted to trade on his own account, by 1766 he bought his freedom. Equiano's subsequent travels as a free man included a grand tour of the Mediterranean as a gentleman's valet, a voyage in 1773–8 on the Phipps Expedition to the Arctic as surgeon's mate, and, as personal servant to the same surgeon, temporary residence among the Miskito Indians on the Caribbean coast of South America.

After collaborating with abolitionist leaders in England, Equiano was appointed to the expedition to establish the Sierra Leone colony for freed slaves; he was dismissed for his complaints of the organizers' incompetence. Equiano then transformed his journals into his autobiography, which was an instant success. He travelled throughout the UK and spoke publicly against the slave trade.

In Equiano's lifetime *The Interesting Narrative* appeared in eight British editions and one American edition, was translated into Dutch, German, and Russian, and continued to be re-issued — in America as late as the 1870s. It was rediscovered by scholars in the 1960s. Paul Edwards edited two abridgements of *The Interesting Narrative — Equiano's Travels: His Autobiography* (1967) and *The Life of Olaudah Equiano or Gustavus Vassa, The African, Written by Himself* (1988) — and a facsimile reprint, *The Life of Olaudah Equiano or Gustavus Vassa, The African, Written by Himself* (1969). Equiano's work has been increasingly valued for its literary qualities. Critics have drawn particular attention to its complex levels of irony and self-masking and, recently, to its roots in Igbo tradition.

PAUL EDWARDS

Further reading: A. Costanzo, *Surprizing Narrative: Olaudah Equiano and the Beginning of Black Autobiography* (1987); Paul Edwards, '"Master" and "father" in Equiano's *Interesting Narrative*', *Slavery and Abolition* 2 (1990); Paul Edwards and D. Dabydeen, *Black Writers in Britain 1760–1890* (1991).

ERI, SIR SEREI VINCENT (1936–93)

Papua New Guinean novelist

Born in Moveave village, Gulf Province, Papua New Guinea, he was educated at Catholic mission schools and Sogeri Central School. After ten years as a teacher, school inspector, and lecturer, Eri enrolled in the University of Papua New Guinea, graduating in 1970. While at university Eri was encouraged by Ulli Beier, then lecturing in creative writing, and also was caught up in the emerging nationalism of the pre-independence period. A government and diplomatic career followed, including appointment as Papua New Guinean high commissioner to Australia from 1976 to 1979. In 1982 Eri resigned from the public service to pursue business interests, but in 1990 he was appointed governor general of Papua New Guinea.

In 1970 Eri published the first novel by a Papua New Guinean, *The Crocodile*. Set in the late 1930s and early 1940s, it is an analysis of the destructive impact on Moveave village of the coming of the missionaries, the kiaps, and the outbreak of the Second World War. It thus invites close comparison with **Chinua Achebe**'s *Things Fall Apart* (1958). In both novels the European administrators fail to understand the culture of the people they are ruling, with devastating results. Like Achebe, Eri is interested in providing an authentic view of the village society to counter distortions by outsiders. His novel is set at a later stage of the imposition of European rule. The protagonist, Hoiri, is born into a Christian family, his father being a convert and a deacon. Eri emphasizes the religious syncretism of Papua New Guineans; Christianity does not replace traditional beliefs and customs, but supplements them.

The Crocodile has been immensely influential on later works, precisely because Hoiri's situation makes him a Papua New Guinean Everyman. Western education has alienated individuals from their villages without offering an alternative society into which they can move. Thus modern Papua New Guineans find themselves in a cultural no-man's-land.

BERNARD MINOL

Further reading: John Lloyd, 'Vincent Eri', *Australian External Territories* 10 (1970); F. D. Glass, 'Between two cultures: interpreting V. Eri's

The Crocodile', in S. Nandan (ed.) *Language and Literature in Multi-Cultural Contexts* (1983).

EROTICA

EROTICA (Australia)
Australia boasts neither a Donne nor a Rochester; it has never had a flourishing tradition of erotic art or literature. The satiric poetry of the Augustans and the auto-erotic poems of the Romantics were early but unhelpful models for Australian erotic writing. Novelists, venturing to write of the erotic, had to wait until the latter part of this century for a suitably permissive climate. Closeted in the Fisher Library's rare books room at the University of Sydney is a distinguished collection of erotica, but almost all of it is drawn from overseas. Perhaps something in Australian society, besides its literary heritage, is to blame for this dearth. **James McAuley** grumbled in his poem 'In the Twentieth Century' how its loves were merely 'processes / Upon foamrubber beds', while **Barry Humphries** remarked how 'The Australian male never makes love to his wife without asking her if she is awake.'

While these comments sketch a myth of the unerotic antipodes, Australia has not been spared controversy over allegedly 'obscene literature' (a legal category that may be intended to subsume and disgrace the erotic). Between 1929 and 1939 an estimated two thousand publications were banned by the Trade and Customs department. Australian readers and writers were denied licit and instructive access to the erotic pleasures of the work of Colette, Defoe, Dos Passos, Hemingway, and Joyce among many. **Max Harris** was fined for the publication of the **Ern Malley** hoax poems in 1944; at the trial, Detective Jacobus Vogelsgang testified for the prosecution, 'I don't know what incestuous means but I think there is a suggestion of indecency about it.' (See **Hoaxes and Jokes**, Australia.) Robert Close was sentenced to jail for the use of such unseemly phrases as 'rutting moll' in his novel *Love Me Sailor* (1945). Even by the end of the 1960s American Philip Roth's innocuous *Portnoy's Complaint* (1969) was banned. This dedicated repressive activity suggests an official fear of what the erotic might be, rather than a clear notion of what it is. (See **Censorship**, Australia.)

There were playful essays in the erotic written in Australia — chiefly by men — in the early decades of the twentieth century. **Jack Lindsay** translated Aristophanes' *Lysistrata* (1925) and wrote the volume of verse *Fauns and Ladies* (1923), illustrated with woodcuts by his father **Norman Lindsay**. Bert Birtles's imitative self-published book of poems, *Black Poppies* (1924), led to his expulsion from the University of Sydney. Besides collecting erotica, the noted soldier and administrator Sir John Monash also wrote a number of lyrics, modelled on *Fauns and Ladies*, concerning his experiences in London in 1917–19. Later he destroyed the manuscript.

Norman Lindsay's novel *Redheap* (1930), concerning the lives of boys growing up in a country town, was banned, probably more because of his reputation as an artist than because of its content. *Micomicana* (1979), Lindsay's collection of bawdy tales, was not published until ten years after his death. Frank Dalby Davison spent twenty-two years writing *The White Thorntree* (1968), a very long novel dealing with the conflict between responsibility and passion in marriage and the place of sexuality in modern culture, but struggled to find a publisher. From the late 1960s, however, Australian writers had begun gleefully — if not to produce erotica — to deal with erotic experiences in their works and to have it published freely. Poetry has little of this to show, although there are exceptions, such as **A. D. Hope**'s description in 'Imperial Adam' (1951) of Adam 'taking Eve from behind' as the 'clean beasts' had taught him.

Frank Moorhouse and **Michael Wilding** were among those whose short fiction dealt with the purportedly greater sexual freedoms of the 1960s and 1970s. The magazines *Man* and *Playboy* were two of Moorhouse's places of publication. Unlike numerous contemporaries who drove themselves to write about sex (an enterprise that McAuley, in an essay 'Sex and Love in Literature', *Quadrant*, 4, 1972, had argued was inimical to the novel), Hope, Moorhouse, and Wilding at least allowed humour into their accounts of sexual congress, thus ventilating a vital aspect of the erotic.

In **Helen Garner**'s *Monkey Grip* (1977) the pains and pleasures of promiscuity and postmarital life are treated in a frank if sometimes sentimental fashion — 'our bodies remembered each other without strain' — that encouraged other women writers. Lesbian attractions feature in several of the fictions of **Elizabeth Jolley** and in **Beverley Farmer**'s *Alone* (1980). Decades before, **Katharine Susannah Prichard** treated sexual relations and desire across racial barriers in her novel *Coonardoo* (1929) and in her play *Brumby Innes* (1940), which was not performed until 1975. Male fears of female eroticism have concerned a number of novelists, for instance **David Ireland** in *The Glass Canoe* (1976). The employment of scatological language and the depiction of sexual acts in fiction, film, and on stage became commonplace from the early 1970s. This may be best understood as a coarse tactic for the avoidance of the erotic.

In 1962 Stephen Murray-Smith and Ken Gott (as 'Simon Ffuckes' and 'Sebastian Hogbotel') edited and themselves published *Snatches and Lays: Songs Miss Lilywhite Should Never Have Taught Us*; the book was commercially published in 1973. Two recent collections of erotic writing by women — *Women's Erotica* (1988), edited by Lyn Giles, and *Moments of Desire* (1991), compiled by Margaret Reynolds — expose the paucity of work in this mode. The most daring and unusual exploitation of the range of erotic impulses is **Eric Rolls**' *Celebration of the Senses* (1984), a book — neither embarrassed nor determined to affront — that may eventually point to new and unexpected directions for erotica in Australia.

JOHN ARNOLD
PETER PIERCE

EROTICA (Canada)

To most Canadians the phrase 'Canadian erotica' is an oxymoron. 'How do you make love in a new country?' asks **Robert Kroetsch**; **Irving Layton** has called Canada 'a cold country in more ways than one'. But while it is true that the moral-religious climate of Canada does not welcome open discussion of sexual enjoyment and that the banning of books — especially by school boards — still occurs, erotica is flourishing in Canadian literature. As critic Claude T. Bissell notes, 'Canadians move slowly, but when they are aroused they move with remarkable speed. Our way of life is puritanism touched with orgy.'

Erotic literature may be described as literature that expresses sexual pleasure; experiences are sensuously described and emotionally expressed, thus stimulating a response from the audience of desire and pleasure. Although few Canadian works before 1960 can be termed erotic, there are exceptions. **John Richardson**'s novel *Wacousta* (1832) contains strong undercurrents of sexuality, the imagery of **Isabella Valancy Crawford**'s poetry conveys a subtle sexuality, and **Martha Ostenso**'s novel *Wild Geese* (1925) has a Lawrentian sensuality. John Glassco, Canada's pre-eminent writer of erotica, began writing in this genre in the 1930s, but only in the 1960s and later were these works widely published. His erotic masterpiece is *Harriet Marwood, Governess* (1976), a work in the manner of Sacher-Masoch. Glassco's other erotic writings include *The English Governess* (1960), also published as *Under the Birch: The Story of an English Governess* (1965), and *Fetish Girl* (1972).

The growth of erotic literature in Canada since

the 1960s is the result of a number of developments — the unlocking of the voices of women and of peoples of various cultures, social classes, and sexual orientation; a growing focus on the body; and new theories concerning the physicality of language and text. **Leonard Cohen**'s novel *Beautiful Losers* (1966), for example, mingles the mystical, humorous, and satirical with a powerful sexuality; **Dorothy Livesay**'s *The Unquiet Bed* (1967) records her emotional and physical response to sexual experiences; **Phyllis Webb**'s *Naked Poems* (1965) is sensuous and personal; and **Elizabeth Smart**'s *By Grand Central Station I Sat Down and Wept* (1945) is a poetic account of her victimization in a love relationship.

Canadian women's fiction of the 1960s and 1970s, especially that of **Margaret Laurence** and **Alice Munro**, expresses the sensual and emotional responses of women to their sexual experiences. Of special note are Laurence's *The Diviners* (1974), which was banned by a number of school boards, and Munro's *Lives of Girls and Women* (1971). Male writers, notably Ray Smith in *Lord Nelson Tavern* (1974), also write graphically of sexual encounters. Sexual relations between human beings and animals form part of the thematic strategies of **Marian Engel**'s *Bear* (1976) and Robert Kroetsch's *What the Crow Said* (1978).

Not until the 1980s did male homosexual experience find expression in Canadian literature. Notable are Scott Symons' *Helmet of Flesh* (1986) and works by **Timothy Findley**. Lesbian experience, however, was written about much earlier in **Jane Rule**'s novel *Desert of the Heart* (1964) and in her ground-breaking collection of essays, *Lesbian Images* (1975). Women novelists of the 1980s such as **Aritha van Herk**, Ann Rosenberg, and Susan Swan challenged male attitudes to women's sexuality by creating female protagonists who seek sex for its own sake. Male novelists such as Laurence Garber, **Matt Cohen**, **Leon Rooke**, **Michael Ondaatje**, **Jack Hodgins**, and David Arnason use earthy language to describe lively exotic scenes.

Canadian poetry since the 1950s provides much variety in erotic material and language. Of special importance is the work of Irving Layton, **Earle Birney**, Michael Ondaatje, Leonard Cohen, Phyllis Webb, **bill bissett**, Joe Rosenblatt, **D. G. Jones**, and **Gwendolyn MacEwen**. **Daphne Marlatt** writes in a language that 'returns us to the body, a woman's body', as part of a movement modelled on the innovations of Quebec lesbian poets, notably Nicole Brossard. Other examples of lesbian poetry are Erin Mouré's *Furious* (1988) and **Dionne Brand**'s *No Language is Neutral* (1990). Lorna Crozier's 'The Sex Lives of Vegetables' (in *The Garden Going on without Us*, 1985) and her 'penis poems' sequence (in *Angels of Flesh: Angels of Silence, Poems,* 1988) humorously flaunt sexuality while mocking convention.

There is little Canadian drama that can be characterized as erotic. Michael Hollingsworth's *Clear Light* (1973) and the collectively written *I Love You, Baby Blue* (1976) both encountered difficulties with the Toronto police. Other plays that include erotic elements are Brad Fraser's *Unidentified Human Remains and the True Nature of Love* (1990) and the 1992 dramatization of Timothy Findley's *Not Wanted on the Voyage*.

The repressive rationality of Canadian culture continues to be challenged — and contradicted — by its erotic literature as Canadian writers increasingly recognize and celebrate the importance of the erotic.

JOY KUROPATWA
MARIANNE MICROS

Escoffery, Gloria (1923–)

Jamaican poet

Born in Gayle, St Ann, Jamaica, she was educated at St Hilda's High School, Jamaica, McGill University, Montreal, Canada, and the Slade School, London, England. She worked for the Jamaican weekly *Public Opinion* and trained as an English teacher. In 1976 the Jamaican government awarded her the Order of Distinction and in 1985 she received the Institute of Jamaica's Silver Musgrave Medal for art.

Available in two publications — a chapbook, *Landscape in the Making* (1976), and *Loggerhead* (1988) — as well as in journals — *Bim, Kyk-over-al* — and anthologies — *The Penguin Book of Caribbean Verse* (1986), *From our Yard* (1987), *In the Gold of Flesh* (1990) — her poetry considers landscape, people, and painting. Its assurance and its confident creative hand find full expression in *Loggerhead.* Poems such as 'Thoughts of a Self-Employed Pensioner' and 'Lines to a Friend and Fellow Survivor Rediscovered after a Space of Twenty Years' confirm that Escoffery recognizes personal strength and poetic/painterly craft as the fruits of age.

Still a resident of rural Jamaica, Escoffery makes easy, apolitical use of nation language. Her poetry does not eschew political or social issues, but these are not its primary concerns. In addition, critics such as Annie Greet and Michael Sharp have noted the sensuousness of the verse and its preoccupation with colour and the visual world. Poems such as 'The Letter Bell', 'The Serendipitous Sixties', 'Secret Geometry', and 'Sun Wheel' betray a brash irreverence and wry humour. If 'somewhere, at this moment, / there are people having a good time', she is clearly part of the fête.

Escoffery comes early in a line of multifaceted Caribbean artists — **Derek Walcott, Dennis Scott, Lorna Goodison,** for example — who paint and/or dance and/or act. With **Louise Bennett** she links Una Marson to the present generation of anglophone Caribbean women poets.

PAMELA C. MORDECAI

ESPINA MOORE, LINA (1919–)

Filipino novelist, short-story writer

Born and raised in Cebu, the Philippines, she took up law studies in Manila's Far Eastern University, but had to stop because of the Pacific War. During the Japanese Occupation she became a courier for the underground resistance movement, eventually spending part of 1943 in a Japanese prison. After the war Espina Moore resumed her studies, this time in the Foreign Service. She married an American lumber company executive. For seventeen years, Espina Moore lived among tribal minorities in the Cordillera mountains of northern Luzon. In the 1950s and 1960s she wrote for various newspapers and magazines, including a farmers' cooperative journal and a fashion magazine. She lives in Metro Manila, but frequently returns to Cebu City, where she heads the Cebu chapter of the Philippine Center of International PEN. Espina Moore has won several awards, including the Pan-Pacific South East Asian Association Award for the English Novel in 1965 and the South East Asian Writers Award (SEAWRITE) in 1989.

Espina Moore's passion for writing began at an early age. In seventh grade, she wrote and directed a play on Rizal's life, 'Rizalina', in which she also acted. At sixteen, she published her first short story. Shortly after arriving in Manila from Cebu, she won a cash prize for another story. Even during the Japanese Occupation, she continued to write stories, publishing one in the *Manila Shimbun.* Espina Moore's short stories in English are collected in *Cuentos: An Anthology of Short Stories* (1985).

Espina Moore has published three novels: *Heart of the Lotus* (1970), *A Lion in the House* (1980), and *The Honey, the Locusts* (1992). In *Heart of the Lotus*, a novel set in the Visayas during the idyllic 1920s and 1930s, she evokes a golden age of gentility and relative prosperity, a world that seemed to combine the best of two worlds — the genteel traditions of nineteenth-century Spanish Philippines and the modern excitement of newly discovered American ways. That brief period of bliss is shattered all too soon by the outbreak of the Second World War.

In *A Lion in the House* Espina Moore studies the traditional 'querida system' in the Philippines, a cultural complex that allows married men to keep mistresses, often establishing second families, in a socially acceptable cult of machismo. She questions the system's insidious, corrupting effects on the moral fabric of Filipino society, leading to the disintegration of otherwise respectable families. The novel has moralistic implications, but its use of black comedy, humour, and well-placed irony renders any didactic intentions less unpalatable.

In *The Honey, the Locusts* Espina Moore follows a number of urban families who are evacuated from Cebu City to rural areas when war reaches the island province and Japanese forces occupy the city. The novel narrates their experiences in the scenic countryside towns and barrios as they try to cope with the realities of war and occupation.

Espina Moore belongs to that early generation of Filipino writers who learned English from American teachers. These writers understandably developed a deep passion for the colonial language and honed their creative skills by reading Anglo-American literature. Although a bilingual writer equally proficient in her native Cebuano, in which she started writing in 1956, Espina Moore believes that the best writers in Cebuano are those trained in English. She confesses to thinking in English while writing in English, and thinking in Cebuano while writing in Cebuano. Typical of her generation, she has gone on record in Roger Bresnahan's *Conversations with Filipino Writers* (1990) as believing that the Filipino writers' training in 'Western technique and tradition' enables them to exercise the necessary control over the media, to tone down the Filipino penchant for emotionalism or sentimentality, to minimize the tendency towards florid and turgid rhetoric, and to handle masterfully 'construction, story line, characterization'.

Long before feminism valorized women writers and women's values in literature, Espina Moore's fiction was already steadily focused on women — the quiet, invisible complexities beneath the surface simplicity and serenity of their lives. Her work focuses on the Filipino woman — her special, unique circumstances, the evolution of her consciousness from the 1920s to the 1980s, conflicts arising when certain residual nineteenth-century attitudes and values confront twentieth-century exigencies, and, above all, the strength and endurance of the Filipino woman who emerges battle-scarred but proud. One notable and laudable feature of Espina Moore's fiction is the toughness of her female characters. Regardless of their social class, her women are street-smart — a result of holding their own in a man's world.

The second factor distinctively marking Espina Moore's fiction is a definite, palpable sense of region or location. She may have left her native Cebu as a young woman and lived most of the rest of her adult life in Luzon, but Cebu is ever-present in her fiction, not only because many of her stories are set there. The setting, however, is not merely physical; Espina Moore evokes the many facets of Cebuano's culture — local customs and traditions, specific socio-political and cultural effects of Cebu's historical developments, and the distinctive Cebuano personality and outlook.

THELMA E. ARAMBULO

ESPINO, FEDERICO LICSI (1939–)

Filipino poet, short-story writer

Born in Pasig, Rizal, a suburb of Metro Manila, the Philippines, he earned an AB in journalism (1959) from the University of Santo Tomas. He writes poetry in English, Pilipino, Spanish, Bikol, and Ilokano, although most of his writing is in English. His facility with languages is demonstrated in his two-volume collection of poems, *In Three Tongues* (1963 and 1964). Confinement in a mental institution produced *Apocalypse in Ward 19 and Other Poems* (1965). Espino has won the Palanca Memorial Award for his poetry collections *From Mactan to Mendiola* (1971), *Tinikling: A Sheaf of Poems* (1972), and *The Ricebird Has Brown Wings* (1973). His short-story collections are *Country of Sleep* (1969), *Percussive Blood* (1972), and *Geometries, Bright and Dark* (1981).

Known primarily as a poet, Espino has moved from being a poet of a private world landscaped with anguish and 'the thorny forests of the id' to one more open to the external world of Philippine reality. His early poetry collections, *Dark Sutra* (1963), *The Shuddering Clavier* (1965), and *Counterclockwise* (1969), show the poet grappling with contrasts and paradoxes: past and present, spirituality and sensuality, innocence and concupiscence, love and lovelessness, man as angel and as fallen ape. His award-winning collections, written in the turbulent period of the early 1970s, immediately before the declaration of martial law in 1973, define the paradoxes in the context of the westernized Filipinos' alienation from their own culture. Thus the title poem in *Tinikling* gives a lesson on survival, using as symbol the national folk dance in which nimble feet must evade a pair of clapping bamboos. *Puente del Diablo: A Poem in Three Movements* (1973) is a retelling of a local legend. In a reversal of the conventional invocation to the Muse, the poet begins with a repudiation of his western literary influences.

Espino's poetry and fiction have been strongly influenced by other art forms such as dance, music, and the visual arts. *Dark Sutra* is divided into four parts: Cantabile, Scherzo, Scherzando, Finale. *Counterclockwise* includes poetic studies on the works of Picasso, Klee, Van Gogh, Chagall, and Duchamp. Despite the sweep of Espino's myriad interests and his forays into the dark libidinal world, his works are always tempered by a classical restraint.

ROSARIO CRUZ LUCERO

ESSAYS

ESSAYS (Australia)
Although conditions of early colonial society were not always conducive to writing and reading contemplative essays, Australian colonial essays fall into the usual categories of reflections on general themes of life and culture, good quality journal articles, and literary discussion. The first collections published in Australia were **Henry Savery**'s *The Hermit in Van Diemen's Land* (1830), lively commentaries on Hobart life after the style of Addison and Steele; and *The Australian Sketch Book* (1838) by the eighteen-year-old James Martin, inspired by, but not imitating, Washington Irving and comprising fifteen attempts to delineate traditional themes in the Sydney setting 'for the amusement and encouragement of my fellow-countrymen'. William Woolls' *Miscellanies in Prose and Verse* (1838) and Richard Rowe's *Peter Possum's Portfolio* (1858), although informed by their colonial setting, are less original than the thoughtfully satiric essays of Daniel Deniehy, published in his journal the *Southern Cross* (Sydney), some of which formed the political satire *How I Became Attorney-General of New Barataria* (1860). Foremost among the journalist essayists was **Marcus Clarke**, whose reputation grew steadily after his first collection, *The Peripatetic Philosopher* (1869), accounts of Melbourne life and literature. Clarke's introduction to **Adam Lindsay Gordon**'s *Sea Spray and Smoke Drift* (1867), adapted from his descriptions accompanying *Photographs of Pictures in the National Gallery, Melbourne* (1875), became a seminal appreciation of the aesthetic qualities of the Australian landscape. While encouraging a new understanding of colonial cultural and natural environment, Clarke's essays and articles in the *Colonial Monthly*, *Argus*, *Australian*, *Melbourne Review*, and *Victorian Review* also covered general cultural and literary commentary on European and American topics. In

greatly varied forms, the essay continued to promote aspects of national culture and identity, including the reflective *Essays: Social, Moral and Political* (1879) of Richard Birnie, and Francis Adams' *Australian Essays* (1886) and *The Australians* (1893). Adams, a socialist and republican in politics and a disciple of Matthew Arnold in cultural values, lived only six years in Australia, to 1890, but his contributions to the Brisbane *Courier* and **William Lane**'s *Boomerang* had some influence on Australian nationalism. **A. B. Paterson**, better known as a poet, contributed articles and sketches to a number of journals including the *Sydney Morning Herald*, the ***Bulletin***, and the *Australian Magazine*, and some sketches he wrote as a war correspondent and as a journalist in China and the Philippines were collected in *Happy Dispatches* (1934). Among the general essayists is John le Gay Brereton, whose collections of essays in *Landlopers* (1899) and *Knocking Round* (1930) are studies of Australian life, countryside, and writers. M. Barnard Eldershaw's *Essays in Australian Fiction* (1938) offers significant discussions of writers such as **Katharine Susannah Prichard**, **Henry Handel Richardson**, and **Christina Stead** and provide a benchmark for assessing other essays on Australian writing, for example Desmond Byrne's *Australian Writers* (1896) and F. T. Macartney's *Australian Literary Essays* (1957). **Nettie Palmer**'s collections, *Talking It Over* (1932) and *Fourteen Years: Extracts from a Private Journal 1925–1939* (1948), indicate her insight and graphic, fluent style, but not the extent, range, and influence of her contributions to journals and other publications. Her husband, **Vance Palmer**, wrote prolifically as a journalist, novelist, poet, and dramatist, but as an essayist is best known for his *National Portraits* (1940), biographical sketches of Australian figures. Walter Murdoch, an academic critic, was also the most consistent exponent of the relaxed literary essay in the style of Charles Lamb, although, as his major collections including *Seventy-two Essays* (1947), *Selected Essays* (1956), and *Answers* (1953) show, his style is personal and witty. Murdoch's work illustrates the qualities he himself described as desirable in a good essay: 'brevity, a personal flavour, light and familiar but mannerly, wise but not pontifical, satisfyingly knowledgeable without pretending to treat a subject exhaustively'. **A. A. Phillips'** *The Australian Tradition: Studies in a Colonial Culture* (1958) includes the essay 'The Cultural Cringe', introducing a concept that has been much used in assessing the validity of Australian deference to European standards and traditions. In the second half of the century essays on literary, social, and cultural themes have been written by many poets and critics, including the influential collections of **Judith Wright** (*Preoccupations in Australian Poetry*, 1965; *Because I Was Invited*, 1975), **A. D. Hope** (*The Cave and the Spring*, 1965; *Native Companions*, 1974), **Vincent Buckley** (*Essays in Poetry: Mainly Australian*, 1957; *Poetry and Morality*, 1959), **James McAuley** (*The End of Modernity*, 1959), and Dorothy Green (*The Music of Love*, 1984; *The Reader, the Writer, and the Critic in a Monoculture*, 1986; rev. 1990). Exponents of essays on more general and social themes include **Geoffrey Dutton** in *Australia and the Monarchy* (1966) and **Max Harris** in *The Angry Eye* (1973). Among other writers on literary, social, and cultural themes are **Fay Zwicky**, *The Lyre in the Pawnshop: Essays on Literature and Survival* (1974); **Chris Wallace-Crabbe**, *Melbourne or the Bush* (1974); **Les Murray**, *Persistence in Folly* (1984); Don Anderson, *Hot Copy* (1986); **Eric Rolls**, *Celebration of the Senses* (1984); **Christopher Koch**, *Crossing the Gap: Novelist's Essays* (1987); Bernard Smith, *Death of the Artist as Hero: Essays in History and Culture* (1988); and Meaghan Morris, *The Pirate's Fiancée: Feminism Reading Postmodernism* (1988). Many essays by literary and cultural critics such as **Donald Horne**, Geoffrey Dutton, and David Carter are still available only in the journals in which they were published. Several journals, such as *Arena, Island, Meanjin, Overland, Quadrant*, and *Westerly*, as well as publishing strictly literary critical articles, attract more general essays, which at their best are stylistically interesting, engaged but not polemical, and maintain the reflective quality characteristic of the genre. Aboriginal writers who have appeared as essayists include **Oodgeroo Noonuccal** (Kath Walker), **Kevin Gilbert, Jack Davis**, and **Mudrooroo Narogin** (Colin Johnson). The Australian essay remains a vehicle for the discussion and dissemination of changing concepts of national and cultural identity, its many themes frequently mediated through current aesthetic and socio-literary philosophy and ideology.

ELIZABETH PERKINS

Further reading: H. M. Green, *A History of Australian Literature* 2 vols (1961; rev. 1984).

ESSAYS (Canada)

Observing that the essay 'is the traditional form by which criticism has expressed itself', Edward W. Said argues (in *The World, the Text, and the Critic*, 1983) that criticism is 'defined once and for all by its secondariness, by its temporal misfortune in having come after the texts and occasions it is supposed to be treating'. Said's points can be extended to the essay as a genre. The essay, the traditional form of many discourses, is as secondary, as invisible to analysis, as its use is widespread. Many studies of the genre, which themselves often take the form of the essay, begin with attempts to distinguish that genre from other prose forms, including the letter, the sketch, the short story, and the critical article.

The argument for a pure form of the genre is tempting; however, the emergence of the genre is inextricably related to the rise of the professional classes and to the concomitant changes in the fundamental organization of knowledge. Since its appearance, along with the novel and the biography, in the sixteenth and seventeenth centuries, the essay has become the traditional form of expression in a great many emergent discourses, from the political to the academic, from the journalistic to the psychoanalytic; in each instance, it is 'defined once and for all by its secondariness'.

The emergence of the essay in the Renaissance is inseparable both from Gutenburg's invention of moveable type and from the great age of British and European expansion, including the exploration and settlement of Canada, and the idea of discovery that informed it. With the development of the literary periodical in the early eighteenth century, the essay attained both its modern form and its primary means of circulation. As critic George Parker notes, 'although the Jesuits had petitioned for [a printing press] as early as 1665 to educate the savages', that technology was slow to arrive in this country: Bartholomew Green shipped the first press from Boston, USA, to Halifax, Canada, in 1751; William Brown and Thomas Gilmore established the second in Quebec City in 1764. The gradual development of newspapers, magazines, and book publishing in the following decades helped create at least three of the conditions favourable to the development of essayists in this country: a periodical press, a reading public, and a publishing industry. (See **Publishing**, Canada.) Although the early periodicals, such as *The Nova Scotia Magazine* (1789–92) and *The Quebec Magazine* (1792–4), Canada's first bilingual periodical, consisted primarily of reprints from foreign periodicals, the editors invited and printed writing, including essays, from contributors in the colonies. In addition, many early Canadian essays — for example, John Day's *An Essay on the Present State of the Province of Nova-Scotia* (1774), Richard Cockrel's *Thoughts on the Education of Youth* (1795), and John Simpson's *Essay on Modern Reformers* (1818) — took the form of pamphlets. Significantly, a printer's son, the poet and journalist turned politician **Joseph Howe**, who bought

The Novascotian, a Halifax newspaper, in 1828 and who made it the leading journal in Nova Scotia, is most frequently cited as Canada's first essayist. A two-volume collection of his political writing, *The Speeches and Public Lectures of the Hon. Joseph Howe*, was published in Boston in 1858; a selection of his poetry and non-political speeches, *Poems and Essays* (1874), was published in Montreal a year after his death.

Although public orations, particularly political speeches, constitute one source of the essay in Canada, the development of the genre in Canada is in large measure an account of the growth of periodical publication and of journalism in the nineteenth century. In the 1820s Montreal could boast no less than three English-language magazines: *The Scribbler* (1821–7), a weekly; the *Canadian Magazine and Literary Repository* (1823–5), a monthly; and the quarterly *Canadian Review and Literary and Historical Journal* (1824–6). By mid-century, Fraser Sutherland notes, 'counting both Canadas . . . there were magazines in Montreal, York, Kingston, Brockville, Cobourg, and Hamilton'. Undoubtedly the most important literary periodical prior to Confederation, and certainly the longest lasting, was *The Literary Garland* (1838–51), published monthly in Montreal and edited by John Gibson. Although like all Canadian magazines of the period it reprinted material from foreign periodicals, most of the writing in *The Literary Garland* was by contributors resident in the colonies. Some of the non-fiction prose pieces in *The Literary Garland* are identified as essays (for example, 'Self Education. An Essay to Young Men in Commercial Business', 'Thoughts on Poetry and the British Poets'); many more, however, are sketches. While the best-known sketches are undoubtedly the six that **Susanna Moodie** published in *The Literary Garland* in 1847 (subsequently reprinted in *Roughing It in the Bush*, 1852), Moodie's sister, **Catharine Parr Traill** ('Floral Sketches'), the novelist **John Richardson** ('A Trip to Walpole Island and Port Sarnia'), Anna Jameson ('The Falls and Rapids of Niagara'), and many others also contributed sketches or what critic Graham Good terms 'travel essays' to this and other periodicals. (See **Travel Literature**, Canada.)

The sketch, probably the most popular prose form in nineteenth-century Canada, is an outgrowth of the eighteenth-century periodical essay. Its development is attributed to at least three factors: the increasing ability of the expanding middle-class to travel as 'tourists'; the development of a periodical press; and a growing interest in the local, the rural, native peoples and, increasingly, in the 'natural' world. Anna Jameson's *Winter Studies and Summer Rambles in Canada* (1838) perhaps best exemplifies the increasing tourism of the middle-class and its interest both in the wilderness and in aboriginal peoples. Interest in the form remained strong throughout the nineteenth century and well into the twentieth. Many well-known nineteenth-century Canadian writers took up the form: **Archibald Lampman**, for example, published 'Fishing at Rice Lake' in *Forest and Stream* in August 1882; **Sara Jeannette Duncan** wrote 'A Visit to a Carmelite Convent' for *The Week* in November 1887; Archibald MacMechan published 'The Last of the Hostelries' for *The Dominion Illustrated* (1888–91) in July 1890; and **Pauline Johnson** wrote 'Indian Medicine Men and Their Magic' for *The Dominion Illustrated Monthly* (1892–5) in April 1892.

The tradition of the nature essay, which in the nineteenth century developed in close relation to the sketch, flourished in the twentieth. Its best-known practitioners include Peter McArthur, a *Globe* journalist whose farm columns are collected in *In Pastures Green* (1915), *The Red Cow and her Friends* (1919), and *Around Home* (1925); **Frederick Philip Grove**, who brings a novelist's eye and a naturalist's interest to his descriptions in *Over Prairie Trails* (1922) and *The Turn of the*

Year (1923); and William Hume Blake, who, in *Brown Water and Other Sketches* (1915), *In a Fishing Country* (1922), and *A Fisherman's Creed* (1923) celebrates the Laurentian wilderness and those who live close to nature. Roderick Haig-Brown builds on the tradition of both Grove and Blake: like Grove's *The Turn of the Year*, Haig-Brown's first book, *Measure of the Year* (1950), centres on close observation of the seasonal cycle; like Blake's work, Haig-Brown's subsequent books, including *Fisherman's Spring* (1951) and *Fisherman's Summer* (1959), developed out of his passion for fishing.

In the *Literary History of Canada* Brandon Conron rightly argues that 'the greatest single source of the essay in Canada . . . lies in journalism' and immediately moves to a discussion of *The Week*, 'An Independent Journal of Literature, Politics and Criticism' (1883–96) published in Toronto, which, he observes, 'saw the first appearance of many articles later collected as essays'. It is worth noting, however, the importance of an earlier Toronto journal, *The Canadian Monthly and National Review* (1872–8), later reorganized as *Rose-Belford's Canadian Monthly and National Review* (1878–82). Many of the writers published in *The Week*, including Graeme Mercer Adam, Sara Jeannette Duncan, Agnes Maule Machar, **Charles G. D. Roberts, Goldwin Smith**, and Daniel Wilson, first appeared in the monthly. Six of the essays in Goldwin Smith's *Lectures and Essays* (1881) are taken from *The Canadian Monthly and National Review*. Duncan, who wrote extensively for *The Week*, was the first woman employed full time in the editorial department of a Canadian newspaper, *The Globe*; a selection of her writing has been gathered in *Sara Jeannette Duncan: Selected Journalism* (1978), edited by Thomas E. Tausky. The essays of Archibald MacMechan, another frequent contributor to *The Week*, are gathered in six volumes, most notably *The Porter of Baghdad and Other Fantasies* (1901) and *The Book of Ultima Thule* (1928). Although **Bliss Carman**'s poetry was frequently printed in *The Week*, his essays do not appear there. They are to be found in numerous volumes, including *The Kinship of Nature* (1903), *The Poetry of Life: Longfellow, Emerson, Swinburne* (1905), and *Talks on Poetry and Life* (1926).

The closing decades of the nineteenth century and the early decades of the twentieth saw the rise of university periodicals in Canada, the increasing identification of essay writing with the professoriate, and the gradual redefinition of the essay as a form to be taught to students. Both Goldwin Smith and Archibald MacMechan were university professors. George M. Grant, the Principal of Queen's University, Kingston, founded the *Queen's Quarterly* in 1893; and in 1907 Sir Andrew MacPhail assumed the editorship of *The McGill University Magazine* (1901–6), renamed simply *University Magazine* (1907–20) and directed by an editorial board drawn from Dalhousie University, McGill University, and the University of Toronto. MacPhail's essays, many of which first appeared in *University Magazine*, are gathered in three volumes, *Essays in Puritanism* (1905), *Essays in Politics* (1909), and *Essays in Fallacy* (1910). Other university periodicals followed: *The Dalhousie Review* was founded in 1921; the *University of Toronto Quarterly* in 1931. While these periodicals printed essays on a wide range of subjects, more specialized journals, often university-based, also began to appear.

Two other turn-of-the-century developments shaped the Canadian essay in the twentieth century. The first was the rise of mass-circulation magazines both in Canada, and, earlier, in the USA. The advent of such magazines as *Saturday Night* (1887–), *Maclean's* (1896–), *Canadian Home Journal* (1905–59), and *Chatelaine* (1928–) involved the redefinition of audience from an intellectual élite or a group defined by class, region, and church to the literate majority. That the informal essay flourished in the middle decades of the century or that some of its best-known practitioners worked in the editorial departments or wrote for such magazines should hardly be surprising. W. A. Deacon, who edited *Saturday Night* for six years (1922–8), published two influential collections of essays, *Pens and Pirates* (1923) and *Poteen* (1926), B. K. Sandwell, editor of the same magazine from 1932 to 1951, published *The Privacity Agent and Other Modest Proposals* (1928). A second collection of Sandwell's essays, *The Diversions of Duchesstown and Other Essays* (1955), was published posthumously with an introduction by **Robertson Davies**. Peter Donovan's sketches from *Saturday Night* were collected in *Imperfectly Proper* (1920), and Newton MacTavish's writing in *Canadian Magazine* can be found in *Thrown In* (1923). The success of Canada's best-known writer in the early decades of the century, **Stephen Leacock**, rests to some extent on the publication of his humorous sketches and essays in the mass-circulation periodicals. No Canadian writer more successfully adapted the sketch to his own uses than Leacock, who averaged more than a book each year beginning with *Literary Lapses* (1910). The second development that shaped the essay in Canada was the emergence of little magazines. Virtually a new phenomenon at the turn of the twentieth century, the little magazine was in many ways the obverse of the mass-circulation magazines: a low budget, special-interest periodical, often connected to a movement and frequently intent on changing the status quo. Undoubtedly the most important little magazine in the early decades of the century was *The Canadian Forum* (1920–), founded by a group of faculty and students at the University of Toronto. The journal favoured essays, such as Douglas Bush's 'Making Literature Hum' and **A. J. M. Smith**'s 'Wanted — Canadian Criticism', that were terse, argumentative, and often irreverent. Little magazines proliferated in the early decades and frequently provided a forum for dissenting views. Many, such as *The Canadian Forum*, *The McGill Fortnightly Review* (1925–7), and its successor, *The Canadian Mercury* (1928–9), originated on university campuses.

At least two developments following the Second World War accelerated the growing institutionalization of the essay within universities. The first was the demise of many mass-circulation magazines in Canada in the 1950s under the combined weight of competition from American magazines such as *Time* and *Reader's Digest* and from the growing popularity of television. The second was the rapid expansion of Canadian universities in the 1950s and 1960s and the increasing importance placed on post-secondary education. This trend is apparent in the careers of two Canadian writers who published their first book of essays in the immediate post-war period; although neither had his eye set on an academic career, by the end of the 1960s both were professors of English. The first was Robertson Davies, who served as literary editor of *Saturday Night* under B. K. Sandwell and subsequently became editor of the family-owned Peterborough *Examiner*. Davies' humorous weekly columns in the *Examiner* and other papers developed into three books written under the pseudonym of Samuel Marchbanks. Other collections by Davies, published after he joined the University of Toronto (1960), include *One Half of Robertson Davies* (1977), *The Enthusiasms of Robertson Davies* (1979), and *The Well-Tempered Critic* (1981). The second writer was **Hugh MacLennan**, who taught at Lower Canada College until, encouraged by the financial success of his novel *Two Solitudes* (1945), he opted for a career as a freelance journalist and broadcaster; he subsequently took up part-time teaching at McGill University where he became a full professor in 1968. He won Governor General's Awards for his first two collections of essays, *Cross Country* (1949) and *Thirty and Three* (1954). He also published *Scotchman's Return and Other Essays* (1960) and perhaps his best-known collection, *Seven Rivers of Canada* (1961), based on a series of essays he wrote for *Maclean's*.

The best known and most frequently cited practitioner of the scholarly essay in Canada is the critic **Northrop Frye**. His numerous essay collections include *The Educated Imagination* (1963), *Fables of Identity* (1963), *Spiritus Mundi* (1976), and *Divisions on a Ground* (1982). The rapid expansion of the universities resulted in the publication of many more collections of scholarly essays than it is possible to mention. There was also considerable experimentation with the scholarly essay, from the *essais concrètes* of **Marshall McLuhan** in such books as *The Medium is the Massage* (1967) and *War and Peace in the Global Village* (1968) to the poetic evocations of **Robert Kroetsch** in collections such as *The Lovely Treachery of Words* (1989) and the 'crypto-frictions' of **Aritha van Herk** in *In Visible Ink* (1991).

The rapid expansion of the universities was more than matched by the remarkable development of Canadian writing in the same period. Numerous writers emerged in the 1960s and 1970s and many found that the essay form suited both their needs and their talents. For some, including **Margaret Laurence** and **Margaret Atwood**, the essay was an occasional form: Laurence's essays are gathered in *Heart of a Stranger* (1976), Atwood's in *Second Words* (1982). For others, such as **Mordecai Richler**, the essay was a more central concern. Richler's essays can be found in numerous collections, from *Hunting Tigers under Glass* (1968) through *Shovelling Trouble* (1972) to his recent, much debated *Oh Canada! Oh Quebec!: Requiem for a Divided Country* (1992). Notable among experimenters in the essay are **George Bowering** (*Errata*, 1988) and Gail Scott, whose writing emerges out of the remarkable flowering of feminist, postmodern writing in Quebec; her essays are gathered in *Spaces Like Stairs* (1989).

Journalism remains of fundamental importance to the essay in Canada and the writing of many journalists, including Pierre Berton, Gregory Clark, Alan Fotheringham, Robert Fulford, Richard Needham, Peter Newman, Eric Nicol, and Marjorie Nichols, are gathered in book form. (See **Cultural Journalism**, Canada.) Science and technology, particularly the development of computers, is rapidly changing not only journalism but the world in which we live; the essay, which emerged with the invention of moveable type, the discovery of the Americas, and the rise of the professional classes, is changing with it.

PAUL HJARTARSON

Further reading: George Parker, *The Beginnings of the Book Trade in Canada* (1985); Graham Good, *The Observing Self: Rediscovering the Essay* (1988); Fraser Sutherland. *The Monthly Epic: A History of Canadian Magazines* (1989).

ESSAYS (The Philippines)

The first general anthology of Filipino essays, short stories, plays, and poems in English, *Philippine Prose and Poetry*, edited by the Bureau of Education, appeared in 1927. *Dear Devices* (1933), edited by Antonio Estrada, Alfredo Litiatco, and Francisco Icasiano, is considered the first anthology devoted solely to Philippine essays in English. *The Bamboo Flower* (1949) by Alfredo Gonzalez presents a substantial number of his essays. They are characterized by religious feeling and meditation and by a love of nature akin to that of Rousseau, Wordsworth, Thoreau, and Emerson.

In *Filipino Essays in English* (1954) Leopoldo Yabes gathered representative essays by well-known writers in the genre. Yabes' *The Filipino Struggle for Intellectual Freedom* (1957) reveals his nationalist views. *The Background of Nationalism and Other Essays* (1965), by Horacio de la Costa, shows the author's love for his country, and especially for the city of Manila. *Literature at the Crossroads* (1965), collected and published by **Alberto S. Florentino**, presents papers, or essays, read by well-known writers in English at three symposia sponsored by the Congress for Cultural Freedom on the subjects of the Filipino novel, Filipino poetry, and Filipino theatre. (These writers include **Edilberto Tiempo, Severino Montano, Wilfrido Maria Guerrero, Francisco Arcellana,** and Edith Lopez Tiempo.) *The Filipinos in the Philippines and Other Essays* (1966) by Renato Constantino presents a picture of Filipino times and society intended to help Filipino readers know more about their country. *Brown Heritage: Essays on Philippine Cultural Tradition and Literature* (1967), edited by Antonio Manuud, presents interesting and informative dialogues between historians and literary critics. The essays are on Philippine cultural tradition, vernacular literatures, Philippine literature in Spanish, and Philippine literature in English. *Philippine-American Literary Relations 1898–1941* (1969), by Lucila Hosillos, is a scholarly and well-documented work. It is a history of Philippine literature 'as art during a particular stage of its development, its origins and growth in a complex of sources, social conditions, influences, and the Filipino writer's awakening to his artistic needs and powers'. *Philippine Fiction* (1972), edited by Joseph Galdon, gathers together literary criticism from the journal *Philippine Studies* (1953–72). Canonical writers and works are discussed in this collection.

Outline History of Philippine Literature in English (1981), by Asuncion David-Maramba, presents, in an informal way, Philippine literature in English from 1900 to 1972. *Revaluation: Essays on Philippine Literature, Cinema and Popular Culture* (1984), by **Bienvenido Lumbera**, advocates a reassessment of Philippine writing in the light of significant twentieth-century literary and political movements, especially as they affect Philippine literature. Lumbera's writings suggest that he is a nationalist like the historian Renato Constantino.

The Romance Mode in Philippine Popular Literature and Other Essays (1991), according to the author, Soledad S. Reyes, is a collection of essays 'that have sought not only to describe the complex movements and trends that have shaped much of literature, but as importantly, to problematize certain taken for granted assumptions regarding such critical projects'.

ESTRELLITA V. GRUENBERG

ESSAYS (West Africa)

The Gambia, Ghana, Nigeria, Sierra Leone

On the evidence of the contents of Lalage Bown's retrospective anthology of non-fictional African-English prose, *Two Centuries of African English* (1973), the essay form was initially used by Africans mainly in the production of political tracts. This was, of course, in consonance with the mainly political nature of the colonial experience. Most of the first generation of West African nationalists and intellectuals believed that they should first 'seek political freedom and other freedoms shall follow'.

A retrospective survey of the essay form in West Africa must inevitably start with the vanguard generation of nationalists/pan-West Africanists such as Kobina Seyki, J. E. Casely-Hayford, Raphael Armattoe, and Abraham William, all of Ghana (Gold Coast), **Abioseh Nicol** of Sierra Leone, and Nnamdi Azikiwe, Obafemi Awolowo, and Mbonu Ojike of Nigeria. Many of these West Africans were in one way or another connected with pan-West African bodies such as the National Congress of British West Africa (1920–9) and the West African Students' Union of London, England, of the 1930s and 1940s. They tried to articulate in their writings the groups' political and cultural ideals. Casely-Hayford, for example, championed the cause of a University of West Africa, whose main aim would be the promotion of race consciousness, nationalism, and the study of African languages and customs. Such was his conviction that even in his novel, *Ethiopia Unbound* (1911), the view is presented that 'no people could despise its own language, customs and institutions and hope to avoid national death'. This view of the centrality of culture in national and racial survival can also be said to have informed Mbonu Ojike's *My Africa* (1946), Raphael Armattoe's *The Golden Age of West African Civilization* (1946), W. E. Abraham's *The Mind of Africa* (1962), and Kwame Nkrumah's concept of the 'African Personality' — anglophone West Africa's response to francophone West Africa's Negritudinist views.

Increasingly, West African creative writers employ the essay form to contemplate the socio-historical and the cultural backgrounds from which they derive their literary material and vision. These essays may be divided into two broad groups: the light-hearted, satirical, and witty and the specialized, by the cultural scholars.

The first group is basically the outcome of radio talks and newspaper pieces. The most representative of this kind of essay is perhaps Peter Enahoro's *How To Be A Nigerian* (1966), in which he examines, in witty and sarcastic essays, various aspects of Nigerian life. In his *You Gotta Cry To Laugh* (1972), he adopts the same comic style to examine various dimensions of race prejudice. **Mabel Segun**'s *Sorry, No Vacancy* (1985, originally published in 1977 as *Friends, Nigerians, Countrymen*), is a collection of satirical radio essays broadcast between 1961 and 1974. In style and focus it belongs to the same tradition as *How To Be A Nigerian*. (See **Humour and Satire**, West Africa.)

Generally known as one of West Africa's most perceptive academic critics, Emmanuel Obiechina has also written a number of light-hearted socio-cultural essays. In both *Africa Shall Survive, Essays, Tales and Lay Sermons about Africa and the African* (1980) and *Mammon Worship* (1983), Obiechina, employing a relaxed and anecdotal style, reflects on the African condition. In more recent times, **Ken Saro-Wiwa**, poet, playwright and novelist, has also found essays (both the serious and the comical varieties) as viable instruments for his contribution to both political and cultural debates. His *Nigeria: The Brink of Disaster* (1991) provides a sampling of his views about Nigeria's material and political culture. **Elechi Amadi**'s *Ethics in Nigerian Culture* (1982), a modest contribution to literary/cultural essays, attempts an enquiry into the moral and philosophical framework of Nigerian life and culture.

The major exponents of the literary/cultural essay, however, are **Chinua Achebe, Kofi Awoonor, Chinweizu**, and **Wole Soyinka**. (See **Criticism**, West Africa.) In *Morning Yet on Creation Day* (1975), *Hopes and Impediments: Selected Essays 1965–1987* (1988), and the basically political *The Trouble With Nigeria* (1983), Achebe tackles issues ranging from the role of the African writer through the language of the African writer to the relationship between North and South. A consummate stylist, Achebe's essays are critically controlled, self-assured, confident, articulate, pan-Africanist. Because of the transparent simplicity of his prose and his ability to distill the profound from the mundane, Achebe is perhaps the most often invoked African essayist. Awoonor's *The Breast of the Earth: A Survey of the History, Culture and Literature of Africa South of the Sahara* (1975) provides a sensitive interpretation of African history, art, philosophy, music, and literature, with examples drawn from both oral and scribal sources.

The views of Chinweizu and Soyinka, two of West Africa's most controversial essayists, are constantly opposed, although, in principle, they are both committed to a pan-Africanist view of civilization and culture. While Chinweizu often limits his positive cultural spectrum to the black world, Soyinka recognizes that his loyalty to Africa and African tradition should not foreclose his appreciation of the strength of other cultures.

Chinweizu is a prolific, controversial, and irreverent essayist. In addition to several journal articles, especially in *Okike*, his views on West

African culture and literature are contained in *The West and the Rest of Us* (1975), *Toward the Decolonization of African Literature* (1980), and *Decolonising the African Mind* (1987). Chinweizu's views and opinions are often both pertinent and timely, but his style is generally petulant. In contrast to Chinweizu's uncomplicated and pristine African world, Soyinka, drawing examples from his own Yoruba culture and from other African cultures, cautions that African culture is a multifaceted and multilayered phenomenon from which the contemporary creative African must be free to choose. While Chinweizu views things as white or black, Soyinka concentrates on grey areas, believing that to be more representative of the complexity of life. In both *Myth, Literature and the African World* (1976) and *Art, Dialogue and Outrage: Essays on Literature and Culture* (1988), Soyinka displays the combative, erudite, and cosmopolitan temper that has become the hallmark of his work. But even as he answers the charge of obscurity in some of these essays, he tends to pitch the language of his discourse a degree or two removed from the general reader.

There are many other West African essayists whose works have not been collected, but who have contributed views and opinions to the pages of such newspapers as the *Daily Mail* of Sierra Leone, the *Daily Graphic* of Ghana, and the *Daily Times*, *Vanguard*, and the *Guardian* of Nigeria. Similarly, journals such as *Black Orpheus*, *Nigeria Magazine*, *Transition/Ch'indaba*, and *Okike* have published many essays, by a wide range of West Africans, that have initiated a number of cultural debates.

FUNSO AIYEJINA

Cameroon

Given Cameroon's unusual history, it should be no surprise that the essay is the most vigorous written form of literature produced by anglophones. The predominance of this form is also conditioned by the relatively low cost of local newspapers and magazines in which essays appear. Books are costly and publishing houses ephemeral. Also, school texts draw almost exclusively on foreign material, leaving the formation of a national literature to the press.

Cameroon's most influential writer, even several years after his death, is **Bernard Nsokika Fonlon**. For three decades his writings did more than any other's to inspire common identity and purpose among anglophones. Appearing in pamphlet form and in many periodicals, especially in the bilingual English-French review *Abbia*, which he launched in 1963 and edited until he died, Fonlon's articles carried titles that are self-explanatory (but, which, like Montaigne's, often strayed into fascinating asides), for example, 'The Role of Intellectuals and the Authorities in Cultural Development', 'A Case for Early Bilingualism', 'The Idea of Cultural Integration', 'The Language Problem in Cameroon', 'To Every African Freshman, or the Nature, End and Purpose of University Studies', 'The Task of Today', 'The Idea of Literature', and 'The Philosophy, the Science and the Art of the Short Story'.

Deeply influenced by his Catholic seminary education and steeped in echoes of nineteenth-century British literature, Fonlon's style is elegant, rotund, latinate, and archaic to non-Cameroonians' ears, but is much emulated in his country's traditions. Another essayist of considerable reputation is Albert Mukong, a bookseller and political figure from Bamenda who was allied with the revolutionary 'UPC' (Union des Populations Camerounaises), which since the 1940s has led the struggle for genuine independence. His *Prisoner Without a Crime* (1985) is an account of his six years in detention without charges (1970–6), during which he was offered freedom for the price of a loyalty oath, but refused. Other influential writings by Mukong are *The Problems of New Deal* (undated) and the pamphlet 'An Open Letter to the First

Ordinary CNU Congress of the New Deal' (1985). Far leaner than Fonlon's prose, Mukong's has become in recent years increasingly based on his love of the Bible.

Obenson Tataw (d. 1979) is still a force in Cameroon literature. Under the pen name Ako-Aya, which was also the title of his regular column in the *Cameroon Outlook*, he mixed Pidgin and English in acerbic, raucous, satirical essays — frequently censored — that devastated the highest officials in government and their policies. His successor is Rotcod Gobata (also an alias), a columnist for the *Cameroon Post*. A constant victim of censorship, 'Gobata' is more widely read in world literature than any other anglophone commentator except Martin Jumbam and is a significant guide to increased literary, not just political, consciousness in his country. His 'The Two Faces of Mongo Beti' — Beti is his francophone countryman recently home from more than three decades in exile — is a model of astute literary analysis that is politically contextualized. His provocatively titled *The Past Tense of Shit* (1993, a collection of essays from his weekly column 'No Trifling Matter') was seized from the printer by police for political, not moral reasons. Nevertheless, it has a vast underground readership.

George Ngwane (1960–), a journalist and literature teacher, has published three books that follow in the Fonlon tradition, though they are less lofty and learned and more pragmatic. *The Mungo Bridge* (1990) — the Mungo river divides anglophone and francophone zones — analyses anglophone problems under an integrated republican state. In spite of its positive attitude towards a non-federalist arrangement, it landed Ngwane in trouble, and when Bate Besong reviewed it, Besong was detained. In the work Ngwane decries the failure of anglophones and francophones to unite in common cause: 'From 1961, the two provinces [across the Mungo] have built a tower of Babel between them and thereby lost the Garden of Eden'. *Fragments of Unity* (1992) is a history of South West Cameroon and yesterday's heroes; in it Ngwane criticizes contemporary leaders and challenges his people to greater militancy. Himself a leader of 'CAM' (Cameroon Anglophone [sometimes action] Movement), his latest work is *Bate Besong (or the Symbol of Anglophone Hope)* (1993), the first booklet devoted entirely to an anglophone Cameroonian author, which celebrates the most stridently nationalist Cameroonian writer, Bate Besong.

Other essayists of note are Gorji Dinka and Martin Kongnyuy Jumbam. Dinka's eloquent work began appearing in 1985 in French translation when Mongo Beti opened the pages of his radical review *Peuples noirs peuples Africains* to students in a show of solidarity with the anglophones and their plight. Jumbam, a translator for an oil company, publishes fearless essays in many outlets, especially the bi-monthly *Cameroon Life*. His erudite but accessible articles range from literary criticism to political satire and even to non-generic contributions to the literary scene, such as his pamphlet *The Interchange Between the Flesh and the Word: The Dialogue Between Medicine and Literature in Africa* (1993).

STEPHEN H. ARNOLD

Further reading: Richard Bjornson, *The African Quest for Freedom and Identity: Cameroonian Writing and the National Experience* (1991).

ESSEX EVANS, GEORGE (1863–1909)
Australian poet
Born in London, England, and educated in Wales and the Channel Islands, he immigrated to Australia in 1881 and worked successively as farmer, tutor, journalist, and public servant, including publicist for the Government Tourist Bureau. He was a member of the Johnsonian Club and founded

the Austral Society for the cultural improvement of Toowoomba.

Essex Evans was sending poems to newspapers by 1883, and in 1891 published his first volume, *The Repentance of Magdalen Despar*. This was followed by *Loraine and Other Verses* (1898) and *The Secret Key and Other Verses* (1906). His verse was collected posthumously. In 1893–4 he and John Tighe Ryan edited a short-lived journal, *The Antipodean*.

Essex Evans wrote in a variety of styles, from extended narratives to whimsical lyrics. His most popular poem is 'The Women of the West', a gracious tribute to the endeavours and sufferings of pioneer women in the bush. He also wrote two pantomimes for the Brisbane stage. Essex Evans saw himself as a sort of unofficial poet laureate and wrote a series of public poems on events and prominent people. Despite the protests of the ***Bulletin***, his 'Ode for Commonwealth Day' won the fifty-guinea prize offered by the New South Wales government for a celebratory Federation poem. Of more significance is the claim that his earlier 'Federation Song' was instrumental in uniting the colonies.

Essex Evans faced the same dilemma as other colonial writers as their countries approach independence: whether to support a future in a partnership of Greater Britain (later the Commonwealth) or whether to adopt the nationalist, republican option and shake off all colonial controls and connections. Essex Evans' answer was the former, and his imagery for the virtues and potential of the new nation draws heavily on the traditional iconography of Britain as defiant sea-fortress. Although seen now as a minor poet of the period, Essex Evans is still remembered in Toowoomba by an annual pilgrimage and lecture.

CHRIS TIFFIN

Further reading: Chris Tiffin, 'Metaphor and emblem: George Essex Evans's public poetry', *Literary Criterion* 4 (1991).

ESSON, LOUIS (1878–1943)

Australian dramatist

Born in Edinburgh, Scotland, his family immigrated to Australia when Esson was four years old. He became a journalist after leaving the University of Melbourne, Australia, without a degree. The most distinguished Australian playwright of the first half of the twentieth century, Esson is seen as the most conspicuous casualty of a 'cultural cringe' that ensured that imported plays and performers dominated the stage. (See **Drama**, Australia.) Moreover, Esson's association with the Pioneer Players (1922–6) seemed to demonstrate how depressingly inhospitable to pioneers and local products the Australian theatre could be. It was an experience confirmed still more bitterly for Esson by the years of almost total neglect that followed.

However, the stereotype of doomed idealism simplifies not only the matter of Esson's achievement, but also the nature of the difficulties he faced. Esson certainly tasted the pleasures of popularity, particularly with his Shavian political satire *The Time Is Not Yet Ripe* (1912), which wittily deflated the pomposities of all ideologues, whatever their persuasions; despite its success and its dramatization of his own, elegantly theoretical socialism, Esson came to have a great aversion to the play.

Instead, Esson sought to develop myths of Australian cultural distinctiveness. The one-act plays *The Drovers* (1920) and *Dead Timber* (1911) reflect the influence of Ireland's Abbey Theatre in locating Australian images in the archetypal conflicts of the Outback. But despite their power, these plays run into some dramatic obstacles that make their brevity a necessity. Not only are the plot catalysts — a stampede and a flood — unstageable within the conventions of Esson's naturalism, but the phlegmatic bushman stereotype leaves most of the emotional responses to them unexpressed. The outback mythology proves more eloquent, if less clearly focused, when galvanized by domestic melodrama, as in *Mother and Son* (1946), or deflected into rustic comedy, as in the 'The Battler' (premièred 1922).

Esson's quest for a uniquely national identity also involved the culture of the urban working and criminal classes, and this proved rather more fruitful. The rich vernacular of the larrikins in the one-act play *The Woman Tamer* (1911) and the full-length *The Bride of Gospel Place* (1946, first performed 1926) provides a good deal of local colour, while the spectre of actual or potential violence gives some guaranteed momentum to the plot. There is also some room in these plays for Esson's considerable talents as a comic writer, though their dialogue has more vigour than wit.

Esson had a great fondness for the bohemian intellectual life and was a fine writer in a number of forms; his verse, his journalism, and his literary criticism are among the most impressive of the period. The quest for a theatre of the people led him away from those things, and away too from the suburban reality that for most audiences was the source of an identifiable Australianness; ironically, it ended in the marginalization that so often is the fate of the self-conscious pioneer.

PETER FITZPATRICK

Further reading: Vance Palmer, *Louis Esson and the Australian Theatre* (1948); Leslie Rees, *The Making of Australian Drama* (1973); David Walker, *Dream and Disillusion* (1976).

ESSOP, AHMED (1931–)

South African/Indian novelist, short-story writer

He was born in Dabhel, Surat, India, and educated at Johannesburg Indian High School, Fordsburg, Johannesburg, South Africa. He studied at the University of South Africa, Pretoria, earning a BA in English and philosophy (1956) and a BA in honours English (1964). Essop has followed a dual career as schoolteacher in the Johannesburg area and as fictional chronicler of the life of the Indian community in that apartheid-ridden city. Essop's published fiction includes the short-story collections *The Hajji and Other Stories* (1978) and *Noorjehan* (1990) and the novels *The Visitation* (1980) and *The Emperor* (1984).

Essop's work reveals the marginalized status of the Johannesburg Indian community, living in segregated areas, cut off from both white affluence and black squalor. The small scale of this communal life is its distinctive feature. Essop is a master at capturing its special flavour: the obsessions with old customs, traditional obligations under the strain of materialistic values, and the intrusive power of the white state.

Like other Indian communities scattered across the former British Empire, South African Indian enclaves have been sustained by cultural values that come from the subcontinent and not from the milieu in which they happen to find themselves. What Essop's work shows is the steady intrusion of South African politics into the lives of his characters. Inhabiting the middle ground between the hitherto powerless black majority and the all-powerful white minority, the Indian population has been variously wooed by the apartheid regime as a middle- (albeit second-) class mercantile buffer between the two main contestants in the power struggle and victimized and persecuted by the same regime for an identification with the black, or at least anti-racist, cause.

Essop's tales depict both Indian collaborators with and victims of the white power structure. Even when not themselves directly affected by the degradations of apartheid, some of Essop's apolitical characters, whose main interests are domestic, are shown to be inevitably diminished and tainted by the injustices done to those around them. In this, Essop can be contrasted with **V. S. Naipaul,** who both depicts the attempts of Caribbean communities to preserve their Indian customs by isolating themselves from the society around them, and, in his African novel *A Bend in The River* (1979), creates an Indian protagonist who typifies the ethos of a class of international traders who are always bystanders in their adopted homes. Essop, on the other hand, even in his first and least overtly political collection of short stories, reveals his Indian community to be co-opted as either collaborating with or opposing the South African state. The traditionally cocooned and bypassed Indian enclave is shown to be unavoidably involved in the larger South African struggle, even when it is apparently most self-absorbed and self-contained.

At the same time, Essop pursues his particular cultural symbolism throughout his fiction, integrating images and concepts from Indian and Islamic belief into the personal moral of the tales. In this trait, too, he shows his distinctiveness. There is a unique specificity about his fiction, which is much more tightly focused on its cultural subject than is the work of a writer such as **Alex La Guma**, whose depictions of the Coloured community become more generalized as his texts become more explicitly revolutionary.

The Hajji and Other Stories won the Olive Schreiner Prize in 1979. Dealing with the Indian enclave of Fordsburg, the tales evoke the vitality of that inner-city melting pot in mid-century Johannesburg. The mood of Essop's novels changes with their change in locale from downtown Fordsburg to distant, segregated Lenasia. *The Visitation* ironically depicts the mutual corruption of a landlord and gangster in Fordsburg just before the enforced community move to Lenasia. *The Emperor* bitterly denounces the attempt of an autocratic Indian headmaster to collaborate with the 'correct' educational policies of his white overlords. In some of his tales in *Noorjehan* Essop returns to old Fordsburg, but the didactic element associated with his depiction of a bleaker life in Lenasia informs all these short stories.

ROWLAND SMITH

Further reading: Rowland Smith, 'Living on the fringe: the world of Ahmed Essop', *Commonwealth 8* (1985); Eugenie R. Freed, 'Mr. Sufi climbs the stairs: the quest and the ideal in Ahmed Essop's *The Visitation*', *Theoria* 71 (1988); Antje Hagena, 'Straightforward politics and ironic playfulness: the aesthetic possibilities of Ahmed Essop's *The Emperor*', *English in Africa* 17 (1990).

EVANS, HUBERT (1892–1986)

Canadian novelist, short-story writer

Born in Vankleek Hill, Ontario, Canada, he worked as a newspaper reporter before serving in the First World War. In 1926 he published his first book, *Forest Friends*, a collection of outdoor stories. In 1927 he and his wife moved to Roberts Creek, British Columbia, Canada, where he lived until his death. *The New Front Line* (1927) is a novel about a war-weary veteran who homesteads in British Columbia.

Evans published three novels for juveniles about his Airedale retriever — *Derry, Airedale of the Frontier* (1928), *Derry's Partner* (1929), and *Derry of Totem Creek* (1930) — and another collection of outdoor stories, *The Silent Call* (1930). He took up commercial fishing on the rugged British Columbia coast and managed to write left-wing plays, teach unemployed men to fish, and explore the coast on his twenty-eight-foot boat. In 1932 Evans published *The Western Wall*, possibly the best of his approximately sixty novellas and serials. *The Western Wall* is about the spiritual and political crisis of an unemployed Vancouver garage mechanic.

During the Second World War, Evans, a Quaker, campaigned for pacifist ideals by publishing inspirational short stories and serials for juveniles, mainly in American denominational magazines. In 1942 he published *No More Islands*, the first book to examine seriously the expulsion of Japanese Canadians from the British Columbia coast during the Second World War. (This racially motivated expulsion and incarceration of Japanese Canadians eventually caused the Canadian government to compensate Japanese-Canadians financially in 1989.)

After living almost eight years in Native Canadian villages in northern British Columbia, Evans published his second adult novel, *Mist on the River* (1954). Recognized as a Canadian classic, this unsentimentalized depiction of a Native Canadian, Cy Pitt, torn between two cultures, is the first book to depict realistically Native Canadians as central characters.

Evans' third adult book, *O Time in Your Flight* (1979), is based on his vivid recollections of Ontario as a nine-year-old boy in the first year of the twentieth century. Canadian novelist **Margaret Laurence** lovingly referred to Hubert Evans as 'the elder of our tribe'.

ALAN TWIGG

EVASCO, MARJORIE (1953–)

Filipino poet

She was born in Maribojoc, on the central Philippine island of Bohol, and educated in the Philippines. An editor and arts administrator, Evasco teaches and is undertaking doctoral studies in literature and language at De La Salle University in Manila. Highly regarded in the Philippines, she has won awards at Hawthornden Castle, Scotland, and the Rockefeller Foundation, Bellagio, Italy. Extensive travels in Asia, Europe, and the United Kingdom have informed her theme of feminist spiritual exploration, but the influence of the rich folk traditions of Bohol are also evident. She edited *Filipino Housewives Speak* (1991) and her major poetic work to date is *Dreamweavers: Selected Poems 1976–1986* (1987).

Evasco's work seeks to open space for women in a traditional society. *Dreamweavers* employs an overarching metaphor of women's traditional weaving. Images of woven motifs — human, spider, eye, key, star — connect the sections on 'Birth', 'Daughters', 'Women Voices', 'Wisewomen', and 'Pintadas: Marked Women'.

Evasco's work has been influenced by classical Chinese and Japanese poets such as Tu Fu and Basho and by Filipino women poets **Edith Tiempo** and Grace Monte de Ramos. Her major western influences are contemporary American minority women writers and Spanish-language poets who have opposed dominant ideologies, and she draws poetic and revolutionary sustenance from the Philippines' legacy of colonialism. *Dreamweavers* begins with a short letter to US feminist Chicana Gloria Anzaldúa and contains a poem about Hua Mu Lan (Fa Mu Lan), a legendary swordswoman in Chinese American Maxine Hong Kingston's novel *The Woman Warrior*. Both pieces develop the theme of liberation through the magic and strength of women's words. Evasco's poems offer the vivid telluric imagery of Pablo Neruda and the mystic folk quality of Federico García Lorca.

Like those of Rainer Maria Rilke, Evasco's poems resemble messages to or from spirits. Evasco sees herself in the role of the ancient Filipina *babaylane*, a wise woman healer. A shamanic sense of ritual enactment through naming endows her poems with heightened power and presence. Her best poems, such as 'Animasola', are deeply rooted in the local and particular but attain universality through their spare clarity, vivid natural imagery, and unexpected psychic shifts.

KATHRYN VAN SPANCKEREN

SUSAN M. TAYLOR

Further reading: Wong Phui Nam, 'Poetry as the seer's art', *The New Straits Times* 9 June 1993.

EXPATRIATE WRITERS (India, West Africa, The Caribbean)

The migration to London, Paris, and New York of writers from former colonies such as India, West Africa, and the Caribbean occurred in the absence of a stimulating literary environment at home and because of a lack of local publishing opportunities. The first group of aspiring Caribbean writers — **George Lamming, Samuel Selvon, V. S. Nai-**

paul, **Wilson Harris**, and **John Hearne**, for example — immigrated to London, England, soon after independence was achieved in their countries, and made it their literary home. The situation with Indian writers aspiring to write in English was not the same, even though writers such as **Raja Rao**, **R. K. Narayan**, and **Mulk Raj Anand** had to turn to London and Paris and to novelist friends in the west to help get their work published. Writers from India did not have to immigrate to the metropolitan centres in search of an audience or an intellectual climate in which to write. The Indian literary tradition placed a high value upon literary and linguistic accomplishments, particularly among the high castes to which most Indian writers in English belonged. Consequently, the majority of Indian novelists, poets, and dramatists did not emigrate, but continued to live and write in India. The emigrant novelists include Raja Rao, **Kamala Markandaya, G. V. Desani, Sudhin N. Ghose, Santha Rama Rau, Salman Rushdie, Farrukh Dhondy, Bharati Mukherjee, I. Allan Sealy**, and **Vikram Seth** (also a poet). The poets include **A. K. Ramanujan**, Sharat Chandra, **Meena Alexander**, and H. O. Nazareth.

Expatriation is a complex phenomenon. It is not merely a physical, geographical journey; it is also the virtual snapping of the immigrant's ties with the mother country. It is a movement away from a familiar frame of references and relationships and the entry into a new frame; as sociologist Ronald Taft notes, set-backs and rejections in the new land not only arrest the course of assimilation but also lead to actual regressions.

The experience of expatriate writers is similar to that of most immigrants. They share a faith in assimilation in the earlier phases of their stay abroad. Later they express in ethnic terms a need for a distinctively national/racial identity. The case of Third World immigrants becomes more complex when they encounter racial prejudice in the new land. A prevailing pattern in expatriate writing from India, West Africa, and the Caribbean is the representation of the entire immigrant experience — from the moment of the immigrant's arrival into the host country to the moment of later resolve to discover national/racial identity — through the sexual motif of love, marriage, and divorce between black/brown men and white women. Assimilation as an ideal represented in the 'marriage' of two cultures is portrayed, for example, in Kamala Markandaya's *The Nowhere Man* (1972), Raja Rao's *The Serpent and the Rope* (1960), and V. S. Naipaul's *The Mimic Men* (1967). The relationships in these works, however, do not last. A first indicator is that the marriages are childless. The couples then move into separate bedrooms. In the final stage there is separation or divorce. This happens in the novels cited above and also in Rao's *Comrade Kirillov* (1976), Lamming's *Water With Berries* (1971), and Markandaya's *Possession* (1963).

Interestingly, typical expatriate writers maintain that emigration has not interfered with their growth as artists because they have not lost touch with their mother countries. Migrant writers may also maintain — as do Vikram Seth, Salman Rushdie, and Bharati Mukherjee — that racial and cultural heritage is not something that has 'to obtrude on their writing all the time'. In other words, they are cosmopolitan writers. Seth's *The Golden Gate* (1986) chronicles the life of twentieth-century Californian yuppies, while Mukherjee in *Darkness* (1985) portrays the lives of South Asian immigrants to North America. In *The Middleman and Other Stories* (1988) Mukherjee depicts how Third World migrants to the USA, in the process of being uprooted and rerooted, get transformed while transforming their new country. Mukherjee claims that she has now even begun to use American English. Rushdie's *The Satanic Verses* (1988) similarly attempts the international or cosmopolitan theme.

Although most expatriate writers protest to the

contrary, their work provides significant clues that expatriation does have some impact on all first generation migrant writers. While Henry James could write authentically about both Europe and America, he could never erase the memory of his imperfect America. James Joyce's Dublin pervades his novels — all written outside of Ireland. Similarly, Raja Rao's novels return nostalgically to India despite their international locales and characters (French, English, Russian, African, and Jewish) as do the novels of Farrukh Dhondy and Markandaya. The poet A. K. Ramanujan returns obsessively in his poems to India and to family. The novels of Lamming and Naipaul also hearken repeatedly to the Caribbean. Naipaul's theme in *In a Free State* (1971) is international to some extent, but most of his work — early and late — reveals either a nostalgia for Trinidad or a desperate sense of homelessness expressed metaphorically through endless journeys and life spent in a hotel or a camp. Time alone can tell whether such cosmopolitan writers as Mukherjee, Seth, and Rushdie will continue to break fresh ground with their themes or if they will go the way of most first-generation expatriate writers. Seth's poetry already expresses the dual feelings of nostalgia for India and his attraction to the land of adoption. Sharat Chandra's poetry in *Heirloom* (1982) also reveals a deep sense of exile.

Expatriate writers re-create with remarkable emotion and precision experiences of colonization and racism (in the white man's country): with intensity, as in poet H. O. Nazareth's *Lobo* (1984); with understatement, as in Mukherjee's short story 'Jasmine'; and with depth, as in the work of Rushdie, Rao, G. V. Desani, and Dhondy. It is probable that depicting these experiences makes separation from the mother country more bearable. The perspective provided by distance also prompts Third World exiles to define their racial and national identity through opposition to white society and what they perceive of its value system. In the writings not only of Indian but also of Caribbean and African authors, a confrontation is often set up between the west/England/France and India/the Caribbean/Africa, and the conflict is resolved to the advantage of the mother country. In the work of Indian expatriate writers, spiritual India and her perennial traditions are opposed, and shown to be superior, to the west with its materialistic value system. In Markandaya's *Possession*, the swami (spiritual India) wins over Caroline (the materialistic west). In *The Serpent and the Rope*, Madeleine/France/the west loses out to Savitri/India. In Third World expatriate literature writers celebrate what in their views are the superior, perfect values of their pre-colonial societies. For example, in *A Flag on the Island* (1967), *In a Free State*, *The Mimic Men*, and *Guerrillas* (1975), Naipaul lays at the door of the colonizer/neo-colonizer the blame for destroying indigenous community-oriented value systems and reducing the Caribbean to a set of impotent island nations. Although in *Midnight's Children* (1981) Rushdie challenges static tradition (represented by Tai the boatman), he vehemently attributes many of contemporary India's ills to the divide-and-rule policy of Britain (Methwold, with the centre-parting in his hair) and its neo-colonial policy of forcing the colonizer's political and economic framework (Methwold's mansion) upon free India to ensure dependency on the ex-colonizer. Possibly these writers adopt a political stance in order to rationalize the decision to emigrate.

Third World expatriate writers tend to write allegories, a tendency that increases as the writer's stay abroad is prolonged. Here allegory refers not only to an extended metaphor or symbolic reference observed by a critic from outside the work but also to the structural principle of the work itself. Raja Rao's novels are political as well as metaphysical allegories. Rushdie's *Midnight's Children*, *Shame* (1983), and *Haroun and the Sea of Stories* (1990) are political allegories. *The Satanic Verses* is a religious and political allegory.

The novels of Camara Laye (Guinea, West Africa) and George Lamming are political and historical allegories. Perhaps expatriate writers choose allegory as a form to overcome the aesthetic dilemma that Milan Kundera, the Czech expatriate novelist, has described as one of 'how to situate the novel geographically'.

A negative effect of expatriation on writers in exile is that with the passage of time their characters and the situations that they establish tend to grow repetitive, abstract, and self-conscious. Their language also tends towards de-regionalization and silence. This may be an unpalatable finding, but it is one that cannot be ignored. Expatriate writing, however, also offers exciting experiments with technique, form, and language that the experience of writing in a culture different from one's own generates — at least in the earlier phase of a writer's stay abroad.

VINEY KIRPAL

Further reading: Timothy Brennan, *Salman Rushdie and the Third World: Myths of the Nation* (1989); Viney Kirpal, *The Third World Novel of Expatriation: A Study of Emigré Fiction by Indian, West African and Caribbean Writers* (1989).

EXPERIMENTAL THEATRE (New Zealand)
See **DRAMA** (New Zealand)

EXPLORATION LITERATURE

EXPLORATION LITERATURE (Overview)
It is, of course, a pretence to say that Europeans 'discovered' the non-European world. Native Americans spread throughout their continent millennia before Europeans knew that it existed. Indians and Sri Lankans were familiar with the features of their countries thousands of years before European navigators began to touch their shores. In a great diaspora, Polynesians had spanned the Pacific Ocean from Fiji in the west to Easter Island in the east, from Hawaii in the north to New Zealand in the south, hundreds of years before Europeans first ventured into that third of the globe. Muslims had learned the wind and current systems of the Indian Ocean long before the Portuguese rounded southern Africa. As the European reconnaissance was gathering, a vast Chinese fleet visited east Africa.

None the less, it was Europeans who, by their recordings in charts, maps, and journals, defined space, gradually revealed the extent of the globe, and, via printing, progressively conveyed this space and its myriad features to other peoples. It is from these activities that Europeans derive their pre-eminence as discoverers.

European exploration of the non-European world from the beginning of the fifteenth century to the end of the nineteenth century falls conveniently into two main phases — that up to *c.*1750, when activity was driven by trading motives and was undertaken as much by individuals and private companies as it was by governments — and that from *c.*1750, when governments sponsored expeditions whose members deployed emergent scientific knowledge and to a degree pursued exploration for its own sake. Broadly true as this schema is, however, it is not without flaws. Columbus' voyage was sponsored by the Spanish Crown, and the seventeenth-century buccaneer William Dampier made the first really significant attempt to comprehend the oceans' wind and current systems on a global scale. Further, there were powerful commercial and imperial motives behind the striking scientific expeditions of the second half of the eighteenth century commanded by James Cook, Jean François de Galaup, Compte de Lapérouse, Alessandro Malaspina, Antoine-Raymond-Joseph de Bruni, Chevalier d'Entrecasteaux, and George Vancouver.

The European explorations of those countries and regions from which now derive post-colonial literatures in English share a number of common features. One is that the first European ventures into non-European seas and along non-European shores were haphazard affairs, at least until builders had refined naval technology and sailors had accumulated sufficient empirical information to permit purposeful navigation. A second feature is that the first probings of the interiors of continents were often the work of individuals or of small groups, whose findings were then used by theoretical geographers to identify major goals and to advance proposals for their elucidation. (Compare, for example, James Bruce's search for the headwaters of the Nile with that of Richard Burton and J. H. Speke, or the fur-traders' journeys into western Canada with the systematic searches for the northwest Passage conducted by Cook, Vancouver, Sir John Franklin, and others.) A third is that the major scientific expeditions of the period 1750–1850 gathered a huge amount of information about the earth's geography, geology, climate, coastlines, fauna, flora, and peoples, information that was central to the development of the modern scientific disciplines. Nicolas Baudin's expedition to Australia, 1800–1804, for example, brought back 18,500 zoological specimens, including some 2,500 that were new to science. Robert Brown, the botanist on Matthew Flinders' expedition, 1801–1803, collected some 3,400 specimens, of which some 2,000 were new.

As well, the literature of European exploration has followed a discernible path since the late eighteenth century. First, there was that mode of presentation pioneered by Dampier and refined by John Hawkesworth and Cook, involving encompassing descriptions of places, plants, animals, and people, with the written text augmented by charts, maps, and engravings. This mode was then repeated to a greater or lesser extent in a plethora of collections of voyages and travels, geography books, and popular magazines, until it shaped the consciousness of the reading public. Then, as the various disciplines of geography, geology, zoology, botany, and ethnography developed, came further accounts based on extended observation, more limited in their compass but more extensive in their details. With colonization came more personal accounts that offered a semblance of scientific observation, but whose presentation was largely shaped by the assumptions of the dominant culture. (An Australian example is Karl Lumholtz's *Among Cannibals: An account of four years' travels in Australia and of camp life with the Aborigines of Queensland*, 1889.) In the course of the twentieth century, anthropologists and ethnographers have extended and refined the eighteenth-century explorers' beginnings, moving from belief in the possibility of exact scientific description to the recognition of the ultimate discreteness of the Other. And there have been travellers' accounts beyond number, some of them merely anecdotal, some of them suffused with 'local colour', and occasionally some of them so expressive of the human condition that they have attained the status of literature. (See **Travel Literature**.)

The Abbé Raynal's striking work on the history of European colonization (*A Philosophical and Political History of the Settlements and Trade of the Europeans in the East and West Indies*, 1776; third ed., 1777) begins with the observation that

> No event [s have] been so interesting to mankind in general, and to the inhabitants of Europe in particular, as the discovery of the New World, and the passage to India by the Cape of Good Hope . . . [They have given rise] to a revolution in the commerce, and in the power of nations; and in the manners, industry, and government of the whole world.

European sea-borne discovery certainly did unite the world's political and economic systems as never before; and European inland explorations then continued this process. One large result was the emergence of European empires with all their concomitants — economic exploitation, centres and peripheries of power and culture, racial and economic hegemony and subservience, and the loss of national, racial, and religious identities. The fading of these concomitants in the second half of the twentieth century has given rise to the post-colonial age.

To the post-colonial consciousness, the recognition and acceptance of the integrity of the Other is the only possible moral stance. However, critics of the tyrannies of the past tend to overlook a point that needs to be stressed. The sense of cultural relativity that some of the eighteenth-century European explorers evinced (a sense seen most notably perhaps in Cook's comments on the Australian Aborigines) was a development necessary to the recognition of the Other, and without it we could not have had those compelling modern studies of different realities, such as Greg Dening's *Islands and Beaches: Discourse on a Silent Land: Marquesas 1774–1880* (1980) and Anne Salmond's *Two Worlds: First Meetings between Maori and Europeans, 1642–1772* (1992).

This interconnection between the narratives of European exploration and contemporary outlook appears in another way, too. There are good grounds for finding (with Harold Bloom) the internalization of the quest to be one of the central features of Romanticism, an old literary movement that continues to exert a powerful presence. Among the shoals of the Great Barrier Reef, in imminent danger of being swept against a 'wall of Coral Rock rising all most perpendicular out of the unfathomable Ocean', Cook discovered what it was to be an explorer. 'Was it not', he wrote after they had narrowly escaped destruction a second time, 'for the pleasure which naturly results to a Man from being the first discoverer, even was it nothing more than sands and Shoals, this service would be insuportable especialy in far distant parts, like this, short of Provisions and almost every other necessary.'

To be the first discoverer — but, increasingly as the world was mapped, named, and known, of what? John Ledyard, a junior of Cook on the third voyage, indicated the answer that two hundred years' of cultural and literary development would provide when he wrote from Yakutsk, Siberia, in October 1787 (in *John Ledyard's Journey through Russia and Siberia 1787–1788*, 1966, edited by S. D. Watrous):

> . . . & I will declare that I never was so totaly at loss how to accommodate myself to my situation. The only consolation I have of the argumentative kind is to reflect that him who travels for information must be supposed to want it, & tho a little enigmatical it is I think equaly true that to be traveling is to be in error: that this must more or less necessarily anticede the other, and that an error in judgment only, is always to be forgiven.

To travel is to be in error — but how other than by travelling may we know the falsity of some perceptions and the truth of others? Imaginatively, it is no great step from Cook's exchanging names with Polynesians or his undoing of his hair and his taking off his shirt so as to be able to view the *'inasi* (harvest festival and investiture) ceremony at Tonga in 1777 to those transformations, personal and cultural, that are central to so much post-colonial literature in English, such as Malcolm Lowry's *Under the Volcano* (1947), **Patrick White**'s *Voss* (1957), **Margaret Atwood**'s *Surfacing* (1972), **V. S. Naipaul**'s *The Enigma of Arrival* (1987), and **Janette Turner Hospital**'s *Charades* (1988).

ALAN FROST

Exploration Literature (Australia)
Europeans entertained the idea of a great southern continent for a thousand years before their voyaging brought them to the lesser actuality of Australia. The earliest Dutch descriptions of 'New Holland' presented a reality very different from the imagined populous land mass strewn with spices and precious metals. The officers of the *Arnhem* and *Pera*, which coasted sections of the Gulf of Carpentaria in 1623, related that

> the land between 13 and 17 degrees . . . is an arid and poor tract without any fruit trees or anything else useful to man; it is low and monotonous without mountain or hill . . . there is little fresh water . . . In general the men are barbarians all much alike in build and features, pitch-black and entirely naked . . . and what they live on . . . [are] certain roots which they dig out from the earth.

Repeated regularly thereafter, this cluster of images received definitive form in William Dampier's account in *A New Voyage Round the World* (1697) of his weeks at Cygnet Bay in 1688. Captain James Cook and Sir Joseph Banks found the continent's eastern littoral to have a gentler aspect, and in his *A New Geographical, Historical and Commercial Grammar* (1787) William Guthrie described New South Wales as 'rather barren than fertile; yet in many places the rising grounds are chequered by woods and lawns, and the plains and vallies covered with herbage'.

The perception that the landscape of eastern Australia was akin to an English nobleman's 'park' occurs very frequently in descriptions from the first decades of European colonization, but it scarcely affected the prevailing impression that the country possessed only limited possibilities. 'To men of small property, unambitious of trade, and wishing for retirement,' wrote **Watkin Tench** in *A Narrative of the Expedition to Botany Bay* (1789) after six months' experience in 1788, 'I think the continent of New South Wales not without inducements.' A succession of writers over the next fifty years reinforced negative perceptions of Australia's landscape, as settlers experienced drought, flood, and insect plague and as they found no precious metals.

However, this sense of limited possibility did not attach to the continent's fauna and flora. William de Vlamingh found the mysterious black swan, long postulated as a sport of nature, in Western Australia in 1697; Cook and Banks found the even more mysterious kangaroo at the Endeavour River in 1770; and these discoveries were followed in the first decades of settlement by those of the emu, platypus, and lyrebird. Plants were equally unexpected; Sir J. E. Smith commented on them in *A Specimen of the Botany of New Holland* (1793).

It was with the determined search from the mid-1820s onwards for country over which fine-wooled sheep might graze that Australia became a place of infinite possibility. Major Thomas Mitchell wrote of the western district of what became Victoria — which he explored in 1836 — in *Three Expeditions into the Interior of Eastern Australia* (1838). In 1840 J. L. Stokes waxed lyrical about the 'Plains of Promise' beneath the Gulf of Carpentaria; in 1844 Ludwig Leichhardt found that the 'hollows' bordering the upper reaches of the Burdekin River 'were covered with a dense sward of various grasses, and the forest was open as far as the eye could reach' (*Journal of an Overland Expedition in Australia*, 1847); ten years later, Augustus Gregory found open grasslands in the Northern Territory. Even the star-crossed Burke and Wills expedition found some good grasslands in the Gulf and Channel countries.

But exploration also revealed the arid interior of the continent. For six months in 1845, Charles Sturt's party was confined to Depot Glen near Mt

Poole as all water shrank from the surrounding countryside. Leichhardt and his men disappeared without a trace somewhere in the interior in 1848. Only one of Burke's and Wills' party survived the attempt to cross the continent south to north in 1860–1. J. M. Stuart told how he reluctantly decided to give up his attempt in 1860 in *The Journals of John McDouall Stuart* (1865). The probes into the western deserts by William Gosse, Ernest Giles, Peter Warburton, John Forrest, and Alexander Forrest were likewise extremely harrowing. All of the explorers of the interior, and some of the littoral, suffered greatly from heat, thirst, scurvy, and rough terrain. The need for water is a recurring, emphatic note in their narratives. 'I must go where the water leads me,' Stuart observed poignantly in his *Journals*.

There is also an extra-geographical aspect to these explorers' accounts. Exhibiting that motif of the journey into the underworld common in Victorian literature (for example, Browning's 'Childe Roland to the Dark Tower Came'), the narratives of exploration effectively offer the 'Dead Heart' of the Australian continent as an objective correlative of void (*néant*). In this, they prefigure, and indeed have provided some materials for, such twentieth-century reiterations as **Patrick White**'s *Voss* and **Randolph Stow**'s *To the Islands*.

Three other images of great force reside in the narratives of Australian exploration. The first concerns the hostility of tribal Aborigines to the European parties. Myall blacks harried expeditions mounted by Thomas Mitchell, Sturt, E. J. Eyre, and Leichhardt. Edmund Kennedy was speared when in sight of the ship that would have rescued him. John Forrest's and Warburton's parties were similarly threatened. Northern blacks attacked J. L. Stokes' men and tried to burn out Augustus Gregory's camp on the Baines River.

Paradoxically, a second image concerns co-operation between whites and blacks. Aborigines repeatedly pointed out water holes and pasture to Eyre as he struggled across the Nullarbor Plain in 1840–1. The people of the South Alligator River showed Leichhardt's men how to negotiate swamplands, and then fed them. In 1861 inland blacks repeatedly succoured Burke's and Wills' party, and kept John King alive for three months until a search party found him.

A particular aspect of this co-operation is the presence of Aborigines on many of the exploring expeditions. Eyre had Wylie with him, Kennedy had Jackey. In 1844 Harry Brown and Charley accompanied Leichhardt. G. A. Dalrymple had Lt Marlow (of the Native Police) and Cockey with him. Tommy Windich and Jemmy Mungaro accompanied Forrest in 1869; Dick travelled with Giles in 1872 and 1873. Another Charley accompanied Warburton in 1873. Tommy Windich and Tommy Pierre went with Forrest in 1874, Tommy Oldham with Giles in 1875. The bushcraft, hardiness, and courage of these men were often indispensable to the success of the expeditions. Charley was much more adept than Leichhardt's other men at shooting birds and animals, and the fresh food he provided kept them healthy. Where the whites might wander for days in a futile quest for water, the blacks might find it quickly. In 1873, for example, Charley repeatedly found water for Warburton's party, as did Tommy Windich for Forrest's in 1874. In 1875 at one point Giles' party went for seventeen days without fresh water, until Tommy found Queen Victoria Spring in the middle of the Great Victorian Desert. The blacks were also valuable for tracking straying animals and men. In October 1845, for instance, Charley found two members of Leichhardt's expedition after they had been lost for three days. And they often supported — sometimes literally — their debilitated white companions. The pairings of Eyre and Wylie, Kennedy and Jackey, and Forrest and Tommy Windich are eloquent examples of how whites and blacks were able to come together for survival in the face of the inland's hostility.

The third image has emerged only in the last decades. Voyaging remarkably beyond the confines of his age, in a perception quite distinct from those of such fashionable armchair philosophers as Rousseau, James Cook wrote in 1770 of the Australian Aborigines:

> From what I have said of the Natives of New-Holland they may appear to some to be the most wretched people upon Earth, but in reality they are far more happier than we Europeans; being wholy unacquainted not only with the superfluous but the necessary Conveniencies so much sought after in Europe, they are happy in not knowing the use of them. They live in a Tranquillity which is not disturb'd by the Inequality of Condition: The Earth and sea of their own accord furnishes them with all things necessary for life, they covet not Magnificent Houses, Houshold-stuff &ca, they live in a warm and fine Climate and enjoy a very wholsome Air, so that they have very little need of Clothing and this they seem to be fully sencible of, for many to whome we gave Cloth &ca to, left it carlessly upon the Sea beach and in the woods as a thing they had no manner of use for.

Mutilated by his editor and with its sentiments transferred to the Terra del Fuegians in the 1773 narrative of his voyage, this striking paragraph has really only gained prominence with the publication of **J. C. Beaglehole**'s edition of Cook's *Journals* (1955–67). It has become a potent signifier of the late twentieth century's distrust of western industrial society and fears for the environment.

ALAN FROST

Further reading: Ernest Favenc, *The History of Australian Exploration* (1888); E. H. J. Feeken and G. E. E. Feeken, *The Discovery and Exploration of Australia* (1970).

EXPLORATION LITERATURE (Canada)
Contemporary knowledge of Canada as mapped space derives from a considerable body of writing — very little of it by Canadians — on the exploration of Canada's geographical space. The corpus was initiated by Dionyse Settle's 1577 'report' of Martin Frobisher's second voyage (*A True Report of the Last [or Rather the Second] Voyage into the west and northwest Regions &c* . . .). It was augmented massively with the large number of Arctic exploration accounts written between 1819 and 1856 and is still being rounded off with the production of previously unpublished accounts, often in scholarly editions and/or for various learned societies. While it is probable that few significant sources remain unearthed, critical investigation of exploration as *writing* is just beginning. Readers who seek to find a pattern in this mass of material are more likely to identify series of narratives about discrete projects — conducted in different sectors of the land masses and seas that now constitute Canada and with varying historically and geopolitically determined motivations — than to locate a consistently developing narrative of 'the discovery of Canada'. (See **Canada**.)

In English-language narratives, five (overlapping) phases emerge. The first extends from 1577 to 1635 and chronicles the first European explorations of North America's northeast coast, incidental to the great project of the search for a Northwest Passage to the Indies. Approximately 150 years later the second phase began, with the publication of Samuel Hearne's account of his extensive travels from the shores of Hudson Bay into the prairie interior — *Journey from Prince of Wales's Fort in Hudson Bay to the Northern Ocean* . . . (1795). This phase is characterized by commercially motivated exploration conducted almost entirely under the auspices of trading companies. Although several of the key narratives of this phase remained unpublished until the early twentieth century, classic narratives from the period include the writing of such men as Henry Kelsey (*The Kelsey Papers*, 1929, edited by A. G. Doughty and C. Martin); Anthony Hendry ('York Factory to the Blackfoot country: the journal of Anthony Hendry, 1754–55', in *Proceedings and Transactions of the Royal Society of Canada*, 3rd Series, vol. 1, 1907, edited by L. J. Burpee); Alexander Mackenzie (*Voyages from Montreal, on the River St. Laurence, through the Continent of North America*, 1801); and David Thompson (*David Thompson's Narrative of His Explorations in Western North America, 1784–1812*, 1916, edited by J. B. Tyrrell).

A third phase, associated with British imperial projects in the Pacific, involves the exploration of the Pacific coasts and includes narratives by Captains James Cook (*A Voyage to the Pacific Ocean . . . in 1776–1780*, 1784) and George Vancouver (*A Voyage of Discovery to the North Pacific Ocean and Round the World*, 1798). In the fourth phase, extending from the early to the mid-nineteenth century, the search for a Northwest Passage was renewed.

The voyage literature that resulted from a succession of enterprises to discover the passage, led by Martin Frobisher, Humphrey Gilbert, John Davis, Henry Hudson, William Baffin, Luke Fox, and Thomas James between 1576 and 1632, was published mainly in the travel compendia of Samuel Purchas (*Purchas his Pilgrimes*, 5 vols, 1625, and culminated in the Hakluyt Society edition *Hakluytus Posthumous; or, Purchas his Pilgrimes*, 20 vols, 1905–7), which integrate the Renaissance project of discovery and mapping into a global history and geography.

Besides the more obvious practice of mapping, however, the texts of this phase tend to serve as propaganda urging continuation of the Northwest Passage project. Some advocate colonization while others invite commercial exploitation. The individual texts (journals, letters, and accounts) can be read as a single text in which nascent imperialistic designs are implicated alongside more general exploratory cartographic and scientific interests. These intersections reveal themselves clearly in acknowledgments of patronage: that of the English Crown, on the one hand, and of competing London and Bristol mercantile interests on the other. While these documents sometimes include vivid landscape, seascape, and meteorological description (later to prove useful in such literary productions as Coleridge's 'Rime of the Ancient Mariner') and the beginnings of sketchy ethnographic observation, their major interests lie elsewhere. Luke Fox's *North-west Fox* (1635) shows how maritime exploration has been inserted into a *textual* tradition; in addressing charges that his own book is merely a collection of others' narratives, he asks: 'who can speake or write that which was never done before . . . ?' Two years earlier, Thomas James' *The Strange and Dangerous Voyage of Captain Thomas James* . . . had effectively acknowledged the futility for the time of the Northwest Passage project, so that for more than one hundred years both the voyaging and the tradition of the voyage narrative were interrupted. John Franklin's catastrophic expedition to find the passage has come to symbolize the period. During the 1850s, the many expeditions 'in search of' Franklin issue forth in accounts of varying format and length. (There is, significantly, another body of writing from this time — the French-language narratives of explorations that began with Jacques Cartier's charting of the lower Saint Lawrence River region in 1535 and reached ever further into the prairie interior as part of the Montreal-based enterprises of the North-West Company.)

In the second phase of the documentation of the exploration of 'Canada', 'voyaging' is an overland project, initiated from either the St Lawrence River or the fur-trading forts on the shores of Hudson Bay. This project involved the discovery and charting of the great western river systems, the motivation for which was related to the competitive fur-trading interests of the Hudson's Bay Company and the North West Company, whose dual imperatives were to gain knowledge of the vast territorial expanses of the west and the northwest and to incorporate the indigenous populations into the practices and economies of the fur trade. (The overall exploratory project, which began with Henry Kelsey, culminated in the arrivals of Alexander Mackenzie and David Thompson at the Pacific coast in 1793 and 1811 respectively.)

While the desire of the travellers to articulate their experiences doubtless played a part in the production of narratives, their importance also relates to the institutional drives for record, publicity, and even propaganda of the sponsoring commercial/imperial organizations. Henry Kelsey's journals are interesting for their verse-couplet form; Samuel Hearne's narrative is the closest of these documents to the classic travel book; Alexander Mackenzie's *Voyages from Montreal* is also a readable adventure chronicle. By the early nineteenth century, however, David Thompson could find no publisher for the narratives of his extensive journeys across the Rocky Mountains and to the Pacific coast. Taken collectively, the texts of overland exploration fulfilled an urgent need for first-hand geographic and ethnographic lore and instilled foundational conceptualizations of 'the Canadian land and its peoples' that are now undergoing revision.

In the same period, maritime endeavours again assumed importance, as the British Admiralty dispatched missions to the Pacific coast. Interest in the great continental west coast in some ways replicated earlier interest in mapping the South Pacific islands and continent and, moreover, involved some of the same figures, notably James Cook and George Vancouver. What is true for the earlier phases applies equally to the Pacific phase: there is no 'Canada'; in both aims and methodologies, the exploratory project represents motivations and conceptual frameworks that are broadly European in their assumptions about knowledge and are specifically English in relation to a new imperialism.

Both Cook and Vancouver produced narrative accounts of their serial voyages; Cook's narrative, especially as augmented in the *Journals* (1955, edited by **J. C. Beaglehole**), instituted a new mode of exploration literature in which mapping, naming, and specific observation became central. While conventional wisdom has been that the Admiralty's textual demands inhibited production of interesting reports, a more recent perspective insists that readers have been looking for the wrong things: late eighteenth-century exploration texts suggest a dynamic dictated by neither extraordinary personal investments nor excessively restrictive Admiralty pressure, but rather by the simpler need to textualize 'new' spaces. (See also **Travel Literature**, Canada.)

The second major phase of Arctic exploration, beginning with the John Ross/W. E. Parry expedition of 1818 and culminating in Robert McClure's 'discovery' of the Northwest Passage in 1856, was initiated by the English Admiralty, with the same purposes of mapping and gaining scientific information as impelled the Pacific coast exploration project. Search for the famed Northwest Passage was still central to the project, although the fable of a passage to the Indies no longer enticed. The major shifts in motivation and rationale signalled by the British Navy's involvement are reflected in the accounts of these expeditions of the first half of the nineteenth century (including two accounts by John Ross, four by W. E. Parry, and two by the ill-fated Sir John Franklin, who died on 11 June 1847, west of King William Island). But these of ficial and quasi-official documents, with titles such as Ross' *A Voyage of Discovery* (1819) and Franklin's *Narrative of a Journey to the Shores of the Polar Sea* (1823), were supplemented by the publications of subordinate mission members. Although these generally multivolume narratives conform to what some commentators name an 'Admiralty style', they are none the less often dramatic, contain detailed information about climate, mineralogy, flora and fauna, and are generally sympathetic to the Inuit populations when encounters with them are recorded. Robert McClure's *The Discovery of the North-West Passage by HMS Investigator* (1856) brings this phase to a close in an opinionated account that obscures the posthumous recognition of John Franklin's earlier achievements.

Francis McClintock's *The Voyage of the 'Fox' in the Arctic Seas* (1859) ends with the discovery of the remains of Franklin's party, and it is also the culmination of a postscript to the Admiralty-sponsored phase of Arctic exploration: during the 1850s Arctic exploration continued under the guise of searches for the remains of Franklin's last expedition. At least twenty accounts appeared in the space of little more than a decade and they chronicled additional discoveries. Generally, however, these documents are less formal than the narratives of the preceding phase, as several titles, such as Sherard Osborn's *Stray Leaves from an Arctic Journal* (1852) and John Ross *et al.*'s *Arctic Miscellanies* (1852), suggest.

It was around 1850 that the distinct projects of exploration recorded in this large body of literature could be seen as producing a geopolitical identity named Canada. Until then Canada's land masses and oceanic borders had emerged into mapped form in a roughly circular movement: northwards to the St Lawrence and the Great Lakes, northwest into Hudson Bay, south and west into the Prairies, northwards up the Pacific coast, and — closing the circle — into the Arctic again. Few of the contributors to the collective text of exploration, no matter how significantly they helped define space, shape, and boundary, saw themselves as contributing to the definition of a national or cultural entity. However, narratives of exploration are clearly vital to any understanding of how Canada came to be adequately formulated in space and in time.

As yet, there is no satisfactory study of the discourse of exploration in Canada equivalent to Paul Carter's study of 'spatial history' with regard to Australia (*The Road to Botany Bay: An Exploration of Landscape and History*, 1987). Often, students of literature exposed to the brief accounts of exploration writing available complain about lack of literary merit and stress the mythopoetic function of such narratives. It is nevertheless true that exploration writing has proved its resonance for several contemporary writers, who have eloquently and imaginatively reinterpreted its texts. Exploration texts, however, constitute a genre to which the criteria often invoked in judging a novel are simply not relevant. A significant study would certainly take account of this material as a distinctive genre with various formal aspects, but it would also need to examine it within specific historical and spatial determinations and to maintain a sharp awareness of a range of motivations with reference to both composition and publication.

PATRICK HOLLAND

Further reading: Elizabeth Waterston (ed.), with Ian Easterbrook, Bernard Katz, and Kathleen Scott, *The Travellers: Canada to 1900. An Annotated Bibliography of Works Published in English from 1577* (1989); Germaine Warkentin, ed., *Canadian Exploration Literature: An Anthology* (1993).

EXPLORATION LITERATURE (New Zealand)
Abel Tasman's brief encounter with New Zealand and its indigenous population in 1642–3 is reported in seventeenth-century collections of European

voyages, but the first extensive accounts of the land and people were made by Captain James Cook, who circumnavigated New Zealand in 1769–70, and Joseph Banks, who accompanied him. Banks and Cook, rational and humane men, recorded sympathetically and straightforwardly what they observed. However, the eighteenth-century reading public was not offered the journals in anything like their original form. Dr John Hawkesworth, commissioned by the Admiralty to polish the manuscripts, went beyond editorial emendation: he not only blended the journals into a single narrative and added philosophical digressions and classical allusions, but he effectively glossed the narrative with his own moral perspective so that, as **Bill Pearson** has pointed out in reference to an episode in Tahiti, 'what is implied is a colonial relationship, a prudent handling of a people under tutelage, grateful and tractable'. Thus the Polynesians — New Zealanders as well as Tahitians — were rendered according to metropolitan tastes and, since *An Account of the Voyages Undertaken . . . for Making Discoveries in the Southern Hemisphere* (3 vols, 1773) was for more than a century the standard account of 'Cook', Hawkesworth's encoded version, frequently reprinted, translated, quoted, and paraphrased, continued to exert a major influence upon later exploration literature, fiction as well as non-fiction.

Cook's accounts of several later short visits to New Zealand were less changed before publication; he noted that his journal for the second expedition was designated as 'a work for information and not for amusement'. A little of what was written by his subordinates also found its way into print as, for example, in the substantial and lively narrative of George Forster's *A Voyage Round the World . . .* (2 vols, 1777). Much of J. M. Crozet's *Nouveau Voyage à la mer du sud* (1783) deals with the three months that M. J. Marion du Fresne's expedition spent in northern New Zealand during 1772, when the killing of du Fresne and several other Frenchmen led to a massive French retaliation. Here, again, it is European ideas as well as local *moeurs* that are the subjects of exploration: Crozet inveighs against the idealization of the Noble Savage by the *philosophes*, but his editor, Alexis Rochon, surmises that the Frenchmen were killed as a consequence of their own transgressions. Members of other expeditions — French, British, and Spanish — recorded their calls at New Zealand and published scientific, geographic, and ethnographic data. The most imaginative contribution was made by J. S. C. Dumont D'Urville, who visited New Zealand three times between 1824 and 1840. He supplemented his own observations with those of earlier explorers and missionaries and wove the material together, in a more considered way than Hawkesworth, in *Voyage pittoresque autour du monde* (2 vols, 1834–5).

During the 1890s British publishers provided versions, if unreliable ones, of the journals of Cook and Banks, and a translation of J. M. Crozet's account. These coincidentally but usefully appeared when Pakeha New Zealanders were becoming more conscious of a need to collect information on New Zealand history. Local scholars translated the sections of Tasman's journal and those of French and Spanish expeditions dealing with New Zealand. Robert McNab in particular searched out log-books, journals, and newspaper records of the activities of sealers, whalers, and miscellaneous adventurers as well as scientific explorers; these materials were published in his *Historical Records of New Zealand* (1908, 1914), modelled on the Australian series.

During the same period, amateur ethnologists, especially S. Percy Smith in his *Hawaiki* (1898, 1921), fashioned from Maori traditions a history of heroic Polynesian exploration that brought the first discoverer, Kupe, to Aotearoa (New Zealand) in the tenth century, followed by a 'Fleet' of Polynesian migrant-settlers in the fourteenth century. The year AD 1350 (Smith's estimate from averaging some genealogies) became the accepted date of settlement. This early history of non-European voyaging was given widespread currency by Sir Peter Buck (Te Rangi Hiroa) in *Vikings of the Sunrise* (1938), first published in the USA, and in *The Coming of the Maori* (1949). The popular sequence is enshrined in **J. C. Beaglehole**'s *The Discovery of New Zealand* (1939); preceding the discussion of Tasman and Cook is a chapter entitled 'The Maori Voyagers'.

Beaglehole's interests were not at all insular, but his various writings and his definitive editions of the journals of Cook and Banks fostered, or sometimes provoked, local as well as general scholarship on Pacific exploration. Notable works in the field include: John Dunmore's *French Explorers in the Pacific* (1965, 1969), *The Fateful Voyage of the St Jean Baptiste* (1969), his re-creation of an expedition under the command of Jean de Surville, and an edition of journals from the same expedition, *The Expedition of the St Jean-Baptiste to the Pacific, 1769–1770: From Journals of Jean de Surville and Guillaume Labé* (translated and edited by Dunmore, 1981); Olive Wright's translations of materials by Dumont D'Urville and his officers; **E. H. McCormick**'s *Tasman and New Zealand* (1959), which traces the dissemination of Tasman's accounts; and Michael Hoare's edition of the journals of J. R. Forster, *The Resolution Journal of Johann Reinhold Forster, 1771–1775* (4 vols, 1982). The Canadian scholar Glynn Barratt prepared *Bellingshausen: A Visit to New Zealand: 1820* (1979) in New Zealand, and his emphasis on the value of the ethnographic records is paralleled, on a larger scale, by Anne Salmond's *Two Worlds: First Meetings Between Maori and Europeans, 1642–1772* (1991) and by the publication in the 1980s of the series *Early Eyewitness Accounts of Maori Life*, drawn from French observations.

While this textual elaboration of the Enlightenment enterprise proceeded, Andrew Sharp, in *Ancient Voyagers in the Pacific* (1956), argued that Polynesian exploration had been fortuitous rather than deliberate, a thesis that caused major controversy and much further scholarly activity in attempts to resolve the issue. David Simmons, in *The Great New Zealand Myth* (1976), demonstrated that Percy Smith's methods of historicizing Maori tradition in *Hawaiki* were fundamentally flawed; yet, as Anne Salmond has pointed out, the 'Fleet' had become a crucial part of modern Maori tradition, incorporated into basic cultural rituals. In *Hawaiki: A New Approach to Maori Tradition* (1985), Margaret Orbell suggests that Maori traditions regarding the original homeland of Hawaiki and the migration should be seen as 'religious narratives', not as myths that are 'untrue', but as myths that express a truth more than merely historical. It would seem that here, as in other aspects of the literature of exploration, the potential for the semiotic misunderstanding that led to conflict on Pacific beaches during many initial encounters remains.

PETER GIBBONS

Further reading: Jonathon Lamb, 'A sublime moment off Poverty Bay, 9 October 1769', in Graham McGregor and Mark Williams (eds) *Dirty Silence: Aspects of Language and Literature in New Zealand* (1991).

Exploration Literature (West Africa)
'That country is wonder hot, and that makes the folks thereof so black.' So wrote Sir John Mandeville in the sixteenth century (later published in *Mandeville's Travels: Texts and Translations,* 1953, edited by Martin Letts), thus purveying a popular image of Africa that persisted for centuries. In 1555 first-hand accounts of the west coast of Africa appeared in England with the narratives of Thomas Windham, who travelled to Guinea in 1553, and those of John Lok, who went to Elmina in 1554–5. (These are contained in Richard Eden's English translation of the works of

Peter Martyr of Angleria — *The Decades of the Newe Worlde or West India, Conteyning the navigations and conquestes of the Spanyardes* . . ., 1955.) More first-hand information soon followed; some is contained in the two editions of Richard Hakluyt's *The Principal Navigations, Voyages, Traffiques and Discoveries of the English Nation* (1589, 1599–1600). *The History and Description of Africa* (1896), edited by Robert Brown, contains John Pory's translation of 1600 of the works of Leo Africanus (first published in Italy in 1550); its extensive commentary includes descriptions of African kingdoms such as Mali, Timbuktu, and Bornu. From the mixture of fact and legend available in Elizabethan England emerged the images of Africa and Africans presented by dramatists of the day. (See Eldred Jones' study *Othello's Countrymen: The African in English Renaissance Drama*, 1965.)

The first substantial account of Africa by an Englishman is Richard Jobson's *The Golden Trade; or, A Discovery of the River Gambia* . . . (1623; repr. 1968, introduced by Walter Rodney). Jobson was an agent for a group of London merchants interested in the possibilities of trade in West Africa; his account stresses the potential for trade, but he also records his observations of the customs of the African people among whom he moved. Trade did not develop immediately. When it did, it was trade in slaves, which, because of the demand for labour in the Caribbean plantations, soon overtook other forms of commerce previously established in West Africa. In slave traders' accounts the first pejorative views of Africans were expounded, views designed to legitimize traffic in human cargo.

Such was the exploding interest in Africa in the period between 1623 and 1803 that only a few of the hundreds of published narratives of exploration and navigation into the interior of West Africa can be cited here: A. and J. Churchill's *Collection of Voyages and Travels* (8 vols, 1732–47); *A New General Collection of Voyages and Travels* (4 vols, 1745–47), compiled by John Green; Willem Bosman's *A New and Accurate Description of the Coast of Guinea* (1705); J. Barbot's *A Description of the Coasts of North and South Guinea* (1732); William Snelgrave's *A New Account of Some Parts of Guinea, and the Slave Trade* (1734); and W. Smith's *A New Voyage to Guinea* (1745). This was also a period of scientific enquiry in West Africa, coinciding with progressive settlement by Europeans on the coast. Michel Adanson, for example, published his account of a visit to West Africa between 1748 and 1753 in *A Voyage to Senegal* (1759). A botanist, Adanson also recorded ethnographic information about the Wolof people with whom he spent considerable time. Thomas Winterbottom initiated the study of tropical medicine when, as physician to the colony of Sierra Leone, he published *An Account of the Native Africans in the Neighbourhood of Sierra Leone* (1803), which describes African medical practices and procedures.

During the nineteenth century three distinct strands developed in English accounts of travel, exploration, and settlement in West Africa; these strands reflect the growing, sometimes collaborative, sometimes combative, interests of the English in the region. There is writing relating to the official or political, including: Thomas Joseph Hutchinson's *Narrative of the Niger, Tschadda, and Binuë Exploration* (1855), *Impressions of Western Africa* (1858), and *Ten Years' Wandering among the Ethiopians* (1861); James Africanus B. Horton's *West African Countries and Peoples* (1868), about the 1865 Parliamentary Select Committee Report recommending self-government for West African peoples; and Mary Henrietta Kingsley's *West African Studies* (1899). There is writing relating to religious and philanthropic enterprises — for example, Hope Masterton Waddell's *Twen-*

ty-nine Years in the West Indies and Central Africa (1863) and Henry Roe's *West African Scenes* (1874), and others focusing on trade and commerce, such as Macgregor Laird's and R. A. K. Oldfield's *Narrative of an Expedition into the Interior of Africa* (2 vols, 1837) and Harold Bindloss' *In The Niger Country* (1898).

Following the anti-slavery movement and the founding of Sierra Leone, there was the quest for 'legitimate' trade in the region. The Anti-Slavery Society was formed, its main purpose being the carrying out of 'Commerce and Christianity'. The Society published *The Anti-Slave Reporter* (founded 1839) and it promoted the Niger Expedition of 1841–2 to Lokojä, at the confluence of the Niger and Benuë rivers, for the purpose of establishing a permanent Christian trading and religious centre. The expedition was a disaster. Charles Dickens reviewed it in bitter terms in *The Examiner*, and under the pen-name Boriobhoola-Gha satirized it mercilessly in *Bleak House* (1852–3). (Samuel Adjayi Crowther, a young schoolmaster and former slave who later became the first African Bishop of the Niger, accompanied the expedition.)

The Niger Expedition confirmed the beliefs of Macgregor Laird that the Niger River was navigable from Bonny to Onitsha, and once trading pacts were negotiated with African merchant-traders on its bank (the most notable of whom was King Pepple of Bonny), the interior of the coast swiftly opened up. From this time publication about all aspects of African life and the African landscape proliferated. Some works purport to be ethnographic studies; others reveal attitudes towards trade and the practices of traders, the activities, successes, and failures of the various missionary societies, or the ways in which political treaties were negotiated, sometimes in amicable discussion, sometimes with the threat, or use, of the cannon. With the establishment of indigenous newspaper publication came the beginnings of independence movements.

The number of narrative accounts of travellers to West Africa — explorers, visitors, missionaries, traders, political officials, and the merely inquisitive — seems boundless, indicating the fascination that Africa has had for strangers to its shores for more than four centuries.

G. D. KILLAM

Further reading: G. D. Killam, *Africa in English Fiction* (1968); Alta Jablow and Dorothy Hammond, *The Africa that Never Was: Four Centuries of British Writing about Africa* (1970).

EZEKIEL, NISSIM (1924–)

Indian poet, dramatist

Born in Bombay, India, of Jewish (Bene-Israel) parents, he was educated in India (MA, 1947, the University of Bombay) and in England, where, he later wrote, 'Philosophy, / Poverty and Poetry, three / Companions shared my basement room'. Absent from India between 1948 and 1952, he returned by earning his passage on an English cargo ship. Since retiring from the English department of the University of Bombay in 1985, Ezekiel has managed an advertising firm.

In post-independence Indian-English literature, Ezekiel has wielded enormous influence as a leading poet, as editor of many journals — including *Quest* (which he founded and edited between 1955 and 1957), *Poetry India*, *Illustrated Weekly*, and *The Indian PEN* — and as a critic of literature and art. His *Collected Poems: 1952–1988* (1989), with an introduction by **Gieve Patel**, contains seven collections of verse: *A Time to Change and Other Poems* (1952), *Sixty Poems* (1953), *The Third* (1959), *The Exact Name: Poems: 1960–1964* (1965), *The Unfinished Man* (1960), *Hymns in Darkness* (1976), and *Latter-Day Psalms* (1982), winner of a Sahitya Akademi award in 1983. His *Selected Poems 1965–75* appeared in 1976. Ezekiel is also a dramatist — *Three Plays* (1969) contains

Nalini, a three-act play, *Marriage Poem*, and the one-act farce *The Sleepwalkers*. All three plays satirize various aspects of Indian bourgeois life. With Vrinda Nabar, he translated *Snake-Skin and Other Poems of Indra Sant* (1974) from Marathi.

Ezekiel is a poet of Bombay, and his poems on the city comprise his best collection, *The Unfinished Man*. 'A Morning Walk' describes how poverty makes Bombay a 'Barbaric city sick with slums'. All the poems in this collection evoke a sense of musical delight with their effective use of rhyme. The poems written between 1983 and 1988 lack some of the brilliance of early poems in *The Unfinished Man*. An autobiographical poem, 'The Way It Went', seems pedestrian when it speaks of a 'child on my lap / . . . calling me Grandpapa'. But Ezekiel's erotic zeal has continued unabated in his more mature years. He uses the Radha and Krishna myth to represent his own sexual reverie: 'Radha says she longs for Krishna / As the soul longs for union with God. / Krishna likes the idea.'

Commonwealth poets have used the English language to describe their national aspirations, their unique cultures, and their immediate environments. Thus, **A. D. Hope**'s Australia has five cities, 'like five teeming sores', and **Irving Layton** writes that, although his fellow Canadians are 'dull', the rivers of Canada are 'wise and beautiful'. Similarly, Ezekiel has been consciously Indian in his sensibility. In his sequence, 'Very Indian Poems in Indian English', he uses Indian English and its characteristic continuous present tense to convey a particularly Indian attitude to the state of the world:

> I am standing for peace and nonviolence
> why world is fighting fighting
> why all people of world
> Are not following Mahatma Gandhi,
> I am simply not understanding,
> Ancient Indian wisdom is 100% correct.

'Goodbye Party for Miss Pushpa T. S.' and 'Irani Restaurant Instructions' also re-create the peculiar flavour of Indian English. Ezekiel believes that a poet should belong to his immediate environment and be proud of his country, as suggested in 'Marriage' (in *The Unfinished Man*): 'The Indian landscape sears my eyes / I have become a part of it.' After reading **Ruth Prawer Jhabvala**'s *Heat and Dust*, he said that he could write a similar novel about England entitled 'Cold and Snow'.

Ezekiel's literary and art criticism has been the by-product of his poetry. His essay 'Naipaul's India and Mine' (in **Adil Jussawalla**'s *New Writing in India*, 1974) provides a clue to his personality. While **V. S. Naipaul** feels uneasy in India's crowds, Ezekiel has the humility to be one of the multitude.

Ezekiel has continued to show remarkable dedication to his vocation as a poet. No other Indian-English poet has shown the ability to organize as competently his experience into words. His poems have a certain remarkable finality of form. In 'Poet, Lover, Birdwatcher', he observes that 'the best poets' wait for words like an ornithologist sitting in silence by the flowing river, or like a lover waiting for his beloved until she 'no longer waits but risks surrendering' (*Collected Poems*). A painstaking craftsman, Ezekiel asserts that mere warmth of human emotions is not enough for the creation of great poetry: genius lies in the ability to perceive new resemblances.

One of Ezekiel's strengths is his remarkable sincerity. He is always himself, within his range. His poem 'Marriage' reveals his stark bluntness: the initial excitement of romantic love — 'Our love denied the primal fall' — is inevitably followed by a feeling of satiation — 'the same thing over and over again' — and the poem finishes on a note of paradox. Ezekiel's own words perhaps summarize his achievement most eloquently: 'It is possible to be a good minor poet without major delusions.'

In 1988 Ezekiel was honoured with the Padma

Shri Award for his distinguished contribution to Indian literature in English.

CHETAN KARNANI

Further reading: Chetan Karnani, *Nissim Ezekiel* (1974); *Journal of South Asian Literature* 3–4 (1976), special issue on Nissim Ezekiel; *The Journal of Indian Writing in English* February (1986), special issue on Nissim Ezekiel; Bruce King, *Three Indian Poets: Nissim Ezekiel, A. K. Ramanujan, Dom Moraes* (1991).

F

FACEY, ALBERT (1894–1982)
Australian autobiographer
Born in Maidstone, Victoria, Australia, he wrote only one book, *A Fortunate Life* (1981), in which he created only one memorable character, himself. But that book, written at the suggestion of his family, became a bestseller worldwide, and that character has come to epitomize qualities many like to think of as typically Australian — courage, cheerfulness, kindness, endurance, and a curiously invulnerable innocence. The story tells of decency triumphing over violence and indifference: a boy is virtually orphaned by the death of his father and the desertion of his mother, brought up by a valiant grandmother, and forced to earn his living from the age of eight. He runs the gamut of experience, working for struggling and sometimes brutal farmers, on the railways, droving in the northwest, touring with a boxing troupe, enlisting in the army and being wounded at Gallipoli, taking up land and failing as a soldier settler, working for the tramways, and finally becoming president of the union and a respected member of the community.

The language is simple; Facey learned to read and write only as an adult. The appeal lies rather in the unpretentious dignity of the story, summed up in the last two sentences: 'I have lived a very good life, it has been very rich and full. I have been very fortunate and I am very thrilled when I look back.'

The book is also an achievement for its publishers, the Fremantle Arts Centre Press, in particular for the two editors, Ray Coffey and Wendy Jenkins, who recognized the quality of the manuscript that came to them in a series of school exercise books tied together with string.

VERONICA BRADY

FAIRBURN, A. R. D. (1904–57)
New Zealand poet
He was born Arthur Rex Dugard Fairburn in Auckland, New Zealand, and, apart from two years spent in England between 1930 and 1932, he lived his life in Auckland. He was a lyric poet, a satirist, a critic, and a polemicist who worked variously as a magazine editor, a craftsman, an art lecturer, and a radio script-writer.

Fairburn's first book, *He Shall Not Rise* (1930), is a collection of neo-Georgian lyrics ending with 'Rhyme of the Dead Self' — a repudiation, decked out in rococco poeticisms, of the poetic manner of the rest of the book. At least one critic has suggested that *He Shall Not Rise* contains Fairburn's best writing, though a more conventional view would prefer the later lyrics or the long 'philosophical' poems.

Fairburn's return to New Zealand in 1932 marked a turning point. He had gone to England full of ambition to enter the literary mainstream and determined to leave behind the small-town philistinism of his homeland; on his return he was forced to support his young family on what he could earn on relief work. He became active in the Social Credit movement and began a long poem about New Zealand and the forces of history and economics that acted upon it. Attempting to dispose of his youthful Georgian tendencies evident in *He Shall Not Rise*, Fairburn turned to Ezra Pound and T. S. Eliot as models of poetic practice. *Dominion* (1938), a long poem in five sections, was to be Fairburn's *The Waste Land*; he began it in 1935, several years before **Allen Curnow**'s first work in a similar vein, *Not in Narrow Seas* (1939).

Dominion did not find a publisher at once. T. S. Eliot declined it for Faber and Faber, and it was eventually published in New Zealand. The Social Credit rhetoric and the satire on New Zealand life now seem heavy-handed, but there are striking images: 'we, the destined race, rulers of conquered isles, / sprouting like bulbs in warm darkness, putting out / white shoots under the wet sack of Empire'. In the central section, 'Elements', the New Zealand landscape is powerfully present as nurturer and touchstone, providing images of religious intensity ('the coasts / bear crimson bloom, sprinkled like blood / on the lintel of the land'); elsewhere in the poem the New Zealander's perception of the land as 'the space between the barbed-wire fences . . . measured in sweated butterfat' is an index of cultural and spiritual emptiness.

The poet's relation to society became a preoccupation. Fairburn conceived of his role as 'artist-citizen', and he produced a steady flow of articles, reviews, and poems for publications such as *Tomorrow*, an independent weekly. Impatience with cant, a penchant for the absurd, and a natural wit produced in his prose and verse the whole gamut of satire, from savage invective to comic verse, on any subject from aesthetics to politics. Fairburn collaborated with **Denis Glover** on a collection of mainly literary satires and parodies, *Poetry Harbinger* (1958). There is, however, an eerie self-reflexiveness about 'I'm Older than You, Please Listen', with its advice to the talented young to leave New Zealand while they can: 'Don't be content to live in / a sort of second-grade heaven . . . becoming a butt for the malice / of those who have stayed and soured.'

Poems 1929–1941 (1943) — work by Fairburn, Glover, Allen Curnow, and **R. A. K. Mason** — includes love poems that are among the finest pieces Fairburn wrote. It is as though the pressure of the experiences that lay behind them forced him to find a new language, direct and plain: 'Time smiles and whets his knife, / and something has got to come out / quickly, and be buried deep.'

In the late 1940s Fairburn wrote another long poem, 'The Voyage' (1952). As with *Dominion*, the initial impulse was satirical, but the poem became a disquisition on the ends of human endeavour, 'a poem about faith and works', as he put it. In 'To a Friend in the Wilderness' (1952) he debated whether to exchange engagement with society for withdrawal to a local Arcady. Characteristically, Fairburn opted for engagement. ('The Voyage' and 'To a Friend in the Wilderness' were first published in *Three Poems: Dominion, The Voyage and To a Friend in the Wilderness*, 1952.)

Fairburn's *Collected Poems* was published in 1966. A selection from his *The Woman Problem and Other Prose* (1947), selected by Denis Glover and Geoffrey Fairburn, appeared in 1967; *The Letters of A. R. D. Fairburn* (1981) was edited by **Lauris Edmond.**

ANNE FRENCH

Further reading: Denys Trussell, *Fairburn* (1984).

FARAH, NURUDDIN (1945–)

Somali novelist

He was born in Baidoa, Somalia, and educated in Mogadishu, at the universities of Essex and London, England, and at the Punjab University of Chandigarh, India, where he earned a BA. Appropriately for one who comes from a nomadic tradition, his studies and employments have been nomadic on a global scale, taking in many western and African countries. (English, in which his novels are written, is his fourth language.) Farah's preoccupying subject throughout his writing career, however, has been the oppression of Somalia by the Soviet-backed but Islamic-based totalitarian regime of General Siyad Barre. Specifically, his novels pin-point the negative collusions of family and state authoritarianisms and of tribalism, Islam, and Marxism and feature pioneering studies of the patriarchal subjection of women in the Horn of Africa.

Farah's first novel, *From a Crooked Rib* (1970), is set in the colonial 1950s and focuses on an illiterate Somali woman, Ebla, and her determined flight from bartered marriages. Hers is a society in which a woman's position is negotiated entirely by men; her only alternative to being sold by others as a chattel-wife is to sell herself as a prostitute. This independent woman is driven into marginal groups of propertied widows, landladies, spinsters, and divorcees who anticipate the isolated feminist fringe of the 1970s depicted in the later *Sardines* (1981). (In *Sardines* Ebla reappears twenty years later, as a liberated matron, wise from the lessons of her marriages and divorces.) Farah's second novel, *A Naked Needle* (1976), is set in Mogadishu during the period 1969 to 1972, which saw Siyad Barre's Soviet-backed revolutionary military coup (1969) followed by Somalia's period of political alignment with the USSR. It is a youthful *jeu d'esprit* and stylistic *tour de force* in which the mercurial narrator Koschin simultaneously draws a mental map of the city, a satiric sketch of the new political élite, and a summary of Somalia's postwar history. While Koschin's naïve revolutionary idealism turns a blind eye, the gathering forces of political repression begin to close in menacingly, and the revolution drifts towards the terrorist totalitarian dictatorship — the subject of Farah's next novel, *Sweet and Sour Milk* (1979).

Sweet and Sour Milk (the first of a trilogy of novels including *Sardines* and *Close Sesame*, 1983) presents a demented, deranged world of political corruption, an Orwellian nightmare of unpersons, dawn disappearances, and rearranged history. Under an obscurantist dictator, Somali reality has become an opaque hermetic text that resists interpretation, and the plot to murder and mythologize Soyaan, an economic adviser to the president, proves to be ultimately unravellable. It is, moreover — since the regime's security corps of spies and informers is drawn from illiterates working entirely in the oral medium — unwritten and unwritable. *Sweet and Sour Milk,* like many works of post-colonial fiction, hovers between western and indigenous forms; the definitive, clarifying closure hinted at by the format of the political thriller and detective novel dissolves into the vagaries of oral culture.

In both *Sweet and Sour Milk* and *Sardines,* domestic and political tyranny are mutually reinforcing, invoking each other's authority and sanctioning each other's violence. When Samater, a government minister, throws his tyrannical mother out of the house he brings the wrath of the regime on his head, while Keynaan, as father and policeman, stamps out subversion at both levels. Tribal despotism is but the family's patriarchal and matriarchal authoritarianisms writ large. In *Sardines* Farah switches the focus to embattled Somali womanhood and presents woman as a symbol of the subjugated political self, making the enslavement of Somali women analogous to the political oppression of which it is a part. Rape is used as a political weapon, and female circumcision is an instrument of patriarchal power over women.

The veteran protagonist of *Close Sesame* is a national hero of the anti-colonial struggle, a loving monogamous husband, and a beloved grandfather. He lives harmoniously with children and grandchildren in a non-authoritarian household and devoutly upholds Islamic ideals of brotherhood and neighbourliness that cut across tribal divisions. These qualities, however, are insufficient to issue the 'open sesame' to the closed door of African dictatorship; but, as in the other two novels, active opposition to the general is carried on — albeit futilely — by the sons.

Farah has said in an interview that it is the post-colonial writer's task to redraw the dubious colonial maps of his or her world. The alternative cartographic hegemonies that result from *Maps*

(1986), however, are as much figmentary constructs, as random in their ordering principles and as unstable as signifiers, as the colonial ones. In *Maps* Farah ventures into the postmodernist territory that has proved such a fertile vein for other Commonwealth writers (**Salman Rushdie** and **Wilson Harris**, for example) and for younger African authors (including **M. G. Vassanji**, Kojo Laing, and **Ben Okri**). The narrator, Askar, a child of the disputed territory of the Ogaden, is a liminal creature who straddles sexual, national, and ontological boundaries: he is described as at once male and female, Somali and Ethiopian, a 'half-man, half-child' who holds 'simultaneously multiple citizenships of different kingdoms'. Born to two patriotic martyrs, he is the posthumous mythic offspring of Ogadenese nationalism, his orphaned life an analogue for his parentless nation. Hence, Askar, like Saleem in Rushdie's *Midnight's Children* (1981), and Oskar, his near-namesake in Günter Grass' *The Tin Drum* (1959), identifies his own personal history with that of his country — both are 'creatures brought into being by ideas' — and proceeds to see himself both as a real child and as the epic miracle-child of oral legend, endowed with supernatural insight and fantastic psychic and physical powers. (He even menstruates in sympathy with his adoptive Ethiopian mother and knows her, excruciatingly, through the body, which overrides abstract nationalistic hatreds.) There is, in the usual postmodern way, a puzzling indeterminacy in this novel regarding where metaphor and allegoric meaning end and where literal reality starts, where mindscape and dreamscape pass into landscape, where physiological space moves into topographical space (there is, for example, an erosion of menstrual charts into military maps), and at what point — in what is arguably the first African novel of the body — the personal becomes the public body.

Farah's most recent novel *Gifts* (1992), which places the love-offerings of a suitor against the backdrop of international aid to the famine-struck Horn of Africa, explores the complex psychology of donorship, its binding ties and dependencies, in the modern world.

DEREK WRIGHT

Further reading: 'A symposium on the work of Nuruddin Farah', *Journal of Commonwealth Literature* 1 (1989).

FARMER, BEVERLEY (1941–)

Australian novelist, short-story writer

She was born in Melbourne, Australia, and educated at the University of Melbourne. Known as a short-story writer, Farmer has also published *A Body of Water* (1990), a diary that incorporates short stories, and a novel, *The Seal Woman* (1992). Her intellectual formation is modernist and canonical. She moved from a working-class family to the new world of the university and is strongly influenced by such writers as T. S. Eliot, D. H. Lawrence, James Joyce, Nikos Kazantzakis, and **Patrick White**.

Farmer's short stories are characterized by a plain writing style that leaves her free to concentrate on thematic human issues and aspects of character, particularly the will. She married a Greek man in Australia in the 1960s and many of her stories, such as 'Melpo' and 'Ismini' (in *Milk*, 1983) and 'Place of Birth' and 'Pomegranates' (in *Home Time*, 1985) are fictionalized aspects of the experiences and insights she had as a member of her Greek family, in Australia and Greece. Much like Patrick White, Farmer bonded herself to aspects of Greekness and her Greek extended family, even after her marriage formally ended.

In her stories Farmer is willing to represent 'the other' — here, Greeks, the male partner — as familiar rather than foreign (with the exception of the men in 'A Man in the Laundrette', in *Home Time*, which documents how 'Whenever you talk to a man, it's there'). Place, autobiography, and literary antecedents are also major elements in

Farmer's writing, as in stories selected from *Milk* and *Home Time*, published as *Place of Birth* (1990). She has remarked that 'it is necessary for me to get the place right before I can fit a fiction in a place' and that 'the process of fiction to me is distilling and creating another voice'.

Farmer's longer fiction displays a more wordy, expressionist tonality, offering the reader a journey along language to areas where the tactile and verbal seem to coalesce — the actual body is figured in *Alone* (1980), *A Body of Water*, and *The Seal Woman*. The rough-textured directness of *Alone*, the story of an eighteen-year-old girl working her way through being abandoned by her girlfriend-lover, becomes, in *A Body of Water*, the suggestive fugue-like set of interlocking stories, essays, and diary entries on creativity, the senses, and the spirit. *A Body of Water* seems to lead to the equally autobiographic and daring, but perhaps less satisfactory, set of possibilities in *The Seal Woman*. In this novel Farmer allegorizes a treatment of the Scandinavian myth of one great love by writing from the consciousness of a Danish woman, Dagmar, who revisits Australia after the death of her husband. Dagmar thinks in English, with a voice very similar to the diarist in *A Body of Water*, and a reader unable to accept the 'fugal' tone and pace of the novel might feel that she says *'Ja'* and *'Nej'* once too often.

DAVID ENGLISH

Further reading: Lyn Jacobs, 'The fiction of Beverley Farmer', *Australian Literary Studies* (1990); Ray Willbanks, 'Beverley Farmer: interview', in *Speaking Volumes: Australian Writers and Their Work* by Ray Willbanks (1992).

FEMINISM

FEMINISM (Overview)

The development of post-colonial criticism and theory has made it clear that feminism not only plays a central role within post-colonial practice, creative and critical, but also that post-colonial criticism and feminism have the same objectives. Both post-colonial and feminist criticism aim to reveal the contours of traditional power structures, imperial and patriarchal, and to show how writers have challenged or re-inscribed these often-overlapping and intertwined forms of traditional authority. Post-colonial criticism has been concerned with canon formation, the phases of imperialism and decolonization and the expression of these in literature and orature, and the articulation of forms of resistance within literature — such as revisions and rewritings of traditional narratives, linguistic creolization, and the creation of oppositional voices and hybrid forms. These concerns are also those of feminist critics within the post-colonial field, as they examine the intersections of gender with colonial and post-colonial politics. The gradual emergence of critiques more sympathetic to issues of race and minority experience has marked post-colonial and feminist theory and practice in similar ways. Sensitivity to diversity is crucial to contemporary post-colonial criticism and has become crucial to feminist praxis. (See **Criticism**.)

What women writers have in common in many ex-colonies is their attempt to foreground the particular problems and lives of women, the forms of marginalization or dispossession experienced by women, and the intersections with and differences from the lives of men within the same political structures. Women's writing has often thus operated in an overlapping private and political space, showing how family patterns, traditional power structures and conventions, and male authority have worked hand in hand with colonial politics to disempower women. Writing has often been a vicarious adventure within which women throw off their chains and achieve some degree of autonomy and self-expression.

Even here there are immediately great economic and cultural differences that have resulted in the much later emergence of women's voices from black Africa, India, and the Caribbean. The eighteenth and nineteenth centuries saw the emergence, in Canada, South Africa, Australia, and New Zealand, of a generation of writers who were colonial administrators' wives, relatives, or visitors. Here the focus was on white, middle-class experience, and the genres tended to be memoir, letters, autobiography, and travel writing, though romance narratives could be used to open up social problems, and a type of colonial *Bildungsroman*, the story of an artist as young white woman in a colony, can be detected in, for instance, the novels of **Olive Schreiner** and **Miles Franklin**.

In Africa, India, Pakistan, and the Caribbean, economic factors have meant a slower emergence of women's writing, though performance art has often played a continuing role. When such voices have emerged, they have often been powerful oppositional writers, such as South Africa's **Miriam Tlali**, West Africa's **Flora Nwapa**, **Buchi Emecheta**, and **Ama Ata Aidoo**, India's **Anita Desai** and **Shashi Deshpande**, and the Caribbean's **Jamaica Kincaid**. Such writers have interrogated the norm of middle-class feminism and sometimes prefer Alice Walker's term 'womanism', which emphasizes the celebration of strength, solidarity with sisters and foremothers, and a collectivity rather than the individual. Many women writers from the black post-colonial world have drawn on the roots of slavery to expose a tradition of female pain and have been more inclined to make other forms of marginalization visible, such as the lives of lesbian women, women workers, rural women, and impoverished women. Here, too, there has been a greater experimentation in genre and language, as in the work of **Erna Brodber**, **Olive Senior**, and **Dionne Brand**. The difficulty set up by dialect and regional folklore or legend in itself becomes a challenge to middle-class readers and fractures any hypothetical homogeneity of post-colonial womanhood.

Ex-colonies with well established readerships, publishing houses, and funding agencies or economic support for writers — such countries as Australia, New Zealand, and Canada — have made the whole process of the recovery of the work and lives of women writers, canon formation, the development of a sense of continuity and tradition, and the publication of emergent voices much more fluent. In South Africa and the Caribbean, performance art and the reshaping of oral traditions to politically reformist ends have been more visible. In South Africa, ordinary black women's lives are only now being made visible in literature.

Anthologies of women's poetry and fiction tend to belong to the second wave of the women's movement, from the 1960s and 1970s onwards, as do anthologies of feminist criticism in the post-colonial world and feminist revisions of literary history. (See **Anthologies**.) There is now a much more self-conscious view within feminist criticism of gender and genre, of gender, race, and class, of the earlier marginalization of lesbian experience, and of political and cultural diversity among post-colonial women writers. Many of the writers themselves have resisted assimilation to any feminist or womanist grouping.

Migration and displacement have played their role in women's writing, themes, and textures, as in post-colonial writing generally. While earlier displacements, such as that of Canadian **Mavis Gallant**, tended towards Europe and away from a colony, others, such as the movement of slave ships from Africa to the Caribbean, have played a haunting but crucial role in shaping the voices of poets such as **Lorna Goodison** and Dionne Brand. Modern migrations have more often been between ex-colonies, or, in the case of South Africa, have been due to censorship and other political factors. **Bessie Head**, **Sheila Roberts**, **Fleur Adcock**, and **Janette Turner Hospital** all migrated differently: to Botswana, the USA, England, and Canada. The tension between two cultures and countries has become a topos in women's writing and a source of creative energy, as immigrant memory has been within the multicultural layering of Canada's mosaic.

Feminist theory, criticism, and social praxis, as well as conferences, workshops, publications, and university teaching, have all made women writers in the post-colonial world more visible in their similarities and differences. As well as offering a feminist cutting edge to post-colonial critiques of power, these writers have demonstrated a weaving together of the disparate lives of women, what Elaine Savory (Fido) calls a 'quilting' of literary inheritance that demonstrates a shared commitment even as it calls attention to diversity.

CHERRY CLAYTON

Further reading: Laura E. Donaldson, *Decolonising Feminisms: Race, Gender, and Empire-Building* (1992).

FEMINISM (Australia)

Women writers have always been numerous and prominent in white Australia, and towards the end of the nineteenth century in the context of a lively women's rights movement their fiction, poetry, and journalism took up feminist themes. The novelists **Catherine Helen Spence** and **Miles Franklin**, poet and journalist **Mary Gilmore**, and **Louisa Lawson**, editor of the *Dawn*, were declared feminists; others, such as **Barbara Baynton**, Catherine Martin, **Rosa Praed, Tasma,** and **Ada Cambridge** wrote critically, satirically, sometimes tragically, of women and gender relations in colonial life.

While this tradition is continued in the work of later writers such as **Henry Handel Richardson, Katharine Susannah Prichard**, and many others, they rarely took up overtly feminist positions. The backlash against feminism in the first half of the twentieth century was the context within which older writers such as **Christina Stead, Judith Wright**, and **Dorothy Hewett** established their names. They have expressed reservations about the wisdom of women writers seeing themselves, or being seen, as a group with distinct interests and approaches, as the feminism of the 1970s maintained. Nevertheless, these writers have associated themselves with feminist projects such as anthologies and publishing houses.

The feminism of the international women's movement's 'second wave' has strongly influenced the production and reception of women's writing in Australia since the early 1970s, providing a receptive climate that simultaneously celebrates women's creativity and criticizes patriarchal domination of the literary scene past and present. Feminist journals — most notably *Hecate*, also *Refractory Girl*, *Lip*, and *Australian Feminist Studies* — bookshops, and small presses, as well as women's studies courses, have played a crucial role in creating the current literary climate. Since the mid-1980s, local commercial publishers have taken up feminist writing with enthusiasm.

Anthologies can provide a guide to the aims and impact of literary feminism. In 1975 Kate Jennings published a collection of new and established women poets called, succinctly, *Mother I'm Rooted*. A decade later, *The Penguin Book of Australian Women Poets* (1986), edited by Susan Hampton and Kate Llewellyn, ranged from traditional Aboriginal chants through the neglected 'feminist' poems of such recognized writers as Mary Gilmore to the work of editors Susan Hampton and Kate Llewellyn and their contemporaries. Many of the most innovative writers of this generation appear in *Beyond the Echo: Multicultural Women's Writing* (1988), edited by Sneja Gunew and Jan Mahyuddin, which emphasizes the importance of linguistic experiment to writers culturally dispossessed in various ways. Critical anthologies include *Gender, Politics and Fiction: Twentieth-century Australian Women's Novels* (1985, 1992), edited by Carole Ferrier; *A Bright and Fiery Troop: Australian Women Writers of the Nineteenth Century* (1988), edited by Debra Adelaide; and *Poetry and Gender* (1989), edited by David Brooks and Brenda Walker. (See **Anthologies**, Australia.)

Aboriginal women's autobiographies such as **Sally Morgan**'s *My Place* (1987) and Ruby Langford's *Don't Take Your Love to Town* (1989) find a wide and appreciative audience. Autobiographical writing by women of all cultural backgrounds is the subject of Joy Hooton's *Stories of Herself When Young* (1990). (See **Life Writing**, Australia.)

Critical and historical studies include Drusilla Modjeska's *Exiles at Home* (1981), on Miles Franklin, Katharine Susannah Prichard, and other writers of the 1920s and 1930s; Patricia Clarke's *Pen Portraits: Women Writers and Journalists in Nineteenth-century Australia* (1988); Dale Spender's *Writing a New World* (1988); and Pam Gilbert's *Coming Out from Under* (1988), on the fiction of such writers of the 1980s as **Elizabeth Jolley** and **Helen Garner**, who are represented in the useful anthology *Eight Voices of the Eighties* (1989), edited by Gillian Whitlock. Collected interviews with women writers include Jennifer Ellison's *Rooms of Their Own* (1986) and Giulia Giuffre's *A Writing Life* (1990).

Representations of women in men's as well as women's writing are discussed in *Who Is She? Images of Woman in Australian Fiction* (1983), edited by Shirley Walker, and some theoretical ramifications of this question are explored in Kay Schaffer's *Women and the Bush: Forces of Desire in the Australian Cultural Tradition* (1988).

Feminist literary theory in Australia draws eclectically on other anglophone feminisms including Marxist feminism and contemporary French philosophy — as can be seen in Schaffer's book and in the Australian contributions to *Grafts: Feminist Cultural Criticism* (1988), edited by Susan Sheridan. The influence of Meaghan Morris' work in this area has been considerable — see her essay collection *The Pirate's Fiancée* (1988).

SUSAN SHERIDAN

Further reading: Debra Adelaide, *Bibliography of Australian Women's Literature 1795–1990 (1991)*.

FEMINISM (Canada)

Recent study has shown how women writers were marginalized in (Anglo)Canadian canonical procedures for much of the twentieth century. (See *Re(Dis)Covering our Foremothers*, 1990, edited by Lorraine McMullen.) However, the first Canadian novel, *The History of Emily Montague* (1769), is attributed to a woman (**Frances Brooke**), and the international reputation of Canadian literature has been created in large part by the feminist work of **Margaret Atwood**, **Alice Munro**, and **Margaret Laurence**, whose writing emerges from two inheritances: they are daughters of empire in a settler/invader colony and daughters of patriarchal history. As such, they are also part of a long tradition in women's writing in Canada that articulates the simultaneous mobility and constraint, subversion and complicity, of the position of women in colonial space, particularly that of white, Anglo-Saxon, predominantly Protestant and middle-class women who have (or had) canonical status.

While their reactions to the colony differed, and their degrees of feminist awareness ranged from minimal to explicitly supportive, the nineteenth-century British women Anna Jameson, **Susanna Moodie**, **Catharine Parr Traill**, **Isabella Valancy Crawford**, and **Sara Jeannette Duncan** all found in the colony a degree of gender flexibility that would have been unavailable to them at 'home'. Native-born writers **Nellie McClung** (better known for her suffragist activity than for her didactic prairie settlement romances) and **Lucy Maud Montgomery** (better known by international readers than by Canadian literary academics) were among the bestselling novelists of their time, and while their plots tended to traditional romance endings, their heroines also tended to be outspoken and out of feminine bounds long enough to create gender flexibility in the literary repertoire, just as immigration to the colony imposed dislocation but also alternative gender arrangements.

The work of several of these women also opened a space for viewing the imbrications of gender, class, race, and national constituents of subjectivity — if not by the class necessity of immigration alone, then by the geo-social (or even ancestral in **Pauline Johnson**'s case) necessity of cross-cultural encounter in the formation (or imposition) of nation-making. Jameson, Traill, and Moodie all noted alternative gender arrangements in the indigenous population; **Emily Carr**'s autobiographical writings — out of literary fashion when written in the 1940s and 1950s — recorded in great detail her observations of Native Canadian culture, while the fragmentation of the indigenous population and the difficulty of prairie settlement are inscribed in the women characters of **Sheila Watson**'s *The Double Hook* (1959) and *Deep Hollow Creek* (1992, written in the 1930s); though neither Carr nor Watson can be said to be feminist *per se*, their work is indicative of a pattern of cross-cultural gender interrogation that marks Canadian women's writing in English from Brooke, Jameson, and Traill to Atwood and Laurence and beyond.

Canadian women writers enjoyed a prominence matched by women's activism from the 1880s to the end of the First World War. The Women's Christian Temperance Union and the National Council of Women were only the largest of many women's organizations devoted to acquiring the vote and to social reform, although often the vote was solicited less for women's rights than for representation of the patriarchal and patriotic values of the dwindling Anglo-Saxon power base. (See *A Not Unreasonable Claim: Women and Reform in Canada, 1880s–1920*, 1979, edited by Linda Kealey.) Indeed, the 'New Woman' was greatly outnumbered by 'maternal feminists' and devotees of the 'social gospel'. (For the range of women's concerns of the time, see *New Women: Short Stories by Canadian Women 1900–1920*, 1991, edited by Sandra Campbell and Lorraine McMullen.)

Following the First World War, two factors led to the decline in prominence of women's writing — the legislation of married women out of the work force and into the home, and the reclamation of 'culture' by the élitist modernist movement. The few key Canadian figures to survive this period include **Ethel Wilson** and writers of non-British immigrant backgrounds — **Martha Ostenso**'s *Wild Geese* (1925) is a founding text in the prairie realist tradition, while **Laura Goodman Salverson**'s *The Viking Heart* (1923) and *Confessions of an Immigrant's Daughter* (1939) encouraged the maintenance of cultural specificity within the national mosaic. **Adele Wiseman**'s *The Sacrifice* (1956) shows the collision of a woman's independence with the patriarchal attempt to re-establish a Jewish community following the Second World War. The poetry of **Dorothy Livesay** and **Anne Marriott** through mid-century participates in a tradition of coalitional politics (supporting the rights of women, the working class, and farmers) in the west; this tradition continues through such West Coast socialist feminist presses as Press Gang and such urban writers as Helen Potrebenko; coalitional politics in the east are represented, for example, by Women's Press, Second Story Press, Sister Vision Press, and Williams-Wallace. Because of the dominance of Anglo-Saxon ancestry in central and eastern Canada and the concomitant retrenchment of traditional gender arrangements, virtually no women's writing survived through the world wars period. Jessie Sime's short stories about working-class immigrant women, *Sister Woman* (1919), and her novel, *Our Little Life* (1921), set in Montreal, clearly constitute the first urban fiction in Canada, but they are also clearly written by and about the 'New Woman': these works have remained largely unknown, much like

Elizabeth Smart's modernist *By Grand Central Station I Sat Down and Wept* (1945), until reclamation by second-wave feminist academics.

Second-wave feminist literature has benefited directly from the success of Atwood, Laurence, and Munro, whose works interrogate the compulsory feminization of women, often specifically in the context of colonial inheritance. Other key but lesser-known writers in the early history of second-wave feminism are **Audrey Thomas** (*Ten Green Bottles*, 1967), **Marian Engel** (*Sarah Bastard's Notebook*, 1974, first published as *No Clouds of Glory!*, 1968), Sylvia Fraser (*Pandora*, 1972), Wiseman (*Crackpot*, 1974), Sharon Riis (*The True Story of Ida Johnson*, 1976), and **Betty Lambert** (*Crossings*, 1979). **Phyllis Webb**, **Bronwen Wallace**, **Daphne Marlatt**, Erin Mouré, Betsy Warland, Lorna Crozier, Di Brandt, and **Dionne Brand** are key feminist poets, though several of them write in other genres as well. Indeed, although the short story, autobiography, *Bildungsroman*, and *Künstlerroman* have been the most common genres, cross-genre activity is as common in contemporary feminist writing as cross-cultural gender articulations: many feminist writers are also academics — for example, Lola Lemire Tostevin, **Aritha van Herk**, Donna E. Smyth, Makeda Silvera, Lee Maracle, and Himani Bannerji. Many feminist journals (for example, *Tessera*, *Room of One's Own*, *Atlantis*, and *Fireweed*) and other collective publications (e.g., *Telling It: Women and Language Across Cultures*, 1990, edited by the Telling It Collective) represent diverse creative and scholarly forms and eclectically blend feminist and poststructuralist theory, racial ancestries, and erotic preferences. (See **Criticism**, Canada.) Among the better-known black feminists are Brand, **Claire Harris**, and **Marlene Nourbese Philip**; among the better known lesbian-feminists are Brand, Beth Brant, Marlatt, Warland, and **Jane Rule**. Important aboriginal feminists include Brant, Jeannette Armstrong, J. B. Joe, Lenore Keeshig-Tobias, **Maria Campbell**, Lee Maracle, and Monique Mojica. (See **Aboriginal Literature**, Canada.) Among the better-known dramatists are Sally Clark, Margaret Hollingsworth, Betty Lambert, Ann-Marie MacDonald, **Sharon Pollock**, and **Judith Thompson**. Banuta Rubess' 'Pope Joan' (premièred 1984) has enjoyed international attention rivalled only by Thompson's later work and by MacDonald's *Good Night Desdemona (Good Morning Juliet)* (1990).

Feminist excavation of public and private histories (Sarah Anne Curzon's play *Laura Secord, the Heroine of 1812*, 1887, is perhaps an ur-text here) dominates second-wave feminist writing: Atwood re-creates Susanna Moodie, Susan Swan the giantess Anna Swan, Jane Urquhart both Laura Secord and Margaret Cruikshank, **Joy Kogawa** the internment of the Japanese during the Second World War, Sky Lee the Chinese settlement in British Columbia (the latter two through maternal history), and Joan Crate the indigenous and imperial ancestry of Pauline Johnson. Contemporary feminists have entered and expanded the openings made by actual and literary foremothers and by cultures other than Anglo-Saxon (Canada's **multiculturalism** is perhaps most visible in feminist writing), while new traditions are being established (including men's feminist literature) at a rate too prolific to be identified here.

DONNA PALMATEER PENNEE

Further reading: Shirley Neuman and Smaro Kamboureli, eds, *A Mazing Space: Writing Canadian Women Writing* (1986); Barbara Godard, ed., *Gynocritics/Gynocritiques* (1987); Libby Scheier, Sarah Sheard, and Eleanor Wachtel, eds, *Language in Her Eye* (1990).

FEMINISM (The Caribbean)

The term 'feminism' is complex in the Caribbean context. It is impossible to discuss gender issues separately from those of race and class, which importantly differentiate Caribbean feminism from so-called 'white' feminism, largely associated with North America and Europe. The term 'womanism', derived from Alice Walker's usage to denote black women's cultural experience, is also important. Both terms have been re-defined within Caribbean contexts.

Caribbean feminism is closely reflective of Caribbean reality — its racial diversity and its issues of economic decolonization — and while uniquely sensitive to local issues, is ground-breaking in the feminist world as a whole. In general, there is a necessary emphasis on feminist praxis, responding to the critical situation of many poor women. The Caribbean Association for Feminist Research and Action (CAFRA) has a developed programme of research directed towards social action, as do the Women and Development Unit, headed by Peggy Antrobus, and the Women's Studies Programme, both at the University of the West Indies. The development of the women's movement in the Caribbean, especially in the 1980s, has created a supportive context for women's writing, reflected in the increase in women's texts published and in the development of feminist criticism.

Caribbean feminist literary criticism has addressed certain important issues thus far: the examination of male-authored texts from a feminist perspective; the promotion of women writers, known and unknown, through anthologies and critical articles; the discussion of social contexts that impede or encourage women's writing; the organization of international conferences, which have brought together women writers from the Caribbean world; the scholarly search for origins and forgotten texts. A developing interest is in the growth of writing produced outside the Caribbean by women now living in Canada, the UK, the USA, and Africa.

Diversity remains a major feminist issue, and while anglophone writing by Caribbean women now understandably and importantly reflects a predominantly African-Caribbean experience, Caribbean women of almost all ethnic backgrounds are producing work. Much of it presents a striking complexity of identity — resulting from different racial inheritances or experiences of living in different societies because of migration — and utilizes a linguistic register that shifts easily between international English and Creole. The feminist ideal of a commonality of female experience or culture has interfaced with the need for a critical discourse responsive to this multi-faceted work. Post-colonial theory is another factor in changing perspectives on Caribbean criticism, and in this change feminist criticism remains central.

Caribbean women writers have produced work in all major literary genres, though they have written few plays. Critical response to women's growing role in public performance (calypso, reggae, drama, ritual, festival, for example) is best able to realize the nature of the work it studies when social conditions are fully discussed along with the nature of the form that springs from them.

Because feminism is as concerned with the social circumstances of the production of literature as with its aesthetic quality and character, the career pattern of women writers and their relation to oral or scribal traditions is important. As in the case of **Jamaica Kincaid**, critics can reinforce expectations that a major woman writer will produce a large body of sustained work over a long period of time and that she will designate herself as a professional writer and attempt to earn a living from writing, responding to the demands of an international audience. But many Caribbean women writers are necessarily engaged in earning a living apart from writing, are supporting children alone, and in responding to their local audience are communally 'quilting' a literary inheritance from relatively small bodies of high quality work, sometimes begun seriously in middle age. Some anthologies, such as the recent collection of Caribbean women's poetry *Creation Fire* (1990), edited by Ramabai Espinet and sponsored by CAFRA, reflect commitment to excellence in writing and make a political statement reflective of respect for modes of life and writing patterns that many women share in the Caribbean today.

ELAINE SAVORY (FIDO)

Further reading: Pat Ellis, ed., *Women of the Caribbean* (1986); Carol Boyce Davies and Elaine Savory Fido, eds., *Out of the Kumbla: Caribbean Women and Literature* (1990).

FEMINISM (India)

Indian women writing in English have attempted to portray women as multi-faceted rather than as fitting neatly into such categories as *pativrata* (a chaste woman loyal to her husband) and ideal mother. **Kamala Markandaya**'s early novels, *Nectar in a Sieve* (1954) and *Some Inner Fury* (1955), represent traditional images of women who are self-sacrificing and self-effacing. Markandaya's later novel, *Two Virgins* (1973), however, contrasts the aspirations of two girls growing up in a conservative family — one breaks with conventions and leaves home; the other suppresses her desires and remains there. In *Where Shall We Go This Summer?* (1975), **Anita Desai** deals with a woman who wakes up to her sexual desires, questions motherhood, and becomes an exile on an island. Although she returns to her family, she has questioned, if not resolved, her passivity. **Shashi Deshpande**'s protagonist in *The Dark Holds No Terrors* (1980) is another who protests, although temporarily, against her husband's physical and mental flagellation. Though a doctor capable of financial independence, she chooses to go to her father during her protest but eventually returns to her husband. **Nayantara Sahgal** appears radical when she makes her women characters, who are wage-earners, experience divorce. But these women — in *This Time of Morning* (1965) and *The Day in Shadow* (1976) — face life with optimism and confidence with help from men they respect. Raji Narasimhan, however, in *Forever Free* (1979) depicts a woman who, after experiencing the routine of marriage and a series of affairs, realizes that she does not need a man for emotional fulfilment. She finds freedom through her bond with her mother. There is an emphasis in the novel on female bonding.

More recent novelists such as Shobha De (*Socialite Evenings*, 1989) and Namita Gokhale (*Paro*, 1984) — often dismissed as writers of sensational fiction — emphasize the creativity of women and the act of writing itself. If writing liberates, uninhibited writing liberates more. There is, consequently, a sexual frankness in their work not evident in earlier novelists.

Indian women's poetry in English, beginning with that of **Kamala Das**, has also been concerned with sexuality and the act of writing as liberating — Das' *Summer in Calcutta* (1965), for example. While **Sarojini Naidu** wrote lyrical romantic poetry, and Monika Varma writes about love (in *Across the Vast Spaces*, 1975), it is Das who, through introspection and an uninhibited manner of dealing with sex and her body, pioneered the feminist movement in poetry. She shows how writing in a colloquial language about women's bodies and personal issues and the act of writing itself can be liberating, can make the 'private' woman — a woman condemned to the background — 'public'. **Gauri Deshpande** in *Beyond the Slaughterhouse* (1972) writes on love, sex, and motherhood; Mamta Kalia in *Tribute to Papa and Other Poems* (1970) rebels against a society that is obviously patriarchal and inhibiting; **Suniti Namjoshi** in *Feminist Fables* (1982) is concerned about love; and **Eunice de Souza** in *Fix* (1979) discusses motherhood, sex, and women's problems from a Goan Catholic perspective.

ALLADI UMA

Further reading: Meena Shirwadker, *Image of Woman in the Indo-Anglian Novel* (1979); Sunada P. Chaven, *A Study of Indian Women Poets in English* (1984).

FEMINISM (New Zealand)

The work of women writers has never been absent in New Zealand writing, but it has rarely received the same prominence or attention as the work of men. The work of many women writers, such as the women novelists of the 1880s and 1890s, has remained out of print for long periods. Until recently, significant figures such as **Katherine Mansfield** and **Janet Frame** have been exceptions in a masculinized literary history, while the work of most women writers has been largely contained by generic expectations and boundaries that categorized it as 'minor'. Women writers of the late nineteenth century typically produced romances, memoirs (such as **Lady Mary Ann Barker**'s *Station Life in New Zealand*, 1870), or highly sentimental and ornate poems conforming to expectations of 'refinement' in writing. Women writers who modified conventional expectations or subjects often wrote under pseudonyms that implied masculinity, such as the well-known novelist **G. B. Lancaster**. Some women writers used conventional romance structures to address social questions such as the status of women in marriage or the prohibition of alcohol. These include a number of women temperance novelists at the end of the nineteenth century (Ellen Ellis, Kathleen Inglewood, Susan Mactier, and **Edith Searle Grossmann**, for example). Some fiction, such as Grossmann's *In Revolt* (1893), *A Knight of the Holy Ghost* (1907), and *The Heart of the Bush* (1910), was romance narrative that questioned the legal and social status of women and the moral questions raised by marriage. Although most female novelists before 1920 were not experimental or innovative in their use or choice of genre, many writers, as has been shown by Heather Roberts' *Where Did She Come From? New Zealand Women Novelists 1862–1987* (1989), used romance narratives or family sagas to open up social, moral, and political questions.

The best-known examples of romance novels with a political agenda, however, occur in the slightly later work of **Jean Devanny** and **Jane Mander**. Devanny's novel *The Butcher Shop* (1926), which is a Marxist and sexually frank analysis of the place of women in marriage, was banned both in New Zealand and Germany; Mander's earlier novel, *The Story of a New Zealand River* (1920), which focuses on the economic basis of marriage for women and suggests alternatives, was criticized in New Zealand on its appearance. As Roberts shows, marriage and the family form the central location for fiction by women and the site of far-reaching political and sexual commentary. It seems clear that women, in their often-conventionally articulated preoccupation with gender identity, also provide a continuing critique of social institutions. **Robin Hyde**'s *The Godwits Fly* (1938) is a family novel whose focus on the life of a young girl highlights family structures and gender roles as well as the developing subjectivity of a female artist. An even more stringent critique of marriage and romance is presented in Hyde's fantasy novel *Wednesday's Children* (1937). Hyde's own life and publishing history have come to stand as an example for feminists of the way in which women writers are disadvantaged: none of Hyde's fiction remained in print after her death, whereas the work of her male contemporaries, **John Mulgan**, **A. R. D. Fairburn**, and **Allen Curnow**, has always been available.

It was not until the early 1970s, however, that literary history began to be rewritten by feminism. The recovery of forgotten writers and texts as part of the redrawing of the map of literature has been the major feminist literary project. New Zealand, like Australia, has seen a good deal of this kind of activity, which had its origins in a surge of interest in women writers in the early 1970s when a number of small-press feminist journals (*Spiral*, 1976–85; *Broadsheet*, 1972–) were established. In 1977 Riemke Ensing published *Private Gardens*, an anthology of New Zealand women's poetry similar to the Australian anthology of feminist verse *Mother I'm Rooted* (1975), edited by Kate Jennings. *Private Gardens* collected a number of poets who have since become major writers and a significant presence in feminist literature (**Anne French**, **Lauris Edmond**, for example) and 'discovered' the 1950s' poet Mary Stanley, whose work has since appeared in major anthologies.

In the late 1970s and in the 1980s, a number of collections of short fiction by women appeared and drew attention to the number of women writers who were not represented in anthologies such as the Oxford series. These collections included *Shirley Temple Is a Wife and Mother: 34 Stories by 22 New Zealanders* (1977), edited by Christine Cole Catley; *Women's Work: Contemporary Short Stories by New Zealand Women* (1985), edited by Marion McLeod and Lydia Wevers; and *In Deadly Earnest: A Collection of Fiction by New Zealand Women, 1870–1880s* (1989), edited by Trudie McNaughton. A new outlet for writing by women was provided by the New Women's Fiction series (edited by Cathie Dunsford in 1986, Aorewa McLeod in 1988, and Mary Paul and Marion Rae in 1989). Separatist publishing has provided an opportunity to rewrite literary history, as in the anthologies *Happy Endings* (1987) and *Goodbye to Romance* (1989), both edited by Elizabeth Webby and Lydia Wevers. These collections represent a continuous tradition of short fiction published in journals and collections by women from the 1850s to the 1980s in both Australia and New Zealand.

A regional selection of new writing on both sides of the Tasman Sea is offered in *Speaking with the Sun* (1991), edited by Stephanie Dowrick and Jane Parkin. *Yellow Pencils: Contemporary Poetry by New Zealand Women* (1988), edited by Lydia Wevers, represents poetry by women in the 1980s that was fuelled, as were short fiction collections, by the enormous increase in the published work of women writers in the mid-1970s. Both lesbian writing (*The Power and the Glory and Other Lesbian Stories*, 1987, edited by Miriam Shapira) and writing by Maori women (**Patricia Grace**, **Keri Hulme**, Ngahuia Te Awekotuku), like lesbian writing in Australia and the work of Australian Aborigine **Sally Morgan**, have been given impetus by the feminist emphasis on breaking silence, associating feminist activity generally with minority and indigenous literatures. (See also **Feminism**, Australia.)

As creative work by women writers has found expanded outlets, markets, and readerships, feminist critical activity has provided a context for the reconstruction and re-evaluation of literary history and textual commentary within a feminist framework. The impact of feminism on New Zealand literary production of all kinds is evident in all areas and has affected permanently the canonical and colonialist assumptions of traditional male-based literary history. (See also **Criticism**, New Zealand.) *Women's Studies Journal* (1984–) is a continuing source of feminist critical commentary.

LYDIA WEVERS

Further reading: Sue Kedgeley, *Our Own Country* (1989).

FEMINISM (Pakistan)

Due in part to the religious orientation of the state, feminism is not an ideological plank in Pakistan. However, feminist concerns, including an awareness of the changing role of women and their identity, do exist in Pakistan; these concerns are reflected in Pakistan's literature in English.

In the novels of **Bapsi Sidhwa**, themes of family and communal life and the socio-political upheavals in a pre- and post-partition subcontinent are mediated through the perceptions and interventions of major female characters — of the tenacious elderly in *The Crow Eaters* (1978) and of the precocious young in *Ice-Candy-Man* (1988). Sidhwa's portrayal of women's shrewd adaptability compares with the portrayal of Indian women in the fiction of **Ruth Prawer Jhabvala**. Sara Suleri's semi-autobiographical *Meatless Days* (1989) is stylistically unique in the Pakistani context in its observation, nuance, and response to family relationships and to a society of an educated élite. Its introspective mode is shared in Indian novelist **Anita Desai**'s *Clear Light of Day* (1980).

Unlike the work of Indian women poets such as **Kamala Das** and **Eunice de Souza**, that of Pakistani poets **Maki Kureishi** and Hina Imam is more restrained. Das' 'The Looking-Glass' (in her *The Descendants*, 1967) and de Souza's 'Autobiographical' (in her *Ways of Belonging: Selected Poems*, 1990) are candid and assertive; Kureishi's 'Windows' (in *Wordfall*, edited by **Kaleem Omar**, 1975) and Imam's 'Disenchantment II' (in her *Midnight Dialogue*, 1990) are sensitive sketches of women's experience.

Some Pakistani male poets have registered feminist concerns; **Alamgir Hashmi**, in his 'The Woman at the Lahore G. P. O.' (in his *Neither This Time/Nor That Place*, 1984), presents a sympathetic though detached consideration of women's experience. As shown in 'Mother's Daughter' (in his collection *Arrival of the Monsoon*, 1985), **Taufiq Rafat**, however, tends to portray women as bullied, but shrewish.

S. S. SIRAJUDDIN

FEMINISM (The Philippines)

Filipino women writers, while not uninfluenced by western feminism, seek their roots in Philippine history and tradition. Reclaiming the past, they go back to the tradition of the pre-hispanic *babaylan* or priestess, the spiritual and cultural leader of ancient Philippine society, who set the rhythms of life and work in the community, healed the sick, and served as the repository of tribal lore and wisdom. The prayers she chanted were the beginnings of poetry, the rituals where she assumed the role of the gods who spoke through her the beginnings of drama. Today, Filipino women writers invoke the '*babaylan* spirit' as a source of inspiration.

The literary past similarly provides role models for feminist writers. In the nineteenth century, with patriarchal culture at its most repressive, Leona Florentino (1849–84) courageously left her abusive husband to devote herself to writing poetry; her international reputation was reflected by the inclusion of her work in the *Bibliotheque internationale des oeuvres des femmes* (1889), edited by Andzia Wolska. Early in the twentieth century, Magdalena Jalandoni (1891–1978), against her mother's objections, embarked on a long and productive literary career as the first Filipino woman novelist, publishing such works as *Ang Bantay Sang Patyo* ('The Guardian of the Graveyard', 1925). She lived her feminism by participating actively in the fight for women's suffrage in the 1920s.

Gaining access to an education in English under American rule, Filipino women were among the earliest to write fiction and poetry. Among these writers were **Angela Manalang Gloria**, who was denied a major literary prize because she dared to write a poem, 'Querida' ('Mistress'), on the subject of illicit love, thus going against the grain of conventional morality, and **Estrella Alfon**, who affirms the mother-daughter bonds in 'Magnificence', a story about a woman's magnificent rage as she protects her daughter from a sexual pervert. Essayist **Carmen Guerrero-Nakpil**, writing after the Second World War, dismantled stereotypes of women and celebrated Filipino female consciousness in such works as *Woman Enough* (1983).

Contemporary feminist writers, while forging links with the past, are nevertheless very much aware of the woman question in the context of new realities. **Ninotchka Rosca**'s *The Monsoon Collection* (1983), short stories written under martial law, depicts the brutalization of women under military rule. Poets Marra Lanot (*Dream*

Sketches, 1991), **Marjorie Evasco**, Grace Monte de Ramos ('Brave Woman', in the poetry anthology *Caracoa V: Subversu*, 1984), Fannie Llego ('A Prayer of Great Expectations', in *Caracoa 7: Breaktext*, 1985), Lina Reyes (*Honing Weapons*, 1987), and **Fatima Lim**, to mention only a few, use memory and imagination not just to question the traditional roles of women but to create new and alternative metaphors linking the marginalization of women to issues such as militarization, poverty, migrant labour, and environmental concerns, which profoundly disturb Philippine and other post-colonial societies. Anthologies of poetry and prose offering feminist perspectives include *Caracoa V: Subversu* and the bilingual prose and poetry of *Ani* 1 (1988).

University-based feminist critics, such as those included in *Women Reading . . . Feminist Perspectives on Philippine Literary Texts* (1992), edited by Thelma B. Kintanar, have also helped develop feminist writing in the Philippines by actively publishing critical essays on traditional and modern Filipino texts, by both male and female writers, to uncover possible biases, in the case of the one, and to discover the female consciousness submerged in the text, in the case of the other. Most recently, Filipino women have begun writing in less traditional genres such as autobiography as a way of telling their stories and understanding their lives. (See **Life Writing**, The Philippines.)

THELMA B. KINTANAR

FEMINISM (South Africa)

Women writers have contributed to South African literature since the nineteenth century and include such notables as Nobel Prize-winning author **Nadine Gordimer**. Yet feminism, both as a social movement and as a literary phenomenon, has been almost absent from South African writing until comparatively recently. The reason for this is that in South African writing in English the issues of race and racial oppression have occupied the moral high ground, almost entirely eclipsing the associated issues of gender oppression. While many sensitive writers, both male and female, have explored topics associated with the politics of race, the politics of gender have been considered to be a minor issue in South African society. (See **Criticism**, South Africa.)

There was a women's movement in South Africa in the late nineteenth century and early twentieth centuries. It focused its energies on securing the vote for women in the colonies, and later, in the Union of South Africa. The most prominent South African feminist of this time was **Olive Schreiner**, whose novel *The Story of an African Farm* (1883) includes Lyndall's impassioned speech against the narrow confines of education for girls and women in the Cape colony. Schreiner's unfinished novel, *From Man to Man* (1926), includes an exposé of the social dishonesty and double standards that force one of the major characters, Bertie, into a life of prostitution. Her non-fictional *Woman and Labour* (1911) argued strongly for women to give up their parasitic lives of dependence within middle-class marriages and to assume their own identities through productive labour. While Schreiner's primary literary topic was gender, she was also sensitive to its association with race, especially in later years. She withdrew from the women's suffrage movement because of its focus on white women only: she wanted *all* women to get the vote.

After white South African women were given the vote in 1930, the energy of the women's movement dissipated. In the 1930s and 1940s there is evidence of a consciousness of gender issues among the socialist and communist workers who were active in the Garment Workers Union. There are poems in English expressing solidarity among women as well as a larger body of writing in Afrikaans that has been documented by Elsabe Brink. However, the draconian political oppression that followed the National Party's assumption of power in 1948 and the implementation of apartheid soon silenced these voices in South African literature.

In the 1970s, when the second wave of the women's movement was a major influence on writing by women in post-colonial societies such as Canada and Australia, it continued to be a very low-key issue in South Africa. This can be attributed to two factors: first, the racial oppression imposed by apartheid continued to provide the major focus for protest writers, and secondly, key feminist works such as Kate Millet's *Sexual Politics* and **Germaine Greer**'s *The Female Eunuch* were banned as 'undesirable' texts in South Africa. This latter action meant that seminal feminist ideas were suppressed by the dominant racist and patriarchal government, along with other 'subversive' ideas. Government paranoia saw feminism as another radical assault on the so-called civilized and Christian norms that Afrikaner nationalism perceived itself to be struggling to uphold on the 'dark continent'.

The suppression of key texts, coupled with the androcentric bias of English departments within South African universities, meant that it was only in the 1980s that the idea of feminism became viable both for writers and for academics. The first feminist anthology to appear was a compilation of creative writing and visual imagery called *LIP from Southern African Women* (1983), edited by Susan Brown, Isabel Hofmeyr, and Susan Rosenberg. This was followed by *Vukani Makhosikazi: South African Women Speak* (1985), edited by Jane Barrett *et al.*, *Women in South Africa: From the Heart* (1988), edited by Seageng Tsikang and Dinah Lefakane, and *Women in Southern Africa* (1987), a collection of essays edited by exiled political activist Christine Qunta. These in turn were followed by work produced by academic feminists — Cherry Clayton's collection of essays *Women and Writing in South Africa* (1989) as well as two revisionist anthologies of women's work, *Breaking the Silence: A Century of South African Women's Poetry* (1990), edited by Cecily Lockett, and *Raising the Blinds: A Century of South African Women's Stories* (1990), edited by Annemarie van Niekerk. (See **Anthologies**, South Africa.)

Although the impetus of much of the feminist theorizing and anthologizing of the late 1980s was towards formulating the concept of women as an oppressed group within South Africa, what has become apparent in the 1990s is that the term 'feminism' has different meanings for women of different racial groups. Women of colour tend to see 'feminism' as a concern of middle-class white women, something imported from Europe and the USA that has little relevance to their lives. Their own struggle for gender equality is expressed in different terms and is associated with their struggle for racial liberation. There is, in South African writing, an emerging tradition of black women writers who concern themselves with gender issues but refuse the label of 'feminist'. These include **Bessie Head**, whose short-story collection *The Collector of Treasures and Other Botswana Village Tales* (1977) describes the oppression of women in Tswana society, as do her novels *Maru* (1971) and *A Question of Power* (1974); **Miriam Tlali**, whose *Muriel at Metropolitan* (1975) and *Soweto Stories* (1989) describe the lives of ordinary women in South African under apartheid, and Sindiwe Magona, whose *To My Children's Children* (1990) is an autobiographical perspective on the life of a woman whose strength of character and determination enable her to rise from the position of a South African domestic servant to that of an employee of the United Nations in New York, USA.

Feminism, defined as a focus on gender politics and the writing of women, is yet to be established as a category in South African literature in the way that it has in Australia and Canada. It is to be hoped that as democracy is introduced into South African political life, feminism and the politics of gender will come to be seen as valid issues to be explored by future generations of writers and academics.

CECILY LOCKETT

FEMINISM (West Africa)

Early West African creative writing in English was dominated by male writers, maintaining the tradition of female voicelessness in predominantly patriarchal social structures. In the twentieth century, however, the liberalizing impact of western education has helped African women to give voice to their experiences. They have begun to question their second-class status in society, reclaiming through creative work their rights as autonomous, independent selves.

Nigeria's **Flora Nwapa** followed **Chinua Achebe**'s example in exploring African communal experience. In *Efuru* (1966) and *Idu* (1970) her focus is not primarily feminist — in fact, in a 1988 interview she declared that she is not a feminist. Like many African female writers, such as **Buchi Emecheta**, Nwapa is wary of labels because of an inherent scepticism about some controversial dimensions of European feminism. (African women writers, critic Chukwenye Okonyo argues, prefer to be called womanists.) Nevertheless, *Efuru* and *Idu* explore women's emotional and social experience and their refusal to be limited by marriage, which they view as a patriarchal institution. Efuru is an astute and successful businesswoman who has inherited the attributes of Uhamiri, the 'woman of the Lake' who endows her with the gifts of foresight and intellectual and physical beauty. The use of this mythic pattern provides a metaphor for Nwapa's exploration of women's essential genius and gifts, seen as superior to those of the dominant male class. Nwapa's heroines are both beautiful and gifted and, contrary to patriarchal demands, refuse to accept arranged marriages and insist on marrying for love. It is here and in her exploration of female eroticism that Nwapa reveals her feminism.

In her later novels Nwapa becomes more iconoclastic, rejecting patriarchal moral standards that deny female selfhood. Her heroines are increasingly rebellious and reject marriage, but accept motherhood as the fulfilment of their destiny as female. Nwapa's later heroines are more egotistical, overthrowing morals that restrain and negate them. In *One Is Enough* (1981) the heroine, Amaka, rejects marriage and uses her sexuality both as a pleasure principle and for economic advancement. This becomes the pattern of female exploration of selfhood in the novel *Women Are Different* (1986), where the omniscient narrator traces the related lives of four women as they build themselves and their careers, forging a new morality in an essentially amoral post-independent Nigeria.

Nigeria's Buchi Emecheta is the first major African female novelist to articulate the perpetuation of patriarchal injustice. Her compelling *The Joys of Motherhood* (1979) poses the central question: 'God, when will you create a woman who will be fulfilled in herself, a full human being not anybody's appendage?' The novel narrates the experiences of Nnuego — beautiful, intelligent, generous, psychic even. Her first marriage fails because she cannot produce children; as a consequence, she is brutalized physically and emotionally. Although in her second marriage she has several children and sacrifices herself in compliance with the socially accepted role of mother, she dies lonely and unattended. Emecheta questions motherhood, women's abdication of self in relation to sons and husbands, and patriarchal views of women as nothing but producers of children; she rejects a patriarchal sexual morality that applies strict sanctions on women while allowing men sex ual freedom.

In *Double Yoke* (1982) Emecheta's heroine Nko is a university woman who indulges in sexual adventures for pleasure and uses sex as a weapon in power politics. Debbie Ogedengbe, in Emecheta's historical novel *Destination Biafra* (1982), is a counterpoint to Nnuego in *The Joys of Motherhood.* Debbie adopts a male sexual morality that allows her sexual experimentation; she joins the army and is a political activist.

Ama Ata Aidoo, who comes from a matrilineal society among the Akan Ghana, is an articulate feminist. Her now-classic play *Anowa* (1969) explores the dilemma of the gifted woman in a patriarchal society. The play is structured from a popular folk myth, common in Nigeria and Ghana, about a headstrong, beautiful girl who chooses her own husband, Kofi Ako, a seeming gentleman who turns out to be a devil. She helps him to become wealthy, but he then becomes true to his male egoistic self — he buys slaves and uses his fellow human beings, including Anowa, as commodities. Anowa is alienated and Kofi becomes symbolically and physically impotent. The tragedy of male greed leads inexorably to the destruction of both Anowa and Kofi.

Aidoo's novel *Our Sister Killjoy* (1979) explores how African politics, colonization, European cultural imperialism, and European bourgeois values lead to women's emotional agony. The novel traces the journey of the heroine, Sissie, from Ghana through London, England, to Germany. The journey motif allows Sissie to provide an ongoing commentary on the fallacies of western pretensions to cultural and moral superiority. It ends with a moving love letter that is an articulation of the female self and of the female emotional landscape similar to Ramatoulaye's monologue on her life in Senegal's Mariama Bâ's *Une si longue lettre* (1980), translated by Modupe Bode Thomas as *So Long a Letter* (1981).

Aidoo's poetry ranks with the most important women's poetry in English to emerge from Africa. Her collected poems, *Someone Talking to Sometime* (1985), offer a sustained exploration of her response to her world and its realities — female, social, and political. Aidoo has always insisted that love is a luxury the African writer cannot afford to investigate in the face of dire political mismanagement and rural pauperization. And while it is a woman of love who surfaces at the conclusion of *Our Sister Killjoy*, Aidoo is not a narrow feminist in the manner of Emecheta, whose focus is on women's agony alone. Rather, Aidoo's perspective is both feminist and humanist.

Catherine Obianuju Acholonu has emerged as an important Nigerian poet with her volumes *The Spring's Last Drop* (1985) and *Nigeria in the Year 1999* (1985). Her work ranges through pathos to humour, but her images of the female body prove most memorable. Her imagistic gift for evoking personal response to life is revealed in 'Spring's Last Drop', a celebration of the gifted woman.

West African women's writing is young, but it has shown surprising maturity and a strong feminist impulse. It has moved quickly from descriptions of emotional and physical mutilation in patriarchal society to the identification and articulation of women's selves and their goals.

EMILIA OKO

Further reading: Lloyd Brown, *Women Writers in Black Africa* (1981); Carole Boyce Davies and Anne Adams Graves, eds, *Ngambika, Studies of Women in African Literature* (1986); Henrietta Otukunefor and Obiageli Nwodo, *Nigerian Female Writers* (1989).

FENNARIO, DAVID (1947–)

Canadian dramatist

Born David Wiper, he achieved success with three angry plays that document the oppression of working-class families in the Pointe St Charles area of

Montreal, Canada, where he was born and raised. On the basis of his autobiographical novel *Without a Parachute* (1972), he was commissioned by Centaur Theatre to write a play. The result was *On the Job* (1976), a social-realist drama in which anglophone workers in a garment factory stage a drunken wildcat strike on Christmas Eve while their union representative drinks with the bosses. Fennario reworked this situation in *Nothing to Lose* (1977), this time placing the strike in a tavern and introducing the character of a working-class writer who fears losing touch with his community.

Although Fennario admires his working-class characters, he acknowledges their self-destructive drunkenness, sexism, and racism. His most popular play, *Balconville* (1980), focuses on three families, one francophone and two anglophone, that share both a tenement balcony and the despair of unemployment. Set at the time of the Parti Québécois campaign for separatism, *Balconville* advanced the unpopular proposition that the politics of nationalism and language conceals the real issues of class struggle. Commonly considered the first bilingual Canadian play, it won the 1979 Chalmers Award for best Canadian play.

Fennario's dialogue is marked by an extraordinary gift for violent rage and idiomatic humour. The simplicity of his plots has developed in his later work into a more epic style that recalls the agitprop theatre of the 1930s.

A committed Marxist, Fennario renounced the professional theatre for what he considered its hostility to political drama, and founded a community drama group for which he has written a series of plays tracing the history of working-class Montreal — 'Joe Beef', 'Doctor Neill Cream', 'The Murder of Susan Parr'; several of them have played in Toronto to indifferent response. In 1991 Fennario returned to the professional theatre with 'The Death of René Lévesque', in which he accuses Quebec's separatist Parti Québécois of selling out its socialist roots.

ALAN FILEWOD

Further reading: Robert C. Nunn, 'The interplay of action and set in the plays of David Fennario', *Theatre History in Canada* 9 (1988).

FERLAND, BARBARA (1919–)

Jamaican poet

Born in Jamaica and educated at Brampton and Wolmer's Girls' School, Jamaica, she lives in England. Ferland has not been prolific, but what she has produced has been outstanding. Her song 'Evening Time' has been so successful that it is often wrongly called a folk song. She wrote the songs and music for the first all-Jamaican pantomime, 'Busha Bluebeard', first performed in 1949. She worked for thirteen years for the British Council, Jamaica, and collaborated with one of its officers, Tom Murray, who had settled in Jamaica, on the collection *Folk Songs of Jamaica* (1952).

A contributor to the British Broadcasting Corporation's (BBC) **'Caribbean Voices'** programme, Ferland's work has been broadcast in Jamaica and Canada, and by the BBC in Jamaica and overseas. Examples of her work appear in *Focus*, *Bim*, *Caribbean Voices* (vol. 2., 1970, edited by **John Figueroa**), and the Open University's Third World Studies course materials. A poet of great sensitivity, Ferland's concerns reach to the poor children of Jamaica reciting the Hail Mary, as in the poem, 'Ave Maria', in the Open University's *Caribbean Sampler* (1983, 1985), edited by John Figueroa: 'Bend low the laden bough / Child-high; sweeten her incense flavoured breath / With food good Mary . . . ' Ferland's writing reaches, too, to the peasant boy painted in a moment of stasis by Modigliani, as in 'Le Petit Paysan (Modigliani)' (in *Caribbean Voices*, vol. 2):

It is quite strange for him to have to sit so;

Nor turn his head to watch a cart go by.
But he accepts the moment as it passes —
And does not dream that it will never die.

Still in close contact with Jamaica, Ferland continues to write poetry.

JOHN J. FIGUEROA

FERNANDO, GILDA CORDERO (1929–)
Filipino short-story writer
Born Gilda Cordero in Quiapo, Manila, the Philippines, to scientist Narciso Cordero and his wife Consuelo Luna, she was raised in Manila and attended St Theresa's College and the Ateneo de Manila University. Fernando was one of the first Filipino short-story writers of the 1950s who did not come from the University of the Philippines, but from a convent school, bringing with her a fluid command of English, an eye for the nuances of relationships, and a sense of irony.

Fernando's stories won both literary prizes from the *Philippines Free Press* and Palanca Memorial Awards and have been collected in *The Butcher, The Baker, The Candlestick Maker* (1962) and *A Wilderness of Sweets* (1973). Although she stopped writing short stories in the 1970s, her stories are remembered for their sensitivity to the minutiae of living and especially to women's lives.

Novelist and critic **N. V. M. Gonzalez** divides Fernando's stories into three groups: 'incisive stories of suburbia with its dowdy, glamor-starved housewives, their status symbols, and their money-anxious husbands' (as in 'The Dust Monster'); 'stories enlisted with some cause' (i.e., corruption in the public school system, as in 'The Visitation of the Gods'); and stories about children ('The Eye of a Needle'). Her best stories are 'People in the War' and 'A Wilderness of Sweets', both delicately painful renderings of war, close up, and 'The Dust Monster', a bittersweet account of a woman's disappointments and aspirations.

Fernando has written essays and columns for magazines and a children's book, *Horgle and the King's Soup* (1965). She edited and wrote for the ten-volume Filipino Heritage: The Making of a Nation series (1977), *The Culinary Culture of the Philippines* (1976), and *Philippine Food and Life* (1992). Most importantly, she conceptualized, edited, wrote for, and did pictorial research for books she published under her imprint, GCF Books. These include *Streets of Manila* (1977), *Turn of the Century* (1978), *Philippine Ancestral Houses* (1980), *Being Filipino* (1981), *The History of the Burgis* (1987), *Folk Architecture* (1989), and *The Soul Book* (1991). The GCF books, about Philippine culture, are imaginatively presented and innovatively designed and illustrated.

DOREEN G. FERNANDEZ

FERNANDO, LLOYD (1926–)
Malaysian novelist, critic
Born in Ceylon (now Sri Lanka), he immigrated to Malaysia in 1938. He earned two undergraduate degrees at the University of Malaya (then situated in Singapore) and earned his Ph.D. (1964) at the University of Leeds, England. He was professor of English and head of the department of English, University of Malaysia, Kuala Lumpur, Malaysia, from 1967 to 1978, subsequently practising law in Kuala Lumpur.

Fernando's novel, *Scorpion Orchid* (1976), is a significant landmark in Malaysian literature. Set in pre-independence Singapore, it depicts the experiences of four university undergraduates — each representative of one of the four major ethnic communities in the Malaysian region: the Malays, Chinese, Indians, and Eurasians — whose friendship and political idealism are tested as inter-ethnic conflict breaks out in the wider society. The novel, peppered with literary quotations from Malaysia's past (all from Asian sources), counters widely accepted Eurocentric perceptions of the history and the literature of the region and provides a localized sense of literary and historical tradition. *Scorpion*

Orchid grapples with questions of post-colonial nation-building, the (de)construction of history, cross-cultural conflict, detribalization anxiety (the common individual response to 'bicultural' realities), the immigrant experience, and the social, political, moral, physical, sexual, and emotional coming of age of the individual in a turbulent and dynamic historical period. It concludes with a positive commitment to the development of a cultural identity that is both national and broadly regional. This identity is ultimately capable of accommodating the aspirations of existing ethnic communities, in contrast to the essentially alien, neo-colonial identity that European hegemony attempts to impose.

Fernando's critical and theoretical essays are collected in *Cultures in Conflict* (1986), which includes the influential 'Open and Closed Cultures in Literature: A Note from the Third World towards the Redefinition of Culture' (1975) and 'The Social Imagination and the Functions of Criticism in Asia' (1976). He explores, in particular, both the phenomenon of co-existing cultural heritages, beliefs, logics, customs, and institutions within the political boundaries of an individual society, such as that of Malaysia, and the question of how this phenomenon relates to the character of Southeast Asian literature. Fernando also stresses the importance of reviving or retrieving the essentials of a submerged 'Asian' cultural heritage for incorporation into Southeast Asian literatures in order to help re-create an integrated and dynamic 'Asian', or at least Southeast Asian, cultural identity. Such an identity, in his view, might assist in drawing together the disparate ethnic communities that make up the Southeast Asian population and might help to protect against the corrupting influence of the worst of mass culture emanating from the west.

Fernando has also been influential in fostering the development of English-language literature in Malaysia as an editor and compiler of anthologies. These include *Twenty-two Malaysian Stories* (1968), *New Drama One* (1972), *New Drama Two* (1972), and *Malaysian Short Stories* (1981),

PETER-JOHN LEWIS

Further reading: Koh Tai Ann, 'The empire's orphans: stayers and quitters in *A Bend in the River* and *Scorpion Orchid*', in Peter Hyland (ed.) *Discharging the Canon: Cross-Cultural Readings in Literature* (1986).

FERNANDO, PATRICK (1931–82)

Sri Lankan poet

Born in Kalutara, Sri Lanka, he was educated at Holy Cross College in Kalutara and at St Joseph's College and the University of Ceylon in Colombo. A Roman Catholic, he read western classics at the university; this background provides the context for his poetry. From 1952 to 1979 Fernando was a tax officer in the department of Inland Revenue, where he rose to the position of commissioner. He was a lecturer in tax law at the Institute of Chartered Accountants and at the University of Ceylon. From 1979 until his premature death, he was a tax consultant.

'A Ceylonese writing to be read by anybody anywhere cannot move in a field that is exclusively Ceylonese or "oriental",' Fernando said. Perhaps he arrived at this point of view deductively: the framework for his poetry is not Sri Lankan as such, and his poems have been published abroad. Not only was his first collection, *The Return of Ulysses* (1955), published in London, England, but his *Selected Poems* was issued posthumously in Delhi, India, in 1984; his poems have also appeared in foreign anthologies. However, it can be argued that, contrary to his pronouncement, he does, in fact, write for a Sri Lankan-educated public.

Fernando's poems fall into several categories. His personal poems, such as 'For a Boy of Eight', and genre pictures of Negombo fisherfolk, such as 'The Fisherman Mourned by His Wife' and 'Sun and Rain on the West Coast', are among his weaker efforts, though popular with both critics and readers. Satirical poems such as 'The Late Sir Henry', 'Chorus on a Marriage', and 'Obsequies of the Late Anton Pompirellim Bishop' are first-rate. While it may appear as if the satire inhibits feeling, the case is more complex: Fernando, concerned with feeling, satirizes the lack of it. In fact, feeling is present in poems in all the categories. The classical poems, written early in his career, are also fine; they capture the spirit of the originals, and those versed in the classics will understand and appreciate them best. These poems, however, do possess a contemporary interest — Fernando is really writing of such permanent themes as the enduring power and tragic destiny of love in a poem such as 'The Lament of Paris'. Like T. S. Eliot, he has 'a perception, not only of the pastness of the past, but of its presence'. Later in his career, Fernando grew increasingly fond of writing symbolic poems, usually investing nature with symbolic meanings as in the theme of procreation in 'Survivors', or the destruction of things beautiful and splendid by violent and incongruous forces in 'Life and Death of a Hawk'; he became a fabulist in verse, somewhat like the American poet Marianne Moore.

At every stage in his career, irony is crucial to Fernando's work; it is a feature of his technique as well as that which shapes his vision of life. It enables him to see contradictions as inherent in and central to life and to reconcile himself to these. He was also much preoccupied with death. His language, like that of the American poet-critic John Crowe Ransom, is polished, minted, yet familiar and conversational, and his forms well-crafted and orthodox.

Fernando's is an uncommon kind of sensibility; he and **Yasmine Gooneratne** remain Sri Lanka's most talented poets.

D. C. R. A. GOONETILLEKE

Further reading: Dennis Bartholomeusz, '"Master of the subtle stylus" — the poetry of Patrick Fernando', *Phoenix: Sri Lankan Journal of English in the Commonwealth* 1 (1990).

FIELD, BARRON (1786–1846)
English poet
Born in London, England, he was a descendant of Oliver Cromwell. He became a lawyer and in 1817 moved to Sydney, Australia, to serve as judge of the Supreme Court of New South Wales until his return to England in 1824. He served as Judge of Civil Pleas at Gibraltar (1829–*c.*1835), then retired to Torquay, England. He was a gregarious literary man, a shrewd, quirkish lawyer, and an observant traveller, this explaining his many fiery yet honest contributions to *belles-lettres* and to legal publications. Literary companion of Charles Lamb and Leigh Hunt, and friend of Coleridge, Wordsworth, and Henry Crabb Robinson, he was drama critic for *The Times* and contributor to Hunt's *Examiner*; he wrote on Robert Herrick in 1810, various prose (voyage) pieces for the *London Magazine* (published between 1822 and 1825), and excellent memoirs of Coleridge (1835) and Lamb (1836). A correspondent with Wordsworth from 1828 to 1846, Field wrote a manuscript, 'Memoirs of the Life and Poetry of William Wordsworth', hoping to be the poet's posthumous biographer. He edited many of Thomas Heywood's plays (1842–6) and in this period published a collection of verse, *Spanish Sketches* (1841).

Field's 'Narrative of a Voyage to New South Wales' (1816–17) is the first such voyage account not written by either a navigator or a convict. He edited **J. H. Vaux**'s convict/rogue memoirs, *The Memoirs of James Hardy Vaux* (1819), and his own *First Fruits of Australian Poetry* (1819), which contains the poems 'Botany Bay Flowers' and 'The Kangaroo' — the first poetic descriptions of Australia's flora and fauna. Field's 1822 paper, 'The Aborigines . . . ', is an uneven ethnographic essay on the indigenous Australians' hunting and fishing life style; he also edited/largely wrote

Geographical Memoirs on New South Wales (1825). These works express a number of important, early British attitudes to Australia: the call to rescue the study of flora and fauna from the specialists; the assertion of Australia's need for Romantic nature poetry; a hatred for Australia's lonely landscape; and a concern for the Aborigines, convicts, and religious and public education. (See **Foreign Writers**, Australia.)

Field's best critical writing conveys both enthusiasm and discrimination, making him a valid precursor of **Charles Harpur** and **Henry Kendall**.

J. S. RYAN

Further reading: C. H. Curry, 'Barron Field (1786–1846)', in Douglas Pike (ed.) *Australian Dictionary of Biography* Vol 1 (1966); Geoffrey Little, 'Introduction', *Barron Field's Memoirs of Wordsworth* (1975).

FIGUEROA, JOHN (1920–)

Jamaican poet

Born in Kingston, Jamaica, of Panamanian and Cuban parents, he attended St George's College, a Jesuit boys' school. Beginning his professional life as a secondary schoolteacher, he was appointed professor of education at University College of the West Indies in 1958. He left UWI for other universities — first in Puerto Rico, then Nigeria, and finally the UK, where he now lives with his wife, Dorothy. Figueroa has published three collections: *Blue Mountain Peak* (prose and poetry, 1944) and the poetry collections *Love Leaps Here* (1962) and *Ignoring Hurts* (1976). He has written on Caribbean literature and edited four volumes of Caribbean poetry.

Figueroa's youth, spent close to the Jamaican countryside, his Latin parentage, his Catholicism, his Jesuit education, his travel — all have shaped his work. It is no surprise that his poetry is preoccupied with aesthetic and religious concerns, is often classical in form — (he has adapted Horace and Virgil), and, in its use of allusions to other literatures and cultures, is imbued with the sensibility of one bred on mortal sin in the tropics and employs all his languages (English, Latin, Spanish, Jamaican Creole) for its purposes. Poems such as 'At Home the Green Remains', 'Christmas Breeze', and 'Hartlands/Heartlands' articulate his engagement with Jamaican life and landscape. Other poems record his experiences in other places — 'Spanish Dancer in New York', 'Two from Cidra', 'The Ladies of Spain'. Versions I and II of 'Brou, Philibert le Beau', describing the church at Brou in late morning sunlight, are vintage Figueroa. His best poetry is also his most simple poetry. Figueroa's difficulty has perhaps been in recognizing that the 'high' universal concerns that are often his subject would best be conveyed in the least elaborate ways.

Figueroa's homages to the masters are often fine poems, succeeding in being his as well as theirs. 'Hespera (after Sappho)', 'Goodbye (after Lorca)', 'To Pyrrha/From Horace, Odes 1, 5', 'Pastores', and 'El pecho del amor muy lastimado' (these last two 'after St John of the Cross') can all stand scrutiny. His religious poems are equally persuasive: 'Psalm 120: A Song for Pilgrims', 'Hymn at Evening', and 'Too Late . . . ' are spare, honest, moving.

Influential critics have been negative towards Figueroa's work: **Mervyn Morris** terms some poems 'palpable frauds', **Derek Walcott** writes of 'a naïve sentimentality that is mistaken for compassion and an occasional gaucherie that is nothing less than laziness', and Lloyd Brown characterizes Figueroa's poetry as 'mere word-painting'. Gerald Guinness, in defence of the poetry, pertinently raises the issue of ethnicity and the question of whether a black Figueroa would have been as harshly received. Figueroa's oeuvre and contribution are limited. Still, despite its apprenticeship to classical masters, his voice is his own. More generously received, it might have said more, better.

PAMELA C. MORDECAI

Further reading: Pamela Mordecai, 'John Joseph Maria Figueroa', in Daryl Cumber Dance (ed.) *Fifty Caribbean Writers: A Bio-bibliographical Critical Sourcebook* (1986).

FILM AND LITERATURE

FILM AND LITERATURE (Australia)
Conventional film industry wisdom is that about three out of four feature films are based on published works. In Australia the proportion seems lower, but the pattern is similar with adaptations from all literary genres. This pattern emerged early, with Australia's second feature film, *Robbery under Arms* (director, Charles MacMahon, 1907) based on **Rolf Boldrewood**'s bushranging novel.

During the silent phase of Australian film-making, filmmakers consistently used literary sources for adaptation into film scripts. Preferred themes included bushranging, convictism, and aspects of pioneering and life in the bush. *Robbery under Arms* was remade several times, as was *For the Term of His Natural Life*, based on **Marcus Clarke**'s novel; its definitive silent version is the meandering 1927 epic directed by Norman Dawn.

Raymond Longford, the greatest of Australian silent directors, with collaborator Lottie Lyell, adapted **Steele Rudd**'s stories *On Our Selection* (1920) and *Rudd's New Selection* (1921). Longford directed the classic Australian silent film, *The Sentimental Bloke* (1919), based on **C. J. Dennis**' verse narrative *The Songs of a Sentimental Bloke*. In less memorable adaptations, some **Henry Lawson** stories were brought to the screen in *While the Billy Boils* (1921) and *Joe* (1924) by director Beaumont Smith. Other silent adaptations included **Katharine Susannah Prichard**'s *The Pioneers* (in 1916 and 1926) and Steele Rudd's *The Romance of Runnibede* (director, Scott K. Dunlap, 1927).

During the first sound film phase from 1930 to 1960, a different trend emerged. Until 1950, most films were from original screenplays, though they were sometimes loosely based on literature — the four Dad and Dave movies directed by Ken G. Hall for Cinesound, for example. Hugely popular, these films bore little resemblance to Rudd's original characters.

After 1950 literary adaptations became more frequent. A pattern of foreign-controlled co-productions developed through the decade 1950–1960. *Robbery under Arms* was remade in 1957 by British director Leslie Norman, who also directed films of **D'Arcy Niland**'s *The Shiralee* in 1957 and **Ray Lawler**'s *Summer of the Seventeenth Doll* in 1959. American companies, too, made location films in Australia based on local literature. Stanley Kramer directed the film of Nevil Shute's *On the Beach* (1959), while Fred Zinnemann had more success achieving an Australian tone in *The Sundowners* (1960), based on **Jon Cleary**'s novel. One notable local production, *Three in One* (director, Cecil Holmes, 1956), was largely based on stories by Lawson and **Frank Hardy**.

While the 1960s saw a decline in Australian productions, overseas filmmakers continued adapting Australian fiction in location films, with Michael Powell directing John O'Grady's *They're a Weird Mob* (1966) and **Norman Lindsay**'s *Age of Consent* (1969). However, the most notable foreign contributions came in 1971 with Ted Kotcheff's version of *Wake in Fright*, based on Kenneth Cook's 1961 novel, and Nicholas Roeg's version of James Vance Marshall's children's story *Walkabout*.

These films influenced the young directors who would spark the Australian film revival, such as Peter Weir, who filmed **Joan Lindsay**'s 1967 novel *Picnic at Hanging Rock* in 1975. This film marked the start of the 'new wave' of Australian films, foreshadowed in such earlier films as Tim Burstall's *Stork* (1971), scripted by **David Williamson**, and Michael Thornhill's *Between Wars*

(1974), scripted by **Frank Moorhouse**.

David Williamson's credits extend from *Stork*, through a range of adaptations of his plays in the 1970s and the original screenplay *Gallipoli* (director, David Weir, 1981), to *Travelling North* (director, Carl Schultz, 1986) and *Emerald City* (director, Chris Thomson, 1989). Along with Bob Ellis, Cliff Green, Peter Yeldham, Tony Morphett, and Eleanor Witcombe, Williamson is in the front rank of Australian screen writers.

The halcyon days of the revival, in the later 1970s and early 1980s, included adaptations of Ronald McKie's *The Mango Tree* (director, Kevin Dobson), **Patrick White**'s *The Night, the Prowler* (director, Jim Sharman), **Thomas Keneally**'s *The Chant of Jimmie Blacksmith* (director, Fred Schepisi), **Miles Franklin**'s *My Brilliant Career* (director, Gillian Armstrong), **A. B. Paterson**'s *The Man from Snowy River* (director, George Miller), **Helen Garner**'s *Monkey Grip* (director, Ken Cameron) and **Christopher Koch**'s *The Year of Living Dangerously* (director, David Weir).

During the later 1980s, some weightier works of fiction about Australia such as D. H. Lawrence's *Kangaroo* (director, Tim Burstall, 1987) and **Christina Stead**'s *For Love Alone* (director, Chris Thomson) were filmed, without great success. The use of more popular fiction as sources for adaptation continues with **Peter Corris**' *The Empty Beach* (director, Chris Thomson, 1986) and Criena Rohan's *The Delinquents* (director, Chris Thomson, 1989).

BRUCE MOLLOY

Further reading: Brian McFarlane, *Words and Images: Australian Novels into Films* (1983); Bruce Molloy, *Before the Interval: Australian Film 1930–1960* (1990).

FILM AND LITERATURE (Canada)

English-language film-making in Canada has always been a fragile enterprise, under competing influences from both the USA and Britain. While Hollywood shaped and controlled the mass entertainment market, Canadian public policy drew on British models and experience to use film to develop a distinctive cultural identity. Contacts between Canadian literature and film, however, have been sporadic. Early film-makers appealed to nationalist sentiment with undertakings to adapt Canadian stories, but although themes and locations were Canadian, writers and film-makers were usually American. One exception was Ernest Shipman's series of Canadian adaptations of popular pioneer novels in the early 1920s.

One alternative to a faltering private industry lay in federal cultural institutions, inspired by British models but mandated to propagate a national cultural identity. In 1939 John Grierson, the father of British documentary, founded the National Film Board (NFB). In 1952 the Canadian Broadcasting Corporation (CBC) expanded to include television. The NFB first concentrated on documentary and so literary content was limited to filming authors' biographies and interviews. For many years CBC's television drama was broadcast live from the studio. Some Canadian plays reached a wide audience and writers such as **David French** and **George Ryga** wrote for television. (See **Broadcasting**, Canada.)

As the NFB developed fictional film-making in the 1960s, it began adapting Canadian short stories with strong regional content by writers such as **W. O. Mitchell** and **Sinclair Ross**, and this has continued intermittently. When CBC Television began to use film for drama production, location shooting and documentary techniques combined with the social purpose of the national mandate to produce social realism and topical 'docudramas' (dramatized documentaries) in anthology series such as 'For the Record' (1975–86). Examples include **David Fennario**'s *On the Job* (1976), **Rick Salutin**'s *Maria* (1977), and **Carol Bolt**'s *One Night Stand* (1978), all directed by documentarist Allan King. Novelists **Margaret Atwood** and **Timothy Findley** also contributed screenplays. Experimental theatre appeared — for example, the improvised 'docudrama' *The Farm Show*, whose 1973 tour became the basis of **Michael Ondaatje**'s 1974 film *The Clinton Special*. Costume drama series based on dynastic novels such as *The Forsyte Saga* found a Canadian equivalent in the ill-fated 'The Whiteoaks of Jalna' (1971–2), from Findley's scripts of **Mazo de la Roche**'s novels; in the 1980s, adaptations of **Lucy Maud Montgomery**'s *Anne of Green Gables*, and other works directed by Kevin Sullivan, were internationally successful.

In 1967 federal investment became available for private-sector theatrical production, and literary works offered prospects of commercial success. Adaptations included both plays (**John Herbert**'s *Fortune and Men's Eyes*, Harvey Hart, 1971; William Fruet's *Wedding in White*, Fruet, 1972) and novels (**Mordecai Richler**'s *The Apprenticeship of Duddy Kravitz*, Ted Kotcheff, 1974; **Hugh Mac Lennan**'s *Two Solitudes*, Lionel Chetwynd, 1978; Atwood's *Surfacing*, Claude Jutra, 1981; Findley's *The Wars*, Robin Phillips, 1983; and Joan Barfoot's *Dancing in the Dark*, Leon Marr, 1986).

More recently, closer integration of film-making and television distribution has led to new forms: television mini-series that spawned shorter theatrical versions, and short stories packaged as television series and as educational films. The former most notably includes Richler's *Joshua Then and Now* (Kotcheff, 1985). Atlantis Films of Toronto adapted short stories by Callaghan, **Hugh Garner**, **W. P. Kinsella**, **Margaret Laurence**, **Alice Munro**, Richler, and Sinclair Ross.

English-Canadian writers have worked more closely in television drama and film than in theatrical film-making. One exception is dramatist Ted Allan, whose film scripts include *Lies My Father Told Me* (Jan Kadar, 1975) and *Bethune* (Borsos, 1990).

DAVID CLANDFIELD

Further reading: David Clandfield, *Canadian Film* (1987).

FILM AND LITERATURE (India)

Although India has become the biggest producer of films in the world, Indian film-makers, by and large, have seldom looked to literature to provide the subjects of their films. A striking exception to this is Satyajit Ray, by common consent India's greatest film-maker. With the sole exception of the Bengali-language *Ganashatru* ('An Enemy of the People', 1989), based on Henrik Ibsen's *An Enemy of the People* (1882) but wholly Indianized in content, nearly all of Ray's major films — for example, his famous Apu Trilogy, consisting of *Pather Panchali* ('Song of the Little Road, 1955), *Aparajito* ('The Unvanquished', 1956), and *Apur Sansar* ('The World of Apu', 1959) — are based on classics of Indian literature. The Apu Trilogy is based on two novels by Bibhutibhushan Banerjee (*Pather Panchali*, 1929, and *Aparajito*, 1932), but the filmic adaptations involve not only dramatic compression, elision, and omissions but also additions. The now-celebrated train sequence in *Pather Panchali*, for instance, so cleverly intercut with the death of old Indir, is Ray's own dramatic gloss on the seemingly random sequence of events in the novel. *Apur Sansar* shows an even freer adaptation from Banerjee's *Aparajito*, for Ray's Apu is an altogether more refined and sensitive character than that of the original. While in the novel Apu reacts with an almost exaggerated calm to the death of his young wife in childbirth, Ray's hero is so convulsed with grief that he strikes his brother-in-law in a rare gesture of violence for a Ray film.

Control of emotion, however, is central to Ray's aesthetic, which is unashamedly classical, as he himself states in his critical collection *Our Films, Their Films* (1976): 'If classical implies an orderly unfolding of events with a beginning, a middle and an end — *in that order*; a firm rein applied to emotion; and an avoidance of disorientation for its own sake, then I will only be too happy with the label.' Sometimes, however, this 'reining in' of emotion increases the aesthetic distance so markedly that a certain cerebral coldness follows. This happens in *Ashani Sanket* ('Distant Thunder', 1973), based on yet another Banerjee novel, *Asani Sanket* (1959), in which a studied avoidance of the suffering of the victims of the devastating Bengal famine of 1943 (which claimed an estimated three million lives) gives the impression that Ray is more concerned with causes than effects.

More frequently, however, Ray's emotional restraint leads to some of his greatest triumphs. In *The Postmaster* — the first of the three-part *Teen Kanya* (1961), containing 'The Postmaster', 'Monihara' ('The Lost Jewels'), and 'Samapti' ('The Conclusion'), all three of which are based on some early turn-of-the-century short stories by India's lone Nobel laureate for literature, **Rabindranath Tagore** — Ray's restraint is masterly. Instead of making the little girl, Ratan, plead with the departing postmaster, begging him to take her with him as in the Tagore original, Ray admirably underplays her hurt, opting instead to focus on the hero's dilemma. The effect is a rather subdued, yet crushing pathos. Significantly, in the same year (the Tagore centenary year), Ray produced a full-length documentary, *Rabindranath Tagore* (1961), signalling the start of a lifelong commitment to the work of the Bengali literary giant. *Charulata* ('The Lonely Wife', 1964) is vintage Ray and marks the peak of his cinematic career; yet another Tagore work, the novella *Nastanirh* (1901), provides the basic story material. A few psychological weaknesses and gaps in the original are neatly ironed out in Ray's near-perfect screenplay, which reveals the essentially tragic nature of human love. One weakness of the original is the lack of appropriate buildup for a crucial plot turn — Umapada's treachery — and the other is the husband's 'marathon incomprehension' (the phrase is Ray's own) of his wife's involvement with his own brother, Amal. At the end of the Tagore story, Bhupati, the husband, leaves his wife, Charu, for ever, but in Ray's film there is more than a hint of imminent reconciliation, if essential alienation, between the estranged couple.

After a lapse of nearly twenty years, Ray returned to Tagore for the subject of his film *Ghare Baire* ('The Home and the World'), based on the novel of the same title, published in 1915 and sadly the least satisfactory of his literary adaptations. Perhaps he is not entirely to blame. Opinions about the Tagore original have always been divided: Bertolt Brecht approved, but his contemporary Georg Lukacs loathed the novel when it first appeared in English translation. Because the action is insufficiently dramatized, the characters appear as mere mouthpieces of the author's philosophy. These faults are hardly mitigated in Ray's wordy screenplay, but the chief difficulty lies in the portrayal of the protagonist, Nikhil. In the Tagore original he is presented as flawed but all-too-human; in the film Nikhil seems a veritable plaster saint set on an impossibly high pedestal.

Several other noted Indian film-makers have produced adaptations from literature, in various Indian and European languages. Some of the best films on Indian subjects have been produced by the Ismail Merchant-James Ivory team, and at least two of them — *The Householder* (1963) and *Heat and Dust* (1983), which had an international cast, including Greta Scacchi and Julie Christie — are entirely based on the novels of the German-born **Ruth Prawer Jhabvala** (*The Householder*, 1960, and *Heat and Dust*, 1975), who has lived in New Delhi, India, for many years.

Aside from Jhabvala, **R. K. Narayan** is the only contemporary Indian novelist of distinction whose work has provided the basis for Indian films. Four of his novels have been made into films; the best known of them, *The Guide* (1958), was adapted to film in 1965, both in Hindi and English (the English version titled simply *Guide*).

The film was co-produced by Bombay movie mogul Dev Anand and Nobel laureate Pearl S. Buck, who also wrote the screenplay. Narayan was assured 'a hundred-percent-Indian story, with a hundred-percent-Indian cast, and a hundred-percent-Indian setting for an international audience'. The Indo-American film was widely publicized, since it was made in wide screen and in colour and at great cost. However, Narayan took exception to the film in a hilariously satirical essay, 'Misguided Guide', published in *Life* magazine (15 May 1969). He was appalled by the extravagance of the locations (princely Jaipur and Udaipur amid the arid deserts of the state of Rajasthan instead of humble, fictitious Malgudi whose 'geography and sociology' were known to thousands of Narayan's admirers all over the world). To Narayan's further chagrin, the plot also underwent 'drastic changes', and two of the major characters suffered a minor metamorphosis. Rosie, for example, appears suddenly at the end of the film to throw herself at the feet of the dying hero. In the event, the film is rather unsatisfactory and the tantalizing ambiguity at the end of the book is wholly lost.

The 1988 film *Swamy* (based on a Hindi television serial of Narayan's earliest book, *Swami and Friends*, 1935), directed by the late Shankar Nag, was shown at the London Film Festival. *Banker Margayya*, the 1984 film version (in Kannada) of Narayan's *The Financial Expert* (1952), has elicited unstinted praise for its director, T. S. Nagabharana, from Narayan himself, who found the storyline 'fully achieved'. Perhaps Narayan's views on the relation between film and literature may strike one today as rather conservative. Aesthetically, he clings to a strict bourgeois realism in the portrayal of both people and places. For him, violation of the unities of action and place is a serious matter. Narayan's reflections on cinema (scattered throughout his two recent collections, *A Writer's Nightmare: Selected Essays, 1958–1988*, 1988, and *A Story-Teller's World*, 1989) reveal a neo-classical outlook wholly at variance with that of most contemporary Indian film-makers, with the sole exception of Satyajit Ray, who would appear to share much of Narayan's orthodox outlook.

T. G. VAIDYANATRAN

FILM AND LITERATURE (New Zealand)
Because of the nation's relatively small population and its fitful production of feature films, the term 'film industry' in reference to New Zealand can be used accurately only when discussing the new wave of film-making from 1977 onwards. More than sixty feature films were made between 1975 and 1985, whereas only three had appeared in the previous thirty years. While the percentage of New Zealand feature films that are adaptations of literature is currently about average (twenty-five per cent), this rate was higher in the late 1970s, when there were even fewer scriptwriters and less confidence in original screenplays than is the case in the 1990s. Holding up an existing book in front of reluctant investors made it easier to get financial backing, a situation typical in a new film industry.

Initially, television was important. When television broadcasting began in New Zealand in 1960, it was under government control. As a result, there was some opportunity during the period for objectives other than commercial ones to hold sway; there was the possibility that adaptations of serious literary works could be approved. The first television adaptation of New Zealand literature was the trail-blazing Winners and Losers series — adaptations of short stories by **Katherine Mansfield**, **John A. Lee**, **Maurice Duggan**, **Barry Crump**, **Maurice Shadbolt**, and **Witi Ihimaera** screened in 1975 and 1976. Winners and Losers set high standards of cinematography, editing, and acting. However, in comparison with countries such as Australia, which has a tradition of turning its classic popular novels into miniseries, not much literature has been adapted for television in New Zealand. (See **Film and Literature**, Australia.) *The God Boy* (1976), from **Ian Cross**' 1957 novel of the same title, is a notable exception; it is, in fact, the only adult novel ever fully adapted on New Zealand television. The film was made at a time when, briefly, commercial pressures were absent from the government-funded channel responsible.

During the 1980s government policy was to lessen public involvement in many activities, including television, by turning government enterprises into public corporations or State Owned Enterprises (S.O.E.s). Television New Zealand (TVNZ) is now an S.O.E. required to be businesslike, to compete with private channels, and to make a profit. This has meant that decisions to produce adaptations from serious literature are far less likely than under the old order. With this 'corporatisation', private investment is now necessary, and the economic downturn has effectively vitiated that avenue of sponsorship. Attempts to make major series out of classics of New Zealand realism such as **Bill Pearson**'s *Coal Flat* (1963) and Maurice Shadbolt's *Strangers and Journeys* (1972) have never raised sufficient money. A very successful 1981 series was made from the children's novel *Under The Mountain* (1979), by **Maurice Gee**, the one New Zealand novelist who has turned to writing original film scripts.

One potential new source of finance is 'New Zealand on Air', a government body empowered to spend some $25 million NZ a year in compulsory broadcasting fees collected from owners of TV sets. 'New Zealand on Air' is charged with encouraging the portrayal of New Zealand 'culture' on television. However, it has yet to invest in any literary adaptations other than *An Angel at My Table* (1990), a three-hour version of **Janet Frame**'s autobiographical trilogy. Director Jane Campion won widespread international acclaim and several film festival awards for this work.

Following their Winners and Losers, directors Ian Mune and Roger Donaldson turned to films, making *Sleeping Dogs* (1977) from **C. K. Stead**'s *Smith's Dream* (1971; rev. 1973). As the first film of the new wave, *Sleeping Dogs* was very important in film history, despite its fudging of the novel's political analysis in its adherence to the conventions of the buddy-movie genre. Other notable adaptations in succeeding years included Timothy White's and Vincent Ward's 1978 film *A State of Siege*, of Janet Frame's 1966 novel of the same title, made while they were university students, and **Sue McCauley**'s *Other Halves* (1984), the only example of a novelist adapting her own work (*Other Halves*, 1982) for the screen. In *Came A Hot Friday* (1985), a highly successful version of **Ronald Hugh Morrieson**'s 1964 novel of the same title, director Ian Mune ruthlessly pared away the book's complexity, emphasizing its comedy. Morrieson has in fact been the most adapted of all New Zealand authors; his novels *The Scarecrow* (1963) and *Pallet on the Floor* (1976) were released as films, with the same titles, in 1982 and 1986, respectively.

BRIAN McDONNELL

Further reading: Nicholas Reid, *A Decade of New Zealand Film* (1986).

FILM AND LITERATURE (South Africa)

Historically, South African literature and cinema in English and Afrikaans have been closely related. Between 1916 and 1922, when African Film Productions made thirty-seven epic features of high technical quality rivalling those of D. W. Griffith, narratives were rooted in jingoism. Boer and Briton stood together under the flag of 'unity' and civilization against 'barbaric' tribes. *De Voortrekkers/Winning a Continent* (1916, Dutch/English intertitles), about the 1836 Great Trek by Afrikaners to escape British occupation of the Cape, was scripted by Afrikaner historian and language activist Gustav Preller. This film inspired the making of *The Covered Wagon* (1923). *Symbol of*

Sacrifice (1918), about the 1879 Zulu-British wars, employed 25,000 Zulu warriors. Films based on **Henry Rider Haggard**'s novels were *King Solomon's Mines* (1918) and *Allan Quatermain* (1919); other films adapted from novels include John Buchan's *Prester John* (1920) and H. de Vere Stacpoole's *The Blue Lagoon* (1923).

An amateur movement of Afrikaner Nationalists in the late 1930s mobilized cinema to oppose jingoism. By filming memorials and venerating folk heroes, the Nationalists attempted to re-create a nostalgic pastoralism destroyed by the two Anglo-Boer Wars and the resulting Afrikaner trek to the cities between 1880 and 1940. The second war (1899–1902) specifically forced them to labour for the enemy in the cities. *'n Nasie Hou Koors* ('A Nation Holds Course', 1939) documented the centennial re-enactment of the Great Trek in 1938, an event that re-kindled the Afrikaner cause. Working within the *Reddingsdaadbond* ('Salvation Brotherhood'), these amateurs saw themselves as the saviours of Afrikaner culture. They were the first to film the novels of hallowed Afrikaner writers such as C. J. Langenhoven's *Donker Spore* ('Dark Trails', 1944). These film-makers derived their aesthetic inspiration from Soviet cinema of the 1920s, but took their political cue from German Nazi cinema. Arising out of this moment is Jamie Uys' only serious film, *Doodkry is Min* ('They Can't Keep Us Down', 1961), made to commemorate the 'Wonder of Afrikaans' and the economic defeat of British imperialism with the establishment of a Republic in 1961.

A state subsidy scheme introduced in 1956 generated a spurt of production that lasted well into the late 1970s. Most were cheap films aimed at small-town Afrikaan-speaking viewers and the uncritical patrons of drive-ins. Of the 289 films made between 1967 and 1979, those by Emil Nofal and Jans Rautenbach stand out. *Wild Season* (1967) trashed the *Reddingsdaadbond* cultural stereotype of the Afrikaner. *Die Kandidaat* ('The Candidate', 1968) shredded the idea of Afrikaner unity and purity. *Katrina* (1969), from Basil Warner's play 'Try for White' (premièred 1959), exposed traumas of love across the colour-line. Rautenbach's *Jannie Totsiens* ('Goodbye Johnny', 1970) derived from the *Sestiger*'s era — the 1960s, when aesthetically radical Afrikaans writers questioned received political myths, genres, and conventions. Rautenbach tried to pull the imperatives of this 1960s' writers movement into 1970s' film-making by naming his company *Seventig* ('Seventy'). *Jannie Totsiens*, aesthetically derived from this short-lived movement, is an expressionist allegory confronting the psychological and physical prisons within which white South Africans had chained themselves.

Ross Devenish's and **Athol Fugard**'s dramas, *Boesman and Lena* (1969), *The Guest* (1971), and *Marigolds in August* (1980), offer neo-realist interpretations of interracial issues. *The Guest* exposes a drug-racked episode in the life of Eugene Marais, an Afrikaner folk hero and 'founder' of the Afrikaans-language. Their television film about the making of the play, *Athol Fugard: a Lesson from Aloes* (1980), documents in stark *cinéma vérité* the trials of cross-racial play-making under apartheid. To most white audiences of the time, however, the characterizations, motivations, and images offered by Rautenbach and Fugard failed to match white racial stereotypes and world views. The use of expressionism and neo-realism to which they had been previously exposed was another alienating factor. Condemnation by fanatical, influential watchdogs and arbitrary state censorship intimidated financiers and distributors. Fugard's fourth feature is *The Road to Mecca* (1990), directed by Peter Goldsmid. It narrates the story of an eccentric woman sculptor in the Karoo who becomes alienated from the conservative religious townspeople.

The dominant genre in Afrikaans cinema began with *Debbie* (1965), ending with *April '80*

(1980). Symbolically rooted in the social upheaval of Afrikaners during the urban trek, the trajectory of this genre can be traced through early twentieth-century high Afrikaans literature, mid-century popular Afrikaans (similar to Mills and Boon) genres, radio soaps, film, and television. The city locates the site of struggle between pastoral Afrikaners and 'alien' industrial forces symbolized by English-speakers in the city. Afrikaners are 'insiders'. 'Outsiders' are English-speakers who represent imperialist domination, or communism. These themes are symbolically resolved through love affairs between insiders and outsiders. Class restructuring of a maturing economy in the 1960s and 1970s saw a *rapprochement* between English and Afrikaner from the early 1970s on. The cinematic insider-outsider axis shifted correspondingly. With the onset of the militarist state, the outsider became black, allied to naïve English-speaking liberal student activists. The emphasis was no longer on insider-outsider relationships, but on relations between insiders in the context of a war against the 'outside'. Like early South African cinema, English and Afrikaner again stand together under the flag of 'unity' against a barbaric — now communist — destroyer of white civilization.

The late 1980s witnessed a cinema consistently critical of apartheid and South African history. Examples are *Jock of the Bushveld* (1986), directed by Gray Hofmyer and based on **Percy Fitzpatrick**'s 1907 novel of that title, and two films based on works by Daleen Mathee — *Fiela's Child* (1987), directed by Katinka Heyns, and *Circles in the Forest* (1988), directed by Regardt van den Bergh. Mathee's films, set in the Knysna forest, deal with the early racist British administrations. *The Honey Bird* (1980), a made-for-television film directed by Alan Nathanson and based on the **Stuart Cloete** short story of that title, brings death to a white farmer who refuses two Bushmen water. *The Native Who Caused all the Trouble* (1989), directed by Manie van Rensburg from the play by Nicholas Haysom, deals with dispossession. White working-class racial prejudice is the theme of *Saturday Night at the Palace* (1987), directed by Robert Davies, from the play scripted by Bill Flynn and Paul Slabolepszy.

KEYAN G. TOMASELLI

Further reading: Keyan G. Tomaselli, 'Capital and culture in South African cinema: jingoism, nationalism and the historical epic', *Wide Angle* 3 (1986); Keyan G. Tomaselli, *The Cinema of Apartheid: Race and Class in South African Cinema* (1988).

FILM AND LITERATURE (West Africa)
Film production in West Africa, as with much of contemporary African culture, has been greatly influenced by institutions created in the colonial period. In 1935 the British created the Bantu Educational Cinema Experiment for the purpose of educating Africans. By 1939 the British had expanded the operation, establishing Colonial Film Units in their colonies, including Ghana and Nigeria. These units initially distributed propaganda films during the Second World War, but later they produced films on British manners and technology. In 1949 a film school was founded at Accra, Ghana, for the purpose of creating an indigenous production unit that would make films more palatable to African tastes. Still under British direction, the Ghana Gold Coast Film Unit produced various films, including Sean Graham's *The Boy Kumasenu* (1952), a successful portrayal of city life. With independence in 1957 President Nkrumah nationalized the film industry and employed a group of foreign directors to produce a series of documentaries and propaganda films, all of which were confiscated when Nkrumah was overthrown in 1966. One of the classics of this period was *Tongo Hamile* ('The Tongo Hamlet', 1965), an adaptation of *Hamlet*.

The Ghana Film Corporation was established in 1969; its director, Sam Aryetey, produced and directed *No Tears for Ananse* (1968), drawing upon popular folk mythology. Other film-makers who followed include Egbert Adjesu (*I Told You So*, 1970), King Ampaw (*They Call It Love*, 1972), and the most successful of all, Kwaw Ansah, whose film *Love Brewed in an African Pot* (1981), in which the common theme of the clash between modern and traditional values highlights a love romance, enjoyed wide popularity. Both Ampaw and Ansah established their independence, seeking to make entertaining films, although Ansah's historical *Heritage Africa* (1987) gives a more serious treatment of Africans' conflicts about identity.

Film production in Nigeria also emerged out of the crucible of the Colonial Film Unit. With the creation of television programming, under the direction of Segun Olusola, adaptations of plays by Jean-Paul Sartre, **Wole Soyinka**, **Duro Lapido**, and J. P. Clark (**Bekederemo**) were aired. Olusola co-produced the original script of *Son of Africa* in 1970. At the same time, the independent film-maker Francis Oladele adapted Soyinka's play *Kongi's Harvest* (1967), directed by Ossie Davis and starring Soyinka in the role of Kongi. Oladele's second adaptation, *Bullfrog in the Sun*, based on **Chinua Achebe**'s *Things Fall Apart* (1958) and *No Longer at Ease* (1960), followed in 1972. One of the more interesting state productions was Amadu Halilu's *Shaihu Umar* (1967), an epic history of the Hausa religious leader, based on the 1955 Hausa novel of the same title, written by Nigeria's first prime minister, Sir Abubakar Tafawa-Balewa. These early Nigerian efforts are not considered durable works.

The most prominent director, Ola Balogun, has also produced films, creating a large and respectable corpus, including *Black Goddess* (1979), about ex-slaves who returned to Nigeria after gaining freedom; *Cry Freedom* (1981), about the liberation movement in Kenya, based on **Meja Mwangi**'s novel *Carcase for Hounds* (1974); *Aiye* (1979), co-produced with Chief Herbert Ogunde and based on a play written by Ogunde, about the struggle between a traditional healer and an evil sorcerer; *Orun Mooru* (1982); and *Money Power* (1984).

The popular films of Eddie Ugbomah include *The Rise and Fall of Dr. Oyenusi* (1977), the story of a Lagos gangster, and other films of suspense. Wole Soyinka has also produced a feature film of his own, *Blues for the Prodigal* (1985).

A large and successful national industry has been created in Nigeria, with directors appealing to popular tastes, while government support for distribution and production has made it possible to resist the monopolistic conditions of western control that continue to prevail in much of the rest of Africa.

KENNETH W. HARROW

Further reading: Manthia Diawara, *African Cinema: Politics and Culture* (1992).

FINDLEY, TIMOTHY (1930–)

Canadian novelist, dramatist, short-story writer

Born in Toronto, Canada, he grew up in the city's moneyed district of Rosedale, attending Rosedale Public School, St Andrew's College (a prestigious private school in Aurora, Ontario), and Jarvis Collegiate (Toronto). In his initial career as an actor, he was a charter member of the Stratford (Ontario) Festival company, a graduate of London's Central School of Speech and Drama, and a contract player with H. M. Tennent (London, England); he played on Broadway and on national (USA) tour with Ruth Gordon in Thornton Wilder's *The Matchmaker*.

After a prolific and award-winning period as a script-writer (mainly documentaries) for the Canadian Broadcasting Corporation (CBC), Findley began writing fiction and plays full-time and moved into his present home (outside Toronto) with William Whitehead (co-author of several CBC scripts, including *The National Dream*, based on Pierre Berton's history of the Canadian National Railway). His short stories, collected in *Dinner Along the Amazon* (1984) and *Stones* (1988), appeared as early as 1956, and he began writing novels in the 1960s, but *The Wars* (1977) established his reputation as one of Canada's best writers. His many awards include a Governor General's Award for Fiction (for *The Wars*), the Canadian Authors' Association Literary Award, the Canadian National Institute for the Blind Talking Book of the Year Award, the Canada-Australia Literary Prize, and the Mystery Writers of America Edgar Allan Poe Award. He has received honorary degrees and writer-in-residence appointments from several Canadian universities; he was the chair of The Writers' Union of Canada, president of the English-Canadian Centre of PEN International, and is an Officer of the Order of Canada.

Findley is of a generation of Commonwealth writers who were born into the dying days of empire and 'old world' wealth; as such, he writes both out of and against a colonial inheritance, and as a Canadian, he writes out of and against American imperialism. He is also of a generation who came of age in a world of war on an unprecedented scale; his writing is located, then, in a complex politico-cultural matrix of disintegrating master narratives, the effects of which are still with us.

While *The Last of the Crazy People* (1967) and *The Butterfly Plague* (1969; rev. 1986) remain largely unknown, they are consistent with his later work and with his plays — *The Paper People* (television drama, 1967), *Can You See Me Yet?* (1977), and 'John A. Himself!' (premièred 1979) — in their obsession with politics past and present and in their exposure of the actual and discursive violence done by masculine, imperial, colonial, and fascist systems. The first novel deconstructs, through a child's eyes, the exclusionary practices of the colonial Canadian upper-middle class. *The Butterfly Plague* juxtaposes Germany's Third Reich and the Hollywood film industry from the 1920s through the 1940s to demonstrate that the line between nationalism and fascism may be indistinguishable.

The Wars (made into a film in 1983) deconstructs the world of empire through a young Canadian soldier's experience at the front in the First World War. Against the backdrop of familial conflict and disintegrating Edwardian elegance (it gives way to alcoholism, madness, and violence), the novel powerfully indicts the 'glory' of empire and the 'heroism' of war, and graphically depicts the rape of land, animals, and youth that such national (and masculine) discourses perpetrate. Through diaries, tape-recorded oral histories, descriptions of personal photographs, and feminine/feminist narrators, the novel articulates a discourse counter to 'official' history.

Famous Last Words (1981; adapted as a CBC radio drama in 1988) uses filmic and historical intertexts as sites for exposing the ideological operations of German and Italian fascism and American imperialism in the Second World War. It boldly fictionalizes a fascist cabal, among whose members are the Duke and Duchess of Windsor, Charles Lindbergh, and Ezra Pound's Hugh Selwyn Mauberley, to show how cultural texts (including royal personages) are part of the operations of ideology; no one remains unscathed in this exposure, perhaps not even the novel itself, which self-consciously relies on the artifices of film and mythology that the world powers, especially the USA, used during the Second World War.

Not Wanted on the Voyage (1984) is a humorous but angry rewriting of the biblical story of the Flood and Findley's most powerful indictment of the western world's arbitrary hierarchization of the genders, the species, and their corresponding modes of response to history. The royal 'we' of the biblical (and colonial) patriarchy replicates aboard the ark the apparatus of church, state, and armoury; the novel's anachronistic style shows how the 'developed' world's androcentrism, anthropocentrism, heterosexism, racism, and imperialism are continuous with biblical and colonial systems. The plebeian 'them' who are kept below decks are clearly (but not utopianly) privileged as members of a community where difference is embraced and where horizontal relations rather than vertical laws motivate action and sustain life.

The Telling of Lies: A Mystery (1986) is a detective story set in the 1970s and 1980s, but the murders are multiple and have been committed much earlier: Findley explores 'how' (not 'who') the nuclear murders committed in Hiroshima and Nagasaki and the brainwashing military experiments conducted in a Canadian hospital are a result of imperialism and racism, of the criminal egotism of 'progress' and the American 'salvation' of the 'free world', and of the equally criminal collusion of an apathetic populace.

Findley's political commitment and vision are reminiscent of those of South Africa's **J. M. Coetzee**, **André Brink**, and **Doris Lessing**, while his style is sometimes similar to the mannered social criticism of Australia's **Patrick White**, the easy theatricality of New Zealand's **Maurice Gee**, but also the evocative precision and horror of South Africa's **Nadine Gordimer**. As these names suggest, Findley is of that primarily white, middle- to upper-class generation of post-colonial writers in English who are aware of the contradictory position they occupy as privileged observers of history's injustices. His homosexuality mediates that privilege, however, while his fiction remains accessible, more versatile and self-reflexive, and his politics simultaneously more local and more searching of the relations between personal and public histories than those of his more canonized contemporaries.

His autobiographical writings are collected in *Inside Memory: Pages from a Writer's Workbook* (1990).

DONNA PALMATEER PENNEE

Further reading: Diana Brydon, 'Timothy Findley: a post-holocaust, post-colonial vision', in Robert L. Ross (ed.) *International Literature in English: Essays on the Major Writers* (1991).

FINLAYSON, RODERICK (1904–92)
New Zealand short-story writer
He was born in Auckland, New Zealand, and, except for occasional visits abroad, he lived there all his life. In his youth he was close to several extended Maori families who lived near an uncle's farm where he stayed. His first stories were on Maori themes, and his characters, in contrast to those in earlier New Zealand fiction, were notable in being neither romanticized nor comic. In recent decades Maori writers have told their own stories. It was not so then, and Finlayson's were the first to embody a bleak view of the effect on Maori society of landlessness, tribal disintegration, and urban migration, notwithstanding the resilience and good humour of many individuals. These stories were published in *Brown Man's Burden* (1938) and *Sweet Beulah Land* (1942) and reprinted in *Brown Man's Burden and Later Stories* (edited by **Bill Pearson**, 1973).

Finlayson was one of two writers who, in the 1930s, set the New Zealand short story on a new path — the other, **Frank Sargeson**, was the major talent and better-known name. Finlayson began publishing stories two or three years after Sargeson and had a more modest career and reputation, but in more than half a century he remained remarkably consistent in his vision and technique, both of which are more direct and less artful than Sargeson's.

Finlayson held that industrial capitalism was equally inimical to warmth and spontaneity in Pakeha life and to the health of the natural environment. An early conservationist, his views were expressed in a brief essay, *Our Life in This Land* (1940), in a number of stories, and in a serio-comic novel, *Tidal Creek* (1948). The impact of Europeans and especially of evangelical missionaries on Polynesian islanders is the theme of his other novel, *The Schooner Came to Atia* (1952). Finlayson's later stories and novellas include *Other Lovers* (1976) and *In Georgina's Shady Garden* (1988); he also wrote a historical novel for children, *The Springing Fern* (1965).

DENNIS McELDOWNEY

FITZGERALD, R. D. (1902–87)

Australian poet

Born Robert David FitzGerald at Hunters Hill, Sydney, Australia, he lived there for most of his life. After briefly studying science at the University of Sydney, he worked as a surveyor, an occupation that provided resource material for some of his extended poems. One of Australia's leading poets of his generation, Fitzgerald was named an officer of the Order of the British Empire in 1951; in 1982 he was made a member of the Order of Australia. In 1965 he shared the Encyclopaedia Brittanica Award. In 1985 he was awarded an honorary Doctor of Letters degree from the University of Melbourne.

FitzGerald's work spanned fifty years and includes *The Greater Apollo: Seven Metaphysical Songs* (1927), *To Meet the Sun* (1929), *Moonlight Acre* (1938), *Heemskerck Shoals* (1949), *Between Two Tides* (1952), *This Night's Orbit* (1953), *The Wind at Your Door* (1959), *Southmost Twelve* (1962), *Selected Poems* (1963), *Of Some Country* (1963), *Forty Years' Poems* (1965), and *Product: Later Verses* (1977). He also published two collections of essays on poetry: *The Elements of Poetry* (1963) and *Of Places and Poetry* (1976).

FitzGerald's work is crucial to an understanding of Australian poetry from the 1930s to the 1950s, a period of decisive change and a great onrush of confidence in Australian writing. Although less spectacular in his technical and imaginative claims than his contemporary **Kenneth Slessor**, FitzGerald continued to develop his poetic talents long after Slessor abandoned poetry, and his persistence and dedication yielded not only major late works — 'The Wind at Your Door' is indisputably one of the major poems in Australian literature — but also an example of lifelong commitment to his craft that had no precursor in Australian literature and has been paralleled only by the careers of **A. D. Hope** and **Judith Wright**.

FitzGerald's attempts at lyrical writing — the dominant mode in Australian poetry for much of the twentieth century — are overshadowed by his meditative and semi-narrative works. 'Essay on Memory' — in *Moonlight Acre* — won the Australian Literature Society Gold Medal in 1938 and is generally considered the major Australian poem of the 1930s. The same volume contained another long poem, 'The Hidden Bole', a meditation on the quality of beauty. FitzGerald's knotty, compressed style can be seen to follow the line of Australian poetry initiated by **Christopher Brennan**, but in his two major narrative sequences, *Heemskerck Shoals* and *Between Two Tides*, his own personal means of expression reached maturity. Uncompromising and full of a shaggy sort of strength, this was a poetry that avoided glitter. Instead, it tugged and chewed on its material, and its very anti-lyricism showed an alternative to easier and more ingratiating verse styles.

FitzGerald's influence has been far-reaching and writers such as J. M. Couper, **Bruce Beaver**, **John Blight**, **Vincent Buckley**, and, to a certain extent, **Thomas Shapcott** and Grace Perry have reflected in varying degrees something of the architectural strength and determined thoughtfulness of FitzGerald's best writing. His preoccupation with time, a renegotiation with the past, and a consciousness of his role in defining an evolving Australian literature remained landmarks of the late poetic works, though the fascination with specific ancestry, so brilliantly explored in 'The Wind at Your Door', was to occupy him more and more. One of his most astonishing poems, 'The Face of the Waters' (in *This Night's Orbit*), remains unparalleled in his output for its genuine lyrical impulse coupled with the more characteristic meditative determination.

The common influence upon both FitzGerald and Slessor was the vitalist philosophy of artist **Norman Lindsay** in the 1920s. If Slessor's work imbibed some of the dandyism and self-conscious rollickry of Lindsay's attempt to graft onto the Australian environment what he thought of as a Greek hedonism, FitzGerald gained by accepting aspects of vitalism's determinist and anti-mystical mode, as well as through an access to poets admired by Lindsay such as Robert Browning and the medieval French poet François Villon. FitzGerald took what he needed from vitalism and imbued it with his own pragmatic surveyor's personality, but it was a personality that was acutely aware of environment and geography; to this he added his own increasing preoccupations with genetic mutations and inheritances.

THOMAS SHAPCOTT

Further reading: G. A. Wilkes, *R. D. FitzGerald* (1981); Julian Croft, ed., *Robert D. FitzGerald* (1987).

FITZPATRICK, SIR JAMES PERCY (1862–1931)
South African novelist, short-story writer

Born in King William's Town, Cape Colony, South Africa, of Irish parents, he completed his schooling in Cape Town. The son of a judge, he began his career in a Cape Town bank, but finding the work tedious and confining, Fitzpatrick seized the first opportunity to exchange his city job for a frontier existence in the newly established goldfields of the Transvaal Lowveld. The narrator of his most enduring work, the autobiographical *Jock of the Bushveld* (1907), recoils from the recollection of a city-bound existence: '"Not back to the cage! Not that!"' The image of the caged beast aptly reflects Fitzpatrick's major literary preoccupations: the romantic depiction, in his fiction, of pioneering imperialism, and the explicit support, in his political writing, of British expansionism.

In addition to *Jock of the Bushveld,* Fitzpatrick's other major literary success was a political pamphlet, *The Transvaal from Within: A Private Record of Public Affairs* (1899), which played a significant role in influencing British public opinion against the Transvaal in the crucial period prior to the Anglo-Boer War. His association with the Jameson Raid, an attempt by British-backed Rand mining magnates to seize the Witwatersrand goldfields from the Transvaal, led to a treason charge and a three-year abstinence from political activity. The publication of *The Transvaal from Within* represented a dramatic termination of Fitzpatrick's enforced silence.

Fitzpatrick's first book recounted an expedition through Mashonaland (now part of Zimbabwe) in 1891 and was a pioneering work both in theme and as a literary phenomenon. *Through Mashonaland with Pick and Pen* (1892) described a journey preparing the way for later expansionist ventures into the territory of the Mashona chief, Lobengula; it also became the first book to be printed and published on the Witwatersrand.

Fitzpatrick's pre-Boer War years on the eastern Transvaal gold diggings provided the material for *Jock of the Bushveld*, a South African classic and a classic animal story. The book has had a phenomenonally successful publication history, having remained in print since its first edition in 1907. (A film version was produced in 1986.) Episodic in structure, the book draws on Fitzpatrick's knowledge of the characters of the mining settlements and on his experience as a transport rider (ox-wagon haulier) between the Mozambican port of Lourenço Marques (now Maputo) and the eastern Transvaal mining towns of Barberton and Lydenberg. Rudyard Kipling, a close acquaintance, persuaded him to publish the stories of his experiences and to have artist Edmund Caldwell provide the illustrations.

Jock of the Bushveld belongs to a genre of animal stories written in the early 1900s primarily for children but infused with the spirit of pioneering virtues. Comparisons may be made with Jack London's *The Call of the Wild* (1903), which is located in the Klondike region, Canada, and although stylistically more accomplished, has a dog as protagonist, as well as with Rudyard Kipling's *Just So Stories* (1902) and **Ernest Thompson Seton**'s *Wild Animals I Have Known* (1898).

GRAHAM STEWART

Further reading: C. Niven, *Jock and Fitz* (1968).

FLORENTINO, ALBERTO (1931–)
Filipino dramatist

Born in Santa Rosa, Nueva Ecija, the Philippines, he attended the University of the East and the Far Eastern University, both in Manila. Florentino wrote his first play, 'The Memento', in 1953, and soon afterwards the well-known *The World Is an Apple* and *Cadaver*, which won the first prize and the first honorable mention, respectively, in 1954, the first year of the Palanca Memorial Awards for Drama. In 1957 he received another Palanca award for *The Dancers* and, in 1959, Arena Theater Playwriting Contest prizes for *Oli Impan* and 'Cavort with Angels'. *The World Is an Apple*, *Cadaver*, *The Dancers*, and *Oil Impan* were first published in *The World Is an Apple and Other Prize Plays* (1959).

Florentino's five award-winning plays brought to the attention of theatre audiences the denizens and slums of Tondo, and their struggle and poverty. According to **Severino Montano**, Florentino's drama offers a 'poetic vision of social protest'. Critic Leonard Casper writes in *The Wounded Diamond* (1964) that the appeal of Florentino's plays

> is not to organized charity nor to the Social Welfare Agency, but to any man with self-respect and self-knowledge who would be lessened by the symbolic death of any other man. Florentino is concerned with what the haves have not, and what the have-nots sometimes have.

Clear proof of the dominance of the English language in the theatre of the Philippines was the fact that Florentino's audiences accepted without question or discomfort the fact that his stevedores, prostitutes, and slum children were speaking correct and idiomatic English. Years later, these plays could be credibly staged only in Tagalog translation, and Florentino himself declared an end to writing in English. (See **Drama**, The Philippines.) He wrote plays for the Tagalog television drama series 'Balintataw', seventeen of which were published in 1973 as *Panahon ng Digma* ('Wartime'), *Memento Mori*, and *From Book to Stage*.

Florentino published some forty-five 'Peso Books', collections of poems and stories by Filipino writers in English and Filipino, thus making them available to a wide public at low prices, and a Storymasters series of slim collections of stories. These series include works by **Jose Garcia Villa**, **R. Zulueta da Costa**, Amador Daguio, **Francisco Arcellana**, **Arturo Rotor**, and Sinai Hamada. He currently writes on books for *The Manila Chronicle*.

DOREEN G. FERNANDEZ

FOGARTY, LIONEL (1957–)
Australian poet

He was born on the Aboriginal reserve of Cherbourg, in Queensland, Australia. Described by **Mudrooroo Narogin** as 'the most original Aboriginal poet in Australia', Fogarty rejected the white system that had imprisoned his people and enforced an education that denied their cultural existence. Resistance to white indoctrination is such a strong element in Fogarty's work that the few critics (Aboriginal and non-Aboriginal) who have grappled with his poetry have focused upon the demands it makes upon the reader. This approach, while apparently constructive in accommodating the meaning and significance of his words, is largely an abnegation of the writer's value in expressing the Aboriginal perspective. The language is justifiably difficult, for it is Fogarty's often-stated objective to exploit the limitations of white Australian English in explaining the dimensions of the suffering and abuse endured by Aborigines. Fogarty's publications include the poetry collections *Kargun* (1980), *Yoogum Yoogum* (1982), *Kudjela* (1983), and *Nguti* (1984).

The regional focus in Fogarty's verse is evoked by a continual reworking and reformulating of local themes directed at the (Murri) Aborigines' sense of spirituality (Aboriginality), which draws upon an affinity and identification with the land. It is to this extent that white readers problematize Fogarty's work at the level of semantics and grammatical constructions. Words for Fogarty become as manipulable as clay, creating distortions of the white-imposed reality. (To comprehend Fogarty's verse without conceding to the dominance of his perspective is to risk becoming abandoned in a wilderness of one's socialized ignorance.) The associative imagery exploited so well through **Wilson Harris**' metaphoric fusions of landscape and character are evident in Fogarty's willingness to project Aboriginal thought into the antagonistic setting of the English language.

Fogarty is one of several Aboriginal poets (from the more experienced **Kevin Gilbert** to the lesser-known Selwyn Hughes, also collected in *Inside Black Australia*, 1988, edited by Gilbert), whose uncompromising persistence provokes the white establishment to confront its cultural schizophrenia, as it struggles to affirm a spatial and spiritual identification with Australia (Aboriginaland).

CLIFF WATEGO

FOLKLORE

FOLKLORE (Australia)

Folklore is the unofficial practice and expression of distinctive social groups sharing common interest(s). It exists interdependently with the more formal, official aspects of any society and generates forms that often articulate points of view, situations, and linguistic configurations considered to be 'vulgar' or otherwise unacceptable. Folklore may be transmitted orally, by imitation or example, through mass media, and through art forms of all kinds, including literature. Australian writers who have utilized folklore in some contrived way are legion and include such diverse writers as **Henry Lawson**, **A. B. Paterson**, **David Malouf**, and **David Ireland**. Folklore also features in less meditated modes in other genres, particularly autobiography, where it is often presented as historical fact, as in **Albert Facey**'s *A Fortunate Life* (1981).

Folklore is persistent, tending to continue within a culture as 'tradition' even when the impulses and contexts that originally gave rise to it have long disappeared. The past and the present are thus continually drawn together in folklore, a fact that helps to account for its existence as an important element of human relations and goes some way towards explaining its cultural functions in all Australian cultural and ethnic groups. Writers in particular are frequently drawn to utilize such 'grass-roots' material in their works.

The earliest serious collection of Anglo-Celtic folklore in Australia appears to be the work of A. B. ('Banjo') Paterson, who actively solicited folk ballads for what was to become his anthology *Old Bush Songs* (1905). Paterson's aim was to salvage the remnants of what he saw as a bygone way of life, the days of the shearers, gold-diggers, and overlanders. His influence ensured that subsequent collecting activity, beginning in the 1950s, would also concentrate almost exclusively on the Anglo-

Celtic aspects of bush life, seen as the source of 'authentic' Australian folklore. Folk song, music, and dance collectors have continued Paterson's impulse. (See **Songs and Ballads**, Australia.) To a lesser extent, the difficult-to-define narrative form of the bush 'yarn' has also been recovered through these collecting activities.

Since the 1970s considerable investigation of ethnic traditions has taken place. Though not often undertaken from a folkloric point of view, such investigations have incidentally increased our knowledge of the folk traditions of multicultural Australia. This expansion of understanding has also involved an expansion of the Australian understanding of the term 'folklore'. In addition to music, song, and dance traditions, folklore now embraces material forms, such as arts and crafts, cuisine, costume, a variety of verbal forms and narrative traditions, and behavioural forms, such as customs and beliefs.

Recent work has also extended the purview of folklore in accordance with modern practice, particularly with regard to knowledge of new folklore forms that have developed and older forms that have flourished in the era of international travel and electronic communication. These forms include topical jokes, graffiti, modern legends, and folklore produced on, and transmitted by, the electronic photocopier. Such material is mostly international in its diffusion, though usually localized for Australian conditions. It is frequently critical of authority, racist, sexist, or otherwise scabrous. Its enormous popularity in Australia confirms the country's status as a typical polyethnic, overwhelmingly urban-dwelling, industrial/technological modern nation-state.

The diversity implicit in the foregoing summary makes generalization about style, content, and even function of Australian folklore impossible. What can be said is that folklore in Australia tends to exhibit the characteristics of folklore elsewhere in the world.

Verbal folklore in Australia, as in other countries, is strongly humorous, often deals with the deflation or undermining of authority and, consequently, is often held to be typically or 'authentically' Australian. (See **Humour**, Australia.) Study of both older and more recent folklore forms shows that, in fact, most of the elements present in Australian folklore are found in the folklores of other countries, leading to the conclusion that folklore has more to do with general socio-cultural processes and conflicts than with expressions of real or supposed 'national character'. Such learned observations, however, are not likely to affect popular perceptions that folklore somehow contains the essence of cultural identity. While this continues, folklore will continue to feature in all forms of literature, the other arts, and everyday life.

GRAHAM SEAL

Further reading: *Folklife Our Living Heritage: Report of the Committee of Inquiry into Folklife in Australia* (1988); Graham Seal, *The Hidden Culture: Folklore in Australian Society* (1989).

FOLKLORE (Canada)

English-speaking Canadians have more often associated the unofficial, oral-based, and traditional aspects of culture known as folklore with others than with themselves and have rarely, except in distinct regional or ethnic groups, asserted identity through such cultural artefacts. Since 1970 the federal multicultural policy has clearly promoted this identification, but the roots of English-Canadian folklore lie in historical circumstances that fostered community and regional identity above national identity. (See **Multiculturalism**.) There are notably few oral-based traditions that enjoy recognition as national lore, even if they are to be found across the country. Rather than specific lore, generally it is forms or types of traditions that tend to be national in distribution. Examples include ethnic jokes, monster legends, and pseudo-Native lore (such as place-name legends for aboriginal words). Recurrent themes in such material derive from the social and physical conditions of Canada: for instance, the use of multiple characters of different ethnicity in many jokes reflects the country's diverse population, while the ubiquity of water in legends exemplifies the importance of waterways to all Canadians, both indigenous and post-contact. This national lore has also taken various literary forms, such as **Pauline Johnson**'s famous poem, 'Legend of the Qu'Appelle' (first published in *Flint and Feather*, 1912), extremely popular booklets of jokes, and extensive journalism related to monsters.

Rather than documenting their pioneer past or celebrating their peasant conditions, English-speaking Canadians from early on identified with folklore through the encounter with others' roots rather than with their own. The documentation of 'foreign' folkways as noteworthy exotica entered English-Canadian literature with early travel accounts, including such Canadian classics as Anna Jameson's *Winter Studies and Summer Rambles in Canada* (1838). (See **Travel Literature**, Canada.) The appropriation of patterns as well as content from other cultural groups (particularly Native and French Canadians) typifies English-Canadian publications involving folklore throughout the nineteenth century as well as the first half of the twentieth century. Romantic fascination with the peasantry inspired many such works — for instance, W. H. Drummond's 'L'il Ba'tiste' poems in *The Habitant and Other French-Canadian Poems* (1897) — presenting habitant folk speech in English. These works, through their regular inclusion in textbooks, coloured English-Canadian ideas about folklore and French Canadians for several subsequent generations.

Some writers demonstrated an informed sensitivity to actual French-Canadian folk traditions (**William Kirby** in *The Golden Dog*, 1877, and Paul A. W. Wallace in *Baptiste Laroque*, 1923, for example); still others directly presented important documents of Canadien lore — **Sir Charles G. D. Roberts** translated P. A. de Gaspé's fictionalized account of Quebecois folklife at the time of the Conquest, *Les Anciens Canadiens* (1863), as *The Canadians of Old* (1880). Such works, including some by French Canadians in English, are all the more remarkable owing to the relative paucity of comparable ones dealing with English-Canadian traditions. Their abundance is, however, exceeded by the works that present the oral literature and traditions of Canada's aboriginal peoples — a considerable literature that spans the genres and centuries. (See **Aboriginal Literature**, Canada, and **Legends**, Canada.) Particularly significant in terms of representing folklore and affecting its understanding are works about first encounters with the indigenous other. Such works include John R. Jewitt's captivity narrative, *The Adventures and Suffering of John R. Jewitt* . . . (1824; reprinted in 1974 as *The Adventures and Sufferings of John R. Jewitt, Captive Among the Nootka, 1803–1805*, edited by Derek G. Smith), and James Houston's *White Dawn* (1971), told as if from a Native viewpoint. There is also a profusion of books presenting Native myths and aetiological tales for the young, comprising a substantial proportion of Canadian children's literature. (See **Children's Literature**, Canada.)

English-speaking Canadians have been largely concerned with their own traditions rather than with those of the Native peoples. Even in the Atlantic provinces, now so widely associated with folklore, serious collecting only began around the 1920s and required external stimulus from scholars in quest of 'old' traditions (such as Maud Karpeles seeking ballads) or from students trained by outsiders to value the lore of their home regions (for example, W. Roy Mackenzie, who documented his return in *The Quest of the Ballad*, 1919). The generic and regional concentration of this outside interest focused subsequent scholarship, directing the greatest attention on song and on the east of Canada. (See **Songs and Ballads**, Canada.) The many works by Helen Creighton (from 1932 into the 1980s, including a widely popular volume on the supernatural, *Bluenose Ghosts*, 1957) reinforced public association of folklore with the Atlantic region. Meanwhile, activities of the Folklore Division of the National Museum (now the Canadian Centre for Folk Culture Studies) and its director, Marius Barbeau, encouraged all Canadians to recognize folklore. From the 1950s onwards, Edith Fowke endeavoured to document the folklore of all Canadians across the country through media programming and by collecting (mostly songs of the Central Canadian lumberwoods) and publishing numerous books, many of them with a national focus, such as *Canada's Story in Song* (1960) and *Folklore of Canada* (1976). Since the late 1960s scholarship in specific areas (most notably Newfoundland) and on ethnic groups in particular has overshadowed such works of national scope. The recent scholarship documents the sense of continuity that most typifies Canadian tradition, much of which traces its ancestry to foreign sources but has assumed particular characteristics, uses, or significance in Canada.

Since the middle of the twentieth century, authors in search of an authentic Canadian voice have turned increasingly to common Canadians and their ways. Works by such writers as **Margaret Laurence**, **Alice Munro**, **W. O. Mitchell**, Anne Konrad, and **Robertson Davies** often rely upon the presentation of supposed or actual traditional texts, patterns, and themes drawn from their own heritage and illuminate these folk ways. The most prevalent stories in Canada are family legends — the narratives of how people came to be in Canada, their experiences in migrating and settling there, and of making Canada their home. Much of the best of Canadian literature, from **Susanna Moodie**'s *Roughing It in the Bush* (1852) through **Mordecai Richler**'s St. Urbain Street novels to Nino Ricci's contemporary works, focus on this theme. Such works, combined with an ever-increasing body of scholarship, continue to document folklore in English and to promote a greater understanding of it as a significant aspect of Canadian culture.

CAROLE H. CARPENTER

Further reading: Carole H. Carpenter, *Many Voices: Folklore Activities in Canada and Their Role in Canadian Culture* (1979).

FOLKLORE (The Caribbean)

Caribbean folklore combines elements derivative of African, European, Indian, and Amerindian traditions.

Belief Systems

In the Caribbean there is an array of Christian religions, including establishment and non-conformist European and American churches, the Ethiopian Orthodox Church, and syncretic African-Christianity. Other religions include Hinduism, Islam, and African traditional belief systems.

In addition to Christianity, Hinduism, and Islam, there are other beliefs that colour Caribbean peoples' world views. For example, Amerindians and Africans once believed that talismans protected their wearers against offensive missiles; Africans believed that souls of departed slaves made return flights to Africa, called Guinea. Currently, both Amerindians and Africans regard spirits of the dead as powerful. They believe such spirits linger in the vicinity of their living relatives or that the spirits are hurt and need placation by offerings and rituals. Libations of liquor or water are still made at boat launchings or at the start of house construction.

The intersection of the temporal and visible world with the spiritual dimension underlies the astrological consultation made by Hindus prior to important rites of passage and financial undertakings. This intersection also predicates that for many people, dreams, colours, objects, and actions have spiritual resonance or are conduits for spiritual messages. The utterance of curses, wishes, even assumptions, can cause them to be actualized; in its negative realization, this is to 'put goat mouth on' something or someone. Evil can also be transmitted through the eye: young growing things are particularly vulnerable. Plants and farm plots are therefore protected by the suspension of blue bottles from trees and fences. The professional involved in obeah — manipulation of spirit force for good or evil — is variously called an 'obeah man' or 'obeah woman', a 'lookman' or 'seer'. Antidotes to negative obeah include charms hung in homes or gardens, worn on clothes or as rings and bangles, adornment in specific colours, the rubbing of the body or the sprinkling of specific locations with oils and waters, and the immersion of the body in sea or herbal water.

Spirit Beings

Among spirit beings are the ghost/duppy/*jumbi*; in Guyana, the Dutchman, spirit of an early European colonizer; *fantom* or moongazer, a taperingly tall man bestriding roadways; treasure guardians lingering over sites of buried native American, Dutch, and Spanish loot; the rolling calf with fiery eyes and noisy chains; prankish *dwen* or *bolom* — babies who have died before being christened; and *baku* — dwarfs confined in jars and released by their greedy masters to carry out vengeful tasks. Wealth is believed to lead a man to sell his soul to the Devil, who lodges the soul in a dog — the *loup garou* or *lagahoo*. Wealth in exchange for childlessness is the bargain struck with the mermaid/fairmaid/'water muma'/'river muma'/*mama dlo* ('Mother Water') who inhabits rivers and occasionally the sea. The old *haig/sukuya* is the configuration of an old woman who sheds her skin, transforms into a fireball, and becomes a vampire, while *la jablesse* is a beautiful female who encounters men along lonely pathways and lures them to death or misfortune. Papa Bois (Father Forest) frightens humans by his appearance, but protects animals from hunters.

Some of these creatures are distinguished by cloven feet; some are repelled by the Christian cross, or, in the African tradition, by salt, bundles of herbs, or brooms of coconut leaf spines.

Customs

The main rites of passage in the Caribbean are christenings, weddings, and funerals. Wakes take place on the nights of death, and the funeral at nine and forty nights after burial and at a year after death. Eating, drinking, socializing, games, storytelling, hymn-singing, and the recitation of the rosary and other prayers characterize wakes. Some also include concreting of the grave and commemorative services in church.

Weddings feature much speech-making and music. Some African groups in Guyana precede weddings with *kwekwe* (an African-based prenuptial dance/drumming occasion, featuring songs with sexual overtones), while Hindus in Guyana and Trinidad hold several prenuptial ceremonies to initiate separately the bride and groom into their new roles.

Other home-based celebrations are elaborate family meals for Christmas and for Moslem Eid (celebration at the close of the Ramadan season of fasting); African-derived rituals such as *shango/orisha*, *kumfa*, *kumina*, and Koromanti play — all variants of African-based danced religions in the English-speaking Caribbean; and African *saraka* and Hindu *puja* — thanksgiving or intercession prayer occasions. *Jhandi* (Hindu religious flags) aloft bamboo poles bear the insignia of the deity invoked in the *puja*, while flags in the colour/s of deities honoured are planted at an earthen shrine where *orisha* (Yoruba deities) rituals are held. Catholics undertake vehicular pilgrimages to church shrines; African-Christians and Hindus go to seaside and waterfall sites.

Other public activity includes masked dancing processionals variously called *kambule*, *gumbe*, *jonkonu*, masquerade, carnival, *seu*, and *rara*. These are accompanied by drum and/or metal percussion to the singing of topical and satiric songs known variously as *kaiso*, calypso, *mento*, *tambu*, *makamba*, and *rara*. These parades take place either at Christmas, in August, or, under Catholic influence, on the days immediately preceding Lent, or, in Haiti, immediately preceding Easter. The latter time is when St Lucian and Trinidadian children flog effigies of the Devil/Judas. On occasion, mutual-aid Friendly Society members process through the streets in military-like manner, and sodalities dedicated to the rose and marguerite flowers hold colourful competitive processions and cultural activities in St Lucia. The joyous Hindu processional of Phagwa marks the rice harvest. The Moslem Hosay commemorates the murder of Hosein and the political abdication of Hassan, both grandsons of the Prophet, the brothers symbolized by elaborately decorative tombs called *taja* pushed through streets to the accompaniment of male drum ensembles, women's dirges, and crowds.

Fire rituals are dimly recalled in the open-flame torches of *kambule*; candlelight enlivens house-fronts and graveyards for the Catholic festival of *La Toussaint* (All Souls). Cotton wicks lit in oil-filled diminutive clay *deya* (small bowls serving as votive oil lamps) for the Hindu festival of Divali acclaim the bounty of goddess Laskhmi together with Lord Ram's recovery of his abducted wife, Sita, symbolizing the triumph of justice over evil.

MAUREEN WARNER-LEWIS

Further reading: Satnarine Persaud, 'Names of folk-spirits in Guyana', in John Rickford (ed.) *A Festival of Guyanese Words* (1978); John Nunley and Judith Bettelheim, *Caribbean Festival* Arts (1988).

FOLKLORE (East Africa)

Folklore is one of the cornerstones of East African literature. It expresses the traditional values that form a basis for the contemporary East African culture. Since literature is an artistic expression of the social reality, it follows that folklore provides a firm foundation for written East African literature. In the 1970s and 1980s scholars and researchers in the region made great efforts in encouraging the preservation of folklore and in furthering its pursuit as an academic subject. Apart from researchers and scholars, East African creative writers have breathed new life into folklore by manipulating it to contribute to the creativity of their works. The preservation and study of folklore have occurred on the theoretical level and on the level of collecting and recording folklore material.

Okot p'Bitek of Uganda makes a most valuable contribution to the study of folklore in his *Africa's Cultural Revolution* (1973). In this theoretical work he underlines the didactic and social value of folklore and calls for its serious consideration by his fellow scholars. p'Bitek also acts as a pace-setter for East African folkorists in his collection of Acholi songs *The Horn of My Love* (1974). As he states in the preface, he engaged in the process of recording these songs in response to his compatriot **Taban lo Liyong**'s statement in *The Last Word: Cultural Synthesism* (1969) that East Africa was a literary desert. p'Bitek's intention was to demonstrate that East Africa had a wealth of literary material by including and studying folklore as a form of literature in its own right. Indeed, p'Bitek does prove his point, since *Horn of My Love* is the richest collection of folk songs in East Africa. The work comprises an introduction and numerous children's songs, work songs, love songs, wedding songs, and satirical and funeral dirges, among others. Each song is recorded in the original Acholi language, and a translation faithful to the original is given in English.

p'Bitek influenced East African scholars to

give folklore the serious attention it deserves, and scholars such as Penina Muhando Mlama of Tanzania began encouraging the study of folklore. Mlama's efforts, for example, led to the current popularity of the study of folklore as a foundation of Tanzanian theatre.

In Kenya, apart from the introduction of folklore as an academic area in secondary school and university, p'Bitek's theories led to interest in the preservation of folklore through the collection and publication of various literary materials. The first such publication was Rose Gecau Mwangi's *Kikuyu Folktales* (1970), followed by B. Onyango-Ogutu's and A. A. Roscoe's *Keep My Words: Luo Oral Literature* (1974). Each of these early publications has an introduction and literary materials in English translation.

Later Kenyan folklore researchers have deviated slightly from their predecessors' methodology in terms of the scope, content, and form of their publications. There is still a tendency to base each publication on the folklore of a single ethnic group — for example, Naomi Kipury's *Oral Literature of the Maasai* (1983), Karega Mutahi's and Wanjiku Kabira's *Gikuyu Oral Literature* (1988), and C. Chesaina's *Oral Literature of the Kalenjin* (1991). Unlike the earlier publications, where the literary materials are recorded solely in English translation, current publications follow p'Bitek's model in *The Horn of My Love* and record each literary text in its original language, followed by its equivalent English translation. Furthermore, instead of concentrating on one genre, as did earlier researchers, the current researchers incorporate selections of the four major genres of folklore — oral narratives, songs, proverbs, and riddles.

Some folklore texts, though they appeal to university and other older readers, bear titles suggesting that they are aimed at the school market. These texts include comprehensive notes and recommended questions as guides for studying the folklore material. Examples are S. Akivaga's and A. B. Odaga's *Oral Literature: A School Certificate Course* (1982) and Jane Nandwa's and **Austin Bukenya**'s *African Literature for Schools* (1983). A publication that also deserves mention is *Kenyan Oral Narratives* (1985), edited by Kavetsa Adagala and Wanjiku Kabira, which attempts to incorporate folklore stories from more than one ethnic Kenyan group.

Contemporary East African creative writers have shown significant dependence on folklore for enriching both the form and content of their works. This is demonstrated in the drama, poetry, and prose fiction of the region. In *The Contest* (in *The Barbed Wire and Other Plays*, 1977) Mukotani Rugyendo of Tanzania uses two techniques borrowed from folklore — the storytelling tradition and traditional contests in oratory. Through these two techniques the playwright dramatically condemns individualism and selfishness while promoting communalism and altruism, which he views as enshrined in Tanzania's brand of socialism. **Ebrahim Hussein**, Rugyendo's compatriot, uses the recitation tradition to underscore the intensity of serious moments in *Kinjeketile* (1970) and to give dramatic life to the historical progression of his play. In Uganda, **Robert Serumaga** and John Ruganda make use of myth and the storytelling tradition in *Majangwa* (1974) and *The Floods* (1980), respectively.

The backbone of Okot p'Bitek's long poem *Song of Lawino* (1966) is the folklore of the Acholi of Uganda. Though too long to be an orally transmitted poem, *Song of Lawino* has borrowed form, imagery, and its satirical voice from Acholi folklore songs. The strength of Lawino, the persona in p'Bitek's satire on the sterility of superficial modernization, springs mainly from her stance as a character from Acholi folklore and the traditional milieu.

The best example of the contribution of folklore to contemporary East African prose fiction is the work of **Ngugi wa Thiong'o**, Kenya's and, indeed, East Africa's leading novelist. Ngugi makes extensive use of folklore in his early short stories and novels. In the story 'And the Rain Came Down' (in *Secret Lives*, 1975), Ngugi examines his protagonist's predicament against the background of Gikuyu mythology. The major point of conflict is built around the heroine's suspicion that she is barren. This conflict and its final resolution in the heroine's eventual discovery that she is in fact pregnant can only be fully understood in the context of Gikuyu values on procreation. The most important role of a women is that of a mother, a factor that implies that a barren woman is a misfit. After creating a traditional environment, Ngugi then uses Gikuyu religion and mythology to emphasize the psychological tension his heroine undergoes while battling with the possibility of barrenness. The writer uses the folkloric mode of supplication for the heroine's prayer to the Gikuyu god to intervene in her predicament.

In his first novel, *The River Between* (1965), Ngugi's dependence on folklore is notable. The major theme of cultural conflict is examined against a background of a traditional society undergoing change. The creation of the traditional environment in the novel is achieved through the use of folklore. In many parts of the novel, Ngugi borrows the voice of a traditional storyteller to narrate the historical progression of the events.

A Grain of Wheat (1967) is perhaps Ngugi's best novel to date. The Gikuyu myth of creation gives meaning to the freedom fighters' commitment to the war for political independence. It is the Gikuyu myth that explains the close, almost sacred, relation of these people to the land for whose liberation the freedom fighters are ready to die. In addition to alluding to this myth as a background to the war, Ngugi creates his hero and heroine from the characters of the mythical father and mother of the Gikuyu, respectively.

CIARUNJI CHESAINA SWINIMER

Further reading: Okot p'Bitek, *Africa's Cultural Revolution* (1973); E. Gachukia and S. Akivaga, eds, *Teaching of African Literature in Schools* (1978).

FOLKLORE (India)

Indians are nourished on fables, parables, and legends during their childhood, and they cannot but carry a deep impress of them in their subconscious. From **Toru Dutt**'s *Ancient Ballads and Legends of Hindustan* (1882) to **Ruskin Bond**'s *Tales and Legends from India* (1990), many Indian writers have presented Indian folklore in English.

Though the flavour of folklore and the magic of myth can be found in the work of almost all Indian writers writing in English, very few have shown the powerful influence of folklore on contemporary minds. (See **Myth in Indian-English Literature**.) An atypical example is **Manoj Das**' title story from *The Crocodile's Lady: A Collection of Stories* (1975). A western scholar on a visit to a remote Indian village hears the story of a woman who had been temporarily metamorphosed into a she-crocodile and married her abductor, a crocodile. The woman, now almost a hundred years old, is herself the narrator. Such is the intensity of her narration that for a moment the scholar unconsciously believes the story. The point the author tries to make is that the woman herself lives in her own make-believe world and totally believes it to be true. This overlapping of reality and fantasy derives from the pervasive presence of folklore in the Indian imagination.

While the title of **Raja Rao**'s novel *The Serpent and the Rope* (1960) refers to the famous Sanskrit dictum warning that a serpent can be mistaken for a rope, the main story describes rituals that are both scriptural and related to folk practice. **R. K. Narayan**'s Malgudi is in one sense a typical Indian village of today, but it is, in fact, a world pervaded by an atmosphere of folklore. His characters are recognizable partly as men and women and partly as shadows of a rural past that survives in folklore.

Among the stories that fall into the twilight zone between mythology and folklore is the story of Savitri. While the original story is narrated in the epic *Mahabharata*, there are many folk ballads, plays, and operas on the subject. The legend receives an unexpected re-creation in the hands of **Sri Aurobindo**, who elevates it to the level of a symbol in his epic *Savitri* (1954). **Girish Karnad** also bases the main plot of his experimental play *Hayavadana* (1975) on the 'Story of the Transposed Heads' from the eleventh-century collection of folk tales *Katha-Sarit-Sagthara* ('Ocean of Stories') to treat the existential theme of the fundamental ambiguity of the human condition.

A few writers have made use of folklore to poke fun at traditional customs and beliefs, festivals, and rites. **Nissim Ezekiel**'s poem 'Night of the Scorpion' (from *The Exact Name*, 1965) is an ironic presentation of the contrast between popular superstition and sceptical realism. In *All About H. Hatterr* (1951, first published in 1948 as *All About Mr. Hatterr, A Gesture*), **G. V. Desani** shatters the belief that Godmen can help us reach God. Thus Indian writers writing in English find folklore extremely useful, however differently they use it.

P. RAJA

FOLKLORE (The Philippines)

Folklore has contributed to the beauty of Philippine fiction in English, giving it local colour, naturalness, and authenticity. Two outstanding writers, **N. V. M. Gonzalez** and **Nick Joaquin**, have been particularly successful in using folklore in their fiction. Both of them grew up in homes and neighbourhoods where folklore is an integral part of life. Gonzalez grew up in Mindoro, where folk stories are part of life and where the people's religious practices blend with superstitious beliefs. Gonzalez uses a wide variety of folk materials in his fiction — folk religious beliefs and superstitions, customs, rituals, legends, proverbs, and folk songs — especially in his early short stories contained in *Seven Hills Away* (1947) and *Children of the Ash-Covered Loam* (1951) and in his novel *A Season of Grace* (1954). Because they believe that spirits inhabit the forest in which they make their clearing, farmers have to befriend and appease these spirits with rituals. In 'The Planting', before he and his wife plant seeds, Paulo petitions the spirits to be kind to them and to protect the crop that they hope to raise. Another farmer makes a food offering of chicken and pork meat, wine, and betel chew before felling trees. Young boys who work for him are made to wear amulets (ginger and garlic sewn into tiny bags of red cloth) to protect them from evil spirits.

Folk customs mark every stage in the lives of Gonzalez's characters in these works. When Sabel in *A Season of Grace* gives birth, the midwife performs all the customary practices connected with childbirth. For instance, she presses hot ashes on the baby's brow, temples, and chin, thus making the sign of the cross to keep away the Evil One. When old Tomas dies, death and funeral customs are observed: there is the vigil, with drinking and guitar-playing to keep the mourners awake; the making of the coffin; the taking of the coffin head-first down the house for the funeral; and the novena prayers with the ninth night celebrated with a big feast. All this done to wish the departed God-speed. Courtship customs are portrayed in 'Lupo and the River'. Lupo's parents make a *pamanhikan* or formal asking for the hand of Paula in marriage to their son. After they agree to provide a hut and twenty-five cavans of uncooked rice for the young couple, Lupo begins to render personal services to Paula's family. In the course of the story, Paula is serenaded (another rural custom) and she obliges the serenaders by singing a folk song. Proverbs are also quoted by the older characters in the story.

Joaquin was born and grew up in legend-rich Manila in a home steeped with culture, tradition, and folklore. As he himself put it, 'I drank folklore with my mother's milk.' He uses only a few types of folklore — legends, folk beliefs, and rituals — but he uses them intensively and exhaustively. Four of his short stories are literary re-creations of legends: 'The Legend of the Dying Wanton', 'The Legend of the Virgin's Jewel', 'Doña Jeronima', and 'The Order of Melkizedek'.

One of Joaquin's best-loved stories, 'May Day Eve', is woven around the folk belief that on the night of the first day of May, anyone who observes certain conditions might look into a mirror and see the face of the person he or she is fated to marry. The plot of 'Guardia de Honor' revolves around the custom in which young daughters of two generations of the same family participate as Guard of Honor in the annual procession in honour of the Virgin of the Rosary. The plot of 'Summer Solstice' revolves around the celebration of the pagan fertility rite of the *Tadtarin*, which somehow became mixed up with the feast of St John the Baptist. The ritual asserts and demonstrates the superiority of woman over man.

Joaquin artistically reworks his folk materials, transforming them into beautiful and deeply meaningful short stories. For instance, he injects a theological dimension into 'The Legend of the Dying Wanton' by tracing the protagonist's spiritual development to the point where he merits the forgiveness of his sins and a visit from Our Lady and her Child.

DAMIANA EUGENIO

FOLKLORE (West Africa)

Folklore permeates the fiction, poetry, and drama of West African literature in English. For some writers, its use means a symbolic return to the past or an occasion to give their work freshness and originality. Others utilize folkloric elements, such as proverb, in terms of their audiences' needs and depend on what their locality offers. This is the case of **Amos Tutuola** and **Chinua Achebe** in their prose narratives. Through folklore the authors offer a rural setting, attitude, or mode of discourse that generates amusement and controversy.

Achebe's *Things Fall Apart* (1958) and his later novels set in village life are enriched by his use of folktales and proverbs. As Achebe says, among Nigerian (Igbo) people there exists a mature art of conversation based on 'proverbs . . . the palm oil with which words are eaten'. He seems to value traditional custom, as the Kenyan novelist **Ngugi wa Thiong'o** defines it in his early stories.

Achebe's interest in folklore is enhanced by his reverence for a glorious pre-colonial African civilization, which he conveys in Igbo folklore. Okonkwo, the protagonist of *Things Fall Apart*, laments the disintegration of communal life in the villages: 'Living fire begets cold, impotent ash'. This utterance expresses Okonkwo's sadness, generalized for other Africans, when his son embraces the Christian religion. Okonkwo, however, is portrayed as an inflexible traditionalist, which leads to his downfall in the face of colonization.

This link between creative writing and immediate social problems is modest in *The Palm-Wine Drinkard* (1952) by Amos Tutuola, whose interest lies chiefly in wit, irony, and fantasy. Here folktale provides the essential narrative form and linguistic innovation — most of the novel's thirty episodes are based on Yoruba folktales. The Drinkard delegates hard work to others as he inhabits a timeless universe of leisure-mongering and questing for identity. The Drinkard's journey to the Deads' Town to find his palm-wine tapper, who died mysteriously, reveals him as an individualist, like the Tortoise in Nigerian folktales. He is selfish, since he violates all or most of his ancestral social norms. The humorous word 'drinkard' suggests an archetypal image of the rare nonconformist who is indispensable: he never fails to uphold common existence, but only out of sheer necessity. His egoism yields at last to the popular demand for community service after his wide and reckless adventures. He moves from drunkenness to wisdom and self-realization via discipline.

One notices in this novel an inversion of the Christian idea of chastity. The Drinkard's youth is marked by sensuality and thoughtlessness, which he outgrows on his journey; significantly, too, he leaves the palm-wine tapper behind in Deads' Town and takes home a magic egg, with which he rescues his town from famine. Although wine attracts the townspeople, they have a contemptuous word for the drunkard — *omutin*, meaning somebody without commonsense and politeness. The Drinkard's salvation and reunion with his kinsmen serve as a warning to wrongdoers like himself and as a lesson in morality. Actually, Tutuola blends fantasy and social criticism in the right proportions. He has enough faith in humanity that endures hardships to see the light.

In Tutuola's writing, like Achebe's, folklore mirrors the state of pre-independent Africa. Contemporary literary works from Nigeria and Ghana emphasize current issues. There is a recurrent story of the 'assimilated' individual unable to enjoy life among his or her relatives. **Wole Soyinka**'s *The Lion and The Jewel* (1963) and **Ama Ata Aidoo**'s *Dilemma of a Ghost* (1965) retell the 'Nikun' folktale, which appears in **Timothy Aluko**'s *One Man, One Wife* (1959). Soyinka's Sidi and Aidoo's Eulalie, 'a ghost', fall in love with strangers who nearly ruin them. The acceptance of this story in West Africa owes nothing to western traditions, such as the Genesis story of fallen Beauty and Earth, or of humankind that disobeys God to invite suffering plus mortality.

Folklore registers effectively the protest against the ills of colonization, including acculturation, which converts settled villagers into poor and ambitious townspeople. In **Efua Sutherland**'s play *The Marriage of Anansewa* (1975), for example — *Ananse* is a Ghanaian (Akan) word for 'tortoise' — Ananse replies to his educated daughter, Anansewa: 'Yes, it's raining. It's rain combining with life to beat your father down . . . My daughter, it isn't well with the home . . .' In Soyinka's *The Trials of Brother Jero* (1963), **Isidore Okpewho**'s *The Victims* (1970), **A. K. Armah**'s *The Beautyful Ones Are Not Yet Born* (1968), and **Kofi Awoonor**'s *This Earth, My Brother . . .* (1972), Ananse is re-defined as someone who subverts normative ideas and beliefs of civilized society. Like the snake or owl, Brother Jero symbolizes a natural instinct to cheat and destroy his victim. He is both individual and representative of a life-style that survives, partly because of its innate complexity. African writers tend to portray the trickster realistically, as a modern intellectual or politician ('a man of the people'), whose ways are enigmatic. T. M. Aluko's Benjamin Benjamin and Soyinka's Professor are vivid examples of this figure.

Some resemblance exists between Ananse or Tortoise and Abiku, a spirit-child traversing both the human and non-human realms at will and causing endless fear in society. He stands for the principle of oppression and mutability. Abiku is individualistic and uncontrollable, so the problem of how to maintain order and continuity may not be solved by those who adopt rational methods to check his malice. Initially, Soyinka and **Bekederemo** utilize the myth in their poetry. The African audience knows its moral and psychological implication for country people faced with certain dilemmas regarding child mortality. The Abiku myth is also linked to the legend of the Yoruba and Ogun in Soyinka's works, including *The Road* (1965). It supports the narrative style of **Ben Okri**'s *The Famished Road* (1991), a comic tale about the people of Lagos and Nigerian town dwellers. Through the fantasy Okri examines such themes as poverty, violence, retribution, fatalism, and sacrifice.

Folklore contributes aesthetically to West African prose and verse. Behind all this achievement is a strain of political awareness that, unlike that of Romantic and Negritude artists, stems from no clear-cut ideology or philosophy of life. Folklore moderates West Africans' sense of commitment, ensuring the high quality of literary productions. But except in Tutuola's and Soyinka's writings, there are little or no variations on the theme of the black people's dilemma; no deep and lasting thought transcends a racialist impulse on which it is based. In fiction Achebe and his imitators are always valued because of the tragic utterance they build around tradition, its loss due to colonization, and issue relevant to modern experience. Although colonialism is gone, its multiple effects refuse to vanish easily into history.

E. A. BABALOLA

FOLK SONGS (The Caribbean)

See **SONGS AND BALLADS** (The Caribbean)

FONLON, BERNARD NSOKIKA (1924–86)

Cameroonian essayist, poet

Fonlon was born in Nso in the North West Province, the Southern British Cameroons (now Cameroon). He walked and canoed for weeks through rainforests and swamps to reach Christ's College in Onitsha, Nigeria, where he studied from 1942 to 1945. From 1948 to 1953, he was a seminarian at Bigard Memorial Seminary in Enugu, Nigeria. A few weeks prior to his ordination as a priest, Fonlon wrote a now-famous letter to his bishop, demanding to know why there were so few Africans in leadership positions in the Catholic Church in Africa. Rome replied to his letter, denying him ordination. For the rest of his life Fonlon lived as a priest, without the title, devoting his energy to the spiritual and material betterment of his countrymen's lives. He took degrees at Oxford University, England, and at the Sorbonne, France, and on receipt of his Ph.D. (1961) from the National University of Ireland became the first anglophone Cameroonian to earn a doctorate. His thesis was one of the first scholarly works written on literature authored by Africans. He is universally acknowledged by anglophone Cameroonians as their greatest national figure and the father of their distinct literature. His published works include *To Every Son of Nso* (1965), *Under the Sign of the Rising Sun* (1965), *The Task of Today* (1966), and *An Open Letter to the Bishops of Buea and Bamenda* (1973).

Had Fonlon not been an anglophone, and therefore unacceptable to the French who controlled the majority of Cameroon and its population, many Cameroonians think he would have been the country's first president. Completely and elegantly fluent in both English and French, he was moved from the post of assistant secretary to the prime minister of the Southern Cameroons to become the personal secretary of newly 'independent' Cameroon's first president, Ahmadou Ahidjo. He became, sequentially, Cameroon's deputy minister of foreign affairs, minister of transport, posts and telecommunications, and minister of public health and social welfare. In the late 1960s and early 1970s, his friendship with Canadian Prime Minister Pierre Trudeau led to discussions that had a significant influence on biculturalism and bilingualism policies of their respective governments. (Cameroon's proportion of anglophones to francophones is nearly exactly the reverse of Canada's.)

While still in government, Fonlon launched *Abbia* (in 1963), a widely read, bilingual, English-French cultural review that he edited until his death; it was the main forum for educated discussion on many issues of prime importance to his developing country. In its pages many of his finest writings are found. Leaving government in the 1970s, Fonlon moved to the national University of Yaounde, where he headed the world's only department of comparative African literatures, a post he kept until about two years before his death, when a wary President Biya wanted him removed from all positions of influence. Because of his ferocious independence and unimpeachable integrity, *Abbia* was the only Cameroonian publication for more than two decades that could be printed without prior review by government censors. Fonlon's own essays published there were on many topics, as suggested by such titles as 'African Writers Meet in Uganda', 'The Idea of Cultural Integration', 'The Language Problem in Cameroon', and 'To Every African Freshman, or the Nature, End and Purpose of University Studies'. His books include *Random Leaves from My Diary* (1976) and *The Genuine Intellectual* (1978). (See **Essays**, West Africa.)

With such an enormous range of topics in his oeuvre, it is difficult to foresee what distant posterity will identify as Fonlon's most important contributions to history. Today, Cameroonians seek quotations from his work that assist them in their struggle against francophone dominance over anglophones; they comment most frequently on his refusal of an ostentatious life-style and on his integrity, both of which are especially significant in a climate of oppression, greed, and corruption. From his writings the most often quoted passages are on the subject of language, which is symptomatic of a whole range of national concerns that unite anglophone sentiment. In 'Will We Make or Mar?' (*Abbia* 5 March 1964) he wrote:

> unless the East Cameroun francophone leader in whose hands cultural initiative lies, is prepared to share this authority with his brother from West of the Mungo [anglophone], unless he is prepared to make the giant effort necessary to break loose from the strait-jacket of his French education, unless he will show proof of his intellectual probity and admit candidly that there are things in the Anglo-Saxon way of life that can do his country good, there is little chance of survival, neither for English influence, nor even for African values in the Federal Republic of Cameroon. With African culture moribund, with John Bullism weak and in danger of being smothered, we will all be French in two generations or three!

A decade and a half later, in 'To Every African Freshman Ten Years After' (*Abbia* 34-37, 1979), Fonlon wrote that he still supported bilingualism, but that he no longer believed in 'the equality of the two languages': 'My firm conviction now is that English . . . should increasingly become the first language of instruction in the University; indeed that it should be elected as the first official language of Cameroon.' His reasons for favouring English were practical, not chauvinistic or sentimental, and near the time of his death he declared in several places that the language battle had been won, observing that the majority of élite francophones in Cameroon had begun making certain that their children learned English as well as French.

Fonlon's style was archaic, reflecting his deep love of classical European culture. His writings are replete with quotations drawn from vast reading, especially in Latin. The cadences of his finely crafted poetry are reminiscent of much nineteenth-century British verse. He was also a lover of the African proverb, which provided concrete imagery as a counterpoint to the florid, verbose, abstract style he had absorbed from European letters of previous centuries.

STEPHEN H. ARNOLD

Further reading: Dan L. Lantum, ed., *Dr. Bernard Nsoskika Fonlon (1924–1986) is now a Legend (Funeral Addresses, Tributes, and Eulogies* (1988).

FORBES, JOHN (1950–)
Australian poet
Born in Melbourne, Australia, he spent his youth in Malaysia, Papua New Guinea, and Sydney, Australia, and now lives in Melbourne. He was taught

by the De La Salle Brothers and graduated from the University of Sydney. Despite a thesis on the American poet John Ashbery, close reading of American writers Kenneth Koch, Ted Berrigan, and Frank O'Hara, and the conversational influence of Laurie Duggan, Martin Johnston, and Carl Harrison-Ford, Forbes maintains that he was most affected by his study of philosophy and fine arts. He was deeply influenced by the logical positivist aestheticist Donald Brook. In Sydney Forbes worked as a furniture removalist; in Melbourne and Geelong he has taught creative writing and published reviews of nonfiction that are always carefully written, despite his disclaiming their importance.

Forbes co-edited *Leatherjacket* magazine (1973) and edited *Surfers Paradise* magazine (1947; 1979). His poetry collections are *Tropical Skiing* (1976), *On the Beach* (1977), *Stalin's Holidays* (1980), and *The Stunned Mullet* (1988).

Forbes claims that most of the world's poetry is not poetry. His own writing appeals to both the casual reader and the student. The reader discovers humorous, sceptical, and intelligent work that takes almost nothing seriously, least of all the poet's opinions. The reader finds many references to the historical and contemporary world — where life often imitates art and the mass media — via a satirical relativism filled with ideas, images, slang, slogans, arguments, travel advertisements, and tourist traps. By contrast, the student insists on Forbes' only serious commitment — poetry. The student learns that the poet will not use language as a tool to impose his own ego and attitudes. Forbes' poetry is a serious game played through many drafts. He explores his societally-constructed self in the hope of reconstructing it, showing the process rather than providing analysis and explanation. Despite exceptions in the modes of lyricism, tall stories, social criticism, deliberately unpopular rhetoric, and even mainstream 1970s and 1980s Australian poetry, Forbes' intellectual aesthetic preserves a uniformity of purpose that obviates the need for development.

GRAHAM ROWLANDS

Further reading: Martin Duwell, ed., *A Possible Contemporary Poetry* (1982).

FORDE, ALFRED NATHANIEL (1923–)
Barbadian poet, short-story writer
Born in Martindale's Road, in the parish of St Michael, Barbados, he became one of the editors of the literary magazine *Bim* in 1959, prior to serving as permanent secretary in the Ministry of Education. Forde's short stories have appeared in: *From the Green Antilles: Writings of the Caribbean* (1967), edited by Barbara Howes; *Response: A Course in Narrative Comprehension and Composition* (1969), compiled by Cecil Gray; *Sunshine and Shadow: An Anthology of Short Stories* (1980), edited by Roy Narinesingh and Clifford Narinesingh; and in *Perspectives* (1982) and *Wavelengths* (1982), both edited by Cecil Gray. His poetry has appeared in *Caribbean Voices* (vol. 1, 1966), edited by **John Figueroa**, and *Aftermath: An Anthology of Poems in English from Africa, Asia, and the Caribbean* (1977), edited by Roger Weaver and Joseph Bruchac. His one-act play, *The Passing Cloud*, was published in 1966. Forde's major concerns are with the landscape, the nostalgia of community life, and the experiences of boyhood. His characters are essentially sketches — which may explain why he writes primarily in the genres of the short story and poetry. For critic **Wayne Brown**, Forde's poetry in particular fits into the pastoral mode, deriving much influence from the nature poetry of the nineteenth-century British Romantics.

In the introduction to his anthology of poetry for secondary schools, *Talk of the Tamarinds* (1971), Forde alludes to his own propensity to juxtapose human and inhuman states of quality and of being. 'Sea Bird' is a fair representation of Forde's style. It is a poem of nature (bird) and humanity (the poet) and of the latter's longing to transcend the restrictions of a mundane existence. Like a majority of poems by the Ghanaian R. F. Armatoe, some of Forde's can often seem so self-conscious, so given over to approximating another's form, that meaning seems to come only as an accompaniment. He is not regarded as a major Caribbean writer, perhaps because his writing is personal and lacks any real ideological or other strong philosophical commitment.

CURWEN BEST

FOREIGN WRITERS

FOREIGN WRITERS (Australia)

First Impressions

Even before the First Fleet sailed, Australia had been documented by observers, notably Sir Joseph Banks and Captain Cook, and in the early years of settlement several accounts were published: *The Voyage of Governor Phillip to Botany Bay* (1789, 1970), **Watkin Tench**'s *A Narrative of the Expedition to Botany Bay* (1789), and his *A Complete Account of the Settlement at Port Jackson in New South Wales* (1793). These and similar reports fired the fertile imaginations of stay-at-home writers whose subsequent imaginative descriptions influenced world views of the new colony and prejudiced the response of future settlers to the actuality of their new environment.

The Early Years

Barron Field, who stayed in Australia from 1817 to 1824, claimed, inaccurately, to be Australia's first harmonist. He was personally acquainted with Coleridge, Charles Lamb, and Leigh Hunt and was a particular admirer of Wordsworth. But Field's own *First Fruits of Australian Poetry* (1819), consisting of two poems, is a scholar's *jeu d'esprit* on antipodean flora and fauna. It does not further the spirit of Romanticism.

Although contemporary books were imported and read, Augustan diction and conventions, especially in describing landscape, continued to serve the writers of occasional verse published along with short stories and articles in the *Sydney Gazette*, founded in 1803. The Romantic movement was well under way in Europe when **Charles Tompson**'s *Wild Notes, from the Lyre of a Native Minstrel* appeared in 1826. This, the first Australian-published book by a native-born poet, marks a transition. The subject and style of Tompson's 'Black Town', for instance, are like Goldsmith's *The Deserted Village*, but the spirit is Wordsworthian and the verse is pervaded by romantic melancholy.

The colony's first distinctive ventures into narrative form take nothing new from abroad. Thomas Wells' life of the bushranger Michael Howe (*Michael Howe: The Last and Worst of the Bush Rangers of Van Diemen's Land*, 1818) and **James Hardy Vaux**'s own convict *Memoirs* (1819) begin a series of splendid new additions to the existing eighteenth-century tradition of Newgate confessions.

Foreign Novelists, Prose Writers, and Australia

Charles Dickens wrote when much was already known about conditions in Australia. *Great Expectations* (1860–1) presupposes familiarity with the ticket-of-leave system: Magwitch, a convict who makes a fortune in Australia, cannot legally return to England. The Micawbers and Little Em'ly, free settlers, are able to lead a prosperous life in the new country, but hard-hearted villains such as Wackford Squeers transported to Australia can be forgotten. Indeed, mid-century English writers showed a marked reluctance to accept reformed convicts back into society. Thackeray was disturbed by the fact that bad characters could prosper in Australia, and in George Eliot's *Adam Bede* (1859), Hetty Sorrel, transported for infanticide, serves out her time but dies on the way home, a sop to Victorian morality.

Dickens' close friend, the writer Edward Bulwer Lytton, was Secretary for the Colonies in 1858–9 and depicts Australia in his own novel, *The Caxtons* (1849), as a place where fortunes can be made. This book became popular in Australia and was adapted there for the stage. Both novelists drew heavily on the accounts of Samuel Sidney, whose *A Voice from the Far Interior of Australia* (1847) was published under the pseudonym 'a Bushman' and was written at second hand from material supplied by a younger brother who spent several years in New South Wales. Sidney also contributed articles on Australia to Dickens' *Household Words* (1850–9), a major channel for disseminating ideas about bush life to Europeans, Americans, and even urban Australians.

Another writer who never visited Australia owed one of his popular successes to world interest in the gold rush. Charles Reade's melodrama *Gold!* opened in London in 1853, was subsequently expanded into the novel *It Is Never Too Late to Mend* (1856), and then reworked again for the theatre in Australia.

Sir Walter Scott was the acknowledged source of inspiration for **Rolf Boldrewood**, who wrote novels, especially *Robbery under Arms* (1882–3), in Scott's romantic historical adventure mode convincingly transposed into the Australian setting. Much later, in the early years of the twentieth century, **William Gosse Hay** took Scott as the model for his historical novels about Tasmania.

In spite of never visiting the country, Dickens was an enormous influence on the fiction writers of Australia. His books were found congenial because they dealt with working-class people in a predominantly urban environment rather than with romantic love or upper-class marriage. And he wrote about his own lifetime or the recent past. **Henry Lawson**, undoubtedly influenced by Dickens, vividly re-created the settings of his own early years and wrote credible dialogue. His people need to work for their living and they share a common sense of humour. Lawson, however, wrote short sketches developing out of the oral tradition of the Australian yarn and his characters are usually flawed human beings rather than the saints and villains of Dickens.

Dickens, more than Scott or Charles Reade, influenced the work of **Marcus Clarke**, which shows the utter depravity of some aspects of criminal behaviour. Dickens was also the model consciously imitated in Benjamin Farjeon's novels of the goldfields. His influence is acknowledged at present by such disparate writers as **Thea Astley**, Nicholas Hasluck, and **David Malouf**.

Anthony Trollope travelled widely in the 1860s and 1870s. His *Australia and New Zealand* (1873) is a careful observation of such matters as land tenure and labourers' rations. It includes, however, the infamous judgement that 'the Australian black man has to go'. Trollope's novels of upper-class and ecclesiastical society were widely read; the Palliser sequence served as model for **Martin Boyd**'s family chronicles, the Langton tetralogy (1952–62).

As a seaman, Joseph Conrad made four visits to Australia, and he incorporated Australian settings into some of his works, including *Youth* (1902) and *The Mirror of the Sea* (1906). Conrad's influence has been acknowledged by David Malouf and by **Christopher Koch**. Havelock Ellis, who spent four years in Australia, 1875–8, as a very young man, wrote of his impressions in a novella, *Kanga Creek: An Australian Idyll*, not published until 1922, a year before D. H. Lawrence's *Kangaroo*. The contrast with Lawrence is extreme: Ellis found the bush exhilarating, not ominous. But Ellis' influence on Australian writing was minor.

Lawrence spent fifteen weeks in Australia in 1922. He missed seeing **Katharine Susannah Prichard**, who had been very impressed by his *Sons and Lovers*, but he met Mollie Skinner, advised her to 'write an Australian book about things you actually know', and partly rewrote her *The Boy in the Bush* (1924), which they published jointly. His novel *Kangaroo*, written in New South Wales, reveals extraordinary familiarity with the secret right-wing revolutionary New Guard and vividly but ambivalently presents Australian characteristics and the tug of **mateship**. The two novels and his letters show hearty appreciation of the ferocious seascape and the abundant beauty of the flowering season, tempered by alienation from the brooding mystery of the bush. **Rex Ingamells** objected to this spreading of the 'weird, melancholy' portrayal of the bush, earlier promulgated by Marcus Clarke. Members of the **Jindyworobak Movement** considered it an imported foreign prejudgement, not a true reaction. Lawrence knew **Jack Lindsay** and **P. R. Stephensen** in England, and his influence is still widely acknowledged by contemporary writers. He is cited in Candida Baker's *Yacker* volumes (1986–) by writers as different as David Malouf, **Barbara Hanrahan**, Christopher Koch, and **John Tranter**. Even some of Peter Sculthorpe's music is inspired by Lawrence, and David Allen's play *Upside Down at the Bottom of the World* (1981) is based on *Kangaroo*.

Other writers who visited Australia briefly in the days of sea voyages included Kipling, Mark Twain, Zane Grey, R. L. Stevenson, and Agatha Christie, all fêted as popular writers.

With the advent of air travel, and more especially with the availability of government and private funding, the trickle of visitors to Australia has swollen to a flood. The workshops run by visiting American Ursula Le Guin have encouraged science fiction writers. **Chinua Achebe, Wole Soyinka,** and others have brought the African voice to Australia. Yevgeni Yevtushenko from the USSR, **Margaret Atwood** from Canada, **David Rubadiri** from Uganda, and **George Lamming** from the Caribbean have visited, as have writers from China, Egypt, and Singapore. Their influence on budding writers in Australia is incalculable. In addition, an upsurge of second-generation migrant work in English enriches mainstream Australian literature. (See **Migrant Writing**, Australia.)

Foreign Poets, the Nineteenth Century

Several Australian writers found inspiration in the American transcendentalist movement of the 1830s as filtered through the verse of Walt Whitman. Tom Bury (1838–1900), an immigrant writer from Dublin, Ireland, frequently quoted Whitman in the *Ballarat Courier* in the 1880s. This introduction to Whitman so impressed Bernard O'Dowd (by confirming his own radical and socialist views) that he always carried a copy of *Leaves of Grass* with him and kept up a correspondence in which he addressed the American as 'master', though his own work lacks the fluency and lyrical power of Whitman. Opposing the sterility of 'art for art's sake', O'Dowd pursued the poetry of 'politics, sex, science and social reform' to art's detriment. John le Gay Brereton (1827–66), Francis Adams (1862–93), and William Gay are others who found a kindred spirit in Whitman.

New vitality entered Australian poetry when **Charles Harpur**, inspired by Wordsworth, began to publish verse in the 1840s. 'The Creek of the Four Graves' in (*The Bushrangers, A Play in Five Acts, and Other Poems*, 1853) shares with Wordsworth's 'Michael' the sanctification of the land by a monument to grief. Harpur was also drawn to the American transcendentalists Emerson and W. E. Channing, developing their anti-orthodox, individualistic idealism in the direction of radical politics. But he disliked Swinburne and Tennyson for being 'too nice and dainty' in contrast to the more robust Wordsworth.

Apart from the popular bush balladists, most Australian poets continued in the pattern of Wordsworth and Tennyson — right up to the modern period in some cases. But other influences can be seen. Victor Daley (1858–1905), for example, who emigrated from Ireland in 1878, became the centre of Sydney's Celtic twilight of lyrical romanticism. **Christopher Brennan,** on the other hand, tried many role models. A Francophile who studied in Germany, he was influenced by his discarded Catholicism and by Keats, Tennyson, and Swinburne. He took a scholarly interest in Greek and Continental philosophy and translated Novalis and Nietzsche. But the French symbolists were the main influence on his verse, Stéphane Mallarmé becoming his chief mentor and correspondent. Yet, no amount of influence could make up for Brennan's deficiencies of talent. His diction remains 'poetic', often slackly late-Victorian, even sentimental, and it is ill-suited to the philosophic bent of his verse.

Others besides Brennan were interested in Nietzsche. **Christina Stead** knew the whole of *Thus Spoke Zarathustra* by heart, for its 'chant', not its philosophy. O'Dowd and P. R. Stephensen read him, the latter undoubtedly strengthened in his increasingly nationalist, anti-communist, anti-Semitic views. The direct and well-documented influence of Nietzsche on the minor writer William Baylebridge (W. Blocksidge) is less important to Australian culture than the idiosyncratic distortions of Nietzsche's philosophy in the vitalist theories propounded in the magazine *Vision* (1923–4), edited by Jack Lindsay, **Kenneth Slessor**, and Frank Johnson. Lindsay, for example, asserted 'the dynamic continuity of the self', 'the junction of being and becoming', and 'creative exaltation'. These ideas imbue the works of the Lindsays, but the greatest of Slessor's poems, 'Five Bells' (*Five Bells*, 1939), while retaining the vitalist rejection of mechanically measurable time, includes near-nihilistic questioning of human existence.

Further examples of philosophers' influence on Australian writing include that of A. N. Whitehead on **R. D. FitzGerald**'s 'Essay on Memory' and of Wittgenstein's aesthetic theories on **Gwen Harwood**'s poetry. **Patrick White**'s fiction has been seen variously as Freudian and Jungian, while in his early plays, especially *The Ham Funeral* (in *Four Plays*, 1965), there is a strong influence of German expressionism. European naturalism affected **Henry Handel Richardson,** who translated B. Bjornson and J. P. Jacobsen, but *The Fortunes of Richard Mahony* (1930) is more particularly coloured by Swedenborg's idea of the essential harmony of the spiritual and bodily without which the inner being fails and dies. Communism and social realism inform the works of many mid-twentieth-century writers such as Katharine Susannah Prichard, **Dorothy Hewett**, and **Frank Hardy**.

Foreign Influences on Poetry, 1920 Onwards

In the 1920s and 1930s few Australian poets were receptive to the modernism represented by Ezra Pound and T. S. Eliot. The anti-modernist stance adopted in the work of the Jindyworobaks and by the poet-critics **James McAuley** and **A. D. Hope** further limited modernist influence. The search for an authentic personal and national voice led the magazine *Angry Penguins* (1940–6) to European expressionism, surrealism, and the new romanticism of Dylan Thomas. Liberation finally came from the USA. During the 1940s American servicemen poets, notably Harry Roskolenko, had moved in *Angry Penguins* circles, and Roskolenko facilitated the Australian publication of works by the Americans Karl Shapiro, Kenneth Rexroth, and Harold Rosenberg. But it was not until the late 1960s that a younger generation of Australian poets discovered the vast potential of American poetry. Inspiration came from a variety of sources: Wallace Stevens, Robert Lowell, and Galway Kinnell; Allen Ginsberg and Lawrence Ferlinghetti (both of whom visited Australia); the West Coast 'drug poets'; the projectionist Black Mountain poets, especially Charles Olson, Robert Creeley, Denise Levertov, and Robert Duncan — the last three gave readings while visiting Australia — and pre-eminently the New York School of poets, notably John Ashbery and Frank O'Hara. The Generation of '68 in Melbourne and similar poetry reading workshops in other state capitals gave new regional responses to the spread of American experimental verse. **Thomas Shapcott**'s anthology *Contemporary American and Australian Poetry* (1976) illustrates the extent of Australian poets' debt to America in loosening up poetic forms and offering a wide variety of vernacular voices.

Foreign Influences on Crime Fiction

One of the earliest crime novels in Australia is **Fergus Hume**'s highly successful *The Mystery of a Hansom Cab* (1886), which was closely modelled on the style of the French writer Émile Gaboriau. The English immigrant Arthur Upfield began writing in 1928 and created a part-Aboriginal detective, Napoleon Bonaparte, who, like Agatha Christie's Hercule Poirot and E. D. Biggers' Charlie Chan, is culturally apart from the group mores of the characters he investigates. **Peter Corris** admits to modelling his work on the laconic, breezy mode of American Ross Macdonald. Corris is also credited with transferring Raymond Chandler's sense of a living city's topography to Sydney. The more recent crime fiction in America has been predominantly feminist, and a similar trend is observable in Australia in the works of Marele Day and Jennifer Rowe. (See **Crime and Mystery Fiction**, Australia.)

Foreign Influences on Australian Theatre

The influence of foreign drama on Australian theatre was for a long time extraordinarily negative. Managements have put on proven successes from overseas rather than risking money on locally written plays. The convict-built Emu Plains Theatre opened in 1825 with a triple bill of old plays that included *The Mock Doctor*, Henry Fielding's adaptation, first produced in 1732, of Molière's *Le Médecin malgré lui* (1666). In the record of plays performed in Barnett Levey's Theatre Royal in Sydney (1833–8), all except seven ballets or pantomimes and one title of unknown provenance had been previously performed in England. Eight of Levey's productions were mounted in Sydney the year following first performance in England. The arrival in 1874 of J. C. Williams from the USA brought little change in this respect; he claimed that locally written scripts were of inferior quality and continued to favour overseas successes.

Only in the realms of pantomime and melodrama were local themes supreme, but these were under the guidance of three writers originally from England. George Darrell ('Gentleman George'), in Australia from 1868 to approximately 1905, wrote, acted, and produced more than fifty topical, lively, comic, and melodramatic plays on Australian themes. During the 1860s in Melbourne, W. M. Akhurst, in Australia from 1849 to 1871, devised regular pantomimes and burlesques on mainly Australian themes, and from 1873 onwards Alfred Dampier wrote and acted melodramas and adapted works by Marcus Clarke and Rolf Boldrewood for the stage.

It was not until the 1920s that **Louis Esson** succeeded in creating a competitive Australian drama. Esson, a friend of Lady Gregory, W. B. Yeats, and J. M. Synge, was encouraged by the success of the Dublin Abbey Theatre to write of local Australian characters and customs, which he did with antipodean wit and irony. He admired many emerging European, American, and Russian dramatists who were in the process of creating their own national styles, having particular enthusiasm for Anton Chekhov and Eugene O'Neill.

From the 1930s communism characterized much Australian experimental drama. Spreading from the American New Theatre movement and from the enthusiastic reception of the works of Bertolt Brecht, it encouraged a group of dramatists, notably **Dorothy Hewett** and Oriel Gray.

Recent writers are indebted more to the USA

than to Europe, particularly to the American-type drama workshops introduced by Betty Burstall in 1965 at the Melbourne Pram Factory. **Jack Hibberd, John Romeril, Barry Oakley,** and **David Williamson** have all benefited from this experience of close contact with the audience. From the USA, too, came the impetus to free the stage from censorship, allowing nudity and the vernacular voice complete with obscenities.

In spite of some notable successes, however, such as **Ray Lawler**'s *Summer of the Seventeenth Doll* (1957) and the enthusiastic overseas reception of Steve Spears' *The Elocution of Benjamin Franklin* (1977), it remains fairly true now, as in the beginning, that managements regard Australian plays as something of a risk to be avoided in favour of overseas box-office draws. (See **Drama**, Australia.)

DOROTHY COLMER

FOREIGN WRITERS (Canada)

The writers who have come from abroad to Canada and in some way have entered or reflected its culture can be divided into three groups. There are the immigrants, who remain and become Canadians by residence, citizenship, or feeling; these cannot be called foreign writers. But there are two categories to which that description genuinely applies: the sojourners, who stay for a while, perhaps write a book or two and temporarily join the country's literary life; and the travellers, those who stay for days or months, gathering impressions and perhaps, back at home or later in their travels, write something enlightening on their experience. Within these two groups, which could include every foreign writer who was somehow connected with Canada, regardless of quality, many important or at least interesting writers have contributed to the understanding of Canada and the development of its literature.

From the beginning, in both New France and the British North American colonies, there was a clear division between the sojourners, mainly garrison soldiers and their families, and the settlers who had come to stay. Until the coming of the **Loyalists**, it was the people of the garrisons, with their amateur theatricals and musical gatherings and their pens coursing over empty pages in idle hours, who created an island of culture in what seemed to them the Canadian wilderness and initiated a Canadian literature. The first novel that can be called Canadian, *The History of Emily Montague* (1769), was written by **Frances Brooke**, wife of the chaplain to the Quebec garrison, who lived in Canada from 1763 to 1768. The first poetry from English Canada was *Quodlibets Lately Come Over from New Britaniola, Old Newfound-land* (1628) by Ben Jonson's friend Robert Hayman, who intermittently administered a settlement in Newfoundland for a consortium of Bristol merchants.

These are indeed single swallows, for a real literature in English did not begin to take form in Canada until the second quarter of the nineteenth century, after the Loyalists had begun to arrive in the 1780s and after the War of 1812–14 had clearly defined the concept of Canada in the minds of its people. The years following the Napoleonic wars dramatically changed the population of the British North American colonies with an influx of English half-pay officers and insolvent gentry on the one hand, and of the landless and unemployed — largely Irish and Scottish — on the other. Most of the men and women who first established an anglophone literature in Canada were immigrants who remained, such as the members of the Strickland family (see **Moodie, Susanna**) and Tiger Dunlop. But there were still individuals who appeared, sojourned awhile for personal or business reasons, and then departed, having gathered material for books Canadians still read about their predecessors. Anna Jameson came to Canada in the 1830s in the hope of salvaging a lurching marriage with a colonial official, travelled for eight months in Upper Canada, and in her *Winter Studies and Summer Rambles in Canada* (1838) left one of the best accounts of Canadian colonial society at high tide. **John Galt**, who had arrived in 1825 as a land agent of the Canada Company just at the time when he was making a name for himself as a writer rivalling Walter Scott in Britain, went home in 1829, but out of the years in Canada he reaped not only two immigrant novels, *Lawrie Todd* (1830) and *Bogle Corbet* (1831), but also a lively *Autobiography* (1833), dealing extensively with Canadian personalities and politics.

Among the most interesting nineteenth-century sojourning scribblers were the colonial officials and their families, who came out from England on their turns of duty and often returned home with journals published in their lifetimes and later. Lady Dufferin, venturing across the country with her governor-general husband in the 1870s, kept a fascinating diary of visits to Canadian communities, published as *My Canadian Journal 1872–78* (1891), while Sir Francis Bond Head, who may have been a less-than-ideal governor of Upper Canada at the time of the 1837 rebellion, published two years afterwards a lively *Narrative* of the events. Perhaps the most interesting of the unofficial observations by official personages were the diaries that appeared after their deaths, notably the lively journal kept by Lord Dalhousie when he officiated at Halifax after the Napoleonic wars, published as *The Dalhousie Journals* (1979), edited by Margery Whitelaw, and the fascinatingly irreverent narrative of social-political life at the time of Confederation preserved in the journal of Frances Monck, daughter-in-law of the incumbent governor general: *Monck Letters and Journals, 1863–1868* (1970), edited by W. L. Morton.

Increasingly in the nineteenth century, and especially after the completion of the Canadian Pacific Railway in 1885, Canada became one of the favoured destinations of writers who were interested in the adventure and challenge of imperial expansion. This applied particularly to the writers of boys' stories so popular in that age. Captain Frederick Marryat came to Canada not long after the rebellion of 1837 and kept *A Diary in America* (1839) that made interesting comparisons between American drive and Canadian steadfastness, and in *The Settlers in Canada* (1844) combined vigorous narrative with immigration propaganda. R. M. Ballantyne based his writing about Canada on direct experience, for as a youth in 1841 he became a clerk to the Hudson's Bay Company and remained in the fur trade for six years before returning to Scotland in 1847. His first book was the autobiographical *Hudson's Bay* (1848), and among the many novels of the North that followed it were *Snowflakes and Sunbeams; or, the Young Fur Traders* (1856) and *Ungava: A Tale of Esquimaux Land* (1857). Two other noted boys' authors who used Canada as a setting were G. A. Henty (*With Wolfe in Canada*, 1887) and Mayne Reid (*The Young Voyageurs*, 1854).

The first of a long list of British and American literary figures to include Canada in American grand tours was the Irish poet Thomas Moore, who arrived in 1804 and commemorated his visit with the famous 'Canadian Boat Song' (1806) and other sentimental verses. Charles Dickens arrived in 1842 and gave Canada a minor place in his *American Notes* (1842); his third son, Francis Dickens, joined the North-West Mounted Police, played an undistinguished role in the 1885 rebellion, and left a diary of the times, published by the journal *Queen's Quarterly* in 1930. Anthony Trollope was as summary as Dickens in dealing with Canada in his *North America* (1862).

It was at the midpoint of the nineteenth century that American writers began seriously to direct their attention and their steps to Canada. In 1850 Henry David Thoreau found his way north, and in *A Yankee in Canada* (1866) his democratic sneers at English official pomp were balanced by a sympathetic response to Québécois village life. Thirty years later Walt Whitman arrived, convinced that he was treading the future soil of the USA as he went from London to the Saguenay; his *Diary in Canada* (1904) contains lyrical descriptions of harvest days in both Upper and Lower Canada. But in terms of the interpretation of Canadian history, the most important figure from south of the border was undoubtedly Francis Parkman, whose vast nine-volume work *France and England in North America* was published between 1851 and 1892. Just as he ventured over the territory before writing *The Oregon Trail* (1847), Parkman travelled the Laurentian terrain so that he was treading on known territory when he wrote of Canadian history.

Other American writers exploited in different ways the romantic side of Canadian history. Henry Wadsworth Longfellow's travesty of Acadian history, *Evangeline* (1847), was partly redeemed by Harriet Vaughan Cheney's competent historical novel, *The Rivals of Acadia: An Old Story of the New World* (1827). William Dean Howells, whose influence **Sara Jeannette Duncan** acknowledged, used the Canadian setting as a background for examining American conflicts in books such as *Their Wedding Journey* (1872), *Chance Acquaintance* (1873), and *The Quality of Mercy* (1892). And during this period the legendary master himself, Henry James, came discreetly over the border and noted his impression, in *Portraits of Places* (1883), that Niagara Falls is 'the most beautiful object in the world', and that 'Quebec must be a city of gossip; for evidently it is not a city of culture.' This impression was anticipated a few years before by Samuel Butler, who in 1878 visited Montreal, claimed to have seen a maimed plaster cast of the Discobolus in a local museum, and wrote his 'A Psalm of Montreal' with its famous refrain, 'O God! O Montreal!' Between Butler and James, Oscar Wilde arrived on his grand American tour, visiting both Whitman and Canada; he condescended to declare Homer Watson 'the Canadian Constable', declared that 'Niagara Falls must be the second major disappointment of American married life', and delivered a sensitive, forgotten lecture on the poetry of D'Arcy McGee, the tragic Irish-Canadian politician who had once been a Dublin literary associate of Wilde's mother, Speranza.

The expansion of Canada from Confederation onwards, including the opening of the Prairies, the Métis rebellions, and the gold rushes in the Fraser Valley in 1858 and the Klondike in the late 1890s, provoked a stream of vigorous, male-oriented writing about adventure and endurance in the wilderness that was being steadily explored, tamed, and destroyed. This writing included such hyperbolically stirring accounts of prairie and mountain travel as Captain William Francis Butler's *The Great Lone Land* (1872) and *The Wild North Land* (1873). Less sensational in their reporting were the Earl of Southesk and Viscount Milton, wandering aristocrats who partially retraced the overland route across the Prairies followed by gold miners going from eastern Canada to the Cariboo region in the west. Southesk's *Saskatchewan and the Rocky Mountains* appeared in 1875 and Milton's *North-West Passage by Land* (co-authored with W. B. Cheadle) in 1865. The heroics of the latter were ironically diminished many years later by the account of Milton's companion, Dr Walter Butler Cheadle, *Cheadle's Journal of Trip Across Canada, 1862–1863* (1931). (See **Travel Literature**, Canada.)

A more imaginative level was reached when the Klondike attracted a number of American adventure writers, notably Jack London, who developed there his theories of the ultimate role of altruism in a world based on the universal struggle for existence. His early short stories of the Klondike led to major works such as *The Call of the Wild* (1903) and *White Fang* (1906), which are perhaps the best books to come out of the gold rushes. Neither his imitators, such as James Oliver

Curwood (*The Danger Trail*, 1910), nor his parodists, such as Sinclair Lewis (*Mantrap*, 1926), equalled London in his role of the manly yet compassionate adventurer. Another American writer, Wallace Stegner, spent part of his early childhood in Saskatchewan and remembered it in *Wolf Willow* (1963), an eloquently written memoir. One of the best historical novels on Canada, a sombre tale of late seventeenth-century Quebec, *Shadows on the Rock* (1931), is by an American, Willa Cather.

The procession of English writers continued as the century turned. Algernon Blackwood spent most of the 1890s wandering in Canada and the USA, describing his experiences in *Episodes before Thirty* (1923) and later using Canadian settings for some of his Gothic tales. Mrs Humphry Ward took the rail trip across the country and wrote a fictionalized travel account, *Canadian Born* (1910), full of shrewd observations stuffed into a stilted plot.

T. E. Hulme, the English poet and father of Imagism, spent several months in 1907 roughing it across the country, living by casual jobs. Later, in one of his lectures on modern poetry, he remarked: 'Speaking of personal matters, the first time I ever felt the necessity or inevitableness of verse was the desire to reproduce the peculiar quality of feeling which is induced by the flat spaces and wide horizons of the virgin prairies of western Canada.' Two very different poets from Hulme arrived during the years before the First World War, the veteran imperialist Rudyard Kipling and the young dilettante Rupert Brooke. Kipling was so taken with western Canada that he contemplated settling in Vancouver, and his recollections of Canada found their places in several books, notably *Letters of Marque* (1889) and *Letters to the Family: Notes on a Recent Trip to Canada* (1908); he greatly favoured the idea of Canada emerging as a sovereign nation within the Commonwealth. Brooke's *Letters from America* (1916) and the letters in Geoffrey Keynes' edition of his correspondence show a condescending disgust at Canada's colonial life.

Before the First World War, British writers tended either to settle or to travel for relatively short periods; true sojourners were comparatively rare. The best known of them was probably William Cobbett, who spent some years at the end of the eighteenth century in New Brunswick and left an account of that still barely settled region in his *Advice to Young Men* (1829-30). But it was not until the mid-twentieth century that any number of distinguished sojourners appeared and took some part in Canadian literary life. Malcolm Lowry, a remittance man trapped by wartime monetary restrictions, lived on Burrard Inlet, near Vancouver, from 1937 to 1954, writing one incomplete, brilliant novel, *October Ferry to Gabriola* (1970), and a collection of short stories, *Hear Us O Lord from Heaven Thy Dwelling Place* (1961), which show how deeply the experience of life in British Columbia affected him. Wyndham Lewis, the great modernist writer and painter, was likewise trapped — in Ontario — during the Second World War; after a period of poverty in Toronto, he taught at the University of Windsor, and out of his experiences wrote *Self Condemned* (1954), a bitter novel about Canadian society and Canadian academics that Canadians have since somewhat masochistically accepted as a kind of classic.

Another kind of sojourning was that of John Buchan, the Scottish popular novelist who, as Lord Tweedsmuir, served as governor general from 1935 until his death in 1940. During that time Buchan wrote one heavily moralistic novel about Canada, *Sick Heart River* (1941). The Irish writer Brian Moore arrived in 1948 and worked for four years as a reporter on the *Montreal Gazette*. Two of his best novels about Ireland, *The Lonely Passion of Judith Hearne* (1955) and *The Feast of Lupercal* (1957), were written in Canada, but the only novel Moore wrote with a Canadian setting was *The Luck of Ginger Coffey* (1960). By the time it appeared he had already moved on to the

USA, where he has since lived.

The postwar expansion of Canadian universities, especially in the late 1950s and the 1960s, brought many British and American writers to take up teaching posts; the majority remain as immigrants. Among the sojourners who departed, perhaps the most notable were the American novelists Joyce Carol Oates and **Clark Blaise**, the Indian novelist **Bharati Mukherjee** (Blaise's wife), and the American poet Robert Creeley, who taught in Vancouver and was involved in the 1963 Vancouver Poetry Festival, which centred on a group of visiting American poets from the San Francisco Beat tradition and the Black Mountain school.

GEORGE WOODCOCK

Further reading: James Doyle, 'Foreign writers on Canada in English', in William Toye (ed.) *The Oxford Companion to Canadian Literature* (1983).

FOREIGN WRITERS (Hong Kong)

Colonial Hong Kong has fascinated foreign writers by being doubly marginal, a city at the edge of China that was also an eastern outpost of the British empire. It has been experienced and understood as a place of contrasts, as a few examples must suffice to show.

Rudyard Kipling travelled to Hong Kong in 1889, *en route* from India to England, and he sent dispatches back to *The Pioneer* in Allahabad, India, that were later collected in the volume *From Sea to Sea* (1899). Kipling's Hong Kong is a triumphant miniature of the empire itself, stoutly defended, efficiently run, and commercially vigorous. He finds much in the life of the colony to remind him of British India, but is so impressed by the skilful and industrious working people of Hong Kong that he announces mischievously to his Anglo-Indian readers that they have conquered the wrong country. The tempting prospect of a British China is soon dispelled by a visit upriver to Canton, 'a big blue sink of a city full of tunnels, all dark and inhabited by yellow devils'. In Canton Kipling feels overwhelmed: after a moment of racial panic, he is glad to hurry back from this Chinese underworld to Hong Kong, with its reassuring British garrison, its bullish taipans, its excellent shopping, and the expatriate wives in their opulent houses on the Peak, whose social round and endless gossip make the visitor feel he might be back in Simla, India. The only thing wrong with Hong Kong, in Kipling's view, was its vice, which he found disgusting — not because there were prostitutes in the city, but because some of them were white women.

W. Somerset Maugham's sketches of China and China-coast life and characters, *On a Chinese Screen* (1922), were followed in 1925 by *The Painted Veil*, a novel set almost entirely in Hong Kong and China, though it contains only one named Chinese character and no speaking parts for Chinese. In the novel, Walter Fane, a government bacteriologist in Hong Kong, learns of his wife Kitty's adultery with the assistant colonial secretary and forces her to accompany him to the cholera-stricken Chinese city of Mei-tan-fu, where it is quite likely she will die in the epidemic. Kitty, a colonial Emma Bovary, realizes in her ordeal that her lover Charlie Townsend is a cad and she has been a fool. The cholera does not kill her (it carries off the brooding and enigmatic Walter) and though she briefly succumbs to Townsend again in Hong Kong, she returns home to England a less selfish woman who has learned compassion and charity. Here the contrast is deployed again, but to un-Kiplingesque ends. Conditions in China are frightful, but life is serious there and wisdom can be purchased at a price, whereas colonial Hong Kong is the playground of self-important philistine mediocrities with not enough to do. Maugham got into legal trouble over the book and had to change Hong Kong to the imaginary colony of Tching-Yen.

W. H. Auden and Christopher Isherwood spent time in Hong Kong in 1938 *en route* to

China to write about the Sino-Japanese war. Their *Journey to a War* (1939) records Isherwood's impression of Hong Kong as a frenetic in-between place, a dream-like blur that gives off a pervasive sense of unreality that he hoped would dissipate when they arrived in China and the 'real' world. Auden's sonnet on Hong Kong picks up the theme of the unreality of the place and of its marginality: 'Its leading characters are wise and witty', expatriate life is like an urbane domestic comedy, but the real drama is going on offstage, across the border, where life is 'neither comic nor a game'.

Edmund Blunden, professor of English at Hong Kong University from 1953 to 1964, saw in Hong Kong a gentler prospect: poems in his *A Hong Kong House* (1962) can still find it simple and untroubled (though 'development' threatens), an Oriental pastoral — a Hong Kong now as remote, in its way, as Kipling's.

DOUGLAS KERR

FOREIGN WRITERS (India)

The Influence of Foreign Writers on Indian Writers

Indian writing in English is of relatively recent growth. It began after the introduction of the English language in India by the British colonial government. The earliest Indian expression in English was discursive rather than narrative, reversing the natural sequence. As a result, the early growth of Indian poetry in English was parasitic, depending largely on recognition by British scholars and critics. Thus, **Toru Dutt** owed her emergence to Edmund Gosse, and **Rabindranath Tagore**, at least for his work in English, to W. B. Yeats. This feature has dominated Indian writing and continues to do so. **Mulk Raj Anand** was introduced to readers by E. M. Forster, and **R. K. Narayan** by Graham Greene; **Salman Rushdie** and **Vikram Seth** achieved fame partly because of awards won in Britain and the USA. Early Indian poetry in English was also derivative in character, as may be seen in the poetry of **H. L. V. Derozio** and Dutt. **Sri Aurobindo** shows clearly the influence of Tennyson and Matthew Arnold. Only in 1971 could critic V. K. Gorak claim that Indian poetry in English was 'no longer tied to the apron strings of English creative writing'.

The novel as a literary form is not native to India. Philip Meadows Taylor (1808–76) modelled his novels on the romances of Sir Walter Scott, as did Bankim Chandra Chatterjee (1838–94). Although Indian-English fiction preceded fiction in Bengali and other Indian languages, the first significant Indian-English novel, Anand's *Untouchable* (1935), appeared half a century after the Bengali novel was well established. Anand's fiction is like the painting of Amrita Shergill (1913–41); the techniques are borrowed but the content is native. Anand's earlier novels were written under the influence of socialist realism while the later novels are autobiographical.

Raja Rao claims in his foreword to *Kanthapura* (1938) that the structure of his novel is puranic, that is, episodic, implying that it should not be judged by the norms of western fiction. But the story is told by the grandmother and it is difficult to believe that Rao would have adopted this narrative device had he not been familiar with Emily Brontë or Joseph Conrad. Rao's *The Serpent and the Rope* (1968) shows the influence of Aldous Huxley and the discursive novel, and *The Cat and Shakespeare* (1965) the influence of Ionesco and the Absurdist movement.

R. K. Narayan, India's most prolific novelist, is very much rooted in his native soil, which he has fictionized as Malgudi. Comparable to Thomas Hardy's Wessex, it is a microcosm subject to changes brought about by modernity. A contemporary parallel is **V. S. Naipaul**'s Miguel Street, or Trinidad as represented in his early stories. Narayan's narrative technique is somewhat more sophisticated than Anand's. In his novels and stories there is a consistent 'point of view' in

Henry James' sense. In this respect again he is like Naipaul.

Indian writers in English are well-read not only in English fiction and poetry but also in literary criticism. Many of them teach in universities in India or abroad (**Nissim Ezekiel** and **A. K. Ramanujan**, for example). Movements in western critical theory are therefore reflected in their writings. Some outstanding writers of Hindi, Urdu, and Kannada are also teachers of English.

The language of Indian-English fiction has undergone a slow change. As Indian writers begin to migrate to Britain and the USA or to marry natives of English-speaking countries, as **Kamala Markandaya** and **Bharati Mukherjee** have done, their idiom becomes less 'native'. Even those who have not migrated, such as **Nayantara Sahgal** and **Anita Desai**, are distinctly less Indian in their use of the English language. This movement runs counter to the development of a native dialect of English in the Caribbean and among black Americans. (See **Language**, The Caribbean.)

The experimental novel makes a tentative beginning with **G. V. Desani**'s *All About H. Hatterr* (1951, first published under its lesser-known title, *All About Mr. Hatterr, A Gesture*, 1948), which was influenced by James Joyce. It was not followed either by any innovative use of language or by any bold experiments in the stream-of-consciousness technique. **K. R. S. Iyengar** traces Anita Desai's interior monologues to the influence of Virginia Woolf. But recently Indian fiction has caught up with the magic realism of Gabriel García Márquez in Salman Rushdie's novels *Midnight's Children* (1981) and *The Satanic Verses* (1988). **Amitav Ghosh**'s experiments are less ambitious. The self-reflexive novel is exemplified by **Shashi Tharoor**'s *The Great Indian Novel* (1989), reminiscent of novels by John Fowles.

The present generation of poets reflects the changing tastes and critical attitudes prevalent in the USA, Britain, and possibly Australia. The publication of Nissim Ezekiel's *Sixty Poems* (1953) coincided almost with the anti-romantic, ironic poetry of 'The Temperate Zone', which was current in the 1950s in Britain (for example, D. J. Enright and John Wain). The wordiness of Dylan Thomas or Gerard Manley Hopkins, however, is more congenial to the average Indian poet, who lacks their spell-binding incantatory effect. Other interesting poets such as **Keki Daruwalla** and **Kamala Das** reflect the manner of Ted Hughes and the confessional poets respectively. The contemporary trend is to present experience in the raw, almost without mediation.

R. K. KAUL

The Influence of India on Foreign Writers

During the last four hundred years, India has exercised a powerful influence on the English literary imagination. Initial British perceptions of India as a land of riches, spice, pearls, magic, ropetricks, and mysticism found literary expression in Christopher Marlowe's *Doctor Faustus*, in which Faustus cries, 'I'll have them fly to India for gold,' and in Shakespeare's *As You Like It*, where India's riches are referred to again: 'From the east to western Ind, / No jewel is like Rosalind.' In Andrew Marvell's 'To His Coy Mistress', the lover promises his mistress, 'by the Indian Ganges side / Should't rubies find'.

Sir William Jones, Robert Southey, and Thomas Moore are among the writers of the late 1700s and early 1800s who were fascinated by Indian religion and philosophy and used India as a setting for their works. Jones' nine hymns addressed to various Hindu deities (published between 1784 and 1788), Southey's long poem *The Curse of Kehama* (1810), and Moore's *Lalla Rookh: An Oriental Romance* (1817) display an admirable knowledge of Indian religions, philosophy, and history. The influence of India on the British Romantic poets, most notably Shelley and

Coleridge, is similar. This continuing interest in India is a result of the 'exotic' appeal of India and the 'inscrutability' of the land and its people. Early British travellers and residents in India also wrote diaries, travelogues, and memoirs of their experiences there — a tradition that continues today.

Orientalists projected an image of India as a country with a glorious past, full of ripe wisdom embodied in its religion and philosophy. Their theories of Indian civilization and their publication of translations of classical Sanskrit works in the journal *Asiatick Researches* created a sensational reaction in Europe and produced images of India that persist today. Friedrich Max Müller's study of the Vedas — ancient Hindu scripture — sparked his love for the ancient civilization of India and furthered orientalist interests outside of England, both in Europe and North America. Only British imperial rule in India offers an explanation for the comparative neglect in England of India and its civilization.

Anglocentricism marks the characteristic response to India of British historians, Indologists, and art critics. In the writings of these historians, Britain's rule in India is of exclusive interest, and India's entire past is evaluated only to justify British rule. Similarly, the work of British Indologists, who were convinced of their inherent cultural superiority, reveals a bias for British critical canons in literary evaluations. British art critics typically made purely aesthetic responses to Indian art, ignoring its cultural context or comparing it to ancient Greek art. This refusal to view India in its own terms, and this insistence on judging it from an English viewpoint also characterize the literary response to India by Anglo-Indian writers prior to Rudyard Kipling (1865–1936).

The exoticization of India by early British writers was followed by attempts by British writers to explore Indian realities. These stages can be compared to the responses of British writers in other Commonwealth countries; British writers of the nineteenth century used Africa as a setting to excite in the English reading public the interest in the exotic and the 'primitive', whereas later writers such as Joyce Cary and Graham Greene used the novel to explore the realities of African life. Leonard Woolf, who used Ceylon (now Sri Lanka) as a setting for some of his work, and George Orwell, some of whose works are set in Burma (now Myanmar), are other examples.

Sir Walter Scott, Philip Meadows Taylor, and William Delafield Arnold are the major British nineteenth-century literary figures, prior to Rudyard Kipling, whose works deal specifically with India. Scott's novel *The Surgeon's Daughter* (1827) presents a romantic view of British imperialism in India. Taylor, who lived in India as soldier and administrator, wrote *Confessions of a Thug* (1839), known for its vivid and realistic portrayal of Indian life. His trilogy — *Tara* (1863), *Ralph Darnell* (1865), and *Seeta* (1872) — can best be described as historical romance. Arnold's *Oakfield; or, Fellowship in the East* (1853) is the most significant work to emerge during this period. Arnold's preoccupations in the novel — his healthy respect for India despite his assertion of its inferiority, his scathing criticism of British officialdom, his view of the British in India as living in exile, his disarmingly frank exposure of the empire as a commercial enterprise, and his concern for better understanding between the two cultures — constitute the main features of the tradition of Anglo-Indian fiction. The Australian John George Lang (1816–64), who spent the last twenty years of his life in India, wrote many novels set there. The best known of his writings are his novel *The Wetherbys* (1859) and the travelogue *Wanderings in India* (1859). His presentation of India is marked by wit, humour, and gentle satire.

Although Rudyard Kipling is often portrayed as an imperialist, his writings on India contain many significant insights. While he wrote stories emphasizing the nobility and sacrifices of the colonizer, he also recognizes the darker side of imperialism, as, for example, in 'The Man Who Would Be King' (1888). Here the imperialist myth is unmasked, and its real motives — avarice, greed, and ambition — are revealed in sordid detail. In his exploration into discovering meaningful relationships between the rulers and the ruled within the imperial system, Kipling finds that love is one of the significant emotions that makes such a relationship — however brief, remote, and tragic — possible. He is perhaps the only Anglo-Indian writer who was aware of the profound truth that India cannot be understood without the possession of an abiding interest in its religion and metaphysics. Such an awareness on Kipling's part produced two great stories, 'The Bridge-Builders' (1893) and 'The Miracle of Purun Bhagat' (1894).

Kipling's classic of India, *Kim* (1901), is concerned mainly with the quests of two individuals: Kim, a fourteen-year-old Irish orphan, and Teshoo Lama, a holy man from Tibet. Kim's quest is for both his parentage and identity, while Lama, 'a follower of the Middle Way', is in search of an all-healing river. Though Kim belongs instinctively to the world of action, and the Lama to the world of renunciation, there is a deep attachment between the two. In the end it is the Lama who brings to Kim the profound truth of life, namely, that 'there is neither black nor white'. Kim is truly a figure of synthesis who is able to absorb the best of both worlds represented by England and by India. Kim's development can also be taken to stand for the making of an ideal sahib.

Among Kipling's contemporaries were many women novelists who wrote fairly extensively on India. They offer a superficial response to India, their works eulogizing Anglo-Saxon virtues and British rule in India. Although Flora Annie Steel (1847–1929), for example, came under Kipling's influence, she continued to associate India with fanaticism, passivity, inertia, and violence. What distinguishes her work is the occasional attempt to probe Indian reality in some depth and the evidence of a greater complexity that is absent in the others. Another important figure is the Canadian **Sara Jeannette Duncan**, who lived in India for more than twenty years and wrote ten novels and a few short stories set in India. Although she was basically a defender of the raj, her work is characterized by a realistic depiction of Anglo-Indian life in Calcutta and Simla. Despite its melodrama, her last novel, *The Burnt Offering* (1909), is interesting for its depiction of Indian nationalism, as represented in the character of Bal Gangadhar Tilak, and of the possibility of an interracial marriage.

Edmund Candler (1874–1926) is the only British novelist of Kipling's era whose work deals centrally with Indian nationalism. In *Siri Ram, Revolutionist: A Transcript from Life, 1907–1910* (1912) and *Abdication* (1922) the protagonists are presented as young men who are misled into sacrificing their lives for a hopeless cause, a conscious acknowledgement of the novelist's reluctance to come to terms with a movement that was to give India independence in another twenty-five years.

In describing the Anglo-Indian world, *A Passage to India* (1924), by E. M. Forster (1879–1970), takes into account India's social, political, and religious aspects. The novel's division into three sections — 'mosque', 'cave', and 'temple' — gives it a structural and symbolic unity. While the mosque represents Islam — the unity and brotherhood of humanity — caves signify primeval darkness, negation, and the breakdown of human relationships. The temple, on the other hand, suggests harmony and regeneration. Despite his liberal stance, Forster finds India and its people to be both a mystery and a muddle. For him 'the Mediterranean is the human norm' and from this standpoint it is inevitable that India should seem amorphous and formless. Whereas Kipling responds to India with a loving understanding, Forster stands at a distance passing critical judgements. In *Kim*, Kipling is able to illuminate the different facets of the multifarious reality of India that clearly lie outside Forster's interests; *A Passage to India* captures, at best, a passing phase in the history of British-Indian relations. *Kim* projects a fuller and more comprehensive image of India and its people.

The British writer Edward Thompson (1886–1946) wrote a trilogy — *An Indian Day* (1927), *A Farewell to India* (1931), and *An End of the Hours* (1938) — that dramatizes the British dilemma in India. By juxtaposing the world of contemplation, represented by the east, against the world of action, represented by the west, Thompson seems to suggest that attempts to bring the two together are doomed to failure. (See **East-West Encounter**.)

In his tetralogy, *The Raj Quartet* (1977) — *The Jewel in the Crown* (1966), *The Day of the Scorpion* (1968), *The Towers of Silence* (1971), and *A Division of the Spoils* (1975) — Paul Scott (1920–78) explores in great detail the Indo-British encounter in the last days of the raj. He asserts at the outset that the *Quartet* 'is the story of a rape, of the events that led up to it and followed it and the place in which it happened'. While Anglo-Indian novelists of the nineteenth century used sexual assault as an alleged external manifestation of the depravity of Indians as a race, both Scott and Forster make rape a central theme in order to highlight the problems encountered in interracial understanding. In Scott's *Quartet*, Daphne Manners, in love with an Indian, Hari Kumar, is raped by a group of unknown Indians. A variation of this rape occurs on the same day in the abusive and physical attack on Edwina Crane by Indian rioters. In Forster's novel, Adela Quested also believes that she has been sexually molested by Aziz inside the Marabar Caves. While Forster criticizes the British for their role in the investigation of this imagined rape, Scott goes beyond criticism to reiterate that, despite the brutality of the attack, interracial love is desirable and even beautiful.

British outsiders writing on India wrote not so much as individuals but as representatives of the ruling race. Hence, the emphasis in Anglo-Indian writing is on the British in India and not on the India they occupied. In addition to the colonial relationship, the European mind insisted, to use **Nirad Chaudhuri**'s description, on three principles, 'that of reason, that of order and that of measure'. The empirical and the rational often act as a hindrance in understanding the complex social, philosophical, and metaphysical components of the Indian actuality. Furthermore, imperialist ideology engendered in these writers an attitude of condescension and superciliousness. Finally, there was the proverbial British insularity. To achieve some degree of success both artistic detachment and self-effacement are necessary; these qualities were achieved by Kipling, Forster, Thompson, and Scott in varying degrees.

K. C. BELLIAPPA

Further reading: A. G. Bhupal Singh, *A Survey of Anglo-Indian Fiction* (1934); Allen J. Greenberger, *The British Image of India: A Study of the Literature of Imperialism 1880–1950* (1969); Benita Parry, *Delusions and Discoveries: Studies on India in the British Imagination, 1880–1930* (1972); K. C. Belliappa, *The Image of India in English Fiction: Studies in Kipling, Myers, and Raja Rao* (1991); M. K. Naik, *Mirror on the Wall: Images of India and the Englishman in Anglo-Indian Fiction* (1991).

FOREIGN WRITERS (South Pacific)

Among the foreign, English-language writers of the eighteenth and nineteenth centuries whose works are associated with the South Pacific are Robert Louis Stevenson, Beatrice Grimshaw, and Herman Melville. Stevenson, author of *Kidnapped* (1886) and *Treasure Island* (1883), also wrote several other books set in the South Pacific, such as *In The South Seas* (1896), *An Inland Voyage* (1878), and *Island Nights' Entertainments* (1893). Grimshaw wrote several books set in the South Pacific, including *The Terrible Island* (1920), *The*

Coral Queen (1921), *The Valley of Never-Come-Back* (1923), and *Black Sheep's Gold* (1927). Melville, best known for *Moby-Dick* (1851), also wrote *Omoo: A Narrative of Adventures in the South Seas* (1847) and *Typee: A Peep at Polynesian Life. During a Four Months' Residence in a Valley of the Marquesas* (1846).

In an ironic way these writers contributed to the emergence of South Pacific literature because it is in reaction to their presentation of the region in their novels and travel books that Samoan **Albert Wendt** began to write. His anger at the image presented by these foreign writers provoked his desire to set the record right and to counteract what they wrote. **James Baxter**, on the other hand, exerted a more positive influence on Wendt and **Witi Ihimaera** by actively encouraging them to write.

Indigenous writing in the South Pacific is closely linked with the creative writing and the 'Literature of New Nations' courses that were offered in the late 1960s and the 1970s under the direction of Ulli Beier at the University of Papua New Guinea and at the University of the South Pacific. Writers such as Sir **Serei Vincent Eri**, **John Kasaipwalova**, Arthur Jawodimbari, **Russell Soaba**, John Kaniku, Nora Vagi-Brash, Jully Sipolo, and Vanessa Griffen were all products of these universities.

The influence of **Chinua Achebe**'s *Things Fall Apart* (1958) on Vincent Eri, the writer of the first Papua New Guinea novel, *The Crocodile* (1970), is unmistakable. The theme of the negative influence of contact with the west and the attempt to depict a vivid and viable traditional culture are common to both novels.

There was strong interest in the South Pacific in African writers, but, closer to home, influential literary works emerged. Albert Wendt's *Sons for the Return Home* (1973) and *Flying-Fox in a Freedom Tree* (1974) and Witi Ihimaera's *Pounamu, Pounamu* (1972) and *Tangi* (1973) served as models for other Pacific writers. Cross-fertilization was encouraged by meetings and writers' conferences organized in the region.

The dynamism of Kasaipwalova's and Leo Hannet's protest writings stems mainly from the anti-colonial activism that was the underlying message of the early post-colonial writings in Africa and elsewhere. Wendt discusses the inappropriateness of intrusive western culture in his essay 'In a Stone Castle in the South Seas' (first published in *Mana Review* 2, 1976).

Literary criticism in the South Pacific has become more informed, placing these writers within their own oral literary tradition. Although some western critics have suggested French existentialist influence on the works of Wendt and Soaba, it is a question of converging interest rather than one of direct influence. (See **Criticism**, South Pacific.)

ADEOLA JAMES

Further reading: S. Nandan, ed., *Language and Literature in Multicultural Context* (1983); Subramani, *South Pacific Literature: From Myth to Fabulation* (1985).

FOREIGN WRITERS (Sri Lanka)

Sri Lanka's strategic position athwart the sea routes to the east has attracted an extraordinary assortment of foreigners. It was known to the Greeks as Taprobane, and references from early times created an image of the island as a tropical paradise. The first book in English about the island was Robert Knox's *An Historical Relation of Ceylon* (1681). Based on Knox's almost twenty years spent as a captive of King Rajasingha II, it is a comprehensive and accurate account of Sinhala life in the seventeenth century, couched in plain yet gripping prose. Published between part one of John Bunyan's *Pilgrim's Progress* (1678) and Daniel Defoe's *Robinson Crusoe* (1719), it is a source for the latter: Knox's Puritanical piety and commercial, practical sense resemble Crusoe's. The book deserves a place in Sri Lanka's literature.

As British imperialism expanded in the nineteenth century (the whole of Ceylon came under British rule in 1815), the tendency to regard the colonies as places of advancement became more pronounced. Memoirs such as Major Forbes' *Eleven Years in Ceylon* (1840) and Samuel Baker's *Eight Years' Wanderings in Ceylon* (1855) provided useful information. John Capper collected his stories in *Old Ceylon: Sketches of Ceylon Life in Olden Times* (1877). The only creative work of value in this century, however, was William Knighton's *Forest Life in Ceylon* (1854). It is 'a collection of light sketches' on colonial life, like William Arnold's *Oakfield; or, Fellowship in the East* (1853), set in India. Knighton, however, responds more actively to his alien setting, his writing has more verve, and he includes a 'native', Marandhan, as an important character worthy of respect in his own right.

In his novel *The Village in the Jungle* (1913), a minor masterpiece based on his Ceylon experiences and written in the heyday of imperialism but from an anti-colonial position, Leonard Woolf comes closer to the common people of the empire than any other British writer. Woolf's vision is tragic: life is presented as a terrible struggle for existence with human beings indomitably fighting a losing battle. His *Stories of the East* (1916) includes two tepid tales of Ceylon.

The outstanding work published during the decline of empire is John Still's *The Jungle Tide* (1930). Written with intimate knowledge, perceptiveness, and verbal skill, it is a creative interpretation of the jungles of Ceylon, their inhabitants, and their buried cities, and of Sinhala culture of the time. In poetry the most important name is W. S. Senior, whose *Vita-Magistra* (1937) was reprinted in 1983.

Though such writers as Mark Twain, Nikos Kazantzakis, Pablo Neruda, D. H. Lawrence, and André Malraux passed through or lived temporarily in Ceylon and wrote cameos of it in prose or verse (Lawrence's 'Elephant', Neruda's 'Monsoon in May'), there is no such corpus of works by major and minor writers as there is about India (Rudyard Kipling, E. M. Forster, Paul Scott, Maud Diver) or Africa (Joseph Conrad, Joyce Cary, Graham Greene, Elspeth Huxley). Nevertheless, British writing about Sri Lanka helped prepare the development of a tradition of Sri Lankan writing in English.

D. C. R. A. GOONETILLEKE

FOREIGN WRITERS (West Africa)

The development of English-language fiction presenting West Africa drew its energy from an image of Africa that began to emerge in the 1780s — in information provided by coastal travellers and explorers into West Africa's interior, in the refinements and syntheses of this information by stay-at-home scholars and publicists, in the popular presses, in boys' adventure books, and in Sunday School tracts. (See **Exploration Literature**, West Africa.) According to Philip D. Curtin in his *The Image of Africa* (1964), the major affirmations of this body of writing were the 'common knowledge' of the educated classes. Thereafter, when new generations of explorers and administrators went to Africa, they went with a prior impression of what they would find. Most often they found it, and their writings, in turn, confirmed the older image — or, at most, altered it only slightly.

Desultory publication of novels between 1865 and 1898 gave way in the twentieth century to a more or less consistent production of fiction in English about West Africa. With only a few exceptions, novels written about West Africa represent mere commercial exploitation of popular sentiment about the region and are not concerned with presenting an analysis, in fictional terms, of the views that are incorporated into their pages. The better writers — Joyce Cary, David Caute, Saul Bellow — make an appeal to intelligence as well as feeling and offer an analysis of the situations they describe; this fiction, however, has value more for the way it elucidates the society that produced it than for the accuracy of its representation of Africa. Some of this fiction, while exploiting popular sentiment about West Africa, contains descriptions of historical events: for example, George Alfred Henty's novels about the campaigns against the Ashanti on the Gold Coast — *By Sheer Pluck* (1883) and *Through Three Campaigns* (1903) — Sir Harry Johnston's *The History of a Slave* (1899), W. Somerset Maugham's *The Explorer* (1907), and Stanley Portal Hyatt's *Marcus Hay* (1907).

Most of the novels published between 1884 and 1920 are romances — either adventure stories that exploit the 'strangeness' and remoteness of the setting and depict stirring and exciting adventures in which characterization is generally slight and stereotyped, or those dealing with sentimental love. These novels tell the stories of men who, having suffered devastating reversals of fortune and moral degeneration, apply to, and are accepted by, the Colonial Office for service in Africa. The novels dramatize their adventures in Africa, where they recover their moral and financial reputations through acts of bravery and endurance. Typically, the male protagonist is tempted by some 'dusky maiden', but he never commits the socially unacceptable act of marriage to her. Rather, the protagonist is 'saved' by the sudden appearance of the European fiancée by whom he had been spurned, and a happy resolution of their affairs (and the plot) is effected. Novelists who regularly published books of this kind (none of them surviving in popularity) include Lady Dorothy Mills, Mary Gaunt, Robert Simpson, John Ridgewell Essex, and Louise Gerrard.

By 1920 the use of the romance form for depicting West Africa gave way to attempts at more realistic presentation because more writers had spent time in West Africa and could write their descriptions with more accuracy. Examples of these works include *Dark Gods* (1925) and *Master!* (1927) by Lady Dorothy Mills, an intrepid world traveller; *Hoodman-Blind* (1927) and *Gone Native* (1928) by A. C. G. Hastings, an officer of the British political service in Nigeria; and *The Whispering Bush* (1924) and *Jackson's Ju-Ju* (1929) by A. E. H. Southon, of the Ilesha Baptist Mission in Western Nigeria. These and other works of the period describe and dramatize the problems related to colonial administration and the contending, even antagonistic, forces within the colonies — those of politicians, businessmen, and missionaries.

The most prominent of this type of writing is that of 'the white man's burden' — the concept of the responsibility of the imperialist-colonialist nations to the 'subject races'. It was to the advantage of both political officials and traders to maintain views of African 'inferiority' — it made the task of ruling easier and the share of profits larger. Yet herein lies the fundamental duplicity: the aim of the officials and traders was to provide the experience and capacities that would eventually make Africans independent of whites. Even missionaries, who preached equality of both Africans and whites before God, insisted also on the essentially inferior evolutionary status of Africans, as evoked in Albert Schweitzer's remark that 'the African is my brother; but he is a junior brother.'

In fact, few writers whose works are set in West Africa had either sufficient interest in, or sympathy with, Africans to offer a realistic view of their life. From Henty onwards, Africans and their society were presented in a series of stereotyped views that derived from the pre-Victorian period and were enhanced by the social Darwinism of Victorian times. In such works, Africans are persistently viewed as 'primitive', vulgar, and mentally inferior to Europeans, their society as chaotic, and their religious practices as demonic. Joyce Cary's four African novels — *Aissa Saved* (1932), *An American Visitor* (1933), *The African Witch* (1936), and *Mister Johnson* (1939) — are much praised in some quarters, but they confirm such stereotypes and lapse into melodramatic endings that vitiate whatever credible presentations preceded them. There is only one possible exception to this pattern in the hundreds of novels published during the period — R. S. Rattray's *The Leopard Priestess* (1931), which proceeds from the enquiries of the author, a Colonial Office anthropologist, into Ashanti law and custom.

In terms of the ethical and aesthetic values it possesses, this body of fiction on West Africa is hollow at the core. It is bad literature because it pretends to present Africa, African life, and European association with Africa in realistic terms, but it relies, in fact, on a system of stereotypes and fosters a reality totally at variance with the actual situation.

It is against the legacy of these views of the legitimacy of European activity on the West Coast of Africa — in political administration, in trade, and in the Christian Church — that contemporary African writers continue to react. Fiction presenting West Africa during the colonial period purveys a bitter legacy.

G. D. KILLAM

Further reading: M. M. Mahood, *Joyce Cary's Africa* (1964); C. L. Innes, *Chinua Achebe: Cambridge Studies in African and Caribbean Literature* (1990).

FOSTER, DAVID (1944–)

Australian novelist

Born in Sydney, Australia, he studied science at the University of Sydney and the Australian National University in Canberra before turning to writing. His scientific background is readily apparent in his interest in concepts such as entropy and in his vast and eclectic vocabulary, which includes many abstruse and technical words. For instance, Foster's first book, three novellas titled *North South West* (1973), contains sentences such as 'We will fall before their arrows as before the nematocysts of a coelenterate.' Nevertheless, his prose is energetic, idiomatic, full of tension, and often witty in its attack on whatever is fashionable.

Foster made a number of false starts early in his career — a book of verse, *The Fleeing Atalanta* (1975), an unsuccessful science-fiction novel titled *The Empathy Experiment* (1977), which he co-authored with D. K. Lyall — though he did have some success with *The Pure Land* (1974), a kind of parody of that great Australian fictive stand-by, the generational epic. His early works are full of outsiders and drop-outs, fringe figures who search for a meaning and significance in life and finally settle, more or less willingly, for the conviction that there is none.

But Foster made his real reputation in the 1980s with a series of novels that characteristically exhibit a bizarre, almost surreal wit, an inventive and satiric imagination, and a delight in playing with language for its own sake. He employs modes of farce and parody that recall American novelists such as John Barth, though in his technical knowledge and density of detail he is more like Thomas Pynchon. Probably his best novel is *Moonlite* (1981), a highly inventive and amusing account of the picaresque adventures of one Finbar MacBuffie, adventures that seem to amount to something like an allegorical account of the history of immigration to Australia. Foster plays with language, using arcane or invented words, punning vigorously, giving the characters names like 'The Marquis of Moneymore', and providing a variety of dialects as well as a multitude of satiric targets from pseudo-scholarship and Christianity through advocates of temperance to Australian myths of heroism and identity.

Moonlite was followed by *Plumbum* (1983), which starts off coherently enough with a group of young musicians gathering to form the Blackman Brothers heavy metal rock band in Canberra, but as the band travels overseas the medley of voices and sounds that crowd the novel becomes increasingly frenetic, the action more surreal and indecipherable. *Dog Rock* (1984) is a parody of the detective quest with an abundance of improbable clues and a plot of Byzantine complexity. Foster returned to the territory of *Dog Rock* with the slight but witty *The Pale Blue Crochet Coathanger Cover* (1987).

Among Foster's other works are the novellas *The Adventures of Christian Rosy Cross* (1986), set in the Middle Ages, and *Hitting the Wall* (1989), one of which had been previously published in the collection of stories *Escape to Reality* (1977).

LAURIE CLANCY

Further reading: Helen Daniels, *Liars* (1988).

FRAME, JANET (1924–)

New Zealand novelist, short-story writer, autobiographer

Born in Dunedin, New Zealand, she grew up in the Otago/Southland region of New Zealand's South Island. In the first volume of her autobiography, *To the Is-land* (1982), Frame accounts for a childhood marked by poverty and alienation. Two further volumes, *An Angel at My Table* (1984) and *The Envoy from Mirror City* (1985), continue the story of female artistic development in the face of harrowing physical, spiritual, economic, and psychological vicissitudes. Here, Frame constructs herself as 'ordinary', but determinedly marginal in her desire to amalgamate the world of fact with the world of imagination. The three volumes were reprinted as one volume, *An Autobiography* (1989).

Frame is characteristically described as the writer of 'intense, idiosyncratic and visionary perceptions' and/or as the most brilliant writer New Zealand has produced. Her first volume of short stories, *The Lagoon: Stories* (1951), introduced a number of Frame's typical thematic concerns — an obsession with time, change, and death as inevitable. Her first novel, *Owls Do Cry* (1957), portrays dysfunctional family life in a small-town New Zealand setting. *The Edge of the Alphabet* (1962) extends these concerns, exploring the western world during the Cold War years as a culture so loveless and death-driven that the only 'rational' option seems to be global suicide through nuclear holocaust. These novels are concerned with aspects of death and decay, especially of bodies, with none of the positive, regenerative associations she develops in her later work.

The Lagoon, published while Frame was incarcerated in New Zealand mental institutions, won the Hubert Church Memorial Award for literature. It also won her a remittal from an impending leucotomy. As she says in her autobiography, 'it is little wonder that I value my writing as a way of life when it actually saved my life'. Writing-as-subject and an attention to the role of the artist in local and global society are Frame's consistent concerns.

Frame focuses on words. The language of euphemisms, clichés, and advertising is shown as poisonous, as a corrupting edifice or a deceptive lushness that covers the hollowness and emptiness that form the common condition of life. A character in *Scented Gardens for the Blind* (1963) laments the 'tattered bargain-price words'; another in *Faces in the Water* (1961) seeks to avoid the 'kind of phrases which people use like mothballs to try and preserve a period of time'; a computer salesman's speech in *The Carpathians* (1988) comes 'fully manufactured in precast phrases and sentences', while the real estate agent has a 'large supply of useless, sparkless words', straight off the 'assembly line', delivered without care. Thus, characters are often ordinary, conformist, unexceptional, untalented, lonely. The inability to communicate is the norm, not the exception, in Frame's vision of a decaying culture.

Frame's novels suggest that the individual's delineation of inner feelings and truths can lead to a form of significant communication; however, as she notes in her *An Autobiography*, one's use of language can prove dangerous. While a patient in the mental hospital, her description of gorse as having a 'peanut-buttery smell' (quoting Virginia Woolf) was considered ample proof of Frame's verbal schizophrenia. Indeed, she found that when she 'began to say what (she) really felt, using a simile or metaphor, an image', she recognized the listener's conditioned response: 'Here was the mad person speaking.'

Frame's work exposes as an urgent problem the inadequacies of current systems of communication. In novels such as *A State of Siege* (1966), *The Rainbirds* (1968, published in North America as *Yellow Flowers in the Antipodean Room*, 1969), and *Intensive Care* (1970), Frame is an advocate of the individual's need, and right, to create meaningful patterns of identity, to use language to communicate positive and independent patterns of otherness without fear of punishment or exclusion (represented by the mental institutions or by the deadly patterns imposed by a conformist society).

Frame's early and middle work reflects a concern with the problems of knowing and of articulating, of asking such questions as: what are the limits of the knowable? what are the limits of its expression? This concern results in her fiction in typically modernist devices that transfer the epistemological difficulties of the character to the reader. Techniques such as the multiplication and juxtaposition of perspectives and virtuoso variants on interior monologue simulate for the reader problems of accessibility, reliability, and limitation of knowledge that plague the characters in such novels as *Owls Do Cry*, *Faces in the Water*, *The Edge of the Alphabet*, and *Scented Gardens for the Blind*.

Frame's later fiction appears to abandon the inextricable (modernist) problem of attaining reliable knowledge and, instead, explores modes of being, foregrounding such questions as, 'What kinds of world are there?' 'How are they constituted?' 'What happens when boundaries between worlds are violated?' These questions are explored with a sharp sense of outrageous humour in *The Carpathians*, where narrative and 'real' boundaries collide cataclysmically. Typically, Frame deliberately toys with narrative expectations; her narrators specialize in upsetting expectations of who is telling the story and to what end.

Because of its patent metafictionality and language-oriented nature, Frame's latter work has been appraised as postmodern; however, not all critics agree. For some, a novel such as *Living in the Maniototo* (1979, winner of the New Zealand Book Award for Fiction in 1980), only *seems* to conform to a postmodernist celebration of the abyss when, in fact, it remains caught within the lexicon of an earlier (modernist) perspective. In fact, Frame's work resists categorization; labels such as 'postmodern', 'post-colonial', and feminist refuse to stick.

Critic David Dowling has compared as apocalyptic novels *Intensive Care* and Canadian **Hugh MacLennan**'s *Voices in Time*. Susan Ash compares *The Carpathians* to **Margaret Atwood**'s *Bodily Harm*. Frame's concern with time and history and with interchangeable signifiers links her work to that of **Wilson Harris**, **Salman Rushdie**, and **Gerald Murnane**, who share an interest in what can be recuperated from an imperial past and what has to be begun anew.

SUSAN ASH

Further reading: Margaret Dalziel, *Janet Frame* (1980).

FRANKLIN, MILES (1879–1954)

Australian novelist

Born near Tumut, New South Wales, Australia, Stella Maria Sarah Miles Franklin was a fifth-generation Australian who spent her early life — detailed in *Childhood at Brindabella* (1963) — on properties around Tumut and Goulburn, New South Wales. She published nine works under her own name, six under Brent of Bin Bin, and one under Mr and Mrs Ogniblat L'Artsau.

Although she was a committed pacifist, socialist, and feminist, Franklin's works demonstrate conflicting attitudes towards national identity. Her most famous novel, *My Brilliant Career* (1901), published in the year of Federation, is fiercely Australian, yet it rejects the easy optimism of the nationalist tradition. It celebrates the beauty of the bush in rhapsodic terms, but demonstrates the harshness of bush life for women and children. It reveals, too, the extent to which Australian bush life was still dominated by English notions of class, for the station Caddagat replicates the social hierarchy and activities of an English country estate, and the six pastoral romances, written under the pseudonym Brent of Bin Bin, idealize the pseudo-English way of life on Australian properties. At the same time Franklin resisted the dependence upon Britain that was perpetuated in the terms of Federation, denouncing in both *My Career Goes Bung* (1946) and *Cockatoos* (1954) the involvement of Australia in the Boer War.

My Brilliant Career, written when Franklin was sixteen years old, depicts the struggle of Sybylla Melvyn, its young heroine and an aspiring writer, against the constrictions of female life in the bush. The institutions of marriage (seen as degrading) and **mateship** (why is it exclusively male?), and above all the sexual imperative, are brought into question as Sybylla violently rejects the advances of a handsome and eligible suitor to whom she is obviously attracted. In its passionate plea for personal and sexual freedom, *My Brilliant Career* has been likened to **Olive Schreiner**'s *The Story of an African Farm* (1883), to Thomas Hardy's *Jude the Obscure* (1896), and to **Rosa Praed**'s *Affinities* (1886), suggesting that the pressure for sexual autonomy for women at the end of the last century was as intense in colonial as in metropolitan cultures. Meanwhile, the sexual ambivalence of *My Brilliant Career* is reflected in Franklin's literary career (she almost always wrote under a male pseudonym) and in her personal life. Though she warmly encouraged suitors such as the poet **A. B. Paterson**, she apparently retreated smartly from any sexual or material commitment, seeing it as simply another form of imperialism.

Franklin worked in Chicago, USA, for the National Women's Trade Union League from 1908 to 1915, and served in Macedonia with a nursing unit from 1917 to 1918. She worked for public housing in London, England, until 1925 and returned permanently to Australia in 1932. In her will she created the prestigious Miles Franklin Award for Australian Fiction.

SHIRLEY WALKER

Further reading: Verna Coleman, *Her Unknown Brilliant Career* (1981).

FRASER, KEATH (1944–)

Canadian short-story writer

Born in Vancouver, Canada, he took his BA and MA at the University of British Columbia, Canada, and a Ph.D. at the University of London, England. He taught at the University of Calgary, but later returned to Vancouver to devote himself to writing. A gardener in his story 'The Emerald City' says, 'Few of us, loyal to the city, have lived anywhere else. We wouldn't want to.'

Fraser's travels, however, have been extensive. Like the Vancouver soil and climate, where plants from everywhere take root, he includes the exotically native and foreign in his stories, and his characters preserve a consciousness a cut above the ordinary — an East Indian waiter will yearn for 'the cognisance of customers', a gardener cultivates asters and the friendship of a Persian poet.

Fraser has published two books of short fiction, *Taking Cover* (1982) and *Foreign Affairs* (1985), in which two novellas, *Foreign Affairs* and *The History of Cambodia*, also published in *Canadian Fiction Magazine* (49, 1984), exemplify his themes. In *Foreign Affairs* a former Canadian diplomat to India, retired on disability for multiple sclerosis, lives in the near-imprisonment of his body and his apartment. He struggles between wanting to be out and about, pushed into a relapse by the unconventional daughter of his former mentor, and staying safe at home in the care of his long-time housekeeper. Here is the theme of confinement and of fatal opposite attractions for what is near to home and what lies outside. In *The History of Cambodia* the fate of Aleta Macvey, a Canadian reporter captured by the Khmer Rouge, echoes this theme. The novella swings back and forth in time, between Aleta's childhood and her teenage explorations of sex on Wreck Beach in Vancouver, and Cambodia where, instead of finding a story, Aleta is forced to marry a cadre leader and live out the real horrors with his guerrilla group. Fraser's art in the novella affirms the high morality of his work and his main ability as a writer, which is to bring suffering from remote places home.

GEORGE McWHIRTER

FREDERICK, RAWLE (1945–)

Trinidadian poet, short-story writer

Born in San Fernando, Trinidad, he travelled to Canada in 1967 to study English at McGill University. It was during this period of changing social norms and political dissent that his first published works appeared — in the *McGill Journal of Education* and in an anthology entitled *Let the Niggers Burn* (1972), edited by Dennis Forsythe. A volume of poetry, *Transatlantic Cargo*, was published in 1973. These poems gave voice to the rage felt by a generation of young black people striving to redefine themselves and confronting the challenge of institutionalized racism. While dialectic was paramount at this phase of Frederick's work, there was also a vivid awareness of the subtleties of experience. The duality of the political versus the personal is a feature that continues to inform his writing.

In 1973 Frederick took up a teaching post in Iringa, Tanzania. The Tanzanian years were a fallow period for Frederick's writing, enriched by a profound appreciation of the traditional cultures surrounding him. The encounter with Africa proved fruitful, extending the range of his material and bringing a reflective quality to his style. In 1977, a year after leaving Tanzania, he won first prize in the Trinidad and Tobago Creative Awards for his short story 'Homecoming'. That same year he moved to Bermuda, where a career in teaching intertwined with a lively participation in the local literary scene as a newspaper features writer, as co-editor of the *Bermuda Education Journal*, and as a founding member of the Bermuda Writers' Collective, which published a book of short stories *Palmetto Wine* (1990). His collection *The Vendor of Dreams and Other Stories* was published in 1992.

Frederick's life and work reflect the travels and psychological searchings of countless people from the Caribbean during the second half of the twentieth century. However, his writing defies easy categorization, being marked by a highly individual consciousness.

ANGELA BARRY

FREEMAN, DAVID (1945–)

Canadian dramatist

Born in Toronto, Canada, a victim of cerebral palsy, he attended a school for handicapped children and was later sent to a sheltered workshop. Rejecting this way of life, he studied political science at McMaster University, Canada (BA, 1971). Freeman is one of the Canadian dramatists who between 1971 and 1975 created a substantial, continuing body of plays, mostly staged in new alternative theatres — a phenomenon analogous to the development of Australian drama at the time.

Freeman's first play, *Creeps* (1972), was staged at Factory Theatre Lab, Toronto, in 1971. An angry, painful, moving, and powerful drama, it is set in the men's washroom of a sheltered workshop and dramatizes the plight of five men, all suffering from cerebral palsy. While they squabble among themselves, they unite to oppose do-gooders who are presented in three short hallucinatory scenes. Freeman argues that *Creeps* is more than semi-documentary, being about 'freedom and having the guts to reach for it'. *Battering Ram* (1972) is a *danse macabre* featuring a widowed mother, her daughter, and the paraplegic youth whom the mother invites to stay. Freeman dramatizes the sexual frustration of the disabled, the unresolved mother-daughter tension, and the mixed motives of those helping 'the disadvantaged'. *Creeps* and *Battering Ram* can be categorized with other 'dramas of disability' such as Brian Clark's *Whose Life Is It Anyway?* (1979), Bernard Pomerance's *The Elephant Man* (1979), and Mark Medoff's *Children of a Lesser God* (1980). Canadian plays that deal with mental and physical disability include **W. O. Mitchell**'s *Back to Beulah* (1982) and Joan MacLeod's *Toronto, Mississippi* (1989).

You're Gonna Be Alright, Jamie Boy (1974) is an over-extended satire on a blue-collar family obsessed with television; the family is observed through the eyes of the sensitive son who may escape. Freeman attempts to extend his range again in the slight *Flytrap* (1980), about a middle-aged couple that takes in a young man as lodger. When possessive rivalries develop, the young man becomes the couple's victim.

Silent since 1980, Freeman receives little critical attention, although in 1990 *You're Gonna Be Alright, Jamie Boy* received a minor production in London, England, and *Creeps* has been anthologized.

MALCOLM PAGE

FRENCH, ANNE (1956–)

New Zealand poet

Born and educated in Wellington, New Zealand, she emerged as a poet of considerable talent with her collections *All Cretans Are Liars* (1987), winner of the 1988 New Zealand Book Award for Poetry, *The Male as Evader* (1988), and *Cabin Fever* (1990).

All Cretans Are Liars shows considerable sophistication and technical skill, but also a relaxed and witty personal voice. These poems, often addressed to others, cleverly subvert the clichés of love and fidelity: '& now / language mere speaking / undoes us.' *The Male as Evader* is more concentrated in subject and tone, pursuing, with comic relish and satiric venom, questions of truth and knowledge in relations between the sexes. Here poems are small fictions, dialogues, and character sketches that expose unrelentingly the stylish insouciance of male evasion. French's ever-present sense of the literary traditions of both New Zealand and England makes many of these poems implied criticisms of a male-dominated literature of romantic love: 'writing well is the best revenge.'

Cabin Fever takes a fresh turn, though some poised love poems connect it to earlier work. In an impressive sequence of poems on sailing, French, always fascinated by the power of words to create reality, uses yachting terminology and the language of geography, geology, and history to create a self-contained and idyllic world of sky, sea, and landfall. Other poems in the book show her exploring, in tones of the 1980s, the problems of national identity so absorbing to the New Zealand poets of fifty years before.

ELIZABETH CAFFIN

FRENCH CARIBBEAN CONNECTIONS IN CARIBBEAN LITERATURE

Francophone communities in the Caribbean are as distinct from their anglophone neighbours as they are from each other.

The term 'Francophone Caribbean' is used to describe the islands of Martinique and Guadeloupe, the former prison colony of French Guyana in South America, and the Republic of Haiti.

Whereas Haiti became independent in 1804, the rest of the French Caribbean has relations with France dating from the seventeenth century and remaining unbroken to the present. Since becoming Overseas Departments in 1946, Martinique, Guadeloupe, and Guyana have become officially integrated into the French cultural and educational system. The Overseas Departments are totally dependent on France and are as politically somnolent as Haiti is volatile. Haiti, with a majority of monolingual creole speakers, remains fiercely independent of its former metropole. Both are different from the former British West Indies, which non-violently gained independence in the 1960s.

French Caribbean literature has traditionally demonstrated a range and vitality that often anticipate and overshadow movements that appear later in the rest of the region. Arguably, Caribbean literature began in Haiti with the declaration of independence in 1804. As **C. L. R. James** writes in *The Black Jacobins* (1938), 'West Indians first became aware of themselves as a people in the Haitian revolution.' While the anglophone Caribbean remained relatively silent even after emancipation, Caribbean self-awareness produced a surge of literary activity in nineteenth-century Haiti. In this early nationalist phase, poets attempted to create an authentic Haitian literature. For instance, 'Choucoune' by Oswald Durand (1840–1906) is the first successful experiment in writing poetry in Creole. Haiti's early essayists are also the first to discuss issues of sovereignty and neo-colonialism. The works of Baron De Vastey and Anténor Firmin elaborate an anti-colonial ideology before the milder *Froudacity* (1889) by the Trinidadian J. J. Thomas.

In the 1930s the other French Caribbean countries joined Haiti in giving a new thrust to the region's literature. The Negritude movement and its Haitian equivalent, *noirisme*, celebrated the Caribbean's African past. Martinique's Aimé Césaire and Haiti's Jean Price-Mars are leading figures in a movement to which only the Jamaican novelist **Claude McKay**, then part of the Harlem Renaissance, seemed sensitive.

If French Caribbean writers were the first to promote black consciousness, they were among the first to challenge its excesses. By the 1940s, with an anglophone Caribbean literature just emerging, younger francophone writers were already questioning Negritude. Frantz Fanon's use of Sartrean existentialism, Jacques Roumain's Marxism, Haiti's marvellous realism, Edouard Glissant's 'Antillanité', and a post-Negritude feminism represent new departures for the French Caribbean.

Awareness of French Caribbean literature is first apparent in the 1950s in the literary magazines *Bim* and *Caribbean Quarterly*. These links are strengthened with an early play by **Derek Walcott**, *Henri Christophe* (1950), and with his later essay 'The Muse of History' in *Is Massa Day Dead?* (edited by Orde Coombs, 1974). Both **George Lamming** and **E. K. Brathwaite** used Haitian religious ritual in *Season of Adventure* (1960) and *The Arrivants* (1973) respectively. The irregular but important Carifesta celebrations, an increasing availability of translations, and growing regionalism further intensify relations between francophone and anglophone Caribbean.

J. MICHAEL DASH

Further reading: J. Michael Dash, 'The French connection', *Bim* 17 (1983).

FRENCH, DAVID (1939–)

Canadian dramatist

Born in Coley's Point, Newfoundland, Canada, he moved with his family to Toronto in 1945, a migration that established the poles of his dramatic universe: the rural, quasi-mythic, pre-Confederation outport experience of his parents' generation, and the urban, postwar, central Canadian environment that shaped his own. Trained as an actor, he wrote and performed in television for the Canadian Broadcasting Corporation through the 1960s before turning to the stage with *Leaving Home* (1972), the first play of his semi-autobiographical Mercer family tetralogy.

The success of *Leaving Home* and its sequel, *Of the Fields, Lately* (1973), did much to legitimize Canadian playwriting. At a time of strong nationalism and a newly booming professional theatre, French dramatized Canadian cultural tensions in a popular and accessible theatrical form (the naturalistic family play). His association with Toronto's Tarragon Theatre helped make it a flagship of the 'alternate' theatre movement, which opposed the neo-colonialist structures and programming of the larger regional companies. Chris Johnson has usefully compared *Leaving Home* with **Ray Lawler**'s *Summer of the Seventeenth Doll* (1957) in terms of the two plays' explorations of their respective national 'legends' and their somewhat similar positions in the historical development of Canadian and Australian drama.

Leaving Home and *Of the Fields, Lately* focus on the alienation of the family patriarch, Jacob Mercer, in late-1950s Toronto as his sons grow up and leave home. He and his wife Mary, brother-in-law Wiff, and friend Minnie retain the salty dialect and colourful narrative impulse of the native Newfoundlander (whose Irish heritage gives these plays more than a little of the flavour of Sean O'Casey). In contrast, the teenaged sons Ben (French's own persona) and Billy, and Minnie's daughter Kathy are bland, assimilated Canadians. Minnie's boyfriend Harold, a dour undertaker, silent but sexually potent, becomes a complex comic prototype in the eyes of the expatriate Newfoundlanders: 'What is he, Minnie? Newfie?' asks Jacob. 'No, boy — Canadian.'

The later Mercer plays move backwards in time. *Salt-Water Moon* (1985) interrogates the nostalgic Newfoundland mythologized by Jacob in the early plays. Romantically detailing the courtship of Jacob and Mary in Coley's Point in 1926, it also exposes the semi-feudal nature of the society and economy from which they will later flee. *1949* (1989), the most epic and heavy-handed of the Mercer plays, returns to Toronto on the eve of Newfoundland's entry into Confederation to explore the ambivalence of an entire culture's leaving home.

French has had limited success with his forays outside the Mercer saga. *Jitters* (1980) is the major exception; it is his most commercially successful play, a hilarious backstage comedy about Canadians' sense of artistic inferiority and their ambivalent relation to American cultural imperialism. His 1978 translation of Chekhov's *The Seagull* opened on Broadway in 1992.

One of the most critically respected and most frequently produced Canadian playwrights, French has broken no new ground with his traditional dramaturgy rooted in domestic realism. But his best plays skilfully marry stage populism with incisive analyses of Canadian cultural insecurity.

JERRY WASSERMAN

Further reading: Chris Johnson, 'Is that us?: Ray Lawler's *Summer of the Seventeenth Doll* and David French's *Leaving Home*', *Canadian Drama* (1980).

French, Stanley (1937–)

St Lucian dramatist

Born in Castries, St Lucia, he was educated there and in London, England, where he studied civil engineering. French is both a civil engineer and one of St Lucia's foremost playwrights. His plays explore his ongoing concerns about the influence of Christianity in the lives of Caribbean people, the confrontation between the traditional and the modern, the relationship between the rulers and the ruled, and the legacy of class attitudes in the colonial context.

French's stance is highly critical of authority, of both church and state, and is sympathetic to the plight and aspirations of the lower classes. *The Rape of Fair Helen* (1983), for example, is a bitter allegory in which a politician sexually abuses a young girl, and a priest turns a blind eye. 'No Rain, No Play' (premièred 1972) uses the context of a cricket match to examine the clash of values between social classes.

Stylistically, French works within the framework of realism, but not rigidly so. In attempting to portray the typical Kweyol-speaking St Lucian, he has to some degree fashioned a dialogue that allows his characters to express vivid emotion. French has also incorporated devices such as the chorus and the use of song. His most complex play, *Under a Sky of Incense* (1981), is a play-within-a play; using the setting of the rehearsal of a play about Martin Luther, French skilfully constructs a scathing criticism of the Roman Catholic church in colonial St Lucia.

French has written in other forms, but his plays constitute a significant body of work that has helped to shape a St Lucian tradition of the playwright as social critic. His other plays include 'Ballad of a Man and Dog' (premièred 1970), 'The Light and the Dark' (premièred 1972), and the radio play 'The Interview' (broadcast 1976).

KENDEL HIPPOLYTE

FRIGGIERI, JOE (1946–)

Maltese poet, dramatist

Born in Lija, Malta, cousin of **Oliver Friggieri**, he studied at the University of Malta and earned two Ph.D. degrees, from the Universita' Cattolica del Sacro Cuore, Milan, Italy, and Oxford University, England, respectively. Since 1972 Friggieri has been a professor of philosophy at the University of Malta. He is a specialist on the philosopher J. L. Austin, on whom he has published *Actions and Speech Actions in the Philosophy of J. L. Austin* (1991).

A bilingual writer whose major work is poetry, Friggieri has also written plays in Maltese and is a well-known director in Maltese theatre, directing plays from the classical repertory to contemporary Maltese works by such dramatists as **Francis Ebejer**. Some of his earliest verse appeared in the form of broadsheets designed by Maltese artist Norbert Attard. Friggieri has edited an arts magazine, *Arts* (1971–4), and, in the years 1975 to 1980, a monthly Maltese-language newspaper, *Illum*. He has also presented arts programmes on Maltese television.

Friggieri's poetry is in the mainstream of the European lyrical tradition, but reflects Maltese society as still undergoing the conflict of spiritual and political values experienced much earlier by other European countries. Like his contemporaries Mario Azzopardi, **Daniel Massa**, and Victor Fenech, Friggieri writes in reaction to both the values and the rhetoric of tradition; unlike them, he has never been drawn to the experimental use of form and language. Even in his early pieces, such as those anthologized in *Malta: The New Poetry* (1971), edited by Mario Azzopardi, he rarely uses even the free unrhythmic verse that is commonplace of the modernist movement. Friggieri has always aimed at transparency in his style and because of this — and his preoccupation with time and change — he has a kinship with seventeenth-century poet Robert Herrick. Friggieri himself admits an affinity with English poet Philip Larkin, whose work betrays the same gentle irony and deeply rooted pessimism. Friggieri's poetry implies the need to understand, and accept unprotestingly, the human condition.

Some of Friggieri's poetry, translated into English, appears in *Cross Winds: An Anthology of Post-War Maltese Poetry* (1980), compiled by Oliver Friggieri, Konrad Hopkins, and Ronald von Roekel.

PAUL XUEREB

FRIGGIERI, OLIVER (1947–)

Maltese poet, novelist, critic

He was born in Floriana, Malta, into a deeply religious family. Cousin of **Joe Friggieri**, he studied philosophy and theology in Malta's Catholic seminary, a religious formation that until recently has coloured much of his creative output. Friggieri has been an angry intellectual linked to campaigns for the wider recognition of Maltese language and culture, first as a founding member of the Movement for the Promotion of Literature, and more recently as professor and head of the department of Maltese in the University of Malta.

Steeped in the humanist tradition, Friggieri is extremely well-read in Italian literature. He is a great admirer of Dante, Baudelaire, and Marcel Proust, whose works have exerted an influence on his craft and imagery. Since his first poetry collection, *Dhahen fl-Imhuh* ('Smoke in the Mind', 1967) — many poems from which have been published in English in *Malta: The New Poetry* (1971), edited by Mario Azzopardi, and in *Cross Winds: An Anthology of Post-War Maltese Poetry* (1980), co-edited by Friggieri with Konrad Hopkins and Ronald van Roekel — Friggieri has been a prolific writer of poetry, short stories, novels, critical articles, and books. Nationally recognized as the critic most consistently committed to Maltese literature, Friggieri has not only published full-length studies on Malta's national poet Dun Karm, on Ruzar Briffa, Gwann Mamo, and Guze' Ellul Mercer, but he has written extensively in Maltese, English, and Italian on literary theory and practical criticism and has edited a number of anthologies and introductions.

Friggieri's works strive to activate the common individual's potential, to give a voice to the voiceless. Widely translated, his writing has a consistent patriotic basis that seeks to destabilize the present by referring to the patriotic intensity of the past, as, for example, in his poetic drama *Rewwixta* (1990). However, the distinctive tone in his creative work — prose as well as hendecasyllablic poetry (which he regards as one cycle) — is one of great personal emotional intensity filtered through an intellectual detachment that permits the creation of an artefact 'both permanent and stable', as in his shared poetry collection *Analizi '70* ('Analysis '70', 1970), edited by Victor Fenech, and his collections *Call of the Drums* (1971), *Poeziji ta' Mhabba* (1981), *Your Look Lights up the Lantern* (1988), and *A Distraught Pilgrim* (1991). Here, as well as in his novel *L- Istramb* (1980, translated by Grazio Falzon as *A Turn of the Wheel*, 1987), Friggieri is ostensibly addressing the common person, but the recurring central themes are basically philosophical and religious: the tyranny of time, the fragility of humanity's pretentious search and feeling for God, and 'love and death as aspects of man's basic existential angst'. Much of this work is imbued with a religious pessimism similar to that of Leopardi, suggesting that the writer can only find refuge in art. Art, in turn, is seen as being useful only at the level of the creative individual, an illusion that provides 'the writer's own pathetic way of salvation . . . a sublime way of killing time as time kills you'.

DANIEL MASSA

Further reading: Peter Serracino-Inglott, 'The poetry of propitiation', introduction to *A Distraught Pilgrim* by Daniel Massa (1991).

FRYE, NORTHROP (1912–91)
Canadian critic
Born in Sherbrooke, Canada, he attended school in Moncton before enrolling at Victoria College, University of Toronto, in 1929. After graduating in 1933, he studied theology at Emmanuel College and was ordained as a United Church minister in 1936. He earned an MA at Merton College, Oxford, England, and began his teaching career at Victoria College, where he taught until his death. At the time of his death he was also chancellor of Victoria University.

Frye is best known as the author of *Anatomy of Criticism: Four Essays* (1957). His systematic approach to world literatures, however, was always inseparable from his sympathy for particular and local creative expressions. Although Frye demonstrates that Blake's visions follow a systematic pattern (*Fearful Symmetry*, 1947), he also joins Blake in recovering the power projected into the old patterns, a power invested in the tyrannical old sky god. This potentially redemptive power is made available to the dispossessed.

The romantic appeal of the marginalized figure is at the heart of Frye's critical thought, and it militates against the building of closed systems. This may explain Frye's preference for the essay form. Many of his books, *Fables of Identity: Studies in Poetic Mythology* (1963) and *A Study of English Romanticism* (1968), for example, are collections of essays. Often these essays were first given as public lectures: *The Educated Imagination* (1963), *The Well-Tempered Critic* (1963), *The Modern Century* (1967), *The Secular Scripture: A Study of the Structure of Romance* (1976), and *Creation and Recreation* (1980), for example. Frye was, first and foremost, a teacher. His books on Shakespeare, similarly, usually consist of essays or lectures: *A Natural Perspective: The Development of Shakespearean Comedy and Romance* (1965); *Fools of Time: Studies in Shakespearean Tragedy* (1967); *The Myth of Deliverance: Reflections on Shakespeare's Problem Comedies* (1983). It is fitting that Frye should have won a long overdue Governor General's Award for *Northrop Frye on Shakespeare* (1986), a book based on lectures given to his students.

While Frye's most narrow imitators have sometimes applied his approach rigidly to specific texts, he himself never followed up on the implicit promise to provide practical applications of the system worked out in *Anatomy of Criticism*. The reason for this is surely at least in part a product of Frye's understanding of his Canadian and Commonwealth context. His work on Canadian writing demonstrates his fascination with voices that refuse assimilation. He observed repeatedly that culture, in contrast to political ideologies, moves towards decentralization. Although strong separatist feelings are a fact in many parts of Canada, cultural pluralism muted Frye's inclination to develop cohesive systems. Canada, moreover, is alone among Commonwealth countries in having to deal with the proximity of the USA. Frye's frequent visits to universities in the USA and his membership on the Canadian Radio-television and Telecommunications Commission, 1968–77, gave him an affectionately ironic perspective on Canadian-American relations.

Contemporary responses to Frye, particularly in the USA, are often ahistorical, turning a blind eye to the fact that Frye's voice emerges from a specific place and time. Frye's own writings, in contrast, demonstrate a strong historical awareness. Although he wrote on individual authors (*T. S. Eliot*, 1963; *The Return of Eden: Five Essays on Milton's Epics*, 1965), he was more often concerned with the task of addressing the relation of literature to society, a preoccupation reflected in his titles: *The Stubborn Structure: Essays on Criticism and Society* (1970), *The Critical Path: An Essay on the Social Context of Literary Criticism* (1971); and *Spiritus Mundi: Essays on Literature, Myth, and Society* (1976).

Frye's numerous writings on Canadian literature do not lend themselves to easy generalizations. He served as editor of *The Canadian Forum* from 1948 to 1952, and from 1950 to 1960 he wrote the poetry criticism section for the annual 'Letters in Canada' issue of the *University of Toronto Quarterly*. His most influential essay on Canadian writing is also the one that has the most potential for application to other Commonwealth literatures that have gone through a colonial period. In the 'Conclusion' to the first edition of the *Literary History of Canada* (1965), he introduced the now familiar image of the 'garrison mentality'. This and other essays are collected in *The Bush Garden: Essays on the Canadian Imagination* (1971) and in *Divisions on a Ground: Essays on Canadian Culture* (1982). In the years immediately preceding his death, Frye's energies were concentrated on completing two books on the Bible: *The Great Code* (1982) and *Words With Power* (1990).

MAGDALENE REDEKOP

Further reading: John Ayre, *Northrop Frye: A Biography* (1989); A. C. Hamilton, *Northrop Frye: Anatomy of His Criticism* (1990).

FUGARD, ATHOL (1932–)
South African dramatist

He was born to an Afrikaans-speaking mother and an Anglo-Irish father in arid Middelburg, Cape Province, South Africa; shortly thereafter he and his family moved to the coastal Port Elizabeth, landfall of the British settlers of 1820 who formed the frontier of the colony of the Eastern Cape. (Today a bleak industrial city, because of its underdeveloped and depressed circumstances, Port Elizabeth is the centre of black resistance politics.) Fugard was educated at Marist Brothers College and at Port Elizabeth Technical College, and, from 1950 to 1953, at the University of Cape Town. Failing to complete his arts degree, he set off in 1953 on a hitch-hike up Africa, then worked his way around the world on a tramp steamer.

On his return to Port Elizabeth in 1956, he married Sheila Meiring, who is well known as the poet and novelist Sheila Fugard. In Cape Town and then in Johannesburg during the Sophiatown Renaissance period (1958–60), they produced experimental plays, including two for black casts, *No-Good Friday* and *Nongogo* — both published with *Dimetos* in *Dimetos and Two Early Plays* (1977). A third work from this time is the novel *Tsotsi* (not published until 1980), detailing the exhilarating mixed cultural life of the Renaissance, a life soon after demolished by the engineers of apartheid. The most performed playwright South Africa has produced, Athol Fugard has more than twenty works to his credit. While in Europe in 1960, where the Fugards had some experience of experimental and avant-garde theatre, the news of the Sharpeville massacre drove the couple home for a decade of work, including the writing and production of four small-scale chamber plays, jokingly referred to as the Port Elizabethan plays — *The Blood Knot* (1963), *People are Living There* (1969), *Boesman and Lena* (1969), and *Hello and Goodbye* (1971). Fugard himself played in and directed most of their first productions, and although these works have become frequently performed in the repertory of several countries, in English and in translation, their origins were modest and low-budget, calling on few theatrical resources aside from skilful performance.

In the 1970s, arising out of his experience as director of the black Serpent Players Company in Port Elizabeth and the opening of South Africa's first professional fringe theatre, The Space (in Cape Town), Fugard worked in collaboration with his leading players, John Kani and Winston Ntshona, to write and produce two workshop plays — *Sizwe Bansi Is Dead* and *The Island*, first published in *Statements* (1974), a trilogy of highly engaged political dramas. These plays, with their original two-man casts, turned slender resources to great advantage and toured for many years within South Africa, in the UK, in the USA, and in several Commonwealth countries. The former is an indictment of the pass-law system of controls on black migrancy, and the latter a scathing and poignant attack on the inhuman and divisive punishments meted out to political prisoners detained on the infamous Robben Island. The third play of the trilogy is *Statements after an Arrest under the Immorality Act*.

Subsequently, Fugard has ventured into the feature-movie field. In 1974 he produced a film adaptation of *Boesman and Lena*. The film, also entitled *Boesman and Lena*, was directed by Ross Devenish and starred Fugard and his frequent leading lady, Yvonne Bryceland. He also produced *The Guest: An Episode in the Life of Eugène Marais* (1971) and *Marigolds in August* (1980); all three films have proved enduring with film-festival audiences. With his play *A Lesson from Aloes* (1981), Fugard has reverted to more formally scripted work, analysing the cost of survival in South Africa in terms of the penalties paid by dissidents, and making the controls and distortions exercised by the security police actively felt on stage.

Fugard's most explicitly autobiographical work, *'Master Harold' . . . and the Boys* (1982), deals with an incident between his younger self and the two black waiters of the café his mother managed at Saint George's Park in Port Elizabeth. Set during a rainy afternoon, this touching and bitter parable is about white privilege and the disadvantaged state of blacks.

Fugard's next play, *The Road to Mecca* (1985), was made into a film in 1990 and featured Yvonne Bryceland, Kathy Bates, and Fugard. The play is based on the true story of Helen Martins, the self-taught sculptress who scandalized her remote and upright community by persisting in her production of eccentric objects. The play is commonly read as an allegory about the maintenance of artists' freedom during the darkest days of apartheid.

In 1983 Fugard published his *Notebooks* of the years 1960–77, selected by **Mary Benson**. In its own right a documentary history of his South Africa, the collection also offers sidelights on a career that distinguished Fugard not only as a writer but as a practical and influential man of the theatre whose view of life in South Africa is uncompromising and unsparing and might now be called 'Fugardian'.

Fugard's output has oscillated between public and private utterance. Some of his works are 'objective', rich in social commentary, and contain strong agitprop elements. *Sizwe Bansi Is Dead*, for example — one of the most frequently performed plays of the last two decades and at the origin of the Black Theatre Movement of the 1970s and 1980s — uses the style and techniques of workshop theatre in exploring the dilemma of a black work-seeker forced by the cruel absurdity of apartheid to abandon his own identity in favour of the security of a false one. The gritty script, derived from the actual language of its two original performers and their stories, is an example of a theatre of confrontation squarely challenging both South African audiences and, subsequently, those overseas who may have been construed as passively supporting the appalling South African dispensation. The battle lines in the play are drawn clearly enough, but that does not mean the script lacks subtlety and often-explosive humour. The African performance style of direct address and ongoing editorializing is refreshing for western audiences and makes for a rousing and novel theatrical experience.

By contrast, Fugard also devises introspective, private works that are often frustratingly obscure, as though he is insisting on the right to pursue his own demon, come what may. His *A Place with the Pigs* (1987), described by one critic as a 'personal parable', analyses a marriage of entrapment and the changed conditions needed to release the pair into a liberated state. Intractable and wrapped in philosophical riddles, the work has not proved to have mass appeal.

My Children! My Africa! (1989) is one of Fugard's most 'public' plays to date and, indeed, is organized as an inquest or open hearing on the torching to death of an obscure black schoolteacher. The play proceeds as a debate, with the theatre as forum for discussion of an achingly relevant issue: the levels of murderous violence that erupt in the name of the freedom struggle in South Africa. Aspects of *My Children! My Africa!* are frankly didactic, and Fugard's 'lesson' is that thwarted aspirations inevitably turn in on themselves, that repression breeds explosive acts of destruction of self and of others, and that peace can be achieved only on the basis of justice. These vintage Fugard messages are delivered in virtuoso and fresh ways in this script; within his auditorium, violence acts as therapy. *Playland* (1992) uses the same techniques.

Fugard is difficult to situate in Commonwealth literature, as he seems to have no feeling for parallel events in the English-speaking world outside South Africa and remains indifferent to his English history and heritage. In many interviews, he describes himself as a white Afrikaner who writes in English (as opposed to an English-speaker). His experience of the European avant-garde in the late 1950s was brief — Sartre and the British Angry Young Men had a glancing impact on his first plays, as did the poetic realism of Eugene O'Neill and Tennessee Williams. Fugard's lasting affinity, however, is with Albert Camus — raised in an outlying, colonized province of the metropolis, cut off and yet privileged — and Fugard's *Dimetos* is really about such masters on the periphery of power. Another affinity is with Bertolt Brecht, perpetually in flight from Fascist tyranny, just as Fugard himself has been persecuted at times by the South African system. (One is inclined to forget that, under segregated theatre conditions in South Africa, plays with mixed casts such as *The Blood Knot* were performed illegally, and that within the country Fugard's role has always perforce been oppositional.) From William Faulkner, Fugard picked up the richness and usefulness of exploring 'one little corner of the world' in depth — in his case, unglamorous, backwater Port Elizabeth and its unpromising environment.

Although Fugard has had faithful support from the professional theatre infrastructure and from the liberal establishment within South Africa, he has had no real professional challenge or rival. Single-handedly he has pulled South African stages into prominence and produced drama at the cutting edge of contemporary experience, while introducing his uniquely cruel and compelling country to the rest of the world like no other writer before him. He is a loner, an original. (See also **Drama**, South Africa.)

STEPHEN GRAY

Further reading: Dennis Walder, *Athol Fugard* (1984); Russell Vandenbroucke, *Truths the Hands Can Touch: The Theatre of Athol Fugard* (1985); Stephen Gray, *Fugard on File* (1991); John Read, *Athol Fugard: A Bibliography* (1991).

FURPHY, JOSEPH (1843–1912)
Australian novelist
Born at Yering (now Yarra Glen), Victoria, Australia, he was the son of Protestant Irish parents who immigrated to Australia in 1841. He married Leonie Germaine in 1867 and had a series of itinerant jobs before working in his brother's foundry at Shepparton from 1883 to 1904. It was while he was at Shepparton that he began writing and publishing stories in the ***Bulletin***, first as Warrigal Jack and, after 1893, as Tom Collins. He moved to Swanbourne, Perth, Australia, in 1904, and lived there until his death. His Swanbourne house has been memorialized in Justina Williams' *Tom Collins and His House* (1973).

Such is Life: Being Certain Extracts from the Diary of Tom Collins, set in the Riverina and defined by Furphy as being of 'temper, democratic; bias, offensively Australian', was written at Shepparton and published by the *Bulletin* in 1903. It began as a 'neatly' written manuscript of 1,125 pages, which he sent to the *Bulletin* for its appraisal in 1897. **A. G. Stephens**, the literary editor, accepted the manuscript but recommended major editing. *Rigby's Romance* (1946) and *The Buln-Buln and the Brolga* (1948) resulted from these excisions. *Rigby's Romance* was serialized in the *Barrier Truth* in 1905–6.

Deriving in part from Furphy's antagonism to the type of colonial romance popularized by **Hen-**

ry **Kingsley**'s *The Recollections of Geoffry Hamlyn* (1859), *Such is Life* draws its form and subject matter, Furphy explained to Stephens, from the 'jumble of incident, dialogue, reflection *etc*. (Such *is* Life)'. Accordingly, Tom Collins, the novel's narrator and putative author, who is wholly given over to the randomness of life and allows this to determine the structure of the novel — by randomly choosing to chronicle the events of one day per month — becomes the novel's ironic vehicle, exposing what Furphy called 'the patchwork web of life'. He finds, like Henry Fielding, that some days do not offer suitable material for his narrative and rearranges the dates to suit his plot, even as he repeatedly asserts the plotlessness of life. To compound the irony, the plot also contains a submerged romance to which Tom is oblivious. While the novel is experimental and self-conscious about form in the way of much contemporary writing, its closer affiliations are to eighteenth-century explorations into the technical problems of realism. Such a preoccupation is understandable in a writer who was trying to unshackle novels written in Australia from English models and expectations.

Although Tom is a dissembler, the deeper ironies and ambiguities of the novel lie not so much in the protagonist's divided sensibility as in the tension between the ideals of socialism and the self-interest of the individual. Just as an element of the novel's 'meaning' lies in its relationship (ironic and serious) with earlier writing — absorbing or denying **Rolf Boldrewood**, Henry Kingsley, Dickens, Walter Scott, Laurence Sterne, Fielding, Cervantes, Shakespeare, and the Bible — in other respects it initiates a dialogue with theories of socialism and with exploration into free will and determinism in novels by writers such as George Eliot, Henry James, and Thomas Hardy.

Less complex than *Such is Life*, *Rigby's Romance* and *The Buln-Buln and the Brolga* are also woven out of loose (but never random) conjunctions of yarns and stories. *Rigby's Romance* (formerly chapter five of the original manuscript) also features Tom as the ironic vehicle as it explores contrasts between theory and practice and belief and experience in the context of Christian socialism. *The Buln-Buln and the Brolga* comprises stories exploring issues of fact and fiction in narrative. (It substantially reworks sections of chapter two of the original manuscript.)

Although it sold only just more than 1,100 copies in 'a slow, dropping sale' during Furphy's lifetime, by 1947 **Douglas Stewart** was speaking of the 'deification of Joseph Furphy'. *Such is Life* was reissued in 1917, an edition of his poems in 1916, and an abridged version of *Rigby's Romance* in 1921; an abridged version of *Such is Life* was edited by **Vance Palmer** and **Nettie Palmer** in 1937; the 1903 version was re-released in 1944 to commemorate the centenary of Furphy's birth. J. K. Ewers' study *Tell the People!* (1943) was followed by **Miles Franklin**'s *Joseph Furphy: The Legend of a Man and His Book* (1944); a special 1945 issue of *Southerly* was devoted to Furphy. Recognition of Furphy's achievement was furthered by Kate Baker and a small group of enthusiasts. In the 1940s criticism focused on questions concerning Furphy's craft and on exegesis of the plot of *Such is Life*; during the 1960s the metaphysical potential of the work was tapped; more recently, the novel has been subjected to various post-structuralist readings.

JAMES WIELAND

Further reading: John Barnes, *The Order of Things: A Life of Joseph Furphy* (1990); *The Annotated Such is Life: Being Certain Extracts from the Diary of Tom Collins* by Joseph Furphy; introd. by Frances Devlin-Glass, Robin Eaden, Lois Hoffman, and G. W. Turner (1991); Julian Croft, *The Life and Opinions of Tom Collins: A Study of the Works of Joseph Furphy* (1991).

FURTADO, JOSEPH (1872–1947)
Indian/Goan poet
Born in Furtadovaddo, Palierne, Bardez, in Portuguese Goa, now in India, he was educated in Goa before attending, for a few years, boarding and arts schools in India. Furtado worked in India as a draughtsperson, agent, and chief engineer, usually for railway companies. He often moved between Goa and the cities of Bombay, Calcutta, and Poona, where there were better opportunities for employment.

Although well-read in English and European literature, Furtado followed the conventions of Romanticism in adopting the persona of a self-educated poet who wrote in simple, sincere words and produced ballad-like nature poems on the flowers, fauna, and landscape of his native Goa. In 'A Fiddler' (first published in his volume *A Goan Fiddler*, 1927), for example, the speaker pretends to be a musician who lives in the city, but whose music is nostalgic of the past and of rural life. *Poems of Joseph Furtado* (1895) claims to express emotion without regard to versification. Although Furtado's early volumes received little recognition in India, *Lays of Goa and Lyrics of a Goan* (1922) was widely reviewed in India and abroad, and *A Goan Fiddler* (with a preface by Edmund Gosse) and *The Desterrado* (1929) were published in England.

Furtado's Goan Catholic interests can be seen in his pamphlet *A Guide to the Convent and Churches of Old Goa* (1922), in his short critical study, *Principais Poetos Goanos* (1927), which includes nine of his own poems in Portuguese, and in the historical romance *Golden Goa* (1938). His *Selected Poems* (1942) was revised before his death and republished in 1967.

While Furtado is best known as a rare early instance of an Indian writing poetry in dialect and pidgin, a practice less common in India than in West Africa or the Caribbean, such poems are rare among his nine volumes of verse. Furtado deserves attention because of his bilingualism and because, in a purposefully self-limited way, his poetry is often good. Working within late Victorian and Edwardian conventions, his work reveals a sense of humour, the treatment of a variety of topics, including the spiritual, and lively personae.

BRUCE KING

Further reading: R. Parthasarathy, ed., *Ten Twentieth Century Indian Poets* (1976); Philip Furtado, 'Poet Joseph Furtado', *Journal of South Asian Literature* 1 (1983).

G

GALLANT, MAVIS (1922–)

Canadian short-story writer

Born in Montreal, Canada, Gallant began her education at the age of four in a Jansenist boarding school. On the death of her father she was sent to some seventeen schools in Canada and in the USA, but never attended university. She has been bilingual in French and English from early childhood. Passionately anti-fascist as a young woman, she has satirically metamorphosed her political experience during the war years in Canada in her play *What Is to Be Done?* (1983). Nevertheless, a strong yet subtle political sense and a profound sympathy for the oppressed and exploited — whether children or prisoners-of-war — are the hallmarks of her writing. From 1944 to 1950 she worked as a journalist for the *Montreal Standard*, covering economic, cultural, political, and social issues. After publishing a handful of stories in Canadian journals, she sold a story to *The New Yorker*, quit her job, and gave herself three years in Europe to establish herself as a writer. She has been there since 1950, travelling widely and living for a time in Italy, Austria, and Spain before settling in Paris. She has returned often to Canada, giving readings across the country and in 1983–4 served a term as writer-in-residence at the University of Toronto.

Unlike expatriates such as **V. S. Naipaul**, who have repudiated their countries of origin, Gallant has always been quick to identify herself as a Canadian abroad. On the other hand, she refuses to bring nationality into any discussion of her fiction — indeed, she has said that nationalism is something to be distrusted and rejected absolutely. 'I'm a writer in the English language,' she once told an interviewer. 'Was Katherine Mansfield a New Zealand writer to you?' The term 'post-colonial' does little to illuminate the nature or focus of Gallant's writing, since she has always been a 'citizen of the world', equally at home in English and French, especially fond of the best in American culture, and more amused than incensed by the imperialist trappings and socio-cultural icons of the British. Indeed, a decided coolness of tone, a pervasive narratorial detachment, and a flair for social satire are typically Gallant.

Certain critics have attempted to argue that those of Gallant's fictions that deal with her Canadian experience are more satisfying or authentic than those set in Europe, but this would seem to tell more about the limitations of such critics than about the true strengths and significance of Gallant's writing. As far as her Canadian fiction is concerned, she is in the enviable position of being able to treat Québécois and English-language culture with equal authority. She is, for example, as perceptive in a story such as 'Bernadette', about the paralytic ethos of pre-*révolution tranquille* Quebec, as she is in 'Its Image on the Mirror', which explores the stultifying effect of Scots-Presbyterianism on the emotional lives of certain English Canadians. But the most important aspect of Gallant's writing is its illumination of the lives of the dispossessed and deracinated, at home or abroad. For many Canadian writers of the present generation, Gallant's engagement with the 'international theme', her opening up of fictive territory that could be convincingly explored by those born and bred in Neepawa, as well as New York, has been a revelation.

Gallant has written about Canadians, Americans, Australians, and the English abroad, as well as of Europeans at home; the geographical range of her fiction, however, is resolutely European and North American. The Commonwealth writer who most readily springs to mind *vis-à-vis* Gallant is the equally well-travelled and politically acute **Christina Stead**. Gallant's seemingly effortless translation from Montreal to Paris is comparable to that of her compatriot Anne Hébert although it has taken Canadians appreciably longer to discover Gallant's work and to accord her due recognition as one of the country's finest artists. **Margaret Laurence**, **Mordecai Richler**, and **Norman Levine**, who have also spent extended periods of their writing lives outside Canada, seem to have been more readily 'forgiven' by certain kinds of Canadian nationalists, largely because these writers did eventually return to settle in Canada. One can argue that it is a sign of Canada's cultural maturity that writers like Gallant, who choose to live outside the country, are as appreciatively read as are those who, like **Alice Munro**, have never 'left home'.

Gallant's mastery of the French language and her sophisticated knowledge of French culture, society, and politics have allowed her to produce invaluable 'social narratives', among them the notebook that she kept during the student uprisings of 1968 in Paris, and a lengthy introduction to the affair of Gabrielle Russier, a lycée teacher who was romantically involved with one of her students and who committed suicide after being imprisoned as a consequence of the affair. Both narratives were first published in *The New Yorker* and were subsequently collected in her collection of essays and reviews, *Paris Notebooks* (1986).

It is, however, for her consummately elegant and incisive literary prose that Gallant has won international recognition. Her exceptional command of narrative voice and mastery of language, her preoccupation with what she calls 'abstract justice' — the need to extend imaginative understanding to those whom it is fashionable or 'politically correct' to ignore or to consider pariahs — and her delicious and far-reaching comic sense are as evident in her first collection of short fiction, *The Other Paris* (1956), as in her later work, for example, *In Transit* (1988). Her profound concern for those who suffer rather than make history, and her delineation of the ambiguous role of memory in both revising and uncovering the truth of experience, are best revealed in what is arguably the finest of her eight short-fiction collections, *From the Fifteenth District* (1979), although they also inform such other European-centred works as *The Pegnitz Junction* (1973) and *Overhead in a Balloon* (1985). Her novels, *Green Water, Green Sky* (1959) and the comic *tour de force A Fairly Good Time* (1970) deal with the appalling experiences of women irremediably trapped within the feminine mystique. The 'Linnet Muir' sequence collected in *Home Truths* (1981) — for which she won a Governor General's Award — is one of Gallant's rare portrayals of a woman who refuses imprisonment inside the female 'kitchen in a slum' (*Green Water, Green Sky*) and who attains personal, intellectual, and emotional independence. The stories that make up this extraordinary sequence can be described as a kind of enchanted prose. Gallant's evocation of childhood in a vanished Montreal, and her account of a writer coming into her vocation, create a vision of reality at once elusive and immediate, poignant, and disturbing.

JANICE KULYK KEEFER

Further reading: Neil K. Besner, *The Light of Imagination* (1988); Janice Kulyk Keefer, *Reading Mavis Gallant* (1989).

GALT, JOHN (1779–1839)
British/Canadian novelist

The son of a trader and sea-captain, he was born in Irvine, Scotland, where he was raised in the afterglow of the Scottish Enlightenment. Widely travelled, he was one of the first novelists from Great Britain to visit Canada, and one of the first to set a novel there based on first-hand experience. He is also known as the founder of the Canada Company, which played a vital role in colonizing the region now known as Ontario. Practical and protean, Galt not only supervised the building of actual communities in Canada, but also helped to write the 'new world' into cultural existence. Because he was both a colonizer and a novelist, and because so many of his writings on the 'new world' have survived in every genre and in government records, Galt provides a unique vantage point from which to view the most important phase of cultural transfer in the modern history of the English-speaking peoples.

Lawrie Todd; or, The Settlers in the Woods (1830), Galt's popular Defoe-like novel of pauper emigration and urban and backwoods life in New England, did for a vanishing and crucial era of American pioneer life what his Scottish 'Tales of the West' did for eighteenth-century Ayrshire. His *Bogle Corbet; or, The Emigrants* (1831), the fictional autobiography of a genteel emigrant who settles in the Ontario region, is unusual because of the distinctions drawn between Canadian and American society and habits of speech. The novel also shows how Canada, the Caribbean, and New England were linked in the minds of those looking out from Britain. Galt's *Autobiography* (1833) chronicles his experiences in Canada in the late 1820s; his 'American Traditions' articles in *Fraser's Magazine* (1830–2) illustrate his interest in the creation of new national identities by building new literatures out of shared or invented aboriginal and immigrant folklore and traditions. Although he was particularly sensitive to issues involving aboriginal people and highly critical of some aspects of his own civilization, Galt was an unashamed if complex imperialist, convinced of the rightness of British expansion.

NICHOLAS McCARTHY WHISTLER

GAMALINDA, ERIC (1956–)

Filipino novelist, poet, short-story writer

Born in Manila, the Philippines, he attended the University of Sto. Tomas and the University of the Philippines. He has been a fellow of the University of the Philippines Creative Writing Center, the Hawthornden Castle International Retreat for Writers, the Bellagio Study and Conference Center, and the Philippine Literary Arts Council. Gamalinda has written articles on art, rock music, and current events and won Palanca Memorial Awards for a one-act play (1981), poetry (1985, 1988), and short fiction (1988). He works at the Center for Investigative Journalism in Metro Manila as staff writer and broadcast co-ordinator.

Gamalinda's work includes the novels *Planet Waves* (1989), which received the National Book Award for Fiction, *Confessions of a Volcano* (1990), and *The Empire of Memory* (1992). He has also published *Lyrics from a Dead Language* (1991), a collection of poems written between 1977 and 1991, and *Peripheral Vision* (1992), a volume of short fiction. Poet **Ophelia Dimalanta** calls Gamalinda's poetry 'loopings of lyric and lore mediating between memory and feelings'; **Gemino Abad** calls it a 'fugitive antiphon', in which a 'syntax of illusion and rhetoric of habitation become a strange new alphabet of our blood'.

Considering that in the past nine decades (starting in 1901 with the establishment of the educational system by Americans) only some 120 Philippines novels have been written in English, Gamalinda's three novels represent an energetic bid to capture Philippine experience in novel form and in an adopted language. Gamalinda calls *Planet Waves* 'a palimpsest of quarter-truths and fictions'; he moves beyond the novel's family (mothers, children, grandfather, and a grandson who 'wakes up one morning to discover that he has a seraph's wings' and meets his grandfather floating in space) to explore time and space. *Confessions of a Volcano* focuses on two Filipinos in Japan, while exploring much contemporary Japanese literature and sensibility. *The Empire of Memory* is ambitious and sprawling, exploring recent events (the Marcos years), politics, social history, and family skeletons.

Poet Danton Remoto calls *Peripheral Vision* a mind-bender, citing especially 'Women and Apparitions', 'a long, postcolonial fiction that questions our notions of institutions, of empires', and naming Gamalinda 'one of the most talented writers of his generation'.

DOREEN G. FERNANDEZ

GANDHI IN INDIAN-ENGLISH LITERATURE

For **Mohandas Karamchand Gandhi**, writing was not an end in itself, but rather one of the means to living the good life — both the outer life in society and the inner life of the spirit. He did not subscribe to the doctrine of art for art's sake; for him art was for truth's sake also. In the several non-violent battles that he waged, first in South Africa and later in India, Gandhi used language with an almost biblical simplicity and directness. Writing was for self-knowledge as well as for communication and for converting people to one's point of view. In his famous 1921 appeal to **Rabindranath Tagore**, Gandhi advised the poet to lay down his lyre temporarily and plunge into political action.

When Gandhi became the leader of the nation on its march from subjection to liberation, the press in India — in English and in the regional languages — acquired a modernity and force as it reached out to the masses. Gandhi's own English-language journals *Young India* (1919–30) and *Harijan* (1933–*c*.51) set the standard, and English in India, following the Gandhian revolution, has been broadly utilitarian, cultivating the virtues of simplicity and native force.

Gandhian inspiration has likewise made an impact on creative writing in the languages of India, including English. In his *Murugan the Tiller* (1927) and *Kandan, The Patriot* (1932), **K. S. Venkataramani** projects Gandhian economics and Gandhian politics on the respective protagonists, Murugan and Kandan. Other novels in which Gandhi figures or where his presence can be inferred are **Mulk Raj Anand**'s *Untouchable* (1935) and *The Sword and the Sickle* (1942), Venu Chitale's *In Transit* (1950), **K. A. Abbas**' *Inquilab: A Novel of Indian Revolution* (1955), **R. K. Narayan**'s *Waiting for the Mahatma* (1955), **K. Nagarajan**'s *Chronicles of Kedaram* (1961), and **Raja Rao**'s *Kanthapura* (1938).

More significant even than Gandhi's presence or recorded speech was the Gandhi-charged political, socio-ethical, and spiritual atmosphere of the 1920s, 1930s, and 1940s that made the Gandhi years India's latter-day heroic age. The impact was felt everywhere — in art, dress, an austere lifestyle, and an acceptance of the 'Sarvodaya' ideal of the sunrise of the good of all, a social order based on love and achieved by fighting hatred and violence with suffering and faith in God.

Gandhi is very much a felt presence in the more than one hundred volumes of the Collected Works of Mahatma Gandhi, begun in 1958, but also in a great many other works of prose and verse, drama, and fiction. Biographical studies such as N. K. Bose's *My Days with Gandhi* (1953) and Krishna Kripalani's *Gandhi: A Life* (1968), autobiographies such as *Jawaharlal Nehru: An Autobiography* (1936) and S. C. Bose's *An Indian Pilgrim* (1848), a panel discussion such as P. A. Wadia's *Mahatma Gandhi* (1935), and a comparative study such as B. R. Ambedkar's *Ranade, Gandhi and Jinnah* (1943) fairly indicate the range of this literature in non-fiction prose. Fictional presentation of Gandhi has been fairly continuous since Venkataramani's work; there are also plays: K. S. Rangappa's *Gandhi's Sadhana: A Play in Three Acts* (1969) and S. K. Ojha's *Riding the Storm: A Play on Mahatma Gandhi*, (1990), for example. Tributes in verse are legion, ranging from **Sarojini Naidu**'s rhapsody 'O Mystic Lotus, Sacred and Sublime' to R. R. Sreshta's 'A Light unto Our Path', a long poem on the Mahatma's martyrdom.

Most ambitious of all is **Chaman Nahal**'s 'Gandhi Quartet', covering the period 1915–48 — from the year of Gandhi's return to India from South Africa to his martyrdom. The four novels are *Azadi* ('Freedom', 1975), *The Crown and the Loincloth* (1981), *The Salt of Life* (1990), and *The Triumph of the Tricolour* (1993). They cover, respectively, the independence-partition holocaust of 1947–8, the non-co-operation movement of 1920–2, the salt-satyagraha movement of 1930–2, and the final 'Quit India' movement of 1942–5. The 'Gandhi Quartet' almost invites comparison with epic narratives such as Tolstoy's *War and Peace* or Thomas Hardy's *The Dynasts*. Novels such as **Manohar Malgonkar**'s *A Bend in the Ganges* (1964) recall the vicissitudes of the Gandhi era, and **Khushwant Singh**'s *Train to Pakistan* (1956) evokes the terror and pity, bestiality, and heroism of the post-partition horrors of 1947.

K. R. SRINIVASA IYENGAR

Further reading: C. D. Narasimhaiah, *The Writer's Gandhi* (1967); K. R. Srinivasa Iyengar, *Indian Writing in English* (5th ed., 1987).

GANDHI, MOHANDAS KARAMCHAND
(1869–1948)

Indian statesman, essayist, autobiographer

He was born at Porbandar, Kathiawar, in Gujarat State, India; his father and grandfather, of the 'Vaishya' (trading) caste, were both chief ministers in Kathiawar princely states. Married at the age of twelve to Kasturbai, also twelve, Gandhi matriculated from Alfred High School, Rajkot, India, at the age of eighteen. He spent three years in England (1888–91), studying law at the Inner Temple, London. Having practised in Bombay and Rajkot with little success, Gandhi sailed for South Africa in 1893 in search of a better career, but instead discovered his life's philosophy and mission. Following his return to India in 1915, he led the 'Quit India' movement whose goal of independence for India was achieved largely through campaigns based on Gandhian principles of truth, non-violence, and passive resistance. His moral leadership earned him the title Mahatma (Great Soul).

The influence of his devout mother, Putlibai, and his readings of the Bible, the Upanishads, the *Bhagavadgita*, the Koran, Ruskin's *Unto This Last*, and Thoreau's essay 'Civil Disobedience' were important shaping factors in Gandhi's life. He soon put into practice his own political, social, and economic theories by launching 'Satyagraha' (the force that is born of truth, love, and non-violence) movements.

Gandhi's ideas were not embodied in a systematic treatise. Most of his writings are to be found scattered in his journalistic articles, his letters, and memoranda. His early writings, such as *London Diary* (undated, estimated to have been written between 1888 and 1894), a record of his life in London, and such essays as 'Foods of India', are of slight literary importance.

Gandhi's South African writings, including the pamphlets 'An Appeal to Every Briton in South Africa' (1895), 'The Indian Franchise' (1895), and 'Grievances of the British Indians in South Africa' (1896), make a fervent plea for the betterment of the lives of South African Indians. In 1904 Gandhi took over a weekly publication *Indian Opinion* (published in Gujarati and English) with a view to fighting the Indian settlers' cause.

Gandhi's seminal work, 'Hind Swaraj' ('Indian Home Rule'), appeared in the columns of *Indian Opinion* in 1909. Originally written in his mother tongue, Gujarati, it was translated into English by Gandhi and published as *Hind Swaraj or Indian Home Rule* in 1910. It is the first direct statement of his principles of truth and non-violence and concludes with both the remark that he bears 'no enmity towards the English but . . . towards their civilization' and with his commitment to Swaraj (self-rule).

In India Gandhi founded two journals, *Young India* (1919–30) and *Harijan* (1933–*c.*51). His *An Autobiography or The Story of My Experiments with Truth* (vol. 1, 1927; vol. 2, 1929, translated from Gujarati by Mahadev Desai) is the most significant of his works in English. As the title suggests, it is essentially a spiritual quest, an absorbing, honest self-portrait. *Satyagraha in South Africa* (1928), *Discourses on the Gita* (first published in Gujarati in 1930 and translated into English and published under this title in 1960), based on Gandhi's theories of non-violence and non-attachment, and *From Yeravada Mandir* (letters written from prison containing mostly Gandhi's teachings) were translated by V. G. Desai. Gandhi also wrote *Constructive Programme: Its Meaning and Place* (1941; rev. 1945) — his ideas on political, social, economic, and cultural activities — and *Key to Health* (1948), translated by Sushila Nayar. The Collected Works of Mahatma Gandhi series, which began publication in 1961 and is edited by the publications division of the government of India, already contains more than seventy-five volumes and is not yet completed. *The Selected Works of Mahatma Gandhi* (6 vols), edited by Shriman Narayan, was published in 1968.

Gandhi was neither a great scholar nor an original thinker, but his writings are a treasure-house of knowledge on political, social, economic, cultural, and spiritual issues and are written in clear, direct prose. He rediscovered the ethical values of the ancient Indian tradition and aligned them with similar values from the western tradition. As he himself acknowledged, 'I have nothing new to teach the world. Truth and non-violence are as old as the hills. All I have done is to experiment in both on as vast a scale as I could do.'

P. A. ABRAHAM

Further reading: Louis Fischer, *The Life of Mahatma Gandhi* (1950); S. N. Bhattacharya, *Mahatma Gandhi: The Journalist* (1965); Bhabani Bhattacharya, *Gandhi, the Writer* (1969); Ved Mehta, *Mahatma Gandhi and His Apostles* (1976); Glyn Richards, *The Philosophy of Gandhi: A Study of his Basic Ideas* (1987).

GARNER, HELEN (1942–)

Australian novelist, short-story writer

Born in Geelong, Victoria, Australia, and educated at Melbourne University, she worked as a high school teacher until in 1972 she was dismissed for being too frank with students about sexual matters. Her first novel, *Monkey Grip* (1977), was an equally controversial winner of the 1978 National Book Council Award, more conservative readers being horrified by its detailed presentation of inner city, counter-culture life-styles, with an emphasis on drug taking and sexual freedom. For its female characters, most notably the novel's narrator, Nora, 'free love' does not bring happiness. Nora's obsession with Jacko is shown to be as strong a 'monkey grip' as is his heroin addiction. An apparently unstructured, rambling book, criticized on first appearance as a mere transcript of its author's diaries, *Monkey Grip* can now be seen as a work of considerable art as well as the definitive account of alternative life-styles in Australia during the 1970s.

Garner used her award money to live during 1978 and 1979 in Paris, where she wrote *Honour and Other People's Children* (1980). Though the least popular of Garner's works and the only non-prize-winner, the two novellas that constitute the book clearly indicate the direction her later fiction was to take. Eschewing the more heightened passion and drama of *Monkey Grip*, she focuses here on the tensions and emotions of everyday life: the breakup of a marriage, the divided loyalties of a child, the uneasy relationship between children and adults. This content is accompanied by a concentration and refinement of form and style, with Garner striving to get the maximum effect from the minimum number of words.

Both the pared style and the focus on family life are seen at their best in *The Children's Bach* (1984), one of the finest pieces of recent Australian fiction. Winner of the 1986 Adelaide Festival Award, this novella concentrates on the Fox family — Dexter, Athena, and their two sons. We are shown the impact on their life of various outsiders: Elizabeth, a former girlfriend of Dexter's; her younger sister Vicki; Philip, a rock musician. When Athena leaves for a brief affair with Philip, Dexter is horrified to find himself in bed with Vicki. But Athena returns to restore order to the house and resume her playing of Bach, tossing 'handfuls of notes high into the sparkling air!' Music is integral to this novel, both thematically and structurally, with voices, styles, images, and tones being woven contrapuntally together.

Postcards from Surfers (1985), a collection of stories, won the 1986 New South Wales Premier's Literary Award for Fiction. While many of its stories, including the title piece, continue Garner's exploration of the telling details of everyday and family life, others, such as the much anthologized 'The Life of Art', show her experimenting with a more patterned formal structure and a more stylized prose. She has continued to work in this less naturalistic vein in *Cosmo Cosmolino* (1992), a novella and two interlinked stories, while also achieving success as a script writer for film and television.

ELIZABETH WEBBY

Further reading: Pam Gilbert, *Coming Out from Under: Contemporary Australian Women Writers* (1988).

GARNER, HUGH (1913–79)

Canadian novelist, short-story writer, journalist

Born in Batley, Yorkshire, England, he was taken to Canada in 1919. Most of his life was spent in working-class and then middle-class neighbourhoods of downtown Toronto, which he re-created in detail in his essentially autobiographical novels, short stories, and magazine articles. Garner was heavily influenced by Hemingway and Dos Passos and his abrasive candour and championing of 'the common man' earned him a degree of popular success unusual for a Canadian writer of his period.

Garner's *Cabbagetown* (abridged, 1950; in full, 1968) is his most autobiographical as well as his most accomplished novel. Its frank, sympathetic depictions of working-class life are echoed in the novel *The Silence on the Shore* (1962) and in many of his short stories. From the mid-1960s on, Garner's increasing alcoholism resulted in a sharp decline in his writing abilities, although some of the later fiction, particularly the mystery novel *The Sin Sniper* (1970), exhibits traces of his earlier flair for dramatic realism.

Garner's short stories comprise a wildly uneven but at times stunningly powerful body of work in which he often takes greater risks than in his novels. His short-story collections include *The Yellow Sweater* (1952), *Hugh Garner's Best Stories* (1963), which is representative of his talent for the short story, *Men and Women* (1966), *Violation of the Virgins* (1971), and *Hugh Garner Omnibus* (1978). 'The Conversion of Willie Heaps' (1951), for example, is a psychologically sophisticated examination of religious mania, and 'One-Two-Three Little Indians' (1952) is a sensitive portrayal of the plight of Canada's Native peoples (both stories are included in *The Yellow Sweater* and *Hugh Garner's Best Stories*). As in his novels, Garner's sympathy for the underdog imparts a fierce, passionate tone to the best of his short stories, which more than compensates for their occasionally awkward syntax and limited vocabulary.

Garner's non-fiction writing is of very high quality. His *One Damn Thing After Another* (1973) is a remarkably frank autobiography; *Author, Author!* (1964) collects his deservedly esteemed magazine journalism. Although Garner's aversion to conventional literary society made him a lifelong outsider and has resulted in a degree of posthumous neglect, his work is at its best a forceful and evocative record of a largely ignored stratum of Canadian life.

PAUL STUEWE

Further reading: Doug Fetherling, *Hugh Garner* (1972); Paul Stuewe, *Hugh Garner and His Works* (1985); Paul Stuewe, *The Storms Below: The Turbulent Life and Times of Hugh Garner* (1988).

GEDDES, GARY (1940–)

Canadian poet, anthologist

Born in Vancouver, Canada, he studied at the University of British Columbia and in the UK before completing a Ph.D. at the University of Toronto, Canada, in 1975. He has taught in universities across Canada, edited *Studies in Canadian Literature*, and operates Cormorant Press on his farm near Ottawa. A self-proclaimed 'missionary' of Canadian culture, he is the best-known poetry anthologist in Canada, as well as the author of more than twenty books of his own poetry and prose. His *Twentieth-Century Poetry and Poetics* (1985) and the anthology that first appeared as *Fifteen Canadian Poets* (1970, with Phyllis Bruce) — later revised as *Fifteen Canadian Poets Plus Five* (1978) and *Fifteen Canadian Poets Times Two* (1988) — have been widely used in Canadian schools and universities. As an anthologist, Geddes has helped to define a Canadian poetic canon and to demonstrate its variety and growth. (See **Anthologies**, Canada.)

Intensely sensitive renditions of human conflict, as well as thoughtful reconsiderations of other artistic reactions to conflict, give Geddes' poetry a place with the writings of other Canadian writers such as **Rudy Wiebe**, who have attempted to jolt Canadians into meaningful connections with the ethical dilemmas of struggles elsewhere. This theme may best be seen in *Hong Kong Poems* (1987), written out of research he did on the disastrous Canadian military expedition to Hong Kong in 1941, and in *The Terracotta Army* (1984), written after leading a writers' tour to China. Travel, particularly to Latin America, continues to stimulate Geddes' poetry.

The theme of suffering and conflict can be found throughout his earlier work, especially in *Letter of the Master of Horse* (1973). **George Woodcock** has highly praised Geddes' explorations of history's pain and chaos, calling him Canada's best political poet. In other works, such as *Divided We Stand* (1977), which offers a mixture of genres, Geddes has concentrated on Canadians' preoccupation with defining a national identity. In short stories in *The Unsettling of the West* (1986), Geddes worked at deconstructing western Canada's myths. In his various roles as editor, publisher, reviewer, teacher, anthologist, and writer, Geddes has stimulated poetry in Canada and has done much to make it accessible abroad.

TERRENCE CRAIG

GEE, MAURICE (1931–)

New Zealand novelist, children's writer

Born in Whakatane township, New Zealand, but raised in Henderson, he was educated at Avondale College, the University of Auckland, and Auckland Teachers' College. From 1955 he worked as a schoolteacher and casual labourer before going to England in 1961. During those years he wrote short stories, some of which are collected in *A Glorious Morning, Comrade* (1975). Gee returned from England in 1962. His first novel, *The Big Season* (1962), looks back to earlier 'man alone' fiction in pitting the nonconformist individual against the puritan community. His second novel, *A Special Flower* (1965), is more subtle in charting the impact of an uninhibited woman on a repressed hero and his proper mother and sister, developing further the method of multiple perspectives that Gee began in the earlier story, 'The Losers' (first published in the journal *Landfall* in

1959 and since widely anthologized).

With *In My Father's Den* (1972), written during a year off from his work as a librarian, Gee began to find his voice as a novelist. There, like **Maurice Shadbolt** and **Maurice Duggan**, but more explicitly, he questions the 'man alone' rebellion against puritanism, showing that the terms of the protagonist's 'liberated' revolt are actually set by the puritanism against which it is aimed. With its juxtaposition of the scarcity-society of the 1940s and the affluent 1960s, *In My Father's Den* is Gee's first major exploration of 'post-provincial' New Zealand. This exploration is continued in *Games of Choice* (1976), a sharply-drawn picture of the breakup of a suburban family focusing on a protagonist caught between the puritanism of his father, with his memories of the Depression, and the illusory freedom of his daughter, who is at home in an affluent world where sex is another consumer experience. The juxtaposition of the emotionally and stylistically different first-person points of view of the protagonist and his father is a further advance in Gee's method, anticipating the Plumb trilogy which followed.

In 1976 Gee moved with his family from Auckland to Nelson and became a full-time writer, depending on his writing of children's fiction and film and television scripts to supplement his income as novelist. It was only then, he has said, that he 'was able to use material [he]'d been sitting on which [he] didn't want to use until [he] was absolutely settled and had the time to do it.' The 'material' was the life of his grandfather, James Chapple, and the literary result was his finest work to date, the Plumb trilogy — *Plumb* (1978), *Meg* (1981), and *Sole Survivor* (1983). The first novel traces the life of George Plumb — courageous in his idealism as rebel clergyman and pacifist, a visionary nevertheless blind to much of himself and his family. Plumb narrates his own story as an old man in 1949 and in the process begins to come to terms with his life while preparing for death. *Meg*, not so well-known but as fine a novel, is told in 1965–6 by Plumb's favourite daughter as she looks back upon and accepts her life. *Sole Survivor*, less successful as an independent novel, is told in 1982 by Meg's cynical, disillusioned journalist son. The three novels overlap; the same events may be told two or even three times and the different points of view correct and corroborate each other. The narrative method, adapted from that of Joyce Cary's trilogies, succeeds fully in presenting Gee's critical, compassionate, relativistic vision. Providing the fullest picture of New Zealand life and history yet created in fiction and with a rich range of memorable characters, the trilogy is the most successful work in the tradition of New Zealand realism.

Gee followed the trilogy with *Prowlers* (1987) and *The Burning Boy* (1990). The first resembles *Plumb* in its use of an aging first-person narrator looking back on his life and changing in the process of remembering. The central character of *Prowlers*, however, with his dry, sceptical, scientist's vision of both his scientific and his sister's political careers, is very different from both George Plumb in what he sees and in how he sees it. *The Burning Boy* is another departure, almost Victorian in its scope, with a wide range of characters interacting within a small city, but almost postmodern in its play with an omniscient point of view. These works show that Gee, a major novelist in his range and growth, is still developing.

LAWRENCE JONES

Further reading: Bill Manhire, *Maurice Gee* (1986).

GHANA

The Republic of Ghana lies on the west coast of Africa, approximately 650 kilometres north of the equator. It shares its borders on the west with Côte d'Ivoire (Ivory Coast), on the east with Togo, and on the north with Burkina Faso (formerly Upper Volta). Ghana has a land mass of approximately

240,000 square kilometres, and its climate ranges from tropical in the south-west to savannah in the north. Its population of 15,656,000 (1991) comprises forty-four per cent Akan, sixteen per cent Mole-Dagbani, thirteen per cent Ewe, nine per cent Ga-Adangbe, and eighteen per cent others. English is the official language. By estimation, forty-six per cent of the population is Christian, thirty-eight per cent practises traditional religions, and sixteen per cent is Muslim.

The first black African nation to regain independence from colonial rule (6 March 1957, becoming a republic on 1 July 1960), Ghana derives its name from Old Ghana (AD fifth to thirteenth centuries), the earliest of Sudanese states, which Arabic scholars Al Fazari (AD eighth century) and Al Yaqubi (AD ninth century) described as the land of gold. Basil Davidson and Kwamena Dickson contend that, following the collapse of ancient Ghana in the twelfth century, the ancestors of the Akans migrated from the Niger belt to settle in territories within present-day Ghana and Côte d'Ivoire, joining settlements that had existed at the edge of the forest region since Neolithic times. An early wave of Neolithic groups from the Mediterranean region had reached northern Ghana by 1000 BC, followed by migrant groups from the Congo, Central Africa, and the Niger bend in 900 BC. The acquisition of iron technology made it possible to penetrate the forest region and establish settlements around family and clan units, which ultimately became enlarged communities. These groups were strengthened by waves of incoming migrants from the Sudanese belt during major population dispersals between the twelfth and sixteenth centuries. These movements resulted in the consolidation of Gur-speaking settlements (the Kokomba, the Nanumba, Lobi, and Grunsi) north of the Black Volta, and Kwa-speaking settlements (Akan, Ga-Adangbe, and Ewe) in the southern half of the country.

The earliest Akan speaking group in Ghana, the Guans, migrated across the Volta gorge and Akwapim ridge to settle along the Afram and coastal plains. They merged with other migrant Akan groups who dispersed throughout the southern half of Ghana as they pressed for territories. One of the earliest settlements to attain statehood, Bono, in the Techiman area, gained political and economic influence as a major source of the trans-Saharan gold trade that attracted Mande Dyula traders from the north-west and Hausa traders from the north-east. By the fifteenth century, another major commercial centre flourished at Begho, north-eastern Ashanti, where Mande traders obtained gold for markets in North Africa and Europe. These traders introduced Islam and their material culture (the weaving of kente strips and the dyeing of cloth). The growth of trade spurred the expansion and consolidation of territories, some of which formed the nuclei of major Akan states such as Denkyira, Adansi, Fanti, and Akwamu.

A wave of Ga migrants from Benin, the Niger delta area, joined aborigine Kpesi (Guan) settlements along the Accra plains in approximately AD 1300. By the sixteenth century, Ga (Accra, Osu, Labadi, Nungua, Tema, and Kpone) and Adangbee groups (Shai, Mla, Manya, and others) had settled in the Greater Accra area, Shai Hills, and parts of the eastern region.

Like the Gas, the Ewes migrated westward from Ketu (Yoruba and Edo regions) through Tado (on Mono river, Benin Republic) and Nuatji (Notsi, Togo) to join settlements in the eastern and lower Volta regions. These migrants formed clusters of settlements in the north-west (Kpandu, Kpalime), west (Ho and Adaklu), and south-east (Anlo and Tongu).

From ancient times, aborigine groups of Konkomba, Nanumba, Lobi, and Gurunshi had occupied territories in Upper North, and indigenous Guan tribes of Gonja (Ntafo in Twi), Dompo, and Krachi had settled north of the Black Volta. By the mid-fifteenth century, however, these settlements were routed by invaders from the Suadanese belt, Lake Chad, and Hausaland who established their own kingdoms. Thus, the Maprusi dominated the tribes of the Upper East (Wa), while the Dagomba defeated the Konkomba and extended their influence over settlements toward the north-western Côte d'Ivoire frontier. Following that trend, Mande-speaking groups from Mali also invaded the Northern and Upper regions, causing aboriginal Guan groups and the Nanomba and Kokomba to seek refuge in central Ghana and Togo.

Competition with the trans-Saharan gold trade came from the Portuguese, who established a direct maritime commercial link with the Guinea Coast in the late fifteenth century. Consequently, the Portuguese built the Elmina Castle in 1482 as well as forts at Accra, Shama, Axim, and Keta to protect their trade with the Gold Coast. However, they were joined by the Spaniards and the Dutch (sixteenth century), and the English (1631), followed by Sweden, Denmark, France, and Brandenburg (Prussia) by the end of the seventeenth century.

The initial contact of Europeans with the Guinea coast occurred coevally with their arrival in the Americas, where they established plantations and forced enslaved Africans to cultivate products such as sugar and cotton for markets in Europe. In Ghana, the crippling factional wars to capture slaves to exchange for guns in order to safeguard the homestead resulted in massive depopulation and realignment of small tribes behind the powerful kingdoms of Akwamu and Denkyira, both of which were superseded by the Asante Empire by 1710. For the next two hundred years the Asantes were the dominant group, wielding influence beyond the borders of modern Ghana.

Concurrently, and following its declaration to abolish slavery (1807), Britain gained considerable political and commercial influence in Ghana. Britain sought to undermine the grip of its European competitors on the Gold Coast through vigorous commercial campaigns and missionary activities. The British also attempted to curb the growing power and independence of the Asantes, against whom they waged war relentlessly throughout the nineteenth century.

The British appropriated territories in accordance with such unilaterally conceived documents as The Bond of 1844 and the Berlin Conference (1885). Local opposition to British imperialism was articulated by Ghanaians (Attoh Ahumah, John Mensah-Sarbah, Kofi Asaam, Kobina Fynn Asaam, and others) who were educated in mission schools, but who saw beneath the veneer of white pretension. The dominant issues of the early protest movement by Ghanians were the devaluation of the indigenous tradition, the arbitrary appropriation of the traditional land by the colonial government, and the tightening grip of colonialism.

In the early decades of the twentieth century, nationalism in the Gold Coast was led by J. E. Casely-Hayford, Kobina Sekyi, and Kwaggir Aggrey, whose protest against colonial rule was articulated as part of the global liberation movement of black people. Casely-Hayford's *Ethiopia Unbound* (1911; repr. 1969), which addresses issues of African identity and cultural nationalism, also strengthened the commitment to Pan Africanism. Sekyi's play *The Blinkards* (premièred 1915, first published in 1974), a criticism of educated Ghanaians who depreciate their indigenous culture, is in the tradition of celebrating racial pride.

After the Second World War, nationalism benefited from improved socio-economic conditions in the Gold Coast and from the leadership of J. B. Danquah and Kwame Nkrumah. Danquah's party, United Gold Coast Convention (UGCC), failed to garner national support as Ghanaians increasingly rallied to Nkrumah's call for mass action, confrontation, and the slogan 'Independence Now'. Nkrumah was active in the Pan African movement, drawing inspiration from Casely-Hayford, W. E. B. Du Bois, and George Padmore. Nkrumah saw Ghana's independence as a landmark in the struggle for the total liberation of Africa.

Nkrumah built cultural and educational institutions and implemented accelerated educational programmes that have remained the most far-reaching educational reform in Ghana. He also expanded existing rail, road, and telecommunication networks and built hydro-electricity facilities to stimulate industrialization. From a literary historical perspective the climate of general optimism led to the publication of such works as the anthology *Voices of Ghana* (1958), edited by Henry Swanzy, and the journal *Okyeame*, which are artistic expressions of a national cultural awakening.

The 1966 overthrow of Nkrumah in a coup by the army and police set the country on a downward spiral marked by political and social instability. There are obvious parallels between the economic and political *malaise* and Ghanaian literature since the mid-1960s, which is dominated by a feeling of *Angst*. **Ayi Kwei Armah**'s novel *The Beautyful Ones Are Not Yet Born* (1968) is an eloquent reflection of Ghana's social and economic malady.

The National Liberation Council, which removed Nkrumah's government, handed political control to K. A. Busia's civilian government, which was itself replaced on 13 January 1972 by the National Redemption Council. This body reorganized itself in October 1975 as the Supreme Military Council, only to be removed from power by J. J. Rawlings and the Armed Forces Revolutionary Council in 1979, which relinquished power, three months later, to Hilla Limann's civilian elected government. Rawlings returned to power through another coup (31 December 1981) and for more than a decade ruled through the Provisional National Defence Council (PNDC). On 3 November 1992, Ghana became a civilian-ruled country with the election of Rawlings as president of the Fourth Republic. He succeeded in halting the downward slide in Ghana's economy by instituting bold measures that have stimulated business and industry, thereby improving the lot of Ghanaians.

Ghana's annual gross national product growth of more than five per cent between 1984 and 1989 and of 2.7 percent in 1990 is among the highest in sub-Saharan Africa. The country has had a sober assessment of its social-economic problems, its resources, and its commitment to the well-being of Ghanaians. The growth in economy and political stability has served as an impetus for Ghanaian culture, which has seen an increase in the volume and quality of literary productions. It seems that since the late 1970s Ghanaian literature has taken a new direction with fresh voices such as those of **Kofi Anyidoho** and Meshack Asare, whose optimistic outlook represents a major departure from the disquiet, disenchantment, and cyncism that define Ghanaian writing in the second decade after independence. Another recent trend in the culture is the use of mass media and public performances for the dissemination of Ghanaian literature. The combined positive developments in the economy and Ghana's political and social structures have produced a healthy climate that augurs well for the future.

CHRIS KWAME AWUYAH

Further reading: Robert A. Myers, *Ghana* (1991).

GHOSE, AUROBINDO

See **AUROBINDO, SRI**

GHOSE, MANMOHAN (1869–1924)

Indian poet

Born in Bhagalpore, Bengal, India, he, along with his elder brother Benoy Ghose and his younger brother Aurobindo Ghose (**Sri Aurobindo**), studied at the Grammar School, Manchester, England, and at St Paul's School, London, England. Manmohan Ghose began writing poetry at St Paul's, where Laurence Binyon became his close friend.

He went to Christ Church College, Oxford, England, in 1887.

Five of Ghose's poems appeared in *Primavera* (1890), a small collection of poems by Laurence Binyon, Stephen Phillips, Arthur Cripps, and Ghose; his work evoked an appreciative comment from Oscar Wilde. In 1893 Ghose returned to India and joined the educational service of the government. In 1903 he became professor of English at the Presidency College, Calcutta. In this period Ghose developed an intimate contact with **Rabindranath Tagore**, who admired his poetry.

Ghose's *Love Songs and Elegies* was published in 1898; a posthumously published collection of his work, *Songs of Love and Death* (1928), was edited by Binyon. Nature and love are the dominant themes in the early lyrics, while a meditative vein and a sense of loss are pervasive in the later ones. The poet's gift of imagination, his mastery of the English language, and his feeling for verbal music are evident in all. The death of Ghose's wife in 1918 led to two lyric sequences, 'Orphic Mysteries' and 'Immortal Eve'; five choric odes on the story of Orpheus were added to these in the last year of the poet's life.

Ghose's major effort is the unfinished 'Perseus, the Gorgon-Slayer', based on the legend of Perseus and structured as a Homeric epic. Begun in 1898, the poem was abandoned in 1916. Ghose began the poetic drama 'Nollo and Damayanti', based on the *Mahabharata*, but only five scenes were written. *Adam Alarmed in Paradise*, an epic begun in 1919, expresses both the poet's anguish at the holocaust of the First World War and his abiding faith in God. The poet addresses Europe and the Christian world and affirms that the crucifixion of Christ will not be in vain. In 1970 the *Collected Poems of Manmohan Ghose*, edited by Lotika Ghose, was published.

L. S. R. KRISHNA SASTRY

Further reading: Lotika Ghose, *Manmohan Ghose* (1975).

GHOSE, SUDHINDRA NATH (1899–65)

Indian novelist, journalist, essayist

Born in Burdwan, Bengal, India, into the distinguished Christian family of Sir Bipan Bihari Ghose and Lady Mahila (Palit) Ghose, he earned a bachelor of science degree from Presidency College, University of Calcutta, India, in 1920. From 1922 to 1926 Ghose was a research scholar at the universities of Geneva, Switzerland, and Paris, France. He then obtained his Doctor of Letters degree from the University of Strasbourg, France (1929). He was a foreign correspondent (1924–31) for the *Hindu* of Madras, and associate editor (1929–31) of YMCA's *World's Youth*, Geneva. This was followed by service in the League of Nations secretariat at Geneva between 1931 and 1940. Ghose travelled to England in 1940, worked as a lecturer in the Education Section of the British armed forces until 1946, then lectured on education for various institutions in London.

Ghose returned to India in 1957 as professor of English at Visva-Bharati University, Santiniketan; his appointment was abruptly terminated in early 1958 following his caning of a colleague and a brutally violent assault on him by a group of students. Ghose returned to England embittered and disillusioned and continued to lecture in adult education.

Ghose's major literary achievement is his tetralogy of novels — *And Gazelles Leaping* (1949), *Cradle of the Clouds* (1951), *The Vermilion Boat* (1953), and *The Flame of the Forest* (1955). A long autobiographical fiction, the tetralogy traces the narrator-protagonist's personality through four stages (childhood, adolescence, university experience, confrontation with the world) that coincide in many respects with Ghose's experiences of growing up. The settings in the novels, the descriptions of the Santal village in the Penhari Parganas (*Cradle of the Clouds*), and the Chandernagore scenes and family history (*The Vermilion Boat*) further suggest that Ghose wrote from personal experience.

Actual and hypothetical connections between Ghose's oeuvre and his life most likely would have featured more assertively in assessments of his work had it not been so undeservedly neglected. Ghose, by all accounts, was of a passionate, eccentric, volatile, and romantic nature. The infusion of these and other traits in the characterization of the fictional narrator, as well as his narrative style, imply a powerful imaginative bonding of Ghose and his persona. The 'sardonic humour' that critics Shyamala Narayan and **M. K. Naik** have observed in Ghose's fiction is cited by critic D. McCutchion (who knew Ghose and who uses the same phrase) as one of Ghose's compulsive, personal characteristics. McCutchion's profile of Ghose, stylistically metamorphosed, is recognizable in the tetralogy: the narrator is 'extravagant', 'nervously excited', 'sentimental', 'furiously busy', 'fantastic', 'whimsical', 'outrageous', 'anecdotic', and 'lyrical', with 'a fundamentally generous but temperamental heart'. Generosity in the tetralogy is affirmed by the contrast between the 'lovable' characters and the selfish rogues, and by the (excessively innocent) narrator's romantic, idealistic quest for love, beauty, truth, and spirituality.

The structuring of the tetralogy's collective narrative as cultural odyssey, and the resulting eclecticism of form and theme are more substantial than vicarious autobiography. Narayan, for example, has read the tetralogy allegorically, as 'a twentieth century *Pilgrim's Progress*', and has used the namelessness of the narrator and many of the characters in support of this reading. In *Cradle of the Clouds*, moreover, the protagonist does acquire for a time a name that reverberates with allegoric and mythic resonance — that of Balaram, the elder twin brother of Krishna. (The protagonist, born on the anniversary of Balaram's birth, performs Balaram's role in the fertility ritual of the ploughing ceremony.)

The so-called 'allegorical' cruxes of the novels derive mainly from pre-Indo-Aryan, Hindu, and Bengali mythopoeic visions of life. The Balaram figure's quest for personal and cultural identity (he suffers from orphan loneliness) is supported and sublimated by animal and supranatural archetypes. For example, a pet elephant makes his victimized childhood tolerable, a dolphin saves him from drowning and precipitates him into a new *ashrama* (life-stage, or, read in another light, a Joycean epiphany), a fierce bulldog helps him circumvent Calcutta corruption. As embryo avatar of Krishna, the narrator's karmic desire (erotic/spiritual) is for a Radha consort, who epitomizes sublime beauty (Urvashi); he finds two consorts: Roma, a Eurasian (*The Vermilion Boat*), and the superior Myna, dancer, singer, 'Flame of the Forest', and woman of 'mystic moods' (*The Flame of the Forest*). The narrator discovers that he had tenuously encountered these tantalizing, enigmatic young women as girls in his earlier lives.

Roma is supplemented by the snake goddess Manasa, earth's divinity, and by the Tantric idea of salvation through sensual joy rather than through renunciation. She later rejects the narrator, however, in favour of western-style material comfort uncomplicated by religious learnings, and Myna becomes his guru. As a Radha-Krishna team worshipping the Lord through the Beloved, the protagonist and Myna celebrate the world as divine creation and undertake a pilgrimage in quest of the Absolute — a conjunction of joy and holiness, of *matra* (measure, balance) and the feminine principle.

These (and other) governing patterns of myth and archetype give the tetralogy symbolic qualities that also have a characteristic fluidity; his narrative method is one of flamboyantly mixing genres and traditions. This formal heterogeneity, for example, includes elements of the *Bildungsroman*, of the picaresque, of fantasy, realism, romance, satire (including such satiric name puns as 'Kolej Huzoor' and 'Foni Dhar'), as well as cynical caricatures of political demagogues and activists. The predominant models and examples, however, derive from Indian literary and oral cultures. Ghose's consumption of these influences is evident in his array of linguistic devices: the use of epigrams, mottos, conventional metaphors, ornate phraseology, invocations, chants, rhetorical questions, and intertextuality; the incorporation of quotations (from sacred texts and from poems by **Rabindranath Tagore** and **Sarojini Naidu**, for example) and visual signs (musical notation, illustrations); the retelling of fables and myths; and the use of narrative digressions such as *upakathas* (subsidiary tales) and *sthala-purana* (legendary origin of place).

In his engagement with tradition and mythology, Ghose has been compared with **Raja Rao**. The comparison entails their experimental adaptations of Indian storytelling, which, in combination with an appetite for the picaresque and episodic, recalls **G. V. Desani**'s *All About H. Hatterr* (1951, first published as *All About Mr. Hatterr, A Gesture*, 1948). In some respects, Ghose's portrayal of the Bengal psyche anticipates **Amitav Ghosh**'s fiction. Ghose's amalgam of fantasy and realism, politics and myth, may also be viewed as a prelude to Ghosh's and **Salman Rushdie**'s explorations of India. Further afield, Ghose's fiction can be rewardingly contemplated alongside that of such artists of the mythopoeic as **Wilson Harris**, **Amos Tutuola**, Camara Laye, **Ben Okri**, and **Keri Hulme**.

SYD HARREX

Further reading: Shyamala A. Narayan, *Sudhin N. Ghose* (1973); M. K. Naik, *A History of Indian English Literature* (1982).

GHOSE, ZULFIKAR (1935–)

Pakistani novelist, poet, short-story writer

He was born in Sialkot, India (now in Pakistan), and moved to Bombay, India, with his family when he was seven years old, and from there to England following the partition. Finishing his studies at Keele University, England, Ghose worked as a reporter for *The Observer* and then as a schoolmaster in London. Since 1969 he has been teaching at the University of Texas at Austin, USA.

Although Ghose began by writing short stories and poetry, his significant development and output as a novelist have earned his fiction a certain priority. His first novel, *The Contradictions* (1966), follows such realistic writing as 'The Zoo People' (in Ghose's short-story collection *Statement Against Corpses*, 1964, with B. S. Johnson) and deals with Indo-British cultural hypotheses — the cumulative perceptions, notions, and theories about each other held by the parties in contact and generalized as culture. Rationality, barrenness, and fertility are observed to be both real and figurative, and the narrative is resolved by finding a pattern of fulfilment and complementarity in the lives of the characters as of the countries. Land is again a major theme and metaphor in *The Murder of Aziz Khan* (1967), in which the protagonist faces both humiliation and expropriation of his land by the new industrialist classes in post-colonial Pakistan.

Ghose became interested in Brazil and in Latin America following his marriage to a Brazilian artist, and his creative canvas becomes broader as he takes up the imperial theme in the trilogy *The Incredible Brazilian — The Incredible Brazilian: The Native* (1972), *The Beautiful Empire* (1975), and *A Different World* (1978). Four hundred years of Brazilian history are re-created convincingly in the picaresque lives and times of his hero Gregório Peixota da Silva Xavier, who in his multiple reincarnations lives through to our own day. But with this work and *Crump's Terms* (1975) Ghose signals a liberation of the form. *Crump's Terms* is a change in Ghose's writing, moving from oppressions of history to the private obsessions and everyday life of a west London schoolteacher, who combines his observations of civilization and of the schoolchildren with gross puns and mechanical routines. The narrative (the medium) itself appears to be the final object of narration. In fact, since the publication of *The Contradictions*, Ghose's writings have displayed a consistent concern with language as the stuff of fictive life, which transcends both time and material reality of which history is constituted. The metafictional commentaries in *Crump's Terms* are redirected messages to frame the stream-of-consciousness from the reader's standpoint. Although *The Incredible Brazilian* trilogy is effective as a historical romance, its major concern is with the 'poetry of language . . . a mystical breathlessness' (*A Different World*), because 'life is a constant process of elaborating a language' (*The Beautiful Empire*), a process in which the main plot is encased.

Further, *Hulme's Investigations into the Bogart Script* (1981) asserts language to be the only tangible reality and the fiction to be an ironic history of self and society; for only fiction, it is proposed in Ghose's critical book *The Art of Creating Fiction* (1991), can achieve perfection, which is its main concern. *Figures of Enchantment* (1986), a superb post-colonial novel, in its dislocations of time and material reality leaves only language as a textual figuration of survival amidst all other human matter 'decomposing . . . on the beach' at the end of the book.

Ghose's *The Triple Mirror of the Self* (1992) creates a variable and complex identity for the 'shadow man' who must suffer such narrative burdens as he lives in his own and others' memories. Urim, Shimmers, and Roshan are transformations of the 'same' person in various places, and he attempts to evolve backwards, so to speak, in order to be all at once. Starting up in South America again, Urim works up his memory and desire back into being also an English Shimmers and a subcontinental Roshan. The replications and extensions across time and space only accentuate the tragicomedy of the situation and are themselves considered to be an aspect of the universal soul.

The main rehearsal for the technique in this novel was provided by *A New History of Torments* (1982), *Don Bueno* (1983), and *Figures of Enchantment*. They involve a search for an El Dorado and an exploration of the self with a psychological detailing of the landscapes of Malcolm Lowry, whom Ghose has mentioned in his writing. A semblance of reality is created to set off historical echoes and disguise the intertextual structures. Legend, however, takes over quickly, and however imposing the human agents, their own personalities are subsumed under the pressure of circumstances in which the characters face (and partly create) as well as fulfil their individual but repetitive destiny. Fiction triumphs over social logic and fact in the text, whose real concerns are with obsession, destiny, and mystery. In *Figures of Enchantment*, the love story, adventure yarn, and family romance make up the subtexts for a super-narrative that fuses them together as it revises earlier *écriture*, rewriting Shakespeare's *The Tempest* to re-vision the questions of exile, identity, language, sexuality, and power. All these novels, including *The Triple Mirror of the Self*, employ shifting temporal frames, leitmotifs, and syntactic involutions to create the text's figurative drive and to flaunt the illusion of reality in a timeless dimension — a poignant symbol of a world remade and fallen beyond repair.

The symbolic is rooted in the autobiographical and historical hold on reality. In his autobiography, *The Confessions of a Native-Alien* (1965), Ghose, the 'triple' exile, has noted the paradoxical character of an uprooted existence, the essence of which is time rather than space, and the need for the worlds that will yield to a sense of belonging. Less categorical as a 'Native-Alien' about the 'pleasures' of exile or identity than **George Lamming,** Ghose shares with **Robert Kroetsch** the problematics of creating a language for 'uncreated' land, fearing its self-sufficient condition. Yet he must continue to make equivalents — even if language appears to sustain only the illusion of reality, as a subtle artifice, and thereby indulges fine imagination but deceives the heart. Ghose has discussed these issues, as well as those related to silence, (Hamlet's) insanity, and representation in his critical volumes *Hamlet, Prufrock, and Language* (1978) and *The Fiction of Reality* (1983). The argument continues yet in other forms.

Ghose's poetry has corresponding themes and paths of formal development. The poems in his first book, *The Loss of India* (1964), established the loss of innocence, order, 'home'. England substitutes, and France adds a zest in *Jets from Orange* (1967). The prosaic diction hardens to its subjects in poems such as 'The Lost Culture' and 'Kew Bridge' without losing the lush balances of 'The Picnic in Jammu'. *The Violent West* (1972) followed Ghose's move to Texas. Philosophical weights are applied to the search for home there, almost dissembling a celebration of homelessness. The poems in this book test the hypotheses about dreams, land, and the universe — as in 'On Owning Property in the U.S.A.' and 'View from the Observatory'. The clear discursive shift of *A Memory of Asia* (1984) focuses on the relations of language and perception to memory. 'Flying over the Extinct Volcanoes' has transparent images and symbolic resonances (religion, stock market, weather chart, etc.) denying the narrative comfort. The later poems carry forward this style. The mood is sombre when not bitter. The medium itself is the main theme and a recompense. As in Ghose's fiction, being an outsider to the society describes an angular conception of experience, questioning and confirming the separate iden ity of the self. Each emptying out is measured agɐinst value and desire.

For Ghose, language alone is the life-principle in the *données* of art, powered by memory and by a compelling need to understand the self, relationships, and beliefs; all his writings in various forms offer a remarkable example of the unity of ideas. A seamless body of work has been created, working consistently and ostensibly after such models as Flaubert, Proust, Machado de Assis, and Nabokov, with furtive glances to Wittgenstein, Beckett, and Stevens. But some of the major concerns in his oeuvre — the place of emotion in human life and the relationship of the mind to the matter, of the reality to the art of dealing with it, of appearance to reality, of the mind to the heart, and of the language to the subject — are essentially part of a greater Muslim and Pakistani tradition in world letters.

ALAMGIR HASHMI

Further reading: Alamgir Hashmi, 'Tickling and being tickled à la Zulfikar Ghose', *The Ravi* (Lahore) 2 (1982) and in *Commonwealth Novel in English* 2 (1982); 'Zulfikar Ghose', in Daniel G. Marowski and Roger Matuz (eds) *Contemporary Literary Criticism* Vol. 42 (1987); C. Kanaganayakam, 'Unreal reel and the unreeled real: *Hulme's Investigations into the Bogart Script*', *The Journal of Indian Writing in English* 2 (1988); Jussawalla Feroza and Reed Way Dasenbrock (guest eds), 'Zulfikar Ghose', *The Review of Contemporary Fiction: Milan Kundera/Zulfikar Ghose Number* 2 (1989); Alamgir Hashmi, 'A stylized motif of eagle wings woven: the selected poems of Zulfikar Ghose', *World Literature Today* 1 (1992).

GHOSH, AMITAV (1956–)
Indian novelist

He was born in Calcutta, India, and in his early years witnessed the varied cultural life of Calcutta, Dhaka, and Colombo. He graduated from the University of Delhi, India, before taking his Master of Philosophy in social anthropology at Oxford University, England. During the Emergency (1975–7) Ghosh worked as a journalist with the Indian Express group of newspapers. He lives in Delhi.

It is perhaps early to arrive at any proper evaluation of Ghosh as novelist; to date he has published only two novels, *The Circle of Reason* (1986) and *The Shadow Lines* (1988). These, however, have received popular attention and critical acclaim. Like **Ruth Prawer Jhabvala**'s *The Householder* (1960), *The Circle of Reason* is grounded in a traditional Indian conceptual framework. The difference, however, is that where Jhabvala chooses one of the four *ashramas* or stages (of *Grihasta* or the householder) as an organizational device, Ghosh seeks to structure his novel with reference to the three cardinal qualities that, according to Indian philosophy, make individuals what they are: *Tamas*, *Rajas*, and *Satwik*, the order indicative of a soul's gradual and upward evolution. Curiously, in *The Circle of Reason* the order is reversed. Part One is entitled 'Satwa: Reason'; Part Two, 'Rajas: Passion'; and Part Three, 'Tamas: Death'. The novel presents the fantastic story of Alu, a master weaver, who on giving up his profession attains some kind of a revelation. The action of the novel takes place in different parts of the world, including the imaginary city of Al Gazaria. Ghosh balances the character Alu, whose real name is Nachiketa Bose, with Nachiketa, of the *Katha Upanishad*, who confronts the baser qualities in his own father and, with the help of Yama, the lord of the dead, moves on to attain the *Satwik*, the highest stage of being.

If at the conceptual level the novel's reversal and balancing suggest a circle, words, phrases, and symbols (such as carbolic acid, sewing machines, Pasteur, and birds) placed in different contexts and played against one another weave further circles that remind one of the complex patterning of T. S. Eliot's *The Waste Land* (1922). The innumerable stories within the story of Alu — the Indian *Upakatha* or subsidiary story — and the solicitude for the art of narration and for community experience also suggest how well Ghosh has drawn on Gunadhya's *Kathasaritsagara*: realism and fantasy live comfortably together in the novel.

Though *The Circle of Reason* has some lively and memorable characters such as Balaram, Torudebi, Kulfi, Zindi, and Jyoti Das, and though it has some splendid lyrical passages, including those on weaving, its main thrust is towards an understanding of the mystery of reality. The characters grapple with the mystery by narrating and placing their experiences both in time and, through enactment, outside of time.

In its handling of time frames and experiences of men and women who belong to different generations and cultures, *The Shadow Lines* calls to mind Jhabvala's *Heat and Dust* (1975). Though *The Shadow Lines* appears to narrate merely one more story of the raj and of the east-west encounter, it is very much a continuation of the central themes of *The Circle of Reason*: the nature of reality, time, history, myth, language, and imagination. The narrator lives in Calcutta, but through the fantastic Tridib and Ila, his cousin, he makes voyages — both real and imaginary — to England, Pakistan, and throughout India. This novel has more clearly realized characters than *The Circle of Reason* and is more strongly rooted in recognizable cultural locales. As in William Faulkner's *The Sound and the Fury* (1929), events and incidents are presented through multiple perspectives and attain a dramatic objectivity. Memories of events and incidents shape the characters; Tridib, Maya Debi, the unnamed first-person narrator, and his grandmother are the sum total of the physical and imaginative responses they evoke in others. *The Shadow Lines* won the 1989 Sahitya Akademi Award.

Ghosh is a talented writer who has a gift for making new and vitally meaningful metaphors. He can play creatively with the English language and has a genius for transforming the general and the abstract into arresting concretions.

D. A. SHANKAR

Further reading: Lalitha Jayaraman, 'A new literary landscape: Indo-English fiction in the eighties', in Shivaramakrishna *et al.* (eds) *tenor* September (1990).

GIBBON, REGINALD PERCEVAL (1878–1926)
South African novelist, short-story writer, poet
Born Reginald Percival Gibbon in Trelech, Wales, he attended the Old Mill School in London, England, and the Moravian School at Koningsfeld, Baden, Germany. Gibbon arrived in South Africa in 1897 and left permanently in 1903. He worked as a free-lance journalist and was subsequently employed by *The Natal Witness*, *The Rand Daily Mail*, and *The Rhodesian Times*. He published short stories in this period: 'Van der Linde's Dying', in *The Natal Witness* in 1901 (entitled 'The Good End' in his story collection *The Vrouw Grobelaar's Leading Cases*, 1905), and 'The Post Cart' and 'Dissipation in Dopfontein' in *The Rand Daily Mail* in 1902.

Gibbon's South African experience is reflected in his short fiction, his poetry collection *African Items* (1903), and in his novels *Souls in Bondage* (1904) and *Flower of the Peach* (1911, republished as *Margaret Harding*, 1983), all set in South Africa. A fifth work, *Salvator* (1908), is set in what was then known as Portuguese East Africa. Later works, such as the short-story collections *The Adventures of Miss Gregory* (1912), *The Second-Class Passenger* (1913), *Those Who Smiled* (1920), and *The Dark Places* (1926), have international settings.

In the 'African' works Gibbon shows an ideological shift from colonialist bigotry to dawning liberalism. *Souls in Bondage* is permeated with racism and shows the influence of social Darwinism. *The Vrouw Grobelaar's Leading Cases* locates the racial bigotry in the storyteller, a rural Cape Dutch woman. *Flower of The Peach*, written after Gibbon had left South Africa, suggests that relationships are possible between people of different races when they are of equal intellectual and moral stature. Even in this work, however, Gibbon suggests that black culture is essentially unknowable and transient.

Following his return to England, Gibbon contributed to magazines in England and the USA, further establishing his reputation as a writer. He had a wide circle of literary friends, among whom were Joseph Conrad and Ford Madox Ford.

GERALDINE D. E. CONSTANCE

Further reading: Jenny de Reuck, 'Race and gender: a study of the artistic corruption of Perceval Gibbon's *Souls in Bondage*', *Journal of Literary Studies* 1 (1988); P. D. Williams, 'Introduction', *Margaret Harding* by R. P. Gibbon (1911; repr. 1988).

GIBBS, MAY (1877–1969)
Australian children's writer
Born in Surrey, England, she went to Australia at the age of four and spent her early years in Western Australia. It was there that she encountered the flora and fauna that are the basis of her bush mythology — the gumnut babies and the Bad Banksia Men, images that express both the sturdy charm of the Australian bush and its dangers. Gibbs studied art in London, England, and in 1913 returned to live in Sydney, where she illustrated children's books and drew twenty-five covers for the *Sydney Mail*. In 1916 her *Gumnut Babies* and *Gum Blossom Babies* showed a talent for writing as well as illustration — the floral babies Bib and Bub having first appeared as an illustrated bookmark in the shape of a gum leaf in 1913. Gumnut expressions such as 'deadibones' are now part of Australian vocabulary. Gibbs' most enduring books feature the gumnuts Snugglepot and Cuddlepie, whose adventures reached a wider audience through radio broadcasts and a ballet produced in 1988. The characters Bib and Bub featured in a cartoon strip drawn by Gibbs from 1924 to 1967.

From early in her career, Gibbs' images have been popularized, first by wartime pictorial propaganda and later by merchandising in the Beatrix Potter style. There could scarcely be an Australian child who, seeing the seed-head of a banksia in the bush, has not been told by an adult of Gibbs' Bad

Banksia Men, hairy nightmare creatures with grasping elongated fingers and hoarse voices. Like Potter, Gibbs avoided sentimentality and sought accuracy in her depiction of Australian bush life, depictions that are also a plea for conservation. Unlike Australian contemporaries Ida Rentoul Outhwaite and others of the Melbourne school, Gibbs rejected delicate European fairy images as unsuitable for a setting she saw as suggesting 'things grotesque, mirthful, cunning, and quaint'.

Gibbs' Sydney harbourside home, Nutcote, is being restored as a gallery and museum after a national campaign for its preservation.

KERRY WHITE

Further reading: Maureen Walsh, *May Gibbs, Mother of the Gumnuts: Her Life and Work* (1985); Robert Holden, *A Golden Age* (1992).

GIBRALTAR

The literary history of Gibraltar, a British dependency at the western end of the Mediterranean, is not as colourful as its military history, but there are works worthy of note partly as a result of this eventful past. Gibraltar was known to the Phoenicians, who left evidence of their presence in caves around the Rock, but there is evidence in the form of a Neanderthal-age skull of much earlier habitation. The Romans knew it as Mons Calpe, and with Mt Abyla on the other side of the Straits of Gibraltar it formed one of the Pillars of Hercules. The Rock, rising sharply out of the sea to a height of nearly 425 metres, has fascinated writers for many centuries. It stands at the eastern end of the Straits and, approached from the west, it appears out of the mist with a shape like a crouching lion. Many significant historical events have happened in and around its small area of 5.8 square kilomometres.

The first settlement on the Rock was of Moorish forces under Tarik ibn Ziyad in AD 711 when the Moors invaded southern Spain. For the next 750 years Gibraltar was under Moorish occupation except for a short period between 1309 and 1333. There is no surviving literature produced in Gibraltar from this period, nor from the period of Spanish occupation between 1462 and 1704. The present population of Gibraltar can be traced back to the capture of the Rock by an Anglo-Dutch force in 1704 and its cession by Spain to Britain by the Treaty of Utrecht in 1713. For many years after this event, writing about Gibraltar was mainly by persons serving there in the British garrison who cannot be classified as Gibraltarians. During the eighteenth century an indigenous Gibraltarian population developed, which, by the end of the century, numbered around five thousand persons. The century saw three sieges, in which Spanish forces tried without success to recapture the Rock. The third of these, which lasted for four years, 1779–83, became known as the Great Siege. Of the voluminous literature about this siege the most notable is *A History of the Late Siege of Gibraltar* (1785) by John Drinkwater, a member of the garrison as a captain of the 72nd Regiment, who was present throughout the siege. More closely associated with the Rock than most servicemen, Drinkwater was instrumental in establishing the Garrison Library. It opened in temporary premises in 1793 and moved to its present building in 1804. During the course of the century a number of books were published by members of the garrison and, in some cases, by their wives.

There was a rapid increase in population at the beginning of the nineteenth century as a result of the Napoleonic Wars; the increase arose from the development of Gibraltar as a British port when British ships were excluded from European ports under the control or influence of Napoleon's armies. During the rest of the century the size of Gibraltar's civilian population fluctuated between fifteen and twenty thousand. Epidemics affected the total numbers from time to time, and there were changes in the composition of the population through immigration. By the end of the century the population was composed of British, Spanish, Portuguese, Minorcan, Maltese, Genoese, and Jewish residents. The Jewish community, many of Moroccan descent, has remained the most cohesive in Gibraltar and is prominent in the development of a local literature, although its writers have not been prolific. The Roman Catholic church has also been a source of writing about Gibraltar.

Important events between the world wars were the development of institutions with Gibraltarian representation in this British-governed colony and, because of the Spanish Civil War, some isolation of the Rock from Spain between 1936 and 1939. These events contributed to a more distinctly Gibraltarian culture; the evacuation of much of the civil population during the Second World War hastened the process. A few years after the war all aspects of life in Gibraltar were greatly affected by Spanish claims for the return of Gibraltar. This circumstance led to complete closure of the frontier between 1969 and 1982, with lesser restrictions applying for nearly nineteen years between 1964 and 1985. This period became known as the fifteenth siege and, like previous sieges, it led to some historical literature. On this occasion, however, there was much more writing by Gibraltarians, and subjects covered extended also to the Rock's unique and interesting natural history, particularly that related to plant life and bird migrations. The tradition of serving officers contributing to Gibraltar's historical literature has continued with the publication of *The Rock of the Gibraltarians* (1987); written by General Sir William Jackson, governor of Gibraltar (1978–82), it recounts the history of the Rock from Moorish times to the 1980s. Jackson's *The Governor's Cat* (1992) is a work in a lighter vein, focusing on his time as governor. (See **Historical Writing**, Gibraltar.)

Serving officers of the garrison and others who are not Gibraltarians have contributed to knowledge of Gibraltar, and a few of their works can be regarded as part of the literature of Gibraltar, particularly when the authors have been closely associated with the Rock, but the literary culture is to be found in the works of Gibraltarians. At one time Spanish was the language of Gibraltarian literature and was also the lingua franca of the area, especially after the immigration from Spain during the nineteenth and early twentieth centuries. Hector Licudi, for example, wrote a novel, *Barbarita* (1929), in Spanish, and translated *Conversations with Oscar Wilde* into Spanish and Benito Mussolini's novel *The Cardinal's Mistress* from Italian to Spanish. Before this time, however, a local culture had developed based on immigration from many places, particularly Genoa; the culture was also related to British rule. This was strict as befitted a fortress, but at the same time British laws and customs respected individual rights and reduced friction between different races and religions. Modern developments have been affected by cultural moves away from Spain. English has become the language most often used by Gibraltarian writers, who have greatly increased the production of local writing, although there are only about twenty thousand resident Gibraltarians on the Rock. There is a dictionary of local usage by Cavilla entitled *Diccionario Yanito* (1990).

To date there are only two English-language volumes of poetry of significance: Leopold Sanguinetti's *The Calpean Sonnets* (1957) and Peta Pryor's *From Gibraltar with Love* (1985). Mario Arroyo's *Destiny Is the Name of a Woman* (1989) contains English and Spanish poems.

Gibraltarian novels in English include *The Mating Cry of the Dodo* (1977), a political satire with cartoon illustrations published by Mesod Benady under the pseudonym Giannito Benady (he is generally known as Tito Benady), and *Sherlock Holmes in Gibraltar* (1990) by Sam Benady. The latter, like many recent works by Gibraltarians, was published by Gibraltar Books Ltd.

Gibraltarian children's literature in English is

rare, but includes Marie Bensusan's *Sonia el Mono Llanito* (1986), translated into English as *Sonia and Her Rock Ape* (1989). Others are Henry Chichon's *The Story of the Rock* (1990) and Charlotte Rosado's *Melissa from Gibraltar* (1992), which has an appendix on the natural history of the rock.

PHILIP DENNIS
ANNE TAYLOR

GIFKINS, MICHAEL (1945–)
New Zealand short-story writer
Born in Wellington, New Zealand, he was educated at the University of Auckland, where he earned a first-class honours BA in English literature. Gifkins was a university teacher, fisherman, waterside worker, and stonemason before becoming a free-lance writer and publishing consultant. He has held several fellowships, including that of writer-in-residence at the University of Auckland and the Katherine Mansfield Memorial Fellowship at Menton, France.

Gifkins' first collection of stories, *After the Revolution and Other Stories* (1982), contains fiction previously published in literary journals. Like the work of his Australian contemporaries **Michael Wilding**, **Frank Moorhouse**, and **Murray Bail**, the collection reflects a culturally specific contemporary environment, where characters take drugs, lead itinerant unstructured lives, and are aware of limitations, shifts, and expansions in their perception and in the medium, especially language, in which it is conveyed.

Gifkins' stories are generally non-realist with incomplete contexts of narration. In his later collections *Summer is the Côte d'Azur* (1987) and *The Amphibians* (1989), however, his fiction has become more postmodern in its techniques, using collage and pastiche as narrative strategies. While the stories in *After the Revolution* were mostly recognizable within a New Zealand environment, Gifkins' later stories move into an international context and culture, mostly with a European setting, full of characters who establish unexplained but global networks of connections and who participate in a universally recognized culture of consumer goods and materialist ambitions. Like Murray Bail, Gifkins both records and satirizes the transactions of internationalist culture.

LYDIA WEVERS

GILBERT, KEVIN (1933–93)
Australian dramatist, poet, anthologist
He was born on the banks of the Lachlan River near Condobolin, New South Wales, Australia, in the heart of Wiradjuri tribal country. One of eight children, he was orphaned at the age of seven. He never forgot the sense of alienation which he felt as a child, pushed to the fringe of non-Aboriginal society in Australia. All of his work — poetry, prose, drama, and polemic — reflects a simultaneous sense of alienation from the dominant European culture and a celebration of his pride in Black Australia.

Gilbert became the first Aboriginal dramatist with his play, *The Cherry Pickers*, drafted in 1968 while he was in prison and first performed in 1971 at the Mews Theatre in Sydney. This landmark in Aboriginal literature was not published until 1988, when Gilbert totally revised it to reflect the revolution in Black Australian political activity since the early 1970s.

Gilbert stated in his introduction to the work that it 'is a play of humanity, of the search for justice, of a return to spirituality'. It achieves this by focusing on the trials — and resilience — of a closely-knit group of Aboriginal fruit-pickers who counter the non-Aboriginal world with humour, pride, and cultural power.

The author's first non-fiction work was published by Angus and Robertson in 1973. Entitled *'Because a White Man'll Never Do It . . .'*, Gilbert's is an incisive, restless, and questing text. He seeks for solutions, for a definition of what he calls the 'Aboriginal patriot', but a strong sense of impatience also runs through the book.

Probably Gilbert's most important work is *Living Black* (1977), the first major Aboriginal oral history recorded, transcribed, and edited by a Black Australian. In the mid-1970s the author spent nearly two years travelling the length and breadth of Australia, visiting small outback towns, fringe camps, missions, and urban black communities, all the while interviewing other Aborigines about their experiences.

The pages of *Living Black* are a testament to the trust which Gilbert established and to the richness of Aboriginal culture which he uncovered, despite the intense hardships which many of his interviewees had endured. Two themes keep resurfacing in *Living Black*: the ideal of keeping the Aboriginal nation spiritually and politically healthy and the concept of Aboriginality — what it means to be a 'First Australian'.

Gilbert demonstrates in *Living Black* the keen powers of observation, the empathy, and the sense of justified outrage that also characterizes much of his poetry, especially in *People Are Legends* (1978). Although he records much suffering and pain, the collection is also uplifting and a powerful exhortation to examine what he calls in its introduction the 'root causes of Aboriginal despair'.

This is not to typecast Gilbert as a 'protest poet'. The author's verse is as noteworthy for its irony and satire as for its passion and critique; it defies simple categorization and gains redoubled strength from this complexity. In 1988 Gilbert demonstrated once again his talent as a poet and anthologist with the seminal collection, *Inside Black Australia: An Anthology of Aboriginal Poetry*. The first national anthology of Aboriginal verse, it is a classic text: a pointed yet nuanced reflection of the richness of Black Australian poetry from every state and territory of Australia, accompanied by an introduction which is an example of the author at his most impressive.

The definitive Gilbert poetic text is *The Blackside* (1990), a collection that republishes much of his previous work and adds new material that reflects in a searing way upon post-bicentennial Australia. It does justice to an author for whom justice was always the most important goal: an Aboriginal poet, spokesperson, dramatist, artist, and philosopher who is one of the key figures in Black Australian literature.

ADAM SHOEMAKER

GILKES, MICHAEL A. (1933–)

Guyanese dramatist, poet

He was born and raised in Georgetown, British Guiana (now Guyana), more than a decade after the birth of most of the members of the *Kyk-over-al* group, from which came so many of Guyana's first generation of writers. Gilkes qualified as a pharmacist before his interest in arts and literature steered him into becoming a teacher of English and a university academic. He quickly became known as an authority on Caribbean literature and an important figure in the theatre of the region.

The most important of Gilkes' plays is *Couvade: A Dream Play of Guyana* (1974), performed at the first Caribbean Arts Festival (Carifesta) held in Georgetown in 1972. Reminiscent of the plays of **Dennis Scott**, *Couvade* is a complex drama in which a Caribbean artist-intellectual (Lionel) undergoes a ritual encounter with both the past (particularly the Amerindian past of Guyana) and the future — represented by Lionel's unborn child, whose safe birth is curiously endangered by his father's social and creative obsessions. The title refers to an Amerindian custom whereby the husband performs certain rituals during his wife's pregnancy and labour in order to ensure the spiritual well-being of the child; this suggests the regionally important themes of identity and cultural independence that are prominent in Gilkes' work. **Wilson Harris** regards the play as 'one of the most significant' to have emerged from the Caribbean. Gilkes' other plays include 'Young Aesop' (premièred 1962), 'In Transit' (premièred 1968), 'A Pleasant Career' (premièred 1988), and 'This Island Now' (premièred 1989).

Since leaving the University of Guyana in 1974 for the University of the West Indies, Barbados, Gilkes has pursued his interest in Caribbean theatre as actor, director/dramaturge, and playwright. He has also turned his talents to the task of adapting Caribbean literary works for film and videotape; his video production of **Jean Rhys**' *Wide Sargasso Sea* (1966) has been telecast throughout the region.

Gilkes has written a number of fine poems, including nostalgic re-creations of childhood (for example, 'Woodbine', in *Graham House Review* 14, 1991) as well as incisive meditations set in his adopted Barbadian landscape ('Littoral', in *Graham House Review* 14, 1991, and 'Tutorial', in *AGS* 2, 1978).

MARK McWATT

GILMORE, DAME MARY (1865–1962)
Australian poet, journalist

Born Mary Jean Cameron near Goulburn, New South Wales, Australia, she was educated at a small private school at Wagga. In the Broken Hill mining district, where she taught, she learned working-class politics and joined the labour movement. Friendships with the writer **Henry Lawson**, the social philosopher **William Lane**, and the ***Bulletin*** editor **A. G. Stephens**, when she came to Sydney in 1890, strengthened her already independent mind and belief in social equality and justice. From 1896 to 1902 she worked in Cosme, Lane's socialist settlement in Paraguay, marrying an Australian shearer, William Gilmore, before returning to Australia.

Married life on an isolated farm in western Victoria, together with her need to participate in the struggle for a better society, provided material for poems published in the literary Red Page of the *Bulletin*. From 1908 to 1931 Gilmore edited the women's page of the Sydney *Worker*, providing sensible domestic reading and advice and intellectual stimulus on a wide range of topics, and she also wrote for other journals. *Marri'd and Other Verses* (1910) was followed by *The Passionate Heart* (1918), poetry on war themes, *The Tilted Cart* (1925), ballads for recitation, *The Wild Swan* (1930) and *Under the Wilgas* (1932), including Aboriginal themes, *The Rue Tree* (1931), on religious themes, *Battlefields* (1939), *The Disinherited* (1941), *Pro Patria Australia* (1945), *Fourteen Men* (1954), and several collections and selections. Gilmore's prose includes *Hound of the Road* (1922), observations on family life and religion, and two volumes of recollections, *Old Days, Old Ways* (1934) and *More Recollections* (1935). Gilmore acquired an informed understanding of Aboriginal life before European invasion from acquaintance with Aborigines in her childhood environment and from study at a time when little about Aborigines was known or understood by most Australians. When her husband took up farming in north Queensland she moved to Sydney with her son; her poetry shows the conflict between the demands of family and a woman's need for a wider career.

In recent years evaluation of Gilmore's poetry for its relevance to nationalist, Aboriginal, and social justice concerns rather than as art has broadened to include greater appreciation of its intrinsic poetic achievement. Beneath an apparently clear surface her lyrics hold a balance between opposing values and impulses, the more illuminating because unresolved. These oppositions include national pride in pioneering achievement and concern for the tragic destruction of Aboriginal culture, married and maternal love and the need to serve society in a wider sphere, and a deep religious impulse balanced by an acute awareness of human material needs. A focus of literary activity during her long retirement in Sydney, she is the subject of several dramatic works, including *To Botany Bay on a Bondi Tram* (1984) by Beverley Dunn.

ELIZABETH PERKINS

Further reading: Sylvia Lawson, *Mary Gilmore: A Tribute* (1965); W. H. Wilde, *Courage a Grace: A Biography of Dame Mary Gilmore* (1988); W. H. Wilde and T. Inglis Moore, eds, *Letters of Mary Gilmore* (1980).

GILROY, BERYL (1924–)

Guyanese novelist, poet, children's writer

Born in Berbice, Guyana, she was never forced to attend school and spent her early childhood educating herself and talking to the older generation in the village where she lived. Gilroy later trained as a teacher in Guyana and worked for UNICEF. In 1951 she attended London University, England, where she gained a diploma in child psychology and a bachelor of science degree; she later earned an MA in education at the University of Sussex, England, and a Ph.D. in counselling psychology. In the 1980s she became a child psychotherapist and research fellow at the London University Institute of Education.

Gilroy's experiences as a black woman in London in the 1950s (she had to work as a factory clerk and a maid before finding suitable employment as a teacher) made an important impression on her and are documented in her autobiographical work *Black Teacher* (1976). Gilroy was the first black headteacher of a London primary school, and from 1970 onwards was mainly preoccupied with writing a series of children's stories based on the multicultural experiences of the children that she encountered. These stories reflect her commitment both to the psychological development of children and to the issues of multiracialism prevalent in British society.

Although Gilroy's adult fiction has won several literary awards — she won the Greater London Arts Creative Writing Prize in 1982 — there has been little substantial criticism of her work to date. This is regrettable, as both *Frangipanni House* (1986) and *Boy-Sandwich* (1989) are powerfully written novels. The first deals with the theme of women and old age. Set in Guyana, it tells the story of Mama King, who, trapped by age and infirmity, is left by 'well-meaning' relatives in an old people's home. She eventually escapes but not before she has been almost stripped of her dignity as a grandmother and driven close to madness. The novel protests against a society in which the traditional roles of women have been undermined by alien cultural forces and that denies its responsibility to its own traditions.

Boy-Sandwich examines change in the lives of three generations of immigrants and questions the nature of the meaning of 'home' to both the old and the young. As with Gilroy's other works, her approach to characterization reflects her interest in psychology and the effects of cross-cultural encounters. The novel *Stedman and Joanna — A Love in Bondage* (1991) fictionalizes the historical journals of John Stedman, who met and married a slave while serving the Dutch government as a soldier in the eighteenth century. The novel is a moving historical romance that rewrites an important moment in colonial history and points to the many stories in Caribbean history that are still unwritten.

Gilroy has also published poetry; the poems in *Echoes and Voices (Open-heart Poetry)* (1991) reflect Gilroy's desire to heal through writing and are drawn mainly from her own life experiences as a young woman, wife, and widow.

SUSHEILA NASTA

Further reading: Beryl Gilroy, 'I write because . . . ', in Selwyn Cudjoe (ed.) *Caribbean Women Writers: Essays from the First International Conference* (1990).

GLEN, ESTHER (1881–1940)

New Zealand children's writer

She was born in Christchurch, New Zealand, and became a journalist. Her contribution to New

Zealand children's literature has been recognized in the naming of the most prestigious New Zealand literary award for children's literature — the Esther Glen Award. She wrote only three major novels, but was influential in encouraging the publication of New Zealand children's writing, first in the *Christchurch Sun*, and then in the *Christchurch Press*.

Glen's novels are family stories. *Six Little New Zealanders* (1917) was obviously influenced by the Australian **Ethel Turner**'s *Seven Little Australians* (1894) in its depiction of ordinary children who were neither good nor bad, but simply high-spirited. The 'six little New Zealanders' are the Malcolm children who stay on their bachelor uncles' farm when their parents go to England for a year. Excellent capital is made from a situation in which the uncles are ignorant of the ways of children, and the city children know nothing of the country.

The sequel, *Uncles Three at Kamahi* (1926), exceeds *Six Little New Zealanders* in humour and vitality and follows the family on its return to the farm for the next summer vacation. Individual characters are well drawn, and many incidents are dependent upon their respective foibles. *Robin of Maoriland* (1929) concerns a family of older girls, but is more sentimental than the previous novels. An authoritative treatment of sisterly relationships is nevertheless evident in all three books.

BETTY GILDERDALE

GLOVER, DENIS (1912–80)

New Zealand poet, publisher

Born in Dunedin, New Zealand, he was educated at Auckland Boys Grammar School, Christ's College, and the University of Canterbury, where he studied Greek and English. He decided early to become a publisher. (At school he met Bob Lowry, who shared his passion for type and printing and who later became an influential editor/publisher.) Glover bought a small printing press and published a student newspaper, *Oriflamme*, which was immediately banned. Undeterred, he founded the Caxton Press and began to print and publish works of literature.

Glover spent the Second World War in the Royal Navy, mainly on Arctic convoys, and took part in the D-Day invasion, winning a Distinguished Service Cross. After the war he returned to New Zealand and to typography, printing, and publishing, first at Caxton Press, later at Pegasus and Wingfield Press. His selected poems, *Enter Without Knocking*, was first published in 1964; an enlarged edition appeared in 1971, and a further edition, *Selected Poems*, was published posthumously in 1981 and contains an introduction written by his friend **Allen Curnow**. Glover began writing poetry as a schoolboy — he was to publish more than twenty volumes of his own writing — but the impulse to print and publish other people's work also came early. At Caxton Press he published before 1940 the work of **A. R. D. Fairburn**, Curnow, **Ursula Bethell**, **Frank Sargeson**, and **M. H. Holcroft**, and, though his literary publishing lost money, it was both distinguished and well produced.

Glover's early poems, such as 'Scab Loaded' and 'All of These' (both first published in *Thirteen Poems*, 1939), reflect the social concerns of the 1930s — Day Lewis was perhaps the strongest influence on Glover's work. His best-known poem, 'The Magpies', dates from this time. Still fondly quoted and remembered in popular memory as a simple pastoral poem, its subject is rural poverty in the Depression: 'But all the beautiful crops soon went / To the mortgage man instead, / And quardle oodle ardle wardle doodle / The magpies said.' 'Sings Harry', first published in full in *Sings Harry, and Other Poems* (1951), contains Glover's best work. Through Harry, the poet found a way to express what he could not say *in propria persona*. The poems are full of love for the South Island high country and nostalgia and regret for lost youth; they are simple and expressive. Typically, and in an image vivid to New Zealanders, they disclaim significance: 'Not I but another / will make songs worth the bother: / The rimu or kauri he, / I'm but the cabbage tree.' *Arawata Bill* (1953) similarly celebrates the solitary life of a gold prospector who spent his life fossicking in the mountains of north-west Otago. Though the sequence is more fully developed than the *Sings Harry* poems, it is only partially successful.

Glover's great love of the sea found expression in *Towards Banks Peninsula* (1979), a sequence inspired by an old sea-dog of his acquaintance and by a familiar cruising ground. Imagery of the sea is used in *To a Particular Woman* (1970), a sequence of love poems. This book, and the longer and more explicit account of a love affair that followed in *Diary to a Woman* (1971), reveal an unexpected side of Glover, who previously had written few love poems and had hidden any hint of personal disclosure.

At school Glover had been diagnosed as being 'of incurably frivolous disposition'; in his literary life this trait took the form of an impulse to write satire. One of his best-remembered pieces, the title poem of *The Arraignment of Paris* (1937), written in heroic couplets, lampoons an anthologist who promoted what Glover later referred to as the Menstrual School of poetry (referring to work of women poets that appeared in the annual *New Zealand Best Poems*, 1932–43, edited by C. A. Marris); like Dryden's *MacFlecknoe*, Glover said, it will outlast its subject. A collection of Glover's light verse and satire, *Sharp Edge Up*, was published in 1968.

Glover had a sensitive ear and was a meticulous craftsman, but he was not technically innovative, and he disliked the formlessness of contemporary poetry. He enjoyed using full rhyme, though in his serious writing he preferred to vary it with half-rhyme, and he commonly used a short line with variable stresses, giving his writing a vernacular freshness. Above all, Glover valued direct and simple utterance and was constitutionally suspicious of the high-flown. His best work celebrates the barely articulate man of action, whose plain thought and speech may achieve a rough-hewn wisdom and a lyrical grace.

ANNE FRENCH

Further reading: J. E. P. Thomson, *Denis Glover* (1977).

GODFREY, DAVE (1938–)

Canadian novelist, short-story writer

Born in Winnipeg, Canada, he received an MA (1961) from Stanford University, USA, a master of fine arts degree in creative writing (1963) from the University of Iowa, USA, and a Ph.D. in English (1967) from Iowa. Godfrey served as the acting head of the English department of Adisadel College, Cape Coast, Ghana, while with the Canadian University Service Overseas from 1963 to 1965. He taught creative writing in Canada at the University of Toronto (1966–76), York University (1977–8), and the University of Victoria (1978–). He was instrumental in starting three publishing houses — House of Anansi Press (1967), New Press (1969), and Press Porcépic (1973). His nationalistic stance is revealed in his many works of non-fiction. *Gutenberg Two* (1985), co-edited with Douglas Parkhill, examines the cultural impact of computer technology in Canada and contains 'Power, Communications and the People', Godfrey's seminal essay on the 'crofter' tradition.

Godfrey's short-story collections, *Death Goes Better with Coca-Cola* (1967) and *Dark Must Yield* (1978), and his Governor General's Award-winning novel, *The New Ancestors* (1970), are concerned with twentieth-century imperialism and particularly with the domination of Canada by the USA. Godfrey's attack on the Coca-colonization of the world aligns him with writers such as Australian **Frank Moorhouse**, whose book of stories, *The Americans, Baby* (1972), also deals with the effect of post-colonial conditions on the individual. In their more progressive fictions, these two writers use a juxtapositional, self-reflexive, and process-oriented style that foregrounds language as a form of rebellion against existing value systems that have succumbed to the material in lieu of the spiritual. Godfrey's more disjunctive stories — 'River Two Blind Jacks', 'Binary Dysfunction', and 'The Hard-Headed Collector', for example — raise epistemological issues through embedded narratives, contradictory reports, and appropriated news items that blur 'fact' and 'fiction'. *I Ching Kanada* (1976) deconstructs and 'Canadianizes' the sixty-four oracles of the largely Confucian 'Book of Changes'. In *The New Ancestors* physics and fiction are convoluted until events viewed through shifting perspectives become undefinable and take on a multiplicity of possible interpretations. For Godfrey, 'empirical truths' are secondary to 'mythic truths' and the socializing role of the mythmaker.

KARL JIRGENS

GOH POH SENG (1936–)

Singaporean novelist, poet, dramatist

Born in Kuala Lampur, Malaya (as it was then known), he trained as a doctor in Dublin, Ireland. He subsequently wrote and staged some of the earliest Singapore plays in English — 'The Moon is Less Bright' (premièred 1964), 'When Smiles Are Done' (premièred 1965), and 'The Elder Brother' (premièred 1966). He published one of the first Singapore novels in English, *If We Dream Too Long* (1972; translated into Russian, 1974), followed by *The Immolation* (1977). He has written poetry — *Eyewitness* (1976), *Lines from Batu Ferringhi* (1978), and *Bird with One Wing* (1982) — and his short stories have appeared in various magazines.

Goh understands the desire of the post-colonial Singapore writer in English to develop a language that conveys 'a recognisably local sense and sensibility' and a 'prose style . . . that depicts life here, authentically'. But his attempts to reproduce the local variety of English in his writing are unconvincing, partly because of a faulty ear and inconsistent literary technique, partly because Singaporean English had not in the 1960s and 1970s established many of the recognizably standard and distinctive features so well captured in the speech of **Catherine Lim**'s characters.

Despite an evident commitment to writing and a seriousness of purpose, Goh's work has received relatively little critical acclaim. His plays exist only in typescript and, except for *The Immolation* and *Eyewitness*, his other works were self-published. His poems, especially the self-published volumes, tend to be self-indulgently meditative and prolix. Goh's main preoccupations are responses to contemporary political causes and events such as anti-colonialism and the Vietnam War — best exemplified in *The Immolation* — and a sense of alienation and marginality commingled with romantic idealism. The latter is represented by the situation of an English-educated clerk in *If We Dream Too Long* who, incapacitated by an unusable colonial education and traditional past, finds the new, thrusting, post-independent Singapore uncongenial. *Eyewitness* combines both these preoccupations in what may be considered his best poem, 'Exile in a Cold Land', where the 'lone man' in a winter landscape can be read as a metaphor for the linguistic, cultural, and spiritual alienation of the post-colonial writer.

KOH TAI ANN

GOLDFIELDS LITERATURE (Australia)

In the first decade of the gold rushes — between 1851 and 1861 — Australia produced more than one-third of the world's total output. Gold discovery generated immediate social dislocation and prodigious immigration: the population of Australia doubled in ten years, while Victoria's increased seven-fold. Critics such as **Russel Ward** argued that the existing tradition, the bushman's ethos — **mateship**, anti-authoritarianism, 'obliteration of class barriers' — intensified; **Humphrey McQueen**, that 'acquisitive competition' was strengthened and 'gross materialism' resulted; and **Manning Clark**, that xenophobia infected the diggers' ideal of mateship.

Three decades of sporadic reports preceded the first official discovery of gold by Edward Hargraves near Bathurst, New South Wales, in 1851. Faced with a mass movement of workers to the goldfields, the government, unable to control the mining of gold — legally Crown property — imposed licence fees to finance policing of the diggings and discourage wholesale abandonment of employment. Further finds were made in Victoria, at Clunes, Ballarat, and Bendigo. By 1853, alluvial gold depleted, diggers searched for ancient riverbeds, auriferous 'gutters' beneath old lava flows. Digger teams dug shafts and removed clay, water, and basalt by bucket, using windlasses, horses, and steam engines. After months of labour, physical danger, carbon dioxide inhalation, and heat, they might fortuitously unearth 'jeweller's shops'; usually, shafts were 'shicers' or 'duffers'. 'Balaarat', Raffaello Carboni wrote, was 'a Nugety Eldorado for the few, a ruinous field of hard labour for many.'

Englishman William Howitt, druggist and author, was a goldseeker for two years from 1852. *Land, Labour and Gold* (1855) chronicles his impressions of celebrated diggings and unwashed diggers with 'grim beards', 'strong fustian trowsers', and 'dirty battered cabbage-tree' hats, their language 'measled with vileness and vulgarity'. Instant fortunes he dismissed as romance; more probable were dysentery, fevers, rheumatism, or death; 'gigantic labour' in shafts deluged with 'Stygian water'; and 'arbitrary, Russian' police tyranny. Charles Thatcher, a London flautist who arrived at the Victoria diggings in 1852 or 1853, affords similar vivid pictures of Ballarat and Bendigo. In halting verse, his songs distil serious preoccupations — vanishing 'days of tub and cradle', misappropriated mining claims, Sinophobia, intransigent digger independence, and abhorrence of licence raids.

Inevitably, licence fees incited revolt, 'blueshirts' confronting 'gold-lace' on the Turon River and at Bendigo in 1853. In 1854 licences were ceremonially burned at Ballarat, allegiance was pledged to a Southern Cross-emblazoned flag, and thirty miners and five soldiers died when troops attacked their roughly constructed fortifications (the Eureka stockade) on 3 December. Carboni, Ballarat insurgent and Italian Risorgimentist, wrote in effervescent, laboured English *The Eureka Stockade* (1855), a source-book for later authors such as **Marcus Clarke**, **Louis Esson**, and **Henry Handel Richardson**. The rebellion was transmuted into the mythical birth pains of Australian democracy; Eureka's 'god-like' heroes, **Henry Lawson** eulogized, 'broke the nose of Tyranny'.

Catherine Helen Spence published her first novel in the year of the Eureka rebellion. Romantic and didactic, *Clara Morison: A Tale of South Australia during the Gold Fever* (1854) describes major goldfields indirectly through letters and diggers' retrospection. Economically depressed, the city of Adelaide was readily consumed and depopulated by 'all-engrossing gold-fever'. Fortunes are made, but the atmosphere of the diggings in Spence's novel is threatening, with unsavoury grog shops, ex-convicts, horse stealing, 'midnight robberies and bowie knives', illness, and disturbing egalitarianism. While Spence foresaw technological and cultural benefits, she viewed gold as a God-sent curse for the 'colonial sin of worldly-mindedness', replacing nation-building qualities with 'fondness for unearned money'.

Rolf Boldrewood was police magistrate and gold-mining commissioner in the Gulgong area and **Henry Kingsley** prospected throughout Victoria. Because English readers demanded romance of the goldfields, writers such as these purged the diggings of drudgery, populated them with heroes and villains, and motivated dramatic action with love, mateship, and heroism rather than acquisitiveness. Local colour in Boldrewood's *The Miner's Right: A Tale of the Australian Goldfields* (1890) ranges from mining techniques to the shooting of a notorious bushranger. In Marcus Clarke's *His Natural Life* (1870–2), the protagonist Rufus Dawes purportedly unearths Ballarat's first gold; he is entangled in pre-Eureka upheavals and the rebels' flag is embroidered in his store, while Carboni, Thatcher, and Peter Lalor, Irish-born leader of the Eureka Stockade, dominate Ballarat's tumultuous life. In both works, however, all of this activity is peripheral: the core romantic action begins and ends in aristocratic England.

Joseph Furphy, prey to 'gold-witchery', subsisted on 'worn-out goldfields'; Lawson was raised on Gulgong; and Edward Dyson, born on Ballarat's diggings, hauled trucks in company-operated deep sinkings. In their fiction, diggers continually confront injury, shaft-collapse, falls, and explosions. Romanticization of the proletarian digger, the archetypal Australian, followed romanticism of setting. Lawson mythologizes first-generation diggers: their mateship, 'manly independence', 'reckless generosity', 'dogged determination and courage' were the stuff of which the Australian nation was made. In *The Fortunes of Richard Mahony* (1930), however, Henry Handel Richardson consciously broke from the tradition of goldfields fiction. Richardson's father, an unsuccessful Ballarat digger, became Mahony, and her goldfields, meticulously and exhaustingly described, are Breughelian in their realism. The diggings and the quest for gold are symbols in Richardson's trilogy of failure and exile, disillusion and dissolution.

Gavin Casey's mining stories are celebrations of common men; on this celebration **Katharine Susannah Prichard** impastoed political overtones. Prichard's trilogy — *The Roaring Nineties* (1946), *Golden Miles* (1948), and *Winged Seeds* (1950) — chronicles the Kalgoorlie mines of Western Australia from a 'clutter of tents' to a town fringed by poppet heads, from prospecting to deep-mining for British companies, from classlessness to class war. Mateship, egalitarianism, and anti-authoritarianism evolve into militant unionism, demands for rights for alluvial diggers, safe timbering, ventilation and sanitation, or resistance to company despotism. Casey's approach in such short-story collections as *It's Harder for Girls* (1942) and *Birds of a Feather* (1943) is humanistic. Kalgoorlie's treacherous earth groans; marriages crumble; each morning the miner tastes 'the Twelve-hundred-foot Level on his tongue', presaging the deadly silicosis. But compensations exist: good wages, proud masculinity, and camaraderie. In **Randolph Stow**'s *Tourmaline* (1963) a drought-ridden mining town becomes the surrealistic stage for a psychic-theological drama where progression from idealized individualism to fraternal solidarity is reversed.

NOEL HENRICKSEN

Further reading: Geoffrey Blainey, *The Rush That Never Ended: A History of Australian Mining* (1963).

GOLDSMITH, OLIVER (1794–1861)

Canadian poet

Born at St Andrews, New Brunswick, Canada, the child of United Empire Loyalists, he spent his working life in the commissariat of the British Navy, first in Halifax, but eventually throughout the world at such postings as Hong Kong and the island of Corfu during the Crimean War (1854–6). He retired to England and died at Liverpool. Goldsmith was the author of the long narrative poem *The Rising Village* (published first in England in 1825; revised and published with other poems at Saint John, New Brunswick, in 1834), the first book-length poem published by a native English-Canadian.

Goldsmith's intention in *The Rising Village*

was to continue the story of the displaced English cottagers that was told by his grand-uncle and namesake, the Anglo-Irish Oliver Goldsmith (1728?–74), in *The Deserted Village* (1770). In 560 lines (1834) of accomplished heroic couplets that show the influence of Alexander Pope, James Thomson, and Goldsmith, *The Rising Village* describes the pioneering activities of the British in 'Acadia's [Nova Scotia's and New Brunswick's] woods and wilds'. Already looking backward some fifty years in 1825, *The Rising Village* recounts the 'civilizing' of the New Brunswick wilderness: the banishment of beasts and indigenous inhabitants (probably Micmacs and Malecites); the first cultivation of the soil, which in Goldsmith's view entailed right of possession; the establishment of 'society'; and the ensuing prosperity, 'Till empires rise and sink, on earth, no more', as the last line of the poem proclaims. In the poem Goldsmith also tells the hapless tale of Flora and Albert, two youths who pledge their troth only to have Flora left at the altar when skittish Albert runs off. This interpolated tale of abandonment serves as an exemplum, as a coded warning to the inhabitants to persist in the colonial enterprise, to remain faithful both to their harsh and promising new land ('Flora' being the emblem of Acadia), and to the mother country.

GERALD LYNCH

Further reading: *The Autobiography of Oliver Goldsmith* (1985); Gerald Lynch, ed., *The Rising Village* by Oliver Goldsmith (1989).

GOLDSWORTHY, PETER (1951–)

Australian poet, novelist, short-story writer

Born in Minlaton, South Australia, he grew up in various other South Australian country towns and finished his schooling in Darwin. He graduated in medicine from the University of Adelaide, has been awarded writing grants and residencies, and works part-time in a general practice shared with his wife. He was a member of the Friendly Street Poets' committee that produced fourteen poetry collections in the 1980s. His work comprises poetry, short stories, literary journalism, and a novel.

Goldsworthy's short poetry collection *Readings from Ecclesiastes* (1982) won the 1982 Commonwealth Poetry Prize, the 1983 Fellowship of Australian Writers Anne Elder Award, and the 1984 South Australian Biennial Literary Award; his second poetry collection, *This Goes With This* (1988), shared the Bicentennial Grace Perry Poetry Prize. His Adelaide-based story collections *Archipelagoes* (1982), *Zooing* (1986), and *Bleak Rooms* (1988) were followed by his short, Darwin-based novel *Maestro* (1989).

Despite Goldsworthy's many journalistic references to international literary modernism, his own writing is comparatively traditional. He writes well-made poems about people, places, fauna, and things. His stories and novel are conventional narratives filled with both caricatures and recognizable characters. Some poems are witty (particularly the parodies); some stories are savage realism ('The Reunion'). Mainly, however, his poetry comprises emotional response restrained by irony, while his stories are exaggerated developments of contrary responses, zany and/or obsessive satires on trends and trendiness of all kinds. Although sometimes slight, slick, or corny, the stories are often wildly funny for their entire lengths.

The autobiographical *Maestro* suggests Goldsworthy's dissatisfaction with what he sees as his own shortcomings. Restricted by wit, irony, success, intelligence, and social skills as well as by the absence of oppression and suffering, he chooses to portray his adolescent vulnerability and non-medical curiosity about great pain. He is nagged by doubts about his ability to write long, flawed, unrevised works of tormented genius. The novel does not grow out of his stories but returns to some themes from *Readings from Ecclesiastes*.

If *Maestro* does not reveal artistic development, it is nevertheless of biographical interest.

GRAHAM ROWLANDS

GONZALEZ, ANSON JOHN (1936–)

Trinidadian poet, critic

Born in Mayo, Trinidad and Tobago, he founded the literary journal *The New Voices* in 1973. He was a facilitator in the birth of the Writers' Union of Trinidad and Tobago (1980), serving as president between 1988 and 1990. In 1988 he was the recipient of the first WUTT Writer of the Year Award.

Gonzalez has published several volumes of poetry: *Score* (with Victor D. Questel, 1972); *Love Song of Boysie B. and Other Poems* (1974); *Collected Poems 1964–1979* (1979); *Postcards and Haiku* (1984); and *Moksha: Poems of Light and Sound* (1988). His nonfiction publications include *Self-Discovery Through Literature: Creative Writing in Trinidad and Tobago* (1972) and *Trinidad and Tobago Literature: On Air* (1974).

Gonzalez began writing during the turbulent late 1960s and the 1970s. As one of the group of 'new' post-independence poets that includes **Anthony McNeill**, **Mervyn Morris**, and **Dennis Scott**, Gonzalez brings to his poems the conflicts of a young, multicultural, post-colonial nation caught in the midst of nation-building. Kenneth Ramchand has recognized Gonzalez as among the writers 'who are genuinely involved in building upon our complex traditions'; Gonzalez's Trinidadian contemporaries include Abdul Malik and **Wayne Brown**.

The critical, unromantic eye that Gonzalez's 'nationstate' poems casts on efforts to attain a national identity and autonomy is typical of the 'new' generation group. Not swayed by the mass philosophies of the black consciousness and nationalist movements, he maintains a unique perspective and uses symbols of the nationalist and black liberation movement — the steel band, in 'Cadence', and jazz, in 'Hey, Alfie' — to expose their shortcomings and failures. Music — its tones, rhythms, and moods — forms an interesting feature of Gonzalez's poetry, an influence that perhaps originated in the 'dub' poetry tradition of the 1960s and 1970s.

Other concerns — such as love and sex, religion and death, all rendered from a distinctly personal standpoint — also appear in Gonzalez's writing. The spiritual search for God and self-realization that dominates Gonzalez's later work adds a relatively new dimension to the already-complex tradition of the region's poetry.

JENNIFER RAHIM

Further reading: Jennifer Rahim, *The Work of the Spirit — Moksha: Poems of Light and Sound* (1989).

GONZALEZ, N. V. M. (1915–)

Filipino novelist, short-story writer, poet, critic

He was born Nestor Vicente Madali Gonzalez on the island of Romblon, the Philippines, to a Visayan-speaking family. Gonzalez spent his early years in what he calls a 'small harbour town' before moving at the age of four, with his family, to Mindoro, an island in the Tagalog region. The backwoods of Mindoro became the world of his early fiction.

Gonzalez received his early schooling in Romblon and Mindoro, and in 1933 began studies at the National University and Manila Law College, both in Manila. This formal higher education was not to reach its logical conclusion, as other roads led the young Gonzalez to work at the *Graphic*, a leading magazine. In 1940 he won a Commonwealth Literary Award for his first novel, *The Winds of April* (1941). Gonzalez took up a teaching position at the University of the Philippines and travelled internationally, particularly in Asia, which nurtured his feeling of kinship with writers in other colonized countries. He had a tenured position at the University of California at Hayward, USA, and later returned to the University of the Philippines, which conferred on him the Doctor of Humane Letters in 1987 and named him first International Writer-in-Residence.

Gonzalez's fictional works include the novels *The Winds of April*, *A Season of Grace* (1954), and *The Bamboo Dancers* (1959) and the short-story collections *Seven Hills Away* (1947), *Children of the Ash-Covered Loam and Other Stories* (1951), *Look, Stranger, on This Island Now* (1954), *Selected Stories* (1964), and *Mindoro and Beyond: Twenty-One Stories* (1979).

Gonzalez sees the Philippines as 'one nation made up of three countries': Manila, the City, is the first country; the Barrio is the second; the Mountain, the third. *Seven Hills Away* established his concern for the people of the Barrio, people of the most rural margins of the Philippines, with whom he identifies. In the Gonzalez Barrio, which is forest, mangrove swamp, and clearing, the concerns are primal: survival, subsistence, making it through another day or another harvest. The characters are peasants whose deepest links are to nature and to a code of their own making. While the backwoods in these stories represent a self-contained world, they are not untouched by the pull of such imperialistic forces as education, commerce, and material progress. The last story in *Seven Hills Away*, 'The Happiest Boy in the World', dramatizes the moral implications of this incursion for the tenant-farmer Julio, who, with great effort, writes his landlord a letter asking that his son be allowed to serve in his household in exchange for an education in the town school. It is a dearly bought future for the boy, and the story raises large questions about what is gained and what is lost.

In *Children of the Ash-Covered Loam and Other Stories* and *A Season of Grace* Gonzalez problematizes further the situation of barrio folk confronted with the possibility of progress in some form. The imperialist in these works appears in several disguises — peddler, government official, school inspector, merchant, concessionaire. He is a seller of promises, and the farmer, fisherman, or schoolteacher either buys the goods, paying the price, or, reading the hidden agenda, rejects them, paying the price of that choice.

The dilemma of the native confronted by the political and economic power of an outsider is fully rendered in *A Season of Grace*, the story of *kaingin* ('slash-and-burn') farmers who become the object of the designs of those in power. In his autobiographical essay *Kalutang: A Filipino in the World* (1990), Gonzalez says that 'an imagination, a sensibility, that emerges out of a Third World environment must fend for itself, for it is easy prey to the rabid charity of other worlds'; for the most part, Doro and Sabel and the other peasants in *A Season of Grace* fend for themselves. If there is a tyranny or power they accept, it is what to an outsider would be that of nature over their crops, and therefore their lives. This acceptance of nature is not a surrender, however, but an affirmation of the code by which they choose to live. It is also resistance to colonization.

In Gonzalez's two succeeding books, *The Bamboo Dancers* and *Look, Stranger, on This Island Now*, the protagonists inhabit a bigger world; in many cases they make the expected move from barrio to city. Against the backdrop of a larger, more complex world, however, they also feel, and seem, smaller. Exceptions perhaps are the young protagonists — the boy narrator in 'The Bread of Salt' and the central characters in 'The Wireless Tower' and 'The Eternal Fort' — who have the future before them.

In these stories, the middle-class characters would be in good company with those in **R. K. Narayan**'s Malgudi. They are small-time bureaucrats, schoolteachers, sailors. However ordinary they are, Gonzalez treats them, and their lives, seriously. He does not hide his respect for his poorest characters, who are dignified even in their despair. If Narayan's hallmark is understated comedy, Gonzalez's is understated reverence for his characters. It is an attitude he shares with Anton Chekhov and Sherwood Anderson.

Ernie Rama, the protagonist of *The Bamboo Dancers*, is perhaps Gonzalez's most westernized character. The author calls the novel a confession, a series of illuminations for Rama, an artist who visits Japan and Taipei on his way home to the Philippines from a scholarship in the USA. Significantly, Rama's most crucial illuminations about truth, art, and tradition come to him in his home country.

Two non-fictional works, *The Father and the Maid: Essays on Filipino Life and Letters* (1990) and *Kalutang: A Filipino in the World*, are crucial to an understanding of Gonzalez the writer. These essays reveal a writer deeply aware of the imperialist agenda and conscious of the need to examine closely this agenda and to seek the path one might travel in integrity and dignity and in kinship with all colonized peoples.

BERNADETTE S. OLOROSO

Further reading: Miguel A. Bernad, *Bamboo and the Greenwood Tree* (1961); Edilberto N. Alegre and Doreen G. Fernandez, *Writers and Their Milieu* (1987); Florentino B. Valeros and Estrellita V. Gruenberg, *Filipino Writers in English* (1987), Gemino H. Abad and Edna Z. Manlapaz, *Man of Earth* (1989).

GOODISON, LORNA GAYE (1947–)

Jamaican poet, short-story writer

She was born in Kingston, Jamaica, and after graduating from high school studied at the Jamaica School of Art and at the school of the Art Students' League, New York, USA. Goodison's paintings have been exhibited internationally and have been used on the covers of all her books. She has worked as a teacher, in advertising, and in public relations.

Goodison has been a leading contributor to an impressive output of writing by Caribbean women since the 1970s. Her published works include the poetry collections *Tamarind Season* (1980), *I Am Becoming My Mother* (1986), *Heartease* (1988), and *Selected Poems* (1992) and the short-story collection *Baby Mother and the King of Swords* (1990). *Tamarind Season* bore witness to a fresh, fertile imagination, represented with sensuous immediacy in a relaxed yet subtly controlled variation of speech rhythms. The poems show an identification with the disadvantaged, a sharply satirical eye for social pretentiousness, and a refreshing willingness to address the particularities of women's sensibility and culture, to lay frank claim to her sexuality, and to question societal constraints on that sexuality. (See **Feminism**, The Caribbean.) The collection also marked the beginning of a significant achievement in extending and subtilizing the use of the vernacular in Caribbean poetry, by the way in which it moved up and down the Jamaican speech continuum.

Tamarind Season includes Goodison's most widely known poem, 'For My Mother (May I Inherit Half Her Strength)'. It encompasses various Goodison themes that relate to her depiction of women's lives, including the social context of a gender code that has traditionally disadvantaged women. The poem also celebrates women's strength and inventiveness in adversity. Reprinted in *I Am Becoming My Mother*, 'For My Mother' finds there sister pieces that advance a female line of cultural descent as represented in resilient, nurturing black women. These women not only embody the idea of sisterhood and female independence of spirit, but are also leaders of the 'tribe' as a whole and exemplars of woman's role in the history of black struggle.

Goodison's talent for finding richly suggestive images to embody the condition of her female persona is seen in a poem such as 'Tightrope

Walker', where the precarious delight of the woman giving herself to a heady, secret love is imaged in the high-wire performer displaying her skill and finery, ostensibly to the crowd but really for her lover. 'The Mulatta as Penelope' contributes to feminist revisioning of androcentric mythology by positing a Penelope who refuses to acquiesce in the role of the forever-waiting woman, living only for her wandering man's uncertain return.

Heartease evokes the blessed calm of a place, 'Heartease', of illumination and soul-satisfaction reached only after a difficult, contentious journey. The collection is suffused with a mystical light, which transfigures the poet's pervasive water imagery. The dominant rhythm is incantatory, breathing benediction, although it can also lay a holy curse on the oppressor. The quality of transcendence is all the more convincing for being instinct with a sense of the rough world. Nor is the winning-through merely personal. The poems still speak with a communal resonance.

Baby Mother and the King of Swords is about the problems of romantic relationships between women and men. With two possible exceptions, the stories constitute a recital of the woes of women in love. The lament is sharpened and varied by glimpses of the potential of man-woman relationships and by instances of women's rejection of the status of victim. Among the more vivaciously nuanced, subtly resonant pieces are 'I Don't Want To Go Home in the Dark' and 'Moon', which evoke, from the ironic point of view of a sophisticated female consciousness, the impossibility of true communication between the woman and her egocentric, proprietorial, man-of-the-world lover.

EDWARD BAUGH

Further reading: Edward Baugh, 'Goodison on the road to Heartease', *Journal of West Indian Literature* 1 (1986); Velma Pollard, 'Overlapping systems: language in the poetry of Lorna Goodison', *Carib* 5 (1989); Edward Baugh, 'Lorna Goodison in the context of feminist criticism', *Journal of West Indian Literature* 1 (1990); Elaine Savory Fido, 'Textures of third world reality in the poetry of four African-Caribbean women', in Carole Boyce Davies and Elaine Savory Fido (eds) *Out of the Kumbla* (1990).

GOONERATNE, YASMINE (1935–)

Sri Lankan poet, critic

Born in Colombo, Sri Lanka, she attended Bishop's College, Colombo, later graduating in English from the University of Ceylon, and earned a Ph.D. from the University of Cambridge, England. She was a lecturer in English at the University of Ceylon from 1959 until 1972, when she immigrated to Australia. She has since been in the School of English and Linguistics, Macquarie University, where she is professor of English and the founding director of its Post-Colonial Literatures and Language Research Centre. In 1981 Macquarie conferred on her its first Doctor of Letters degree.

In her doctoral dissertation, published as *English Literature in Ceylon 1815–1878* (1968), Gooneratne, like the older generation of critics in Sri Lanka and elsewhere, extended the application of 'Cambridge English' to the new field of Commonwealth literature. She was the pioneer critic of Sri Lankan literature in English and performed a valuable service in launching a journal, *New Ceylon Writing*, in 1970, to replace the last in the line of Sri Lankan literary journals in English, *Community*, which had ceased publication in 1963. Her critical studies *Jane Austen* (1970) and *Alexander Pope* (1976) continue to hold the interest of both general reader and scholar. The most sophisticated of her studies of individual writers is *Silence, Exile and Cunning: The Fiction of Ruth Prawer Jhabvala* (1983). *Diverse Inheritance: A Personal Perspective on Commonwealth Literature* (1980) is a collection of essays.

Gooneratne is probably best known, especially

outside Sri Lanka, for her work as a critic, but her first two collections of poetry, *Word Bird Motif* (1971) and *The Lizard's Cry and Other Poems* (1972), are equally valuable. A member of the upper class, she is at times rather aristocratic in her poetry, like W. B. Yeats in his Coole Park poems. But she is able to transcend the limitations imposed by her origins to become a critic of her class. In 'Post-office Queue' her affluent but apologetic persona addresses a 'sister' of lower class. Aware of the problems of crossing class barriers, she still makes an attempt; the poem's irony is targeted at upper-class attitudes. In 'Peace-Game', while Gooneratne satirically and allegorically contemplates class conflict, the tension of the poem suggests another dimension — international power politics. Satire and wit, befitting her familiarity with the Augustans, are her strengths. Gooneratne, however, is capable of combining these elements with deep feeling, as in 'The Second Chance'; she also writes effective love poetry, as in 'Rocks on Marine Drive' and 'White Cranes'. In her poetry Gooneratne has mastered an alien language and alien forms, moulding them with ease to the experiences she wishes to express. Critic M. C. Bradbrook judged the fifty-three poems of *Word Bird Motif* to be 'masterly in their range and ease'.

In 'The Lizard's Cry', her most ambitious and longest poem, Gooneratne attempts to combine the convention of the *sandesaya* or message poem of Sanskrit and Sinhala traditions with an eighteenth-century 'imitation' of Pope's *Dunciad*, replacing Pope's content with local material while retaining the form and spirit of the original. Gooneratne's poem works only in patches; her satire, which is not sufficiently objective or positive, deteriorates into vituperation.

Although alienation prevented Gooneratne from relating to the concerns of the mass of the people and has limited her range, it did not staunch her creativity while she remained in Sri Lanka. Driven to immigrate to Australia — partly because of the 'solemn dons and grave administrators' she satirizes in 'Masks in the University Senate Room' — she experienced a different kind of alienation. *Six Thousand Foot Death Dive* (1981) contains poems written in Australia, Honolulu, USA, and Sri Lanka between 1972 and 1981. Nine years is a long interval to precede a slim volume of twenty-nine short poems, and it is a disappointing performance for a poet who had been so prolific, though explicable in the light of what she says about her immigration in the poems themselves. Australia has diminished her satiric fire and has wrought changes. Her technique has altered; while she had earlier exploited clarity and precision of style, 'she is now exploring the resources of resonance, the depths and echoes that rim the edges of a poet's line,' according to critic Lakshmi de Silva. More significant, however, is her preoccupation with exile, especially the difficulty of writing poetry in Australia. Like Coleridge in 'Dejection: An Ode', Gooneratne expresses her inability to communicate. Her alienation in a foreign country is responsible for the poetry in this volume failing to achieve the quality of her earlier verse. 'Big Match, 1983', while reflecting her concern for ethnic harmony, suggests an awareness that the Sri Lankan milieu from which her poetry had taken value and strength has been irrevocably changed by civil war and is, in fact, no more. Gooneratne has reached a crisis in her career as a poet.

Relative Merits: A Personal Memoir of the Bandaranaike Family of Sri Lanka (1986) is perhaps a substitute for the poetry Gooneratne did not or could not write after 1983. In it she chronicles the history of her family. While expatriate Sri Lankan **Michael Ondaatje** in *Running in the Family* (1982) selects a semi-factual, semi-imaginative mode, Gooneratne is wholly factual. Both authors surrender partially to the blandishments of their community — the Burghers (people of mixed Sri Lankan and Dutch or Portuguese ancestry) and the

Sri Lankan upper class, respectively — while being critical of it. Both write well and offer a personal odyssey as well as a history of a segment of Sri Lankan society.

Gooneratne's achievement is many-faceted: she is a critic, poet, memoirist, and university teacher. For her distinguished contribution to Sri Lankan and Australian literature and education she was awarded the Order of Australia in 1990.

In 1991 Gooneratne published a novel, *A Change of Skies*, about South Asian immigrants in Australia.

D. C. R. A. GOONETILLEKE

GOONEWARDENE, JAMES (1921–)

Sri Lankan novelist, short-story writer

Born in Pannala, Sri Lanka, he spent his early childhood in Matara and was educated at St Peter's College, Colombo. Though Goonewardene has produced radio dramas and documentaries and has written on such subjects as Lankan writing in English and the rock fortresses of Sri Lanka, he is primarily a writer of fiction. He has published five novels, a collection of short stories, and numerous short stories in Lankan and foreign journals, all in English.

The interplay and contrast between urban and rural societies is a dominant theme of Goonewardene's early fiction. Disillusioned with the materialism and artificiality of urban life, the protagonists of both *A Quiet Place* (1968) and *Call of the Kirala* (1971) turn to life in the villages for spiritual inspiration. While these protagonists find village life more satisfying than the urban life-style that they reject, the village is seen to have its own problems — jealousy, superstition, and intrigue, among others. These early novels anticipate Goonewardene's later fiction in suggesting that Lankan society is in general hostile to 'human intelligence' and freedom. The sensitive individual feels uneasy in this society.

This view is examined in detail in the title story of Goonewardene's collection of stories, *The Awakening of Doctor Kirthi and Other Stories* (1976). Dr Kirthi, the story's protagonist, is a surgeon who is honest and dedicated to his work. But these qualities are not appreciated in Lankan society; what is required for success is cunning and ruthlessness, which the surgeon lacks. The point that the story enforces when Dr Kirthi leaves the country for good is that those who are upright and disciplined find it difficult to survive in Lankan society.

Goonewardene's portrayal of Lankan life becomes even grimmer in *An Asian Gambit* (1985) and *One Mad Bid for Freedom* (1990). Like **Ediriwira Sarachchandra**'s *Curfew and a Full Moon* (1978) and **Raja Proctor**'s *Waiting for Surabiel* (1981), *An Asian Gambit* is a novel about the Lankan insurgency of 1971. Goonewardene's view of the insurgency is harsher than Sarachchandra's and Proctor's. The insurgent leaders in Goonewardene's novel are unprincipled and opportunistic, their youthful followers politically naïve. And the socio-political system that the insurgents attack is itself unjust and corrupt. Intelligent and humane men such as Deva and Ariya (the novel's principal characters) can identify themselves with neither the insurgents nor the 'establishment'.

Equally pessimistic is the view of Lankan society found in *One Mad Bid for Freedom*. The society depicted here is sterile, violent, and hostile to the creativity that Korale (the novel's main character) represents. The chauvinism and intolerance of the 'Bhasha Peramuna', an extreme Sinhala-language movement that attacks Korale's 'followers' in the novel's surreal climax, emerge as this society's dominant trend.

Though in *Dream Time River* (1984), a story of childhood in colonial Sri Lanka, Goonewardene has written a novel that is not primarily satirical, his forte as a writer is social satire. His most recent novel confirms his status as Sri Lanka's most talented and important writer of satiric fiction in English.

NIHAL FERNANDO

GORDIMER, NADINE (1923–)

South African novelist, short-story writer, essayist

Born in the small mining town of Springs, on the gold-bearing reef that runs through Johannesburg, South Africa, she attended private schools and the University of Witwatersrand, South Africa. Gordimer has spent most of her life in South Africa, although she has made frequent visits abroad and travels extensively.

Gordimer's childhood was atypical. Her parents were immigrants: her father a Jewish watchmaker-become-jeweller who had emigrated from Lithuania in adolescence, her mother a native of England. What distinguished Nadine Gordimer's youth from that of similar white children in comparable small mining towns was not the ethos of her family, but the fact that her mother took her out of school at the age of eleven on the pretext of a heart ailment and kept her at home until she was sixteen. The daughter lived entirely within the social orbit of her parents, particularly of her mother, had private lessons at home, and developed a passion for reading and writing. She published her first short story (a children's story) at the age of thirteen, and her first adult story in 1939. Her first collection of short stories, *Face to Face*, appeared in 1949, and her first novel, the autobiographical *Bildungsroman*, *The Lying Days*, in 1953.

When Gordimer was awarded the Nobel Prize for Literature in 1991 there was worldwide approval of the choice. The warmth of that reaction entailed a recognition of her two lifelong preoccupations: the craft of writing and a commitment to opposing, in her writing, the evil of South African apartheid.

For Gordimer, the Nobel Prize is the most significant of a series of awards dating back to 1961, when she won the W. H. Smith Literary Award for her short-story collection *Friday's Footprint* (1960). *A Guest of Honor* (1970) won the James Tait Black Memorial Prize in Britain and the CNA (Central News Agency) Literary Prize in South Africa. *The Conservationist* (1974) won the Booker Prize in the UK and the CNA prize in South Africa. *Burger's Daughter* (1979) also won the CNA prize in South Africa. Vice-president of PEN International (1986–7), Gordimer has received several honorary degrees, as well as prizes in the USA, France, Italy, and Germany.

Until the 1980s Gordimer was known primarily as a writer of fiction and as a tireless worker for, and advocate of, free expression in South Africa, particularly for black writers, who were most vulnerable to censorship laws and arbitrary judicial powers. Recently, however, her critical writing and her political comments published in journals outside South Africa have become increasingly influential. The publication in 1988 of her collected essays, *The Essential Gesture: Writing, Politics, and Places*, edited by Stephen Clingman, and in 1990 of a collection of her previously published interviews, *Conversations with Nadine Gordimer*, edited by Nancy Topping Bazin and Marilyn Dallman Seymour, illustrate the growing interest in all aspects of her writing.

Many South African whites resent the authoritative role Gordimer plays outside the country as a critic of the South African regime. For many whites the pride at a local woman who has made good in the world is balanced by anger at a local busybody-traitor who consistently and self-righteously misrepresents the situation to that external audience. At the same time, Gordimer's refusal to submit her fiction to the simple demands of revolutionary action has alienated her from many black commentators totally committed to a political programme. By remaining in South Africa when so many other writers of her generation — **Dan Jacobson**, **Lewis Nkosi**, and most of the writers for ***Drum*** magazine in the 1950s — emigrated, Gordimer shares with white writers such as **Alan Paton** and **J. M. Coetzee** a determination not to become a distant observer — either of the hitherto inexorable tightening of apartheid, or of the current, violence-ridden groping towards a new kind of political order. Whereas Gordimer's decision to stay in South Africa in the 1960s and 1970s was seen by some to entail a desire to enjoy the privileged status of whiteness even when protesting the evils of apartheid, the resolve with which she and writers like her continue to record and comment on the turbulent present can only be regarded as steely rather than indulgent.

These stresses in Gordimer's life are typical of the society she depicts. While much of her early fiction deals with the intractability of the political situation in mid-century South Africa and with the impasse (political, cultural, moral) created by white possession and control of the land, her latest works deal with the complex demands made on those living in a society in transition. The role open to whites in the struggle to change South Africa has always been one of Gordimer's preoccupations. As the situation there crystallizes into a confrontation between entrenched white rulers and a determined black 'people', options available to well-meaning, non-racist whites are shown to have become increasingly limited.

Gordimer has always believed in the 'truth' of the creative imagination. 'Nothing I say here will be as true as my fiction,' she commented in her celebrated 1982 public address 'Living in the Interregnum' (published in *The New York Review of Books*, 20 January 1983). Her brand of realism, conceptually influenced by George Lukacs, relies on vivid evocations of surface, texture, and nuance to reveal social and public truths through a penetratingly accurate representation of private lives and moments. In her later works she shows an increasingly complex use of fictional form. Recurring patterns of language or image combine with shifts in narrative perspective or voice to create extraordinary richness and cohesiveness.

The Lying Days traces the protagonist's development from small-mining-town girl to member of the bohemian Johannesburg set as she lives through the turmoil of the early days of National Party rule and of incipient, systematic apartheid. On the eve of a long-desired journey to Europe, the protagonist realizes that she will return to South Africa in spite of its darkening political scene. Themes encapsulating much of Gordimer's early fiction are the erosion of liberty and self-respect, not only for the victims of apartheid but also for whites who dislike systemic racism but are inevitably tainted and compromised in segregated South Africa, and the appropriateness of a commitment to stay on rather than to take refuge in a less complicated society overseas.

Most of Gordimer's early novels and short stories deal with the corrosive effects of racism on the lives of all. Her work of this period has often been compared to the early writing of **Doris Lessing**, who describes the stifling and claustrophobic effects of colonial life in what was then Rhodesia. Gordimer's early and middle work chronicles a growing disillusion with liberalism as a creed to combat apartheid. In *A World of Strangers* (1958) and *Occasion For Loving* (1963), which brilliantly capture the mood of politically volatile Johannesburg at the time, even promising relations among black and white intellectuals and artists founder on the entrenched inequities of opportunity in the nascent police state. In *The Late Bourgeois World* (1966) the egotistical shortcomings of an incompetent 'liberal' white saboteur are revealed in the thoughts and recollections of his ex-wife after she hears of his suicide. His ineffectual revolutionary posturing is contrasted with the terrifying request for aid made to the female protagonist by a real revolutionary from the black underground.

A commitment to action — even from a 'guest' in Africa — becomes a prominent theme in *A Guest of Honor*, Gordimer's only book set entirely outside of South Africa (in a composite east-central state). The effect of all-encompassing political commitment is the central theme in *Burger's Daughter*, and the need for effective commitment informs *A Sport of Nature* (1987) and *My Son's Story* (1990). In these last two novels, politically active characters are often treated ironically, but the texts show a veneration for activism that typifies her latest writing.

Gordimer's short stories, and particularly her *Selected Stories* (1975), demonstrate a startling clarity of detail and a haunting resonance. Her most significant novels are those produced in mid-career: *The Conservationist* (1974), *Burger's Daughter*, and *July's People* (1981). *The Conservationist* evokes the arid world of a white Johannesburg industrialist who can buy land, but not belong to it. *Burger's Daughter* deals with the unsuccessful attempt of its protagonist (the daughter of a celebrated communist) to 'defect' from political action. *July's People* analyses a typical master-servant relationship during an imagined, future civil war when members of a white family take refuge in the village of their servant.

In all her work Gordimer creates vivid characters, actions, and locales. Through these 'truthful' depictions, and their interlocking images and motifs, she evokes broader truths about human behaviour and about her specific fictional milieu.

ROWLAND SMITH

Further reading: Stephen Clingman, *The Novels of Nadine Gordimer: History from the Inside* (1986); John Cooke, *The Novels of Nadine Gordimer: Private Lives/Public Landscapes* (1985); Judie Newman, *Nadine Gordimer* (1988); Rowland Smith, ed., *Critical Essays on Nadine Gordimer* (1990).

GORDON, ADAM LINDSAY (1833–70)
Australian poet
Born in the Azores, he was educated at Cheltenham, England. In 1853 he was sent in disgrace to South Australia, where he worked successfully as mounted policeman, horse-breaker, and parliamentarian. He also attempted unsuccessfully to raise sheep near Bunbury in Western Australia. Gordon contributed verse to South Australian and Melbourne sporting papers. His first book, *The Feud: A Ballad* (1864), was followed in 1867 by two volumes, *Ashtaroth: A Dramatic Lyric* and *Sea Spray and Smoke Drift*, and a move to Victoria. Financial problems intervened, however. Gordon lost money on the publications, a fire destroyed a livery stables business, and a claim he had made on a Scottish estate was rejected. In the midst of pressing financial difficulties he brought out a fourth volume, *Bush Ballads and Galloping Rhymes* (1870), but on the day after its publication he committed suicide.

More than any other nineteenth-century Australian writer, Gordon became a cult figure because of the flamboyance of his horse-riding, his breezy, memorable poetry, and the pathos of his death. Several biographies were written in the succeeding fifty years, a monument was erected in Melbourne, and in 1934 his bust was included in Poets' Corner, Westminster Abbey, London.

Marcus Clarke suggested that Gordon's poems contained the beginnings of an Australian school of poetry. Gordon's is not a lyric, descriptive talent like **Henry Kendall**'s, however. If he initiates an Australian school it is one of horsy action, exuberant speed, and taciturn stoicism. His famous quatrain is given a Christian context, but is equally available to the sceptic and epitomizes the simple bush ethic that the ***Bulletin*** writers were to adopt as a national lay religion:

Life is mostly froth and bubble,

Two things stand like stone —
Kindness in another's trouble,
Courage in your own.

Gordon had little interest in nationalist agendas, however. Only a few of his poems have a strongly Australian inflection; for the most part he was as content to evoke a gallop up an English country lane or across a brutal medieval battlefield as around a Victorian racetrack.

CHRIS TIFFIN

Further reading: Ian McLaren, *Adam Lindsay Gordon: A Comprehensive Bibliography* (1986).

GOULD, ALAN (1949–)

Australian poet, novelist

Born in London, England, of British-Icelandic parents, he lived in Ireland, Iceland, Germany, and Singapore before immigrating to Australia in 1966. He graduated from the Australian National University, Canberra, in 1971 and has since been widely regarded as one of the leading figures in Canberra literary circles. Gould has received a number of creative writing fellowships from the **Literature Board** of the **Australia Council** and was a founding editor of both *Canberra Poetry* and The Open Door Press. In 1991 he was made the founding Poetry Editor of *Voices*, the quarterly journal of the National Library of Australia.

Gould is known chiefly as a poet who has drawn effectively upon his Icelandic heritage and his close affiliation with the sea. His publications of verse are: *The Scald Mosaic* (1975), *Icelandic Solitaires* (1978), *Astral Sea* (1981) — which won the New South Wales Premier's Poetry Award — *The Pausing of the Hours* (1984), *The Twofold Place* (1986), and *Years Found in Likeness* (1988).

Gould has published two volumes of fiction — *The Man Who Stayed Below* (1984), which won the Foundation of Australian Literary Studies Award for Best Australian Book of the Year, and a collection of three novellas, *The Enduring Disguises* (1988).

As a poet, commentator, and critic, Gould made an initial impact as one of the most ardent followers of the ideas of **Les Murray**, particularly as they related to developments in Australian poetry. Gould's own work has always been highly idiosyncratic and, although its sense of a rigorous formal component might be seen to relate to the influence of the elder Canberra poet **A. D. Hope**, Gould's own personal feeling for language and sound has always been distinctive. His choice of poetic subject matter also stems from a far broader concept of relationships with the sea and with ships than is apparent in the prevailing 'voyager tradition' of Australian poetry defined in the 1950s by **Douglas Stewart**.

Gould's ventures into prose suggest that, like **Rodney Hall**, he may well find in this medium an avenue for later developments, whereas his recent poetry suggests consolidation rather than advance.

THOMAS SHAPCOTT

GOW, MICHAEL (1955–)

Australian dramatist

Born in Sydney, Australia, he has worked as an actor and director with major state and experimental companies and in films and television. In 1982 his first stage play, *The Kid* (1983), was workshopped at the Australian National Playwrights Conference and subsequently widely produced. Gow's most successful play, *Away* (1986), won many awards. The State Theatre Company of South Australia produced his *1841* (1988), for the 1988 Adelaide Festival and Australia's Bicentennial, where it was disliked for its uncelebratory view of Australia's colonial history. He has written for radio and television, notably his acclaimed 1989 screenplay of **Sumner Locke Elliott**'s novel *Edens Lost* (1969).

Gow is considered Australia's leading young playwright, a possible successor to **David Williamson**. His plays have met with considerable popular success and critical acclaim for their comic and poignant observation of generational relations and for their affectionate evocation of suburban Australian rituals among the newly affluent post-war generation. Critical attention has focused on his sure theatricality and his intertextual references to Greek theatre, Shakespeare, and Ibsen. His comedy-romance *Europe* (1987) dramatizes Australia's fascination-resentment for European culture. Like **Louis Nowra**, Gow appropriates the classic repertoire and styles as a distinctive feature of post-colonial theatre; he quotes canonical mythologies such as Wagner's *Ring* (*The Kid*), the Atreidae (*On Top of the World*, 1987), romantic melodrama (*1841*), or Hollywood movies.

Gow's pervasive themes are the family and its cohesions and fractures, and the death of the young. *The Kid*, set among dispossessed urban youth, combines a parodic quest with the alienated lyricism of Sam Shepard. The bleakness of the kids' fate persists in the hugely popular *Away*, set in 1968 amid the beach culture of the annual Christmas family holiday, where reconciliations are effected by a young boy's fatal illness. *On Top of the World* takes place atop a Gold Coast apartment block, where a shattered family precariously regroups around its dying father. However, the depoliticizing acclamation of Gow as a celebrator of healing and consensus ill prepared critics for the accusatory tone of *1841*, a dystopic view of Australia's convict past and client-state present.

VERONICA KELLY

GRACE, PATRICIA (1937–)

New Zealand short-story writer, novelist

Born in Wellington, New Zealand, of Ngati Raukawa, Ngati Toa, and Te Ati Awa descent, and affiliated by marriage with Ngati Porou, she regularly visited her extended family at tribal land on the Porirua Harbour during her childhood. Educated at local schools in Wellington and at Teachers' Training College there, Grace subsequently taught in primary and secondary schools in the King Country, Northland, and in Porirua; since the 1970s she has lived on ancestral land. She is a teacher and the mother of seven children.

In the 1960s and 1970s Grace began publishing short stories in magazines and periodicals, primarily in *Te Ao Hou*, *Landfall*, and *Islands*. Her first collection, *Waiariki* (1975), like her first novel, *Mutuwhenua: The Moon Sleeps* (1978), deals with the effects on individuals' lives, particularly Maori lives, of the tensions between Maori and Pakeha life-styles. *Mutuwhenua* focuses on the predicament close to Grace's own experience — the dislocation suffered by a young woman, Ripeka, who, when newly married and pregnant, moves with her Pakeha school-teacher husband to an urban environment, an inner-city house 'somewhere and nowhere at all'. Only the intervention of Ripeka's extended family, which interprets her nightmares and anxiety attacks as the result of the house being built on an old burial ground, allows her to recover.

Two further collections of Grace's stories appeared in the 1980s: *Dream Sleepers and Other Stories* (1980) and *Electric City and Other Stories* (1987), as well as two children's books, *The Kuia and the Spider* (1981) and *Watercress Tuna and the Children of Champion Street* (1984; published in Maori as *Te Tuna Watakirihi Me Nga Tamariki o te Tiriti o Toa*, 1985). The latter two are illustrated by Maori painter and illustrator Robyn Kahukiwa, who also collaborated with Grace on the production of *Wahine Toa: Women of Maori Myth* (1984), a pictorial representation for adult readers of stories about women from Maori mythology. The text is in Maori and English and Grace's version is based closely on traditional renderings of these stories.

Grace's writing is integrated with her work as a teacher and with her role in her community as the initiator of creative and other work projects centring around the Marae. This conscious regeneration of a community is the subject of her novel *Potiki* (1986). The novel inscribes itself within a Maori history, represented by the stories of a lineage of 'carvers' who depict the passing generations in their work. The novel begins with an empty place on a carving, a space between the legs of another figure; it ends with that space filled with a carved representation of Toko, the physically damaged child who becomes the 'potiki', the precious little one, of the community. He grows to be the wise young man who understands 'the old stories' and who can inspire the village to resist the duplicitous pressures of a commercial subsidiary wishing to purchase and develop the ancestral land, upon which the community is physically and spiritually based. Toko dies in that struggle, but after his death he watches from the wall of the meeting house: 'And from this place of now, behind, and in, and beyond the tree, from where I have eversight, I watch the people.' The novel ends with a verse in Maori, reinforcing the connection between the people of now and their ancestors, whose images are carved on the meeting house wall. These final words are untranslated; this departure from the earlier works, which are accompanied by glossaries, represents a changing attitude among Maori writers who now insist that Maori language and things Maori take a central place in New Zealand society.

Grace's style is unornamented yet passionate. Her early work is clearly influenced by both **Frank Sargeson**'s commitment to capturing the rhythms of local and colloquial speech and by the unpretentious plainness that characterizes so much New Zealand writing of the Sargeson tradition. The resonance of Grace's writing has been expanded by a more generous use of images and stories from Maori religious and poetic tradition.

In *Electric City* Grace continues to use the personal and subjective perspective as a way of countering historically grounded European attitudes towards Maori; she counters stereotypes by creating inner worlds of her characters that simultaneously reveal the cultural aspects of personal point of view.

A number of interviews and a film documentary (*Ruia Taitea: The World Is Where We Are*, 1990) recount Grace's attitudes to her work.

MARY PAUL

Further reading: Peter Beatson, *The Healing Tongue* (1989).

GRAY, ROBERT (1945–)

Australian poet

Born at Coffs Harbour, New South Wales, Australia, he worked in Sydney, Australia, as an advertising copy-writer, bookshop assistant, and freelance journalist and reviewer. He has received numerous senior writing fellowships from the **Literature Board** of the **Australia Council**.

Gray's verse publications are *Creekwater Journal* (1974), *Grass Script* (1978), *The Skylight* (1983), *Selected Poems* (1985), and *Piano* (1988). An expanded version of *Selected Poems* was published in 1990; the earlier edition of this collection won the National Poetry Award at the Adelaide Arts Festival, the New South Wales Premier's Literary Award, and the Grace Leven Poetry Prize.

Gray's poetry has gained increasing attention and respect as the work of a striking imagist who has focused on the particularities of things, of place, and of incident in order to express a Zen view of the world. His work has avoided the self-conscious internationalism of some of his contemporaries, and if one were to seek influences from the generation of American poets immediately prior to his — an almost ubiquitous phenomenon among Australian poets in the late 1960s and early 1970s — they would be in the work of Hayden Carruth, Wendell Berry, or perhaps Robert Bly. Among Australian poets to whom Gray might be seen to hold allegiance are **David Campbell**, **Les A. Murray**, in his early work, and **Geoffrey Lehmann**.

Although Gray has written many poems based upon experience and observation in Sydney, his poems of regional precision perhaps most effectively define him. His work presents a valid alternative to that of **John Tranter**, whose espousal of a language of admass urban culture is in striking contrast to Gray's use of apparently anecdotal particularities. Gray's influence can be discerned in the work of Australian poets such as **Geoff Page**, Jamie Grant, and **Kevin Hart**.

Underlying all of Gray's writing has been his absorption of Zen Buddhist concepts of creative passivity. He took, however, a more-or-less assertive stance in relation to current poetic practice when editing, with Geoffrey Lehmann, the anthology *The Younger Australian Poets* (1983), which was a direct response to Tranter's *The New Australian Poetry* (1979).

THOMAS SHAPCOTT

GRAY, STEPHEN RICHARD (1941–)

South African novelist, poet, dramatist, essayist

Born in Cape Town, South Africa, he was educated at St Andrew's College, Grahamstown, and at the University of Cape Town. As a post-graduate student at Cambridge University, England, Gray took a BA and an MA in English, edited *Granta* magazine, and directed the touring Cambridge Shakespeare Group. In this latter capacity he visited Aix-en-Provence, France, and stayed on for two years as a *lecteur* in English. He spent another two years at Iowa State University, USA, gaining a further MA in creative writing. From lecturer Gray rose to professor of English at the Rand Afrikaans University, Johannesburg, South Africa, gaining a D.Litt. et Phil. there in 1978 for his work on South African English literature. In 1982 he spent a year as writer-in-residence at the University of Queensland, Australia, and in 1991 retired from university lecturing to become a full-time writer. Gray, however, continues various 'militant' teaching activities, giving courses on creative writing to budding black dramatists, poets, and novelists.

Gray's *Southern African Literature: An Introduction* (1979) is a major work, with cross-cultural references to all writing produced in and about southern Africa. Gray has published numerous editions and critical studies, notably of the works of **H. C. Bosman**, **Stephen Black**, **Athol Fugard**, **William Plomer**, and C. Louis Leipoldt, and anthologies of the area's poets and dramatists: *Theatre One* (1978), *Theatre Two: New South African Drama* (1981), *Modern South African Poetry* (1984), and *The Penguin Book of Southern African Verse* (1989). Gray is probably the best-known researcher and promoter of a real literary identity for southern Africa.

Gray's own creative output is sometimes unjustly overlooked. He is a brilliantly inventive poet; his works include *The Assassination of Shaka* (1974, with woodcuts by Cecil Skotnes), *Hottentot Venus and Other Poems* (1979), and *Apollo Café and Other Poems* (1989). As playwright he has dramatized (with Barney Simon) Bosman's *Cold Stone Jug* (1982) and has written a comedy about Jules Verne's connections with South Africa, *An Evening at the Vernes* (published in *Contemporary South African Plays*, 1977, edited by Ernest Pereira). His *Schreiner: A One-woman Play* (1983) was widely praised. Gray's best-known novels, *Local Colour* (1975), *Caltrop's Desire* (1980), *John Ross: The True Story* (1987), *Time of Our Darkness* (1987), *Born of Man* (1989), and *War Child* (1991) deal with both the everyday life of South Africa and the myths of the making of the nation. Some of the novels have frequently been a subject of scandal for their revealing, and sometimes burlesque, analyses of gay life in the subcontinent, but as one critic states: the novels open 'the debate on issues of class, gender, race and sexual orientation as inseparable from political imperatives'. Gray's work is subversive from within.

ANNE FUCHS

Further reading: Robert Greig, 'Gray matters', *Living July* (1989); Dieter Welz, interview with Stephen Gray, in National English Literary Museum, 1097, *Writing Against Apartheid* (1989); Stephen Gray, 'An author's agenda: re-visioning past and present for a future South Africa', *Kunapipi* 1 and 2 (1991).

GREER, GERMAINE (1939–)

Australian feminist writer

Born in Melbourne, Australia, she was miserable as a child, 'imprisoned in a bookless house, bored at school', while at home the 'only relief from tedium was trouble'. With relatives in Australia, residences in Essex, England, and Tuscany, Italy, emotional attachments in Asia and academic ones in America, and intimate with the broad spectrum of English literature, Greer is self-consciously internationalist. A university teacher and lecturer for a time, she has contributed articles to, or has edited, controversial periodicals and underground London newspapers; as a 'groupie' she has followed rock musicians; and she has led well-publicized international feminist campaigns. She has described herself as 'really just an intellectual superwhore'.

Greer has edited an anthology of seventeenth-century verse and has published eight books. Her first book, *The Female Eunuch* (1970), established her reputation as a polemicist. *The Obstacle Race* (1979) and *Sex and Destiny: The Politics of Human Fertility* (1984) continued, more cogently but less popularly, her 'second-wave' feminist apologia. Especially in *The Female Eunuch*, Greer is an apologist in the contemporaneous mould of Desmond Morris, Robert Ardrey, and even Erich von Daniken; she argues 'from her convictions to her evidence', eclectically seeking examples from anthropology, sociology, psychology, and literature, from extended Calabrian families to sexually aroused lads in industrial England, to substantiate a constellation of dogma united by the text: 'Women represent the most oppressed class of life-contracted unpaid workers . . . They are the only true proletariat left.' Greer's indebtedness to the English literary tradition is everywhere evident: Shakespeare's immortality-through-progeny motif, Mary Wollstonecraft's eighteenth-century ideas on female emancipation, tension between fertility and sterility in T. S. Eliot's *The Waste Land*, and Bob Dylan's vacillation between romanticization and exploitation of women are all transmuted into an argument for social and psychic revolution.

Greer's feminism has progressively been incorporated into compassion for all who are exploited or indigent and into hatred for paternalism, capitalism, and consumerism. In *Daddy, We Hardly Knew You* (1989), her crusade became personal. Belligerence gave way to sensitivity as she sought to clothe the skeletal memory of her father with biographical flesh.

In 1991 Greer published *The Change: Women, Ageing and the Menopause*.

NOEL HENRICKSEN

GRENVILLE, KATE (1950–)

Australian novelist, short-story writer

She was born in Sydney, Australia, and was educated at the University of Sydney (BA, 1972) and at the University of Colorado, USA (MA). She published three novels with strong and effective feminist themes in a short period of time, leading up to the Australian Bicentennial celebrations of 1988 — *Lilian's Story* (1985), *Dreamhouse* (1986), and *Joan Makes History* (1988). Perhaps the most powerful of these is *Lilian's Story*, an episodic narrative based loosely on the life of a well-known Sydney eccentric, Bea Miles. Like all of Grenville's writing, *Lilian's Story* writes out 'the body' in a range of suggestive ways. Lilian puts on weight from an early age and is subject to the tyrannies of her father's turn-of-the-century patriarchy. The novel also acceptably allegorizes the relationship between the newly independent colony and England. Lilian's father is named 'Albion', and it is his rape of his daughter that sends Lilian off into a life of eccentric and necessary self-assertion. Lilian is a literary first cousin of **Patrick White**'s 'vernacular illuminates' who walk the same streets of Sydney in novels such as *The Vivisector*, to which *Lilian's Story* bears a strong resemblance.

While it had a blaze of publicity and popularity, *Joan Makes History* is a less successful novel. Its techniques and themes are too notional and seem forced for the occasion of the bicentennial. Joan writes in her head a history of white Australia for its first 200 years to 1988, in which another Joan takes part. The aim is to put women into male history to make it 'her story', but what had been the successful first-person narrative and latent allegorizing of *Lilian's Story* appears forced here.

The short novel *Dreamhouse* received academic attention because of its highly crafted literariness and Gothic symbolism. It developed from an earlier short story, 'Country Pleasures', from the collection *Bearded Ladies* (1984). The novel sets up a self-consciously pastoral interlude, complete with satyr figures, and a nature so animated that it is almost fetishistic. Rennie and Louise journey from England for a summer in Tuscany, Italy. Louise's hatred for her egotistic ambitious academic husband and the male world he represents is the mainspring for the heavy tension in the novel. Husband and wife form a foursome with Hugo and Viola, a brother and sister couple in the next farmhouse (relations of Rennie's patron), and the plot unfolds through suggestive labyrinths of buggery, incest, monks, goats, and castles until Louise releases herself at the end in a triumphal act of independence. *Dreamhouse* exemplifies Grenville's insistence, as a woman and feminist, on her right to activate ideologies of the body and carnality; male readers relying on genteel aestheticism to legitimate their own literary language may regard this as heavy pessimism.

DAVID ENGLISH

Further reading: Gerry Turcotte, '"The ultimate oppression": discourse politics in Kate Grenville's fiction', *World Literature Written in English* 1 (1989); Brenda Walker, '"Sweetest and best in womanhood"?: equivocal representations of maternity in Australian women's fiction', *Westerley* 4 (1989).

GREY OWL (1888–1938)

Canadian essayist, conservation writer

Born Archibald Stansfeld Belaney, he was abandoned as a child by his English parents. He had a lonely and unhappy childhood in Hastings, Sussex, England, but found refuge in a fantasy world of his own making, centring on the North American Indian. By the time he died in Saskatchewan, Canada, he had created for himself a different heritage and was known to the world as Grey Owl, one of Canada's greatest conservationists. Grey Owl's four books remain in print and have been translated into numerous languages — *The Men of the Last Frontier* (1931), a collection of essays about the Canadian wilderness; *Pilgrims of the Wild* (1934), an account of how he became a conservationist; *The Adventures of Sajo and Her Beaver People* (1935), a children's book about the beaver; and *Tales of an Empty Cabin* (1936), a second collection of stories about the Canadian wilderness.

Only after his death did the press discover that Grey Owl, who claimed to have been raised by an Apache Indian mother and Scots-American father near the banks of the Rio Grande, was actually born in Hastings, where he lived with his two maiden aunts and his grandmother. He attended Hastings Grammar School, and immigrated to Canada at age seventeen. (See **Hoaxes and Jokes**, Canada.)

Much of the inspiration for Belaney's conservationist ideas came from Native Canadians. In 1907 he arrived at Lake Temagami in northern Ontario, and there met the Ojibwa. During the next thirty years he heard many stories from the North American Native peoples about their universe and its inhabitants.

In the mid-1920s, Anahareo, his Iroquois wife — his third wife — convinced him of the need for conservation. He began to write as Grey Owl, and made conservation the central theme of his writings. He was appointed in 1931 to look after a beaver conservation programme in western Canada. He completed his last three books at Prince Albert National Park in Saskatchewan.

DONALD B. SMITH

Further reading: Lovat Dickson, *Wilderness Man: The Strange Story of Grey Owl* (1973); Donald B. Smith, *From the Land of Shadows: The Making of Grey Owl* (1990).

GROSSMANN, EDITH SEARLE (1863–1931)
New Zealand novelist
Born at Beechworth, Victoria, Australia, she was taken to New Zealand in 1878 and educated at Invercargill Grammar School, Christchurch Girls' High School, and Canterbury College of the University of New Zealand, where she graduated with an MA in 1885. Grossmann worked as a university tutor, wrote articles for newspapers and magazines in New Zealand and abroad, travelled extensively, and was active in women's causes. Her four novels all focus on the status and treatment of women. *Angela: A Messenger* (1890) — which was published under the name Edith Searle — is a melodrama of martyrdom caused by male lust, violence, and drinking. *In Revolt* (1893) and *A Knight of the Holy Ghost* (1907) trace the development of the Australian protagonist, Hermione, from an unhappy marriage, through her becoming a prophet of feminism and the Religion of Humanity, to her final martyrdom at the hands of her husband and unjust laws. *The Heart of the Bush* (1910), Grossmann's last novel, turns to an ideal reconciliation of male and female within a marriage of complementary equals. All four novels are didactic and are written in a mode of heightened symbolic moral melodrama. The two Hermione novels, with their emphasis on equal rights for women, their fierce attack on sexual double standards, their depiction of a women's commune, and their fervent faith in moral evolution, are the most important literary works to emerge from the first wave of New Zealand feminism. (See **Feminism**, New Zealand.)

LAWRENCE JONES

Further reading: Heather Roberts, *Where did She Come From? New Zealand Women Novelists, 1862–1987* (1989).

GROVE, FREDERICK PHILIP (1879–1948)
Canadian/German novelist
Born Felix Paul Berthold Friedrich Greve, at Radomno, East Prussia, he was educated at Bonn and Munich, but left university without a degree. During 1903 he travelled in Italy with Elsa, wife of the architect August Endell, until he was arrested for fraud. Released from prison in June 1904, he met with André Gide; the interview is the subject of Gide's 'Conversation avec un Allemand'. For five years Greve tried to repay his debts and support Elsa by means of numerous translations. He also wrote impressionistic criticism, notably of Oscar Wilde, and published two novels, both of them, Elsa claimed, 'dictated by me — as to content'.

Despite almost incredible productivity — he told Gide that he had proofed sixty-two volumes in two years and nine months — Greve could not succeed economically as a translator. In September 1909 he pretended suicide and fled to the USA, where Elsa joined him. For two years they attempted farming in Kentucky, until he abandoned her. Grove, as he now called himself, became a teacher in Manitoba, Canada, where in 1914 he married Catherine Wiens. They taught in various small communities until he retired in 1924. Their daughter, born in 1915, died suddenly in 1927 — Grove's later poetry struggles with that grief. A son, Leonard, was born in 1930. Catherine died in 1972.

Grove's first Canadian book, *Over Prairie Trails* (1922), records a series of near-epic drives by carriage and sleigh. The emphasis is on observation of the natural world, and on the challenge it offers the person prepared to face it. Grove's usually Olympian prose derives a warmth in this volume from the goal of the 'island of domestic bliss' of wife and child he struggles to reach despite darkness, fog, and snow. A companion volume, *The Turn of the Year* (1923), is also in the tradition of the local-colour essay practised by such American nature writers as Henry David Thoreau and John Burroughs.

Settlers of the Marsh (1925) is the first of the four western novels on which Grove's reputation as a realist rests, but its elements do not always blend: the chronicle of settlement, the psychological exploration of the emotional collapse of the district strong man, the almost feminist Clara's avowal of her rights as a woman and of her sexual needs, and the balancing of primal forces that operate equally in external nature and within humankind.

The prairie novels have been studied as tragedies, and Grove's own critical essays, in *It Needs to Be Said* (1929) and elsewhere, emphasize the tragic in all great literature — tragic in the Nietzschean sense that their protagonists are often supermen in their capacity for work, in their inherent superiority to their communities, and in their autocratic indifference to democratic processes. With the exception of the young Len Sterner of *The Yoke of Life* (1930), all are patriarchs whose disillusionment with success matches their growing alienation from their families and communities. *Our Daily Bread* (1928) depicts the decline of John Elliot (considered by Grove a 'Lear of the Prairie') into isolation after his wife's death, as his family disintegrates and the fertility of the land is lost. (The concluding symbolism of the empty house may anticipate **V. S. Naipaul's** *A House for Mr. Biswas*.) In a draft of *Fruits of the Earth* (1933) the autocrat Abe Spalding kills the man who seduces his daughter, and then invites his own death from the guns of the posse, upon which he looks symbolically from his straw stack. In the published novel, however, the Nietzschean finale is replaced by Abe's sober acceptance of his own failure as a parent, as he takes up also the burden of civic responsibility.

In 1929 the Groves moved to Ottawa, where Grove was to be an executive with Graphic Press, which had published *A Search for America* (1927), his first-person account of the struggle of a young European to adjust to America's blatant exploitation of the immigrant. Unhappy in the role of business executive, Grove bought a small dairy farm near Simcoe, Ontario, where he spent the rest of his life.

The belated acceptance of the social burden typifies the later Grove protagonists, notably Sam Clark of *The Master of the Mill* (1944) and even the anti-heroine of *Consider Her Ways* (1947). The sense of the great cycles of cosmic time rendering human pretensions futile — a concept by no means unique with Grove, but important to him — is explicit in *The Master of the Mill*. In *Consider Her Ways*, Grove satirizes human pretension, as a colony of highly evolved ants undertakes an epic quest from Venezuela to New York City to study humans, a species considered to have degenerated after choosing the capitalist way of slavery instead of the agricultural way of creative leisure and intellect.

In his last years Grove's sense of neglect was ameliorated in part by literary awards and public honours, including a Governor General's Award for his autobiography *In Search of Myself* (1946).

Since his death Grove has been generally accepted as the first major realist in modern English-Canadian literature; now that realism itself is being critically called in question, that role may be re-assessed.

In some ways Grove typifies the immigrant writer in post-colonial societies: in his sense of isolation, his feeling of rejection or of grudging acceptance, and the conviction of personal failure. In the essay 'Rebels All' Grove claims that the autobiographer's aim is to 'justify his present', if necessary, by revising his past, a process that may be integral to the immigrant experience. He is less representative, perhaps, in that English is not his first language. He is not a Voss, however, either in relation to his fellows or in his idealism. In the naturalistic tradition, Grove's achievers achieve materially; no transcendence awaits them, but at best a belated self-knowledge.

The Grove papers, held at the University of Manitoba, include a number of unpublished works.

D. O. SPETTIGUE

Further reading: Ronald Sutherland, *Frederick Philip Grove* (1969); D. O. Spettigue, *Frederick Philip Grove* (1969); D. O. Spettigue, *F. P. G.: The European Years* (1973); Paul Hjartarson, *A Stranger to My Time: Essays By and About Frederick Philip Grove* (1987).

GUERRERO, WILFRIDO MARIA (1911–)

Filipino dramatist

Born in Manila, the Philippines, to the Guerrero family of Ermita, known for being doctors, poets, scientists, writers, and diplomats, his early formal education was under the American Jesuits of the Ateneo de Manila. His first play was written in Spanish, his home language, when he was in the fifth grade.

Guerrero's first play in English, 'Half an Hour in a Convent' (1934), was written while he was a sophomore at the University of the Philippines; since then he has written some eighty plays, variously assembled in seven volumes including *13 Plays* (1947), *12 New Plays* (1971, with a foreword by **Nick Joaquin**), *My Favorite 11 Plays* (1976), and *Retribution and Eight Other Selected Plays* (1990). His works have been performed at the University of the Philippines (where, despite not having a college degree, he taught drama) and throughout the country, by the University's Mobile Theater, and by other school and community groups.

The theatre critic and historian Nicanor Tiongson noted (in the *U. P. Newsletter*, 1978) that Guerrero was a pioneer in writing Filipino plays that focused on the specific issues of middle-class Philippine society, using English in a way that 'did not destroy the realism' of his plays.

As director for sixteen years of the University's Dramatic Club and for nineteen years of the University's Mobile Theatre, Guerrero trained the actors, directors, and audiences of his time. His best-known works — one-act plays such as *Wanted: A Chaperone* (premièred 1940, published in *13 Plays*) and *Three Rats* (in *Evening News*, 1948) and such full-length plays as *Forever* (1947), *Condemned* (1947), and *The Forsaken House* (1939, in *Herald Midweek Magazine*) — form part of the national repertoire. Their lasting quality, writes critic Edilberto Alegre (in Alegre's and Doreen Fernandez's *Writers and Their Milieu*, 1987), rests 'in their ability to capture the flavor of the life and livelihoood of . . . the genteel class to which he belongs'.

When theatre swung back into the vernacular in the 1960s, eighteen of Guerrero's plays were translated into Filipino and other languages and toured by the Mobile Theatre, thus keeping them in circulation and currency.

DOREEN G. FERNANDEZ

Further reading: Edilberto N. Alegre and Doreen G. Fernandez, *Writers and Their Milieu II* (1987); Wilfrido Ma. Guerrero, *The Guerreros of Ermita* (1988).

GUERRERO-NAKPIL, CARMEN (1922–)
Filipino essayist
Born Carmen Guerrero in Manila, the Philippines, among the Guerreros of Ermita, a distinguished family of doctors, scientists, and writers, she was educated at St Theresa's College. A young war widow, Guerrero-Nakpil entered journalism in 1947 as staff member and proof-reader and rose to writer, magazine editor, and editorial page columnist. She wrote daily and weekly columns for the *Manila Chronicle*, the *Sunday Times Magazine*, and the *Times-Journal*, among others. Guerrero-Nakpil was for several years chair of the National Historical Commission and of the Cultural Committee of the Philippine Commission for UNESCO. She has won many awards and is recognized as one of the most respected, skilled, and insightful essayists in the country.

Guerrero-Nakpil's newspaper columns have been collected in *Woman Enough and Other Essays* (1963), *A Question of Identity* (1973), and *The Philippines and the Filipinos* (1977). Among them is the much-quoted and discussed piece 'Cultural Roots and Foreign Influences', which explores the Malay matrix and foreign influences (Chinese, Indian, Spanish, Mexican, American) in Philippine culture and argues that 'Filipino culture, buffeted and exposed more than most others is still . . . only and entirely itself'.

Guerrero-Nakpil has written memorably, wittily, and sometimes acerbically about the Filipina, whom she describes as:

> a woman with a past — a long, unburied, polychromatic, delicious past which is forever returning to color her days. There have been three men in her life: her Asiatic ancestor, the Spanish friar, and the Americano, and . . . she echoes all the men she has known in her person.

Guerrero-Nakpil also writes about men, politics ('Politics may make us, but it is for us to shape it'), language ('Because it is so distinctive, Filipino English has developed another paradox. It has become a vehicle for nationalism, rather than . . . Americanism'), education, tradition, life-style, and history. Her latest book of essays, *The Philippines* (1989), contains eleven essays on culture, the current scene, art, and history.

Her first novel, *The Rice Conspiracy* (1990), is a spy story set in contemporary Philippines, with actual, recognizable power-players as fictional characters.

DOREEN G. FERNANDEZ

GUNN, JEANNIE (1870–1961)
Australian novelist
Born in Melbourne, Australia, she recounts her brief experience as the wife of Aeneas Gunn on a Northern Territory cattle station, Elsey, in two books that have become part of Australian pioneer folklore. *The Little Black Princess: a True Tale of Life in the Never-Never Land* (1905) was written for children and tells of the relationship between the 'Missus' (Gunn) and Bett-Bett, a lively young Aboriginal girl. Gunn's book for adults, *We of the Never-Never* (1908), details the thirteen months spent on Elsey, where the front gate is seventy kilometres from the homestead (itself barely habitable), and the Missus has to overcome the station hands' hostility to a white woman intruding in their world. The book ends in tragedy when Aeneas Gunn, the Maluka (boss), dies of malarial dysentery and his wife returns to life in Melbourne. A film of *We of the Never-Never* was released in 1982, and the novel was adapted for children by Nance Donkin in 1983.

The charm of both books lies in their affectionate portraits of various outback characters and in their details of a remote place few Australians would ever see for themselves. Unadventurous city folk no doubt took comfort from the fact that a fellow urbanite could cope with the vicissitudes of outback life. Despite her genuine interest in and respect for Bett-Bett, Gunn portrays Aboriginal people as naïve and childish, although, in regard to their customs and beliefs, she does concede 'that under every silly nonsense was a great deal of good sense'. Her relatively slight and leisurely encounter with pioneer conditions can be compared to the different situation of Karen Blixen's Kenyan experience in *Out of Africa*.

KERRY WHITE

Further reading: Ira Nesdale, *The Little Missus: Mrs Aeneas Gunn* (1977); Margaret Berry, 'Memoir of Jeannie Gunn', in *We of the Never-Never* by Jeannie Gunn (repr. 1983).

GUSTAFSON, RALPH (1909–)

Canadian poet, short-story writer

He was born and has lived most of his life in the Eastern Townships of Quebec, Canada. Educated at Bishop's University, Lennoxville, Quebec, and at Oxford University, England, Gustafson lived in New York, USA, in the 1940s and 1950s, bringing Canadian literature to international attention with anthologies such as *The Penguin Book of Canadian Verse* (1958). In 1960 he returned to Canada and became professor of English at Bishop's.

Gustafson's development as a poet provides a miniature history of Canadian literature. He has been called the 'heir of civilized centuries in a country without myths' and has been hailed as 'one of the most complete Canadian poets'. Author of more than twenty-five books of poems, including *Fire on Stone* (1974), which won a Governor General's Award, Gustafson remains less well known than contemporaries such as **A. J. M. Smith** or **F. R. Scott** because of his dense allusiveness and complex verbal textures.

Poems such as 'Carta Canadensis', 'At Moraine Lake', and 'In the Yukon' are studies of landscape and national identity. Like St Lucian poet **Derek Walcott**, Gustafson acknowledges the 'historylessness' of his country (in comparison with the UK and other European countries) and looks instead to the land for continuity and grandeur. Stories such as 'The Pigeon' focus on an imaginative child, prototype of the artist, trapped in a stultifying society 'aggressively dedicated to demanding "utility"', as Gustafson writes in the essay 'Poetry Can't Wind Clocks, but . . .'. This links him thematically to Canadian author **Sinclair Ross** and Australians **Vance Palmer** and **Patrick White**.

Cultured and widely travelled, Gustafson depicts a world composed of both debris and miracle, fire and stone. Ultimately, he affirms the humble satisfactions of daily living and the astonishing endurance of human love. His poems, like W. H. Auden's, offer a rare celebration — 'The praise of love, the humour read, / The permanence of temporary gods'.

WENDY ROBBINS

Further reading: Wendy Robbins Keitner, *Ralph Gustafson* (1979); Dermot McCarthy, *Ralph Gustafson and His Works* (1989).

GUTHRIE-SMITH, WILLIAM HERBERT (1861–1940)

New Zealand naturalist

Born at Helensburgh, Scotland, and educated at English schools, he immigrated to New Zealand in 1880 and, apart from occasional visits to Britain and ornithological excursions to various parts of New Zealand, his life after 1882 was spent farming his sheep station at Tutira in Hawkes Bay. He reported sympathetically on the avifauna of Tutira in *Birds of the Water, Wood and Waste* (1910), the first of his four ornithological books. Guthrie-Smith's powers of observation, developed from his need to understand how to manage his property effectively as well as his keen interest in natural history, are most fully displayed in *Tutira: The Story of a New Zealand Sheep Station* (1921; rev. 1953). It begins with the geological shaping of the landscape and proceeds to recount in detail the establishment of the 'primeval' vegetation, the period of Maori habitation, and the deleterious impact of introduced species — birds, sheep, plants, and colonists. The account is enlivened by Guthrie-Smith's rueful disclosures of his own inadvertent dislocations of the ecosystem, but the appeal of the work for New Zealanders undoubtedly lies in its microcosmic account of the ambiguities, even tragedies, of colonization, and the implicit autobiography of the colonist's acclimatization to the rhythms of a 'new' land. By the 1930s, *Tutira* was regarded as a classic of New Zealand literature. In general, Guthrie-Smith's oeuvre signals the change from topographical writing to an ecological perspective.

PETER GIBBONS

GUTTERIDGE, DON (1937–)

Canadian poet

Born in Point Edward, Ontario, Canada, he has lived and worked in southern Ontario (as a professor of education) for most of his life. The author of more than a dozen volumes of poetry and fiction, Gutteridge's reputation was made by his long poem *Riel: A Poem for Voices* (1968; rev. 1972), an ambitious work that incorporates documentary material within a lyric framework in order to reveal vividly and within a mythic dimension the figure of the Métis hero Louis Riel. *Riel* is part of a historical tetralogy that includes *Coppermine: The Quest for North* (1973), *Borderlands* (1975), and *Tecumseh* (1976).

In the late 1970s Gutteridge turned away from the poetic and fictional exploration of Canadian history and embarked on an autobiographical probing that he called 'true history'. In the poetic sequence *A True History of Lambton County* (1977) and in subsequent volumes he has paid particular attention to excavating his own life, particularly his childhood. Here again Gutteridge's aim is to augment fact and notation with the resonance of myth.

Gutteridge has acknowledged the influence on his work of **Northrop Frye**'s theory of literature as mythopoesis; he is also indebted generally to the approach to Canada and Canadian literature provided by **Margaret Atwood**'s *Survival: A Thematic Guide to Canadian Literature* (1972). *Riel* shows how a sense of myth, coupled with a strong historical subject, can result in significant poetry; *A True History of Lambton County* employs similar techniques and draws upon a sense of region that has characterized so much Canadian writing. These two strains — exploited most forcefully in contemporary writing by Irish poet Seamus Heaney — helped make Gutteridge a timely voice through the 1970s.

Despite his practice of interleaving lyrics with documentary material, Gutteridge's work is conventionally late modernist, using free verse in short-line, brief strophe sequences. While his confidence in language as a means for 'realizing' Canada conceptually and mythically is persuasive, his poetic project seems confined somewhat by its own phenomenological assumptions, by the particular nature of its mythopoeic romanticism, and, finally, by the conventionality of its language.

PATRICK HOLLAND

GUY, ROSA (1928–)

Trinidadian children's writer

Born Rosa Cuthbert in Diego Martin, Trinidad, she spent most of her childhood in Harlem, New York, USA, following her family's emigration there in 1932. Guy is primarily an author of young adult fiction. Her early work draws upon her experiences in New York, where African Americans and West Indian immigrants saw themselves as victims of poverty and racism. Guy has published thirteen major works of fiction, a play (*Venetian Blinds*, 1954), and a translation for young children of a fable by the Senegalese author Birago Diop as *Mother Crocodile: An Uncle Amadou Tale from Senegal* (1981) and edited *Children of Longing* (1970), a collection of responses by young African

Americans to their plight in the 1960s.

Throughout the 1940s Guy worked with the American Negro Theatre. Influenced by the activism of Black Garveyites, Martin Luther King, Jr., and Malcolm X, she began writing seriously in 1951 when she became founding president of the Harlem Writer's Guild, but her first book, *Bird at My Window*, was not published until 1966.

Though not overtly didactic, Guy's young-adult fiction, including *Mirror of Her Own* (1981), *My Love, My Love: or, The Peasant Girl* (1985), and *The Ups and Downs of Carl David III* (1989), is both entertaining and instructive. Readers can easily identify with the characters who, though black, have universal concerns. Focusing on her young protagonists' search for love and their struggles to cope with social and economic deprivation, Guy censures, often angrily, a society that permits discrimination. Her anger is in contrast to the pervasively gentler tone of **Michael Anthony**. In *Ruby* (1976), Ruby Cathy, whose family moved to Harlem from the West Indies, endures discrimination and social abuse. She finds love and security temporarily in a lesbian relationship, which Guy describes with openness and sensitivity.

Guy has also written a number of young adult mysteries. These novels, such as *New Guys Around the Block* (1983), whose protagonist is a street-smart young detective, examine problems of drug abuse, violence, crime, and the inability of adults to understand adolescents. Guy renders setting and experience with stark realism using authentic street language and Caribbean dialect.

SHARON RAMRAJ

Further reading: Jerry Norris, *Presenting Rosa Guy* (1988).

GWALA, MAFIKA PASCAL (1946–)

South African poet

He was born in Verulam, near Durban, South Africa, of an African father and a Coloured mother. He matriculated in 1965 from the Catholic high school in Inkamana, Natal, and read for his BA (law) at the segregated University of Zululand. Gwala dropped out of university after a year when he was labelled a communist by white lecturers because he challenged some of their ideas. He then worked in a variety of capacities: as a legal clerk, factory employee, secondary-school teacher, trade union organizer, free-lance reporter, and researcher. He was a founding member of Black Consciousness and worked for the movement in its Research and Publications Unit, with Stephen Biko and **Mongane Wally Serote**, and edited *Black Review* (1973). He became one of the movement's leading theoreticians and literary exponents.

Gwala's first poetry collection, *Jol'iinkomo* (1977), contains poems written mainly between 1969 and 1975. His work is critical of the black middle class for its ambivalence and opportunism. He is wary of its empty rhetoric — 'Hitler used socialist rhetoric and economic planning to fight socialism', he has stated — and what he describes as its 'dashiki cult'. In his poems Gwala also strives to 'dis-alienate' blacks by teaching them not to remain slaves to white archetypes and by urging them to stop seeing themselves in negative terms as non-Europeans, non-whites, and non-beings ('Black Status Seekers'). Other poems (such as 'Paper Curtains' and 'Election Pincers') expose the hoax that was South Africa's policy of separate development. Without rejecting western culture outright he asserts the primacy of his own cultural heritage ('The Children of Nonti').

His other collection, *No More Lullabies* (1982), contains poems written after 1976 and a few earlier ones. In poems such as *'Old Man Nxele's Remorse: 20 June 1976'* and 'The ABC Jig' Gwala responded to the Soweto massacre, the murder of Biko in police detention, and other atrocities perpetrated by the apartheid regime with a sense of outrage that was typical of the black community's response. The tone of the later poems is grimmer, as the political situation in South Africa deteriorated.

Gwala gradually drifted away from Black Consciousness, which emphasized the primacy of race, and came to embrace a class analysis. 'The South African struggle is a class struggle tubed into a racial pipeline,' he explained. He found himself increasingly at odds with Inkatha, led by Gatsha Buthelezi in Natal, and, when his life was endangered, fled the area in 1987 to take up a scholarship at the University of Manchester, England, to do post-graduate studies in politics and labour relations.

MBULELO VIZIKHUNGO MZAMANE

Further reading: Nadine Gordimer, *The Black Interpreters* (1973); Jacques Alvarez-Pereyre, *The Poetry of Commitment in South Africa* (1984).

H

HAGEDORN, JESSICA (1949–)
Filipino novelist, poet, dramatist
She was born in Manila, the Philippines. When she was twelve years old, her family moved to San Francisco, USA. She now lives with her husband and family in New York. She has made a reputation for herself as a performance artist, lyricist, dramatist, poet, and novelist. She has also worked as a radio commentator, screenwriter, and journalist.

Hagedorn began writing at an early age and, with the encouragement of Kenneth Rexroth, published her first poems in 1973 in a collection he edited, *Four Young Women: Poems. Dangerous Music* (1975), her first book of poetry and short fiction, combined powerful, lively, and biting language with dramatic and socially incisive wit. *Pet Food and Tropical Apparitions* (1981) included a novella, poems, and stories. Maxine Hong Kingston, Ntozake Gange, and Garland Jeffries were among those who hailed her strong, surprising clarity and captivating humour. Some of these early works were reprinted in *Danger and Beauty* (1993).

Hagedorn's flashy first novel *Dogeaters* (1992) catapulted her into the mainstream. It was nominated for the American National Book Award and garnered wide critical acclaim and phenomenal commercial success. This 'sharp-eyed, sharp-tongued', complex, richly detailed, imaginative and accomplished collage of a novel arrestingly conveys 'a world on quiet fire', in the words of John Updike. The plot lines and complex relationships of characters are woven together rather loosely and are often interrupted by bits and pieces of news reports (some actual, others fictional), extracts from historical documents and radio scripts, thus creating a chaotic pastiche in the postmodern manner. Unravelling the knotty plot through the use of multiple points of view, Hagedorn succeeds in bringing out the tragic, yet comic, elements of the fantastic but real world for the Manila of the Marcos era.

MA. TERESA LUZ DE MANUEL

HAGGARD, HENRY RIDER (1856–1925)
English novelist
Born among landed gentry at Bradenham, Norfolk, England, he was sent to South Africa at the age of nineteen; his eight years there inspired many of his fifty-eight romance tales. Experiences with the Zulu while under the fatherly Theophilus Shepstone, whom Haggard accompanied during the 1877 British annexation of the Transvaal, spawned his non-fictional book, *Cetywayo and His Neighbours* (1882).

The defence of imperialism in *Cetywayo and His Neighbours* is echoed in Haggard's fiction and in his autobiography, *The Days of My Life* (1926). Haggard is not unsympathetic towards the Africans, particularly if, like the Zulus, they appealed to his typically Victorian militarism. *Nada the Lily* (1892), for example, was a minor breakthrough in its projection of the Zulu point of view. However, in its simplified, archaic rendition of 'native speech' and its overlay of European motifs, it does not ring true, and the 'noble savage' hero Umslopogaas is more Viking than Zulu.

Haggard achieved immense popularity with *King Solomon's Mines* (1885). He inspired writers, from his close friend Rudyard Kipling through Bertram Mitford to Graham Greene, and manufactured an image of Africa often unquestioningly believed. His fiction, however, propagated the racial paternalism of his class, notably through his indestructible, two-dimensional hero, Allan Quatermain.

Haggard's eighteen tales of Quatermain indulge atavistic fantasies of searches for (significantly) fair-hued heroines, mythical cities, and sheer adventure in the face of 'stern policeman Fate'. Quatermain epitomizes imperialism's contradictions. He is cynical about the very occultism through which Haggard inscribes the irreducible mystery of Africa (critic Patrick Brantlinger calls this 'Imperial Gothic'); he spurns degenerate commercialism, but enriches himself with treasure; he is unrepentantly murderous of Africans but faultlessly, if bluffly, genteel towards fellow whites, chivalrously upholding the almost-misogynist morality of muscular Christianity.

Haggard's 'fine weird imagination', as his contemporary romancer R. L. Stevenson noted, generally redeemed his slapdash prose, though his final Zulu trilogy, concluding with *Finished* (1917), seems deadened by personal tragedy and forty frenetic years as traveller and agriculturalist.

DAN WYLIE

Further reading: Morton Cohen, *Rider Haggard: His Life and Work* (1968); Wendy Katz, *Rider Haggard and the Fiction of Empire* (1987).

HALEY, RUSSELL (1934–)

New Zealand poet, short-story writer, novelist

Born in Dewsbury, England, he grew up in Leeds before immigrating with his family to Australia in 1961. He moved to New Zealand in 1966. He holds an MA in English (1970) from the University of Auckland.

Haley published the poetry collections *The Walled Garden* (1972) and *On the Fault Line and Other Poems* (1977) before switching to short fiction with *The Sauna Bath Mysteries and Other Stories* (1978). Like the work of Australians **Murray Bail**, **John Tranter**, **John Forbes**, and **Michael Wilding**, Haley's fiction signals the emergence in New Zealand writing of postmodernist or 'New' fiction. The stories in *The Sauna Bath Mysteries* represent experience as an intellectual or perceptual puzzle, placing emphasis on the reader's role in constructing meaning.

The story collection *Real Illusions* (1984) remains in the postmodern mode, focusing on the construction of identity through family, place, history, and migration, referencing Haley's own past in a way similar to that of Australian **Frank Moorhouse**. Like Moorhouse, Haley uses discontinuous narrative, as in his collection *The Transfer Station* (1989), to suggest both perceptual complication and incomplete knowledge. His novels *The Settlement* (1986) and *Beside Myself* (1990) focus on male subjectivity and the construction of subjectivity in language. Difficult relationships with women and the subject's perception of contemporary culture also feature in Haley's narratives.

Haley co-edited with Susan Davis *The Penguin Book of Contemporary New Zealand Short Stories* (1989) and has written a biography of the artist Patrick Hanly — *Hanly: A New Zealand Artist* (1989).

LYDIA WEVERS

HALIBURTON, THOMAS CHANDLER (1796–1865)

Canadian humorist, historical writer

Born and educated in Windsor, Nova Scotia, Canada, where he lived most of his life, he practised law from 1821 to 1829 in Annapolis Royal, Nova Scotia. Haliburton served as MLA for Annapolis County from 1826 to 1829. After the death of his father in 1829, he accepted his father's position as an Inferior Court circuit judge, moved his family back to Windsor, and built 'Clifton', the family home. In 1841 Haliburton became a Supreme Court Judge, a position he held until he resigned in 1856. In 1856 he married Sarah Harriet

Hosier Williams, a widow. He lived the last years of his life in England and from 1859 to 1865 was Member of Parliament for Launceston in North Cornwall.

Haliburton's first two books — *A General Description of Nova Scotia* (1823) and his two-volume *History of Nova Scotia*, published by **Joseph Howe** in 1829 — describe Nova Scotia's past and present. Haliburton continued to publish works of a historical nature throughout his life, issuing *The Bubbles of Canada* (1839) in response to what he termed 'the present state of agitation in Lower Canada' and to the shortcomings of Lord Durham's mission to Canada. His *Rule and Misrule of the English in America* (1851) is an account of the development of the American colonies.

In 1835 twenty-one of Haliburton's sketches, 'Recollections of Nova Scotia', were serialized in Joseph Howe's newspaper *The Novascotian*. The completed series of sketches was published in 1836 as *The Clockmaker or, The Sayings and Doings of Samuel Slick, of Slickville*. Richard Bentley, the London publisher, pirated it, and Haliburton's international career as the creator of the Sam Slick sketches was launched.

Haliburton continued *The Clockmaker* in a second series in 1838 and a third series in 1840. The first three series detail the journeys on horseback around Nova Scotia of a loquacious Yankee pedlar, Samuel Slick, in the company of a resident, the Squire, who acts as narrator. British readers thought Slick an original. Haliburton's originality lay in bringing alive the stock figure of the 'Stage Yankee' and in creating for him a vigorous dialect, full of Americanisms.

In the following two series (two volumes each), entitled *The Attaché; or, Sam Slick in England* (1843, 1844), Sam visits England. Haliburton's strategy was to amuse first, then to deliver moral lessons on the proper relationship of England and her colonies — a relationship he later described very much in terms of the modern Commonwealth in the chapter entitled 'Colonial and Matrimonial Alliances' in *The Season-Ticket* (1860).

Haliburton first broke from the figure of Slick in *The Letter Bag of the Great Western* (1840), twenty-seven letters (most in dialect) from passengers and crew on the celebrated steamship the *Great Western*. In 1849 he published another work without Slick: *The Old Judge*; *or, Life in a Colony* (1849), now generally regarded as his finest achievement. *The Old Judge* is a fascinating, reflective, occasionally sentimental, but none the less impressive portrait of colonial life. The narrator, a visitor to Illinoo, Nova Scotia, has two local guides: Thomas Barclay, a lawyer, and old Judge Sandford. He eventually meets Stephen Richardson, a larger-than-life woodsman, whose tall tales energize the narrative.

Haliburton edited two three-volume collections of American humour for the British reading public: *Traits of American Humour* (1852) and *The Americans at Home* (1854). He also revived Sam Slick, successfully, in *Sam Slick's Wise Saws and Modern Instances* (1853), allowing Slick to relate the narrative himself as 'Commissioner of Fisheries on the Shores of the British Province'. The change in format helped considerably; Slick matures into a shrewd observer of human nature. *Nature and Human Nature* (1855) concludes the Sam Slick series.

After moving to England, Haliburton gave public speeches on the state of the North American colonies and tirelessly promoted investment in North America. His literary output was prodigious and the number of editions of his books in print during his lifetime phenomenal. Haliburton's posthumous reputation plunged in 1924 when V. L. O. Chittick labelled him a 'provincial Tory'. The assessment is somewhat mean-spirited. As the creator of the most famous comic Yankee of the day, Haliburton's fame was anything but provincial.

RICHARD A. DAVIES

Further reading: V. L. O. Chittick, *Thomas*

Chandler Haliburton ('Sam Slick'): A Study in Provincial Toryism (1924); Richard A. Davies, ed., *On Thomas Chandler Haliburton, Selected Criticism* (1979); Frank Tierney, ed., *The Thomas Chandler Haliburton Symposium* (1985); Richard A. Davies, ed., *The Letters of Thomas Chandler Haliburton* (1988).

HALL, RODNEY (1935–)

Australian poet, novelist, editor

Born in Solihull, Warwickshire, England, he immigrated in 1948 to Australia, where he was educated at Brisbane Boys' College and the University of Queensland. He was youth officer for the Australian Council for the Arts prior to its restructure in 1973, poetry editor (1967–78) of the *Australian*, and poetry adviser (1972–5) to publishers Angus and Robertson. Hall has edited several important collections of Australian verse, including *New Impulses in Australian Poetry* (1968, with **Thomas Shapcott**), *Poems from Prison* (1973), and *The Collins Book of Australian Poetry* (1981), which was the first anthology to include a significant proportion of Aboriginal writing. He has for a long period been actively involved in Aboriginal affairs. His writing has always demonstrated his social and political conviction.

Hall has been a prolific writer, initially as a poet and later a novelist and social observer. His chief verse publications are 'Statues and Lovers' (in *Four Poets*, 1962), *Penniless till Doomsday* (1962), *Forty Beads on a Hangman's Rope* (1963), *Eyewitness* (1967), *The Autobiography of a Gorgon* (1968), *The Law of Karma* (1968), *Heaven, in a Way* (1970), *Romulus and Remus* (1971), *A Soapbox Omnibus* (1973), *Selected Poems* (1975), *Black Bagatelles* (1978), and *The Most Beautiful World* (1981). His novels are *The Ship on the Coin* (1972), *A Place among People* (1975), *Just Relations* (1982), *Kisses of the Enemy* (1987), and *Captivity Captive* (1988). Other books include a monograph on the artist Andrew Sibley (1968), the text of the photographic collection *Australia: Image of a Nation* (1983), and *Journey Through Australia* (1988). His editing of two volumes of the posthumous poems of **Michael Dransfield** — *Voyage into Solitude* (1978) and *The Second Month of Spring* (1980) — were crucial to the full evaluation of that poet's work. In 1968 Hall was the first writer to be awarded a residency at the Australian National University in Canberra.

Hall's chief novels constitute his major claim to literary achievement. *Just Relations* was awarded the prestigious Miles Franklin Award, as well as the Barbara Ramsden Award and the Australian Natives' Association Literature Award in 1982. *Captivity Captive* was awarded the Victorian Premier's Literary Award in 1988. He was made a member of the Order of Australia in 1990.

From the outset of his writing career Hall adopted a quizzical, almost confrontational stance towards the reader, challenging expectations and assumed responses. His delight in virtuoso formal techniques and the use of persona added to the game in which the reader was taken as a fully operative participant. He fragmented lyric forms and responses into splinters, or 'progressions', that in poem sequences such as *The Law of Karma* foreshadow his later large-scale prose works in their use of (often savage) irony and an underlying satiric intensity. Perhaps his most remarkable poem sequence is *Black Bagatelles*, which achieves a sensuous immediacy coupled with a playful and dramatic intelligence in a series of virtuoso variations on the subject of death. It is a work that bears comparison with another verse sequence on the same subject published around the same time, **Bruce Beaver**'s *Death's Directives* (1978).

Hall's award-winning third novel, *Just Relations*, is one of the key works of Australian fiction in the 1980s; it gave Hall an international reputation and was the first Australian book to be included in *King Penguin* editions. Possibly as a result of this book and its two successors, *Kisses of the Enemy* and *Captivity Captive*, Hall has been more highly praised overseas than in Australia. Certainly *Kisses of the Enemy* was received with grudging praise in Australia, though it drew enthusiastic reviews in the USA. Its subject, an American-monitored political take-over of Australia, with military, economic, and social ramifications, is one that has little precedent in Australia, whereas overseas the influence of Gabriel García Márquez and other Latin American writers in such genres has long been prominent. *Captivity Captive*, however, was immediately acclaimed in Australia for its power, its originality, and its poetic intensity. It deals with an ingrown Irish pioneer family and a puzzling triple murder — based on a factual Queensland incident at the turn of the century. Hall's command of his material and the reader complements his love of virtuosity with a deeply felt exploration of the bonds of family and the nature of man's relationship with his environment.

THOMAS SHAPCOTT

Further reading: Jim Davidson, 'Rodney Hall' (Interview) *Meanjin* 40 (1981); 'Rodney Hall', in Martin Duwell and Laurie Hergenhan (eds) *The 'ALS' Guide to Australian Writers: A Bibliography 1963–1990* (1992).

HALL, ROGER LEIGHTON (1939–)

New Zealand dramatist

Born in Woodford Wells, Essex, England, he immigrated to New Zealand in 1958 where he received his tertiary education. He was an energetic contributor to television and stage revues before his emergence as the country's most commercially successful playwright with *Glide Time* (1977), which received fourteen productions in its first year. Hall has since been generous in his support of emergent writers through both his dramaturgy course at Otago University, New Zealand, and national theatre workshops.

Glide Time is largely satire directed against the New Zealand public service, but there is also a human drama of some complexity, skilfully foreshadowed in the earlier action, that becomes poignant towards the end. *Middle-Age Spread* (1978) is a domestic dinner-party comedy about a schoolteacher nervously in retreat from the only extra-marital relationship of his life (dramatized through flashbacks). As well as having many professional productions, the play was filmed and had a long West End run, which drew attention to the satirical, stylistic, and structural similarities between the work of Hall and that of British dramatist Alan Ayckbourn and the Australian **David Williamson**.

An underlying filament of social awareness is detectable even in *Glide Time*, but Hall had less success in developing this in his next plays. *State of the Play* (1979) shows a has-been dramatist heightening consciousnesses during a play-writing seminar, but seems fundamentally a dramatic cliché, while the comedy *Prisoners of Mother England* (1980) uses revue methods to satirize immigration. *Fifty-Fifty* (1982) is set in London, England, and is relatively subtle in its character portrayal, but Hall's propensity towards serious themes becomes overt in the short play 'The Rose' (premièred 1981), dealing with the 1981 Springbok rugby tour of New Zealand. 'Multiple Choice' (premièred 1984) is a serious critique of the educational system, and 'Dream of Sussex Downs' (premièred 1986) is a subtle study of English expatriates in New Zealand. However, in most of his later work Hall's undeniable gift as an entertainer has led him towards farce and musicals, notably in *Footrot Flats* (1984), a theatricalization of a local cartoon series.

That Hall is a shrewd observer and manipulator of his society is clear, for many of his plays appear to generate their own momentum: radio and television spin-offs from *Glide Time* continued for nearly ten years, while the stock-market farce,

'After the Crash' (premièred 1988), used the same characters as *The Share Club* (1988); they too had extended lives in television series.

HOWARD McNAUGHTON

HAMILTON, JUDITH (1952–)

Jamaican poet

Born in Spanish Town, St Catherine, Jamaica, she describes herself as 'emerged from the matrix of a loving, creative family' — her father once crafted fine furniture; an uncle writes poetry and is an accomplished photographer. It is that keen eye and sure sense of form that she brings to the re-creation of states of nature, her record of people and events, and her occasional social commentary. Her poems have appeared in journals and anthologies; *Rain Carvers* (1990) is her first collection. Hamilton's poetry is Eastern, haiku-like. (Her religious inclination is Eastern.) Utilizing both Creole and standard languages, it is spare, working simple powerful images to its purposes. Her poem 'epitaph' — 'house vacant. / tenant get im green / card' — manages historical reference, irony, humour, and social comment in eight words. In its economy Hamilton's poetry recalls **Mervyn Morris**' writing; in the power of its imagery, the work of **Anthony McNeill** — Hamilton cites both as influences. She also cites **Dennis Scott**, who directed her in Arthur Miller's play *The Crucible* when she was fourteen. The event proved a turning point in her life, leading her away from theatre to poetry. Occasionally there is a glimpse of the theatrical and the surreal in Hamilton's rendering of images, but Scott's influence is perhaps best seen in her careful lineation, something about which he was obsessive. The most persistent images in her poetry are light — as the promise of hope and the new — and the interplay of light and dark; these clearly derive from her religious focus.

PAMELA C. MORDECAI

HAN SUYIN (1917–)

Hong Kong novelist, historian

Born in Chengtu, Szechuen, China, to a Chinese father and a Belgian mother, she completed pre-medical education in China and continued her studies at the University of Brussels, Belgium. (She uses the pseudonym Han Suyin for her published works, but is also known by the name Mrs Elizabeth Comber.) In 1938 she returned to China, married an ex-Sandhurst Chinese officer, and practised midwifery in the Chinese interior during the Sino-Japanese War. This experience is the basis of her first novel, *Destination Chungking* (1942). Han later qualified as a medical doctor in London, England. After her husband was killed in 1947, she spent a year as house surgeon at the Royal Free Hospital before going to Hong Kong. There she wrote *A Many-Splendoured Thing* (1952), which established her reputation as a writer. The novel tells the tragic story of the love between a Eurasian female doctor and a British journalist.

Following the success of *A Many-Splendoured Thing*, Han published the novels *. . . and the Rain my Drink* (1956), *The Mountain Is Young* (1958), *Cast But One Shadow* (1962), *Winter Love* (1962), and *The Four Faces* (1963). Her best-known works of non-fiction are those that combine autobiography and Chinese history: *The Crippled Tree* (1965), *A Mortal Flower* (1966), *Birdless Summer* (1968), *My House Has Two Doors* (1980), and *Phoenix Harvest* (1980). Han has written voluminously on China and the Chinese, often intertwining her personal history with that of China, as in *China in the Year 2001* (1967) and *Asia Today, Two Outlooks* (1969). She has also written on Mao Tse-tung and on the Chinese Revolution, in *The Morning Deluge: Mao Tse Tung and the Chinese Revolution (1893–1953)* (1972) and *The Wind in the Tower: Mao Tse-Tung and the Chinese Revolution (1949–1975)* (1976).

MIMI CHAN

HANCOCK, SIR KEITH (1898–1988)
Australian historian
Born in Melbourne, Australia, he studied at the universities of Melbourne and Oxford, England, and held a post at the University of Western Australia before being appointed to the chair of modern history at the University of Adelaide, Australia, in 1926. In 1933 Hancock took up the chair of history at the University of Birmingham, England, and thereafter had a most distinguished academic career in England at Oxford and the University of London before his return to Australia in 1957, where he was for some time director of the Research School of Social Sciences in the Australian National University.

In common with a number of Australian historians of the period, Hancock's first substantial work, *Ricasoli and the Risorgimento in Tuscany* (1926), dealt with European circumstance. His second, *Australia* (1930), a single-volume account of the development of the nation, is still praised for its grasp of the essential processes, variously geographical, demographic, economic, social, by which an initially derivative society diverged from its metropolitan parent, and for the lucidity of its prose. Subsequently, Hancock massively extended this interest in colonial issues with his *Surveys of Commonwealth Affairs* (3 vols, 1937–42), with his extended advice on political and economic circumstances in Africa, with his directorship (1949–56) of the Institute of Commonwealth Studies at the University of London, and with his acclaimed two-volume biography of Jan Smuts, *The Sanguine Years, 1870–1919* (1962) and *The Fields of Force, 1919–1950* (1968). As his career indicates, though, Hancock saw himself equally as a citizen of the metropolis, a fact reflected in his long residence in England, in his work in the War Cabinet Offices (1941–5), in his editing the official histories of that war, and in his autobiographical *Country and Calling* (1954).

After his return to Australia, Hancock continued his memoirs with *Professing History* (1976), in which he reflected on a lifetime of writing and involvement in academic and public affairs. A dedicated ecologist, his interest shows strongly in *Discovering Monaro* (1972). Built on multidisciplinary footings, this eloquent evocation of the history and character of the high plains south of Canberra, Australia, that Hancock had come to love exhibits well his essential qualities as a historian.

ALAN FROST

HANRAHAN, BARBARA (1939–91)
Australian novelist, short-story writer
Born in Adelaide, Australia, she was by education and practice a painter and print-maker. In 'Beginnings', an autobiographical essay in *Eight Voices of the Eighties* (1979), edited by Gillian Whitlock, Hanrahan speaks about the development of her writing career when she was an expatriate in England during the late 1960s and the nostalgia for Australia that fuels all the early novels: *The Scent of Eucalyptus* (1973), *The Albatross Muff* (1977), and *Where the Queens All Strayed* (1978). She returned to live in Adelaide, explaining, 'I felt with **Janet Frame** that: "If a writer lives in exile and writes for ever of his native land, his work may fail to develop and mature, or it may be restricted to a narrow period of memory."' She writes about a girl growing up in the 1950s and leaving Adelaide to become an artist in England in a series of novels that become a loosely connected *Bildungsroman — The Scent of Eucalyptus*, *Sea Green* (1974), and *Kewpie Doll* (1984). Some critics have suggested that Hanrahan's most persistent attitude to Adelaide is the need to depart. However, this *Bildungsroman* can also be read as a post-colonial reckoning with 'home' and 'away', centre and periphery, in much the same manner as **Jessica Anderson**'s *Tirra Lirra by the River* (1978), or Canadian **Margaret Laurence**'s Manawaka series.

Like a number of other post-colonial women writers such as Janet Frame, **Margaret Atwood,** and **Audrey Thomas**, Hanrahan has used the gothic mode to represent home and domesticity. In particular, her descriptions of Adelaide, both in the novels and in essays such as 'Weird Adelaide' (*Eight Voices of the Eighties*), are reminiscent of Atwood's descriptions of Toronto, Canada — beneath a superficial conservatism and constraint lurk dark emotions and fantastic impulses. Like Frame and Atwood, Hanrahan frequently draws upon the child's perspective to escape the authoritarian view and enter the world of fantasy and subversion.

This pursuit of the non-heroic, the everyday, is particularly evident in *Annie Magdalene* (1985), which deliberately turns aside from 'the big things of history' and pursues the 'very small', the life of one obscure woman and the domestic culture of women in the working-class suburbs of Adelaide. Hanrahan suggested that in her pursuit of the regional, working-class voice of Annie she was influenced by what black women writers of the USA were doing — writing against the stereotypes and getting behind the silences. Many of the stories of the *Dream People* (1987) collection also pursue the small, private life. A number of publications appeared posthumously in 1992: a novel, *Good Night, Mr. Moon*, and the autobiographical works *Iris in Her Garden* (short stories) and *Michael and Me and the Sun*.

Hanrahan was a skilled artist with a number of exhibitions of her print-making in Australia and overseas to her credit. In her study of Hanrahan's prints, Alison Carroll argues that there is a close relationship between Hanrahan's writing and art. In both, women are usually the centre of interest in the work, and the child-like view is often privileged.

GILLIAN WHITLOCK

Further reading: Diana Brydon, 'Barbara Hanrahan's fantastic fiction', *Westerly* 3 (1982); Alison Carroll, *Barbara Hanrahan: Printmaker* (1987); Annette Stewart, 'Barbara Hanrahan's grotesquerie', *Quadrant* 32 (1988); Alrene Sykes, 'Barbara Hanrahan's novels', *Australian Literary Studies* 11 (1983).

HAQ, KAISER (1950–)
Bangladeshi poet
He was born in Dhaka, Pakistan (now in Bangladesh), attended Dhaka University and the University of Warwick, England, and teaches in the English Department of Dhaka University. Considered one of the best young poets in the former East Pakistan, he has continued to write both prose and poetry and since the early 1970s has developed a distinctive style and idiom in his work.

In his two published collections, *Starting Lines* (1978) and *A Little Ado* (1978), and in his poems published in *The Worlds of Muslim Imagination* (1986), edited by **Alamgir Hashmi**, Haq captures in a few lines the essentials of a social landscape, whose lineaments are drawn by a deep feeling for place and by a self-conscious relation to the poetic medium. 'Master Babu', for example, presents a series of shifts of language and brings out both the irony and pathos of the life of a schoolmaster as he conducts himself through his work and family life. Haq has written some moving poems about people, family, and place — 'Cousin Shamsu, Darzi', 'My Village and I', and 'Tourist Sahib', for example — and he gives them a living character through the subtlety of his close observation and the use of the specific spoken idiom. His general portraiture and humour resemble the manner of Pakistan's **Taufiq Rafat**, though Haq's material is more densely packed. Haq can also combine his derisive imagery with moving writing and unforgettable images of his country. His writing (published also in *London Magazine*) recalls such poems written in Indian English as Indian poet **Nissim Ezekiel**'s 'Goodbye Party for Miss Pushpa, T. S.' (in his *Hymns in Darkness*, 1976), but bears both a Bangladeshi stamp and Haq's larger social sympathies.

Haq is never unmindful of his poetic calling,

its compulsion, and its problems, and declares a fresh discipline for poets and their subject-matter; in 'Moon' this declaration is directed at the moon itself, ' . . . You don't belong / here, I tell it sharply.' Earlier in the same poem the general romantic attitude in the poetic tradition is undercut by a critical and self-mocking look at the writer himself: 'Self-immured, hands / to the head, elbows / on a creaking escritoire, / I've missed dinner to imagine / the real terrors behind rumours . . . '

Haq has edited the literary magazine *Form* (1982–6) and *Contemporary Indian Poetry* (1990) and has translated contemporary poetry from Bengali, including *Selected Poems of Shamsur Rahman* (1985). His occasional essays and his more recent biographical writing have also drawn considerable interest and include 'Forgotten Fred: A Portrait of Frederic Manning' (*London Magazine* Dec. 1983–Jan., 1984), 'More in the Water than in the Air: Notes from the 3rd Class World' (*London Magazine* April–May, 1986), and 'By the Crumbling Wall: Berlin Notes' (*Chapman*, Scotland, 61-2, 1990).

ALAMGIR HASHMI

HARBOURFRONT CENTRE (Canada)

Harbourfront Centre is an arts, cultural, and community centre in Toronto, Canada. It was formerly known as Harbourfront, a federally owned, non-profit Canadian crown corporation established in 1972 whose mandate was to provide cultural, educational, and recreational activities on 100 acres of land on Toronto's central waterfront. The corporation developed the site to include commercial and private real estate, with part of the revenue from the development subsidizing Harbourfront's varied cultural activities, often offered free to the public. Harbourfront Centre was formed on 1 January 1991 with the purpose of adapting the original mandate to the needs of the 1990s; it remains a non-profit organization.

The Centre's facilities include the 450-seat Premiere Dance Theatre; the 420-seat du Maurier Theatre Centre, used for music and theatre; and York Quay, home to ten performing and exhibition centres, including the Brigantine Room, where the Harbourfront Reading Series takes place. (The literary readings began in the early 1970s.) The first International Festival of Authors took place in 1980; under artistic director Greg Gatenby the annual festival has grown to become the most important event of its kind in the world (some two hundred writers gave readings in 1992–3) and the centrepiece of the Reading Series.

Harbourfront Centre attracts more than 3.5 million visitors annually, showcases some 450 community-based arts organizations, and hosts major international cultural events.

EUGENE BENSON

HARDY, FRANK (1917–)

Australian novelist, short-story writer

Born at Bacchus Marsh, Victoria, Australia, he has lived since 1937 in Melbourne and Sydney, Australia, and in France. Experience of rural work, unemployment, and Depression poverty provided material for *The Man from Clinkapella* (1951) and *Legends from Benson's Valley* (1963). These often-humorous stories also reveal his commitment to Communism — he joined the Communist Party in 1939 — and to versions of the laconic, stoic, or anti-authoritarian Australian character.

Hardy's first novel, *Power Without Glory* (1950), remains his best known, partly because of the court case that followed publication, in which he was charged with criminal libel. After a nine-month trial, Hardy was acquitted. *Power Without Glory* crosses documentary and fictional genres; centred on a man who rises to wealth and power, partly through criminal influence, it invites both local historical and general political readings. Its broad social canvas bears comparison with **Ralph**

de Boissière's *Crown Jewel* (1952); both authors were members of the Melbourne Realist Writers' Group.

Hardy's *Journey into the Future* (1952) — in the genre its title announces — recounts a trip to the Soviet Union. His later attitudes were revealed in controversial articles such as 'The Heirs of Stalin' (1969), published in *A Frank Hardy Swag* (1982).

Although *Power Without Glory* and Hardy's stories can be labelled social(ist) realism, his subsequent work develops distinctive stylistic and thematic concerns. Hardy returns obsessively — his word — to the story of the writing of *Power Without Glory* and the subsequent trial, most notably in *The Hard Way* (1961) and *Who Shot George Kirkland*? (1980). This 'rewriting-with-difference' thematizes the relation among fiction, truth, and history and among questions of political and artistic motivation, responsibility, and guilt. Hardy's works typically have multiple narrators and narratives, a fictional text and metatext, as in *The Four-Legged Lottery* (1958) and *But the Dead Are Many* (1975), a study of Marxist/Party intellectuals and his most complex novel.

Hardy's other works include an account of a strike by Aboriginal stockmen, *The Unlucky Australians* (1968), incorporating lengthy 'transcriptions' of Aboriginal English; *The Outcasts of Foolgarah* (1971); *The Obsession of Oscar Oswald* (1983); *The Loser Now Will Be Later to Win* (1985); and collections of yarns as told by Hardy's creation Billy Borker.

DAVID CARTER

HARLOW, ROBERT (1923–)

Canadian novelist

Born in Prince Rupert, British Columbia, Canada, he grew up in the mill town of Prince George. After four years as a pilot in the Royal Canadian Air Force, Harlow entered the University of British Columbia in 1945, where he studied creative writing with **Earle Birney**. On Birney's recommendation he was accepted into Paul Engle's Writers' Workshop at the University of Iowa, completing an MFA degree in 1950. In 1959 he founded *Prism International* (with Earle Birney and others). He joined the Canadian Broadcasting Corporation in 1951, but left in 1965 to head UBC's newly established creative writing department. He continued to teach at UBC until his retirement in 1988.

Like **Thomas Keneally** and **Patrick White**, Harlow is essentially a moralist. Contingency, moral ambiguity, sexuality, and violence are recurrent subjects in his novels. *Royal Murdoch* (1962), *A Gift of Echoes* (1965), and *Scann* (1972) explore the conflicts of a colonial society in transition. *Scann*, the most ambitious, starts from the assumption that fiction, like colonialism, is an attempt to control chaos by a process of expansion; the novel achieves a dialogic richness that resists closure. 'Only bad writers go in for endings. Or beginnings,' says the narrator, Scann. At the same time, 'The act of advancing, freeing, conquering, brings only the illusion of mastery over contingency while it distracts the mind from the certainty of tyranny and bondage.' In its insistence on the act of writing as a means of shaping experience, *Scann* is something of an anomaly for Harlow. The novels that follow — *Making Arrangements* (1978), *Paul Nolan* (1983), and *Felice: A Travelogue* (1985) — return to the linear realism of his first works. *Making Arrangements*, a comic foray into the *demi-monde* of the race track, lacks the seriousness and the subversiveness of true carnival. *The Saxophone Winter* (1988) is an intensely realized study of sexual awakening. Its adolescent hero gradually learns that teachers and parents are not always in control. The burning school that opens the novel images the contradictions of adult life: 'The violence of the fire inside the school was masked by the shell around it.'

HILDA L. THOMAS

HARPUR, CHARLES (1813–68)

Australian poet

Born in New South Wales, Australia, he was educated by his father, who was then the schoolmaster of the Government School at Windsor. Wide reading in English literature, especially poetry, gave Harpur an appreciative and critical understanding of language and aesthetics, and his involvement in the political and moral issues of colonial society prompted him to take the role of poet and prophet for the emerging nation. From 1833 to his death Harpur wrote more than 600 poems, including political satire critiquing events in Europe from a colonial perspective as well as urgent political and social issues of New South Wales. Among his major poems commemorating and celebrating colonial life are 'The Creek of the Four Graves', 'A Storm in the Mountains', 'The Bush Fire', 'A Coast View', and 'The Kangaroo Hunt'; his shorter, deftly original lyrics include 'A Mid-Summer Noon in the Australian Forest', 'A Musical Reminiscence', and 'To an Echo on the Banks of the Hunter'. Other works include *Thoughts: A Series of Sonnets* (1845), *The Bushrangers, A Play in Five Acts, and Other Poems* (1853), and *The Tower of the Dream* (1865).

Harpur's poetry, always endowed with an eclectic philosophical awareness, includes specifically metaphysical pieces such as 'The Witch of Hebron', 'The World and the Soul', and 'To a Comet', together with meditations on death and the permanence of the soul that have an idiosyncratic Christian resonance. His love poetry is often trite, but a sequence of thirty-four sonnets, 'Nora or Records of a Poet's Love', contains some sensitive lyrics.

Harpur, a committed Republican, left many prose essays, often on political and social issues and often attached as notes to poems; but there are several commentaries on aesthetics, including 'A Discourse on Poetry' and the prose notes to 'Poetical Studies or Rhymed Criticisms', a survey of English poets from Chaucer to Shelley. Knowing little about Aboriginal culture, he showed in his work an ambivalent relationship with the Aboriginal people, but he deplored their mistreatment by settlers in poems such as 'An Aboriginal Mother's Lament' and 'The Spectre of the Cattle Flat'. 'The Slave's Story' and his formidable five-act, blank verse play *Stalwart the Bushranger* (1987), inspired by the bushranger John Donohoe, embody his hatred of oppression.

ELIZABETH PERKINS

Further reading: James Normington-Rawling, *Charles Harpur, An Australian* (1962).

HARRIS, ALEXANDER (1805–74)

Australian writer

Born in London, England, he spent a secluded childhood in an atmosphere of non-conformist religion; during adolescence, however, he developed 'uncontrolled dissipation'. Harris enlisted in the Horse Guards, but deserted when reprimanded for having unsatisfactorily polished buttons; he absconded to Australia in 1825, possibly under an assumed name, thereby frustrating later attempts to validate his several and contradictory autobiographies. Articles written by Harris described his life in Australia as a series of diverse employments — clerking, sawmilling, shell-burning (for lime), and sundowning. Several close encounters with death in the bush directed his thoughts towards the 'Omniscient Manager of all things'. He returned to England in 1840, becoming a missionary to London's East End indigent.

Under the pseudonym An Emigrant Mechanic, Harris published *Settlers and Convicts; or, Recollections of Sixteen Years' Labour in the Australian Backwoods* (1847). For the English reader, he combined guidelines for prospective colonists with an account of an exciting and exotic new country, immediate because written in the first person. Frontier life in other British colonies engendered thematic (although hardly temperamental) analogies in the writings of **Susanna Moodie**, Isabella Aylmer, William Bartram, and Hugh Henry Brackenridge, for example. Harris amplifies his own experiences with related anecdotes and moralizations. The brutality of the penal system, corruption of the New South Wales police, the intemperate drinking habits of the colonists, and white extermination of the Aboriginal population are authorially and frequently damned.

Testimony to the Truth; or, The Autobiography of an Atheist (1848) — anonymous, autobiographical, religious in nature, and warmly commended by Charlotte Brontë — ignited greater public enthusiasm; in 1849 there followed a romantic fiction exploiting similar colonial material, *The Emigrant Family; or, The Story of an Australian Settler* (1849). Wholeheartedly part of the Anglophilic genre that **Joseph Furphy** would later denounce, this novel nevertheless includes an Australian-born hero, Reuben Kable.

In 1851 Harris immigrated to the USA, writing for the *Saturday Evening Post* (Philadelphia) a series of articles that, with sermons deleted, became his final autobiography, *The Secrets of Alexander Harris* (1961). During the American Civil War he settled in Canada; he died in Copeland, Ontario.

NOEL HENRICKSEN

HARRIS, CLAIRE (1937–)
Trinidadian/Canadian poet

Born in Port of Spain, Trinidad and Tobago, she has taken degrees at University College, Dublin, Ireland, at the University of the West Indies, Jamaica, and at the University of Nigeria, Lagos. She immigrated to Canada in 1966 to teach in Calgary, Alberta. Harris travels widely and participates actively in Alberta's literary community. Her volumes of poetry include *Fables from the Women's Quarters* (1984), *Translation into Fiction* (1984), *Travelling to Find a Remedy* (1986), *The Conception of Winter* (1988), and *Drawing Down a Daughter* (1992). She has received various awards, including the regional award (Americas) of the Commonwealth Poetry Prize (1985) for *Fables from the Women's Quarters*; her poems are often anthologized.

In a personal letter, Harris listed the influences on her work as, in addition to Fanon, Sartre, Césaire, bel hooks, and **Doris Lessing**, 'the great European surrealists and prose poem writers . . . among the French, Baudelaire, Rimbaud, and Claudel; among the Americans, Ashbery; among the Spaniards, Lorca, Alexandre, and Machado'. She writes that all of these influences had 'seeped into the soul before I was 16'. Harris' essays articulate the dilemma of being a black writer in Canada. For example, in an early version of the essay 'Working with/out a Net' (revised and published in *Crisis and Creativity in the New Literatures in English: Canada*, 1990, edited by Geoffrey Davis), she writes, ' . . . either one must abandon personal experience and personal myth to adopt the mythology and aesthetic of the larger society, or one must accept marginalisation.'

Harris' work is comparable to that of her Trinidadian compatriots **Marlene Nourbese Philip** and **Dionne Brand** in its engagement with the issues of racism, sexism, and the minority writer in Canada. Specifically, Harris' writing is a poetics of identity. Never simplistically autobiographical, her poetry articulates a search to find, through memories of the Caribbean, experiences of different cultures, ethical involvement in political issues, and, especially through the act of writing itself, a location for a self to occupy. The experience of expatriation is central; complexity of vision is constant.

Harris' poems are often experimental. Characteristic features are haikus, experiments with line length and prose poetry, and poems in which two approaches, usually factual and imaginative, to the same events appear in different forms on the same page. Poems enter into others' experience, whether that of family, Latin American revolutionaries, or a wide variety of women travelling or living in foreign cultures. Recently Harris has moved to longer narrative forms composed of lyrics, prose poetry, and prose. Probing and analytical, Harris' work examines the many hard choices available to any individual who would construct a conscious identity.

CAROL MORRELL

Further reading: Monty Reid, 'Choosing control: interview with Claire Harris', *Waves* 1 (1984); Barbara Godard, 'A writing of resistance: black women's writing in Canada', *Tessera* 12 (1992).

HARRIS, MAX (1921–)

Australian novelist, poet, editor

Born and educated in Adelaide, Australia, from his undergraduate days onwards he was a controversial and pivotal figure in several artistic and literary movements that promoted left-wing politics and radical experiments in expression. In later life Harris became more conservative, but the former strain of anarchic individualism still survives. Author of *The Vegetative Eye* (1943), a precocious experimental novel, and several volumes of verse, he edited or coedited the quarterly journal *Angry Penguins* (1940–6), *Ern Malley's Journal* (1952–5), *Australian Letters* (1957–68), and the *Australian Book Review* (1961–73, 1978–). As a broadcaster and regular newspaper columnist over many years Harris has become a national personality.

Both his novel and first two volumes of verse, *The Gift of Blood* (1940) and *Dramas from the Sky* (1942), illustrate a determination, not entirely successful, to assimilate European expressionism and surrealism. His main aim in *Angry Penguins* — with John Reed and Sidney Nolan — was to provide a cultural base for all advocates of change in the arts and society in opposition to the conservative forces that were as entrenched in Australia as in Canada and New Zealand in the 1940s. However, the **Ern Malley** hoax, of which he was the chief victim, arrested the modernist cause, and he did not publish his third volume of verse, *The Coorong and Other Poems*, until 1955. *A Window at Night* (1967) contains the best poems from earlier volumes, together with an introduction by fellow poet Robert Clark. A late volume with the mocking title *Poetic Gems* (1979) contains a typical blend of sardonic wit and disenchantment.

The publication of *The Vital Decade* (1968), a selection of writing and painting from the journal *Australian Letters*, clearly established for a wider public the innovative role of this journal. The various collections of Harris' journalism, including the aptly titled *The Angry Eye* (1973), illustrate his self-proclaimed role: 'trying to define what is happening in the Australian ethos at any given moment, and establishing what it means'. He is a colourful, maverick figure who has never fully discarded the anarchist stance he first championed in the 1940s after reading **George Woodcock** and Herbert Read.

JOHN COLMER

HARRIS, WILSON (1921–)

Guyanese novelist

Born in New Amsterdam, Guyana, he worked for many years as a surveyor in the South American interior. He immigrated to England in 1959 and married Margaret Whitaker, a Scottish writer. They lived for more than twenty years in London before moving to Essex. His experience in the rain forest greatly influenced his perception of the spirit of place in a land repeatedly invaded and peopled by different races. London provided the setting for the novels he wrote in the late 1970s and 1980s, although like the Guyanese novels, they illustrate the cross-culturalism of which he was one of the earliest exponents.

Harris' considerable opus — nineteen novels,

two volumes of novellas, four of criticism, and many essays — presents an unending exploration of humanity's psyche in dialogue with its eclipsed ancestry, with the landscape (a 'living text'), and with the vanished peoples — Amerindians and slaves — of Guyana's tragic past. His work explores humanity's inexhaustible potential for creativity and is an 'unfinished genesis of the imagination' whose regeneration, the central theme of all his fiction, he sees as the answer to the crises of the contemporary world. His novels range from the re-creation of the 'New World' conquest to the fictionalization of astronomical features, such as black holes, and quantum physics in an attempt to reconcile art and science and convey a perception of reality in keeping with our present-day understanding of the universe. They present humanity as capable of great imaginative and intellectual daring yet also very limited by a one-track mind and will-to-power.

Unlike **V. S. Naipaul**, who sees western myths as alien and irrelevant to the Caribbean because they are incompatible with its allegedly unheroic past, Harris sees them as the legacy of a common human ancestry and has re-created many of them through local personae in a Caribbean setting. His first novel, *Palace of the Peacock* (1960), the opening book of the *Guyana Quartet*, fictionalizes the West Indian and European myth of El Dorado, using it as a metaphor for the conquest of the 'new' world, the meeting between Europeans and dispossessed Amerindians, and the symbolic re-enactment of all conquering expeditions into the heartland of Guyana. The main character, Donne, evokes at once Renaissance ambition and the poet's imagination (**Derek Walcott**'s 'ancestral murderers and poets'), which could have produced a new kind of society. With his multiracial crew Donne pursues Amerindians on a dangerous river to get cheap labour for his plantation. Most of the crew die, and when Donne reaches the waterfall above which his Amerindian mistress and her people have taken refuge, the narrative is transformed into a visionary sequence in which Donne becomes at last fully conscious of the hell he has built. The resurrected crew and the Amerindian people are momentarily united in the 'Palace of the Peacock' and an alternative to disaster and enmity is offered through consciousness and imagination. By breaking the mould of ingrained prejudice and stasis, in spite of, and through, the resulting void, Harris suggests that the catastrophic past offered a largely neglected potential for reconciliation and development. He differs from other Caribbean writers in rejecting the notion of a distinct West Indian identity, which he considers as partial and limited.

Together with the *Quartet*'s other novels, *The Far Journey of Oudin* (1961), *The Whole Armour* (1962), and *The Secret Ladder* (1963), *Palace of the Peacock* emphasizes the need for a genuine multiracial community. Harris also differs from many Caribbean writers by rejecting realism because it is inadequate to render the 'dismembered psychical world' of the Caribbean and 'persuades' the reader that the selected elements it presents (historical and social situations, manners, fashionable conventions, and even moral attitudes) belong to an inevitable order of things.

After *Heartland* (1964), a sequel to the *Quartet*, his fiction — *The Eye of the Scarecrow* (1965), *The Waiting Room* (1967), *Tumatumari* (1968), *Ascent to Omai* (1970), and *Companions of the Day and Night* (1975) — becomes increasingly self-reflexive. It shows a double preoccupation with the state of loss incurred in the past and the kind of fiction the artist-narrator-protagonist attempts to conceive. The dynamic behind these novels is one of 're-vision' of both content and form as Harris creates a 'fiction that consumes its own biases': re-vision of an individual and historical past; re-vision of the make-up of characters, who form a nucleus of selves and are 'agents of personality' through whom the past is re-enacted while they progress by intuitive thrusts rather than participation in a conventional plot; re-vision also of their mode of perception and style through 'convertible imageries', protean metaphors whose meanings change with the protagonist's altering vision. This was to lead to 'the novel as painting' as illustrated in *Da Silva da Silva's Cultivated Wilderness* (1977) and its sequel *The Tree of the Sun* (1978), in which painting is an exploratory metaphor to grasp the 'inimitable'.

After *The Sleepers of Roraima* (1970) and *The Age of the Rainmakers* (1971), which reinterpret Amerindian myths and show that myth, as opposed to historiography, is a carrier of renewal and can 'breach the mimicry of fact', *Black Marsden* (1972) and *The Angel at the Gate* (1982) are informed by an inner movement towards otherness, though Harris always carefully shows that the deprived 'other' can become possessive in turn and dangerously hypnotic. The quest in which his characters are involved leads to disorientation and uncertainty as positive prerequisites to the transformation of the characters' apprehension of events. The narratives follow a pattern of dislocation and reconstruction, not in a linear process but in a canvas of partial crumblings interwoven with partial re-visions. The traditional forms of allegory, comedy, tragedy, and epic are also revised, particularly in his latest trilogy, *Carnival* (1985), *The Infinite Rehearsal* (1987), and *The Four Banks of the River of Space* (1990). The 'carnival' of individual life and history with its interplay of hiding and revelation is a 'divine comedy of existence' that shows the Inferno (here of the middle passage but also of the modern industrial state), Purgatorio, and Paradiso not as separate finite states but as fluid, overlapping categories, while 'carnival' allows for the repeated partial unmasking of the contradictory faces of reality. *The Infinite Rehearsal*, a phrase that epitomizes Harris' writing process and has greatly influenced recent post-colonial criticism, is a spiritual autobiography that 'rewrites' Goethe's *Faust* (associated with Quetzalcoatl) and presents the survival of modern civilization and the conception of a new kind of fiction as aspects of the same allegorical quest. *The Four Banks of the River of Space* explores the creative and regenerating potential of epic and myth as the figure of Ulysses, once a great and vengeful hero, is fragmented into several figures whose revisionary self-analysis makes more conciliating.

The originality of Harris' writing lies not only in his thought-provoking fiction but in his use of language and symbolism, the poetic density of his narratives, and their rich intertextual allusions. Like the masterpieces he revises, they are rooted in the 'unconscious' and the 'universal' imagination. The deep and genuine cross-culturalism of his writing makes him hard to classify. He belongs with the great innovators who make us look at our world in a new light and see it as a global landscape in which conflicts are interdependent but can only be solved through the individual consciousness and imagination.

HENA MAES-JELINEK

Further reading: Hena Maes-Jelinek, ed., *Wilson Harris: The Uncompromising Imagination* (1991).

HARRISON, SUSIE FRANCES (1859–1935)

Canadian poet, novelist, belletriste

Born Susie Frances Riley in Toronto, Canada, she was one of the most active members of the literary and musical life of the city in the late nineteenth century; she often published under the pseudonym Seranus.

The large theme that pervades Harrison's fiction and letters is the desire for a distinct Canadian literature; she uses Quebec society and culture, as well as the Canadian landscape, to epitomize the distinctions of Canada. She also defines the Canadian national character in relation to English characters (particularly in her short stories) and American characters (particularly in her novels), a common literary device of her day, in the tradition of Henry James. Harrison's novels are also concerned with the forces of Americanization that threaten to undermine the Canadian identity. In her poetry — *Pine, Rose and Fleur de Lis* (1891), for example — and several chapbooks, Harrison celebrates *habitant* life, favouring the French villanelle form.

The title story of the semi-autobiographical *Crowded Out and Other Sketches* (1886) presents in a dramatic first-person narrative the mental and spiritual deterioration of a Canadian writer, living in London, England, who is unsuccessful in finding an English publisher for his tales of French-Canadian life. The novel *The Forest of Bourg-Marie* (1898), set in Quebec, explores the lure of Canadians to the USA by the promise of financial reward, and the cultural deracination, corruption, and estrangement that result. *Ringfield* (1914) continues the theme of American corruption of Canadian values, this time through industrialization. The novel explores the dark side of male-female relations, particularly passion and obsession, in a *demi-monde* of decadence.

Harrison's letters reveal that she felt ignored or undervalued at home and abroad, illustrating the cultural insecurity of 'colonials' and of women in her day. In the 1920s she regretted that her contribution to the presentation of Quebec in English literature had been forgotten, superseded by writers such as **Duncan Campbell Scott** and William Henry Drummond. She was bitter that the modernists dismissed her writing, failing to see its accuracy and to appreciate its symbolic and romantic qualities.

CARRIE MacMILLAN

HARROWER, ELIZABETH (1928–)

Australian novelist, short-story writer

Born in Sydney, Australia, she spent her early years in the industrial town of Newcastle, which she vividly evokes in *The Long Prospect* (1958). Harrower studied psychology, worked in publishing, lived in London, England (1951–9), and is the author of numerous stories and four very distinguished novels, all published between 1957 and 1966. Essentially an urban writer with a sensitive insight into evil and paranoid states, she has been compared by early critics with **Patrick White** and later championed by feminists, who tend to simplify her complex vision by a too-rigid gender classification into male dominance and female passivity.

The short story 'The Beautiful Climate' offers a paradigm of Harrower's fictional universe, a world characterized by a conflict between people with a blind, insane desire for power and those who are doomed to be passive victims; some of the latter provide the innocent seeing eye: the daughter in the short story, the child Emily in *The Long Prospect*, and Clare in *The Watch Tower* (1966).

In her remarkable first novel, *Down in the City* (1957), Harrower establishes subtle links between place, climate, and states of mind. The figure of evil in the next novel, *The Long Prospect*, is a woman not a man, but in *The Catherine Wheel* (1960), which is set in London bed-sitterland, she again studies the conflict between male dominance and female suffering. Her fourth novel, *The Watch Tower*, is her masterpiece. The creation of Felix Shaw climaxes early studies and is comparable in subtlety with **Christina Stead**'s portrait of Sam in *The Man Who Loved Children*, except that Felix lacks any redeeming features. His bursts of petty pique and rage, his resentment of others' success, his dark nihilism, brutal aggression, latent homosexuality, and alcoholism all point to a profound psychic disorder. His passive wife illustrates the danger of acquiescent pity, while her sister Clare wins through to escape from this Australian Bluebeard's castle. What distinguishes all Harrower's writing is the combination of psychological insight into personal relations with an effortless expansion of this insight into a searching critique of modern urban society.

JOHN COLMER

HART, JULIA CATHERINE (1796–1867)

Canadian novelist

Born Julia Catherine Beckwith in Fredericton, Canada, she is best known as the author of *St. Ursula's Convent; or, The Nun of Canada* (1824). This two-volume novel, the first novel published in British North America written by a native-born author, is a highly episodic, moralistic, and romantic tale designed to be read aloud. Reflecting Hart's New England and French ancestry, *St. Ursula's Convent* is set in Quebec and Europe. Kidnappings, shipwrecks, exchanged infants, and characters of false identity make up this sensational yet sentimental story. Despite the seemingly complicated plot, the work is extremely well written.

Contemporary critics, failing to recognize *St. Ursula's Convent* as a novel for juveniles, dismissed it as the naive and sentimental outpouring of a colonial writer. It remains, however, an important literary artefact and an example of early nineteenth-century Canadian writing and reading tastes.

Hart's second published novel, *Tonnewonte; or The Adopted Son of America* (1824–5), was published in two volumes in three different editions in the USA. As in her first novel, the author examines two contrasting cultures, in this case those of France and New York state. The novel makes an appeal to American patriotic feelings by providing a contrast between the American democratic way of life and what Hart saw as class-conscious French society. Again her interest in life in the 'new world', its history and landscape, is evident. Hart completed a third novel, 'Edith; or, The Doom', which was never published. It has been well described as focusing 'on a family curse and its expiation during the time of the American Revolution'.

In the modest preface to her first novel Hart expressed her feelings about her country and its literature: 'it is gradually rising into notice . . . the time may come, when British America will be as noted in "song" or "deeds" as any kingdom of Europe; but to attain that eminence, she must cherish native genius in its humblest beginnings.'

DOUGLAS G. LOCHHEAD

Further reading: Douglas G. Lochhead, ed., *St. Ursula's Convent* (1824; rev. 1991).

HART, KEVIN (1954–)

Australian poet

Born in London, England, he was educated at the Australian National University; he teaches at Deakin University, Australia. Following graduation in philosophy, Hart spent eighteen months writing in Europe and the USA. His poetry — *Nebuchadnezzar: A Sequence of Poems* (1977), *The Departure* (1978), and *The Lines of the Hand: Poems 1976–9* (1981) — reflects this duality, balancing intelligence with deep feeling for the intimate and ordinary and drawing on recollections of working-class England and on his experiences as a migrant in Brisbane as well as on his philosophical reading. There is also a strong sense of tradition that is unusual in Australian poetry, a sense of being somehow on trial before the jury of the dead, 'queuing behind each one of us', and of the unborn, 'assembling in the jury room'. This makes not only for irony but for the poise with which Hart handles the religious feeling that informs his work, a feeling that runs from adolescent enthusiasm — watching 'the rim of dust / halo the silent city' and stepping 'into a day of grace' walking to the Missionary Baptist Church — to the later ambiguous but powerful belief expressed in a series of poems about the great 'god-haunted philosophers' — Spinoza, Pascal, Nietzsche, Martin Heidegger, and Dietrich Bonhoeffer. This religious feeling, however, is not at odds with his interest in the human, the historical, and the political evident in poems such as 'Prague 1968' and 'The Twenty-first-century'. For Hart, as for the German philosopher Ludwig Feuerbach, quoted in one of the epigrams to his second book, *The Departure*, 'only community constitutes humanity'. The God he believes in is part of that community 'in and out of history / like needle through cloth'.

Confessional and religious in its subject matter, Hart's poetry has none of the rawness of a Robert Lowell or a Sylvia Plath. Interested in form, master of coolly precise yet passionate language, he is concerned rather with 'the silence between words / that cannot bear then to burn alone'.

VERONICA BRADY

HART-SMITH, WILLIAM (1911–90)

Australian poet

Born in Tunbridge Wells, England, he lived in New Zealand (1923–36, 1948–62, 1978–90) and Australia (1936–48, 1962–78). His poetry is represented in anthologies of both countries, but he is known mainly as an Australian poet.

In 1932 a chance discovery of D. H. Lawrence's verse stimulated a passion for poetry. Moving to Sydney in 1936, Hart-Smith delighted in the local landscape and discovered **David Unaipon**'s retelling of Aboriginal legends. 'I was always looking for something basic and primitive,' he said, and his interest in romantic mysticism and animism led to poems that were published in the Jindyworobak anthologies. He became associated with the **Jindyworobak Movement**, co-editing an anthology in 1944. In 1943 Jindyworobak Publications published his first volume, *Columbus Goes West*, which contains a number of lyrics adopting Aboriginal personae as well as poems that, like 'La Perouse', consider the plight of the Aborigine in the modern industrial city.

The title poem, 'Columbus Goes West', provided the seed for Hart-Smith's most important work, first published by **Denis Glover**'s Caxton Press as *Christopher Columbus* (1948) and completed with the addition of 'The Death of Columbus' when the forty-three-poem sequence was published by Angus and Robertson in *Poems of Discovery* (1959). **Allen Curnow** criticized the 1948 sequence for presenting characters as 'exhibits rather than fellow-creatures'. Hart-Smith's interest in Columbus is not, however, for 'psychological realism' but in Columbus as a type of voyager who leaves 'materialistic Europe' for a visionary golden realm, who rounds the circle of West and East to discover the terrestrial paradise. 'He was an alchemist but didn't realise it,' Hart-Smith commented. The remarks indicate an abiding interest in mysticism that would lead Hart-Smith away from the Jindyworobaks, although he continued to draw upon Aboriginal legends.

Hart-Smith's poetry, praised for its precise imagism by **Judith Wright** and **Vivian Smith**, among others, has been better served than that of other Jindyworobaks, although his *Selected Poems 1936–1984* (1985) suffers the appalling fate of being organized alphabetically.

Hand to Hand: A Garnering (1991), edited by Barbara Petrie, contains Hart-Smith's own selection of his work. It also offers a bibliography, two interviews, and a number of essays on Hart-Smith, and nearly ninety of his poems previously unpublished in book form.

LAWRENCE BOURKE

HARWOOD, GWEN (1920–)

Australian poet

Born in Brisbane, Australia, she moved to Tasmania when she married in 1945 and has lived there ever since. Her first book, *Poems* (1963), marked the emergence of a mature and original poet who has continued to increase in stature with subsequent work. Trained as a musician, Harwood has written numerous works for music, including opera libretti, set by Australian composers. Many early poems published under pseudonyms —

Francis Geyer, Walter Lehmann, T. F. Kline, and Miriam Stone — have appeared under her own name in *Selected Poems* (1975; rev. 1990). Earlier books include *Poems, Volume Two* (1968), *The Lion's Bride* (1981), and *Bone Scan* (1988).

Music is a recurring motif in Harwood's poetry, whether in an early poem, 'Beethoven, 1798', the later 'New Music', dedicated to her operatic collaborator, the composer Larry Sitsky, or in a suite of four poems, each with a musical subtitle, called 'Divertimento'. Music — as an image of all art — is both a solace and a challenge. 'Only Mozart, perhaps, found the right tone / to make things bearable,' she writes in 'Beyond Metaphor'. An acute sense of the painfulness of life, which inevitably involves loss and sacrifice, is set against the capacity of art to 'make things bearable' — but not always. Art, especially for the practitioner, is therefore a challenge and a trial. Her own poetry continues to adhere loosely to an easy metrical formality that has grown increasingly colloquial while retaining many of poetry's traditionally 'musical' elements such as metre, stanzaic regularity, and an occasional use of rhyme or muted half-rhyme.

Music as an image of art is also central to a continuing series of poems about the exploits of Professor Kröte, an alcoholic ex-Viennese pianist and one-time prodigy now working as music teacher and occasional salon performer in Australia. Kröte appeared in Harwood's first book, but the theme of the tormented, frustrated, and failed artist adrift in a philistine world has also provoked his appearance in more recent collections. These poems are often occasions for accurate and at times very funny satire on the pretensions of the vulgarly 'arty' as well as the unleavened proletariat. But they are also gently critical of the comically pathetic Kröte himself, a second-rate, self-pitying artist who none the less knows and values art in a way that Australian society does not. In the more recent poems in which he figures, an ageing Kröte acquires pathos and dignity as he accepts his own failure as an artist and his own mediocrity, while those around him remain unaware of theirs.

Professor Eisenbart, a nuclear physicist, is another figure in Harwood's early poetry. Academically powerful, intellectually in command of forces that could destroy the world, Eisenbart would seem in stark contrast to the bumbling and often drunk Kröte. Both, however, are forced to face their shortcomings when confronted with youth — embodied in a young woman — and genuine artistic ability.

A continuing force in Harwood's poetry is the philosophy of Ludwig Wittgenstein, to whose *Tractatus* Harwood frequently alludes. Other German philosophers, such as Martin Heidegger, as well as European writers such as 'Hölderlin, Nerval, Lenz, Novalis, Trakl' ('Mappings of the Plane'), also figure in her poetry, which has an intellectually sharp concern with language and its relation to the world, and consequently with its own limitations and possibilities.

Pain and loss are frequent subjects but are as often redressed by a sense of fellowship with other intellectuals and artists such as the poet **James McAuley**, or by communion and sympathy with other women — her mother and grandmother, for example. Harwood's poetry shows great trust in the strength, endurance, and capacities of women, as in 'An Impromptu for Ann Jennings', a tribute to women who, contemplating their own lives and their children's, can claim that 'Time has given again / a hundredfold those lives that we surrendered'. More recent poetry moves from the suburban milieu of her first book to a quiet celebration of the natural landscape and its creatures, hearing in 'the seawind breathing . . . the pure, authentic speech / that earth alone can teach' ('Threshold'). This shift, however, is accompanied by no diminution in intellectual power and authority.

ANDREW TAYLOR

Further reading: 'Gwen Harwood', in Martin

Duwell and Laurie Hergenhan (eds) *The 'ALS' Guide to Australian Writers: A Bibliography 1963–1990* (1992).

HASHMI, (AURANGZEB) ALAMGIR (1951–)
Pakistani poet, critic
Born in Lahore, Pakistan, he holds degrees from the University of the Punjab and the University of Louisville, USA, and is a professor of English and Comparative Literature. As can be seen from his *Commonwealth Literature: An Essay towards the Re-definition of a Popular/Counter Culture* (1983), Hashmi is part of a modern, western-educated Pakistan that, by its knowledge of, and familiarity with, the wider world, finds itself threatened by reactionary fundamentalism and authoritarian forms of nationalism. Hashmi is a non-political writer whose poetry is concerned with the personal. For years his essays and writings — anthologized in *The Worlds of Muslim Imagination* (1986) — have demonstrated the variousness and tolerance of his Islamic heritage.

Although he has also written about western culture and literature, Hashmi's most important lectures and essays call attention to the richness and variety of classical and contemporary Pakistani and Muslim literature, whether in Persian, Urdu, English, or other languages. He edited *Pakistani Literature: The Contemporary English Writers* (2 vols, 1978; 2nd rev. ed., 1987), and his 1987 lecture 'A Groundnote for a Comparative and Common Study of English Literatures: Seven Hypotheses' (first published in his *The Commonwealth, Comparative Literature and the World*, 1988) argues for equal recognition of the non-European contribution to literary studies. He asserts that a truly decolonized perspective would not perpetuate theories of dependency in which the so-called Third World is constructed through European theory. When, in his lecture 'Muslim Literary Imagination and the Shape of the Contemporary World' (1988), Hashmi speaks of 'spiritual dialogue', it is to give emphasis to the liberal, humanistic side of Muslim literature, its inclusiveness rather than its exclusiveness. Whereas writers such as **Salman Rushdie** dramatize and heighten political, religious, ethnic, or ideological conflict, Hashmi keeps a low profile. He discusses significant issues without causing controversy and provides a useful corrective to simplified notions of nationalism and the relationship of the post-colonial world to contemporary European and American cultures.

Hashmi's poetry reflects his life and experience in Pakistan, the USA, and Switzerland. In *The Oath and Amen: Love Poems* (1976) he is haunted by a bilingual muse and contrived forms and language that translate and blend the traditions of the Urdu *ghazal* (originally a Persian poetic form) and English poetry. His American years are reflected in the long poem *America Is a Punjabi Word* (1979). Concerned with language and the conventions of poetry in different societies, it amusingly juxtaposes clichés of orientalism with the stereotypes of the west. American stereotypes of being 'on the road' are parodied as the speaker travels through the USA with the perspective of a Pakistani journeying with a camel (his muse and foreignness). It is an alien country seen as humorous analogy to the Islamic world: 'I was in New York. / I went up an / updated pyramid.' Hashmi brings to the language and the nakedness of American poetry his own sensibility; he considers himself to be like language — arbitrary, exiled from reality, like a camel in the USA.

In *My Second in Kentucky* (1981) the comic mask is often dropped to reveal a quiet sadness as the poet — nostalgic for Lahore and his family — is no longer at home anywhere. There is increasing obliqueness as modernist juxtaposition and the compression of the *ghazal* create a poetic, leaping sort of logic. Unusual expressions and purposely non-American English contribute to the feeling of exile and the ways in which language is associated with society and environment, as in the title poem: 'Shredded in the cold / winds of Kentucky for days, / women pass around incentive: / make bold.' The mood in the four *ghazals* is autumnal and associated with Lahore; they conclude with rejection: 'This place is too old for me. This sun is too old for me.'

Hashmi shares with St Lucian writer **Derek Walcott** a concern with the varied sources of the authentic self. The title poem of *This Time in Lahore* (1983) treats the temptation to make peace, to give up the quest, to settle for the possible rewards of the prodigal son. But during a visit home the poet notices that his father is unshaved, his mother greying, his own books worm-eaten and wet from the last monsoon, and the military now in command. Unlike the youthful joyfulness in earlier collections, *This Time in Lahore* celebrates the normality of failure, the impossibility of harmony. These poems are sober, determined, expressing the calm, knowing voice of experience; in 'Poem in Pakistan', for example, it is the poem itself that is important at the end of the day: 'I forget now what it was. / The poem is nevertheless.'

Many poems in *This Time in Lahore* refer to locations; the style flows naturally in a continuous movement as part of the thought. Hashmi's concern with time and place is shown in most titles of his books, including *Neither This Time/Nor That Place* (1984). Travel, age, time, storms, observing women, many cities, many countries, foreigners, writing poetry — there is a pattern in the mosaic. No place is the right place, no time is the right time for wholeness, unity, continuity, or Eden; but all places are the right place and time for experience, for consciousness, for poetry. 'Bahawalpurlog' (in *Neither This Time/Nor That Place*) brings together the vision scattered through these poems. Even at Panjnad — where Pakistan's five main rivers come together and which should be a symbol for a new unity, a new national language — the dust-storm blows, time silts the river, and the poet feels alienated. Language, like reality, exiles one from the unity of oneness, of belonging.

In *Inland and Other Poems* (1988), the speaker is often alone, isolated, usually in a romantic, picturesque place. He reads letters, comments wryly on books, and indulges in punning. There are fantasies about people discovered in newspaper stories, reflections on love and marriage, and self-mockery about his temporary celibacy while visiting Pakistan. While the volume begins with rejection and the oddments of a life without purpose, it builds towards renewal as the stories become comic and playful. The philosophical and psychological themes of Hashmi's mature poetry owe much to his years abroad; they speak of human experience across cultural and political boundaries.

The Poems of Alamgir Hashmi and *Sun and Moon and Other Poems* were published in 1992.

BRUCE KING

Further reading: Hina Babar Ali, 'Alamgir Hashmi's wandering soul', *Journal of South Asian Literature* 23 (1988); Bruce King, 'Alamgir Hashmi's poetry: Pakistan, modernity and language', The *Journal of Indian Writing in English: Writing in English From Pakistan, Sri Lanka and Bangladesh* 16-2 (1988); Michael Sharkey, 'Let's celebrate: Alamgir Hashmi's *My Second in Kentucky*', *New Literature Review* 15 (1988); Shaista Sonnu Sirajuddin, 'Three contemporary poets: a study of their use of language', *Explorations* (Lahore) 1 (1991).

HAU'OFA, EPELI (1939–)

Papua New Guinean novelist, short-story writer

Born in Salamo, Papua New Guinea, of Tongan missionary parents, he was educated in Papua New Guinea, Tonga, Fiji, Australia, and Canada. Hau'ofa's perspective is genuinely pan-Pacific and international. He is a trained social anthropologist who, during his field study in Trinidad for an MA from McGill University, Canada, was profoundly influenced by **V. S. Naipaul**'s early satirical writing. He completed a doctorate in anthropology at the Australian National University in 1975. Hau'ofa's dissatisfaction with anthropology and a fixed job is evident in his career: he started as senior tutor in anthropology at the University of the South Pacific's Centre for Applied Studies in Development; from 1978 to 1981 he was deputy secretary to the King of Tonga and the Keeper of the Palace Records; and since 1981 he has held various academic and administrative positions at the University of the South Pacific, finally being awarded a personal chair as professor in sociology. Hau'ofa's main ambition has been to write full-time.

Hau'ofa's early writing is non-fictional, comprising chiefly monographs that showed his predilection for subjects of general interest. He is the author of *Our Crowded Islands* (1977), *Corned Beef and Tapioca: A Report on the Food Distribution System in Tonga* (1979), and *Mekeo, Inequality and Ambivalence in a Village Society* (1981). Hau'ofa's objection to empiricist and rationalist thinking is expressed in an early poem, 'Blood in a Kava Bowl' (1976), and in his prose works *Tales of the Tikongs* (1983) and *Kisses in the Nederends* (1987).

In *Tales of the Tikongs*, Hau'ofa's first fictional work, the twelve tales are linked by the familiar subjects of racism, poverty, corruption, education, and Christianity and by the Thersites figure of Manu, who warns against progress and development in the fictional island state of Tiko: 'Tiko can't be developed until the ancient gods are killed.' Like **Albert Wendt**, Hau'ofa employs both oral and literate modes, but unlike Wendt's cold melancholic humour, Hau'ofa's style is characterized by exuberant Rabelaisian laughter, aimed at absurdities both in traditional culture and post-colonial life. His style consists of regional vignettes, drolls, jokes, tall tales, sketches, and brief essays.

Hau'ofa has been compared to Evelyn Waugh and **R. K. Narayan**. There are also interesting parallels between O. V. Vijayan's 'excremental satire' in *The Saga of Dharmapuri* (1988) and Hau'ofa's depiction of corruption and his protagonist's search for relief from the pain in his posterior in *Kisses in the Nederends*. The bizarre adventures of the novel's protagonist, Bomboki, allow the author to masquerade in institutions and conventions, both secular and sacred, and to turn them upside-down to create laughter as well as to comment on the pain created in the Pacific by colonialism and neo-colonialism. No authority or convention is spared, not even the author behind the narrator. The cyclical structure of the novel rejects any closure; the last line, 'Kiss my Arse', resonates and responds to the epigraph: 'What we call the beginning is often the end.'

SUBRAMANI

Further reading: Subramani, *South Pacific Literature* (1985); Subramani, Interview with Epeli Hau'ofa in *Landfall* 9 (1989).

HAY, WILLIAM GOSSE (1875–1945)

Australian novelist

Born into a well-to-do family, he grew up in Adelaide, Australia, and spent his life there and in nearby Victor Harbour, except for visits to Tasmania, the setting for most of his six novels. By nature (he was prickly and reclusive) and by historical placement at odds with the changing values of the turn of the century, he made his main themes out of isolation and the endurance required by dedication to his art in an unsympathetic colonial environment. His novels include *Stifled Laughter* (1901), *Herridge of Reality Swamp* (1907), *Captain Quadring* (1912), *Strabane of the Mulberry Hills* (1929), and *The Mystery of Alfred Doubt* (1937).

All Hay's heroes undergo a lonely ordeal. In his most notable novel, *The Escape of the Notorious Sir William Heans and the Mystery of Mr Daunt* (1919), the hero, a gentleman convict on parole in Hobart, moves through a world of menace that is unusual and powerful because it is ambiguous rather than overt. Heans undergoes an ordeal of consciousness that is not dramatized internally but rather deflected through symptomatic but ambiguous externals in which things may not be what they seem. If there is something of the colonial romancer's debt to Sir Walter Scott there is also an affinity with the psychological dualities, where outer threats echo inner ones, of Nathaniel Hawthorne and of the R. L. Stevenson of *The Master of Ballantrae*.

Like other post-colonial writers, Hay uses melodrama (with mixed success) and gothic to push towards extremes. He also uses a painstaking realism, but it is a transfiguring realism, full of overtones. Indeed Hay is again typical in that he reminds us that post-colonial writers have periodically rebelled against restrictions of realism on the one hand or against romance or romanticism on the other. Long before **Patrick White** scornfully dismissed 'dun-coloured offspring of journalistic realism', Hay aimed to raise Australian literature out of the desolate bog of boring novels of the paddock and stockyard variety, turning, as many before him and since, to Australia's ballad-like and tragic history. In the remarkable *Heans* he succeeded.

LAURIE HERGENHAN

HAZZARD, SHIRLEY (1931–)

Australian novelist, short-story writer

Born and educated in Sydney, Australia, she married the scholar Francis Steegmuller and settled in New York, USA, after travels with her parents to Hong Kong, New Zealand, Europe, and the USA. Hazzard worked as a secretary with the United Nations before becoming a full-time writer, and her UN experience formed the basis for her novel *People in Glass Houses* (1967) and for *Defeat of an Ideal* (1973), a critique of the UN.

Hazzard's collection of short stories and her four novels rarely touch Australian experience, being mainly concerned with morality and love in postwar Europe, England, and America. Her two short novels set in Italy, *The Evening of the Holiday* (1966) and *The Bay of Noon* (1970), follow an established tradition in which English or American women encounter the exotic and rich culture of Italy in the course of love affairs. Henry James, E. M. Forster, and the Australian novelist **Martin Boyd** have written in this tradition, though critic Algerina Neri has argued that Hazzard's novels are distinguished from these traditional Anglo-Saxon treatments of Italy by Hazzard's closer knowledge of Italians and their language and by the way in which Italian attitudes and values are essential to their plots.

Hazzard's longest novel, *The Transit of Venus* (1980), has attracted widespread critical attention for its complex discussion of love and the uncertainty of its expectation or consummation. In this novel, Hazzard presents love as a difficult moral question and an aspect of life in which even her best-intentioned characters make mistakes. Love is linked to natural disasters, war, and accidents of time and technology so that the novel leaves a sense of human fragility and powerlessness. Several critics have praised Hazzard's emphasis on the importance of individual morality in a chaotic and uncaring world, and some have placed her within the tradition of moral writing in English.

The critical debate about Hazzard's work stems largely from different readings of this placing of her work in traditions of high culture. Her stylish writing has won both admiration and the charge of over-deliberate self-consciousness. Her world is overwhelmingly middle-class, cultured, and international, and her moral position sometimes suggests a correspondingly conservative outlook. Paradoxically, it is the sheer elegance and control in her writing that has led to caution on the part of some critics.

Hazzard's work is richly allusive to other

English writers such as Thomas Hardy as well as to European writers such as Giacomo Leopardi. Yet this allusiveness tends to blur the specific historical context of her writing. Among her contemporaries she may have more in common with such English writers as Margaret Drabble than with North American or Australian writers.

SUSAN LEVER

Further reading: William J. Scheick, 'A bibliography of writings by Shirley Hazzard', *Texas Studies in Literature and Language* 25 (1983); Algerina Neri, 'Ripening in the sun: Shirley Hazzard's heroines in Italy', *Westerly* 28 (1983).

Head, Bessie (1937–86)

South African/Botswanan novelist, short-story writer

Born in Pietermaritzburg, South Africa, she was raised by foster parents and educated at a mission school; her illegitimacy, her mixed parentage, and the brutal manner in which these facts were revealed to her provided impetus for the themes of her writing. After four years teaching in South Africa and a short period writing for *Golden City Post* (she had a regular column for teenage readers called 'Home Post'), Head took up a teaching position in Botswana in 1964.

Head's work forms a closely knit corpus marked by consistent threads of autobiographical detail, characterization, and thematic preoccupation; yet, especially towards the end of her career, her writing shows considerable formal variety. In most of her work she is not directly concerned with colonialism or apartheid (exceptions are the handful of stories set in South Africa, the story 'Heaven is not Closed', and the account of Botswana's historical development in *Serowe, Village of the Rain Wind*, 1981). In the novel *Maru* (1971), Head condemns an institutionalized racism that predates colonialism — that of the Batswana for the San (Bushmen). In her short stories especially — *The Collector of Treasures and Other Botswana Village Tales* (1977), for example — she emphasizes the harshness of the land and the damaging impact of traditional observance of witchcraft and medicine murder. Central themes that run throughout Head's work include: the breakdown of the nuclear family in Botswana in the second half of the twentieth century (*Serowe*); the tyranny of a venal chieftaincy; the social transformation caused by the emergence of a bureaucratic and technical class after independence; and the repression of women.

In her first novel, *When Rain Clouds Gather* (1969), a black South African nationalist flees to Botswana; Head describes his responses, and those of a British agricultural expert, to the challenges of exile/expatriation and the attempt to establish a model farming project against opposition from the local chief. Maru, whose central character is a Masarwa (San) woman living in Botswana, employs an elaborate parallelism in narration and characterization, exploring racism, women's oppression, and the components of male identity through the interlocking love relations of two couples.

In *A Question of Power* (1974), her most complex novel, Head moves beyond the realist mode of *When Rain Clouds Gather*, employing emblematic action and a prose that often recalls D. H. Lawrence in its preference for short, firm statement and in its use of categorical abstractions and bald paradox. *A Question of Power* in a sense extends the themes of Head's first two novels. In a terrifyingly authentic account of mental breakdown, the central character, Elizabeth, a Coloured woman, experiences the fragmentation of her personality and its extension into the projected personae of two males, Dan and Sello, and their victims. Elizabeth's hallucinations reveal a complex of anxieties regarding gender roles, sexuality, race, and the status of the exile; the novel ends, however, with a persuasive demonstration of the disintegration of these anxieties and a realization of the ultimate power of selfless love.

The international success of *A Question of Power* was one factor in the long-delayed granting of Botswanan citizenship to Head in 1979. The last period of her life was one of relative stability and happiness; this is reflected in the confident projection of a community's shared aspiration in *Serowe*, a work that establishes a history of Botswana's development from approximately 1880 to 1970, through some fifty recorded interviews with citizens of the village in which Head settled. Her last novel, *A Bewitched Crossroad: An African Saga* (1984), also gives an account of Botswanan history. Two posthumous volumes (the contents overlap) gather together short stories not included in *The Collector of Treasures*, essays, and autobiographical sketches: *Tales of Tenderness and Power* (1989) and *A Woman Alone* (1990).

Head's work establishes a clear-eyed notation of brutality through a language that ranges from caustic sarcasm (dealing with religiosity and hypocrisy in the story 'The Village Saint' and with racism in the closing lines of *Maru*) to the directness of *A Question of Power*.

CHRIS DUNTON

Further reading: Lloyd W. Brown, *Women Writers in Black Africa* (1981); Lee Nichols, 'Bessie Head', in Lee Nichols (ed.) *Conversations with African Writers* (1981).

HEARNE, JOHN (1926–)

Jamaican novelist

He was born to Jamaican parents in Montreal, Canada. The family returned to Jamaica in 1928 and Hearne entered Jamaica College in 1937. He left Jamaica to join the Royal Air Force during the Second World War, after which he entered Edinburgh University, Scotland, to study history. He returned to Jamaica in 1950 to teach at Jamaica College, travelled to England for two years, returned to Calabar High School, Jamaica, until 1957, then went back to England until 1962. Hearne was resident tutor in the extra-mural department at the University of the West Indies from 1962 until 1967. From 1967 to 1974 he was secretary of the Creative Arts Centre (the university's theatre company) and since 1976 has been its director. He is a well-known columnist for *The Gleaner*.

Hearne's novels, unlike those of **George Lamming**, are concerned with the adjustments of middle-class individuals, sometimes intellectuals, to an evolving society on the verge of, or shortly after, national independence. His first novel, *Voices Under the Window* (1955), is concerned with a young 'brown' lawyer, Mark Lattimer, who has been fatally injured while rescuing a black boy during a riot. On his deathbed he recalls, through flashbacks, his loss of innocence — from the moment he is told by servants that he is not white, to that in which he commits himself politically and socially to the black working class and to his black mistress, Brysie. In this loosely written novel the major image is the gash, the gulley, the wound — the psychic wound that is never healed. (Lattimer dies of a massive haemorrhage as he recalls the killing of a boar in a gully in the Blue Mountains.) *Voices Under the Window* is unique among Hearne's novels in that political commitment is seen as more important than personal commitment.

In *Stranger at the Gate* (1956) another middle-class lawyer, Roy McKenzie, tries to start a communist party in Cayuna — the fictional island of the next four novels, which bears a striking resemblance to Jamaica. (In early Spanish maps, what became Port Royal was called Caguna, which in Spanish pronunciation is close to 'Cayuna'.) McKenzie gives his life as an act of political commitment, while Carl Brandt, a plantocrat who appears more importantly in later novels, embodies the outmoded ideals of decency, respect, and personal commitment. These ideals nevertheless become more important in Hearne's later work.

The Faces of Love (1957) concentrates on

romantic love as a means of finding what Hearne calls in his 1961 novel *Land of the Living* a 'territory the heart can occupy'. Lovelace (the cavalier poet?), an English expatriate, finds a home when he finds a woman who can return his love.

In *The Autumn Equinox* (1959) political commitment is represented by the American Jim Diver, who is in Cayuna to help the anti-Baptista revolution in Cuba. The novel's centre of intelligence and moral commentary, however, is the ageing Nicholas Stacey, a member of the plantocracy who has been involved in a number of earlier Latin American revolutions. His world-weary observations on politics are in no way disproved by Diver and in no way trouble the deep, almost incestuous relationship with his adopted daughter.

Land of the Living presents the most crucial political challenge of all of the Cayuna novels, as the central character, Stephan Mahler, an educated dispossessed Jew, feels a bond with the antagonist, black peasant Marcus (Garvey?) Heneky. Here, personal commitment massively outweighs political commitment. Unlike Lattimer, the white Mahler deserts his black mistress for a suitable match in terms of class and colour.

The Sure Salvation (1981) differs radically from Hearne's earlier novels in both form and content. The book's concern is the voyage of a slave ship, from Africa, across the middle passage, to South America. The form is deeply allegorical and symbolic. The only noble people here are the black slaves, especially Mtishta, whom the evil Reynolds attempts to seduce. *The Sure Salvation* is Hearne's most pessimistic book and perhaps his final comment on this flawed experiment that is the Caribbean. It contains no friendship, no redeeming love, but only the beginnings of chasms of race, class, and colour and the wasteful love of Hogarth, the captain, and his wife, Eliza. Hearne has also co-authored with **Morris Cargill** — under the joint pen-name John Morris — three thrillers: *Fever Grass* (1969), *The Candywine Development* (1970), and *The Checkerboard Caper* (1975).

BARRIE DAVIES

Further reading: Barrie Davies, 'The seekers', in Louis James (ed.) *The Islands in Between* (1968).

HEATH, ROY A. K. (1926–)
Guyanese novelist
Born Roy Aubrey Kelvin Heath in Georgetown, British Guiana (now Guyana), he attended Central High School and Queen's College there. Heath immigrated to London, England, in 1950, when **George Lamming** and **Sam Selvon** made the same journey, but he did not become known as a writer until two decades after his more famous fellow exiles. Heath read modern languages at the University of London. Upon graduation he began his long career in London teaching French. Although he studied law and was called to the bar both in England (1964) and in Guyana (1973), he never practised, preferring instead to remain a teacher at a London comprehensive school.

Heath writes in *Art and Experience* (1983) that it was Guyana's achievement of independence in 1966 that aroused in him the desire to become a writer. Paradoxically, however, although Heath's fiction has fed richly upon his obsessive and meticulous memories of Georgetown and the coastland, his novels cannot be called celebrations of the place and its people. They seem to reveal instead the failures and shameful inadequacies of individual and community. In *A Man Come Home* (1974), Foster raises the national flag each day, proud of his country's independence, but the flag flies over a household that is hopelessly divided and filled with violence and predatory sexuality. This is true of nearly all of the households in Heath's fiction, and there are those who would argue that in any case these ills accurately symbolize the political corruption and economic failure of post-independence Guyana.

It is clear that one of Heath's primary strategies is the use of irony. In *The Murderer* (1978) and in the Armstrong family trilogy — *From the Heat of the Day* (1979), *One Generation* (1981), and *Genetha* (1981) — the meticulous, realistic details of setting and action intensify the ironic lack of cause or motivation for the characters' behaviour and fate. It has been argued that Heath's writing is in the realm of tragic irony, the fiction of victims and scapegoats. Galton, in *The Murderer*, and the members of the Armstrong family, for example, are diminished characters, derided and victimized by large, anonymous forces that they do not understand.

In the novels the domestic household is the sinister locus of these destructive forces. Galton, for example, becomes disturbed as a child because of the way he is treated at home, and Armstrong's irritability at home and hostility against his wife (which are never explained) convey to the reader an oppressive sense of the power of historical forces and of the envy generated by class divisions in colonial Georgetown. In the works of other Caribbean writers these forces would be carefully defined, but in Heath they are not even stated. It is easier to understand the motives for the actions of Mrs Singh in *The Shadow Bride* (1988). As critic Jeff Robinson points out, she is an Indian matriarch in the mould of **V. S. Naipaul**'s Mrs Tulsi, who is denied the power and control, even over her own son, that her great wealth should ensure; she is also in revolt against a culture that requires submissiveness in women.

The victimization of women is another prominent theme in Heath's writing. Like the heroines of **Jean Rhys**, women in Heath's novels illustrate the ways in which they are doubly victimized — by society and by men. Maiden aunts, wives, mistresses, domestic servants, and prostitutes all share a common and unhappy dependence upon men. Mrs Singh rebels against this situation, Galton's mother takes cruel revenge upon her son, and Gladys Armstrong allows the moral deformity of the situation to infect her own personality; she tells one of the servants: 'Sometimes I feel like giving myself to the ugliest man that passes by.'

Except for *Kwaku* (1982), a novel much lighter in tone and one that strings together a number of fantastic stories in the manner of **Amos Tutuola**, Heath's work is reminiscent of that of **Edgar Mittelholzer**, especially in its treatment of sexuality and the fascination with the supernatural, elements that push the work of both novelists in the direction of the crudely sensational. *The Murderer*, which won the *Guardian* prize for fiction, however, is an accomplished psychological portrayal of a disturbed personality, and, despite flaws, the Armstrong family trilogy is an impressive artistic achievement.

MARK McWATT

Further reading: Mark McWatt, 'Tragic irony, the hero as victim: three novels of Roy A. K. Heath', in Erika Smilowitz and Roberta Knowles (eds) *Critical Issues in West Indian Literature* (1984); Mark McWatt, 'Wives and other victims in the novels of Roy A. K. Heath', in Carole Boyce Davies and Elaine Savory Fido (eds) *Out of the Kumbla* (1990).

HEAVYSEGE, CHARLES (1816–76)

Canadian poet, dramatist

The location of his birthplace is undocumented, but he was probably born near Liverpool, England. In 1853 he immigrated to Montreal, Canada, where he continued to work as a wood-carver, the trade he had practised in England; from 1860 he was employed as a journalist, an occupation with higher social status.

Heavysege's place in the Canadian canon is illustrative of literary history problems common to all Commonwealth countries. He was accepted as Canada's greatest writer in his own time only after his work had been praised abroad. In the mid-nineteenth century, when Canadian writing was perceived as part of the mainstream of English literature, a successful 'Canadian' author was one whose works were as good as those written elsewhere on similar, non-national themes. In the twentieth century his works have become the butt of satire (as in **Robertson Davies'** *Leaven of Malice*, 1954). Moreover, the fact that Heavysege had no formal education beyond the age of nine allows modern critics to regard his works as examples of a rough and primitive pioneer period.

Heavysege's principal publications include the poems *The Revolt of Tartarus* (1852), *Jephtha's Daughter* (1865), and *Jezebel* (1868); two dramas, *Saul* (1857) and *Count Filippo; or, The Unequal Marriage* (1860); and one novel, *The Advocate* (1865). The dominant characteristic of his works is a strong sense of drama. Even *The Advocate*, which is generally considered to be a pot-boiler, contains scenes and characters that linger in the memory. *Count Filippo*, with themes of marital jealousy, revenge, and seduction, is notable today for erotic imagery that was certainly uncommon in 1860. *Saul* was his most famous work in his own time, and remains so today. Critics have focused on the Byronic rebellion of the principal protagonist, a characteristic of many of Heavysege's works.

Heavysege was reported by one of his daughters as having a great love of the Canadian landscape, yet none of it is described in any of his drama or poetry. Only *The Advocate* is set in Canada. We do not know whether his use of classical and biblical subjects was the result of an inability to deal with the complexities of a new land in a creative way, or whether he simply accepted themes that the Canadian society of his day regarded as suitable.

MARY LU MacDONALD

Further reading: George Woodcock, 'Charles Heavysege (1816–1876)', in Robert Lecker, Jack David, and Ellen Quigley (eds) *Canadian Writers and Their Works* Poetry Series 1 (1988).

HELU THAMAN, KONAI (1946–)

Tongan poet

She was born and educated in Nuku'alofa, Tonga. She received a BA (1968) from the University of Auckland, New Zealand, an MA in international education (1984) from the University of California, USA, and a Ph.D. in education (1988) from the University of the South Pacific. She taught at Tonga High School before becoming a senior lecturer in education and a pro vice-chancellor at the University of the South Pacific.

Helu Thaman, the major poet in the South Pacific, has published four collections: *You, the Choice of My Parents* (1974), *Langakali* (1981), *Inselfeuer* (1986), and *Hingano* (1987). Four main themes recur in her verse: the valuing of Tongan tradition; regret at the passing of some of those traditions because of modernization; conflict between the individual's drives and society's demands for conformity; and the valuing of personal relationships. *'Ofa*, the Tongan equivalent of the Polynesian concept referred to as *aloha* in Hawaii, as *aroha* in Maori, and *alofa* in Samoa, Tokelau, and Tuvalu, is translated by Helu Thaman as 'kindness, concern, compassion, and other good feelings towards others'; this concept pervades her poems exploring personal relationships.

While Helu Thaman's criticism of the changes wrought by westernization links her voice with those of other Pacific poets, especially **Albert Wendt**, in his early and influential work, and **John Kasaipwalova**, hers is a sad rather than an angry voice. Furthermore, she also criticizes elements of Tongan tradition, such as the system of arranged marriage. Her work is rich in Pacific imagery. The flora of Tonga, for example, feature prominently as symbols. Hence the titles of her two collections: *Langakali* is derived from a culturally important, sweet-smelling flowering tree rarely found in Tonga today, and *hingano* is Tongan for the highly fragrant pandanus flower, closely associated with love (high-ranking women once used its dust to make themselves more attractive to men). Helu Thaman's recent unpublished work reveals her interest in writing verse for children and in such issues as literacy, women's rights, and the environment.

CLIFF BENSON

Further reading: K. Goodwin, 'A review of *Langakali* by Konai Helu Thaman', *SPAN: Journal of the South Pacific Association for Commonwealth Literature and Language Studies* 13 (1981).

HELWIG, DAVID (1938–)

Canadian novelist, poet, editor

Born and raised in Toronto, Canada, he has been associated with the city of Kingston, Canada, for most of his adult life. After studies at the University of Toronto (BA, 1960) and the University of Liverpool, England (MA, 1962), Helwig started teaching at Queen's University, Kingston, where he remained for nearly twenty years, with a brief break in the mid-1970s to act as literary manager at the Canadian Broadcasting Corporation. Since 1980 he has been working full-time as a professional writer.

In nearly two dozen books of poetry and fiction, Helwig has captured a loyal following. He is not among the best-known writers of his time, not through lack of talent, nor meagre output, but because his many fine works are so exquisitely low-key and intimate, quiet and precise, beautiful, muted, and strangely intricate that they command respect more than celebration, appreciation more than celebrity. It could also be that Helwig, in choosing to be associated with Kingston rather than Toronto and with small publishers rather than large, has intentionally placed himself on the margin.

It is ironic that a writer who is somewhat of an aesthetic populist remains at the edge of the mainstream. In *The Sign of the Gunman* (1969) and in the tetralogy of novels that includes *The Glass Knight* (1976), *Jennifer* (1979), *A Sound Like Laughter* (1983), and *The Bishop* (1986) he has consistently tried to write for the broadest readership possible, without compromising taste, intelligence, or art. The same impulse, perhaps, has led him more and more in his writing to stress fiction over poetry, although he is an accomplished poet.

Helwig has also edited a number of books. His collections of essays, *The Human Elements* (1978) and *The Human Elements II* (1981), gather almost at random a selection of pieces on Canadian culture, on the basis of their quality rather than for specific subject-matter or rhetorical position. His several short-story anthologies similarly display an eye for quality rather than a mind given to editorial adjudication. It is not for taste or judgement, however, but for his own creative sensitivity that Helwig ultimately deserves wider recognition.

JOHN MOSS

HENDRIKS, A. L. (1922–92)

Jamaican poet

Born in Kingston, Jamaica, to a Jamaican businessman father and a French mother, he was educated in Jamaica, except for a year at Ottershaw College in Surrey, England. His schooling at Ottershaw was cut short by the Second World War and he completed his studies in Jamaica. Hendriks also educated himself by reading widely. He worked as a sales manager and then general manager, successively, of each of the two broadcasting stations in Jamaica. He became director of Thomson Television International, of Caribbean Broadcasting of Barbados, and of Trinidad and Tobago Television. He retired in 1971 to devote his time exclusively to writing.

Widely travelled in the Caribbean, the UK, and the USA, Hendriks lived in Germany, France, Spain, and England. He was thus able to regard the Caribbean dispassionately; it should not be overlooked that none of his several wives were from the Caribbean. But Hendriks did not ignore his birthplace. His collections of poetry — *On This Mountain* (1965), *Muet* (1971), *These Green Is-*

lands (1971), *Madonna of the Unknown Nation* (1974), *The Naked Ghost* (1984), *The Islanders* (1984), *To Speak Simply* (1986), and *Check* (1988, written with the English poet Alan Harris) — include several poems set in the Caribbean and some in Jamaican dialect.

The frequently anthologized 'An Old Jamaican Woman Thinks about the Hereafter' (*On This Mountain*) shows Hendriks' humanity and his understanding of the mind of a simple, uneducated Jamaican. 'Jamaican Small Gal' (*To Speak Simply*) demonstrates his skilful handling of Jamaican dialect: 'Small gal, Jamaican, she came to me, / Said, "Lissen mi, Baas, Look what wi see! / Hard time dah ketch wi, eh Missa D?"'

In contrast with later work, Hendriks' earlier poems contain few examples of dialect verse, suggesting that he wished to be known as a poet rather than as a Caribbean poet. Having achieved that ambition he later seemed more willing to emphasize his roots. His versatility — and perhaps his French descent — is shown in 'St. Paul de Vence' (*The Islanders*), which he wrote in both English and French. Hendriks' poetry is distinguished by a nearly impeccable sense of rhythm and by a remarkable clarity. That so many of his poems have been chosen for inclusion in anthologies intended for use in schools is proof of the latter.

Hendriks was a poet of deep thought and one who put into practice what he wrote about poetry in the English poetry magazine *Agenda* 29 (1990):

> Unless verse is produced out of a compulsive and wholly irresistible need to relate the writer's vision of reality with the intention of bringing clarity of perception and delight in the real world to others, and expressed in terms that are skilful, significant and perceptible, not arcane or stultifying, then it is not the valid article; it is not poetry.

CEDRIC LINDO

HENNING, RACHEL (1826–1914)

Australian letter-writer

Born in Bristol, England, she is noted for her family letters, written between 1853 and 1882 but not published until 1952, when they were edited by David Adams in the ***Bulletin***, appearing in book form in 1963. The early letters are addressed to her brother and sister who immigrated to New South Wales, Australia, where Rachel joined them in 1854; the others record her journeys to England in 1856 and back to Australia in 1861, where she remained permanently, marrying Deighton Taylor. Some letters are written from her brother's Queensland property, and others from a variety of locations in NSW.

As a historical document, *The Letters of Rachel Henning* provides a wealth of information on pioneering domestic life from a middle-class, Anglo-oriented viewpoint. Henning writes about social attitudes, household tasks, the 'servant problem', gardening, and the difficulties of maintaining a fashionable appearance in the bush. But the letters are also a significant literary text. In her reading Henning sought to keep abreast of current English fiction and poetry, especially that of her favourite, Tennyson, and a keen literary sensibility informs her writing as she creates an image of herself and her new surroundings, while readers can observe how the author herself is gradually reconstructed by colonial experience.

Initially she finds Australia completely alien, comparing life there to a term of imprisonment. Gradually she adjusts to Australian life, however, eventually admitting her great enjoyment of 'the lovely climate, good health and free outdoor life that we have here', also acknowledging the beauty of the countryside while continuing to express nostalgia for the English landscape. Yet Henning never seems to have regarded herself as Australian, for even in 1877 she praises her Australian-born nephew for lacking 'the colonial coolness and assurance that we English all hate so'. The letters offer graphic insight into the deep ambivalence of colonial life in nineteenth-century Australia. (See also **Letters**, Australia.)

DOROTHY JONES

Further reading: Dorothy Jones, 'Ladies in the bush: Catharine Traill, Mary Barker and Rachel Henning', *SPAN* 21 (1985); Paul Hamilton and Dorothy Jones, '"Watering geraniums and feeding dogs": the letters of Rachel Henning', *Journal of Australian Studies* 19 (1986).

HENSHAW, JAMES ENE EWA (1924–)
Nigerian dramatist
Born in Calabar, eastern Nigeria, he was educated at King College, Onitsha, and at the National University of Ireland (1943–9), where he studied medicine. Following his return to Nigeria, Henshaw held senior positions as consultant and controller in the medical services and ministry of health.

Henshaw is one of the pioneer West African dramatists whose plays were performed prior to national independence. He favours progress and modernization and attacks corruption and tribalism, while at the same time wanting to reconcile the progressive, western-educated young with their traditionalist elders. In Henshaw's works progress usually wins, but consistently there is a happy ending allowing the elders to save face. *This is Our Chance* (1957, first performed in 1948 by an African students' association in Dublin, Ireland) attacks tribalism and prejudice against intertribal marriages. *Jewels of the Shrine*, the best one-act play in the 1953 All Nigeria Festival of the Arts, asks for respect and care for old people. Both plays are included, along with *A Man of Character*, which attacks bribery, corruption, and blackmail, in the collection of Henshaw plays *This is Our Chance*: *Three Plays from West Africa* (1957).

The title play in the collection *Children of the Goddess and Other Plays* (1964) portrays a conflict between Christian missionaries and a juju priest in a nineteenth-century African village. *Companion for a Chief* (in the same collection) criticizes the ritual killings accompanying the burial of important chiefs and might be contrasted to **Wole Soyinka**'s *Death and the King's Horseman* (1965). The third play in the collection, *Magic in the Blood*, satirizes the drunkenness and inefficiency of a village court and the privileges of African royalty.

Medicine for Love (1964, first produced in 1956 by the West African Drama Group in London, England) is a satire on polygamy, traditional medicine-men, and the bribery and corruption that accompany supposedly democratic elections in West Africa. *Dinner for Promotion* (1967) is a comedy about the newly rich, favouritism, and the ambitious who wine and dine their superiors. *Enough is Enough: A Play of the Nigerian Civil War* (1976) concerns prisoners and their guards during the Nigerian Civil War. Henshaw's most recent play is *A Song to Mary Charles* (*Irish Sister of Charity*) (1984).

BRUCE KING

HERBERT, CECIL LIONEL (1924–)
Trinidadian poet
Born in Belmont, Trinidad, he graduated in 1943 from Queen's Royal College, the Alma Mater of several distinguished Caribbean writers. Herbert trained with the Royal Air Force in Moncton, Canada. When the war ended he became a land surveyor for the Trinidadian government, a profession he still practises. Unlike several of his literary colleagues, Herbert did not immigrate to England, preferring instead to remain in Trinidad, where he found his poetic voice.

Herbert was one of several young and gifted writers who contributed to the Caribbean literary renaissance of the 1940s and 1950s. His poems, many of which were published in the journal *Bim* and later collected in 1981 as *The Poems of Cecil Herbert*, edited by Danielle Gianetti, show a disciplined fusion of tenor and form. His poetry marks an important departure from the gratuitous landscape painting of earlier Caribbean poets. While Herbert's imagery is sensuous, it does not degenerate into gratuitous voluptuousness, and his landscape, dominated by the Poui, Immortelle, and Saman trees, is charged with symbolic resonances. For Herbert, the Poui and its vibrant flowers, which appear only during the dry season, symbolize blossoming creativity as well as the survival and the regeneration of the Caribbean people.

Although they are rooted in a palpable Caribbean matrix, Herbert's sensibilities and themes — for instance, the loss of youth, and lust bearing its own implosive seed of death — transcend West Indianness. Furthermore, Herbert's skilful combination of intellectual honesty and emotional truth — perhaps his poetry's most engaging quality — assures him a solid place in the development of Caribbean poetry.

HAROLD BARRATT

Further reading: O. R. Dathorne, 'Introduction', in O. R. Dathorne (ed.) *Caribbean Verse: An Anthology* (1974); Paula Burnett, 'Introduction', in Paula Burnett (ed.) *The Penguin Book of Caribbean Verse* (1986).

HERBERT, JOHN (1926–)
Canadian dramatist
Born John Herbert Brundage in Toronto, Canada, he attended public schools (1932–43), the Ontario College of Art (1947–9), the New Play Society School of Drama (1955–8), and the National Ballet School (1958–60). Since 1960 he has been a playwright, actor, dancer, set and costume designer, prop man, lighting, stage and house manager, artistic director of Toronto's Adventure Theatre (1960–2) and New Venture Players (1962–5), founder of the Garret Theatre Studio (1965–70) and the Medusa Theatre Club (1972–4), and associate director of the Smile Company (1984). He was associate editor of the arts magazine *Onion* when it published his novel, *The House That Jack Built* (1975–6). Herbert has lectured intermittently on drama and writing at New College, University of Toronto, at Ryerson Polytechnical Institute, and the Three Schools of Art, Toronto.

Although Herbert has produced and directed many plays in Canada and the USA, he has published only three titles, all of which betray obvious American models: *Fortune and Men's Eyes* (1967), *Omphale and the Hero* (1974), and the anthology *Some Angry Summer Songs* (1976), which includes *Pearl Divers*, *Beer Room*, *Close Friends*, and *The Dinosaurs*. All explore the tensions and complexities of life on the margins (embodied most powerfully for Herbert in gay male relationships); most show the influence of Edward Albee, Eugene O'Neill, and Tennessee Williams.

Fortune and Men's Eyes is justifiably Herbert's greatest critical success. A prison drama of unusual intensity, it was adapted for film by Harvey Hart and released in 1971. Remarkably similar to the New Zealand play *Outside In* (1984) by Hilary Beaton, and reminiscent of the Australian plays by Jim McNeil, it is typical of the post-colonial prison play. Brutal, frank, and outrageous in its coarse punning and camp overacting, it develops a stinging social satire through incomparable verbal playfulness and inexhaustible literary parodies. Typically, it traces the entry, initiation, and corruption of a congenial adolescent, Smitty, inside the claustrophobic, hierarchical, predatory world of the prisoner community. The play presents a pointed allegory of an aggressive outer society, contaminated by its puritanical and capitalist neo-colonial legacies.

GARY BOIRE

Further reading: Ann P. Messenger, 'Damnation at Christmas: John Herbert's *Fortune and Men's Eyes*', in W. H. New (ed.) *Dramatists in Canada* (1972).

Herbert, Xavier (1901–84)
Australian novelist
Born at Port Hedland Walkaway, near Geraldton, Western Australia, he was wet-nursed by Aborigines. Mistreated by his parents, Herbert, an indifferent scholar, left school at the age of fourteen, subsequently qualified as a pharmacist, unsuccessfully attempted medicine, and began to write newspaper articles and short stories. While recurrently practising pharmacy and writing, Herbert took up numerous other vocations that were frequently the stuff of fiction — pearl fishing, crocodile hunting, superintending an Aboriginal compound, droving, and prospecting. In 1930, financed by money earned physicking gonorrhoea-infected Chinese in Darwin, Herbert sailed to London, England, where, in penurious circumstances, he wrote *Capricornia.* The book was rejected by London publishers because its 'Australian flavour' was 'too strong'. Moneyless and disillusioned, he returned to Australia in 1932, where, radically revised, *Capricornia* was finally published in 1938, winning the Commonwealth sesquicentenary literary competition and the Australian Literature Society's Gold Medal. *Capricornia* is an impetuous novel, savage and satirical, an examination of miscegenation and a damnation of social attitudes to Euraustralians or 'yeller-fellers'.

In 1942 Herbert served as sergeant, first in the North Australia Observer Unit, a guerrilla group prepared to discourage Japanese invasion of the sparsely inhabited northern Australian coast, and subsequently in British intelligence. *Soldiers' Women* (1961), an atypically urban novel, dramatizes and melodramatizes the love-lust spectrum among Australian women under the social pressures and distortions of the Second World War. Herbert's final novel, the 850,000-word *Poor Fellow My Country* (1975), combines themes of miscegenation and the pressure of war, from which combination issues an urgent nationalistic, anticolonial doctrine for his compatriots. In addition to his three novels, Herbert published an autobiography, *Disturbing Element* (1963); a collection of short stories, *Larger Than Life* (1963); and a novella, *Seven Emus* (1959).

For most of his life, Herbert avoided cities, preferring the frontiers of Australian society; he claimed to have prolonged the literary preoccupation in Australia with the Outback. Herbert's veneration of the 'unsettled' areas of his country and his correlative denunciation of its urban areas governed his bitter, scornful, and meiotic style and were fundamental to his nationalism.

In Herbert's vision, pre-European Australia was Edenic — his phrase *Terra Australis del Espiritu Santo* names the southern land of the holy spirit. In this land Aborigines lived as a simple brotherhood, practising natural communism, beneficiaries of the fecundity and luxuriance provided by the spirit of the land. Ultimately Herbert described the spirit as the Koonapippi-Tchamala dyad, representing creativity and destructiveness, order and chaos, and surrounded by a pantheon, the whole spiritually galvanizing Australia. This perception is analogous to the creed of the **Jindyworobak Movement**: Aborigines are at the core of a workable nationalism. Herbert's observations echo those of D. H. Lawrence, although Herbert had never read *Kangaroo.*

Into this Australian paradise, Herbert argues, entered the 'disturbing element', the immigrant, with his alien institutions, mythology, legends, and deities. Herbert's writing lives through the tension between the inherent and indestructible national spirituality and the exploitative materialism of the colonizers. Herbert originally saw resolution in the creation of a creole nation through which immigrants might be transmuted into Australians, and the British colony into a near-utopian nation. In life, he inaugurated a Euraustralian League in 1936; in fiction, he enthusiastically advocated miscegenation, lamenting the progressive persecution, dispossession, and consequent desacralization of part-Aborigines, which eroded their noble spirituality. In Herbert's fiction, European dispossession of Aborigines is thematically central. Colonization of Australia, he argues, began with bloody massacre and invasion; it continued when pastoralists occupied Aboriginal land and spoiled their hunting grounds; throughout Australian history Aborigines were infected, raped, enslaved, and demoralized. The persistence of colonialism and rejection of nationhood were indicated by the continued exploitation and subordination of Aboriginal people and the refusal of white Australians to acknowledge their corporate guilt. Herbert's lifelong advocacy on behalf of the Aborigines had a nationalistic as well as a humanitarian basis. He believed that his writing was, in this regard, effective and that '*Capricornia* did in Australia what *Uncle Tom's Cabin* did in the United States'.

The establishment of the Commonwealth of Australia in 1901, in Herbert's view, offered the 'Australia Felix people' a second utopian opportunity — integrity with their country 'by right of vision'. The colonial mentality, however, extinguished the national potential with Australia's commitment to Britain's war in 1914. Herbert's conception of the 'true Commonwealth', whenever it might emerge, owed much to American subliterati such as Edward Bellamy or Henry George. Its government was socialist and republican; its policy, isolationist and anti-imperialist; and the object, the common good of all patriots.

Contrasting the true commonwealth with Australian reality, Herbert became bitter, misanthropic, and negativistic. The animus of his sustained hatred was colonialism, inherent in such bulwarks of continuing Anglocentricity as institutionalized Christianity, reverence for the British monarchy, and Australia's participation in international political movements. Herbert's Anglophobia did not blunt his attack on the colonizing intentions of the USA through economic imperialism, or of Russia through political expansion. British indicators of Australia's colonial status, however, were ubiquitous — absentee landlordism, aristocracy, architecture, and even clothing — and Herbert excoriated them. As strong as his Anglophobia was Herbert's detestation of Australians too apathetic to grasp independence, at the cost of rebellion if necessary.

Herbert's work shows little aesthetic stasis, but much didactic kinesis. Critic John McLaren suggests that 'in its intentions and achievements' it is in the tradition of the eighteenth-century controversialists. Herbert's writing is erosive, his humour sardonic, the satire acidic. His is a demythologizing literature, sparing the legends of neither Anzac nor Eureka, violent and iconoclastic, destructively critical of his society. The didactic aim of his negativism was 'to create so much despair that positive people will be driven to rectify the anomalies of the reality'.

Formally and didactically, Herbert's fiction is Australocentric. Thematically, it is his quest for *Terra Australis del Espiritu Santo.*

NOEL HENRICKSEN

Further reading: Harry Heseltine, *Xavier Herbert* (1973); Marianne Ehrhardt and Lurline Stuart, 'Xavier Herbert: a checklist', *Australian Literary Studies* 8 (1978); Laurie Clancy, *Xavier Herbert* (1981); John McLaren, *Xavier Herbert's 'Capricornia' and 'Poor Fellow My Country'* (1981).

HERCULES, FRANK E. M. (1917–)
Trinidadian novelist
He was born in San Fernando, Trinidad and Tobago, and educated in Trinidad and England, where he read law. He immigrated to the USA in the 1940s, becoming a US citizen in 1959. Hercules has published the novels *Where the Hummingbird Flies* (1961), *I Want a Black Doll* (1967), and *On Leaving Paradise* (1980), as well as a non-fiction study, *American Society and Black Revolution* (1972), and various articles. As a result of the variety of influences on his life, Hercules brings to his writing an objectivity and global

sensibility that inform his subject-matter and allow him to report with expertise, in both his fiction and non-fiction, on sociological and psychological conditions in the Caribbean and the USA.

Hercules' work falls into the broad categories of Caribbean experience and African-American experience. He makes English colonialism in the Caribbean his subject-matter in both *Where the Hummingbird Flies* and *On Leaving Paradise*. In the former novel Hercules addresses the ills of imperialism and points to the need and potential for change. In *On Leaving Paradise*, however, he depicts the disintegration of colonialism and the rise of a healthy Caribbean identity. In the evolution of his treatment of this issue, Hercules may be compared to **Chinua Achebe**, whose fiction also depicts a society's progress from its colonial beginnings to its development of an autonomous national character. Hercules' African-American concerns are expressed in *I Want a Black Doll* and *American Society and Black Revolution*, which focus on the devastating effects of racism.

Critics have responded favourably to Hercules' recording of the human condition, rendered in a Juvenalian mode. Hercules is to be celebrated for his expression of a humanistic vision and for his political insight.

CAROL P. MARSH-LOCKETT

Further reading: Carol P. Marsh, 'Frank E. M. Hercules', in Daryl C. Dance (ed.) *Fifty Caribbean Writers: A Bio-bibliographical Critical Sourcebook* (1986).

HERENIKO, VILSONI TAUSIE (1954–)

South Pacific dramatist

He was born Vilsoni Tausie on the Polynesian island of Rotuma, a somewhat reluctant member of the Fiji group. (He took on his father's surname following the elder Hereniko's death.) After attending the University of the South Pacific in Fiji (BA, 1977), he studied under one of the major pioneers in drama-in-education, Dorothy Heathcote, at the University of Newcastle-upon-Tyne, England (1982). He returned to the University of the South Pacific, where he taught and completed a Ph.D. on the traditional Rotuman clown. Hereniko was appointed to the University of Hawaii, USA, in 1991 and is probably the best known of the small group of South Pacific playwrights writing in English.

Hereniko, ultimately, is a moralist in whose plays personal decisions must be made in the context of social paradox. He has published four full-length plays and produced several one-act plays. *Don't Cry, Mama* (1977, under the name Vilsoni Tausie; repr. 1986, under the name Vilsoni Tausie Hereniko), written while he was at university, presents an upwardly mobile, recently urbanized family, imitating manners it only partially understands and fixed upon material acquisitions as emblems of social achievement. *The Monster and Other Plays* (1989) contains the early one-act plays *One Family*, *Hanisi Ofien* ('Love Has Gone'), *The Scarecrow*, and *Good Morning Class*.

A Child for Iva (1981, published under the name Vilsoni Tausie) explores ethnic and generational differences, arranged marriages, and infanticide. In *Sera's Choice* (1986), two undergraduates — a Fijian woman and an Indo-Fijian man — decide to marry and to transgress the unyielding social barriers that pattern the social map of Fiji.

The 1987 *coup d'état* in Fiji jolted Hereniko out of a preoccupation with domestic issues and produced what is probably his most intensive stage piece, the one-act *The Monster*. Part parable, part Beckett, the play presents an inter-ethnic friendship under attack by a destructive militaristic creature. *The Shadow*, first performed with *The Monster* in 1987, was a return to domestic realism with the familiar Fiji dilemma of a woman whose husband has just returned from an extended stay as part of the United Nations peace-keeping force in the Middle East.

In *The Last Virgin in Paradise* (1991) Hereniko takes a comic swipe at the responses of both tourists and Eurocentric foreign social researchers to Polynesian society and culture.

ANDREW HORN

HEWETT, DOROTHY (1923–)
Australian dramatist, poet

Born in Wickepin, Western Australia, she grew up on her father's farm in the isolated wheat belt and was educated by correspondence. When she moved to Perth to further her education, she also dramatically furthered her life experience to include sexual experimentation and membership in the Communist Party. As was said of her bestselling volume, *Wild Card: An Autobiography* 1923–1958 (1990), 'Hewett has lived out a soap opera of a life. If she were a man, her life would be described as Rabelaisian, and she, a hell-raiser.' Hewett moved to Sydney in 1948. Her novel *Bobbin Up* (1959), based on her factory experiences, was reprinted in Virago Modern Classics in 1985. Because much of her writing — in prose, drama, and poetry — has been based on personal experience, this has led to instances of legal action instigated by her first husband, the Western Australian writer Lloyd Davies.

Regarded for many years as a colourful figure on the periphery of Australian writing, Hewett has become increasingly recognized as a major figure whose work stands in contradistinction to many of the literary developments in poetry and drama that have tended to be seen in relation only to male practitioners. Her essentially lyrical voice, her use of myth and archetype, and her freely rhapsodic games with time and persona relate her to a view of creativity that was at one time unfashionable, but which is increasingly accepted as an alternative to 'dun realism' (**Patrick White**'s phrase) and psychological 'micropinning'. Because Hewett's writing, while maintaining lyrical subjectivity, has constantly explored ways of approach and an endless series of masks or projections, its lyric base has accrued an astonishing elasticity. The sum of her achievements is in many ways greater than the individual parts. Hewett forced into the post-Brechtian world of Australian drama of the early 1970s a less cut-out political stance, plangent rather than strident; her acknowledged masterpiece in this genre is *The Man from Mukinupin* (1979). Her other plays include: *This Old Man Comes Rolling Home* (1976), *The Chapel Perilous* (1972, banned in Western Australia but widely used as a teaching text elsewhere), *Bon-Bons and Roses for Dolly* (1976), *The Tatty Hollow Story* (1976), 'Joan' (premièred 1975), *The Golden Oldies* (1976), *Susannah's Dreaming* (1981), and 'Fields of Heaven' (premièred 1982). *Golden Valley* and *Song of the Seals* were published in the volume *Golden Valley, Song of the Seals* (1985). Hewett wrote the libretto for the 1983 opera 'Christina's World' by Ross Edwards, premièred by the Seymour Group in Sydney.

Hewett's collections of verse are *What About the People* (1961, with her husband, Merv Lilley), *Windmill Country* (1968), *Rapunzel in Suburbia* (1975), *Greenhouse* (1979), *Alice in Wormland* (1987), and her *Selected Poems: A Tremendous World in her Head* (1989).

Although she has not been a prolific poet, Hewett established with *Rapunzel in Suburbia* not only a *succès-de-scandale* but an important breakthrough in technical command, influenced to a certain extent by the writings of Anne Sexton and contemporary American poets who came into her field of reference through her association with **Robert Adamson** and his Sydney magazine *New Poetry*. The scandal related to one poem from that collection, 'Uninvited Guest', because of which her former husband took legal action; a second printing, omitting the poem, had to be published. Hewett's later verse collections demonstrate an exhilarating increase in sweep and dramatic power as well as a playful, satiric, and sensual energy that has no parallel in Australian literature. A sometimes reckless willingness to take risks pays off in these poems, where eloquence and passion are counterpointed by a hard-won wisdom.

The publication of the first volume of her autobiography, *Wild Card*, has led to widespread anticipation that this will be succeeded by further volumes and revelations. Its literary style is rich and full of surprises, selecting candid details and outlining a difficult, courageous life.

Hewett was awarded a life emeritus fellowship by the **Literature Board** of the **Australia Council** in 1989.

THOMAS SHAPCOTT

Further reading: Margaret Williams, *Dorothy Hewett: The Feminine as Subversion* (1992).

HIBBERD, JACK (1940–)

Australian dramatist

Born in Warracknabeal, Victoria, Australia, he was educated in Bendigo and studied medicine at Melbourne University. He was a leading spirit of the 'New Wave', 'fringe' Australian drama of the late 1960s and the 1970s — specifically of the Melbourne side of this movement — that centred on the work of the Australian Performing Group at the La Mama and Pram Factory theatres (which have also produced his later plays). His work shares the zesty larrikin spirit of the movement as a whole, its preference for knockabout, cabaret-style theatricality, and the aggressively iconoclastic Australianism of its themes and character stereotypes. Hibberd is distinct, however, in his inventiveness within the variety of non-naturalistic theatrical forms of twentieth-century European avant-garde dramatists, particularly Bertolt Brecht and Samuel Beckett, and in his success in fusing these styles with his Australianism. Also unique to Hibberd is the vivaciously literary language of his plays, dubbed 'ocker baroque' by one critic. This language, indebted both to James Joyce and **Barry Humphries**, blends the mimicry and delighted celebration of the vernacular with a playful ornateness of phrasing that relishes the effects of juxtaposed registers.

Within these parameters Hibberd has explored a variety of forms: quasi-naturalistic satire in *White with Wire Wheels* (1970); satiric, episodic Brechtianism in *Peggy Sue* (1982), first performed in 1974; the re-creation of populist mythology through adaptation of the comically summarizing properties of Brechtian style in *A Toast to Melba* (1976) and *The Les Darcy Show* (1976); experimental reworking of Gogol's *The Overcoat* (1977); and ingeniously carnivalesque mock-ceremony in *Dimboola* (1974), first performed in 1969. His début in prose, *Memoirs of an Old Bastard* (1989), equally bears the familiar Hibberd trademarks.

Hibberd's best play is arguably *A Stretch of the Imagination* (1973), where he powerfully re-creates the masculinist legend of Australian tradition in the figure of Monk O'Neill. The use of the Beckettian monologue, with its dramatically and philosophically significant alternation of speech and silence, achieves in *A Stretch of the Imagination* a uniquely clear focus for the celebration of the larrikin ocker persona and for the mockery of its scatologically obsessed misogyny and final negativism. The play achieves a full emotional resonance somewhat lacking elsewhere in Hibberd's work. As a whole his work is perhaps implicated in the emotional denial of the ocker persona that is its main character.

DIRK DEN HARTOG

Further reading: John Hainsworth, ed., *Hibberd* (1987).

HICKS, BONNY (1968–)

Singaporean novelist

Born in Singapore, she studied at the Singapore Chinese Girls' School and Hwa Chong Junior College. She is a model by profession. Her first book is essentially her autobiography. *"Excuse me, are you a model?"* (1990) is written in the style of a *Bildungsroman* and tells the story of a young girl growing into maturity in fast-paced Singapore. The honesty and frankness of the work caused much controversy, and several public forums and discussions about the book were organized. One in particular, 'The Bonny Hicks Revolution', organized by the National University of Singapore Society, attracted hugh crowds. Because of the book's enormous success, a Chinese edition was published, with additional chapters detailing Hicks' experiences and those of her family after the launch of the English edition.

Hicks' second book, *Discuss, Disgust* (1992), addresses the relationship between a high-class call-girl and her daughter and raises questions of social importance. Again, the author chooses to be candid in her narration, sparing no one involved in the business of hypocritical existence. The book is also a kind of fantasy, with its protagonist establishing a link with a kind of alter-ego for her daily sustenance. It is a disturbing book and one that perhaps asks more than it answers.

NG WEE LI

HIGHWAY, TOMSON (1951–)

Canadian dramatist

Born on a reserve in Manitoba, Canada, and raised in the Cree language, he is the pre-eminent Canadian Native playwright. Like many Native children of his generation, he grew up in a residential school and foster homes, but unlike most he entered university, taking degrees in music and English at the University of Western Ontario, Canada. There he collaborated with **James Reaney**, whose exuberant theatrical techniques influenced Highway's own dramatic writing. In 1989 he cofounded Native Earth Performing Arts, Toronto's first professional Native theatre.

Highway established himself as a major voice in Canadian drama with two plays, *The Rez Sisters* (1988) and *Dry Lips Oughta Move to Kapuskasing* (1990), both set on a Native reserve in northern Ontario. In *The Rez Sisters*, a group of women put aside their differences and travel to Toronto to the world's biggest bingo. In *Dry Lips* the men of the reserve confront their political impotence as first the women of the reserve, then all aboriginal women in the world, invade the men's domain and form a Native women's hockey league. Both plays demonstrate that the emancipation of Native peoples proceeds from the empowerment of women.

In Highway's plays, comedy of character and community life expands to mythic proportions as a simple situation is transformed into a theatrical metaphor. The agent of transformation is Nanabush, the trickster of traditional Native religion, who, in Highway's words, 'can assume any guise he chooses. Essentially a comic, clownish sort of character . . . He straddles the consciousness of man and that of god, the great spirit.' Because the Ojibway and Cree languages do not differentiate gender, Nanabush is both male and female.

Unlike many aboriginal playwrights, Highway avoids overt political analysis in his plays, preferring to reclaim myths and spirituality erased by colonialism. This absence of militant politics may in part explain why *Dry Lips* was revived for a commercial tour at the Royal Alexandra Theatre, Toronto, in 1991.

In 1989 Highway was the recipient of the Wang International Prize for Canadian writing; his plays have won major national awards.

ALAN FILEWOD

Further reading: Daniel David Moses, 'The trickster theatre of Tomson Highway', *Canadian Fiction* 60 (1987); Denis Johnston, 'Lives and circles: the Rez plays of Tomson Highway', *Canadian Literature* 124/125 (1990).

HILL, BARRY (1943–)

Australian short-story writer, novelist, poet

Born in Melbourne, Australia, he was educated at the universities of Melbourne and London, England. He has worked as a secondary-school history teacher, an educational psychologist, and as a literary journalist for *The Times Educational Supplement* and the Melbourne *Age*.

Since 1975 Hill has devoted most of his time to writing. *The Schools* (1977) is a study of some Australian 'alternative' schools offering 'open education' and aiming to act as 'community resources'. *A Rim of Blue* (1978) and *Headlocks and Other Stories* (1983) contain short fiction; *Near the Refinery* (1980) is a short novel. In these works Hill is concerned with characters who recognize their psychological captivity but strive for freedom and/or love; there is often a strong sense of institutional social injustice, and philosophical questions about the nature of reality are raised.

Hill's novel, *The Best Picture* (1988), draws on both European and eastern philosophical concepts. Wittgenstein, Bertrand Russell, A. J. Ayer, and other western philosophers in the tradition of logical positivism intersect with mantras and the Vedic scriptures. At an ashram in Queensland, Australia, the characters seek truth, love, goodness, and inner peace, though the search is full of anguish and betrayal. The style is Joycean, lyrical, and fissured; more prominence is given to the philosophical dialectic than to coherence of plot or characterization.

'Ghosting William Buckley', a stage play, was produced on radio by the Australian Broadcasting Commission in 1988 and entered for the 1988 Prix Italia. *Raft: Poems 1983–1990* (1990) indicates that Hill's poetry is less experimental in form than is his prose. The poems concern love, family, and Buddhist understandings of life and death; there is an abundance of images of flowers, land, and water. *Sitting In* (1991) is a free-flowing, stream-of-consciousness account of a 1979 sit-in at a Union Carbide factory near Melbourne, a protest about wages and conditions in which Hill's mother and father were both deeply involved.

Hill's philosophical concerns and his discontinuous psychological narratives bring him into comparison with other contemporary Australian fiction writers, such as **David Foster**, and with non-Australian writers such as Canada's **Robertson Davies** and Uganda's **Taban lo Liyong**.

KEN GOODWIN

Hill, Errol (1922–)

Trinidadian dramatist, theatre historian

Born in Port of Spain, Trinidad, he is largely responsible for propagating the theatre as a vital aspect of Caribbean nationalism. He is one of three Trinidadian artists whose work in the mid-1950s strongly influenced the direction and development of their respective art forms. (The others are Beryl McBurnie in dance and Mighty Sparrow, King of Calypso.)

Hill's principal ideas on theatre in the Caribbean centre around its potential as a national institution, its centrality in the development of a Caribbean community or consciousness, and the role of Carnival in the development of such a theatre. Carnival and its associated arts (masquerade, calypso, and the steel band) provide in Hill's own words 'the largest resource of indigenous materials for use by our graphic and performing artists'. Hill develops this thesis in his book *The Trinidad Carnival: Mandate for a National Theatre* (1972). His play *Man Better Man* (in *Three Plays from the Yale School of Drama*, 1964, edited by John Gassner), is based on stickfighting, a martial art linked with the Carnival celebrations. Hill's dialogue is fashioned in rhymed couplets or 'calypso verse' in an attempt to evoke the rhythm of the calypso and the rhetoric of Carnival warrior figures. Among his ten one-act plays, 'The Ping Pong', on the subject of steel bands, and 'Dance Bongo', which uses the dead-wake tradition, reflect Hill's use of indigenous dramatic elements.

In his critical writing and crusading lectures as the extra-mural tutor in drama at the University of the West Indies, Trinidad, Hill has argued in forthright and uncompromising terms for an institutionalized Caribbean theatre.

Hill's substantial contribution to black theatre scholarship extends beyond the Caribbean. He has written *Shakespeare in Sable: A History of Black Shakespearean Actors* (1984) and edited the two-volume *The Theatre of Black Americans* (1980), the collection *Black Heroes: Seven Plays* (1989), and *Bulletin of Black Theatre*, a journal.

RAWLE GIBBONS

HILLIARD, NOEL (1929–)

New Zealand novelist, short-story writer

Born in Napier, New Zealand, and educated at Gisborne Boys' High School and Victoria University of Wellington, he has published several non-fiction works but is best known for his fiction. At the centre of his work is the Netta Samuel-Paul Bennett tetralogy — *Maori Girl* (1960), *Power of Joy* (1965), *Maori Woman* (1974), and *The Glory and the Dream* (1978). The first and best of these deals with Netta's rural Maori childhood and her unhappy experiences of racism and sexual and economic exploitation in Wellington, while the second deals with Paul's growing up under the repressive forces of puritanism and the Depression. The later two novels bring Paul and Netta together through a difficult interracial courtship and early marriage to eventual happiness. Throughout, the method is that of proletarian social realism and the emphasis is on the racism and repressiveness of New Zealand society. Hilliard's other novel, *A Night at Green River* (1969), also focuses on race relations, as do most of the stories in *A Piece of Land* (1963) and *Send Somebody Nice* (1976).

The first writer of fiction to concentrate on the plight of the urban Maori, Hilliard has been doubly disadvantaged in being ahead of fashion in his social vision and behind it in his traditional social realism. Both factors, however, have probably contributed to his popularity in Russia and China, where his work has been translated and widely circulated.

LAWRENCE JONES

Further reading: Lawrence Jones, *Barbed Wire and Mirrors: Essays on New Zealand Prose* (1990).

HIPPOLYTE, KENDEL (1952–)

St Lucian poet, dramatist

Born in Castries, St Lucia, the Caribbean, he was educated there and at the University of the West Indies, Jamaica. Hippolyte spent a year (1987–8) with the Lee Strasberg School in New York, USA. With his wife, poet Jane King, he directs the Lighthouse Theatre Company and teaches literature at the St Mary's College, St Lucia. Hippolyte's published works include the poetry collections *Island in the Sun, Side Two . . .* (1980), *Bearings* (1986), and *The Labyrinth* (1991) and the play *Drum-maker* (first published in *Caribbean Plays for Playing*, 1981, edited by Keith Noel). He edited *Confluence* (1988), the first collection of St Lucian poetry, and *So Much Poetry in We People* (1990), an anthology of eastern Caribbean performance poetry.

Hippolyte's earliest published poems (for example, 'euroscape' and 'monday', both first published in *Caribbean Quarterly* 1, 1976) show that he had set himself free from what critic Gordon Rohlehr called the inherited colonial 'crypt of the lyric' — the discomfort of pentametered language and the cold distance of condescending intellect. Hippolyte's poetry in the early 1970s was a literary manifesto of an unyielding commitment to 'roots-culture'. His forms, subtly wrought and technically adventurous, gave the idiomatic nuances of Caribbean nation-language their rightful place as the bedrock of a confident literature. Hippolyte presents the perspective of the 'shocking madman' — the reject of society, the oppressed — with a witty, grim, ironic realism that strips away pretension.

Hippolyte is a spiritual compatriot of poets **Mervyn Morris, Dennis Scott,** and **Anthony McNeill,** whose influences are more Rastafarian soul-rebel dread-beat than any discernible school of literati. He was also part of a critical community that developed a relevant paradigm for perceptive artistic analyses of contemporary Caribbean life.

In St Lucian writing, where **McDonald Dixon** and **John Robert Lee** have broadly followed the 'classical model' line of **Derek Walcott,** Hippolyte has been the 'modern', preferring the freedom of American Allen Ginsberg. Hippolyte always surprises by taking words suddenly away from the expected direction and into a startling configuration.

JOHN ROBERT LEE

Further reading: Gordon Rohlehr, 'The problem of the problem of form: the idea of an aesthetic continuum and aesthetic code-switching in West Indian literature: "futuriginal: Kendel Hippolyte's poetry"', *Caribbean Quarterly* 1 (1985).

HISTORICAL NOVEL (India)
See **NOVEL** (India)

HISTORICAL WRITING

HISTORICAL WRITING (Australia)

As has commonly been the case in colonial societies, the earliest histories of European Australia concentrated on such topics as exploration and settlement and the growth of a civil society that the metropolitan culture could proudly include within its orbit. In this phase of historiography, pioneering effort and political and economic achievement were elevated, and such unsavoury aspects as the foundation with convicts and the oppression of the Aborigines were skated over or ignored entirely. Writing of the convict aspect, David Blair announced sorrowfully in his *History of Australasia* (1878) that he would pass over it 'as lightly as the exigencies of true narration will permit. Better, a thousand times, would it be for the world, if the entire record were buried in eternal forgetfulness.'

Lasting into the twentieth century, this kind of history was slowly supplanted by the 'scientific' one. Chief among its methods were the collation and close analysis of documents and the growth of academic training in these techniques. In Australia the collection of documents preceded the growth of the history schools. From the late nineteenth century onwards private and public funds have been used to build up rich library holdings, particularly in the State Library of New South Wales and the National Library of Australia. Concomitant were the gathering and publication of records in England and elsewhere relating to Australian history, most notably *Historical Records of New South Wales* (8 vols, 1892–1901) and *Historical Records of Australia* (31 vols, 1914–25). Since the Second World War these collections have been massively enlarged by that of the Australian Joint Copying Project, which now runs to some six thousand microfilm reels.

As the teaching of academic history spread from the universities of Sydney, Melbourne, and Adelaide to other state institutions, and as all sent students to Oxford, Cambridge, and London, England, works unmistakably in the new mode appeared. The first truly notable national history was **Sir Keith Hancock**'s *Australia* (1930), which was followed by R. M. Cradford's *Australia* (1952), A. G. L. Shaw's *The Story of Australia* (1955), and **Manning Clark**'s *A Short History of Australia* (1963) and *A History of Australia* (6 vols, 1962–87). In general, these works were largely political and economic in their orientation, the author often seeking in the past the beginnings of those features such as legislative structures and unionism that had come to dominate Australian society. They established an approach that has continued into the present, with F. K. Crowley's collection by various hands, *A New History of Australia* (1974), and *The Oxford History of Australia* (5 vols, 1986–).

Within this framework of general history, particular aspects have been extensively pursued. Reflecting the older view that great figures determine events, there has been an emphasis on biography, with founding governors (Phillip, Bligh, Macquarie, Darling, Bourke, Arthur) and the fathers of Federation (Parkes, Deakin, Barton, Griffith) receiving attention. The significance of certain spectacular events has also been analysed, with **C. E. W. Bean** in his official histories presenting the First World War campaigns at Gallipoli and in France as crucibles in which the nation's steel was forged and, more recently, Bill Gammage — *The Broken Years: Australian Soldiers in the Great War* (1974) — and others seeing the consequences from a post-Second World War anti-heroic stance.

Since the need to explain the mysterious emergence of a civil society is perhaps the single greatest challenge to historians of Australia, there has been an abiding interest in the convict beginnings, with Eris O'Brien's *The Foundation of Australia* (1937) and A. G. L. Shaw's *Convicts and the Colonies* (1966), and, more recently, Portia Robinson's *The Hatch and Brood of Time* (1985) and J. B. Hirst's *Convict Society and its Enemies* (1983) standing out. Running parallel has been a strong concern with labour and unionism in such works as Robin Gollin's *Radical and Working Class Politics: A Study of Eastern Australia, 1850–1910* (1974) and John Merritt's *The Making of the AWU* (1986).

Regional history — M. Kiddle's *Men of Yesterday: A Social History of the Western District of Victoria 1834–1890* (1961) and G. C. Bolton's *A Thousand Miles Away: A History of North Queensland to 1920* (1963) — and literary and cultural history — G. Serle's *From Deserts the Prophets Come: The Creative Spirit in Australia, 1788–1972* (1973) — have also been major interests.

Since 1970 Australian historiography has reflected the great diversity of European and American interest in urban history — G. Davison's *The Rise and Fall of Marvellous Melbourne* (1979), for example — demography and political analysis becoming more prominent than before. There has also been a plethora of studies of working-class circumstance in the manner of E. P. Thompson and his school. With perhaps the exceptions of **Geoffrey Blainey** and O. H. K. Spate — *The Pacific Since Magellan* (3 vols, 1979–88) — historians have not much attempted studies along the lines of the Annales school; nor, rather surprisingly, have there been thoroughgoing interdisciplinary studies with an ecological focus such as Alfred Crosby's *The Columbian Exchange* (1972).

However, the past decades have been notable for the vigorous attention given to the Aborigines, both concerning their prehistory, with a school led by John Mulvaney pushing back their occupation of the continent from a few thousand years to 60,000 BC, and their contact with European culture, with Henry Reynolds and others detailing the widespread frontier violence and subsequent oppression.

Accompanying this last development has been that of ethnographic history. While its two most singular practitioners, Greg Dening (in *Islands and Beaches: Discourse on a Silent Land, Marquesas, 1774–1880*, 1980) and Rhys Isaac (*The Transformation of Virginia*, 1982), have dealt with non-Australian circumstance, they have been instrumental in developing and disseminating to a rising generation of scholars new modes of conceptualizing and writing, and their influence will be increasingly reflected in studies of the many ethnic and religious groups who have migrated to Australia in the twentieth century and whose presence was emphasized during the bicentenary in *The Encyclo-*

paedia of the Australian People (1988), edited by James Jupp.

ALAN FROST

Further reading: Stuart MacIntyre, 'The writing of Australian history', in D. H. Borchardt (ed.) *Australians: A Guide to Sources* (1987).

HISTORICAL WRITING (Canada)

For four centuries the history of Canada has attracted the attention of scholars and publishers. Since European penetration and early settlement, each generation or age, reflecting its own concerns, has written its history. From the period prior to the Second World War onwards, the quality and quantity of Canadian historiography have grown tremendously. Academic writers, located mainly at the expanding universities, have focused on nation-building, on political developments and controversies, and on English-French relations, but they have also concerned themselves with economic development and staples production. In the late twentieth century the collective concern of writers on Canada's past has both broadened and specialized to encompass diverse aspects of social, intellectual, and economic history, including issues concerning women, children, families, public health, business, law and order, ethnicity and, not least, Native peoples and aboriginal affairs.

The French Foundations

The first Canadian histories were compiled in French by priests, lay brothers, and colony-builders, including Marc Lescarbot, Gabriel Sagard, and Samuel de Champlain. Some histories were written by individuals who never visited Canada, such as André Thevet, whose *Les Singularitez de la France Antarctique* was published in Paris in 1557. Lescarbot, a Parisian lawyer, is regarded as the first historian of Canada; his *Histoire de la Nouvelle-France* was published in three Paris editions, in 1609, 1611–12, and 1617–18. The Jesuit Pierre-François Charlevoix is credited with writing the first perspective on French development in Canada to 1736. His *Histoire et description generale de la Nouvelle France* (1744) was based heavily on documentary sources, not the least of which was the *Jesuit Relations* — the collective name given to a series of reports sent by Jesuit missionaries in Quebec to the Society of Jesus in Paris, some of which were published in 1858 (73 volumes, covering the period 1610–1791, were published between 1896 and 1901). For some time Jesuits continued as the premier Canadian historians, a trend identified later in the significant work of the secular Quebec national historian François-Xavier Garneau, writing in the mid-nineteenth century. These histories provide information about Canada's Native peoples and habitations, and its geography, flora, and fauna; they also exemplify the zeal of the Roman Catholic Counter-Reformation. They are also regarded, critically, as pious attempts to justify French imperialism.

The Colonial and Early National Periods

The first English-language histories of Canada date from the period following the Conquest of 1759, when the British gained control of French colonies in Canada. The war of 1812–14, fought between the British and Canadians and American invaders, accentuated the desires of Upper Canadians and Maritimers to write new histories of British North America. As the nineteenth century progressed, historians of what later became Canada glorified the British Empire and wrote what could be called Britannic Canadian history. This is best exemplified by W. H. Kingsford's ten-volume *The History of Canada*, written between 1887 and 1898. This work, despite its bias, is a comprehensive account of the political and constitutional development of diverse provinces prior to and following the Confederation of Canada, brought into existence by the British North America Act of 1867. J. C. Dent's *The Last Forty Years* (1881), in mild contrast, carefully eulogizes moderate reform.

Changing international relations and Canadian military activities overseas (first in the Anglo-Boer War, then in the First World War) accentuated Canadian nationalism. In addition, the economic development of Canada — in forestry, mining, agriculture, railways, and shipping — invited Canadians to rewrite their history in more structural terms. Joseph Pope edited the memoirs of John A. Macdonald. Oscar Douglas Skelton compiled lengthy biographies of two great Canadians: A. T. Galt and Wilfrid Laurier. (See **Life Writing**, Canada.) W. P. M. Kennedy wrote distinguished histories of the Canadian constitution. Works on labour, by H. A. Logan, on Canadian-American relations, by H. L. Keenleyside, and on Commonwealth relations, by R. G. Trotter and Chester Martin, were part of the diversification of scholarly historical research in English that marked the 1920s.

The Classical Period: 1930–67

In the years before and after the Second World War, English-Canadian historiography blossomed in the writings of several well-known, colourful, and nationally committed — if divided — university teachers. These include Harold Adam Innis, Donald G. Creighton, Arthur R. M. Lower, Frank Underhill, W. L. Morton, C. P. Stacey, and, towards the end of this era, Maurice Careless, Margaret Ormsby, William J. Eccles, Kenneth McNaught, and Peter B. Waite.

Innis was the most important scholar to write histories on the economic development of what became Canada. His works on the staples theory and on communications are fundamental to an understanding of Canada's economic history and the nation's continuing difficulties as a world trader. Innis wrote histories of the Canadian Pacific Railway and the cod fisheries, but his most important was *The Fur Trade in Canada* (1930). In it, and elsewhere, Innis claimed that the fur trade and its voyageur canoeing and trekking routes marked out the future political boundaries of Canada. He also argued that because Canada's staples economy was dominated on a world stage, it would remain both northern and marginal rather than continental and dominant. Innis also wrote histories about the pulp and paper industry and evolving bases of communications. He highlighted the pervasive influence of the USA in Canada's more recent development. By his many works, exemplary as pioneering social science in Canada and reflective of American scholarly influences, Innis became recognized as a truly international scholar.

In his *The Commercial Empire of the St. Lawrence: 1760–1850* (1937), Donald Creighton explained how a merchant class, based in urban Montreal, developed the infrastructure of the modern Canadian nation state. Creighton extended his theme in other works, including *Dominion of the North* (1944) and *The Road to Confederation* (1964). Widely read by high-school and university students, Creighton is regarded by some as the dean of Canadian historians. His two-volume biography of John A. Macdonald — *The Young Politician* (1952) and *The Old Chieftain* (1955) — while overly eulogistic, is regarded as one of the finest political biographies written in the English language. Creighton feared the aggressive power of the USA and stressed the national need for a centralized federalism and a powerful and continuing British conservative tradition; he was extremely critical of French-Canadian historical leadership and of liberal *ententisme* and continentalism.

In contrast, Arthur R. M. Lower became an expert on Canada's hinterland, on the history of Canadian forests and timber trades. His great whiggish text, *Colony to Nation* (1946), stresses moderate reform, North American nationalism, and the reconciliation of the two (French and English) linguistic communities. His *Canadians in the Making* (1958) pioneered the writing of Canadian social history.

While Innis, Creighton, Lower, and many others wrote history from an Ontarian or a Montreal perspective, W. L. Morton stressed the importance of the **Canadian North** and the West, each with its own legitimate perspectives, in *The Progressive Party in Canada* (1950) and *Manitoba* (1957). With *The Kingdom of Canada* (1963), Morton became the great 'Red Tory' of Canadian scholarship, stressing Canada's unique experience as a nordic people, very different from the Americans, with a state interventionist economy and strong government support for economically weaker groups and regions. The western Métis and the French-speaking Canadians outside of Quebec were his heroes; separatists and neo-conservative continentalists were his villains.

Other writers followed to reinterpret Canada's past. Maurice Careless, in his brilliant two-volume biography of George Brown of the *Globe* newspaper, *Brown of the Globe* (vol. 1, 1959; vol. 2, 1963), and in his many other books, stressed the positive role of Toronto-led Upper Canadian Reform in building the country and nurturing its economy. He also developed a vital thesis on multitiered metropolitanism, analysing the efficacy of regionalism and multiculturalism and showing the futility of searching for a single Canadian identity or culture. Also of note is Craig Brown's *Robert Laird Borden: A Biography* (vol. 1, 1975; vol. 2, 1980), on one of Canada's prime ministers. William Eccles, the greatest English-language writer on the French regime (his *Frontenac, the Courtier Governor*, 1959, for example), stressed France's geopolitical and military interest in North America, criticized Innis' staples approach, and later emphasized the ongoing positive role of aboriginal First Nations in Canada. Margaret Ormsby turned her attention to British Columbia and the Pacific in *British Columbia: A History* (1958), while Kenneth McNaught stressed the legitimacy and strength of an English-based social democratic tradition in Canada in his *A Prophet in Politics: A Biography of J. S. Woodsworth* (1959). C. P. Stacey wrote and supported studies of Canada's contributions in the Second World War; his *Canada in the Age of Conflict* (vol. 1, 1977) is the standard account of Canada's external relations from 1867 to 1948.

The period prior to the centennial of Canadian Confederation (1967) sparked a number of significant works. P. B. Waite wrote *The Life and Times of Confederation, 1864–1867* (1962) and W. L. Morton wrote *The Critical Years: The Union of British North America, 1857–1873* (1964). In 1963 Creighton and Morton together launched the multi-volume Canadian Centenary Series, which appeared well into the late 1980s. It currently contains nineteen volumes; taken together, these volumes constitute a comprehensive, multi-authored history of Canada from Norse explorations to the contemporary period.

Beginning in the 1950s, Quebec secular historians, after the corporatist-clerical historiography of L'abbé Lionel Groulx (1878–1967), took an increasing interest in their own history. Particularly important are the works of Michel Brunet, Gustave Lanctot, and Fernand Ouellet.

Recent Decades

The quantity of Canadian historiography exploded in the 1970s and 1980s as history departments in the country's universities grew very rapidly and new scholarly societies and journals were founded. Attention diversified and often became more fragmented, more regional, more social-, class-, and gender-oriented. Recently, Gerry Friesen's *Canadian Prairies: A History* (1984), and Ken Coates' and William Morrison's writings on the Yukon and on other northern themes, inspired by the work of Morris Zaslow, have reflected a growing consciousness of regional affairs. Similarly, the Atlantic Shipping Project, funded by the **Canada Council** and based on British Board of Trade papers, examined the role of shipping and seaborne trades in the history of Atlantic shipping and ports; it resulted in works by David Alexander, L. R. Fischer, Eric Sager, G. Panting, and others. The history of the Maritime provinces has also been served by writers such as Ernest Forbes, Ken Pryke, George Rawlyk, Judith Fingard, and, earlier, W. S. MacNutt; Barry Gough wrote histories of Pacific-coast maritime activities. H. Viv Nelles, Christopher Armstrong, Michael Bliss, Peter Oliver, and many others have written widely on Ontario regionalism and resource problems. Gilbert Tucker, Gerald Graham, Desmond Morton, and S. F. Wise made significant contributions to histories of the Canadian army, navy, and air force. Blair Neatby, Jack Granatstein, Robert Bothwell, and John English have written voluminously on mid-twentieth-century political and administrative problems and personalities.

Ramsay Cook and, later, Susan Mann Trofimenkoff have written widely and brilliantly of French-Canadian nationalism and other cultural movements; representative of their work are Cook's *The Politics of John W. Dafoe and the Free Press* (1963) and Trofimenkoff's *Action Française: French-Canadian Nationalism in the 1920s* (1975). Cook has also delved into aspects of Canadians' belief systems, including religion. Many historians have stressed the long story of aboriginal groups and their relationship with 'settler' societies; these scholars include Bruce Trigger, Cornelius Jaenen, Sylvia Van Kirk, Jennifer Brown, Robin Fisher, J. R. Miller, Olive Dickason, Brian Slattery, John Milloy, David McNab, and Bruce Hodgins. In particular, Douglas Cole and Trigger have made distinctive contributions to Native studies and to cross-cultural history. Hodgins, with others, has also focused on the comparative aspects of federalist Canada and federalist Australia.

Historians such as Douglas McCalla have confronted and challenged the staples approach to Canadian economic history, substituting a concept of complex internal activity that generated growth from expanding commercial and agrarian roots. Carl Berger and many more have written extensively on Canada's intellectual past, while Greg Kealey, Bryan Palmer, and a host of colleagues have delved deeply into labour and other aspects of Canadian working-class history.

Many non-academic popular historians have written a great deal of quality work. They include **Farley Mowat**, Pierre Berton, Barry Broadfoot, and Peter C. Newman. The Hudson's Bay Company's *Beaver* (1920–) is a popular historical journal. The *Canadian Historical Review* (1919–) and *The Journal of Canadian Studies* (1966–) are two important national scholarly publications; *Acadiensis* (1970–), *B. C. Studies* (1969–), and *Ontario History* (1908–) are also excellent historical periodicals.

Surveys of Canadian historical literature are to be found in Norah Story's *The Oxford Companion to Canadian History and Literature* (1967) and its *Supplement* (1973), and in the three volumes of the *Literary History of Canada* (2nd ed., 1976), edited by C. F. Klinck, and in the 1990 fourth volume. Carl Berger's *The Writing of Canadian History* (1976; 2nd ed., 1985) is also especially important. Finally, begun in the late 1950s, the ongoing multi-volumed *Dictionary of Canadian Biography*, currently edited by Ramsay Cook, is an indispensable source for Canadian historiography.

BARRY GOUGH
BRUCE W. HODGINS

HISTORICAL WRITING (The Caribbean)
The classic era of mercantilism, settlement, and plantation development in the seventeenth and eighteenth centuries produced the first histories of the British colonies in the Caribbean, ranging from early island histories such as Richard Ligon's *A True and Exact History of the Island of Barbados* (1657) and Edward Long's *The History of Jamaica*

(1774) to Bryan Edwards' ambitious *The History, Civil and Commercial, of the British Colonies in the West Indies* (2 vols, 1793). These, and others of the same era and genre, written by British residents or by local (Creole) whites, attempt to celebrate the achievements of the settlers and to defend the brutally materialistic society they had created. Early in the nineteenth century, as the British anti-slavery movement matured, more critical 'histories' reflected the spirit of the religious and secular enlightenments — for example, Thomas Coke's *A History of the West Indies* (1808–11) and Thomas Southey's *A Chronological History of the West Indies* (1827).

With the decline of anti-slavery and the ascendancy of imperialism, histories of the Caribbean from the mid-nineteenth century tend to focus on the islands' place in the epic of British expansion overseas. Caribbean history was considered important because the region had been the great theatre for the Anglo-French duel, and books in this genre are suffused by a nostalgia for past glories. Slavery is ignored as far as possible and the islands' history appears to have ended with the noble gift of freedom in 1838. Works of this kind range from J. A. Froude's *The English in the West Indies* (1887) to Alan C. M. Burns' *History of British West Indies*, published as late as 1954. In addition to the 'Imperial' histories, mainly but not exclusively the work of British scholars or popular writers, whites resident in the islands developed in the same era a tradition of writing local histories and (in some cases) publishing primary sources. Though much of this work is antiquarian and narrowly focused, among its better products are island histories such as W. J. Gardner's *A History of Jamaica* (1873) and L. M. Fraser's *History of Trinidad* (1891–6), institutions such as the Institute of Jamaica and the Barbados Museum and Historical Society, and publications such as the series of documents produced by the Trinidad and Tobago Historical Society in the 1930s.

Gradually the writing of Caribbean history became more scholarly. American and British academics publishing between the 1920s and 1940s — notably Lowell J. Ragatz, Frank Pitman, Richard Pares, Vincent Harlow, and C. S. Higham — produced important studies of the islands in the heyday of sugar and slavery. Towards the end of this period two Trinidadian scholars published seminal works: **C. L. R. James** — *The Black Jacobins* (1938) — and Eric Eustace Williams — *Capitalism and Slavery* (1944). These books — along with the establishment of the University of the West Indies, which began to teach Caribbean history in the early 1950s — ushered in the modern era of Caribbean historiography. The era was marked by a decisive shift from the 'Imperial' genre through the recognition that Caribbean history must be studied in its own right and on its own terms, not as an arena for European 'expansion', and by a determination to 'creolize' the region's past by focusing on the experiences and achievements of the people who had inhabited it during the last 500 years.

Since the publication of *Capitalism and Slavery* these trends have been progressively developed in a plethora of historical studies. Many have focused on the slave era (1640–1838). The now-classic studies by E. V. Goveia (*Slave Society in the British Leeward Islands*, 1965) and **E. K. Brathwaite** (*The Development of Creole Society in Jamaica, 1770–1820*, 1971) pointed the way by defining 'slave society' as embracing all the groups resident in the Caribbean during slavery. Increasingly, however, historians focused on the Afro-Caribbean population, especially in studies of slave resistance, such as Michael Craton's *Testing the Chains* (1982), and slave demography, such as B. W. Higman's exemplary *Slave Populations of the British Caribbean: 1807–1834* (1984). The development of the plantation as the dominant mode of production in the Caribbean since 1640 has attracted several historians who, following a line first developed by Williams, have been particularly interested in the period of 'decline' between 1783 and 1834 and its relationship to the British movements to abolish the slave trade and slavery.

Problems of adjustment to emancipation between the 1830s and the 1860s have been the theme of several important works, notably Douglas Hall's *Free Jamaica: 1838–1865* (1959) and W. A. Green's *British Slave Emancipation* (1976). Until recently, the decades between 1865 and 1937 were something of a 'dark age' in Caribbean historiography, but since 1970 studies of social, economic, and political developments in this era have appeared, notably those by B. Brereton, P. Bryan, T. Holt, K. O. Laurence, C. Levy, W. K. Marshall, B. Moore, B. Richardson, W. Rodney, D. V. Trotman, and D. Wood. Attention has also focused increasingly on the period of decolonization since the labour unrest of the late 1930s, with Ken Post's *Arise Ye Starvelings* (1978) perhaps the major contribution. Relatively little has yet been attempted on cultural or religious history of the *Annales* type, but Gordon Lewis' magisterial *Main Currents in Caribbean Thought* (1983) is of note.

Scholars have investigated particular groups or events in individual territories in considerable detail, as in Barry Gaspar's *Bondmen and Rebels* (1985) — on the Antigua slave rising of 1736 — and good general histories of some islands have appeared, most recently Hilary Beckles' *A History of Barbados* (1990). In complete contrast are a few works that seek to integrate the history of the English-speaking lands into the whole regional story: F. W. Knight's *The Caribbean: The Genesis of a Fragmented Nationalism* (1978, 2nd ed. 1990) is a distinguished example of the latter genre; the proposed six-volume UNESCO 'General History of the Caribbean' will devote a whole volume to historiography and methodology.

B. BRERETON

Further reading: Elsa V. Goveia, *A Study on the Historiography of the British West Indies to the End of the Nineteenth Century* (1956; repr. 1980); W. K. Marshall, 'A review of historical writing on the Commonwealth Caribbean since *c.* 1940', *Social and Economic Studies* (Jamaica) 3 (1975); B. W. Higman, 'Theory, method and technique in Caribbean social history', *Journal of Caribbean History* 1 (1985–6).

HISTORICAL WRITING (Gibraltar)

Although the early history of Gibraltar is the subject of J. J. Alcantara's *Medieval Gibraltar* (1979), there is little historical writing about this important period. The Jewish community in Gibraltar, however, has been active in publishing works about its history and current situation. Abraham Serfaty's *The Jews of Gibraltar* (1933) traces the history of the Jews in Gibraltar from the time of the Treaty of Utrecht (1713) — a treaty that specifically prohibited Jews and Moors from residing within the town and fortress. The Jews had been subjected to some persecution in Roman Catholic Spain, as had Moors during a period when a resurgence of Moorish power was feared. In the 1930s, when Serfaty was writing his account, events in Europe — particularly in Hitler's Germany — were exposing Jews to persecution once again. While Spain did not single out Jews for persecution, the generally turbulent state of the country led to a feeling of insecurity among Jews; consequently Gibraltarian Jews had an interest in establishing their own identity under British rule. The story of the Jewish community in Gibraltar has been developed more recently in Mesod Benady's *The Settlement of Jews in Gibraltar 1704–1783* (1979) and *The Jewish Community of Gibraltar* (1989), by the latter under the name of Tito Benady. Benady has also edited a handy *Guide Book to Gibraltar* (1985; rev. 1991), a guidebook, *A Guide to the Gibraltar Museum* (1988), and *The Royal Navy at Gibraltar* (1992).

The publication in Gibraltar of H. W. Howes' *The Gibraltarians* (1951) was a great step forward in gaining a general acceptance of a Gibraltarian identity. Working from census reports and other official documents from the beginning of the British occupancy of Gibraltar, Howes shows how the Gibraltarian people are descended from British, Genoese, Spanish, Portuguese, Minorcan, Maltese, and Jewish elements — particularly those of Moroccan Jewish descent. (See **Gibraltar**.) About the same time Dorothy Ellicott began recording her extensive knowledge of Gibraltar. Her contributions include *Tarik's Hill* (1953), *Bastion Against Aggression* (1968), *Our Gibraltar* (1975), and *Gibraltar's Royal Governor* (1981). The latter deals with the governorship of the Duke of Kent, which began in 1802. Governor in title until his death in 1820, he did not return to active governorship after his recall in 1804, when his attempts to apply strict discipline among the troops led to mutinies. *Our Gibraltar*, written when the Spanish frontier was closed and the Franco regime was making claims to sovereignty of the Rock, was designed to show that Gibraltar should belong to its people under existing arrangements with the UK. Ellicott was also associated with her husband Jack Ellicott in writing *An Ornament to Almeida* (1950), about Gibraltar's city hall, originally built as a mansion by Aaron Cardozo.

Another writer on historical and current affairs, George Palao, has written *The Guns and Towers of Gibraltar* (1975), *Gibraltar: Our Forgotten Past* (1978), *Gibraltar: Our Heritage* (1979), *Gibraltar: Tales of Our Past* (1981), and *Gibraltar: Genesis and Evolution* (1982). His books are well illustrated with his own line drawings. Palao also provided some drawings for William Jackson's *The Rock of the Gibraltarians* (1987).

Other works relating to twentieth-century events are Luis F. Bruzon's *Gibraltar Problem Español* (1971), Joe Garcia's *Operation Felix: Hitler's Plan to Capture Gibraltar* (1979), and Helen C. Mazauram's *Rock Siege 1964–1985* (1986). Joe Garcia's *Dateline Gibraltar* (1990) draws on his work as a reporter for British papers during a period of thirty years. Charles Caruana's *Rock under a Cloud* (1989) traces the history of the Roman Catholic Church on Gibraltar from its early difficult days under Father Romero immediately after the British capture in 1704. The story of the evacuation of the civilian population during the Second World War is told in T. J. Finlayson's *The Fortress Came First* (1991).

PHILIP DENNIS
ANNE TAYLOR

HISTORICAL WRITING (Hong Kong)

There are few histories of Hong Kong written in English. G. B. Endacott's *A History of Hong Kong* (1958) remains a standard reference, as does his *Government and People in Hong Kong: A Constitutional History of Hong Kong* (1964), based on Colonial Office records. Though he has been criticized for concentrating on the colonial administration, thus overlooking many important aspects of Hong Kong's social, economic, and cultural development, Endacott's contribution is still significant.

An effort to update Endacott's work was not made until the publication of Nigel Cameron's *An Illustrated History of Hong Kong* (1991). Despite the title, the book's text is substantial, though based on secondary sources, much of them anecdotal. By contrast, Alan Birch's *Hong Kong: The Colony that Never Was* (1991) may be regarded as a pictorial history with a long interpretative essay, passionate and often thought-provoking.

Interestingly, all three writers begin their histories with the Opium War and the cession of Hong Kong in 1841. A general history of Hong Kong prior to the arrival of the British is still to be written, but there are several monographs covering this earlier period. The main impetus has come from the Sinologist Maurice Freedman, whose *Lineage Organization in Southeastern China* (1958) inspired a long-running debate on the structure of

Chinese rural society. (With the Chinese mainland inaccessible from the 1950s to the late 1970s, field-work was carried out mainly in Hong Kong's New Territories.) Works drawing on ethnographic materials, and often using sociological and anthropological methodologies, nevertheless provide much information and insights into early Hong Kong history. James Hayes' *The Hong Kong Region 1850–1911: Institutions and Leadership in Town and Countryside* (1972) is a fine example of how rural life can be reconstructed. Other worthy examples include Hugh Baker's *A Chinese Lineage Village: Sheung Shui* (1968), Rubie Watson's *Inequality among Brothers: Class and Kinship in South China* (1985), and David Faure's *The Structure of Chinese Rural Society: Lineage and Village in the Eastern New Territories, Hong Kong* (1986).

The scarcity of general histories of urban Hong Kong is likewise compensated for by monographs. Ng Lun Ngai-ha's *Interactions of East and West: Development of Public Education in Early Hong Kong* (1984) is the first of a series of heavily documented historical works, some more readable than others, that appeared in the 1980s. Norman Miners' *Hong Kong under Imperial Rule, 1912–1941* (1987), for example, analyses the tensions between the Colonial Office in London, England, and the colonial government in Hong Kong. Steve Yui-Sang Tsang's *Democracy Shelved: Great Britain, China, and Attempts at Constitutional Reform in Hong Kong, 1945–1952* (1988), while examining a critical moment of Hong Kong's constitutional history, also provides what is so far the most comprehensive picture of postwar social and economic conditions. Elizabeth Sinn's *Power and Charity: The Early History of the Tung Wah Hospital, Hong Kong* (1989), drawing on the hospital's rich archival sources, discusses the role a local Chinese social-political élite played in a British colony, and *China, Great Britain and Hong Kong* (1991), by Chan Lau Kit-ching, is an intensive study of the triangular relationships so fundamental to Hong Kong's existence.

There are some popular histories on different periods of Hong Kong's past; of these the war years (1941–5) have a special fascination. Many works on the siege of Hong Kong, on anti-Japanese resistance, and on life inside and outside of the internment camps have been published. The most generally informative book on this period is Endacott's *Hong Kong Eclipse* (1978), published posthumously and edited by Alan Birch.

No report on Hong Kong's historians can be complete without mentioning The Revd Carl Smith, whose encyclopedic knowledge of local source materials has helped numerous scholars with their research. His own writings have appeared in many journals, and some appear in his *Chinese Christians: Elites, Middlemen and the Church in Hong Kong* (1985).

ELIZABETH SINN

Further reading: Alan Birch, 'Approaches to Hong Kong history', in David Faure, James Hayes, and Alan Birch (eds) *From Village to City: Studies in the Traditional Roots of Hong Kong Society* (1984).

Historical Writing (New Zealand)

A major feature distinguishing New Zealand historiography from that of other anglophone settler societies is evident in the first substantial work on the colony's history, A. S. Thomson's *The Story of New Zealand: Past and Present — Savage and Civilized* (1859). Thomson, an army surgeon stationed in the country for several years, gave great emphasis to relationships between Maori and Pakeha, which he saw as having political and moral dimensions. Even in later narratives of conquest and colonization that were much cruder than Thomson's careful account, the colonizers acknowledge the existence of the colonized, if only by way of justifying dispossession of the indigenes. Nevertheless, Australian historian G. W. Rusden's attempt to argue consistent injustice by the settlers, in his *History of New Zealand* (1883) and *Aureretanga: Groans of the Maoris* (1888), was very unpopular. The orthodoxy was essentially a story of progress in civilization through the articulation of British political, economic, and social institutions, set out briefly in E. M. Bourke's *A Little History of New Zealand* (1881), and, at greater length and sententiously, in Alfred Saunders' two-volume *History of New Zealand* (1896, 1899).

In *The Long White Cloud: Ao Tea Roa* (1898), **William Pember Reeves** transformed the narrative of colonization into a distinctive New Zealand history. His emphasis on the importance of progressive politics established a central mythology for many later historians and the 'short history' became a significant literary-historical form, used to good effect later by such major writers as J. B. Condliffe, **J. C. Beaglehole**, W. T. G. Airey, **Keith Sinclair**, and W. H. Oliver. The single most accomplished historical work published in the generation after Reeves' *Long White Cloud* was Condliffe's economic history, *New Zealand in the Making* (1930). Other major contributions in the first forty years of the twentieth century were made by **James Cowan**, who celebrated the interaction of Maori and settlers, Lindsay Buick, who strove to give colour to major incidents and characters, especially of the 1830s and 1840s, and Eric Ramsden, whose interest was similarly concentrated on the period before the imposition of British sovereignty. What J. B. Hirst has called the 'pioneer legend' in Australia was recounted in New Zealand through numerous works of local history. Often 'untainted' by approval for progressive politics or bicultural sympathies, such local histories have continued to proliferate throughout the twentieth century.

The influence of university-based historians since the 1940s is manifest in the contributions of Beaglehole, F. L. W. Wood, W. P. Morrell, and James Rutherford — all of whom had in various ways an interest in the relationship between New Zealand and Britain — and in the work of their students. There was also a considerable development in the writing of regional history, with such important works as W. J. Gardner's *The Amuri: A County History* (1956), A. H. McLintock's *The History of Otago* (1949), Philip Ross May's *The West Coast Gold Rushes* (1962), and W. H. Oliver's *Challenge and Response: A History of the Gisborne East Coast Region* (1971). Two short histories, Keith Sinclair's *A History of New Zealand* (1959) and W. H. Oliver's *The Story of New Zealand* (1960), provided the standard interpretations of the New Zealand past for new generations of general readers as well as scholars; these works emphasized 'race relations', questions of identity and culture, and the impact of progressive political movements. Also influential, nevertheless, were the contributions of historians working outside academia: W. B. Sutch, Dick Scott, and Tony Simpson told a story of class conflict, Pakeha racism, and political betrayal.

The growth of postgraduate studies in New Zealand, an increase in the number of historians working within universities on New Zealand research topics, and the revivification of the government's Historical Branch have resulted in the production during the 1970s and 1980s of a considerable range of specialized monographs by academics or university-trained historians. As well as work in the traditional fields of political, diplomatic, constitutional, and economic history, there have been major innovations in other areas, including business history — R. C. J. Stone's *Makers of Fortune: A Colonial Business Community and its Fall* (1973); intellectual history — M. P. K. Sorrenson's *Maori Origins and Migrations: The Genesis of Some Pakeha Myths* (1979); labour history — Erik Olssen's *The Red Feds: Revolutionary Industrial Unionism and the New Zealand Federation of Labour 1908–14* (1988); social policy — Margaret Tennant's *Paupers and Pro-*

viders: Charitable Aid in New Zealand (1989); women's history — Charlotte Macdonald's *A Woman of Good Character: Single Women as Immigrant Settlers in Nineteenth-century New Zealand* (1990); and cultural history — Rachel Barrowman's *A Popular Vision: The Arts and the Left in New Zealand* (1991), which provides social and political contexts for understanding works of fiction, non-fiction, and drama. These works are all revisionist to some extent, but there have been no significantly new synoptic works, though Miles Fairburn's iconoclastic recalculation of nineteenth-century settler history in *The Ideal Society and its Enemies: the Foundations of Modern New Zealand Society, 1850–1900* (1989) has inaugurated debate about the nature of Pakeha society. These studies have been informed in varying degrees by the insights of scholars in other countries, but David Hamer's *New Towns in the New World: Images and Perceptions of the Nineteenth-Century Urban Frontier* (1990) has been unusual in taking a range of settler societies as its focus.

The encounter of Maori and Pakeha remains a central concern of many New Zealand historians, and this has been heightened by major political debates during the 1980s. Revisionist works by Alan Ward — *A Show of Justice: Racial 'Amalgamation' in Nineteenth Century New Zealand* (1974); John Owens — *Prophets in the Wilderness: The Wesleyan Mission to New Zealand 1819–27* (1974); James Belich — *The New Zealand Wars and the Victorian Interpretation of Racial Conflict* (1986); Claudia Orange — *The Treaty of Waitangi* (1987); and Hazel Riseborough — *Days of Darkness: Taranaki 1878–1884* (1989) — exemplify the reworking of records to incorporate more extensively Maori cultural perspectives. The prospect of a post-colonial historiography has been brought closer to reality with the publication of Maori accounts of the past in the reports on claims before the judicial Waitangi Tribunal and by Ranginui Walker's *Ka Whawhai Tonu Matou: Struggle Without End* (1990), which decentres the Pakeha narrative and installs the indigenous people as the normative presence, while the politics of representation and the complex strategies of colonial discourse have been freshly illuminated by art historian Leonard Bell's *Colonial Constructs: European Images of Maori 1840–1914* (1992).

PETER GIBBONS

Further reading: Jock Phillips, 'Of verandahs and fish and chips and footie on Saturday afternoon: reflections on 100 years of New Zealand historiography', *New Zealand Journal of History* 24 (1990).

HISTORICAL WRITING (Pakistan)

Historiography in Pakistan has been primarily concerned with tracing and explaining the rise of Muslim nationalism in India and the establishment of Pakistan. Certain broad approaches have been adopted by Pakistani historians writing in English. Some general histories claim an ancient heritage for the modern state of Pakistan and offer interpretations of a Muslim polity in terms of a religious, cultural, and political separateness underlying Pakistani consciousness and identity. Such histories include: S. M. Ikram's and P. Spear's *The Cultural Heritage of Pakistan* (1955); Aziz Ahmad's *Islamic Modernism in India and Pakistan: 1857–1964* (1967) and *An Intellectual History of Islam in India* (1969); A. H. Dani's *A Short History of Pakistan: Pre-Muslim Period* (1967), the first volume of the four-volume 'A Short History of Pakistan' series edited by I. H. Qureshi; and Hafeez Malik's *Sir Sayyed Ahmad Khan and Muslim Modernization in India and Pakistan* (1980).

The predominance and authority of nationalist historiography in Pakistan can be explained partly by the ideological orientation of the state. However, a recognition of the issues attendant on the diversity that Pakistan shares with India, Canada, and Nigeria has prompted the exploration of different historical methods. In India and Nigeria, for example, where ethnic and linguistic polarities abound alongside nationalist history, a more pluralistic and less rigidly integrationist approach has been necessitated. Sumit Sarkar's *Modern India: 1885–1947* (1989) and Elizabeth Isichei's *A History of Nigeria* (1983) combine the emergence of non-élitist perspectives and historical analysis based on a cross-section of socio-economic groups. Similarly, historiography in Pakistan has shifted its focus from purely nationalistic, dynastic, and biographical themes to more eclectic and broadly based assessments. The political development of the state and nation, with a variously dated origin and including the Bangladeshi secession, is discussed by Khalid bin Sayeed in *Pakistan, the Formative Phase: 1857–1947* (1960; 2nd ed., 1968) and *Politics in Pakistan: The Nature and Direction of Change* (1980), and by Safdar Mahmood in *Pakistan Divided* (1984) and *Pakistan: Political Roots and Development* (1990).

Intellectual and literary histories of Pakistan include: K. K. Aziz's *A History of the Idea of Pakistan: 1885–1947* (1989); Muhammad Sadiq's *A History of Urdu Literature* (1964; rev. 1984); and Khizar Humayun Ansari's *The Emergence of Socialist Thought among North Indian Muslims: 1917–1947* (1990).

S. S. SIRAJUDDIN

HISTORICAL WRITING (The Philippines)

In the early 1900s Philippine history textbooks were actually editions of American textbooks, and, strangely enough for Filipinos, were about aspects of United States history or American heroes such as Washington and Lincoln — all alien to Filipino experience. It was American education policy to make Filipinos attuned to American democracy and social and cultural values, in attempts to make them good American vassals. (See **Philippines**.) As a result, Filipino schoolchildren knew more about American history and American heroes than they did about their own.

Filipino historians wrote textbooks reflecting the philosophy and biases of their mentors, trained as they were in the American educational system in the Philippines or in the USA. These works were nothing but mere chronicles of events and personalities with no attempt at analysis, interpretation, colourful writing, or use of the imagination.

Early successful attempts in Philippine historical writing using narrative skill and imagination were the works of eminent Filipino historians Teodoro A. Agoncillo and Horacio de la Costa, S.J. In his now-classic work *The Jesuits in the Philippines, 1581–1678* (1961), de la Costa traces the emergence, development, and growth of the Jesuit congregation in the country up to its expulsion from the Philippines. His narration is not confined to lifeless, unimaginative historical narration, however. Rather than merely stringing together historical data, de la Costa places historical figures in a dramatic situation and, through them, narrates historical events by means of understandable frames of reference containing aspects of present-day culture. He imaginatively translates seventeenth- or eighteenth-century realities using similar or analogous contemporary situations. A creative writer in English in his own right, de la Costa the historian has successfully combined his historical and technical training with narrative and creative narrative skills.

Agoncillo's *The Revolt of the Masses: The Story of Bonifacio and the Katipunan* (1956), on the other hand, is a biography of Andres Bonifacio, revolutionary hero, who led what turned out to be the first nationwide uprising against the Spanish rule in the Philippines. The uprising, in turn, initiated a series of events that ultimately led to the establishment of the first republic in the whole of Asia. Following a hastily called court martial, Bonifacio was sentenced to death, a sentence carried out by his own countrymen. At the hands of Agoncillo, the narration of this episode comes alive. It is told from the perspective of Bonifacio, around whom all other characters revolve. Through the skilful use of dramatic narration, Agoncillo succeeds in bringing to the fore events and individuals that make up the first phase of the Philippine revolution against Spain, with all the intrigues and internecine fights of young inexperienced men.

Much contemporary historical writing in English in the Philippines is confined to textbooks, which promise financial gain to the publisher. Serious historical writing, on the other hand, mainly refers to the dry-as-dust historical works of the members of the academe — ponderous prose and kilometric bibliographical notes.

MARCELINO A. FORONDA, JR.

HISTORICAL WRITING (St Helena)

St Helena's pre-settlement literary heritage dates from Jan Huygen van Linschoten's illustrated accounts of 1589, published in his *Itinerario* (Dutch, 1596; English, 1598; Latin, 1599). The earliest fiction set in St Helena is that precursor of modern lunar fables, *The Voyage of Domingo Gonsales to the World in the Moon* (1638) by Bishop Francis Godwin. The first book solely about St Helena, *A Description of the Island of St. Helena; Containing Observations on Its Singular Structure and Formation; and an Account of Its Climate, Natural History, and Inhabitants* (1805), was published anonymously by surgeon Francis Duncan. St Helena's first chronicler was Thomas Henry Brooke, nephew and secretary to Governor Robert Brooke (1787–1801) and himself twice acting governor (1821–3 and 1828), whose *A History of the Island of St. Helena from Its Discovery by the Portuguese to the Year 1806* (1808) was compiled from the Castle records, with an enlarged edition in 1824 covering Napoleon's exile. Ten years later, Ackermann printed more than a hundred copies of Robert Seale's surrealistic study of the Island's volcanic structure, *The Geognosy of the Island St. Helena, Illustrated in a Series of Views, Plans and Sections; Accompanied with Explanatory Remarks and Observations* (1834). Darwin, who met Seale on St Helena in 1836, praised both this and his magnificent model of the Island at Addiscombe Military College, destroyed by a London, England, museum a century later for its case! But the classic work remains John Charles Melliss' *St. Helena: A Physical, Historical, and Topographical Description of the Island, Including Its Geology, Fauna, Flora and Meteorology* (1875), with more than sixty plates, many showing endangered endemic flora. (Melliss' wife Anne, who sketched some of them, was probably the author of a slim volume of verse, *A Few Thoughts for the Stranger and the Resident in St. Helena with Illustrations*, 1868, chromolithographers Vincent Brooks, Day and Son.)

Benjamin Grant of *The St. Helena Guardian* was eager to foster St Helenian literature. Apart from Hudson Janisch's *Extracts from the St. Helena Records*, he printed Captain J. R. Oliver's *Geology of St. Helena* (1879), a work praised by Harvard University professor R. A. Daly in 1927. Grant also wrote *A Few Notes on St. Helena* (1881); *Some Considerations Concerning St. Helena as a Health Resort* (1881), repeated in his seventy-five-page *Descriptive Guide through St. Helena* (1883); *The Citadel of the South Atlantic* (1888); and a twenty-two-page 'General Description of St Helena and Its Literature' for the *Almanac* (1876), reprinted with his 1881 *Notes*, though without mentioning any local works. At the turn of the century, Emily Jackson compiled *St. Helena, the Historic Island* (1903), a mine of ill-organized material, with seventy-five photographs by her husband, chemist Thomas Jackson who, with her brother, E. J. Warren, had six booklets of Island views printed between 1900 and 1937.

In the 1960s two booklets written by visitors to interest Islanders in their homeland were issued by the government press: H. E. Walsh's *St. Helena: An Outline Account of a Famous Island* (1960), and *An Outline of Geography and Local*

Study (undated) by D. A. Hall and D. A. Jeffs, the first attempt to provide a local school-book for South Atlantic scholars, otherwise taught exclusively from English textbooks.

Ascension Island publications include John Parker's *The Ascension Handbook, A Concise Guide to Ascension Island, South Atlantic* (1968; 3rd ed., 1983) and Jeffery Cant's *Wideawake Field: The Story of Ascension Island's Airstrip in World War II* (1973). (See **Publishing**, St Helena.)

TREVOR W. HEARL

HISTORICAL WRITING (West Africa)

The earliest English historical writing on West Africa, as that on the Caribbean, was directly connected with the controversies about slavery in the late eighteenth century. Anthony Benezet's *Some Historical Account of Guinea* (1771) was an anti-slavery tract, while Archibald Dalzel's *The History of Dahomy, an Inland Kingdom of Africa* (1793) was written mainly to justify the slave trade. A few travellers, however, such as T. E. Bowdich, in his *An Essay on the Superstitions, Customs, and Arts Common to the Ancient Egyptians, Abyssinians, and Ashantees* (1821), included historical chapters that were less marked by ideological considerations. (See also **Exploration Literature**, West Africa.)

Not until the colonial period did West Africans themselves, educated at mission schools, take a lead. They often drew upon (but never simply reproduced) oral tradition, as in Carl Christian Reindorf's *History of the Gold Coast and Asante* (1895; 2nd ed., 1966), Samuel Johnson's *The History of the Yorubas from the Earliest Times to the Beginning of the British Protectorate* (1921, but completed in 1897), and J. U. Egharevba's *A Short History of Benin* (1936). Other local historians, mostly Yoruba, preferred to publish in the vernacular.

Several colonial officials, such as Sir John Gray and W. W. Claridge, wrote histories, albeit from a Eurocentric viewpoint, of the territories in which they worked, such as Gray's *A History of the Gambia* (1940) and Claridge's *A History of the Gold Coast and Ashanti from the Earliest Times to the Commencement of the Twentieth Century* (2 vols, 1915). The professionalization of the discipline did not begin until the late 1940s, when a lectureship in African history was created at the University of London, England, and steps were taken towards creating what eventually became the universities of Ghana and Ibadan, Nigeria. In Britain the leading figure was J. D. Fage, whose *An Introduction to the History of West Africa* (1955) went through five editions.

The first university-trained West African historians emerged in the 1950s. The majority were from southern Nigeria, like the 'amateur' local historians who preceded them. K. O. Dike's *Trade and Politics in the Niger Delta 1830–1885* (1956) was based primarily on archival material; other works, such as E. J. Alagoa's *The Small Brave City-State: A History of Nembe-Brass in the Niger Delta* (1964), made effective use of oral traditions. Both Nigeria and the Gold Coast (Ghana) founded a historical journal in 1956 and went on to create a series of historical monographs.

By 1980 the essential outlines of West African history had been established, and monographs had appeared on most of the major pre-colonial states, as well as on various aspects of colonial and post-colonial rule. In terms of quantity the publications of North American historians had gained a leading position. Fage's *Introduction* had been superseded by the *History of West Africa* (2 vols, 1971; 3rd ed., 1985–7), edited by J. F. Ade Ajayi and Michael Crowder. As this collaborative venture indicates, anglophone historians of West Africa have tended to rely less on oral tradition than their francophone counterparts or the historians of East and Central Africa.

Perhaps the major recent development has been a more cautious attitude towards sources, coupled with a questioning of the historicist paradigms that once influenced nationalist, liberal, and neo-Marxist historiography.

ADAM JONES

Further reading: J. D. Fage, 'Continuity and change in the writing of West African history', *African Affairs* 70 (1971); Caroline Neale, *Writing 'Independent' History. African Historiography, 1960–1980* (1985).

HOAXES AND JOKES

Hoaxes and Jokes (Australia)

One way of distinguishing between a hoax and a joke is to consider the words' etymologies. Both are derived from the medieval Latin *jocus*, but whereas a joke originally meant a verbal game, a jest, hoax descends from 'hocus-pocus' (probably a juggler's term), where the element of deception predominates. Of hoaxes, there has been one notorious example in Australian literature — the **Ern Malley** affair of 1944, the avowed aim of which was to discredit modernist poetry. The editor of the journal *Angry Penguins*, **Max Harris**, was prosecuted for publishing the Ern Malley poems.

A second scandalous hoax was the work of the poet **Gwen Harwood**, who concealed her identity in the 1950s and 1960s under various pseudonyms, including 'Frances Geyer', 'T. F. Klyne', 'Walter Lehmann', and 'Miriam Stone'. 'Timothy Kline' merits a spurious 'biographical' note in **Thomas Shapcott**'s anthology, *Australian Poetry Now* (1970), but it was 'Walter Lehmann' who achieved notoriety with two seemingly innocent, perfectly regular sonnets published in the ***Bulletin*** (5 August 1961) before it was realized that they were acrostic in nature and contained a rude message addressed specifically to that paper's editor.

A more entertaining literary joke is the dramatic monologue *Scanlan: A Monologue in One Act*, by **Barry Oakley**, first performed in 1978 at the inaugural conference of the Association for the Study of Australian Literature and first published in *Meanjin* (1, 1978). It is in the form of a lecture on the nineteenth-century Australian poet **Henry Kendall**, delivered by one Scanlan, as addicted to drink as was his subject. As the lecture progresses, the speaker's obsession with his academic rival, Dr Grigsby, becomes apparent; in the end Scanlan is unable to disentangle his life from Kendall's.

Numerous writers have hidden behind pseudonyms, including **Joseph Furphy**, who, as 'Tom Collins', was the author-narrator of *Such is Life* (1903) and *Rigby's Romance* (1921; rev. 1948). For more than two decades a mystery surrounded the identity of Brent of Bin Bin, whose six novels bore a remarkable resemblance to those of **Miles Franklin**, even to the point of the manuscripts having been typed on a machine with the same peculiarities. Franklin would never admit to being the author of the 'Brent' novels, the best-known of which are *Up the Country* (1928), *Ten Creeks* (1930), and *Back to Bool Bool* (1931).

Miles Franklin's friend Mary Fullerton (1868–1946) published poetry and fiction under her own name as well as two novels under two different male pseudonyms (*Rufus Sterne*, 1932, by 'Robert Gray', and *The Murders at Crabapple Farm*, 1933, by 'Gordon Manners'), but in the 1940s she adopted the initial 'E' for her last two books of verse, *Moles Do So Little with their Privacy* (1942) and *The Wonder and the Apple* (1946). The identity of 'E' was not known until after Fullerton's death.

A pseudonym may indicate writing in a different genre, or may be intended to deceive an editor or prove a point. **Nettie Palmer** notes in her journal *Fourteen Years* (1948) that Frank Wilmot invented the name 'Furnley Maurice' because as Wilmot he could not get his verse published in the magazine the *Bookfellow*, whereas that of 'Furnley Maurice' was accepted. Thereafter he was always known by that name.

John O'Grady (1907–81) adopted the persona of an Italian migrant, 'Nino Culotta', when he wrote *They're a Weird Mob* (1957), in which he looked at Australian society through a newcomer's eyes. **B. Wongar** is the name used by Sreten Bozic for his apocalyptic fiction dealing with the destruction of Aboriginal tribal life by the white man.

The 'tall story' in verse or prose, whether literary or passed on by word of mouth, forms a large category of Australian jokes. The city slicker versus the man from the bush, the trials and tribulations of life in the country, jokes played on the 'new chum', usually an Englishman, are perennial sources of humour, particularly in the nineteenth century. **Geoffrey Lehmann**'s *Comic Australian Verse* (1972) and Bill Scott's *The Penguin Book of Australian Humorous Verse* (1984) are anthologies that draw on such traditional material. There are characters such as **Alan Marshall**'s 'Spewa Jack' and **Frank Hardy**'s 'Billy Borker'. It is noteworthy that practically all Australian humorists of this kind are male, writing about an all-male environment. (See **Humour**, Australia.)

PATRICIA EXCELL

HOAXES AND JOKES (Canada)

In Canadian literature only the **Grey Owl** hoax is as central to the national tradition as the **Ern Malley** episode is in Australia. Represented as a Native Canadian, Grey Owl was proved after his death to be Archie Belaney, a British immigrant, a revelation that led to an instant devaluing of his environmentalist writing. Only recently have the texts themselves been recognized for their importance in Canadian nature writing apart from the race of their author. Unlike the Australian **Banumbir Wongar**, whose texts are of interest only through their claims to be Aboriginal, Belaney used his 'Indianness' to gain status for pronouncements that reflected the keen observations of an amateur naturalist.

Although too small to be regarded as a full-fledged hoax, an event that connects the 1920s and the 1970s has received much critical attention. In 1970 John Glassco published his *Memoirs of Montparnasse*, a vivid account of his experiences as an expatriate North American in Paris, France, between 1929 and 1932, claiming that the manuscript was unchanged since he completed it in 1933. Some critics, however, pointed to major differences between the 1970 version and a chapter published in 1929. The affair's significance lies probably in Glassco's attempt to create the image of a youthful aesthete to support his later reputation as Canada's only literary pornographer. Glassco created the persona as a specific corrective to the norm of Canadian life.

The most notable hoaxes in Canada are recent. One is the product of a continuous literary joker, **George Bowering**. At its base, it is just a pseudonym. Bowering's main pseudonym, E. E. Greengrass, is only that, but a later version becomes a true hoax. When Pier Giorgio Di Cicco published *Roman Candles: An Anthology of Poems by Seventeen Italo-Canadian Poets* (1978), one contributor was Ed Pratoverde, 'Greengrass' in Italian, who later decided to drop the 'dumb pen name' and be listed as Ed Prato, complete with fictionalized contributor's biography. This is especially interesting today when the appropriation of voice is a major issue in Canada, and WASP ('White Anglo-Saxon Protestant') imitation of ethnicity has been often attacked.

Something closer to the Ern Malley tradition is the Crad Kilodney hoax. One newspaper report accurately termed Kilodney 'a self-publishing author who hawks his books on downtown corners'. When Kilodney's submissions to the Canadian Broadcasting Corporation's literary competitions were rejected three times he decided, in 1988, to test the competition by submitting stories by William Faulkner, Jack London, Franz Kafka, Luigi Pirandello, Sherwood Anderson, O. Henry, and Maxim Gorky. None made the short list. Kilodney claimed that this shows 'the incompetence of the preliminary screening process'. In the furore immediately after Kilodney's revelation no one suggested that the stories might not have deserved to win: as Kilodney himself admitted, he chose 'fairly obscure' examples, which might not have fitted the Canadian temper. But, most significantly, they would inevitably be subtly if not blatantly out-of-date.

More joke than hoax is the Toronto Research Group, which, through the journal *Open Letter* (6 and 7, 1980–81), created an extended commentary on pataphysics, 'the science of imaginary solutions and the source of answers to questions never to be posed . . . '. The issue refers to 'three known institutes in Canada: L'Institut Onto-Genetique, the Institute of Humanitarian Studies and the Institute for Creative Misunderstanding. There is rumour too, of the pending existence of a Centre for Marginal Studies and some acknowledgement of a non-College of Epistemological Myopia.' *Open Letter*, always the home of the Canadian avant garde, is an appropriate venue for such a serious farce. (Crad Kilodney is mentioned as a non-participating pataphysician, and George Bowering was at the time on the board of *Open Letter*.) The Canadian literary hoax remains the game of a select few.

TERRY GOLDIE

HODGE, MERLE (1944–)

Trinidadian novelist

Born in Carapichaima, Trinidad, she earned a BA in French and a master of philosophy degree (with a thesis on the Negritude Movement's Leon Damas, a French Guyanese poet) from the University of London, England. Hodge has worked in various countries of the Caribbean, including Jamaica and Grenada, and now lectures at the University of the West Indies, Trinidad.

Hodge is best known internationally for her novel *Crick Crack, Monkey* (1970), a key text in Caribbean literature. The novel particularly rewards feminist critical approaches, and, because it bridges the gap between adolescent and adult literature, it is used as a text in Caribbean secondary schools. Since the publication of *Crick Crack, Monkey*, however, Hodge has focused her energy on critical work, which is connected with her urgent activist approach to education, gender, and development in Trinidad and the English-speaking Caribbean. Consequently, only a few short stories have appeared: 'Millicent' (1973), 'Inez' (1975), and 'Jeffie Lemmington and Me' (1980).

Hodge's work explores the complex relationships among education, language usage, creative writing, folk traditions, gender relations, family structures, and political and economic development. Fruitful comparison may be made between *Crick Crack, Monkey* and **Erna Brodber**'s *Jane and Louisa Will Soon Come Home* (1980).

Crick Crack, Monkey synthesizes Hodge's politics and art and is marked by skilful use of satire, humour, and an intimate and accomplished knowledge of Trinidadian English-based Creole and its contrastive uses with Standard English. Hodge's use of language counterpoints a reconstructive stereotyping of black and brown women that enables her to mount powerful and sweeping challenges to Eurocentric notions of race and colour, class, gender, and the validity of certain cultural patterns over others. Hodge's work deals with pre-independence Trinidad and externalizes the complex dynamic of cultural conflict as it impinges on the attempt of young black women to forge a confident and self-aware identity.

HELEN PYNE TIMOTHY

Further reading: Ena V. Thomas, '*Crick Crack, Monkey*: a picaresque perspective', in Selwyn R.

Cudjoe (ed.) *Caribbean Women Writers: Essays from the First International Conference* (1990).

HODGINS, JACK (1938–)

Canadian novelist, short-story writer

Born to a family of loggers and farmers in the Comox Valley on Vancouver Island, British Columbia, Canada, he attended the University of British Columbia, where he pursued his interest in creative writing by studying with the Canadian poet **Earle Birney**. The author of four novels, two collections of stories, and a children's book, Hodgins currently teaches at the University of Victoria.

Hodgins' fiction has been frequently discussed within the context of Latin American 'magic realism'. While critics have amply documented his indebtedness to Colombian novelist Gabriel García Márquez — noting, for example, the ease with which Hodgins, in both *The Invention of the World* (1977) and *The Resurrection of Joseph Bourne* (1979), moves between a locally inflected realism and a powerfully imaginative discourse of myth and magic — little work has been done exploring Hodgins' writing within a Commonwealth context. This is an unfortunate oversight since, as Canadian critic Stephen Slemon has convincingly argued, many of Hodgins' thematic preoccupations and discursive strategies — including his involvement with 'magic realism' — overlap suggestively with the predominant concerns of a number of contemporary post-colonial writers.

Commenting in an interview on the influence of Latin American writers on his work, Hodgins gestures towards a recognition of the extent to which he might be considered a post-colonial writer by explaining that 'all literatures were equally foreign' to someone who grew up in a small rural community in western Canada. In an interview in the journal *Kunapipi* (1, 1990), Hodgins reflects on the lack of literary models on his own home ground: 'I had to invent my own kind of novel to deal with a people and an island that had not been written about before in serious fiction.' Just as his teacher, Birney, was one of the first poets to put western Canada on the literary map, Hodgins has become one of the first fictive chroniclers of Vancouver Island. Defining himself not only against the dominant cultural traditions of Britain and the USA but also in opposition to other regions of Canada, Hodgins is engaged throughout his fiction in an attempt to map out sites of interaction between self and place.

Hodgins' fictional world is peopled with figures who, like the characters in many transcultural texts, often find themselves on a quest for belonging. In *Innocent Cities* (1990), the interaction between self and place is played out through an exploration of linguistic dislocation. One key figure experiences cultural displacement when she moves from the comfortable world of things in England into a new continent, Australia, made up of nothing but beautiful and exotic words. The discomfort occasioned by this shift from a world of things to a world of words signals Hodgins' involvement in probing the relationship between a transplanted English language and a new place.

Hodgins' other texts similarly explore patterns of rootlessness. In *The Resurrection of Joseph Bourne*, which won the Governor General's Award for Fiction in 1980, many of the town's inhabitants engage in overtly uncharacteristic behaviour in attempts to overcome their fear of not belonging to the community. The notion of home for these characters has been rendered unstable as a result of various adjustments and transformations. Like the displaced Irish villagers in *The Invention of the World* who escaped one form of domination only to find themselves re-colonized in the 'new world', these characters, in their search for something they can call home, serve as emblems of Hodgins' continuing engagement with the cultural meanings of place and belonging.

The fear of not belonging, of not being able to define and articulate home, is repeatedly played out alongside Hodgins' thematic and structural insistence on the value of community. Stylistically, Hodgins' foremost achievement may well be his ability to give expression to his Vancouver Island community. With the possible exception of *The Honorary Patron* (1987), Hodgins' novels seek to re-create and emphasize communal, rather than individual, experience. Such an emphasis relates him to such Commonwealth writers as **Chinua Achebe** and **Raja Rao**, who reject the Eurocentric cult of the individual in favour of formulations that enable articulation of the values of their own cultural heritages.

AJAY HEBLE

Further reading: David Jeffrey, *Jack Hodgins and His Works* (1989).

HOLCROFT, MONTAGUE HARRY (1902–93)
New Zealand novelist, journalist, critic
Born near Christchurch, New Zealand, he set out to be a professional writer — an almost unknown career at that time and place — at the age of nineteen. His autobiography, *The Way of a Writer* (1984), tells of his precarious life in Christchurch, in Australia, and in London, England, during the 1920s and 1930s. Early in his career he wrote mostly formula stories for popular magazines, graduating to Conradish novels set in faraway places including *Beyond the Breakers* (1928), *The Flameless Fire* (1929), and *Brazilian Daughter* (1931). During the 1930s Holcroft's writing diverted to criticism and philosophical reflection, and a long essay, *The Deepening Stream: Cultural Influences in New Zealand* (1940), was a prize-winner in the New Zealand Centennial Literary Competition. It was followed by *The Waiting Hills* (1943) and *Encircling Seas* (1946) to form a trilogy collected as *Discovered Isles* (1950). The books ranged widely, through education, politics, social habits, the place of a writer in New Zealand, and studies of particular writers, but were chiefly notable for developing, in near-mystical language, a theory of the influence of a still largely primeval landscape on the lately arrived humans scattered precariously on its surface. This view had affinities with the work of a number of South Island poets at the time, including **Ursula Bethell, Denis Glover, Allen Curnow**, and **Charles Brasch**, and was an acknowledged influence on some of them. It was less compelling to North Island writers, whose landscape was more lush and contained more reminders of a thousand years of Maori habitation.

Holcroft turned to newspaper editing for a living in the late 1930s and was editor of the *New Zealand Listener* from 1949 to 1967 and again briefly in 1972–3. A literary as well as broadcasting journal, the *Listener* in Holcroft's time published virtually every well-known New Zealand writer, most of them repeatedly. After his retirement he published many more books, including collections of his *Listener* editorials, local histories, criticism, and further autobiography — *A Sea of Words* (1986).

DENNIS McELDOWNEY

HONG KONG
Hong Kong is situated on the south-east coast of China. It comprises the island of that name, the small district of Kowloon on the mainland just opposite, and a larger area of the mainland called the New Territories. The island of Hong Kong, which has given the territory its name, is less than one-tenth of the size of the New Territories and has an area of 51.5 square kilometres. Kowloon has an area of only nine square kilometres.

Hong Kong became a British colony in the nineteenth century. Britain concluded with China three treaties relating to Hong Kong: the Treaty of Nanking, signed in 1842 and ratified in 1843, under which Hong Kong island was ceded in perpetuity; the Convention of Peking in 1860, under which the southern part of the Kowloon peninsula and Stonecutters Island were ceded in perpetuity;

and the Convention of 1898, under which the New Territories were leased to Britain for ninety-nine years.

According to the terms of the Sino-British Joint Declaration signed in December 1984, British administration and jurisdiction over Hong Kong will continue until midnight 30 June 1997, when Hong Kong will become a Special Administrative Region (SAR) of the People's Republic of China. The Joint Declaration provides that for fifty years after 1997 Hong Kong's form of government will remain unchanged and that China's socialist system and policies will not be practised in the SAR.

If, for the vast majority of the local population, the end of British rule in Hong Kong is a source of apprehension, it is not because of any cultural ties or feelings of affinity with the British. The local population is concerned with the preservation of prosperity, stability, and civil and other liberties; British literature and culture are of little interest. The material advantages of knowing the English language have long been recognized, but, with the exception of a small minority of western-educated returned students and anachronistic remnants of more Anglophilic times, there is no particular love of English for its own sake. (See **Historical Writing**, Hong Kong.)

From the colony's beginnings, the local population and the British colonizers developed separately. They literally lived apart, with special zones such as the Peak and a part of Tsimshatsui in Kowloon declared off-limits to the Chinese. In the conduct of business, English-speaking Chinese middlemen were employed. The European community developed a strong social life, centring on amateur theatricals, the Hong Kong Club (established in 1846), and various sporting activities. Throughout the nineteenth century the Chinese continued to support their own vernacular schools in Chinese. Only a very small number received what was known as a 'European education in a European language' in the government-funded schools. Some wealthy, local Chinese sent their children to be educated in the UK, but for years the University of Hong Kong — until 1967 the only tertiary institution in the territory — provided Hong Kong with the vast majority of its bilingual civil servants as well as with educators, physicians, engineers, and other professionals. Until the late 1960s, with the establishment of The Chinese University of Hong Kong, tertiary education was restricted to a privileged few. It was left to the missionary schools, run by different religious denominations, to make the English language and western culture available to a larger number.

Thus, Hong Kong has remained essentially a Chinese city. Chinese, which here refers to both Cantonese, the spoken southern Chinese dialect, and written Chinese, is used for a range of everyday purposes. In this respect Hong Kong is very different from Singapore, where English serves as a lingua franca for the various ethnic and linguistic communities.

The separate development of the communities has resulted in a virtual absence of a local literature written in English. In an interview in *All Asia Review of Books* (4, 1989), **Timothy Mo** focuses on the linguistic obstacle to such a literature and advances a simplistic reason for the dearth of Hong Kong writers in English: 'Indians have no problem writing good English but no Cantonese or Chinese has that expertise.' There is a more cogent reason for the dearth, one that is closely related to, and perhaps the partial cause of, alleged linguistic incompetence: links with China go far beyond the sharing of a standard written language. There are deep cultural ties between overseas Chinese communities and the motherland; because of Hong Kong's geographical position, these ties are particularly strong. The long-standing popular view of Hong Kong as a cultural desert, where the pursuit of literature and the arts are sacrificed to the worship of money and material success, persists. Yet it has always been considered a mark of cultivation among the older, upper-class Chinese to write poetry in Chinese, to paint a little, and to produce good calligraphy.

As 1997 draws nearer there has been a tremendous increase in the output of, and interest in, 'Hong Kong literature' in Chinese, in spite of continued controversy over its definition, quality, and critical approaches and criteria. The editors of *Renditions* (1973–), a Chinese-English translation magazine, attempted, through English translation, to show a wider readership the richness and diversity of this literature in a special issue (*Renditions: Hong Kong*, 29 and 30, 1988).

In the field of local writing in English, however, the reverse is true. The Chinese — and Hong Kong Chinese today (if they do read anything in English) — have always tended to respond negatively to writing in English about China and the Chinese. This type of resentment of what can been seen as invasion of privacy is probably not unique; in Hong Kong society, about to enter into a postcolonial era, there is a growing psychological resistance to the idea of writing in a foreign language, presumably for a reading public that does not understand Chinese. There may be some Hong Kong Chinese who have both the desire and the linguistic ability to write in English, but they lack creativity. With such a small catchment area as Hong Kong, there is less likelihood of the convergence of such desire, ability, and creativity.

One should qualify the statement that Hong Kong Chinese, on the whole, have never identified with their colonial masters. Until 1950, many graduates from local secondary schools, indeed some of the wealthiest ones, attended universities on the Chinese mainland. The situation changed after 1949 with the Communist takeover. Children growing up in Hong Kong, many of them refugees from the mainland, saw their future as lying in British Hong Kong or in western English-speaking countries. The severing of links with mainland China became particularly marked after 1957 because of the upheavals caused by the Great Leap Forward and the Cultural Revolution. It was not until the late 1970s that Hong Kong people began to visit China again in great numbers. Thus, the 1950s and 1960s have been described as a 'true colonial period' that coincides with the 'golden age' of writing in English in Hong Kong. What English writing there is tends to come from local Chinese writers, for whom the 1950s and 1960s were formative years, although some of their writing was produced, or at least appeared in print, after the 1960s.

If the definition of 'Hong Kong literature' were broadened to include works by western visitors or residents who have written about the colony, then one could include such writers as Somerset Maugham, James Clavell, and Christopher New. (See **Foreign Writers**, Hong Kong.) The English language in Hong Kong is experiencing difficult times; consequently, the Hong Kong 'voice' in English will be heard even more rarely.

MIMI CHAN

Further reading: David Bonavia, *Hong Kong: Living with the Future* (1985); Jan Morris, *Hong Kong: Xiang-gang* (1988); Alan Birch, *Hong Kong: The Colony that Never Was* (1991).

HONNALGERE, GOPAL R. (1943–)

Indian poet

Born in Bijapur, India, he was raised in Mysore and Bangalore, taking a university degree in science. A follower of Zen Buddhism, he works as a teacher.

Honnalgere began writing seriously in the 1960s when a change in sensibility became evident both in the substance and form of Indo-Anglian writing. His poetry collections include *A Wad of Poems* (1971), *A Gesture of Fleshless Sound* (1972), *Zen Tree and the Wild Innocents* (1973), *The Nudist Camp* (1978), *The Fifth* (1980), and *Intermodes* (1986). While the majority of contemporary Indian poets writing in English have cultivated a lyric idiom following contemporary British and American poets, Honnalgere has consciously distanced himself from this imitative tendency. He chooses to follow instead the Bhakti cult and folk style of the oral tradition; the influence of the Indian saint-poets is quite obvious in his work, as are regional influences.

In the early phase of Honnalgere's writing, abstract nouns such as self, love, time, God, eternity, and faith abound; they are largely eliminated from his later poems. The long poems of the early period sound pompous, but the shorter ones have the stamp of authentic experience. *Zen Tree and the Wild Innocents* demonstrates a gathering maturity. Here one glimpses a new-found metaphysical density, and Jesus is a recurring presence. In *The Nudist Camp* Honnalgere, using humour and humility, challenges the 'civilized' sexual standards of his society. The volume also suggests a rebellious creative spirit. *The Fifth* is a companion volume to *The Nudist Camp*, containing surrealist prose pieces. Most of the volume's poems are potential short stories reminiscent of the art of James Thurber. Honnalgere often uses three or four haiku-like verses to make a complete poem, and his specialized knowledge of biology and biochemistry is evident in his imagery. *Intermodes* displays an unusual breadth of sympathy, like that seen in Indian Bhakti poetry. Honnalgere has not published a volume of poetry since 1986.

PURNIMA MEHTA

HOOD, HUGH (1928–)

Canadian novelist, short-story writer

Born in Toronto, Canada, of a Nova Scotian father and a French-Canadian mother, he was educated in Roman Catholic schools and at the University of Toronto, where he received his Ph.D. in 1955. He taught at St Joseph's College, Connecticut, USA, from 1955 to 1961 when he joined the English department of the mainly francophone Université de Montréal, Canada. He is married to Noreen Mallory, a former theatre designer turned painter. These biographical details and his Catholic and bicultural Canadian background are reflected in his prolific works — four non-fiction books, seven short-story collections, a novella, and twelve novels.

Hood is a 'conservative' writer in the Christian humanist, allegorical tradition of Dante and Spenser; he claims 'influences' from Wordsworth, Coleridge, Joyce, Proust, and Anthony Powell (but not from Canadian writers — even his mentor, **Morley Callaghan** — because 'they're not good enough'). His aesthetic, expressed in essays in *The Governor's Bridge Is Closed* (1973) and *Trusting the Tale* (1983), he calls 'superrealism' — an exhibition of the transcendent essence of things, 'the spirit in the flesh', the holy in the daily. This 'secular analogy to Scripture' rejects the 'psychological novel of character and incident' to synthesize the cultural and occupational details of his characters' lives with metaphorical incidents and allegorical 'emblems'. This aesthetic is brilliantly realized in the condensed iconography and stylistic virtuosity of his short stories, particularly in the title story of his 1971 collection, *The Fruit Man, the Meat Man and the Manager*, where 'the Fruit Man is God proffering the apple, and the Meat Man is Christ incarnate, and the Manager is the Holy Spirit moving the world.'

In his novels Hood has sought, with less success, for a fictional form to embody his religious vision: *White Figure, White Ground* (1964) is a parable, *The Camera Always Lies* (1967) a romance, *A Game of Touch* (1970) a realistic psychological study, and *You Can't Get There From Here* (1972) a fantasy satire. *The New Age/ Le nouveau siècle* is a projected twelve-volume series of novels (the first of which, *The Swing in the Garden*, was published in 1975, the last projected for 2000), a 'documentary fantasy' or 'social mythology' of Canada in the twentieth century. In this genre, which combines 'the novel' with 'fully-developed Christian allegory', Hood claims to be '*both* a realist and a *transcendentalist allegorist*'. While praising the latter accomplishment, critics have disputed the former. Despite the neatly compartmentalized Dachau sections in *Black and White Keys* (1982), Hood has still failed to engage, dramatically and consistently, the problem of existential evil. And his 'spots of time', while evoking the noumenal, tend to subvert coherent structure and realistic characterization, creating neither a modernist nor a postmodernist discourse, but simply a cold pastoral. Nevertheless, this 'one bright book of the redemption and atonement' audaciously challenges Canadian critical stereotypes with its distinctive vision and form.

BARBARA PELL

Further reading: J. R. (Tim) Struthers, 'Hugh Hood: an annotated bibliography', in Robert Lecker and Jack David (eds) *The Annotated Bibliography of Canada's Major Authors* 5 (1984).

Hope, A. D. (1907–)

Australian poet, critic

The son of a Protestant clergyman, he was born Alec Derwent Hope at Cooma, New South Wales, Australia, and was educated at the University of Sydney and at Oxford University, England. He became a lecturer at Sydney Teachers' College in 1937, and after moving to Melbourne and later to Canberra, became professor of English at the Australian National University. He retired in 1968, but has maintained a close relationship with the university, which has named one of its buildings in his honour.

Throughout his career, Hope has published with great distinction both as a poet and as a critic. His collections of essays, *The Cave and the Spring* (1965), *A Midsummer Eve's Dream: Variations on a Theme by William Dunbar* (1970), *Native Companions: Essays and Comments on Australian Literature, 1936–66* (1974), *The Pack of Autolycus* (1978), and *The New Cratylus: Notes on the Craft of Poetry* (1979), demonstrate his commitment as a poet and reveal as much about his own craft and vocation as they do about their ostensible subject matter. Hope's capacity to be both a stimulating academic and a leading poet has been an example to many younger writer-academics.

Although he began writing poetry in 1930, Hope's first book, *The Wandering Islands*, was not published until 1955. Its mixture of eroticism and satire is reminiscent of W. H. Auden, but with a tone that was to become distinctly Hope's own. The voice is reasonable yet committed, witty yet sensuous, intellectual yet capable of great emotional resonance. In 'William Butler Yeats' Hope praises the Irish poet for having found 'that noble, candid speech / In which all things worth saying may be said'. Hope's own poetry is forever motivated by the search for such a speech, and in his espousal of what he called 'the middle way' he can rightly claim to have found, or made, it. By the 'middle way', Hope meant the voice that was typified by seventeenth and eighteenth-century English poetry, such as that of Dryden and Pope. It did not aspire to the heights or depths of Elizabethan or Romantic poetry, but could, as the occasion demanded, achieve them both. It was 'The poetry of the great commonplaces . . . making an act of celebration'.

Hope has achieved and sustained such a voice, but at the expense of isolating himself from other developments in Australian poetry. Metrical formality was prevalent in Australian poetry in the 1940s and 1950s, but Hope has kept to this mode while other poets have explored free verse and other more experimental modes. Readers outside Australia may find Hope academic or even antiquarian in his formalism. But those familiar with the rhythms and cadences of Australian speech will admire the way he has re-fashioned and transformed traditional verse forms, accommodating within them a capacity to speak directly and naturally, yet with a sustained dignity and authority.

Hope's poetry displays a cosmopolitan, urbane

sophistication and a wide, even erudite, breadth of reference. Unlike the work of many of his contemporaries, his poems are rarely concerned with anything obviously Australian, nor do Australian landscape or history play much part in them. Rather, they frequently take as their starting point something read in a book, or some out-of-the-way fragment of scientific or social history. Frequently myths or biblical stories are re-fashioned or re-interpreted in order to shed a new and unfamiliar light on experience. Myth is an important element in Hope's poetry, testifying to the enduring forms of human experience as well as to the richness of human culture. These myths, in such poems as 'The Return of Persephone' or 'Apollo and Daphne', provide the dramatic framework for an exploration of passion and loss. 'Apollo and Daphne, II', a later poem, turns to the theme of art as that activity in which 'men share in the divine'.

For Hope, poetry is a vocation of the highest order. Like many Australian writers, he displays no traditional Christian or other religious belief. Yet his poetry seeks to reveal 'in man . . . A splendour, which his human virtues mask' and to celebrate the harmony that he feels exists at the core of the universe. An early poem, 'Standardization', praises the rightness with which nature endlessly replicates an almost identical shape for the leaf. The much anthologized 'The Death of the Bird' testifies to the pattern and rightness — even if it seems pitiless — of the workings of the natural world. Numerous poems revel in a joyous yet decorous eroticism that, in the straight-laced years in which they were written, provoked considerable stir. Today the effect is one of sane and dignified sensuality, warm sensuousness, and a moving but unsentimental willingness to praise. In a later poem, 'Pervigilium Veneris', Hope pays tribute to the great lover-poets, 'Ovid and Pushkin, Byron and Ronsard, / Gongora, Goethe'. For these poets, he claims, 'Apollo [was] their source, Aphrodite their guide, / And Zeus their avatar.'

As 'On an Engraving by Casserius' states, 'An artist's vision . . . links the person and the abstract cause.' Many poems resonate with this sense of the coherence and the dignity of life. However, Hope is also a sharp and unrelenting critic of folly and mediocrity, although the bite of some early satires has been replaced by a mellower note in the later poetry. Still, a poem such as 'The Sacred Way' (1970) bitterly laments the replacement of former heroes by figures such as Frankenstein and Dracula. As a critic and reviewer, Hope has been both witty and trenchant in his defence of what he deems acceptable standards of intelligence and lucidity in Australian writing. While perhaps conservative in his literary values, and little in sympathy with Australia's ventures into postmodernism, he has been a constant and much respected champion of Australian writing who instituted the first university course in Australian literature. He has won many literary prizes, and was made a Companion of the Order of Australia in 1981.

Hope's poetry is found in *Collected Poems 1930–1970* (1972), *A Late Picking: Poems 1965–1974* (1975), *A Book of Answers* (1978), *Antechinus: Poems 1975–1980* (1981), and *The Age of Reason* (1985).

ANDREW TAYLOR

Further reading: 'A. D. Hope', in Martin Duwell and Laurie Hergenhan (eds) *The 'ALS' Guide to Australian Writers: A Bibliography 1963–1990* (1992).

HOPE, CHRISTOPHER (1944–)

South African poet, novelist, short-story writer

He was born in Johannesburg, South Africa, and educated at the universities of Witwatersrand (BA, 1965; MA, 1971) and Natal (BA Honours, 1970). He settled in 1975 in London, England, where he established himself as one of the most significant writers emerging from the turbulent contemporary South African milieu. As a poet Hope has received the Thomas Pringle Prize (1972) and the Cholmondeley Award for Poetry (1974); his collections of poetry are *Whitewashes* (with Mike Kirkwood, privately printed, 1971), *Cape Drives* (1974), *In the Country of the Black Pig* (1981), and *Englishmen* (1985). His work has appeared in a number of magazines, journals, and anthologies including *London Magazine*, *Les Temps Modernes*, *The New Statesman*, *New York Times*, *The Times Literary Supplement*, *The New Yorker*, *the transatlantic review*, and *Best British Short Stories*.

A Separate Development (1980), which was temporarily banned in South Africa, received the David Higham Prize for Fiction. Hope's other published works include a selection of short stories, *Private Parts and Other Tales* (1981; revised as *Learning to Fly and Other Tales*, 1990), the novella *Black Swan* (1987), and the novels *Kruger's Alp* (1984), which won the Whitbread Prize for Fiction in 1985, *The Hottentot Room* (1986), *My Chocolate Redeemer* (1989), and *Serenity House* (1992). The autobiographical *White Boy Running* appeared in 1988 and the travel commentary *Moscow, Moscow* in 1990. For children, Hope has written *The King, the Cat and the Fiddle* (1983, with Yehudi Menuhin) and *The Dragon Wore Pink* (1985). He has also written a number of plays for radio and television, including *Ducktails* (1976), *Bye-Bye Booysens* (1979), and *An Entirely New Concept in Packaging* (1983). He reviews regularly for the British Broadcasting Corporation radio, weekly newspapers and journals, and lectures and reads internationally for the British Council.

From *A Separate Development* onwards Hope rejects the sentimental, melodramatic, or tragic modes to which the liberal white writers of South Africa were often drawn. Rather than assault his readers with moral exhortation, he emphasizes the cruel absurdity of the racial system, ridiculing its contradictions and creating satire that never trivializes the horror nor reduces the moral impact of his probing of apartheid. He recognizes that a major difficulty confronting the novelist seeking to write social satire is the fact that this role has been appropriated, unwittingly, by the conventional news media, which, by reporting directly the South African actuality, constantly provides examples of the absurdity inherent in the cumbersome race classification system that is apartheid. In his writing Hope weds subject-matter to form, the slightly surreal, bizarre nature of incidents and characters suggested through comic exaggeration (burlesque) or caricature, or through ingenuous characterization, in which characters reveal attitudes endemic in South Africa.

Kruger's Alp offers a blackly comic allegory, parodying Bunyan's *The Pilgrim's Progress*, about the abuses of power in South Africa. The hapless protagonist, the disabled priest Blanchaille, on pilgrimage to Switzerland to investigate Kruger's mythical millions, is exposed to the various forms of corruption tainting all who are touched by the politics of apartheid. Hope writes to subvert the distortions of everyday reality in South Africa by indicating that the conspiracies of its political life are unexceptional and are built into the very fabric of social life.

A similar corruption is revealed in the world of political exiles and police agents who people the London club after which *The Hottentot Room* is named. The club is frequented by South African exiles and expatriates and is run by Frau Katie, a German-Jewish refugee who was once married to a Nazi and who suffered moral contradictions and dilemmas similarly experienced by the novel's protagonist, Caleb Looper, a left-wing journalist spying for the regime. Looper seeks absolution by returning Frau Katie's ashes to her original home in East Berlin, and Hope's romantic double-agent, reminiscent of Conrad's Razumov in *Under Western Eyes*, exposes the moral and emotional ambiguities of alienated South Africans, making the novel Hope's bleakest vision of the homelessness of the exile.

White Boy Running is the last work in which

Hope focuses on his country of origin. In it, the writer returns to South Africa to record his impressions of the May 1987 white election while exploring and revisiting his past. Hope highlights Afrikaner Nationalists' continuing struggle, like that of Humpty Dumpty, to make words mean just what *they* want them to mean; the linguistic deformations of the politicians, technocrats, and South African public who arbitrarily separate signs from the things they represent are exposed throughout this lively text.

Like many exiled writers following a decade and more of writing to come to terms with origins, Hope moves on from his engagement with the country of his past. In *My Chocolate Redeemer* he offers the story of chocolate-obsessed Bella Dresseur, a fifteen-year-old teenager abandoned by her neurotic mother to live with humourless, xenophobic, fascist relatives in the French lakeside village of La Frisette, where she meets the chocolate-coloured exiled and deposed African leader of Zanj. Like Idi Amin and Baby Doc Duvalier, the one-time redeemer of his people is now known as the Beast of Zanj. Having lost her father in this African country, the orphaned protagonist (who derives her comfort from the chocolate she stashes under her bed) transfers her affection to Monsieur Brown, as she calls him, a 'most likeable fellow', and she saves him from those racist Frenchmen who seek to destroy him. The novel is a polished, surreal comedy that obliquely interrogates the ironies of the colonial claim to superiority while illuminating the many levels of self-deception inherent in the relationship between Europe and Africa.

In *Serenity House* Hope develops fertile, sometimes-bizarre links between seemingly unrelated events and institutions. In this dark fable he subverts the tale of Jack the Giant Killer by linking Florida's Magic Kingdom, Poland's Auschwitz, and Serenity House, a suspect retirement home for the elderly in London's Highgate, to present a powerful satire on contemporary life in modern England and the USA. Hope is a South African writer who has become fully international.

PHIL JOFFE

HOPKINSON, SLADE (1934–)

Guyanese poet, dramatist

Born in New Amsterdam, British Guiana (now Guyana), the son of Leonard Arthur Hopkinson and his wife Niebert (aunt of the poet **Martin Carter**), he grew up in colonial British Guyana and has lived in Barbados, Jamaica, Trinidad, and Canada, where he makes his home in Toronto. He was educated at schools in Guyana and Barbados and between 1952 and 1956 earned his BA and a diploma in education at the University College of the West Indies, Mona, Jamaica. Hopkinson is a poet, playwright, fiction writer, teacher, actor-director, and essayist whose handling of dialects and cultural details reveals a deeply pan-Caribbean outlook. A convert to the Muslim faith, he has taken the name Baakoo Abdur-Rahman. His work includes *The Four and Other Poems* (1954), *The Madwoman of Papine* (1976), *The Friend* (1976), and the plays *The Onliest Fisherman* (1957) and 'A Spawning of Eels' (premièred 1968), as well as selections in anthologies of Caribbean poetry and prose. Many of his poems appeared in the journal *Bim*.

As an undergraduate, Hopkinson belonged to a group of budding literati that included such writers as **George Lamming**, **Mervyn Morris**, and **Derek Walcott**, an association that fostered his view of the Caribbean as a diversified yet cultural whole. Hopkinson taught in Jamaica, coedited the People's National Party newspaper, *Public Opinion* (1958-9), and married a Jamaican. Increasingly interested in theatre, he moved to Trinidad to work with Walcott as actor-director in the Trinidad Theatre Workshop. In 1971 Hopkinson founded the Caribbean Theatre Guild in Trinidad. At this point his career seemed to be that of director and playwright; his poetic craft, however, continues to dominate his literary life.

JEAN D'COSTA

HORNE, DONALD (1921–)

Australian novelist, journalist

Born in Muswellbrook, New South Wales, Australia, he was educated at Sydney University where, influenced by the radicalism of the philosopher John Anderson, he adopted extreme left–wing views. Following service in the Australian Air Force (1941–4) and in the diplomatic service (1944–5), amusingly recorded in his second autobiography, Horne adopted a variety of careers. After undergraduate journalism, editing the journal *Honi Soit*, he worked for Australian and British newspapers, edited the ***Bulletin*** (1961–2 and 1967–72), and co-edited the conservative *Quadrant* (1963–6). In 1973 Horne became an academic and, on his retirement, was appointed chair of the **Australia Council**.

Horne's writing is as versatile as his career: three novels, three volumes of autobiography, a biography of the Australian prime minister Billy Hughes, and numerous works of popular history and social commentary. The novels, *The Permit* (1965), *His Excellency's Pleasure* (1977), and *But What If There Are No Pelicans?* (1971), deal respectively with the follies of officialdom, the anachronistic post of governor general, and a vision of the future. Of the autobiographies — *The Education of Young Donald* (1967), *Confessions of a New Boy* (1985), and *Portrait of an Optimist* (1988) — the first, and best, gives a memorable account of the genesis of a young intellectual and his physical and social milieu, comparable with **Hal Porter**'s *The Watcher on the Cast-Iron Balcony* (1963) and **Wole Soyinka**'s *Aké* (1981).

Horne is best known for *The Lucky Country* (1964) — a critique of Australian society in the 1960s — and the stream of popular sociological works that recycled and developed his analysis of Australian culture. He consistently attacks Australia's dependence on the UK and the monarchy, argues the case for republicanism, and condemns the country's political and cultural élites for lack of vision. In such later works as *Ideas for a Nation* (1989) his analysis is more optimistic. Always a provocative and challenging writer, as versatile as the Canadian **George Woodcock**, Horne commands a witty, paradoxical style that owes much to his early career as a journalist. That he is widely read points not only to his engaging style and arresting titles but to an extensive Australian preoccupation with national identity and social change.

JOHN COLMER

HORROR FICTION (Singapore)

See **NOVEL AND SHORT FICTION** (Singapore)

HOSAIN, ATTIA (1913–)

Indian short-story writer, novelist

Born into an orthodox Muslim feudal family in Lucknow, India, she studied at Isabella Thoburn College in Lucknow and was the first Muslim woman from the family of a *Taluqdar* (landlord of the raj) to graduate in English liberal education, graduating in 1933 from the University of Lucknow. In the 1930s Hosain came under the influence of the nationalist movement as well as the Progressive Writers' Group; she worked as a journalist, broadcaster, and fiction writer. In 1947 she and her husband and their two children immigrated to England, where she presented her own women's programme on the British Broadcasting Corporation's Eastern Service and associated herself with television and the West End stage. Hosain also lectured on the fusion of eastern and western cultures. Her published fiction comprises the collection *Phoenix Fled and Other Stories* (1953) and the autobiographical novel *Sunlight on a Broken Column* (1961).

The stories in *Phoenix Fled* are marked by sharp observation, humanistic vision, a reminiscent mood, and stylistic mastery. The title story deals with the horrors of India's partition in 1947. 'The First Party' dramatizes the effect of an ironic confrontation between traditional simplicity and modern sophistication. Elements of suspense and surprise, moments of truth, and a fine web of significant circumstance generally characterize Hosain's short stories, all of which thematically date to pre-independence India.

The artistic and cultural value of Hosain's *Sunlight on a Broken Column* can be better understood in comparison with such 'period' novels as Cornelia Sorabji's *Love and Life Behind the Purdah* (1901), Iqbalunnisa Hussain's *Purdah and Polygamy: Life in an Indian Muslim Household* (1944), **Humayun Kabir**'s *Men and Rivers* (1945), Zeenth Futehally's *Zohra* (1951), and Rama Mehta's *Inside the Haveli* (1977). Hosain's *Sunlight on a Broken Column* (the title is a phrase from T. S. Eliot's 'The Hollow Men') encapsulates the turbulence of Indian social and political conditions of the 1930s. Largely reminiscent, and only occasionally nostalgic, the novel renders imaginatively and realistically the tragic aspects of the end of the British raj. It succeeds in providing an 'objective correlative' for the poignant, but not pessimistic, love story of the narrator-protagonist as 'the poetic rebel'.

A. V. KRISHNA RAO

Further reading: Anita Desai, 'Introduction', *Sunlight on a Broken Column* by Attia Hosain (repr. 1992).

HOSAIN, SHAHID (1934–)

Pakistani poet

Born in Aligarh, India, he was educated in Pakistan and the UK and worked in Pakistan's media bureaucracy. He edited the first anthology of Pakistani poetry in English — *First Voices: Six Poets from Pakistan* (1965). His own poetry is representative of a post-partition Pakistani liberal and urbane cosmopolitanism, with its firm emotional and intellectual commitment to an indigenous culture and society.

Hosain's modernized romantic idiom is capable of a lyricism that eschews sentimentality, as in 'A Gift of Stones' and 'Anniversary' (in *Pieces of Eight: Eight Poets from Pakistan*, 1971, edited by Yunus Said). In 'The Oriental Poet Comes to Tuscany' (in *First Voices*), however, the need for roots prompts a return from foreign climes to the speaker's 'rancid and acrid country' that lies with 'heat and squalor' in his 'heart'. Hosain's frequently objective stance and realistic description — as in 'A Speculation' and 'The Housewife Dreams . . . ' (*First Voices*) — are nevertheless tinged by a highly personalized response to scene and situation, as in 'A Prospect of Desire' and 'Across the Indus' (*Pieces of Eight*) and 'A Nightmare for My Time' (*First Voices*).

'Karbala' (*First Voices*) offers a quasi-dramatic rendering of a tragic event in Muslim history with, as in T. S. Eliot's *Murder in the Cathedral* (1935), the tacit assumption of shared cultural and religious values and experience. This approach is also evident in the mildly sardonic tone used to convey experience in such poems as 'Concerning the Difficulties of Faith in Hot Climates' (*First Voices*) where, instead of formal devotion, vivid evocations of an inhospitable landscape and a primitive will for survival make human piety a fragile gesture.

In his detached irony and unsentimental responsiveness to traditional values in a contemporary world, Hosain may be compared with Indian poets **Gieve Patel** (for example, 'Naryal Purnima' and 'Servants', in *Poems of Gieve Patel*, 1966) and **Arun Kolatkar** ('Makarand' and 'The Blue Horse', in Kolatkar's *Jejuri*, 1976). In Hosain's later work — for example, 'Prescription', in *Pakistani Literature: The Contemporary English Writers* (2nd ed., 1987, edited by **Alamgir Hashmi**) — there is a marked disillusionment and a rejection of glib 'honed solutions'.

S. S. SIRAJUDDIN

HOSEIN, CLYDE (1940–)

Trinidadian short-story writer, poet, film-maker

Born in Couva, Trinidad, he had his early schooling there before moving to England in 1954. He studied at the London School of Economics from 1959 to 1962, but returned to Trinidad soon afterwards, where he worked in television, as a reporter for the Trinidad *Guardian*, and as managing director of an advertising agency. In 1976 Hosein immigrated to Canada and studied film-making at Ryerson Polytechnical Institute, Toronto.

Hosein's fiction and poetry have appeared in journals in Canada, Britain, and the Caribbean. His collection of thirteen short stories, *The Killing of Nelson John and Other Stories* (1980), provides a panoramic view of Trinidad as a colonial society with a legacy of exploitation, cultural and racial diversity, poverty, and injustice. In a typical story, a woman recalls the household where she worked as a maid. She was made pregnant by her boss, and although she raised her daughter through sacrifice and dedication, the girl has gone abroad and has never written to her. The children of the household whom she helped to raise have also moved away. In the end, she is left with a sense of isolation and abandonment. In another story a Trinidadian employee protests against his English boss' sexual exploitation of women secretaries in a soap-manufacturing firm. The secretaries, however, do not support his protest; he is made to look like a liar and is dismissed.

The prevailing tone in Hosein's stories, however, is not one of protest or lament. Although these stories convey a pervasive feeling of dereliction, loss, and futility, this feeling is often mixed with examples of resistance, ambition, and folly. The result is a densely peopled, colourful, and compelling portrait of Caribbean colonial life that reflects both the social documentation of **Samuel Selvon** and the ironic insights of **V. S. Naipaul.**

FRANK M. BIRBALSINGH

HOSPITAL, JANETTE TURNER (1942–)

Australian novelist, short-story writer

Born in Melbourne, Australia, she was educated in Brisbane before moving to the USA in 1965. She has lived in India and England, and is now working as a full-time writer in Ontario, Canada. Many of the titles of Hospital's work — a collection of short fiction, *Dislocations* (1986), the novels *Borderline* (1985) and *Charades* (1988) — indicate both her position as an expatriate Australian writer, suffering from what she has called 'a case of dislocated perspective', and her narrative preoccupation with contemporary political questions and postmodern philosophies, evident in both the subject-matter and the formal properties of her writing.

Hospital's upbringing in a closely knit, fundamentalist, Pentecostal family influences her work, with its religious themes of guilt and redemption not used, she says, in the narrowly theological, but in the richly symbolic sense. Enhanced by her academic training as a medievalist, these themes are central to *Borderline*. The Queensland rainforest environment is also a continuing influence.

A strong feminist politics is central to Hospital's work. It is evident in her characteristic fictional use of a two-woman motif: the strong woman who combats and resists the limitations her society seeks to impose on her, often by escaping from it; and the damaged woman who succumbs to or is trapped by these social forces. A narrative interest in the family as the source of both security and threat for its individual members, especially women, is specific in *The Tiger in the Tiger Pit* (1983). In *Charades*, with its clear references to Scheherazade, Hospital examines the potential of female storytelling.

Hospital won the Seal Award, the major Canadian prize for an unpublished first novel, for *The Ivory Swing* (1982); in 1987 *Dislocations* won the Fellowship of Australian Writers Australian Natives' Association Literature Award, and *Charades* was the only Australian novel on the long 'short list' for the Booker Prize in 1989.

A second collection of short fiction, *Isobars*, was published in 1990, and a novel, *The Last Magician*, in 1992. A complex work with a Chinese-Australian photographer as the last magician, the novel uncovers intersecting structures of corruption in contemporary Sydney, as it deals with questions of personal and social guilt and responsibility.

Increasingly, Hospital's writing is concerned with the illusory nature of reality and with multiple time perspectives. In these and other ways her work is like **Salman Rushdie**'s. Most recently, Hospital has been fascinated by contemporary physics, stimulated especially by reading Werner Heisenberg, Niels Bohr, and Albert Einstein.

DELYS BIRD

HOVE, CHENJERAI (1956–)

Zimbabwean poet, novelist

Born in Gwern, Zimbabwe, he lives in Harare, where he has been a writer-in-residence at the University of Zimbabwe since 1991. Hove writes in both English and Shona. His poetry constantly concerns itself with the lives and predicaments of the peasantry and the masses; the voice projected in his volume of poetry *Red Hills of Home* (1985) and the collection of war poetry *Up in Arms* (1982) is angry, compassionate, and, at times, celebratory.

Hove searches for a poetic idiom that carries the weight of both Shona and Zimbabwean English, but only achieves this comfortably in his pathbreaking war novel, *Bones* (1988), experimental in its language and in its move away from realism. The same desire to create narrative structure around the inner lives of his characters is evident in his second novel, *Shadows* (1991), a story of the struggle for land and of lost love that is patterned as much around dream and memory as it is around external events. A central theme is the conflict between generations; a secondary theme is that of the strain and poverty of both urban and rural life for many Zimbabweans.

A major achievement of *Bones* is its foregrounding of the experience of rural women through the struggling and resilient figure of the farm worker, Marija, whose son went to fight in the liberation war and never returned. *Bones* is also significant in its combination of the spirit of nationalism and its questioning of the achievements of the years of independence. Both novels use madness as a device for exploring areas of social and personal tension and frustration in both the old, pre-independence and the new, post-independent political dispensations.

LIZ GUNNER

Further reading: Annie Gagiano, '"I do not know her, but someone ought to know her": Chenjerai Hove's *Bones*', *World Literature Written in English* 2 (1992).

HOWE, JOSEPH (1804–73)

Canadian poet

Born in Halifax, Nova Scotia, Canada, the son of a Loyalist printer from Boston, USA, he was an apprentice at the *Royal Gazette* newspaper at the age of thirteen. Howe educated himself in all of the best models of English literature and rhetoric. When he was twenty-four years old he bought *The Novascotian*, and during the next twelve years made it arguably the best newspaper in the colonies. He became the centre of The Club, a group of influential young writers that included **T. C. Haliburton**.

Howe led Nova Scotians in achieving the first responsible government in the colonies and served as premier and lieutenant governor. His editorializing constituted the beginning of political literature in Canada. He is hailed as the first Canadian champion of freedom of the press — in 1835 he successfully defended himself against a libel charge in a six-hour speech exposing the evils of government by Council.

Notwithstanding his reform stance, the Howe revealed in the collected *Poems and Essays* (1874, compiled by his son Sydenham; repr. 1973, compiled by Malcolm Parks) is conservative and didactic. His poetry, like much colonial poetry, is formed on second-rate traditional models and is disappointing even in its attention to local detail. Among his more interesting writings are his travel sketches of Nova Scotia, edited by Parks as *Western and Eastern Rambles* (1973). In these, politics and moral sentiments are secondary, and Howe's broad interests in his province and its people are shown to advantage.

Howe was an Empire 'loyalist' above all else, opposing Confederation and advocating a scheme of empire federation. The real force of his character is best displayed in his speeches and in his public and private letters, particularly those to his half-sister Jane, but a definitive edition of these materials is yet to come. Literary criticism of Howe is scant.

ANDREW SEAMAN

Further reading: J. A. Chisholm, *The Speeches and Public Letters of the Hon. Joseph Howe* (1909); Ray Palmer Baker, *A History of English-Canadian Literature to the Confederation* (1920); Carrie MacMillan, 'Colonial gleanings: "the Club papers" (1828–31)', *Essays in Canadian Writing* 31 (1985).

HOWES, EDITH (1874–1954)

New Zealand children's writer

Born in London, England, she was educated at schools in Kaiapoa and Christchurch, New Zealand. She became a teacher whose major interest was nature study, and many of her stories have the strongly didactic intention of telling New Zealand children about their country's bush, beach, and marine life.

Like those of England's Cecily Barker and Australia's **May Gibbs**, Howes' stories centre around 'flower fairies'. Unlike Barker and Gibbs, however, Howes did not illustrate her own work. Her most famous book during her lifetime was *The Cradle Ship* (1916), which ran into numerous editions and was translated into French, Italian, and Danish. Daringly advanced for the period, it aimed to teach children 'the facts of life'. When twins want to know where babies come from, they are taken by their mother on a 'Cradle Ship', on which they see a wide variety of creatures and come to understand that babies, as mammals, grow 'beneath the mother's heart'.

When liberated from the sentimental 'flower fairy' syndrome, Howes wrote directly and well, as in the first indigenous adventure story, *Silver Island: A New Zealand Story* (1928), in which children live off the land when marooned on an off-shore island, and in *Young Pioneers* (1934), a well-researched story about early settlers. These are the books that still appeal. Howes' fairy stories, although well told, can only be regarded as interesting period pieces. Her other published works include: *The Sun's Babies* (1910), *Fairy Rings* (1911), *Rainbow Children* (1912), *Maoriland Fairy Tales* (1913), *Wonderwings and Other Fairy Stories* (1918), *Little Make-Believe* (1919), *The Singing Fish* (1921), *The Dream Girl's Garden* (1923), *The Enchanted Road* (1927), *More Tales of Maori Magic* (1928), *Sandals of Pearl* (1929), *The Golden Forest* (1930), and *Mrs Kind Bush* (1933).

BETTY GILDERDALE

HUDSON, FLEXMORE (1913–88)

Australian poet, short-story writer, editor

He was born in Charters Towers, Queensland, Australia, of a Baptist minister father and Jewish mother. The family moved to Sydney and then to

Adelaide, where Hudson graduated from the University of Adelaide. He worked as a teacher in rural South Australia and later in Adelaide. Despite recurring ill health, he enjoyed outdoor sport and leisure activities, which included a year under sail.

Hudson published the poetry collections *Ashes and Sparks: Forty-three Poems* (1937), *In the Wind's Teeth* (1940), *Indelible Voices: A Poem* (1943), *With the First Soft Rain* (1943), *As Iron Hills* (1944), and *Pools of the Cinnabar Range* (1959). He edited the important, internationally oriented quarterly, *Poetry* (1941–7) and the *Jindyworobak Anthology* (1943). Other work includes his autobiographical collected short stories *Tales from Corytella* (1985), literary journalism, educational works, radio plays broadcast by the Australian Broadcasting Corporation, and the unperformed early play 'Asoka', in which the mad scientist Brahma invents atomic weapons before Nagasaki and Hiroshima. Unpublished work includes a novel and an autobiography.

Finding no justice in an indifferent universe, Hudson struggled to believe in the moral improvement of the human race. He evoked both harsh and beautiful landscapes in his poetry. However, the cruelty and prejudices of rural life in the broader context of the Second World War provided him with the societal dimension of his short-story writing. Dislike of rural values and behaviour also affected the directions of his lyric, rhetorical, and lyric-rhetorical poetry. He either ignored society, lapsed into a geo-political nationalism over-influenced by his Jindyworobak friend **Rex Ingamells** and Walt Whitman, or explored issues through microcosmic and macrocosmic images of nature. While Hudson's socialism amounted to no more than educated compassion in the stories, it merged with his religio-philosophical views in the poetry. Study of Asian cultures developed his atheism into a modified Hinayana Buddhism via Arthur Schopenhauer's philosophy, suffusing accomplished poems such as 'To a Cuttlefish' and 'Birds in the Dawn'.

GRAHAM ROWLANDS

Further reading: Paul Depasquale, *Flexmore Hudson* (1981).

HUFANA, ALEJANDRINO G. (1926–)
Filipino poet, dramatist

He was born in a northern Philippine province and educated in local schools before entering the University of the Philippines where he earned an AB in English in 1952 and an MA in comparative literature in 1961. He taught literature at the University of the Philippines for fifteen years before he was sent on a Rockefeller fellowship to study art librarianship at Columbia University, USA, which awarded him a master's degree in 1969. Upon his return to Manila he was appointed director of the Cultural Center of the Philippines Library and held this position until 1985, when he immigrated to California, USA.

Hufana is a bilingual (English and Ilocano) writer. His early collections of poetry include *13 Kalisud* (1955), *Sickle Season: Poems of a First Decade, 1948–1958* (1959), which won the University Golden Jubilee Prize for Poetry, and *Poro Point: An Anthology of Lives* (1961), poems of the period 1955 to 1960. *Curtain Raisers* (1964), a collection of plays, earned Hufana the Republic Cultural Heritage Award in 1965.

In 1961–2, while on a Rockefeller creative writing fellowship at the University of California, USA, Hufana finished *Sieg Heil: An Epic on the Third Reich*, published in 1975. His other volumes of poetry include *The Wife of Lot and Other New Poems* (1971), *Obligations: Cheers of Conscience* (1975), and *Shining On: Collected Poems, 1950–1985*. He has also published *The Unicorn: A Dance Drama* (1971), *Notes on Poetry with Integrated Critique and Verse Compilation* (1972), *Mena Pecson Crisologo and Iloko Drama* (1965), and *Introduction to Literature* (1964), co-authored with Elmer A. Ordonez, Rony V. Diaz, and Edilberto P. Dagot.

Also a painter, Hufana belonged to an artists' group called the Primitives, which has held several exhibits in Manila.

ELMER A. ORDONEZ

HULME, KERI (1947–)
New Zealand novelist, short-story writer, poet
Born in Christchurch, New Zealand, of Maori, Scottish, and English ancestry, she began a law degree at Canterbury University, which she abandoned in favour of various jobs such as tobacco picker and post office worker while writing in her spare time. She lives in a self-built octagonal-shaped home on the west coast of the South Island.

Hulme's first book, the poetry collection *The Silences Between: Moeraki Conversations* (1982), explores relations among the Maori self, other people, the land, and the past. It reflects Hulme's deliberate identification with her Maori ancestry, an act that aroused heated debate about her status as a Maori writer after the publication of her novel *The Bone People* (1983), winner of the Pegasus Award for Maori Literature and the Booker Prize.

Hulme says that in *The Bone People* she wanted to suggest that everyone in New Zealand has suffered by the repression of Maori spirituality. For some critics, the novel succeeds as an 'optimistic blueprint for future race relations', with 'images of women' that can provide 'new visions of individual and shared power that can inspire the transformation of a culture and society'. Other critics, however, argue that the 'last quarter of the novel extends itself too far and that 'the characters cannot stand up under the mythic burden placed on them'. One critic claimed that there is 'something black and negative deeply ingrained' in *The Bone People*'s 'imaginative fabric' that implies an authorial 'imaginative complicity' with the novel's violence.

Hulme has resisted affiliation with the European literary tradition: 'I haven't much liked it — not from any idea that I'm special, just simply because it doesn't nourish or seem good to get involved with.' It is the response from within the Maori community that Hulme values. For her, receiving the Pegasus Award meant that the work was 'accepted as a Maori thing'.

Hulme's collection of short fiction, *Te Kaihau: The Windeater* (1986), was written contemporaneously with *The Bone People*. Stylistically and thematically the two books have much in common. The Maori myths that fuel the novel also fuel the short fiction; but where the novel's ending intends to reconcile tensions, the short fiction lays these tensions wide open. Where the 'negative element' is apparently resolved in *The Bone People*, *Te Kaihau* is unrelentingly negative. Viciousness is rarely mitigated with *aroha*, and images of alienation dominate over community in a matter characterized by what poet **Ian Wedde** has called a mixture of a 'bleak vision' with 'garrulous humour'.

Hulme published the poetry collection *Strands* in 1992.

SUSAN ASH

Further reading: Judith Dale, '*the bone people*: (not) having it both ways', *Landfall* 39 (1985); Susan Ash, '*The Bone People* after *Te Kaihau*', *World Literature Written in English* 29 (1989).

HUME, FERGUSON WRIGHT (1859–1932)
English/Australian detective fiction writer
Born in Worcester, England, of Scottish parents, his family immigrated to New Zealand in 1863 and he trained in law there. He immigrated to Australia in 1885 and finally settled in England in 1888. Known as Fergus Hume, he published some 140 works of popular fiction between 1886 and 1929 and perhaps twenty (lost) plays, various lyric

poems, and hymns. His numerous and complex detective narratives — early examples from which his contemporary, Conan Doyle, may well have borrowed mode and motifs — had their origins in French literature's crime stories by Émile Gaboriau and Fortuné Du Boisgobey. Hume's *The Mystery of a Hansom Cab* (1886), set, written, and first published in Melbourne, largely launched in Australia the non-convict, non-bush-ranging crime novel. Its sequel volumes, *Madame Midas* (1888) and *Miss Mephistopheles* (1890), pursued gold rush themes and are partly derivative from **Rolf Boldrewood**, Victor Hugo, and French Romanticism.

Hume's early work in England was largely for the gentlemen's magazines; it is colonial in its nostalgia for the Pacific and linguistically fascinating for its knowledge of modern Greek, Spanish, Maori culture, and opera. His long sequence of popular novels (1890–*c*.1930) has certain distinctive characteristics: a fascination with Free Presbyterian, theosophical, occult, and spiritualist belief systems; a relatively complex psychology; a love of Chinese, Polynesian, gypsy, and other minority groups; a Dickensian fascination with east London and the lower Thames; early delineation of railway murders, bohemian Chelsea, Edwardian theatre, town planning, and other hitherto neglected themes.

Although thought of as colonial, Hume moved in, and influenced, many English literary circles through such friends as Bram Stoker and G. K. Chesterton. In Australian and English lighter fiction he was influential for clue puzzles, early amateur detectives, and mining mysteries — features now found in the work of Canada's Howard Engel. Hume is also the classic case of the man of letters who lost his copyright and was then widely published — in Germany, the USA, Sweden, and elsewhere. Large collections of Hume's perhaps 900 editions have been assembled where he is best remembered — in New Zealand, Australia, and the USA — and his work savoured for its social content and quiet charm.

J. S. RYAN

Further reading: J. S. Ryan, *Literary Detection: Towards a Bibliography of the Works of Fergus Hume* (1989).

HUMOUR AND SATIRE

HUMOUR (Australia)

If a nation, in critic Benedict Anderson's definition, is an 'imagined political community', then traditional Australian humour — strongly linked to national myths developed by the ***Bulletin*** writers in the 1890s — has greatly contributed to imaginings of nationhood. It draws on historical experiences of convictism, pioneering, and the bush and is bound up with perceptions of the Australian character as egalitarian, anti-authoritarian, and irreverent towards social pretension, for, as Anderson indicates, nations are conceived 'as a deep, horizontal comradeship' despite inequalities and exploitation prevailing within them.

Australian humour is dominated by irony and often sounds a note of fatalistic resignation, with individuals protesting their plight while wryly acknowledging their impotence, as, for example, the wounded soldier who urges the comrade piggybacking him through no man's land to start walking backwards: 'You're getting the V. C., but I'm getting all the flamin' bullets.' A waterside worker drinking with a reporter from the *Bulletin* in a pub in Wyndham, Western Australia, is recorded as saying: 'So you are up here to write about us . . . Put this in mate. Cambridge Gulf is the arsehole of the world, and Wyndham is 65 miles up it!' This blend of protest, resignation, and pride characterizes much Australian humour — protest at a harsh environment, resignation to the impossibility of change, and pride in being able to endure it all. But fatalism and stoic endurance are frequently offset by bursts of riotousness when the sense of bleak confrontation between individuals and the injustices of fate erupt sporadically into anarchic disorder, as in **Henry Lawson**'s story 'The Loaded Dog', where events take on a quality of preposterous and total absurdity. Although such eruptions usually subside, with the *status quo* reestablished, the brief collapse into anarchy offers temporary relief, or at least a distraction from the intransigent situations in which people find themselves trapped.

Humour has been used to construct the landscape of a country that seemed to contradict everything the first arrivals from Britain might have reasonably anticipated. Tall stories — often incorporating motifs from European folklore — with their deadpan accounts of grotesque impossibilities, were one means of coming to terms with what **Marcus Clarke** called the 'phantasmagoria of that wild dream-land termed the bush'. Fantasies were generated in gatherings where, as Lawson writes in 'Stragglers', men 'tell lies against one another sociably'. Tales were told of the fabulous Speewah station, located variously in Queensland, the Kimberleys, and Back o' Bourke, where everything was larger, more abundant, and more spectacular than anywhere else. So many men worked there that the cook and his assistant had to row out in a boat to sugar the tea while the station hands were gargantuan figures such as Crooked Mick who used Ayers Rock to stone the crows.

Oral culture plays an important part in Australian humour through an idiom that blends dry irony with fantasy and riotousness, generally expressed in energetic outbursts of abuse and profanity. In early convict usage, bread that contained more chaff than flour was a 'scrubbing brush', and 'wearing a red shirt' described a back lacerated from flogging. A black eye was a 'Botany Bay coat of arms' and freed convicts were 'Botany Bay swells'. Exclamations about 'weather so hot it's a hundred in the waterbag' or drought country 'you couldn't flog a flea over', contain within them the seeds of more elaborate inventions such as the story of a stockman who sent his dog after a strayed bullock, waiting patiently for years until the animal returned with a boot in his mouth, the leather marked with the brand on the hide of the lost beast. Invective also generates its own kind of comic energy — 'May your chooks turn into emus and kick your dunny over' — and the abundant profanity of vernacular speech, with its blend of exuberance and defiance, can have a similar effect.

Colloquial idiom contributes to what John Docker identifies as a 'carnivalesque' element in Australian culture that mocks accepted hierarchies. But while Australians appreciate irreverence, its implications make them nervous. They admire the defiant gesture and enjoy the idea of challenging holders of power and status, yet are unprepared to accept the degree of social change a genuinely successful challenge might provoke. The attraction of figures such as **Ned Kelly** or an event such as the Eureka Stockade, representing a heroic stand against authority, lies partly in the fact that they failed. While the swagman hero of 'Waltzing Matilda' defies both squatter and troopers, it is surely significant that he drowns, leaving only a ghostly voice to sing defiance from the billabong. Would the song be so dearly cherished had he triumphed over the squatter and escaped with his stolen jumbuck?

Mingled irony and irreverence invest much Australian humour with a dismissive quality. An Australian parliamentarian is reputed to have interrupted a long-winded colleague in midspeech with a note saying 'Pull out, dig. The dogs are pissing on your swag.' Such reductivism succeeds in puncturing pretensions, but it can also represent a denial of individual aspiration and the possibility of personal triumph. Outsiders of various kinds are derided by demolition experts to reinforce group solidarity and while this may expose the tensions of class conflict, as in some 'newchum' jokes used by nineteenth-century outback workers to test and reject newcomers (often portrayed as upper-class

Englishmen), it also reveals a strain of exclusiveness and xenophobia. Aborigines and Asians — particularly the Chinese who immigrated to Australia in large numbers during the gold rushes — have been the butt of many racist jokes in traditional Australian humour, which has also reflected and reinforced highly masculinist myths of place and national identity whose power and persistence are revealed in the success of a film such as *Crocodile Dundee* (1986).

Women, perceived at best as outsiders and at worst as enemies, are often represented as 'God's police', relegated to that region of bourgeois gentility, the domestic sphere, where values are at odds with the freedom and male camaraderie supposedly experienced in the bush. Women seeking to enter the male world, or to assert themselves independently of it, are likely to be dismissed as absurd monsters, often cast in the role of termagant who presides over suburbia — for example, Jack Gudgeon's mother-in-law in **Lennie Lower**'s *Here's Luck* (1930) and **Barry Humphries**' creation, Edna Everage. Australian women humorists have sought ways of circumventing or subverting a tradition of national humour in which women are either ridiculed or ignored. **Thea Astley** satirizes the male world of outback myth — 'the basic decency of blokes' — in her novel *An Item From the Late News* (1982), and Mary Leunig creates cartoons where women, rather than men, are trapped in the horrors of domestic life, snapped at by furious domestic appliances and furniture red in tooth and claw.

Australian humour, deeply rooted in the disjunctions of colonial life — English and Currency, upper class and lower class, old hands versus new chums, the bush versus the city, and an assertively male view of the world that sought to render women peripheral — has contributed significantly to Australians' sense of national identity. But proletarian bias and jaunty irreverence often obscure its discriminatory nature and narrow world view.

DOROTHY JONES

Further reading: Dorothy Jones, '"It's no good farting against thunder": resignation and exaggeration in Australian humour', *Span* 25 (1987); Dorothy Jones and Barry Andrews, 'Australian humour', *The Penguin New Literary History of Australia* (1988); Dorothy Jones, 'Serious laughter: on defining Australian humour', *Journal of Commonwealth Literature* 23 (1988); *Thalia: Studies in Literary Humor 10* (1989) — special issue on Australian humour.

HUMOUR AND SATIRE (Canada)

Colonial humorous writing began with Revd **Thomas McCulloch**, a Presbyterian minister and Scottish immigrant. Author of *Letters of Mephibosheth Stepsure*, published between 1821 and 1823 in the *Acadian Recorder*, he responded to poor economic times by creating the persona of Stepsure, a frugal farmer with right values who satirized the moral laxity of Nova Scotians. McCulloch's model of the industrious farmer introduced to colonial humour and culture the 'back to the land' myth, identified by **Northrop Frye** as appropriate to a rising middle class. This convention subsequently informed the reflective pastoral humour of Peter McArthur, who celebrated Ontario farm life in such works as *In Pastures Green* (1915) and *The Red Cow and Her Friends* (1919), and **Stephen Leacock**'s sketch of the ideal farmer in *Arcadian Adventures with the Idle Rich* (1914), an ambiguous satire against a commercial plutocracy, predictably set in the USA.

Early colonial humorists also introduced a notable theme in Canadian humour, that of ambivalence towards the USA. While McCulloch deplored Americans as a 'showy race' and the cartoonist J. W. Bengough (1851–1923) caricatured the threatening presence of the USA, **Thomas Chandler Haliburton**, a Nova Scotian judge whose forbears were Loyalist, created the archetypal Sam Slick, an audacious, clock-peddling Yankee. Both celebrated and satirized, Slick paradoxically earned his author the title 'father of American humour' for *The Clockmaker, or, The Sayings and Doings of Samuel Slick of Slickville* (1836) and *The Attaché; or, Sam Slick in England* (1843). These volumes also established what critic R. E. Watters identified as a Canadian colonial habit of looking inwards while looking outwards at John Bull and Uncle Sam. In the character of Haliburton's Squire Poker, first introduced as a British traveller, later transformed into a native Nova Scotian, Watters uncovers the quiet, double-edged mode of ironic humour typical of the colonial Canadian, *in medias res*. As in Australian humour, the ironic mode dominates in the colonial context. (See **Humour**, Australia.) Unlike Australian humour, however, where individuals resign themselves to their own powerlessness, Canadian colonial humour reveals an ironic ambivalence, with humorists playing, as does Haliburton's squire, the ironic middleman or, as Leacock does in his famous essay 'Oxford as I See It' in *My Discovery of England* (1922), by cleverly lambasting both British and American systems of education simultaneously.

British-born Stephen Leacock, a university professor and Canada's most canonized and prolific humorist, contributed, like McCulloch and Haliburton, to the definition of a paternalistic Anglo-Canadian official culture. Leacock's central voice, like Haliburton's, was that of the Tory squire, the educated, ironic, if seemingly naïve, commentator of his best work, *Sunshine Sketches of a Little Town* (1912), a pastoral, regional, and sentimental idyll based on Orillia, Ontario, where Leacock had a country estate. A genial humorist of Victorian sensibilities, he celebrated the humour of sentiment in typically colonial recognition of both British and American models in such critical works as *Mark Twain* (1932) and *Charles Dickens: His Life and Work* (1933). He also anticipated post-colonial trends. His remarkable popular sketch 'My Financial Career', from *Literary Lapses* (1910), introduced the twentieth-century American comic prototype of the little man overwhelmed by bureaucracy and technology. Leacock's intimidated bank customer was a comic model for American humorist Robert Benchley, although Watters has argued that Leacock's little man is a Canadian archetype, with full ironic comprehension of self, reflective of the inner strength of a small nation surviving imperialism.

The colonial legacy of Leacock's persona — the conservative, Anglo-Canadian man of letters — took stronger satiric and élitist shape with **Robertson Davies**, whose misanthropic character Samuel Marchbanks, of Loyalist sympathies and imperialist standards, critiques Canada and Canadians in *The Diary of Samuel Marchbanks* (1947), *The Table Talk of Samuel Marchbanks* (1949), and *Marchbanks' Almanack* (1967).

Leacock's parodies and burlesques also illustrate a colonial tendency to comic imitation rather than comic invention. His parodic volumes, *Nonsense Novels* (1911), *Further Foolishness* (1916), and *Winsome Winnie* (1920), are broad comic imitations of literary genres that display an underlying mockery of American and European culture. Also in this tradition is Paul Hiebert's *Sarah Binks* (1947), a genial mockery of the transplantation of European literary conventions to Canada through the 'Sweet Songstress of Saskatchewan', a ludicrously bad poet whose poetic forms are elevated and imported and whose subject-matter is rural, low-brow, and native. The humour of self-deprecation here is also consistent with colonial status.

As in Australia, both oral and 'bush' culture also contribute to Canadian humour. In Australia, the desert, the Outback, the 'bush' created exuberant bush liars and legendary comic figures such as Crooked Mick, reputed to have used Ayers Rock to stone crows. In Canada, masculine culture on the frontier established a similar tradition of greenhorn trickery through the tall tale and a long list of legendary comic heroes such as Angus MacAskill, the Nova Scotian giant, Joe Montferrand (Joe Mufferaw) of the Ottawa Valley, and Twelve Foot Davis of the Peace River country. The oral tradition of sky-breaking humour has been absorbed by western literary culture. The tall-tale context is important in the humour of **W. O. Mitchell**'s *Jake and the Kid* (1961), a short-story collection based on his popular Canadian Broadcasting Corporation radio series (1950–8), *The Kite* (1962), and the play *The Black Bonspiel of Wullie MacCrimmon* (1966). **Robert Kroetsch** extends western tall-tale telling into the fabulous and comic surrealism in such works as *The Studhorse Man* (1969), *Gone Indian* (1973), and *What the Crow Said* (1978). **Jack Hodgins** on the West Coast also turns the humour of exaggeration into high art as he fantastically reinvents the world in *The Invention of the World* (1977).

Unlike Australian humour, however, where 'convict culture' bred an acceptable pervasive oral tradition of comic abuse and profanity, Canadian humour is comparatively more genteel. The early authority of British colonial élites and of clerical paternalism, typified by missionaries expurgating the bawdy, scatological, and erotic humour of the aboriginal peoples, has been long-standing. Native humour is notably being reclaimed in literature in non-Native H. T. Schwarz's bawdy collection *Tales From the Smokehouse* (1974), in the current reworking of Native legends by Native writers, with an emphasis on the trickster figure and in the satires of Native authors **Basil Johnston** in *Moose Meat and Wild Rice* (1978) and cartoonist-writer Everett Soop in *I See My Tribe Is Still Behind Me* (1990).

The humorous fiction of non-Native **W. P. Kinsella**, which takes as subject the Native peoples — *Dance Me Outside* (1977), *Scars* (1978), and *The Fencepost Chronicles* (1986) — is both popular and controversial. There are, however, many good comic collections about regional and national life at the popular level. Official literary and national culture, traditionally emanating from central Canada, includes various serious authors with satirical/ironical dimensions. A classic work, *The Blasted Pine: An Anthology of Satire, Invective and Disrespectful Verse* (1957), includes early colonial and modern writers such as **F. R. Scott**, **Earle Birney**, **A. M. Klein**, **Irving Layton**, **Margaret Atwood**, and **Leonard Cohen**. *Barbed Lyres* (1990) is a recent tribute to this text. Although American critic Edmund Wilson identified the lack of bitterness in *The Blasted Pine* as typical of English Canadians with little to complain about, poet Layton and novelist **Mordecai Richler**, both of Jewish ancestry, have written aggressive satire about mainstream culture and the colonial mentality; Richler, for example, attacks Canadian cultural mythology with post-colonial black humour and mordant satire in *The Incomparable Atuk* (1963) and *Solomon Gursky Was Here* (1989). Post-colonial literary humorists/satirists of multicultural backgrounds and national interests are slow to emerge, although there is some ethnic regional humour, such as Maara Haas' *The Street Where I Live* (1976), a comic treatment of immigrants in Winnipeg's north end, and Armin Wiebe's *The Salutation of Yasch Siemens* (1984).

The tradition of humour in Australia and Canada is clearly masculine. In Australia women are perceived as outsiders, even enemies, and have always been the butt of jokes: 'No kids, dogs or women in this bar.' Similarly, Sam Slick explains, 'A woman, a rug, a walnut tree. The more you beat 'em, the better they be.' If, as critics Dorothy Jones and Barry Andrews suggest, female sexuality is a threat to male bonding and achievement in Australia, as expressed in **Barry Oakley**'s satiric *A Salute to the Great McCarthy* (1970), Canada is ruled by a paradox. **Hugh MacLennan** explained in 1947 that while men and masculine values dominate Canadian society, Canada, in its subordinate national position to the Americans, is 'feminine' — peace-keeping, accommodating, the 'good wife'. This has allowed for nationally recognized female authors whose values do not seem to contradict the nation's ideals. Such authors as **Alice Munro**, Margaret Atwood, and **Aritha van Herk**, none the less, currently write feminist novels and short stories with strong ironic/satiric undercurrents about female status. Erika Ritter, a singular comic voice, has written a daring satirical play, *Automatic Pilot* (1980), with a female comedian as subject, that underlines female and Canadian marginality. Similarly, her *Ritter in Residence* (1987) is a comic collection from a female point of view.

Although the history of Canadian political cartooning has a rich satiric tradition of grass-roots origins, Canadian literary humour has, like Australian humour, depended on the ironic mode rather than on reformist satire. The colonial psychology is that of ironic acceptance of the incongruity between the ideal and the real; as Leacock said, 'The true humorist must be an optimist.'

BEVERLY J. RASPORICH

Further reading: R. E. Watters, 'A special tang: Stephen Leacock's Canadian humour', *Canadian Literature* 5 (1960); Margaret Atwood, 'What's so funny? notes on Canadian humour', *Second Words* by Margaret Atwood (1982); Beverly Rasporich, 'Canadian humour and culture: regional and national expressions', *Culture, Development and Regional Policy*, Canadian Issues Series, Vol. 9 (1988).

HUMOUR AND SATIRE (East Africa)

In the mid-1970s, many symptoms of the development of East African societies indicated that life under colonialism was being replaced, contrary to expectations, by a 'home-made' variant that was no less unattractive. This paradoxical fact created in writers an attitude of rejection that, when accompanied by certain temperamental qualities, incited them to reach for Juvenal's whip. Pure, light-hearted humour is hardly characteristic of East African literature, possibly because the reality on which it draws generally lacks the qualities that favour such humour. But some successful examples prove that a hostile environment need not stifle completely the development of humour. The most notable example is the Ugandan writer **Barbara Kimenye**'s collections of short stories *Kalasanda* (1965) and *Kalasanda Revisited* (1966). The portrait of the life of a typical village community in Buganda that the sixteen connected stories create is made vivid and attractive mainly through the sustained mildly comic approach of the author to characters and situations. Despite the denser social motivation behind Ugandan **John Ruganda**'s play, *Black Mamba* (1973), it is mainly humour that serves to highlight the characters and to expose the chief protagonist, a university professor with double moral standards. Humour seems to come naturally to Tanzanian writer Vianey Timothy, as evidenced in his short story 'A Bachelor on the Loose' (in Dar es Salaam's *Sunday News* 28 July 1991).

Satire in East African literatures has always been social in character. Its writers have been influenced by Kenyan author **Ngugi wa Thiong'o**'s article 'Wole Soyinka, Aluko and the Satirical Voice' (in Ngugi's collection *Homecoming: Essays on African Literature, Culture and Politics*, 1972). Ngugi specifies the object of satire to be 'society's failings', and points to its function — to criticize society when it departs from the norms the satirist upholds and to arouse in readers a sense of moral indignation at the violation of these norms. The aim of satire, in his view, is to 'correct', and the means to achieve it is through 'painful, sometimes malicious laughter'.

The first satirical novels in East African literature in English were Ugandan Godfrey Kalimugogo's *The Department* (1976) and Kenyan Joshua N. Mwaura's *He Man* (1977). The satire of the bureaucracy in both novels exposes and illuminates the conflict between the people and the local bourgeoisie. Kalimugogo's favoured satirical tools are the hyperbolization of the physical features of characters, the perverse substantiation on the part of protagonists of their inane behaviour, stylization, and parody. Notable in both novels is the calm, neutral tone in which the subjects of satire are made to pronounce things extravagantly preposterous and the occasional metamorphosis of the personages as they unconsciously expose themselves. Mwaura's style of narration is in the main low-keyed and impersonal, while Kalimugogo has a distinctive satirical voice.

Ugandan Cyprian Karamagi's *Bulemu the Bastard* (1980) and Kenyan **Francis Imbuga**'s play *Betrayal in the City* (1976) expose the despotic nature and anti-popular character of political power in some African countries. Reality in Imbuga's play is presented as a lifelong tragedy experienced by an enormous mass of people gripped in a vice by some wicked foolery against which the author directs his indignation, biting humour, and brilliant wit.

The ending of *Bulemu the Bastard*, which presents a picture of an ideal society, brings to mind a characteristic not infrequently observed in satirical art — the co-existence of such opposite tendencies as satirical denunciation and utopian affirmation. The power that marks Ngugi's novel *Devil on the Cross* (1982, in English) is concentrated in its satire. It presents a bizarre competition initiated by the Kenyan élite with the aims of assessing the progress made in robbing the masses of their possessions and of selecting the most expert swindler in its ranks. The grotesque is employed to lay bare flagrant injustices in Kenyan society and the moral bankruptcy of the ruling class.

In poetry, **Okot p'Bitek**'s *Song of Lawino* (1966) became a model of East African satirical skill. The caustic laughter of the Ugandan poet is aimed mainly at what he sees as negative tendencies in the ongoing moral and ethical transformation of Africa, while the satire of most East African poets (**Taban lo Liyong**, **Richard Ntiru**, E.-C. Atieno-Adhiambo, **Meja Mwangi**, **Jared Angira**, S. Mbure, A. Kassam, M. O. -Maggoye, and Micere Githae-Mugo) is socially motivated.

What might explain the practical absence of the satirical spirit in Tanzanian literature is the view writers used to hold — associated with the ideology of *ujamaa* — of the necessary evolution of a more humanized form of life in their country than in those that are capitalist.

The development of satire in East African literatures is related to the dynamics of social life and the writers' intellectual evolution. But its power is invariably determined by the magnitude of the individual talent.

EMILIA V. ILIEVA

HUMOUR AND SATIRE (India)

The first Indian humorist to write in English was Nagesh Vishwanath Pai. His *Stray Sketches in Chakmakpore* (1894) gives an amusing picture of Indian life, while his *The Angel of Misfortune* (1904) is a narrative poem of five thousand lines on the misadventures of King Vikramaditya under the baleful influence of Saturn. **Sri Aurobindo**'s *The Viziers of Bassora* (1957), written at the turn of the century, is a romantic comedy, Shakespearean in character. V. V. Srinivasa Iyengar's *Dramatic Divertissements* (1921) explodes with effervescent fun. **R. K. Narayan** makes use of gentle humour and irony in almost all his novels, while **G. V. Desani**'s *All About H. Hatterr* (1951, first published in 1948 under its lesser-known title, *All About Mr. Hatterr, A Gesture*) is a major novel that relies almost totally on improbable pronouncements, word play, and catchy idioms. Among recent writers who have taken to Desani's style are **I. Allan Sealy** (*The Trotter-Nama*, 1988, winner of a Commonwealth Writers Prize for the Eurasia region) and **Boman Desai** (*The Memory of Eleph-*

ants, 1988). In order to avoid religious and caste confrontations, writers are careful about the targets of their humour; thus, for example, a book that touches on the foibles of Parsis will probably be written by a Parsi — Desai, **Rohinton Mistry**, for example — and one about Sikhism by a Sikh — **Khushwant Singh**, for instance.

Satire, however, has been a more effective weapon in the hands of Indian writers in English, most of whom have been political activists and social reformers. One of the earliest satires is Subramania Bharati's *The Fox with the Golden Tail* (1914), which lampoons Annie Besant's espousing the cause of theosophy. Sri Aurobindo's political journalism was laced with biting satire, making his journal *Bande Mataram* very popular in the first decade of the twentieth century.

While political satire is usually ephemeral, a few classics do transcend the immediate context. S. Gopalan's *Jackal Farm* (1949), for example, is a sharp satire on the extraordinary bureaucracy indulged in by the various Indian ministries in the name of planning; it is also directed against the Indian government's approach to political non-alignment. Obviously inspired by George Orwell's *Animal Farm* (1945), the novel lays bare the corruption that has overtaken social, political, and educational institutions in India.

Bhabani Bhattacharya's *He Who Rides a Tiger* (1954) and *A Goddess Named Gold* (1960) are carefully crafted satires on urban sophistication and religious superstition. While the former novel exposes the ostensible pillars of society through a blacksmith masquerading as a brahmin priest, comedy and farce lessen the direct indictment of the latter. To this genre also belong the more recent *Fowl-Filcher* (1987) by **Ranga Rao** and *The Great Indian Novel* (1989) by **Shashi Tharoor**, both of which make use of fantasy and a no-holds-barred style. Tharoor's novel may be seen as a culmination of a spate of novels on the political regime of Prime Minister Indira Gandhi, beginning with **Nayantara Sahgal**'s *A Situation in New Delhi* (1977).

Although Indian drama in English is necessarily a hot house plant because its audience is almost non-existent, writers have not been deterred from exploiting the medium for some vigorous ironic glances at the foibles of contemporary society. **A. S. P. Ayyar**'s *The Slave of Ideas and Other Plays* (1941), Puroshottam Tricamdas' *Sauce for the Goose* (1946), **Asif Currimbhoy**'s *The Tourist Mecca* (1961), and **Murli Das Melwani**'s *Deep Roots* (1970) are some of the plays that attack upper-class pretensions and prejudices.

Indians writing in English have not used poetry as much as fiction for satirizing contemporary follies. Only since independence have some poets laid aside their romanticism and passed caustic comments on life; their objects of satire are the educated middle and upper classes. V. Y. Kantak's *The Dome* (1982) is a satiric attack on the evils that have eroded the bases of India's academies. Among other poets who have used satire are Arnab Guha, **K. R. S. Iyengar**, and **Vera Sharma**. **Nissim Ezekiel**'s *Very Indian Poems in Indian English* (1989) has a friendly but ironic flair that has ensured it a wide readership.

PREMA NANDAKUMAR

HUMOUR AND SATIRE (Pakistan)

Apart from some jocose rhyming in **Shahid Suhrawardy**'s poems, there was little laughter or 'smile' in Pakistani poetry in English until the 1960s. However, observation of incongruities and ironical perception of event, object, and character create fresh, and detached, perspectives in several poems by **Zulfikar Ghose** ('The Crows', 'History Lesson', in his *The Loss of India*, 1964), **Taufiq Rafat** ('Once upon a Time', in *Pieces of Eight: Eight Poems from Pakistan*, 1971, edited by Yunus Said), and **Alamgir Hashmi** ('An Old Chair', 'The Telegram', 'Parking Meter', and 'Pro Bono Publico — in Pakistani English', in his *An Old Chair*,

1979, *My Second in Kentucky*, 1981, *Inland and Other Poems*, 1988, and *Sun and Moon and Other Poems*, 1992, respectively). Experience is analyzed from an unconventional or moral standpoint and reconstituted to gain a sympathetic appraisal of that which is missing or has been spoiled.

In fiction, **Bapsi Sidhwa**'s *The Crow Eaters* (1978) makes use of both situational and verbal humour to make certain crucial points about the characters and their community. Her *Ice-Candy-Man* (1988) exploits language for comic relief, though vulgarized to the extent of a match with the horrible events of partition, which provides the background to its action. Tariq Ali's *Redemption* (1990) builds on his stage experience and offers a hilarious comedy of both situations and ideas in unlikely places; the bawdy jokes, which are the subplot, punctually propel the book to its ideological purpose. This is a satirical work, but no more serious and undiluted than **Ahmed Ali**'s *Rats and Diplomats* (1986), which directly attacks vice, corruption, and the inhumanity of those who manage countries and societies. Adam Zameenzad's black humour, as in *Cyrus Cyrus* (1990), has a strange humanizing effect on his brutalized and robotic subjects.

From a genial tone and pathos to a sharp rebuke or the tongue-in-cheek, the many varieties of humour and satire in Pakistani literature convey the distinctive Pakistani personality, much as the method is used by **R. K. Narayan** and **Samuel Selvon** in their fiction. Some of this writing also uses Pakistani English as Selvon uses a particular dialect to make the points of dialogue.

ALAMGIR HASHMI

HUMOUR (Singapore)

Singaporean humour is as cosmopolitan as its native city, which is composed of a population diverse and international. Singapore's diet of humorous material ranges from Irish jokes, through Cantonese slapstick and satire, to the black humour of American Woody Allen. However, one distinct feature distinguishes its humorous literature from others: Singaporean slang known as 'Singlish'. The undercurrents of dialect in Singlish reflect a mixed heritage derived from Malay, Chinese, and Indian roots. Some appreciate the authenticity of Singlish; others deplore its grammatical impropriety, considering it an inferior form of English. Singlish words such as 'oi' ('hey, you!'), 'lah' (a frequent tag-on, often to give emphasis), and 'alamak' ('oh dear!') are generously littered throughout locally published best sellers, although Singlish has yet to find public acceptance as a linguistic tool for the portrayal of the Singaporean 'everyman' who is so often inept in English.

Nevertheless, this has not prevented the publication of novels celebrating the idiosyncratic properties of Singlish. Singaporean literary favourites such as Michael Chiang's *Army Daze* (1985), Adrian Tan's *The Teenage Textbook, or the Melting of the Ice Cream* (1988) and *The Teenage Workbook, or the Passing of an April Shower* (1989), and Colin Goh's and Lawrence Loh's *The Buaya Handbook* (1990) are just a few examples. In general, Singaporean fiction has given rise to several comic stereotypes of Singlish-speaking locals; the stereotypes invite the reader's empathy and also allow Singaporeans to laugh at themselves and at the stereotypical blunderers they recognize without too much effort.

Singaporean humour books frequently utilize titles with hints of Singlish: for example, the Singaporean joke series *Mr Kiasu* (1991), by 'the Kuppies' — Yu Cheng, Johnny Lau, and James Suresh — *Shiok!* (1990, author not cited), and *The Solid Singapore Joke Book* (1990), by Ben Mathews, among others. The linguistic filter colours all forms of comic writing, whether it focuses on teenage love, military experiences, schooling problems, or politics. In terms of content, there is a tendency in Singapore to exploit subjects popular among teenagers, who form the majority of readers in the country. Only occasionally does Singaporean humour rise above the blatantly ludicrous to wit and subtlety. One notable exception is George Nonis' *Hello Chok Tong, Goodbye Kuan Yew* (1991), a satirical cartoon collection poking fun at Singaporean politics and politicians. It ushers in a new venture into the outrageous that suggests, perhaps, richer and more courageous humorous fiction to come.

JOASH MOO

HUMOUR AND SATIRE (South Africa)

Early nineteenth-century entertainment at the Castle in Cape Town, South Africa, included impromptu skits and comic sketches; however, greater press freedom in the 1830s saw a proliferation of satiric verse and farces. A. G. Bain's *Kaatjie Kekkelbek*, first performed in 1838 and printed in the *South African Sentinel* newspaper in 1839, exploited Cape 'Coloured' humour in a medley of tongues; C. E. Boniface perpetuated an eighteenth-century tradition of comedy in *Kockincoz, or The Pettifogging Lawyers' Plot* (1843), and W. L. Sammons conducted a satirical weekly, *Sam Sly's African Journal* (1843–51). The pioneering years of exploration, hunting, and mining produced an anecdotal type of literature where humour, sometimes crudely racist, often involved the duping of some credulous greenhorn by an old-timer. Tensions between the Boer government of the Transvaal and the largely foreign mining community led to the Anglo-Boer War of 1899, producing a spate of satires in Kiplingesque vein. The 'backveld' or unsophisticated Boer became the butt of such humorists as Douglas Blackburn, whose *Prinsloo of Prinsloosdorp* (1899) exposed the corruption of Transvaal officialdom, **Perceval Gibbon**, author of *The Vrouw Grobelaar's Leading Cases* (1905), and **Herman Charles Bosman**, creator of the memorable Oom Schalk Lourens, whose stories were collected in *Mafeking Road* (1947). Bosman's humour, based on shrewd observation and an undercutting irony, found an echo in the writings of his contemporary, A. J. Blignaut. The versatile Leonard Flemming also found a ready market for his amusing accounts of farm life, as in *A Fool on the Veld* (1916).

Stephen Black, in plays such as *Love and the Hyphen* (premièred 1908 and first published in *Stephen Black: Three Plays*, 1984, edited by **Stephen Gray**) and *Van Kalabas Does His Bit* (1916), displayed a flair for social and political satire; his weekly newspaper *The Sjambok* ('Bullwhip', 1929–31), like **Roy Campbell**'s *Voorslag* ('Whip-lash', 1926–7), was intended to sting South Africans out of their moral turpitude. Campbell's *The Wayzgoose* (1928) is a savage verse satire on the provincialism of his countrymen; a similar attack on the Bloomsbury group, *The Georgiad*, followed in 1931. Anthony Delius ridiculed in verse and prose both English-Liberal and Afrikaner-Nationalist ideologies in *The Last Division* (1959) and *The Day Natal Took Off* (1963). Journalists such as Joel Mervis and Leo Marquard, and writers for ***Drum*** magazine, including Nat Nakasa and Casey 'Kid' Motsisi, found increasing scope for satire. Even in the 1970s, despite bannings and censorship, **Pieter-Dirk Uys**, Robert Kirby, and **Athol Fugard**, as well as such black playwrights as Ronnie Govender, Gibson Kente, and Percy Mtwa, continued to expose — in theatres, music-halls, and on makeshift township stages — the inhuman folly of Nationalist policies. Satiric verse flourished in the hands of Wopko Jensma, **Mongane Serote**, **Sipho Sepamla**, and **Christopher Hope**, who has excelled also at prose satire. Sylvester Stein's *Second-Class Taxi* (1958), Tom Sharpe's *Riotous Assembly* (1971), and Stephen Gray's *Local Colour* (1975) made savage fun of racial policies and prejudices. Humour and satire, however, proved increasingly inadequate in the face of the grim consequences of apartheid: in the late 1970s many writers turned to political sloganeering and strident propaganda. With apartheid now on the way out in the 1990s, there may again be room for humour and fresh targets for satire.

ERNEST PEREIRA

Further reading: Stephen Gray, 'Honest liars: parody in Southern African literature before 1820', *Unisa English Studies* XVI:1 (1978); 'Humour and satire', in David Adey, Ridley Beeton, Michael Chapman, and Ernest Pereira (eds) *Companion to South African English Literature* (1986).

HUMOUR AND SATIRE (West Africa)

West African humour is generally of the robust type with a tendency towards banter and slapstick, as evidenced by radio and television drama sketches. Most of it is unpublished, although there are one or two joke books. One of the few humour books is *No Time to Die* (1976), a collection of amusing poems by Kojo Kyei and Hanna Schreckenbach, based on slogans displayed on passenger trucks in Ghana.

In traditional West African societies satire was generally used for social control. At a time when people lived in close communities, and conformity was important for the survival of the clan, satire was particularly effective in dealing with unwholesome behaviour by individuals and by communities. Loss of dignity and the opprobrium of having one's peccadilloes exposed to public ridicule often acted as a deterrent or corrective. Contemporary oral satire manifests itself in satirical poetry sung or chanted at festivals by non-professional entertainers, masquerades, women-song-and-dance groups, and teenagers. The subjects range from infidelity and premarital sex to laziness and neglect of one's family.

Most of the subregion's satirical writings have their origin in the media. **Mabel Segun**'s *Sorry, No Vacancy* (1985, first published as *Friends, Nigerians, Countrymen*, 1977) is a narrow selection from her weekly broadcasts (1961–74) on the national radio network. Written in a vivid conversational style and with an anthropological eye for detail, the collection is lively, witty, and anecdotal and contains amusing vignettes of Nigerians. The medical profession's cult-like behaviour, lawyers' quibbling, hypocrisy in the church, the vanities of extended burial ceremonies, nepotism, civil servants' insolence, polygamy (ancient and modern), the lethal Lagos traffic — all are the butt of the author's wit. Similar in themes to Segun's work is Peter Enahoro's less-detailed social satire *How To Be a Nigerian* (1966), which appears to have been influenced by Segun's radio broadcasts, some of which were also published in the *Daily Times*.

Ken Saro-Wiwa's *Four Farcical Plays* (1989) also derives from the broadcast medium. The one-act plays were first aired as a television comedy series *Basi and Company*, which satirized the get-rich-quick propensity of Nigerians. His *Prisoners of Jebs* (1988), a cleverly written satire on the Nigerian political scene and its twists and turns, was first published serially in *Vanguard* between 1986 and 1987. It is a highly amusing allegorical account of the happenings in a prison, located on an artificial island off the Nigerian coast, directed by a rogue and peopled by all sorts of miscreants, including defaulting contractors, embezzlers of public funds, drug peddlars, a kangaroo judge, an esoteric professor, and a moronic journalist.

Not so successful are J. K. Randle's *The Godfather Never Sleeps* (1980) and *Who's Fooling Who?* (1985), which comment on various events in Nigeria and abroad. Compiled from newspaper articles, they suffer from wordiness, although parts are very amusing. *Points of Disorder* (1990), by Safe Adewunmi, satirizes the preoccupation of Nigerian legislators with trivialities.

MABEL SEGUN

HUMPHRIES, BARRY (1934–)

Australian satirist

Born in Melbourne, Australia, he began his theatrical career in Melbourne University revues and plays in the early 1950s. Since then he has lived in Melbourne, Sydney, England, and Portugal.

In 1955 Humphries created Edna Everage, the average suburban housewife from the Melbourne suburb of Moonee Ponds, unhappily but indissolubly married to Norm (as in 'normal'). Initially obsessed with the minutiae of daily Melbourne life and the beauties of her suburban home, Edna Everage has since 'developed' into the frantic matriarchal megastar Dame Edna Everage, probably Humphries' most popular character in Australia and overseas.

His best-known creations, especially in England, include the foul-mouthed but deeply puritanical Bazza McKenzie, an anarchistically non-naturalistic male Australian archetype initially featured as a comic-strip character in *Private Eye*. Deliberately anachronistic, Bazza of the wide-brimmed hat and gratuitously vulgar language appeared in the feature films *The Adventures of Barry McKenzie* (1972) and *Barry McKenzie Holds His Own* (1974). Many of Humphries' linguistic creations for Bazza have been absorbed into the Australian vernacular.

Other Humphries creations are the corrupt, dribbling diplomat Les Patterson, and Sandy Stone, a bewildered, desiccated, desexualized suburban male first created in 1959. Stone, surviving as a ghost from a predominantly Anglo-Saxon and 'innocent' Australia, bears significant similarities to Mr Pooter in George Grossmith's and Weedon Grossmith's late Victorian comic novel *The Diary of a Nobody*. Many of Humphries' creations gorge themselves on food, alcohol, and sex; they are almost all loud and rowdy larrikins, fearful of silence. Unlike John Belushi and Tony Hancock, Humphries is able to act out radical and self-destructive forces solely through his characters.

Humphries' one-man shows often savagely lampoon Australia and Australians; they include *A Nice Night's Entertainment* (1962), *At Least You Can Say You've Seen It* (1974–5), *An Evening's Intercourse with Barry Humphries* (1978–9), and *Tears before Bedtime* (1985–7). His books include *Bizarre* (1965), *The Barry Humphries Book of Innocent Austral Verse* (1968), *A Nice Night's Entertainment: Sketches and Monologues 1956–1981* (1981), *The Traveller's Tool* (1985), and *My Gorgeous Life: An Adventure* (1990). Humphries was awarded the Order of Australia in 1982 and judged the most popular performer in the UK in 1989–90.

ROSS FITZGERALD

HUNT, SAM (1946–)
New Zealand poet

Born in Auckland, New Zealand, he attended briefly the University of Auckland and Victoria University of Wellington, but dropped out without graduating. He completed teacher training at Wellington Teachers' College. An exuberant modern troubadour, Hunt has done more than any other New Zealand poet of his generation to create a popular audience for poetry. He produced five bestselling collections in the 1970s, of which the most successful was *South into Winter: Poems and Roadsongs* (1973). His *Collected Poems: 1963–1980* (1980) was followed by *Running Scared* (1982), *Approaches to Paremata* (1985), and *Selected Poems* (1987).

Hunt's most consistent persona is that of the freewheeling ordinary bloke, a kind of Kiwi Jack Kerouac, laconic — somewhat gauche — whose poems or 'roadsongs' are direct and simple, surprised by their own powerful emotion. Hunt's poems tell tales of love and loss and possess a raw energy in performance that they may lack on the page. As a lyric poet Hunt is rather more at ease; given a love affair, a cold wet night, and a bottle, he can construct a poem.

Despite his demotic intentions, Hunt is surprisingly literary. **James K. Baxter** is a pervasive influence, but other New Zealand poets can be discerned — **Fleur Adcock**, for instance, in 'Ice on the Jetty' (in the collection *From Bottle Creek*, 1972), and **Katherine Mansfield** in 'Just Like That!' (*South into Winter*). Hunt is habitually economic, as in 'Those Eyes; Such Mist' (in *Drunkard's Garden*, 1978): 'I have lost all voice. I kiss / those eyes, our voyaging; such mist.'

ANNE FRENCH

HUSSEIN, EBRAHIM (1943–)
Tanzanian dramatist
Born at Lindi, Tanzania, he studied theatre arts at the universities of Dar es Salaam, Tanzania, and Humboldt, Germany, and is generally considered to be the leading East African playwright. In 1988 he won the Tanzania Writers Union Prize for Drama. Hussein is often compared to the Nigerian playwright **Wole Soyinka**; like Soyinka, he is a pioneer of the experimental African theatre, based on a fusion of western and African dramatic elements. His works are, like Soyinka's, erudite, enigmatic, soul-searching, and artistically well-wrought. However, unlike Soyinka, who writes in English and addresses universal existential problems, Hussein writes in Kiswahili and addresses the African condition in a more concrete socio-economic sense. Since he writes in Kiswahili and his work has not been widely translated into other languages, Hussein is less known internationally than Soyinka. Hussein's plays in Kiswahili — social dramas based on the theme of cultural conflict and change — exhibit parallels with the works of **Ngugi wa Thiong'o**, **Gabriel Okara**, **Bekederemo**, and a host of other African writers of the 1950s and 1960s.

In *Kinjeketile* (1969), which Hussein translated into English in 1970, he uses a historical episode, the Maji Maji war against German invaders in Tanzania (1905–7), to probe the problematic of liberation and the role of the leader, the political prophet, in the process. At another level the play is an allegory on African visionary leaders such as Julius Nyerere and Kwame Nkrumah.

M. M. MULOKOZI

HUTCHINSON, LIONEL (1923–)
Barbadian novelist
Born in the parish of St Michael, Barbados, and raised and educated in Barbados, he has spent most of his life there. Retired from government service, he runs workshops for aspiring writers.

Hutchinson's tendentious first novel, *Man from the People* (1969), paints a graphic picture of Barbadian politics in the 1960s before the single-constituency system was introduced in 1966, when the island achieved independence. It is an uncompromising picture in which politicians are self-seeking, sexually exploitative, vulgar, and corrupt. Sam Martin, the hero, is able to keep his moral probity and idealism intact, while Ardware and Green, first colleagues, then adversaries, become increasingly opportunistic and unscrupulous. Even after his loss at the polls, Sam remains confident in his belief that morality and politics, too often strange bedfellows, can and ought to be married. In the presentation of its protagonist, this comic political novel differs from novels by such Caribbean writers as **V. S. Naipaul**, **Shiva Naipaul**, Don Walther, and Peter Alexander; *Man from the People* approves its hero's honesty and idealism.

One Touch of Nature (1971) explores the forgotten 'Red-Legs' who for centuries have occupied the lowest level of Barbadian society. The novel offers incisive social commentary and a fine character study of its 'Red-Leg' heroine Harriet Jivenot, who believes she was born for a better life than that offered by her native society. She develops strong prejudices against East Indians, blacks, and her own 'Red-Leg' men. By no means promiscuous, she becomes involved with five men who change her life. She is courted, abandoned, given her first orgasm, raped, and comforted. Chasing an elusive dream, she misses the obvious, and when she finally acquiesces to Robert's proposal of marriage, the reader senses that she has at long last found herself. Barbados' Lambert's Lane, with its many sights, sounds, aromas, and characters, is a fully realized setting for the novel and comes dramatically alive.

ROYDON SALICK

Further reading: Roydon Salick, 'Lionel Hutchinson: Barbados' forgotten novelist', *Bim* 69 (1985).

HUYGHUE, DOUGLAS SMITH (1816–1891)
Canadian novelist
Born in Charlottetown, Prince Edward Island, Canada, and educated in Saint John, New Brunswick, he began publishing in periodicals in the 1840s. Huyghue co-hosted an exhibition on Native peoples in Saint John in 1843 and worked with the Boundary Commission (charged with settling the border between Maine, USA, and New Brunswick, following the Aroostook War) from 1843 to 1845. After trying to establish himself as a writer in London, England (from the late 1840s to 1852), he immigrated to Australia, where, in August 1853, he went to the Ballarat goldfields as a clerk. There he witnessed the Eureka Stockade uprising in 1854, recording his impressions in watercolours (some published) and drawings and in the unpublished 'The Ballarat Riots', written under the pen-name Pax. (These are now held at the Mitchell Library, of the State Library of New South Wales, Australia.) Huyghue held various civil-service posts before retiring in Melbourne in 1878.

In Canada, Huyghue's novel *Argimou. A Legend of the Micmac* (1847; first serialized in 1842 in the journal *Amaranth*, under the pen-name Eugene) is one of the first to denounce the destructiveness of European settlement on Native life. It contrasts the hypocrisy and preoccupation with progress found in European society to the values of forest dwellers. Huyghue's romantic primitivism and concern for Native peoples also inform his novel *Nomades of the West; or, Ellen Clayton* (1850), in which he calls upon the philanthropic spirit of the age 'to devise some plan to rescue those perishing tribes'.

A sense of conscience also informs 'The Ballarat Riots', which, in spite of Huyghue's position as a government employee, is critical of the bureaucratic policies and class insensitivity that had led to the uprising. Although Huyghue felt his prose account to be more temperate in tone than Raffaello Carboni's *The Eureka Stockade* (1885), there none the less lurks behind his literary control the persona of a man committed to identifying social injustice whether in novels about Native peoples in Canada or in memoirs about diggers in Australia.

GWENDOLYN DAVIES

Further reading: Gwendolyn Davies, 'Douglas Huyghue', *Dictionary of Canadian Biography* 12 (1990); Gwendolyn Davies, 'Sailing for the goldfields: the Ballarat-Maritime provinces connection', in Gwendolyn Davies (ed.) *Studies in Maritime Literary History* (1991).

HYATT, CHARLES (1931–)
Jamaican short-story writer
He was born in Kingston, Jamaica, and his childhood during Jamaica's pre-independence period is the subject of his only publication to date, *When Me Was a Boy* (1989). This collection of anecdotes is the natural offspring of Hyatt's twin careers in theatre and radio broadcasting. His early success on the local stage won him a scholarship to England, where he remained for fourteen years appearing on stage and television. His work with the British Broadcasting Corporation also equipped him to become a dominant figure in radio drama and theatre in Jamaica. Hyatt's writing skills have been honed by the exigencies of oral performance as stand-up comic, storyteller, and broadcaster.

The narrative tone of *When Me Was a Boy*

has echoes of Pa Ben, the storyteller in **Trevor Rhone**'s play *Old Story Time* (1981), a role Hyatt memorably performed on the local stage for more than four years. Material for the book was first tested as a series of five-minute radio broadcasts. The anecdotes are therefore of equal length, beginning and ending with the formula of the title, *When Me Was a Boy* (pronounced 'bwy'). Hyatt has a command of both English and Creole; though he was forbidden to speak 'badly' as a child, he knew and enjoyed the language he heard in the market-place. Putting this language into print was a primary motive for the text, for Hyatt feels it is as valid as dominant dialects of English.

With its accurate and vivid detail, *When Me Was a Boy* is a reliable document of social history and is part of a body of Caribbean writing dealing with growing up in the turbulent period that saw the end of colonial rule.

CAROLYN ALLEN

HYDE, ROBIN (1906–39)

New Zealand poet, novelist, journalist

Born Iris Guiver Wilkinson, she grew up in a number of impoverished suburbs of Wellington, New Zealand. She attended Wellington Girls High School, receiving a number of literary prizes. From the age of seventeen she worked as a journalist on various newspapers in New Zealand and as parliamentary reporter. A brief affair at the age of twenty left her pregnant; she spent seven months in the slums of Sydney, Australia, where she gave birth to a still-born child whom she named Robin Hyde and whose name she later adopted as her pseudonym.

Hyde's range of tasks as a journalist sharpened her understanding of social divisions and she became skilled at adopting many voices; she wrote high-society fashion pieces as well as subversive articles about unemployment, city prisons, and the 1932 Queen Streets riots in Auckland, New Zealand. These multiple voices are also evident in her fiction: those of First World War nurse and of renegade soldier in *Passport to Hell* (1936) and *Nor The Years Condemn* (1938); of French colonial settler in *Check To Your King* (1936); of female fortune-teller and English upper-class gentleman in *Wednesday's Children* (1937).

Until recently critics have concentrated on the mental anguish apparent in Hyde's work. In his introduction to *A Book of New Zealand Verse 1923–45* (1945; rev. 1951), **Allen Curnow** claimed that Hyde 'wrote impulsively and did her best' unaware that her writing 'was near hysteria, more often that not'. Such public and influential opinions effectively depoliticized Hyde's work. She was almost invariably presented in very personal terms as a neurotic, self-absorbed, rather pathetic woman. However, recent critics have shown that the psychic distress evident in Hyde's work is a comprehensible response to the experience of family and New Zealand society. Where middle-class male writers defined problems encountered by New Zealand writers in the 1930s as caused by the distance from metropolitan English culture and the absence of a New Zealand past, Hyde saw the central problems of a colonial society as racial, sexual, and economic in a society whose foundations were built on the expropriation and exploitation of the land.

In contrast to New Zealand poet **Charles Brasch**, who claimed that 'in this raw colonial society, poets have to create order for the first time, in a wilderness that is without form and very nearly void', Hyde located a rich indigenous culture in the Maori. Her essay on New Zealand literature, 'The Singers of Loneliness' (1938?), argues that although the pakeha pioneers were in 'contact with an immense wealth of native myth and poetry', most of this was 'grossly wasted'.

Hyde conceived of writers as 'serving' their audience. She criticized the 'moderns' (as 'young men') for their lack of social involvement, viewing their work as unnecessarily obscure and élitist. She felt that women writers might tap a nerve in the national consciousness, which the 'serene male' cannot hope to reach because he 'has never been obliged to look at life with a perpetual crick in his neck'. This interest in writing and gender manifests itself in both *Wednesday's Children* and in her autobiographical novel *The Godwits Fly* (1938). *Wednesday's Children* deliberately revises contemporary notions about female identity and potential, exploring the validity of fantasy as a strategy for scrutinizing and subverting prevailing cultural images and assumptions. *The Godwits Fly* more explicitly explores the girlhood of a writer growing up in a restrictive colonial society. Although some claim that technically there is nothing new in *The Godwits Fly*, Hyde believed her novel marked a narrative innovation, at least in New Zealand fiction.

Hyde was a prolific writer. Before she committed suicide, she had produced three volumes of poetry, five novels, and two books of non-fiction as well as articles and daily journalism. Two major collections of poetry, *Houses by the Sea, and Later Poems* (1952) and *Selected Poems* (1984), edited and with an introduction by Lydia Wevers, and an autobiography, *A Home in This World* (1984), were published posthumously. Hyde wrote that it was her poetry that 'mattered more than anything else'. Her early verse reflects a preoccupation with the world of dream associated with the Romantic poets whom she admired, as well as a self-conscious use of 'poetic' language associated with the Georgian poets. *Houses by the Sea, and Later Poems* includes a long sequence of imagistic, sharply detailed evocations of childhood and is generally assessed as her finest work. A selection of Hyde's journalism, *Disputed Ground: The Journalism of Robin Hyde*, edited by Gillian Boddy and Jacqueline Matthews, was published in 1991.

SUSAN ASH

I

IDRIESS, ION (1889–1979)
Australian travel writer
Born in Sydney, Australia, he became by turns an assayer, prospector, rabbit poisoner, boundary rider, surveyor, and explorer. After serving as a trooper abroad during the First World War and travelling widely in outback Australia as well as in New Guinea and the Torres Strait, Idriess settled in Sydney as a free-lance writer. In the early 1930s his books of description, travel, biography, and adventure about outback life became bestsellers in Australia. A rapid and prolific writer, he produced forty-seven books between 1927 and 1969. *Lasseter's Last Ride* (1931), the story of the tragic search for a legendary gold reef in central Australia, sold seventeen thousand copies in its first year. *Flynn of the Inland* (1932), on the founder of the Australian Inland Mission, and *The Cattle King* (1936), about a successful pastoralist, also presented an ideology of heroic colonization of inland Australia.

Idriess' writing is vivid, entertaining, and good-humoured, based on first-hand experience, diaries, and interviews. His concern was generally to use popular forms to promote public and government awareness of the potential of the Australian interior and of issues such as untapped mineral resources, communications, irrigation, conservation, defence, and the importance of Aboriginal culture. There were many inconsistencies in Idriess' lay theorizing on political, social, and economic issues. These contradictions, along with his publishing success and penchant for the sensational, made his work generally unpopular with the Australian literary intelligentsia, who viewed his wide popularity — which included international and foreign-language publication — as detrimental to the reputation and development of a serious national literary culture.

Despite the success of travel writing elsewhere in the Commonwealth, no other writer in this genre achieved such influence as Idriess. He promoted national pride through his descriptions of the vastness, beauty, and potential wealth of inland Australia. His importance also lies in his evocation of an Australian self-image of ironic and stoic independence and practicality.

MARGRIET BONNIN

Further reading: Margriet Bonnin, 'Ion Idriess: "rich Australiana"', in Susan Dermody, John Docker, and Drusilla Modjeska (eds) *Nellie Melba, Ginger Meggs and Friends: Essays in Australian Cultural History* (1982).

IHIMAERA, WITI TAME (1944–)
New Zealand novelist, short-story writer
Born in Gisborne, New Zealand, he is of Maori descent, with tribal affiliations to Te Aitanga A Mahaki, Rongowhakaata, Ngai Tamanuhiri, Ngati Porou, Tuhoe, Whakatohea, Te Whanau A Apanui, and Kahungunu. He received tertiary education at Auckland and Victoria universities, New Zealand. Ihimaera has worked as a journalist, an information officer with the New Zealand ministry of foreign affairs, as New Zealand's consul to the USA in New York, and as counsellor (public affairs) at the New Zealand embassy, Washington, USA.

Ihimaera's *Pounamu, Pounamu* (1972) was the first published volume of stories by a Maori writer, and his *Tangi* (1973) the first published novel by a Maori writer. Ihimaera writes about Maori people and contexts, seeking in his early writing to redress the lack of familiarity with the Maori side of New Zealand's dual cultural inheritance; Ihimaera's later texts are often more overtly polemical.

Characters, settings, motifs, and themes, including the character Tama Mahana, the village of Waituhi, and the meeting-house Rongopai, are shared across Ihimaera's fictions. His works are characterized by the contrast of Maori and Pakeha values, represented through the conflict of rural community values and urban, individualistic, materialistic values and figured in the motif of literal or metaphorical journeys between Waituhi and Wellington. Ihimaera's major themes include the importance of the land to the Maori, the centrality of history and genealogy to an understanding of the present, and the importance of both the spiritual presence of the ancestors and the *whanau* ('extended family') as constitutive of the 'self'. Such concerns are shared by Aboriginal Australian writer **Sally Morgan** in her autobiographical *My Place* (1987).

The stories in *Pounamu, Pounamu* address issues of cultural difference, though with less anger than in Ihimaera's later collection, *The New Net Goes Fishing* (1977), which deals more explicitly with racial tension and confrontation. The Emerald City motif framing the collection points to the effect on Maori youth and culture of the insistence of Pakeha aspirations to urban material success. The collection *Dear Miss Mansfield: A Tribute to Kathleen Mansfield Beauchamp* (1989) marks the centennial of **Katherine Mansfield**'s birth and offers stories that are specifically Maori variations on some of Mansfield's works.

Tangi was developed from a story of the same title in the collection *Pounamu, Pounamu*. Structured in alternating episodes of Tama Mahana's journey from Wellington to Waituhi after the death of his father, it traces Tama's response to the loss and his gradual recognition and acceptance of the spiritual inheritance from his father. The novel *Whanau* (1974) evokes the life of a village, its range of characters and their relationships focused by the disappearance of the village's oldest inhabitant, Nanny Paora.

Ihimaera's most complex and critically controversial novel to date is *The Matriarch* (1986). Its scope and size have resulted in critical discussion of it as post-colonial epic. The text is pervaded by the violence of colonization's historical and cultural fragmentation and by the problematic position of the indigenous (writing) subject of white-settler, post-colonial society. There are continuities of character, setting, theme, and motif with Ihimaera's earlier writing. However, the textual fragmentation — abrupt shifts of tone and a discourse that is variously rhetorical, polemical, didactic, and domestic — represents a departure from the earlier writing. Reference and intertextuality include Maori cosmology and mythology, the Biblical Exodus, colonial New Zealand history, the Italian Risorgimento, the Parliamentary *Hansard*, and the operas of Verdi.

The matriarch of the novel is Artemis, a powerful, charismatic woman tracing her descent from Te Kooti Rikirangi and Wi Pere Halbert, both of whom fought for Maori land rights, the former in guerrilla confrontation, the latter as a Member of Parliament. Artemis teaches her grandson Tama his ancestral and historical inheritance, preparing him to follow her life's work, despite opposition from both her husband and Tama's mother. While *The Matriarch* has been praised for its ambition and achievement, other responses have pointed to an alleged failure of narrative coherence and imaginative credibility, and Maori feminists have disputed the representation of Artemis.

Ihimaera's other works include *The Whale Rider* (1987), the opera 'Waituhi' (premièred 1984), the collection *Into the World of Light: An Anthology of Maori Writing* (1982), which he coedited with Don Long, and *Te Ao Marama: Contemporary Maori Writing. Volume I: The Whakahuatanga O Te Ao. Reflections of Reality* (1992), which he edited.

CHRIS PRENTICE

Further reading: Hartwig Isernhagen, 'Witi Ihimaera's fiction: from indigenous myth to late modernist city myth?' *World Literature Written in English* 1 (1984); Alex Calder and John Beston, 'Two responses', reviews of *The Matriarch, Landfall* 161 (1987); Trevor James, 'Lost our birthright forever? the Maori writer's re-invention of New Zealand', *SPAN* 24 (1987); Umelo Ojinmah, *Witi Ihimaera: A Changing Vision* (1993).

IKE, VINCENT CHUKWUEMEKA (1931–)
Nigerian novelist
Born in Ndikelionwu village in Eastern Nigeria, he was educated at Government College, Umuahia, University College at Ibadan, and Stanford University, USA, where he earned an MA for a study of Nigerian universities. (The study was later published as *University Development in Africa: The Nigerian Experience*, 1976.) Ike has held several important administrative positions in universities in West Africa. He retired from public service in 1979.

Ike is the author of seven novels — *Toads for Supper* (1965), *The Naked Gods* (1970), *The Potter's Wheel* (1973), *Sunset at Dawn* (1976), *Expo '77* (1980), *The Chicken Chasers* (1980), and *The Bottled Leopard* (1985) — all satires. In 1990 he published *Our Children Are Coming.*

Toads for Supper deals with the indiscretions of the protagonist Amadi who, while an undergraduate, engages in amorous relationship with several women; *The Naked Gods* centres on the intrigues that characterize the appointment of a vice-chancellor of Songhai University; *The Potter's Wheel* humorously highlights the problem of over-indulging an only son in the family.

In *Sunset at Dawn* Ike chronicles the tragic experience of the **Nigerian Civil War**, while in *Expo '77* he lambastes the corrupt examination malpractices prevalent in some West African institutions. *The Chicken Chasers* laments the attempt to prevent the secretary general of the African Cultural Organization from assuming a second term of office. In *The Bottled Leopard* Ike examines the misconception often held in traditional African societies that male children are intellectually superior to their female counterparts.

Ike employs humour, dialogue, sarcasm, and proverbs — which are drawn mostly from Igbo mythology and folklore — both to interest his audience and to enrich his work. He is a satirist who, while lampooning the foibles and failings of people and their institutions, reveals sympathetic insight in delineating his characters. Much like **Chinua Achebe**, Ike is concerned with the problems confronting his people and the ways in which these problems can be addressed for the ultimate good of society.

ISAAC I. ELIMIMIAN

Further reading: Ezenwa-Ohaeto, 'Chukwuemeka Ike', in Yemi Ogunyemi (ed.) *Perspective on Nigerian Literature: 1700 to the Present* 2 (1988); Ezenwa-Ohaeto, 'The historical dimension of Chukwuemeka Ike's female characters', *A Current Bibliography on African Affairs* Vol. 22 (1990).

IMBUGA, FRANCIS DAVIS (1947–)
Kenyan dramatist
Born in Chavakali, Kenya, he was educated at Nairobi University, Kenya, where he graduated with a bachelor of education degree and an MA. He holds a Ph.D. in drama from the University of Iowa, USA. Imbuga is professor of literature and dean of the faculty of arts at Kenyatta University, Kenya.

Imbuga is the most prolific playwright in Kenya. (See **Drama**, East Africa.) Within a period of two decades he has published nine plays. He has also written, directed, and acted in numerous published scripts for Kenyan television. The younger Imbuga was interested in family drama and traditional issues and his early plays revolve around interpersonal relations and the conflict between the 'old' and the 'new' Kenyan culture as it relates to family interaction.

The Fourth Trial (1972) examines the predicament of the younger generation of couples facing traditional demands on procreation. To the older generation a marriage is null and void if there are no children, and the blame is always levelled against women, as the voice of tradition contends in the play: 'Women were made to flower the world with children. A woman who cannot contribute to this might as well have been born into something else.' *Kisses of Fate* (1972, published with *The Fourth Trial*) laments the disintegration of family relationships. The playwright warns against the possibility of perverted relations, such as incest, once the family base is broken.

Imbuga typically blends comedy with tragedy, as in *The Married Bachelor* (1973), which castigates the moral sterility of the new generation of the educated élite and exposes the tragic consequences of its disregard for traditional values. He revisits the conflict between traditional and modern cultural values in *Burning of Rags* (1989), a revision of *The Married Bachelor*.

Critics have characterized the work of Imguba as 'Literature of disillusionment'. In this respect, Imbuga and Uganda's **John Ruganda** meet. Just as Ruganda's work shows his disillusionment with the political situation in Uganda after the attainment of independence, so Imbuga, in *Betrayal in the City* (1976) and *Man of Kafira* (1984), reveals his thorough disappointment with Kenyan independence, and what he sees as the betrayal of the people's hopes.

One of the most thorny issues to which Imbuga the dramatist reacts with particular sensitivity is that of the devaluation of human life in post-independence Kenya in particular, and in Africa in general. As in *Betrayal in the City* and *Man of Kafira*, Imbuga ridicules the power hunger that leads to the perpetration of a tragic *status quo* in *Game of Silence* (1977) and *The Successor* (1979), satirical dramas enhanced by motifs of dreams and madness.

An important development in Imbuga's drama that appears to have roots in his earlier family drama is his interest in gender politics. In *Aminata* (premièred at the End of Women's Decade Conference in Nairobi in 1985 and first published in 1988), Imbuga calls for a re-examination of traditional practices and attitudes that deter the progress of women and African society in general.

CIARUNJI CHESAINA SWINIMER

Further reading: Ciarunji Chesaina Swinimer, *Notes on Francis Imbuga's 'Man of Kafira'* (1984).

INDIA

More than three thousand years ago, when the nomadic Aryans came to the banks of the Ganga in search of food for themselves and fodder for their cattle, their immediate reaction to nature's fury — fierce winds, pouring rain, thunder and lightning, primeval darkness, and oppressive silence — was, predictably, one of awe and wonder. Unable to rationalize these mysterious phenomena, they imagined them to be the work of some hidden hand and sought to propitiate the 'Shining Ones' — believed to be presiding over the elements — by chanting hymns that became the poetry of the Rig-Veda, called by scholar Max Müller 'the first utterance of Aryan man'. As time passed, questions about existence and reality were embodied in the poetry of the Upanishads (Sanskrit philosophical treatises) and in the Sutras (a set of aphorisms in Hindu literature). The Vedas (the most ancient Hindu scriptures), the Upanishads, and the Sutras laid the foundations of Indian culture.

The Aryans invested every rock, tree, and river with divinity, and they peopled the Himalayas with gods and goddesses, visualizing Siva and his spouse Gowri as having their abode on Gowrisankara (Mount Everest). The land the Ayrans occupied they variously called 'Aryavarta', 'Brahmadesa', and 'Punyabhumi'; the peoples living in west Asia referred to those living on the other side of the river Indus as '(H)Indus', whose way of life gradually acquired the name Hinduism. What was

'India' to outsiders was for the insiders 'Bharatadesa' or 'Bharat', after the mythical founder Bharata — myth more real than facts of history. (Although India has been accused by western historians of having no sense of history, some of them are beginning to look upon history as myth.)

Modern archaeological excavations have unearthed an advanced urban society, the Harappa-Mohenjodaro civilization, which flourished in the Indus Valley (now in Pakistan) at least one thousand years before the Aryans arrived. This was the creation of dark-skinned Dravidians, the original inhabitants of the land who were pushed south by the invading fair-complexioned Aryans. There was extensive intermingling, though, of Aryans and Dravidians as is evident not only in the indistinguishable shades of complexion and facial features of their descendants today but in the pervasive presence of Sanskrit terms in the Dravidian languages of Tamil, Kannada, Telugu, and Malayalam, though Tamil claims antiquity with Sanskrit. Sanskrit — the word is a synonym for culture — is an Indo-European language and the present-day Hindi is its chief descendant, though more than six variations of it under different names are also spoken in the states of north India.

The Aryans and the Dravidians built up the composite Indian civilization that originated on the banks of the Ganga, where a succession of empires flourished. It is widely acknowledged that the Ganga holds India's patrimony — *Vyapini Jnana Ganga* ('Ganga pervading with Knowledge') — and flows in the veins of all Indians. Ganga is the generic name for all water, hence the myth of the 'Ganga and Her Sisters', the title of an unpublished novel by **Raja Rao**. Through the ages the Ganga has drawn to its banks for discourse and debate not only thinkers such as Buddha, in the sixth century BC, and Sankara, in the eighth century AD, but India's millions seeking purification — hundreds of people to this day go there to bathe, worship, and some even await their deaths, in the belief that it ends the cycle of births for them. **Jawaharlal Nehru**'s lyrical 'will' sums up the river's lasting vitality in the Indian psyche: 'The Ganga, especially, is the river of India, beloved of her people, round which are intertwined her racial memories, her hopes and fears.' In keeping with the hilarious tone of **G. V. Desani**'s significantly titled narrative *All About H. Hatterr* (1951, first published in 1948 under its less-known title, *All About Mr. Hatterr, A Gesture*), its author also writes of the river: 'She dwelleth, dwelleth the Babe Dwelleth midst murmur and gurgle, gurgles over gurgles, coiling ever-coiling . . . the resounding Glory of Ganga, the hymn of the hills.' But the most celebrated account of the Ganga in recent English prose is found in Raja Rao's *The Serpent and the Rope* (1960), which expresses Rao's conceptual thinking and profound awareness of the river's impact:

> The whole of the Gangetic plain is one song of saintly sorrow, as though Truth began where sorrow was accepted. So sorrow is our river, sorrow our earth, but the green of our trees, and the white of our mountains is the affirmation that Truth is possible. Truth is the Himalayas and Ganges humanity. That is why we throw the ashes of the dead into her. She delivers them to the sea, and the sun heats the water so that, becoming clouds, they return to the Himalayas.

Plurality, or unity in diversity, has always characterized Indian life and thought. The physical features of India — covering more than three million square kilometres — underline this characteristic, with the Himalayan mountains and their dense forests in the north, with the vast Ganges plain (with potential for feeding India's some 850 million people) extending down to the southern peninsular plateau, bound by the Arabian Sea in the west, the Bay of Bengal in the east, and the Indian Ocean to the south. Conducive to seafaring, south India carried on extensive trade with the countries of Asia and the Roman Empire. North-east India has the world's highest level of rainfall, 12,700 millimetres annually, while the arid deserts of Rajastan and parts of Gujarat, with their extremes of cold and heat, have the lowest — 76.2 millimetres annually. India's mineral wealth includes gold, silver, copper, iron, diamonds, and precious stones.

The country's forests, like its mountains and rivers, have also given character to Indian civilization. The great teachers of Vedic times and later ages dwelt in their forest hermitages, and kings and emperors made long journeys to sit at their feet. As told in the Upanishads and epics, these teachers gathered pupils from far and near and offered guidance to the good people when they were exiled to wander in the woods. Voluntary withdrawal into the forest by the householder in his old age in order to contemplate — *Vanaprasta* ('forest-dwelling') — was a necessary stage in a Hindu's life and is still esteemed. (See **R. K. Narayan**'s *The Vendor of Sweets*, 1967.) Certain trees acquired special significance, because, for example, the Buddha received enlightenment under the peepul tree, and Sita, the heroine of the *Ramayana*, sat under *Asoka* waiting for her release from the demon Ravana.

Different flowers were dear to different gods and are still offered in worship. Even today green leaves are used in Hindu homes on all festive occasions. Poetry of the Vedic and the Classical ages is replete with descriptions of trees and flowers by name; such descriptions were not considered 'pathetic fallacy' until they became the stock-in-trade of inferior poets. Celebration of plants and flowers was not a reaction against city life, as in English Romantic poetry, but was spontaneous, having its origin in the forests. Tribals in India still ask to be excused by the woods for cutting a tree or killing a fowl. Members of the Chipkos tribe in India's north-east are still said to hug a tree to ward off danger.

India has a wide variety of fauna ranging from elephants, lions, and tigers to the jackal and the deer. The birds are of every shade, size, and song and some serve as emblems of royal dynasties. While the cow has earned the epithet 'sacred', most other animals are also connected with gods, notably the mouse, the vehicle of the elephant god, Ganesa. The seven-hooded cobra provides the couch for the god Vishnu, hence the practice of cobra worship. In the epic *Ramayana*, the demon Ravana abducts Sita, the heroine; a vulture fights Ravana, squirrels build a bridge, and the monkey god Hanuman leads an army of monkeys to rescue Sita. In the *Mahabharata*, Pandava King Yudhistara refuses to enter heaven unless his dog can accompany him. Even today, the Jains, a major religious sect comprised of prosperous business people, do everything possible to avoid treading on a worm. **M. K. Gandhi** was indebted to the Jains in his doctrine of non-violence. The term *Vasudaiva Kutumbakam* ('Earth Family') is no pretentious claim. *Panchatantra*, said to be the source of Aesop's *Fables*, consists of numerous stories in which animals are characters. R. K. Narayan's *The Man-Eater of Malgudi* (1961) and *A Tiger for Malgudi* (1983) are in that tradition. The cat in Raja Rao's *The Cat and Shakespeare* (1965) is a traditional symbol of God as Mother.

It is these concepts that have given a sense of cultural unity to India, underlined by the founding of cultural centres in the four corners of India (on mountain, seashore, or river bank) by Sankara in the eighth century. The entire country is dotted with thousands of pilgrim centres, some considered 'golden', most 'leaden', others, like Varanasi (Benares), 'silver', which explains the title of **M. Anantanarayanan**'s remarkable novel, *The Silver Pilgrimage* (1961). Absorbent like the ocean, Hinduism has allowed in its fold thousands of castes while claiming exclusive virtue and a 'holier than thou' attitude, which nevertheless helped to preserve Hindu society against the onslaughts of invaders. The nation's religions include Hindu (approximately eighty-three per cent of the population), Muslim (approximately eleven per cent), Christian (approximately three per cent), and Sikh (approximately two per cent). India also enjoys a great diversity of languages. Its constitution recognizes fifteen languages, plus English, Konkani, Manipuri, Maithili, Nepali, and Rajasthani.

Recent Indian writing in English, influenced by 'progressive' western ideas, as well as by writing in regional languages, has emphasized the 'social ills' of the caste system, but little of this writing has celebrated its contribution to cultural variety and richness in ceremonial rituals, costumes, jewellery, dietary habits, and dialectical vigour in language. What has given social cohesiveness to Indian society through the ages are caste, joint family, and the village community, in each of which the group and not the individual is of primary importance, as in traditional African society; in India even great poets, composers of music, architects, and sculptors once remained anonymous. The *Mahabharata* speaks of expanding spheres of duties rather than of rights, and of the sacrifice of the good of the individual for the sake of the family, of the family for the village, of the village for the country, and of the country for the good of humanity. If the king is God's deputy on earth, his first concern must be the good of the people; he can be killed if he proves despotic. Again, it is not the king, according to Manu, the law-giver, but the *Sudra* ('the lowest caste') that can do no wrong. This well-organized society provided for vertical mobility of the individual based on merit in moral and spiritual matters — hence Gandhi, a trader by caste, could command universal respect. Many poets and philosophers were from the caste of untouchables, hence **Mulk Raj Anand**'s efforts to confer identity on Bakha in *Untouchable* (1935) (where the misbehaviour of the Brahmin priest is held to ridicule) and on the cobbler in his short story 'The Cobbler and the Machine'. In Rao's *The Cat and Shakespeare*, the lowly tobacco-chewing Nayar is represented as a wise man, and in R. K. Narayan's *The Guide* (1958), Raju, who becomes a swami, is a shopkeeper's son.

The rebel is no outlaw in Indian society; he has always identified himself with the good of large sections of people — thus the Buddha, Sankara, and Ramanuja (twelfth century AD) commended a life of renunciation. However, renunciation practised for one's own salvation is considered another form of selfishness and is not approved. Gandhi wished if there were rebirth to be born an untouchable. **Sri Aurobindo**, a Cambridge-educated Indian, withdrew from active politics to write his *magnum opus*, *Savitri* (1954), an epic in which a king wanders the three worlds and comes back to earth with a prayer, not for the birth of a son (as was usually desired) but for the birth of a daughter. When she comes of age, Savitri marries Satyavan against the warning of a sage who predicts his death in twelve months after the marriage. Savitri keeps her vigil on the fateful day and enters into a prolonged dialogue with the God of Death, who gives him back to her. The first important Indian poet writing in English, **Toru Dutt**, a convert to Christianity who died at the age of twenty-one, celebrates in her short poems (*Ancient Ballads and Legends of Hindustan*, 1882) the lives of such young rebels as Dhruva, Prahlad, Buttoo, and Savitri.

Dutt was in the line of celebrated women poets such as Akkamahadevi (twelfth century AD), who wrote in Kannada, and Mira (sixteenth century AD), who wrote in Hindi. If **Nayantara Sahgal**, **Anita Desai**, **Santha Rama Rau**, and **Shashi Deshpande** have become reputed novelists in English in the late twentieth century, and if thousands of women have received higher education in arts, sciences, medicine, and engineering and have occupied positions of power and responsibility, they owe it to a tradition of freedom enjoyed by women in India. It is also true, however, that throughout the ages division of labour in society led to the segregation of the sexes and to secondary roles for Indian women.

Why then did India fall behind the west? How did it allow a succession of invaders — the Greeks, Afghans, Mongols, Turks, Moghuls, and finally the British — to rule? Except for the British, who ruled India from the early seventeenth century until 1947, those invaders were absorbed into the country. The Moghuls especially contributed to India's cultural richness in painting, poetry, and architecture (notably the Taj Mahal). The people of India who lived in small village communities took little notice, however, of what happened outside their villages. The absence of a strong political centre to match a strong invader was a major cause of foreign domination. There also grew a gap between the inner life and the outer life of the individual and, even more, between the individual and society. The people lost contact with the vibrant world outside, thanks to their 'holier than thou' attitude. The technological west stole a march on India despite India's early contribution to mathematics (zero being her greatest gift), medicine, engineering, sculpture, temple architecture, jewellery, and, from the Muslims, weaving (the Muslin, notably).

It is also true that there were far-sighted Indians such as Raja **Rammohun Roy**, who, at least ten years before Macaulay set foot on Indian soil, petitioned India's Governor General to instruct Indian youth in European science in the English language. While Persian was the court language during the 400 years of Moghul rule, the people at large used their own languages. Those who worked for Britain's East India Company — the barber, cobbler, errand boy, shopkeeper, postman, and policeman — had to know some English. Because of their admiration for their English rulers, who represented modernity in their eyes, Indians demanded English education even before universities were founded in 1857 in Calcutta, Bombay, and Madras.

Indian nationalism grew after the First World War, promoted by the Indian National Congress. Gandhi's call for self-rule and for the removal of untouchability, and his 1930 non-violent civil disobedience campaign, spurred the independence movement. The head of the Muslim League, Muhammad Ali Jinnah, however, demanded the creation of a new nation for the Muslims — Pakistan.

Indian culture asserted its astonishing vitality in its response to Gandhi's call for non-violent non-co-operation with the British. The meeting of the east and the west during the raj and the resultant clash of cultures provide material for considerable fictional writing in English, notably Raja Rao's *Kanthapura* (1938), **Bhabani Bhattacharya**'s *So Many Hungers!* (1947), and, peripherally, Mulk Raj Anand's *Untouchable* and R. K. Narayan's *Waiting for the Mahatma* (1955).

The British government partitioned the subcontinent into India and Pakistan on 15 August 1947 when India became a self-governing nation, a 'democratic republic' which, thanks largely to Jawaharlal Nehru's initiative, chose to enter the Commonwealth, with the Queen as its head. Partition and its attendant sectarian violence gave rise to some important novels, notably **Khushwant Singh**'s *Train to Pakistan* (1956), **Kamala Markandaya**'s *Some Inner Fury* (1955), and **Chaman Nahal**'s *Azadi* (1975). Tensions among subcastes found literary expression in **K. Nagarajan**'s *Chronicles of Kedaram* (1961).

Although Indians are known for their self-effacement, they have produced a crop of autobiographies, notably Gandhi's *The Story of My Experiments with Truth* (vol. 1, 1927; vol. 2, 1929), Nehru's *An Autobiography* (1936), R. K. Narayan's *My Days* (1975), **Nirad C. Chaud-**

huri's *The Autobiography of an Unknown Indian* (1951), and numerous fictionalized autobiographies. (See **Life Writing**, India.)

What has distinguished Indian society through the ages is the place of religion in the life of the individual and the group, and the primacy of the inner life over the outer, with a desire to live according to dharma ('right conduct') — that which holds the individual intact and society together, with emphasis on correct behaviour. (See **Religion and Caste**, India). Art and literature, for example, have always been looked upon as aids to a philosophical way of life. They both share the same *Purusharathas* ('ends'), dharma, *Artha* ('wealth'), *Kama* ('desire of senses'), and *Moksha* ('self-realization'), or release from the *Maya* of attachment to the world, traditionally described as an image seen in a mirror. One has a right to acquire wealth and to enjoy the pleasures of the senses, but, according to dharma, art and literature help in seeing oneself and others better. The arts were expected to engage the emotions of readers or spectators so deeply that they would be absorbed in them while the experience lasted. With the repetition of such experiences the individual grows less and less self-centred and relates more and more to the world outside, hence the immense popularity of the *Bhagavadgita* among the élite, and of the epics *Ramayana* and *Mahabharata* among the common people. It is astonishing how unlettered masses can still cite large sections from their popular versions of the epics, and draw attention in ordinary conversation to a character, situation, and conduct from the epics, commonly referred to as the 'culture of the masses'. These works have sunk into the consciousness of the Indian people and shaped their outlook, as is abundantly proved by the extraordinary success in the early 1990s of televised series of India's epics. An amazing continuity has characterized Indian civilization, as it has the Chinese.

C. D. NARASIMHAIAH

Further reading: K. M. Panikkar, *A Survey of Indian History* (1947); Jawaharlal Nehru, *The Discovery of India* (1946); A. L. Bhashan, *The Wonder That Was India* (3rd ed., 1968).

INGAMELLS, REX (1913–55)
Australian poet
Born in Orroroo, South Australia, he was educated and worked in Adelaide before moving to Melbourne in 1951. With twelve books of poems, two novels, five general books, and several anthologies published in his lifetime, Ingamells is now known mainly for one prose manifesto, *Conditional Culture* (1938), and for creating the **Jindyworobak Movement**. His poetry has long been out of print — the only 'collected works' is *Selected Poems* (1944) — reflecting and furthering critical dismissal; Brian Elliott's *The Jindyworobaks* (1979) has brought it back to attention.

Ingamells' early lyric poetry celebrates the South Australian desert country and wildlife. Introducing Ingamells' first collection, *Gumtops* (1935), L. F. Giblin wrote of Australia's need for a new Adam to name the land and proposed Ingamells as candidate. *Forgotten People* (1936) continues to 'name' the Outback while reflecting growing interest in earlier 'namers', the Aborigines. Poems such as 'Voice for the Wilderness' (*Sun-Freedom*, 1938), anticipate **Les Murray** in celebrating a wild landscape set against the industrial city.

Ingamells soon saw that the need was not for a new Adam to name the land, but to recover the original names and legends. Developing the Jindyworobak thesis, he began including Aboriginal references in his poetry. The propagandist came to overpower the lyricist. Too often Ingamells labours his lesson in capitalized generalities. This habit, criticized by **A. D. Hope**, seriously damages *The Great South Land: An Epic Poem* (1951). The epic reflects a contemporary interest in 'voyager' poems — see **Douglas Stewart**'s *Voyager Poems* (1960) and **Allen Curnow**'s work, for example; it delivers much information with earnest enthusiasm and contains a number of striking passages. Its admiration for European explorers and the technology enabling the voyages offers a useful corrective to the view that Ingamells denied the European heritage and escaped into primitivism. The epic shows how mutual incomprehension can arise between two radically different cultures, a theme explored by Murray and **Vincent O'Sullivan**, among others; but it lacks specific focus or insight, and the writing is pedestrian.

Ingamells' brief, impressionistic nature lyrics are livelier, and these, well-represented in Elliott's *The Jindyworobaks*, remain the highlight of his poetry.

LAWRENCE BOURKE

INGRAM, KENNETH N. (1921–)

Jamaican poet

Born in St Ann, Jamaica, he attended Jamaica College and the University of London, England. After leaving school he wrote several poems and short stories, mainly between 1940 and 1944. His professional life has been devoted to research and librarianship; his publications are largely in bibliographical, archival, and historical studies.

By his own account, Ingram's literary interests were stimulated by his schoolteachers so that he 'became part of that wave of creativity and surge of national sentiment which . . . owed much to the catalytic effect of Edna Manley and the circle of young writers and artists which gathered around her'. Ingram's published oeuvre includes about twenty-five poems, several of which appeared in early issues of *Focus*, in the weekly *Public Opinion*, in an issue of *Life and Letters*, and in various anthologies. He mentions D. H. Lawrence, G. M. Hopkins, and T. S. Eliot as possible influences.

History has been kinder to Ingram than to his contemporary (and fellow Catholic) **John Figueroa**. The poems of Ingram that are overly sentimental, gauche, that strain to achieve their 'literary' effects or contort diction and adopt archaisms for no apparent reason, have been forgotten in favour of some quite fine pieces such as 'It Is a Rose-Red Morning' and 'Sheep'. Thanks to recitation at annual festivals and inclusion in anthologies, these have become virtual Jamaican classics. Ingram feels (correctly) that his poems are largely 'characterized by . . . an awareness of the sensuous beauty and vitality of the natural world; awareness of its transitory nature; and a . . . sense of the sadness of the human condition'. The best are well-crafted and marked by a distinctive voice. Though his work has received little critical comment, Ingram, along with writers such as **George Campbell**, Una Marson, **Vivian Virtue**, and Basil MacFarlane, helped indigenize Jamaican poetry.

PAMELA C. MORDECAI

IRELAND AND IRISH VALUES IN AUSTRALIA

Prior to massive post-1947 immigration to Australia, people of Irish origin formed about a third of the population of Australia and the country's only significant non-English factor, particularly given their predominantly Catholic religious culture. The early convict Irish, often minimally literate in English, nevertheless produced one popular convict rhymster, Francis MacNamara, who wrote 'A Convict's Tour to Hell' (1839), and they supplied, mainly anonymously, an indelible Irish influence on a tradition of Australian popular songs and ballads, carried forward by the Irish element in the period of gold rushes and bushranging, from the 1850s to the 1870s. (See **Songs and Ballads**, Australia.) This crudely vigorous anti-authority, socially critical verse commentary originated in a blend of convictism and pioneering not shared by other Commonwealth countries and dominated the tradition of 'protest literature' that celebrated the common working man. (See **Convict Literature**, Australia.)

A strong Irish-Australian subculture lasted from the 1820s to the 1960s, based on Irish-Catholic leadership and education. In its disintegration after the 1960s the subculture became, to an extent not duplicated elsewhere in the Commonwealth, raw material for an explosion of novels, plays, and reminiscences written in the main by ex-Catholics of Irish descent.

In its prime, from the 1880s to the 1950s, the culture of Irish Catholic Australia, intensely religious and church-controlled, claimed to be truly Australian, as distinct from the servile imitation Englishness of the establishment. Its major literary vehicle was journalism. A network of Irish-Australian weekly newspapers and periodicals flourished from the 1870s to the 1960s. Mainly church-owned and religious in emphasis, all carried substantial Irish news and magazine sections, which serialized popular Irish fiction such as the many novels of Canon P. A. Sheehan and locally written novels such as those by Marion Miller Knowles — women were prominent in 'popular' colonial Catholic authorship. Often the verse contributed by the host of minor Irish poets — from Victor Daley to Bernard O'Dowd — who populated the literary scene from the 1880s to the 1920s lumped together an Irish past and a romanticized Australia, with little real encounter with either. The most serious Irish-Australian talent of the time, **Christopher Brennan**, paid little attention to his 'Irishness', an attitude shared by later Irish-Australian writers, notably **James McAuley** and **Gerald Murnane**. The work of poet **Vincent Buckley** and novelist Gerard Windsor partially reverses this rejection: both see Ireland, to some degree, as their imagination's home.

The most successful identification of the Irish with the Australian bush experience is represented by the verse collection *Around the Boree Log and Other Verses* (1921) by John O'Brien (Father P. J. Hartigan), still in print, with half a million copies sold. Hartigan reconciled and amalgamated Irish and Australian rural cultures and embodied the harmonious integration with environment to which Irish Australia aspired. Less idealized but in the same optimistic tradition is **Ruth Park**'s clan novel of the Sydney slums, *The Harp in the South* (1948). The positive view of the Irish lent itself also to the saga tradition, to which the realities of Irish family pioneering, notably that depicted in **Mary Durack**'s *Kings in Grass Castles* (1959), provided a factual base. Sagas range from **Miles Franklin**'s *All That Swagger* (1936) to the commercialism of **Colleen McCullough**'s *The Thorn Birds* (1977) and include a colonial trilogy by Lola Irish linking Australia and Canada, of which the last volume is *The House of O'Shea* (1990).

Australian literature offers other portraits of the Irish that are much more ambivalent: the complexities of **Henry Handel Richardson**'s *The Fortunes of Richard Mahony* (1930) darken in the four major novels analysed by Vincent Buckley — **Joseph Furphy**'s *Such is Life* (1903), **Xavier Herbert**'s *Capricornia* (1938), **Patrick White**'s *The Tree of Man* (1955), and **D'Arcy Niland**'s *Dead Men Running* (1969). These 'serious' novels, in which the Irish are perceived as outsiders, catch them in the historical process of seeking an Australian role and identity, at odds with both their new world and their old. Contemporary writers are much more at home with the ambivalence, resolving it through farce — **Thomas Keneally** in the novel *Three Cheers for the Paraclete* (1968) and **Barry Oakley** in the play *The Feet of Daniel Mannix* (1975), for example — but more often through a tradition of celebratory and historical writing that goes back to J. F. Hogan's *The Irish in Australia* (1887) and Cardinal Moran's *History of the Catholic Church in Australia* (1895).

PATRICK O'FARRELL

Further reading: P. O'Farrell, *The Irish in Australia* (1986); Vincent Buckley, 'The Irish presence in the Australian novel', in Colm Kiernan (ed.) *Australia and Ireland 1788–1988* (1986).

IRELAND, DAVID (1927–)

Australian novelist, dramatist

Born in Lakemba, New South Wales, Australia, he is one of Australia's most controversial novelists. His novels are often overtly political, savagely attacking what he sees as the alienating and dehumanizing nature of capitalist society as symbolized in the title of one of his best-known works, *The Unknown Industrial Prisoner* (1971). Ireland has experimented with different styles, from the more or less straight naturalism of his first novel, *The Chantic Bird* (1968), which lies somewhere between J. D. Salinger's *The Catcher in the Rye* and Anthony Burgess' *A Clockwork Orange* as a bleak account of adolescence, to the surrealism of *A Woman of the Future* (1979), in which one character finds a coffin growing out of his side.

The Chantic Bird is the story, told in his own words, of a teenage boy's record of random acts of violence against human beings and animals, of his subversion of a society that he views with revulsion and contempt, and with which he can deal only by remaining solitary and apart. Repulsive as many of the boy's actions are, Ireland seems to come close to suggesting that the youth merely represents in more honest terms the qualities — violence, selfishness, aggressive competitiveness — that capitalist society embodies but refuses to acknowledge.

The Unknown Industrial Prisoner is an angry work that has much in common with such American novels of the 1950s as *One Flew Over the Cuckoo's Nest*, with their determinist view of history. Ireland alternates between sympathy and rage at the workers at Puroil, the world's second largest company, and the spinelessness with which they accept their condition of industrial exploitation. *The Flesheaters* (1972) pushes the argument further.

Although Ireland is known largely for his fiction, he began his writing career as a playwright, and *Burn* (1974) is actually a fictional adaptation of a stage play, *Image in the Clay* (1964; premièred 1958). *The Glass Canoe* (1976), a novel, shows the beginnings of Ireland's interest in male and female roles in Australia, with its ironic celebration of the all-male subculture of drinking — the glass canoe is a glass of beer — and pubs.

A Woman of the Future (1979), arguably Ireland's best novel, is the story of Alethea Hunt, a young girl growing up in an Australia of the not-too-distant future who disappears mysteriously at the age of eighteen, having been transformed into a leopard. The concept of Alethea, 'a healthy girl-plant, growing in the Australian sun', is strong enough to give the book a coherence and narrative drive that Ireland's often cerebral novels sometimes lack. In contrast to earlier works, it takes a surprisingly optimistic view of Australia.

The novel was followed rather oddly by *City of Women* (1981), in which Ireland develops both his interest in the macabre and surreal and his complex and ambivalent relationship to women; it polarized feminist opinion especially. It is an account of Sydney, again some time in the near future, when it has become a city of women; men have been reduced to the status more or less of ravaging guerrillas. Although it contains comic and even poignant moments, it is by far Ireland's most disturbing and violent novel, filled with images of disease and aggression. It does, however, begin to postulate the notion of art as a palliative against despair: 'Hang on to words, words can arrange your life, words were invented to arrange our lives.'

In *Archimedes and the Seagle* (1984), however, Ireland returns to his more benign mood. Archimedes, the red setter who narrates the novel, views his adopted family with a kind of tolerance and accommodating affection, aware of their limitations but managing to forgive and love them nevertheless. Ironically, it may be the case that only in working through the consciousness and persona of a 'dog person' can the author express faith in humanity. In a strange way, however, his novel *Bloodfather* (1987) continues his movement towards reconciliation. Dedicated 'to the liberation of God', it is a kind of latter-day *Portrait of the Artist as a Young Man* and Ireland's most manifestly personal work.

LAURIE CLANCY

Further reading: Helen Daniel, *Double Agent* (1982).

IRELAND, KEVIN (1933–)

New Zealand poet

Born Kevin Jowsey in Auckland, New Zealand, in his twenties he found a literary mentor in the fiction writer **Frank Sargeson** and spent some time living in the army hut in Sargeson's garden in which **Janet Frame** wrote her first novel, *Owls Do Cry* (1957). Ireland, with John Yelash, founded a brash new literary magazine, *Mate* (1957–77), but in 1959 left New Zealand for England, where he was to spend the next twenty-five years. He worked briefly in Bulgaria, translating Bulgarian poetry into English. On returning to London, England, he took a job as printer's reviser at *The Times* and worked there for nearly two decades. Ireland has published more than ten volumes of verse and has written several libretti. Since his return to New Zealand in 1985 he has held several writing fellowships.

While in England, Ireland considered himself a New Zealand writer. All his collections of poetry were published in New Zealand, and his work first appeared in New Zealand magazines. He maintained contact with New Zealand literary life and did not seek to enter the English literary mainstream, unlike his contemporary and fellow expatriate, **Fleur Adcock**. Ireland's first volume, *Face to Face: Twenty-Four Poems* (1963), with an introduction by **Barry Crump**, showed the influence of **R. A. K. Mason**, whose work Ireland admired for its short, spare, unpunctuated lines and its gruff unsentimentality. Ireland found Mason's religious and philosophical subject matter rather less congenial, but not until his second collection, *Educating the Body* (1967), did he find his own subject and distinctive voice: an ironic, urbane, self-deprecating anatomy of love and lovers' folly.

Literary Cartoons (1977), which won the New Zealand Book Award for Poetry, successfully marries irony about love to irony about writing. The Literary Man provided Ireland with the perfect mask: 'the only way he could confess / the true man he felt he was at heart / was to set down a sequence of troubled jests.' For most of his poetic career Ireland has been a resolute minimalist. In the mid-1980s, however, he began to write longer poems and to use a much longer, punctuated line. He turned his attention to the past, from slapstick evocations of boyhood cinema heroes (in *The Year of the Comet*, 1986) to serious poems about his colonial ancestors (scattered throughout *Practice Night in the Drill Hall*: *Poems*, 1984, and *Selected Poems*, 1987). *Tiberius at the Beehive* (1990) is a sustained satire on recent New Zealand political life, with much of the verve and wit of *Literary Cartoons*.

ANNE FRENCH

IROH, EDDIE (1946–)

Nigerian novelist

Born in Nigeria, he has described his childhood as one in which he was 'born on banana leaves and partially orphaned at eight'. Iroh was trained in the military, worked for the Biafran War Information Bureau and Reuters Limited news reporting agency, and headed the features and documentary department of Nigerian Television, Enugu, before moving to London, England, to work as a journalist for Nigerian publications. He has published four novels — *Forty-eight Guns for the General* (1976), *Toads of War* (1979), *Without a Silver Spoon* (1981), and *The Siren in the Night* (1982), the latter three forming a trilogy of historical fiction about the **Nigerian Civil War**.

If the first generation of Nigerian novelists was concerned with cultural assertion, cultural conflict, and the disillusionments of independence, Iroh is of the second generation, which, using more popular, action-packed, fictional genres, took the Biafra-Nigeria Civil War as its subject. The war showed how the corruption, lack of vision, tribalism, and other failures of Nigerian politicians invited foreign intervention, increased the distance between the leadership and the masses, and contributed to a callous disregard for the people by the élite. In *Forty-eight Guns for the General*, *Toads of War*, and *The Siren in the Night*, the details and military language are carefully researched. *Forty-eight Guns* shows how forty-eight foreign white mercenaries paid by the Biafrans become a group above the law acting in its own interest. *Toads of War* is a love story set in Owerri, where a group of favoured civilians enriches itself through the black market, threats, and bureaucratic power during the final days of Biafra. *The Siren in the Night* is set shortly after the war's end, when open fighting is replaced by fear, suspicion, and more subtle reprisals against those on opposite sides during the war. Part of the attraction of such novels is their similarity to thrillers and spy stories in their realistic detail, technical language, and appearance of insider knowledge.

BRUCE KING

ISVARAN, MANJERI S. (1910–66)

Indian poet, critic, short-story writer, translator

Born in Tanjore, Tamil Nadu, India, he had a chequered and probably underestimated career as a pioneering Indian writer in English. Associated with the literary and cultural journals *Short Story* (1934–5), *Swatantra* (1953–8), and *Triveni* (1928–), he also translated several literary masterpieces from Malayalam into English. Isvaran's publications include nine volumes of poetry, nine volumes of fiction, and two plays.

A transitional figure linking the Indian Renaissance and post-independence periods, Isvaran reflected the prevailing poetic trends in language and style. While his early poems are flawed by the use of tired diction and ornamental imagery, his later poems are marked by maturity in style and wisdom of experience. *Saffron and Gold and Other Poems* (1932) celebrates in the title poem the traditional ideal of wifehood. *Altar of Flowers* (1934) comprises twenty-seven lyrics on south Indian themes. *Catguts* (1940) is justly famous for its vitriolic attack on 'paracritics' and for its affirmation of Isvaran's convictions. If *Catguts* clearly marks a departure from the style of his early poems, *Brief Orisons* (1941) defines poetry, in the impersonal tone of a detached poet, as 'an utterance of the whole blood'. *Penumbra* (1942) reveals the poet's increasing preoccupation with contemporary socio-political issues.

Like **Raja Rao**, Isvaran sought to create his own identity as an Indian English writer inspired by India's 'usable past' yet influenced by western ideas. *The Fourth Avatar: Poems* (1946), an ironic allusion to the Avatar of *Nara-Simha* ('the Man-Lion'), is comparable to W. B. Yeats' 'The Second Coming'. *Oblivion* (1950) reveals Isvaran's maturer style and philosophical vision, in contrast to the anguish and angst of the early poems. *Rhapsody in Red* (1954) indicates a variety of moods and a consummate virtuosity of technique. Isvaran's greatest poetic treatment of the theme of innocence is found in *The Neem Is a Lady and Other Poems* (1957). Isvaran was keenly concerned with the imponderables of life; his later poems — confessional in tone, imaginative in their use of irony, and philosophical in outlook — anticipate the work of **A. K. Ramanujan** and **R. Parthasarathy**.

Isvaran's short-story collection *Naked Shingles* (1941) uses ornate words and phrases, as was the vogue during the Indian Renaissance. *Siva Ratri*

(1943) offers a reminder of the creative usability of India's mythological past and underscores Isvaran's technical virtuosity in achieving formal synthesis. *Angry Dust* (1944) demonstrates his sophisticated technique in experimenting with a narrative point of view. *Rickshawallah* (1946) contains stories with a proletarian bias that are inspired by Dostoevsky, Chekhov, and Gorky. Isvaran's other volumes of stories include *Fancy Tales* (1947), *No Anklet Bells for Her* (1949), *Immersion* (1951), *Painted Tigers* (1956), and *A Madras Admiral* (1959). *Immersion*, a novella with Freudian insights, is an imaginative exploration of the psyches of a rape victim (a culturally conditioned, puritanical woman), her victimizer, and her orthodox but totally innocent husband.

Isvaran's other published works include two plays — the dramatic narrative *Song of the Gypsymaiden* (1945) and *Yama and Yami* (1948) — and the monograph *Venkataramani; Writer and Thinker* (1932).

A. V. KRISHNA RAO

Further reading: Uma Parameswaran, 'An Indo-English minstrel: a study of Manjeri S. Isvaran's fiction', *Literature East and West* 1 and 2, June (1969); K. Ayyappa Paniker, *Manjeri S. Isvaran* (1983).

IYAYI, FESTUS (1947–)

Nigerian novelist

Born in Benin-City, Nigeria, he was educated at Annunciation Catholic College, Irrua, Government College, Ughelli, the Kiev Institute of National Economy, USSR, and the University of Bradford, England, where he earned a Ph.D. For many years Iyayi was a lecturer in business administration at the University of Benin. His radical political views have often resulted in his detention without trial, culminating in his eventual dismissal from the university in 1988. Iyayi is generally seen as Nigeria's ideological equivalent to Kenya's **Ngugi wa Thiong'o**, especially in his passionate belief that literature should be employed for the liberation of the oppressed. His novels include *Violence* (1979), *The Contract* (1982), and *Heroes* (1986).

In each of his novels Iyayi examines the nature of class relationships and class struggles within the context of a neo-colonial Nigeria. Their plots involve naïve heroes who are persuaded by the realities of their societies to join forces with the oppressed. Iyayi defines what he considers to be the main issues of his time and invents characters and adapts contexts to illustrate both the contradictions contained in such issues and possible resolutions. *Violence* and *The Contract* examine the various levels of violence in a society predicated on social inequality and exploitation. *Heroes* — winner of the Commonwealth Writers Prize in 1988 — is set in the context of the **Nigerian Civil War** and suggests that both sides in that war were equally barbaric and that the real casualties were the soldiers, workers, and peasants, while the beneficiaries were the officers, traditional rulers, and business tycoons on both sides.

FUNSO AIYEJINA

IYENGAR, K. R. S. (1908–)

Indian critic, poet, translator

Born Kodaganallur Ramaswami Srinivasa Iyengar at Sattur, Tamil Nadu, India, he took his MA and D. Litt. from the University of Madras, India. He taught at Belgaum and Bagalkot before moving to Andhra University, Waltair, as professor of English (1947–66) and vice-chancellor (1966–8). He subsequently served as vice-president (1969–77) and acting president (1977–8) of Sahitya Akademi, the Indian National Academy of Letters. An honorary member of the Modern Language Association of America (1984) and Fellow of the Sahitya Akademi (1985), Iyengar has also received honorary doctorates from Andhra, Sri Venkateswara, and Nagarjuna universities as well as numerous awards, including the Kalidsnag Memorial Medal (1959).

Iyengar's published works include studies of Shakespeare, G. M. Hopkins, Lytton Strachey, **Rabindranath Tagore** (*Rabindranath Tagore*, 1965), and François Mauriac and important critical and biographical studies of **Sri Aurobindo**, including *Sri Aurobindo: A Biography and a History* (2 vols, 1972). His *On the Mother: The Chronicle of a Manifestation and Ministry* (2 vols, rev. 1978) won the 1980 Sahitya Akademi Award for work in English. (The first, much smaller edition was published in 1952.) Iyengar's other critical works include *The Adventure of Criticism* (1962), *Mainly Academic: Talks to Students and Teachers* (1968), *Two Cheers for the Commonwealth* (1970), and *A Big Change: Talks on the Spiritual Revolution and the Future of Man* (1970). His poetic works in English include *Tryst with the Divine* (1974), *Microcosmographia Poetica* (1978), *Leaves from a Log* (1979), and *Australia Helix* (1984). He has also rendered into English verse the Sundarakanda of Valmiki's *Ramayana*, in Sanskrit, as *The Epic Beautiful* (1983), Tiruvalluvar's *Tirukkural*, in Tamil, as *Tirukkural: Lights on the Righteous Life* (1988), and, in collaboration with S. S. Basawanal, Basava's *Vachanas*, in Kannada, as *Musings of Basava: A Free Rendering* (1940). Iyengar's *Sitayana* (1987) is a retelling of the Ramayana story with Sita as the central figure, while *Satisaptakam* (1991) is a re-creation in verse of select tales from the *Mahabharata*, the *Bhagavata*, and the Tamil epic *Silappadhikaram* in which seven archetypal classical heroines represent woman as force.

For more than six decades Iyengar has been at the forefront of the shaping of new connections in English studies in India. His *Indian Writing in English* (1962; rev. 1973, 1982, and 1987) is a landmark publication, placing Indian literature in English in context with American, Commonwealth, and comparative literatures.

D. V. K. RAGHAVACHARYULU

Further reading: M. K. Naik, *Aspects of Indian Writing in English: Essays in Honour of Professor K. R. Srinivasa Iyengar* (1979).

J

JABAVU, NONI (1919–)

South African autobiographer

Born in Alice, Cape Province, South Africa, in what is now the 'homeland' of Ciskei, she is also known as Noni Nontando, Noni Helen (or Helene) Nontando, Alexandre (or Alexandra) Nothemba, but publishes under the name Noni Jabavu. Her grandfather, John Tengo Jabavu, was the first black editor/owner of a South Africa newspaper, *Imvo Zabantsundu* (1884–). Her father was chair of Latin and Bantu Languages at Fort Hare University, the first 'black' university in South Africa and Alma Mater of such political figures as Nelson Mandela, Robert Sobukwe, Gatsha Buthelezi, Kaiser Mantanzima, Seretse Khama, and Charles Njonjo. Jabavu left South Africa at the age of thirteen to be educated in England — at Mount School, York, and Church of England College for Girls, Birmingham — and married Michael Cadbury Crosfield.

Jabavu's two autobiographical novels, *Drawn in Colour* (1960) and *The Ochre People* (1963), reflect her upbringing in a highly educated and self-conscious rural élite (unlike the urban background from which most African writers emerge). She retains a strong sense of tribal identity as a Xhosa and is able to analyse herself and her nation from a perspective somewhat distanced from the usual deeply involved view of the contemporary black South African writer. In her language there is less evidence of the oral residuality found in the work of such writers as **Mtutuzeli Matshoba** and Todd Matshikiza.

Jabavu's writing focuses on short episodes in her life instead of attempting epics of 'black' life in South Africa. *Drawn in Colour* is an account of Jabavu's return to South Africa following her brother's death. *The Ochre People* describes her return and visits to family in the Eastern Cape Province in 1962, emphasizes both her alienation from and identification with the culture of her people, and details the impact of the west on East and South Africa.

In 1976 Jabavu returned to South Africa to research a biography of her father. At the time she wrote a weekly article for England's *Daily Despatch* in which she included extracts from a projected second novel, describing the indignities to which she had been subjected as a black visitor to South Africa. Jabavu has not yet published the biography or the novel.

JENNY WILLIAMS

Further reading: Harold Loeb, 'The literary situation in South Africa', *Southern Review* 8 (1972).

JACKMAN, OLIVER (1929–)

Barbadian novelist, poet

Born in Black Rock, in the parish of St Michael, Barbados, he attended St Stephen's School, Combermere; Harrison College, St Michael; and Magdalene College, Cambridge University, England. After completing legal studies at Sir Hugh Wooding Law School, Trinidad, he served in the diplomatic corps in Washington, USA, from 1967 to 1984. He maintains a successful law practice and is also a regular columnist with *The Nation* newspaper in Barbados.

Jackman's published work comprises several poems in the literary magazine *Bim*, the short story 'A Poet of the People' — first published in *Amistad I* (1970), edited by John A. Williams and Charles F. Harris — and the novel *Saw the House in Half* (1974). 'A Poet of the People' is a contracted form of the novel and is superior to *Saw the House in Half* in several ways. Jackman's narrative style tends to over-elaborate the setting and the psychological state of his characters; his fiction tends to pronounce a kind of self-conscious literariness perhaps less troubling in the short story than in the novel. At the end of the short story, for example, the narrator, St Clair Brathwaite, decides against revealing the calypsonian's identity. However, in the novel Brathwaite says, 'I know Beguiler. He's a Bajan I used to know in London and Nigeria. Dacosta Payne. That's his name.' The decision to refrain from unmasking the Mighty Beguiler in the short story demonstrates an understanding of the black man's strategy of survival in a hostile, racist world; it is an understanding that is compromised and betrayed in the novel. Jackman's concern with the West Indian in exile is also found in **V. S. Naipaul**'s *The Mimic Men* (1967) and **Sam Selvon**'s *Moses Ascending* (1975), but Jackman's writing lacks the incisiveness of Naipaul's satire and the sublimity of Selvon's wit.

GLYNE A. GRIFFITH

JACOBSON, DAN (1929–)
South African novelist, short-story writer
Born in Johannesburg, South Africa, he spent his school days in Kimberley and later studied at the University of the Witwatersrand (BA, 1949). Soon afterwards Jacobson left for Israel, where he spent two years on a kibbutz. He then went to London, England, where he began writing. Returning to South Africa in 1951, he spent the next three years working in business and journalism. In 1954 he returned to London and has lived there since, working as a writer and university lecturer. He has received numerous literary awards, including the Rhys Memorial Prize (1959), the Somerset Maugham Award (1964), and the H. H. Wingate Award (1978).

The Trap (1955) and *A Dance in the Sun* (1956) marked Jacobson early as a writer of ability and are still the works for which he is best known (new combined editions of these novels were released by several publishers in the 1980s). Both novels concern life on a South African farm and engage with problems in the relationships between white employer and black employee in which tension and violence cannot be kept below the surface.

In *The Trap*, the farmer Van Schoor discovers that his trusted 'boy' Willem is stealing his sheep. In an attempt to purge himself of this betrayal, he pounds his fists into Willem's badly beaten face. Ironically, he later drinks coffee with Willem's accomplice, a white man who betrayed Willem to the police. In *A Dance in the Sun* the young narrator and his companion bear witness for the black servant Joseph against his employer Fletcher, who is guilty of crimes against Joseph's family. In a peculiarly South African twist, Joseph uses their testimony to blackmail Fletcher into taking him back into employment. At the end, the demented Fletcher is left dancing like a madman at the knowledge that his whole life will be fashioned by the power that Joseph now exerts over him. Clearly discernible is an allegorical dimension to these novels: the implication is that South Africa is trapped in relationships of dominance and subordination and is destined to act out a ritualistic 'dance in the sun'.

Jacobson's third novel, *The Price of Diamonds* (1957), is set in Lyndhurst, a fictionalized Kimberley. As the title implies, the story concerns the temptations of acquiring wealth by illicit means — in this case illegal diamonds. *The Evidence of Love* (1960) deals with miscegenation, a recurring theme in South African literature. The fair-skinned Kenneth Makeer, who is officially classified 'coloured', dates and later marries a white woman. The consequence is a prison sentence for the couple. *The Beginners* (1966) is an autobiographical novel that deals with the lives of members of a South African Jewish family.

The Rape of Tamar (1970), which retells the Old Testament story of an incestuous rape, marks a departure from overtly South African themes. This and later novels by Jacobson, including *The Wonder-Worker* (1973) and *The Confessions of Josef Baisz* (1977), evince the author's increasing fascination with the creative process; these later works have distinctively postmodern or reflexive qualities. *The Confessions of Josef Baisz* invites comparisons with **J. M. Coetzee**'s *Waiting for the Barbarians* (1981) in that it is set in an indeterminate region (middle Europe or, obliquely, South Africa) and is a recounting of the life of a servile state functionary in a totalitarian country.

Jacobson's abilities as a novelist are matched by those as a short-story writer. His stories have appeared in several collections through the years, including *A Long Way from London* (1958), *Beggar My Neighbour* (1964), *Through the Wilderness and Other Stories* (1968), *A Way of Life and Other Stories* (1971), and *Inklings: Selected Stories* (1973). One of Jacobson's best-known stories, 'Beggar My Neighbour', is about a young white boy who befriends two black children and later has to come to terms with the harsh implications of rigid racial segregation, which consigns the children to disparate futures largely determined by race.

Jacobson's later work includes *Time and Time Again: Autobiographies* (1985), *Adult Pleasures: Essays on Writers and Readers* (1988), and the novels *Her Story* (1987), *Hidden in the Heart* (1991), and *The God-Fearer* (1992).

CRAIG MacKENZIE

Further reading: Anne Fisher, 'Dan Jacobson', *Dictionary of Literary Biography* 14 (1983); Sheila Roberts, *Dan Jacobson* (1984); Stephen Gray, 'The private landscape of meaning or the public landscape of politics: Stephen Gray interviews Dan Jacobson', *Kunapipi* 2 (1989).

JAMES, C. L. R. (1901–89)

Trinidadian historian, political theorist, novelist

Born Cyril Lionel Robert James in Tunapuna, Trinidad, and educated in Port of Spain, Trinidad, he was the author of *Minty Alley* (1936), *The Black Jacobins: Toussaint L'Ouverture and the San Domingo Revolution* (1938), *Beyond a Boundary* (1963), and many lesser-known works. He had an extraordinary talent for bringing art, sports, history, and philosophy into the stream of political thought and action. Although he never held a university degree, he served as a political mentor to politicians, a guide to social historians and writers, an activist-sage to grass-roots organizers, and a theoretician to Marxist intellectuals. He influenced such post-colonial writers as the historians Eric Williams and Walter Rodney and the novelist **George Lamming**, whose works also illuminate the historical struggle of West Indians to overcome colonial oppression.

James acquired an insistence on moral leadership from his upbringing and education in classical thought. Victorian honour and the school code were part of his early formation, as was cricket, a game that stood as much for character as it did for endurance, teamwork, and technique. William Hazlitt and William Thackeray were the writers he most cherished throughout his life; it was to them, and to Aristotle and Marx, that James turned for a vision of humanity that interrelated art, ethics, politics, and psychology. His historical work sought to override the myth that historical accomplishments are products of mere individual achievement. To stimulate revolutionary consciousness he used all available means of persuasion: fiction, history, essays, lectures, sports, short stories, and plays. *The Black Jacobins* was the first major historical study to popularize a Third World hero and the first to show the vital role of mass populations in the process of national liberation. At the heart of the history lies an intense concern with the emancipation of modern colonial peoples.

Much of James' appeal is related to his active involvement in social movements. A literary pacesetter in the late 1920s, he drew his inspiration from black working-class culture in Port of Spain.

As an advocate of West Indian independence, he published *A Case for West Indian Self-Government: The Life and Times of Captain Cipriani* (1933), an indictment of British imperialism. During the 1930s, he became a committed Pan-Africanist and Marxist activist in London, England. In 1936, not only did his novel, *Minty Alley*, appear in print, but his play, 'Toussaint L'Ouverture', was also performed on the London stage with Paul Robeson in the leading role. (The play was later published in *A Time and a Season: Eight Caribbean Plays*, 1976, edited by **Errol Hill**.) In 1939, James discussed (with Leon Trotsky in Mexico) plans for an independent black movement. For fifteen years he led a group of North American Marxists, the Johnson-Forest Tendency and was part of a group called 'Facing Reality', which undertook an intensive re-examination of Hegel's dialectic. 'Facing Reality' published *Mariners, Renegades, and Castaways* (1953), a Marxist analysis of Herman Melville aimed at the proletariat, and *Facing Reality* (1958), written by James, Grace C. Lee, and Pierre Chaulieu (a pseudonym for Carlos Castoriadis), an ambitious work that sets forth editorial committees as a means of 'assisting' the working class in its 'spontaneous' rebellions. James would later assert that *Facing Reality* indicated the future route of intellectuals within Poland's Solidarity movement. From 1958 to 1960, as secretary to the newly formed West Indian Federation, he travelled throughout the islands lecturing on its behalf. He argued that with all of its flaws, the Federation offered the potential to establish in the West Indies the modern equivalent of the Greek city-states.

Unlike **V. S. Naipaul**, who denied West Indian cultural achievement, James emphasized West Indian contributions to literature, sports, music, and politics. As editor of *The Nation* (1958–62), the organ of Eric Williams' People's National Movement, and *We, the People* (1965), of his own Workers' and Farmers' party, he educated the Trinidadian public on issues of social and political significance. To encourage a national community, *We, the People* carried poetry, essays, speeches, and short stories written by some of the most talented writers of the Caribbean. In 1962, he completed *Beyond a Boundary*, an intricate autobiographical tale seasoned with cultural history and told within the context of a national sport, cricket. Throughout the next two decades, he travelled within the USA, the UK, the West Indies, and Africa, lecturing mainly to student groups. Eloquent, intellectually versatile, and passionately militant, he argued that resistance to oppression was the essence of Caribbean history. 'There is one dominant fact and that is the desire, sometimes expressed, sometimes unexpressed, but always there,' he argued, 'the desire for liberty, the ridding oneself of the particular burden which is the special inheritance of the black skin.'

CONSUELO LÒPEZ SPRINGFIELD

Further reading: Paul Buhle, ed., *C. L. R. James: His Life and His Work* (1986).

JANES, PERCY (1922–)

Canadian novelist, poet, short-story writer

Born in St John's, Newfoundland, Canada, he grew up on the island's west coast. From early adulthood to middle age, Janes lived away from Newfoundland, in Ontario and in England, and travelled extensively; his first novel, *So Young and Beautiful* (1958), is set in Ontario. In the mid-1960s, however, he returned to Newfoundland and to the harrowing experiences of his own upbringing for the inspiration of *House of Hate* (1970). Janes has published six novels, a collection of short stories (*Newfoundlanders: Short Stories*, 1981), and two volumes of poetry (*Light and Dark: Poems*, 1980, and *Roots of Evil: Para-Political Verse*, 1985), but his outstanding achievement continues to be *House of Hate*.

The achievement of *House of Hate* is paradoxical, for although the narrator, Juju, attempts in the end to find a societal cause for the abusive situation he and his siblings suffered at the hands of a tyrannical father, the novel does not support such an analysis. Its power, rather, stems from its devastating portrayal of a pathologically insecure man, filled with self-loathing and paranoia, who physically and psychologically brutalizes his wife and children, maiming them to such an extent that his hatred reverberates tragically even after he is dead. Although the narrator heroically summons up compassion and humour in recounting the story, the novel's intensity is due, as **Margaret Laurence** pointed out, to Janes' refusal to turn away from the terrible events that inspired it. Janes' verse contains some of the honesty and outrage of *House of Hate*, but is uninventive in diction and hackneyed in theme. His subsequent novels (*Eastmall*, 1982, *Requiem for a Faith*, 1984, *No Cage for Conquerors*, 1984, and *The Picture on the Wall*, 1985) are all set in Newfoundland and are flawed by a tendency to reduce narrative to the illustration of ideas about society.

ADRIAN FOWLER

Further reading: Patrick O'Flaherty, *The Rock Observed: Studies in the Literature of Newfoundland* (1979).

JEKYLL, WALTER (1849–1929)
English/Jamaican folklorist
He was born in Surrey, England, educated at Harrow and Cambridge, England, and entered holy orders, serving in Worcester, England, and Malta. He later left the church to study music in Milan, Italy. He returned to England and gave music lessons, charging the poor a penny a lesson. Because of ill health, Jekyll lived in many different parts of Britain and observed different regions and classes of people. In summer he hiked in Norway. His extraordinary linguistic skills and his interest in folklore probably developed from these experiences. He settled permanently in Jamaica in 1895. His great collection, *Jamaican Song and Story: Annancy Stories, Digging Sings [sic], Ring Tunes, and Dancing Tunes* (1907), provides folkloric material that demonstrates the interrelationship of song, story, and dance-mime unique to Jamaican creole culture.

Jekyll's material also represents the distinctive culture of Jamaica's Blue Mountain region, where he first settled. Regretfully, Jekyll published no material representative of eastern Jamaica, where he later lived. Regional and temporal distinctions between his material and that of later folklorists appear when one compares his work with Laura Tanna's *Jamaican Folk Tales and Oral Histories* (1984), which makes careful regional distinctions, and Daryl C. Dance's *Folklore from Contemporary Jamaicans* (1985), which reveals the effects of decreolization, urbanization, and time. Yet we remain indebted to Jekyll's methodical accuracy: 'The stories and tunes of this book are taken down from the mouths of men and boys in my employ,' he writes in the preface to *Jamaican Song and Story*. Jekyll's method was in every case to sit with his sources during their recitals and to make them dictate slowly; the stories are in their *ipsissima verba*. His notes form one of the richest resources on Jamaican and Afro-Caribbean language and folk culture even today.

JEAN D'COSTA

JENKINS, GEOFFREY (ERNEST) (1920–)
South African novelist
Born in Port Elizabeth, South Africa, he was educated at Potchefstroom, where his first publication — an award-winning essay entitled *A Century of History: The Story of Potchefstroom* (2nd ed., 1971), written while still at school and with a foreword by Jan Smuts — appeared in 1939. Before the commercial success of his first novel, *A Twist of Sand* (1959), Jenkins worked as a journalist in South Africa, Rhodesia, and England, where he became a close friend of novelist Ian Fleming. Jenkins' readership is international, his

fifteen novels since 1959 having sold more than ten million copies in some twenty-three languages.

A common element in many popular adventure thrillers, and dominant in those of Jenkins, is a fascination for exhaustive technological detail, and Jenkins' journalistic 'nose' claims a mildly prophetic topicality for some of his themes — pre-Chernobyl nuclear pollution in *In Harm's Way* (1986), for example — and opportune settings — the Falkland Islands, for example, in *A Ravel of Waters* (1981).

Jenkins' earlier thrillers show an unformulated desire to come to terms with 'Africa', which in a novel such as *The River of Diamonds* (1964) poses an exotic problem that is only superficially technological. There is in Jenkins' writing a heroic quest for rational explanations of the irrational, with the 'Africa' of the Namib Desert representing the unknowable primeval and an archetypal 'Africanness' contained in the symbol of the diamond. Similar formulations, where a significant object functions fetishistically to encapsulate the 'essence' of the story, can be found in Jenkins' other sea and desert adventures.

Despite Jenkins' express intention to write wholly 'unpolitical' novels — the plot of *A Hive of Dead Men* (1991), perhaps because of its Cape Town setting, abandons credibility in its avoidance of the socio-political realities of contemporary South Africa — his later novels generally reflect with fidelity the established South African attitudes to the Cold War. In *Fireprint* (1984) the Cold War is won for the west through a blend of selective misogyny (also an element in *A Hive of Dead Men*), heroic homophobia, and a brand of cosmopolitan derring-do that, for some of his South African reviewers, seems lacking in plausibility in (or despite) its fictional South African setting.

JOHN A. STOTESBURY

JEWISH WRITING (Australia)

In the nineteenth century, in newly colonized countries such as Australia and New Zealand, anyone whose written script was other than roman or language other than English had a meagre chance of seeing print. Accordingly, most of the small amount of nineteenth-century Australian writing known to be by Jews was in English, and indeed most of the early Jewish settlers came from western Europe and spoke, or quickly learned to speak, reasonably fluent English.

John George Lang (1816–64) was the first Australian-born writer of fiction. His collection of Australian-based stories, *Botany Bay* (1859), and his novel, *The Forger's Wife* (1855), were published in England. Lang was of Jewish descent; his grandfather, John Harris, an English Jew and transported convict who later became Australia's first policeman, arrived in 1788 with the First Fleet. *Shalom* (1978, 1983, 1988), a collection of Australian Jewish short stories compiled by **Nancy Keesing**, contains a story by Lang and one by Nathan Spielvogel (1874–1956), who was a well known and widely published writer. The other writers represented belong to the twentieth century; many were born in Australia or New Zealand, but a number were born overseas or to recent immigrants from eastern Europe, chiefly Russia and Poland.

Two Jews, **Judah Waten** and **David Martin**, can be said to have pioneered in the early 1950s excellent writing by immigrants, though Eric Schlunke (1906–60) and Colin Thiele (1920–), descendants of a large nineteenth-century influx of Lutheran settlers, also began to publish widely at that time. Since the 1970s, writers of Greek descent have, with Jews, dominated migrant poetry and fiction. (See **Migrant Writing**, Australia.)

Morris Lurie and **Serge Liberman** can be viewed as the successors of Waten and Martin (in some of his books). They are close in age, their families have an east European origin, they both live in Melbourne, and they share many preoccupations, particularly migrant families and parent-child relationships; their methods, styles, and approaches are, however, different.

Lily Brett, Nancy Keesing, **Judith Rodriguez**, and **Fay Zwicky** are also among the large number of Jewish writers. Marjorie Pizer (1920–) has had twelve volumes of poetry published, including *Seasons of Love* (1975) and *Selected Poems 1963–1983* (1984); with her late husband, Muir Holburn, she founded Pinchgut Press (1947; re-established with the late Anne Spenser Parry in 1975). Maria Lewitt (1924–), born in Poland, learned English after arriving in Melbourne in 1949. Her autobiographical novels, *Come Spring* (1980) and *No Snow in December* (1985), have won major prizes. Other works include educational books for adolescents such as *Just Call Me Bob* (1976) and *Grandmother's Yarn* (1986). Alan Collins (1928–), born in Sydney, has written *Troubles: Tsorres* (1983) and a novel, *The Boys from Bondi* (1987). Mal Morgan (1936–), born in England, the co-organizer of 'La Mama Poetica' poetry readings at La Mama Theatre in Carlton, Melbourne, has published four volumes of poetry: *Poemstones* (1976), *Statues Don't Bleed* (1984), *A Handshake with the Moon* (1987), and *Once Father and God* (1992). Alex Skovron (1948–), born in Poland, won the Fellowship of Australian Writers Anne Elder Award and the Association for the Study of Australian Literature Mary Gilmore Award for his volume of poetry, *The Rearrangement* (1988). Ron Elisha (1951–), born in Jerusalem, works as a medical practitioner in Melbourne. His play *Einstein* (1986) won Australian Writers' Guild Awards (AWGIES) for best stage play and most outstanding script. Other plays include *In Duty Bound* (1983), *Two* (1985; AWGIE for best stage play, 1984), *Safe House* (1985), *The Levine Comedy* (1987), and *Pax Americana* (1990). Yvonne Fein (1953–), editor of the literary journal *Melbourne Chronicle*, is a short-story writer and author of the play *On Edge* (1992). The books of Michele Nayman (1956–), born in London, England, include poetry (*Where You Love You Are*, 1977) and fiction (*Faces You Can't Find Again*, 1980, and *Somewhere Else*, 1989).

Jewish literary creativity is not limited to fiction and poetry; in the equally important areas of factual and critical writing, Julius Stone, Cyril Pearl, Zelman Cowen, and **A. A. Phillips** have made excellent contributions to ideas and knowledge in the fields of history, law, science, biography, and criticism.

NANCY KEESING

Further reading: Serge Liberman, comp., Laura Gallou, ed., *A Bibliography of Australian Judaica* (1987; rev. 1991).

JEYARATNAM, PHILIP (1964–)

Singaporean novelist, short-story writer

Born in Singapore, to an English mother and an Indian father, both lawyers, he took a law degree (1986) at Cambridge University, England, and first attracted public notice when 'Campfire' won second prize in Singapore's National Short Story Competition in 1983, and 'Evening under Frangipani' took first prize in 1985. These were published in *First Loves* (1987), a collection of nineteen short stories featuring the central character, Ah Leong, his relatives, and friends; the stories, Jeyaratnam feels, 'should be read in sequence'. In an English book market dominated since colonial days by fiction and bestsellers imported from the west, *First Loves* was remarkable as the first Singaporean fictional work in English to top the local bestseller list of prose works in English and to remain a bestseller for more than a year. Within eight months it was reprinted five times, and by early 1990 was into its tenth impression. Jeyaratnam quickly followed *First Loves* with a novel, *Raffles Place Ragtime* (1988). Launched appropriately at Raffles Place itself, it was reprinted twice by 1989.

Although *First Loves* attracted attention initially because of Jeyaratnam's father's prominence as Singapore's lone, outspoken opposition member of parliament, Jeyaratnam's stories, like **Catherine Lim**'s, 'constitute an appreciable slice of Singapore life' (as the publishers cannily note) with which its reading public could immediately identify. But whereas Lim's popular earlier stories focus on the lives of characters drawn from a cross-section of Singaporean society, particularly the Chinese, Jeyaratnam's deal with the experiences and worries of young Singaporean adults of his generation born after Singapore became self-governing in 1959. An English-educated generation, it is comfortable with the 'Singlish' that his (and Lim's) characters use unself-consciously. It has also grown up in a stable, increasingly affluent, but tightly-run, disciplined society, governed since 1959 by the same ruling party, and his stories perceptively represent and express the generation's middle-class life experience, preoccupations, and some of its restiveness. The men are about to enter, are performing, or have just completed National Service, while both men and women are preoccupied with job prospects, careers, emergent sexuality (or bitter-sweet first loves), interracial and love relationships (sometimes the two coincide), social class, and the 'quality of life' in a hard-driving, cosmopolitan, contemporary Singapore. Jeyaratnam's fiction reflects a characteristic tendency towards earnest, idealistic, socio-political comment, both overt and implicit, expressed by the author, his characters, and his plots. Typically, characters from the lower end of the social scale have difficulty relating to members of the moneyed middle class. The latter live in posh districts and produce chic, confident, aggressive, highly-educated career women — there is a misogynist strain in Jeyaratnam's fiction — suggesting a serious class division and young male inadequacy in a meritocratic society. But the overt socio-political criticism is a minor, even engaging, weakness in a writer whose work reveals a literary talent that one hopes early success will encourage rather than overwhelm.

KOH TAI ANN

JHABVALA, RUTH PRAWER (1927–)

Indian novelist, short-story writer, script-writer

Born in Cologne, Germany, she immigrated with her Jewish family to England in 1939. She completed her English education with an MA in English from the University of London. She married Parsi architect Cyrus S. H. Jhabvala in 1951 and returned with him to his home in Delhi, India.

Developing her characteristic mode of ironic comedy, Jhabvala's first four novels were set in Delhi, focusing in turn on the Indian arranged marriage (*To Whom She Will*, 1955), corruption in Indian public life (*The Nature of Passion*, 1956), an Englishman stranded in India (*Esmond in India*, 1957), and the growth of love within an arranged marriage (*The Householder*, 1960). After 1960, Jhabvala's fiction became grimmer in tone. *Get Ready for Battle* (1962) condemns dishonesty, hypocrisy, and exploitation of the poor; *A Backward Place* (1965) lashes self-serving western expatriates and Indian urbanites; *A New Dominion* (1972) satirizes the chauvinism of independent India; and *Heat and Dust* (1975) contrasts east-west personal relationships in British India with those possible in the 'free' India of the 1970s.

Though she is sometimes compared with E. M. Forster, Paul Scott, and **Salman Rushdie**, Jhabvala's experience as a triple exile renders her work on India unique in contemporary literature. She has theoretically justified her changing attitudes to India in a well-known essay that prefaces the second of her four collections of short stories: *Like Birds, Like Fishes* (1963), *An Experience of India* (1966), *A Stronger Climate* (1968), and *How I Became a Holy Mother* (1976).

Moving to a new milieu in New York, USA, in 1976, Jhabvala explored American life in several short stories and in the novels *In Search of Love and Beauty* (1983) and *Three Continents*

(1987). She has meanwhile consolidated a complementary and very distinguished career as a screen writer, which began in India with the film of her own novel *The Householder* (1963), and includes *Shakespearewallah* (1965), *The Guru* (1969), *Bombay Talkie* (1970), *Autobiography of a Princess* (1975), *Roseland* (1977), *Hullabaloo over Georgie and Bonnie's Pictures* (1978), *Jane Austen in Manhattan* (1980), *Heat and Dust* (1983), and *Madame Sousatzka* (1989), all but the last stemming from her thirty-year partnership with the American director James Ivory. Among the film scripts Jhabvala has written for Merchant-Ivory Productions are adaptations of novels by **Jean Rhys** (*Quartet*, 1981), Henry James (*The Europeans*, 1979, and *The Bostonians*, 1984), Evan Connell (*Mr and Mrs Bridge*, 1990), E. M. Forster (*A Room with a View*, 1986, and *Howard's End*, 1992).

Jhabvala has received a number of awards for her literary work, including the Booker-McConnell Prize (for *Heat and Dust*), 1975; a John Simon Guggenheim Memorial Fellowship, 1976; the Neil Gunn International Fellowship, 1979; and a Macarthur Foundation Fellowship, 1984. In 1983 she was awarded the honorary degree of Doctor of Letters by the University of London and both Britain's National Film Critics Award and the British Academy of Film and Television Arts Award for the screenplay *Heat and Dust*.

In 1993 she published the novel *Poet and Dancer*.

YASMINE GOONERATNE

Further reading: H. M. Williams, *The Fiction of Ruth Prawer Jhabvala* (1973); James Ivory, *Autobiography of a Princess: Also Being the Adventures of an American Film Director in the Land of the Maharajas* (1975); Nicola Bradbury, 'Filming James', *Essays in Criticism* 29 (1979); Yasmine Gooneratne, *Silence, Exile and Cunning. The Fiction of Ruth Prawer Jhabvala* (1983, 1990); Fritz Blackwell, 'A European emigre in India', *Asiaweek Literary Review* 15 February 1985; Robert Emmet Long, *The Films of Merchant Ivory* (1991).

JINDYWOROBAK MOVEMENT

Described by **A. D. Hope** as 'the Boy Scout School of Poetry', it was an expression of Australian nationalism in the 1930s and 1940s. Inspired by **P. R. Stephensen**'s *The Foundations of Culture in Australia* (1936), **Rex Ingamells** formed the Jindyworobak Club, publishing a manifesto, *Conditional Culture* (1938), in which he explained that 'Jindyworobak', taken from James Devaney's *The Vanished Tribes* (1929), means 'to annex, to join', and that 'The Jindyworobaks . . . are those individuals who are endeavouring to free Australian art from whatever alien influences trammel it.' Ingamells asserted three points needed to free Australian art: a clear recognition of environmental values; the debunking of much nonsense; an understanding of Australia's history and traditions, primeval, colonial, and modern. The most important point was the first, which for Ingamells meant a perception of the environment without the 'alien influences' or 'pseudo-Europeanism' that came from figurative language 'such as English writers apply to a countryside of oaks and elms and yews.' Ingamells argued that 'writers and painters must become hard-working students of Aboriginal culture' if they would achieve this 'clear recognition', also termed 'thought-contact with nature', 'imaginative truth' — the multiplication of terms suggests uncertainty over the relation of the key terms 'nature' and 'culture'.

From 1938 to 1953 an annual anthology of poetry and various titles by associated poets carried the Jindyworobak publishing imprint. The club became a looser movement involving, in addition to Rex and John Ingamells, **Ian Mudie**, **W. Flexmore Hudson**, **William Hart-Smith**, and **Roland Robinson**. The anthologies included contributions from most important poets then writing in Australia, even from those, like **Judith Wright** and

James McAuley, who never subscribed to the full creed.

By the 1950s the Jindyworobak poets took separate directions, and the movement had served its purpose. It remained an important influence for Wright and **Les Murray** in urging sympathetic study of Aboriginal culture, although the Jindyworobaks could be insensitive in taking Aboriginal mythology as a product of the landscape rather than of a social group, stripping the mythology of metaphysics to recycle it as secular symbols.

LAWRENCE BOURKE

Further reading: Brian Elliott, ed., *The Jindyworobaks* (1979).

JOAQUIN, NICK M. (1917–)

Filipino short-story writer, novelist, essayist, dramatist, poet, biographer

Born in Paco, Manila, the Philippines, he quit school after three years of secondary education because classroom work bored him; he discovered that he could learn more by independent reading. In 1934 Joaquin began writing short stories, poems, and essays, many of which were published in Manila magazines such as the *Philippine Free Press* and *Graphic*; a few found their way into foreign journals such as *Hudson Review* and *Partisan Review*.

In 1940 his story 'Three Generations' was published in the *Graphic* and was named to **Jose Garcia Villa**'s Roll of Honor for short stories that year. This short story and Joaquin's most important play, *Portrait of the Artist as Filipino* (1952), testify to the Filipinos' search for identity by looking back into the past and observing its continuing impact in the present and the future.

Joaquin's story 'La Naval de Manila' (1943) won a contest sponsored by the Dominicans, whose institution, the University of Santo Tomas, awarded him, on the strength of his literary talents, an Associate in Arts certificate. The Dominicans also granted him a two-year scholarship to Saint Albert's College, Hong Kong. Unable to follow the rigid rules imposed upon those studying for the priesthood, however, he left the seminary in 1950.

In 1949 'Guardia de Honor' was judged the best story of the year in the *Philippine Free Press*; it also won first prize in the 1950 Carlos Palanca Memorial Awards for Literature. The stories 'La Vidal' and 'Doña Jeronima' won first prizes in the 1958 and 1965 Palanca contests, respectively.

For his prize-winning entry *The Woman Who Had Two Navels* (1961), Joaquin was awarded the first Stonehill Annual Fellowship for the Filipino Novel in English in 1960. For his contribution to Philippine literature, he was given the Republic Cultural Heritage Award for Literature in 1961 and was named National Artist in 1976. For his journalistic writings, published under the byline Quijano de Manila (an anagram of his name), he received the Philippine Journalist of the Year Award. He has travelled on a two-year Rockefeller Foundation Fellowship through Europe, the USA, Mexico, Australia, China, Taiwan, and Cuba.

Joaquin's published books include *Prose and Poems* (1952), *The Woman Who Had Two Navels, Selected Stories* (1962), *La Naval de Manila and Other Essays* (1964), *Portrait of the Artist as Filipino, Tropical Gothic* (1972), *Reportage on Crime* (1977), *Nora Aunor and Other Profiles* (1977), *Ronnie Poe and Other Silhouettes* (1977), *Reportage on Lovers* (1977), *Amalia Fuentes and Other Etchings* (1977), *Gloria Diaz and Other Delineations* (1977), *Doveglion and Other Cameos* (1977), *Joseph Estrada and Other Sketches* (1977), *A Question of Heroes* (1977), *Pop Stories for Groovy Kids* (1979), *Almanac for Manileños* (1979), *Tropical Baroque: Four Manileño Theatricals* (1979), *Manila: Sin City and Other Chronicles* (1980), *Language of the Street and Other Essays* (1980), *Reportage on the Marcoses* (1981), *Cave and Shadows* (1983), *The Aquinos of Tarlac* (1983), *Joaquinesquerie: Myth a la Mod* (1983), *The Quartet of the Tiger Moon: Scenes from the*

People-Power Apocalypse (1986), *The World of Rafael Salas: Service and Management in the Global Village* (1987), *Culture and History: Occasional Notes on the Process of Philippine Becoming* (1988), *Jaime Ongpin the Enigma: A Profile of the Filipino as Manager* (1990), and *Manila, My Manila: A History for the Young* (1991).

The Woman Who Had Two Navels is considered canonical by most critics and scholars of Philippine literature. (See **Novel**, The Philippines.) His only other novel, *Cave and Shadows*, is a mystery thriller, and unlike *The Woman Who Had Two Navels*, is written in a language closer to that of the peoples. Joaquin's work has been anthologized in many literary collections, and numerous critical articles on his work have been written. A full-length critical study utilizing contemporary Marxist approaches is *Subversions of Desire: Prolegomena to Nick Joaquin* (1988), by Epifanio San Juan, Jr.

In his introduction to Joaquin's *Prose and Poems* (1952), Teodoro M. Locsin described Joaquin as 'the first literary artist of the country. No Filipino now writing matches his stories in power and beauty; their wedding of primitive emotions with sophisticated treatment is beyond the power of local practitioners of the arts.' Jose Garcia Villa, moreover, has stated that 'Nick Joaquin is, in my opinion, the only Filipino writer with a real imagination — that imagination of power and depth and great metaphysical seeing — and which knows how to express itself in great language.' In **Manuel A. Viray**'s view, 'Nick Joaquin, a gifted stylist, has used his sensitive style and his exciting evocations in portraying the peculiar evil, social and moral, we see around us, and in proving that passion as well as reason can never by quenched.'

Irked by the prevailing social, moral, and religious disorientation he sees in the Philippines, Joaquin has taken a hard look into the past, particularly at the last few decades of the Spanish regime in the Philippines. He believes that the past has curative values that can be retrieved and reinvigorated to help Filipinos correct the prevailing situation in society and thus strengthen the moral fibre of the people and make them religious again.

ESTRELLITA V. GRUENBERG

JOHN, ERROL (1924–88)
Trinidadian dramatist
Born in Port of Spain, Trinidad, he achieved international recognition when his play *Moon on a Rainbow Shawl* (1958) won the 1957 London *Observer* Prize for drama.

Before he immigrated to England in 1951, John had written at least two one-act plays that were produced by Trinidad's first local amateur theatre company, the Whitehall Players — 'How Then Tomorrow' (1947), a fantasy, and *The Tout* (1966, premièred 1949), a melodrama on poverty and crime, later rewritten as the screenplay *The Dispossessed* (in *Force Majeure, The Dispossessed, Hasta Luego: Three Screenplays*, 1967).

Moon on a Rainbow Shawl (premièred in London, England, in 1957) demonstrates, without the sentimentality of *The Tout*, how immorality, racism, and class exploitation make any dream of self-fulfilment from urban slum life nothing but fantasy. Because of the voice it provides, not only to a class, but to a whole civilization anxious to make its mark on the world, the play's impact on Caribbean drama is similar to that in England of John Osborne's *Look Back in Anger* (1957), with its frank, naturalistic portrayal of working-class life, and to that in Australia of **Ray Lawler**'s *Summer of the Seventeenth Doll* (1957). *Moon on a Rainbow Shawl* has been translated into several languages and was produced internationally, including a 1962 New York production starring James Earl Jones and Cecily Tyson.

John's screenplays include *Force Majeure* and *Hasta Luego*; for television he has written 'The Exiles' (broadcast 1968) and the script 'Uhuru'.

John is also regarded as one of the finest actors Trinidad has produced. Dynamic and intelligent, he displayed a controlled authority and resolute determination. He formed his own Company of Five in which he acted and directed meticulously. In England he became a professional stage and screen actor.

RAWLE GIBBONS

Further reading: J.A. Ramsaran, review of *Moon on a Rainbow Shawl*, *Black Orpheus* 5 (1959).

JOHNSON, COLIN

See **NAROGIN, MUDROOROO**

JOHNSON, LINTON KWESI (1952–)

Jamaican poet

Born in the parish of Clarendon, Jamaica, he immigrated to England in 1963. His initial reaction to the racism he experienced there was to become the kind of anomic young rebel who emerged as the subject of much of his poetry. He channelled his anger more politically, however, through his association with the Black Panther party of England and later with the Race Today Collective. Although these associations were eventually discontinued, Johnson remains indebted to the ideas on colonialism, race, and culture developed by the intellectual mentor of the Race Today movement, **C. L. R. James**.

Johnson's early reading of W. E. B. DuBois and Frantz Fanon served to focus his experience as a young colonial born black in the metropole. More important in his genesis as a writer was his discovery of a Caribbean literary heritage, particularly the protest tradition as represented by the poems of **Martin Carter** of Guyana and **George Campbell** of Jamaica, and by the new Rastafarian poetry of the late 1960s. He was further impressed by the poems of the Congolese Tchicaya U Tam'si and the Nigerian **Christopher Okigbo**.

Responding to these inspirations in the early 1970s, Johnson wrote the long dramatic title poem of his first book, *Voices of the Living and the Dead* (1974), and the sequence, originally titled 'Notes on Brixton', that developed into his second book, *Dread, Beat and Blood* (1975). The third volume, *Inglan Is a Bitch*, followed in 1980. His poems have also appeared in numerous anthologies in the UK and the Caribbean. The main theme has been that of black working-class life and daily struggle in England.

Johnson is known worldwide mainly through performances in more than twenty countries and six recordings of his poems set to music of his own composition. The poems in his 1991 album *Tings an' Times* were subsequently published in his fourth book, *Tings an' Times* (1991).

His decision to write primarily in Jamaican Creole and to base his rhythms on those of Jamaican music have caused him to be considered part of a group of reggae or 'dub' poets that includes **Mutabaruka**, **Mikey Smith**, Oku Onuora, and **Jean Binta Breeze**, all of whom Johnson promoted. Although they all published, performed, and recorded, Johnson has been the most insistent on the craft of writing poems rather than the simple scripting of performances. Moreover, he has been the most successful in linking the personal voice and the political voice in his writing. His poems reward study and re-reading for their use of Creole, rhythmic structure, patterns of imagery and as a cumulative chronicle of the struggles of blacks in the UK in the last two decades.

Johnson has received several honours and awards, among which are the C. Day Lewis Poetry Fellowship and Associate Fellowship in Warwick University's Centre for Caribbean Studies, England.

ROBERT J. STEWART

Further reading: Mervyn Morris, 'Interview with Linton Kwesi Johnson', *Jamaica Journal* 20 (1987), extracted in E. A. Markham, ed., *Hinterland: Caribbean Poetry from the West Indies and Britain* (1989).

JOHNSON, LOUIS (1924–88)
New Zealand poet
Born in Wellington, New Zealand, and raised in Feilding, Johnson published fifteen volumes of poetry between 1946 and 1986; a posthumously published volume, *Last Poems*, appeared in 1990.

From the late 1940s until 1968, Johnson lived in Wellington, working as a teacher, then as an editor of publications in the department of education. He became a leading figure in a Wellington-based group of younger poets (including **James K. Baxter** and **Alistair Campbell**) through his editorship of the *New Zealand Poetry Yearbook* (eleven issues, 1951–1964) and his founding of *Numbers* (1954–60). Both journals generated vigorous literary debate. Arguing that narrow nationalist and landscape-oriented prescriptions for New Zealand poetry were no longer sufficient, Johnson contended that a less provincial poetry might open itself to more 'universal' impulses, to a poetry of human relationships (especially of love and domestic life) in the increasingly international context of New Zealand's burgeoning postwar cities and suburbs.

During this period, Johnson's most important volumes of poetry were *New Worlds for Old* (1957) and *Bread and a Pension* (1964). The main subdivisions of the latter, 'The Human Position', 'Compositions with Children', and 'Maps of the Heart', indicate how closely his poetry reflected his critical concerns. The irony of the title poem drew attention to his insistent preoccupation with the contemporary social context. Satire and compassion are mixed in poems that explore the pleasures and (more often) the frustrations of human relationships in a benevolent state promising the good life to conforming citizens locked into nine-to-five commuters' jobs and suburban domesticity. Johnson speaks from *within* this world and introduced a style of urbane Audenesque personal utterance that has remained influential in New Zealand poetry into the 1990s.

In 1968 Johnson left New Zealand (he later spoke of the 'slow poisonings' of his life as a 'New Zealand urban worker and suburban liver'), spending one year in New Guinea, then teaching creative writing at Mitchell College in Bathurst, New South Wales, Australia. *Fires and Patterns* (1975), which includes poems set in New Zealand, New Guinea, and Australia, marked a significant advance in his control of the personal voice, achieving a freer interplay of observation, memory, and reflection and fewer of the 'inert, avuncular homiletics' that he saw as 'the main danger to the didactic personality'.

Returning to New Zealand in 1980, Johnson embarked on a second literary career, more as an outsider this time. There were four late volumes of poems — *Coming and Going* (1982), *Winter Apples* (1984), *True Confessions of the Last Cannibal* (1986), and *Last Poems* — rich products of a second marriage and family and of an increasingly acerbic response to the 'aspects of human reality here' that are denied 'for the sake of safety and conformity'.

TERRY STURM

Further reading: Kendrick Smithyman, *A Way of Saying* (1965); James K. Baxter, *Aspects of New Zealand Poetry* (1967).

JOHNSON, PAULINE (1861–1913)
Canadian poet
Born on the Six Nations Reserve near Brantford, Ontario, Canada, of an English mother and a Mohawk father, she received a cultured Victorian upbringing. From 1893 to 1909, billed as Tekahionwake, the Mohawk Princess, she held audiences across Canada and in parts of the USA and England spellbound with recitations of her own poems and achieved international acclaim as a concert entertainer and poet.

Johnson's poetry, which appeared in *The White Wampum* (1895), *Canadian Born* (1903), and *Flint and Feather* (1912), ranged from melodious verse celebrating love and the beauties of the Canadian landscape to dramatic and energetic pieces on Native and patriotic themes. In *Legends of Vancouver* (1911) she romanticized tales told her by Chief Joe Capilano. Two volumes of prose were published posthumously — *The Shagganappi* (1913), a collection of boys' adventure stories, and *The Moccasin Maker* (1913), a collection of short stories, many of which idealize women and portray the trauma that her Native heroines experience when they fall in love with white men.

As a mixed-blood, middle-class woman writer faced with the need to earn her own living in Victorian Canada, Johnson was compelled to accept the popular tastes of her white audiences. She was both intensely British and Canadian in her loyalty and passionately Native in her sympathies. This predicament and ambiguity created the complex, fascinating persona that drew people to her. Today much of her literary output is considered dated and trite, highly melodramatic, and sentimental. Nevertheless, she articulated the experiences and emotions of women and Canada's Native people at a time when their voices were rarely heard.

S. PENNY PETRONE

Further reading: Betty Keller, *Pauline: A Biography of Pauline Johnson* (1981); A. LaVonne Brown Ruoff, *The Moccasin Maker: E. Pauline Johnson* (1987).

JOHNSTON, BASIL H. (1929–)

Canadian mythographer, short-story writer, essayist

Born on the Parry Island Indian Reserve in Ontario, Canada, he is primarily interested in the Ojibwa culture and language. He has produced Ojibwa language courses on tape and in print and has written numerous short stories, essays, and articles that have appeared in Native and mainstream journals, newspapers, and anthologies. Four of his books — *Ojibway Heritage* (1976), *How the Birds Got Their Colours* (1978), *Tales the Elders Told: Ojibway Legends* (1981), and *Ojibway Ceremonies* (1982) — record ancient Ojibwa narratives, ceremonies, and rituals and explain the religious beliefs and social customs that have given the Ojibwa their mythology. His most popular book, *Moose Meat and Wild Rice* (1978) — a collection of twenty-two stories — deals with life on and off the fictional Moose Meat Point Reserve. Johnston focuses on the relationships between Moose Meaters and white government officials and clergymen in scenes of hilarious adventure that satirize the inconsistencies of Native acculturation. With a gift for comic outrageousness, he punctures the pretensions of Natives and whites alike. Many of the community's protagonists are conventional characters, but Johnston exposes their absurdities with such good-humoured caricature that the reader soon forgets their stereotypical behaviour and enjoys their life-affirming exuberance.

In *Indian School Days* (1988) Johnston recalls his youth during the 1940s at a church-run, government-funded residential school for Native Canadian children in the Northern Ontario town of Spanish. Despite boring routines, heavy chores, exacting discipline, institutional food, frustrations, and rebellion, Johnston manages to evoke a wonderful camaraderie among the boys as they try to cope with or outwit their white teachers. Utilizing an episodic and anecdotal structure, he is preoccupied more with comic situations than with any censure of the residential school system, as some readers might have expected.

Johnston has an unerring ear for Indian-English speech patterns and pronunciation, and he delights in language, sometimes getting so carried away with his own extravagance that his idiosyncratic dialogue can become tedious and his banter exhausting. Nevertheless, Johnston is a master storyteller with a love of humour and drama in the manner of his Ojibwa ancestors.

S. PENNY PETRONE

JOHNSTON, GEORGE HENRY (1912–70)
Australian novelist, journalist
Born in Melbourne, Australia, he became a journalist with the Melbourne *Argus*. He was a war correspondent in Papua New Guinea (1942–3), Asia (including Tibet), Italy, and the North Atlantic (1944–5). He also wrote free-lance articles for American magazines, which admired the journalistic modernity of his style, with its impressionistic images, witty similes, and long, floating sentences.

Grey Gladiator (1941) and *Battle of the Seaways* (1941) are about the war at sea. Other books from this time are *Australia at War* (1942, a piece of patriotic jingoism), *New Guinea Diary* (1943), and *Pacific Partner* (1944, explaining the Australian war effort for Americans).

In Sydney, Australia, working on the *Sun* newspaper, Johnston produced his first novel, *Moon at Perigee* (1948, published later in the USA and the UK as *Monsoon*). It is set in India against a background of nationalist protests. *High Valley* (1949), on which he collaborated with his second wife, **Charmian Clift**, is based on his Tibetan experiences. *The Big Chariot* (1953), another jointly written novel, is set in seventeenth-century China; it was written while Johnston and his wife lived in London, England, where he headed an Australian news bureau. Later novels were mostly written on the Greek islands of Kalymnos and Hydra, where Johnston and Clift lived, supporting themselves as writers, from 1954 to 1964: *The Cyprian Woman* (1955), *The Darkness Outside* (1959), *Closer to the Sun* (1960), *The Far Road* (1962), *The Far Face of the Moon* (1964), and the jointly written *The Sponge Divers* (1955). During this period Johnston also wrote, under the pseudonym Shane Martin, five mystery novels about the adventures of an archaeologist.

My Brother Jack (1964) was Johnston's first aesthetic and financial success. Launched with considerable publicity in England and Australia, it has sold almost four hundred thousand copies and was adapted for television. It is an autobiographical novel in which the narrator, David Meredith, recalls his boyhood and early manhood. After rejecting his family and his first wife, his scale of values, and his country, he comes into contact towards the end with Cressida Morley, a thin disguise for Charmian Clift. The character of Meredith, many of the themes (such as jealously towards his wife, doubt about the value of his writing, unease at the competitiveness of society), and the two controlling images of the voyage and the kaleidoscope can be found more clumsily worked in *Closer to the Sun* and *The Far Road*. *Clean Straw for Nothing* (1969) and *A Cartload of Clay* (1971) continue the semi-autobiographical account of *My Brother Jack*. They are concerned with the sense of failure in marriage, career, and life, and the consolation that the only meaning is the search for meaning.

Johnston collaborated with the American photographer Robert Goodman on a wide-ranging book about Australia, *The Australians* (1966). Johnston's and Clift's stories are collected in *Strong Man from Piraeus* (1984), and his wartime notes in *War Diary 1942* (1984). His fictionalizing of biography is paralleled by **David Malouf** in *Johnno* and **Wole Soyinka** in *Aké*.

NESS SHANNON

Further reading: Gary Kinnane, *George Johnston* (1986).

JOLLEY, ELIZABETH (1923–)
Australian novelist, short-story writer
Born in Birmingham, England, to an English father and Viennese mother, she trained as a nurse in London and Birmingham; in 1959 she immigrated to Western Australia with her husband, Leonard Jolley, and their three children. While pursuing her career as a writer, she worked at a variety of occu-

pations — nurse, domestic cleaner, door-to-door salesperson. She teaches creative writing at the Fremantle Arts Centre and Curtin University of Technology. In fourteen years following the appearance of her first book, *Five Acre Virgin and Other Stories* (1976), Jolley published two further books of short fiction and ten novels, winning numerous literary awards including the *Age* Book of the Year Award for *Mr. Scobie's Riddle* (1982), the New South Wales Premier's Literary Award for Fiction for *Milk and Honey* (1984), and the Miles Franklin Award for *The Well* (1987). Her novels have been translated into French, German, and Hebrew, and she is the subject of a film, *The Nights Belong to the Novelist* (1987), directed by Christina Wilcox.

Although Jolley claims the landscape of her writing is not to be found clearly on any map, she acknowledges the influence of 'a small portion of Western Australia' upon her work. The contrast between Australia and Europe is also important in her fiction; many characters are represented as exiles experiencing loss, dislocation, or even excitement through changing countries. But time and experience, rather than geography, may also exile characters — for example, Jacob in *Milk and Honey*, and Vera in *My Father's Moon* (1989) — from their youthful, more innocent selves. The theme of exile is reinforced by characters who occupy a marginal position in society — the very old, middle-aged spinsters, European migrants, lesbians — as Jolley aims to reveal value in the lives of 'those who fail to meet expected social achievement'.

Echoes reverberate throughout Jolley's fiction. Narrative material is recycled, as in the short story 'The Libation' and *Miss Peabody's Inheritance* (1983), or 'Pear Tree Dance' and *The Newspaper of Claremont Street* (1981). Characters from a novel — Miss Porch and Mrs Viggars in *Foxybaby* (1985), for example — may reappear in a short story, while *My Father's Moon* and *Cabin Fever* (1990) share the same protagonist. Individual images and more substantial motifs, such as the much-desired plot of land (vineyard, orchard, small farm) keep reappearing, described by the author as 'consolations' and compared to phrases of music that can be 'repeated, perhaps with slight changes of rhythm or key'.

Despite claiming that she is not drawn to writing that finds its subject in writing, Jolley frequently teases her readers with the self-reflexive devices of metafiction and by creating unreliable narrators to challenge readers' faith in her narrative. Jacob in *Milk and Honey* recounts his past life from a mental hospital, though whether as patient or merely as employee is unclear. Like Jacob, Vera Wright in *My Father's Moon* dissimulates, making disastrous moral choices.

Mordant comedy both illumines the darker side of human behaviour and helps make it bearable. Jolley's delight in the absurd and the grotesque is also linked to the gothicism that features so prominently in her fiction, offering interesting comparisons with the work of New Zealand writer **Janet Frame** or the Canadian novel *Bear* by **Marian Engel**. A favourite setting is the enclosed institution with its own power structure — an old people's home, boarding school, or nurses' home. In *Milk and Honey* family life generates a yet more tightly enclosed world in which individuals are impelled into weird, even horrific actions partly dictated by the tortured constraints of their lives.

Critics, not always recognizing Jolley's use of gothic fantasy, have sometimes dismissed her characters' behaviour as wildly improbable or have accused her of sensationalism and morbidity. But choosing a mode in which naturalism and fantasy merge and external events become a projection of the characters' inner world enables her more readily to explore their moral dilemmas. The inability to escape the consequences of past actions casually and irresponsibly undertaken is a major concern of Jolley's fiction, presented with mingled humour and pain, and this moral vision contributes much to her substantial literary achievement.

DOROTHY JONES

Further reading: Pam Gilbert, *Coming Out from Under: Contemporary Australian Women Writers* (1988); *Westerly* (1986), special issue on Elizabeth Jolley.

JONES, DOUGLAS GORDON (1929–)

Canadian poet, critic

Born in Bancroft, Ontario, Canada, he took his BA (1952) and MA (1954) at McGill and Queen's Universities respectively, subsequently teaching at Bishop's University and the Université de Sherbrooke. In *Butterfly on Rock: A Study of Themes and Images in Canadian Literature* (1970), Jones wrote a largely mythopoeic meditation on the nature and themes of Canadian literature in English that, alongside **Northrop Frye**'s *The Bush Garden* (1971) and **Margaret Atwood**'s *Survival* (1972), helped shape Canadian studies for the next crucial decade. His translations — notably of Paul-Marie Lapointe's *The Terror of the Snows* (1976) — and founding editorship of the bilingual literary journal *ellipse* have established him as an ambassador for the bilingual nature of Canadian literature and culture. He has also written poems that are wholly or partly in French and illustrate the consistent 'multicultural' quality of his work.

Jones is almost as fascinated by the visual arts as by poetry, and his writing has painterly qualities. Indeed, in the early poem 'A Problem of Space', he regrets that language cannot merely create 'and leave an image, / And a space', as Chinese paintings do. Other poems include painters from Cézanne to Klee, David Milne to Alex Colville. Not surprisingly they also show the imagist influence of Ezra Pound, on whom Jones wrote his MA thesis.

Yet John Donne, Robert Duncan, **Ralph Gustafson**, Anne Hébert, and **Archibald Lampman** also inhabit Jones' poems, as do Odysseus, Orpheus and Eurydice, Persephone, and Eve. And the poems are equally notable for their 'syllabic grace' and an increasingly flexible partnership of syntax and form. In 'Phrases from Orpheus', for instance, Jones indents his lines differentially so as to allow two or three voices to speak at once, not marching in parallel columns that, like John Ashbery's, never meet, but intertwining as in a fugue. And his Lampman poems are charmingly unobtrusive acrostics.

The detachment that Jones achieves in his fragmentary imagist poems or in 'The River: North of Guelph', and also the sheer literary dexterity of this most subtle of Canadian poets, has led some reviewers to deplore a lack of 'vigour and robustness' in his work. His first two collections, *Frost on the Sun* (1957) and *The Sun is Axeman* (1961), may well seem to be playing deftly over the surface of things and shying away from darkness and depth. But those poems in *Phrases from Orpheus* (1967) that grapple with his brother's death and the break-up of his marriage are truly mythic explorations and reshapings of depth and pain and darkness. And those in *Under the Thunder the Flowers Light Up the Earth* (1977), winner of a Governor General's Award for Poetry, are equally truly songs of a man who has come through — wise, witty, lyrical, subtle, strong. *A Throw of Particles* (1983) combines a selection from three earlier collections with more of much the same. Finally, the title sequence of *Balthazar* (1988) is a poetic response to the work of the painter Balthus (pseudonym of Balthazar Klossowski).

JAMES HARRISON

Further reading: E. D. Blodgett, 'D. G. Jones', in Robert Lecker, Jack David, and Ellen Quigley (eds) *Canadian Writers and Their Works*, Poetry Series 9 (1985).

JONES, EVAN (1931–)

Australian poet

Born in Preston, Victoria, Australia, he studied at

the University of Melbourne, where he edited *Melbourne University Magazine* in 1953. After taking up a Stanford University writing scholarship, he returned from the USA to teach in the history and English departments of the Australian National University and the University of Melbourne. In 1969 he published the monograph *Kenneth Mackenzie*, and he edited, with Geoffrey Little, *The Poems of Kenneth Mackenzie* (1972). His four volumes of poetry are *Inside the Whale* (1960), *Understandings* (1967), *Recognitions* (1978), and *Left at the Post* (1982).

'A Commemoration of Professor Hope' reflects Jones' and **A. D. Hope**'s common allegiance to traditional verse forms. Jones has been a consistent and skilful user of rhyme and of a variety of stanzaic models ranging from ballad quatrains and refrains to sonnets to tercets, while his diction and tone have developed the playing off of colloquial idioms against more conventional rhetorics of intellect and emotion. Like **Peter Porter**, to whom he dedicates 'Grand Illusion', Jones writes primarily of the human behaviour displayed in his social environment, although he has found in fairytales and ballads, with their mixture of the magical and the matter-of-fact, a congenially unpretentious way of gaining access to the realm of myth.

In naturalistic mode, he turns a sharp eye on contemporary academic and domestic mores: sceptical about the striking of heroic attitudes, he sees 'romantic slipshod bravura' in art or in life as constantly reproved by 'the green world's swift laconic song: / *O turn it up, old sport*' (*'Ars longa, vita brevis est?'*). At the same time he retains considerable sympathy for a humanity too often faced with the question: 'would you rather / love in mutual delusion, nursing your silly stories, / or live in clear wit, alone with your cat and the furies?' In similar fashion, scepticism about the transcendental cannot completely obliterate the idea that 'somewhere else / the traceries of light burn on' nor persuade him to be deaf to moments when 'Bach weaves that shining / web of perfect order which I can neither / comprehend or disbelieve' ('A Letter from the House-Mouse to the Beavers').

JENNIFER STRAUSS

JONES, MARION PATRICK (1934–)
Trinidadian novelist

Born Marion Glean O'Callaghan in Woodbrook, Trinidad, she was educated at St Joseph's Convent, Port of Spain. She is known by her pen-name, Marion Patrick Jones. She left Trinidad for New York, USA, in the mid-1950s, obtained a diploma in library science, and returned home to become a chartered librarian. In the 1960s Jones graduated with a bachelor of science degree from the University of London, England; she also did post-graduate studies in social anthropology at the London School of Economics, writing a thesis on the Chinese community in Trinidad. She worked in Paris, France, for several years, and now lives in Woodbrook, Trinidad.

Jones has published two novels — *Pan Beat* (1973) and *J'Ouvert Morning* (1976). These reflect her Catholic, middle-class upbringing as they deal with the lives of post-independence Trinidadians who 'benefited', for better or worse, from their prestigious Catholic secondary education and from the sacrificial labour of their status-oriented parents. The author's invaluable contribution to the region's literature is her sensitive analysis of the Trinidadian middle class, as it strives to escape poverty and anonymity. Her novels levy a rather harsh judgement on this sector because of its enslavement to a materialist ethic.

The emotional and spiritual void that Jones' characters (male and female) suffer because of their desperate reach for upward social mobility recalls **Merle Hodge**'s Aunt Beatrice (in *Crick Crack, Monkey*, 1970), **George Lamming**'s Fola (in *A Season of Adventure*, 1960), and **Erna Brodber**'s Nellie (in *Jane and Louisa Will Soon Come Home*, 1980). Indeed, Jones' novels may be seen as offering a disturbing investigation of the precarious search by post-colonial societies for empowerment. Her truncated narrative technique, which has often been misunderstood, at its best produces a moving correlation with the interior fragmentation of her characters. Along with Brodber's Nellie, **Jean Rhys**' Antoinette (in *Wide Sargasso Sea*, 1966) and Myriam Warner-Vieyra's Juletane (in *Juletane*, 1982, English version, 1987), Jones' Elizabeth, in *J'Ouvert Morning*, makes powerful use of the Caribbean madwoman's discourse as feminist protest.

JENNIFER RAHIM

Further reading: Joycelyn Loncke, 'The image of the woman in Caribbean literature: with special reference to *Pan Beat* and *Heremakhonon*', *Bim* 64 (1978); Harold Barratt, 'Marion Patrick Jones', in Daryl C. Dance (ed.) *Fifty Caribbean Writers: A Bio-bibliographical Critical Sourcebook* (1986).

JORDAN, ARCHIBALD CAMPBELL (1906–68)
South African novelist, poet, short-story writer, critic
The son of an Anglican minister, he was born at Mbokothwana, Transkei, South Africa. A Xhosa, he was educated locally and at St Cuthbert's Higher Boarding School. He took his BA (1934) and MA (1942) at the University of South Africa, and his Ph.D. (1956) at the University of Cape Town. Jordan became a schoolteacher and lecturer. He left South Africa permanently in 1961 when the government refused him a passport and later became professor of African languages and literature at the University of Wisconsin, Madison, USA. Jordan was dedicated to African studies and his writings reflect his interest in Xhosa history, language, and literature. He wrote creatively in Xhosa and translated some works into English. His novel *Ingqumbo Yeminyanya* (1940), which, with Priscilla P. Jordan, he translated into English as *The Wrath of the Ancestors* (1980), is a classic of modern Xhosa literature.

Ingqumbo Yeminyanya deals with history and the changing traditions of the Mpondomise people and with the familiar themes of conflict between the new and the old, between westernized 'school' Africans and traditional 'red ochre' people, and between mission religion and traditional beliefs. However, critic Harold Scheub has argued that *Ingqumbo Yeminyanya* is a novel of character. The novel concerns a prince who leaves university to claim leadership of the Mpondomise. A complex novel of great merit, the English translation preserves the original Xhosa expression and idiom.

Jordan's collection of critical essays, *Towards An African Literature: The Emergence of Literary Form in Xhosa* (1973), explores Xhosa literature in a social context. Jordan shows the effect on traditional forms of social changes after the advent of literacy, which resulted from the arrival of European missionaries.

Jordan was interested in the performance of traditional oral tales (*iintsomi*), which have a strong communal element. He attributed the survival of these tales to their artistic value, each 'symbolizing something of permanent meaning'. A collection of oral tales, translated into English and retold by Jordan, was published posthumously in 1973 as *Tales from Southern Africa*. Although he did not publish a volume of his poetry in English, Jordan is considered to be among the forerunners of the South African black consciousness poets.

PATRICIA HANDLEY

JOSÉ, FRANKIE SIONIL (1924–)
Filipino novelist, short-story writer, poet, editor
Born in Rosales, Pangasinan, a poor rural province on the island of Luzon in the Philippines, he was one of five children of an impoverished landless family. José studied as a medical student at the University of Santo Tomas, Manila, and began writing in 1949. He supported his studies by selling stories and journalistic pieces and graduated in English literature. A journalist for much of his

life, he worked in increasingly important editorial positions for *The Commonweal*, the United States Information Service in Manila, *The Manila Times Sunday Magazine*, *Progress*, *Comment*, and *The Asia Magazine* in Hong Kong (as managing editor). He was also correspondent to *The Economist* from 1968 to 1969. In these positions and as a member of the Filipino diplomatic corps, he moved with his family to many international posts. José taught at the University of the East Graduate School (1974) and at De La Salle University (1984–5) and received an honorary doctorate from the University of the Philippines in 1992.

José's background of peasant poverty is central to his themes, whether as journalist, editor, or fiction writer. Many of his editorial essays are concerned with land reform and social justice and have become increasingly pro-feminist. His later publications have dealt more with the crisis of poverty and corruption, especially centred in Manila, that afflicts the increasingly urbanized Filipino population.

José's first published novel, *The Pretenders*, appeared in 1962, and his first collection of short stories, *The God Stealer and Other Stories*, in 1968. In 1966 José founded *Solidarity*, a journal devoted to publishing on ideas and cultures from Southeast Asia. In his position as *Solidarity* editor he has published essays, his own and those of others, that are critical of state corruption and push for further democratic and progressive reforms in the Philippines. But it wasn't until he founded his bookstore and art gallery Solidaridad (in 1967) that he was able to concentrate on his writing career. Since then, he has published prolifically. His publications include two novellas (*Two Filipino Women*, 1981, and *Three Filipino Women*, 1992), eight novels, a book of poems (*Questions*, 1988), and four short-story collections: *The God Stealer and Other Stories*, *Waywaya*, *Eleven Filipino Short Stories* (1980), *Platinum*, *Ten Filipino Stories* (1983), and *Olvidon and Other Short Stories* (1988). He is best known for his five-novel narrative cycle of Filipino characters, conflicts, and history — the Rosales quintology — comprising *The Pretenders*, *Tree* (1978, first serialized as *The Batete Tree* in 1956), *My Brother, My Executioner* (1979), *Mass* (1982), and *Po-on* (1984). Other novels include *Ermita* (1988) and *Gagamba* (1991).

Although never part of the Filipino academic intellectual circle, José's art *engagé* has exercised considerable influence, frequently opposing the status quo and élitism rampant in the universities that contribute, he argues, to the Philippines' economic and cultural problems.

Beginning with the position that literature's value resides in the dynamic evolutionary nexus of individuals and experiences called society, José's essays persist in asking the fundamental question: What is art? Sometimes his answer comes close to arguing for literature as instrumentality, stressing its usefulness in achieving social change and its polemical nature; as he noted in an unpublished paper, literature should 'portray the agony of a people and voice their aspirations'. As such, his work participates in the production of that 'imagined community', the Filipino nation. His work shares reflections similar to those produced by other Filipino writers, particularly on what **N. V. M. Gonzalez** has called the 'crossroads syndrome' — a culture of collisions of Asia and the west, leading to a sense of discontinuous history and cultural hybridization.

Because José's practice steers away from reification of the relation between art and society, his fiction is not simply protest literature. We can see a dialectical process in his pronouncements on fiction and in his novels. Breaking away from objectivist and aesthetical definitions of literature dominant in the Americanized Philippines of the 1950s and 1960s, José's novels achieve a 'national' stance through their insistence on specificities of subjects, themes, and style, founded on a theoretical recognition of the material basis of Filipino history and culture; that is, through an ideology of cultural nationalism. A similar critical cultural nationalism constructed on oppositional identity politics can be said to run through much post-colonial writing, as seen in the novels of **Ngugi wa Thiong'o**, Nawal El Sa'Adawi, and **Mudrooroo Narogin**.

José's attempts to innovate and revitalize certain literary forms and techniques shape part of the dialectic. Arguably, his narratives, committed to social comment and criticism, demonstrate their communicative vitality in specific form.

According to José, the subjects and characters of the Rosales quintology have their source in an over-arching determination already in place when he was a young man studying at university. He wrote passages of various novels within the same period of time; thus, despite the different chronological ordering of the novels' publication, he insists that the quintology forms one comprehensive and organic totality. According to their internal chronology, the first work of the quintology is *Poon*, set in the Revolutionary 1890s, but published last in the series. The second, *Tree*, deals with injustices suffered by peasants under the nineteenth-century Spanish colonial *encomedia* ('plantation') system and during the peasant revolutions against land corruption. *My Brother, My Executioner* explores the polarization of Filipino society into Ilustrados, the landed aristocracy, and disenfranchized peasants who were the major supporters of the 1950s Huk Rebellion. *The Pretenders* possesses crucial references to the history of peasant revolution and treats the conflicts within a US-dominated, socially mobile, middle-class, divided between its origins in peasant and working-class communities and the corrupt temptations offered by the Ilustrados. *Mass* is set in the civil disorders that took place under martial law in the 1980s. The narratives move from an agrarian background of pioneering activists, through settled (albeit tenant) farming, to the plantation system and a westernized urban middle-class and proletarian environment. This oeuvre mirrors the sweep and range of Filipino geo-economic and social history, testifying to José's ambition and the scope of his historical imagination. The quintology attempts a fictional re-narrativization (filtered through a subjective authorial presence) of Filipino national history. While the Rosales novels abound with polemical digressions, these features are constituted on a frame of national ideology.

The Pretenders focuses on themes of social injustice and class struggle and their internalized reflections and refractions in the anti-hero's spiritual paralysis and self-destruction. Despite the apparent Marxist criticism of capitalism, the novel operates chiefly through psychological analysis while offering polemical criticisms of contemporary Filipino society. *Tree*, similarly, oscillates between psychologized interior dramas and materialist critiques of Filipino feudalist society; the narrative focus on the protagonist's guilty sufferings weakens its social criticism to privilege instead the private dimensions of individual experience. *My Brother, My Executioner* shows José more in control of his political materials, with the ideological polarities allegorized in the struggle between the two half-brothers, the dark-skinned revolutionary hero and the land-owning mestizo.

Because of these three novels, José was viewed, as late as 1981, as chiefly interested in contemporary middle-class Philippine society. By 1983, however, the Swedish scholar Artur Lundkvist was noting 'his descriptions of the rural environment [for their] intense glow and lyrical shine'. In fact, the last two novels of the Rosales cycle portray both Manila's slum inhabitants (*Mass*) and the ancestral pre-Revolutionary peasants in Luzon (*Poon*). The linked novels' versatility and broad nationalistic concerns allow a variety of themes, social issues, and literary effects that exceed the category of protest literature. Instead, it is the unwavering nationalist orientation in these novels, doubly polished for being reiterated so often, that characterizes them.

The Rosales quintology has its full significance when read as a national epic. Its conception and production point to an evolutionary process, incipient in the young author's intentions. The development of the Filipino hero in the five novels marks the increasing clarity of the epic ambition and displays a responsiveness to material Filipino socio-political circumstances.

Still, although José claims that in the 1940s he already had in place a basic core of Filipino history and society as his subject, internal evidence indicates that José did not begin with the epic form in mind: the first expression of his oeuvre was closer to the short story. For example, while the construction of a locality as representative of Filipino national identity is present in *Tree*, its loosely strung chapters are more akin to short narratives than to the novel's sustained development of theme and character. His collections of short stories cover the range of his social concerns, from the loss of native culture in the early story, 'The God Stealer', to the sexual degradation that epitomizes political corruption in the stories in *Platinum*. In his novellas, *Two Filipino Women* and *Three Filipino Women*, sympathy for the urban destitute and fascination with the intersections of sex and politics result in a sharp critique of the economic exploitation of women's bodies and also in the humanization of the figure of the prostitute.

The note to *Wawaya* indicates that most of the stories in the collection are allegorical. As Kenneth Burke argues, language is symbolic action; like his novels, José's short stories function symbolically to persuade the readers to certain moral values. Plots and characters are highly stylized rather than realistically individualized, in keeping with the narrative satirical intentions. Fantasies of rural pastoralism and innocence and sentimental portrayals of family ties are recurrent features in his fictions.

Despite the constraints of writing in the English language in a nation where the national language is Pilipino (Tagalog-based Filipino) and where the present trend is towards writing in the native languages, José continues to publish prolifically. His last two novels, *Ermita* and *Gagamba*, are tenuously related to the Rosales quintology through intertextual references to characters and actions, but they push his subjects to fresh territory. In *Ermita*, José finally gives centre-stage to a female character who is as resilient, striving, and heroic as are his nationalist heroes. Beginning with Gagamba, the spider-like, legless, lower-depth centre-of-consciousness, *Gagamba* pulls the reader into the social maelstrom of Manilan society through a collage of picaresque vignettes; the central device of an earthquake that levels, literally and figuratively, the myriad social and economic classes who meet in the fatal Ermita restaurant underlines a bleak authorial vision of historical contingency and moral chaos.

José's works have been translated into twenty-two languages. His steady literary production, the steadfastness of his commitment to a vision of social justice simultaneously produced with a tragic sense of human corruption, and his elegiac celebrations of the natural world have brought him deserved national and international acclaim. Acknowledging him in *The New York Review of Books* as 'the foremost Filipino novelist in English', Ian Buruma also underscores the breadth of José's appeal. Paradoxically, even as José has worked and reworked the myths of Filipino national identity, he has become the Philippines' first internationally recognized writer.

SHIRLEY LIM

Further reading: A. T. Morales, ed., *F. Sionil Jose and His Fiction* (1989); Shirley Geok-lin Lim,

Nationalism and Literature: English-language Writing from the Philippines and Singapore (1993).

JOSEPH, MICHAEL KENNEDY (1914–81)
New Zealand novelist, poet
Born in Chingford, Essex, England, he first went to school in France, and lived from the age of ten to twenty in New Zealand. He took two degrees at Merton College, Oxford, England, served throughout the Second World War in a British artillery unit, and returned to New Zealand in 1945 to write and to teach English at the University of Auckland, where he remained for the rest of his working life. Although he was emphatically a New Zealand writer, his background shows in the urbane, Europeanized surface of all his work, as did his Catholicism in his moral concerns.

As a poet Joseph's output was small. He published three collections — *Imaginary Islands* (1950), *The Living Countries* (1959), and *Inscription on a Paper Dart: Selected Poems 1945–72* (1974) — but the last repeated much of the first two. He began with well-turned lyrics that often work a single image into a moral application. His later writing included evocations of New Zealand landscape and reflections on New Zealand society (some sharply satirical) and literature. In form his writing became progressively looser, and sometimes almost surrealist, as in the erudite and witty 'The Rosy Cats of Doctor Paracelsus'. All of his poetry, whatever the form, is distinguished by a high degree of technical accomplishment.

This is equally true of Joseph's fiction. Mastery of the form seemed his principal aim. Once he had achieved the desired form, which he always did 'first go', he moved on to another. None of his six novels is much like any of the others. In an almost cinematic, semi-documentary mode *I'll Soldier No More* (1958) follows an artillery unit through the Second World War; *A Pound of Saffron* (1962) is a fable about the manipulation of people in an academic setting; *The Hole in the Zero* (1967) is science fiction set in a random universe without cause and effect; *A Soldier's Tale* (1976) returns to the Second World War in a metafictional anecdote of horrifying violence. *The Time of Achamoth* (1977), also science fiction, pursues purposeful evil through past and future; the posthumously published *Kaspar's Journey* (1988), written for younger readers, is a tour through Europe and Moslem North Africa at the time of the Children's Crusade. In all his fiction a dazzlingly vivid surface overlies a moral, metaphysical, or technical intent.

Joseph's one published work of criticism is an accomplished, if rather gentlemanly, study, *Byron the Poet* (1964).

DENNIS McELDOWNEY

Further reading: M. K. Joseph, 'Beginnings', *Islands* 5 (1979); K. K. Ruthven, 'Joseph's tale', *Islands* 5 (1979).

JOSHI, ARUN (1939–93)
Indian novelist
Joshi is among the most significant Indian novelists writing in English, meriting ranking only after the great trio of fiction-writers **Mulk Raj Anand**, **R. K. Narayan**, and **Raja Rao**. His novels are *The Foreigner* (1968), *The Strange Case of Billy Biswas* (1971), *The Apprentice* (1974), *The Last Labyrinth* (1981), and *City and the River* (1990). *The Foreigner*, in spite of its indebtedness to Camus' existentialism, has a native, Indian angle in mediating an experience that is not merely social but metaphysical. The protagonist does not belong to any specific place and time; in philosophical terms his foreignness is analogous with the human predicament.

Finding one's roots and exploring human values, however, is the theme of what may be Joshi's best novel, *The Strange Case of Billy Biswas*. It is the story of Bimal Biswas, who, belonging as he does to the upper crust of Indian society, gets infinitely bored by it and flees only to find his roots in the integrity of the tribal world. It is a tale told with excellent craftsmanship, maintaining the contrast between the impulsive and seemingly eccentric behaviour and actions of Billy and the cool, collected account of his friend Romi (Ramesh) Sahai. What makes the story fascinating and convincing is Billy's brilliant, rational outlook and the primitive force that triggers his creative energy and prompts his actions. Billy's most crucial act is his disappearance from home, family, and the civilized world; whatever he says or does is a manifestation of immense faith in the creative energy of the primitive world, as opposed to the duplicity and hypocrisy of the civilized world. The efforts of his family and his friend Romi (the narrator of the story) and the police in their search for Billy Biswas in the jungle among the tribals results in the police killing Billy by mistake. His pointless death is testimony to Billy's view of the stranglehold civilization exerts. (Billy's final utterance before death is about betrayal by this bastard civilization.)

The Apprentice, with its gripping narrative technique and strikingly relevant theme, is an extraordinary achievement. It is a crushing and poignant tale told with brutal frankness about the corruption of our civilized world — a theme not very different from that of *The Strange Case of Billy Biswas*. *The Apprentice* is the story of a conscience-stricken man with a curious mixture of idealism and docility and a vague sense of values that he flouts for the sake of his career. Rathan Rathor, the narrator and protagonist, is the apprentice who evolves into a product of the corrupt society in which he lives. He succumbs out of an innate moral weakness that makes him an Everyman of modern times. He loses his identity but cleverly climbs up the ladder of success.

Rathan is bribed into passing defective war material during the Chinese aggression, not knowing the grievous consequences. He is horrified by the atrocity of his act when he realizes that a friend has become a victim. It is this intense sense of guilt that leads him to a strange act of expiation of his sin — the strangest apprenticeship in the world — namely, wiping the shoes of the congregation sitting on the steps outside the temple every morning on his way to his office. What is evident in the novel is Joshi's compassionate vision of life, nourished by Indian legends and tales of sin and expiation. That it is perhaps the most appropriate comment to appear on the contemporary Indian scene is not to diminish its artistic merit, but to admire the handling of such didactic material within the framework of a novel.

The Last Labyrinth carries echoes of Joshi's earlier preoccupations, but lacks the artistic achievement of *The Strange Case of Billy Biswas* or *The Apprentice*. There is a seeming indulgence in the labyrinthine spheres of human experience it explores in contrast to the natural narrative of *The Strange Case of Billy Biswas. The Last Labyrinth* is a novel about the failure of a successful businessman in grappling with the complexities of life. Som Bhasker, a millionaire industrialist, has unsatiated yearnings, which he thinks to quench by possession — be it of women, business, or material things. Anuradha, his lover, becomes the focal point of Som's existence, which is like all human existence — riddled with mysteries of love, death, and God. The secret of the realization of the ultimate reality is hidden in the last labyrinth, and Som's exploration is not really different from Bismal Biswas' exploration of the corrupt world of civilization in *The Strange Case of Billy Biswas*, and Rahan Rathor's exploration as an insider in the corrupt world of contemporary society. Though their paths cross, the goals are the same, and it is Joshi's distinction that his social and moral concerns always lead to an exploration of the metaphysical.

City and the River is a modern parable that unfortunately loses the drive, concern, and passion of Joshi's earlier fiction, in which the rich experience of the novelist shapes his vision. In this work that vision itself becomes the subject-matter and hence abstract, and the exercise of uniting the city with the river appears contrived.

The Survivor (1975) is a slim volume of short stories that proves Joshi's forté to be the novel.

C. N. SRINATH

JURGENSEN, MANFRED (1940–)
Australian poet, editor
Born in Flensburg, Germany, of Danish and German parents, he immigrated to Melbourne, Australia, in 1961. His first poems in English were lyrics in which the concepts of language and exile assumed a mystical as well as an emotional connotation that characterizes much of his mature work. Like many of his contemporaries, Jurgensen was preoccupied with the political corruption of language and with the identity of the speaking voice in verse and prose. His poetry, plays, short stories, and novels transcend personal origins to represent the emotional and metaphysical experiences of his generation. Prolific as a creative writer in both German and English, he has also published extensively in both languages in his academic role as professor of German at the University of Queensland. His writing in English includes nine volumes of poetry, from *Signs and Voices* (1973) to *The Partiality of Harbours* and *My Operas Can't Swim* (both 1989) and *Selected Poems 1972–1985* (1987), selected and introduced by the poet **Dimitris Tsaloumas**. Although influenced by such poets as W. B. Yeats, T. S. Eliot, and Paul Celan, Jurgensen has a unique voice, creating a constantly enriched world of signs and symbols and experimenting with themes and language, as in the passionately ironic volume *The Skin Trade* (1983) and the prose monodrama *The Unit* (1984). The poem cycle *A Winter's Journey* (1979) is a tribute to Schubert's *Winterreise* in which he reverses the sequence of musical form in the *Lieder* and presents an intensely experienced history in complex mimetic writing.

Jurgensen has published two novellas in English, *A Difficult Love* (1986) and *Break-Out* (1987), of which *A Difficult Love* is a story of obsessive love mediated through an ambivalent reaction to the Australian environment. While the narrative voices and socio-political concern of his prose recall the novels of Swiss author Max Frisch, Jurgenson's work also contains impressionist and surrealist elements. Through editing and publishing the journal *Outrider*, publishing work by Australian writers, including those whose native language is not English, in his Phoenix Press, and as general editor of the *German-Australian Studies* series, Jurgensen contributes greatly to the encouragement of Australian literature.

ELIZABETH PERKINS

JUSSAWALLA, ADIL (1940–)
Indian poet
Born into a Zoroastrian family in Bombay, India, he was educated at Cathedral School, Bombay, and University College, Oxford University, England. Jussawalla spent thirteen years in England, teaching at a language school, before returning to India in 1970, where he taught at St Xavier's College, Bombay, between 1972 and 1975. He has published two volumes of poetry — *Land's End* (1962) and *Missing Person* (1976). He edited *New Writing in India* (1974) and, in collaboration with **Eunice de Souza**, edited an anthology of Indian prose in English, *Statements* (1976). For many years Jussawalla has written free-lance for newspapers and magazines.

The poems in *Land's End* that were written abroad are largely experimental; sharp and powerful, they deal with a sense of isolation, resulting from cultural displacement. Jussawalla says of these poems that he had 'tried to show the effect of living in lands I can never leave nor love properly to belong to'. Caught between two cultures and languages, he reveals in his early poems both an emotional need to become part of the society in which he lives and the desire to be away from it. He returned to India only to find himself a misfit.

The poems in *Land's End* are loaded with images of sterility, as in 'November Day', which utilizes the seasonal fading and falling of leaves as symbols of barrenness. 'The Moon and Cloud at Easter', '31st December '58', 'The Suburb', and 'The Dolls' are poems indebted to a tradition moulded by T. S. Eliot and employed by novelists such as Evelyn Waugh and Graham Greene. In these poems, according to critic Bruce King, the futility of modern life is juxtaposed with Christian symbols 'to show the vitality and superiority of a former sacred to a present secular culture'.

In *Missing Person* Jussawalla emerges as a poet of Indian sensibility in his exploration of his relationship to India. The exile's return, memories of his foreign experiences, his reaction to his native milieu, and his continued quest for self-knowledge form the collection's chief concerns. The poems have become more politicized and depersonalized than those in *Land's End*, and such devices as masks, impersonations, and juxtaposed ironies are used to disguise the self.

The many voices in *Missing Person* are difficult to identify, and the form of the poetry is highly fragmented and without a structural centre. The Missing Person is depicted as a victim of colonialism, mass culture, the English language, the attractions of foreign land, the east-west conflict, and a middle-class morality. With no sense of belonging, he is a fragmented personality shaped by various contradictory cultural influences. Ignorant of his own identity, an exile, the Missing Person becomes a metaphor that sparks the poet's exploration of self and society.

P. A. ABRAHAM

Further reading: Bruce King, *Modern Indian Poetry in English* (1987; rev. 1989).

K

Kabir, Humayun (1906–70)

Indian poet, novelist, critic

Born in Faridpur, Bengal (now in Bangladesh), he had a brilliant academic career in philosophy and English at the universities of Calcutta, India, Oxford, England, and Andhra, India. In his illustrious career as a gifted writer and secular politician, Kabir helped post-independence India develop its educational policy. A Gandhian nationalist, creative writer, erudite scholar, and effective communicator, he published more than twenty books in Bengali and English.

Kabir's Sir George Stanley public lectures were published in *Poetry, Monads and Society* (1941). His poetry is rich in imagery and lyrical in form and content. Noteworthy are such poems as 'The Padma', 'Mahatma', and 'Trains', in his collection *Mahatma and Other Poems* (1944). These poems bear the unmistakable stamp of the English Romantics and Victorians. *Three Stories* (1947), a representative collection of Kabir's short stories containing 'Prestige', 'Marzeena', and 'Sardar', is a slice of life from the Muslim Bengal of the 1920s and 1930s. His themes are varied, his technique realistic, and his language late Victorian. Kabir's stories generally illustrate his impressive imaginative powers in plot construction, dialogue, characterization, socio-cultural setting, and humanistic moral vision. 'Prestige', for example, is a frontal attack on the chauvinistic practices of purdah and of burqa (the dress or veil worn by orthodox Muslim women, which covers the entire body) among the conservative Muslims of his day. Kabir's vision is anti-fundamentalist, secular, and critical; in this sense it anticipates the artistic values of **Salman Rushdie**. If 'Prestige' indicts the superstitious observance of the *Shariat* (the Muslim Personal Law), 'Marzeena' postulates an alternative value system centred on the western concept of individualism. Aloneness as the existential condition of all non-conformists is symbolized by Marzeena. Though somewhat pessimistic, the story prophetically projects the image of the 'New Muslim Woman' emerging from the cultural backwaters of Bengal. 'Sardar' is the story of Bazil Sardar, a worker in a Calcutta factory of the 1930s, who, oppressed by the degrading system enforced by colonial masters, finally decides to strike for better wages and treatment.

It is, however, the fictional classic *Men and Rivers* (1945) that earns Kabir a place in the history of Indian English fiction. The novel, with its locale in the undivided rural Bengal, develops the river Padma into a forceful metaphor for the ephemerality and endurance of life and for the vicissitudes of fortune that beset its rustic men and women. Deftly dovetailed into the novel's tight structure is the tragic intimation of adolescent love between Malek and Nuru, who, however, are frustrated by the final ironic revelation of their 'blood-relationship' as brother and sister who cannot marry.

Kabir's other works include a collection of speeches and addresses entitled *Of Cabbages and Kings* (1948), a volume of essays, *Science, Democracy and Islam* (1955), as well as *The Indian Heritage* (1946), *Studies in Bengali Poetry* (1962), *Indian Philosophy of Education* (1965), and *Britain and India* (1980).

A. V. KRISHNA RAO

Further reading: Dipankar Datta, *Humayan Kabir: A Political Biography* (1969); K. G. Sayidain, *Professor Humayun Kabir* (1970); Amaresh Datta, ed., *Encyclopaedia of Indian Literature* Vol. 3 (1989).

KACHINGWE, AUBREY (1926–)

Malawian novelist

He was born in Malawi, educated in Malawi and Tanganyika (now in Tanzania), and is a print and radio journalist. Kachingwe's only novel, *No Easy Task* (1966), is a landmark in the early literary production of East and Central Africa. Having worked in Kenya, Tanzania, and Malawi (then Nyasaland), Kachingwe re-creates in a fictional country, Kwacha, the atmosphere prior to political independence, as a national organization exerts pressure to accelerate the handing over of power from colonial masters. The novel shows the initiation into political action of a wide range of citizens — church ministers, taxi drivers, villagers, retired soldiers, a few professional politicians — who work together with mounting confidence and hope. Pride in achievement is echoed in the plot, with several births announced for new couples. The social diversity, a source of potential divergence, is not glossed over: the protagonist, a journalist, sets the tone, which is that of sober reporting. The tensions and compromises between newspapers and politics are particularly well defined.

If the novel's cool, clear demonstration creates a certain emotion, it is through restraint and a dignity of tone that is not without human warmth. Some characters, such as the efficient but ambiguous politician Dan Dube and the very powerful illicit night-club owner 'Sleepy Aunt', recur in many other African novels; it is interesting to compare the evolution of these stereotypes in later works such as **Chinua Achebe**'s *Anthills of the Savannah* (1987) or **Ben Okri**'s *The Famished Road* (1991).

J. BARDOLPH

KADHANI, MUDERERI (1952–)

Zimbabwean poet

He was born in Mhondoro, Zimbabwe, and studied at St Ignatius College and the universities of Zimbabwe and York, England. Kadhani is co-editor, with **Musaemura Zimunya**, of *And Now the Poets Speak* (1981). He has published one poetry collection, *Quarantine Rhythms* (1976).

Kadhani's distinctiveness lies in his combination of political themes and careful attention to form. He writes of life under the Rhodesian government in a stylistic mixture of literary cosmopolitanism and indigenous poetic forms. In this regard, his work is similar to **Dambudzo Marechera**'s.

Kadhani is a master of vivid and compact imagery. In 'When it Came', the first poem of *Quarantine Rhythms*, he conveys the suffering endured by blacks in Rhodesia through an exceptionally condensed image of 'arid' tears, 'clotted on the cheeks of the land'. The personification of the land brings out the intensity of a particular instance of human suffering while, through allusion, it places it in the context of the biblical story of the children of Israel.

Kadhani's quest to diversify his poetic expression is illustrated by his borrowing from non-standard registers, as in his poem 'Born in the Nation's Orphanage'. Kadhani's predilection for transcultural borrowing is further evident in his use of the conventions of concrete poetry. Nevertheless, his interest in foreign poetic traditions is not at the expense of local forms. His praise-poem, 'Rekayi Tangwena', gives epic proportions to the story of Chief Rekayi Tengwena's dispossession of his land by the Rhodesian government.

Kadhani is an experimental poet who is ceaselessly searching for different ways of representing human suffering.

MPALIVE-HANGSON MSISKA

Further reading: Adrian Roscoe and Mpalive-Hangson Msiska, *The Quiet Chameleon: Modern Poetry from Central Africa* (1992).

KAHIGA, SAM (1943–)

Kenyan novelist, short-story writer

He was born in Uthiru Village, Central Province,

Kenya. The brother of **Leonard Kibera**, Kahiga grew up in the stormy period of the Mau Mau rebellion — a factor that has dominated his fiction. His protagonists — whether freedom fighters, home guards, or colonial administrators — are portrayed as people who are neither wholly good nor wholly bad. The emptiness of their existence is attributed to war and the absence of love and understanding. Referring to the indiscriminate murder of people by the freedom fighters, a character in 'Esther' (a short story in the collection *Potent Ash*, 1968, co-authored by Kahiga and Kibera) cries, 'who are they fighting, I want to know? the villagers they have burnt! the innocent lives they have taken! everywhere they go they kill their own because they can't get at the white people, and those are the thieves of the land!' (A similar reaction to the freedom fighters is also found in Kenneth Watene's *Dedan Kimathi*, 1974.) Kahiga's *Dedan Kimathi, The Real Story* (1991) attempts to reconstruct the character of the freedom fighter; unlike **Ngugi wa Thiong'o**'s portrayal of the freedom fighter in *Weep not, Child* (1964) and *A Grain of Wheat* (1967), Kahiga does not mythologize the character, but depicts him with normal human weaknesses.

In the novels *Lover in the Sky* (1979) and *When the Stars Are Scattered* (1979) Kahiga explores cultural conflicts in love relationships and the moral decadence that pervades social life. Kahiga's other published works include the novel *The Girl from Abroad* (1974) and the short-story collection *Flight to Juba* (1979).

EGARA KABAJI

Further reading: Helen Mwanzi, *Notes on 'Potent Ash'* (1985).

KAILASAM, THYAGARAJA PARAMASIVA

(1884–1946)

Indian dramatist

Born in Bangalore, India, he was a geologist by training — a student of the Royal College of Science (now Imperial College, London, England) and a Fellow of the Royal Geological Society — and a playwright by choice. He was the author of twenty-one plays in Kannada; in English he wrote five plays and, in *Little Lays and Plays* (1933), a number of short plays and poems. During his years in London (1908–15), and quite apart from his academic achievement as a geologist, Kailasam came under the influence of British drama and theatre, especially of Bernard Shaw and Oscar Wilde and of the great Shakespearean actors he had seen on the stage, including Beerbohm Tree.

Kailasam the man was as fascinating as the writer. Born rich, but with a disregard for money, he was an amiable eccentric, an athlete, a compulsive bohemian, a brilliant wit, and a legend in his own lifetime. With his irrepressible high spirits, his incredible feats of memory, his flair for parody, his verbal fireworks, his superb command not only of the spoken idiom but of all its dialectal variations in Kannada and in English, his versatility in acting, and his uncanny knowledge of music, both Karnatak and western, Kailasam was a total man of the theatre. His singular contribution to the language of the theatre was, as he called it, 'Kannadanglo' — Kannada mixed with English words — which has become common currency in everyday speech, especially that of the Indian educated middle class.

While Kailasam's social realist Kannada plays emphasize character rather than plot, his English plays — *Fulfilment* (1933), *The Purpose* (1944), *Keechaka* (1949; Kannada version, 1948), and *Karna: The Brahmin's Curse* (1946) — are based on the *Mahabharata*, while *The Burden* (1933) is based on the *Ramayana*.

Kailasam's deeply compassionate vision of humanity resulted in a totally credible gallery of characters in his Kannada plays — especially in *Tollu Ghatti* (1923), *Poli Kitti* (1923), *Home Rulu* (1930), and *Bandavalavillada Badayi* (1935). His achievement as a playwright is such that actors have always found it a delight to perform in his plays.

S. RAMASWAMY

Further reading: L. S. Seshagiri Rao, *T. P. Kailasam* (1984).

KALMAN, YVONNE (1942–)

New Zealand novelist

Born in Hawera, New Zealand, she turned from schoolteaching to a professional writing career in the late 1970s, achieving success in the American blockbuster market (like her Australian counterpart, **Colleen McCullough**) with a three-volume historical saga set in colonial Auckland: *Greenstone Land* (1981), *Greenstone Land: Juliette's Daughter* (1982), and *Greenstone Land: Riversong* (1985).

Kalman's novels are primarily spectacular entertainments, tracing the romantic and marital destinies of her spirited heroines against a background of internecine dynastic power struggles in a raw colonial environment, interspersed with erotic sexual episodes and graphic scenes of violence. In two equally successful later blockbusters, *Mists of Heaven* (1987) and *After the Rainbow* (1989), Kalman used the same formula, turning this time to colonial Christchurch for her raw materials.

Kalman's interest in New Zealand history as a subject coincides with the revival of historical consciousness in many more 'serious' novelists of the 1980s, such as **Maurice Shadbolt**; she was also the first New Zealand popular novelist after **G. B. Lancaster** in the 1930s to revive the New Zealand historical romance as a major genre. Although Kalman is highly skilled in the conventions of the genre, her image of colonial New Zealand — with its emphasis on the struggles of isolated pioneering women and on racial conflict and prejudice and with its iconoclastic attitude to 'official' history — belongs very distinctly to the 1980s.

TERRY STURM

KAMAL, DAUD (1935–87)

Pakistani poet, translator

He was born in Abbottabad, Pakistan, into a family that followed academic, administrative, and business professions. He was professor of English at the University of Peshawar, Pakistan.

Kamal's is a poetry of romantic interest and residual suggestion. He had begun to compose early, but was a latecomer among the poets of his generation. Translation of Urdu poetry and, further afield, transcreation in English preoccupied him a great deal before he found his own voice. After an apprenticeship with the work of the Urdu master Mirza Asadullah Khan Ghalib — Kamal published his free verse translation *Ghalib: Reverberations* in 1970 — he found in Faiz Ahmed Faiz's poetry (which he translated as *Selected Poems of Faiz in English*, 1984, and *The Unicorn and the Dancing Girl: Poems of Faiz Ahmed Faiz*, 1988) both the translator's challenge and the creative artist's trim. These translations and renderings were an important part of Kamal's creative output and will be usefully studied by the reader of his poetry.

Although *Compass of Love and Other Poems* (1973) is not strictly a collection of translations, the book comprises renderings — departures evidently based on the writings of well-known writers, in the manner of Kamal's earlier renderings from Ghalib. However, the book is informative about Kamal's early interests and development; also, unlike his later work, several poems in the volume contain direct allusions and comments on everyday events. Some of the early poems did filter into the later collections, but the obvious socio-political aspects are later expunged as compression substitutes for range. In any case, Kamal's two poetry collections, *Recognitions* (1979) and *A Remote Beginning: Poems* (1985), represent his original and best work.

The poems in *Recognitions* largely contradicted the modernist as well as narrative work of the period and referred, both in their technique and sentiment, to the more traditional sources of art, although some poems have the descriptive quality of **Edwin Thumboo**'s early poetry (for example, in Thumboo's 'Ayer Biru' in *The Second Tongue*, 1976, and *Rib of Earth*, 1956). *A Remote Beginning* was also a version of imagist practice joined to the poetics of the Urdu *ghazal* and the haiku; it proved the utility of the paths trodden earlier. Of how a poet's work does not develop or change essentially, Kamal's is one solid example. He continued to contemplate a rather static world of muted images, which his mythographic imagination made into shapes of art, preserving therein a personal meaning. Words are used in his poems with economy and speciality; themes do not matter — not so much at any rate. But image and phrase, as they induce a mood or hint at a feeling, are all-important. Early poems such as 'Crow' and 'A Toy Cart in Taxila Museum' (*Recognitions*) are good examples of Kamal's technique, which rarely failed to reproduce itself. He had seen his subject in a certain way and expressed himself so in the poem titled 'Reproductions' (*Recognitions*). Later, too, as a pervading sadness alternates with outrage, two main styles remain discernible: lyric-narrative, as in the fine poems 'The Street of Nightingales' and 'Water-Carrier' and in the staccato telegraphese of 'Rivermist' (*A Remote Beginning*).

ALAMGIR HASHMI

Further reading: Peter Dent, ed., *The Blue Wind: Poems in English from Pakistan* (1984).

KANNAN, LAKSHMI (1947–)
Indian poet, short-story writer
Born in Mysore, India, she is a bilingual writer who uses the pen-name Kaaveri for her fiction in Tamil. She holds a Ph.D. in English (1973) from Jadavpur University, Calcutta, India. After some fifteen years of teaching English, Kannan became a free-lance advertising consultant. Her published work includes three volumes of poetry — *Impressions* (1974), *The Glow and the Grey* (1976), and *The Exiled Gods* (1985) — and two volumes of short stories, *Rhythms* (1986) and *Panjata and Other Stories* (1992).

Kannan's forte is the short, striking lyric, marked by a meditative vein. Her preoccupations in *Impressions* and *The Glow and the Gray* are with a woman's search for true identity, nature's place in human life, and the ambivalence of one's cultural inheritance. Her perspective encompasses the need for wholeness (integrity), best illustrated in the poem 'Fruits': 'Fruits I like either whole or not at all.' Some striking poems in the second volume clinically examine the distorted images of women in Indian society. 'Shakti', an overtly feminist poem, and 'Shock Absorber' exploit the Indian iconographic figures of Ardhanareswara (a half-female, half-male deity in Hindu temples) and Durga (a martial goddess) to highlight the chasm between ideology and reality relating to women's position. 'Comrade' takes a surprising angle on the feminist perspective — an erotic situation of mutual incomprehension is turned into a spiritual quest for the true self.

The Exiled Gods is more strident and political in tone. Post-feminist poems such as 'Kanyakumari' (meaning the eternal virgin) and 'Draupadi' affirm a faith in the inviolable self in woman. The pain of being born female is also poignantly explored in 'Woman with a Past' and 'Woman to Woman'. In 'Burnt Brown by the Sun', the denunciation of social injustice heard in the agony of the nameless 'She' becomes the denunciation of Aryan racial discrimination against Dravidians.

Rhythms is Kannan's own translation of her collection of Tamil short stories. The central focus is on the gamut of women's experience — drawn mostly from the middle classes — in modern India and abroad. An exception is 'Muniyakka', which deftly combines metaphysical complexity and a lower-class social milieu. Kannan's heroines search for an inclusive ideal of harmony while chafing under hidebound tradition. Man is not regarded as the sole enemy.

C. T. INDRA

KARAKA, DOSABHAI FRAMJI (1911–74)
Indian novelist, autobiographer, biographer
Born in Bombay, India, into an aristocratic family, he was Zoroastrian by faith and a versatile personality. He studied at Oxford University, England, and was the first Indian to become the President of the Oxford Union in 1934. His mother tongue was Gujarati. Karaka was stimulated to write by G. B. Shaw's *Candida* and in 1938 published his autobiography *I Go West*, which envisages a free India. A later autobiography, *Then Came Hazrat Ali*, was published in 1972. After eight years' stay in England, Karaka returned to India, where he worked variously as a magistrate, member of the Bombay Legislative Council, chair of the Bombay Municipal Corporation, and as the sheriff of Bombay.

A brilliant journalist, Karaka was initially a war correspondent with the *Bombay Chronicle*; his writings, ranging from travelogue to novel, have a journalistic flavour. His historical and biographical works include *Out of Dust He Made Us Into Man* (1940) on **M. K. Gandhi**, *Nehru: The Lotus-Eater* (1953), and *The Famous Mogul Nizam VII of Hyderabad* (1955). *The Pulse of Oxford* (1933), *Oh! You English* (1935), and *New York with its Pants Down* (1948) contain ironic sketches of English and American life. Karaka highlights, often ironically, the weakness of western civilization.

Karaka published three novels. According to critic **M. K. Naik**, *Just Flesh* (1941) is, perhaps, 'the only novel by an Indian set wholly in the west and representing only British characters'. *There Lay the City* (1942) is a love story set in Bombay during the Second World War. *We Never Die* (1944) has Muslim and Hindu characters. Karaka's talent as a storyteller is conspicuous, but he seems to be lacking in creative imagination. He will be best remembered for his lively thumbnail sketches and his pungent satire on contemporary situations.

PURNIMA MEHTA

KARNAD, GIRISH (1938–)
Indian dramatist
Born in Matheran, near Bombay, India, but raised and educated in Dharwad, Karnataka State, he graduated in 1958, later attending Oxford University, England, as a Rhodes Scholar. On returning to India he worked for Oxford University Press, Madras, for six years. A respected film and television director, actor, and script-writer in both Hindi and his mother tongue, Kannada, Karnad played the lead in *Samskara* (1969), the movie that heralded the new wave in Kannada cinema. In 1974–5 he was director of the Film and TV Institute of India, in Pune. He is chair of Sangeet Natak Akademi, India's national academy of the performing arts, New Delhi.

A typical example of the bilingual fluency of many Indian authors, Karnad writes first in Kannada and translates his own work into English, although his first play, *Yayati* (1961), remains untranslated in English. Encouraged by a critic's remark about the absence of good historical drama in Kannada, Karnad turned to medieval Indian history for the plot of *Tughlaq* (1964, English 1972). His characterization of Muhammad Tughlaq, fourteenth-century sultan of Delhi, awed audiences with its delineation of Tughlaq's initial idealism degenerating into tyrannical despotism. Karnad agrees that the play manifests a disillusionment with post-Nehru politics in India. He claims that commercial theatre also influenced *Tughlaq* with its vast canvas and such devices as a comic duo — the rogue Aziz is almost a Fool to Tughlaq's Lear.

Drawn by the perennial vitality of indigenous folk theatre, Karnad began experimenting with form in *Hayavadana* (1971, English 1975). He incorporated such traditional props as masks and half-curtains, as well as the meta-theatrical Indian convention of the director introducing and performing in the play. The use of folk techniques has become widespread in urban Indian theatre, following Karnad's lead in this respect. The play itself originates in a Sanskrit tale, though Karnad freely utilized Thomas Mann's version, *The Transposed Heads* (1940). Through a curious set of circumstances, the heads and bodies of two friends get interchanged, confusing all as to who is the real husband of the first man's wife. Thus, Karnad examines human identity, incompleteness, and even adultery.

Anjumallige (1977) failed perhaps because of its theme of incest. *Nagamandala* (1988, English 1990) conflates two Kannada folk tales in another play-within-a-play. It explores storytelling as a concept: the dramatic frame shows how the oral tradition has an independent life, while the dramatic narrative reveals a lonely woman talking to herself to stay alive. Neglected by, but devoted to, her husband, she finds a lover in a snake that takes his form, enabling Karnad to delve further into the meanings of infidelity, fantasy, and wish fulfilment. Karnad terms the method 'simultaneous presentation of alternative points of view', comparing it to Brecht's 'complex seeing'.

Karnad's plays have achieved great success on stage in various Indian languages, Alyque Padamsee's *Tughlaq* by Theatre Group in Bombay (1970) being the best-known English production. Karnad's later works display even more imaginative theatricality, with speaking roles given to a goddess, dolls, and a half-man, half-horse (in *Hayavadana*) or even to flames, a story, and a snake (in *Nagamandala*).

ANANDA LAL

Further reading: 'Girish Karnad', interview, in Paul Jacob (ed.) *Contemporary Indian Theatre* (1989).

KASAIPWALOVA, JOHN (1949–)

Papua New Guinean poet, dramatist

He was born in Okaikoda, his father's village, on Kiriwina Island in the Trobriand Islands, Papua New Guinea; his mother's subclan, the Kwenama, had chiefly prominence. Kasaipwalova's uncle, the pre-eminent chief of the Kwenama clan, took John at an early age to be raised as a chief, but after a custody battle he was sent to a Catholic boarding school in Sideia, Milne Bay District. At both this school and at St Brendan's College in Yeppoon, Queensland, Australia, Kasaipwalova's performance was outstanding, earning him a Commonwealth scholarship.

Moving to the University of Queensland, Australia, to study arts and law, Kasaipwalova became actively involved with radical groups on campus, notably the Revolutionary Socialist Students Alliance. He failed his exams, however, and lost his scholarship and, consequently, his visa. Kasaipwalova's politics at this time were strongly nationalist, inevitably perhaps in the early movement towards decolonization. Attending the University of Papua New Guinea in 1970, he launched immediately into anti-colonial campus politics. The polemic stance of Kasaipwalova's radicalism was supported by a strong histrionic and theatrical disposition. When ordered not to chew betel nut by an airport official, he loudly defended his right to do so. This incident was the basis of his short story, 'Betel Nut is Bad Magic for Aeroplanes'.

It was from this radical temperament and dislike for formal education that Kasaipwalova's creative energies grew. Like so many young writers of this period of pre-independence (the early 1970s) — a period some have seen as the flowering of Papua New Guinea writing — Kasaipwalova was deeply influenced by Ulli Beier, a professor of English at the University of Papua New Guinea. His published and unpublished writing is almost all the result of the intense creativity of one year, 1971, during which Kasaipwalova explored a wide range of literary forms — poetry, short story, drama, and the novel — and published the poetry collections *Reluctant Flame* (1971) and *Hanuabada* (1972). Several of his best-known poems, such as 'Reluctant Flame' and 'Return to My Native Land', are denunciations of colonialism and racism. Kasaipwalova returned to the Trobriand Islands in 1972 and threw himself into the work of the Kabisawali Association, a self-help movement founded by his uncle, which attempted to adapt commercial, political, and social projects to traditional patterns of co-operativeness. He wrote of the interrelatedness of such traditions in the journal *Gigibori* (1975): 'To us the *valu*, or village, goes beyond the physical number of people, the number of houses . . . It is the political, social and spiritual personality of our basic communal unit.'

Kasaipwalova's writing is most significant in its conscious employment of English variants. In his view, English, which is adapted and changed by the exigencies either of *tok pisin* ('pidgin') or mother language, becomes a more flexible and appropriate artistic medium. (See **Language**, South Pacific.) An excerpt from Kasaipwalova's unfinished novel, 'Bomana Kalabus O Sori O' ('Bomana Prison, Oh Sorry'), in the anthology *Voices of Independence* (1980), edited by Beier, is perhaps the writer's best demonstration of appropriated English.

BILL ASHCROFT

KAYIRA, LEGSON (1942–)
Malawian novelist
He was born in Nthalire, Karonga district, Nyasaland (now northern Malawi), of the Tumbuka tribe and was educated at the Presbyterian Church's Livingstonia mission school before setting out to walk 3,200 kilometres to Khartoum, Sudan, carrying a Bible and *The Pilgrim's Progress*, in search of further education and fame. Following studies at Skagit Valley Junior College, Washington, USA, and the University of Washington, USA, where he received a BA in 1965, he moved to the UK for postgraduate studies at the University of Cambridge. Kayira remains Malawi's most productive internationally published novelist, though this distinction has been achieved entirely out of the country.

Something of the sheer guts of this remarkable man is captured in the title of Kayira's first book, his autobiography *I Will Try* (1966), which **Es'kia Mphahlele** felt captured well the surface of Malawian village life. Four novels followed — *The Looming Shadow* (1968), *Jingala* (1969), *The Civil Servant* (1971), and *The Detainee* (1974). As a group these reveal amused detachment slowly yielding to social concern. For the most part they show Kayira as a man of the broad middle ground, like, for example, Canada's **Stephen Leacock**, for whom life proceeds in a pragmatic cheerful way and in whose work the comic spirit thrives.

Critic Charles Larsen rightly called Kayira's work pastoral, and it does capture very well the special feel of rural Malawi, its landscape, and its people. With *The Civil Servant*, however, the prose begins to cut deeper. Kayira's gently comic vision darkens, and *The Detainee*, which explores the oppression that his fellow writers had been attacking in verse, trades pastoralism for satire and a mood of deep disillusion. While Kayira shows a definite sensitivity for traditional belief, much in his work suggests that there are aspects of the traditional that he dismisses with both a shrug and a supercilious smile.

ADRIAN ROSCOE

Further reading: Adrian Roscoe, *Uhuru's Fire: African Literature East to South* (1977).

KEARNS, LIONEL JOHN (1937–)
Canadian poet
Born in Nelson, British Columbia, Canada, and educated in poetic theory and structural linguistics at the University of British Columbia and the

School of Oriental and African Studies, London, England, he has published eight books of poetry and two 'cine-poems'. A member of the 'Tish-group' in the 1960s, he was influenced by fellow poets **George Bowering**, **Frank Davey**, and **bp Nichol**, and his teacher, **Earle Birney**. Kearns pioneered the exploration of interactive communications technology and taught at Simon Fraser University for twenty years, resigning in 1986.

By the Light of the Silvery McLune: Media Parables, Poems, Signs, Gestures, and Other Assaults on the Interface (1969), a tribute to **Marshall McLuhan**, first showed Kearns' fascination with media. *Practicing up to be Human* (1978) and *Ignoring the Bomb: New and Selected Poems* (1982) reflect strong social concerns. 'The Birth of God', his most anthologized poem, has appeared as wall-hanging, T-shirt design, and computer poem. His interactive stack poem 'Hhmmm' is widely distributed through computer bulletin boards. *Convergences* (1984), an ambitious post-modern treatment of Captain Cook's arrival among the Mooachahts of British Columbia in 1778, interweaves points of view and time frames through the present, including the composition of the poem and its being read by future readers. Its non-linear literary form prefigured Kearns' growing interest in interactive 'hypertext' and the computer screen as a superior medium for poetry.

Never definitive, because he revises published texts in response to reactions, Kearns' work is typically clear, with a strong sense of order and marked endings. Themes of memory and mutability flow from growing up in a small town and being with his father (also a writer). Love relationships are presented playfully, as in 'Takeover', reminiscent of Thom Gunn's 'Carnal Knowledge'. Kearns' poems may be funny or philosophical or may celebrate ordinary moments of experience. Poetry, he says, 'can somehow wake us up to the fact that we are still here, alive, and free to act'.

BILL SCHERMBRUCKER

Further reading: George Bowering, *A Way With Words* (1982); Lianne Moyse, 'Dialogizing the monologue of history and lyric: Lionel Kearns' *Convergences*', *Open Letter* (Summer, 1989); Manina Jones, *Beyond TISH* (1991).

KEE THUAN CHYE

Malaysian dramatist, poet

Born in Penang, the Federation of Malaya (in what is now Malaysia), he graduated from the Universiti Sains Malaysia, Penang, in 1976 and obtained an MA (1988) in drama from the University of Essex, England. Kee is currently the literary editor of the *New Straits Times*. He has organized four annual, national short-story competitions and is a regular theatre columnist for the *New Sunday Times*, a film reviewer for the *New Straits Times*, and an arts columnist for *Business Times*. He also writes for *Asiaweek*, *Far Eastern Economic Review*, and *The Asia Magazine*.

Kee is best known for his contribution to theatre. Since the early 1970s he has written such plays as 'Oh, But I Don't Want To Go. Oh, But I Have To . . . ' (premièred 1974), 'Eyeballs, Leper and a Very Dead Spider' (premièred 1977), and 'The Big Purge' (premièred 1988). His *1984 Here and Now* (1987) was the first agitprop drama in English to be written and performed in Malaysia, where it premièred in 1985. Based loosely on George Orwell's novel *Nineteen Eighty-Four* (1949), the play appropriates the imagery of class hegemony to comment on local racial politics. 'The Big Purge', which premièred at the University of Essex, England, under Kee's direction, develops his earlier concerns with how racial and religious issues are manipulated in the perpetuation of the political status quo.

Kee's poems have been published in local newspapers, in regional journals (*Pacific Quarterly Moana*, *Southeast Asian Review of English*, and *Focus*), and in the bilingual *An Anthology of Malaysian Poetry/Antologi Puisi Pelbegai Kaum*

(1988), edited by **K. S. Maniam** and M. Shanmughalingam. He has also edited a collection of the winning entries of the 1987 *New Straits Times* — Shell Short Story Competition — *Haunting the Tiger and Other Stories* (1991).

Kee's other works include a biography of Sabah expatriate Joseph Wolf — *Old Doctors Never Fade Away* (1988) — and a collection of writings on the arts and other topical issues in the region — *Just In So Many Words* (1992).

JACQUELINE LO

KEENS-DOUGLAS, PAUL (1942–)

Trinidadian poet, storyteller

Born in Silver Mill, San Juan, Trinidad, where he now lives, he spent most of his childhood and early adult life in Grenada. He trained as a broadcaster in New York, USA, studied sociology at Sir George Williams University (now Concordia University), Montreal, Canada, and did postgraduate work in sociology at the University of the West Indies, Jamaica.

Keens-Douglas' published books include *When Moon Shine* (1975), *Tim Tim* (1976), *Tell Me Again* (1979), *Is Town Say So* (1981), *Lal Shop* (1984), and *Twice Upon A Time* (1989). Keens-Douglas, however, is primarily an oral performer, at his most effective before an audience or when recorded in performance. His work falls into three overlapping categories: celebrations of folk beliefs and customs, critical (usually humorous) commentary on Trinidadian life, and extravagant comedy. He has created a number of memorable characters, such as Tanti Merle and Dr Ah-Ah.

Exaggeration is a frequent Keens-Douglas device, as shown in his references to the woman who puts on lipstick with a broom and to the cricketer bowling so wide, 'He out a fella playin' in a nex' match. / On de followin' day!' Particularly in some of the later pieces, the performer is often laughing also at himself, at the man who 'say he bringing culture to the people. But remember, de people ain't sen' an' call him!' Keens-Douglas' timing and vocal control are impressive and often subtle. His body language is sometimes essential to his meaning. As he said in a 1989 performance: 'you must remember that West Indians talk with their bodies, with their hands. Now if you want to hush up a West Indian you don't tie he mouth, you tie he hand, and he can't talk.'

Keens-Douglas' achievement — like that of Louise Bennett, **John Agard**, **Linton Kwesi Johnson**, **Mikey Smith**, Oku Onuora, and **Jean Binta Breeze**, for example — raises questions about the need, particularly in the context of a Caribbean culture that is still predominantly oral, for criteria of assessment that give adequate weight to performance.

Keens-Douglas' recordings include *The Dialect of Paul Keens-Douglas: 'Tim Tim'* (1976), *Savannah Ghost* (1977), *One to One* (1978), *Fedon's Flute* (1980), *Is Town Say So* (1982), *Bobots* (1983), *Fete Match* (1984), *More of Me* (1987), *Carnival Is Marse* (1989), *Selected Works of Paul Keens-Douglas* (1990), and *Live A Little Laugh A Lot* (1991).

MERVYN MORRIS

KEESING, NANCY (1923–93)

Australian poet, critic, editor

Born in Sydney, Australia, she graduated from the University of Sydney. Initially a social worker at the Royal Alexandra Hospital for Children (1947–51), Keesing became widely known as a free-lance writer and active executive member of numerous literary organizations, including the English Association of New South Wales and the Australian Society of Authors. She was a founding member (1973–4) of the **Literature Board**, serving as its chair (1974–7), and was active with the National Book Council and the journal *Overland*. She was made a member of the Order of Australia in 1979.

Initially known as a poet, Keesing published *Imminent Summer* (1951), *Three Men and Sydney*

(1955), *Showgrounds Sketchbook* (1968), and *Hails and Farewells* (1977) and edited, with **Douglas Stewart**, the important anthologies *Australian Bush Ballads* (1955) and *Old Bush Songs* (1957). Keesing's other books include criticism, *Elsie Carew* (1965) and *Douglas Stewart* (1965); social commentary, *The White Chrysanthemum* (1977) and *Lily on the Dustbin: Slang of Australian Women and Families* (1982); children's novels, *By Gravel and Gum* (1963) and *The Golden Dream* (1974); and historical books, *Gold Fever* (1967), *The Kelly Gang* (1975), and *John Lang and 'The Forger's Wife'* (1979). Her two books of memoirs are *Garden Island People* (1975) and *Riding the Elephant* (1988). Her collection of Australian Jewish short stories, *Shalom* (1978), was not only a widely admired text; it was also one of the most important collections to illustrate the 'multicultural' nature of Australian society and writing. She was a tireless supporter of writers in languages other than English in Australia.

Keesing's poetry remains the key to her literary activity. She was one of a generation of poets who emerged in the 1940s under the shadow of the Second World War and who revitalized language and craft, combining lyrical exactitude with a quality of wit and playfulness notably absent in the work of many writers of that period. Keesing's later interest as an observer and collector of literary and verbal curiosities gained vividness by her warm concern for people. In 1986 she provided one of the most significant Australian literary endowments — the Nancy Keesing Studio in the Cité Internationale des Arts, Paris, to offer short-term accommodation to young Australian writers.

THOMAS SHAPCOTT

KELLY, NED (1855–80)

Australian folk hero

Born at Beveridge, Victoria, Australia, he spent most of his short life in north-eastern Victoria, the 'Kelly country' of folklore, tourist promotion, and Bertram Chandler's 1983 fantasy novel of that name. Imprisoned several times during the 1870s for assault, horse stealing, and receiving, Kelly was outlawed at the end of 1878 for killing three policemen at Stringybark Creek. His bushcraft and police incompetence helped him to evade capture until 1880 when he was taken at Glenrowan, where other gang members died. Last and most famous of Australian bushrangers, Kelly was hanged on 11 November 1880.

Unlike the gentlemen outlaws of novels to which his career gave impetus, notably *Robbery Under Arms* (1882–3), by **Rolf Boldrewood**, and **Rosa Praed**'s *Outlaw and Lawmaker* (1893), Kelly's legend was that of an underdog, Irish and convict in origin, proverbially 'game', who heroically resisted authorities that he portrayed as unjust. This is the burden of the piece of literature that survives *by* him, the outlaw manifesto known as 'the Jerilderie Letter'. Studded with invective against the 'parcel of big ugly fat-necked wombat headed big bellied magpie legged narrow hipped splay-footed sons of Irish bailiffs' — that is, the Victorian police — the letter was also a statement of grievance. Towards its conclusion, Kelly histrionically characterized himself as 'a widows [*sic*] son outlawed'.

His fame fostered by Australian sympathy with larrikin figures of resistance to order, Kelly has been the subject of ballads, folk songs, stage melodramas, six films, many novels — among them Nat Gould's *Stuck Up* (1894) and Eric Lambert's *Kelly* (1964) — poems by **David Campbell**, **Douglas Stewart**'s play *Ned Kelly* (1943; first produced on radio in 1942), as well as two series of paintings by Sidney Nolan. Historian **Manning Clark** compared him with Robin Hood, another outlaw who was a supposed benefactor of the poor, and spoke of the bushranger hero as 'a colonial Ishmael . . . He was also a colonial Cain'.

PETER PIERCE

Kempadoo, Peter (1926–)
Guyanese novelist

Born in Port Mourant, Guyana, he immigrated to England in the late 1950s. Under the pseudonym Lauchmonen he wrote two novels, *Guiana Boy* (1960) and *Old Thom's Harvest* (1965). Kempadoo returned to the Caribbean and lived in Barbados for some years before moving to Zimbabwe, where he now lives as a virtual ascetic.

Kempadoo's writing is notable for its authoritative study of rural Indo-Guyanese society. Details of speech, work, food, dress, domestic duties, family relationships, and religious observance are vividly described in wholly authentic circumstances. *Guiana Boy* is a loosely structured, episodic novel in which each chapter consists of related scenes in the life of an Indo-Guyanese boy. Events are reported from the boy's point of view, his chief observations being about his parents, friends, and his teacher, Mr Last. Guyanese dialect and expressions mingle with standard English to reinforce the local flavour of the narrative. Expressions such as 'paddy boosie' (rice husks) and 'I felt like a cent ice melting away' are vivid, original, and lend added authenticity.

Old Thom's Harvest covers similar terrain, though the plot focuses more steadily on the career of the protagonist, Old Thom, and his family. The deaths of Thom and his wife provide a tragic finale to an already sad story. *Old Thom's Harvest* is notable not only for the tragic nature of Thom's 'harvest', but also for revealing a stronger sense of diversity both among Indians themselves — for example, in their different forms of religious worship — and within the multi-ethnic society of Guyana as a whole.

Up to 1960, except for **Edgar Mittelholzer**'s *Corentyne Thunder* (1941), there were no reliable, full-length fictional studies of Indians in Guyana, although Indians form the largest ethnic group in the country. Kempadoo's novels help correct this deficiency.

FRANK M. BIRBALSINGH

Kendall, Henry (1839–82)
Australian poet

Born at Kirmington, New South Wales, Australia, to indigent parents, he was christened Thomas Henry after his grandfather, but never used his first name. His father died when he was thirteen years old, and three years later he worked as a cabin boy on a ship owned by an uncle. In 1857 Kendall worked in Sydney as a delivery boy, shop assistant, and then clerk. Despite having had little formal education, his literary bent was encouraged by his mother and by wealthier friends, and by the early 1860s he was submitting poems to both Australian and English journals. A friend, J. Sheridan Moore, the first of a number of patrons, sponsored the publication of Kendall's first book of verse, *Poems and Songs*, in 1862.

Kendall secured a civil service position as clerk in 1863 and married in 1868. The following year he resigned to try to earn a living in Melbourne by writing, in part to escape the financial impositions of his mother and siblings that had put him deeply into debt. Despite the warm support of Yorick Club members such as **Marcus Clarke** and Hugh McCrae, and the critical success of his second volume, *Leaves from Australian Forests* (1869), Kendall could not make a living and returned to Sydney in 1870 depressed, desperate, and drinking. After a miserable two years of poor health and separation from his wife and children, he was befriended by the Fagan family, timber millers at Gosford, north of Sydney, who nursed him back to health, helped him over his drinking and depression, and installed him as clerk in a branch of their timber business near Port Macquarie, where he was rejoined by his wife and children. Kendall won a prize for a poem commemorating the Sydney Exhibition in 1879, and the following year saw his third book, *Songs from the Mountains*, published and well received. (He also earned a little extra money writing for Sydney papers.)

In 1880 Kendall applied to the poet-politician Henry Parkes for a civil position and was made Inspector of Forests. The job was no sinecure, however, and in 1882 he died of tuberculosis, probably exacerbated by the rigours of his trips of inspection.

Kendall was predominantly a lyric poet of the attractive mountain country north of Sydney, but his range extends much further. He wrote biting satires — including one on a local politician, 'The Song of Ninian Melville', that was suppressed — horsy action poems ('The Song of the Cattle Hunters'), humorous bush character sketches ('Jim the Splitter'), and meditative and public pieces ('The Sydney International Exhibition'). His nature poetry is broadly celebratory, but, as critic Adrian Mitchell has argued, the essence of Kendall's lyric landscape of mountain-stream-sea is not minute description of the palpable, but rather evocation of the unseen, which is symbolized or suggested by the physical. In 'Orara' the focus is on what can only be imagined: 'A radiant brook, unknown to me / Beyond the upper turn'. On occasion this absence lies in the past, and in 'The Last of His Tribe' Kendall superbly moulds the contemporary 'soothe the dying pillow' attitude to Aborigines into a haunting and dignified lament.

Kendall was a second-generation Australian poet. He had in **Charles Harpur** an older local poet whom he championed and in whose tradition he could situate himself. Despite his use of English literary models such as Tennyson and Swinburne and his occasional inappropriate English poeticism for features of landscape, he suffered little confusion of values or allegiances and strove to rework his language to serve local ends. His extravagances of alliteration and rhythm do not connote any cultural change. Kendall believed in a natural music that should be mimicked in verse. He defended Harpur against charges of unmelodiousness on the grounds that Harpur was recording a landscape with a different melody and attacked Whitman and Longfellow for not really developing an American native music in their poetry. He was a staunch nationalist who for a while called himself Henry Clarence Kendall ('Clarence' being the local river) and rather charmingly signed himself 'Henry Kendall NAP' (National Australian Poet).

CHRIS TIFFIN

Further reading: Ian F. McLaren, *Henry Kendall: A Comprehensive Bibliography* (1987); Russell McDougall, ed., *Henry Kendall: The Muse of Australia* (1992).

KENEALLY, THOMAS (1935–)
Australian novelist
Born in Sydney, Australia, he worked for a time as a schoolteacher after abandoning study for the Roman Catholic priesthood. Since the late 1960s he has been able to live as a full-time writer, supplemented by university teaching and residencies. Keneally won the first of two Miles Franklin Awards with his third novel, *Bring Larks and Heroes* (1967), and the British Booker Prize for *Schindler's Ark* (1982), after having previously been three times short-listed. Other awards and the strong sales of his works around the world have done little to consolidate academic regard for Keneally's fiction as distinct from its popularity. He has been criticized by feminists for his depiction of women, by others for stylistic carelessness.

Nevertheless, Keneally's is the most varied and ambitious, if uneven, oeuvre of any living Australian novelist. The enduring divisions of Australian society, beneath the ostensible will to conform and depend on other countries' armies and cultures, have been a perennial subject. Keneally has portrayed sectarian and racial prejudices, notably in *The Chant of Jimmie Blacksmith* (1972), an account of murders committed at the turn of the century by an Aborigine who is oppressed for seeking advancement in European terms. Keneally's fiction traces — from the days of the first settlement of Australia as 'the world's worse end' to the present — the antagonism of Australians of Irish descent (like Keneally himself) for those originally from England. The social fissures that different national heritages and memories create is a central issue in *A Family Madness* (1985). The miscellaneous peopling of Australia and the polyphony of voices there, as well as the conflicts that these have engendered, have been a primary concern for Keneally, notably in *Women of the Inner Sea* (1992).

Persistently he has made war his subject. *The Fear* (1965, reissued as *By the Line* in 1989), his second novel, is set on the home front during the Second World War. Other novels, *Season in Purgatory* (1976) — for which one of his sources was New Zealander Lindsay Rogers' memoir of service with partisans in Yugoslavia, *Guerilla Surgeon* (1957) — and *The Cut-Rate Kingdom* (1980) are set during that war. Keneally has been especially preoccupied with 'the monstrous nature' of civil war. Although Australians have been spared such conflict, Keneally reconstructed the bitter rending of society by civil war in the USA in 1862 in *Confederates* (1979), in contemporary Eritrea in *Towards Asmara* (1989), and in *Blood Red, Sister Rose* (1974), a novel of the Hundred Years' War. The latter's heroine, Joan of Arc, appears fleetingly in other novels. Recurrent characters, themes (such as battle), and motifs (for instance, blood, lost in various ways) add to the unity of texture of what might otherwise appear as an improbably diffuse body of work. Keneally's numerous historical novels are always in vital senses war novels: the intense jeopardy to selfhood and to nationhood that war poses excites his attention. As William Coyle, Keneally has published two novels of the Second World War: *Act of Grace* (1988), which interweaves the moral dilemmas of a bomber squadron in England and Catholic clergy in Australia, and *Chief of Staff* (1991), the background of which is the war in the Pacific.

Two of his novels, *The Survivor* (1969) and *A Victim of the Aurora* (1977), are set in Antarctica. Promiscuous in his choice of settings, Keneally greedily engorges as many of the climacterics of family and national history as he can. The wide extent of his subject matter and his choice of genres seem at times nearly reckless. Besides the historical fictions are thrillers — his first novel, *The Place at Whitton* (1964); the poised social comedy of seminary life based on his youthful experiences, *Three Cheers for the Paraclete* (1968); the portentous fable, *A Dutiful Daughter* (1971); anatomies of contemporary Australia, notably *A Family Madness*, but also the delightful comic experiment with a fetus narrator, *Passenger* (1979). This is a bold, restless project that has some affinities with the work of the Irish-born novelist Brian Moore. An apter comparison is more exotic. Keneally is an antipodean Balzac, constructor of tragicomedies on a national scale. His stylistic echoes of himself mark him as a mannerist. The temper of his fiction (in common with such authors as **Marcus Clarke**, **Christina Stead**, and **Patrick White** in a central tradition of Australian literature) is melodramatic.

Keneally's novels are thronged with persecutors (from the Ethiopian Air Force to illiterate Australian farmers) and the persecuted (any of his protagonists). All inhabit a superstitiously charged, imperilled world in which their survival is random and at hazard. Sexual congress, the field of battle, and the recurrence of historical and tribal nightmares all threaten to destroy the fragile integrity of his characters. As a melodramatist, Keneally courts, and does not always avoid, risible rhetorical excess, but this is the price paid for his version of the shaping of Australia by the threats, pressures, and opportunities of remote and recent historical events. Despite the cruelties and senseless waste that his novels depict, he remains an optimistic patriot of the abiding utopian possibilities of Australia.

His fame as a novelist accessible to a heterogeneous, international audience obscures Keneally's work in other areas, although the ambition to embrace any subject and perhaps the fear of his own silence remain common features. He has written plays, television and film scripts, a book on Moses, a book for children about **Ned Kelly**, and an impressionistic account of the 'customs, secrets, ironies and landscapes' of Australia's Northern Territory, *Outback* (1983). In 1992 he published two travel books — *Now and in Time to Be*, about Ireland, and *The Place Where Souls Are Born*, on the American south-west.

As hindsight is never archly employed in his historical fiction, so Keneally has brought a sense of wonder and the illusion of new discovery to his accounts of Australia, in particular to his portrayal of the European languages first spoken there, the ideologies (such as Hearn's republicanism in *Bring Larks and Heroes*) that it has skewed, and the immemorial acts strangely re-performed by Europeans in a land new to them. These were matters freshly handled in another of Keneally's novels of Australian settlement, *The Playmaker* (1987), which was reworked by Timberlake Wertenbaker as the play *Our Country's Good* (1988). In his unlikely blending of jocularity, moral earnestness, and historical span, Keneally has been a maverick interpreter of the myths and legendary figures by which Australians might orient themselves.

PETER PIERCE

Further reading: Peter Pierce, 'The sites of war in the fiction of Thomas Keneally', *Australian Literary Studies* 12 (1986); Patrick Buckridge, 'Gossip and history in the novels of Brian Penton and Thomas Keneally', *Australian Literary Studies* 14 (1990); Peter Quartermaine, *Thomas Keneally*, Edward Arnold Fiction Series (1991).

KENNA, PETER (1930–87)

Australian dramatist

He was born in Balmain, Sydney, Australia, into a Catholic working-class family. From this background and his lifelong experience as an actor on stage and radio came the sympathetic understanding of Australian Irish Catholic working-class family life and the technical expertise that characterize his plays. His first major success was his third play, *The Slaughter of St. Teresa's Day* (1972; produced 1959), which won the General Motors-Holden national playwrights' competition. Although using more melodrama and violence (admiration for Eugene O'Neill and Sean O'Casey left its mark) than his later work, *Slaughter* demonstrates Kenna's ability to create memorable characters (underworld queen Oola Maguire is the first of a line of strong matriarchs culminating in Aggie Cassidy in *A Hard God*), to spin yarns — he calls his character-building monologues his arias — and to write convincing dialogue, catching with compassion and humour aspects of Australian urban life.

Talk to the Moon (1977; produced 1963) and *Listen Closely* (1977; produced 1972) also explore working-class family relationships. Their titles reflect Kenna's increasing interest in the related themes of unfulfilled lives and failure of communication, themes chillingly transmuted in *Trespassers Will Be Prosecuted* (1977; produced 1965) in which a young boy and a derelict trapped in a culvert play out vicious, Pinteresque games in a power struggle that exposes their social and psychological vulnerability.

In *A Hard God* (1974; produced 1973) the loss and dislocation experienced by the Cassidy family, uprooted originally from Ireland and now driven by the Depression from their land into the city, might be compared with the experience of immigrant life in England depicted by West Indian novelists **George Lamming** (*The Emigrants*, 1954) and **Samuel Selvon** (*The Lonely Londoners*, 1956, and *Moses Ascending*, 1975). In *A Hard God* Kenna experiments with juxtaposed scenes — he has pointed out in interviews that criticism of his work as outmoded realism disregards his experiments with form and the poetic intensity of much of the language — to dramatize the generation gap. Here too he begins the treatment of the theme of homosexuality he continued in *Mates* (1977; produced 1975) and the two plays he wrote later to join *A Hard God* as 'The Cassidy Album'.

REBA GOSTAND

KENYA

Kenya is bordered by Tanzania on the south, the Indian Ocean on the south-east, Somalia on the east, Ethiopia on the north, Sudan on the north-east, and Uganda on the west. It occupies an area of 582,646 square kilometres. Its population comprises twenty-five million people, made up of Kikuyu, Luyha, Luo, Kalejin, Kamba, Kisii, Meru, and Masai. Thirty-eight per cent of the population are Protestants, twenty-eight per cent Roman Catholics, twenty-six per cent traditional religions, and six per cent Muslim. Its largest city and capital is Nairobi, with a population of 1.5 million.

It is believed that Bantu tribes from West Africa entered Kenya in approximately 1000 AD, followed by the Nilotu peoples in approximately the end of the fifteenth century, when the Portugese took possession of the coast. British control of Kenya was established by the Berlin conference in 1885. The British East African Protectorate was established in 1895 and this opened the way to European settlers, especially in the area known as the White Highlands. Kenya became a British colony in 1920. African participation in Kenyan politics was permitted in 1944. The war of independence, popularly known at the time as the **Mau Mau War**, lasted from 1952 until 1960 and prompted negotiations that resulted in the granting of independence in 1963.

English was the official language immediately after independence, but in 1969 a constitutional amendment instituted the use of Swahili in the National assembly. Jomo Kenyatta became prime minister in 1963 and president of the republic in 1964. After Kenyatta's death in 1978, Daniel Arap Moi became president and was re-elected in 1983 and 1988.

Agriculture is central to Kenya's economy, contributing one third of the nation's gross domestic product, two-fifths of national exports, and a quarter of all wage employment. Much of the country is not suitable for cultivation, restricting farming to the highlands, western plateaux, and part of the coast. The main cash crops are coffee, tea, sisal, wattle, and sugar. Since independence, the agricultural economy has been marked by the move towards African ownership of the land and the development of farm co-operatives. Kenya's mining industry, though small, has potential for expansion.

In 1974 Swahili replaced English as the official language of Kenya. President Kenyatta at that time stated that 'the basis of any independent government is a national language, and we can no longer continue aping our former colonizers . . . Those who feel they cannot do without English can as well pack up and go.' However, English remains the language of most senior administrators, of the military, and of higher education and the professional classes. The mixing of Swahili, English, and indigenous languages is now common. Kenyan English, in terms of its linguistic features, is considered part of East African English, but the authenticity and homogeneity of both the national and the regional variety are controversial matters. The first newspaper in Kenya, the *African Standard*, was established in 1902 and is now known as the *Standard*. Other English-language publications are the *Daily Nation*, established in 1960, and the *Weekly Review*. The Voice of Kenya radio and Kenyan Television broadcast in English as well as Swahili.

Kenya's best-known writer, in English, Kikuyu, and Swahili, is **Ngugi wa Thiong'o**.

G. D. KILLAM

Further reading: N. Miller, *Kenya* (1984).

KHAN, ISMITH (1925–)
Trinidadian novelist
Born in Port of Spain, Trinidad, to Faiez and Zinab Khan, he is a descendant of the Pathans of the Indian subcontinent through both parents and of indentured immigrants on his mother's side. He grew up under the influence of the ardent nationalism and anti-colonialism of his grandfather, Kale Khan, a proud Pathan warrior. A young Muslim, Ismith Khan attended an elementary Anglican Church school and later the then-élitist Queen's Royal College, early introductions to the realities of social and economic exclusion. Working later as a reporter on the *Trinidad Guardian* reinforced this sensibility. All these shaping experiences and his urban upbringing near the island's central political theatre meet in Khan's work, where, like **Sam Selvon**, he becomes a 'creole' novelist (as distinct from an Indian novelist), after a first novel examining the destiny of Indian migrants and their offspring.

Khan holds a BA in sociology from the New School for Social Research in New York, USA, and an MA in creative writing from Johns Hopkins University, USA, his thesis becoming the kernel of his third novel. He has since lived in the USA, teaching creative writing and literature at various institutions, and since 1986 as an adjunct professor at Brooklyn's Medgar Evers College.

Khan's first novel, *The Jumbie Bird* (1961), uses family history as a point of departure to examine the Trinidad East Indian predicament. Trinidad's only novel with extended treatment of this subject, *The Jumbie Bird* draws on history to explore the ambivalences of British officialdom and the consequent confusion among the migrant population. Khan presents, through three generations, syndromes of exploitation, bewilderment, and misery, of wavering transition, and of problematic but possible integration; this last, however, is not as expansively treated as in **V. S. Naipaul**'s *A House for Mr. Biswas*. The Indian nationalism the historical Kale Khan sought to bequeath to his grandson is implicitly criticized in this novel and is already being transmuted into a local nationalism. The resultant anti-colonial discourse becomes pervasive in the second novel, *The Obeah Man* (1964), where, as in *The Crucifixion* (undated, 1987?) the characters are presented not in terms of their ethnicity but as end-products, living reduced lives characterized by an emptiness endemic to colonialism. In both novels the characters' attempts to transcend this emptiness are explored empathetically, thus imparting to them a certain nobility negating the popular stigma attaching to the likes of an obeah man, an upstart preacher, a prostitute, and a parasitic cripple. The alternation of standard and vernacular registers for the narrative of *The Crucifixion* constitutes a further anti-colonial signification.

ARTHUR D. DRAYTON

Further reading: Arthur Drayton, 'Ismith Khan', in Daryl Cumber Dance (ed.), *Fifty Caribbean Writers: a Bio-bibliographical Critical Sourcebook* (1986).

KHAN, RAZIA (1935–)
Bangladeshi poet
She was born in Dhaka, India (now in Bangladesh), and educated in East Pakistan and abroad. She has followed an academic career at Dhaka University, Bangladesh, where she is a professor of English. Khan has established in Bangladesh a firm reputation as a poet with her two collections of poetry, *Argus under Anaesthesia* (1976) and *Cruel April* (1977). Khan is generally considered to be one of the country's best writers.

Khan's poems are marked with the apt use of familiar images evoked in an educated plain style, often in contrast to the strong emotional content of her subject-matter. The loss of childhood's joys is a recurrent theme, sometimes celebrated in 'the shape of stone-tears' ('The Grave of Time'). Poems such as 'This Land of Golden Grass' and 'My

Journey' describe the irretrievable beauty and safety of early youth that adolescence and further growth will destroy. 'The House Revisited' is an important poem in this context, as if serving as a bridge between youth and adulthood, when so much (in this case the father's house and a youthful affair) should be sacrificed in order to grow up. Love, as such, is also a denial of happiness and fulfilment, both within and without marriage; this point is made rather explicitly in 'The Old Man and the Girl'. 'Cruel April', with its Eliotesque overtones, presents two unfulfilled lovers who have lived 'elsewhere' and decide to trade wishes for something other than desired thus far — 'the right prayer'.

Khan's poetry often describes city life and the habits and tantrums of the urban rich, particularly of westernized women — 'Time to Grow Young', 'Death of Phoenix', and 'Euphony of Eugenics', for example. 'The School Wall' and 'The Fire Flower' show the contrasts as well as the possibilities of a convergence, however transient, between the socially separate worlds of the rich and the poor, although in 'The Fire Flower' this possibility is ruled out.

In the set of poems named after Mount Carmel, a spiritual quest and the struggle to realize the personal self are greatly in evidence, yet the refusal to be passively traditional or empty and modern actually leads to a lack of choice. In this sequence, feelings are suppressed so that a rebirth is envisioned by a different path, perhaps one of religion. Khan conveys the experience in direct though quiet tones similar to those of India's **Eunice de Souza**, but the limited scope of Khan's poetic form and limiting social textures of her language disallow any breakthrough towards the newness sought. Jamaican **Velma Pollard**'s poems in *Crown Point and Other Poems* (1988) and *Considering Woman* (1989) show that having the verbal and rhythmic resources of Standard and Jamaican English and a grip on the life of the community can lead to an art balanced between the poet's own history and its fictive shaping — indeed, a communal myth. Khan's poems, in Standard English, nevertheless speak to us effectively and seek out the consolations of form and society within.

ALAMGIR HASHMI

KIBERA, LEONARD N. (1942–83)
Kenyan novelist, short-story writer
He was born at Kabete, near Nairobi, Kenya, and educated at Kangarû High School, Embu, Kenya, at the University of Nairobi, where he obtained a BA in English. Kibera was at Stanford University, USA, and at the University of California (Berkeley), USA, before teaching full-time at the University of Zambia (1972–5) and at Kenyatta University, from 1976 until the year of his death.

Kibera is probably best known for his novel *Voices in the Dark* (1970) and for the short-story collection, *Potent Ash* (1968), co-authored with his brother **Samuel Kahiga**. His play 'Potent Ash' was aired by the British Broadcasting Corporation; his articles have appeared in several East African literary journals, including *Zuka*, *Busara*, *Transition*, and *African Literature Today*. Kibera's work compares well, thematically and ideologically, to that of his contemporary and close associate, **Ngugi wa Thiong'o**.

The **Mau Mau War** of national liberation (and its continuing effects, especially on the psyches of the Kenyan masses) informs most of the short stories in *Potent Ash*. It is also the predominant theme in *Voices in the Dark*, whose dense metaphorical language explores and deplores social and political conditions in post-independence Kenya, in particular the horrible betrayal of peasant and working-class aspirations. 'The Spider's Web' is Kibera's most anthologized short story; it resonates constantly in *Voices in the Dark* as Kibera caustically depicts the emergence and temporary triumph of a national middle-class and its role in the devastation of the national economy through its collaboration with foreign corporate interests.

Both 'The Spider's Web' and *Voices in the Dark* emphatically assert the spuriousness of Kenya's independence, declaring that the 'new' black masters/mistresses are infinitely worse than the white colonial ones. *Voices in the Dark* subtly hints at the beginnings of a police state and the insidious incorporation of the church and its agents into the coercive machinery of the state. The ubiquitous drought symbolizes the lack of social justice, especially as this applies to the victims of both colonial and post-independence state violence in its various forms.

Voices in the Dark also questions the role of the 'dissident' artist in the rehumanization of the post-independence wasteland, while posing the question of interpersonal relationships, especially those between the sexes. With its highly successful 'experimental' style, it remains one of East Africa's most profound novels.

GĨTAHI GĨTĨTĨ

KIDMAN, FIONA (1940–)

New Zealand novelist, short-story writer, poet

Born in the rural region of Northland, New Zealand, she spent her early life there, attending country schools and Waipu District High School. She worked as a librarian, a media writer, and critic before becoming a full-time writer. Kidman has published the poetry collections *Honey and Bitters* (1975), *On the Tightrope* (1978), and *Going to the Chathams: Poems 1977–1984* (1985) and a radio play (*Search for Sister Blue*, 1975), but is best known for her short stories and novels. Kidman has twice received the New Zealand Scholarship in Letters, and in 1988 won the New Zealand Book Award for fiction for her novel *The Book of Secrets* (1987).

In the novel *A Breed of Women* (1979), set in 1950s Northland, Harriet rebels against repressive respectability. In each of the novels *Mandarin Summer* (1981), *Paddy's Puzzle* (1983, also published as *In the Clear Light*, 1985), and *The Book of Secrets* is a female protagonist struggling to assert independence against repressive patriarchal, puritanical, or small-town values; each novel employs the motif of the house, both as image of containment and definition and as a symbol of the difference within (the self). In *Mandarin Summer* and *Paddy's Puzzle* the buildings are also inhabited by an array of socially marginal characters who represent 'difference' in relation to the social norms of the Depression and the postwar era. Kidman's protagonists must often negotiate the terms of individual and social identity and difference, including their status within patriarchal society. In this, Kidman's writing is reminiscent of the Manawaka novels of Canadian **Margaret Laurence**.

Kidman's short-story collections, *Mrs Dixon and Friend* (1982) and *Unsuitable Friends* (1988), share some of the preoccupations of her novels. Family relationships, particularly among women, are another site of Kidman's exploration of identity and difference. Such relationships tend to be difficult, as for example, in *Paddy's Puzzle*, in which Clara Bentley is contrasted with her 'respectable' sister. In *The Book of Secrets*, generational differences alienate a mother from her conventional daughter, who, in turn, rejects her own daughter; the granddaughter identifies with her grandmother.

The novel *True Stars* (1990) explores echoes between national and family relationships, the tensions of issues of race, class, and gender, and specific historical events such as the Springbok rugby tour and the subsequent protests.

CHRIS PRENTICE

Further reading: Elizabeth Rosner, 'Silencing the ventriloquist: *The Book of Secrets*', *World Literature Written in English* 1 (1990).

KIMENYE, BARBARA (1939–)
Ugandan short-story writer
Well known as a writer of children's books — for example, her Moses series, from *Moses* (1966) to *The Gemstone Affair* (1978) — Kimenye made her name with two collections of short stories that were among the first works of fiction from East Africa: *Kalasanda* (1965) and *Kalasanda Revisited* (1966). These two works are striking, particularly with the passage of time, as radically different from the mood and format of the early publications in that region. Using the same set of characters, the two collections create a timeless Buganda village, given to gossip and to the gentle censuring of local figures, traders, and small officials whose mild eccentricities are brought back to order at the end of each story. The ladies of the Mother's Union achieve a modest degree of modernization, without encroaching on the power of the church, the local chiefs, or the representatives of the Kabaka. Kimenye's style is smooth, her humorous tone adapted to a slightly patronizing stance.

This atmosphere of mild comedy is rare in African fiction. It is based on an amused observation of the details of women's lives, as found in women's magazines, combined with a lack of verisimilitude for wider issues: like the work of Karen Blixen, the format of Kimenye's short stories resembles at times European folk tales and conveys a fundamentally conservative vision in praise of a post-colonial stability that was not to be. *Kalasanda* and *Kalasanda Revisited* deserve to be read as testimonials to a certain type of middle-class Anglicized aesthetics of the 1960s and for some well-handled humorous characters.

J. BARDOLPH

KINCAID, JAMAICA (1949–)
Antiguan novelist, short-story writer
She was born Elaine Potter Richardson in St John's, Antigua, the Caribbean. In 1966 she went to the USA and has been a staff writer with the *New Yorker* since 1976.

Like most Caribbean writers in English, Kincaid is drawn to the shorter forms of fiction. Her first publication is a collection of poetic sketches — *At the Bottom of the River* (1983). It evokes growing up and the conditioning effects of small-island life upon a girl whose head is filled to the point of hallucination with sights and sounds and memories and, most of all, with the shaping and controlling voices of community in chorus with that of a dominating mother. The high literariness, to the eye, of *At the Bottom of the River* is matched and balanced by the author's acute sense of the rhythms of the Caribbean speaking voice, to such revolutionary effect that one might well speak of 'literary orality', yet another flowering of Caribbean language after the decisive experiments by **Sam Selvon** in *The Lonely Londoners* (1956).

Kincaid comes, almost episodically, to the novel form in the eight chapters of *Annie John* (1985), fleshing out with people (fishermen, carpenters, and schoolteachers), places (cemetery, school, church, undertaker's establishment, and jetty), and natural features (sea, sky, light, heat, colour) the social and physical round and the limitations upon flesh and spirit of island life as experienced by a young girl. Kincaid makes fantastically true and convincing the paradox of an environment that gives an inner sustainment that can never be withdrawn and then becomes tyrannous and oppressive to those it so surely nourished. Annie John is presented, with all the enjoyment and typicality that comes from selective memory, as a girl among girls at school. At the same time, we are made to feel the pain and the passions of a gifted and unusual child. This most affecting account of girlhood and of a girl's growing in a particular place is complex, involving the acceptance and at least partial understanding of change, separation, sexuality, and death as necessary elements of the mortal state. It is this context that makes the treatment of the mother-daughter relationship in *Annie John* so rich and so justly celebrated, even by those not intimate with the Caribbean or with the Caribbean sensibility embodied in the main character. *Annie John* is an example of how Caribbean women writers turn to the form of fictional autobiography and to fictions of childhood to explore the repression of the female and to articulate the silent half of the population. (See **Feminism**, The Caribbean.)

A Small Place (1988), a collection of short stories, is a demonstration of the freedom with which women can see the condition of the islands precisely because they are not part of the system of power and privilege that invests in the status quo. Here Kincaid explores the colonial mentality and its exploitation after 'Emancipation' and 'Independence' by corrupt politicians who have conspired with foreign investors, international crooks, drug dealers, and international financial agencies to re-peripheralize (after slavery and colonialism) the economy and culture of Antigua and the other islands of the Caribbean.

The narrator of *Lucy* (1990) has gone to the USA 'mourning' the end of a love affair, 'perhaps the only true love in my whole life I would every know'. Lucy's experiences during one year in the household of Lewis and Mariah, who hire her to care for their children, are counterpointed by memories of the mother she hates (Mrs Judas) and of the island she has left for good. The work carries those themes related to race, gender, class, and colonialism beyond the treatment given them in *Annie John*. The theme of the relationship between mother and daughter is complicated by the parallel between the mother on the island and Mariah and by the implications of the role of Mariah as imperial foster mother. *Lucy* is a novel about female sexuality, about the oppressiveness of family (experienced by a female with three male siblings), and about the hollowness of family (observed by Lucy in her new home). It is a tale of two places and of the placelessness of the narrator, who is full of nostalgia for a paradise she was never considered eligible to dream of.

In the final (or beginning) chapter, the force of memory, anger and despair, and the integrity of the heroine begin to take positive shape:

> I understood I was inventing myself, and that I was doing this more in the way of a painter than in the way of a scientist. I could not count on precision or calculation; I could only count on intuition. I did not have anything exactly in mind but when the picture was complete I would know.

KENNETH RAMCHAND

Further reading: Selwyn Cudjoe, 'Jamaica Kincaid and the modernist project: an interview', in Selwyn Cudjoe (ed.) *Caribbean Women Writers: Essays from the First International Conference* (1990); Allan Vorda, 'An interview with Jamaica Kincaid', *Mississippi Review* 1-2 (1991); Kay Bonett: 'An interview with Jamaica Kincaid', *The Missouri Review* 2 (1992).

KING, HUGH (1951–)

Jamaican dramatist

Born in the small town of Old Harbour, St Catherine, Jamaica, he was educated in Jamaica, the USA, and England, and currently spends most of his time between Jamaica and England writing, producing, directing, and performing his own plays. Ten of these were written between 1977 and 1990 and they have been performed in Jamaica, the USA, Canada, England, and the Cayman Islands. King's first play, 'The Resurrection of Jonathan Digby', dealing with the effects on a family of paternal delinquency, premièred in Jamaica in 1977. 'Body Moves' (premièred 1984), about the romance of a young Rastafarian boxer and the daughter of a bigoted boxing-gym owner, was adapted to film. 'Nightwork' (premièred 1978), about a good-hearted prostitute, is King's most successful play to date.

King has stated that he does not 'embark on a work where there is no spirituality and the hope of moral enlightment for mankind'. His plays are an unusual mix of a high moral tone and vulgarity, covering a wide range of popular themes. Critic Keith Noel has written: 'King has his ear to the ground and is always able to select topics of genuine interest to the theatre-going public. He has treated prostitution, social prejudice, mental illness, child abuse, incest, the criminal underworld, religion, the generation conflict, the national guard, drug abuse and other social and psychological issues of concern to the nation.' 'Ramrod' (premièred 1987), for example, explores the marijuana trade and its effects on the friendship of two men. King's weaker work — about half of his first ten plays — is melodramatic and poorly plotted; and even his more accomplished scripts have a strong soap opera quality, which, of course, does not prevent them from being popular. Humorous situations and witty dialogue have been consistent components of his plays.

MICHAEL RECKORD

KING, MICHAEL (1945–)
New Zealand historian
Born in Wellington, New Zealand, he attended Victoria University of Wellington. King subsequently worked as a journalist in the Waikato and developed an interest in Maori society and history, an interest expressed in newspaper and magazine articles, television programs, and several books. The work that established him as a major writer is *Te Puea* (1977) — a biography of the Tainui leader Te Puea, whose struggles to revivify a physically impoverished people (their land had been confiscated by Pakeha in the 1860s) encompass most of the first half of the twentieth century. King's study was authorized by Tainui elders and his knowledge of Maori language and protocols enabled him to deploy with previously unparalleled sensitivity not only documentary evidence, but also oral testimony.

Like *Te Puea*, King's later studies — *Whina: A Biography of Whina Cooper* (1983), an account of the prominent and controversial Maori woman's work in urban welfare and protest movements, and *Maori: A Photographic and Social History* (1983) — were applauded by Pakeha and Maori, but some Maori were by then openly critical of what they regarded as Pakeha exploitation of Maori culture. In his memoir, *Being Pakeha: An Encounter with New Zealand and the Maori Renaissance* (1985), King traces the development of his own cultural consciousness and his career as a writer, defending his procedures as a cross-cultural communicator and reporting his decision to stop writing on Maori subjects. *Moriori: A People Rediscovered* (1989), a history of the people of the outlying Chatham Islands, was written at the instigation of Moriori descendants.

King's other explorations of New Zealand history and culture include: two pictorial histories — *New Zealanders at War* (1981) and *After the War: New Zealand Since 1945* (1988); a finely-rendered example of investigative journalism that recounts the sinking of an anti-nuclear ship by French agents — *Death of the Rainbow Warrior* (1986); and *The Collector: A Biography of Andreas Reischek* (1981). *The Collector* is an account of how, in the 1880s, the Austrian naturalist Reischek stole two corpses from a Maori burial site and spirited them away to a European museum, a theft that continues to have cultural reverberations a century later.

PETER GIBBONS

KINGSLEY, HENRY (1830–76)
Australian novelist
Born in Northamptonshire, England, brother of the novelist Charles Kingsley (1819–75), he studied at

Oxford but left without a degree, immigrating to Australia in 1853. After some time in the gold-fields of Victoria and a short spell as a police trooper, he returned to England in 1858. *The Recollections of Geoffry Hamlyn* (1859) and *The Hillyars and the Burtons* (1865) — Kingsley's most significant contribution to Australian fiction — and *Ravenshoe* (1862), which embraces the Crimean War, are the most successful of his nineteen prose works, which show a progressive decline after his 'Australian' novels of 1859 and 1865.

A precursor of Australian fiction, Kingsley's prose explores imaginatively, but not romantically, the fortunes of English families whose members emigrate to live 'the best stories of station life in the golden age of squatterdom'. He can tell of the frontier life of the British empire without sentimentality, contemplative of land, bird life, flora, and bushland silence. His is a prose of personal growth and sympathetic observation rather than of heroic action, and his characters have family and class culture — German, clerical, gypsy, or convict — his work thus filling the gap in Australian literary history between lurid convict tales and the frontier novels of a **Rolf Boldrewood**. Kingsley struggled to create fiction on the basis of the facts, seeing clearly, reporting accurately, and passing far beyond the immigrant's vade-mecum. His achievement easily surpasses that of New Zealand's W. M. Baines or Alexander Bathgate, although all strive to catch their colony's development, appeal, and manners.

Although limited, both *The Recollections of Geoffry Hamlyn* and *The Hillyars and the Burtons* are sensitive records of experience, satiric of political organization, and imaginatively aware that Australia would call forth 'great sacrifice of human life' in its taming. More perceptive criticism rejects the canard of 'clever journalism', preferring rather to stress Kingsley's eye for character, his peculiar talent for lively story, his warm humanity, and power to hold his audience. His deep compassion towards a colonial society remains memorable, not least for its being the obverse of his brother Charles' propensity to uncharitable dogmatisms.

J. S. RYAN

Further reading: J. S. D. Mellick, *The Passing Guest: A Life of Henry Kinglsey* (1983).

KINSELLA, W. P. (1935–)

Canadian novelist, short-story writer

Born in Edmonton, Canada, he was raised on a remote Alberta homestead for ten years before moving back to Edmonton with his parents. As a young boy Kinsella developed a lifelong fascination with baseball. His other chief fictional subject is Native Canadians, with whom, he maintains, he has had relatively little contact.

In 1967 Kinsella moved to Victoria, British Columbia, where after stints at odd jobs, including taxi driving, he enrolled in the University of Victoria (BA, 1974). He studied under his mentor, **W. D. Valgardson**, who urged him to do post-graduate work in the USA at the University of Iowa's Writers' Workshop (master of fine arts degree, 1978). When his first collection of Silas Ermineskin stories, *Dance Me Outside* (1977), appeared, most readers assumed Kinsella was a Native Canadian. Other popular short-story collections about Canada's First Nations people are *Scars* (1978), *Born Indian* (1981), *The Moccasin Telegraph* (1983), and *The Fencepost Chronicles* (1986), which received Canada's Stephen Leacock Medal for Humour.

Kinsella's first novel and perhaps his most famous work, *Shoeless Joe* (1982), was expanded from a short story of the same name. Set in Iowa, the novel received the Houghton Mifflin Literary Fellowship Award and was voted novel of the year by the Canadian Authors' Association. In 1989 *Shoeless Joe* was adapted to film as *Field of Dreams.* Although Kinsella claims he has never played organized baseball, he continues to write successful fiction related to the game: *The Thrill of the Grass* (1984) and *The Iowa Baseball Confederacy* (1986).

Kinsella has claimed that a collection of thirteen stories unrelated to baseball or Indians, *Red Wolf, Red Wolf* (1987), is one of his best books. *The Alligator Report* (1985) is a collection of twenty-six stories, many pertaining to Vancouver. *Box Socials* (1991) is a novel about life in a non-Indian northern Alberta backwater in the 1940s.

Kinsella lives in White Rock, British Columbia, with his wife, writer Ann Knight, with whom he has published a collection of poetry, *The Rainbow Warehouse* (1989).

ALAN TWIGG

KIRBY, WILLIAM (1817–1906)
Canadian novelist, poet
Born in Kingston-upon-Hull, England, the son of a tanner, he moved with his family to the USA in 1832 and to Upper Canada in 1839, settling finally in Niagara-on-the-Lake, where he carried on his trade as a tanner. As Kirby rose among the English establishment, he became editor of the *Niagara Mail*, a collector of customs, and in 1882 a member of the Royal Society of Canada.

It is by virtue of his novel *The Golden Dog* (1877) — a historical romance set in Quebec in 1748 — that Kirby's place in the annals of early Canadian literature is assured. However, he also wrote much politically inspired narrative poetry, such as *The U. E.: A Tale of Upper Canada* (1859), an epic poem in which Loyalist values are celebrated, exaggerated, and manipulated into the writing of an establishment view of Canadian history — a patriotic and English tribal view. This work and others, such as *Canadian Idylls* (1894) and *Annals of Niagara* (1846), enact a form of literary Canadian nationalism that is suspicious of Americans, moderately tolerant of French Canadians, and is grounded in a form of British imperialism that later, progressively more sensitive Canadian nationalists would find constricted in its glance and more imperial than culturally broad-minded. The aesthetic quality of Kirby's poetry is low and his ideological vision is more remarkable for its stimulative role in the emergence of early Canadian nationalism than for its thoroughness as accurate Canadian history.

The Golden Dog is clearly Kirby's best work, and while, like many early works of other colonies, it suffers from a tendency to rely on 'Old World' models for the recipe of its historical romance, it is nevertheless a well-written, often crisp, and unique novel; more recent critics have praised it for such strengths as its dignified prose and carefully crafted sense of pace and suspense. Like Kirby's narrative poetry, *The Golden Dog* is more melodrama, romance, simplified and nostalgic morality, and establishment ideology than credible history or highly explorative art. Kirby's work remains more interesting as historical artefact than complex fiction.

TERRY WHALEN

Further reading: Lorne Pierce, *William Kirby: Portrait of a Tory Loyalist* (1929).

KISSOON, FREDDIE (1930–)
Trinidadian dramatist
Born in St James, Trinidad, he was an actor during the 1950s, when a distinct Caribbean drama was developing. Kissoon travelled to London, England, on a British Council scholarship and in 1962–3 studied theatre there. Returning to Trinidad, he founded the Strolling Players in 1957, which, still under his leadership in the 1990s, is one of the oldest theatre companies in Trinidad and Tobago.

Kissoon has written some fifty-eight plays for stage, radio, and television. These are mostly humorous sketches of folk life, some based on topical issues ('Common Entrance', on the primary school examination, and 'Crash Workers', about a state project for casual labourers, for example), while others are well-structured comedies ('Mamaguy', 'Calabash Alley', and 'Zingay'). Kissoon's longer dramatic works include 'God and Uriah Butler' (premièred 1967), on the 1937 labour riots in Trinidad, the passion play 'We Crucify Him', and his serialization for radio of his popular 'Calabash Alley', a comedy of urban folk life.

With an actor's ear for the spoken word, Kissoon celebrates the local 'dialect' in his plays. His situations may be naturalistic or farcical, but, like Baba Sala, the 'Father of Humour' of Nigerian folk opera, Kissoon's theatre, rudimentary and, by policy, always affordable, appeals to a popular audience. His plays have broadened the popularity of what has been traditionally seen in Trinidad as an élitist pastime and must be seen as a response to the starchy, middle-class theatre groups of the 1950s. However, audiences have grown in sophistication since Kissoon started working in drama and many of his plays have not gone beyond giving their audiences the opportunity to laugh at themselves, presenting self-parodies without, at times, the instruction of satire.

Kissoon was awarded the Humming Bird Medal in 1987 for his contribution to Trinidadian drama and theatre.

RAWLE GIBBONS

KIYOOKA, ROY KENJIRO (1926–)

Canadian poet, artist

Born in Moose Jaw, Saskatchewan, Canada, widely travelled in Canada, Mexico, and Japan, but centred in Vancouver since the 1960s, he is an iconoclastic and experimental artist (painting, photography, and writing, often mixed). He traces his crossing of the borders of genre to Group of Seven painter J. E. H. MacDonald: 'in early 50s im reading his West by East and think yeah — why not why not "paint" and "write" poems — ; had read my Whitman — wanted to praise the open road.' Strongly postmodern in the self-referential nature of their texts, Kiyooka's published journals and letters combine photography with writing and display a childlike curiosity and wonder, undimmed through his career, typical of 1960s romanticism.

Retiring in 1991 after two decades as professor of fine arts at the University of British Columbia, Kiyooka published many nakedly self-revelatory texts. Like Joyce Cary's *The Horse's Mouth* (1944), his *Nevertheless These Eyes* (1967) employs the persona of the erotic English painter Stanley Spencer to expose tensions in the artist's life. *The Fontainebleau Dream Machine* (1977) is an ambitious deconstruction of some conventions of western art. In his richest and most interesting book, *Transcanada Letters* (1975), Kiyooka documents crossing the nation on a voyage of self-discovery. In the chapbook *Wheels: A Father and Son Trip Through Honshu's Backcountry w/Photographs* (1987) and in *Pacific Windows* (1990), he focuses on his identity as a Canadian of Japanese origin, and on relationships between generations. *Pear Tree Pomes* (1987) is a moving lament for a past relationship.

Kiyooka's influence on other writers and artists has been catalytic, without creating a following. Luke Rombout, prefacing a twenty-five-year retrospective at the Vancouver Art Gallery, records how 'almost each time . . . a comment [acknowledging Kiyooka's influence] was made, in Regina, in Halifax, in Montreal, in Toronto — Kiyooka had just left.' His dynamic writing circle includes **George Bowering**, Gladys Hindmarch, Gerry Gilbert, Carole Itter, **Fred Wah**, and **Daphne Marlatt**; yet he remains the quintessential individualist of the Vancouver literary scene.

A selected bibliography appears in the *Capilano Review*, second series, 2 (1990).

BILL SCHERMBRUCKER

KLEIN, A. M. (1909–72)

Canadian poet, novelist

Born Abraham Moses Klein in Ratno, the Ukraine, he moved with his parents to Montreal, Canada, in

1910. Educated in Protestant and Jewish schools, Klein pursued his academic studies at McGill University, Montreal, and the Université de Montréal. Admitted to the bar in 1933, he earned his livelihood as a lawyer while pursuing a literary career as poet and writer. From 1938 to 1955 Klein edited *The Canadian Jewish Chronicle*, to which he contributed numerous editorials, essays, book reviews, poems, and stories. After a mental breakdown in the mid-1950s, Klein ceased writing and ultimately withdrew from public life.

Although he failed to gain wide critical recognition in his lifetime, Klein's distinctive and uninhibited voice recorded a remarkable chapter in the history of Canadian letters. While Klein's writing insists upon Jewish thematics, its wide-ranging references demonstrate the extent of his cultural affinity with his adoptive country. Much of Klein's work focuses on the nature of Canadian Jewish experience; moreover, his poetics reflects the ambivalent attitudes of Canadian literature towards its European roots. An erudite Joycean scholar raised on British literature, Klein none the less shows an increasing tendency to question the world view promoted by the 'major culture'. For instance, his mock-epic *The Hitleriad* (1944), the first Canadian literary response to Nazi terror, opens with a refutation of Milton's notion of Providence.

Klein's first volumes of poetry, *Hath Not a Jew* (1940) and *Poems* (1944), illustrate his intention to combine seemingly incompatible cultural traditions. Both volumes invoke the rituals and folklore of the east European *shtetl*, which the poet assimilated through his immigrant parents. Some of the poems reflect Klein's Zionist sympathies and his concern about the worsening situation of Jews in Europe. Stylistically, the poems reflect the strong influence of Elizabethan poetry, English Romanticism, and Imagism. One of Klein's most striking cross-cultural amalgams emerges in the poem 'Autobiographical': while relating to Wordsworth's postulation of 'emotion recollected in tranquillity', the poem is a reminiscence of childhood in which the city of Montreal assumes the mythical aura of Jerusalem.

The Rocking Chair and Other Poems (1948), for which he received a Governor General's Award, is considered Klein's best poetic achievement. The poems are a sensitive treatment of French-Canadian tradition and an astute observation of the quality of life in Quebec. Rooted in an authentic Canadian locale, the collection reaches beyond literary trends embedded in colonial attitudes, aiming at a global vision of the world's moral and cultural disintegration. It presents a metaphoric depiction of a society in which excessive materialism and ruthless exploitation breed alienation and despair. The concluding 'Portrait of the Poet as Landscape', which subverts Miltonic and Joycean world pictures, offers a striking image of the poet in a world that has banned poetry.

The Second Scroll (1951), Klein's only novel and his ideological signature, envisions a humanistic redemption that eliminates the notion of colonial parochialism altogether. The novel is a response to the Holocaust in which the rebirth of the state of Israel is both a re-enactment of the story of Exodus and the actualization of the biblical eschatological prophecy. The link with Canada, however, is emphatically maintained through the Canadian protagonist-narrator. His quest for his European uncle, a Holocaust survivor, not only re-establishes the tragically severed links of Jewish culture and tradition, but presents the Canadian Jew, the product of Canadian humanistic ideology, as instrumental in the restoration of humanistic ethics.

Klein's particular contribution to Canadian letters lies in his dynamic world view, in which Canadian Jewish experience is a source of inspiration that engenders visions of universal dimensions. Klein inspired a generation of Canadian Jewish writers and poets, such as **Henry Kreisel**, **Irving Layton**, and **Miriam Waddington**. Affectionately remembered in the poetry of **Eli Mandel**,

Leonard Cohen, **Seymour Mayne**, and others, Klein is considered the father of Canadian Jewish literature. The University of Toronto Press began publishing his collected works in 1982.

RACHEL FELDHAY BRENNER

Further reading: Usher Caplan, *Like One That Dreamed: A Portrait of A. M. Klein* (1982); Rachel Feldhay Brenner, *A. M. Klein, the Father of Canadian Jewish Literature* (1990).

KNISTER, RAYMOND (1899–1932)

Canadian novelist, short-story writer, poet

Born and raised in farming country immediately north of Lake Erie, Ontario, Canada, Knister wrote extensively before being appointed associate editor of the Iowa City, USA, literary magazine *The Midland* in 1923. During eight months with *The Midland* he finished a first regional novel examining the lives of the older children in a tobacco-growing family in south-western Ontario just after the First World War. He also composed a second regional novel focusing on a young male farmer and a young female writer in southwestern Ontario in the early 1920s. Both novels remain unpublished. After spending four months in Chicago, USA, Knister returned to Canada in 1924 and continued to contribute poems, stories, and criticism to international and Canadian periodicals.

Knister edited *Canadian Short Stories* (1928), the first stock-taking of its kind. The anthology contains a valuable introduction by Knister, seventeen stories by writers such as **Duncan Campbell Scott**, to whom the volume was dedicated, as well as a useful appendix of Canadian stories published during the preceding thirty-five years. Knister's third attempt at a regional novel, *White Narcissus* (1929), a poetic narrative depicting a young male writer who returns to the south-western Ontario farming community of his childhood and courts a woman oppressed by her parents' deadly relationship, earned favourable notices following publication in London, Toronto, and New York. *My Star Predominant* (1934), a densely textured fourth novel portraying the final years of John Keats, was published in London and Toronto two years after Knister's death by drowning.

Recognition for Knister has come slowly but steadily with the posthumous publication of selections of his poems, short fiction, and essays under the editorship of **Dorothy Livesay**, Michael Gnarowski, David Arnason, Peter Stevens, and Joy Kuropatwa. *White Narcissus* has been reprinted twice, in 1962 and 1990 (the 1990 edition with a memoir-afterword by **Morley Callaghan**). A small but significant body of scholarship, criticism, and biography has appeared, including two monographs by Kuropatwa, one on Knister's poetry and one on Knister's fiction, published in 1987 and 1991, respectively, under the same title, *Raymond Knister and His Works*.

J. R. (TIM) STRUTHERS

Further reading: Brian Trehearne, *Aestheticism and the Canadian Modernists: Aspects of a Poetic Influence* (1989); W. J. Keith, *Literary Images of Ontario* (1992).

KOCH, CHRISTOPHER JOHN (1932–)

Australian novelist

Born in Hobart, Tasmania, Australia, he has lived in Europe and America and travelled widely in Asian countries, particularly India. He has worked as a producer for the Australian Broadcasting Commission, resigning in 1973 to write full time. He now lives near Sydney. Apart from four novels and a collection of essays, Koch has written poetry and a number of radio and television scripts. *The Year of Living Dangerously* (1978) won the National Book Council Award in 1979, and in 1982 it was made into a film. (The screenplay was jointly written by the director Peter Weir, by playwright **David Williamson**, and Koch.)

The Boys in the Island (1958), like **Randolph**

Stow's *The Merry-Go-Round in the Sea* (1965), is an account of boyhood and early adolescence in provincial Australia. Both novels deal with the impact of the Second World War, the confusing relationship between 'homes' — Britain and Australia — and with adolescent yearning for the metropolis. Like **George Lamming**'s *In the Castle of My Skin* and **Austin Clarke**'s *Growing Up Stupid Under the Union Jack,* Koch's novel points up many of the ironies inherent in the transfer of Anglo-education to vastly different colonial environments.

Writing in terms that echo the sentiments of the many post-colonial settler-colony writers, Koch notes the perennial problems of 'trying to match' the 'spirit' of the environment with the 'spirit of the ancestral land . . . the lost northern hemisphere . . . but matching them up isn't easy: the task of a lifetime, in fact'. *Across the Sea Wall* (1965; rev. 1982) and *The Year of Living Dangerously* are both part of this quest, and like a number of other Australian writers — Randolph Stow, **Robert Drewe**, and **Blanche d'Alpuget** — Koch explores and deploys Asian philosophies as enabling and mediating terms in the post-colonial construction of Australian identity.

In *Across the Sea Wall* Robert O'Brien embarks on the reflex-like journey to that northern 'homeland' of England. But *en route* he is diverted to India, and the classic voyage home remains incomplete. O'Brien is deflected by the seductions of Indian travel and by Ilsa Kahlins, who embodies for him both the nostalgia of the 'lost' European past and the Indian goddess Kali in her manifestation as dancer, weaver of *maya.* Together these figurations suggest the ways in which the illusion of a sophisticated European 'origin' haunts the colonial imagination, producing the 'shadows on the screen' of the colonial psyche.

In *The Year of Living Dangerously* it is the Indonesian *Wayang Kulit* (shadow puppetry) on which Koch draws to continue his investigation of the complex relationship among Australia, Asia, and Europe. The emphasis on shadows, puppets, and on memory and the creation of illusion are not incidental to Koch's vision. They provide, as he explains, the almost inevitable tropes of the settler-colonial condition:

> The society that had produced us, so far away from what it saw as the centre of civilization, made us rather like the prisoners in Plato's cave. To guess what that centre was like, that centre . . . for which we yearned, we must study shadows on the wall as our parents and grandparents had done . . . shadows, clues to the real world we would one day discover in the Northern hemisphere.

The Year of Living Dangerously again connects Europe, Asia, and the question of colonial and a post-colonial Australian identity, investigating this through an account of the private and public lives of a group of journalists in Djakarta in the months leading up to the PKI (Perserikaton Kommunist di Indies — Indonesian Communist Party) coup of 1965, which eventually resulted in the downfall of charismatic Indonesian President Sukarno. The novel has a 'double hero': Billy Kwan, the 'divided Chinese-Australian, and Guy Hamilton, the English-Australian'. Both, as Koch notes, are 'aspects of the one', products 'of a dying colonial world'. Doubles, like shadows (and the colonial inflections these tropes facilitate), recur throughout Koch's oeuvre. In *The Doubleman* (1985), however, the setting is primarily Australian and in this exploration of the contemporary post-colonial consciousness Koch draws on Gnostic rather than Indian philosophy.

Koch's essay collection, *Crossing the Gap: A Novelist's Essays* (1987), explores many of the issues raised in his novels.

HELEN TIFFIN

Further reading: 'Christopher Koch', in Martin

Duwell and Laurie Hergenhan (eds) *The ALS Guide to Australian Writers: A Bibliography 1963–1990* (1992).

KOGAWA, JOY NOZOMI (1935–)
Canadian novelist, poet
Born in Vancouver, Canada, she spent her childhood there until 1942, when her family, with some twenty-two thousand other Japanese Canadians, was forcibly uprooted, a tragic event of injustice and racism in Canada. Her father, an Anglican minister, was sent to Slocan, one of many internment camps in the British Columbia interior. In 1945 her family relocated again, this time to Coaldale, Alberta. She studied music and theology in Toronto, then returned to Vancouver, where she married David Kogawa in 1959. She lived in various Canadian towns before moving to Toronto in the late 1970s, after separating from her husband.

The delicate poems in Kogawa's slender first book, *The Splintered Moon* (1967), were followed by a radical transformation in craft and content in her substantial second book, *A Choice of Dreams* (1974). In the brilliant opening sequence the poet travels to her ancestral home in Japan only to find herself curiously in and out of place: in appearance she is 'Japanese', but she sees herself as a 'foreigner' — a Canadian. Later, in Ottawa, Canada, she uncovers in an attic trunk remnants of her mother's prewar years on British Columbia's coast. The archival impulse leads to another remarkable sequence, 'Forest Creatures', in which the poet confronts a childhood shaped by bigotry. This introspective power shimmers in the less-focused but mature voice of *Jericho Road* (1977), speaking with a ruthless honesty about collapsed values and with a refined sympathy for the victimized: 'it's creaturely concern / keeps me sleepless.'

This concern combines with Kogawa's own past in the novel *Obasan* (1981), winner of the Books in Canada First Novel Award in 1981 and the Canadian Authors' Book of the Year Award in 1982. The narrator, Naomi Nakane, responding to her uncle Isamu's death, re-enacts the painful memories of childhood uprooting and thereby breaks the silence of the past. As victims of racism, Japanese Canadians endured the shame of being branded 'enemy aliens', and like Obasan (Japanese for 'aunt') and Isamu, they acquiesced in a muted life. Naomi moves between the passive silence of Obasan and the vocal anger of Aunt Emily, who never stops pestering her with documents corroborating the injustices. *Obasan* stunningly interweaves the lyric gift of Kogawa's poetry with autobiography, history, and fiction. This liberation from generic boundaries places it within a Canadian postmodernism that moves beyond the conventional separation of literary forms.

In the 1980s *Obasan* gained popularity as a narrative of Japanese Canadian internment. Kogawa has also published a children's version, *Naomi's Road* (1986), and her fourth book of poems, *Woman of the Woods* (1985). Kogawa was swept up in the Japanese Canadian movement to seek redress for the injustices suffered during the Second World War and witnessed the historic 1988 Redress Settlement in the House of Commons. The novel *Itsuka* (1992) — the title, loosely translated, means 'someday' — is a sequel to *Obasan* and traces Naomi's participation in the redress movement.

ROY MIKI

Further reading: Marilyn Russell Rose, 'Politics into art: Kogawa's *Obasan* and the rhetoric of fiction', *Mosaic* 21 (1988); Mason Harris, 'Broken generations in *Obasan*: inner conflict and the destruction of community', *Canadian Literature* 127 (1990).

KOLATKAR, ARUN BALAKRISHNA (1932–)
Indian poet
He was born in Kolhapur, India, and raised and educated there. Early in life Kolatkar developed a keen interest in painting and was introduced to the finest achievements of Baroque and Renaissance art and architecture through his father's collection

of picture post-cards. He took a diploma in painting from the J. J. School of Art, Bombay. He lives in Bombay, pursuing the profession of a graphic artist.

Kolatkar began writing poetry at the age of sixteen. Many of his poems appeared in respected poetry journals and have been much anthologized. He writes both in English and Marathi and often translates from one language to the other. He has published two books — *Jejuri* (1976), a long poem in English that won the Commonwealth Poetry Prize, and *Arun Kolatkarchya Kavita* (1976), a collection of poems in Marathi.

Like the Jamaican poet **Derek Walcott**, Kolatkar is essentially a painter-poet and shows a penchant for experimental constructs. He often transfers the techniques of visual arts — photographic delineation, animation, montage technique, calligraphic representation, and cinematographic use of individual stills — to the verbal medium, turning a poem into a visual frame. Kolatkar's 'boatride', a poem in eleven sections, best illustrates his skilful use of visual effects. Further, his poetry reveals the unmistakable influence of western art movements — Dadaism and Surrealism, in particular. These experimental forms, with their rejection of conventional realist art, provide suitable models for an effective projection of a Hindu view of life, in which the reality of existence itself is neither ultimate nor absolute but relative and even illusory.

Some of Kolatkar's shorter poems, such as 'Crabs', 'The Hag', and 'Woman', abound in surrealist imagery, but it is in his more mature work, *Jejuri*, that he is able to adapt these new forms to communicate an authentically Indian vision of life. *Jejuri* is a narrative sequence depicting the participant-narrator's journey to the holy shrine of Khandoba at Jejuri, a small town in western India. The pilgrim undertakes the journey in a non-spiritual mood, goes through the experience with emotional non-attachment, and emerges without the slightest change in his attitudes. He is a disinterested witness observing and noting the details with photographic accuracy. The world of Jejuri seethes with contraries: gods and beasts, temples and cowsheds, priests and beggars, icons and heaps of rocks, shrines and stations, nullifying the distinction between the sacred and the profane. This has often led critics to conclude that *Jejuri* is an Indian version of T. S. Eliot's *The Waste Land* and a poem of scepticism. But actually the poet conceives Jejuri as 'a non-event', as he himself put it. In *Jejuri*, there is neither fear nor excitement, neither reverence nor irreverence, neither acceptance nor rejection, but rather a detached observation of the essential incongruity of life itself. The entire observation is rooted in a pervasive sense of the comic, conforming to the Hindu vision of life as 'a play'. It is this successful transmutation of life into art that makes Kolatkar's achievement so important.

C. VIJAYASREE

Further reading: M. K. Naik, 'Arun Kolatkar's Jejuri and the three value systems', *Dimensions of Indian English Literature* by M. K. Naik (1984).

KOLIA, JOHN (1931–)

South Pacific novelist

He was born John Collier in Sydney, Australia, and was educated in Sydney and in England. He studied medicine at the University of London, England, later working as a medical assistant in Australia. In 1956 he moved to Papua New Guinea to take up similar work. In the following years, Collier moved between England and Papua New Guinea, studying and teaching. He earned a BA from the University of Papua New Guinea in 1971, changed the spelling of his name to a local phonetic form (Kolia), by which he is known, and in 1976 became a naturalized citizen. In that year he earned his Ph.D. in oral history from the University of Papua New Guinea.

Kolia published eight novels between 1978 and 1980; these were written, he claims, in a 'compulsive frenzy' fuelled by his anxiety for the welfare of the peoples of Papua New Guinea, both indigenous and expatriate. The novels are *The Late Mr Papua* (1978), *A Compulsive Exhibition* (1978), *Up the River to Victory Junction* (1978), *My Reluctant Missionary* (1978), *Traditionally Told* (1979), *Close to the Village* (1979), *Without Mannerisms* (1980), and *Victims of Independence* (1980).

Kolia's novels confront the reader with the violent male chauvinism of Papua New Guinean societies. They foreshadow the breakdown of law and order, as Papua New Guineans react with increasing aggression to any frustration or apparent indignity. While he is critical of Australia for its self-interested presence and its imposition of an inappropriate legal system, Kolia deplores the tendency of Papua New Guineans to retain many of the less desirable elements of their traditional culture and to aspire to those of western civilization.

Unlike Australia's **B. Wongar**, Kolia never adopts the authorial perspective of the unsophisticated indigenous writer; rather, like **Chinua Achebe** of Nigeria, he sees his role as didactic and culturally re-integrative. However, a rumbustious good humour often counterbalances the didacticism and alleviates the more grimly lurid aspects of his narration. *Victims of Independence* is particularly memorable for the carnage that litters its scenarios, but it also confronts the reader with the ideational possibilities of the spirit world of animism. *My Reluctant Missionary* endorses racial and religious syncretism. *Without Mannerisms* proposes an egalitarian society based on reciprocity and made viable by the self-assertion of each individual.

LYNETTE BAER

KON, STELLA (1944–)

Singaporean dramatist

She was born in Edinburgh, Scotland, and took up Singaporean citizenship in 1966. Kon describes her fictional *The Scholar and the Dragon* (1986) as 'the rags-to-riches story of a 16-year old Confucian student who arrives in Singapore in 1906'. Her short fiction has appeared in various Singaporean magazines, but it is Kon's work as a dramatist that has earned her the most significant public and critical attention. Two collections of her short plays for schools have been published — *The Immigrant and Other Plays* (1975) and *Emporium and Other Plays* (1977). She is a three-time winner of Singapore's National Playwriting Competition — in 1977 for *The Bridge* (1977, also published in *Prize Winning Plays III*, 1981, edited by **Robert Yeo**), in 1983 for *Trial* (1983), and in 1985 for *Emily of Emerald Hill* (1990).

In *The Bridge* Kon presents the activities of inmates of a contemporary drug rehabilitation centre as they stage their own musical drama based on episodes from the Indian epic *Ramayana*. The play's 'bridgings' — past and present, the sacred and the secular, mythic anguish and contemporary social problems — are explored through an adventurous deployment of a range of theatrical idioms from east and west, from realistic methods to the conventions of epic dance-drama. Kon works the mythic narrative of the capture of Princess Sita and her rescue by Rama into an interesting metaphor for the ravages of, and struggle against, drug addiction.

In *Trial* the trial of Socrates is juxtaposed against scenes set in contemporary Singapore in an exploration of generational conflict and themes of integrity, duty, and responsibility. The audience is implicated in the action by being made to function as Socrates' jury and to vote on his guilt or innocence.

The success of *Emily of Emerald Hill* at the Singapore Drama Festival of 1985 was widely heralded as a significant breakthrough for indigenous Singaporean drama in English. The play is a monodrama in which the protagonist, Straits Chinese matriarch Emily Gan, enacts the story of her rise to eminence within the domestic empire of the

Gan household. *Emily of Emerald Hill* is a compellingly evocative microcosm of a Singaporean past, and, in the character of Emily Gan, Kon has produced what remains the most powerfully realized character in Singapore theatre in English to date.

Kon's later work for the stage includes 'Dragon's Teeth Gate' (premièred 1986), in which soulless materialism, embodied in business huckster Freddy Tan, vies with mythological figures such as the Chinese goddess of mercy for the soul of Singapore. In 'Butterflies Don't Cry' (premièred 1989) two performers playing lovers in the Chinese opera 'The Butterfly Romance' conduct a backstage affair. 'The Towkay's Daughter' (premièred 1989) is a short comedy, while 'The Martyrdom of Helena Roderigues' (premièred 1991) is described by Kon as 'a dramatisation of my own short story (1969) about mother and son locked into symbiotic guilt and domination'.

F. M. G. (MAX) LE BLOND

KONADU, ASARE (1923–)

Ghanaian novelist

Born at Asamang, Ashanti Region (now in Ghana), he attended Abuakwa State College and studied journalism in London, England, and Strasbourg, France. He worked with various government news agencies before establishing Anowuo Educational Publications, which primarily published his works. Anowuo published *Don't Leave Me Mercy* (1966) and *A Husband for Esi Ellua* (1968) under Konadu's pseudonym, Kwabena Asare Bediako (which should not be confused with the name of Ghanaian novelist **Bediako Asare**). Konadu's *The Lawyer Who Bungled His Life* (1965) is a weak treatment of the 'been-to' theme, a recurrent subject of the return of foreign-trained Ghanaians to the local tradition, which is fully developed in Kobina Sekyi's play *The Blinkards* (written in 1915; first published in 1974) and **Ayi Kwei Armah**'s *Fragments* (1970).

Konadu follows the conventions of popular literature that developed in urban areas in Africa after the Second World War, stimulated by growth in the economy and by the spread of mass literacy. Its trademarks of melodrama, gratuitous plot, cliché, and bombastic language have won a large readership. Popular writers amplify common themes of love, crime, and money, offering readers formulaic entertainment. (See **Popular Writing**, West Africa.)

Konadu's marketing strategy involves door-to-door sales and distribution through schools, post offices, the work-place, and street vending. Estimated sales figures of *Come Back, Dora!* (1966; revised and published as *Ordained by the Oracle*, 1969) and *Shadow of Wealth* (1966) are significantly higher than those of works by Armah and **Kofi Awoonor**.

Unlike Benibengor Blay and E. K. Mickson, Konadu occasionally shows literary seriousness. He gives insight into Akan funeral practices and ancestor worship in *Come Back, Dora!* and shows the human implications of the traditional attitude to barrenness in *A Woman in Her Prime* (1967). On the whole, however, there is no winnowing of the chaffs of sociological reportage from the fine grains of imaginative literature. Konadu remains a writer who has yet to attain an individual voice of literary quality.

CHRIS AWUYAH

Further reading: Ime Ikkideh, 'The character of popular fiction in Ghana', in Richard Priebe (ed.) *Ghanaian Literatures* (1988).

KREISEL, HENRY (1922–91)

Canadian novelist, short-story writer

Born in Vienna, Austria, Kreisel escaped from the Nazis to England in 1938. In 1941, after internment in New Brunswick, Canada, he studied English literature at the University of Toronto. He joined the English department of the University of Alberta, Canada, in 1947, became head of the department in 1961, and served as vice-president of the university from 1970 to 1975.

Kreisel decided to immerse himself in the culture of his adoptive country and become a writer in English. His well-known essay, 'The Prairie: A State of Mind' (1968), explores the impact of the forbidding vastness of the Prairie upon consciousness. The story 'The Broken Globe', published in the collection *The Almost Meeting and Other Stories* (1981), examines the degree to which an outsider may assimilate the Canadian landscape through the power of poetic imagination.

Kreisel's determination to become Canadian did not undermine his Jewishness. An admirer of Joseph Conrad's mastery of English, Kreisel nevertheless chose to identify with the Canadian **A. M. Klein**, who, he claimed, 'showed me that it was possible to use within a Canadian context one's total experience'. Thus, in his two novels, Kreisel exposes his Canadian protagonists to the experience of the Holocaust. The protagonist in *The Rich Man* (1948) has to contend with a sense of helplessness and guilt *vis-à-vis* his European relatives. The protagonist in *The Betrayal* (1964) is made witness to the horrifying choices that the victims of the Holocaust had to face, the consciousness of which impels an ethical re-examination of himself.

Kreisel's literary work is informed by an unflinching faith in humanism. His radio drama, *The Man Who Sold His Shadow* (1956), emphasizes the importance of interrelationships based upon responsibility and compassion. Indeed, Kreisel's contributions to Canadian society attest to the strength of his humanist convictions.

RACHEL FELDHAY BRENNER

Further reading: Shirley Neuman, ed., *Another Country: Writings by and about Henry Kreisel* (1985); Rachel Feldhay Brenner, 'Henry Kreisel — European experience and Canadian reality: a state of mind', *World Literature Written in English* 2 (1988).

KROETSCH, ROBERT PAUL (1927–)

Canadian novelist, poet, critic

Born in Heisler, Alberta, Canada, he graduated from the University of Alberta in 1948 with majors in literature and philosophy. Kroetsch worked for six years in the Canadian North, on riverboats on the Mackenzie River, and for the United States Air Force in Goose Bay, Labrador. He returned to formal studies and was awarded an MA from Middlebury College, Vermont, USA, in 1956 and a Ph.D. from the University of Iowa, USA, in 1961. Since 1961 Kroetsch has held academic positions at the State University of New York at Binghamton, USA (1961–78), and, from 1978, with the exception of one year at the University of Calgary, at the University of Manitoba, Canada. His writing is noteworthy not only for its exploratory attention to different generic forms and to the complexities of influence but also for its engagement with questions of folk culture, local and national identity, literary traditions, and strategies of narration.

Kroetsch's early experience of farm life, the prairie landscape, and rural culture became the focus for many of his works, especially those that take account of history as process and story-making — as an exchange not only between writers and readers but also between the allegedly known and the yet-to-be discovered, between, as Kroetsch has suggested in his 1981 essay 'Beyond Nationalism: A Prologue' (republished in his collection of essays *The Lovely Treachery of Words*, 1989) 'the vastness of (closed) cosmologies and the fragments found in the (open) field of the archaeological site'. He places emphasis upon language, on the ambiguous status of definitions and of boundaries, and on the value of interplay.

Kroetsch first won recognition for his novels, then for his poetry — with its special attention, both formal and philosophical, to fragmentation, discontinuity, and dialectical construction — and for the critical essays in which he explores ideas about the (un)making of texts and culture with particular emphasis on the heterogeneity of 'Canadian' writing.

With its presentation of opposed male characters and perspectives, role-playing, ego-competitiveness, quest motifs, and the influence of Homer and Conrad, Kroetsch's first novel, *But We Are Exiles* (1965), introduces interests that recur in his Albertan triptych — *The Words of My Roaring* (1966), *The Studhorse Man* (1969, winner of a Governor General's Award), and *Gone Indian* (1973). Mythologizing the province of Alberta and creating emblematic figures, Kroetsch examines relationships between landscape and cultural history while experimenting with first-person narration and interplays of voice and character in ways that recall Twain and Faulkner, Conrad and Nabokov. Increasingly self-conscious about forms of presentation, focusing on exaggeration, uncertainty, storytelling, and different generic models, Demeter Proudfoot's peculiar biography of Hazard Lepage in *The Studhorse Man* and Mark Madham's editing of Jeremy Sadness' tapes in *Gone Indian* demonstrate the 'decreative' energy and unreliability of texts in playful intersection. These prefigure Kroetsch's emphasis on interpretation and ideological difference in Anna Dawe's revision of William Dawe's field notes in *Badlands* (1975) and in Karen Strike's reconstruction of Dorf's journal in *Alibi* (1983). Kroetsch's novels — including *What the Crow Said* (1978), with its magic realist version of a mythical place on the border between Alberta and Saskatchewan — address the genealogical imperative in transportable Canadian contexts. Intrigued with matters of origin, influence, identity, and exchange, but sceptical about unity and resolution, Kroetsch celebrates narrative variety and invites continuing reconsideration of national culture in some of its diversity. Notably postmodern, Kroetsch's works may be compared with the fiction of **Sheila Watson, George Bowering, Jack Hodgins**, and **Michael Ondaatje**.

Kroetsch has been publishing poetry since 1961, with four volumes appearing in the 1970s. *Field Notes: 1–8, A Continuing Poem* (1981) presents an opportunity for critical analysis of 'the continuing poem' as an intertextual work in progress, a fragmented investigation of personal and western Canadian experience and of problems of knowledge and language procedures in which citation of documentary sources establishes the sense of history just as the emphasis on arrangement, interrogation, and invention serves to displace it: 'I live by a kind of resistance,' says the sad Phoenician. 'Stone Hammer Poem' (1973) offers a strong introduction to Kroetsch's poetry. Focused on the implement, a stone hammer, it presents a discontinuous narrative of cultural layers that invites reflection on landscape, history, change, meaning, and value. 'The Ledger' and 'Seed Catalogue', each commencing in a particular document, also show Kroetsch's success in deconstructive revisions that recover versions of the past as rich narrative glimpses. Incorporating *Advice to My Friends* (1985), *Excerpts From the Real World* (1986), and later writing, *Completed Field Notes* (1989) indicates in one volume the range of Kroetsch's innovation, energy, humour, and compassion. 'How do you grow a poet?' he asks in 'Seed Catalogue'. From 'Stone Hammer Poem' to 'After Paradise' (1989), his writing, in its variety, provides the answer. While Kroetsch acknowledges the influence on his practice of Walt Whitman, Wallace Stevens, and William Carlos Williams, his work invites comparison with other exponents of the long poem in Canada, such as **bp Nichol**, George Bowering, **Daphne Marlatt**, **Eli Mandel**, and Michael Ondaatje.

The Lovely Treachery of Words brings together seventeen critical essays, eight of them published in an *Open Letter* collection (Spring

1983). With Shirley Neuman's and Robert Wilson's *Labyrinths of Voice: Conversations with Robert Kroetsch* (1982), these volumes reveal Kroetsch as an astute critic, indicating again the formal invention, insight, and judgement that characterize his fiction and poetry and demonstrate his commitment to Canadian writing and cultural history. While he acknowledges the influence of Barthes, Foucault, Derrida, and Bakhtin, there is no sudden post-structuralist swerve; judiciously eclectic, from the earliest essays Kroetsch writes a criticism of resistance to uncomfortable binaries, to simple configurations of influence, and to reductive formulations of tradition and nationalism. His re-readings present literature's 'decreative' interrogations of the divided inheritance, both personal and communal, and seek a critical practice that explores achievements, changes, and new directions 'without recourse to an easy version of national definition, and without easy recourse to old vocabularies' ('Beyond Nationalism: A Prologue'). Essays become poem, anecdote, fragment, thesis, story in combinations that signal a lively interest appropriate to the seriousness of the enterprise.

BRIAN EDWARDS

Further reading: Peter Thomas, *Robert Kroetsch* (1980); *Reflections: Essays on Robert Kroetsch, Open Letter* Summer/Fall (1984), issue on Robert Kroetsch; Robert Lecker, *Robert Kroetsch* (1986).

KULYK KEEFER, JANICE (1952–)

Canadian poet, short-story writer, novelist, critic

Born Janice Kulyk in Toronto, Canada, into a Ukrainian and Polish immigrant family, she was educated at the University of Toronto and Sussex University, England. She has taught English literature in Nova Scotia, Canada, at Sussex, and at the University of Guelph, Canada. Kulyk Keefer entered the Canadian literary scene in the 1980s with the publication of a book of poems, a novel, two critical books, and three short-story collections, and by winning numerous Canadian literary prizes.

Kulyk Keefer's criticism, *Under Eastern Eyes: A Critical Reading of Maritime Fiction* (1987) and *Reading Mavis Gallant* (1989), illuminates the polarities of regionalism and internationalism within her own creative writing. (See **Regionalism in Canadian Literature in English**.) Her first book, *The Paris-Napoli Express* (1986), with its stories about Canadians travelling in Europe and European exiles in Canada, signals her characteristic doubleness, where the rich incomprehensibility of Europe is juxtaposed with strong evocations of Canadian locales.

Though her poetry, many of her short stories, and her novel *Constellations* (1988) show acute insights into social conditions in Nova Scotia, Kulyk Keefer resists classification as a Maritime writer. While *Constellations*, set in an impoverished Nova Scotia rural community, is related to traditions of Maritime realism, its dimensions of European lyricism (in references to the poet R. M. Rilke and classical music) and its attention to narrative artifice mark its distance from social documentary and its aesthetic delight in 'fictive correspondences'.

Significant departures are the thematic and formal features of the stories in *Travelling Ladies* (1990), showing Kulyk Keefer's affinities with **Mavis Gallant** and other expatriate Commonwealth women writers such as **Katherine Mansfield** and **Shirley Hazzard**. The journey motif produces subtle dismantlings of definition for her Canadian protagonists in stories such as 'Bella Rabinovich/Arabella Rose' and 'The Grey Valise', where indeterminacy of feeling is contained by fastidious syntactic control within decorously postmodernist narratives.

Within the short-story genre, Kulyk Keefer offers a distinctive redefinition of Canadian national and literary identity, showing the contemporary shift away from singleness of identity towards decentring and cultural pluralism. Switching between Canada and Europe, her stories figure no construction of 'home' but departures for unknown destinations.

Her second novel, *Rest Harrow* (1992), set in Sussex, is a contemporary 'condition of England' novel written from a disillusioned Canadian perspective.

CORAL ANN HOWELLS

Further reading: 'Divided loyalties' (interview), *Books in Canada* 19 (1990); Colin Nicholson, '"Grain of the Actual": Janice Kulyk Keefer and her writing', *British Journal of Canadian Studies* 2 (1992); Coral Ann Howells, 'Janice Kulyk Keefer's *Travelling Ladies*', *British Journal of Canadian Studies* 2 (1992).

KUMAR, SHIV K. (1921–)

Indian poet, novelist

Born in Lahore, India — now in Pakistan — he graduated from Foreman Christian College, Lahore, and took his Ph.D. in English literature from Cambridge University, England, with a dissertation on the impact of Henri Bergson on the stream of consciousness novel in English. He lives with his wife and two children in Hyderabad, Andhra Pradesh, where he was the chair, Department of English, Osmania University, until 1961. His varied career includes: poetry recitations in several countries, including the USA; a Commonwealth Visiting Professorship at the University of Kent, Canterbury, England; a British Council Visitorship at Cambridge; and the position of Distinguished Professor of Literature at the University of Northern Iowa, USA. He was elected to the Fellowship of the Royal Society of Literature, Britain, in 1978.

Kumar is a man of many moods and modes and his writing reflects this in its diversity of themes and forms. Running through all his work is a robust optimism in the joy of life, despite its unavoidable pains. His overall outlook celebrates intuition over reason, primal impulse over conscious action. His poetry has been characterized as confessional in the American mode, but it is, in fact, confessional in a peculiarly Indian sense, its quarry being not the subjective self, but the Vedantic self, a self that shuns all dualities. Sex is one of the major preoccupations of Kumar's poetry, but what attracts him is not the mere flow of physical body into body, but the more subtle experience of the transcendental. Love and death remain the crucial poles of his verse.

Kumar began to write poetry relatively late — past middle age. His poetry collections include *Articulate Silences* (1970), *Cobwebs in the Sun* (1974), *Subterfuges* (1976), *Woodpeckers* (1979), and *Trapfalls in the Sky* (1986). The strength of his poetry derives not only from his technical virtuosity but also from his distinctively Indian articulation of personal experience.

Kumar has published two novels, *The Bone's Prayer* (1979) and *Nude Before God* (1983). Sprawling, autobiographical narrations framed in a metaphysical-comical mode, they are underpinned by a strategy of self-conscious deconstruction of the narrative structure. But the similarity to the post-structural western novel is superficial because Kumar draws his inspiration from the traditional Indian practice of dissolving the dichotomy between the narrative and the metaphysical discourse, best represented by that quintessentially Indian product, the *Mahabharata*. But Kumar himself has emphasized the sheer exuberance of the humour, the rich comic tapestry within the metaphysical matrix of his novels. Even death becomes deconstructed as a joke. Both *The Bone's Prayer* and *Nude Before God* explore the themes of joy in pain and of pain in joy, climaxing in a transcendental bliss.

The nineteen stories of Kumar's only collection of short stories, *Beyond Love and Other Stories* (1980), continue this exploration into the mystery, the agony, and the ultimate hopefulness of life. His characters are not escapists, for they face life and wrestle with its meaning. Kumar's only published play, *The Last Wedding Anniversary* (1975), centres on the breakdown of a two-year old marriage ending with its hero returning to the girl he had loved before the marriage. Kumar has also translated works from Urdu into English and is currently translating the poetry of the Pakistani Urdu poet, Faiz. Whatever the ultimate evaluation of Kumar's work, there is no doubt that it will find a significant place in the history of Indian writing in English.

K. RAGHAVENDRA RAO

Further reading: T. G. Vaidyanathan, 'Between Kali and Cordelia: the poetry of Shiv K. Kumar', in Vasant Shahane and M. Sivaramakrishna (eds) *Indian Poetry in English: A Critical Assessment* (1980).

KUO PAO KUN (1939–)

Singaporean dramatist

Born in Hebei province, China, he moved to Singapore in 1949. He worked for a time in radio, but his interest in the theatre took him to Australia, where he enrolled in Sydney's National Institute of Dramatic Art. As founder (with his wife Goh Lay Kuan) in 1965 of the Practice Performing Arts School (now Centre) and, in 1986, of the Practice Theatre Ensemble, Kuo has been a central force in the quest for an authentically Singaporean theatre. As a bilingual (Mandarin and English) experimental playwright he has produced the most sustained and artistically challenging body of work in the Singapore theatre. (See also **Drama**, Singapore.)

In the 1980s, while continuing to work in, and write for, the Chinese-language theatre (his own plays, the titles of which mean 'The Little White Sailing Boat' and 'Kopi Tiam', were performed at the Singapore Arts Festivals of 1982 and 1986 respectively), Kuo commenced a direct and sustained involvement in the English-language theatre. Between 1985 and 1989 he wrote, directed, and produced two satiric monodramas, *The Coffin is Too Big for the Hole* and *No Parking on Odd Days*, and two full-length dramatic works, *The Silly Little Girl and the Funny Old Tree* and *Mama Looking for Her Cat* — all published in *The Coffin is Too Big for the Hole . . . and Other Plays* (1990). The first three of these were written and performed in both Mandarin and English. The fourth deploys a complete range of Singaporean languages and dialects working in choristic and contrapuntal fashion, harnessed to highly stylized and symbolic physical action as well as to motifs drawn from children's dialect songs and games. The result is a powerfully moving parable of alienation between generations, of the disruptive and dehumanizing encroachments of the modern upon traditionally stable family and personal relations.

Kuo's minimalist settings, his movement away from traditional dialogue, his harnessing of indigenous folk materials, and his radical use of the enormous linguistic diversity of Singapore have functioned to liberate the English-language theatre in particular from its restrictive allegiance to conventional western forms.

In 1989 Kuo was awarded the Singapore Cultural Medallion for Drama.

F. M. G. (MAX) LE BLOND

KUREISHI, HANIF (1948–)

English/Pakistani dramatist, novelist

Born in London, England, of an English mother and a Pakistani father, he grew up in London when the British National Front was gaining power. In early adolescence Kureishi reacted to the Front's racist ideology, and in his autobiographical essay 'The Rainbow Sign' (in *My Beautiful Laundrette and the Rainbow Sign*, 1986) he recounts how his search for an alternative philosophy took him to the extremist movements of Afro-Americans in the USA and to his roots in Pakistan. In the end, Kureishi seems to have committed himself to a liberal humanism reflected in his drama. His early play, *The King and Me* (in *Outskirts and Other Plays*, 1983), is about the emptiness of life in the west. The same mental condition has suicidal or sadistic effects in *Tomorrow-today!* (in *Outskirts*), in which the characters appear to be dehumanized. In *Outskirts*, this pathological dehumanization, a consequence of desperation, is expressed through racist attacks on Pakistani immigrants.

The theme of Kureishi's later plays is race relations in the UK, as in the novels of the Caribbean writer **E. R. Braithwaite**. 'Borderline' (premièred 1981), for example, is about racial tension, but, unlike the works of Braithwaite, it suggests that both the immigrant Asians and the British are responsible for this state of affairs and that they can also transcend it. In 'Birds of Passage' (premièred 1983), Kureishi is especially critical of Pakistani entrepreneurs who force Londoners from their homes.

In Kureishi's most powerful play, *My Beautiful Laundrette*, the homosexual relationship between a Pakistani youth and an English youth is the central symbol for the possibility of a social relationship between the two groups. This relationship transcends racial antagonism in a way that the friendship between an Englishman and an Indian cannot in E. M. Forster's *A Passage to India* (1924). While this play is successful, *Sammy and Rosie Get Laid* (in *Sammy and Rosie Get Laid: The Script and the Diary*, 1988), in which copulation symbolizes the attempt to form human relationships, is not. It appears that Kureishi endorses individualism and freedom, but fails to understand that the fragmentation of relationships and the lack of consensus about social norms of behaviour are the consequences of these ideas. (*Sammy and Rosie Get Laid* was adapted for film in 1988. Kureishi also wrote the script for the film *London Kills Me*, 1991.)

The weakness of Kureishi's first novel, *The Buddha of Suburbia* (1990), derives from the same lack of understanding. Like his early plays, the novel is about the emptiness of British life. The narrator, Karim Amir, is born of an Indian Muslim father and a British mother. His father deserts him and his mother to live with another woman. This desertion is perceived as the supreme betrayal by the narrator, who tries to find happiness in sex and drugs. Although the nihilism of youth in contemporary Britain is portrayed realistically, the novel fails to rise to the level of Kureishi's best plays.

TARIQ RAHMAN

Further reading: 'Hanif Kureishi: mocking liberal taboos' (interview), *Inside Asia* 7 (1986); Philipp Dodd, 'Requiem for a rave', interview with Hanif Kureishi, *Sight and Sound* Sept. (1991); Alamgir Hashmi, 'Hanif Kureishi and the tradition of the novel', *The International Fiction Review* 2 (1992).

KUREISHI, MAKI (1927–)

Pakistani poet, educator

Born in Calcutta, India, and educated at D. J. Sind College, Karachi, Pakistan, and at Smith College, USA, she taught English at Karachi University until her retirement.

Although Kureishi has not published a collection of her own work, her poetry has been widely anthologized. In her writing there are echoes of W. B. Yeats and Emily Dickinson — in her view of nature's relentless cycles of procreation and decay, as, for example, in 'Windows', and in the intimate yet restrained evocations of death, as, for example, in 'Kite' (both published in the anthology *Wordfall*, 1975, edited by **Kaleem Omar**). The imperatives of the flesh are recognized, but rarely personalized, in Kureishi's work. A preoccupation with detachment is paramount, and she is drawn to the Buddha figure in poems such as 'The Buddhist Monk' and 'The Sculptor' (*Wordfall*); yet, a burgeoning physical world of 'blood heat' and 'summer honey itch' in the 'breeding cell' impinges on the desired but 'desireless' meditative calm ('The Buddhist Monk').

Kureishi's poems usually chart a series of poised moments designed to cultivate a disciplined content ('Windows', 'Marriage', in *Wordfall*), but the interior monologue form and inscaping mediated by the persona of a detached observer are frequently subject to disruption, as in 'The Moment' and 'The Fire Temple' (*Wordfall*). The fragile order and balance of the perceived world are underlaid by natural and human violence as well as by archetypal fears in 'Day' and 'Air Raid' (*Wordfall*) and the poetry gains in conviction because this primal world is acknowledged alongside the craven need to keep it buried.

In some of Kureishi's later work ('Curfew Summer', in *The Worlds of Muslim Imagination*, edited by **Alamgir Hashmi**, 1986) her essentially private world admits inclusion of Pakistan's political upheavals. In her needlepoint style and her often-ironic detailing of everyday existence Kureishi's work compares with Malaysian **Shirley Lim**'s 'Monsoon History' (in her collection *Crossing the Peninsula and Other Poems*, 1980) and Indian **Eunice de Souza**'s 'Women in Dutch Painting' (in de Souza's *Women in Dutch Painting*, 1988), though Kureishi's writing is characterized by the relative absence of a contemporary feminist emphasis and assertiveness.

S. S. SIRAJUDDIN

KUZWAYO, ELLEN KATE (1914–)

South African short-story writer, autobiographer

Born in Thaba Patchoa, the Orange Free State, South Africa, she was raised chiefly by her maternal grandparents. By them she was called Motlalepule ('one who arrives on a rainy day'). Kuzwayo completed her schooling in Natal and trained as a teacher at Lovedale College. After five years of marriage, her husband's behaviour compelled her to escape from her home, abandon her children, and seek refuge with her father in Johannesburg. There she taught, remarried, and had a third son before training as a social worker; among her fellow students was Winnie Mandela. Kuzwayo's life has been dedicated largely to the welfare of her people; shortly after the uprisings of 1976 she was detained without charge for five months. She is now regarded as a 'mother of Soweto'. The first black writer to be awarded the CNA (Central News Agency) Literary Prize, she was awarded an honorary doctorate by the University of the Witwatersrand in 1987.

In her autobiography, *Call Me Woman* (1985), Kuzwayo records how her family's farm was 'wrenched' away in 1974. The film *Tsiamelo: A Place of Goodness* (1987) records this dispossession. Such legalized appropriation of land leads Kuzwayo to one of her main themes: the homelessness of her people in the land of their birth. Supported by the ethos of Black Consciousness, she frames the narrative of her efforts to re-create for herself and her family a 'home my mind could turn to' with a forceful protest against the imposed poverty of life in townships like Soweto and with examples of the courage with which women in particular combat their oppression.

Kuzwayo's interest in teaching self-reliance to others is the basis for *Awake From Mourning* (1980), the first of the two films she produced with Betty Wolpert. Kuzwayo's belief that education is vital in the national struggle for liberation also informs her collection of short stories, *Sit Down and Listen* (1990).

M. J. DAYMOND

Further reading: Dorothy Driver, 'Women as mothers; women as writers', in Martin Trump (ed.) *Rendering Things Visible* (1990).

L

Lacambra Ayala, Tita (1931–)
Filipino poet, short-story writer, journalist, essayist
Born in Ilocos Norte, the Philippines, she grew up in neighbouring Benguet, her playmates belonging to the Igorot tribe of that mountain province. While studying for a degree in education at the University of the Philippines, Lacambra Ayala supported herself by free-lance writing for metropolitan magazines. During the mid-1950s she moved to the southern region of Mindanao, where she simultaneously taught journalism at a private university and worked at a pineapple canning factory.

Attendance at a writers' workshop and a course under Philippine novelist **N. V. M. Gonzalez** led Lacambra Ayala to explore her talent for writing in forms other than journalism. Her first collection, *Sunflower Poems* (1960), consisted of twenty-eight poems printed on chipboard used to pack newspapers rolls. Encouraged by its favourable reception by fellow writers and by critics, she published another collection of thirty poems, *Ordinary Poems* (1967). American critic Leonard Casper praised her poems for their emotional intensity, which he traced to the poet's deliberate diminution of scale and scope.

A long-time resident of Davao City, Lacambra Ayala has committed herself to drawing together and publicizing the works of artists of that region. Herself a visual artist whose works have been exhibited both in Mindanao and Manila, she is the editor of the Road Map Series, a folio on art and poetry featuring local writers. Number 21 of the Series was a collection of her essays, *This Side of Bananas: Ten Familiar Essays* (1985). Her *Pieces of String and Other Stories* (1984) is a collection of seventeen prize-winning short stories. Though these volumes demonstrate the considerable range of her writing skills, Lacambra Ayala's reputation is most secure in the area of poetry, as examplified in *Poor Boy Poems and Others* (1987), published as volume two, number two of the Road Map Series.

EDNA ZAPANTA MANLAPAZ

Ladoo, Harold Sonny (1945–73)
Trinidadian/Canadian novelist
Born in Couva, Trinidad, and raised amid Trinidad's plantations by descendants of indentured East Indians, he was educated by Canadian Church Mission Schools and his own reading of Victoriana. He immigrated to Canada in 1968, working at odd jobs while he completed his BA at Erindale College, University of Toronto, and feverishly produced numerous manuscripts that resulted in two published novels: *No Pain Like This Body* (1972) and *Yesterdays* (1974).

Released by **Dennis Lee**'s House of Anansi Press, these novels exhibit the then-fashionable obsession with the elemental and with asserting a strong minority voice in response to a paralysing American cultural domination — an approach evaluated by Lee in his long poem 'The Death of Harold Ladoo'. Like other Anansi works — especially French-Canadian Roch Carrier's *La Guerre, Yes Sir!* (1968) — the novels employ Ernest Hemingway's dramatic style and William Faulkner's grotesque realism, along with a brusque cinematic structure. As in Carrier, there is satire, black comedy, allegory, and magic realism, although the latter quality especially is more muted here than in its South American incarnations.

Ladoo himself professed Hemingway's creed of rendering experience in all of its immediacy and saw as his task the accurate presentation of rural

Caribbean life. Although he definitely intends a critique of colonialism, his main concern is to immerse the reader in the particularities of his people's speech and customs in a manner that is less mediated than in the work of his East Indian Trinidadian contemporaries such as **V. S. Naipaul** (in his early novels) and **Sam Selvon**, both of whom are more overtly universalist and desire to bridge the gap between cultures by either assimilating minorities into a dominant western cultural mainstream (Naipaul) or by creating a fluid cultural cosmopolitanism (Selvon).

No Pain Like This Body expresses its minority voice by replacing Carrier's omnipresent Catholicism with a Hindu fatalism grounded in the *Dhammapada*. An unrelenting rain parallels Carrier's ubiquitous snow as a manifestation of both nature's antipathy and humanity's indomitable spirit. Focusing, again like Carrier, on death and a wake, the novel reveals a human degradation and chaos that is countered only by the beauty and orderly rhythms of its female characters. Emile Espinet describes it as a classical tragedy but also as a timeless folk parable similar to Nigerian **Amos Tutuola**'s *The Palm-Wine Drinkard* (1952), noting that it avoids romanticizing both the tropics themselves and the anguish of its colonized inhabitants.

In *Yesterdays*, human degradation becomes even more prominent as excrement replaces rain as the dominant metaphor, and scatological comedy replaces tragedy as the dominant mode. A pastiche of a number of Ladoo's short stories, the novel is a Bakhtinian carnivalization that satirizes religious oppression and human ambition, exploiting a boisterous Indo-Caribbean dialect in place of the tempered poetry of the earlier novel as it more stridently attacks colonialism.

JOHN LeBLANC

Further reading: L. R. Early, 'The two novels of Harold Ladoo', *World Literature Written in English* 15 (1976).

LA GUMA, ALEX (1925–85)

South African novelist

Born in the Coloured ghetto of District Six, Cape Town, South Africa, to Jimmy and Wilhelmina La Guma, he was raised in a home steeped in left-wing politics. In 1948 La Guma followed his father's example by joining the Communist Party (outlawed two years later by the Nationalist government's Suppression of Communism Act). As a listed Communist, La Guma was from that date an official enemy of the apartheid state. He became actively involved in trade union and opposition politics while employed as a factory hand, a clerk, and eventually as a journalist. In 1954 La Guma married Blanche Herman and the following year became chair of the anti-apartheid South African Coloured People's Organization. He was one of the 156 accused in the famous Treason Trial of 1956–60; after his acquittal he was on three occasions detained for several months for suspected underground political activity. La Guma and his family left South Africa on an exit permit in 1966. After working as a journalist in London, England, he was posted to Havana, Cuba, in 1978, as chief representative of the African National Congress in the Caribbean, a position he occupied until his death.

La Guma began writing fiction in the mid-1950s while employed as a columnist and feature writer (1955–62) for the left-wing Cape Town weekly, *New Age*. A handful of his short stories was followed by his three novels written in South Africa: *A Walk in the Night* (1962), *And a Threefold Cord* (1964), and *The Stone Country* (1967). In exile, La Guma published a further two novels, *In the Fog of the Seasons' End* (1972) and *Time of the Butcherbird* (1979), several short stories, and a travelogue, *A Soviet Journey* (1978). In 1969 he was awarded the Lotus Prize by the Afro-Asian Writers Association.

La Guma's fiction documents the suffering under oppression and the growth of revolutionary consciousness of the black, particularly Coloured, South African community. In the absence of an appropriate local literary tradition, he forged a terse, elegantly tough narrative style that has been labelled journalistic, but which may owe more to late nineteenth-century Naturalism, mediated through such American literary champions of the underdog as John Steinbeck and James T. Farrell. A loyal Stalinist, La Guma characterized his work as socialist realism; 'revolutionary romanticism' (Gorky's term) is a more apt characterization, given La Guma's tendency to sentimentalize the political aspirations of his working-class characters.

A Walk in the Night depicts a few decisive hours in the lives of a handful of characters in the sleazy underworld of District Six. The plot is slight and appears to depend upon an ironic, but arbitrary, series of coincidences. Closer inspection reveals that La Guma is giving fictional form to a rigorous Marxist analysis of the South African social formation, anticipating much later resistance writing by privileging the category of class rather than race. All of La Guma's characters, lacking the means of collective self-representation, are doomed by the social order to be little more than links in a chain of cause and effect, their consciousness radically determined by the material forces of a coercive political system. In *And a Threefold Cord* La Guma suggests the dawning of political awareness in the realization of the central character that 'you can't stand up to the world alone'. The charitable bonds that sustain the Pauls family in poverty and tragedy anticipate the wider affiliations of social class, in which, it is implied, any hope for the future of the oppressed must lie.

La Guma's subsequent novels advance the dialectic of his thesis towards revolution. *The Stone Country* is set within the walls of Roeland Street jail in Cape Town, the 'stone country' that is a metaphor for apartheid South Africa at large. In the course of the narrative the activist protagonist succeeds in politicizing his fellow inmates. In *In the Fog of the Seasons' End* the resistance movement regroups its forces in the post-Sharpeville state of emergency. The narrative traces the fortunes of two movement cadres on the run from the authorities: one dies a martyr's death at the hands of the security police, but the other successfully smuggles three young men over the border for training in guerrilla warfare. *Time of the Butcherbird* is more schematic and symbolic than its predecessors. Against the background of a rural community's attempts to resist forced removal, an individual act of revenge is made to stand for the violent redress that inevitably awaits the political oppressor.

Through the evolving political awareness of its major characters, La Guma's fiction graphically evokes the gathering momentum of revolutionary consciousness in South Africa. The passive resentment on display in *A Walk in the Night* gradually develops in subsequent novels into a commitment to armed struggle. In this process *The Stone Country* marks the transfer of consciousness of class identity and political purpose from the interpreting mind of the reader to that of the fictional characters. Perhaps because he is more deliberate and accomplished than most other black South African 'protest' writers, La Guma's didacticism is generally unobtrusive. Critics have made use of the metaphor of the camera to characterize the detailed manner in which he evokes the textures of his worlds, but representation in La Guma is never purely documentary or 'objective'; moreover, the sentiment of moral disgust that informs the act of seeing may in its intensity seem to reach beyond the abjection of a particular social order awaiting political redemption to embrace the human condition itself. In La Guma's later work, presumably as a result of his long exile, the focus of the observing eye is considerably less sharp.

While La Guma's reputation outside South Africa is high, his writings were banned and virtually unknown within South Africa until the late

1980s. New assessments of his achievement are awaited as his work — its function as political protest now receding into history — is assimilated into the domestic literary and critical tradition.

GARETH CORNWELL

Further reading: Abdul R. JanMohamed, *Manichean Aesthetics: The Politics of Literature in Colonial Africa* (1983); Cecil A. Abrahams, *Alex La Guma* (1985).

LAL, PURUSOTTAM (1929–)

Indian poet, critic, translator

Born at Kapurthala, the Punjab, India, he moved with his family to Calcutta, where he received his early education. He later taught in colleges, occasionally lecturing at American universities. In the advancement of Indian-English poetry Lal holds the central place. Besides writing verse, he is a founder of the Writers Workshop (1958–) of Calcutta, whose members' work appeared in *Modern Indo-Anglian Poetry: An Anthology* (1960), co-edited by Lal and K. R. Rao. The volume marked a revolt against the fuzzy, spiritual spasmodicism of earlier 'Aurobindonian' verse. It advocated the modern Pound-Eliot ideals of concrete terms and experience, denying spiritual ecstasies a place in the human scheme. Most subsequent verse-making in India has followed the direction of the Writers Workshop. In the 1970s the Indian government awarded Lal the title Padmashri, recognizing his work as poet, translator, and scholar.

Lal's own verse stands in contrast to the ideals he has promoted. His earliest collection, *The Parrot's Death and Other Poems* (1960), is his most characteristic. Following its publication he ventriloquized several other voices with considerable success, but his own voice is represented clearly in this first work. He is a Sanskritic lyricist delicately attuned to the beauty of nature — bees, roses, 'peeling moonlight', rain. He writes poems of love, but his control of stylized emotion and echoic language ('syllables more splendid than life', 'the hunched bee') shows a classical self-discipline, not romantic impetuosity. Undercutting the rather cerebral preface to *The Parrot's Death and Other Poems*, Lal stresses the 'moral tenderness' holding his poems together. Picturesque images such as 'the golden bee / Nuzzling her lip and nose' linger in the memory. The persistent urging of friends that he write socialist realist poetry is revealed in the title of Lal's next collection, *'Change!' They Said: New Poems* (1966). Writing such poetry made him uncomfortable; he called it 'as unsatisfactory as 14-carat gold'. But he did write such perfect satires as 'Friend'. Lal turned with relief to Sanskritic classicism in *Draupadi and Jayadratha and Other Poems* (1967), *Yakshi from Didarganj and Other Poems* (1969), and *The Man of Dharma and the Rasa of Silence* (1974). Social realism recurs in *Calcutta: A Long Poem* (1977); *Collected Poems* (1977) marks the end of this phase. Grace, controlled earnestness, and sincerity characterize his lyricism. Lal brings to his translations from Pali, Sanskrit, Urdu, and Punjab a disciplined use of language. *The Golden Womb of the Sun* (1965) opens with intimate address, 'What now, storm gods?', until then unknown in Vedic translation. Easy-flowing, unrhetorical metrics make his translation of the Upanishads — *Bhagawad Gita* (1965) and *Dhammapada* (1967) — eminently readable. His *Mahabharata* translation was published between 1968 and 1980. Far more challenging are Lal's translations of Sanskrit plays: *Great Sanskrit Plays* (1965) and *The Farce of Drunk Monk* (1968). Exquisite sensuousness marks his translations of Sanskrit love poems, and his Punjabi religious songs in *Jap-ji* (1967) are solemn and devotional.

Lal has sponsored publication of the work of more than a hundred little-known Indian poets. His most eloquent monument is *Modern Indian Poetry in English: An Anthology and a Credo* (1969; 2nd ed., 1971), which demonstrates that Indians can write creatively in English. His awareness of this ideal is best represented in *The Concept of an Indian Literature: Six Essays* (1968; 2nd ed., 1969), which shows that Indo-English poetry is primarily Indian in character.

SHANKAR MOKASHI-PUNEKAR

Further reading: S. Mokashi-Punekar, *P. Lal: An Appreciation* (1968).

Lambert, Betty (1933–83)

Canadian dramatist

Born in Calgary, Canada, she moved in 1952 to Vancouver, earned a BA from the University of British Columbia, and taught English at Simon Fraser University from 1965 until her death. She wrote many radio and television plays for the Canadian Broadcasting Corporation but became best known for her stage work, first as a children's playwright in the late 1960s, later for one of Canada's most successful sex comedies and for two powerful dramas about the abuse of women.

'I accuse you, Canada . . . of the crime of innocence,' says a young Canadian woman involved in an educational but abusive relationship with a Holocaust survivor in the 1979 radio play *Grasshopper Hill* (1985). Similarly, in the novel *Crossings* (1979) a young woman writer pays heavily for her sexual awakening by a logger. In Lambert's work 'the crime of innocence' is invariably committed by otherwise strong, capable women who conspire with the patriarchy that victimizes them. Nationality and gender are implicitly equated in the deferential colonial mentality that learns the hard way the lessons of sexual imperialism.

Sqrieux-de-Dieu (1975) treats these issues comically as a suburban housewife tries sexual experiments to enliven her dull marriage until she discovers her husband's infidelity. With *Jennie's Story* (1982), Lambert found her mature dramatic voice in the Depression-era tale of a simple-minded farm wife who, with her mother's consent, has unknowingly been sterilized to conceal her seduction by the parish priest. An affirmative ending follows Jennie's suicide (she swallows lye, 'the lie about herself', said Lambert) in a structure Lambert called 'female tragic form'.

Under the Skin, posthumously performed in 1985 and first published in *Jennie's Story and Under the Skin* (1987), and — like *Jennie's Story* — factually based, focuses on the mother of a missing girl whose kidnapper turns out to be a male neighbour. His own cowed and abused wife is caught between her terrible knowledge of the truth and her fear of upsetting the comforting lie she has swallowed. The play confirmed Lambert's position as perhaps the foremost dramatic chronicler of the end of Canadian innocence.

JERRY WASSERMAN

Further reading: 'Battling Aristotle: a conversation between playwright Betty Lambert and director Bonnie Worthington', *Room of One's Own* 8 (1983).

Lamming, George (1927–)

Barbadian novelist, essayist

Born and raised in Carrington Village, near Bridgetown, Barbados, he attended Roebuck Street Boys' School, then won a scholarship to attend Combermere High School, where he was encouraged to write poetry by **Frank Collymore**, a member of the faculty and editor of the journal *Bim*. In 1946 Lamming went to Trinidad where he taught at the College of Venezuela and acted as an agent for *Bim*. In 1950 he left Trinidad for the UK, travelling on the same ship as Trinidadian novelist **Sam Selvon**; they were part of a larger migrating labour force that went to England in search of opportunities not available at home.

In England Lamming quickly established himself as a writer and intellectual. His first novel, *In the Castle of My Skin* (1953), was well received in the UK, Europe, and the USA. Lamming published three more novels in quick succession: *The Emigrants* (1954), *Of Age and Innocence* (1958), and *Season of Adventure* (1960). He also published *The Pleasures of Exile* (1960), a pioneering collection of essays on intellectual history and cultural politics that gave impetus to the development of post-colonial discourse in and out of the Caribbean. Lamming's later novels are *Water with Berries* (1971) and *Natives of My Person* (1971). His *Conversations: Essays, Addresses and Interviews 1953–1990* (1992), edited by Richard Drayton and Andaiye, contains his most important statements on the literature and culture of the Caribbean.

During the 1950s Lamming worked on overseas programming for the British Broadcasting Corporation and travelled extensively. He visited the USA in 1955 on a Guggenheim Fellowship and in 1956 was one of the participants in The Congress of Negro Writers and Artists. In 1962 he was awarded a fellowship from the **Canada Council**. Lamming has travelled throughout the Caribbean and in 1975 was writer-in-residence at the University of Nairobi, Kenya; he also held this position at the University of DaresSalaam, Tanzania. In 1976 he was awarded a Commonwealth Foundation grant and travelled to six major universities across India and Australia. In the USA he has taught literature and creative writing at the University of Pennsylvania, Cornell University, and many others. In 1980 Lamming was awarded an honorary doctorate by the University of the West Indies. He lives in Barbados, but he continues to travel extensively and accepts many teaching and lecture engagements abroad.

Lamming's novels tell the collective story of the modern Caribbean. The essential mystery of the Caribbean's cultural past is retold in a series of novels rooted in the social and political reality of the area. Their unifying theme is liberation from colonialism, broadly conceived of as a continuing psychic experience 'long after the actual colonial situation formally ends'. The sequence of the novels suggest an allegorical master narrative of Caribbean liberation.

In the Castle of My Skin begins with the Caribbean of Lamming's childhood and adolescence from the mid-1930s through the 1940s, a period marked by social unrest and the mobilization of labour that was the beginning of the independence movement in the English-speaking Caribbean. The work is brilliantly conceived as an autobiography of childhood and adolescence on one level and as a novel of decolonization and ideological demystification on another. While *In the Castle of My Skin* ends with the impending departure of the central character, Lamming's second novel, *The Emigrants,* begins with emigration and arrival. The novel is crowded with a variety of characters from many islands who seek to redefine themselves in the 'mother country', an ideal landscape that they have been taught to revere. They settle uncomfortably in England's industrial cities, discovering the meaning of their marginality in an environment that is unexpectedly hostile and strange. The disillusionments of metropolitan England are followed by return to the Caribbean in *Of Age and Innocence*, where return coincides with the withdrawal of the British Empire and the advent of an independent Caribbean. The psychological drama of collapsing social relationships and identity reconstruction in a time of revolutionary social change is drawn with great sensitivity to the politics of race and class in the economic and social life of the Caribbean. *Season of Adventure* follows logically from the preceding novels; it envisions a popular uprising among the poor and dispossessed that brings about the collapse of the first independent republic in a fictive Caribbean island. The mechanism for renewal is rooted conceptually in the peasant and African base of the society, and in a newly formed alliance between the artist and a revolutionary new female presence.

Water with Berries returns to the themes of emigration and exile previously explored in *The Emigrants*. Set in the UK as racial hostility towards Caribbean immigrants reaches critical proportions, the novel speaks to a new militancy among immigrants unaccepting of their peripheral status. *Water with Berries* is broadly based on Lamming's interpretation in *The Pleasures of Exile* of *The Tempest* as a colonial text. *Natives of My Person* adds a new dimension to the unfolding drama of the Caribbean writer's 'quarrel' with history; it tells the story of a sixteenth-century voyage from the fictive European kingdom of Lime Stone, the goal of which is the establishment of a more just and equitable society in the Americas. In an interview with George Kent (1973), Lamming describes the novel as 'the whole etiology of *In the Castle of My Skin, The Emigrants* and *Season of Adventure*'. *Natives of My Person* is elaborately conceived to locate the most pressing issues of the late twentieth century in the beginnings of colonialism. It sustains the allegorical vision and weight of other great novels of the Americas such as Herman Melville's *Moby-Dick* (1851) and Gabriel García Márquez's *One Hundred Years of Solitude* (1967). *Natives of My Person* is of special interest to the discourses of feminism and decolonization, the politics and poetics of transgression, and post-colonial reconstruction.

Lamming's grand narrative of Caribbean liberation engages core themes of modern Caribbean writing and the literature of decolonization everywhere — colonialism and nationalism, emigration and exile, tradition and modernity, identity in the context of race, class, gender, and ethnicity, cultural hybridity, the interdependence of oral and written cultural traditions, and the role of the writer in a time of revolutionary social change. Lamming's essentially historicist perspective and reinvention of a mythic past link his work to that of the great literary architects of cultural decolonization beyond the Caribbean, from Africa, India, Ireland, and the Americas. Comparisons are most frequently drawn with African writers, among them **Chinua Achebe**, **Ayi Kwei Armah**, Camara Laye, **Ngugi wa Thiong'o**, and **Ezekiel Mphahlele**. Lamming's novels, however, may also be compared with those of black American writers such as James Baldwin, Ralph Ellison, **Paule Marshall**, and Richard Wright, and with novels of writers from the French- and Spanish-speaking Caribbean, such as Alejo Carpentier, Aimé Césaire, Jacques Roumain, and Joseph Zobel.

One of the architects of the post-colonial appropriation of *The Tempest*, Lamming, in *The Pleasures of Exile* and in other essays on cultural politics, anticipates the post-colonial critic's preoccupation with hegemony, language, place and displacement, abrogation, and appropriation as strategies of cultural decolonization and national reconstruction.

SANDRA POUCHET PAQUET

Further reading: Sandra Pouchet Paquet, *The Novels of George Lamming* (1982); Patrick Taylor, *The Narrative of Liberation* (1989); Joyce Jonas, *Anancy in the Great House* (1991).

LAMPMAN, ARCHIBALD (1861–99)
Canadian poet

Born in Morpeth, Canada West (now Ontario), he acquired a thorough education in the classics and modern literature at Trinity College, Toronto. His employment in the Post Office Department in Ottawa from 1883 until his death proved both frustrating in its pettiness and tedium and advantageous in providing ample opportunity to read and write. Lampman played an important part in the intellectual life of the new nation, as a poet and as a contributor to 'At the Mermaid Inn', a literary column that appeared in the Toronto *Globe* from 1892 to 1893. His letters, essays, and lectures, most of them published posthumously, reveal much about his poetics and his cultural milieu. As a socialist and a supporter of women's emancipation, Lampman was one of the few nineteenth-century Canadian writers to profess radical political views. His poetry, widely published in Canadian and American periodicals, was well received in both countries and appeared in two volumes, *Among the Millet and Other Poems* (1888) and *Lyrics of Earth* (1895).

As one of the leading Canadian writers of a period that was 'post-colonial' in a very immediate sense, Lampman offers a study in paradox. He is often grouped with his contemporaries **Charles G. D. Roberts, Bliss Carman**, and **Duncan Campbell Scott** under the name **'Confederation Poets'** — an allusion to their birth in the decade of Confederation and to their interest in fostering a national literature in the wake of the political union of 1867. The label is misleading in so far as it may imply uniformity in their work, but it does usefully suggest their determination to constitute, against the formidable literatures and publishing industries of Great Britain and the USA, a centre of literary achievement that would have mass, substance, and a character of its own. Lampman devoted much of his energy as a critic to struggling against 'a general mental and spiritual depression which necessarily results from the maintenance of an inferior colonial position'; he clearly understood that 'beyond a certain point — that point, viz., when the national spirit begins to show itself, as it is now distinctly doing with us — it is impossible for a people to remain in the attitude of colonists without intellectual deterioration.' At the same time, his fundamentally Romantic point of view and his eclectic practices as a writer resulted in a poetry imbued with the rhetoric and ideas of his British and American precursors.

Lampman's Romanticism is evident in his faith in the regenerative virtue of nature, his belief in the transforming power of imagination, and his view that writers should assess the real in the perspective of ideal truth and beauty. It is apparent also in his preferred genres: meditative landscape poetry ('Among the Timothy', 'The Frogs', 'Heat'), symbolic parable ('The City of the End of Things'), and Romantic narrative ('The Monk', 'Ingvi and Alf', 'At the Long Sault: May, 1660'). Lampman also produced some of the finest sonnets ever written in Canada, demonstrating great versatility in form and subject matter. His promptness to embrace Romantic values is at once subversive in principle and conservative in his recourse to the models of a distant era. Attracted to the transcendental vision of early nineteenth-century British and American writers, he was impelled by the intellectual and social crises of his own time to call that vision into question. The resulting tensions traverse much of his poetry, in its variable emphasis upon unity and diversity, space and time, the symbolic and the mimetic, primitivism and progress.

During his career, Lampman moved from an almost obsessive concern with nature to a greater involvement with social and ethical questions. His realistic modification of the pastoral reflects his perception of a society that was in transition from a frontier to an agrarian nation with a growing urban population. In his most accomplished long poem, 'The Story of an Affinity', he rewrites Wordsworthian pastoral and Tennysonian domestic idyll to affirm an optimism still possible for a young writer in a new country, even in the last decade of the nineteenth century. While Lampman's reputation suffered during the modernist period, recent critics have recognized that he adapted the resources of the Romantic tradition with a skill unprecedented in English-Canadian poetry.

LEN EARLY

Further reading: George Wicken, 'Archibald Lampman: an annotated bibliography', in Robert Lecker and Jack David (eds) *The Annotated Bibliography of Canada's Major Authors* 2 (1980); L. R. Early, *Archibald Lampman* (1986).

LANCASTER, G. B. (1873–1945)
New Zealand novelist, short-story writer
Born Edith Joan Lyttleton in Epping, northern Tasmania, Australia, and raised on the family sheep station in North Canterbury, New Zealand, she became New Zealand's first successful popular fiction writer (writing under the pseudonym G. B. Lancaster). She published thirteen novels and several hundred short stories after 1900 — mostly set in New Zealand, Australia, and Canada — during a career that took her to London, England, in 1909, and, after 1925, on an unsettled twenty-year pilgrimage through New Zealand, Australia, Canada, and the USA.

The mid-career novel that established Lancaster's reputation in England and the USA was *The Law-Bringers* (1913), a romantic action novel set in north-west Canada, but her best work consists of a later trilogy of 'dominion-historical' sagas: the bestseller *Pageant* (1933), set in colonial Tasmania, *Promenade* (1938), set in colonial Auckland and Canterbury, and *Grand Parade* (1943), set in eighteenth-century Halifax, Nova Scotia, Canada.

Lancaster's central theme is the civilizing mission of Empire, viewed initially through high-minded Anglican evangelical values in action-packed narratives that subject her male colonial protagonists to fierce tests of physical endurance and moral integrity. However, the emphasis falls less on the achievements of Empire than on failure and demoralization. The romance pattern in her early novels acts as a metaphor for the larger theme of territorial conquest, but the pattern is rarely fulfilled, such is the level of corruption, violence, and exploitation of indigenous peoples.

In the later novels the tragic intensities of the earlier romance pattern are left behind, and the vision of colonial history, presented through a succession of highly intelligent, compassionate but 'un-illusioned' female protagonists, becomes deeply ironic. The pageant, promenade, and grand parade of Britishness, strutting self-importantly across the stage of imperial ambitions, resolves itself, for Lancaster, into a comedy of repeated errors.

TERRY STURM

LANE, WILLIAM (1861–1917)
Australian novelist, journalist
Born in Bristol, England, he worked for a period in the USA and Canada, where he became a journalist. He immigrated to Queensland, Australia, in 1885, imbued with notions that in a new environment might be forged a new social order based on equality and shared resources and free of the entrenched privilege of the old. Sustained by such works as Marx's *Das Kapital*, this dream dominated the next fifteen years of his life.

In Brisbane, Lane worked as a reporter, producing provocative articles on social issues, including feminism. In 1887 he founded the *Boomerang*, like its Sydney counterpart, the ***Bulletin***, a vehicle for radical political and racist views. He also played a leading part in populist politics; in 1890 he became editor of the *Worker*, which was henceforth the organ of unionist causes. Out of these circumstances he wrote, under the pseudonym John Miller, *The Working Man's Paradise* (1892), a novel less interesting for its literary accomplishment than for the author's passionate commitment to the cause of improving society.

Influential as he was in public forums, Lane was at heart a mystic who believed that love — and he — might bind humankind together. From at least 1890 onwards, he meditated the formation of a primitive communistic society. After inquiring about sites in New South Wales and Western Australia, the New Australia Co-operative Settlement Association chose one near Asunción in Paraguay, where Lane sailed in July 1893 with a band of enthusiasts, with others, including **Mary Gilmore**, arriving subsequently.

Based partly on the ideas of Edward Bellamy's *Looking Backwards* (1887), and of John Ruskin and William Morris, this venture was another manifestation of the irrational utopianism so prominent in western thought at the end of the nineteenth century. Inevitably, it failed, with the pioneers losing their cohesion as a consequence variously of physical hardship, quarrels, jealousies, and Lane's uncompromising attitudes.

Lane founded Cosme, a second settlement in Paraguay that slowly went the way of the first and that he himself left in 1899 for New Zealand, where he grew steadily more conservative in outlook.

ALAN FROST

LANGLEY, EVE (1908–74)
Australian novelist
Born in New South Wales, Australia, she lived for some years in New Zealand and married unhappily there. After a period of living in institutions, she returned to Australia, where she lived out the rest of her extraordinary and tragic life. Oppressed by sexual tensions and uncertainties and the assumptions of a patriarchal society, Langley fought unsuccessfully to establish her own sexual identity, dressing often in men's clothes and changing her name by deed poll to Oscar Wilde. By the time she died in a hut in Katoomba in the Blue Mountains of New South Wales, she had long become a recluse. Little of this tragic fate is prefigured, however, in *The Pea Pickers* (1942), the first of only two novels Langley published, though she wrote many more which remain in various stages of completion in manuscript together with plays, poems, and other writings. When it first appeared, readers were charmed by its youthful ingenuousness and good humour, and most also mentioned its 'poetical' qualities. If the poetical qualities now seem rather thin and uninteresting — the actual poems included, like most of Langley's verse, are atrocious — the book retains its engaging freshness. It is the story of two young girls who, disguised in male clothing, wander through Gippsland, in eastern Victoria, living precariously off any jobs they can find. Rambling and picaresque, the novel is loosely unified by the contrast between the romantic yearnings and illusions of the narrator Steve and the systematic and sardonic puncturing of them by the hard-headed bushmen she meets.

The White Topee (1954) is a kind of sequel, set two years later but revealing much more openly the strains and tensions that were only obliquely apparent in the earlier novel. It is a meandering, actionless book with little discernible narrative or coherence. Steve is drawn towards various males, such as her long-suffering boyfriend Macca, but, as she says revealingly, 'What I really wanted was to be a man, and free for ever to write and think and dream.'

LAURIE CLANCY

Further reading: Joy L. Thwaite, *The Importance of Being Eve Langley* (1989).

LANGUAGE

LANGUAGE (Australia)
Australian language ecology
Australia's seventeen million inhabitants speak more than two hundred immigrant and indigenous languages, the most important — by number of speakers — being English, the official and *de facto* national language spoken by eighty-three per cent of the population as its primary language; next come Italian, Greek, Yugoslavian languages, German, Dutch, Polish, and Chinese. This ranking reflects the composition of postwar immigration, which has influenced not only Australia's language ecology and current language policy but also the evolution of Australian English.

Despite the fact of a multilingual Australia, a myth of Australian monolingualism and monoculturalism was sustained for almost two hundred years of Anglo-Celtic settlement. But Australia was never a monolingual country: linguistic and cultural diversity existed before and after British colonization. It is estimated, for example, that some 250 Aboriginal languages were spoken at contact, only fifty of which remain viable. Today, fifty thousand indigenous Australians speak two English-lexifier creole languages, a legacy of colonial contact. During the first settlement at Port Jackson in 1788, an Aboriginal pidgin arose, the first of several that accompanied European invasion of Aboriginal territory. Pacific Islander indentured workers in the nineteenth century brought with them varieties of Pacific Pidgin English. From these pidgins developed the two Australian creoles, Northern Territory Kriol, spoken in Aboriginal communities across northern Australia, and Torres Strait Creole, the lingua franca of the Melanesian Torres Strait Islanders. These creoles also index black ethnic identity, especially among the young, and continue to influence varieties of Black Australian English.

Australian English

Australian English, which was accorded 'positive recognition' in 1987 by the *National Policy on Languages*, has its primary linguistic origins in the southeastern regional dialects of nineteenth-century England, the geographical source of most early migration to the new 'southern' colonies of Australia, New Zealand, and South Africa. Thus, while it is a distinct variety, it shares with the other 'southern colonial Englishes' the bulk of its phonology, morphology, syntax, and vocabulary. The latter, however, evidences a more diverse origin in a multiplicity of British dialects. Although accused of being predominantly Cockney — a working-class London dialect — Australian English has a more eclectic provenance. The convicts, although sentenced in London courts, were not necessarily Londoners. They included a sizeable proportion of Celtic (Irish, Scottish, Welsh, and Cornish) peoples; yet, despite this, there is little influence from Celtic languages on Australian English, apart from a few vocabulary items, minor morphosyntactic forms, and possibly the pronunciations of words such as *fillum* (film) and *growun* (grown).

Studies

For most of its development, Australian English has been studied with reference to the norms of British Received Pronunciation, the most prestigious British class dialect. Early commentators were preoccupied with the differences between the two varieties, stigmatizing Australian forms as inferior and adducing all kinds of extralinguistic reasons for its 'peculiarities'. For example, spectrographic studies show that Broad Australian speech — the most distinctive variety, popularly known as 'Strine' (Australian) — occupies a relatively smaller vowel space than other varieties. This was said to stem from Australians' need to speak with their mouths almost shut to keep out the flies.

Also stressed was the uniformity of Australian English, again taking as a yardstick the heterogeneity of British regional dialects. While social and geographical variation in Australian English often remains opaque to speakers of other varieties, such variation does exist and is susceptible of linguistic and sociolinguistic analysis.

The first serious studies of Australian English dealt with its vocabulary, with lexical processes such as word compounding and noun phrase formation, and with the semantic processes of broadening, narrowing, amelioration, and pejoration, as English vocabulary evolved to meet the demands of a new physical, social, and psychological context. The first dictionary of 'Austral English' was published in 1898. After the Second World War emphasis shifted from the lexicon to phonology. *The Speech of Australian Adolescents* (1965) by A. G. Mitchell and Arthur Delbridge proposed a three-way classification of Australian English on the basis of diphthong pronunciation: Cultivated,

General, and Broad. Although the authors denied any correlation with social class, Cultivated speech is associated primarily with middle-class females, whereas Broad is associated with working-class males. Methodologically flawed, this work nevertheless provided a framework for much subsequent analysis and remains the most influential study of Australian English.

The establishment of linguistics departments in Australian universities from the late 1960s, although dominated by British ideology, began to produce linguistically trained graduates with an interest in describing not only indigenous Australian languages but also Australian English. This has led to more sophisticated descriptions in phonetics, phonology, morphology, and syntax, often using a variationist model, which allows linguistic features to be correlated statistically with sociological factors such as class, gender, age, and ethnicity and reveals interrelationships between these and geographical factors. Popular interest in the subject has also increased with a wave of new books and the provision of Australian materials for instruction in English as a second language.

Lexicon

Certain words are recognized throughout the English-speaking world as distinctively Australian: *barrack* (cheer on), *cobber* (friend), *dinkum* (genuine), larrikin (mischievous person). Although these words originated in various British regional dialects, they disappeared from British English but were retained in Australian English, eventually to be repatriated as Australianisms.

Many English words were semantically modified in order to express the colonists' relationship with an environment they found both exotic and threatening. The 'beautiful names of an intimate countryside' were displaced by harsher terms, more appropriate to the new land: bush (forest-covered land); never never (desert country); outback (remote country); property (farm); pastoralist (owner of a large property). Perhaps surprisingly, Aboriginal languages have left few traces in Australian English. Only about 220 borrowed words exist, almost all of them place and topographical names and terms for indigenous flora, fauna, and material culture: Cunnamulla, Murrumbidgee, Woolloomooloo, Woolloongabba, billabong, coolabah, kangaroo, kookaburra, didgeridoo, and woomera, for example.

Four major 'lexical regions' of Australian English have now been mapped: New South Wales and Queensland; Victoria and Tasmania; southeast South Australia; and Western Australia. These reflect early settlement patterns rather than later political boundaries. The unobtrusiveness of lexical differences, their association with objects of everyday life, their apparent idiosyncrasy, and the fact that they are not closely associated with class differences, as they are in the UK, ensured that they remained peripheral to mainstream linguistic analysis until recently.

One unmistakably Cockney influence on Australian English is rhyming slang. Cockney expressions such as China (plate) — mate; trouble and strife — wife; and butcher's (hook) — look (as in 'to have/go for a butcher's') are still heard in working-class pubs, where males order a dog's eye and dead horse (pie and sauce) with their beer. It also assumed a local flavour: Captain (Cook) — look; Dad and Dave — shave; Noah's (Ark) — shark; Kembla (Grange) [a village near Wollongong] — change/money, as in 'Give us some Kembla!'; Greta (i.e., Garbo) — garbage [garbo] collector; and even Old Jack (Lang) — rhyming slang. Australian war prisoners used rhyming slang in the prison camps to avoid being understood by their Japanese guards, who could not decode the complex interplay of sound, meaning, and cultural context.

From time to time there is an outcry about foreign — usually American — influence on Australian English. Located within the American sphere of political, economic, and cultural influence, Australians borrow American terms, which have prestigious connotations, and adopt simpler American spellings: 'color' rather than 'colour'; 'finalize' rather than 'finalise'; 'pediatric' rather than 'paediatric'. Australian lexicon (and cuisine) has also been enriched by the borrowing of gastronomic terms from Italian, Greek, and Chinese, which tend to have variable pronunciations as they progress towards nativization. *Cappuccino* has become so nativized that it is sometimes written as *cuppaccino* — from *cuppa* (cup of tea) — with a plural form, *cupsaccino.*

Morphosyntax

Australian English syntax differs little from pan-English syntax, with some minor exceptions, such as the familiar appellations for Woolloongabba, Mount Isa, and Alice Springs as *the Gabba, the Isa, the Alice*. Recent syntactic innovations, found also in other varieties of English, involve transferring words from one grammatical category to another. Thus, nouns are used as verbs: 'They letter-boxed the town'; verbs as nouns: 'I'm just going for a little relax'; and verb-plus-noun object combinations become compound verbs: 'He decided not to prawn-trawl all his life.'

More distinctively Australian is felt to be the abundance of abbreviations; word play has long been a feature of Australian English. A frequent practice is to attach the suffixes '-ie' and '-o' to truncated nouns — as in actor Paul Hogan's call to 'Put another shrimp on the *barbie* [barbecue]!' — and by hundreds of similar forms in common use: *mozzie* (mosquito), *muffie* (muffler), *Tassie* (Tasmania), *compo* (compensation/payment), *relo* (relative), *muso* (musician). So stereotyped is this process that it was satirized in the following passage:

> Thommo, a commo journo, who lived with his preggo wife from Rotto in a fibro in Paddo, slipped on the lino taking a dekko at the nympho next door . . . ['Thompson, a communist journalist, who lived with his pregnant wife from Rottnest Island in a fibrocement house in Paddington, slipped on the linoleum taking a look at the nymphomaniac next door . . . ']

A. Wierzbicka (*Language in Society* 15, 1986) analyses the '-ie' here as a depreciative suffix, and '-o' as a suffix connoting familiarity. She also suggests that the well-known 'Australian love of abbreviations' reflects Australian anti-intellectualism and informality.

Today the use of swear words before stressed syllables within words — 'fan-bloody-tastic' and 'in-fuckin'-credible' — and the coining of exotic similes — 'flat out like a lizard drinking' (very busy) — are less common than previously and more typical of older working-class male speech.

The examples in this section are associated with particular registers rather than with social class, the major division in Australia being between working class (blue-collar or manual occupation) and middle-class (white-collar or professional occupation). In the following dyads, however, the first item is associated with middle-class speech, the second with working-class speech: gave/give, did/done, saw/seen; we (you) were/we (you) was; you/youse; ran quickly/run quick; more modern/more moderner; more than/more than what; those people/them people.

Phonology

The following phonological features are not necessarily unique to Australian English; in many cases they continue centuries-old historical trends. However, they are considered to be characteristic because of their association with particular social groups, their frequency of occurrence, and their use in popular stereotypes. Some of them are also beginning to be diagnostic of urban regional varieties, as urban accents become more divergent, perhaps reflecting a new localism in the face of postwar immigration. (Examples are borrowed or adapted from Alistair Morrison's bestselling *Let's Talk Strine*, 1965.)

Certain vowel pronunciations are thought to be particularly characteristic of Australian English, especially the 'broad' pronunciation of diphthongs, represented orthographically as *mite* (mate), *noice* (nice), *flair* (flower). Today these occur most often in rural and 'Ethnic Broad' varieties, tending to become simple vowels elsewhere: *Didger rilly riedabat it in the piper?* ('Did you really read about it in the paper?'). The raising of lax vowels, a feature also of New Zealand, South African, and Southern English speech, is increasingly frequent in Australian English: *It's jessa flesh in the pen* ('It's just a flash in the pan').

Also extremely common are consonant pronunciations that result from simplificational processes, such as palatalization, consonant cluster deletion, and intervocalic voicing, especially in the casual speech of young adults and working-class males: *Hancher gotcher key?* ('Haven't you got your key?'); *Jeggoda the tennis? Nar, dingo. Sorten TV.* ('Did you go to the tennis?' 'No, I didn't go. I saw it on TV.'); *Chiddim*? ('Did she hit him?').

Popularly identified with young people's speech are two stereotyped features: the pronunciations *nothink, somethink, everythink, anythink* (nothing, something, everything, anything), and the so-called 'rising inflection', also found in North American and British English, which refers to the raising of the voice pitch at the end of a statement in a way more typical of questions or requests for confirmation. However, it almost always occurs in narratives and as answers to questions to which only the replier has the relevant information: 'Q: Where were you born? A: In the Mater [Hospital]?'.

Agencies of standardization

No academy or other official normative body exists to oversee the standardization of Australian English. Until recently, spelling and grammatical standards were set by British English dictionaries, grammars, and style manuals, and pronunciation norms were those of Received Pronunciation.

In 1954 the Australian Broadcasting Commission established a Standing Committee on Spoken English to advise on pronunciation and general matters of usage, including sexist language and style, and in 1966 the first of four editions of the *Australian Government Style Manual* was published with the aim of exercising a normative influence over aspects of the written language.

Extremely important in establishing local standards was the 1981 publication of *The Macquarie Dictionary*, which based its forms squarely on Australian usage. Originally scorned by purists, it has now become the major authority for the pronunciation and spelling of Australian English.

Conclusion

English remains the major institutional language and lingua franca of Australia, and widespread knowledge of English is generally considered essential to national cohesiveness, interaction among different ethnic communities, provision of equal rights, and access to higher education. Australian English, the cover term for a range of national varieties, reflects Australians' unique geographical, social, cultural, and historical experience.

ANNA SHNUKAL

Further reading: George William Turner, *The English Language in Australia and New Zealand* (1972); David Blair, 'An Australian English bibliography', *Working Papers of the Speech and Language Research Centre, Macquarie University* 2 (1978); G. A. Wilkes, *A Dictionary of Australian Colloquialisms* (1978); Joseph Lo Bianco, *National Policy on Languages* (1987); Peter Collins and David

Blair, *Australian English: The Language of a New Society* (1989).

LANGUAGE (Canadian English)

Although English is only one of Canada's two official languages, it has, in fact, been the working language of the federal government until recent years, since French is limited to the province of Quebec and a few areas concentrated in the provinces of New Brunswick, Ontario, and Manitoba. While the status of English and French was protected in several acts, especially in the British North America Act (1867), the status of French has declined at all levels, a decline promoted by language policies in the provinces. Manitoba, for example, abrogated its official bilingualism in 1890 in favour of English, an act declared illegal by the Supreme Court of Canada in 1979; Ontario abolished French schools in 1912. An attempt to arrest the domination of English began in the 1960s when the federal government introduced measures to safeguard French. The Official Languages Act (1969) gave both languages equal status in all federal matters, and this provision was included in the 1982 Constitution and was pursued in federal programmes. Provincial governments were urged to implement similar policies, but they responded according to their political interests. New Brunswick complied with a similar Official Languages Act, but Quebec, taking more extreme measures in an attempt to reverse the decline of French, adopted a charter in 1977 making French its only official language. Ontario has implemented its own limited language policy providing for schools and government services in French without explicitly recognizing French as an official language.

The result of such varied legislation is that Canada has no uniform language policy. The attempt to establish bilingualism in all the provinces has failed, and the trend is now towards territorial unilingualism. The need for a clear policy and positive response to all language groups in Canada is becoming more urgent, especially since Quebec is seeking greater independence, and the First Nations are demanding more self-government.

Significantly, distinct regional varieties of Canadian English (CE) exist, especially in Newfoundland and the Maritime provinces of Nova Scotia, New Brunswick, and Prince Edward Island, but a recognized urban and educated accent, often labelled 'General Canadian', is prevalent across Canada. CE is similar to American English, the other major variety of North American English, but it also includes features from varieties of British English. It has a number of characteristics that distinguish it from both American and British English even though it seems to be losing its more distinctive features and merging with Northern and Midland American.

The actual usage of CE demonstrates a great deal of regional and social flexibility: the 'a' in 'tomato' might be pronounced as in 'ate', 'at', or 'ah'. One of the characteristics of the usage is the existence of the many dual forms that occur in grammar (Have you any/Do you have any), vocabulary (chesterfield/couch), pronunciation (the 'u' in words such as 'duty', 'assume' rhyming with either 'beauty' or 'booty'), and spelling (cheque/check).

Some scholars emphasize the American influence on CE, some the British, and others independent developments. The prevalent view among scholars is that the national variety of CE is based on the language of the immigrants to the Canadas from the rebellious American Thirteen Colonies, the Loyalists and post-Loyalists of the 1780s and 1790s. These settlers did not speak 'American' English — they were part of British North America before 1776 and spoke the same varieties of British dialects.

Another view argues that the history of CE

begins with the dialects of British English brought by settlers in the nineteenth century who overwhelmed the language of the earlier Loyalists. This view points out that many items that seem to derive from American English actually came from the early British dialects that subsequently changed. For example, the Canadian pronunciation of 'grass' [æ] came from British English, since [æ] existed in British English as a different vowel from the one in 'farther' before the end of the eighteenth century. (The new vowel, as in 'farther', did not exist in British English until the end of the eighteenth century, according to M. H. Scargill.) Also, the use of the phrase 'in back of' as a variant for 'behind' was common in British English.

The development of the vocabulary that is distinctive in the national variety of CE is represented in the *Dictionary of Canadianisms on Historical Principles* (1967). The *Gage Canadian Dictionary* (1983), a major revision of school dictionaries such as the *Canadian Senior Dictionary* (1979), in spite of its limitations as a desk dictionary, is the most scholarly, purely Canadian dictionary for adult use. Increasing numbers of Canadianized versions of American dictionaries have also been appearing, but the cloning process has not produced a fully adequate dictionary of Canadian English. Some of the major regional varieties are recorded in the *Dictionary of Newfoundland English* (1982) and the *Dictionary of Prince Edward Island English* (1988).

The phonology, grammar, regional variations, and usage have not been studied as fully as the lexicon but are the subject of much recent scholarship.

The different settlement patterns of English-speaking immigrants are significant for the creation of CE and its major dialect regions. The variety of CE that critic J. K. Chambers calls heartland Canadian, spoken from Quebec westward, was established in southern Ontario by the Loyalist refugees and post-Loyalists from midland America. Their varieties of English must have homogenized after they arrived and acted as a norm for later settlers. This form of English, although it includes many variables, spread throughout the rest of Ontario, the prairie provinces, and British Columbia. Southern Ontario was a major source for the English-speaking settlements, and the English of these settlers became the linguistic model for the major cities in spite of regional, rural, and other variations.

The dialect variations in the Maritime provinces and in Newfoundland are more pronounced as a result of a different settlement history, but General Canadian is also prevalent there. The Acadian region that became the Maritime provinces of Prince Edward Island, New Brunswick, and Nova Scotia was settled by various groups: first the Acadian French and later, after the Treaty of Utrecht in 1713, the British. Following this period, increasing numbers of New Englanders moved into the region, especially after the expulsion of the Acadian French in 1755. New migrants from England, Scotland, and Ireland continued to have a marked influence on the diversity of the language. The influence of the Loyalist settlers after the American Revolution was probably not very great since they tended to adapt to the customs and language in the region.

Newfoundland's long history of settlement and the development of English is different. The area was mainly settled by immigrants from Britain, including a large Irish group, and it was isolated from the mainland, becoming part of Canada only in 1949. The enclave dialects in the isolated settlements along the coast, the rich innovations in the vocabulary, and grammatical and pronunciation features contributed to a form of English in Newfoundland markedly unlike that of the rest of the country, but the CE of the mainland is nevertheless becoming dominant, and the enclave dialects are much less varied than was once thought, according to the Newfoundland dictionary. Other dialects in the Ottawa Valley and the Red River district of

Manitoba seem to be losing their characteristic features as they are replaced by General Canadian. A nationally recognizable dialect of English seems prevalent throughout Canada in spite of the regional and social variations. For example, critic Gaelan Dodds De Wolf has shown that while Vancouver English and Ottawa English share a number of significant phonetic characteristics of CE, they vary geographically and sociologically. More older people and more women use the variable diphthong in 'site' and 'side' in both cities, but speakers in Vancouver distinguish them more frequently than speakers in Ottawa. George Anthony Tilly found that the language of English Canadian novels of the 1970s, including those from Newfoundland, does not show significant regional differences but rather emphasizes various sociological differences, depending on differences between rural and urban speakers, generations, social classes, and ethnic groups.

The numerous new words and new or different meanings are the most noticeable innovations, but vocabulary expansion is natural to the English language. The Canadian vocabulary has adapted new words from many sources and developed its own meanings for existing words. Even though more than fifty Native languages were spoken throughout Canada, many over large areas, relatively few words — 'potlatch', 'pemmican', and 'moose', for example — were borrowed from the First Nations, and even fewer from the Inuit: 'totem', 'kayak', and 'mukluk'. Many of the derivations are difficult to confirm precisely, and some are surprising; 'canoe' is actually of Haitian origin from the Arawaks, and 'Eskimo', meaning 'eater of raw flesh', is derived from Algonquian; the term 'Eskimo' is being replaced with Inuit, an Inuktitut word meaning 'the people'.

The practice of using English terminology when referring to aboriginal peoples is more significant than the few derivations. The word 'Indian' is the result of the initial confusion of the Spanish invaders. Commonly used words such as 'squaw', 'noble savage', 'medicine man', and many others emphasize negative colonial attitudes. The dominance of the Anglo-Canadians discouraged borrowing because of deliberate attempts to destroy or suppress Native languages and culture or even whole Indian nations such as the Beothuk in Newfoundland. **Basil Johnston** claims that only three of Canada's original fifty-three aboriginal languages are not in danger of disappearing completely.

CE borrowed from the early French Canadians, who had already developed their own language for exploration, trade, and geography in North America and such words as 'rapids', 'portage', 'depot', 'kettle', among many others. It continues to be influenced in Quebec by French, but at the national level, except for the word order of 'Air Canada', 'Encyclopedia Canadiana', and a limited number of other examples, the influence of French on Canadian English has waned.

The continuing process of adding distinctive lexical items to CE is especially marked by developing new compounds with specific meanings such as 'flight pay', 'chesterfield suite', and 'baby bonus', or by attaching unique significations for existing words.

The pronunciation and grammar differ from General American in only minor ways. CE is distinct because of the particular distribution of the features more than its individual characteristics. A famous feature of CE identified as 'Canadian raising' is a typical example. It involves the regularly variant pronunciations of two diphthongs, a centring and raising of the diphthongs in 'out' and 'kite' compared to a lower and longer pronunciation in 'loud' and 'ride'. This difference is determined by the unvoiced consonants after the diphthong and a few other regular phonetic features. These diphthongs occur in other dialects, but in Canada they occur with other features such as the use of the same vowel sound in words such as 'cot/caught', the occurrence of post-vocalic 'r' in words such as 'part' and 'car', the two pronunciations of 'lieutenant' (i.e., 'leftenant' and 'lootenant'), the Canadian flat 'a' as in 'cat', 'dance', 'class', and 'ask', compared to the so-called British 'a' that developed late in the nineteenth century, and the voicing of intervocalic 't' with optional flapping so that 'matter' sounds like 'madder'. Perhaps the most important aspect of the Canadian accent is that it allows for significant variation; no particular regional form of CE is considered more prestigious than any other or a model for the rest of the country.

General Canadian has few distinctive grammatical items even though CE, like other varieties of English, has many individual and social variations. Useful, increasingly common features, especially in spoken English, involve the selection of a plural pronoun to avoid gender-specific usage in reference to singular antecedents, also common in British English until the nineteenth century, as in 'Everyone will submit their project,' or verb agreement with semantically plural but grammatically singular subjects to emphasize the individual members of a group, as in 'The committee consider their task'.

Canadian spelling frequently allows for many of the variations found in British and American English. Canadians never developed a programme of spelling reform like that introduced by Noah Webster for American English, but it has acquired many American spellings alongside British ones, without a clear preference for either. The degree of preference varies a great deal with individual words, contexts, and people. Common variations involve 'or/our', 'er/re', and 'ense/ence' endings (flavor, fiber, pretense), single or double 'l' (jeweler), and simplification of diagraphs (encyclopedia/encyclopaedia, anemic/anaemic). Some spellings, such as 'tire' and 'curb', seem to follow American usage, but are actually derived from older British spelling. Many newspapers tend to favour American spellings, but policy varies with different publishers.

In spite of the flexibility of CE, there is a general preference for a fairly conservative form that is recognizable throughout the country and generally thought of simply as good English. Many characteristics go unnoticed by Canadians except by dictionary editors and specialists. Those peculiarities of which people are aware are usually considered part of a dialect, a regionalism, or merely poor English. Canadian schools tend to inflict a narrow control on the language of students. This control has the same function as the historical domination of English in Canada over speakers of French, Native, and minority languages. Ironically, CE is a language that allows for diversity and individual flexibility, but English in Canada, as elsewhere, has often been used as a weapon to suppress linguistic freedom.

BERNIE HARDER

Further reading: W. C. Lougheed, *Writings on Canadian English, 1976–87: A Selective, Annotated Bibliography* (1988).

LANGUAGE (The Caribbean)

In the English-speaking Caribbean countries — most of which are former British colonies — history may be traced in language usage and language usage in history. English is the official language of legal documents, textbooks, and formal public use, but it is not the only language used in these cultures. Co-existing with Standard English are dialects of English, creole Englishes, and, in a few cases, other languages such as Hindi, Spanish, French Creole, and other Caribbean Creoles.

The polyglot past has yielded the many language varieties of the present. In Caribbean countries a range of usages — known as a creole continuum — links the standardized English of educated speakers to the true creole speech of the working class. Both groups use partially overlapping language forms and understand one another generally, but the structure of creole English differs from that of Standard English. The syntactic contrast (along with other differences of word formation, semantics, vocabulary, and pronunciation) establishes the creole Englishes as systematically alien to English itself, even though much of their vocabulary is of English stock. Consequently, Caribbean speakers have available to them not only two ranges of vocabulary, but two ranges of grammatical expression. This wealth has proven both a blessing and a curse: it permits rich and complex rhetorical effects as writers and speakers code-switch between the levels of the continuum, but the creole forms also tend to be strange to speakers from other areas. Standard English is a powerful means of international communication, and publishers have been reluctant to issue any text that strays very far from that norm. At the same time, Caribbean writers and readers have a growing appetite for their own words and their own voices. Nothing less can represent the complexity of these cultures.

Anglophone Caribbean writers have typically grown up among dialects and variant language forms. In nineteenth-century British Trinidad, for example, English and English Creole held sway alongside French and French Creole, Spanish, and various African languages; in this setting, every child came in contact with more than one dialect or language. Similar complexities of language usage exist in all other former English colonies; each colony breeds its peculiar opportunities for the recreation of experience through linguistic experimentation. Caribbean folk songs and tales today include traces of this complex linguistic past, while novels such as **V. S. Reid**'s *The Jamaicans* (1976) have attempted to re-create the cultural cross-currents of history by invoking linguistic features from many sources.

Today's Caribbean Englishes reveal a dynamic contest between Standard English and a welter of contending dialects. In the seventeenth century the earliest colonizers brought with them a new phenomenon: a standardized English used for written records and spoken by an educated few, along with a range of regional and class dialects that formed the base of their language community. In the British Caribbean, metropolitan English formed the written language of the literate few. Seventeenth-century documents show few variations from the standard save in private papers. Metropolitan English adorns the notebooks of Welsh, Lancashire, and Somerset overseers who understood that spoken and written style had parted company forever. White colonials of the Caribbean recorded neither their own dialects nor the contemporary Caribbean, African, and pidginized languages of the majority of people, nor even the creole Englishes, which, eventually, everyone spoke. Those creole Englishes are, in fact, the offspring of African languages and the despised non-standard English dialects of the time. Eighteenth-century writers who could have demonstrated other language forms clung to the metropolitan norms. The Nigerian **Olaudah Equiano** wrote in metropolitan English; Francis Williams (1700–70), the black Jamaican graduate of Cambridge University, wrote ornate Latin verse.

As European Romanticism and the cult of the innocent savage highlighted peoples beyond the metropolitan pale, writers such as Jean Jacques Rousseau, Robert Burns, and the brothers Grimm raised ideas that would challenge attitudes to language usage. Yet non-standard usages and the languages of subject peoples remained a matter of record only for missionaries and authors of travellers' journals. For the main, only a stereotypical pidgin availed to represent any non-metropolitan culture. The novelist Mayne Reid (1818–83) shows some skill in writing in the form of black speech of the Americas in his only Jamaican novel, *The Maroon* (2 vols, 1862), but no writers spoke from within Caribbean creole culture itself. Yet all Caribbean peoples, whether descendants of Europeans or Africans, felt the pressure of the languages around them, the strongest being the creole languages themselves. Consequently, the contending forms were forced to interact in order to give voice and shape to Caribbean experience.

Members of the anglophone Caribbean community switch linguistic codes: topic, audience, and speaker mix to produce an appropriate code, whether creole or standard. A speaker, for example, may use a standard code to add formality — satiric or serious — to a remark and then switch into the use of deep Creole to add emotional emphasis or folk humour to the discourse. Speakers of a standardized English may code-switch as readily as speakers of deep Creole, perhaps more frequently. Thus any speech act, however simple it appears, carries in its linguistic form crucial information about situation and speakers. Even in the nineteenth century, however, the Caribbean creole languages seldom appeared in writing save in records of folk tales, songs, or anecdotes deemed quaint by educated whites. Yet the pressure to reveal new voices began to appear in white colonial writing in such experiments as Mark Twain's *The Adventures of Huckleberry Finn* (1884), a parallel to *Tom Cringle's Log*, which was written by a once-popular, now largely-forgotten Jamaican-by-adoption, Michael Scott, and first serialized in *Blackwoods Magazine* (1829). Both novels record the colonial, non-standard speech of whites and blacks; both have been accused of racism; both display the language behaviour of their own and later times; both emphasize the pressure felt by the peoples of these colonial worlds to shape a unique experience in the languages of those worlds.

Tom Cringle's Log, with its graphic creole comedy, demonstrates why the earliest Caribbean poets chose literary English. Within these cultures, the educated assumed that creole language signified ignorance, backwardness, and distance from the metropole. Its tones were believed incapable of lyric and tragedy; one could not write epic or tragic verse in the medium of calypso, folk tale, or digging song. The metropolitan genres existed exclusively — it seemed — in the metropolitan dialect.

To fashion a mode for Caribbean experience, language and genre had to merge and re-emerge in new forms. Early portrayors of original Caribbean experience include Henry G. Murray, whose dramatic monologues blend Creole and standard English. Unlike Scott's generic association of 'creole and comedy', Murray's *Tom Kittle's Wake* (1877) movingly describes the death of a fisherman and the funerary rites that follow. In it, dialogue and inner monologue are in Creole, the narrative in Standard English; tone shifts cross language lines, and genre hesitates. Murray calls his work a 'dramatic monologue', unable to fit it into any standard genre. Other experimenters such as **Claude McKay** in *Constab Ballads* (1912) and **Alfred H. Mendes** in *Pitch Lake* (1934) soon attempted a more daring linguistic realism, linking character and dialogue to mood, tone, and plot development. Within two generations **Jean Rhys**, **Wilson Harris**, **Jamaica Kincaid**, **Erna Brodber**, and others broke from the old rules to shape new literary forms.

Emergent language cultures create new genres and demand new linguistic experiments. **Edward Kamau Brathwaite** mingles Barbadian, Trinidadian, and Jamaican language forms with Standard English. Already accustomed to Creole in dialogue and drama, Caribbean novelists and poets now use it for extended first-person narrative, as in **Sam Selvon**'s *The Housing Lark* (1965) and **Derek Walcott**'s *The Star-Apple Kingdom* (1979). Creole language has moved to the centre, on virtually an equal footing with the metropole's standard, so that the omniscient voice may now speak Creole. Most twentieth-century Caribbean writers depend on a standardized English as their staple, interpolating dialectal, creole, or other linguistic material (as in Brathwaite's *The Arrivants: A New World Trilogy*, 1973) to meet the needs of setting, dialogue, or narrative voice. Satirists such as the Jamaican **Louise Bennett** or the Trinidadian Selvon use Creole or dialect almost exclusively, foregrounding their usage against the felt presence of the standard language.

In the twentieth century the forces of standardization — education, the media — have accelerated the processes of de-creolization whereby English has supplanted all other languages. Languages such as Jamaican Creole and Guyanese Creole have lost more of their distinctive features, producing intermediate forms that finally become little more than dialects of English. That completed process may be seen in Barbadian English and its dialects. A similar process is at work in Trinidad. French Creole is disappearing in places such as St Vincent and Dominica. Yet Caribbean writers remain very aware of the power of the varied past: dialectal and creole forms mingle with Standard English in the works of poets, novelists and — most of all — playwrights. Non-standard forms are now a vital asset to the creative genius of the Caribbean literary imagination.

JEAN D'COSTA

Further reading: Mervyn C. Alleyne, *Comparative Afro-American: An Historical-Comparative Study of English-Based Afro-American Dialects of the New World* (1980); Lawrence D. Carrington *et al.*, eds, *Studies in Caribbean Language* (1983); John Holm, *Pidgins and Creoles*, 2 vols (1988).

LANGUAGE (Indian English)

Indian English (IE) is a cover term for the institutionalized variety of English used by educated Indians across India. IE is essentially a contact language, clearly demonstrating convergence with Indian languages belonging to four major language families (Indo-Aryan, Dravidian, Tibeto-Burman, and Munda). English in India is deeply influenced by the diverse socio-cultural patterns of the subcontinent. These influences, both linguistic and cultural, manifest themselves in two processes, nativization and acculturation, resulting in the Indianization of the English language. The linguistic features of Indianization include pronunciation, grammar, vocabulary, and semantics.

Pronunciation

In pronunciation IE tends to use syllable-timed rhythm as opposed to the stress-timed rhythm of the native varieties of English. The use of vowels shows considerable variation, depending on the mother tongue of the speaker. A system of eleven pure vowels and six diphthongs generally characterizes educated IE speakers: /i:/ (*meet*); /I/ (*sit*); /e:/ (*safe*); /ɛ / (*send*); /æ/ (*mat*); /a:/ (*large*); /ʊ/ (*shot*); /o:/ (*no*); /U/ (*book*); /u:/ (*pool*); /ə/ (*bus*). The diphthongs are /ai/ (*five*); /⊃i/ (*boy*); /au/ (*cow*); /Iə/ (*here*); /eə/ (*there*); /Uə/ (*poor*). An epenthetical vowel is added to consonant clusters such as *sk-*, *sl-*: school is pronounced as *isku:l* in Bihar and Uttar Pradesh, and as *səku:l* in Kashmir and Punjab. The alveolar consonants (t, d) are replaced by retroflex consonants (pronounced with the tongue-tip curled up toward the hard palate); the fricatives /Θ/ and /ð/ are pronounced as aspirated consonants /th/ and /dh/ or /d/, respectively; /f/ is pronounced as /ph/; the distinction between /v/ and /w/ is reduced to /w/; no distinction is made between voiceless palato-alveolar /ʃ/ and its voiced counterpart /ʒ/, and no distinction is made between 'dark l' (in *full*) and 'clear l' (in *luck*). All varieties of IE are rhotic, thus /r/ after a vowel is retained. In south Indian IE double consonants are geminated (*bully* as *bul-lee*). Stress is not used to make phonemic distinctions, but is used for emphasis, and suffixes are stressed. Unstressed vowels are pronounced as full vowels (i.e., in *photography*, all syllables receive full value), and the distinction between strong and weak forms of vowels is neutralized.

Grammar

In grammar, British English continues to provide a yardstick for the norm. There are, however, several grammatical features that mark Indianness. The following are illustrative: considerable variation in the use of the three articles (zero, definite, and indefinite); use of stative verbs (*have*, *know*, etc.) in progressive tenses (*Mary is having two houses*; *You must be knowing that . . .*); use of reduplication for emphasis and distributive meaning (*I want to buy some small small things*; *Give one one pencil to students*; *Who who came to the party?*); reduction of the range of tag questions to one generalized question tag (*Isn't it?*); use of *yes* and *no* as tag questions (*Sheela is going to school, yes?*); formation of *wh*-questions without subject-auxiliary inversion (i.e., *When you would like to go?*); and variation in the use of tenses, such as the use of present perfect for simple past, i.e., *I have bought the shirt yesterday*.

Vocabulary

The lexical stock of IE varies in the degree of assimilation. A large number of assimilated words with Indian socio-cultural and administrative connotations have been transferred to British and American English (*bungalow*, *chutney*, *nirvana*). The number of words from Indian languages in IE is ever increasing, particularly in the media and in various contexts of social interaction (*pukka*, 'real'; *janata*, 'masses'). The lexical borrowing in IE is of several types. Single lexical items are borrowed from Indian languages or from Arabic and Persian via Hindustani and Urdu (*ahimsa*, 'non-violence'; *bhajan*, 'devotional song'; *chapati*, 'unleavened bread'). Hybridized formations are coined in which one component is from English and another from an Indian language (*lathi-charge*, 'to charge with baton'; *swadeshi cloth*, 'home made cloth'). Lexis is also Indianized when contextually appropriate words and idioms from local languages are translated, i.e., *twice born*, 'brahmin'; *dining-leaf*, 'banana leaf used as plate'; *head bath*, 'washing one's hair'; *cousin brother*, *brother-in-law* (as kinship terms); *to eat someone's head*, 'to be a nuisance'. IE extensively exploits code-mixing — mixing English and Indian languages — as a very productive process even in newspaper captions.

Semantics

Semantic shifts of Indian or English words are of the following types: semanic restriction, i.e., purdah is used only in one sense in IE as opposed to its wide range of meanings in Hindi/Urdu/Hindustani; semantic extension, i.e., the use of kinship terms (*mother*, *father*, *brother*, *sister*) in non-kinship contexts to denote respect, honour, closeness (as in **Mulk Raj Anand**'s works); archaisms, currency of words in IE that are considered archaic or are functionally restricted in contemporary British or American English (i.e., *bosom*, *thrice*, *needful*); contextual redefining of lexical items, as in the use of culture specific words such as *intermarriage* (marriage involving persons from two different religions or castes), *interdine* (eating with a member of another religion or caste), *communal* (specific reference involving Hindus and Muslims, i.e., *communal riots*).

IE users express bilingual creativity in discoursal, stylistic, and rhetorical strategies also. It is through such strategies that IE has created its own cultural appropriateness and contextual relevance. This has contributed towards its cultural identity and extension of the canon. These strategies are used for various language functions, from announcements of birth and marriage to matrimonial advertisements.

IE users show variation in their proficiency in English in terms of language acquisition, region of India, and ethnic group. On the scale of proficiency IE forms a cline from educated to a broken variety (pidginized bazaar variety). The regional varieties are defined with reference to the first language of the speaker (Bengali English, Tamil

English), or in terms of larger language families (Dravidian English). One ethnic variety, Anglo-Indian English, has received some attention from scholars. The IE speech community thus comprises a cline of varieties, the two ends of the cline being marked by educated IE at one end and broken English at the other, as they are, for example, in Nigerian English or Singaporean English.

BRAJ B. KACHRU

Further reading: Braj B. Kachru, *The Indianization of English: The English Language in India* (1983).

LANGUAGE (Pakistan)

Several varieties of English are in use in Pakistan. British influence has been quite predominant in the written and spoken registers that have evolved since the nineteenth century. However, there is also evidence of its wearing off in favour of other usage, so that this indigenized Pakistani English language, widely used in its specific (educated) context, shows itself to be distinctive at all linguistic levels — lexicon, morphology, syntax, semantics, and discourse. Since 1947, English in Pakistan has also increasingly incorporated the Islamic ritual and ethos both in its vocabulary and grammar. It has attained, therefore, an *equal* and valid status for cultural and literary expression.

Linguists generally describe the three or four spoken subvarieties in terms of degrees of proximity to the British Standard; the samples most distant from it — and any other variety — are often regarded as 'genuinely' Pakistani. American English, which has gradually infiltrated the spoken and written idiom, is discounted in most studies.

Pakistani English itself draws on various sources, including varieties of English elsewhere (generally British, American, and South Asian Englishes) and other Pakistani languages, and it is the richer every day for this reason. The ordinary written language reflects these trends as much as the spoken dialect(s). Electronic media (radio, television, and so on), newspapers, and popular magazines employ this characteristic mix. Regarding literature, **Alamgir Hashmi** states that 'The language of these [Pakistani] writers is English as naturalised here and now and it is Pakistani'. But, as it flows from sources that are still recognizable, the literary language appears to vary on a large scale, as does the perception concerning language as constituting self-image. Scholarly language, usually closer to the British Standard, also varies towards *authenticity*, though it is rarely acknowledged to be Pakistani English. Poets, novelists, prose writers, and dramatists all frequently provide markers when they employ a mesolectal or another subvariety in their work.

ALAMGIR HASHMI

Further reading: Alamgir Hashmi, 'Preface' in Alamgir Hashmi (ed.) *Pakistani Literature: The Contemporary English Writers* (2nd. ed., 1987); Alamgir Hashmi, 'Prolegomena to the study of Pakistani English and Pakistani literature in English', *Pakistani Literature* 1 (1989); Robert J. Baumgardner, 'The indigenisation of English in Pakistan', *English Today* 21 (1990); Tariq Rahman, 'Linguistic deviation as a stylistic device in Pakistani English fiction', *The Journal of Commonwealth Literature* 1 (1990); Tariq Rahman, *Pakistani English: The Linguistic Description of a Non-Native Variety of English* (1990).

LANGUAGE (The Philippines)

Brought to the Philippines in 1898 by the American colonial forces and government, the English language spread rapidly through the islands by means of the American primary education system and its initial group of American teachers.

The rapid dissemination of English through the government school system is one of the most interesting success stories in English-language teaching in any country, for when the first census was taken in 1901, only a few hundred people claimed some knowledge of English. By the second census of 1918, eighteen per cent claimed to be able to speak and read English. By the 1939 census, seven years before independence, twenty-six per cent claimed competence in English. The last census (1980), when speakers of English as a second language were asked to give self-reports, 64.5 per cent (of thirty nine million Filipinos six years and older) claimed to speak English. Based on extrapolations (not actual census data), this number is expected to increase to 78.7 per cent (of a total population of 79 million) by the year 2000.

The Philippines thus claims to be the third largest English-speaking country in the world, after the USA and the UK. However, the percentages have to be taken with some caution, since the degree of self-reported competence ranges along a cline from a simple repertoire of functionally useful phrases through basic interpersonal communication and more advanced cognitive academic language proficiency to near native proficiency. Usually, competence in the language is a direct function of the years and quality of schooling (using English as the medium of instruction in a bilingual scheme, the other language being Tagalog-based Filipino, an indigenous language), since the language is learned primarily in school, with reinforcement from the mass media (print is still predominantly in English, radio predominantly in Filipino, and television more in Filipino than in English). The domains of English are rapidly ceding to Filipino, so that English is now largely confined to the domain of education (science and mathematics), international diplomacy, and business transactions (at the upper levels).

There is currently activity in creative writing in English and a great amount of code-switching between English and Filipino in the mass media and in informal discourse. Local features of English are being creolized as these features are learned by children growing up in bilingual homes and studying in more affluent schools. These features may be characterized as simplification of the American English vowel system, the collapsing of consonantal distinctions (especially voiced and voiceless sibilants), syllable-timed speech, and local intonation (from Philippine languages). Vocabulary is characterized by the abundant use of local terms, loan translations, and what have been called Filipinisms. Loan translations are direct, word-for-word translations from a collocation (with phrase, clause, or sentence) from the source language. For example, 'I am ashamed to you' is a literal translation from the Filipino sentence '*Nahihiya ako sa iyo*', which in practice means 'I am quite embarrassed by this'. Filipinisms are idioms and figures of speech based on word-for-word translations from the source language (Filipino or any other of the Philippine languages) to the target language (the Philippine variety of English). For example, the Philippine-English term 'onion-skinned' is a direct translation from a figure of speech in Filipino and means 'thin-skinned'. Filipinisms are thus a subvariety of loan translations and are characterized by their idiomatic character. They are figures of speech, unlike ordinary loan translations, which are translations of literal speech.

Writing is most accomplished in expository discourse with the use of a classroom dialect, a formal, semi-antiquated nineteenth-century variety based on Victorian stylistic models and a limited repertoire of styles (largely formal, since for informal usage either Filipino or the code-switching variety is used, with the intimate usually in one's indigenous mother tongue). In addition to the limited styles, there is sometimes style shifting of an unexpected nature (formal with a sudden and unexpected use of informal or colloquial or even vulgar terms), which can sound ludicrous to an outsider.

The situation of English in the Philippines at present is one of domain reduction, but the use of the language is quite stable in these domains.

ANDREW GONZALEZ

Further reading: Teodoro A. Llamzon, *Standard Filipino English* (1969); Andrew Gonzalez, *Studies in*

Philippine English (1985).

LANGUAGE (St Helena)

English has always been the language of St Helenians, if not of St Helena. For 150 years after its discovery in AD 1502, this uninhabited ocean oasis was used variously by Portuguese, Spanish, Dutch, and English seamen returning to Europe from the east. With its settlement by the English East India Company in 1659, the Island's 'mother-tongue' became English. However, its use as a prison has brought other languages: French, during Napoleon's exile at Longwood (1815–21), known as La Domaine française de Ste Hélène since 1858 and staffed by a French vice-consul; and Afrikaans, spoken by its 6,000 prisoners during the Anglo-Boer War (1899–1902). These salient events, evoking extensive literatures overseas, left little linguistic, though some literary, legacies locally. In the second oldest British colony (passing from the Company to the Crown in 1834) and the smallest Anglican bishopric (since 1859), the language and way of life may seem English, yet visitors find the colloquial speech 'so corrupt that only Islanders can decipher it', in an Italian journalist's words (*L'Espresso*, May 1990).

Indeed St Helenian culture is unique. (See **St Helena**.) Since the Island has been a garrison and seafarers' haven for centuries, with the stigma of slavery still sharply felt, racial origins are diverse. Settlers came from Great Britain, of course, as did officials and soldiers of both the Company and the Crown; slaves came from the East Indies and Madagascar until 1792, contract Chinese labourers and artisans from Canton (1810–*c.*1840), and 553 freed slaves from the Island's own Liberated African Depot (1840–64). A few Boer prisoners chose to stay in 1902 (when the Boer War ended) and even the Zulu chief Dinizulu (1890–7), who was exiled on the Island, left descendants there. Conversational English has a Dickensian flavour with some East Indian input and marked district variations, but only a linguistics specialist could identify origins.

TREVOR W. HEARL

Further reading: Arne Zettersten, *The English of Tristan da Cunha* (1969); Vivienne Dickson, 'St Helena place-names', *Names* 21 (1973).

LANGUAGE (South Africa)

While English may be the major language of culture, commerce, and education in South Africa, relatively few South Africans count it as their mother tongue. Zulu is the language spoken most widely in South Africa, followed by the other important African languages — Xhosa, Tswana, and Sotho. Afrikaans is also, of course, another major South African language. None the less, it is English, with its links with other parts of anglophone Africa and the rest of the former Commonwealth, that is the language in the ascendancy in South Africa.

From the earliest manifestations of South African English literature, the English language has been under pressure from other languages and dialects and also from the need to develop an appropriate register for rendering the landscape and experience of Africa. The beginnings of South African literature in English are usually traced to the poetry of **Thomas Pringle** in the 1830s, and some of his most famous poems evince the problems encountered by English-speakers in Africa. Pringle's diction, not surprisingly for one so freshly arrived from Britain, is full of the flourishes of the Romantic poetic tradition and also of Scottish (and English) local and topical idiom. His poems abound in 'glens', 'vales', 'dells', and 'sylvan bowers'; they also, however, employ South African names of Dutch provenance for local fauna ('hartebeest', 'eland') and occasionally whole sentences in the Dutch language. A large part of Pringle's struggle as a writer was to find a linguistic register that matched the African landscape, and here Pringle, as a pioneer colonial writer in South

Africa, first encountered a problem that was to set a pattern for virtually all subsequent South African literature in English.

Late nineteenth-century writers such as **Olive Schreiner**, **W. C. Scully**, Ernest Glanville, and **Perceval Gibbon** all engaged with the multilingual nature of early South African society. In her novel *The Story of an African Farm* (1883), Schreiner included a glossary of untranslated Dutch words used in the novel — an indication perhaps that the English language was not wholly capable of rendering life in South Africa. Scully, a fluent Xhosa speaker, captures the ambience of the Xhosa culture in his stories of the Transkei, *Kafir Stories* (1895), by including a host of Xhosa words and phrases, idioms, and oral narrative styles. On the other hand, Ernest Glanville's well-known 'Abe-Pike' character (in his *Tales from the Veld*, 1897) speaks in a mid-western American drawl, and this reflects the influence of the American frontier 'yarnster' tradition and perhaps points to some similarities between the two settler communities. The storyteller figure in Gibbon's 'Vrouw Grobelaar' tales (*The Vrouw Grobelaar's Leading Cases*, 1905) is a rural Dutch-speaking Boer woman who regales her extended family with tales on the stoep. Like **Herman Charles Bosman**'s Oom Schalk Lourens, the Vrouw's speech is rendered in such a way as to imply that she is speaking Dutch.

Pauline Smith's novel *The Beadle* (1926) and her collection of stories *The Little Karoo* (1925) have been widely acclaimed for their accurate rendering of the distinctive cadences and constructions of the Dutch-Afrikaans language — although, as **J. M. Coetzee** has pointed out, her technique was not simply to transliterate, but rather to construct a unique style of English that gave the appearance of following the contours of the Afrikaans language.

One of South Africa's first black writers, **Sol T. Plaatje**, was eminently placed to reflect the multilingual nature of South African society. While his best-known work, *Mhudi* (1930), at times reflects the stylistic inelegancies of a cultural eclecticism (Shakespearean iambic pentameters, biblical phraseology, and African oral idioms co-exist awkwardly), this novel contains no fewer than five different languages — English, Dutch-Afrikaans, Tswana, Koranna, and Ndebele — and his contribution to evolving a uniquely South African linguistic register is important. The brothers **R. R. R. Dhlomo** and **H. I. E. Dhlomo** are two other early black writers who had to engage with the problem of language. Rolfes Dhlomo's short stories of the late 1920s and the 1930s, for example, combine the quaintly Victorian register of the mission-educated scholar with idiomatic Zulu exclamations and constructions. Herbert Dhlomo was a prolific writer, and his plays and poetry reflect his mixed cultural heritage: he was equally at home imaginatively reconstructing a praise-poet's praise to a king, as he did in his historical play *Cetshwayo* (written in 1937, first published in 1985), as writing an elegant sonnet, 'Ndongeni' (1942), lamenting the lack of recognition accorded the guide who accompanied Dick King on his epic journey to Grahamstown in 1842. These early black South African writers made important inroads into adapting the English language to South African cultural life.

On the other side of the language divide, in his famous novel *Cry, the Beloved Country* (1948), **Alan Paton** attempted to capture in English the oral cadences of the rural, spoken Zulu of his protagonist Stephen Kumalo. This was done chiefly by direct translations into English of Zulu idioms and expressions, a process that **Mbulelo Mzamane** has recently criticized as being stilted in comparison with the register achieved in C. L. S. Nyembezi's Zulu translation of the book.

But perhaps South African English literature's most famous non-English-speaking character is Herman Charles Bosman's Oom Schalk Lourens, a backveld Afrikaans raconteur unequalled for his eloquence and folk wisdom. Oom Schalk's English mirrors the constructions of the Afrikaans language and the famous opening lines of 'Makapan's Caves' (1930) contain a good example of this: 'Kafirs? (said Oom Schalk Lourens). Yes, I know them' (*Kafirs? [. . .] Ja, ek ken hulle.*) As with the inhabitants of Pauline Smith's Little Karoo, the reader is left in little doubt that it is Afrikaans that is ostensibly being spoken.

Under the influence of postwar American culture, the ***Drum*** writers of the 1950s often resorted to American slang and affected the cool of Chicago gangsters. This is especially evident in the 'On the Beat' yarns of Casey Motsisi (collected in *Casey and Co: Selected Writings of Casey 'Kid' Motsisi*, 1978, edited by Mothobi Mutloatse). In these yarns, American slang and Runyonesque 'gangster-talk' and mannerisms are humorously affected. The influence of the English canon, Shakespeare, and of Oscar Wilde, in particular, is evident in the case of **Can Themba**, another *Drum* writer who frequently affected the linguistic nonchalance of the English dandy: 'Fancy, Tilly, I forgot to take my pass'; 'I imagine he hasn't had a morsel all day, the poor devil'; 'Give the old chap a rest, will you, Tilly?' ('The Suit', in *Classic* 1, 1963, and *The Will to Die*, 1972, selected by Donald Stuart and Roy Holland). However, he sometimes reflected the growing influence of American culture, particularly in the form of American slang.

The rising influence of Black Consciousness in the late 1960s and the 1970s was accompanied by a return to African cultural roots. African oral forms, idioms, expression, and attitudes came to dominate black writing in English, and this is especially evident in the poetry of the time. The titles of poetry volumes by **Mongane Serote** (*Yakhal'inkomo*, 1972), **Mafika Gwala** (*Jol'iinkomo*, 1977), and others reflect this tendency and were interpreted at the time to be an overt assertion of African cultural identity. The poetry itself incorporated a wealth of expressions rendered directly in an African language or else following the stylistic traditions set by African oral poets. The 'trade-union poets' of the 1980s completed this cycle by donning the mantle and style of the traditional African praise-poets (*iimbongi*), but sang the praises of trade unions at mass rallies. Alfred Qabula's 'Praise Poem to Fosatu' (in *Black Mamba Rising: South African Worker Poets in Struggle*, 1986, edited by Ari Sitas) is the best-known example of this.

The rendering of *tsotsi-taal* ('gangster-talk') in modern township-based African literature became very marked with the increased political awareness that followed in the wake of Black Consciousness. Rendering a popular idiom came to have both a cultural and political cachet, reflecting as it did the politically conscious writer's sympathies with the oppressed classes. This kind of experimentation with language was not confined to black South African writers, and, indeed, it achieved a very radical form in the poetry of Wopko Jensma.

The stories and poems of **Achmat Dangor** elevated the use of the demotic to aesthetic heights by juxtaposing *skollie-taal* (the Afrikaans-English dialect of the South African Coloured) with an abundance of classical allusions and the finely turned phrase of an educated scholar. Similarly, some contemporary white South African writers have captured the demotic registers of white urban communities. The stories of **Sheila Roberts** and Barney Simon, for example, incorporate a range of South African (largely urban, working-class) slang.

These are merely some well-known examples that reflect the cultural-linguistic diversity of South Africa's multilingual population. Overwhelmingly, it has been the English language as the region's lingua franca that has absorbed and carried these influences by the other languages of South Africa. However, nothing in South Africa is without a conspicuous political resonance, and the use of other languages and linguistic forms frequently reflects an attempt at asserting a social and political distance from white (largely English-speaking) hegemonic culture. And while none of South Africa's major black writers has adopted the stance of Kenya's **Ngugi wa Thiong'o** and reverted exclusively to an indigenous African language, the adaptation — indeed subversion — of Standard English in South Africa has carried the literature of the region into rich and unique veins of linguistic exploration.

CRAIG MacKENZIE

Further reading: J. M. Coetzee, 'Pauline Smith and the Afrikaans language', in Dorothy Driver (ed.) *Pauline Smith* (1983); Jeremy Cronin, '"The law that says / constricts the breath-line (. . .)": South African English language poetry written by Africans in the 1970s', *English Academy Review* (1985); Njabulo S. Ndebele, 'The English language and social change in South Africa', in David Bunn and Jane Taylor (eds) *From South Africa* (1987).

LANGUAGE (South Pacific English)

The Pacific is a region of immense linguistic diversity. There are approximately 850 languages spoken in Papua New Guinea, sixty in Solomon Islands, and more than one hundred in Vanuatu. East, towards Polynesia, and north, towards Micronesia, the degree of diversity is much less dramatic, but most island states and territories there each have an additional language — and sometimes more than one. Fiji, which was part of the Commonwealth until it was expelled in 1987 after the abrogation of the previous constitution, contributes Rotuman, a number of languages originating from the Indian subcontinent, as well as several varieties of Fijian that are in many cases dialectally so distinct that they could almost be considered different languages.

Of necessity, English rapidly became an important means of internal and international communication. After initial contact with Europeans in the late 1700s and early 1800s, the kind of English spoken by islanders throughout the Pacific differed recognizably from any variety of metropolitan English. Often referred to as 'South Seas Jargon', it was probably little more than broken English interspersed with local vocabulary and characterized by a fairly fluid grammar.

As contacts continued in Polynesia and Micronesia, South Seas Jargon gradually merged with Standard English. In Melanesia, however, where linguistic diversity is much more extreme and mission schools were not to have an impact until later, South Seas Jargon developed and became a language in its own right; it is referred to as Melanesian Pidgin. This is spoken in such mutually intelligible varieties as Tok Pisin in Papua New Guinea, Pijin in Solomon Islands, and Bislama in Vanuatu. Although for many years of its history it was referred to as 'broken English', it is now clearly a separate language, and a speaker of English, when hearing Melanesian Pidgin for the first time, will understand no more than if it were Friesian.

Since the introduction of formal education to Melanesia in the early 1900s, English, in addition to Melanesian Pidgin, has taken root as a lingua franca. However, English is largely used as a spoken language only by those with tertiary and upper secondary education, while lesser-educated people tend to use Melanesian Pidgin. Even among those who use English, it is common to alternate between the two to show that the speaker is a Melanesian who is not trying to be a European.

Although English is now widely written and, to a lesser extent, spoken in the Pacific, it is not possible to speak of a unified 'Pacific English' in the same sense in which we can speak of 'Australian English' or 'New Zealand English'. Even these metropolitan models vary according to the state or territory: New Zealand English models predominate in Western Samoa, Tokelau, the Cook Islands, and Niue; Australian English models predominate in Papua New Guinea and Nauru; and

British models predominate elsewhere. However, Pacific Islanders do not actively model their speech on that of their respective former colonial overlords. Some influences from local phonologies are evident in recognizable Pacific accents. Thus, despite the fact that Melanesians initially learned English from a variety of different kinds of Europeans, it is difficult to tell a Papua New Guinean from a Solomon Islander or a ni-Vanuatu on the basis of accent, and the general accent may simply be labelled 'Melanesian'. Although Polynesians can generally be distinguished by their accents, there is no uniformity of accent among Polynesians; one feature that characterizes Tongans in relation to Pacific Islanders, for instance, is the substitution of 'f' for 'th', whereas people from most other parts of the Pacific frequently pronounce 'th' as 't' or 'd'.

There is equally as little uniformity in the lexicon. Typically, each nation or territory incorporates into its English local words not known outside that country, usually spelled as they would be in the local language. Thus, Tongans speaking English will refer to their *ta'ovala* ('mat worn around waist'); i-Kiribati to the *maneaba* ('communal meeting house'); Cook Islanders to the *tamure* ('vigorous traditional dance'); ni-Vanuatu to *laplap* ('baked grated root crop'); and Papua New Guineans to a *mumu* ('earth oven'). The use of such local vocabulary is not extensive, however, and generally does not extend to semantic fields beyond that of traditional culture. **Albert Wendt**'s novels, for example, include a fair number of Samoan words that have to be glossed by the author.

Perhaps more important is the emergence of locally created idioms. One country in which this phenomenon has attracted some attention is Papua New Guinea, where English has in the last generation come to be more widely used than Pidgin as a language of day-to-day communication among the educated élite. For educated Papua New Guineans, trying to speak with an Australian accent is of little social value, and young educated people are developing colourful slang expressions in English (which sometimes then get borrowed into Pidgin as well). For instance, to 'polish someone's floor' means to spend the night at a friend's home sleeping on a mat (or a mattress) on the floor; a 'beer face' is someone overly fond of drinking beer; and someone who is 'waterproof' doesn't shower very often. Anne-Marie Smith's work on the grammar of spoken and written English in Papua New Guinea — abbreviated in the article 'English in Papua New Guinea' in *World Englishes* 7 (1988) — also suggests that non-standard features are becoming fixed. These trends are clearly recognizable to educated Papua New Guineans, and some writers have consciously attempted to imitate these kinds of spoken styles in their written work.

In many places in the Pacific the expression of local identity through English apparently has been cultivated to an extreme. The work of Shem Yarupawa on what he calls 'Milne Bay Informal English' indicates that people from this area, who have for generations used only English rather than Pidgin as their lingua franca, have incorporated many non-standard lexical and grammatical features into their English. Instead of saying, for example, 'Otherwise many guys will try their luck and we won't stand a chance,' people from Milne Bay will say, 'No good too many boys will sidey and our luck will flat.'

Another, even more extreme, case, is that of the Pitcairn Islanders and their close relatives, the Norfolk Islanders. These people, descended from a small group of Tahitians and *Bounty* mutineers, still speak a variant of English very different from Standard English. It includes a number of words of Polynesian origin, as well as many English words used in highly distinctive ways. It is grammatically also very different from Standard English, to the point where the two are mutually unintelligible to the uninitiated. For instance, 'Nain salan worn el fet raun mais tiebl isi' translates into English as 'Only nine people will fit comfortably round my table.'

TERRY CROWLEY

Further reading: Karen Ann Watson-Gegeo, ed., *World Englishes* 8 (1989), special issue on English in the South Pacific.

LANGUAGE (West African English)

West Africa is one of the most linguistically heterogeneous regions in the world. The area's extreme linguistic plurality stems from the indigenous spoken languages, often estimated as numbering between one and two thousand. The linguistic diversity of the region is further intensified by other languages, such as French and English, that became entrenched in some of the countries during and after colonization. For example, English functions as the official language in Nigeria, Ghana, Liberia, Sierra Leone, and The Gambia and as a foreign language in other West African countries; French performs the same official function in Benin Republic and Cote d'Ivoire, among others; both English and French function as the official languages in Cameroon, while the various indigenous languages are often reserved for non-formal linguistic situations.

As in any contact situation between languages, English and French and the indigenous languages have exerted great influence on one another; hence, language-mixing (using different languages in a single construction) and code-mixing (shifting from one language to another) are familiar linguistic experiences. It is common, therefore, to hear utterances such as 'Bue door no mame' ('Open the door for me'), a mixture of Akan and English, or 'Kelechi bialu na nkem. We then went out' ('Kelechi came to my house. We then went out'), switching from Igbo to English.

West African English is not a uniform variety of English. The different countries of the region often have different varieties of the same language. In Liberia and Sierra Leone, for example, English is the mother tongue of some people, while it functions as a foreign language in Benin Republic and Cote d'Ivoire. Even within the same country, geographical, educational, and social factors necessitate differences in the varieties of the language. Hence there are differences in the varieties of English used in the eastern, northern, and western regions of Nigeria.

Varieties of English in West Africa can be discussed in terms of the educational attainment of the speakers, social acceptability, international intelligibility, and in terms of geographical, temporal, and stylistic varieties. The varieties are not mutually exclusive; as Loreto Todd has observed, the varieties form a sort of continuum rather than mutually exclusive categories.

West African English can be described in terms of a pyramid. At the basilectal level (the lowest point of the pyramid — varieties one and two in Ayo Banjo's study) is the variety of English spoken by people with extremely limited access to formal education and conventional methods of acquiring the language and by those with limited exposure to formal acquisition of the language. This variety is neither accepted intranationally nor is it internationally intelligible. According to Banjo, the first group of speakers of this variety (in Nigeria) expresses the thinking process of an indigenous language through English words. Since the second group has some exposure to English, there is a conflation between realizing thoughts in indigenous languages with English words and the speakers' attempt to contextualize their thinking process in English.

This variety is often marked by such a profound level of interference from the speaker's mother tongue that the phonological, syntactic, and lexical rules of the mother tongue are substituted for those of English. For example, it is pervasively syllable-timed instead of stress-timed, as in English; English vowels are rendered in terms of those of the indigenous languages (usually seven), and English diphthongs are rarely used. Furthermore, speakers of this variety often use the third-person plural to refer to older people and respected individuals. Errors of concord and malapropism and tense mixture are also common in this variety.

In the same way, there is usually semantic extension, especially in relation to kinship terms. It is therefore common to have speakers of this variety using 'mother' and 'father' to refer not only to their biological forebears but anyone that is as old as their parents or in a position of authority. On the lexical level, as Ayo Bamgbose has pointed out, many innovative words, such as 'fellow' (any person — male or female), 'branch' (call on one's way to another place), 'drop' (alight), and 'lesson' (private tuition) are predominant.

The mesolectal variety (Banjo's variety three), which is a transitional variety, is used by a significant percentage of the population with different levels of formal education. It is usually intranationally and internationally intelligible and accepted. On the phonological level, many speakers use both the segmental and suprasegmental resources of English, though the realizations are usually West African. Syntactically, it is quite close to the standard varieties of other world Englishes, as syntactic rules are usually followed and the lexicon includes most of the words that are unique to the African environment and other English words. It is therefore common to find some of the lexical items of the basilectal variety appearing in this class.

The acrolectal variety (Banjo's variety four) represents the speech of West Africans whose mother-tongue is English. Because Liberia and Sierra Leone were settled by English-speakers after the abolition of slave trade in Britain and North America, the English spoken there often approximates British and American Englishes. Language use by speakers of this variety is frequently affected by their relationship with other members of the community, and features of the earlier varieties discussed are usually seen in their speeches. There are, however, cases where non-speakers of this variety tend to imitate speakers of this variety.

In other countries such as Nigeria and Ghana, the acrolectal variety describes the use of English by those who, as Banjo observes, grew up in native speakers' speech communities or who have one parent as a native speaker of English. In other words, their initial exposure to language was to English in a mother-tongue situation — the phonological component of this variety is almost British, American, Canadian, or Australian, etc. Though it is internationally intelligible and accepted, it is often rejected intranationally because of its 'foreignness'.

Krio and Pidgin are two languages that are closely related to English spoken in West Africa. While the status of Krio (widely spoken in Sierra Leone) as a distinct language is clear, that of Pidgin has not yet been fully established. As a result, many scholars either discuss Pidgin as a variety of English or as a language on its own. It seems useful, however, to discuss it, like Krio, as a different language with its own varieties. This approach is strengthened by the fact that Krio and Pidgin are the mother tongues of some people (Krio in Sierra Leone, and Pidgin in some parts of the Nigerian Delta and some parts of Cameroon). In addition, both languages are quite different from English on all levels of linguistic analysis and are not usually intelligible to speakers of other varieties of English outside the zones where they are spoken.

Krio and Pidgin result from the interaction between English and indigenous West African languages, at an often casual level. Both languages are widely spoken across the West African region by people who speak any or all of the basilectal, mesolectal, and acrolectal varieties of English. Both Pidgin and Krio can serve as the lingua franca of some West African countries (Krio in Sierra Leone and Pidgin in Nigeria and Cameroon).

West African English occupies a unique position in West African literature, as most West African writers whose works are widely read outside the region often write in English, sometimes along with their mother tongues. As a result, all varieties of West African English appear in the region's literature. Different varieties are usually used to represent the speech pattern of various characters.

ADETAYO ALABI

Further reading: John Spencer, ed., *The English Language in West Africa* (1971); K. A. Sey, *Ghanaian English: An Exploratory Survey* (1973); Loreto Todd, 'The English language in West Africa', in Richard W. Bailey and Manfred Gorlach (eds) *English as a World Language* (1982); Ayo Banjo, 'Varieties of English in a multilingual setting in Nigeria', in Simon P. X. Battestini (ed.) *Developments in Linguistics and Semiotics, Language Teaching and Learning, Communication Across Cultures* (1987).

LAPIDO, DURO (1931–78)

Nigerian dramatist

He was born in Oshogbo, Nigeria, and became a primary-school teacher. In 1962 he was one of the founding members of the Mbari-Mbayo Club in Oshogbo; in 1963 he formed the Duro Lapido Players theatre group. He wrote ten Yoruba folk operas combining music, dance, drumming, mime, proverbs, and praise songs. The audience is often invited to participate in the action of the plays.

Lapido's best known and most successful works are *Oba Koso* ('The King Did Not Hang'), a story about the rivalry between two generals in King Shango's armies, *Oba Moro* ('The Ghost King'), and *Oba Waja* ('The King is Dead'), which displays the tragic consequences on traditional society of adopting westernized ways. (All three appear in English translation in *Three Yoruba Plays*, 1964, translated by Ulli Beier.) *Oba Koso* was performed at the Berlin Theatre Festival in 1964 and at the Commonwealth Festival in the UK in 1965. Critic Adrian Roscoe notes that *Oba Waja* demonstrates 'the strength and adaptability of Yoruba drama'. Lapido's *Moremi*: *An Historical Play* (adapted to English by Ulli Beier in *Three Nigerian Plays*, 1967, edited by Beier) explores how African artists are caught between local traditions and the pressures of outside influence.

G. D. KILLAM

LAURENCE, MARGARET (1926–87)

Canadian novelist, short-story writer

Born Jean Margaret Wemys in Neepawa, Manitoba, Canada, her childhood was touched by several deaths in the family, among them her mother's when she was four years of age, and her father's when she was nine. In 1943 a Manitoba scholarship enabled her to leave Neepawa to attend United College in Winnipeg. She married Jack Laurence, an engineer, in 1947 and moved with him to England in 1949. In 1950 the Laurences moved to Somaliland, now Somalia, Africa, and in 1952 to Ghana, where they lived until 1957. After five years in Canada following their African sojourn, Margaret Laurence separated from her husband and returned to England. In 1969 she began to spend summers at a cottage on the Otonabee River in Ontario, Canada, while living in England during the winters. She served as writer in residence at the University of Toronto, Trent University, and the University of Western Ontario in this period. She was named a Companion of the Order of Canada in 1971. In 1974 she returned to Canada permanently and settled in Lakefield, Ontario. Between 1981 and 1983 she was Chancellor of Trent University and during the next years devoted much of her time to conservation projects.

Laurence began her writing career in Africa. *A Tree for Poverty* (1954) is a translation and retelling of Somali poetry and stories, the first time that Somali poems and folktales had been collected and translated into English. The attention paid to the oral tradition out of which the stories and poems grow is a landmark in the study of African literature. *A Tree for Poverty* also indicates the necessity of probing the oral cultures of Commonwealth countries in order to find the roots of regional literatures. Laurence went on to write a series of stories set in Ghana (then the Gold Coast) about Africans caught between 'old' and 'new' worlds. These stories were later collected in *The Tomorrow-Tamer* (1963). Other books drawn from Laurence's life in Africa are *This Side Jordan* (1960), a novel about Ghana's independence movement; *The Prophet's Camel Bell* (1963), a book created from a journal Laurence kept while living in Somaliland; and *Long Drums and Cannons* (1968), a critical work on English-language Nigerian writers. *This Side Jordan* is considered an apprentice novel, but Laurence's African stories are often viewed as among her best work. At the beginning of her writing career she was in a position to view Canada as a Commonwealth country seeking independence and, like Ghana, Somaliland, and Nigeria, as a nation engaged in a search for its own culture. The perspective she gained on Canada, and especially the Canadian Prairies, was conditioned by her years in Africa and her attention to its native literatures.

Laurence is best known for her Manawaka fiction based on her home town of Neepawa. Her first three Manawaka novels — *The Stone Angel* (1964), *A Jest of God* (1966), and *The Fire-Dwellers* (1969) — were written while living in England, following separation from her husband. In Canada these novels made a strong impact, showing the power of Canadian regionalism and establishing Laurence as one of Canada's foremost writers. *The Diviners* (1974), often seen as her most ambitious work, takes up characters from the other Manawaka novels and provides a closure to the sequence. *The Diviners* and *A Jest of God* both won Governor General's Awards for fiction. After the appearance of *The Diviners,* Laurence wrote only children's books, such as *Jason's Quest* (1970), and essays. A collection of essays appeared under the title *Heart of a Stranger* (1976); after her death her daughter Jocelyn completed and published her memoirs, begun in 1985, as *Dance on the Earth* (1989).

Laurence's interest in the oral cultures of Africa bears fruit in the skilled character portrayals in her Manawaka fiction. The novels provide settings in which the most important fictional element — the characters themselves — can unfold in all their complexities. In her essay 'Gadgetry or Growing: Form and Voice in the Novel', Laurence claims that form was important to her only insofar as it could harbour the characters within it.

Laurence's fiction is about people unlikely to become either heroes or anti-heroes, people who have been largely ignored — single women in middle age and people on the fringes of society. Her writing pushes us to see their full value as human beings and to participate in forms of anti-drama: concerns and events that are traditionally considered boring or trivial. Laurence's characters are the kinds of people who do not ordinarily fascinate us and she emphasizes our tendency to ignore or reject them by surrounding her main characters with people who react similarly. It is a mark of Laurence's genius that wherever her focus rests the result is interesting. Her work can change our perspective by showing what our environment, its people and places, is composed of in terms of human value.

Some elements of Laurence's work are often singled out as central to her vision: the theme of personal and social freedom; the disparity between restraint and self-expression; the liberation of the inner lives of women; the effect of region on character; and the cultural inheritance of a people and of individuals and the combined strength and weakness that such inheritance bears. Her most influential novel, *The Stone Angel,* combines a number of these elements in the character of Hagar Shipley. Not until the end of a long life does Hagar find a kind of personal freedom and inner peace. Her self-discovery is accompanied by insight into how her ninety years have been misspent and by the recognition that she has not before given voice to her true inclinations. She has been constrained by convention and inheritance as well as by the confines of the small town in which she has lived. As Laurence shows, it takes more than mere will-power to overcome the forces that suppress people and to become able to speak truly.

KRISTJANA GUNNARS

Further reading: Clara Thomas, *The Manawaka World of Margaret Laurence* (1976); William New, ed., *Margaret Laurence* (1977); George Woodcock, ed., *A Place to Stand On: Essays by and about Margaret Laurence* (1983); J. M. Kertzer, *Margaret Laurence and Her Works* (1987); Christl Verduyn, *Margaret Laurence: An Appreciation* (1988); Don Bailey, *Memories of Margaret: My Friendship with Margaret Laurence* (1989); Kristjana Gunnars, ed., *Crossing the River: Essays in Honour of Margaret Laurence* (1989); Colin Nicholson, ed., *Critical Approaches to the Fiction of Margaret Laurence* (1990); Patricia Morley, *Margaret Laurence: The Long Journey Home* (1991).

LAWLER, RAY (1921–)

Australian dramatist

Born in Footscray, Melbourne, Australia, he left school early for factory work and went on to a career as actor, director, and dramatist. Lawler's tenth play, *Summer of the Seventeenth Doll* (1957), which in 1955 shared first prize in a Playwrights Advisory Board competition with Oriel Gray's *The Torrents* (first published in 1988), marked a breakthrough for Lawler and for Australian drama that compares with the impact of John Osborne's *Look Back in Anger* (1957).

A successful 1955 run in Melbourne of *Summer of the Seventeenth Doll* (with Lawler playing Barney) was followed by a Sydney production in January 1956. A London production with an Australian cast, again including Lawler, put Australian drama suddenly on the world map; the play won the 1957 *Evening Standard* Award for best play on the London stage. Although the 1958 New York production did not have the same success, *Summer of the Seventeenth Doll* was included in Louis Kronenberger's *Ten Best Plays of the American Season 1957–58* (1959), and in 1960 was made into a film. It is a school text in Australia. Two companion plays, *Kid Stakes* and *Other Times*, were published with *Summer of the Seventeenth Doll* as *The Doll Trilogy* (1978).

Partly on its own merits and partly because of its popular success, *Summer of the Seventeenth Doll* is the most important play in Australian theatrical history. In it, Roo and Barney, Queensland cane-cutters, spend the annual 'lay-off' season in Melbourne with Olive and Nancy, a relationship with established rituals of presents (this is the seventeenth Brisbane 'Ekker' show-doll for Olive), outings, and singsongs round the piano. But time and age have threatened the mateship between the two men, Nancy has opted out to marry a city bloke, and Olive's fantasy world crumbles. Roo's belated marriage offer is fiercely rejected by Olive, and the fragile dolls are destroyed when the men fight.

Lawler's intention was to portray an alternative to marriage, a theme that led to some early condemnation of the play; the play also dramatizes a turning point in the Australian self-image: the outback legend and myths of **mateship** confront the increasing urbanization of Australia. (The disintegration of a way of life is a theme central to much Commonwealth writing: **Chinua Achebe**'s *Things Fall Apart* (1958) and *Arrow of God* (1964) are memorable examples.)

Lawler's powerful symbolism, conveyed through verbal and stage images, and realistic presentation invite comparison with that of Ibsen, Tennessee Williams, and Arthur Miller. His affectionate observation of working-class characters, easy use of authentic speech rhythms, local idiom and slang, and his comic understanding and exuberant gusto all suggest modern Anglo-Irish drama, especially J. M. Synge's *The Playboy of the Western World* (1907).

Lawler lived overseas, mainly in Ireland, for twenty years, writing television plays for the British Broadcasting Corporation, before settling again in Australia as director with the Melbourne Theatre Company. His later stage plays, some premièred in the UK, never captured audiences as did *Summer of the Seventeenth Doll. The Piccadilly Bushman* (1961) raises questions about post-colonial problems, the cultural cringe, the expatriate, and the nature of 'Australianness'.

REBA GOSTAND

Further reading: P. Holloway, ed., *Contemporary Australian Drama: Perspectives Since 1955* (1981; rev. 1987).

LAWSON, HENRY (1867–1922)

Australian novelist, short-story writer, poet

Born on the goldfields at Grenfell, New South Wales, Australia, he moved to Sydney with his mother in 1883. Hampered by deafness (from nine years of age) and conflict between his parents (see 'A Child in the Dark, and a Foreign Father'), he had a lonely and difficult childhood. Between 1887 and 1892, interspersed with trips to Albany (where he worked for the *Albany Observer*) and Queensland (where he wrote for the *Boomerang*), Lawson became known as a writer of verse about bush life and of radical protest verse that often had an urban setting.

In 1892, as well as contributing to the carefully constructed ***Bulletin*** 'debate' with **A. B. Paterson** about appropriate representations of the bush and bush life — antipodean realism versus romanticism — Lawson drew on his experiences working at Hudson Brothers coach factory in Sydney to explore in the Arvie Aspinall series the condition of the urban poor. He also began a rich series of bush stories, writing 'A Day on a Selection', 'The Bush Undertaker', and 'The Drover's Wife'. Confident of Lawson's ability, J. F. Archibald, editor of the *Bulletin,* funded a working and 'research' trip to Bourke and beyond looking for 'copy'. The trip was a revelation, releasing a wry, ironic humour, valorizing endurance, and confirming Lawson's idea of the physical and mental hardship of bush life. 'Hungerford' and 'The Union Buries Its Dead' came directly out of the trip, and the Mitchell figure and the bush workers carefully delineated in 'Send Round the Hat' owe their genesis to this period. Lawson had found his subject-matter and discovered a form that enabled him to explore the essential in the typical.

In Sydney in 1893 he also turned his experiences into journalism, contributing to the *Bulletin, Truth,* and the Australian *Worker* before going to New Zealand in 1894, once more looking for work. His first collection, *Short Stories in Prose and Verse* (1894), although undistinguished, confirmed Lawson's ability. In 1896 he married Bertha Bredt and began a long association with Angus and Robertson, who published a prose collection, *While the Billy Boils* (1896), and *In the Days When the World was Wide* (1896), a collection of verse. In the next five years, the couple spent time in Western Australia and New Zealand, where Lawson taught for a year at a Maori school, before returning to Sydney and a renewal of his drinking problem in 1898 as he re-established his associations with Sydney's bohemia. The prose collections *On the Track* and *Over the Sliprails* and *Verses Popular and Humorous* were published in 1900 when the Lawsons, with their two children, left for London, England, seeking the wider recognition that he had argued for in his polemical essay 'Pursuing Literature in Australia' (the *Bulletin,* 1899).

Although Lawson did not achieve this recognition in London, he published some of his best work while there: *Joe Wilson and His Mates* (1901), which drew on a 1894 visit to New Zealand; a selection of previously published work, *The*

Country I Come From (1901); and *Children of the Bush* (1902). In the ten years after his return to Australia in 1902, Lawson's literary output foundered, his marriage disintegrated, and his drinking landed him in jails and institutions. *The Romance of the Swag* (1907), incorporating *Children of the Bush*, was followed by the repetitive *The Rising of the Court* (1910) and *Triangles of Life* (1913), in which Lawson began to mimic his early voice in a prose that was becoming flaccid, relying on melodrama and a debilitating artifice. Further volumes of popular verse included *When I Was King* (1905), *The Skyline Riders* (1910), *For Australia* (1913), *My Army, O My Army* (1915), and *Song of the Dardanelles* (1916). He wrote regularly for the *Bulletin* during the war, his imperialism and jingoism sitting uncomfortably with those ideals of republicanism and egalitarianism on which his reputation was founded.

A *Selected Poems of Henry Lawson* was published in 1918, and David McKee Wright's *Poetical Works of Henry Lawson* (1925) has proved an enduring collection. Colin Roderick edited the three-volume *Henry Lawson: Collected Verse* (1967–9), *Henry Lawson: Short Stories and Sketches 1888–1922* (1972), and *Henry Lawson: Autobiographical and Other Writings 1890–1922* (1972). Roderick has also edited *Henry Lawson: Letters 1890–1922* (1970) and *Henry Lawson: Criticism 1894–1971* (1972). Although widely criticized, Cecil Mann's *The Stories of Henry Lawson* (1964) initiated continuing interest in Lawson's prose.

Biographical and critical interpretations include Bertha Lawson's *My Henry Lawson* (1943), W. H. Pearson's *Henry Lawson Among the Maoris* (1968), Brian Matthews' highly respected *The Receding Wave* (1972), which convincingly documents Lawson's decline, **A. A. Phillips'** *Henry Lawson* (1970), Stephen Murray-Smith's *Henry Lawson* (1972), **Manning Clark**'s controversial *In Search of Henry Lawson* (1978), and Colin Roderick's *The Real Henry Lawson* (1982). Brian Kiernan's *The Essential Henry Lawson* (1982) includes newly discovered material.

The direction of the critical debate over Lawson in the 1960s is exemplified by the tension between A. A. Phillips' and Harry Heseltine's 'Literary Heritage' articles in *Meanjin* 21 (1962). Phillips sought to locate Lawson firmly in the 'frontier life' of the period, catching in his fiction the life 'men actually live', while Heseltine offers a Lawson confronting the void, establishing affinities with writers such as Franz Kafka, Jean-Paul Sartre, and Albert Camus.

More recent criticism has found Lawson a no less significant site of exploration. Kay Schaffer has made extensive use of Lawson in her study of cultural myths of masculinity and the construction of ideas about masculinity and femininity, *Women and the Bush* (1988); Xavier Pons in *Out of Eden: Henry Lawson's Life and Works, a Psychoanalytic View* (1984) draws on a psychoanalytic analysis to probe the personal and public paradoxes and contradictions that manifest themselves in Lawson's life and oeuvre; such explorations as Lynn Sutherland's *The Fantastic Invasion: Kipling, Conrad and Lawson* (1990) fruitfully locate Lawson in the context of international contemporaries and invite consideration of the pressures of colonialism that helped shape his work.

On his death Lawson was given a state funeral, the first Australian writer to be so honoured; he is generally regarded as Australia's most important writer, and he is the subject of a society and a journal, *The Lawsonian.*

JAMES WIELAND

LAWSON, LOUISA (1848–1920)

Australian poet, journalist

Born in Guntawang, New South Wales, Australia, she married in 1866 Niels Larsen, by whom she had five children (including **Henry Lawson**). She moved with her family to Sydney in 1883. A period as co-publisher of the *Republican* and *Nationalist* newspapers inspired Lawson to found *Dawn* in 1888. Though not the first journal for women, it was the first to be produced and printed entirely by women for women, vigorously addressing the issues of women's rights and canvassing a wide range of women's affairs: political, domestic, recreative. Sometimes using the pseudonym Dora Falconer, Lawson wrote or edited virtually the entire journal, a monthly, for all but ten months (when she was ill) of its seventeen-year life.

By 1890 *Dawn* was campaigning unrelentingly for female suffrage, recording every advance in this respect until its achievement in 1902. While a devout nationalist and champion of Australian writers (although *Dawn* had little to say about other Australian women writers), Lawson undoubtedly felt part of an international sisterhood: she admired and published the work of Elizabeth Barrett Browning, Christina Rossetti, and **Olive Schreiner**.

In some ways Lawson's journalism was unsophisticated, comparing unfavourably to that of contemporary feminists such as Vida Goldstein or Rose Scott; but *Dawn* was a household journal, with no aspirations to intellectualism, and combined topics such as women's employment, education, and marriage reform with household hints, recipes, a children's page, and even crossword puzzles.

Lawson's years in the bush remained with her all her life. Bush subjects dominate her lesser-known poetry (and almost-forgotten stories). *The Lonely Crossing and Other Poems* (1905) contains unpretentious lyrics, such as 'The Squatter's Wife', of quiet yet forceful drama. Her national, patriotic poems are refreshingly unsentimental. Noteworthy too are the confessional poems of love and renunciation, which have reminded several critics of Emily Brontë and Christina Rossetti.

DEBRA ADELAIDE

Further reading: Brian Matthews, *Louisa* (1987); Elaine Zinkhan, 'Louisa Albury Lawson, feminist and patriot', in Debra Adelaide (ed.) *A Bright and Fiery Troop: Australian Women Writers of the Nineteenth Century* (1988); Olive Lawson, ed., *The First Voice of Australian Feminism: Excerpts from Louisa Lawson's The Dawn 1888–1895* (1990).

LAXMAN, RASIPURAM KRISHNASWAMY (1924–)

Indian cartoonist, journalist, novelist

Born in south India, he graduated from the University of Mysore. His love for cartooning took him to the *Free Press Journal* and then to the *Times of India*, where he has worked for more than forty years. He has published more than eight collections of cartoons. Being the brother of **R. K. Narayan** hampered his literary ambitions: 'I was afraid to set foot in the domain of my brother. I felt I would come off poorly in the comparisons that were bound to take place.' Laxman, has, however, published a novel, *Sorry, No Room* (1969); this was reprinted in 1988 as *The Hotel Riviera*, which also contains three short stories from his earlier collection of miscellaneous writings, *Idle Hours* (1982). He has received honorary degrees and awards, including Padma Bhushan from the government of India and a Ramon Magsaysay award.

The Hotel Riviera is a carefully crafted novel, resembling those of Narayan in its conception and execution. With humour and compassion it dramatizes the story of a hotel manager who becomes interested in a woman busy leading her own life of convenience and pleasure. The counsel of a swami convinces him that the time is propitious for him to win her affection, although he does not even speak to her about it. After a series of complications, in which he quarrels with almost everybody, he shuts himself in his room. Later, when the man is beaten in the house of his lady-love, his father is summoned to carry him back to his village.

Laxman gives his novel a strong Indian ambience by painting scenes swarming with life and activity and succeeds in showing how people regulate (or spoil) their lives by pinning faith on forces that appear to defy reason. The novel illustrates Indian community living, in which people participate (sometimes disastrously) in the lives of others.

Idle Hours is a variegated collection. It includes travel pieces about Laxman's visits to Australia, Mauritius, and Khatmandu that combine description with observation; anecdotes about his meetings with fellow cartoonists and celebrities whom he drew for his newspaper; and humorous essays about events, politicians, and professionals. 'The Saga of Ramaswami' memorably illustrates that truth is stranger than fiction. The stories in the collection deal with unusual happenings, adventures, and accidents. 'The Gold Frame' is the best, because of its delicate irony — a person is enthusiastic about putting one of his ancestors in a beautiful frame, though he does not even recognize him.

Laxman invites comparison with O. V. Vijayan, a cartoonist and writer whose work has been translated from Malayalam into English. Although Vijayan's *The Saga of Dharmapuri* (1988) is a trenchant satire on the post-colonial culture of India, both writers laugh at the foibles and perversions of human beings. But if Laxman's humour is like Chaucer's or Fielding's, Vijayan's is Swiftian and Rabelaisian.

T. N. DHAR

LAYTON, IRVING (1912–)
Canadian poet

Born Israel Lazarovitch at Tirgu Neamt, Romania, he moved at the age of one with his parents to Montreal, Canada. He was educated at Montreal's Baron Byng High School, which was also **A. M. Klein**'s and **Mordecai Richler**'s school (it appears as Fletcher's Field High in Richler's novels). He earned a bachelor of science degree in agriculture (1939) at Macdonald College, Ste Anne de Bellevue, Quebec, and an MA (1946) in economics and political science at McGill University. He taught at Sir George Williams College (now Concordia University) and concluded an inspirational teaching career at York University, Toronto. In the forefront of the second wave of Canadian modernist poets, Layton was associated with such seminal journals of Canadian modernism as *First Statement* (1942–5) and *Northern Review* (1945–56) and, in the early 1950s, with his one-time friend and subsequent detractor **Louis Dudek**, was instrumental in the founding of Contact Press. (See **Literary Magazines**, Canada.) He is the winner of numerous awards and honours, including a Governor General's Award for *A Red Carpet for the Sun* (1959).

Since publishing his first book, *Here and Now* (1945), Layton has successfully styled himself as Canada's most publicly controversial poet. Opposed to the high modernist conception of poetry as providing aesthetic pleasure for an élite few, he views the poet and poetry as passionately engaged in the affairs of society. If the moribund masses of enslaved Canadian Gentiles and puritan colonials must be shocked into seeing Layton's truth with language and images that are sometimes vulgar and graphically sexual, so be it. The title of one of his finest lyrics expresses this self-justifying poetic: 'Whatever else poetry is freedom.' And whatever else middle-class Canada might be in its own collective mind, for Layton it is the enemy of freedom and poetry. As the artistic record of a healthy confrontation between the writer and his society, Layton's work can be seen in a Canadian tradition that includes **Bliss Carman**, **Archibald Lampman**, and **Stephen Leacock**. Layton can also be seen to share something intentional with Australia's premier satiric poet of the modern era, **A. D. Hope**. Hope's target is also often the prudish vestiges of colonial gentility; he shares with Layton a Lawrentian belief in the therapeutic virtues of sexual love, and his tactics are frequently as shocking as Layton's, though Layton eschews the Australian's surgical coolness and classical resonances.

Scourge of the bourgeoisie, the Gentile, and the modern Jew, even of the state of Israel itself, Layton, in his sixth decade of continuous activity, remains, like a faithful old volcano, Canada's foremost poet *engagé*. In recent years a number of critics have attempted to devalue his achievement as poet and polemicist/theorist, pointing to the self-styled poet/king's absence of poetic fabric. (There is something typically Canadian in this urge to criticize writers for what they are not, especially Canadian writers who have achieved international acclaim: Carman is dismissed for not being a modernist poet, Leacock for not being a novelist, Richler for not being Bellow, and so forth, in illustration of the genuine colonial attitude.) But such critics who would devalue Layton's achievement — and he helps his detractors by being, as loud and loutish advertiser for himself, often his own worst enemy — must finally confront the numerous superb lyrics, for example, 'A Tall Man Executes a Jig', 'The Birth of Tragedy', 'The Cold Green Element', 'Song for Naomi', 'The Fertile Muck', and at least one perfect poem, 'Berry Picking'. Collectively his poetry is best sampled in *The Collected Poems of Irving Layton* (1971), *The Darkening Fire: Selected Poems, 1945–1968* (1975), *The Unwavering Eye: Selected Poems, 1969–1975* (1975), *A Wild Peculiar Joy 1945–1982* (1982), and *Final Reckoning: Poems 1982–1986* (1987). Layton's fiction can be sampled in *The Swinging Flesh* (1961), and his polemical prose in *Engagements: The Prose of Irving Layton* (1972) and *Taking Sides: The Collected Social and Political Writings* (1977). He has also published two collections of letters — *An Unlikely Affair* (1980), with Dorothy Rath, and *Wild Gooseberries: The Selected Letters of Irving Layton* (1989) — and the autobiographical *Waiting for the Messiah: A Memoir* (1985).

GERALD LYNCH

Further reading: Seymour Mayne, ed., *Irving Layton: The Poet and his Critics* (1978); Elspeth Cameron, *Irving Layton: A Portrait* (1985).

LEACOCK, STEPHEN (1869–1944)

Canadian short-story writer, humorist

He was born in Swanmore, Hampshire, England. From the early years of the eighteenth century, Leacock's family was engaged in the Madeira wine trade, and something of the quality of Madeira may be discerned in the full, cheerful flavour, with a hint of brimstone in the aftertaste, of Leacock's best work. His father, Peter, was a high-spirited ne'er-do-well who married a clergyman's daughter, Agnes Emma Butler, in a runaway match, after which they farmed briefly and unsuccessfully in South Africa and in 1876 immigrated to Canada, to a farm — described by Leacock as 'the damnedest place I ever saw' — near Lake Simcoe in Ontario. There were eleven children of the match, of whom Stephen was the third. In 1887 he drove his father to the railway station, put him on a train, and said, 'If you come back, I'll kill you!'

The mother struggled to maintain the family at a level of gentility; the children had an excellent tutor, and in 1882 Leacock went to Upper Canada College, Toronto, the foremost boys' school in the province. He was head boy when he left, and had been editor of the school paper. To finance his studies at the University of Toronto he became a schoolmaster at UCC and continued in that work for ten years, disliking it intensely. In 1899 Leacock enrolled at the University of Chicago, USA, to work with Thorstein Veblen, and achieved his doctorate in political economy and political science in 1903, *magna cum laude*. In 1900 he married Beatrix Hamilton and their happy union continued until 1925, when she died of cancer. They had one son.

Upon leaving Chicago, Leacock obtained an appointment at McGill University, Montreal, as a sessional lecturer, and in time rose to be William

Dow professor of political economy, ending this work when, to his keen resentment, university regulations compelled his retirement at age sixty-five. He was much admired as a teacher. During 1907 and 1908 he toured the British empire, speaking on imperial organization, and thus began the career as a public speaker that brought him fame and a worldwide audience.

Although Leacock had written a popular work (which was always his chief money-earner) on political science in 1906, and had added a volume to the Makers of Canada series in 1907, he did not begin his career as a humorist until 1910, when his wife and his brother George persuaded him to publish some of his brief pieces as *Literary Lapses* (1910). He paid for publication himself, and the first printing of three thousand copies sold out in two months; the book was purchased for publication in England by John Lane of the Bodley Head. At this time Leacock was forty and had no notion of himself as a popular writer, though he had always been known in his circle as a wit. *Literary Lapses* contained some of his best work, and the road to fame opened before him.

Leacock's next book, *Nonsense Novels* (1911), was made up of ten short parodies of popular forms of fiction. He lacked the ear of the true parodist, but the exuberant fun of the stories, especially 'Gertrude the Governess', in which Lord Ronald 'flung himself upon his horse and rode madly off in all directions', gained him a wide audience. In 1912 he produced his most ambitious effort, *Sunshine Sketches of a Little Town.* Its form is curious, for although it is not quite a novel, its component stories, when taken from the whole, are not self-sufficient. Despite its great success in the English-speaking world, the book gave serious offence in the little town itself (Orillia, Ontario) and Leacock never again drew inspiration for his fiction so directly from life, nor did he experiment further with the novel form.

Instead he devoted himself to providing what he called 'funny pieces, just to laugh at' for the many magazines in the USA and the UK that published such work. He commanded the highest fees and at his peak he earned between $40,000 and $50,000 a year, of which only $6,000 was his McGill salary. Every year he published a book in time for the Christmas trade, in which the previous year's funny pieces were gathered. He also achieved fame and wide popularity as a lecturer, and one of his finest chapters of reminiscence is 'We Have with Us Tonight' in *My Discovery of England* (1922), in which the torments of the public lecturer are described and his failure to kill a man with laughing — a long-held ambition — is recorded.

It was in public lecturing and writing of short comic sketches that Leacock's strength lay. Although his style is colloquial, and the reader may almost hear the inflections of his voice in his prose, the effects of a classical education are to be discerned in the precision and flavour of his vocabulary, and the sureness with which his points are made. He was too impatient of research for the critical work he attempted in *Charles Dickens: His Life and Work* (1933) and a Victorian sense of propriety made him an unsatisfactory biographer. Nor is *How to Write* (1943) a book that his admirers can open with pleasure, for it is foolishly didactic and the chapters on writing humour are painful. Leacock could no more tell anyone else how to write humour than Jove could have told a mortal how to turn into a swan.

The last of his forty-six books, published posthumously in 1946, is *The Boy I Left behind Me*, four chapters of brilliant autobiography.

ROBERTSON DAVIES

Further reading: Ralph L. Curry, *Stephen Leacock: Humorist and Humanist* (1959); Robertson Davies, *Stephen Leacock* (1970).

Leakey, Caroline Woolmer (1827–81)
Australian poet, novelist
Born and educated in Exeter, England, she arrived

in Tasmania, Australia, in 1848; in 1854 she published *Lyra Australis; or, Attempts to Sing in a Strange Land*. The maudlin obsession with death in these poems is understandable in the light of her illnesses at the time, but the cloying religiosity, the stereotyped images, and archaic diction can be explained only by the author's strict evangelical outlook.

The Broad Arrow, Being Passages from the History of Maida Gwynnham, a Lifer (1859) — published under the pseudonym Oline Keese — is Leakey's only novel. Based on information gained about the Tasmanian penal system, Leakey wrote compellingly about the conditions of the female convict. The first novel written by a woman and founded on personal experience of a convict state and the first to have a female hero, it was an important influence on **Marcus Clarke**'s *His Natural Life*, serialized between 1870 and 1872.

The Broad Arrow is remarkable for other reasons. It protests against the brutality of the convict system, but does not find that brutality unspeakable; some of Leakey's passages are horrifically graphic. It deplores the spinelessness of the church and the treatment of the Tasmanian Aborigines; it faithfully documents convict and free life; it takes a committed feminist stance on the vulnerability of women. Constantly republished until the end of the nineteenth century, the novel made a substantial contribution to the growing suspicion in Britain that the so-called convict class was just a myth and that the convicts were themselves victims.

Excessively evangelical, like many women of her time and class, Leakey suppressed her intelligence, passion, pride, and independence. Her personality was dominated by frustration and drama, her daily life by chronic ill health, and her time by fervent penances. Leakey's later years were spent channeling her obvious literary talents into the production of religious tracts and moral tales.

DEBRA ADELAIDE

Further reading: Emily Leakey, *Clear Shining Light: A Memoir of Caroline Woolmer Leakey* (1882); Shirley Walker, 'Wild and wilful women: Caroline Leakey and *The Broad Arrow*', in Debra Adelaide (ed.) *A Bright and Fiery Troop: Australian Women Writers of the Nineteenth Century* (1988).

LEE, DENNIS BEYNON (1939–)

Canadian poet, editor

Born, educated, and employed as university teacher and editor in Toronto, Canada, he is the archetypal urban Canadian poet coming of age in the 1960s. He helped set up Rochdale College, a short-lived educational and housing co-op, co-founded with **Dave Godfrey** the Toronto-based House of Anansi Press, has been editor and friend to many young writers while at Anansi and later at Macmillan and at McClelland and Stewart, and has identified a new generation of Canadian poets in his anthology *The New Canadian Poets, 1970–1985* (1985).

In his first book of poems, *Kingdom of Absence* (1967), Lee, like American poets John Berryman and Robert Lowell and New Zealand's **Ian Wedde**, attempted to rework the sonnet form to his own ends. These were as yet too inchoate to reshape an existing form or conjure a new one into being, however, and the formal measures to which Lee resorted, though put to brilliant use later in his children's verse, were ill-suited to a quest for his own authentic voice. *Civil Elegies* (1968) employs a more flexible form that is not afraid of the long line and feels no need to eschew the sustained syntax that layered thought and feeling demand. Poetically silent thereafter for some years, Lee found philosopher George Grant's pessimistic analyses of the human and in particular the Canadian condition perversely comforting, identifying therein the sources of his *Angst*. With a revised and expanded *Civil Elegies* (1972), exploring public and private aspects to a Canadian version of the colonial dilemma, he won a Governor General's Award for Poetry.

The freedom of form Lee claims in *Civil Elegies* is carried a stage further in *The Gods* (1978) and most notably in his elegy 'The Death of Harold Ladoo', a poem commemorating a Trinidadian immigrant whose work Lee edited for Anansi. The contrast in their styles is revealing: **Harold Ladoo**'s tempestuous prose, 'that raucous, raging thing I'd read' as Lee puts it, is viscerally sensuous and emotional, and Lee's sinuously intellectual syntax seeks and achieves ever-more liberated rhythms in poems such as 'Not Abstract Harmonies But', which renounce yet never escape their abstract roots. Just such abstractions, derived from philosopher Martin Heidegger, inform his analyses in *Savage Fields: An Essay in Literature and Cosmology* (1977) of works by **Michael Ondaatje** and **Leonard Cohen** — analyses that throw more light on Lee than on Cohen or Ondaatje.

Lee does escape his intellectual cage, not in Ladoo-like prose, but in his verse for children. And as if in compensation, he feels free to restrict himself to deftly virtuoso formal rhythms. *Alligator Pie* and *Nicholas Knock* (both 1974) are superb collections for younger and older children, though *Garbage Delight* (1977) and *Jelly Belly* (1983) seem disappointing attempts to repeat those earlier successes. *The Difficulty of Living on Other Planets* (1987) is an uninspired use of the rhythms of his verse for children in verse for adults, its best pieces in fact all stolen from *Alligator Pie* and *Nicholas Knock*. (See **Children's Literature**, Canada.)

JAMES HARRISON

Further reading: Tom Middlebro', *Dennis Lee and His Works* (1984).

LEE, EASTON H. (1931–)
Jamaican dramatist
Born in Trelawny, Jamaica, where he received his early education, he later studied theatre arts in the USA and communication arts in the UK. His primary contribution to cultural and artistic activity in Jamaica is in the field of drama, where he has demonstrated his talents not only as a playwright but also as an actor and director. His work as a drama officer for the Jamaica Social Welfare Commission and as a media specialist has directly influenced his development. As a drama officer, Lee worked with groups around Jamaica, and his early one-act plays such as 'Pretty Medicine', 'Man to Man', and 'Born for the Sea', written and produced between 1962 and 1965, are based on improvisation. He wrote and produced the first play written for Jamaican television, *Paid in Full* (1965), later revised as 'The Full Price' (unpublished). In 1988 Lee was awarded a Silver Musgrave Medal for his contribution to art and culture in Jamaica.

Lee's one-act plays combine art and education. He believes that plays must say something to society that gives positive direction for personal and social choices and difficulties. Some of his plays are directed to children's audiences and many incorporate religious themes. His full-length plays, 'They That Mourn' and *The Rope and the Cross* (1986), produced for Easter 1963 and 1979 respectively, demonstrate the importance of the religious element in his work. *The Rope and the Cross*, for example, was intended to make the Christian story of the Passion meaningful to Caribbean audiences.

In his popular one-act plays, Lee has captured the flavour of Jamaican life. Sometimes, as in *Tarshan Lace and Velvet* (1979), action is set in the past. Lee's works have not been published in a single volume, but *Tarshan Lace and Velvet* can be found in *West Indian Plays for Schools* (1979), edited by Jeanne Wilson.

JOYCE JOHNSON

LEE, JOHN ALEXANDER (1891–1982)
New Zealand novelist
He was born in Dunedin, New Zealand, and his deprived childhood led to petty thieving and brushes with the law — he was sentenced to flogging

and incarceration in an 'industrial school'. In early adulthood he became a 'swagger' — one of the many walking the country in search of casual work — and was introduced to socialist ideas and such writers as Upton Sinclair and Jack London. He served in the First World War, lost an arm, and was decorated for gallantry. In 1922 Lee was elected to parliament as a Labour member and in 1935, in New Zealand's first Labour government, he became under-secretary to the minister of finance with responsibility for a state housing program. In 1940, after he had persistently criticized the ailing prime minister, M. J. Savage, he was expelled from the Labour Party; he formed a breakaway Democratic Labour Party, but was defeated at the next election.

Lee's *Children of the Poor*, a partly autobiographical novel written in the tradition of his early heroes Sinclair and London, was published (at first anonymously) in 1934. When it became known that the author was a member of parliament some electors were scandalized, but the power and passion with which he told the story were soon recognized. *The Hunted* (1936) and *Civilian into Soldier* (1937) are sequels.

Although these novels are set several decades earlier, the occasion of their writing was the Depression of the 1930s. Lee's work is cited by the Australian critic Ian Reid as showing the deep and continuing influence of the Depression on fiction in both Australia and New Zealand.

The books Lee wrote after his parliamentary defeat portray every stage of his colourful career. Some are called novels, some autobiography, but they differ little in style or substance. Among them are stories of swaggers — *Shining with the Shiner* (1944); a compelling if prejudiced account of his conflict with Savage — *Simple on a Soap-Box* (1963); *Rhetoric at the Red Dawn* (1965); *Delinquent Days* (1967); and *Soldier* (1976). He also wrote a number of thrillers. At his best Lee was a vigorous, direct, and eloquent writer, though he was obsessed with justifying his political actions and sometimes seemed to be writing the same book over and over again.

DENNIS McELDOWNEY

Further reading: Erik Olssen, *John A. Lee* (1977); Ian Reid, *Fiction and the Great Depression: Australia and New Zealand 1930–1950* (1979).

LEE KOK LIANG (1927–92)

Malaysian novelist, short-story writer

He was born in Alor Star, Kedah, Malaya, to, in his own words, a father who was a 'stern follower of the British Raj' and fourth-generation Straits-Chinese and 'a saronged woman, quick tempered with a mixture of Siamese, Chinese, Malay culture'. Lee's schooling in Malaya's Chinese, Japanese, English, and Malay education systems in the 1930s and 1940s laid the foundations of the cultural heterogeneity of his sensibility, the core of which is Straits-Chinese. In the early 1950s Lee attended the University of Melbourne, Australia, where he wrote and published short stories; this literary apprenticeship culminated in his first collection, *The Mutes in the Sun and Other Stories* (1963). He studied law at Lincoln's Inn, London, England, and after graduating returned to Malaya to practise law.

Lee's documentary story, 'Return to Malaya' (1944), published in the journal *Encounter*, laid some of the foundations for his fictional method: detached-observer narration and a meticulous rendering of physical, social, and behavioral detail. This method is exemplified in a later hallmark image — that of 'the bar where a group of young men sat like loose-limbed spiders on the stools' (in 'Not So Long Ago but Still Around', in *Death Is a Ceremony and Other Short Stories*, 1992).

Lee's diverse educational experience had important repercussions for him as a Malaysian who wrote in English and chronicled the private lives, phobias, and passions of Malaysians from different ethnic backgrounds. In situating his characters in the Malaysian scene, Lee was subtly mindful of the politics of multiracism. The influence of his family background is also discernible in his fictional studies of Chinese family life and the tenacious traditions and dynastic ambitions that have shaped it. *Flowers in the Sky* (1981), comprising four related stories, conducts a thorough exploration of the belief systems embedded in Malaysia's multicultural society. The novel's theme of the conflict between spiritual values and acquisitive, corrupting materialism is also deftly etched into the plots of many of Lee's short stories.

In Lee's fictional world politics permeates most spheres of human activity and relationships; his work ranges through such issues as sex, marriage, family life, promiscuity, prostitution, religion, the colonial club, racial identity, funerals, violence (which is a psychological as well as a political phenomenon), class hierarchy, and the shadowy nation state. (Lee had practical experience of politics, both as a former member of the Penang State Assembly and as a barrister who has represented oppressed worker groups.)

The Mutes in the Sun presents alarming, powerful profiles of individuals brutalized, ostracized, and alienated by authority figures or fellow victims. These dark effects, paradigms of social evils yet mitigated by gestures of compassion or love, suggest that Lee introduced to South-East Asian literature relevant adaptations of Dickens, Hawthorne, and Dostoevsky. The title story of *The Mutes in the Sun* as well as 'Dumb, Dumb, by a Bee Stung' (in *Death Is a Ceremony*) feature misshapen mutes whose characterizations are symbolic as well as naturalistic. In Lee's metaphoric narrative design, mutes and mutilators inhabit opposite sectors of the psyche and society. Lee's image of the mute (silenced by nature, fear, family, community, or authority) is potent with moral and political *Angst* and articulates a theme of the *malaise* of silence that is echoed, for instance, in **Ee Tiang Hong**'s poem 'Silence is Golden'. *Death Is a Ceremony and Other Stories* extends the social and psychological range of Lee's compassionate melancholy. 'When the Saints Go Marching' and 'A Pack of Cards', for example, are sinister and sad versions of the same situation: they are *Jane Eyre* Gothic without the romance; *études* to complement **Jean Rhys**' symphonic *Wide Sargasso Sea* (1966).

Whereas 'The Mutes in the Sun' is a Poe-like tale of tragic terror and mystery, set in an equatorial Waste Land, its affirmative coda (the mutes discovering the action, speech, and liberation of compassion) anticipates the tragicomedy of cultural reconciliation in *Flowers in the Sky*, in which suffering and celebration enjoy an equipoise previously unsustained in Lee's fictional world. In this novel tales of passion are juxtaposed to probe some of Malaysia's cultural and religious traditions. As a writer of short fictions whose technique of applied introspection reveals the inward brooding of a world and its inhabitants, Lee may be compared with such short-story artists in the new literatures in English as **Albert Wendt**, **Olive Senior**, and **Witi Ihimaera**.

SYD HARREX

Further reading: Syd Harrex, 'Mutes and mutilators in the fiction of Lee Kok Liang', in Daniel Massa (ed.) *Individual and Community in Commonwealth Literature* (1979); Syd Harrex, 'Scalpel, scar, icon', in Bruce Bennett *et al.* (eds) *The Writer's Sense of the Contemporary* (1982).

LEE, JOHN ROBERT (1948–)

St Lucian poet, short-story writer

Born in Castries, St Lucia, the Caribbean, he was educated at St Mary's College. After working for the Royal Bank of Canada from 1967 to 1969, he studied English and French literature at the University of the West Indies. His poetry collections include *Vocation and Other Poems* (1975), *Dread Season* (1978), *The Prodigal* (1983), *Possessions* (1984), *Saint Lucian* (1988), and *Clearing Ground*

(1991). His short stories have appeared in the journal *Bim* (53, 1971), in *Facing the Sea* (1986), compiled by Anne Walmsley and Nick Caistor, and in *Caribbean New Wave: Contemporary Short Stories* (1990), selected by Stewart Brown. Lee is in many ways a bridge between the earlier 'literary' tradition established by **Derek Walcott** and a growing trend among younger Caribbean writers towards the greater use of oral forms. Solidly grounded in mainstream modern English poetry, Lee's imagery has always drawn freely from the St Lucian folk tradition. Further, where necessary, Lee has incorporated in his work the vocabulary and structures of Kweyol, the first language of many St Lucians.

Thematically, Lee's work intertwines a number of related ideas and concerns: poetry as a vocation; the encounter between traditional and modern values; the place of Christianity in the life of the individual and community; and man-woman relationships. Stylistically, Lee's poetry has moved in the direction of 'plain speaking', utilizing more of the rhythms, musicality, and phrasing of natural speech. This trend has naturally brought to the work a more communal dimension. Lee's stance is less that of a lone spiritual voyager and more that of a guide. This has paralleled his own immersion in Christianity.

Once involved in theatre, Lee has turned his attention to writing short stories and cultural journalism. A supporter of local publishing, his work has none the less appeared in international publications and has been the subject of various studies and articles. Lee is now a librarian and has produced a bibliography of St Lucian creative writing, 'St Lucian Creative Writing: An Index of Titles' (in the *Folk Research Centre Bulletin*, 2, 1991).

KENDEL HIPPOLYTE

Further reading: Michael Gilkes, 'Confluences: reconciling life and language — the poetry of John Robert Lee', *Wasafiri* July/Aug. (1992).

LEE, RUSSELL (1964–)

Singaporean horror writer, biographer

She was born Harjeet Kaur in the small Malaysian town of Seramban and graduated with an arts degree from Monash University, Australia, after which she went to Singapore to work in several research positions. She is known by her pseudonyms Russell Lee and H. Sidhu. Her decision to write under a *nom de plume* was prompted, in part, by the sensitivities of her career, a fact borne out by her public acknowledgement of the true identity of Russell Lee immediately after she left her last job.

Lee's *The Almost Complete Collection of True Singapore Ghost Stories* (1989) has sold more than 70,000 copies in English. Ghost stories have always been popular in Singapore, but *The Almost Complete Collection* was the first collection made up almost exclusively of Singaporeans from various walks of life recounting their own encounters with the supernatural. The language of the book is simple, even ungrammatical at times, which only helps the documentary style ring true. Readers felt a sense of sharing, as tales they had heard passed around verbally for generations (e.g., those about some stations in Singapore's new mass transit train system being haunted) appeared in print for the first time.

Lee caused another sensation on the local publishing scene when she sued the company Flame of The Forest, which published *The Almost Complete Collection* as its first book, for unpaid royalties. She also sued the company for royalties from a subsequent Chinese edition.

Lee formed her own publishing company, Native Publications, later Native Communications, and in 1991 and 1992 she released two successful sequels to *The Almost Complete Collection.* Both were well received critically and continue to do well in the market. The bestselling second volume includes contributions from readers, and stylistic but spine-chilling graphics of some local ghosts. Both volumes retain Lee's cynical and witty voice, as she comments on some stories, dismissing them or offering alternative scientific explanations.

Lee has also published other bestsellers, including, under the name H. Sidhu, *The Bamboo Fortress* (1991), a collection of first-hand accounts of the Second World War from prominent Singaporeans, including the former deputy prime minister, Dr Toh Chin Chye.

RAVI VELOO

LEE TZU PHENG (1946–)

Singaporean poet

Born in Singapore, she was educated at Raffles Girls' School, Singapore, and at the University of Singapore, where in 1972 she completed her doctorate on W. B. Yeats. A senior lecturer in the department of English at the National University of Singapore, Lee has published three books of poetry, *Prospect of a Drowning* (1980), *Against the Next Wave* (1988), and *The Brink of an Amen* (1991). Her most frequently anthologized poem, 'My Country and My People', established her status as a poet and her reputation as both a 'national' poet and an advocate of nationalism. The latter honour rests uneasily upon her, however, given the poem's ambiguity and ambivalence.

The subject of Lee's poetry is predominantly the 'inner life'. It draws the reader close in its bid to be heard or understood: 'Can the heart be heard, / being needful and inarticulate?' ('The Stream'). Lee's poetry, intimate and personal, is thus also confessional in its mode of address, although its use of factual autobiographical detail is minimal. This confessional mode, summed up by the poet's direct address to the reader — 'let me show you what I've seen' ('In Sight') — expresses 'the extravagance of our need' ('Telling It Like It Is') and is especially characteristic of Lee's second volume, in which Theodore Roethke is a major influence (as compared to **Arthur Yap**'s influence in the first volume).

Lee's poetry embodies a quest or search that takes on a specifically religious character in her second and third collections. Suffering is allegorized as a spiritual process; love and redemption are figured allegorically in the imagery of the garden, of angels, and of the Word becoming flesh. The opening poem of *Prospect of a Drowning* focuses on the image of a grain of sand inside the oyster shell as a metaphor for artistic creation and expresses a resolve to 'suffer its torment / and harden this sickness / to pearl'. By the second volume the emphasis has changed; the opening poem states: 'Who would find treasure learns to hold / The gift of tears more dear than pearls.' This statement suggests that *Against the Next Wave* foregrounds the place of 'tears' or suffering in the poet's discourse. This is not to say that the 'pearls' are totally neglected; words, the poet's pearls, are the subject of the poet's scrutiny in *Against the Next Wave*. The second volume, in fact, does re-read much of the first, as its allusive title (a line from the titular poem of the first book), the opening poem, and many others clearly demonstrate.

In *The Brink of an Amen* Lee's imagery is frequently symbolic and invokes dichotomies: Silence versus words/language/babble (as in the titular poem) and sight/light/knowledge versus darkness. This third volume pursues the notion of the quest set up in *Against the Next Wave*, and the arrival at or realization of the privileged term of the opposition (silence and sight) figures as an epiphany (as in the title of the collection).

Lee's lyricism is a discourse of mood and feeling. It appears to be an attempt to reify emotion. The poetry, however, is pregnant with the conflicting awareness that language cannot be wholly concrete; its ambiguity and semantic shifts — 'this mesh of intentions / between feeling and speaking' ('Listen') — militate against any such opacity.

ANNE BREWSTER

Further reading: Lucilla Hosilla, 'The inner world of Lee Tzu Pheng's poetry', *Solidarity* 101

(1984); Kirpal Singh, ed., *Critical Engagements: Singapore Poems in Focus* (1986).

LEGENDS

LEGENDS (Australia)

In his poem 'Australia' **A. D. Hope** wrote of the perverse good fortune of a country that lacked 'songs, architecture, history'. By implication, few of the false consolations afforded by national legends were to be found there. Australian culture has not advanced many legendary figures, perhaps from suspicion of those spheres of action that usually furnish women and men for legend, whether as warriors, martyrs, political leaders, pioneers, explorers, or saints. While Canadian literature celebrates the revolutionary separatist Louis Riel (in **Don Gutteridge**'s *Riel: a Poem for Voices*, 1968, and **John Coulter**'s plays, for example), explorer Sir John Franklin (in **Gwendolyn MacEwen**'s verse play, *Terror and Erebus*, in *Afterworlds*, 1987), and the slain missionary Brébeuf (in **E. J. Pratt**'s poem *Brébeuf and His Brethren*, 1940), Australian writers have preferred the invention of flawed, often spurious characters — bushrangers, ratbags, turncoats.

They have also favoured legendary types rather than individuals: the bushwoman and the bushman, **Henry Lawson**'s drover's wife, **Judith Wright**'s Bullocky, bushrangers, the corporate legend of the Anzac soldier, people identified by their legal and illicit work. In the ethos of rural labourers — **mateship**, sardonic humour, anti-authoritarianism — **Russel Ward** found the essence of the legend (*The Australian Legend*, 1958). In such purportedly representative folk could be found the veritable 'matter of Australia', legends that served a multitude of cultural purposes: to reassure, ennoble, guarantee historical continuities. The Canadian *coureurs de bois* and the Boer voortrekkers in South Africa fulfilled similar roles in those countries' literatures.

In the nineteenth century Emily Manning ('Australia'), in her poem 'From the Clyde to Braidwood', lamented that 'no legend old' added 'softening beauty' to the Australian landscape. The paucity of historical materials has led to sporadic confections of legends. Douglas Sladen's recommendation of **Adam Lindsay Gordon** as 'the poet of Australia', which led to his bust being placed in Westminster Abbey, England, was an instance in the 1930s. Four decades later, perhaps in reaction to the Vietnam War, the need to remember or concoct legendary folk quickened in Australia. Beneficiaries included 'Breaker' Morant (in the play by Kenneth Ross that became a film), King O'Malley and Martin Cash (in polemical musicals by Michael Boddy and others), **Ned Kelly** and **Henry Lawson** (in historical works by **Manning Clark**), Nellie Melba, and Les Darcy (in plays by **Jack Hibberd**). This pantheon includes two bushrangers, an alcoholic writer, a court-martialled soldier, a politician, an expatriate singer, and a boxer who, having failed to enlist in the First World War, died in temporary disgrace in America in 1917. The legendary victim of treachery, whether Morant or Victoria Cross winner Albert Jacka, Kelly, Darcy, or the great racehorse Phar Lap (which died in California), is a story that has had a long run in Australian culture.

The Aborigines have infrequently become stuff of literary legend, although G. G. McCrae's poem *Mamba* (1867) made an attempt in the manner of Longfellow, and **K. Langloh Parker**'s *Australian Legendary Tales* (1896) set a fashion for retelling Aboriginal stories by non-Aborigines. An exception is **Mudrooroo Narogin**'s (Colin Johnson's) novel *Long Live Sandawara* (1979), about the life and inspiration of an Aboriginal resistance leader. In the nineteenth century a number of Australian poets, among them **Charles Harpur**, found the Maori opponent of British rule, Honi Heke, a fitter subject than the Aborigines.

Australians have also tried to make a handful

of years into a seminal epoch. **Vance Palmer**'s *The Legend of the Nineties* (1954) reveals how the decade before Federation has become a prime site of legend-making, as a time of nationalist stirrings and literary as well as social radicalism and experiment. This activity centred on the 1890s is another instance of that premature nostalgia for history and literature that the country has not yet had time to produce. This is suggested by the titles of the reminiscent accounts of G. A. Taylor (*Those Were the Days*, 1918) and Arthur Jose (*The Romantic Nineties*, 1933), and **Katharine Susannah Prichard**'s novel *The Roaring Nineties* (1946).

Through disputes over the worth of legendary people and a legendary decade, a history might be willed into being in Australia. This was the assumption of **P. R. Stephensen**, who wrote in *The Foundations of Culture in Australia* (1936) that Australian history was 'packed with love and legend . . . A decade of our own history is more important to us than a century of history from elsewhere.'

PETER PIERCE

Further reading: Manning Clark, 'Heroes', in Stephen R. Graubard (ed.) *Australia: The Daedalus Symposium* (1985); Clem Gorman, ed., *The Larrikin Streak: Australian Writers Look at the Legend* (1990).

LEGENDS (Canada)

Before European immigrants brought written words to the land now called Canada, aboriginal people had been communicating with one another through oral traditions for more than ten thousand years. Their intricately crafted legends, myths, and stories are the first Canadian literature and a continuing source of inspiration to both Native and non-Native writers today. Aboriginal masters of the storytelling art gave voice to masterpieces that can compare with any of the world's great literatures. (See **Aboriginal Literature**, Canada.)

The Native peoples of Canada typically view their world as imbued with human qualities of will and purpose. They study the life cycles of plants, animals, and natural phenomena in the same way that they study the actions and motivations of other people. Their legends connect people of different generations to one another and to the non-humans with whom they share life. They tell about a mythic time of beginnings when people and animals were closer to one another. Like the great books of written literary traditions, legends in an oral tradition challenge people to think with intelligence and compassion about the human condition. A mutually understood legendary vocabulary enables people to communicate creatively with one another while living responsibly within a nourishing and sustaining social order.

To the Haida of Haida Gwaii (the Queen Charlotte Islands of British Columbia, Canada, on European maps), Raven is both a bird and an ancestor whose adventures in mythic time explain the way things are today. Each stream, beach, cove, and island has meaning both in the experience of living people and in the legendary events that Raven and other beings of the Haida cosmos experienced in mythic times. In 1900 anthropologist John Swanton recorded superb tellings of Raven stories from Haida masters John Sky and Walter McGregor. According to Canadian poet **Robert Bringhurst**, 'If there is such a thing as Canadian literature, actually distinct from the literature of Europe, [Sky and McGregor] are two of its earliest and greatest authors.'

The Micmacs of maritime Canada tell of a legendary hero named Glooscap who transformed a mythic world into the one where people live today. His tracks may still be seen in natural features of the landscape. Salish people of Canada's northwest coast have legends of a similar culture hero named Khaals. The Cree and Ojibwa of the eastern woodlands and subarctic look to Nanabush, their culture hero and trickster, for amusement and inspiration. (Cree playwright **Tomson Highway** made Nanabush a central figure in his acclaimed plays, *The Rez Sisters*, 1988, and *Dry Lips Oughta Move to Kapuskasing*, 1990.)

A remarkable account of the beings who populate the legendary Cree/Ojibwa world was set down by a Northwest Company trader, George Nelson, in 1823 and published in 1988 by Jennifer Brown and Robert Brightman as *The Orders of the Dreamed: George Nelson on Cree and Northern Ojibwa Religion and Myth*. Cree writer Stan Cuthand views Nelson's text as important because it 'may remind us of half forgotten tales, ideas and concepts, so that they can be saved for another generation'. Nelson describes how legendary beings instruct shamans 'according to the orders of the dreamed' and how they come to shamans in the ritual theatre of the 'shaking tent' or conjuring lodge. Each legendary character has a familiar voice and personality in the same way that members of a small community have distinctive features that are known to all. Flying Squirrel, for example, speaks in a contrary tongue like that encountered in dreams. 'You must take everything he says,' Nelson tells us, 'as we do our Dreams, i.e., the opposite.' Everyone jokes about Loon's cry — 'I want to have a wife' — but only the conjurer can interpret Buffalo's hoarse and rough speech. In their commentary on Nelson's journal, editors Brown and Brightman write, 'Mythic beings are not confined to another or ancient world, and their revelations are not a closed book . . . Since they participate in the social and mental life of ordinary human beings, they may be thought of as persons and classificatory relatives.'

Aboriginal Canadians tell and hear their legends in ordinary time, but they interpret them in relation to a time of the mind, a mythic time. They experience the characters of myth as real and active in their lives. In *The Rez Sisters* Nanabush dances over seven women as they talk about bingo. Raven looks over the people of Haida Gwaii during their protests over clear-cut logging. Nuu-Chah-Nulth elder Simon Lucas explains that the government of his people resides in *klukwana*, a ceremony in which killer whale transforms himself into wolf. 'You may have trouble understanding our government,' he says to a white audience, 'but let me tell you that we sometimes have trouble understanding yours.' These aboriginal tricksters and transformers survive the transition from tribal to national life just as the people whose traditions they embody have survived. They thrive on making sense of the ambiguities inherent in being tribal in a national setting. They also thrive on making fun of them.

The legends of aboriginal people are more than a relic of the past. They move in a circle between mythic time and the time of ordinary experience. They move in a world that is rich with meaning. They continue to be real. In talking about his dramatic use of Cree legend, Tomson Highway draws a circle and explains: 'This is the way the Cree look at life. A continuous cycle. A self-rejuvenating force. By comparison, Christian theology is a straight line. Birth, suffering, and then the apocalypse . . . Human existence isn't a struggle for redemption to the Trickster. It's fun, a joyous celebration.'

ROBIN RIDINGTON

Further reading: John Swanton, *Haida Texts and Myths: Skidegate Dialect* (1905); Robert Bringhurst and Bill Reid, *Raven Steals the Light* (1984); Julie Cruikshank, *Life Lived like a Story: Cultural Constructions of Life History by Tagish and Tutchone Women* (1990); William New, ed., *Native Writers and Canadian Writing* (1990), special issue of *Canadian Literature*; Robin Ridington, *Little Bit Know Something: Stories in a Language of Anthropology* (1990); Julie Cruikshank, *Reading Voices: Dan Dha Ts'edenintthe'e* (1991).

Legends and Myths (South Africa)

European settlers worldwide approached unknown territories and peoples with mingled trepidation and hope and, naturally, perceived them through the lenses of long-embedded Eurocentric conventions and legends.

No European legends survived translocation unmodified: in South Africa by the 1830s a Cape newspaper mocked travellers for their fears of 'dragons and chimera', and Nathaniel Isaacs laughed at his own abortive search for a Natal unicorn. Transported myths inflected settlers' texts in structure and attitude rather than in content, in ways analogous to early travellers' inscriptions of alien landscapes using Burke's Enlightenment aesthetics. Legend-laden tropes helped formulate, and were chosen to reflect, European settlers' governing ambivalence between arrogance and guilt, conquest and assimilation — ambivalence that critic Abdul JanMohamed has termed colonialism's 'Manichean aesthetic'.

Two interlocking pairs of legends — those of the Lost City and lost Eden and, secondly, those of 'Noble' and 'Ignoble' savages — are prominent metaphoric frames for settlers' reactions to Africa's intractable difference. First, tales of the Lost City and of lost Eden, like America's El Dorado, have exercised the European imagination from Homer's Elysium and Dante's terrestrial paradise to Prester John and present-day Zimbabwe. Zimbabwe inspired multiple romances, from H. M. Walmsley's *The Ruined Cities of Zulu Land* (1869) and **Henry Rider Haggard**'s *King Solomon's Mines* (1885) to John Buchan's fusion of legend and fear of Zulu rebellion in *Prester John* (1910).

The mythical cities function partly as an extension of imperial urban culture; invariably built and governed by whites, they embody a wider derogation of African achievement. Thus, Zimbabwe is attributed to Phoenician enterprise, just as the Zulus, Walmsley's protagonist avers, 'sprang from . . . Pharoah's seamen'; Shaka Zulu's innovative predecessor Dingiswayo is instructed by a stray English doctor; the Xhosa hero Makanna in M. Norbet Morgan's *Bronze Napoleon* (1940) is Persian; and Zulu and Xhosa circumcision customs developed from Jewish rites.

Contradictorily, stories of unreachably beneficent cities implicitly criticize both western 'progress' and its offshoot, colonial urban culture. As **H. C. Bosman** notes in his ironic lampoon, 'Lost City' (1951): 'The expedition doesn't have to leave Johannesburg, if it's a lost city it wants.' Throughout South African literature a utopian element thus intersects with myths of the classical Arcadia, the biblical Eden, and protean varieties of pastoral.

J. M. Coetzee notes that, unlike America's retreating frontier, South Africa's topography has been antagonistic to the Edenic: the ambivalently threatening titan Adamastor, figuratively immanent in Table Mountain for poets from Camoens to **Sydney Clouts**, and the Australia-like desert interior have been the more enduring tropes of a frontier literature simultaneously disillusioned, increasingly uncomfortable with a literary vocabulary inherited from England, and obsessed with race. Though numerous writers, from **W. C. Scully** in the 1890s to Elsa Joubert (in her *The Long Journey of Poppie Nongena*, 1980, first published in Afrikaans in 1978), have assumed an 'African voice', this South African Garden is serpent-infested, and the serpent is generally the black man. The teeming-Eden travelogues of many early hunters such as John Barrow (*Travels into the Interior of Southern Africa*, 1806) and William Burchell (*Travels in the Interior of Southern Africa*, 1822) attempted textually to excise the presence of aboriginals altogether; later Edens were to be reconstructed by Puritanical 'cheerful toil' in the face of non-cultivating and therefore degenerate 'savagery'. South Africa spawns neither a neo-primitivist school like Australia's **Jindyworobak Movement** nor an eco-frontiersman of the stature of American James Fenimore Cooper's Natty Bumppo.

Nevertheless, versions of paradise continue to inform South Africans' inscriptions of their place on the land, from Haggard's adventurers, escaping from tawdry mercantilism, through Bosman's sardonic anti-bucolics and **Jack Cope**'s story 'Power' (in his collection *The Man Who Doubted*, 1967), in which a boy's compassion for a trapped bird halts an entire electricity network, to Dalene Matthee's tragic elephant-and-woodcutter pastoral *Circles in a Forest* (1984).

The tensions among the values of Garden and anti-Garden, humanitarian dream, disappointed dystopia, and exploitative progress are reflected in the second pair of legends: those of the Noble and the Ignoble Savage. Antiquity's Ethiopian Prince and anthropophagi, the medieval Wild Man, and Aphra Behn's Oroonoko are refurbished in South African settler literature to combat the depredations of the slave trade and the exigencies of frontier conflict. Little belief in Noble Savagery survived early contact, however. As with Australia's Aborigines, Chain-of-Being hierarchies and bowdlerized Darwinism justified the extermination of the Khoi-san and the dispossession of the Bantu. Persisting sporadically from Haggard's Umslopogaas to Uys Krige's story 'Death of the Zulu' (in *The Dream and the Desert*, 1953), the Noble Savage was resurrected only with the decisive crushing of African resistance.

In a society dominated by apartheid's ossifying frontiers, the Wild Man — libertine, ungovernable, animal, unintelligible — has greater mythic currency, and popular literature relegates blacks to the clichés of blood-lust. More complexly, the ambiguities of **Roy Campbell**'s poem 'The Zulu Girl' (in *Adamastor*, 1930), for example — where paradisal sensuality suckles the 'old unquenched . . . ferocity of beaten tribes' — echo in the related and recurrent theme of 'going native'. Instances of this theme range from the ethnocentric horror of Captain Frederick Marryat's *The Mission* (1845) to both the sympathetic 'white bushman' stories of **Laurens van der Post** and to **Wilbur Smith**'s *The Burning Shore* (1985). The legendary figure of Robinson Crusoe hovers here, explicit model for innumerable shipwreck fictions and actual colonial careers, from the work of Nathaniel Isaacs, through Henno Martin's *The Sheltering Desert* (1957, translated by William Kimber), to Coetzee's deconstructive *Foe* (1987).

As Coetzee's postmodernist fiction acknowledges, more pernicious than an understandable distortion of African realities by Eurocentric tropes are the hegemonic ends to which those figures are turned. Old legends, appropriated to the context of apartheid, 'transform history into Nature', to use Roland Barthes' phrase, becoming unquestioned local myths essential to social hierarchies and ethnic identities. Nowhere is this clearer than in the myth of Shaka Zulu.

The figure of Shaka (assassinated 1828) dominates the historical landscape of the subcontinent as a thrillingly monstrous tyrant and military genius to generations of whites, as a heroic liberator to blacks from African National Congress (ANC) founder Pixley Seme to present-day Zulu supremo Mangosuthu Buthelezi, as the subject of liberationist dramas from Zambia to Senegal, and as the namesake of a Zulu public holiday, a pop singer, a shoe brand, and a Namibian healer. In 1989–90 alone, Zulu chiefs condemned ANC youth for 'making King Shaka's land dirty'; a self-styled 'white Zulu' invoked him as hero; Afrikaner right-wingers warned of his heritage of violence; a lecturer recommended Shakan organizational methods to Zimbabwean businessmen; and an American university student was dismissed for calling another student 'Shaka Zulu'. Such demotic manifestations are as important as, and nourish, the 'literary'; all things to all people, Shaka has become a primary constituent of both white and black self-consciousness.

Despite the stirring story of illegitimacy, exile, bloodthirsty insanity, and military acumen entrenched in dozens of educational texts, novels, poems, television films, and brochures, little of Shaka's reign is known for certain. Oral traditions are extensive but contradictory; the three white eyewitness accounts are mendacious and inconsistent. The seminal portrait in Nathaniel Isaacs' *Travels and Adventures in Eastern Africa* (1836) of a 'ferocious and unrelenting despot . . . a giant without reason' draws less on demonstrable evidence than on the fictional rhetoric of the Gothic and is clearly an instrument in the book's propaganda campaign for white colonization of Natal. Yet this lurid portrayal is that which is most often plagiarized and quoted, from Cornwallis Harris' *The Wild Sports of Southern Africa* (1839) to James Michener's *The Covenant* (1980).

The appeal of the monstrous, though rooted in often-unrecognized legend, is tenacious because it reconfirms the half-truths of prejudice and serves more pragmatic political structures. In A. T. Bryant's massive and central *Olden Times in Zululand and Natal* (1929), for example, Shaka is a Satanic 'arch-demon' who obliterates a paradisal idyll; whites arrive 'in the nick of time' to rescue the blacks from self-immolation. Himself a priest, Bryant follows nineteenth-century missionaries in commandeering to evangalistic ends a fictionalized Shaka — 'God's scourge to offending nations', as William Holden called him in 1866. Similarly, the baseless notion of Shaka's 'depopulation' of the interior was conjured to conceal the brutality of white incursion.

Fiction easily supersedes evidence. Hence, E. A. Ritter's novel *Shaka Zulu* (1955), the most popular work on the Zulu, interleaves extensive plagiarisms from Bryant with invention, but until recently was cited as a credible source, even in the *Encyclopaedia Britannica.* The 'Battle of Gqokli Hill', repeated in almost every subsequent account as a key demonstration of this 'Black Napoleon's' tactical genius, for example, is a pure fabrication of Ritter's.

Such unquestioning repetition is the myth's hallmark, as are its unexplored contradictions. *Shaka Zulu* partially restores Shaka to 'Noble Savage' status, but also dovetails familiar episodes of sexual abandon and gratuitous violence, reminiscent of both Arcadia and Hades. These antinomies, however, still govern works as recent as Louis du Buisson's 'investigative' *The White Man Cometh* (1987); the narrative structures of heroic adventure and folk tale, necessary components of popular myth, continue to inhibit methodical scholarship. (See **Popular Writing**, South Africa.)

The misconceptions spill into British and American accounts, such as Donald Morris' *The Washing of the Spears* (1965); nor are black South Africans immune. Missionaries' fictionalized, vernacular school-readers contaminated 'oral traditions' collected decades later; at least some current Zulu propaganda owes its lineaments to Ritter. Ritter and other whites in turn owed much to myth-laden African works such as Thomas Mofolo's *Chaka* (first published in Sotho in 1925 and in English, under the same title, in 1931, translated by F. H. Dutton) and **R. R. R. Dhlomo**'s *UShaka* (1937).

This protean projection of complex fears and desires, torn between ethnology and entertainment, Utopia and savagery, thus reflects in many ways the deeper argument in settler literature between personal lyricism and public 'commitment'. The novelist **Ahmed Essop** refers to this tension as South Africans' 'twin temptations,' as the struggle between the desire 'to take up arms against a sea of troubles' and the wish 'to retreat into misanthropy and solipsism'.

DAN WYLIE

Further reading: J. M. Coetzee, *White Writing: On the Culture of Letters in South Africa* (1988); M. van Wyk Smith, ed., *Shades of Adamastor: Africa and the Portuguese Connection* (1988).

LEHMANN, GEOFFREY (1940–)

Australian poet, editor

Born in Sydney, Australia, he graduated in arts and law from the University of Sydney. He practised as a solicitor and later lectured in law at the University of New South Wales. While at Sydney University he co-edited with **Les A. Murray** the magazines *Arna* and *Hermes*, and they co-authored their first verse collection *The Ilex Tree* (1965). Lehmann's subsequent verse publications are *A Voyage of Lions and Other Poems* (1968), *Conversation with a Rider* (1972), *From an Australian Country Sequence* (1973), *Ross' Poems* (1978), *Nero's Poems* (1981), and *Children's Games* (1990). His *Selected Poems* was published in 1976. He has also edited the anthologies *Comic Australian Verse* (1972), *The Flight of the Emu* (1989) and, with Robert Gray, *The Younger Australian Poets* (1983). *A Spring Day in Autumn* (1974) is his only novel. He has published a volume of art criticism, *Australian Primitive Painters* (1977).

When in the 1960s the work of Lehmann and Les Murray first gained attention, they were seen as the natural inheritors of the 'school' of Australian poetry nurtured by **Douglas Stewart** during his period as literary editor of the national weekly the ***Bulletin***. The tradition established was one with a strong consciousness of the rural heritage and the backbone it formed for a developing national expression, though this tradition certainly admitted a great deal of playful city observation and immediacy. Lehmann quickly established his poetic individuality, and in a relatively short space of time he produced a series of thoughtful and often luminous volumes that gave a measured view of his personal world. It included poems of family and regional evocation that drew some of their candour perhaps from the strain of 'confessional' poetry then current, but was also imbued with Lehmann's own sense of elegy for the fragility of things. These poems complemented the ambitious historical series, most notably in the extended 'Monologues for Marcus Furius Camillus, Governor of Africa', with their ancient Roman settings and their opulence and decadence. Later volumes pursued these veins of historical and contemporary meditations on transience. These reach their fullest development in two substantial volumes, *Ross' Poems* and *Nero's Poems*. *Ross' Poems*, based upon anecdotes from Lehmann's first father-in-law, is in seventy-two sections that build up a rich portrait of a farmer, his world, and his family in a way that has assured them of a strong position in the Australian poetry of their period. Together with the poems by Les Murray of this period they provide striking evidence of the legitimacy of a non-urban vein of poetry as an ongoing tradition in Australian culture; it is evident in the work of much later poets such as **Philip Salom** and Tony Lintermans.

Children's Games is a playful and wry exploration of life as a single father, followed — in a quietly virtuoso sequence of five sestinas — by a celebration of a new marriage. The book ends, though, in a curious and almost disturbing expansion of a sequence, 'Simple Sonnets', from his second book *Conversation with a Rider*, tugging that almost surrealistic, folk-like group of poems into a new prominence, this time not youthful and whimsical, but imbued with a painful sense of dislocation and loss, plangent as the most ancient of folk songs are, and as haunting.

THOMAS SHAPCOTT

Further reading: 'Geoffrey Lehmann', in Martin Duwell and Laurie Hergenhan (eds) *The 'ALS' Guide to Australian Writers: A Bibliography 1963–1990* (1992).

LEPROHON, ROSANNA (1829–79)

Canadian novelist

Born Rosanna Eleanora Mullins in Montreal, Canada, and convent educated, she first published poems and five serialized novels (1846–51) in *The Literary Garland* (Montreal), a genteel monthly described by critic Carl F. Klinck as 'Anglo-Bostonian' in tone. However, the primary colonial attachment in Leprohon's early fiction is to England, the setting of all her early tales of high life romance, although there is no evidence she ever visited Europe.

After 1851, when she married Dr Jean Lucien Leprohon, and *The Literary Garland* ceased publication, her work became more specifically Canadian. Motherhood (thirteen children) and her husband's active involvement in French-Canadian cultural affairs directed her attention to the bicultural milieu in which she lived. Growing Canadian nationalism during the pre-Confederation era and concomitant acceptance of Canada as a location for fiction are reflected in the North American setting of most of her subsequent fiction, whose plots continue the interest in the conduct of young women manifested in her earlier work. Recent criticism concentrates on the examination of relations between French and English in *Antoinette de Mirecourt; or, Secret Marrying and Secret Sorrowing* (1864), her only book currently in print. Leprohon's other Canadian novels, *The Manor House of de Villerai* (1859–60) and *Armand Durand; or, A Promise Fulfilled* (1868), received more attention in translation in Quebec than in their original language.

Antoinette de Mirecourt, although set in Montreal in 1763, highlights an enduring Canadian problem in its allegory of bicultural conflict and resolution. When young country-bred Antoinette is beguiled into a secret marriage with a fortune-hunting British officer, her situation parallels the vulnerability of her defeated culture at the hands of the British. Leprohon's adroit resolution disposes of the inappropriate husband and settles her heroine with a more suitable (because Catholic) Englishman, a conclusion to which some French-Canadian critics objected. In her preface, Leprohon presents her 'essentially Canadian' novel as a modest contribution to a nascent national literature.

CAROLE GERSON

Further reading: Carole Gerson, 'Three writers of Victorian Canada', in Robert Lecker, Jack David, and Ellen Quigley (eds) *Canadian Writers and Their Works*, Fiction Series 1 (1983); John C. Stockdale, ed., *Antoinette de Mirecourt* (1989); Lorraine McMullen and Elizabeth Waterston, 'Rosanna Mullins Leprohon: at home in many worlds', in Carrie MacMillan, Lorraine McMullen, and Elizabeth Waterston (eds) *Silenced Sextet: Six Nineteenth-Century Canadian Women Novelists* (1992).

LESLIE, KENNETH (1892–1974)
Canadian poet

Born in Pictou, Nova Scotia, Canada, and educated at Dalhousie University, Canada (BA, 1912), and at the universities of Nebraska, USA (MA, 1914), and Harvard, USA, he was central to the **Song Fishermen**, a coterie of Maritime provinces poets who celebrated the region in their verse between 1928 and 1930. Although Leslie's contributions revealed the influence of Gaelic tradition and Victorian romanticism, he was already beginning to reflect in his work the heightened social sensibility that was to inform his career. After winning the Governor General's Award for poetry in 1938 for *By Stubborn Stars and Other Poems* (1938), Leslie moved to Boston, USA, where he founded and edited the Christian socialist *The Protestant Digest* (1938–49, moved to New York in 1940 and later renamed the *Protestant*), in which he waged a war against Fascism and anti-Semitism and supported causes such as civil rights. In the comic book *The Challenger*, he kept up his attack on Fascism throughout the war years.

Included by *Life* magazine as a suspected 'fellow-traveller' (with Charlie Chaplin, Albert Einstein, and Thomas Mann, among others) during the American McCarthy hearings on communism in the early 1950s Leslie returned to Nova Scotia. There, his Christian socialism continued to find voice in such periodicals as *Protestant* (until 1953), *Man* (1957–9?), and *New Man* (1957–72) and in the monograph *Hungary — Christian or Pagan? An Eye-Witness Report* (1950).

Leslie's poetry in *Windward Rock* (1934),

Lowlands Low (1935), *Such a Din!* (1936), and *By Stubborn Stars* is marked by musical rhythms, poetic diction, and imagery reminiscent of his maritime background. Versatile in various verse forms, he achieved haunting effects in songs such as 'Cape Breton Lullaby', in elegies such as 'Go Lank Rover' (to **Bliss Carman**), and in love sonnets such as 'By Stubborn Stars'. A political poem such as 'Remember Lamumba' is enhanced by the echo of African rhythms, and a satire such as 'Cobweb College' exhibits modernist wit. Leslie's collection *The Poems of Kenneth Leslie* (1971) was followed by *O'Malley to the Reds, and Other Poems* (1972).

GWENDOLYN DAVIES

Further reading: Susan Perly, 'We bury our poets'; Kenneth Leslie: 'a homesick Bluenoser', *The Canadian Forum* June (1975); Burris Devanney, 'Kenneth Leslie: a biographical introduction', *Canadian Poetry* 5 (1979); Burris Devanney, 'Kenneth Leslie: a preliminary bibliography', *Canadian Poetry* 5 (1979).

LESOTHO

Lesotho, a land-locked enclave geographically situated within the Republic of South Africa, measures 30,350 square kilometres. Its population was estimated in 1990 to be 1,754,664 persons. The capital and largest city is Maseru. The Basuto people constitute more then ninety per cent of the population; some seventy per cent are Christian (mostly Roman Catholic), the rest practise traditional animism. The official languages are Sesotho and English.

Lesotho was populated by the San (Bushmen) until the seventeenth century, when various Bantu-speaking peoples began entering the country from adjoining areas. Chief Moshoeshoe led the country between 1820 and 1870; following ten years of war with the Boers (1858–68), who were encroaching on the territory, Lesotho was annexed by the British. It became a protectorate in 1868 and a High Commission territory known as Basutoland in 1884. Independence was achieved in 1966. A member of the Commonwealth, Lesotho is governed by a titular monarch and an elected National Assembly.

With Somalia, Lesotho is one of only two black African countries to be essentially monolingual. Partly for this reason, partly because of the early establishment of a Protestant mission press that stimulated the growth of a written literature in Sesotho, the country has produced relatively little creative writing in English.

Agriculturally highly productive until the 1920s, the country has during the twentieth century become massively dependent on migrant worker income for its survival, the majority of its workers being employed in South African mines. Both the literature and orature in Sesotho reflect this essential reality for the country's self-conceptualization: this is especially clear in the vibrant tradition of migrant workers' narrative poems, *lifela* (pronounced 'difèla'), that have become prominent since the 1920s.

The early acquisition of printing facilities outside mission control (from 1904) resulted in newspapers that were independently edited by Basotho and included some English-language material. During the first half of the twentieth century, however, Sesotho remained massively dominant over English as a medium for literature. There is a substantial output of written poetry and (since the 1940s) drama. Among novelists, the best known — and the best known of all Lesotho writers — is **Thomas Mofolo**, whose third novel, *Chaka* (written 1910, published 1925), is available in English in translations by F. H. Dutton (1931) and Daniel P. Kunene (1981). Mofolo's first two novels are *Moeti oa bochabela* (1907) — translated as *Traveller to the East* (1934) — and *Pitseng* (1910), a Christian allegory and a realistic treatment of life in rural Lesotho, respectively; *Chaka* combines psychological characterization of the titular hero with a large-scale, detailed projection of Zulu culture. From the mid-century, however, Sesotho novels turn much more to a consideration of the lives of migrant workers. The inter-relationship between Lesotho and the Republic of South Africa is reflected in the fact this literature is often considered in the broader context of southern Sotho writing (a reality reflected also in recent publishing practice, a Lesotho novelist such B. M. Khaketla publishing with presses in both Lesotho and the Republic).

Two novels written in English and set, or partially set, in Lesotho are by **A. S. Mopeli-Paulus**, Mosotho-born and living in South Africa. After writing poetry and a short novel in Sesotho, Mopeli-Paulus published *Blanket Boy's Moon* (1953, revised by Peter Lanham) and, with Miriam Basner, *Turn to the Dark* (1956). The former novel deals with the life of a migrant worker both in his home village in Lesotho, where he is involved in medicine murder, and later in South Africa. *Turn to the Dark* is set in northern Lesotho and focuses on rural poverty. Both novels have a strong sociological and historical interest.

Among dramatists writing in English are Masitha Hoeane (1951–) and **Zakes Mda**. Hoeane's plays deal generally, in straight realist terms, with social problems such as urban drift (*Nowhere to Run*, 1987), the exploitation of labour in South Africa, and with AIDS (*A Harvest of Sorrow*, 1989).

CHRIS DUNTON

Further reading: J. E. Bardill and J. H. Cobbe, *Lesotho* (1985).

LESSING, DORIS (1919–)

Zimbabwean/English novelist, short-story writer, memoirist

Born in Kermanshah, Persia (now Iran), she attended the Dominican Convent School, in Salisbury, southern Rhodesia (now Zimbabwe), which she left at the age of fourteen. She immigrated to London, England, in 1949. In 1956 Lessing returned to Rhodesia to write a series of articles for the Soviet newspaper *Tass*; these were published in 1957 as *Going Home*. A prolific writer, Lessing has published eighteen novels and three autobiographical works (*Going Home*, *In Pursuit of the English: A Documentary*, 1960, an account of social and cultural conditions of the British working class in the postwar years, and *Particularly Cats*, 1967). She has also published several volumes of short fiction, including *This Was the Old Chief's Country* (1952), *Habit of Loving* (1958), *A Man and Two Women* (1963), and the selections *The Temptation of Jack Orkney and Other Stories* (1972) and *Stories* (1978); two plays (*Each His Own Wilderness*, 1959, in *New English Dramatists: Three Plays*, edited by E. Martin Browne, and *Play with a Tiger*, 1962); and numerous articles and essays (*A Small Personal Voice*, 1974, edited by Paul Schluckter, *Prisons We Choose to Live Inside*, 1987, and *The Wind Blows Away Our Words*, 1987).

Wide-ranging in her themes, Lessing writes on an epic scale, whether depicting, in social realist mode, colonial, southern Rhodesia or conjuring up cosmic battles between good and evil in the fragmented chronicles she calls her 'space' fiction — a mixture of polemics, allegory, prophecy, and science fiction. These chronicles, which Lessing has entitled Canopus in Argos: Archives, include *Re: Colonized Planet 5, Shikasta* (1979), *The Marriages Between Zones Three, Four, and Five* (1980), *The Sirian Experiments* (1981), *The Making of the Representative for Planet 8* (1982), and *Documents Relating to the Sentimental Agents in the Volyen Empire* (1983).

Lessing attributes to **Olive Schreiner**'s *The Story of An African Farm* (1883) her ability to write 'seriously' about Africa. In her African short stories, in her first novel — *The Grass Is Singing* (1950, adapted to film in 1980) — and in the first four novels of the popular Marxist, feminist, anti-colonial Martha Quest series — *Martha Quest* (1952), *A Proper Marriage* (1954), *A Ripple from the Storm* (1958), and *Landlocked* (1965) — Lessing satirically represents the politics, prejudices, and love affairs of Rhodesia's white colonials between the world wars and during the Second World War. Drawing on her own observations and her broad reading as an energetic autodidact, Lessing deconstructs the romanticism of settler mythopoesis. Despite its anti-colonial stance, Lessing's early work carries traces of Eurocentrism, seen, for instance, in her rendering of the Rhodesian landscape. But her achievement remains; within the chauvinistic and claustrophobic cultural world of a British colony, she developed a vision both oppositional and distinctive.

Perhaps because her political education was in the Communist Party, Lessing has resisted the label 'feminist', deeming it too narrow. She could not, however, prevent women of the 1960s from viewing *The Golden Notebook* (1962), with its fractured form and crisis-ridden hero, Anna Wulf, as representing the condition of modern woman, intent on liberation. Lessing's influence upon feminists and feminist thought, in this novel and others, has been considerable.

Lessing left the Communist Party in 1956, disillusioned by the invasion of Hungary by the USSR and by Stalin's brutalities. In time she adopted Sufism and announced her disbelief in the efficacy of political movements. In her fiction she moved from concern with the relationship between the individual and society to focus on the need for cosmic love. In the late 1980s, however, contemporary social concerns (in London) became her theme once more in such works as *The Diaries of Jane Somers* (1984) — first published separately as *The Diary of a Good Neighbour* (1983) and *If the Old Could . . .* (1984), under the pseudonym Jane Somers — which traces the mid-life trials of a woman who has sacrificed her relationships for her career and who redeems these relationships by devoting herself to a deprived elderly woman. In *The Good Terrorist* (1985) Lessing satirizes amateur militancy at the mercy of more professional agencies (the Irish Republican Army and the KGB come to mind).

Whether her target is colonialism, gender politics, or neglect of London's aged, Lessing's power to stimulate and disturb her readers is due partly to her having remained in touch for three decades with the unsettling, decentring currents of the second half of the twentieth century. But her influence upon her readers has also stemmed (despite the frequent criticism of her lack of attention to style) from her subtle explorations of character and human motives. Perhaps paradoxically for a writer so consistently intent on cultivating suspicion of all labels that might pin down and distort meaning and being, her influence also stems from her ability to suggest, frequently by means of images of great force, the dynamics of the psyche and of behaviours.

EVA HUNTER

Further reading: Jenny Taylor, ed., *Notebooks/Memoirs/Archives: Reading and Rereading Doris Lessing* (1982); Lorna Sage, *Doris Lessing* (1983); Eve Bertelsen, ed., *Doris Lessing* (1985), Southern African Literature Series 5; Katherine Fishburn, *The Unexpected Universe of Doris Lessing* (1985); Katherine Fishburn, *Doris Lessing: Life, Work, and Criticism* (1987); Ruth Whittaker, *Doris Lessing* (1988); Judith Kegan Gardiner, *Rhys, Stead, Lessing, and the Politics of Empathy* (1989).

LETTERS

LETTERS (Australia)

Much early Australian writing takes the form of letters home from eighteenth- and nineteenth-century British settlers constructing a new country and establishing lives there. This great mass of literary material is an important source for Australian colonial history. George Worgan, arriving with the

First Fleet in 1788, describes encounters between Governor Arthur Phillip and Aborigines. The letters of Elizabeth Macarthur, who arrived with the Second Fleet, shed valuable light on political and economic developments in the new colony, while Ellen Viveash's letters from Tasmania in the mid-1830s present interesting information about the economics of farming there. Penelope Selby mentions the Victorian gold discoveries in a letter of August 1851, expressing concern with their effect on the cost of farm labour and gratitude at the rise in bread prices — 'we poor farmers are beginning to hold up our heads.' The great majority of letter-writers were reasonably well-educated and had middle- or upper-class backgrounds; their opinions tend to echo the dominant social and political values of the time. But a few letters survive from people such as Margaret Catchpole, who arrived as a convict in 'the wickedest place I ever was in [in] all my life' and expresses thanks that she is not among those who 'have had their poor head shaved and [are] sent up to the Coal River and there carry coals from day-light in the morning, till dark at night, and half starved'.

Such letters, no matter how artless some may appear, are highly crafted literary documents. It is impossible to tell whether Ellen Viveash, when corresponding with her mother and sisters, was conscious of writing in the same genre as Horace Walpole whose 'delightful letters' she enjoyed so much, but detailed and vivid evocations of life in a new land were a means of holding the interest of overseas correspondents and of bringing them closer. In accordance with nineteenth-century custom, letters were often read aloud within the family circle and then sent on to friends and relatives; a keen sense of audience must have often stimulated the writers' narrative skills. The story of colonial existence presented in letters to England was inevitably dislocated and episodic, sometimes resulting in heightened suspense because mail took so long to arrive. Rachel Henning, for example, announced in a letter to her sister Etta in May, 1865, the startling news of her engagement to one of her brother's overseers, knowing the news wouldn't be received until August.

Settlers brought to Australia a stock of ideas and literary formulations that shaped and directed their observations. George Worgan, for example, describes Sydney Harbour as exhibiting 'a Variety of Romantic Views, all thrown together into sweet Confusion by the careless hand of nature'. The Romantic movement played a significant part in shaping the literary sensibilities of many colonial letter-writers and several descriptions of landscape have a distinctly Wordsworthian ring. Some letters record the ambivalence many colonists felt towards their new land, expressing homesickness for Britain alongside satisfied accounts of prosperity in Australia.

Significant rediscoveries of colonial letters and diaries since the early 1970s have provided greater insight into the personal experiences and inner lives of past Australians. Much of this material is by women and shows their self-creation as they pen the narratives of their lives, constructing in prose an environment that, often without their realizing, subtly reconstructs them. The letters communicate the daily domestic life of past generations, even while the writers apologize for recounting events generally deemed inconsequential. Some writers describe themselves engaged in traditional ladylike pursuits such as needlework and flower collection, although the latter sometimes turned into serious botanizing, as with Georgiana Molloy who corresponded with the director of Kew Gardens, sending him seeds and dried flower specimens from Australia. Many letters lament the difficulty of retaining servants and describe the writer adjusting to domestic chores she would never have contemplated while living in England.

Other letter-writers, besides colonial settlers, have contributed to Australia's cultural and literary heritage. **Ned Kelly**'s Jerilderie letter of 1879 denounces the Victorian police as 'a parcel of big ugly fat-necked wombat headed big bellied magpie legged narrow hipped splay footed sons of Irish Bailiffs or English landlords'. **Henry Lawson**'s letters to his aunt, written while carrying his swag in western New South Wales and Queensland, afford interesting comment on an experience profoundly important to his development as a writer: 'Once in Bourke, I'll find the means of getting back to Sydney — never to face the bush again.' Letters between authors and publisher George Robertson provide interesting glimpses into Australian literary life in the early years of the twentieth century. The First World War also yielded a large crop of letters from Australian soldiers serving at the front in which they seek to construct surroundings and experiences barely imaginable to friends and families half-way across the world, just as the first British settlers had attempted to do on their arrival in Australia.

DOROTHY JONES

Further reading: Lucy Frost, ed., *No Place For a Nervous Lady: Voices From the Australian Bush*, (1984); Dorothy Jones, 'Letter writing and journal scribbling', in Debra Adelaide (ed.) *A Bright and Fiery Troop: Australian Women Writers of the Nineteenth Century* (1988).

LETTERS (Canada)

Canadian literary letters were of antiquarian interest at best until Arthur S. Bourinot, an Ottawa lawyer, poet, and editor, published *Edward William Thomson (1849–1924): A Bibliography with Notes and Some Letters* (1955). This twenty-eight-page booklet includes a memoir, a bibliography, commentary on **Edward Thomson**'s books, a chronology, and a selection of short excerpts from letters by Thomson to William E. Marshall and Ethelwyn Wetherald. 'There is a great field for work here, open to anyone interested; but it would necessarily be a labour of love,' he remarked; he himself carried out this labour by publishing four more small editions of literary letters: *Archibald Lampman's Letters to Edward William Thomson (1890–1898)* (1956); *The Letters of Edward William Thomson to Archibald Lampman (1891–1897)* (1957); *Some Letters of Duncan Campbell Scott, Archibald Lampman and Others* (1959); and *More Letters of Duncan Campbell Scott* (1960). When Helen Lynn published a complete edition of the **Lampman**-Thomson correspondence, *An Annotated Edition of the Correspondence Between Archibald Lampman and Edward William Thomson (1890–1898)* (1980), she criticized Bourinot's selectiveness, his faulty editing, and his inadequate annotation, but she recognized his pioneering spirit. Her own book gives new insight into Lampman and Thomson and the situation of the Canadian writer at the end of the nineteenth century.

Desmond Pacey was the first scholar to realize that Canadian literature could never be studied seriously until responsibly edited editions of the primary materials became available. In the 1940s he began to correspond with **Frederick Philip Grove**, and in the early 1960s he started to gather Grove's letters for a collected edition, *The Letters of Frederick Philip Grove* (1976), published the year after Pacey's death. It is as complete a collection as Pacey could make it; the letters remain as close to the way Grove wrote them as transcription of handwriting to print allows; the provenance of each letter is given; the annotations are exhaustive and cross-referenced; and the letters and introductions are fully indexed. Introductions explain the editorial policies in detail and place the letters in the context of Grove's life and character, his other writing, and world literature.

The Letters of Frederick Philip Grove set a pattern for subsequent editions of letters. The letters, annotations, and introductions in *Susanna Moodie: Letters of a Lifetime* (1985), edited by Carl Ballstadt, Elizabeth Hopkins, and Michael A. Peterman, cast new light on **Susanna Moodie**'s works, her writing and publishing methods, and her relations with her publishers, as well as on Moodie, her husband, and her family. The letters in Richard A. Davies' *The Letters of Thomas Chandler Haliburton* (1988) open up **Haliburton**'s entrepreneurial, legal, and literary activities to historical scrutiny, but few of his personal letters remain. In these editions, Pacey's influence is indirect, but he was the prime mover of Laurel Boone's *The Collected Letters of Sir Charles G. D. Roberts* (1989). While working on the Grove letters, Pacey also collected letters by **Roberts**; Boone's project was finished according to Pacey's ideals. The letters give a clear picture of Roberts' personality; they show his struggle to earn a living as a writer and they document his lifelong effort to encourage Canadian literature.

H. Pearson Gundy had access to all of **Bliss Carman**'s letters, but for reasons of economy he abridged some and omitted others for his *Letters of Bliss Carman* (1981); Gundy eschewed the 'pedantry' of Pacey's painstaking editorial principles. Consequently, the book is not as useful to scholars as it might be. With the short sectional introductions, however, the letters make an illuminating autobiography. Juliana Horatia Ewing, the British children's writer, dramatized for her family in England the very considerable cultural life of Fredericton at the time of Confederation in the letters published in *Canada Home: Juliana Horatia Ewing's Fredericton Letters, 1867–1869* (1983), edited by Margaret Howard Blom and Thomas E. Blom. Thoroughly annotated and indexed, the letters refer to the Carman, Roberts, and Medley families. **Marshall McLuhan**'s agent Matie Molinaro, his widow Corrine McLuhan, and William Toye collaborated on *Letters of Marshall McLuhan* (1987), choosing from thousands of letters to produce an autobiographical summary of McLuhan's career and his intellectual life.

Pacey's contemporary, the Ottawa bibliographer, editor, and critic Robert L. McDougall, published a selection of letters between two of Canada's most significant literary figures: *The Poet and the Critic: A Literary Correspondence Between D. C. Scott and E. K. Brown* (1983). This dialogue about the Canadian literary scene by experts of different generations is a landmark in literary history. Bruce Whiteman's *A Literary Friendship: The Correspondence of Ralph Gustafson and W. W. E. Ross* (1984) gives an inside view of the ferment in Canadian poetry in the 1940s and 1950s, and it remains the best source of information about Ross and his poetry. For *Dear Bill: The Correspondence of William Arthur Deacon* (1988), John Lennox and Michèle Lacombe selected from a voluminous collection of letters to and from a critic who felt caught between the writers in whom he placed his faith and the professors whose positions enabled them to be arbiters of Canada's literary fate. The annotations are a key to Deacon's publishing and writing from 1921 to 1966; the introduction supplies a context for the letters included and directions for finding the letters left out.

Lucy Maud Montgomery was an indefatigable letter-writer; her letters have been published in several volumes. Wilfrid Eggleston edited *The Green Gables Letters, From L. M. Montgomery to Ephraim Weber, 1905–1909* (1960; repr. 1981), and Francis W. P. Bolger and Elizabeth R. Epperly edited *My Dear Mr. M: Letters to G. B. MacMillan from L. M. Montgomery* (1980; repr. 1992); each contains Montgomery's side of a correspondence with a fan — Weber and MacMillan respectively — who became a friend. *The Green Gables Letters* span the creation, publication, and early success of *Anne of Green Gables* (1908); Eggleston summarizes Weber's responses. *My Dear Mr. M* provides glimpses into Montgomery's marriage and family troubles that elucidate her later novels. The first collection of the letters of another prolific letter-writer, **Irving Layton** — *An Unlikely Affair* (1980) — contains both sides of the correspondence between Layton and Dorothy Rath, a poet whose sexual advances he rejected but with whom he remained friends. Francis Mansbridge chose the letters in *Wild Gooseberries: The Selected Letters of Irving Layton* (1989) to show the poet's development and his relationship with Canadian literary culture; Desmond Pacey figures prominently as an intellectually stabilizing influence. Many of the letters in *Irving Layton and Robert Creeley: The Complete Correspondence, 1953–1978* (1990), edited by Ekbert Faas and Sabrina Reed, are long, 'off-the-cuff' essays on Canadian, American, and international literary matters.

The only experiment in facsimile reproduction of letters is George Galt's *The Purdy-Woodcock Letters: Selected Correspondence 1964–1984* (1988), containing letters between **Al Purdy** and **George Woodcock**. To convey the full flavour of the correspondence, Galt's publisher reproduced the letters exactly as they are; much of the book is illegible. Even so, Galt's goal was much like Desmond Pacey's: to set primary materials before Canadian scholars.

LAUREL BOONE

LETTERS (India)

The two sorts of letters discussed here are those written in English and those translated into English from other Indian languages. The writers in the main are the liberal nationalists who brought about the Indian renaissance and worked for the freedom of the country. While most of them were good scholars in Sanskrit, their knowledge of English and powers of discrimination helped them to acquire the finer qualities of the British and educate their conservative countrymen. They rarely wrote the casual personal letters generally associated with such famous English letter-writers as Richard Steele, Lady Mary Wortley Montague, or William Cowper.

Since these writers could never forget their role as 'public' figures and suppressed their private selves, their letters predictably betray a lack of spontaneity. These 'open letters' not only reflect a missionary zeal for education, helping women, and abolishing the evils of caste but also attempt to revive India's spiritual and religious traditions. They serve as footnotes to history and constitute a sort of valuable scrapbook.

Among these letter-writers are three poets — **Toru Dutt**, **Rabindranath Tagore**, and **Sarojini Naidu**. The admirable economy of word and phrase seen in Dutt's letters is almost Keatsian; they are youthful, romantic, and in their concentration of literary gifts expressive of a talent equally at home in English, French, and Sanskrit. Tagore's letters discuss in the vocabulary of a poet such sensitive issues as nationalism, education, and a life transformed by freedom and joy. The aesthetician **Ananda K. Coomaraswamy**'s letters reveal an uncompromising precision that cuts across civilizations and cultures. His letters were written to Buddhist monks and poets, scholars of Sanskrit, and others such as Albert Schweitzer, Eric Gill, Herman Goetz, and George Sarton.

Vivekananda's letters to Sister Nivedita reveal not only his spirituality but his concern for a demoralized people long before Marxism or the feminist movement entered India. His chief distinction lies in the manner in which he concretizes difficult abstract concepts with colloquial vigour.

While G. K. Gokhale's (1866–1915) letters show the influence of progressive western humanitarianism, V. S. S. Sastri's (1869–1946) stylized phrases anticipate their final publication — even letters to his daughter (describing the compliments his English attracted from Lloyd George) are self-righteous and a little too objective. Into this category fall the letters of Sir P. S. Sivaswami Iyer (1864–1946), at once stern and precise; Sir Tej Bahadur Sapru (1875–1949), gossipy and charming; and M. R. Jayakar (1873–1959), rather pompous.

The letters of **M. K. Gandhi**, **Sri Aurobindo**, and **Jawaharlal Nehru** show a refreshing transparency. They take readers into the inner conflicts of the writers. Gandhi's correspondence, which reveals his attempts at self-mastery, became an authentic model for the whole country. Nehru's *Letters from a Father to his Daughter* (1930) — whose education he couldn't directly supervise — was enlarged by him to become a classic, *Glimpses of World History: Letters, 1930–1933* (1934), revealing the thinker-statesman's learning and vision.

MINI KRISHNAN

Further reading: S. Collet, ed., *Life and Letters of Raja Rammohun Roy* (1900); D. G. Karve and Ambedkar, eds, *Gopal Krishna Gokhale: Speeches and Writings* 2 and 3 (1916); T. N. Jagadisan, ed., *Letters of Srinivasa Sastri* (1939); B. N. Banerjee and S. K. Das, eds, *Bankim Chandra Chatterjee: Essays and Letters* (1940); *Rabindranath Tagore: Letters from Russia* by Rabindranath Tagore, trans. Sasidhar Sinha (1960); *Letters of Swami Vivekananda* by Swami Vivekananda (2nd ed., 1964); K. Nelakantan Sastri, ed., *A Great Liberal: Speeches and Writings of Sir P. S. Sivaswami Iyer* (1965); *Letters of Sri Aurobindo*, first series, 1947; second series, 1949; third series, 1949; fourth series, 1951; *Letters of Sri Aurobindo*, trans. from Bengali (1970); Alvin Moore and Rama P. Coomaraswamy, eds, *Selected Letters of Ananda K. Coomaraswamy* (1988).

LETTERS (New Zealand)

In New Zealand, as elsewhere in countries of European settlement, letters are among the most vivid of early literary documents. The urgent need to communicate new experiences, long evenings, and long stretches between mailings were all incentives to write letters, and letters were untrammelled by the literary conventions which proved a straitjacket to those who attempted poetry and novels. Of **Alfred Domett**'s 'epic', *Ranolf and Amohia* (1872), the critic **E. H. McCormick** has written: 'There can be few readers who would not gladly exchange [it] for one volume of memoirs written with the unstudied eloquence of his diaries and correspondence.' 'Unstudied eloquence' was a mark of many settler letters; but although collections in libraries have been mined by historians and biographers, relatively few have been published in their own right. Among the best are those of Thomas Arnold the younger in *New Zealand Letters of Thomas Arnold the Younger* (1966), edited by James Bertram. Brother of Matthew Arnold and close friend of A. H. Clough, Thomas Arnold immigrated to New Zealand in 1847 (and later to Australia) full of enthusiasm to help found a new society, and was quickly disillusioned. Samuel Butler's *A First Year in Canterbury Settlement* (1863) was compiled from his letters by his father. Butler disapproved of the way the book was composed, yet many of his observations on colonial society have become classics. Contrasting women's views appear in the letters of Charlotte Godley and Mary Taylor. Godley, whose husband led the settlement of Canterbury, presents the assured voice of an English gentlewoman in her *Letters from Early New Zealand 1850–1853* (1936), edited by John R. Godley. The letters of Taylor — a downright Yorkshirewoman, friend of Charlotte Brontë, proto-feminist, and shopkeeper in early Wellington — were edited by Joan Stevens and published in 1972 as *Mary Taylor, Friend of Charlotte Brontë. Letters from New Zealand and Elsewhere*.

The most comprehensive selection of Victorian letters is the two-volume *The Richmond-Atkinson Papers* (1960), edited by Guy H. Scholefield, in which the men and women of two extended intermarried families exchange news and views on everything from domestic minutiae and society gossip to political affairs, in which many played a leading part.

The few published collections of twentieth-century letters tend either to record events of special significance (such as the First World War), or to be those of writers. Only the earliest of **Katherine Mansfield**'s letters can truly be called New Zealand letters, but passages scattered throughout her correspondence have become part of New Zealand literary self-awareness. Other writers whose letters have been published are the poets D'Arcy Cresswell — in *The Letters of D'Arcy Cresswell* (1971), edited by Helen Shaw — and **A. R. D. Fairburn** — in *The Letters of A. R. D. Fairburn* (1981), edited by **Lauris Edmond**. There are several others whose letters deserve publication. The letters of the painter Frances Hodgkins are being prepared for publication.

When Maori people began to write in their own language in the early nineteenth century they valued writing especially for exchanging letters with one another and with the colonial authorities. These riches are only just being exploited by bilingual historians. The three volume *Na To Hoa Aroha, From Your Dear Friend* (1986–8), edited by M. P. K. Sorrenson, presents correspondence between two early twentieth-century Maori leaders, Sir Apirana Ngata and Sir Peter Buck (also known as Te Rangi Hiroa). Written mainly in English but with some Maori, the letters are concerned with politics (Ngata became deputy prime minister), Pacific anthropology (Buck was director of the Bishop Museum in Hawaii), Maori traditions, and 'the progress of the race', in an exchange of striking intellectual power.

DENNIS McELDOWNEY

LEVINE, NORMAN (1923–)

Canadian novelist, short-story writer, poet

He was born and raised in Ottawa, Canada. After service in Europe with the Royal Canadian Air Force (RCAF) in the Second World War, Levine attended McGill University, Montreal, graduating in 1948. He moved to England in 1949 and lived at St Ives, Cornwall (with only occasional visits to Canada as writer-in-residence at various Canadian universities), until he returned permanently to Canada in 1980.

Levine set the tone of much of his writing in *Canada Made Me* (1958), a non-fictional account of a 1956 cross-country tour of Canada, viewed from the perspective of a down-and-out writer. Combining autobiographical reminiscence, literary portraiture, historical recollection, social comment, and reportage, Levine describes a Canada where he finds complacency, decadence, social pretentiousness, hypocrisy, futility, dullness, and boredom, in contrast to the quality of life in England, an atmosphere where writers are accepted as writers, whatever other difficulties they may experience. What Levine discovered this early in his writing life was the paradox that while he did not want to go home again, he could not spiritually or imaginatively leave Canada; he also discovered that his natural condition was rootlessness, that he did not belong anywhere. Permutations of this recognition are explored in his subsequent writing.

Levine's work is highly autobiographical. His first novel, *The Angled Road* (1952), recounts its protagonist's desire to escape the oppressive surroundings of a lower-class Jewish neighbourhood in Ottawa. This character decides, while serving in the RCAF during the Second World War, to become a writer as soon as he is able to leave Canada permanently. Most of Levine's subsequent writing explores the consequences of this decision. His second novel, *From a Seaside Town* (1970), and several collections of short stories (*One Way Ticket*, 1961; *I Don't Want to Know Anyone Too Well and Other Stories*, 1971; *Selected Stories*, 1975; *Thin Ice*, 1979; *Why Do You Live So Far Away?*, 1984; and *Champagne Barn*, 1984) describe the difficulties experienced by various writer-protagonists (all of whom, like Levine, are Canadians living abroad) in sustaining themselves as professional writers and their relations with other writers, while coming to terms fully with their decisions to live away from Canada. (In Levine's early years as a writer, Canada held successful authors — like those Levine characters who return to Canada for brief visits — in slight regard.)

From a Seaside Town is typical of Levine's writing. Its tone is self-investigatory and its subject matter bears a strong resemblance to Levine's experiences. Joseph Grand is a middle-aged Canadian writer living in England who has made the move in search of a more expansive and lucrative life. For a time he succeeds as a travel writer, but his fortunes change. He lives in shabby conditions in Cornwall, hounded by creditors, cut off from the writing market that paid his bills. Trapped in poverty and almost-total inertia, Grand turns to autobiography, and the book becomes an introspective examination of his ambivalent relations with family and friends, of his imperfect marriage, of his brief success as a writer, and, most importantly, of his realization, after a visit to Canada, that he belongs there. He also realizes that if he had not left Canada he would have experienced another equally destructive *malaise*.

Levine is concerned with the day-to-day conditions of ordinary people and with trying, usually unsuccessfully, to come to terms with frustration and loneliness. Levine's prose style is simple, plain, detached; there is little descriptive or expository material. The style Levine has perfected is in exact relation to the subject matter. The austere tone prevents the pathos of the stories from descending into sentimentality, and the gentle surface irony sustains this effect.

Levine has also published several volumes of poetry: *Myssium* (1948), *The Tightrope Walker* (1950), and *I Walk by the Harbour* (1976). He has written screenplays for both the British and the Canadian broadcasting corporations.

G. D KILLAM

Further reading: Frederick Sweet, *Norman Levine* (1983), Profiles in Canadian Literature Series 4; Ira Bruce Nadel, '*Canada Made Me* and Canadian autobiography', *Canadian Literature* 101 (1984).

LIBERMAN, SERGE (1942–)

Australian short-story writer

Born in Fergana, Uzbekistan, USSR, he immigrated to Australia in 1951 and later practised medicine in Melbourne. Since 1977 he has been editor of the English section of the *Melbourne Chronicle*, a bimonthly bilingual (English and Yiddish) publication of the Jewish National Library and Cultural Centre 'Kadimah'. He has compiled a bibliography of Australian Judaica containing some 800 authors and subject entries. He has won the Alan Marshall Award three times for collections of short stories: *On Firmer Shores* (1979), *A Universe of Clowns* (1980), and *The Life That I Have Led* (1984). He won the New South Wales Premier's Literary Award for ethnic writing in 1984 for *A Universe of Clowns*. *The Battered and the Redeemed* (1990) is another collection of stories.

Liberman may be described as a literary descendant of **Judah Waten** in his systematic and subtle documentation of a variety of Jewish communities in Melbourne. His stories deal with the worlds of generational turmoil between Jewish migrants and their children, particularly father-son relations. (See **Jewish Writing** and **Migrant Writing**, Australia.) 'Survivors', for example (from *The Life That I Have Led*), begins with the narrator storming away from the unrelenting barrage of his parents' domestic warfare only to end with a revelation of understanding for their situation: 'And yet it was they who had survived, Mother, Father, they who from nothing — and, worse, a legacy of orphanhood, vagabondage and loss — had risen and, all migraines, neuroses and distemper notwithstanding, had clung to decency, responsibility and duty.'

Another version of inter-generational relations in which the son is forced to confront and accept his continuity with his parents' history occurs in an earlier story, evocatively (and ironically) titled, 'Greetings, Australia! To You Have I Come'. Liberman's stories have appeared in numerous anthologies and magazines and his collections have been favourably reviewed; his work, however, has not received any systematic critical attention.

SNEJA GUNEW

LIFE WRITING

LIFE WRITING (Overview)

While life writing in the form of biography has always been more or less honourable and expected in post-colonial literary cultures, autobiography has been something of a poorer relation in many countries and has had to sneak up on respectability and wheedle its way into focus. Part of the reason for this has been the tendency among established metropolitan literary critics to suspect autobiography's intensely personal character, to assume that the committedly subjective cannot pull itself together enough to be taken seriously. The implication in all of this, that biography — that most slippery of literary activities — could be safely taken as a genre in which trust and objectivity were scrupulously served has only recently been subjected to strenuous enquiry and often rigorous dismantling. No doubt, biography's tenacious grasp on an established position in the literary pantheon was aided not so much by important achievements in the genre (though, of course, there *were* many such triumphs) as by important *subjects*, whose eminence and exploits both illumined the work in which they were celebrated and obscured the flaws and tendentiousness of some of the celebration. In the case of autobiography, the eminence of the writers seems rarely to have disarmed potential critics, whose expectations of ego trips and self-aggrandizing distortions were only too often fully met. As the Australian critic **Chris Wallace-Crabbe** has put it (in 'Autobiography', in *The Penguin New Literary History of Australia*, 1988, edited by Laurie Hergenhan):

> Autobiography seems to be a parody, or at least a black and white caricature, of other literary genres. It makes the same claim to refer to life as other genres do, but a good deal more crassly . . . And it brings to the fore all those coarse, nagging questions about whether it is art — formal, aesthetic, beautiful and all that — or merely documentation . . . We are looking here at the admission of a new genre, that of autobiography and memoir, to the category of serious literature. How did it get in? Who left the gate open? How did autobiography disguise itself?

Post-colonial autobiographers provide some answers to Wallace-Crabbe's volley of questions. Much Caribbean autobiography, for example, clung initially to a thin disguise of fiction, while other manifestations of the genre posed the recalling self as both a personal and a political entity: the establishment of the sense of self was made a paradigm of the larger political aspiration towards independence. Australian autobiographers likewise have tended to set up distancing manoeuvres between the recalling self and the self portrayed (while not necessarily moving, like the Caribbean writers, in the direction of fiction) and have tended to use that portrayal as a way of measuring, describing, and evaluating social change. More recently, Australian Aboriginal writers have emerged, using the life writing conventions of a repressive white society to tell their own stories. (See **Aboriginal Literature**, Australia.) Again, Indian autobiography attained a new power (in a literary culture that regarded autobiography as something of an indulgence) under the pressure of political developments. The point is reinforced in the literature of Pakistan, where the most interesting autobiographical writing has been concerned with political and religious issues, and in the rise of New Zealand autobiography, which, partly due to the influence of the women's movement, includes autobiographies by women that are, along with some Caribbean women's autobiographies, among the greatest written in the genre this century.

In short, the seriously introspective post-colonial autobiographer has a built-in safeguard against self-indulgence: the self must be retrieved from colonial hangovers, memories, and actualities before it can be liberated into free-ranging memoir, nostalgia, reminiscence, recall. The post-colonial autobiographical act is, if not always a revolutionary one, at least essentially political; and it is this inevitable tendency that has contributed to the 'rise' and growing acceptance of autobiography in post-colonial literatures by enhancing its seriousness while reducing its capacity for mere self-serving. Where autobiographers have not been so motivated (as, for example, in the work of so many politicians, army generals, and bureaucrats who, in creating their own monuments, are committed to a conservative, non-confronting stance), the autobiography remains undistinguished because self-indulgent. Where the self is recalled, explored, and asserted as part and reflection of a larger complexity of national, religious, and other issues, the autobiography becomes a blow delivered in the cause of one species of freedom or another without losing its quality of personal introspection and self-consciousness. In all the post-colonial literatures it has been the dedication to political, religious, and personal freedom in defiance of and in the wake of the oppressors that has 'opened the gate' and 'let autobiography in', variously disguised . . .

Biography, as earlier mentioned, has had an easier and more accepted path in most post-colonial literatures. In Australia, while light-weight biographies of politicians and sporting figures have proliferated, serious literary and political biography has also flourished, showing an interest not only in refocusing subjects obscured by myth or neglect but also in re-examining the implications of the genre itself. In New Zealand, as in Australia, a Dictionary of National Biography project has given enormous encouragement to biography generally. In all post-colonial countries, the emergence and development of indigenous literature has been central to self-definition and independence and this emergence has likewise encouraged the art of literary biography. In Canada, an initial neglect of writers by biographers gave way to radical re-assessments and a revitalizing of the genre. Post-colonial biography, however, tends to be heavily influenced by what might be termed monumentalism and the founder syndrome. Founding figures, political leaders, and military chiefs (who are sometimes both) are magnetic subjects for biography in most of the countries under review. While the results are sometimes excellent, it is a tendency that does not encourage experiment or questioning of the genre's conventions and vulnerabilities. This was largely the case in Pakistan, Malaysia, Singapore, and Bangladesh. Canadian biography, while conforming generally to this pattern, offered a more substantial version by virtue of biography being seen as crucially contributory to the country's written history.

Post-colonial biography has been to varying degrees at the service of history and the dominant, shaping figures in individual national histories of struggle and foundation. This phase was a necessary precursor, in most countries, to the appearance of more adventurous and experimental biographical writing that, more often than not, was associated not with the national history and its leading protagonists but with the national literature and the writers. In general, it seems that the originally more disreputable genre of autobiography has in the end given rise to the most interesting and innovative life writing in post-colonial countries. (See **Memoirs**.)

BRIAN MATTHEWS

LIFE WRITING (Australia)

Autobiography

The earliest types of autobiography were in the

form of memoirs and diaries, but the art of autobiography was largely neglected until the 1960s, a time that proved conducive to historical retrospection and personal nostalgia and produced a rich outcrop of distinguished works. Many established writers, including **Hal Porter** and **Donald Horne**, adopted the form for exploring the subtle connections between personal and national identity and, like Bernard Smith later, both used sophisticated techniques to create images of the self as it evolves and to distance the present narrator from his past self. Whether consciously written as 'sociography' (Horne's term) or not, most Australian autobiography reveals a greater preoccupation with social change than British autobiography, a feature it shares with writing in other Commonwealth countries. The social emphasis is symptomatic of the urgent need felt by some Commonwealth writers to recapture in words a rapidly changing, now vanished or vanishing, world, and their desire to understand the complex forces that have moulded their lives, including divided loyalties towards external and internal literary traditions. The following are only some of those who have written distinguished autobiographies: **Martin Boyd**, Stella Bowen, **Manning Clark**, **Barbara Hanrahan**, **Xavier Herbert**, **Dorothy Hewett**, Donald Horne, Clive James, **Jack Lindsay**, **Morris Lurie**, **David Malouf**, Graham McInnes, Hal Porter, Bernard Smith, **Kylie Tennant**, and **Patrick White**. Through autobiography two voices are now making themselves heard more powerfully — those of women and Aborigines. *Stories of Herself When Young* (1990), by Joy Hooton, reveals the wealth and variety of women's writing in this genre, while *The Penguin Book of Australian Autobiography* (1987) includes substantial extracts from female autobiographies as well as male, and also passages from such Aboriginal writers as **Dick Roughsey**, Charles Perkins, and **Kevin Gilbert**. The two most popular autobiographies of recent times have been **A. B. Facey**'s racy and unvarnished tale, *A Fortunate Life* (1981), and an Aboriginal autobiography, *My Place* (1987), by artist and writer **Sally Morgan**, a wholly successful attempt to write a multivocal text in which the authentic voices of three generations speak of their struggles to survive in white society. Biography and autobiography in Australia, as elsewhere in the world, are not only rivalling fiction in popularity with the general reading public but assimilating many of the sophisticated techniques perfected by fiction writers in the present century.

Biography

In Commonwealth countries the growth of biographical and autobiographical writing depends on the growth of national consciousness. Arrival in the new land, whether as convict or settler, offered startlingly new experiences and consequently produced sensational convict memoirs such as Martin Cash's *The Adventures of Martin Cash* (1870) or more sober settler accounts. For literary biography to flourish, however, there needed to be national pride in outstanding local figures, appropriate archival material, an active community of scholars, local publishing outlets, and an interested reading public. Most of these conditions were lacking in the colonial period in Australia. Moreover, the education system, through its British-based school readers, extolled British writers and heroic European figures, not local ones. The first biography of an Australian literary figure was Joseph Sheridan Moore's *Life and Genius of James Lionel Michael* (1868), which had no immediate successor and was uncritically laudatory. Even though no major biographies appeared, literary criticism and history in the second half of the nineteenth century, as in Europe, was strongly oriented towards biography. Even so recent a historical work as Manning Clark's mammoth six-volume *A History of Australia* (1962–87), a tale of saints and sinners in the manner of Thomas Carlyle, continues this tradition.

Federation in 1901 and the spirit of nationalism that burgeoned from the 1890s onwards did not immediately produce an indigenous school of biography. There were two main reasons: the most likely subjects were still alive — **Christopher Brennan, Henry Lawson,** and **Joseph Furphy** in literature; Sir Arthur Streeton and Frederick McCubbin in painting; Billy Hughes and Alfred Deakin in politics; moreover, the universities and schools had not yet introduced Australian studies into the curriculum or trained scholars with appropriate research skills. Both **John Shaw Neilson** and Lawson left behind brief manuscript autobiographies, which were not published until many years later, but no definitive biography of either has been written. Beginning in the 1930s, and increasingly since the 1960s, serious biography of statesmen, writers, and others began to appear. Two sources of brief biographical information were published in the postwar period: Percival Serle's two-volume *Dictionary of Australian Biography* (1949) and the vast, ongoing multi-volume *Australian Dictionary of Biography* (1966–), modelled on the British *Dictionary of National Biography*. Numerous books on such national folk heroes as Nellie Melba, Joan Sutherland, and Don Bradman have appeared, but none can claim much literary merit, nor can the popular biographies of such recent prime ministers as R. G. Menzies, Malcolm Fraser, and Bob Hawke. By contrast, three books — on William Light, the founder of Adelaide, Governor E. J. Eyre, and the explorer Ernest Giles, all by **Geoffrey Dutton** — prove that it is possible to combine fine artistry with popular appeal. J. A. Le Nauze's massively researched two-volume *Life of Alfred Deakin* (1965) continues the nineteenth-century 'life and letters' tradition, but his later study of Sir John Monash is more psychologically oriented. Despite Australian egalitarianism and the cult of cutting down the tall poppies, biography escaped the slick post-Lytton Strachey debunking tradition of the 1920s and 1930s. It has also been largely unaffected by modern psycho-biography — Freudian, Jungian, or post-Lacanian — except at the theoretical level through the dissemination of new ideas of biography by the special centre (now inoperative) at Griffith University. The idea of biography as a distinctive art form and not simply a convenient source of factual material is not only somewhat alien to the utilitarian temper of Australian intellectual life, but is only just beginning to be entertained, as the result of recent conferences and visits by distinguished overseas biographers. Moreover, the enthusiastic promotion of oral history by universities, the bicentenerary authorities, and the Australian Broadcasting Corporation tends to minimize the importance of art in re-creating a life through language.

A pioneering work in the field of literary biography was Brian Elliott's *Marcus Clarke* (1958). Notable more recent examples are Dorothy Green's biography of **Henry Handel Richardson,** Axel Clarke's biographies of Christopher Brennan and Richardson, Garry Kinane's of **George Johnston,** and Brenda Niall's of Martin Boyd. For all too long literary scholarship has lacked a solid body of definitive biographies of major authors. Several publishers have now launched new series to fill the gap. Within these, feminist and other new approaches are likely to revolutionize the genre. Already, neglected women such as **Catherine Helen Spence,** a novelist and active publicist for socialism and women's rights, have been the subjects of major biographies. Brian Matthews' biography of Lawson's mother, *Louisa* (1987), in which he dramatizes the relation between author and subject and makes the problematics of the genre an integral part of the work, is likely to prove influential on future practice. No longer will it be easy for naïve ideas about truth and objectivity to prevail in the minds of biographers and readers. Nevertheless, despite the development of more critical attitudes towards the idea of complete objectivity, the existence of abundant archival material remains a basic prerequisite; fortunately, most major libraries have embarked on an enlightened policy of acquisition and preservation of biographical material.

JOHN COLMER

Further reading: Doireann Macdermott, ed., *Autobiographical and Biographical Writing in the Commonwealth* (1984); John Colmer, *Australian Autobiography: The Personal Quest* (1989).

LIFE WRITING (Bangladesh)

Autobiography

The autobiographical merges with the biographical in two memoirs: *Memoirs of Huseyn Shaheed Suhrawardy with a Brief Account of His Life and Work* (1987), edited by Mohammad H. R. Talukdar, and Moulvi Tamizuddin Khan's *The Test of Time: My Life and Days* (1989), edited by Mirza Nurul Huda. Suhrawardy's *Memoirs* contains both a biography of Huseyn Shaheed Suhrawardy, written by the editor, and Suhrawardy's own memoirs. Both sections are concerned with Suhrawardy's political role in the context of Indian independence. Shaista Ikramullah's *Huseyn Shaheed Suhrawardy: A Biography* (1991) provides the Pakistani complement of Suhrawardy's career. While the early chapters of *The Test of Time* were written by Khan himself, the other chapters were compiled by the editor. The more personal sections dealing with Khan's schooling and marriage stand out for their gentle reminiscence and humour. Kazi Anwarul Haque's *Under Three Flags* (1986) and Hamidul Haq Chowdhury's *Memoirs* (1989) are interesting accounts since both authors served the British raj, then Pakistan, and subsequently owed allegiance to Bangladesh.

Biography

Biographies in Bangladesh are generally about political and literary figures and, owing to the slight nature of the narratives, are actually 'life-sketches'. Biographical accounts of Sheikh Mujibur Rahman — who spear-headed the movement that led to the creation of Bangladesh in 1971 and is known as the 'father of Bangladesh' — are limited to a few pages in *Speeches of Sheikh Mujib in the Pakistan Parliament (1955–1956)* (1990), edited by Ziaur Rahman, and to Obaidul Haq's *Voice of Thunder* (1973), which the author calls 'a personality sketch'. Kazi Ahmed Kamal's *Politicians and Inside Stories: A Glimpse Mainly into Lives of Fazlul Haq, Shaheed Suhrawardy and Moulana Bhashani* (1970) is another example of biography that favours the life-sketch. A chapter of this book features Mohammad Ali Bogra, who is also the subject of M. A. Hannan's skeletal *Mohammad Ali (Bogra): A Biographical Sketch* (1967).

Literary Biography

Biographies of poet Kazi Nazrul Islam include Serajul Islam Choudhury's *Introducing Nazrul Islam* (1965), Karunamaya Goswami's 'The Life of Kazi Nazrul Islam' in *Nazrul Institute Patrika* (1, 1989), and *Kazi Nazrul Islam: A Profile* (1989). Roushan Jahan has edited and translated two works by educationist and feminist Begum Rokeya Sakhawat Hossain as *Inside Seclusion: The Avarodhbasini of Rokeya Sakhawat Hossain* (1981) and *'Sultana's Dream' and Selections from 'The Secluded Ones'* (1988); Jahan's introductions contain some biographical information on Begum Rokeya.

NIAZ ZAMAN

LIFE WRITING (Canada)

Autobiography

Since the time of European settlement, autobiography has been a particularly robust literary genre in Canada. Literally thousands of personal narratives exist, taking many different forms, from formal memoirs and travel narratives carefully constructed for public consumption, through more private accounts such as diaries, journals, and personal letters as well as cross-generic productions such as autobiographical poems, plays, and stories. (See **Memoirs**, Canada; **Travel Literature**, Canada;

and **Letters**, Canada.) Women have as frequently been the speaking subjects of Canadian autobiography as have men, nor has class been an insurmountable barrier to publication, as a good number of plain-spoken accounts of Canadian life, whether by pioneers or working-class autobiographers, have survived.

Until very recently, however, Canadian autobiography was dominated by traditional humanist conventions and assumptions, tending to focus on individual lives and stories of personal success as shaped by Anglo-Canadian values and experience. It is only within the past few decades that these conventional expectations with respect to autobiography have begun to yield under pressure of a perceived need to reflect more directly the experience of alterity in Canada, particularly the experience of non-white and aboriginal peoples.

Traditional Autobiography in Canada

As with other nations shaped by British settlement patterns and cultural values in the eighteenth and nineteenth centuries (notably Australia and New Zealand), the earliest Canadian autobiographies reflect the experience of English explorers, administrators, visitors, and settlers as packaged for British readers eager to hear of conquest and survival in the 'new world'. Accounts of public lives by eighteenth-century explorers and administrators, while only marginally autobiographical given their emphasis on factual reportage, do prefigure colonial autobiography in significant ways. Samuel Hearne's explorer narrative, *Journey from Prince of Wales's Fort in Hudson Bay to the Northern Ocean*... (1795), and Hudson's Bay Company representative James Isham's *Observations on Hudson's Bay* (1949), written in 1743, typify the rational, collected, presumably objective observer position that was to characterize much of the autobiography produced in Canada through the next century.

Nineteenth-century autobiographies tend to follow that model, whether in the form of accounts by Canadian agents of Empire (such as Colonel **John Richardson**'s *Eight Years in Canada*, 1847), reports by distinguished visitors to Canada (such as Anna Jameson's graceful *Winter Studies and Summer Rambles in Canada*, 1838), optimistic masculine pioneer narratives (such as John C. Geikie's *Adventures in Canada: or, Life in the Woods*, 1882?), or female-authored settler narratives (including such prominent eastern-Canadian autobiographical accounts as **Susanna Moodie**'s *Roughing It in the Bush; or, Life in Canada*, 1852, **Catharine Parr Traill**'s *The Backwoods of Canada: Being Letters from the Wife of an Emigrant Officer*, 1836, Anne Langton's *A Gentlewoman in Upper Canada*, 1950, edited by H. H. Langton, and *The Journals of Mary O'Brien, 1828–1838*, 1968, edited by Audrey Saunders Miller). In each of these, the posture most frequently assumed by the autobiographer is that of an apparently detached observer of Canadian life, one comfortably severed from its natural or aboriginal elements — which is to say determined to preserve his or her 'old-world' identity or values in the face of potentially 'coarsening' colonial experience.

Early twentieth-century pioneer narratives from western Canada, while generally less clearly focused on English middle-class values and more direct in dealing with the harsh demands placed on homesteaders in the West, none the less retain their focus on the struggles and triumphs of the resilient individual as set against a resistant environment: Mary Hiemstra's *Gully Farm* (1955), Georgina Binnie-Clark's *Wheat and Woman* (1914), H. E. Church's *An Emigrant in the Canadian Northwest* (1929), and Hilda Rose's *The Stump Farm; a Chronicle of Pioneering* (1928) exemplify such chronicles of pioneer endurance in the Canadian west and north-west.

Numerous modern Canadian autobiographies, moreover, retain the contours of colonial autobiography, not only in their emphasis on individualism and Anglo-Canadian ideas of accomplishment and success, but also in their reluctance to question the network of power relations within which these narratives function. Male-authored accounts of public life, such as those of politician Joey Smallwood (*I Chose Canada*, 1973), journalist Bruce Hutchison (*The Far Side of the Street*, 1976), historian C. P. Stacey (*A Date With History*, 1983), and writer **Earle Birney** (*Spreading Time*, 1980), record the autobiographer's individual accomplishments while radiating a sense of general comfort with the society within which he has functioned.

A number of twentieth-century autobiographies by women are similarly focused on individual performance and unquestioning of matters of social orthodoxy: **Nellie McClung**'s *Clearing in the West* (1935) and *The Stream Runs Fast* (1945) are vital and celebratory accounts of her own life as a tireless political activist, but tend to betray unfortunately paternalistic attitudes towards the uneducated and particularly the burgeoning immigrant population of the Canadian west; Florence Bird's autobiography, *Anne Francis* (1974), recounts her important public roles as radio personality and chairperson of the Royal Commission on the Status of Women, but emphasizes her own accomplishments without problematizing the position of social privilege from which she was able to operate.

Indeed, where one might expect to find deviation from this autobiographic paradigm, in autobiographical work by certain twentieth-century non-English immigrants to Canada, the traditional model persists. **Laura Salverson**'s *Confessions of an Immigrant's Daughter* (1939), which deals with Icelandic immigrant life in Manitoba, **Henry Kreisel**'s *White Pelican* (1974), which draws upon the diary he kept, in broken English, as an adolescent German immigrant to Canada, and two memoirs of the Holocaust (Anna Mayer's *One Who Came Back*, 1981, and Eva Brewster's *Vanished in Darkness: an Auschwitz Memoir*, 1984) are forthright and moving in portraying difficult, marginalized lives, but adhere none the less to the dominant autobiographical tradition — given their emphasis on singularity, individualism, and personal triumph over adversity, as well as their untroubled acceptance of Anglo-Canadian cultural norms.

Contemporary Canadian Autobiography

What characterizes contemporary autobiographical writing in Canada is an alternative approach, one rooted in postmodern questions about the constructed nature of the speaking self and post-colonial concerns about power relations as perceived by the disempowered. This paradigm shift is evident in experimental autobiographical work by mainstream writers such as **bp Nichol** (*Journal*, 1978), **Daphne Marlatt** (*What Matters*, 1980), **Robert Kroetsch** (*Field Notes: 1–8, A Continuing Poem*, 1981), and **George Bowering** (*Kerrisdale Elegies*, 1984) — each of whom works against the concept of unitary identity on which traditional autobiography is based. But the shift is equally, and perhaps more affectingly, located in the politically challenging autobiographical works of non-white and Native Canadian writers, whose productions in English are marked by a struggle to express themselves authentically from within the 'master language' that English represents, and through the use of revisionary autobiographical forms that themselves interrogate earlier assumptions about the writing of lives.

One such tendency is a movement toward 'written orality' in contemporary Canadian autobiography. Attempts to reproduce direct, spoken language characterize a number of accounts of the Japanese-Canadian internment during the Second World War, such as Takeo Nakano's diary-based *Within the Barbed Wire Fence* (1980), or Rolf Knight's and Maya Koizumi's direct transcription of an oral account in *A Man of Our Times: the Life-History of a Japanese-Canadian Fisherman* (1976). Wilfred Pelletier's and Ted Poole's *No*

Foreign Land: The Biography of a North American Indian (1973) takes the form of a conversation between a white and a Native man, reproducing not only the words but also the cadence and intonation that characterize unmediated Native speech. **Austin Clarke**'s *Growing Up Stupid under the Union Jack* (1980) incorporates Barbadian dialect into vignettes that reflect his own Caribbean education into British colonialism some twenty years earlier.

Another way of resisting the 'master narrative' model associated with traditional autobiography is to fracture autobiography, constructing texts from deliberately unlinked fragments. Métis Lee Maracle's *I Am Woman* (1988) is a collection of autobiographical essays, while Beth Brant's *Mohawk Trail* (1985) consists of autobiographical miscellany (including short stories, poems, mythology) assembled to reflect her experience and concerns as a Native lesbian feminist. Similarly, multi-authored personal narratives, such as *Days and Nights in Calcutta* (1977) by **Clark Blaise** and **Bharati Mukherjee**, challenge fundamental assumptions about autobiography as a genre that reflects in a unified way a single, unified consciousness.

Some contemporary writers have chosen to produce highly conventioned literary autobiographies, but do so by combining genres in innovative ways. At their most straightforward, such autobiographies fuse autobiography and fiction: **Maria Campbell**'s *Halfbreed* (1973) and Beatrice Culleton's episodically structured *In Search of April Raintree* (1983) are full-length autobiographical fictions in which the act of fictionalizing personal experience serves to de-personalize their stories, to mute the individualism of their cases, as if to generalize or make representational their suffering as Métis women in Canada.

More sophisticated examples of the blending of genres include **Joy Kogawa**'s novel *Obasan* (1981), in which autobiographical elements are combined with fictional characters, extracts from government documents, poems, and surrealistic dream sequences — a tactic that, again, serves to heighten the representational quality of Kogawa's narrative, rendering her story that of a people and not merely the account of an individual's struggle to speak of her own experience. Similarly, **Michael Ondaatje**'s *Running in the Family* (1982) is a complex and sinuous cross-generic exploration of his early life and his family history in Ceylon (now Sri Lanka), as read against his own Canadian-ness and that of his children who accompany his return to Sri Lanka.

Finally, some contemporary autobiographers eschew written language altogether, convinced of the greater relevance and lesser complicity of the spoken word in dealing with alterity and political discontent. Lenore Keeshig-Tobias and John McLeod, for example, are contemporary Native storytellers, who, in telling their own stories and those of their people, see themselves as producing a kind of communal autobiography that enshrines, as traditional autobiographical forms cannot, authentic Native Canadian voices. (See **Aboriginal Literature**, Canada.)

MARILYN RUSSELL ROSE

Further reading: Shirley Neuman, 'Life writing', in W. H. New (ed.) *Literary History of Canada: Canadian Literature in English* vol. 4 (1990).

Biography

As if adopting Carlyle's dictum that 'history is the essence of innumerable biographies' — biographies chiefly of 'heroes' — Canadian biographers in the nineteenth century and well into the twentieth were among the period's chief historians. For nearly a century and a half Canadian biography was mainly an adjunct to, if not, to use Carlyle's term, *the essence* of Canadian written history. With the new nation just beginning to create itself, it was perhaps inevitable and not without justification that it should have seen its emerging history in the context of the lives of those who shaped and influenced its birth and development — the Makers of Canada, as one early series of biographies was named. To judge, moreover, by the bulk of the lives that were chronicled, Canadians saw their dvelopment in terms of two main areas of activity: religion and politics. Other vocations came gradually into their own, though, not surprisingly perhaps, creative artists, particularly writers, were late to be seen as worthy of serious biographical attention.

Biographies of clergymen, mostly of Protestant non-conformists, dominate in the nineteenth century, chiefly because one of the most productive publishers in Canada was the Methodist Book and Publishing House (later Ryerson Press). Scores of clerical 'lives' appeared, often brief 'memorials' gathered into bulky collective volumes, such as John Carroll's *Case and His Contemporaries: Constituting a Biographical History of Methodism in Canada* (5 vols, 1867–77). Often interesting for narrative detail and useful for historical data, these 'lives' are rarely of literary value, their chief purpose being 'piety and usefulness exemplified'.

There were also book-length clerical biographies, notable among them Matthew Richey's *A Memoir of the Late Rev. William Black, Wesleyan Minister* (1839), which provides a valuable history of early Methodism in the Maritimes, and George Patterson's *Memoir of the Rev. James MacGregor . . .* (1859), which does the same for Presbyterianism. Egerton Ryerson (1803–82), a Methodist cleric who helped shape many aspects of Canadian history, especially educational, was the subject of several early biographies, notably J. G. Hodgins' *The Rev. Egerton Ryerson, Founder of the School System of Ontario* (1889). Of clerics of other churches, among the best early biographies both in documentation and literary quality are D'Arcy McGee's *A Life of the Rt. Rev. Edward Maginn, Coadjutor Bishop of Derry* (1857) and Henry Scadding's *The First Bishop of Toronto* (1868), a commemorative biography of John Strachan.

Early collective volumes of secular biographies, despite their often patriotic nationalist fervour, were of a generally higher literary standard than those of clerical lives, mainly because of their less patently didactic purpose. Among the best are H. J. Morgan's *Sketches of Celebrated Canadians and Persons Connected with Canada . . .* (1862), J. C. Dent's *The Canadian Portrait Gallery* (4 vols, 1880–1), J. A. Cooper's *Men of Canada* (1901–2), and, correcting the gender imbalance slightly, W. S. Herrington's *Heroines of Canadian History* (1909).

The chief individual volumes of non-clerical biographies in the nineteenth and early twentieth centuries feature almost exclusively politicians and statesmen. Canada's first prime minister was the subject of an array of celebratory biographies during his lifetime, but the best, Joseph Pope's *Memoirs of the Right Honourable Sir John Alexander Macdonald* (2 vols, 1894), came three years after his death. Other early political figures were suitably, if less abundantly, memorialized: George Brown (by Alexander Mackenzie, 1882), Alexander Mackenzie (by William Buckingham and George Ross, 1892), Sir John Thompson (by J. C. Hopkins, 1895), and **Joseph Howe** (by George Fenety, 1896), to mention a few. Political biographies also dominated the Makers of Canada series (1903–8), published by George Morang. Intended as a history series, it comprises some twenty volumes, mainly of biography of such figures as L. J. Papineau, Howe, Mackenzie, John Graves Simcoe, and Count Frontenac. Unevenly written but usually well researched, they are generally free of the commemorative eulogizing that marked, and often marred, most of the earlier biographies and so signal a significant advance. Another history series, the Chronicles of Canada (32 vols, 1914–16), also includes a number of 'popular' biographies, and the Ryerson Canadian History Readers of the 1920s comprises mostly volumes of political biography.

With the historical motive predominant, it was inevitable that well into the twentieth century most biographers still defined their role as the gathering and recording of facts, sometimes with, often without, critical evaluation and analysis, and with little, if any, probing of motives and emotions, quirks and caprices. The notion that biography as 'the re-creation in written words of a person's life' includes, so far as possible, a re-creation of the inner life, an illumination if not a revelation of the whole person, at rest as well as in action, was generally late dawning upon the minds of most Canadian biographers. The historical motive also largely accounts for the fact that until relatively recently the form of Canadian biography has been mainly that of the linear narrative-chronicle, with the factual data laid out discretely in order rather than seen as an integrated entity, as a *gestalt* rather than a road map.

But the changes came gradually, even from the pens of historian-biographers; examples include R. MacGregor Dawson's probing study *William Lyon Mackenzie King: A Political Biography* (1958); Donald Creighton's exemplary two-volume biography of John A. Macdonald — *The Young Politician* (1952) and *The Old Chieftain* (1955); William Kilbourn's *The Firebrand: William Lyon Mackenzie and the Rebellion in Upper Canada* (1956); and Michael Bliss' *Banting* (1984), by a historian working outside of politics. Good examples of well-rounded political biographies by non-historians are Grace MacInnis' life of her father, *J. S. Woodsworth: A Man to Remember* (1953), Joseph Schull's *Laurier* (1965), Claude Bissell's life of Massey, *The Young Vincent Massey* (1981) and *The Imperial Canadian* (1986), and more recently, Stephen Clarkson's and Christina McCall's *Trudeau and Our Times* (vol. 1, 1990).

For many years the lives of writers were generally neglected by biographers, mainly because there were few Canadian writers considered important enough to enshrine in biographies. The late nineteenth and early twentieth centuries saw a few, brief, rather pedestrian chronicles: F. B. Crofton on **T. C. Haliburton** (1889), L. J. Burpee on **Charles Heavysege** (1901), and James Cappon on **Charles G. D. Roberts** (*Roberts and the Influences of His Time*, 1905). But it was not until the 1920s that Canadian writers began to come into their own as subjects of biography. Lorne Pierce of Ryerson Press was mainly responsible for the change. Though scant space was allowed for biography in the small, neat volumes of the Makers of Canadian Literature series (1923–6), of which Pierce was general editor, they did enable a number of generally competent writers to provide the public with its first small portraits of a dozen Canadian authors from **John Richardson** (by W. R. Ridell) to **Stephen Leacock** (by Peter McArthur). Pierce promoted several other literary biographies, full-length if generally uncritical and two-dimensional: James Cappon's *Bliss Carman and the Literary Currents and Influences of His Time* (1930), Elsie Pomeroy's *Sir Charles G. D. Roberts* (1943), Desmond Pacey's *Frederick Philip Grove* (1945), and H. W. Wells' and Carl Klinck's *Edwin J. Pratt: The Man and His Poetry* (1947).

That these have all been superseded by new biographies — based on new documentation and fresh research and usually adopting a less traditional approach — is indicative of the development and maturation of Canadian literary biography in recent years. These new biographies include Muriel Miller's *Bliss Carman: Quest and Revolt* (1985), J. C. Adams' study of Charles G. D. Roberts, *Sir Charles God Damn* (1986); Douglas Spettigue's *FPG: The European Years* (1973), a major revision of **Frederick Philip Grove**'s life; and David G. Pitt's *E. J. Pratt: The Truant Years* (1984) and *E. J. Pratt: The Master Years 1927–1964* (1987). Of the recent first-time literary biographies — most of them critically objective, well-researched, and often psychologically probing — the best include Clara Thomas' life of Anna

Jameson, *Love and Work Enough* (1967, 1978), Douglas Day's *Malcolm Lowry* (1973), Elspeth Cameron's *Hugh MacLennan* (1981), Usher Caplan's *Like One That Dreamed* (1982), a life of **A. M. Klein,** and Sandra Djwa's *The Politics of the Imagination: A Life of F. R. Scott* (1987).

Dictionaries of Canadian biography have also emerged as important biographical repositories in recent years. The first, edited by C. M. Rose, was *A Cyclopaedia of Canadian Biography* (2 vols, 1886, 1888). This was followed in the next half-century by many similar volumes, most of them competently written if sometimes short on verified fact, the best being W. S. Wallace's *The Dictionary of Canadian Biography* (1926, 1945, 1963). Useful compilations of biographical data in their time, they have all been superseded (at least for subjects deceased before 1901) by the monumental *Dictionary of Canadian Biography* (12 vols, 1966–90 and still in progress). Under competent general editors, particularly Francess G. Halpenny (1969–88, with Jean Hamelin as *directeur adjoint* from 1973), all of whom have ensured both the high quality of the research and writing and a comprehensive scope, the *DCB* is one of Canada's most important historical and cultural repositories.

DAVID G. PITT

Further reading: Clara Thomas, 'Biography', in Alfred G. Bailey, Claude Bissell, Roy Daniels, Northrop Frye, and Desmond Pacey (eds) *Literary History of Canada* 3 (2nd ed., 1976); Ira B. Nadel, 'Canadian biography and literary form', *Essays on Canadian Writing* 33 (1986); Graham Carr, 'Dated lives: English-Canadian literary biography', *Essays on Canadian Writing* 35 (1987); Shirley Neuman, 'Life writing', in W. H. New (ed.) *Literary History of Canada* 4 (2nd ed., 1990).

LIFE WRITING (The Caribbean)

Autobiography

Those who look for traditional or classical forms of autobiography in Caribbean literature in English will sense that autobiography is a genre that Caribbean writers have largely ignored. A straightforward narrative of a life is rare in Caribbean literature. Many authors have deliberately chosen to write the stories of their lives under the guise of fiction, often in the third person. These autobiographies, including such works as **George Lamming**'s *In the Castle of My Skin* (1953), **Paule Marshall**'s *Brown Girl, Brownstones* (1959), **Jamaica Kincaid**'s *Annie John* (1985), and **Wilson Harris**' *The Infinite Rehearsal* (1987), are often called by authors and critics 'fictional autobiographies', a term that suggests the works are not quite authentic accounts of real life experiences. Furthermore, the 'autobiographies' written by Caribbean writers often record the life of an entire community rather than that of a particular individual. The Caribbean autobiography, therefore, is seldom the story of one person's life.

For the author who makes the psychological transition from British subject to free West Indian, for example, the writing of an autobiography is both an essential and a creative act. Much of West Indian literature is concerned with discovering both cultural and national identity and determining what it means to be West Indian. Writers who grew up under colonial rule speak of feeling fragmented and of suffering from what is often called cultural schizophrenia. The act of writing an autobiography, for a former colonial, is a revolutionary act, because it acknowledges an autonomous and independent self. The autobiography usually recounts the colonial experience and records the writer's discovery of the post-colonial self, the independent West Indian self. The autobiography, then, is a personal declaration of independence, genuine and authentic in its rendering of a life experience.

Most Caribbean autobiographies were written by authors in exile. These autobiographies generally take two forms. One is the autobiography of childhood and youth, which comes out of what Frantz Fanon, in *The Wretched of the Earth*

(1961), calls the second phase of the native colonial writer in which a usually disappointing experience abroad causes the exiled writer to recall, and often romanticize, life at home. Lamming's *In the Castle of My Skin* and **Michael Anthony**'s *The Year in San Fernando* (1965) are examples of this form. A second type of autobiography recounts the actual experience of exile, articulating the longing for home and chronicling the awakening to the self and the beginning of the process that **Ngugi wa Thiong'o** calls 'decolonising the mind'. **Sam Selvon**'s *The Lonely Londoners* (1956) and **V. S. Naipaul**'s *The Enigma of Arrival* (1987) are fine examples of this kind of autobiography.

Although Caribbean writers primarily write their life stories as fiction, some use other genres to write autobiographies. **Derek Walcott**'s long poem *Another Life* (1973) is most certainly autobiographical, and Lamming's collection of essays, *The Pleasures of Exile* (1960), offers autobiography in yet another form. **C. L. R. James** has written his autobiography in *Beyond a Boundary* (1963), a work usually classified as a book about cricket.

The newest and most revolutionary forms of autobiography in the Caribbean are those written by women. Their life stories share with autobiographies written by women from other cultures the preoccupation with growing up female in a patriarchal society. The multiple authorship of *Lionheart Gal* (1986), by the Jamaican women's group Sistren Theatre Collective, subverts the notion that an autobiography must be the work of one author. The socio-economic background of its authors causes readers to question the relationship between authorship and social class. *Lionheart Gal* dispels the notion of a 'proper' English literary language in its transfer of an oral language to the printed page.

Some critics claim that autobiography is not a Caribbean literary mode, a puzzling phenomenon when we consider the importance of the genre in the literary traditions of other oppressed and colonized populations. Caribbean writers, however, have simply chosen to tell their stories in their own ways and have challenged readers to reconsider and reformulate definitions of autobiography.

Biography

Not surprisingly, the subjects of Caribbean biographies are normally individuals who made a significant contribution to their island home, the Caribbean, or the world in general. Among the most significant subjects of Caribbean biographies are Trinidadian politician Eric Williams, cricketers Learie Constantine and Sir Frank Worrell, and writers C. L. R. James, Derek Walcott, and V. S. Naipaul.

Williams was the first and only Caribbean leader to take power in government without the backing of a major labour union. He launched the People's National Movement and was head of government from 1956 to 1981. Also a historian and scholar, Williams wrote the definitive history of the Caribbean, *From Columbus to Castro: The History of the Caribbean, 1492–1969* (1970). He is the subject of Ramesh Deosaran's biography *Eric Williams: The Man, His Ideas, and His Politics* (1981).

C. L. R. James has claimed that cricket not only had a great impact on the political and social life of the Caribbean but that it represents the history of the Caribbean in a distinct way. He demonstrates this in his *Beyond a Boundary*, which includes extensive discussion of the lives of Trinidad's Learie Constantine, a famous batsman turned politician, and Barbados' Frank Worrell, the first black captain of the West Indies cricket team. Biographies of Walcott include **Edward Baugh**'s *Derek Walcott: Memory as Vision* (1978) and Robert D. Hamner's *Derek Walcott* (1981); those on Naipaul include Hamner's *V. S. Naipaul* (1973) and Landeg White's *V. S. Naipaul: A Critical Introduction* (1975).

The imposition of colonial British culture onto

the Caribbean created conditions for another, less familiar but important type of biography — histories of the region. (See **Historical Writing**, The Caribbean.) These are histories because of the relationships that many Caribbean writers and historians seem to have to their islands, but they are also biographies because of the unique and inextricable link between person and island, person and earth, that marks Caribbean culture, history, and people. Such links are a reflection of the African heritage that is a reality of Caribbean life. (See **African Connections**, The Caribbean.) These factors account for the intimate and loving ways in which literary figures such as Derek Walcott, George Lamming, **Erna Brodber**, **Lorna Goodison**, and **Olive Senior** write about their island homes, as in Lamming's *In the Castle of My Skin*, Brodber's *Jane and Louisa Will Soon Come Home* (1980), Senior's *Summer Lightning and Other Stories* (1986), Walcott's *Collected Poems 1948–1984* (1986), and Goodison's *Selected Poems/Lorna Goodison* (1992). Embedded in their works are biographies of figures such as Nanny, the Maroons, Cudjoe, and Paul Bogle. (Nanny, or 'N.', was a legendary eighteenth-century Maroon leader in the struggle against slavery. The Maroons were a band of runaway slaves who sustained themselves in the wilds and led a successful revolt against slavery. A Maroon community exists in Jamaica today. Cudjoe was a Coromantee warrior — Coromantee probably refers to an African tribe — who led a slave revolt in Clarendon Parish, Jamaica, in 1690. Bogle was a Baptist deacon and preacher who led the Morant Bay Rebellion in Jamaica in 1865.)

MARGARET KENT BASS

Further reading: Laurence A. Breiner, 'Lyric and autobiography in West Indian literature', *Journal of West Indian Literature* 1 (1989); Helen Tiffin, 'Rites of resistance: counter-discourse and West Indian biography', *Journal of West Indian Literature* 1 (1989).

LIFE WRITING (India)

Autobiography

Ancient Indians had a profound penchant for introspection. However, because their thoughts were governed by a spirit of renunciation, self-effacement, and a merging in the Absolute rather than by one of self-expression, the very idea of writing about oneself would have appeared an indulgence. While this explains the dearth of early Indian autobiographies, there are, nevertheless, examples of early autobiographical writing in India. In the *Rig Veda*'s *Dhanustuti* ('Praise of the Gift of God') the sages speak of their families and the gifts they have received. In *Dhammapada* and *Jataka Tales* Buddha recalls his actions and experiences in previous births; his lessons to his disciples reveal his personality. The inscriptions on rocks and stone pillars of Emperor Ashoka (273–232 BC) promote dharma, express his social concern, and constitute a kind of autobiographical record of his life. Similar concerns are expressed as personal anguish in the mystic poetry of the twelfth-century Saivaite poets of Karnataka.

Muslim invasion and the Muslim rulers' inordinate interest in leaving behind records of their reigns for posterity produced a number of autobiographical writings. The most significant among them is Amir Khasrau's (1250–1325) *Gharratul Kamal* and *Tuhfatus Sighar*. Babur (1483–1530), king of Kabul, is considered the 'prince of autobiographers' because of his *Babur-nama*, while Jahangir (1569–1627), emperor of Hindustan, achieved self-glorification through his memoirs *Tuzuk-i-Jahangiri* (translated by Alexander Rogers as *The Tuzuk-i-Jahangiri*, or, *Memoirs of Jahangir*, 1909).

British rule and the introduction of English education generated in intellectuals, especially Bengalis, a number of autobiographies in English. The first is an autobiographical sketch by Raja **Rammohun Roy** (in *Athenaeum and the Literary Gazette*, 1933), who became famous because of his petition to the governor general demanding that Indian youth be given European scientific education in the English language. Others are Kashiprasad Ghose's autobiography in James Lang's *Handbook of Bengal Missions* (1848), Lal Behari Day's *Recollections of My School-Days* (1969, first serialized in 1876 in the *Bengal Magazine*), and Nishikanta Chattopadhyaya's *Reminiscences of German University Life* (1892). Lutufullah, a tutor in Persian, Arabic, and Hindustani to British officers, published his *Autobiography of Lutufullah, A Mohammedan Gentleman* in 1857.

India's struggle for freedom drew some of its best intellectuals into public life and encouraged autobiographies with a pronounced political perspective, such as Lala Lajpat Rai's *The Story of My Deportation* (1908) and Surendranath Banerjee's *A Nation in Making* (1925). **Jawaharlal Nehru** wrote his *An Autobiography* (1936), he said, in order 'to occupy myself with a definite task so necessary in the long solitudes of gaol life' and to 'clarify myself to myself'. It is easily the best autobiography written by an Indian and resembles **Wole Soyinka**'s prison book *The Man Died* (1973). Subhas Chandra Bose's *An Indian Pilgrim* (1948) is a surprising title for a fiery patriot who aligned himself with Hitler and Mussolini against the British during the Second World War. **M. K. Gandhi**'s *An Autobiography or The Story of My Experiments with Truth* (vol. 1, 1927; vol. 2, 1929) is somewhat like St Augustine's *Confessions.* While 'self-explanation' describes **Mulk Raj Anand**'s *Apology for Heroism* (1946), 'self-projection' characterizes **Nirad C. Chaudhuri**'s *The Autobiography of an Unknown Indian* (1951).

From post-independence India emerged a large number of autobiographies, with interests ranging from politics, religion, and education to social reform, including reformers **Dhan Gopal Mukerji**'s *Caste and Outcast* (1923) and D. K. Karve's *Looking Back* (1936), which describes Karve's efforts to further the education of women. M. A. Malik's (pseudonym Hazari) *An Indian Outcaste: The Autobiography of an Untouchable* (1951) is the first autobiography of an untouchable. Among significant autobiographies by administrators, diplomats, and civil servants are Mirza Ismail's *My Public Life* (1954), Prakash Tandon's *Punjabi Century* (1961) and *Beyond Punjab* (1971), **S. K. Chettur**'s *The Steel Frame and I: Account of Life in the Indian Civil Service* (1962), K. P. S. Menon's *Many Worlds* (1965), Apa B. Pant's *A Moment in Time* (1974), T. N. Kaul's *Reminiscences Discreet and Indiscreet* (1982), and Karan Singh's *Heir Apparent* (1982).

The Story of My Life (1959) by M. R. Jayakar, *Looking Back* (1963) by M. C. Manajan, and *Roses in December* (1973) by M. C. Chagla are autobiographies by eminent jurists. Autobiographies by veteran journalists include K. Subha Rao's *Revived Memories* (1933), K. Rama Rau's *The Pen as My Sword* (1960), and F. R. Moraes' *Witness to an Era: India, 1920 to the Present Day* (1973). Ravi Shankar's *My Music, My Life* (1963) bears comparison with **Rabindranath Tagore**'s *Reminiscences* (1912).

Autobiographies by Indian women are marked by the desire to create self-identity. An early example is *The Autobiography of an Indian Princess* (1921) by Sunity Devi, the Maharani of Cooch-Behar. Cornelia Sorabji's *India Calling* (1935) is a fascinating story of India's first woman lawyer. Vijaya Lakshmi Pandit and Krishna Huthee Sing, Jawaharlal Nehru's sisters, have written their autobiographies: Pandit in *So I Became a Minister* (1936), *Prison Days* (1945), and *The Scope of Happiness* (1979) and Huthee Sing in *With No Regrets* (1944) and *We Nehrus* (1968). **Nayantara Sahgal**, in her autobiographical volumes *Prison and Chocolate Cake* (1954) and *From Fear Set Free* (1962), provides intimate pictures of the Nehru family. Known for their frankness are *Maharani: The Story of an Indian Princess* (1953) by Brinda, Maharani of Kapurthala, and **Kamala**

Das's *My Story* (1976). Other significant autobiographies by women include S. Muthulakshmi Reddy's *Autobiography* (1964), Lady Dhanvanthari Rama Rau's *An Inheritance* (1978), and M. M. Kaye's *The Sun in the Morning* (1990).

Other Indian writers who have published autobiographies include **Santha Rama Rau** (*Gifts of Passage*, 1961), **Ved Mehta** (*Face to Face*, 1963), **Sasthi Brata** (*My God Died Young*, 1967), **Dom Moraes** (*My Son's Father*, 1968), and **R. K. Narayan** (*My Days*, 1974). To suggest that Indian autobiography has attained literary significance is an understatement, although no one has enriched the genre as much as Jawaharlal Nehru.

JAYASHREE SANJAY

Biography

In Sanskrit and other ancient Indian literatures, biographical tradition of a sort existed, but it was too tenuous and irregular to become a significant feature of India's national culture. Quite often, works on the lives of eminent personalities mixed fable and fact and were exercises in hagiography rather than biography. During the medieval and Moghul period, biographical writing existed in the form of court chronicles. However, biography and autobiography, in the modern sense, came to India with the British, and the earliest spurt of biographical writing dealt with founders of the empire. However, Indian biography — that is, lives of Indians written by Indians — made its appearance in the 1870s.

In Indian biography, the subject was invariably a model to be emulated, the focus was mainly on the lives of religious leaders, and the tone was one of total reverence. Several biographies appeared projecting the history of the nation through the stories of individual lives. The tradition of relating lives of important people started in the nineteenth century and at least 2,000 titles have since appeared. In the mid-twentieth century, biography as a blend of scientific observation and imaginative art appeared.

Biographical Collections and Series

Some of the earliest biographical sketches appeared in collections. At the turn of the twentieth century, Natesan, a Madras-based publisher, brought out a low-priced series, Lives and Speeches, which pays rich tributes to nationalist leaders. These are of greater historical than literary value. Other biographical collections of the early period include Govinda Parameswaran Pillai's *Representative Indians* (1897), Manmathanath Dutt's *Prophets of India* (1897), Debendranath Banerjee's *India's Nation Builders* (1919), and Alva Joachim's *Men and Supermen of Hindustan* (1943). All earlier biographical compilations are overshadowed by the *Dictionary of National Biography*, edited by S. P. Sen and published by the Institute of Historical Studies, Calcutta. The first four volumes of this dictionary (1972–4) contain 1,400 biographical sketches of Indians and some foreigners who made valuable contributions to national life. A supplement to the *Dictionary of National Biography*, again in four volumes, was published in 1986. As an ongoing project updating information periodically, the *Dictionary* remains a standard reference book.

Since the 1970s, several institutionally sponsored biographical series have appeared, indicating a growing interest among Indians in historical and biographical research. A large number of short biographies has been published by the Publications Division of the Government of India in its Builders of Modern India series. These are of uneven quality, and though most of them offer a fairly complete narrative in chronological sequence, they do not relate the subject to his or her environment. The Living Biographies series of works on religious leaders, great philosophers, and scientists, published by Bharatiya Vidya Bhavan, caters to school and college students. Sahitya Akademi's Makers of Indian Literature series presents brief but interesting accounts of lives of Indian writers. In addition, the publication of lives of Indian philosophers and saints has been sponsored by institutions such as Ramakrishna math, Advaita Ashram, and Aurobindo Ashram.

Collective biographies containing brief sketches of lives of eminent men often serve as studies of the period. These are works of national rather than personal biography. **Sri Aurobindo**'s *Bankim-Tilak-Dayananda* (1940), S. Radhakrishnan's *Great Indians* (1948), and C. P. Ramaswamy Iyer's *Biographical Vistas: Sketches of Some Eminent Indians* (1968) belong to this category.

Political Biography

Political biography, the most prolific form of biographical writing in India, began in the wake of the Indian nationalist movement primarily as tributes paid to the leaders of the time. H. P. Mody's *Sir Pherozshah Mehta* (1921), N. C. Kelkar's *Landmarks in Lokamanya's Life* (1924), Prithwis C. Ray's *Life and Times of C. R. Das* (1927), and R. P. Masani's *Dadabhai Naroji* (1939) belong to the first wave of political biography. The form, however, acquired greater sophistication in V. S. Srinivas Sastry's *Life and Times of Sir Pherozshah Mehta* (1945) and *My Master Ghokale* (1946). Sastry's subjects are not presented as glorified models, but as individuals rooted in life. Post-independence Indian biography celebrates the achievements of heroes of the freedom movement. **M. K. Gandhi** is the subject of scores of biographies, notable among which are D. G. Tendulkar's *Mahatma* (1951–4), Pyare-lal's *Mahatma Gandhi: The Early Phase* (1956), J. B. Kripalani's *Gandhi: His Life and Thought* (1970), and Mahadev Desai's *Day-to-Day with Gandhi* (1968), translated by Hemantkumar G. Nilkanth. Other prominent political biographies include *Jawaharlal Nehru* (1975), by S. Gopal; *The Nehrus* (1962), by B. R. Nanda; *Jawaharlal Nehru: A Study of His Writings and Speeches* (1960), by **C. D. Narasimhaiah**; *Rajaji* (1975) by Masti Venkatesa Iyengar; and *Dr. Ambedkar* (1954) by A. V. Keer. Biographers in this period adopted a more critical and objective approach to their subjects, evaluating their predecessors' achievements in the light of scientific analysis of fact and documents.

Lives of saints, philosophers, and thinkers continue to engage the attention of Indian biographers. Sri Aurobindo, Sri Ramakrishna, and **Swami Vivekananda** became the subjects of some of the most fascinating biographies. **K. R. Srinivasa Iyengar**'s *Sri Aurobindo: A Biography and History* (1945), Advaita Ashram's *Life of Sri Ramakrishna* (1977), Swami Nikhilananda's *Vivekananda: A Biography* (1953) and *Swami Vivekananda's Life by His Eastern and Western Disciples* (1970) all point to the immanence of God in the lives of specific human beings.

Lives of very few Indian women received biographical attention. Of these the most prominent is Indira Gandhi, whose eventful life has been variously treated by **K. A. Abbas** in *Indira Gandi: Return of the Red Rose* (1966), Zareer Masani in *Indira Gandhi: A Biography* (1975), and **Dom Moraes** in *Mrs. Gandhi* (1980). Padmini Sengupta's *Sarojini Naidu: A Biography* (1966) and Promilla Kalhan's *Kamala Nehru: An Intimate Biography* (1973) merit special mention for their authentic and sympathetic portrayals of their subjects.

Biographies of socially significant people, scientists, and artists form a small component in Indian biography. D. E. Vachna's *The Life Work of J. N. Tata* (1914), A. K. Sen's *Raja Ram Mohan Roy* (1965), **Arun Joshi**'s *Shri Ram: A Biography* (1968), and S. R. Bakshi's *Madanmohan Malaviya* (1991) are notable works of this category. Some thoroughly researched and well-documented historio-biographies that have appeared in recent times are Zubaida Yazdani's *The Seventh Nizam: The Fallen Empire* (1985), Fernandes' *A Biography of Hyder Ali and Tipu Sultan* (1991), and V. K. Bawa's *The Last Nizam: The Life and Times of*

Mir Osman Ali Khan (1992).

Literary biography appears to be the rarest species in Indian writing in English. Among the very few literary biographies written to date, some deserve special mention. These include Krishna Kripalani's *Rabindranath Tagore: A Biography* (1962), Madan Gopal's *Munshi Premchand: A Literary Biography* (1964), T. M. P. Mahadevan's *Subramania Bharathi: Patriot and Poet* (1957), and Pavan Varma's *Ghalib, the Man, the Times* (1989).

C. VIJAYASREE

LIFE WRITING (Malaysia and Singapore)
Exemplars of the historical narrative, the many biographies and autobiographies in English that have appeared in Malaysia and Singapore place the personal within a historical context. Yet, too personal to pass for history, too documentary to qualify as fiction, their generic marginality provides a significant bridge between the formal categories of narrative and history, history and autobiography, biography and memoir, and narrative and autobiography. Employing linear chronologies of birth and development, they usually place the historical impulse of retrieving the past above the aesthetic demands of the literary.

Autobiography

The only Singapore working-class autobiography in English, Tan Kok Seng's trilogy, *Son of Singapore: The Autobiography of a Coolie* (1972), *Man of Malaysia* (1974), and *Eye on the World* (1975), was originally written in Chinese, but was 'rendered into English' in collaboration with Austin Coates, Tan's one-time employer. From the Singapore setting of the first volume, in which Tan lives on a farm and at the age of fifteen begins work as a market coolie (labourer), the autobiography broadens its perspective in the second volume, where Tan becomes chauffeur to a diplomat in Kuala Lumpur. His travels in Malaysia here are augmented in the final volume by visits to other Southeast Asian countries, Europe, and North America.

In *Memories of a Nonya* (1981), Queeny Chang relates her privileged cosmopolitan life, although the work, concentrating heavily on her rich and powerful father, Tjong Ah Fie, and on his life in Sumatra, closes shortly after his death.

Pioneers of Singapore: A Catalogue of Oral History Interviews (1984), compiled by the Singapore Archives and Oral History Department, contains the recollections of seventy-three people. In several other works combining autobiography and memoir, an interest in roots and heritage, as well as in social, cultural, and political history, is also accompanied by nostalgia for a prelapsarian state, represented in the modest *bonhomie* of *kampong* ('village') life. The latter is evoked in *A Kite in the Evening Sky* (1989), Shaik Kadir's recollections of childhood in Geylang Serai. Peter H. L. Wee's *From Farm and Kampong* (1989) begins in 1942 with the uprooting of his family by the Japanese invasion of Singapore and follows the family's settlement in various Malay and Chinese villages. The account of early life concludes with the author's admission as a medical student into university in Singapore.

Lucid and comprehensive, Ruth Ho's *Rainbow Round My Shoulder* (1975) and *Which I Have Loved* (1988) are family memoirs. The account begins with Ho's grandmother's birth in 1870 in Malacca and traces the family's history including Ho's return to Malaya in 1950 from London University, England. In *'Excuse me, are you a model?': The Bonny Hicks Story* (1990), **Bonny Hicks** combines with unprecedented frankness the development of a modelling career and the emotional and sexual awakening of a young woman, while Peter Low's *My Convent Boyhood* (1992) recalls with decorum his eight years as an altar boy to the Archbishop of Singapore.

With the exception of the more personal *Mem-*

oirs of a Menteri Besar: Early Days (1982), by Tan Sri Datuk Dr Mohamad Said, and Ho Rih Hwa's *Eating Salt: An Autobiography* (1991), the memoirs of notable men are characterized by the more aloof personae of public selves, as in Yap Pheng Geck's *Scholar, Banker, Gentleman Soldier: The Reminiscences of Dr. Yap Pheng Geck* (1982), Lee Khoon Choy's *An Ambassador's Journey* (1983) and *On the Beat to the Hustings: An Autobiography* (1988), and Lee Siow Mong's *Words Cannot Equal Experience* (1985).

Biography

Recourse to primary sources has led to 'first-person' biographies, as in the charmingly unaffected *The World According to William Wong Tsap En; 'No Joke, James'* (1985), a compilation by James Wong Kim Min of his late father's letters and papers, the author providing the necessary commentary. Wong Moh Keed's *The Love Letters of Siew Fung Fong and Wan Kwai Pik (1920–1941)* (1988) is an intimate portrait of her maternal grandparents, the granddaughter-editor furnishing introduction and commentary, but otherwise allowing both the English translations of her subjects' letters and her grandfather's diary to speak for them.

The Patriarch (1975) is Yeap Joo Kim's biography of her maternal grandfather, Khoo Sian Ewe, a name initialized throughout in symbolic acknowledgement of his status and wealth in Penang, particularly in the 1940s and 1950s. Sam King's *Tiger Balm King: The Life and Times of Aw Boon Haw* (1992) details the life of the rags-to-riches magnate who spent much of his flamboyant life in Singapore. Interestingly, *A Nonya Mosaic: My Mother's Childhood* (1985) adopts the narrative strategy of a female persona, Gwee Thian Hock becoming surrogate autobiographer for his mother in her first fifteen years. Mixing anecdote, family chronicle, and the public life of her subject, Joan Hon pays tribute in *Relatively Speaking* (1984) to her father, Hon Sui Sen, who had died in office as Singapore's finance minister.

Perhaps no life was as dramatic and tragic as that of the young Maria Hertogh (alias Nadra binte Ma'arof), who was the centre of a legal battle between her adoptive Malay mother and her Dutch parents; the case resulted in religious riots in Singapore and highlighted the divide between Muslim law and colonial law. Hajee Maiden traces Hertogh's life before, during, and after the legal battle in *The Nadra Tragedy: The Maria Hertogh Controversy* (1989).

Although it has become critically fashionable to view autobiography and biography as self-fictionalizing processes, these works are faithful to sources and texts. Ironically, these largely truthful tales make for a documentary artlessness of form and an innocence of stylistic felicity in not a few.

LEONG LIEW GEOK

Further reading: Leong Liew Geok, 'Peranakan society in autobiography and fiction', *Solidarity: Current Affairs, Ideas and the Arts* 119 (1988).

LIFE WRITING (New Zealand)

An early interest in biographical studies in New Zealand is indicated by the appearance of William Gisborne's *New Zealand Rulers and Statesmen 1840 to 1885* and Alfred Cox's *Men of Mark in New Zealand*, both bearing the date 1886. However, despite occasional biographical outlines and deposits of biography and autobiography in histories, memoirs, memorial tributes, and other publications, there was little significant life writing in New Zealand before the 1930s and most major developments have taken place since the Second World War. Since the 1970s autobiography and biography have become important forms of literary expression, reflecting perhaps a decline in cultural and social inhibitions within New Zealand and, for biographical studies, the increased accessibility of archival materials. (See **Memoirs and Reminiscences**, New Zealand.)

Autobiography

The growth of autobiographical writing since the 1950s has been striking in its sheer bulk and in the range of experiences recorded. One important influence has been the women's movement, which, since the early 1970s, has affirmed the significance of women's experiences. An oral history movement, gathering strength since the 1980s, has promoted the view that all lives are interesting and valuable. Not surprisingly, some of the more notable accounts record the lives of women and of the working classes, including: Mary Findlay's posthumously published autobiography, *Tooth and Nail: The Story of a Daughter of the Depression* (1974); **Elsie Locke**'s *Student at the Gates* (1981), which also deals with the Depression and includes her introduction to political activism; and Sonja Davies' *Bread and Roses: Sonja Davies, Her Story* (1984), which details the personal tragedies and political struggles of a feminist. There have also been significant autobiographical contributions from men, including *Sage Tea* (1980), recounting the early life of the painter Toss Woollaston, and **Douglas Stewart**'s depiction of his youth in New Zealand, *Springtime in Taranaki* (1983). In *Off the Sheep's Back* (1986), Bill Richards — bushman, shearer, and farmer — moves from the customarily understated reminiscences of men involved in rural life to a detailed recollection of his travails, including those of his personal relationships. New Zealand autobiographical writing is at its strongest when dealing with childhood and early adult life, and indeed many accounts are thus limited in chronological scope. However, new ground has been broken by **Lauris Edmond**; in *Hot October: An Autobiographical Story* (1989) she tells of her childhood, but goes on to evoke, with the use of contemporary correspondence, the course of her romance that led to marriage. In *Bonfires in the Rain* (1991) Edmond reconstructs her life as a mother and wife, records her initial efforts to write poetry, and plots with some candour the growth and decline of her marriage. *The Quick World* (1992), which, with graceful honesty reveals Edmond's subsequent literary and personal life, completes an outstanding trilogy.

Literary Autobiography

In choosing to be a poet-philosopher, Walter D'Arcy Cresswell certainly rejected cultural and social inhibitions; if the merits of his poetry are arguable, his defence of his vocation and his mannered reports of poverty and bohemia in New Zealand and in Britain — set out in *The Poet's Progress* (1930) and *Present Without Leave* (1939) — make up a virtuoso performance in literary autobiography. The only comparable life writings of this interwar period are **Robin Hyde**'s autobiographical fragments — published as *A Home in This World* (1984) — detailing with great intensity and frankness her pregnancy, single parenthood, ill health, and difficulties as a journalist-writer.

Though writers such as **Ngaio Marsh**, **Nelle Scanlan**, and **Denis Glover** wrote about aspects of their lives, Cresswell's accomplishment in literary autobiography was without peer until the 1970s and 1980s, when several important works were published. In *Indirections: A Memoir* (1980), edited by his friend James Bertram and published posthumously, **Charles Brasch** reflects in a measured way on his search for cultural identification and vocation, a search resolved at the end of his account by the decision to found the literary journal *Landfall* (1947–). The struggles of **Monte Holcroft**, recounted in *The Way of a Writer* (1984) and *A Sea of Words* (1986), are more financial than philosophical, and Holcroft has much to say about journalism and the writing of non-fiction. **Sylvia Ashton-Warner**'s *I Passed This Way* (1979) is the story of a woman fighting for personal and artistic space in a man's world; Ashton-Warner expresses some bitterness for what she sees as tardy recognition of her literary talents by New Zealanders.

The outstanding achievements in literary autobiography are the trilogies of **Frank Sargeson** (*Once is Enough*, 1973, incorporating a piece first published in the early 1950s, *More Than Enough*, 1975, and *Never Enough!*, 1977), and **Janet Frame** (*To the Is-Land*, 1982, *An Angel at My Table*, 1984, and *The Envoy from Mirror City*, 1985). 'To live has been to write,' says Sargeson, a motto that may also be applied to Frame; both autobiographies focus on the life of the writer, and on writing itself, as the essential subject matter. The result in each case is a literary creation at least equal to their finest prose fictions.

Biography

On a journalistic level, G. H. Scholefield's consistent interest in biography, expressed in his studies *Captain William Hobson, First Governor of New Zealand* (1934) and *Notable New Zealand Statesmen: Twelve Prime Ministers* (1946), may be partly explained by his position as parliamentary librarian, but his compilation of *A Dictionary of New Zealand Biography* (1940) in particular drew attention to biographical possibilities. R. M. Burdon's *New Zealand Notables* (three series, 1941, 1945, and 1950) marked a considerable advance: in ten essays dealing with such diverse subjects as a doctor, a boxer, a scientist, and a Maori prophet, Burdon explores personal ambiguities and weighs failure as well as success. His brief study, *The Life and Times of Sir Julius Vogel* (1948), and his more substantial *King Dick: A Biography of Richard John Seddon* (1955) were the first significant political biographies; James Rutherford's *Sir George Grey* (1961) demonstrated how extensive research can assist in delineating a portrait. Two outstanding studies, **E. H. McCormick**'s *The Expatriate: A Study of Francis Hodgkins* (1954) and Antony Alpers' *Katherine Mansfield: A Biography* (1953), utilize literary materials to illuminate the expatriate response to cultural isolation faced by New Zealand artists and writers early in the twentieth century. During the 1950s there were solid accomplishments in autobiography, including Helen Wilson's *My First Eighty Years* (1950), Nancy Ellison's *The Whirinaki Valley* (1956) — both of which depicted, for different eras, the personal tribulations of women and their families — and Dennis McEldowney's *The World Regained* (1957), an account of debilitating illness and surgical revitalization.

Literary Biography

From the 1960s, the growth in critical studies of New Zealand literature resulted in much biographical information as a by-product, especially evident in volumes of Twayne's World Authors Series (the New Zealand volumes of which were edited by Sylvia E. Bowman) and the New Zealand Writers and Their Works series (1975–86), the latter edited by James Bertram. Dennis McEldowney's succinct study, *Frank Sargeson in His Time* (1976), was an important innovation as the literary biography of a still-living writer. Antony Alpers' *The Life of Katherine Mansfield* (1980), a new work rather than a rewriting of his earlier biography, more fully situates the subject among her literary contemporaries in Europe, and the theme of expatriatism, given emphasis in the previous version, becomes relatively unimportant. Several substantial studies in recent years suggest that literary biography now has an important place in New Zealand writing. These include Denys Trussell's *Fairburn* (1984), on **A. R. D. Fairburn**, Lynley Hood's *Sylvia! The Biography of Sylvia Ashton-Warner* (1988), and Frank McKay's *The Life of James K. Baxter* (1990), which provides a richly variegated cultural and political context for the poet.

General Biography and Political Biography

Keith Sinclair's study of **W. P. Reeves**, *William Pember Reeves: New Zealand Fabian* (1965), established a new high-water mark for thoroughly researched and finely written biography. Its critical success influenced scholars to consider biography much more sympathetically than previously had been the case (though two accomplished works that appeared later, E. H. McCormick's *Alexander Turnbull* and **J. C. Beaglehole**'s *The Life of Captain James Cook*, both published in 1974, were the products of intellectual projects going back several decades). It was probably significant, too, that Sinclair's *William Pember Reeves* was not political biography in the narrowest sense; most later studies of politicians have also dealt with the subject's life beyond the corridors of power and have sought to throw light upon the 'times' as well as the life of the protagonist: a particularly fine example is Barry Gustafson's biography of the Labour leader, M. J. Savage, *From the Cradle to the Grave* (1986). Other works that demonstrate in important ways a range of biographical techniques include Judith Binney's *The Legacy of Guilt* (1968), a study of the disgraced evangelical missionary Thomas Kendall; R. C. J. Stone's portrait of the Auckland merchant J. L. Campbell in *Young Logan Campbell* (1982) and *The Father and His Gift* (1987); and Frances Porter's *Born to New Zealand: A Biography of Jane Maria Atkinson* (1989), which depicts not merely the life of Atkinson herself but the manifold activities of the colonial clan to which she belonged. Apart from these works, the inauguration of *The Dictionary of New Zealand Biography* (vol. 1, 1990) has had a considerable impact. The general editor, W. H. Oliver, drew upon contributions from the community at large as well as academic researchers to characterize the lives of 'forgotten' eccentrics, prostitutes, goldminers, and 'homemakers', as well as the country's famous founders. The *Dictionary*'s essays on Maori were republished in a separate volume in the Maori language — *Nga Tangata Taumata Rau, 1769–1869* (1990), also edited by Oliver.

Life Writing and Maori Subjects

Maori identity derives from relationships within *whanau* ('family') and *hapu*, *iwi*, and *waka* ('tribal' units) and is customarily expressed through *whakapapa* ('genealogies') — all somewhat at odds with bourgeois constructions of individualism that have historically informed life writing. The singularity of R. T. Kohere's *The Autobiography of a Maori* (1951) is indicated by the title, though from the 1950s onwards there have been substantial fictional explorations of personal experiences by Maori writers. **Michael King**'s studies of the notable twentieth-century Moari leaders Te Puea and Whina Cooper were a major development in Pakeha biographical treatment of Maori subjects, and Buddy Mikaere has sensitively documented the life of a nineteenth-century Maori leader in *Te Maiharoa and The Promised Land* (1988). Anne Salmond, an anthropologist, collaborated with the autobiographical subjects in *Amiria: The Life Story of a Maori Woman* (1976) and *Eruera: The Teachings of a Maori Elder* (1980), and Judith Binney and Gillian Chaplin have similarly shown concern for the integrity of oral accounts by several Tuhoe women in *Nga Morehu: The Survivors* (1986). One fruitful line of development is indicated by Mihi Edwards' *Mihipeka: Early Years* (1990) and *Mihipeka: Time of Turmoil, Nga Wa Raruraru* (1992), which, while truly autobiographical in their rendering of particular experiences, express a sense of the generally disruptive impact of colonization upon all Maori.

PETER GIBBONS

Further reading: J. O. C. Phillips, ed., *Biography in New Zealand* (1985); Lawrence Jones, *Barbed Wire and Mirrors: Essays on New Zealand Prose* (1987; rev. 1990).

LIFE WRITING (Pakistan)

Autobiography

Among the Pakistan autobiographies written in English, **Zulfikar Ghose**'s *The Confessions of a Native-Alien* (1965) compares well with **George**

Lamming's *The Pleasures of Exile* (1960), R. Mugo Gatheru's *Child of Two Worlds* (1963), and Adewale Maja-Pearce's *In My Father's Country* (1987) in its expression of alienation from both British and indigenous cultures. Equally interesting in theme, though undistinguished in expression, is Bilquis Sheikh's *I Dared to Call Him Father* (with Richard Schneider, 1978), an account of the psychological crisis that led Sheikh, an upper-class Pakistani Muslim woman, to convert to Christianity. Ghose's and Sheikh's autobiographies are exceptions in the genre as practised in Pakistan; others — mostly by generals, politicians, and sports figures — are about the doings of the social persona of the subject and offer no glimpse into either the personal and intellectual life or the intimate recesses of the psyche of the writer. The view offered in such works is from the outside, and taboo areas are rigorously excluded. The family, too, is mentioned only in passing and the interest of the autobiography is restricted to what it reveals about history, general culture, and life in Pakistan. **Hanif Kureishi**'s autobiographical essay 'The Rainbow Sign' (in his *My Beautiful Laundrette and the Rainbow Sign*, 1986), however, is a literary work of distinction.

Autobiographies by generals primarily express conservative views; these include Sher Ali Khan's *The Story of Soldiering and Politics in India and Pakistan* (1978), Muhammad Musa's *Jawan to General: Recollections of a Pakistani Soldier* (1984), W. A. Burki's *Autobiography of an Army Doctor in British India and Pakistan* (1988), Shahid Hamid's *Autobiography of a General* (1988), Faiz Ali Chisti's *Betrayals of Another Kind* (1989), Attiqur Rahman's *Back to the Pavilion* (1989), and Tajammal Hussain Malik's *The Story of My Struggle* (1991).

Politicians such as Firoz Khan Noon, in *From Memory* (1966), and Benazir Bhutto, in *Daughter of the East: An Autobiography* (1988), are liberal by comparison; the latter's treatment of her father's death in 1979 is moving. Other autobiographies by politicians include Mohammad Ali's *My Life: A Fragment* (1942; repr. 1987); former Pakistani president M. Ayub Khan's *Friends, Not Masters: A Political Autobiography* (1967); Abdul Ghaffar Khan's *My Life and Struggle: Autobiography of Badshah Khan* (as narrated by K. B. Narang, 1969); Tariq Ali's *Street-Fighting Years: An Autobiography of the Sixties* (1970); Shaista Ikramullah's *From Purdah to Parliament* (1984); Tamizudin Khan's *The Test of Time: My Life and Days* (1989); and *Inside Baluchistan* (1975), by Mir Ahmed Yar Khan, the ruler of Kalat (a princely state in Pakistani Baluchistan). *Father and Daughter: A Political Autobiography* (1971), by Jahan Ara Shahnawaz, daughter of Muhammad Shafi, a politician from Punjab during the last days of the British in India, is of interest because she, too, is active in politics and social work in Pakistan.

Among sports figures, the cricketer Imran Khan gives an interesting account of cricketing in Pakistan in his autobiography *All Round View* (1988); cricketer Zaheer Abbas' *Zed: Zaheer Abbas* (with David Foot) was published in 1983.

There are no Pakistani autobiographies in English to compare with Indian **Ved Mehta**'s *Daddyji-Mamaji* (1979 — a combined edition of *Daddyji*, 1972, and *Mamaji*, 1979), for example. Such works exist in Urdu, however; Shabbir Hasan Khan Josh's *Yadon ki Barat* (1962), Mumtaz Mufti's *Okhe Log* (1986), and Qudratullah Shahab's *Shahab Nama* (1987) are some of the better-known examples. (None have been translated into English.) It seems that in autobiography, at least, the literary sensibility generally remains anchored to indigenous languages.

Biography

Most biographies of eminent people connected with the history of the creation of Pakistan — M. A. Jinnah (1876–1948), Mohammad Ali (1878–1931), Abdul Ghaffar Khan (1890–1987), and

Muhammad Iqbal (1876–1938) — have been written either by scholars or eulogistic court historians. Those by the scholars include D. G. Tendulkar's *Abdul Ghaffar Khan: Faith Is a Battle* (1967), Afzal Iqbal's *Life and Times of Mohammad Ali* (1974), Stanley Wolpert's *Jinnah of Pakistan* (1984), and Ayesha Jalal's *The Sole Spokesman: Jinnah, the Muslim League and the Demand for Pakistan* (1985). Those by court historians are marred by indiscriminate praise.

Other biographies of politicians include Piloo Mody's *Zulfi My Friend* (1973), a personal and anecdotal biography of Zulfikar Ali Bhutto that is not considered reliable; Salman Taseer's *Bhutto: A Political Biography* (1979), also on Zulfikar Ali Bhutto; Syed Mohammad Jamil Wasti's *My Reminiscences of Chaudhry Rahmat Ali* (1982); K. H. Khurshid's *Memories of Jinnah* (1990); A. H. Batalvi's *The Forgotten Years: Memoirs of Sir Muhammad Zafrullah Khan* (1991); and Tehmina Durrani's *My Feudal Lord* (1991). The latter is a biography of Ghulam Mustafa Khar, one of Zulfikar Ali Bhutto's trusted political associates and the governor of Punjab in 1974–5. Durrani, Khar's third wife, exposes with considerable skill her private life, portraying Khar as a cruel exploiter.

The literary interest of Khalid Hasan's short sketches of eminent people in the arts, politics, and other areas of life (including Faiz Ahmed Faiz, Nasir Ahmad Farooki, Altaf Gauhar, Safdar Mir, and others) in *Scorecard* (1984), however, derives from their originality, wit, and humour. Hamid Jalal's lively account of his uncle, the Urdu short-story writer Saadat Hasan Manto, in 'The Agony of an Ecstasy' (in *Under the Green Canopy*, 1966, edited by Nasir Ahmad Farooki), is of literary merit.

TARIQ RAHMAN

LIFE WRITING (The Philippines)

Autobiography

America is in the Heart (1946) is the quasi-autobiography that catapulted **Carlos Bulosan** to international fame. It has been translated into Danish, Italian, Swedish, French, and Yugoslavian. Bulosan revealed in his book that it was 'hard work and hard living, suffering, loneliness, pain, hunger, hate, pity, joys, compassion — all of these factors made me a writer'. *America is in the Heart* tells how in 1931 Bulosan took steerage passage for North America with only $2.50 in his pocket and recounts key events in his life. He never returned to the Philippines, but he never became a citizen of the USA.

Full Circle (1977) by Conrado V. Pedroche (1909–80) is succinctly summarized by its subtitle, 'Literary journey to this moment'. Pedroche wrote poems, essays, and short stories that are simple and satirically humorous. Like Bulosan, Pedroche uses members of his immediate family in their native surroundings in his stories, thus relating fiction and autobiography. *Memory's Fictions* (1993), the autobiography of **Bienvenido N. Santos**, recaptures memories of his past. It reveals a quiet, almost shy boy, Ben, emerging into young manhood. As Ben grows older, his memories follow him, like shadows — sometimes clear, sometimes fading.

Biography

Manuel L. Quezon: His Life and Career (1948), by Sol. H. Gwekoh (1907–74), is a readable tract on the life of Quezon who, at the time of his departure from the Philippines (when the Japanese invaded the country), was the president of the Philippines Senate. He had a strong hand in the founding of the first Commonwealth Literary Awards in 1940. Other book-length biographies by Gwekoh are *Elpidio Quirino* (1949), *Josefa Llanes Escoda* (1952), *Diosdado Macapagal* (1962), and *The First Pope in the Philippines* (1974). His style is direct and simple, his language forceful. *The First Filipino* (1962), a prize-winning biography of Jose P. Rizal, the Philippine national hero, is considered the most authentic and inspirational presentation on the subject. The author, Leon Ma. Guerrero, Jr. (1915–82), is well known for his essays and biographical sketches.

The Writer and His Milieu: An Oral History of First Generation Writers in English (1984), edited by Edilberto N. Alegre and Doreen Fernandez, is an oral history of fourteen first-generation Filipino writers in English. In the book's preface, the authors state:

> We wanted to find information unavailable in print, and retrieve as well data on how a generation was taught a foreign language, how it reacted to issues, connected with literature, what concerns and aspirations were held by the writers, how these were formed by education and interaction with teachers and colleagues, how they were affected by the dynamics of the writing and publishing worlds, how they had gone beyond the days of writing on the campus.

In 1987 Alegre and Fernandez published *Writers and Their Milieu: An Oral History of Second Generation Writers in English. Filipino Writers in English* (1987) by Florentino Valeros and Estrellita Gruenberg comprises short biographical essays and a bibliographical directory.

ESTRELLITA V. GRUENBERG

LIFE WRITING (South Africa)

Autobiography

Since 1991 South Africa has begun to recover from the censorship and banning under the Nationalist Government of the previous forty years; only now can this history freely be written, and freely read. The country is at present engaged in a process of self-narration — a national recollection of those blanked-out areas of its identity. The current proliferation of South African life stories may be seen as part of the autobiographical impulse of an entire nation finally bringing its past into proper perspective.

That the colonial past has been amply documented can be seen from the various published reminiscences of settlers and visitors, such as Mrs Harriet Ward's two-volume *Five Years in Kaffirland* (1848), H. H. Dugmore's *The Reminiscences of an Albany Settler* (1871), Charles Brownlee's *Reminiscences of Kafir Life and History* (1896), including his recollections of the Frontier War of 1835, and Alfred Whaley Cole's *The Cape and the Kafirs; or, Notes of Five Years' Residence in South Africa* (1852), followed by *Reminiscences of My Life and of the Cape Bench and Bar* (1896). Although not autobiographies in the strict sense of the word, first-person narratives of early life on the frontiers are to be found in the selection of settler writings (diaries and books of reminiscences) edited by **Guy Butler**, *When Boys Were Men* (1969). Wyn Rees' *Colenso Letters from Natal* (1958) provides an arrangement of Frances Colenso's letters with commentary. Nor is *The Diary of Henry Francis Fynn* strictly a diary but a compilation of retrospective accounts by James Stuart published in 1950. Nathaniel Isaacs' *Travels and Adventures in Eastern Africa* (1836) is presented as an autobiographical narrative of the author's residence in Natal during the last years of Shaka Zulu's reign and the first years of Dingane's. Charles Barter, a Member of the Legislative Council and later a magistrate in Natal, recorded his experiences in *Adventures of an Oxford Collegian in South Africa: The Dorp and the Veld; or, Six Months in Natal* (1852), and Francis Statham described his varied journalistic career in *My Life's Record: A Fight for Justice* (1901). Kingsley Fairbridge's *The Autobiography of Kingsley Fairbridge* (1927), published posthumously, is a classic account of his experiences in the Rhodesian bush. (See **Memoirs**, South Africa.)

Among the better-known autobiographical accounts of the Anglo-Boer War are Paul Kruger's

Memoirs of Paul Kruger (published in translation in 1902), the Boer general Ben Viljoen's *My Reminiscences of the Anglo-Boer War* (1902), written in English to win sympathy for the Boers, and Deneys Reitz's *Commando: A Boer Journal of the Boer War* (1929). (The further volumes of his autobiography, *Trekking On*, 1933, and *No Outspan*, 1943, do little more than trace his later career as diplomat.) In *The Boer War Diary of Sol T. Plaatje* (1973) the early black writer offers his perspective on the war. George Munnik's account of his experiences as a Boer prisoner of war appeared in *A Boer in India* (1903), and in his later years he published two further volumes of autobiography: *Reminiscences of 60 Years on Turf and in Sport* (undated) and *Memoirs of Senator the Hon. G. Munnik* (1934). (See **War Literature**, South Africa.)

The majority of autobiographies by white South Africans in the twentieth century conform with the general western paradigm of the singular life story, usually of the public personality, such as the distinguished judge and politician Sir Henry Juta's *Reminiscences of the Western Court* (1912); his son Jan Juta's recollections of his home life, *Background in Sunshine: Memories of South Africa* (1972); the crime writer Napier Devitt's *Memories of a Magistrate* (1934) and *More Memories of a Magistrate* (1935); F. R. Thompson's story of the part he played in the expansion of southern Africa, *Matabele Thompson: An Autobiography* (1936); the Afrikaans writer C. Louis Leipoldt's *Bushveld Doctor* (1937); the war reporter and editor Carel Birkby's *Airman Lost in Africa* (1937); Major P. J. Pretorius' *Jungle Man* (1947); Percival R. Kirby's *Wits' End: An Unconventional Autobiography* (1967); the free-lance journalist and broadcaster Eric Rosenthal's *Memories and Sketches: The Autobiography of Eric Rosenthal* (1969); the educationist E. G. Malherbe's *Never a Dull Moment* (1981); South Africa's best-known racing commentator Ernie Duffield's *Through My Binoculars* (1982); and the heart transplant surgeon Christiaan Barnard's *One Life* (1969), ghost-written by Curtis Bill Pepper, and *A Second Life* (1993, published under the name Chris Barnard).

Literary Autobiography

As in other post-colonial literatures, there is an established tradition of literary autobiography in South Africa, beginning perhaps with **Thomas Pringle**'s *Narrative of a Residence in South Africa* (1835). In 1911 the journalist and novelist Douglas Blackburn published a shared autobiography (with W. Waitham Caddell), *Secret Service in South Africa* (1911). **W. C. Scully**'s *Reminiscences of a South African Pioneer* appeared in 1913, and **Percy Fitzpatrick**'s *South African Memories* was published posthumously in 1932. **William Plomer**'s narrative of his life in South Africa and Japan, *Double Lives: An Autobiography* (1943), had as its sequel *At Home* (1958). **Roy Campbell**'s *Broken Record* (1934), a fanciful volume of reminiscences of his boyhood and early manhood in Natal, his editorship of *Voorslag*, his departure for England, and his years in Spain and Portugal, was followed by the no less fanciful *Light on a Dark Horse* in 1951. Three major twentieth-century South African writers each produced multiple-volume autobiographies: **Sarah Gertrude Millin** tells her story in *The Night Is Long* (1941) and *The Measure of My Days* (1955); Guy Butler tells of his boyhood experiences in *Karoo Morning* (1977), of his war years in *Bursting World* (1983), and of his subsequent life in *A Local Habitation: An Autobiography 1945–1990* (1991); and **Alan Paton** covers his years as teacher and civil servant until publication of *Cry, the Beloved Country* (1948) in *Towards the Mountain* (1980), following it up with a sequel *Journey Continued* (1988).

Also belonging to this tradition of white literary autobiography are **Francis Carey Slater**'s *Settler's Heritage* (1954), **Herman Charles Bosman**'s account of his imprisonment in *Cold Stone*

Jug (1949), Johannes Meintje's story of his farm background, *Frontier Family: A Chronicle of a South African Farm, its Homestead and its People* (1955), the novelist and drama critic Lewis Sowden's *The Land of Afternoon: The Story of a White South African* (1968), the journalist and playwright James Ambrose Brown's *One Man's War: A Soldier's Diary* (1981), and the poet David Wright's special story, *Deafness: A Personal Account* (1969). Despite its title, **Richard Rive**'s *Writing Black* (1981) generically resembles this tradition more closely than that of black South African autobiography.

A number of popular writers have also written their autobiographies: the 'true crime story' writer Benjamin Bennett in *They Crossed My Path; South Africa's Top Crime Writer* (1972); the novelist **Stuart Cloete** in *A Victorian Son: An Autobiography, 1897–1922* (1972) and *The Gambler: An Autobiography, 1920–1939* (1973); the writer of historical romances, Joy Packer, in four volumes of her life story: *Pack and Follow: One Person's Adventures in Four Different Worlds* (1945), *Grey Mistress* (1949), *Apes and Ivory* (1953), and *Home from the Sea* (1963). **Dan Jacobson**'s collection of autobiographical writing, *Time and Time Again* (1985), and **J. M. Coetzee**'s *Doubling the Point* (1992), a collection of his critical essays and interviews with David Attwell, may both be approached as the 'intellectual autobiographies' of these authors.

A complementary tradition of autobiographical writing has developed in response to what **Es'kia Mphahlele** has formulated as a distinctive aesthetic for black South African writing: 'the tyranny of place' — in which the extreme experiences of township life as well as the wider experience of apartheid South Africa produce writing of comparable intensity. **Peter Abrahams**' account of his growth to maturity in Johannesburg's Mayfair in *Tell Freedom* (1954), Mphahlele's story of Marabastad in *Down Second Avenue* (1959), Dugmore Boetie's story of his early life in Sophiatown and his career as a tramp and conman in *Familiarity is the Kingdom of the Lost: The Story of a Black Man in South Africa* (1969), and Bloke Modisane's painful narrative of the death of Sophiatown and of his own psychological undoing in *Blame Me On History* (1963) are classic examples of this tradition. To these should be added the jazz composer Todd Matshikiza's *Chocolates for My Wife* (1961), Naboth Mokgatle's *The Autobiography of an Unknown South African* (1971), **Don Mattera**'s account of his life shaped by the culture of Sophiatown, *Memory Is the Weapon* (1987), Miriam Makeba's *Makeba: My Story* (1988), and the 'Godfather of Soweto' Godfrey Moloi's *My Life, Volumes 1 & 2* (1991; vol. 1 published in 1987) with its account of the shebeen culture of Durban in the 1940s and the gang life of Orlando in the 1950s. Further variations on this tradition may be seen in *The World of Nat Nakasa* (1975), a selection of Nakasa's journalistic writings, edited by Essop Patel, Mark Mathabane's *Kaffir Boy; The True Story of a Black Youth's Coming of Age in Apartheid South Africa* (1986), and in Jay Naidoo's *Coolie Location* (1990).

Worth mentioning, too, is the way much South African narrative production has taken place in an 'autobiographical space' in which most of an author's works may be read in the autobiographical register without the need to reduce them to the stricter categories of either fiction or autobiography. This is the literary space in which Mphahlele's *Down Second Avenue* and his autobiographical novel *The Wanderers* (1971) may be read as co-extensive with *Bury Me at the Marketplace: Selected Letters of Es'kia Mphahlele 1943–1980* (1984), edited by N. Chabani Manganyi, and with *Afrika My Music: An Autobiography 1957–1983* (1984), or Breyten Breytenbach's autobiographical *A Season in Paradise* (1980) and *The True Confessions of an Albino Terrorist* (1984) as co-extensive with his 'fictions' *Mouroir: Mirrornotes of a Novel*

(1985) and *Memory of Snow and of Dust* (1988).

The life story as testimonial document metonymically representing the collective experience of the struggle against apartheid has become an established format for the political autobiography in South Africa, beginning with the Nobel laureate Albert Luthuli's *Let My People Go* (1962) and Z. K. Matthews' *Freedom For My People* (1981). Nelson Mandela's *No Easy Walk to Freedom* (1965), a collection of articles, speeches, letters from the underground, and transcripts of the trials in which he was accused, edited by Ruth First, and *The Struggle is My Life: His Speeches and Writings Brought Together with Historical Documents and Accounts of Mandela in Prison by Fellow-Prisoners* (1978), produced by the International Defence and Aid Fund for South Africa as a tribute on the occasion of Mandela's sixtieth birthday, must serve as his interim autobiographies. Steve Biko's *I Write What I Like* (1978) is a similar compilation of his writings by Aelred Stubbs. Other notable political autobiographies by black South Africans are: *Call Me Woman*, by Ellen Kuzwayo, the first president of the Black Consumer Union; Winnie Mandela's (with Anne Benjamin) *Part of My Soul Went with Him* (1985; revised and published in the same year as *Part of My Soul*); Michael Dingake's, *My Fight Against Apartheid* (1987); Adelaide Tambo's collection of Oliver Tambo's political speeches in *Preparing for Power: Oliver Tambo Speaks* (1987); the religious community leader Frank Chikane's *No Life of My Own: An Autobiography* (1988); Emma Mashinini's *Strikes Have Followed Me All My Life: A South African Autobiography* (1989), with its account of her childhood in Sophiatown and her work as a trade union official; Helao Shityuwete's *Never Follow the Wolf: The Autobiography of a Namibian Freedom Fighter* (1990); *Coolie Doctor: An Autobiography of Doctor Goonam* (1991), one of the doctors who led the Indian Passive Resistance Campaign of 1946; Dr Ysuf Mahomed Dadoo's *His Speeches, Articles and Correspondence with Mahatma Gandhi (1939–1983)* (1991), compiled by E. S. Reddy; and Maggie Resha's *Mangoana o Tsoara Thipa Ka Bohaleng: My Life in the Struggle* (1991).

The autobiographies of white South Africans whose lives have similarly been determined by the struggle against apartheid include: *If This Be Treason* (1963), *Tomorrow's Sun: A Smuggled Journal from South Africa* (1966), and *Side by Side: The Autobiography of Helen Joseph* (1986), the three volumes in which Helen Joseph combined her memoir of the Treason Trial, accounts of banished people, and the biographies of other activists against apartheid together with her own life story; *Where Sixpence Lives* (1986) by Norma Kitson, who founded the City of London Anti-apartheid Group; *White Boy Running* (1988) by novelist **Christopher Hope**; *The World That Was Ours; The Story of the Rivonia Trial* (1989) by Hilda Bernstein; *The Soft Vengeance of a Freedom Fighter* (1990), Albie Sach's account of his recovery from the car-bomb attack on him in Maputo in 1988; *A Far Cry: The Making of a South African* (1989) by **Mary Benson**; *Armed and Dangerous* (1993) by Ronnie Kasrils; and *In No Uncertain Terms* (1993) by Helen Suzman, for thirty-six years a liberal voice in South Africa's apartheid parliament.

Finally, particular developments of the autobiographical form in South Africa need to be recognized. These are so-called non-standard, mediated, quasi-, or even hybrid autobiographies, often presented as anthologies of autobiographical sketches elicited and compiled by researchers and academics. These include *The Diary of Maria Tholo* (1980) by Carol Hermer; *A Talent for Tomorrow: Life Stories of South African Servants* (1985), edited by Suzanne Gordon; *We Came to Town* (1985), edited by Caroline Kerfoot; *Working Women: A Portrait of South Africa's Black Women Workers* (1985), a collection of interviews and photographs edited by Jane Barrett *et al.*; *Sibambene: The Voices of Women at Mboza* (1987), compiled by Hanlie Griesel, E. Manqele, and R. Wilson to portray the lives of women literacy learners in a remote area of north-eastern Natal; and *'Not Either an Experimental Doll': The Separate Worlds of Three South African Women* (1987), edited by Shula Marks.

J. U. JACOBS

Further reading: E. Mphahlele, 'The tyranny of place and aesthetics: the South African case', in C. Malan (ed.) *Race and Literature*, CENSAL-Publication 15 (1987); Jane Watts, *Black Writers from South Africa: Towards a Discourse of Liberation* (1989); *Current Writing: Text and Reception in Southern Africa* 1 (1991), issue on autobiography in Southern Africa.

Biography

South Africa's early colonial history is captured by several biographical works dealing with life at the Cape. An early example is Madeleine Masson's *Birds of Passage* (1950), an account of the lives of several prominent visitors to the Cape in the eighteenth and nineteenth centuries. The 1970s saw the appearance of Hymen Picard's biographical novel on the life of Simon van der Stel, *Man of Constantia* (1973) and his *Lords of Stalplein: Biographical Miniatures of the British Governors of the Cape of Good Hope* (1974). More recently, Peter Philip's *British Residents at the Cape 1795–1819: Biographical Records of 4800 Pioneers* (1981) appeared. The lives of some of the women at the Cape in early colonial times have been dealt with in Thelma Gutsche's *The Bishop's Lady* (1970), the life of Sophy Grey, wife of the first Bishop of Cape Town, and in Jose Burman's *In the Footsteps of Lady Anne Barnard* (1990), which reflects the increasing interest in the women of this period.

A prominent feature of South African biographies is the abundance of writing about the lives of South African statesmen, and particularly Boer leaders. Marjorie Juta's *The Pace of the Ox: The Life of Paul Kruger* (1936), F. S. Crafford's *Jan Smuts: A Biography* (1946), and Eric Rosenthal's *General De Wet: A Biography* (1946) are three early examples. Johannes Meintjies dominated this subgenre with no fewer than four biographies of Boer leaders: *General De la Rey* (1966), *President Steyn* (1969), *General Louis Botha* (1970), and *Paul Kruger* (1974). Major South African writers have also shown an interest in the lives of political leaders: **William Plomer** has written on Cecil John Rhodes (*Cecil Rhodes*, 1933), **Sarah Gertrude Millin** on Jan Smuts (*General Smuts*, 1936), and **Alan Paton** on the Afrikaner intellectual prodigy J. H. Hofmeyr (*Hofmeyr*, 1964). **Stuart Cloete** combined several biographies in his *African Portraits: A Biography of Paul Kruger, Cecil Rhodes and Lobengula, Last King of the Matabele* (1946; rev. 1969), while Phyllis Lewsen's life of the statesman John X. Merriman (*John X. Merriman: Paradoxical South African Statesman*, 1982) and Jeff Guy's *The Heretic: A Study of the Life of John William Colenso 1814–1883* (1983) are two examples of more recent biographies of important and controversial colonial figures.

The lives of important African intellectuals and leaders have also received attention. **Mary Benson** has published important works on the lives of Botswanan statesman Tshekedi Khama (*Tshekedi Khama*, 1960) and African National Congress (ANC) leaders Albert Luthuli (*Chief Albert Luthuli of South Africa*, 1963) and Nelson Mandela (*Nelson Mandela*, 1986). Peter Becker has treated the lives of Mzilikazi, Dingane, and Moshesh, in his series of biographical works — *Path of Blood: The Rise and Conquests of Mzilikazi, Founder of the Matabele Tribe of Southern Africa* (1962), *Rule of Fear: The Life and Times of Dingane, King of the Zulu* (1964), and *Hill of Destiny: The Life and Times of Moshesh, Founder of the Basotho* (1969). Donovan Williams' *Umfundisi: A Biography of*

Tiyo Soga 1829–1871 appeared in 1978 (appropriately enough in a Lovedale Press edition). Fatima Meer's authorized biography *Higher than Hope, Mandela: The Biography of Nelson Mandela* (1989) perhaps caps the recuperation of the lives of important African leaders who have hitherto been denied full recognition. Meer's earlier *Apprenticeship of a Mahatma* (1970) dealt with the South African part of **M. K. Gandhi**'s life. More recently, **Richard Rive** and Tim Couzens have continued this trend in *Seme: The Founder of the ANC* (1991). As its title implies, Diana Russell's *Lives of Courage: Women for a New South Africa* (1989) attempts to place the lives of some of the South African women in politics and public life more firmly on the map.

Literary Biography

Biographical writing on South African authors has become an increasingly popular genre. However, before the 1970s, few works in this genre appeared. Margaret Lane's 1939 biography of the journalist Edgar Wallace (*Edgar Wallace: The Biography of a Phenomenon*) is an early example, and the life of **Henry Rider Haggard** has been treated in a 1951 biography by his daughter, Lilias Rider Haggard — *The Cloak That I Left: A Biography of the Author Henry Rider Haggard KBE*.

The life and work of **Olive Schreiner** has remained an area of fascination for biographers. No fewer than eight works on this pioneer woman writer have appeared over the years. *The Life of Olive Schreiner*, by her husband S. C. Cronwright Schreiner, appeared in 1924. Ruth First's and Ann Scott's 1980 biography, *Olive Schreiner*, was widely acclaimed to be the most authoritative to date. However, three major new works have appeared recently: Joyce Avrech Berkman's *The Healing Imagination of Olive Schreiner: Beyond South African Colonialism* (1989), Karel Schoeman's *Olive Schreiner: 'n Lewe in Suid-Afrika 1855–1881* (1989; translated into English in 1991 as *Olive Schreiner: A Woman in South Africa, 1855–1881*) and his recent *Only An Anguish to Live Here: Olive Schreiner and the Anglo-Boer War, 1899–1902* (1992). Schoeman's painstaking research on Schreiner, coupled with his recent *Missionary Letters of Gottlob Schreiner, 1837–1846* (1991), provides a wealth of meticulously presented biographical information on this major South African writer.

The life of transport-rider, prospector, statesman, and writer **Percy FitzPatrick** in many ways captures the ambience of late nineteenth-century colonial South Africa and has been treated in A. P. Cartwright's *The First South African: The Life and Times of Sir Percy FitzPatrick* (1971) and, more recently, by Andrew Duminy and Bill Guest in their authoritative *Interfering in Politics: A Biography of Sir Percy FitzPatrick* (1987).

The 1980s saw a spate of biographies of major South African writers following Martin Rubin's *Sarah Gertrude Millin: A South African Life* (1977). Some of these are Valerie Rosenberg's *Herman Charles Bosman: A Pictorial Biography* (1981), Peter Alexander's *Roy Campbell: A Critical Biography* (1982, followed in 1989 by his biography of William Plomer), Noel Chabani Manganyi's *Exiles and Homecomings: A Biography of Es'kia Mphahlele* (1983), Brian Willan's definitive *Sol Plaatje: A Biography* (1984), and Tim Couzens' thorough treatment of pioneer South African writer **H. I. E. Dhlomo** in *The New African* (1985).

Biographical writing in South Africa has been well served by several reference works in the genre. Some of these are the pioneering *The African Who's Who*, compiled by T. D. Mweli Skota and published in several editions beginning in 1930, *The South African Woman's Who's Who* (1938), Ken Donaldson's *South African Who's Who, 1951: An Illustrated Biographical Sketch Book of South Africans* (1951), M. E. Manjoo's *The Southern Africa Indian Who's Who* (1972), and, more recently, Mona de Beer's *Who Did What in South Africa* (1988).

Eric Rosenthal's *Southern African Dictionary of National Biography* (1966) and the Human Sciences Research Council's *Dictionary of South African Biography*, which appeared in several volumes between 1968 and 1977, remain the most comprehensive and useful works in the field.

CRAIG MacKENZIE

Further reading: Susan Gardner, 'The methodology of feminist biography', *Hecate* 2 (1981); N. C. Manganyi, 'Biography: the black South African connection', in Anthony M. Friedson (ed.) *New Directions in Biography* (1981); David Maugham Brown, 'Problems of literary biography', *AUESTA* papers (University of Natal) (1986).

LIGHT VERSE (India)
See **POETRY** (India)

LIM, CATHERINE (1942–)
Malaysian/Singaporean short-story writer, novelist
Born in Kulim, Kedah, Malaysia, but a naturalized Singaporean, Lim has been a schoolteacher, deputy director in the Curriculum Development Institute of Singapore, and a language specialist with the Regional English Language Centre. Educated in English, she obtained a BA in literature (1963) and a diploma in education (1964) from the University of Malaya (now the National University of Singapore). Subsequent to her move to Singapore, Lim took an MA (1979) and Ph.D. (1987) in applied linguistics at the National University of Singapore.

Lim has published several short-story collections, two of which, *Little Ironies: Stories of Singapore* (1978) and *Or Else, the Lightning God and Other Stories* (1980), have been selected as secondary-school texts. These were followed by *They Do Return* (1983), *The Shadow of a Shadow of a Dream: Love Stories of Singapore* (1987), *O Singapore! Stories in Celebration* (1989), which received a commendation in the 1990 awards of the National Book Development Council of Singapore, *Deadline for Love and Other Stories* (1992), and *The Woman's Book of Superlatives* (1992). Lim's novel, *The Serpent's Tooth*, appeared in 1982, and her first collection of poetry, *Love's Lonely Impulses*, in 1992.

By her own description, much of Lim's work draws on small experiences, random observations, and casual reflections. She refers to her little square inch of ivory, largely devoted to the common person — mainly the Chinese of her childhood and adult experiences — and the ordinary woof and warp of existence. In this, Lim reflects the predominant tendency among local writers and their common interest in social themes, albeit variously coloured by differences in individual experiences and background. Social realism characterizes her work, which repeatedly explores the relationships between individuals and their environment (human rather than natural) and the negotiation between the old and young, the rich and poor, the traditional and modern, and Asian heritage and western influences — all present in a context that is qualified by its colonial past, conditioned by the present ethos and ideology, and shaped by its vision of the future. Lim maintains that it is the common person's encounter with these issues that generates the essential pulse and pattern of what will emerge as Singaporean culture and identity, upon which the local writer must draw and to the definition of which he or she must contribute, if a truly Singaporean literature is to evolve.

The colonial experience and English education have impinged significantly on Lim. They fed her with a culture, literature, and language that created a natural tendency to write about things English, in Standard English. 'The daffodil fixation' was eventually routed by her growing consciousness of her native heritage and milieu, but making a story told in local dialect 'sound right' in English was a struggle. Lim's attempts to create an authentic message and medium are particularly discernible in her earlier work in its deliberate display and exploitation of local colour and idiom. Her growing maturity as a writer is evidenced by a movement beyond this self-consciousness. The language becomes less insistently Singaporean; the style moves towards a more classical spareness. With better control, the alien and alienating language becomes a tool for exploring local subjects and sensibilities.

Lim's work signals an increasing inwardness, a shift from portraying manners to addressing fundamental human nature and emotions. Apparent, too, is a change from a somewhat moralistic stance to a less simplistic and more artistic objectivity, manifesting a greater understanding and humanity, seen, for instance, in the refinement of her use of irony and the capacity to laugh with, rather than at, her characters.

Lim sees these changes as the inevitable and spontaneous stages of her development as a writer. She asserts that central to her growth is 'fidelity to what I can only loosely call the "creative self" . . . the sum total of a writer's instincts, intuitions and impulses . . . that decides the direction of the writing'. Yet the course is not idiosyncratic; her evolution as a writer follows a fairly characteristic pattern of expansion of perspective and movement from insularity towards what is more universally relevant.

DAPHNE PAN

Further reading: Robert Yeo, 'Catherine Lim and the Singapore short story in English', *Commentary* 2 (1981); Siti Rohaini Kassim, 'An interview with Catherine Lim', *Southeast Asian Review of English* Dec. (1989); Peter Wicks, *Literary Perspectives on Southeast Asia: Collected Essays* (1991).

LIM, MARIA FATIMA V. (1961–)

Filipino poet

Born in Manila, the Philippines, within a Filipino-Chinese family, she attended the Ateneo de Manila University, where she took a degree in English literature (1982). Lim obtained a master of fine arts degree in creative writing from the State University of New York in Buffalo, USA, and her Ph.D. in creative writing at the University of Denver, USA. She won scholarships from universities in Japan, Norway, Ireland, Sweden, Austria, and England. Prior to her doctoral studies she worked in the Philippines in the Office of the President and as assistant to Senator Rene A. V. Saguisag; in the USA she was assistant managing editor of the *Denver Quarterly*. In 1993 she and her husband Adrian Wilson established the Procyon Prize for Poetry, an award aiming to recognize young poets and to promote cross-cultural exchange.

Lim has won many prizes for poetry published in the Philippines and abroad; in 1991 her work was published in two volumes — *Wandering Roots* (poems from the period between 1978 and 1988), and *From the Hothouse* (poems written between 1989 and 1990), both introduced by critic Isagani R. Cruz. Cruz points out the maturity of Lim's craft, calling her 'the most accomplished young Filipino poet of our time. She has the ability to catch the exact nuance, the precise word, even the perfect sound, in her attempts to depict her personal, but always universal, experience.' Cruz notes the skill with which Lim straddles the personal and the social, as in 'Where I am From' (in *Wandering Roots*):

> We are the poor Filipinos
> Richly blessed with malarial squatters,
> Malacanang Palace puppets,
> And inflatable peso bills.
> How can God not be kind to us?
> Surely he sees our lifted faces,
> Wet with the manna
> Of monsoon rain.

Lim also balances in her poetry eroticism and romance, literariness and womanhood. Cruz calls her poems intimate because most public, with the consciousness of many poetic selves: 'She has deconstructed ambiguity itself, in order to transcend the seven types of poetic ecstasy.'

Lim's poetic gift is craft and spirit in seamless union, a voice uniquely female and Filipino.

DOREEN G. FERNANDEZ

LIM, SHIRLEY GEOK-LIN (1943–)
Malaysian poet, short-story writer
Born in Malacca, Malaysia, she was educated at the University of Malaya, Kuala Lumpur (BA, 1967), and at Brandeis University, USA, where she received a Ph.D. in English and American literature (1973). Professor at the University of California, Santa Barbara, USA, Lim has published three books of poetry (*Crossing the Peninsula*, 1980, *No Man's Grove*, 1985, and the selection *Modern Secrets*, 1989) and a collection of short stories (*Another Country and Other Stories*, 1982). She was awarded the Commonwealth Poetry Prize in 1980.

Lim's work reflects her Chinese-Malaysian *peranakan* heritage. Many of her poems and stories are written from the perspective of one returning (either literally or in memory) to the land of childhood. They are often marked by a nostalgia formally inscribed in the realism of the stories, which re-create photographically, as it were, the sights and sounds of the 'other' life, the Asian life of her childhood. It is significant that narrative realism has been the predominant mode of Southeast Asian prose writers in English and expatriate writers alike during the 1970s and 1980s; this suggests that to some extent their efforts were shaped by a common need to identify and authenticate an Asian heritage.

Lim's poetry develops the theme of the writer's relationship with the world of her childhood, foregrounding the poet's identity as an expatriate. Nostalgia is unpacked into its component parts: exile, guilt, the joy of recognition, and a fascination with the exotic. The poet is always aware of the complex nature of her relationship with the people and the land of her past; her poems about her parents, for example, express a poignant sense of grief, guilt, and, sometimes, resentment. They are also marked by a sense of alienation (from her parents and their culture); in 'The Windscreen's Speckled View' (in *No Man's Grove*) she speaks of 'a woman / who was once our mother'. 'Bukit China' (also in *No Man's Grove*), which describes the poet's visit to her father's grave, is characterized by negatives: 'I did not put on straw . . . have not fastened / Grief on shoulder, walked mourning / Behind, pouring grief . . . I pour / No brandy . . . ' Even the joyful affirmation of homecoming in 'Crossing the Peninsula' is the affirmation of the visitor, the explorer/traveller from another world, and repeats in one sense the colonial encounter.

This ambiguity is also evident in the poems that focus on the poet's life in the USA. They highlight Chinese difference and critique the monoculturalism of contemporary USA. The poems 'Modern Secrets', 'Dedicated to Confucius Plaza', and 'Chinese in Academia' depict a cross-cultural interface and reveal linguistic, ethnic, and gender differences that are incompatible with the dominant patriarchal culture. The awareness of difference is respectively ironic, whimsical, and bitter in each of these poems, which highlight the marginalization of an ethnic minority. In 'Lament' the alienation of the non-Anglo-Saxon English speaker is figured in the imagery of a powerless woman; thus, the poet draws a strategic parallel between ethnicity and gender.

Gender issues and feminism are a major concern in Lim's poetry. She writes about women across cultures, looking at their specific conflicts and disadvantages. 'Pantoun for Chinese Women' laments female infanticide in China; 'The Business of Machines' critiques the abuse of women's bodies by western medicine. 'I Look for Women' (*Modern Secrets*) celebrates women — 'the small / Sufficient swans, showers of stars'.

Lim has also published critical work; she edited *Approaches to Teaching Kingston's 'The Woman Warrior'* (1991).

ANNE BREWSTER

Further reading: Anne Brewster, 'Singaporean and Malaysian women poets, local and expatriate', in B. Bennett, Ee Tiang Hong, and R. Shepherd (eds) *The Writer's Sense of the Contemporary* (1982); Anne Brewster, 'The mirror as metaphor in the poetry of Shirley Lim', in John Kwan-Terry (ed.) *Purpose and Direction* (1991).

LIM, SUCHEN CHRISTINE (1948–)

Malaysian/Singaporean novelist, dramatist

Born in Perak, West Malaysia, she holds a BA from the National University of Singapore, a diploma in education from the Institute of Education, and a diploma in applied linguistics from the Regional English Language Centre, Singapore. Lim has worked as a college teacher and as a curriculum materials writer with the Development Institute of Singapore.

Lim's published works include the children's book *The Valley of Golden Showers* (1979), the play *The Amah — A Portrait in Black and White* (1987), winner of the merit award of the National University of Singapore/Shell Company Short Play writing competition, and the novels *Rice Bowl* (1984), *Gift from the Gods* (1990), and *Fistful of Colours* (1992), winner of the Singapore Literature Prize.

Lim's novels centre on the complex relationships between individuals and society. These individuals define their identities in relation to the culture in which they are relentlessly rooted. The protagonist of *Rice Bowl* strives to create thinking students, believing that only through cultivating a larger awareness of issues can accepted norms be examined critically. Interestingly, she eventually becomes an ambiguous character as her idealism clashes with practicality. In *Gift from the Gods* the values of an older generation come into conflict with those of the younger. In this novel Lim also meditates on the identity of women in traditional Chinese society. Its feminist narrative provides a rich point of entry for a reader interested in comparing Asian and western expressions of feminism. *Fistful of Colours* focuses on the experiences of three strong women who defy family tradition and societal conventions in order to define their identities.

WALTER S. H. LIM

Further reading: Varalackshmi Hariharan, 'Earthbound gods', *The CRNLE Reviews Journal* 2 (1990); Ruth Morse, 'A case of (mis)taken identity: politics and aesthetics in some recent Singaporean novels', in Mimi Chan and Roy Harris (eds) *Asian Voices in English* (1991).

LIM THEAN SOO (1924–91)

Singaporean novelist, short-story writer, poet

Born in Penang, Malaysia, his early life and education were disrupted by the Japanese occupation of Singapore (1942–5). The trauma of this period provided Lim with the setting and themes for some of his best writing, particularly the historical novel *Southward Lies the Fortress* (1971), an account of the fall of Singapore, and the spy novel *Destination Singapore: From Shanghai to Singapore* (1976). Another novel, *Ricky Star* (1978), whose central character is a social climber in the late 1960s, was followed by several collections of short stories: *Fourteen Short Stories* (1979), *Bits of Paper and Other Stories* (1980), *The Parting Gift and Other Stories* (1981), *Blues and Carnations* (1985), and *Eleven Bizarre Tales* (1990). A book of poems, *The Liberation of Lily and Other Poems*, was published in 1976.

Three works were published posthumously: *Singaporama* (1991), a novella about a very ambitious young man who aspires to be the richest person in Singapore; *The Towkay of Produce Street* (1991), a family saga set in Singapore between the wars; and a final collection of short stories, *Survival and Other Stories* (1992), in content and style very much like his previous collections.

There is considerable variety in Lim's short fiction, including forays into science fiction and the bizarre, but among his most realized tales are those that focus on the Japanese interregnum. 'Sailboat' (in *Blues and Carnations*), 'Mr. Sindar' (*Fourteen Short Stories*), and 'The Parting Gift' (*The Parting Gift and Other Stories*) sketch vivid pictures of protagonists affected by the war and subsequently haunted by it. Lim's stories are conventional in structure, and he adheres to naturalism's passion and respect for meticulous detail. His characters, however, often speak unconvincing, clichéd (albeit impeccable) English, and his stories are frequently didactic. In plot, style, and moral intention, Lim bears comparison with Goh Sin Tub, his university contemporary. It is tempting to speculate that Lim's delayed entry into university might have given him only a passing acquaintance with modernism, which accounts for his belief about genre and style. At their best, however, Lim's stories are diverse, accurate in locality, and carefully plotted.

ROBERT YEO

Further reading: Robert Yeo, 'I go for a good story', *Asiaweek* 15 March 1985; Robert Yeo, 'Lim Thean Soo's fiction and the Japanese past', in Kirpal Singh (ed.) *The Writer's Sense of the Past* (1987).

LINDSAY, JACK (1900–90)

Australian novelist, critic, editor

Born in Melbourne, Australia, he was the son of **Norman Lindsay**. His parents separated, and Jack's association with his father commenced only after a childhood of voracious reading and academic distinction. Jack was quickly converted to his father's Dionysian-Nietzschean philosophy as expressed in Norman Lindsay's aesthetic manifesto, *Creative Effort* (1920). *Vision*, a magazine Jack Lindsay edited in 1923 and 1924 with **Kenneth Slessor** and Frank Johnson, propounded the Lindsay aesthetic: the modernism of Joyce, Lawrence, the Sitwells, and Van Gogh was denounced as decadent, its stigmata listed as 'physical tiredness, jaded nerves and a complex superficiality'; art should derive from, and communicate, beauty and emotion; nationalism was judged 'absurd', for the artist 'must go deeper into Life for . . . material, and not trifle with the unessential exteriors of fleeting existence'. Denying Australian links, *Vision* proclaimed 'an Australian Renaissance' in art and letters, neo-Hellenic and Eurocentric, based on classical antiquity, the Renaissance, and romanticism.

Lindsay immigrated to England in 1926 to advance the renaissance and disseminate the Lindsay aesthetic. As a principal of the Fanfrolico Press, he published fine and frequently controversial books. With **P. R. Stephensen**, he edited six issues of *The London Aphrodite* (1928–9), in which he argued that the war had driven literature in two deplorable directions. One was characterized by bowelless, aloof, and 'barren intellectuality'; its exemplars were e. e. cummings, James Joyce, and T. S. Eliot. Alternately, there was a primitivism represented by writers such as D. H. Lawrence. The financial collapse of the Fanfrolico Press in 1930 left Lindsay in penurious circumstances, from which he was rescued by the success of a historical novel, *Rome for Sale* (1934). There followed a prodigious collection of publications, influenced since 1936 by Lindsay's espousal of Marxism.

Lindsay's primary devotion was to poetry, from which all his other literary interests radiated. Beginning with *Fauns and Ladies* (1923), a dozen volumes trace the development of his work from a classical-romantic amalgam of imagery-rich lyricism, through *symbolisme* and popularly galvanic mass declamations (with roots in Greek drama and Marxist agitprop), to strong, simple, war poems. Marxist philosophy and technique infuse his thirty-nine novels: his 'British Way' novels focus on contemporary collective struggles against the 'cash nexus' society, while 'revolutionary traditions' and the juggernaut might of the masses underline his historical novels. **Michael Wilding** judged Lindsay's autobiographical trilogy one of the classics of Australian writing: *Life Rarely Tells* (1958) comprises cerebral rather than narrative memoirs, describing the artist's childhood enlistment on the side of poetry and myth against the hostility of the 'actual world'; *The Roaring Twenties* (1960) presents vignettes of celebrated Australian literati and artists against a rumbustious background of post-war, bohemian Sydney; *Fanfrolico and After* (1962) chronicles the 'Australian cultural invasion of Literary London'. Described frequently as a 'Renaissance man', Lindsay also published two collections of short stories, eleven plays, and fifty-nine volumes on matters philosophical, biographical, historical, artistic, and political. He edited and translated with similar prolificacy.

NOEL HENRICKSEN

Further reading: Bernard Smith, ed., *Culture and History: Essays Presented to Jack Lindsay* (1984).

LINDSAY, JOAN (1896–1984)

Australian novelist

She was born Joan à Beckett Weigall in Melbourne, Australia, and educated at the Clyde Girls Grammar School and the National Gallery School, Melbourne. She married Sir Daryl Lindsay in 1922. She was also known as Lady Joan A. Beckett Lindsay and as Joan Weigall.

Lindsay is best known for her *Picnic at Hanging Rock* (1967), which was given additional prominence after the success of the 1975 film of the same title (directed by Peter Weir, screenplay by Cliff Green). By the time she came to write the novel Lindsay had lived an interesting life as a participant-observer in Australia's privileged, old-money semi-bohemian arts élite. Just as the text of *Picnic at Hanging Rock* carries all the themes that preoccupied this group between the wars — libertarian classicism, symbolism, the macabre — so the film carries a vernacular version of the same for the next generation — filmic pastoral and a midsummer visual neo-nationalism.

Picnic at Hanging Rock is the story of a party of schoolgirls who set out for a picnic at a local, suggestively Gothic, volcanic outcrop. Three of the girls and a governess disappear; one of the girls is found by a handsome visitor from England, but is never able to recollect what unspecified horror actually took place, nor does the novel ever explain. Much is made in the novel about concepts of time; the girls seem to have stepped out of time.

An aesthetically unnecessary sequel was published as *The Secret of Hanging Rock: Joan Lindsay's Final Chapter* (1987). Lindsay's cousin Martin à Beckett Boyd wrote the similarly macabre novel *Nuns in Jeopardy* (1940), which tells of the fate of a party of shipwrecked nuns.

Lindsay's interesting autobiographic reminiscences, *Time Without Clocks* (1962), about early married life in the 1930s in semi-rural Victoria, and *Facts Soft and Hard* (1964), a set of social observations of her trip to the USA with her gallery-director husband, reveal a woman content with her partnership but deserving more recognition as an intellectual in her own right.

DAVID ENGLISH

Further reading: Anne Crittenden, 'Picnic at Hanging Rock: a myth and its symbols', *Meanjin* 2 (1976); Terence O'Neill, 'Literary cousins: *Nuns in Jeopardy* and *Picnic at Hanging Rock*', *Australian Literary Studies* 3 (1982).

LINDSAY, NORMAN (1879–1969)

Australian novelist, essayist, painter

One of ten children born to Dr Robert Lindsay and his wife Jane, he was born and raised in Creswick, Victoria, Australia, and quickly displayed the artistic talents that flowed so generously through the gifted Lindsay family. Best known as an etcher, water colourist, pen draughtsman, oil painter, cartoonist, and controversialist, Lindsay also included writing among his many talents. He was anything but a specialist, producing novels, autobiographies, two children's books, critical essays, reminiscences, and treatises on the creative imagination. He had a very long association with the ***Bulletin*** and played an important role in the establishment of the Endeavour Press in the 1930s.

In attempts to characterize the different cultural ethos of Melbourne and Sydney, Lindsay's Nietzschean stress upon the lonely supremacy of the great creative figures has been contrasted with the socialist and reformist spirit attributed to Melbourne's intellectuals. **Douglas Stewart, Kenneth Slessor,** and Norman's son **Jack Lindsay** were among the writers who acknowledged the powerful direct influence he had upon them.

Lindsay developed his views on art and the creative imagination in *Creative Effort: An Essay in Affirmation* (1920). He argued that the great bulk of humanity was concerned with the essentially trivial business of existence — providing food, devising political and moral systems, and so on — whereas it was the task of the exalted few, an aristocracy of genius, to promote the advancement of mind. Lindsay placed Shakespeare and Beethoven at the top of his list of mind-creators, exponents of joy and physical passion; but his ranking system also produced a long list of 'ugly, dirty, depressed minds', among them Milton, Swift, Zola, and Tolstoy. In this schema, genius was the exclusive property of European males. There are no women in *Creative Effort*; their role is to provide not mind but the female form. Though entitled an essay in affirmation, it was also a bristly denunciation of censorious Christians, Jews, calculating moderns, 'half-feminine' minds, 'primitives', orientals, politicians, sociologists, Americans, and humanitarians. Lindsay was a combative soul, full of meaty prejudices and always ready for an argument. As the years wore on, the prejudices intensified, particularly the anti-Semitism, a disorder he shared with his older brother, Lionel. Theories of art and life were also the subject of *Hyperborea* (1928) and *Madame Life's Lovers* (1929).

Lindsay published ten novels, the first, *A Curate in Bohemia* (1913), and the last, *Rooms and Houses* (1968). The novels are heavily indebted to direct experience, particularly his Creswick years. To the end of his life, Lindsay looked back upon the sexual frustrations of late nineteenth-century adolescence with indignant fascination. He loved his feckless, boozy, life-affirming father, but could not find a good word to say for his mother. To his way of thinking, she represented everything repressive, intrusive, and censorious about the Victorian age. She may have found that having ten children knocked some of the fun out of her. In any event, Lindsay became a lifelong anti-wowser.

While this stance often made Lindsay's concerns predictable enough, *Redheap* (1930) and *Saturdee* (1933) are among the best evocations of small-town life in Australian literature. He had a very good ear for colloquial Australian speech and an eye for the humour of youth's passionate entanglements. They are novels written to entertain. However, the Commonwealth censors deemed *Redheap* morally offensive and it remained on the banned list until 1958. It became one of Australia's most famous banned books and confirmed Lindsay's reputation as a dangerous bohemian.

It is very likely that of all Lindsay's writings, the frequently reprinted *The Magic Pudding* (1918) will prove to be the most enduring. This wonderfully told and endearingly illustrated story, featuring an inexhaustible pudding, treacherous behaviour, and a range of rowdy bush figures, has been very successfully adapted to stage production.

Lindsay was a prodigious worker who succeeded in earning a living from his creative talents. While his aesthetic theories dwelt upon the great figures of European culture, he was an indelibly Australian product, often at odds with officialdom and bitterly critical of the wowser mentality. He was nevertheless reluctant to leave Australia for long. He left his home at Springwood in the Blue Mountains to the National Trust, and many of his works are on display there.

DAVID WALKER

Further reading: John Hetherington, *Norman Lindsay: The Embattled Olympian* (1973).

LIPENGA, KEN (1954?–)

Malawian short-story writer, poet

Born into a poor family in the Mulanje district of southern Malawi, he was educated at Nazombe Primary School and Mulanje Secondary School before entering the University of Malawi in 1971. He graduated with distinction in 1976, completed an MA at the University of Leeds, England, then won a scholarship to the University of New Brunswick, Canada, where he read for a Ph.D. before returning to teach at the University of Malawi. Lipenga later became editor of Malawi's national newspaper, the *Daily Times*. He is a formidably talented writer and scholar who is equally at home working in literary criticism, verse, or short fiction.

While an undergraduate, Lipenga was an active member of the University Writers' Workshop, where his verse and short stories were frequently discussed and where his incisive manner and ability to strike off good work with little apparent labour evoked comparisons with the Kenyan poet **Jared Angira**. Lipenga's seeming lightheartedness, however, often masks an outlook that is basically serious. His persona in 'Memorabilia' (an unpublished Writers' Workshop poem), for example, admits that he is 'but a riverside twig / caught in this wild torrent', always at risk of being 'mercilessly tossed ashore'.

Lipenga's collection of short stories *Waiting for a Turn* (1981) brought him public attention, the collection's polish and imagination receiving special praise. The title story is an excellent example of how Lipenga's comic style can cut deeply. In it, a depressed tailor wants to commit suicide by hurling himself off Sapitwa, Malawi's highest peak, only to find that there is a long queue (a whole nation perhaps) and that he must wait his turn. The story so impressed **Felix Mnthali** that it inspired the title for his own collection of verse, *When Sunset Comes to Sapitwa* (1980).

ADRIAN ROSCOE

LITERARY MAGAZINES

LITERARY MAGAZINES (Overview)

The magazine, so frequently used as a resource in literary studies, is rarely examined in its own right. As Bruce Bennett points out in his entry on Australian literary magazines elsewhere in this *Encyclopedia*, definitions on the 'literary', like notions of the 'magazine', have varied widely; in its various guises the periodical press has played a vital role in the colonial and post-colonial context. It is here that we find the first signs of nation-based 'imagined communities' emerging in many Commonwealth contexts. It is also the case that many Commonwealth writers with international reputations began their careers by publishing in local magazines.

Across the Empire periodicals have particular importance as the first sign of a local literary culture. In some cases, and the *Planters' Punch* of Jamaica comes to mind, the journal is the mouthpiece for a particular class or interest. So *Punch* represented the colonialist attitudes of the local affluent whites and high browns (*sic*). In writing of literary magazines published in Sri Lanka elsewhere in this *Encyclopedia*, D. C. R. A. Goonetilleke points out that the early journals were founded in the 1950s and 1960s by graduates of English, with a passion for diffusing the 'best ideas' in the fields of European literature and culture. Specifically Sri Lankan topics were rarely addressed in these magazines; however, despite this such journals helped to create a climate in which writing in English by Sri Lankans might occur.

In the settler colonies of the nineteenth century the numerous and often short-lived magazines are not only records of immigrant nostalgia for the monuments and flora of Europe, they are also the site for the first and tentative engagements with the local landscape and society. In the Canadian *Literary Garland* (1838–51), for example, we find romantic and escapist writing that is very much the product of a first generation of immigrants alongside the sketches of **Susannah Moodie**, who wrote about the frontier of Upper Canada in distinctive and quite radical ways. In Australia in the 1880s and 1890s, the ***Bulletin*** fostered the writing of satirical sketches that were written for and about the local community, one of which was increasingly constructed by the magazine as distinctive and 'Australian'.

Sylvia Lawson has characterized the *Bulletin* as a 'print circus'. This idea of literary magazines in general as heterogenous and diverse is especially important in colonial contexts, where the emergence of a critical commentary that was highly responsive to local considerations both aided and shaped perceptions of a local community. The 'ringmasters' of this print circus, the literary editors who both construct and address a local community, are worthy of attention in their own right. Literary editors of long standing journals (for example John Gibson, editor of the *Garland*, **A. G. Stephens**, editor of the *Bulletin*, **H. G. De Lisser** of *Planters' Punch*, or Albert Gomes, editor of the Trinidadian *Beacon* in the 1930s) produce commentaries that, whilst having little to offer in the way of theoretical consistency or sophistication, are nevertheless fascinating studies of the invention of local communities and constituencies. In Upper Canada, the Caribbean, and Australia a strong sense of Brittanic nationalism is apparent in the writing of Gibson, De Lisser, and Stephens. In contrast, the anti-colonialist stance of Gomes, and his desire to speak to and for a local constituency, leads to difficulties in framing an editorial voice to address the complex cultural mix of the Trinidadian community. In the absence of the dominant Anglo heritage that is so much a feature of the cultural histories of the settler colonies, there is a struggle to reach the threshold at which a sense of communal identity can occur. Gomes had to steer *The Beacon* away from any ethnically based or homogenous idea of national identity. His editorial writings take up the subsequently well-established Caribbean intellectual tradition that celebrates the strength of a community characterized by diversity rather than homogeneity. The idea of being 'beyond nationalisms' is congenial, and promoted by commentaries and editorials in *The Beacon*.

The association of the periodical press with the short story and the sketch has produced particular resonances in the Commonwealth context. This tradition has allowed prose writers to experiment with elementary prose forms and to develop a style that seems appropriate to the representation of what are seen as distinctive social forms in the local community. A particularly interesting example of this occurs in the barrack yard stories promoted by *The Beacon*. More experimental modes of narration and a different perspective were required to write what *The Beacon* group defined as a 'local' short story. Gomes exhorted writers to discard 'English spectacles' and the genres that 'transmogrified [Trinidad] into a land of romance'. Writers were encouraged to read Chekhov and Mansfield, to practise 'modern realism'. 'Realism' in this context was interpreted as focusing on the life of the lower classes, which was seen to be more 'distinctively' local than the culture of the middle and upper classes. As in other post-colonial contexts the writer turned to a world that was alien to his or her experience and class but that nevertheless seemed distinctively local. The sketch and the short story were generically appropriate for experimenting with more open and fragmentary types of narration, for escaping the pressure to produce 'rounded' characters and elaborate plots. The beginning of **C. L. R. James'** barrack-yard story 'Triumph' (1930) makes explicit the shift in perspective and language that is required to begin to represent the 'local': 'Where people in England and America say slums, Trinidadians say barrack-yards . . .' A similar impetus to represent township life inspired **Drum** magazine in South Africa in the 1950s, which also drew on indigenous and American influences.

Much work remains to be done on what one critic has called literary publication 'outside the book' across the Commonwealth literatures. Earlier tendencies to read magazines in terms of the editor's personality or as expressions of an epoch or national spirit are now subject to question. In place of these approaches many critics now focus attention on the literary journal as a distinctive cultural institution or set of institutions. This places more emphasis on the way in which journals and magazines construct and not merely address an audience, and how the competition amongst journals for intellectual and cultural space at any one time can tell us a good deal about a given economy of literary production. These approaches will be particularly fruitful in the Commonwealth literatures.

The significance of periodicals as the front line between writing and the marketplace continues to be felt by writers, readers, critics, and editors. Many Commonwealth writers not only begin their writing careers writing for literary magazines but continue to publish across various genres in the print economy throughout their careers. Literary journals such as *Kunapipi*, *World Literature Written in English*, *Journal of West Indian Literature*, and *New Literatures Review*, among others, have played a seminal role in the development of post-colonial criticism in the Commonwealth context. Unfortunately, it remains the case that few literary magazines enjoy a long and healthy span. As G. S. Balarama Gupta comments in his survey of literary magazines in India elsewhere in this *Encyclopedia*, lack of assistance or irregular assistance from academic and governmental agencies and unsatisfactory marketing and distribution facilities seriously hamper the long term viability of these publications. Fortunately, magazines continue to proliferate as what **Nadine Gordimer** has called 'an unkillable rabbit family of effort and optimism'.

GILLIAN WHITLOCK

Further reading: David Carter, ed., *Outside the Book. Contemporary Designs on Literary Periodicals* (1991).

LITERARY MAGAZINES (Australia)

Definitions of the 'literary', like notions of the 'magazine', have varied widely since the Australian continent was first settled by Europeans in 1788. Combined, the two terms indicate publications ranging from a section of a newspaper containing book reviews and articles to periodicals containing original poems, stories, essays, and scripts. Within such publications, generic emphases have varied greatly across time. The essay and sketch, for instance, were favoured forms before 1850; serialized novels were common in the second half of the nineteenth century; short stories and verse have been staple elements in specialist literary magazines in the post-Second World War period.

Australian literary magazines in the nineteenth century had strong and sometimes overwhelming competition from English periodicals such as the *Edinburgh Review*, *Blackwood's Magazine*, the *Cornhill*, *All the Year Round*, and *Punch*. American literary reviews and magazines such as the *Atlantic Monthly* and *Harper's Monthly Magazine* were also widely bought. Sometimes the solution was to bring out Australian editions of well-known overseas magazines; hence the publication of separate Sydney and Melbourne editions of *Punch* and an Australian edition of *Scribner's*. But Australian-grounded magazines could also be successful, for example the *Australian Journal* (Melbourne, 1865–1962) and the *Australasian* (1864–1946, printed and published at the *Argus* newspaper office, Melbourne). Popular newspapers lent financial and infrastructure support to the most durable of such magazines. Lurline Stuart's *Nineteenth Century Australian Periodicals: An Annotated Bibliography* (1979) lists many magazines that did not survive beyond the year of their inception. Of those that survived more than a year, the Sydney weekly *Atlas* (1844–8) contained the liveliest satire. The *Southern Cross* (1859–60), edited by Daniel Deniehy, gave brief promise of a vigorously populist intellectual content. The *Melbourne Review* (1876–85) was an intelligent journal of 'high' literature, comment, and ideas.

The most successful indigenous literary magazine in Australia's history was the Sydney ***Bulletin***'s Red Page under **A. G. Stephens**' editorship from 1896 to 1906 ('a magazine within a magazine', as H. M. Green described it). Subtitled 'The Australian National Newspaper', the *Bulletin* (1880–) preached an influential brand of nationalism; it is said to have reached a circulation of eighty thousand in the 1890s. Other magazines appeared under the aegis of the *Bulletin: The Bookfellow* (1899–1925) and *Lone Hand* (1907–21), for instance. A radical nationalist outlook was also expressed in other journals, including the Brisbane weekly *Boomerang* (1887–92), founded by William Lane and Alfred Walker. A different radicalism was proposed in the feminist monthly *Dawn: A Journal for Australian Women* (1888–1905), founded and edited by **Louisa Lawson**.

The years between the First and Second World Wars have been presented as a dry period for Australian literary culture, including magazines. More certainly, it represents a neglected period in literary historical analysis. However, some trends can be indicated. The *Bulletin* traditions of Australian humour, gossip, commentary, and criticism continued in the popular *Smith's Weekly* (Sydney, 1919–50), the planning for which was assisted by J. F. Archibald, the *Bulletin*'s founding editor. At a more intellectually testing level was **Jack Lindsay**'s *Vision*, which ran for four issues in 1923 and 1924; it emphasized creative individuality rather than communal values and jousted with European modernism and Australian parochialism. Another brief but noteworthy experiment was **P. R. Stephensen**'s *Australian Mercury* (1935), which was intended to 'encourage any sign of first-class work in Australia, or by Australians, with the idea of fostering or defining indigenous culture'. Its failure to last more than one issue may indicate both the economic difficulties of publishing and Stephensen's temperament, rather than the death of culture in these years.

The years during and after the Second World War saw a stirring of intellectual activity in Australia. **Rex Ingamells**, founder of the **Jindyworobak movement** and editor of the *Jindyworobak Review* (1938–48), observed that 'wartime fervours' led to support of his 'environmental values' and Australian nationalism. However, the war stirred other currents too. *Angry Penguins* (1940–6) was a quarterly journal of literary, artistic, musical, and general interest, edited by Max Harris and John Reed, that stimulated, for a time, international and modernist expectations. Unfortunately, *Angry Penguins* did not survive the publicity surrounding the **Ern Malley** hoax. A combative modernist spirit did resurface for several years in *Ern Malley's Journal* (1952–5), edited by Harris, Reed, and Barrett Reid, but more conservative forces prevailed.

During the 1940s and 1950s, the universities began to play a role in literary magazines, providing editors and, in some cases, institutional support. The quarterly literary magazine *Southerly* (1939–) was founded by the English Association and first edited by R. G. Howarth of Sydney University. After commencing in Brisbane in 1940, *Meanjin Papers* moved in 1945, under the editorship of Clem Christesen, to Melbourne, where the

University of Melbourne provided a base for its broad left, liberal humanitarian approach to literature and society. Subsequent editors Jim Davidson (1974–82), Judith Brett (1982–7), and Jenny Lee (1987–) have charted various 'liberation' movements from the 1970s to the 1990s. *Overland* (1954–) was founded in the Cold War years by members of the student left at the University of Melbourne. Its founding editor, Stephen Murray-Smith, used as *Overland*'s motto a phrase from **Joseph Furphy**'s novel *Such is Life*: 'temper democratic, bias offensively Australian', but by the 1980s the ideological stance and literary preferences were much broader. The impetus for *Quadrant* (Sydney, 1956–) came from the political right: whereas *Overland* had Communist party affiliations, *Quadrant* was published by the Australian Association for Cultural Freedom, an offshoot of the international Congress for Cultural Freedom. From their different political standpoints, *Quadrant* and *Overland* emphasized the value of 'comment', sometimes to the detriment of 'literary' content, but a broader inclusiveness was evident in both from the 1970s.

The quarterly magazine *Westerly* (Perth, 1956–) has offered a more 'regional' approach to literature in Australia. Beginning as a student magazine of the arts at the University of Western Australia, it developed under the editorship of **Peter Cowan** and Bruce Bennett, since the mid-1970s, into a national quarterly based distinctively in the west (and close to southeast Asia), publishing short stories, poems, articles, and reviews. During the 1960s, Adelaide was the home of *Australian Letters*, edited by **Geoffrey Dutton**, **Max Harris**, and Rosemary Wighton. Other magazines have followed the 'regional' lead, notably *Literature in Northern Queensland* (LiNQ, Townsville, 1971–), *Northern Perspective* (Darwin, 1977–), and *Island Magazine* (Hobart, 1979–). As a counterpoint to these magazines, *Scripsi* (Melbourne, 1985–) aims at a sophisticated international audience and syndicates some material from overseas sources.

Literary specialization has led some magazines to concentrate on specific genres. *Poetry Australia* (Sydney, 1964–), edited by Grace Perry and **Les A. Murray**, and *New Poetry* (Sydney, 1971–), edited by **Robert Adamson** and Carl Harrison-Ford, have presented themselves as 'mainstream Australian' and 'international' respectively. Experiments in short fiction found a significant outlet in *Tabloid Story*, devised by **Michael Wilding**, **Frank Moorhouse**, Brian Kiernan, and others in 1972 as a supplement to other 'host' journals. *Australian Short Stories* (1982–), edited by Bruce Pascoe, contains both traditional realist and anecdotal stories, along with more experimental material. Like *Science Fiction*, edited at the University of Western Australia by Van Ikin, *Australian Short Stories* has an enthusiastic, 'club' atmosphere. *Australasian Drama Studies* (Brisbane, 1982–) is more academic, with articles on theatre history and theory.

Contemporary social movements have given rise to new literary magazines. Feminist magazines, for instance, have developed strongly since the 1970s. *Hecate* (1975–), edited by Carole Ferrier at the University of Queensland, is subtitled 'An Interdisciplinary Journal of Women's Liberation'; it publishes creative expression and comment by women across all genres. Unlike *Hecate*, *Luna*, founded in 1976, tried to avoid polemics and political debate, but folded after several issues. *Australian Feminist Studies* (1987–), edited by Susan Magarey in Adelaide, derives from and strengthens women's studies programs in the universities.

Black writing in Australia was well catered for in *Aboriginal and Islander Identity* (1971–82), more commonly called *Identity*. **Mudrooroo Narogin** (Colin Johnson), when canvassing plans to establish a new Aboriginal magazine, observed of *Identity*: 'This periodical was very popular amongst Aboriginal people when it was located in Perth under the editorship of the playwright and poet, Dr Jack Davis, but with its shift to Canberra it underwent a politicization at the expense of cultural matters.'

Australian Literary Studies (1963–), under Laurie Hergenhan's editorship, is a professional journal *par excellence*, providing articles, reviews, and documents on Australian literary history. *Australian Book Review* (1961–73; 1978–) attempts to review a wide range of contemporary Australian publications. An important comparative dimension for Australian literature is provided by journals such as *Australian-Canadian Studies*, (1983–), edited by Malcolm Alexander and Gillian Whitlock, and *Span* (1975–), the journal of the South Pacific Association for Commonwealth Literature and Language Studies. The *CRNLE Reviews Journal* (Flinders University, 1980–) provides a semi-annual review of literary works in the 'new literatures in English', including Australian. From outside Australia, *Antipodes* (1987–), edited by Robert Ross at the University of Texas at Austin, USA, is gaining increasing status and importance. Of more wide-ranging significance are *Kunapipi* (Aarhus, Denmark, 1979–), edited by Australian-born Anna Rutherford, and *World Literature Written in English* (1962–), edited by Diana Brydon at the University of Guelph, Canada. The comparisons fostered by such magazines are crucial for the development of Australian literary studies.

BRUCE BENNETT

Further reading: Bruce Bennett, ed., *Cross Currents: Magazines and Newspapers in Australian Literature* (1981).

LITERARY MAGAZINES (Bangladesh)

Most literary magazines in Bangladesh are published in the Bengali language and have a long publishing history. *Sougat*, for example, was first published in Calcutta in 1918 as a monthly. Following the partition of India in 1947, *Sougat*, like many other magazines, was relocated; in this case to Dhaka (then in Pakistan) in 1952. Many journals of the 1950s and 1960s, although they have not survived, form an important literary and publishing record; among these are *Samakal*, *Kabikanthha*, *Meghna*, *Uttoron*, *Purloomegh*, *Purabi*, *Sanglap*, *Kanthaswara*, *Chhotogalpo*, and *Shilpokala*. Those still flourishing and those that began publishing after the creation of Bangladesh in 1972 are *Kichhudhwani*, *Rupom*, *Shahitya Patrika*, *Uttaradhikara*, *Theatre*, *Gono Shahitya*, *Moitree*, *Ekal*, *Sundarom*, *Mizanur Rahmaner Troimashik Patrika*, *Diponkor*, *Adhuna*, *Nazrul Academy Patrika*, *Shilpo Taru*, and *Nazrul Institute Patrika*. These journals, some monthly, some quarterly, carry varied contents. While *Kichhudhwani* and *Rupom* publish only poetry and short stories, respectively, *Nabarun*, *Shistu*, and *Dhan Shaliker Deshe* are children's journals. Some Bengali-language journals are patronized by the government, but most follow an independent policy. *Samalochana* is devoted entirely to literary criticism.

Among the English-language magazines, the following publish original English writing or translations from Bengali: *Form*, *Bengali Academy Journal*, *Dhaka University Studies*, *Part A*, *Shipokala*, and *Bangladesh Quarterly*. *New Values*, which was an excellent cultural forum, ceased publication in 1965.

KABIR CHOWDHURY

LITERARY MAGAZINES (Canada)

The rise and development of anglophone literary periodicals in Canada followed, by and large, the gradual westward progress of English-language settlement. The latter had taken root in the Atlantic region with some promise of permanence following upon the Treaty of Utrecht (1713) and had, thereafter, crept across the face of North America prompted by history and the geo-political facts of the continent. The Loyalist migrations in the last years of the eighteenth century, the lure of the fur trade in the opening decades of the nineteenth, and the fear of American expansionism following the American Civil War are some examples of the kind of extra-literary push and pull that was influential in the positioning of an anglophone presence first in a French Quebec, then in a sparsely populated Ontario, then in the great prairie lands of the middle west, with a final reaching for the Pacific region in the last decades of the nineteenth century. The periodical press, almost always yoked to a mission of extending and protecting the nascent idea and ideal of a Canada, marched in awkward but determined step with the growth of a national culture. (See **Cultural Journalism**, Canada, and **Publishing**, Canada.)

The early periodicals tended, more often than not, to be sources of general information on various aspects of colonial life. The literary component was likely to be modest and, not infrequently, consisted of reprinted borrowings from magazines originating in England. Local material was a rich and topical mix of news and information on everything from the names and tonnage of recently arrived ships and the detailed nature of their cargoes, to the coming and going of military units and their officers, to accounts of executions and catastrophic fires. However, there is evidence of local literary stirrings, even if these were apt to be ploddingly imitative in style and tone of the literary productions of the Mother Country. Local writing would often take the shape of descriptive sketches of unknown parts of the country, occasional if long-winded poems, some devotional writing, and the odd bit of political polemic trying hard to be witty and entertaining. The overall impression is of a society cautiously observant of its context and reflecting the pious inclinations of pioneers and settlers. These were earnest folk with a down-to-earth sense of themselves and with no great cultural ambitions, although, it must be said, that this same society willingly committed scarce and valuable resources to the founding of colleges and universities, the propagation of their faith, and the creation of a 'civilized' order in what they saw as a 'savage' and chaotic wilderness.

Almost all the better-educated and therefore culturally aspiring members of this young community were recently arrived or were transients destined to move to other postings or charges in the colonial service. Their contribution to the cultural life of the colonies was, however, invaluable. As the English speaking and writing presence extended itself westwards and was helped and reinforced by a measure of stability and success, we see a growing refinement and sophistication in the literary output of what was still a string of insular colonies. Distance, which meant relative isolation and, in later times, the experience of the strong pull of the USA, always seemed to militate against a well-defined sense of national identity. Newly founded periodicals had to struggle to overcome the problems of circulation in a small and scattered population with not a great deal of spare disposable income and to compete with material coming from abroad. The story of literary periodicals in Canada is the story of many magazines launched, but with few surviving beyond the first few issues or the first months or year of publication. Longevity, therefore, was to be a kind of acid test, first of cultural and financial stamina, and then of enduring value. A look at the Canadian 'map' of literary periodicals shows that each and every region, each and every historical period, produced one or two outstanding periodicals that dominated their cultural landscape. The nature of the contribution that these noteworthy periodicals made to Canadian life varied with the needs of the time or place or with the cultural mission, often self-proclaimed, that their editors and their coteries set for themselves. In almost all these cases real advances were made and the literary dimensions of Canadian creativity were enhanced and expanded.

An early example of influence, quality, and success was *The Novascotian* (1824–1926), acquired by **Joseph Howe** in 1828 and raised to pre-eminence by an individual who was destined to become a journalist, poet, and politician of note. His magazine was distinguished for its reportorial innovativeness as well as for its interest in the life, topography, and letters of his native colony of Nova Scotia. Of similar bent, although not as successfully long-lived, was the Montreal-based *Canadian Magazine and Literary Repository* (1823–5), which, by means of a mix of original verse and prose, together with reprinted material, strove to establish a literary tone reminiscent of European models and echoing the popularity of the Byronic tradition.

The opening decades of the nineteenth century had witnessed a shift of the human and economic centre of gravity away from the Atlantic regions to Montreal, where a lively community of increasingly successful gentrified entrepreneurs and colonial administrators was able to support, albeit fitfully, a number of ambitious if short-lived periodicals. An interesting example is *The Scribbler* (1821–7), which showed some staying power and audience appeal due mainly to its editor's quarrelsome and occasionally scandalous insouciance. Such magazines helped to pave the way for the more stable and solid performance of *The Literary Garland* (1838–51), a major cultural force with a claim to national status and clearly living up to the recently crystallized bourgeois ideals of progress, refinement, and gentility expressing themselves in the new middle class of Canada. *The Literary Garland* was done to death by American competition, but it was succeeded in its role by *The Canadian Monthly and National Review* (1872–8), in the name of which the importance of the words 'Canadian' and 'national' should be duly noted even though it continued its life as *Rose-Belford's Canadian Monthly* (1878–82). This periodical attracted (as had *The Literary Garland*) the best talent of its time and ranged widely in its pursuit of material of literary and social value. It should be noted that in the second half of the nineteenth century almost all the periodicals of note expressed or echoed strong national sentiments. In 1883, *The Week* (1883–96), sometimes called 'An Independent Journal of Literature, Politics and Criticism' began to publish in Toronto under the guiding spirit of **Goldwin Smith**, a prominent academic and intellectual of his time. Its role, amply and willingly served by Canada's foremost writers, was to be a showcase of the best writing and thought of the time, an accomplishment that made it a cultural beacon and a point of literary reference.

The advent of the twentieth century, with its growing sense of self-confidence among Canada's cultural élites, produced both the staid and the radical in the world of its periodicals. The university journal, which had made its appearance in the nineteenth century, came into its own with a mix of scholarly, critical, and creative writing. *Queen's Quarterly* (1893–), the *University Magazine* (1901–20, also called the *McGill University Magazine*), the *University of Toronto Quarterly* (1895–1896 and 1931–), and *The Dalhousie Review* (1921–) are prominent examples of this kind of predictably respectable activity. But the early years of the twentieth century were also the years of the rise of modernism, with its attendant radicalization of cultural self-expression. This effect became apparent in the rise of *parti pris* sentiment in those who founded and gravitated to the new periodicals of the times. *The Canadian Forum* (1920–), which absorbed a more staid *Willison's Monthly* and operated at the other end of the critical spectrum from *The Canadian Bookman* (1919–39), is a prime example of a monthly journal of strong opinion devoted to literature and public affairs. Among its scruffier but influential literary cousins in Montreal were *Preview* (1942–5) and *First Statement* (1942–5), which struggled to lift the dead hand of literary convention and to inject the spirit of modernism into contemporary Canadian poetry. They were merged to form a more eclectic avant-garde periodical called *Northern Review* (1945/6–1956), which absorbed the *Canadian Review of Music and Art* and declared its commitment to 'new writing in Canada'.

On the west coast, *Contemporary Verse* (1941–52) pushed a reasoned modernist line, while the Atlantic region relied on *The Fiddlehead* (1945–) as its best outlet first for poetry and later for a wider range of creative writing. Since these periodicals were the work of literary and intellectual coteries, they belong to the little magazine/little press movement in Canada, which is remarkable for the short-lived intensities of a large number of its member periodicals. *Contact* (1952–4) and *Combustion* (1957–60) are, on the other hand, prime examples of the 'one-man' little magazine having a major impact in the shifting of the literary scene from the 'high' or traditional modernism of the mid-century to the new directions of projective verse and later postmodernist indicators. Some, such as *Delta* (1957–66) and *Tish* (1961–9), lasted longer and made a considerable contribution to the literary scene while retaining a strong and individual identity. Others, such as *The Tamarack Review* (1956–82) and *The Malahat Review* (1967–), took a middle-of-the-road approach to publishing, in the case of the former, a wide range of poetry, fiction, and criticism by new and established writers and, in the case of the latter, following the ambitious path of an international journal of life and letters, a role equally well-filled by the literary quarterly *Exile* (1972–).

The postmodernist era has been, if anything, more lively and diverse in the world of Canadian periodicals. A new dimension is the force of regional interest, which pulls and tugs so successfully at the traditional centres of Canadian literary activity that the notion of 'centre' has become irrelevant. (See **Regionalism in Canadian Literature in English**.) Western Canada, in particular, has come into its own and has spawned a great number of regionally focused periodicals. *West Coast Review* (1966) combining with *Line* (1983) to form *West Coast Line* (1990), *Capilano Review* (1972), and *CV II* (1975–; later styled *Contemporary Verse II: A Quarterly of Canadian Poetry/Criticism*), are all excellent examples of this activity. At the same time, journal/periodicals such as *Canadian Fiction Magazine* (1971–), *Open Letter* (several series, beginning in 1966–), and *Room of One's Own* (1975–), describing itself as 'a Canadian feminist quarterly of literature and commentary', are their own cultural centres offering everything from entire issues devoted to one writer's work, to close textual reading and phenomenological discourse, to a discussion of life and writing from an exclusively feminist perspective.

MICHAEL GNAROWSKI

LITERARY MAGAZINES (The Caribbean)
Literary magazines played a vital role when Caribbean literature began to come into its own in the middle of the twentieth century. During the 1930s, 1940s, and 1950s, a handful of magazines, produced mostly on a voluntary basis, provided a nursery for virtually all of the writers who began to gain international recognition, first with the novel in the 1950s and then with poetry in the 1960s.

Before 1930 there were sporadic and mostly brief periodical flowerings. One such, a curiosity now, was *Plummer's Magazine*, 'A Jamaica Literary Magazine' that apparently survived for only two issues, November and December of 1913. Its focus was historical, as was made explicit in an article entitled 'A People Without A History' (author unknown). History, largely in the form of historical romance and social and business history, was a major interest of another Jamaican periodical of the time and one of far greater longevity, the annual *Planters' Punch* (1920–44). As far as literature in the stricter sense was concerned, the journal was mostly a showcase for the novels of its publisher and editor, **H. G. De Lisser**.

De Lisser and his magazine represented the

reactionary, colonialist attitudes of the local affluent whites and high-browns. However, as the last issues of *Planters' Punch* were published, the first issue of *Focus* (1943–60) appeared in Jamaica, as had, more than a decade earlier in other parts of the region, other ground-breaking magazines that represented a new spirit of challenge — anti-colonialist, indigenist, nationalist — to the socio-political establishment.

The pace-setter was the quarterly *Trinidad* (1929–30), which soon gave way to the monthly *The Beacon* (1931–3; 1939). The former had emerged out of a small literary group started by **C. L. R. James** and **Alfred Mendes**. The latter was founded by Albert Gomes, who more or less took over the James-Mendes group and who was to become a leading figure in Trinidad politics. The poetry in *Trinidad* and *The Beacon* was largely old-fashioned and of indifferent quality. It was the short stories — usually realistic portraits of a changing society — that provided the new literary energy, particularly in the work of James, Mendes, and **Ralph de Boissière**.

The publishers of such journals supported others in the region. A note in the November 1933 *Beacon* praised *The Forum*, a Barbadian quarterly begun in 1931; it observed that the journal was produced by the Forum Club, whose members, drawn chiefly from 'the coloured and negro intelligentsia of the Colony', took 'an exceptionally keen interest' in Negro history and literature.

The Forum had a broadly historical and sociopolitical focus and ran for three years, until December 1934, then was briefly revived (1943–5) with much the same range of interests as before. In its latter years, it published poems by **Frank Collymore** and his protégé **George Lamming**, as well as by H. A. Vaughan, who had also contributed poems and historical essays to the earlier *Forum*. **John Wickham**'s talent for the short story also showed itself in the journal. Other notable Barbadian magazines of the period include *The Outlook* (1931–2) and *The Weymouth Magazine* (1943–9).

Three magazines emerged in the 1940s — *Bim* (Barbados), *Focus* (Jamaica), and *Kyk-over-al* (Guyana) — that, along with the British Broadcasting Corporation (BBC) weekly programme **'Caribbean Voices'**, played an important role in the flowering of Caribbean literature. *Bim*, a semi-annual, first appeared in December 1942 and continues to publish; *Focus*, an irregular annual, began in 1943; *Kyk-over-al*, a semi-annual that is still published, and 'Caribbean Voices' appeared in 1945. (The programme ended in 1958.) Each of these ventures was primarily the product of the enthusiasm and vision of one person: Frank Collymore, Edna Manley, **A. J. Seymour**, and the Englishman Henry Swanzy, respectively.

Bim was edited by Collymore until his death in 1980 and has since been edited by John Wickham. Sculptor Edna Manley was the founder and editor of *Focus*, which made four appearances (1943, 1948, 1956, and 1960). It was revived for one issue in 1988, edited by **Mervyn Morris**. *Kyk-over-al* ran from 1945 to 1961 under the editorship of its founder, Seymour. In 1984 he revived it with the assistance of **Ian McDonald**, who has continued to edit it vigorously since Seymour's death in 1989. From the BBC studios in London, England, Swanzy enhanced through 'Caribbean Voices' the inter-territorial scope and character of the new Caribbean literature, employing many of the writers to read and discuss this work on the programme.

It is to these four magazines that one must look in order to get a broad picture of developments in Caribbean literature from the 1940s to the 1960s. For instance, many of those who were to become poets of stature were the most prolific contributors to *Bim* and included **Edward Kamau Brathwaite**, **A. L. Hendriks**, Ian McDonald, Mervyn Morris, **E. M. Roach**, and **Derek Walcott**. Prose fiction contributors of note included **Michael Anthony**, **Timothy Callender**, **Austin Clarke**,

Edgar Mittelholzer, and John Wickham. In *Bim*, too, as in 'Caribbean Voices', one can see Lamming the poet before he became Lamming the novelist.

Later magazines include *Voices* (1964–9), edited by Clifford Sealy in Trinidad; *Now* (1973–4), edited by the British poet Stewart Brown in Jamaica; and *The New Voices*, which continues to thrive under the editorship of its founder **Anson Gonzales** since its appearance in Trinidad in 1973. More sought after than any of these has been the irregularly appearing *Savacou*, originated in 1970 by Edward Kamau Brathwaite and Kenneth Ramchand at the Jamaica campus of the University of the West Indies (UWI).

Caribbean Quarterly (1949–), a cultural journal published by UWI, has provided another valuable forum for critical commentary on Caribbean literature, whose coming of age is underscored by the fact that the region now produces the scholarly *The Journal of West Indian Literature* (1986–), edited by **Mark McWatt**, from the Barbados campus of UWI. Since August 1991 *The Caribbean Review of Books*, published from UWI's Jamaica campus, has appeared to give notice of the increasing volume of writing coming out of the region and its metropolitan diaspora.

EDWARD BAUGH

Further reading: L. E. Brathwaite, '*Kyk-over-al* and the radicals', in George Lamming and Martin Carter (eds) *New World* 3, May (1966), special Guyana independence issue; Edward Baugh, 'Introduction', in Reinhard W. Sander (ed.) *An Index to 'Bim' 1942–1972* (1973); Mervyn Morris, 'Little magazines in the Caribbean', *Bim* 68 (1984); Reinhard W. Sander, *The Trinidad Awakening* (1988).

LITERARY MAGAZINES (India)

India has had a rich, varied, and ancient literary tradition — some of the finest works in Indian languages date back more than a thousand years — but, surprisingly, the country had to wait until almost the middle of the twentieth century to witness the appearance of genuine literary periodicals. In the nineteenth century some newspapers and magazines in India catered to literary tastes by occasionally publishing creative and critical writings and book reviews, but it was only in the 1950s that periodicals concerning themselves mainly with literary matters emerged. In the last forty years, more than a score of them — apart from university journals — have made their appearance, but only a few have survived.

Of the few periodicals that have established a name for themselves, *The Literary Criterion*, edited by **C. D. Narasimhaiah**, takes pride of place. Well produced and of generally high quality, it began as a biannual but is now published quarterly; many useful special numbers deal exclusively with specific literary areas. Another journal from Mysore that has seen nearly three decades of publication is the *Literary Half-Yearly*, edited by H. H. Anniah Gowda. *The Writers Workshop Miscellany* (later issued as the *New Miscellany*), edited by **P. Lal**, has also had a distinguished history, publishing creative and critical articles from emerging as well as established writers. The *Journal of Indian Writing in English*, edited by G. S. Balarama Gupta, is also significant: it is perhaps the only journal in the country exclusively devoted to the promotion and interpretation of Indian literature in English. *Indian Literature*, the official publication of Sahitya Akademi, Government of India, is among the better-produced periodicals (also available at a subsidized price); it covers all the literatures of India. The *Indian Journal of American Studies* promotes Indian scholarship in the area of American literature. *The Book Review*, *Indian Book Chronicle*, and *Review Projector* stand apart from other periodicals in that they concentrate mainly on book reviews.

Other journals have ceased publication, temporarily or for good; they include *Indian Writing Today*, *Quest*, *Poetry India*, *The Indian PEN*,

Chandrabhaga, *East and West*, the *Indian Literary Review*, *Tenor*, the *Literary Endeavour*, *Littcrit*, *Scholar Critic*, *Indian Scholar*, *Commonwealth Quarterly*, *Enact*, *Kavi*, the *Journal of Literature and Aesthetics*, and the *Indian Journal of English Studies*.

Some good work is being done by several universities and state Sahitya Akademies. These journals may not always appear on a strict publication schedule, but they are generally well-printed and economically priced. University journals such as *Karnataka Journal of Humanities*, *Osmania Journal of English Studies*, *Kakatiya Journal of English Studies*, and *Meerut Journal of Comparative Literature and Language* almost exclusively promote research by their faculty and research scholars. Many of these university journals have also brought out excellent special numbers.

The climate for Indian literary periodicals has not been favourable in recent years. Escalating costs, inadequate financial resources, lack of assistance from academic bodies and governmental agencies, and unsatisfactory marketing and distribution facilities are some of the factors that have seriously hampered the growth of literary periodicals in India. Except for a handful of journals such as *Indian Literature*, which is a government publication, and the *Indian Journal of American Studies*, which is an official organ of the American Studies Research Centre, all Indian literary journals in English face the ever-present threat of extinction. If at least some of those periodicals known for their excellence are to survive and flourish, it is imperative that they be patronized not only by serious-minded academics, but also by the state and central governments as well as the universities. (See **Cultural Journalism**, India, and **Criticism**, India.)

G. S. BALARAMA GUPTA

Further reading: G. S. Balarama Gupta, 'English literary periodicals in India', *Literary Horizons* 1 (1986).

LITERARY MAGAZINES (New Zealand)

Literary magazines, in the modern sense of periodicals primarily given to fiction, poetry, and criticism, are a comparatively recent development in New Zealand. Following initial European settlement in the 1840s, hopeful amateurs established monthly or quarterly magazines almost every decade until 1900. *The Southern Monthly Magazine* (1863–6), *The New Zealand Magazine* (1876–7), and *Zealandia* (1889–90), among others, were modelled closely on contemporary British magazines; their content ranged from gardening notes to discussions on Darwinism, but did include some fiction and poetry, either local or imported (and possibly pirated). The longest any of these magazines lasted was three years; three or four issues were more common. They were defeated by a small population and poor communication among the scattered settlements. The earliest periodicals were the voice of British exiles; a conscious New Zealand identity began to be expressed by *Zealandia* in 1890 and more strongly by the *New Zealand Illustrated Magazine* (1899–1905).

Much greater continuity was achieved by daily and weekly newspapers. Both, but especially the weeklies, ran short fiction and serialized novels, nearly all imported; but some local writers were used, often for humorous sketches. The *Triad* (1893–1927), a monthly magazine published in Dunedin from 1893 until 1915, when it moved to Sydney, was the first sustained periodical devoted mainly to the arts. Music was its first interest, but poetry, fiction, and literary criticism were all featured. Paradoxically, the leading New Zealand literary magazine at this time was the famous Sydney ***Bulletin*** (1880–), reflecting a much closer interaction between the two countries than was common later. A New Zealander, **Arthur Adams**, was literary editor of the *Bulletin*, and contributors from New Zealand outnumbered those from any Australian state except New South Wales and Victoria. It was remarked at the time, though, that the

New Zealand contributions tended to be more genteel and 'British' than the Australian larrikinism for which the *Bulletin* was noted.

Apart from *Triad* and some newspapers, the first thirty years of the twentieth century were a barren time for literary publications in New Zealand. *Art in New Zealand*, a quarterly primarily for the visual arts but with some literary content, was established in 1928 and survived until 1946, but the journals published from time to time by the literary societies of the four university colleges were the nearest approach to literary magazines proper. When one of these, The *Phoenix* (1932–3), 'went public' in 1932, reaching beyond the university constituency, it was claimed as the real pioneer of literary magazines in New Zealand. The *Phoenix* lasted two years with only four issues, and halfway through its career, with a change of editor, changed its policy from aestheticism to Marxism. But it was edited with confidence and flair and beautifully printed by Bob Lowry. Most of its contributors moved on to the left-wing weekly (later fortnightly) *Tomorrow* (1934–40), published in Christchurch. Closely associated with the group of writers around the Caxton Press, *Tomorrow*, besides maintaining a lively and iconoclastic commentary on current affairs, was the chief forum for the modernist poets and short-story writers of the 1930s. It was suppressed by government action in 1940 because of its opposition to the Second World War, which it described as 'imperialist'.

Tomorrow's place for writers was taken to some extent by the *New Zealand Listener* (1939–), a weekly established by the state-owned New Zealand Broadcasting Service. The *Listener* has continued to be a market for fiction and poetry and a forum for the discussion of literary matters, at least until its 1990 privatization (the first issues under new ownership appeared in 1991). During the Second World War the infrequently published *New Zealand New Writing* (1942–5) was modelled after John Lehmann's *Penguin New Writing* (1940–50), which was itself hospitable to a number of New Zealand writers. Shortly after the war came New Zealand's first substantial, long-surviving literary magazine: *Landfall* (1947–), published by the Caxton Press and edited by **Charles Brasch**. Brasch formed *Landfall* on exacting models: J. M. Murry's *Adelphi*, T. S. Eliot's *Criterion*, and the Leavises' *Scrutiny*. New Zealand writers responded — the opportunity to publish substantial stories, poetry, and critical studies led to the burgeoning of such work.

Brasch presided over *Landfall* for twenty years. The qualities he sought did not always accommodate more tentative, experimental work; this caused some resentment but also provoked the publication of alternative journals. Most of *Landfall*'s rivals conformed to the usual criteria of 'little magazines', erratic in appearance, experimental, and short-lived. When Brasch retired, his place was taken by Robin Dudding, who had edited the best of the alternative journals, *Mate*. After some years and a disagreement with the management, however, Dudding left *Landfall* to found his own magazine, *Islands* (1972–87), which soon dominated the scene as *Landfall* had done. *Landfall* continued, but for some years seemed to have lost its way; later, under the collective or successive editorship of young academics, it found a new place for itself in the postmodernist advance guard. When *Islands* succumbed to financial troubles, its place was taken by a lively new journal, *Sport* (1988–), published by a group of young Wellington writers. The field continued to be well occupied by other journals, often with a limited agenda and a pre-planned rather than inadvertent short life. Literary studies, rather than literature itself, have taken an increasing role, especially in the annual *Journal of New Zealand Literature* (1983–).

Conscious of the lack of other outlets for New Zealand writers, and coupled, possibly, with an inward-looking sense of nationality among the writers themselves, New Zealand magazines have seldom been open to writers of other countries. The culture of European New Zealanders, in all its aspects, has been inclined to look to the UK and more recently to the USA, rather than to those countries — even Australia — that share its post-colonial experience. The Brasch *Landfall* did publish regular newsletters from Australia and Canada, and a long-running little magazine, *Arena* (1943–75), which was not otherwise of great significance, regularly published work from Australia and Canada, as well as from the UK and the USA, in the 1950s and 1960s. A later magazine, *Pacific Moana Quarterly* (1978–85) — preceded by *Cave* (1972–5) and *New Quarterly Cave* (1975–7) — solicited work particularly from the island nations of the Pacific whose people had begun to migrate to New Zealand in considerable numbers. It was followed by *Crosscurrent* (1986–9). In recent years there have been signs in the larger journals, including *Landfall* and *Sport*, of a greater desire for reciprocal relations with other English-speaking countries. With the number of New Zealanders contributing to, and reading, such journals as *Ariel* (Calgary, Canada, 1970–), *SPAN: Journal of the South Pacific Association for Commonwealth Literature and Language Studies* (1975–), and *ACLALS Bulletin* (1967–), this interest seems likely to increase.

DENNIS McELDOWNEY

LITERARY MAGAZINES (The Philippines)

Since 1593, when printing was first introduced to the Philippines by Spanish colonizers, periodical outlets for writers have never been wanting. One of the highlights of the Spanish colonial period, for instance, was the publication in the Spanish-language periodical *La Solidaridad* of literary essays by Jose Rizal. Since the American colonial period, poets and short-story writers have regularly contributed to literary sections of newspapers and magazines.

The literary magazine properly speaking, however, started only during the American colonial period. Most literary magazines, of course, concentrated on works written in vernacular languages. Among the earliest to accept works written in English were *Expression* (1934), *Story Manuscripts* (1935), and *Veronica* (1937). These were literary magazines in the classic sense of the word, namely, coterie-based, unfunded, commercially unviable, and short-lived. Like many such magazines around the world, they maintained high aesthetic standards, but could not afford high printing quality.

After the Pacific War and to the present, literary magazines run by students have provided the main outlets for non-established writers in English, the established ones being easily invited to contribute to weekly magazines or Sunday supplements of newspapers. Among such student magazines were, or are, *Malate*, *Literary Apprentice*, *College Folio*, *Sands and Coral*, *Flame*, *Heights*, *Dawn*, and *Orion*. Funded by student fees, these magazines tend to have much longer lives than those of the American period. Particularly hospitable today to spending money on literary magazines are the University of the Philippines, De La Salle University, Ateneo de Manila University, University of Santo Tomas, Far Eastern University, University of the East, and Silliman University.

Eventually student writers either finish or drop out of school and join the literary magazines of the 'professionals', such as *Mithi*, published by the Writers Union of the Philippines; *Caracoa*, published by the Philippine Literary Arts Council; *Likha*, published by the Department of Literature of De La Salle University; or *Ani*, published by the Cultural Center of the Philippines, to cite only those that have survived at least five years. Competition for space in these magazines is fierce, particularly since only the poetry journal *Caracoa* has devoted itself exclusively to English writing, the others sharing part of their space with writers in various vernaculars.

Literary magazines are not the main outlets for writers in English. Much more hospitable to English writing are weekly magazines such as *Philippine Graphic* and *Philippines Free Press*, both of which can trace their origins to American colonial times, when the most prestigious outlet for writers was the now-defunct *Philippine Magazine*.

ISAGANI R. CRUZ

LITERARY MAGAZINES (South Africa)
The literary magazine in South Africa has a relatively long history and dates from the second British occupation of the Cape, when **Thomas Pringle** and John Fairbairn produced their *South African Journal* (1824). Pringle and Fairbairn aroused the anger of the then-governor of the Cape, Lord Charles Somerset, thereby proving to be the first of a long line of literary editors who came into conflict with the prevailing establishment. After only two issues, the magazine ceased publication. Other relatively short-lived magazines of the nineteenth century were *South African Grins* (1825), *The New Organ* (1826), and the *South African Quarterly Journal* (published irregularly: first series, 1829–31; second series, 1833–5; third series, 1836). *The Cape of Good Hope Literary Gazette* (1830–5) was another influential venture of the period.

The modern South African 'little' magazine properly begins with *Voorslag* ('whiplash', 1926–7), 'a magazine of South African life and art', edited by the poet **Roy Campbell** with the assistance of fellow writers **William Plomer** and **Laurens van der Post**. As short-lived as Pringle's and Fairbairn's *South African Journal*, *Voorslag* was as successful in rousing the ire of the South African literary establishment. Its combination of corrosive satire and powerful lyric poetry and prose fiction attacked white racism and colonial complacency in a way that brought fierce reaction. *Voorslag* was soon forced to temper its editorial policy, and the trio of authors resigned from editorial control. Most of the copy for the first three issues was written by the three, either under their own names or under pseudonyms. In addition to mounting his *Voorslag* attacks, Plomer crossed the race boundary by publishing verse in John Dube's *Ilanga lase Natal* ('The Natal Sun', 1903–65; renamed *Ilanga*, 1965–).

Two other writers of the 1920s and 1930s, **Stephen Black** and **Herman Charles Bosman,** were instrumental in bringing out literary magazines. Black's *The Sjambok* (1929–31) contained such controversial material that it occasioned four actions for libel. Bosman's *The Touleier* (1930–1) also proved to be alternative and short-lived. It is interesting to note that all of these magazines of the years between the two world wars took their titles from the mystique of the ox-wagon. Colonial metaphor was entrenched, even in the minds of those who were critical of the establishment.

During the Second World War, interest in literature was kept more or less alive as a department in magazines such as *Outspan: South Africa's Weekly for Everbody* (1927–57). Immediately after the Second World War, the Afrikaans writer Uys Krige produced a bilingual magazine, *Vandag* (1946–7), and in 1945 the long life of the Afrikaans magazine, *Standpunte* (1945–92) began. The English-language contributions in *Standpunte* provided a showcase for poetry and creative prose by **Jack Cope**, **Guy Butler**, Anne Welsh, and others.

From 1948, legislation was enacted that steadily put into place what was eventually to become the fully articulated apartheid state. The alternative tendency of the 'little' magazine became even more pronounced. *Vista* (1950) and **Lionel Abrahams**' *The Purple Renoster* (first published in 1956 and sporadically until 1972) were among the magazines that opposed the 'official' South African way of life. *Africa South* (1956–61) was a short-lived magazine edited by a left-wing intellectual, Ronald Segal. Forced into exile, Segal published from England a last issue, *Africa South in*

Exile (1961).

An important phenomenon of the 1950s was the literary work in ***Drum*** magazine (1951–). Inspired by township life in the black Johannesburg settlement of Sophiatown, writers such as **Ezekiel (Es'kia) Mphahlele, Can Themba,** Bloke Modisane, Todd Matshikiza, Nat Nakasa, and Casey Motsisi produced short stories, autobiography, and journalism that proclaimed them as the '*Drum* generation'. The new urban life-style that they reflected was a combination of American and indigenous cultural influences. The spontaneity, freshness, and excitement that this work engendered was very largely stifled during the 1960s by repressive apartheid legislation.

The year 1961 saw the proclamation of the South African Republic and the first issue of a new literary magazine, *Contrast* (1961–90; renamed *New Contrast* in 1990). This publication, edited for twenty years by **Jack Cope** and for a further ten by Geoffrey Haresnape, was to appear at regular intervals until it merged in 1991 with a poetry magazine, *Upstream*. The magazine is a testament by creative writers of what it was like to live under apartheid. The Immorality Act, the Mixed Marriages Act, the Group Areas Act, and other examples of apartheid legislation since repealed are woven into the texture of human experiences recorded in its pages. An ongoing principle in its editorial policy is to combine a search for literary talent with a search for opposition to the negative impulses of bureaucracy and repressive politics.

A more exclusively literary successor to *Drum* was the Johannesburg magazine *The Classic* (1963–71). *The Classic* was closely associated with urban township life, and its first editor was the Johannesburg journalist, Nat Nakasa. The work of leading black writers such as **Bessie Head**, Stanley Motjuwadi, **Mongane Serote**, and **Mafika Gwala** appeared in its pages. The magazine was revived as the *New Classic* in 1975, edited by the Soweto poet **Sipho Sepamla**. *New Classic* ran for five issues, and publication ceased with a 'Short Story Special' in 1978; the magazine reappeared briefly as *Classic* in 1982.

The period between 1960 and 1990 saw the appearance of many 'little' magazines in addition to those cited above. *New Coin Poetry*, *Izwi*, *Ophir*, *Wurm*, *New Nation*, *Front*, *Expression*, *Bolt*, *The Bloody Horse*, and *Staffrider* are some of the members of what **Nadine Gordimer** has called 'an unkillable rabbit family of effort and optimism'. With their small budgets and local readerships the 'little' magazines have been able to give expression to local concerns and nuances of South African English in a way that more substantive literary ventures have not. They have been among the forerunners in the creation of an authentic South African English literature.

GEOFFREY HARESNAPE

Further reading: 'Periodicals', in David Adey, Ridley Beeton, Michael Chapman, and Ernest Pereira (eds) *Companion to South African English Literature* (1986).

Literary Magazines (South Pacific)

Cultural rather than specifically literary enthusiasm was the catalyst for the emergence of the earliest journals in the Papua New Guinea Islands arena and, as with creative texts, the earliest journals appeared in pre-independence Papua New Guinea. (See **Publishing,** South Pacific.) The inception and termination dates of the region's literary magazines are instructive because they parallel the heady literary and cultural activity in the Pacific in the 1970s and early 1980s and its decline in the late 1980s, as governments focused on economic imperatives and individuals moved on to academia or government positions.

In Papua New Guinea, the foundation editors were European academics (for example, Georgina Beier and Ulli Beier of *Kovave*, 1968–76?; Don Maynard of *New Guinea Writing*, 1970, renamed

Papua New Guinea Writing, 1972–8), whose intentions were to provide a model for indigenous successors and to contribute to the generation of national cultural pride. While local editors (**John Kasaipwalova** and Apisai Enos, for example) *did* assume editorial roles, the momentum and finance were not sustained for long.

By contrast, the South Pacific Creative Arts Society espoused a regional approach through its journal *Mana*. Beginning in 1973, *Mana* exploited the distribution potential of the news magazine *Pacific Islands Monthly* (1930–) by appearing there before launching into independent publication in 1977. *Mana*'s founding editors were Pacific writers themselves, and its clever strategy of assembling general and national issues ensured its success in the region, until the political disruptions of 1987 deflected its editors' energies. Local journals include *Bikmaus* (1980–91), *Ondobondo* (1982–91), *The PNG Writer* (1982–91), *Gigibori* (Papua New Guinea, 1985–6), *Faikava* (Tonga, 1978–88?), and *Sinnet* (Fiji, 1980–2?).

Australian, New Zealand, and American literary journals occasionally feature 'Pacific' issues (for example, *Meanjin* 4, 1990; *Manoa* 1, 1975); in the main, Australian journals focus on Melanesia, and the USA and New Zealand on Polynesia.

Emigration, academia, and monograph publishing opportunities have contributed to the death of current journals in the region.

YONI RYAN

LITERARY MAGAZINES (Sri Lanka)

A significant tradition of literary magazines in Sri Lanka began only in the 1940s with the spread of the critical standards of the department of English of the University of Ceylon. Graduates in English, supported by those in other disciplines, founded journals such as *Harvest* (1945–7), *Symposium* (1948–50), *Points of View* (1952), *Community* (1954–8; 1962–3), and *Sankha* (1958) with a 'passion for diffusing . . . the best knowledge, the best ideas of the time' in the fields of European literature and culture. Although the contributions on specifically Sri Lankan topics were meagre, these journals helped to create a climate for writing in English by Sri Lankans.

In 1956, eight years after independence, English was displaced from its pre-eminent position as the official language and as the medium of instruction in schools and universities. The politics of language undermined intellectual and cultural life. In this context, Dick Hensman and Pauline Hensman established the Community Institute in the 1960s and revived the journal *Community*. Their focus became Sri Lanka and its literature, as well as other aspects of national life such as the public service. They reasserted standards and liberalism. Their efforts, however, were short-lived; the journal lasted only from 1962 to 1963.

Their ideals inspired **Yasmine Gooneratne** and Merlin Peiris to launch *New Ceylon Writing* (1970–). *NCW*, however, was conceived as a literary journal and included much more creative writing than its predecessors. With Gooneratne's departure to Australia in 1972, publication became irregular. The journal was followed by *Navasilu* (1976–), the journal of the English Association and the Sri Lanka Association for Commonwealth Literature and Language Studies (ACLALS, founded in 1975). More journals have appeared lately — *New Lankan Review* (1983–) and *Channels* (1989–), for example. In a quest to preserve standards, the Sri Lanka ACLALS, with D. C. R. A. Goonetilleke as founder-editor, launched a new journal, *Phoenix*, in 1990.

The publication of undergraduate magazines primarily concerned with creative work began with the University of Ceylon's *Poetry Peradeniya* (1957–63) and continued with the University of Kelaniya's *Blink* in 1982 and the University of Peradeniya's *Kaduwa* in 1983.

These literary magazines have established a critical tradition without which Sri Lankan literature in English could not have blossomed. Increasingly they have published creative work and thereby encouraged it.

D. C. R. A. GOONETILLEKE

LITERARY MAGAZINES (West Africa)

The work of many leading West African writers was first published in literary periodicals, cultural periodicals with literary supplements or sections, and students' magazines, most of which were or are still published in Nigeria. The earliest student magazine in Nigeria, *University Herald*, began publishing in 1948, when the University College, Ibadan, was founded; it was followed by *The Horn.* These magazines provided budding writers of the 'Ibadan School' with early opportunities for expressing and developing their creativity. *University Herald*, run by the editorial board of the Magazine Club, published short fiction, poetry, and essays. Some of the student contributors, such as its one-time editor **Chinua Achebe**, the advertisement manager Mabel Imoukhuede (now **Mabel Segun**), **Christopher Okigbo**, and **Vincent Chukwuemeka Ike**, have attained prominence in the literary world. *The Horn*, a poetry quarterly run by students of the English Department, produced a rich harvest of poets before it ceased publication in the mid-1960s. Its first editor was J. P. Clark (**Bekederemo**) and the main contributors included the 1986 Nobel Laureate **Wole Soyinka, Christopher Okigbo**, and two of the current best critics in West Africa — Abiola Irele and Emmanuel Obiechina. In 1960, selections from *Horn*, including the pioneer pidgin English poem 'One Wife for One Man' by Frank Aig-Imoukhuede, were published as *Nigerian Students Verse*.

Black Orpheus, the first widely circulating periodical of black writing to appear in the subregion, began publishing in 1957 with Ulli Beier and Janheinz Jahn as founding editors. Later editors included **Es'kia Mphahlele**, Soyinka, Irele, and Clark. Between 1976 and 1980, the journal lay dormant, but it was revived at the University of Lagos in 1981 with Theo Vincent as editor. Now published at irregular intervals, it was for many years the most important organ of literary expression in Africa, with its formidable list of contributors from West, Central, and Southern Africa as well as from the diaspora. *Black Orpheus* publishes fiction, drama, and poetry and also covers music, painting, sculpture, and other art forms.

African Literature Today, an influential periodical published by Heinemann of London, England, is edited in West Africa by Eldred Jones. Its first four issues appeared between 1968 and 1970, but it is now published as an annual survey. Achebe, **Ayi Kwei Armah**, Mongo Beti, **Kwesi Brew**, and Soyinka are some of the writers represented in articles and review. *Nigeria Magazine*, a quarterly cultural periodical founded in 1927 by the Nigerian government, is still flourishing, although it appeared irregularly for a short period in the 1980s. Through the decades its literary supplement has given considerable exposure to poets, novelists, and dramatists.

Most academic literary journals in the subregion tend to be short-lived. One of the longest surviving was *Ibadan*, published by Ibadan University Press from 1959 to 1971. One of the earliest was *Okyeame*, founded in 1964 by the Writers Workshop of the University of Ghana's Institute of African Studies and edited by **Efua Sutherland**. The period 1971–91 saw the birth of a number of academic literary journals in Nigeria: *Opon Ifa* and the *Review of English and Literary Studies* at Ibadan, *Ife Studies in African Literature and the Arts* (*ISALA*) and *Sokoti* at Ife, *Positive Review* from the Ibadan-Ife axis, *Kiabara* at Port Harcourt, *Benin Review*, Ahmadu Bello's *SIAWA Roots* and *Work-in-Progress*, and *Nsukka Studies* at the University of Nigeria. Only the last is still publishing.

Amid the shambles of fallen literary magazines, *Okike*, *Journal of African New Writing*, founded by Chinua Achebe in the aftermath of the

Nigerian Civil War (1967–70), celebrated its twentieth anniversary in 1991. Its considerable success can be attributed to administrative and management policies that ensure quality and continuity in the membership of its international editorial board. *Okike* publishes essays, short fiction, poetry, book reviews, and occasional art work. Most of the well-known African writers and critics as well as new writers have been featured in its pages. *Okike* encourages experimental writing and has established new critical standards for authentic African literature. Although the magazine was conceived of as having three issues per year, it was only able to publish thirty issues in twenty years. But this is an achievement in view of the financial and production difficulties it has faced.

Achebe seems to possess a magic touch. The **Association of Nigerian Authors** (ANA), which he founded in 1981, has not only blossomed into a nation-wide organization, but it also publishes an annual *ANA Review*, whose contents are magazine-oriented although it has the format of a newspaper. Some branches of ANA also publish periodicals.

Only one journal of criticism of children's literature is published in the subregion: *Journal of African Children's and Youth Literature* (*JACYL*), formerly *JACL*, based in Nigeria. Two issues have appeared to date — the first in 1989, the second in 1992.

Children's magazines published in the subregion, like adult magazines, have a high rate of attrition. The pioneer Nigerian *Children's Own Paper*, later renamed *Young Nigeria*, founded by the government in 1944, as well as private enterprise magazines such as *Apollo*, *Playtime*, *Pop and Powerman*, *Kiddie Times*, *Vona*, *Babisco*, *Bazukka*, and *First Magazine* have all passed into oblivion. Three surviving magazines are *Asha*, a teenage magazine, *Binta*, and *Young Ones*, which lays emphasis on school work. Children's magazines have largely been replaced by newspaper and magazine 'corners' and pages, a notion pioneered by the long-running *Daily Times* and the lavishly illustrated but short-lived *New Culture Magazine*.

Back numbers of adult magazines can be found in major university libraries and in some public libraries that maintain sizeable African literature collections. Back numbers of some of the children's magazines are in the archives of the University of Ibadan Library and the Children's Literature Documentation and Research Centre, Ibadan.

MABEL SEGUN

Further reading: Bernth Lindfors, *A Bibliography of Literary Contributions to Nigerian Periodicals 1946–1972* (1975); Hans Zell *et al.*, *A New Reader's Guide to African Literature* (2nd ed., 1981).

LITERARY ORGANIZATIONS (Australia)

Throughout Australia's history there have been writers' clubs and societies that generally combined literary activity with conviviality. Perhaps the most famous of these in the nineteenth century was the Yorick Club, founded by F. W. Haddon in 1868, which included **Adam Lindsay Gordon** and **Marcus Clarke**. The Stenhouse circle in Sydney was less a formal organization than an extensive personal library and an enlightened host, N. D. Stenhouse, who provided financial and moral support to writers such as **Charles Harpur** and **Henry Kendall**. Other groups and associations developed throughout Australia, often associated with Mechanics' Institutes and Schools of Arts; there were German language literary and cultural associations in areas of intensive settlement such as Queensland and South Australia.

In recent years, however, nationally based literary organizations have achieved far greater importance and influence. These are the Australian Society of Authors (ASA), the Australian Writers' Guild (AWG), and the Fellowship of Australian Writers (FAW). The ASA was founded in 1963 to promote and protect the professional interests of writers. It focuses on protection and negotiation of rights for its members; it was closely associated with the lobbying for and eventual adoption of the Public Lending Right scheme that was passed through Parliament in 1976. It also invested heavily, both in capital and promotion, in the Copyright Agency Ltd, which was authorized by the federal government in 1987 to collect photocopying royalty fees from educational institutions for distribution to copyright holders. The ASA produces regular newsletters and a quarterly journal, *The Australian Author*. It has published books and occasional papers of professional interest, and its recommended anthology rates are accepted by the **Literature Board** and most publishers as the standard for negotiation.

The Australian Writers' Guild, founded in 1961 as a 'trade union for script-writers of television, radio, screen, and stage', has become a successful negotiator on behalf of its members. It publishes a monthly journal for members, *Viewpoint*, and presents a well-publicized annual series of Awgie Awards for the best scripts in film, stage, radio, and television as well as specific awards for excellence.

The Fellowship of Australian Writers began as a Sydney-based association founded by **Mary Gilmore** and Roderic Quinn, with J. le Gay Brereton as first president, in 1928; branches were established in other states. In 1955 a federal council was formed, and since then the national presidency rotates among state presidents. The FAW in the various states has fluctuated in activity, largely depending on the calibre of its committees. It has been of particular value to new and beginning writers, and its social functions are an important component in maintaining membership and activities. The Western Australia branch is situated in Tom Collins House, bequeathed to it by **Joseph Furphy**'s son in 1948. In Victoria the FAW administers an important series of literary awards annually. In the 1930s the FAW was influential in causing the government to expand the activities of the Commonwealth Literary Fund.

In the 1980s a new concept in literary organizations developed, the establishment of 'writers' centres'. These have been associated with buildings specifically designed to offer not only a meeting place for writers, but also facilities such as photocopying, fax, and computer access, and for activities such as book launches, workshops, seminars, and conferences. The Literature Board has assisted in the establishment and running of such writers' centres through co-funding, with state governments, the administration costs as well as certain project costs. Victoria, South Australia, and Queensland have established such centres, and New South Wales (NSW) and Western Australia (WA) are (1990) negotiating similar projects.

A further development, a variant on the writers' centre concept, has been the establishment of the Katharine Susannah Prichard Foundation (WA) and the Eleanor Dark Varuna Foundation (NSW), where a specific writer's house has been converted to a venue for writers' residencies as well as meetings, workshops, and other literary activities. State government funding has been essential in both these developments, which also depend on the involvement of an active literary support organization. There are smaller literary organizations such as the Society of Women Writers (Australia), branches of PEN International, and the Poets' Union, which have variously flourished or stagnated, depending largely on the energy of individual committees and members. Other organizations include writers in their activities. For example, the National Book Council, which has a major programme of writers' tours, hosts the annual NBC Banjo literary awards.

THOMAS SHAPCOTT

LITERARY ORGANIZATIONS (New Zealand)
The New Zealand Centre of PEN was established in 1934. Like its counterparts elsewhere, it combines universal ideals with the more practical work

of a writers' union — looking after the general literary interests of its members. The *PEN Gazette* was published from 1937 to 1989. The Centre has occasionally organized literary conferences, but its most significant public achievement was its important part in the representations made to government that led to the establishment of the New Zealand Literary Fund. Although its members must be recognized writers, PEN (New Zealand) founded the Young Writers' Incentive Award in 1972, now open to writers of prose and poetry and awarded annually.

The New Zealand Women Writers' Society was established in 1932. Full membership required three published books, but publication in magazines — the major outlet for New Zealand women's writing — was also recognized. The Society dissolved in 1991, the current healthy demand for women's writing having lessened the need for active membership. Appropriately, activities (largely of a promotional nature) are now centred on an annual Women's Book Festival.

Playwrights are well served by Playmarket (Wellington), which from 1973 has provided expert advice on all playscripts submitted to it. The organization runs biennial workshops at which professional actors, directors, and dramaturgs work on selected scripts, and it also acts as playwrights' agent in placing scripts in theatres. The New Zealand Writers' Guild (Wellington) is essentially a trade union for film and television scriptwriters.

The Book Publishers Association of New Zealand (Auckland) concerns itself with books published overseas as well as with the interests of New Zealand book publishers. It has established three divisions: educational and professional, general, and New Zealand publishing. Booksellers New Zealand (Wellington), formerly the Booksellers' Association of New Zealand, is no longer essentially a trade association. Its focus is almost exclusively on marketing, and membership is open to publishers as well as booksellers. The New Zealand Book Council (Wellington) promotes interest in good writing, arranges lectures on literary matters, sends writers on visits to schools, and hosts British Council visitors.

The Children's Literature Association of New Zealand (Auckland), established in 1969, has strongly influenced public awareness of current writing for children through its various promotional activities and especially through the work of its children's librarian members. The Children's Book Foundation (Auckland) is more closely associated with publishers. (See also **Patronage**, New Zealand.)

JOHN THOMSON

LITERATURE BOARD (Australia)

One of five separate boards of the Australian government's arts-funding statutory authority, the **Australia Council**, the Literature Board (in 1990) consists of five members and a chairperson who normally serve for three years; Board members are selected to cover literary interests, regional distribution, gender, and ethnic balance. In 1990–1 the funds allocated to the Board for distribution were four million Australian dollars. Approximately fifty per cent of these funds go to individual writers by means of fellowships and grants for ongoing writing projects. Formed in 1973, the Board took over the functions of the Commonwealth Literary Fund (CLF), founded in 1908 as the first arts support scheme of the Commonwealth government.

The Board's substantial achievement is in its writers' grants, which have, over a period, underpinned the initial careers of many writers; it has also offered crucial mid-career support for writers. Approximately one hundred fellowships are awarded annually, for one, two, or three-year periods. Through its system of Emeritus Fellowships, offered to some twenty older writers as a life pension, it, alone of boards in the Australia Council, provides a financial support system that honours lifelong contributions to literature. The Board initiated in 1974 a system of writers-in-residence, co-funded with tertiary institutions in Australia, generally for nine- or twelve-week terms. These have subsequently been extended to residencies in other community contexts.

The Board inherited from the CLF a 'guarantee against loss' subsidy scheme to encourage publishers in Australia to produce books of cultural importance that, in the short term, might be of financial risk. This scheme was replaced by a 'per page' outright subsidy to publishers, and some one hundred books a year are thus supported, priority being given to first novels, collections of short stories, verse, and playscripts, as well as non-fiction books of cultural value. In the 1970s the majority of Australian-produced books of fiction, poetry, and drama received such subsidies. By the late 1980s, however, the dramatic increase in Australian support of its own published titles has meant that Literature Board publishing subsidies now cover only the innovative and risk-taking end of publishing ventures. Some 150 publishers are registered with the Board, most of them small regional presses. (See also **Publishing**, Australia.)

The Board has been the substantial sponsor of literary magazines in Australia since its inception; this is a continuing policy priority. Its support of literary festivals was an active factor in the remarkable blossoming of such occasions in the 1980s. The Adelaide Festival Writers' Week, held biennially, has become a major international event. In accordance with the Australia Council's support of Australia as a multicultural society, the Board has given encouragement to writers and audiences in languages other than English, including fellowships, publishing subsidies, workshops, readings, and visits from international authors, as well as translation subsidies. International projects — the appointment of a literary publicist in New York, USA, and **Nancy Keesing**'s endowment of a studio for writers in Paris, France, for example — have been a notable aspect of the Board's work in the 1980s. Support of international exchanges and writers' tours has included the Canada/Australia exchange, the New Zealand/Australia exchange, and major writers' tours of France, the USA, Canada, and countries in Europe and Asia.

A 'brief history' of the Literature Board was published in 1988 by **Thomas Shapcott**, the then director.

THOMAS SHAPCOTT

LIVESAY, DOROTHY (1909–)

Canadian poet

Born in Winnipeg, Canada, to journalist parents who nurtured her literary talents, she was shaped by the Prairies' freedom and multi-ethnicity. The family moved east to conservative, colonial Ontario, where Livesay earned a BA degree in modern languages at the University of Toronto (1931). After receiving a *Diplôme d'études supérieures* at the Sorbonne, France, with a thesis on contemporary British poetry (1932), Livesay, shocked by the Great Depression, rejected many of her England-born father's élitist ideas to become a Marxist and a social worker in Toronto, Montreal, New Jersey, USA, and finally Vancouver. There she married political comrade Duncan Macnair (1937) and had two children. Active in politicized cultural circles and leftist publications in the late 1930s and 1940s, Livesay spent two postwar decades primarily in teaching, direction of adult education programmes, journalism, and other creative writing, in Canada, Europe, and Africa. Livesay has been writer-in-residence at many Canadian universities; she has travelled, published, and lectured extensively. She founded and edited the literary journal *CV II* (1975), nurtured many writers both individually and by editing anthologies, and worked for numerous social, cultural, and environmental causes. Since 1928 Livesay has published more than two dozen volumes of poetry and prose and many hundreds of articles, reviews, short stories, poems, and letters. She has also won numerous awards and distinctions, including a Canadian Authors' Association poetry prize in 1928, two Governor General's Awards for Poetry (1944, 1947), and the Order of Canada (1987), as well as several honorary doctorates.

Livesay's early poetry derived from her immediate worlds of nature and emotion. Precise, spare, introspective, it resembles the imagist verse of American Amy Lowell and Briton Hilda Doolittle (H.D.). During the Depression Livesay came to think such verse socially irrelevant, and, unsatisfied, she ventured into the areas of agitprop drama, exhortatory prose, and proletarian short stories before new literary models — Stephen Spender, W. H. Auden, C. Day Lewis — showed her how to reconcile her social and lyrical impulses. Such powerful poems as 'Day and Night' (1936) go beyond their English models, however, in their combinations of industrial, jazz, and black spiritual rhythms, as well as in their effectively decentring use of multiple voices.

In the 1940s Livesay addressed the plight of minorities such as Japanese Canadians and the Métis of the Prairies; seizing the potential of radio, she composed such verse dramas as 'Call My People Home', first broadcast by the CBC and published in 1949 and reprinted as the title poem of *Call My People Home and Other Poems* (1950). Livesay's poetry also broke ground in its concern with both women's contemporary experience, particularly conflicts of marriage, motherhood, and professional career, and with the neglected perspectives of children. These poems were followed in the 1950s by a cerebral, abstract, increasingly sad voice, until widowhood (1959) freed her to travel and teach in Africa (1960–3). Zambia provided the pounding rhythms and elemental imagery that inspired a flood of poetry; the sexual and emotional honesty of *The Unquiet Bed* (1967) and *Plainsongs* (1969) was stunning to conservative Canada. Returning from another society — tightly organic, oral, and deeply expressive, flushed with new nationhood — had also sharpened her eye for the problems with inhibited, divided, inward-looking Canada. Livesay offered, through verse and essays, rich glimpses of another world, as well as challenges to smug white Anglo-saxon myopia, ageism, racism, and puritanism. In her concerns and their execution she invites comparison with Australian poet and playwright **Dorothy Hewett**.

Since the late 1970s Livesay has concentrated upon three thematic areas: the faces/phases of love; old age; and the endangered condition of the world in environmental, social, and spiritual terms. She continues to reject simplistic solutions or safe stances, and to argue unceasingly the importance of openness to 'Other' (species, cultures, ideas, experiences). In all her poetry, as Livesay herself noted in her preface to the superb *Collected Poems: The Two Seasons* (1972), images recur of house and bed, flower and bird, sun and rain, wind and snow; and in all her writing an ecumenical and humanist spirit and a singing voice prevail.

Livesay's early ambition to excel in prose has repeatedly resurfaced, most recently in a novella, *The Husband* (1990), and a memoir, *Journey With My Selves* (1991). However, as demonstrated by *The Self-Completing Tree* (1986), poetry continues to be the source of her acclaim as one of Canada's finest writers.

LEE BRISCOE THOMPSON

Further reading: Lee Briscoe Thompson, *Dorothy Livesay* (1987).

LIVINGSTONE, DOUGLAS JAMES (1932–)
South African poet, dramatist
Born of Scottish parents in Kuala Lumpur, Malaya, he moved to South Africa at the age of ten and, after completing his schooling near Durban, trained as a bacteriologist in what was then southern Rhodesia (now Zimbabwe). After five years of laboratory work in northern Rhodesia and during the period of Zambian independence, Livingstone left the copper belt and in 1964 returned to Dur-

ban, where he was in charge of marine bacteriological research at a water-research institute. A respected scientist in his field, Livingstone retired from the institute in 1992 and continues to act as a consultant.

In the thirty years since his poems began to appear in literary journals in England and South Africa, Livingstone has published six collections of poetry. His work has also appeared with that of Thomas Kinsella and Anne Sexton in their joint collection *Poems* (1968); with Phillippa Berlyn he translated a number of Shona poems in various literary magazines (see, particularly, 'Eight Shona Poems' in *London Magazine* 10, 1965). A verse play, *The Sea My Winding Sheet* (1971; also in *Theatre One*, 1978, edited by **Stephen Gray**), was followed by two prose plays — *A Rhino for the Boardroom* (in *Contemporary South African Plays*, 1977, edited by Ernest Pereira) and *The Semblance of the Real* (in *Modern Stage Directions*, 1984, edited by Stephen Gray and David Schalkwyk).

Holding honorary doctorates in literature from the universities of Natal and Rhodes, Livingstone is the recipient of several important awards in the UK and South Africa, including South Africa's premier CNA (Central News Agency) Prize for his *Selected Poems* (1984). Recognized by several influential critics as South Africa's leading contemporary poet, Livingstone is regarded by others as 'insufficiently political' to be really significant in the volatile socio-political climate of South Africa.

Written while he was living in Rhodesia, Livingstone's first two poetry collections, *The Skull in the Mud* (1960) and the more substantial *Sjambok and Other Poems from Africa* (1964), focus on aspects of modern life as well as on circumstances in southern Africa that have continued to define his preoccupations and scope: personal isolation and the need for love; religious crisis in an age of science; the veld as a site of struggle in the animal world; the dislocations of transition consequent upon decolonization. The animal poems, with their human analogies, immediately struck readers and critics alike as 'utterly new', and Livingstone has displayed consistently his salient strengths of verbal invention within disciplined metrical and rhyming patterns. Several of his poems utilize animals and the bush as metaphors of human behaviour in uncompromising, almost existential situations, as in 'Stormshelter' (in *Sjambok and Other Poems from Africa*):

> Under the baobab tree, treaded
> death, stroked in by the musty cats,
> scratches silver on fleshy earth.
> . . . .
> Steel spears, slim, yielding and stained
> lightly with water, rattle their points.
> Jointed the hafts swing, tufted brightly,
> maiming invisibly. The shafts reel
> through the streaked Impi from Nowhere.
> There is only one thing to do —
> wheel, stamping, into that brittle rain.

Livingstone's inheritance is modernist: metaphors of complexity and structural principles of juxtaposition predominate over the plain-speaking voice. In reaching towards 'internationalism', especially in the collection *Eyes Closed against the Sun* (1970), Livingstone seeks out the redeeming moment, the enriching fragment, the mythic synthesis amid the detritus of urban experience. *A Rosary of Bone* (1975) explores sexual attraction in a variety of styles so that the collection is as much about the making of poetry as about the making of love. Some may see the overriding theme of these poems as 'masculinity', in which case Livingstone is fair game for feminist critics. Such concerns are emphasized in the selection of his poetry in Italian translation, *Il Sonno Dei Miei Leoni* (1992), translated by Marco Fazzini.

Livingstone's work, however, has never lost connection with southern African reference, and he has remarked that the challenges of living in South

Africa have sometimes made him feel remote, not only from any sense of 'Commonwealth poetry', but from wider debates in English poetry. It is not only that his settings are geographically African, it is also that his concerns take their power and accent from South African localities. In reacting to the 'wind of change' in the early 1960s, for example, Livingstone debunked the heroic image of the colonial hunter while remaining wary of cries of Uhuru ('revolution'). *The Anvil's Undertone* (1978) captures, sometimes directly, at other times subliminally, the crisis of the 'Soweto' years of the 1970s. In responding to the rise of Black Consciousness poets, Livingstone spoke of their rhetoric as lacking form, and in poems such as 'Under Capricorn' (in *The Anvil's Undertone*) he shaped his own intimations of 'living in the interregnum' into allusive evocations of his dilemma both as an individual — what is my role as a white person at a time of massive political action? — and as a poet — can 'art' survive the demands that poetry be a weapon of the struggle?

Livingstone refuses to regard himself as a political poet. Nevertheless, the context of political crisis in the 1970s and 1980s dictated the kind of political criticism that has resulted in ideological rereadings of South African poetry. In a heated debate about 'politics' and 'aesthetics', Livingstone has been both praised as a poet who has remained untendentious and condemned as a poet who has resisted the challenge of political accountability. A more useful approach might be a revisionist one, reading not only Livingstone's commitments but also his ambiguities as indices of what it means to be a 'white African'. The insights gained are rewarding and disturbing: in Livingstone's poetry 'European' values grate against 'African' demands, and a hesitant search for common decency across racial barriers threatens to founder on the scientist's measure of a continent trapped in ignorance and poverty. Livingstone's perceptions offer little comfort to idealizing Africanists or utopian Marxists.

During the state of emergency in the 1980s, Livingstone published very few poems: it was as though silence were his authentic response to the trauma of the times. He continued to write, however, and *A Littoral Zone* appeared in 1991. This is a strong, dense sequence of poems that evinces a 'radical' turning away from the political question to that of human life evolving from the prehistory of an elemental Africa. Sea, sand, and rock are the deep constants against which the poet places the sometimes strident, more often vulnerable, participants in the current human scene, as in 'The Christmas Chefs of Station 1a':

> The mess on the sand incredible:
> scraps, vomit and cartons abound.
> Most redolent of Decembers!
> Here, one has out-sphinctered a newt.
> The approximation to justice,
> the perfectibility of man,
> the conservation of beauty,
> the final attainment of truth
> are salients that ever evade us
> part of our yoke in being human;
> the striving still almost a duty
> and part of the joke on our youth.

The 'scientist', the 'poet', the 'modern', the 'white African' intertwine here in metaphysical image and thought. In its exploration of an uneasy divide between humanity's physical and psychic selves, *A Littoral Zone* poses large questions, particularly to South African readers: Is Livingstone quietly ignoring the tremendous human struggles of the 1980s that forced the South African government to relinquish its policies of apartheid? Is he anticipating a post-apartheid concern with ecologies of destruction and creation? Is his unfashionable rejection of the various 'isms' of current literary argument a constricting or a liberating act? Livingstone's 'South Africanness' may yet be identified in the capacity of his poetry to provoke fundamental debate about the responsibility of the poet in a society of extremely narrow tolerances.

MICHAEL CHAPMAN

Further reading: Michael Chapman, *Douglas Livingstone: A Critical Study of his Poetry* (1981); Michael Chapman, 'Douglas Livingstone', in Michael Chapman (ed.) *South African English Poetry: A Modern Perspective* (1984).

LIYONG, TABAN LO (1939–)

Ugandan essayist, poet, short-story writer

He was born in northern Uganda and educated at Gulu High School, Sir Samuel Baker High School, and the National Teachers College, Kampala, Uganda. He did postgraduate studies in the USA, undertaking political science studies at Howard University and Knoxville College, receiving a master of fine arts degree from the University of Iowa's Writer's Workshop. Liyong has held university positions in Nairobi, Kenya, and Papua New Guinea. He has lived for some years at Juba, south Sudan, and is professor at Juba University, Khartoum.

Liyong's stimulating, provocative approach was immediately noticed in the earnest context of post-independence production. He was an important actor on the early literary scene with the famous cry: 'Why the literary barrenness in East Africa?' When the accent was on authenticity — 'do not uproot the old pumpkin', **Okot p'Bitek** had warned — Liyong would quote Nietzsche and Aristotle and feel duty-bound to question the new sacred cows of post-colonial thinking: 'What we need is more irreverence. We must accept changes and produce changes.' His attacks on the nostalgia for negritude ('crying over spilt milk', he said) are similar to **Wole Soyinka**'s reaction at the time. Later, as national identities were being asserted in essentialist terms, he argued, 'African culture is to be a synthesis and a metamorphosis . . . It picks, it grabs, it carries on.'

Liyong is a prolific and versatile writer, but despite the variety of genres he uses, he expresses recurrent concerns. *Eating Chiefs: Lwo Culture from Lolwe to Malkal* (1970) is a collection of traditional texts that attempt to re-create on paper the vitality of orature. In trying to capture in a modern idiom the spirit of this living popular art, Liyong has written short stories, *Fixions and Other Stories* (1969) and *The Uniformed Man* (1971), that are among the best in African literature. At his best, he can combine the laughter of satirical tales and a desperate humour about modern ills, as in 'It's Swallowing' or 'Fixions'. His poetry is also varied, ranging from brief haiku-like forms to narratives that can be in turn witty or sombre. Collections include *Frantz Fanon's Uneven Ribs with Poems More and More* (1971), *Another Nigger Dead* (1972), and *Ballads of Underdevelopment* (1976).

Liyong has developed a form of 'meditations' in series of short texts that are close both to autobiographical fiction and to essays, particularly in *Meditations in Limbo* (1970), enlarged as *Meditations of Taban lo Liyong* (1978); this 'composite, fictionalised, revised life' (Liyong's description) is intensely personal in a way that is unusual in African literature and is at the same time stylized and nearly abstract. Essays, criticism, and polemic articles constitute *The Last Word: Cultural Synthesism* (1969), *Thirteen Offensives Against Our Enemies* (1973), *Another Last Word* (1990), and *Culture Is Rutan* (1991).

With his use of collage and pastiche and his disregard of boundaries between genres, Liyong is sympathetic to postmodern aesthetics. Yet his most satirical and paradoxical pieces express the moral indignation of passionate commitment. Liyong's fragmentary texts make a coherent whole; his distinctive voice, dizzying verbal gusto, and technical range go hand in hand with an intellectual control that has been a stimulating influence in African letters.

J. BARDOLPH

Further reading: Peter Nazareth, 'Bibliyongraphy [*sic*], or six Tabans in search of an author', in G. D. Killam (ed.) *The Writing of East and Central Africa* (1984).

LOCHHEAD, DOUGLAS (1922–)

Canadian poet

Born in Guelph, Ontario, Canada, he received degrees from McGill University and the University of Toronto, which led to a career as university librarian and professor of English at institutions in Canada and the USA. Among them was Massey College, Toronto, where he developed a research library in association with **Robertson Davies**. Between 1975 and retirement in 1987, Lochhead was director of Canadian Studies at Mount Allison University, Sackville, New Brunswick, Canada. He still lives in Sackville, deliberately placing himself in a specific landscape among cultural continuities that he has inherited through his mother's family, the Van Warts, of Fredericton, New Brunswick.

Lochhead is one of the most energetic, unpredictable, assimilative, lyrically sure-footed and, at the moment, critically underestimated poets in Canada. His first two books, *The Heart Is Fire* (1959) and *It Is All Around* (1960), show the influences of Blake, W. B. Yeats, W. H. Auden, Dylan Thomas, and Theodore Roethke. Friendship with **Raymond Souster** helped Lochhead find a looser colloquialism for his mature work, which begins with *Millwood Road: Poems* (1970). In subsequent volumes, most importantly *The Full Furnace: Collected Poems* (1975), *High Marsh Road: Pages from a Diary* (1980), *A & E* (1980), *The Panic Field* (1984), and *Dykelands* (1989), Lochhead has refined his initial metaphysical preoccupations in work that is both accessible and often archetypally nuanced. In these collections, nature and people, love and the poetic imagination, anecdote and the dance of words, simply for the sake of dancing, are elegantly and concisely wrought into coherence. Sometimes Lochhead's poems and prose poems also enact violent, abrupt collisions that imply a latent coherence now lost to the poet's persona because of guilt and emotional ineptitude. Lochhead's later work, especially the prose poems, has been influenced by Geoffrey Hill's *Mercian Hymns* (1971).

Taking a more overtly religious direction, Lochhead's poetry continues to be lyrically innovative in ways that he sees as analogical to, or even identical with, the processes of earth, which he has always intuited as a feminine presence, a source of wisdom, stability, fullness, and change.

PETER SANGER

Further reading: Peter Sanger, *As the Eyes of Lyncaeus: A Celebration for Douglas Lochhead* (1990).

LOCKE, ELSIE (1912–)

New Zealand children's writer, historian

Born Elsie Farrelly in Hamilton, New Zealand, she earned a BA (1933) from Auckland University. Locke witnessed the hardships of unemployment and poverty caused by the Depression and became indignant that any government could support such inequitable social conditions. Her consequent involvement in politics and her interest in history have combined to connect much of her writing to social issues. Women's rights, injustices against the Maori, the need for conservation, and the importance of reconciliation rather than conflict are articulated in much of her work.

In the first and most famous of Locke's six novels for children, *The Runaway Settlers* (1965), a strong-minded nineteenth-century woman leaves her drunken husband in Australia and brings her family to New Zealand. The hardships endured by this working-class family are always overcome by the woman's indomitable spirit, and the book offers a lively and well-researched picture of early Canterbury. Land disputes between Maori and Europeans feature in two later books, *The End of the Harbour* (1968) and *Journey under Warning*

(1983). In both, Locke's careful research occasionally overweighs and impedes the narrative. In *A Canoe in the Mist* (1984), however, the story flows smoothly and research is more lightly worn. Based upon fact, its central episode is the dramatic eruption of Mount Tarawera in 1866, foreshadowed by the sighting of a Maori ghost canoe, and witnessed by two girls who lived in a nearby village.

BETTY GILDERDALE

LOPEZ TIEMPO, EDITH (1919–)

Filipino short-story writer, novelist

Born in Nueva Vizcaya, the Philippines, she grew up in various regions of the country — where her father was assigned provincial treasurer. In 1940 she married **Edilberto K. Tiempo** and moved with him to Dumaguete City, where he taught at Silliman University. After graduating with an education degree, she became an international fellow at the State University of Iowa, USA, where she obtained an MA in English. Another grant enabled her to earn a Ph.D. from the University of Denver, USA, in 1958.

When American New Critic Leonard Casper edited the landmark anthology *Six Modern Poets* (1954), he included Lopez Tiempo as the only woman in the group. Since then, she has written an impressive body of poems, collected in two volumes, *Tracks of Babylon and Other Poems* (1966) and *Charmer's Box* (1993). Though she has written short fiction (*Abide, Joshua, and Other Stories*, 1964) and three novels (*A Blade of Fern*, 1978, *His Native Coast*, 1979, *The Alien Corn*, 1992) — all of which have been well received — she is most highly regarded for her poetry. She has been a deep influence on the younger generation of poets, all of whom acknowledge the precision and polish that characterize her craftsmanship.

Criticized at times for not writing in her vernacular language, Lopez Tiempo firmly points out that while the introduction of English was 'mostly an accident of history . . . [it] is our language too'. A firm believer in the tenets of Formalism, she is regarded by some contemporary critics as too conservative in both her literary theory and practice. She herself is secure about her position: 'Many people have remarked that my poems, both early and late, all exhibit this influence [of the Romantic tradition]; if a women is true to herself, she will write as a Romantic.'

In 1962 Lopez Tiempo and her husband organized and directed the Silliman University National Summer Writers Workshop, which continues to the present and counts among its alumni most of the country's outstanding writers. An educator who has occupied various administrative posts at Silliman University, Lopez Tiempo has been an exchange visiting professor at several institutions outside the Philippines.

EDNA ZAPANTA MANLAPAZ

LOUKAKIS, ANGELO (1951–)

Australian short-story writer, novelist

Born in Sydney, Australia, of Cretan parents, he has published in English and Greek. He has worked as a teacher, multicultural education officer, welfare officer, and journalist. His first collection of stories, *For the Patriarch* (1981), won the 1981 New South Wales Premier's Literary Award. The film based on his story 'Dancing' was awarded a prize at the Melbourne Film Festival, 1980. Loukakis has been awarded several writers' grants and has recently worked in theatre and script-writing. His second collection, *Vernacular Dreams*, appeared in 1986, and his first novel, *Messenger*, in 1992.

Loukakis' work is primarily concerned with representing the positions of mediation occupied by those second-generation Australians, often Greek, who are caught between the prevailing culture and that of parents whose rituals and languages derive from somewhere designated 'alien' in relation to the public culture. His first story, 'The Boxer and the Grocer', appeared in *Meanjin* in 1976, but probably his most anthologized story is 'Barbecue', in which the narrator is an Australian of Greek extraction who has acquired the necessary accessories of a comfortable middle-class life-style but begins to question his willingness to live out the stereotypes imposed on him by well-meaning friends. Meditating on the contradictions in his life while he is preparing 'authentic' Greek food for his friends gathered for a barbecue, he suddenly decides he needs to shed the various pretensions and expectations to which he is conforming for the sake of others rather than himself. The story ends with the narrator swimming away from all of them, including his Australian wife, at least temporarily.

SNEJA GUNEW

Further reading: George Kanarakis, ed., *Greek Voices in Australia: A Tradition of Prose, Poetry and Drama* (1987).

LOVELACE, EARL (1935–)

Trinidadian novelist, short-story writer

He was born in Toco, Trinidad, but grew up in Tobago with his mother's parents. He attended elementary school in Tobago and high school in Trinidad. During 1953–4 he worked as proof-reader for a daily newspaper, the *Trinidad Guardian*. From 1956 to 1966 he became a field assistant in the department of forestry and later agricultural assistant in the department of agriculture. Between 1961 and 1962 Lovelace studied at the Eastern Caribbean Institute of Agriculture and Forestry. From 1966 to 1967 he studied in the USA at Howard University. He spent a further two years at the University of the District of Columbia and at Johns Hopkins University, where he received an MA in English. In 1977 he was appointed to the English Department at the University of the West Indies to teach literature and creative writing. Lovelace won a Guggenheim Fellowship that took him to the International Writing Program at the University of Iowa, USA, in 1980, and the next year to the International Seminar Program for the Eastern Virginia International Studies consortium. In 1986 he received a National Endowment for the Humanities grant to become writer-in-residence at Hartwick College, Oneonta, New York.

In 1964 Lovelace's first novel, *While Gods Are Falling* (1965), won the British Petroleum Independence Literary Award. *The Schoolmaster*, his second novel, appeared in 1968. From 1967 to 1971, apart from fiction, Lovelace wrote editorials, articles, and reviews for another newspaper, the *Trinidad and Tobago Express*. His third novel, *The Dragon Can't Dance*, was published in 1979 (republished 1981), although it was written after *The Wine of Astonishment*, which appeared in 1982 (republished in 1984).

A volume of stories, *A Brief Conversation and Other Stories*, appeared in 1988. Lovelace also wrote several plays, some of which were collected in *Jestina's Calypso and Other Plays* (1984). Adaptations of *The Dragon Can't Dance* and *The Wine of Astonishment* were also performed as plays in Trinidad.

While Gods Are Falling introduces Lovelace's fundamental theme of regeneration from the adverse social and psychological effects of colonial rule in the Caribbean. This is seen in the experience of Walter Castle, who lives in the town of Port of Spain and is surrounded by the poverty, chaos, and fragmentation that have been produced by centuries of colonial exploitation and oppression in Trinidad. Walter's surname has the ironic force of the title of **George Lamming**'s novel *In the Castle of My Skin* (1953), in which the main character is also surrounded by poverty and disorder despite the dubious protection afforded in the castle of his black skin. Even if Walter is unable to achieve cohesion of the various social factions around him, his efforts confirm his struggle to achieve re-integration out of colonial fragmentation.

The Schoolmaster moves away from the grim social realities of urban Trinidad to the more peaceful, pastoral setting of Kumaca in rural Trinidad. But a plan to build a road that might bring the benefits of modernization and economic progress to Kumaca threatens the settled, traditional values of the village. Supporters of the plan are seen as hostile to Kumaca, as exemplified in the schoolmaster, a newcomer to the village who, at the novel's end, is revealed as responsible for the pregnancy of Christiana, an unmarried young woman who dies in tragic circumstances. The message is that genuine change cannot be attained without regeneration and that regeneration must be based on communal values.

The Dragon Can't Dance returns to the slums of Port of Spain, where Aldrick Prospect plays the carnival dragon figure whose dancing serves as a central metaphor for achieving what the author calls 'personhood' — an awareness of one's humanity and inner resources for surviving and prevailing over problems. In trying to prevail over the sordid conditions in which they live, some characters in *The Dragon Can't Dance* resort to violence and confrontation with the police. They are eventually defeated because their efforts to achieve personhood are not grounded in the healing power of communal values. *The Dragon Can't Dance* is a complex novel with characters representing different social problems, for example, Dolly and Pariag, the Indian couple, who are marginalized in Trinidad society, and Fisheye and Yvonne, who register an underlying conflict between country and city life. But the failed effort to achieve personhood and solve social problems is paramount.

The Wine of Astonishment deals with the persecution of a religious group, the Spiritual Baptists in Trinidad, in the early decades of the twentieth century. The stick-fighter Bolo represents the interests of his community, but he turns against it when it does not support his resistance to the colonial authorities. Bolo's fellow villagers decide to kill him, but they also realize that his misguided efforts have stimulated them to assert their own hidden resources and abilities to resist injustice. One interesting feature of *The Wine of Astonishment* is the first-person narrative in the voice of Eva, whose feminine perspective and peasant sensibility constitute a powerful resource for genuine change.

Jestina's Calypso is about a woman's efforts to find a marriage partner. Jestina sends a male correspondent and prospective husband a picture of Laura, her neighbour, who is more light-skinned than herself. This creates complications that can only be resolved by more widespread acceptance of a broader definition of female beauty, especially by black men.

Altogether, Lovelace successfully evokes the mixed quality of life that the majority of Trinidadians have inherited from colonial rule. His stories do not flinch from reporting these harsh postcolonial conditions, but they also suggest the need for regeneration and the necessity of acquiring personhood based on communal solidarity; but this generally proves elusive in Lovelace's books. Yet the possibility of achieving personhood persists, and it is this fact — of the persistent possibility — that lends a somewhat idealistic tone to Lovelace's fiction and probably explains why his novels are so highly regarded in the Caribbean.

FRANK M. BIRBALSINGH

Further reading: Norman Reed Cary, 'Salvation, self, and solidarity in the work of Earl Lovelace', *World Literature Written in English* 1 (1988).

LOWER, LENNIE (1903–47)
Australian humorist, novelist
One of Australia's leading humorists throughout the 1930s and 1940s, he was born in Dubbo, New South Wales, Australia, and educated in Sydney. He enlisted in the army in 1920 and the navy in 1922, deserting from each in turn. After several years carrying his swag through Queensland and New South Wales, Lower returned to Sydney. He married Phyllis Salter in 1929, having launched his

journalistic career by joining the *Labor Daily* in 1928. He later worked for the *Daily Guardian* and its associate *Smith's Weekly*, moving to the *Daily Telegraph, Sunday Telegraph, Australian Woman's Weekly*, and, ultimately, *Smith's Weekly*, where he remained until his death. Collections of his comic sketches were published during his lifetime and after.

Lower's writing is characterized by vernacular idiom, punning, and a linguistic exuberance that often expands into absurdist fantasy. Much of his work presents a contrast between the world of male solidarity focused on sporting events and pubs — Lower's own drinking exploits were legendary — and the world of domestic suburbia. Home becomes a prison where male freedom languishes under rigorous wifely control, and Lower envisions innumerable grotesque but ultimately ineffectual disruptions to domestic order. While his writing satirizes social pretension and the conformist pressures of suburban living, it also reveals, in **Kylie Tennant**'s words, 'the brutality and masculinity of the Australia of that period'.

In Lower's only novel, *Here's Luck* (1930), which has been reprinted many times, the middle-aged hero, Jack Gudgeon, freed by the departure of his wife, Agatha, forms a precarious alliance against the forces of order and respectability with his teenage son, Stanley, participating in an endless round of drunken binges that steadily demolish the family home, where woman's presence is both longed for and deeply resented. Episodes of anarchy and disorder proliferate, many of them very funny, but no real or lasting change occurs; with Agatha's return at the end of the book, there is a strong suggestion that steady family life will be restored.

DOROTHY JONES

Further reading: Keith Willey, *You Might As Well Laugh, Mate: Australian Humour in Hard Times* (1984).

LOYALISTS (Canada)

At the end of the American Revolution (1775–83), approximately 100,000 civilians and soldiers who had supported the British Crown went into exile from the USA. Representing a cross-section of religious and ethnic backgrounds, these 'Tories' or 'Loyalists' also included black slaves, freedmen, and Iroquois from the Six Nations. While the exiles reflected a significant proportion of the American professional and merchant class and included the survivors of the 19,000 who had served in Loyalist military corps, the vast majority of Loyalists were ordinary farmers, tradesmen, and artisans. Before the end of the conflict, Loyalists had found themselves increasingly subject to mob violence, imprisonment, the confiscation of their property, and physical relocation. New York City had become their last major stronghold, and it was from there that some 50,000 refugees sailed to Britain, the Caribbean, or British North America (Canada) in 1783. Loyalists from Georgia and South Carolina who had taken refuge in Florida in 1782 proceeded to the Bahamas between 1783 and 1785 after the Treaty of Versailles (1783) restored Florida to Spain.

Between 1779 and 1783, approximately 40,000 Loyalists moved to Canada, the majority (30,000) to what are now the maritime provinces. The impact of this mass influx led to the formation of the new provinces of New Brunswick (1784) and Upper Canada (1791, now Ontario). The Mohawks, who felt that the British had sold them out to Congress at the conclusion of the war, settled with their Chief, Joseph Brant, on the Six Nations Reserve near present-day Brantford, Ontario. The 3,000 black Loyalists who went to Nova Scotia experienced broken promises and racial tension. Under the guidance of leaders such as Thomas Peters, formerly a sergeant in the Black Pioneers, and the philanthropic Sierra Leone Company of London, 1,200 blacks, many of them former slaves, sailed from Nova Scotia to Sierra Leone,

Africa, in 1793. Arriving to find only a few tents and two patches of cleared ground, these 'Nova Scotians', as they came to be called, made a distinctive contribution to the development of Sierra Leone. In recent years there has been renewed contact between their descendants and the black community in Nova Scotia.

Of the Loyalists who migrated to the Caribbean, the Bahamian contingent, made up of whites and of black slaves, provides an illustration. While farmers often moved to the Out Islands, merchants, professionals, and the military settled in Nassau, the Bahamas, or on islands such as Abaco. In the Bahamas, as in Canada, where United Empire Loyalist societies founded in the nineteenth century helped sustain a sense of the Loyalist contribution to Canadian history, a Loyalist Association was formed in 1783 'to preserve and maintain those Rights and Liberties for which they left their homes and possessions'. Two hundred years after the arrival of the Loyalists, the Bahamian Post Office issued commemorative stamps to mark the bicentenary of the event, and in 1987 a memorial sculpture honouring black and white Bahamian Loyalists and their descendants was unveiled in Abaco. In a plaque sent by Canada to the Loyalist museum in the Bahamas in 1987, then Canadian Prime Minister Brian Mulroney noted that the 'Loyalists of both our nations made an outstanding contribution to national life in a wide variety of endeavours'.

Those contributions, whether in Canada, the Caribbean, or elsewhere, include the establishment of educational, religious, and cultural structures that contributed to the development of the arts and literature in those countries, although the geographical dispersal of Loyalist writers always militated against the emergence of a Loyalist school of writing. In Canada, however, literary consciousness of the Loyalists emerges not only in the contemporary satires of such Loyalists poets as Jacob Bailey and Jonathan Odell but also in the work of nineteenth- and twentieth-century descendants such as **Bliss Carman, Charles G. D. Roberts,** and **Al Purdy.**

The architectural legacy of the Loyalists can be found in surviving eighteenth-century churches, houses, and public buildings wherever they settled, as can their legacy of town plans and land distribution patterns. Finally, the Loyalists not only reinforced a British infrastructure in the fledgling colonies where they established themselves but, in Canada, they also contributed to the philosophy of evolutionary social process rather than revolutionary social process.

GWENDOLYN DAVIES

Further reading: B. Graymont, *The Iroquois in the American Revolution* (1972); James W. St. G. Walker, *The Black Loyalists* (1976); Gail Saunders, *Bahamian Loyalists and their Slaves* (1983); Neil MacKinnon, *'This Unfriendly Soil': The Loyalist Experience in Nova Scotia, 1783–1791* (1984); Christopher Moore, *Loyalists: Revolution, Exile, Settlement* (1984).

LUMBERA, BIENVENIDO (1932–)

Filipino poet, critic

Born in Batangas province, the Philippines, he studied at the University of Santo Tomas in Manila and took his doctorate in comparative literature at the University of Indiana, USA. A literary scholar and critic, he was a pioneer in the study of indigenous texts, which in the 1960s had not attracted sufficient attention as an area of academic research. Active in various cause-oriented cultural organizations, Lumbera also edited journals, lectured, and wrote on various aspects of Philippine literature and popular culture for journals in the Philippines and abroad. A recipient of a number of national awards for his contributions to cultural studies, he was the Ramon Magsaysay Awardee for Literature for 1993.

Lumbera's *Tagalog Poetry (1570–1898): Tradition and Influences in its Development* (1986) was the first attempt to examine native poetry from a comparative point of view, even as he contextualized the development of the genre against Spanish literary traditions. He eventually made a name for himself as a poet (in Filipino and English), dramatist, and librettist and as the country's foremost literary historian. His works have become models for a generation of Filipino scholars and an inspiration to those working in literary history and criticism in English and in the vernacular.

When martial law was declared in 1972, Lumbera left his post as professor at the Ateneo de Manila University and went underground. He was captured in 1974 and became a political prisoner for one year. In 1976 he joined the state-run University of the Philippines as a professor of literature.

Lumbera's well-known works in criticism include *Philippine Literature: A History and an Anthology* (1982) and *Revaluation: Essays on Philippine Literature, Cinema and Popular Culture* (1984), both of which were responses to the widespread colonialist perspective determined by the country's educational system, largely patterned after the American model.

For Lumbera, criticism cannot be dissociated from politics, and his works have consistently and systematically sought to re-examine texts in their dialectic relationship with socio-historical contexts shaped by the Philippines' colonial past.

SOLEDAD S. REYES

LURIE, MORRIS (1938–)

Australian novelist

Born in Melbourne, Australia, to parents who had emigrated from Poland, he lived abroad for seven years, mainly in England, Denmark, Morocco, and Greece, returning to Melbourne in 1973, where he lives but for frequent visits to New York, USA.

Lurie is a prolific and versatile writer. Most of his work is fiction, including four books for children, but he has written and published stage and screenplays. He has won two National Book Council Awards, an equal second for fiction in 1985 for *The Night We Ate the Sparrow* (1985) and a second in 1988 for his autobiographical *Whole Life* (1987). The latter tells of Lurie's childhood and early adolescence and shows that his fiction for adults is frequently based on the lives of his parents and grandfather or that, in other ways, its sources are, or might be, traceable to events in his life. Novels such as *Rappaport* (1966), *Rappaport's Revenge* (1973), and *Flying Home* (1978) are usually perceived as brilliant comedy, and rightly so, but the obverse of the comic mask is sometimes tragic and often at least poignant. **Serge Liberman**, reviewing *Whole Life* in *Overland* (108), described the book as 'a howl. Not the howl of laughter that the reader who sees Lurie as a humorist may expect; but rather a howl of anguish, of agony, of the most exquisite pain that comes from being repeatedly kicked in the guts by almost everyone within kicking reach'.

Lurie's settings are as often international as Australian. Leo Axelrod, the central character in *Flying Home*, explores the emotional possibilities of Israel, but is unable to re-create his parents' and grandfather's attachment; like many of Lurie's characters he experiences cultural displacement. Lurie's humour, so often derived from the intensely self-aware failure of doomed ambition or pretension, can be compared to that of Isaac Bashevis Singer, Saul Bellow, and Philip Roth.

NANCY KEESING